FOURTH EDITION

PROGRAMMING WITH MICROSOFT® VISUAL BASIC® 2008

DIANE ZAK

COURSE TECHNOLOGY
CENGAGE Learning™

Australia • Brazil • Japan • Korea • Mexico • Singapore • Spain • United Kingdom • United States

Programming with Microsoft® Visual Basic® 2008, Fourth Edition

Diane Zak

Executive Editor: Marie Lee

Acquisitions Editor: Amy Jollymore

Managing Editor: Tricia Coia

Editorial Assistant: Julia Leroux-Lindsey

Marketing Manager: Bryant Chrzan

Senior Content Project Manager: Jill Braiewa

Art Director: Marissa Falco

Cover Designer: Cabbage Design Company

Cover Photo: Cabbage Design Company

Print Buyer: Julio Esperas

Proofreader: Wendy Benedetto

Indexer: Broccoli Information Management

Compositor: International Typesetting and Composition

ISBN-13: 978-0-324-78276-9

ISBN-10: 0-324-78276-4

Course Technology
20 Channel Center Street
Boston, MA 02210
USA

Printed in the United States of America
1 2 3 4 5 6 7 15 14 13 12 11 10 09

Brief Contents

Contents

Preface

Programming with Microsoft Visual Basic 2008, Fourth Edition uses Visual Basic 2008, an object-oriented language, to teach programming concepts. This book is designed for a beginning programming course. However, it assumes students have learned basic Windows skills and file management from one of Course Technology's other books that cover the Microsoft Windows operating system.

Organization and Coverage

Programming with Microsoft Visual Basic 2008, Fourth Edition contains an Overview and 13 chapters that present hands-on instruction; it also contains 3 appendices. In the chapters, students with no previous programming experience learn how to plan and create their own interactive Windows applications. GUI design skills and OOP concepts are emphasized throughout the book. By the end of the book, students will have learned how to use TOE charts, pseudocode, and flowcharts to plan an application. They also will learn how to work with objects and write Visual Basic statements such as If...Then...Else, Select Case, Do...Loop, For...Next, and For Each...Next. Students also will learn how to create and manipulate variables, constants, strings, sequential access files, structures, classes, and arrays. In Chapter 12, they will learn how to create Web pages using ASP.NET 3.5. Chapter 13 shows students how to connect an application to a Microsoft Access database, and then use Language Integrated Query (LINQ) to query the database. Appendix A recaps the GUI design rules mentioned in the chapters, and Appendix B lists the Visual Basic conversion functions. Appendix C, which can be covered after Chapter 3, teaches students how to locate and fix syntax and logic errors in their code. The appendix shows students how to step through their code, as well as create breakpoints.

Approach

Programming with Microsoft Visual Basic 2008, Fourth Edition teaches programming concepts using a task-driven rather than a command-driven approach. By working through the chapters, which are each motivated by a realistic case, students learn how to develop applications they are likely to encounter in the workplace. This is much more effective than memorizing a list of commands out of context. The book motivates students by demonstrating why they need to learn the concepts and skills covered in each chapter.

Features

Programming with Microsoft Visual Basic 2008, Fourth Edition is an exceptional textbook because it also includes the following features:

READ THIS BEFORE YOU BEGIN This section is consistent with Course Technology's unequaled commitment to helping instructors introduce technology into the classroom. Technical considerations and assumptions about hardware, software, and default settings are listed in one place to help instructors save time and eliminate unnecessary aggravation.

VISUAL STUDIO 2008 METHODS The book focuses on Visual Studio 2008 methods rather than on Visual Basic functions. This is because the Visual Studio methods can be used in any .NET language, whereas the Visual Basic functions can be used only in Visual Basic. Exceptions to this are the Val and Format functions, which are introduced in Chapter 2. These functions are covered in the book simply because it is likely that students will encounter them in existing Visual Basic programs. However, in Chapter 3, the student is taught to use the TryParse method and the Convert class methods rather than the Val function. Also in Chapter 3, the Format function is replaced with the ToString method.

FIGURES Figures that introduce new statements, functions, or methods contain both the syntax and examples of using the syntax. Including the syntax in the figures makes the examples more meaningful.

CHAPTER CASES Each chapter begins with a programming-related problem that students could reasonably expect to encounter in business, followed by a demonstration of an application that could be used to solve the problem. Showing the students the completed application before they learn how to create it is motivational and instructionally sound. By allowing the students to see the type of application they will be able to create after completing the chapter, the students will be more motivated to learn because they can see how the programming concepts they are about to learn can be used and, therefore, why the concepts are important.

LESSONS Each chapter is divided into three lessons—A, B, and C. Lesson A introduces the programming concepts that will be used in the completed application. The concepts are illustrated with code examples and sample applications. The user interface for each sample application is provided to the student. Also provided are tutorial-style steps that guide the student on coding, running, and testing the application. Each sample application allows the student to observe how the current concept can be used before the next concept is introduced. In Lessons B and/or C, the student creates the application required to solve the problem specified in the Chapter Case.

APPENDICES A, B, AND C Programming with Microsoft Visual Basic 2008, Fourth Edition contains three appendices. Appendix A summarizes the GUI design tips taught in the chapters, making it easier for the student to follow the guidelines when designing an application's interface. Appendix B lists the Visual Basic conversion functions. See the following "New to this Edition" section for details on Appendix C.

GUI DESIGN TIPS These contain guidelines and recommendations for designing applications that follow Windows standards. Appendix A provides a summary of the GUI design guidelines covered in the chapters.

SUMMARY Following each lesson is a summary, which recaps the programming concepts, commands, and objects covered in the lesson.

REVIEW QUESTIONS Each lesson concludes with meaningful, conceptual questions that test students' understanding of what they learned in the lesson.

New to this Edition!

OPTION STATEMENTS All programs include the `Option Explicit On` and `Option Strict On` statements. In addition, all programs (except for the ones in Chapter 13) contain the `Option Infer Off` statement. The programs that use LINQ in Chapter 13 contain the `Option Infer On` statement.

NAMING CONVENTIONS Hungarian notation is used when naming controls and variables.

CHAPTER 12 Chapter 12 shows how to create Web applications using ASP.NET 3.5.

CHAPTER 13 Chapter 13 teaches students how to connect an application to a Microsoft Access database and then use LINQ to query the database.

APPENDIX C Appendix C, which can be covered after Chapter 3, teaches students how to locate and fix syntax and logic errors in their code. The appendix shows students how to step through their code, as well as create breakpoints.

HELP These notes anticipate the problems students are likely to encounter and help them resolve the problems on their own. This feature facilitates independent learning and frees the instructor to focus on substantive conceptual issues rather than on common procedural errors.

TIP These notes provide additional information about a procedure, such as an alternative method of performing the procedure.

KEY TERMS Following the Summary section in each lesson is a listing of the key terms found throughout the lesson, along with their definitions.

EXERCISES The Review Questions in each lesson are followed by Exercises, which provide students with additional practice of the skills and concepts they learned in the lesson. The Exercises are designated as INTRODUCTORY, INTERMEDIATE, ADVANCED, Discovery, and Swat The Bugs.

DISCOVERY EXERCISES The Discovery Exercises encourage students to challenge and independently develop their own programming skills while exploring the capabilities of Visual Basic 2008.

SWAT THE BUGS EXERCISES The Swat The Bugs Exercises provide an opportunity for students to detect and correct errors in an application's code.

Instructor Resources and Supplements

All of the resources available with this book are provided to the instructor on a single CD-ROM. Many also can be found at the Course Technology Web site (*www.cengage.com/coursetechnology*).

ELECTRONIC INSTRUCTOR'S MANUAL The Instructor's Manual that accompanies this textbook includes additional instructional material to assist in class preparation, including items such as Sample Syllabi,

Chapter Outlines, Technical Notes, Lecture Notes, Quick Quizzes, Teaching Tips, Discussion Topics, and Additional Case Projects.

EXAMVIEW® This textbook is accompanied by ExamView, a powerful testing software package that allows instructors to create and administer printed, computer (LAN-based), and Internet exams. ExamView includes hundreds of questions that correspond to the topics covered in this text, enabling students to generate detailed study guides that include page references for further review. The computer-based and Internet testing components allow students to take exams at their computers, and also save the instructor time by grading each exam automatically.

POWERPOINT PRESENTATIONS This book offers Microsoft PowerPoint slides for each chapter. These are included as a teaching aid for classroom presentation, to make available to students on the network for chapter review, or to be printed for classroom distribution. Instructors can add their own slides for additional topics they introduce to the class.

DATA FILES Data Files are necessary for completing the Lesson applications and Exercises in this book. The Data Files are provided on the Instructor Resources CD-ROM and also may be found on the Course Technology Web site at *www.cengage.com/coursetechnology.*

SOLUTION FILES Solutions to the Lesson applications and the end-of-lesson Review Questions and Exercises are provided on the Instructor Resources CD-ROM and also may be found on the Course Technology Web site at *www.cengage.com/coursetechnology*. The solutions are password protected.

DISTANCE LEARNING Course Technology offers online WebCT and Blackboard courses for this text to provide the most complete and dynamic learning experience possible. When you add online content to one of your courses, you're adding a lot: automated tests, topic reviews, quick quizzes, and additional case projects with solutions. For more information on how to bring distance learning to your course, contact your local Course Technology sales representative.

Acknowledgments

Writing a book is a team effort rather than an individual one. I would like to take this opportunity to thank my team, especially Tricia Coia (Managing Editor), Jill Braiewa (Senior Content Project Manager), and Nicole Ashton (Quality Assurance). Thank you for your support, enthusiasm, patience, and hard work. I could not have completed this project without you. Last, but certainly not least, I want to thank the following reviewers for their invaluable ideas and comments: Cliff Brozo, Monroe College; Neil Dunlop, Vista Community College; and Bill Sypawka, Pitt Community College.

Diane Zak

About the Inside Front Cover

Check out our interviews with recent graduates who are now working in the IT field. One is featured on the inside front cover of this book. If someone you know recently landed a job in IT, we'd like to interview them too! Send your suggestions via e-mail to Amy Jollymore, Acquisitions Editor, at Amy.Jollymore@Cengage.com.

Read This Before You Begin

Technical Information

Data Files

You will need data files to complete the tutorial-style steps and exercises in this book. Your instructor will provide the data files to you. You also can obtain the files electronically from the Course Technology Web site (*www.cengage.com/coursetechnology*), and then navigating to the page for this book.

Each chapter in this book has its own set of data files, which are stored in a separate folder within the VB2008 folder. The files for Chapter 1 are stored in the VB2008\Chap01 folder. Similarly, the files for Chapter 2 are stored in the VB2008\Chap02 folder. Throughout this book, you will be instructed to open files from or save files to these folders.

You can use a computer in your school lab or your own computer to complete the steps and exercises in this book.

Using Your Own Computer

To use your own computer to complete the material in this book, you will need the following:

- A Pentium® 4 processor, 1.6 GHz or higher, personal computer running Microsoft Windows. This book was written and Quality Assurance tested using Microsoft Windows Vista.
- Microsoft Visual Studio 2008 installed on your computer. This book was written using Microsoft Visual Studio 2008 Professional Edition, and Quality Assurance tested using Microsoft Visual Basic 2008 Express Edition and Microsoft Visual Web Developer 2008 Express Edition. If your book came with a copy of Microsoft Visual Studio 2008 (Express or Professional), then you may install that on your computer and use it to complete the material.
- If you are using the Express Edition of Visual Basic, you won't be able to complete Chapter 12 unless Visual Web Developer 2008 Express Edition is installed on your computer. At the time of this writing, you can download a copy of Visual Web Developer 2008 Express Edition from *www.microsoft.com/express/download*.

Figures

The figures in this book reflect how your screen will look if you are using Microsoft Visual Studio 2008 Professional Edition and a Microsoft Windows Vista system. Your screen may appear slightly different in some instances if you are using another version of Microsoft Visual Studio, Microsoft Visual Basic, or Microsoft Windows.

Visit Our Web Site

Additional materials designed for this textbook might be available through the Course Technology Web site, *www.cengage.com/coursetechnology.* Search this site for more details.

To the Instructor

To complete the tutorial-style steps and exercises in this book, your students must use a set of data files. These files are included on the Instructor's Resource CD. They also may be obtained electronically through the Course Technology Web site at *www.cengage.com/coursetechnology*. Follow the instructions in the Help file to copy the data files to your server or standalone computer. You can view the Help file using a text editor such as WordPad or Notepad. Once the files are copied, you should instruct your students how to copy the files to their own computers or workstations.

The material in this book was written using Microsoft Visual Studio 2008 Professional Edition and Quality Assurance tested using Microsoft Visual Basic 2008 Express Edition and Microsoft Visual Web Developer 2008 Express Edition on a Microsoft Windows Vista system.

Course Technology Data Files

You are granted a license to copy the data files to any computer or computer network used by individuals who have purchased this book.

OVERVIEW

An Overview of Programming

After studying the Overview, you should be able to:

- Explain the tasks performed by a programmer
- Understand the employment opportunities for programmers
- Define some of the terms used in object-oriented programming
- Run a Visual Basic 2008 application
- Understand how to use the chapters effectively

Programmers

Although computers appear to be amazingly intelligent machines, they still rely on human beings to give them directions. The directions given to a computer are called **computer programs** or, more simply, **programs**. The people who write the programs are called **programmers**. Programmers use a variety of special languages called **programming languages** to communicate with the computer. Some popular programming languages are Visual Basic, C#, C++, and Java. In this book, you will communicate with the computer using the Visual Basic 2008 programming language.

When a company has a problem that requires a computer solution, typically it is a programmer that comes to the rescue. The programmer might be an employee of the company; or he or she might be a freelance programmer, which is a programmer who works on temporary contracts rather than for a long-term employer. First the programmer meets with the user, which is the person (or persons) responsible for describing the problem. In many cases, this person or persons also will eventually use the solution. Depending on the complexity of the problem, the programmer may need to meet with the user several times. The purpose of the initial meetings is to determine the exact problem and to agree on the desired solution. After the programmer and user agree on the solution, the programmer begins converting the solution into a computer program. During the conversion phase, the programmer meets periodically with the user to determine whether the program fulfills the user's needs and to refine any details of the solution. When the user is satisfied that the program does what he or she wants it to do, the programmer rigorously tests the program with sample data before releasing it to the user. In many cases, the programmer also provides the user with a manual that explains how to use the program. As this process indicates, the creation of a good computer solution to a problem—in other words, the creation of a good program—requires a great deal of interaction between the programmer and the user.

According to the 2006-07 Edition of the Occupational Outlook Handbook (OOH), published by the U.S. Department of Labor's Bureau of Labor Statistics, "When hiring programmers, employers look for people with the necessary programming skills who can think logically and pay close attention to detail. The job calls for patience, persistence, and the ability to work on exacting analytical work, especially under pressure. Ingenuity, creativity, and imagination also are particularly important when programmers design solutions and test their work for potential failures. ... Because programmers are expected to work in teams and interact directly with users, employers want programmers who are able to communicate with nontechnical personnel." The Bureau of Labor Statistics predicts that employment of programmers will grow up to 8% between 2004 and 2014. "As organizations attempt to control costs and keep up with changing technology, they will need programmers to assist in conversions to new computer languages and systems. In addition numerous job openings will result from the need to replace programmers who leave the labor force or transfer to other occupations such as manager or systems analyst." There is a great deal of competition for programming jobs, so jobseekers will need to keep up to date with the latest programming languages and technologies. According to the OOH, median annual earnings of computer programmers were $62,890 in

May 2004. The OOH also reports that "According to the National Association of Colleges and Employers, starting salary offers for graduates with a bachelor's degree in computer science averaged $50,820 a year in 2005." You can find more information about computer programmers on the Bureau of Labor Statistics Web site at www.bls.gov.

Visual Basic 2008

As mentioned earlier, you will use the Visual Basic 2008 programming language to communicate with the computer. Visual Basic 2008 is an **object-oriented programming language**, which is a language that allows the programmer to use objects to accomplish a program's goal. An **object** is anything that can be seen, touched, or used. In other words, an object is nearly any *thing*. The objects used in an object-oriented program can take on many different forms. For example, programs written for the Windows environment typically use objects such as check boxes, list boxes, and buttons. A payroll program, on the other hand, might utilize objects found in the real world, such as a time card object, an employee object, or a check object. Every object used in an object-oriented program is created from a **class**, which is a pattern that the computer uses to create the object. An object created from a class is called an **instance** of the class and is said to be **instantiated** from the class. You will learn more about object-oriented programming throughout this book.

Visual Basic 2008 is available as a stand-alone product (called Visual Basic 2008 Express Edition) or as part of Visual Studio 2008. (Also included in Visual Studio 2008 are the Visual C++ 2008 and Visual C# 2008 programming languages.) You can use Visual Basic 2008 to create programs, called **applications**, for the Windows environment or for the Web. You also can use it to create applications for mobile devices, called smart devices, such as pocket PCs, cell phones, and PDAs (personal digital assistants). You will learn how to create Windows, Web, and smart device applications in this book.

A Visual Basic 2008 Demonstration

In the following set of steps, you will run a Visual Basic 2008 application that shows you some of the objects you will learn about in the chapters. For now, it is not important for you to understand how these objects were created or why the objects perform the way they do. Those questions will be answered in the chapters.

To run the Visual Basic 2008 application:

1. Press and hold down the **Windows logo** key on your keyboard as you tap the letter **r**, then release the logo key. The Run dialog box opens.

2. Use the **Browse** button to locate and then open the VB2008\Overview folder on your computer's hard disk or on the device designated by your instructor. Click **Monthly Payment Calculator** (**Monthly Payment Calculator.exe**) in the list of filenames. (Depending on how Windows is set up on your computer, you may see the .exe

If a Security Warning dialog box appears, click Run.

extension on the filename.) Click the **Open** button. The Browse dialog box closes and the Run dialog box appears again. Click the **OK** button. After a few moments, the Monthly Payment Calculator application shown in Figure 1 appears on the screen. The interface contains a text box, list box, buttons, radio buttons, and labels. You can use the application to calculate the monthly payment for a car loan.

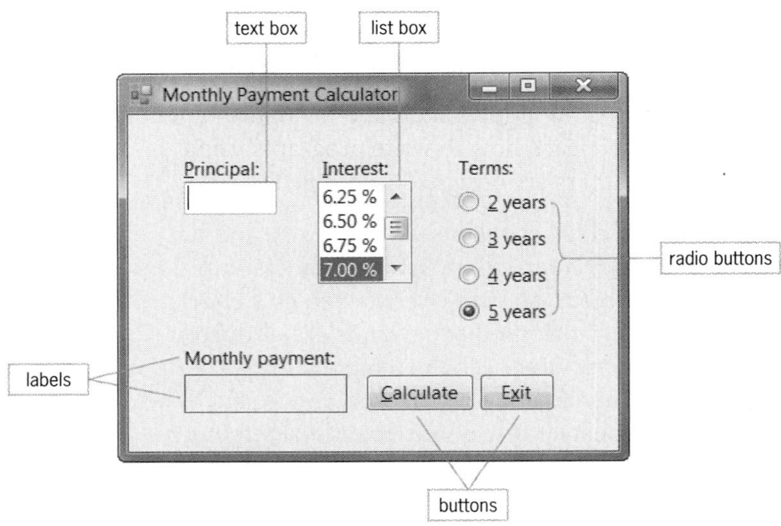

Figure 1 Monthly Payment Calculator application

3. Use the application to calculate the monthly payment for a $20,000 loan at 6.75% interest for five years. Type **20000** in the Principal text box, and then click **6.75 %** in the Interest list box. The radio button corresponding to the five-year term is already selected, so you just need to click the **Calculate** button to compute the monthly payment. The Monthly Payment Calculator application indicates that your monthly payment would be $393.67, as shown in Figure 2.

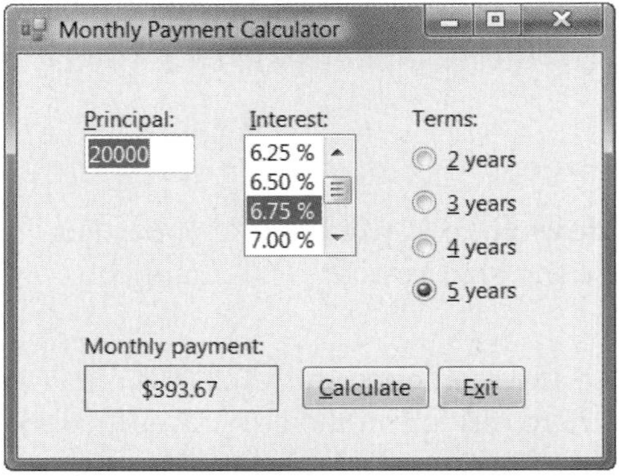

Figure 2 Computed monthly payment

4. Now determine what your monthly payment would be if you borrowed $10,000 at 8% interest for four years. Type **10000** in the Principal text box. Scroll down the Interest list box until the 8.00 % rate is visible, and then click **8.00 %**. Click the **4 years** radio button, and then click the **Calculate** button. The Monthly payment box shows $244.13.

5. Click the **Exit** button to close the Monthly Payment Calculator application.

Using the Chapters Effectively

This book is designed for a beginning programming course; however, it assumes students are familiar with basic Windows skills and file management. The chapters in this book will help you learn how to write programs using Microsoft Visual Basic 2008. The chapters are designed to be used at your computer. Begin by reading the text that explains the concepts. When you come to the numbered steps, follow the steps on your computer. Read each step carefully and completely before you try it. As you work, compare your screen with the figures to verify your results. The figures in this book reflect how your screen will look if you are using the Professional Edition of Visual Studio 2008 and a Microsoft Windows Vista system. Your screen may appear slightly different in some instances if you are using a different edition of Visual Studio, or if you are using the Express Edition of Visual Basic, or if you are using another version of Microsoft Windows. Don't worry if your screen display differs slightly from the figures. The important parts of the screen display are labeled in each figure. Just be sure you have these parts on your screen.

Do not worry about making mistakes; that's part of the learning process. HELP notes identify common problems and explain how to get back on track. TIP notes provide additional information about a procedure—for example, an alternative method of performing the procedure.

Each chapter is divided into three lessons. You might want to take a break between lessons. Following each lesson is a Summary section that lists the important elements of the lesson. After the Summary section is a listing of the key terms (including definitions) covered in the lesson. Following the Key Terms section are questions and exercises designed to review and reinforce the lesson's concepts. You should complete all of the end-of-lesson questions and several exercises before going on to the next lesson. It takes a great deal of practice to acquire the skills needed to create good programs, and future chapters assume that you have mastered the information found in the previous chapters. Some of the end-of-lesson exercises are Discovery exercises, which allow you to both "discover" the solutions to problems on your own and experiment with material that is not covered in the chapter. Some lessons also contain one or more Debugging exercises. In programming, the term **debugging** refers to the process of finding and fixing any errors in a program. Debugging exercises provide debugging tips and allow you to practice debugging applications.

Throughout the book you will find GUI (Graphical User Interface) design tips. These tips contain guidelines and recommendations for designing applications. You should follow these guidelines and recommendations so that your applications follow the Windows standard.

Overview Summary

- Computers rely on programmers to give them directions.
- The creation of a good program requires a great deal of interaction between the programmer and the user.
- The job opportunities for programmers are expected to grow in the next several years.
- Visual Basic 2008 is an object-oriented language. You can use it to create applications for the Windows environment, the Web, and smart device applications.
- The objects in an object-oriented program are instantiated (created) from classes.

Overview Key Terms

Applications—programs created for the Windows environment, the Web, or smart devices

Class—a pattern that the computer uses to create an object

Computer programs—the directions given to a computer by a programmer; also called programs

Debugging—the process of finding and correcting the errors in a program

Instance—an object created (instantiated) from a class

Instantiated—the process of creating an object from a class

Object—anything that can be seen, touched, or used

Object-oriented programming language—a programming language that allows the programmer to use objects to accomplish a program's goal

Programmers—the people who write programs

Programming languages—the languages used to communicate with a computer

Programs—another term for computer programs

CHAPTER 1

An Introduction to Visual Basic 2008

Creating a Splash Screen

In this chapter, you will create a splash screen for Country Charm Inn, a small bed and breakfast located in rural Kentucky. You will create the splash screen using Visual Basic 2008, Microsoft's newest version of the Visual Basic programming language. A splash screen is the first image that appears when an application is started. It is used to introduce the application and to hold the user's attention while the application is being read into the computer's memory.

Previewing the Splash Screen

Before you start the first lesson in this chapter, you will preview a completed splash screen. The splash screen is contained in the VB2008\Chap01 folder.

To preview a completed splash screen:

The Windows logo key looks like this: .

1. Press and hold down the **Windows logo** key on your keyboard as you tap the letter **r**, then release the logo key. The Run dialog box opens.
2. Use the **Browse** button to locate and then open the VB2008\Chap01 folder on your computer's hard disk or on the device designated by your instructor. Click **Splash** (**Splash.exe**) in the list of filenames. (Depending on how Windows is set up on your computer, you may see the .exe extension on the filename.) Click the **Open** button. The Browse dialog box closes and the Run dialog box appears again.

If a Security Warning dialog box appears, click Run.

3. Click the **OK** button in the Run dialog box. The splash screen shown in Figure 1-1 appears. The splash screen closes when eight seconds have elapsed.

Figure 1-1 Splash screen for the Country Charm Inn

Chapter 1 is designed to help you get comfortable with the Visual Studio 2008 integrated development environment. An **integrated development environment (IDE)** is an environment that contains all of the tools and features you need to create, run, and test your programs. As do all the chapters in this book, Chapter 1 contains three lessons. You should complete a lesson in full and do all of the end-of-lesson questions and several exercises before moving on to the next lesson.

LESSON A

After studying Lesson A, you should be able to:

- Start and customize Visual Studio 2008 or Visual Basic 2008 Express Edition
- Create a Visual Basic 2008 Windows application
- Manage the windows in the IDE
- Set the properties of an object
- Restore a property to its default setting
- Save a solution
- Close a solution
- Open an existing solution

The Splash Screen Application

In this chapter, you will create a splash screen using Visual Basic 2008. As mentioned in the Overview, Visual Basic 2008 is available as a stand-alone product (called Visual Basic 2008 Express Edition) or as part of Visual Studio 2008. Before you can use Visual Basic 2008 to create an application, you first must start either Visual Studio 2008 or the Express Edition of Visual Basic 2008.

To start Visual Studio 2008 or Visual Basic 2008 Express Edition:

1. Click the **Start** button on the Windows taskbar, then point to **All Programs**.
2. *If you are using Visual Studio 2008*, click **Microsoft Visual Studio 2008**, then click **Microsoft Visual Studio 2008**. (If the Choose Default Environment Settings dialog box appears, choose Visual Studio Development Settings, then click Start Visual Studio.) The Microsoft Visual Studio 2008 splash screen appears momentarily, and then the Microsoft Visual Studio window opens.

   If you are using Visual Basic 2008 Express Edition, click **Microsoft Visual Basic 2008 Express Edition**. The Microsoft Visual Basic 2008 Express Edition splash screen appears momentarily, and then the Microsoft Visual Basic 2008 Express Edition window opens.
3. Click **Window** on the menu bar, then click **Reset Window Layout**. When you are asked whether you want to restore the default window layout for the environment, click the **Yes** button. If necessary, click the **Maximize** button on the Microsoft Visual Studio title bar. Your screen will appear similar to Figure 1-2 if you are using the Professional Edition of Microsoft Visual Studio 2008; however, your Recent Projects section might include some additional information. If you are using a different edition of Visual Studio, or if you are using the Express Edition of Visual Basic, your startup screen might look slightly different than the one shown in Figure 1-2. The startup

screen in Figure 1-2 contains three windows: Toolbox, Start Page, and Solution Explorer. You will learn about the Solution Explorer window in this lesson. The Toolbox window is covered in Lesson B.

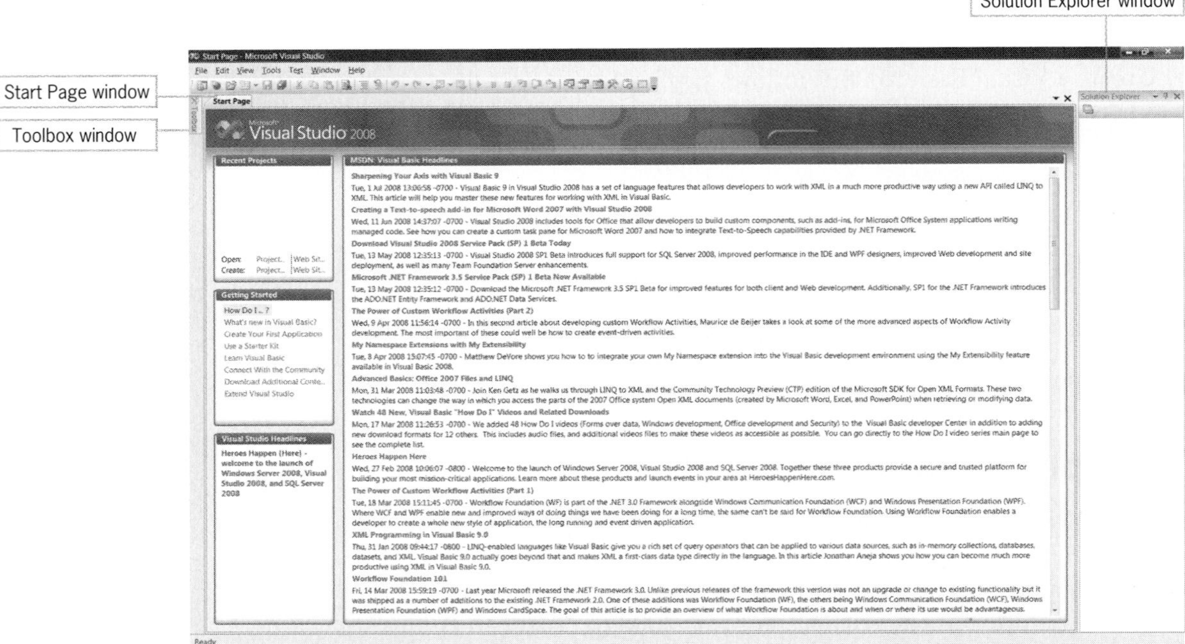

Figure 1-2 Microsoft Visual Studio 2008 Professional Edition startup screen

The splash screen will be a Windows application, which means it will have a Windows user interface and run on a desktop computer. A **user interface** is what the user sees and interacts with while an application is running. Windows applications in Visual Basic are composed of solutions, projects, and files. A solution is a container that stores the projects and files for an entire application. Although the solutions in this book contain only one project, a solution can contain several projects. A project also is a container, but it stores only the files associated with that particular project.

To create a Visual Basic 2008 Windows application:

1. This first step is necessary so that your screen agrees with the figures and steps in this book. Click **Tools** on the menu bar, then click **Options** to open the Options dialog box. If necessary, expand the **Projects and Solutions** node, then click **General**. If necessary, select the following three check boxes: **Always show Error List if build finishes with errors**, **Always show solution**, and **Save new projects when created**. If necessary, deselect the **Show Output window when build starts** check box. See Figure 1-3.

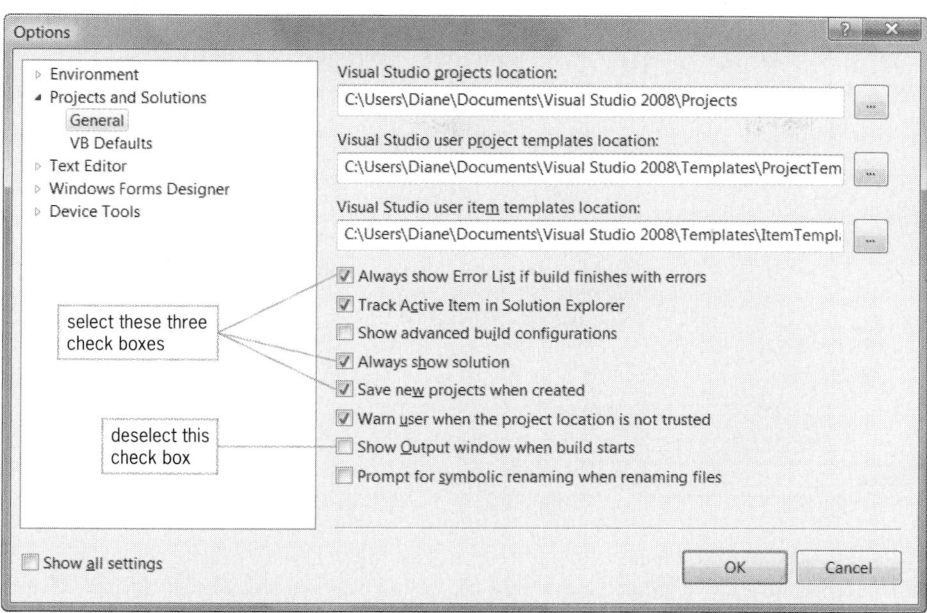

Figure 1-3 Options dialog box

2. Click the **OK** button to close the Options dialog box. Click **File** on the menu bar, then click **New Project**. The New Project dialog box opens. If you are using Visual Studio 2008, expand the **Visual Basic** node in the Project types list, if necessary, then click **Windows**.

You also can use the Start Page to open the New Project dialog box. To do so, click Project..., which appears next to Create in the Recent Projects list.

3. If necessary, click **Windows Forms Application** in the Visual Studio installed templates section of the Templates list. A template is a pattern that the computer uses to create solutions and projects. Each template listed in the Templates list includes a set of standard folders and files appropriate for the solution or project. The folders and files are automatically created for you when you click the OK button in the New Project dialog box.

4. Change the name entered in the Name box to **Splash Project**.

5. Click the **Browse** button, which appears next to the Location box. The Project Location dialog box opens. Locate and then click the **VB2008\Chap01** folder, then click the **Select Folder** button.

6. If necessary, select the **Create directory for solution** check box in the New Project dialog box. Change the name entered in the Solution Name box to **Splash Solution**. Figure 1-4 shows the completed New Project dialog box. The drive letter will be different if you are saving to a device other than your computer's hard drive—for example, if you are saving to a flash drive. In addition, your dialog box will look different if you are using the Express Edition of Visual Basic.

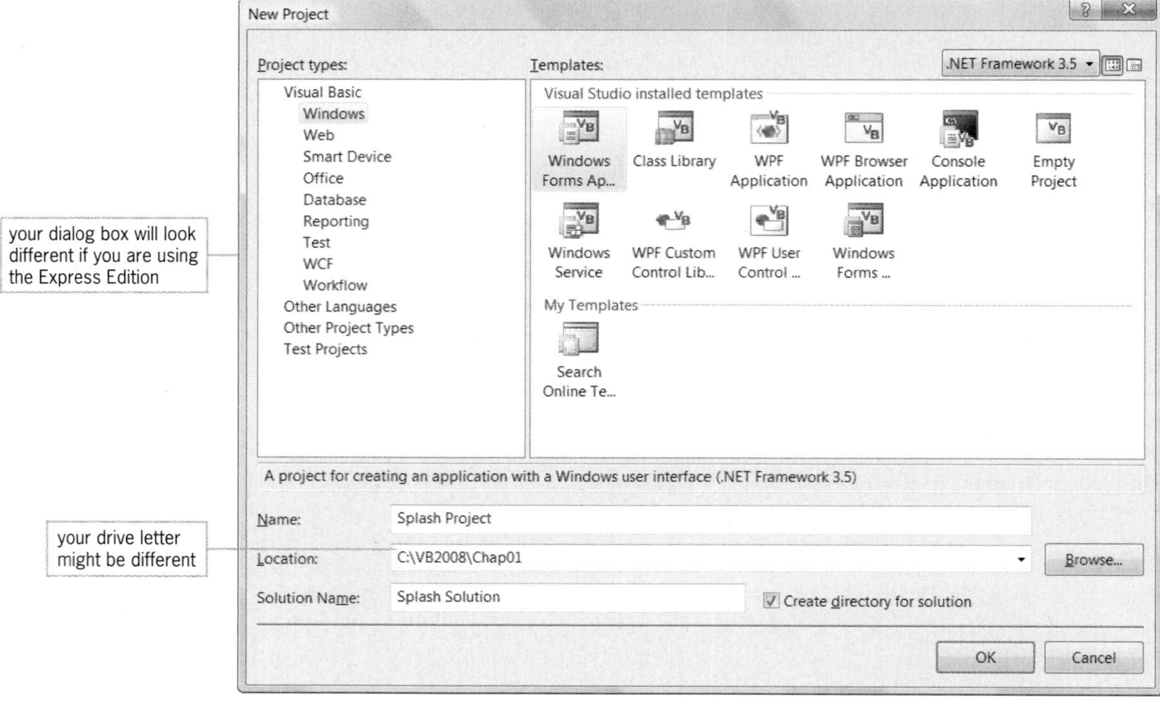

Figure 1-4 Completed New Project dialog box

7. Click the **OK** button to close the New Project dialog box. When you click the OK button, the computer creates a solution and adds a Visual Basic project to the solution. The names of the solution and project appear in the Solution Explorer window. See Figure 1-5.

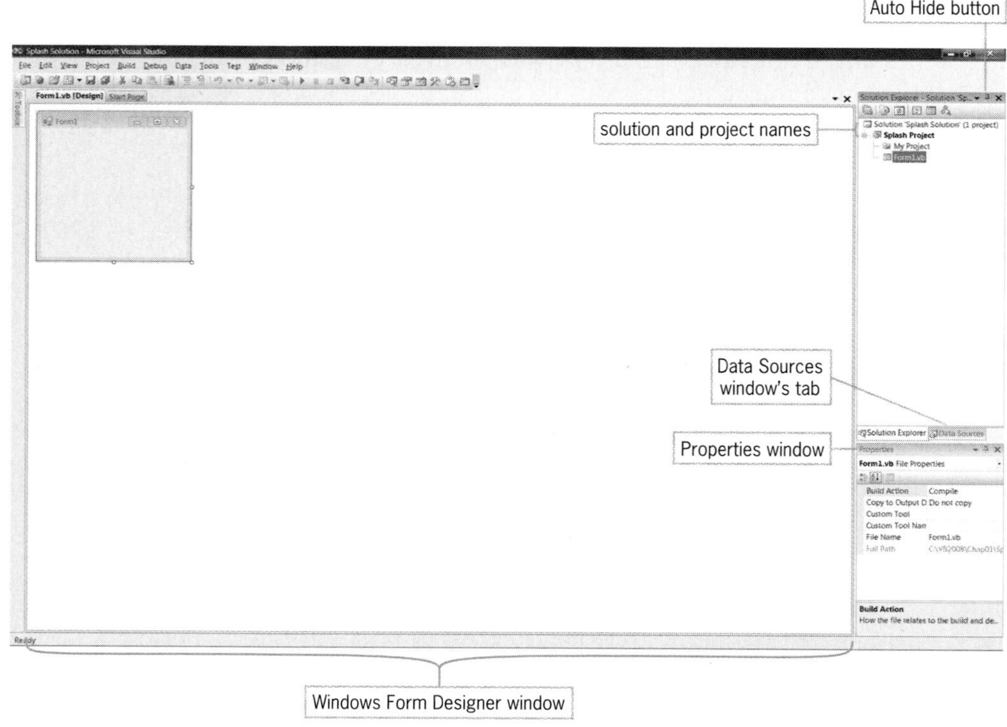

Figure 1-5 Solution and Visual Basic project

8. If you want to widen the Solution Explorer window to match Figure 1-5, position your mouse pointer on the window's left border until the mouse pointer becomes a sizing pointer, then drag the border to the left.

The sizing pointer mentioned in Step 8 looks like this: ↔.

Managing the Windows in the IDE

In addition to the Toolbox, Start Page, and Solution Explorer windows mentioned earlier, three other windows are open in the IDE (Integrated Development Environment) shown in Figure 1-5: Windows Form Designer, Data Sources, and Properties. Having so many windows open at the same time can be confusing, especially when you are first learning the IDE. In most cases, you will find it easier to work in the IDE if you either close or auto-hide the windows you are not currently using. The easiest way to close an open window is to click the Close button on the window's title bar. In most cases, the View menu provides an appropriate option for opening a closed window. You auto-hide a window using the Auto Hide button (refer to Figure 1-5) on the window's title bar. The Auto Hide button is a toggle button: clicking it once activates it, and clicking it again deactivates it. The Toolbox window in Figure 1-5 is an example of an auto-hidden window.

To close, auto-hide, and display windows in the IDE:

1. Click the **Start Page** tab to make the Start Page window the active window, then click the **Close** button on its title bar. Click the **Data Sources** tab to view the Data Sources window, then click the **Close** button on the window's title bar.
2. Now practice auto-hiding a window. Click the **Auto Hide** button (the vertical pushpin) on the Solution Explorer window's title bar. The Solution Explorer window is minimized and appears as a tab on the right edge of the IDE.
3. Now practice temporarily displaying a window. Place your mouse pointer on the Solution Explorer tab. The Solution Explorer window slides into view. The horizontal pushpin on the Auto Hide button indicates that the window is being displayed temporarily. Move your mouse pointer away from the Solution Explorer window. The window is minimized and appears as a tab again.
4. Next, you will practice permanently displaying a window. Place your mouse pointer on the Solution Explorer tab. When the Solution Explorer window slides into view, click the **Auto Hide** button (the horizontal pushpin) on its title bar. The vertical pushpin replaces the horizontal pushpin on the button. Figure 1-6 shows the current status of the windows in the IDE. Only the Windows Form Designer, Solution Explorer, and Properties windows are open; the Toolbox window is auto-hidden. If the items in the Properties window do not appear in alphabetical order, click the **Alphabetical** button.

To reset the window layout in the IDE, click Window on the menu bar, click Reset Window Layout, and then click the Yes button.

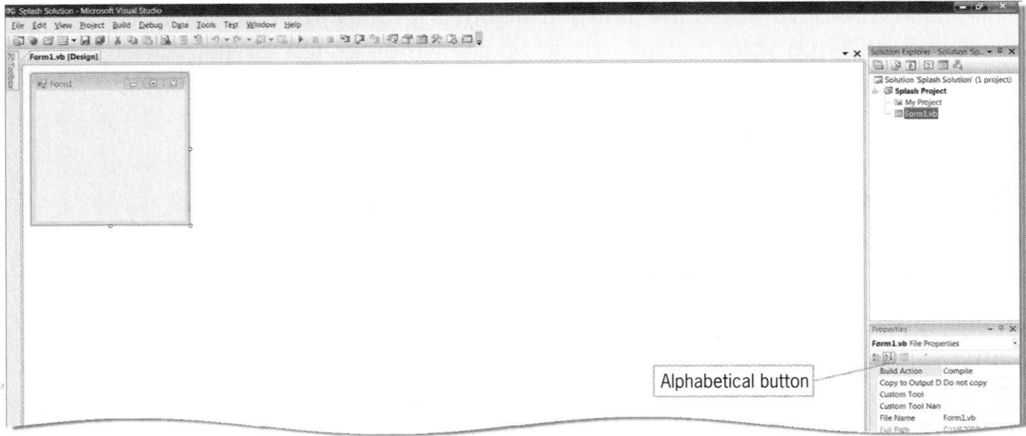

Figure 1-6 Current status of the windows in the IDE

In the next several sections, you will take a closer look at the Windows Form Designer, Solution Explorer, and Properties windows. (Recall that the Toolbox window is covered in Lesson B.)

The Windows Form Designer Window

Figure 1-7 shows the **Windows Form Designer window**, where you create (or design) the graphical user interface, referred to as a **GUI**, for your project. Recall that a user interface is what the user sees and interacts with when using an application. Only a Windows Form object appears in the designer window shown in the figure. A **Windows Form object**, or **form**, is the foundation for the user interface in a Windows application. You create the user interface by adding other objects, such as buttons and text boxes, to the form. Notice that a title bar appears at the top of the form. The title bar contains a default caption—in this case, Form1—as well as Minimize, Maximize, and Close buttons. At the top of the designer window is a tab labeled Form1.vb [Design]. [Design] identifies the window as the designer window. Form1.vb is the name of the file (on your computer's hard disk or on another device) that contains the Visual Basic instructions associated with the form.

As you learned in the Overview, all objects in an object-oriented program are created (instantiated) from a class. A form, for example, is an instance of the Windows Form class. The form is automatically instantiated for you when you create a Windows application.

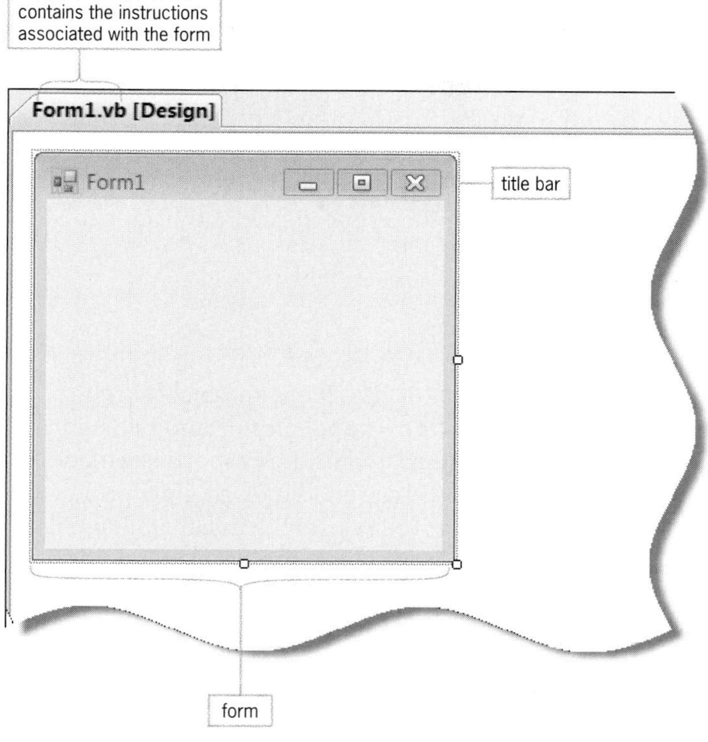

Figure 1-7 Windows Form Designer window

The Solution Explorer Window

The **Solution Explorer window** displays a list of the projects contained in the current solution and the items contained in each project. Figure 1-8 shows the Solution Explorer window for the Splash Solution, which contains one project named Splash Project. Within the Splash Project are a My Project folder and a file named Form1.vb. The .vb on the filename indicates that the file is a "Visual Basic" source file. A **source file** is a file that contains program instructions, called **code**. The Form1.vb file contains the code associated with the form displayed in the designer window. You can use the Code Editor window, which is covered in Lesson C, to view the contents of the Form1.vb file.

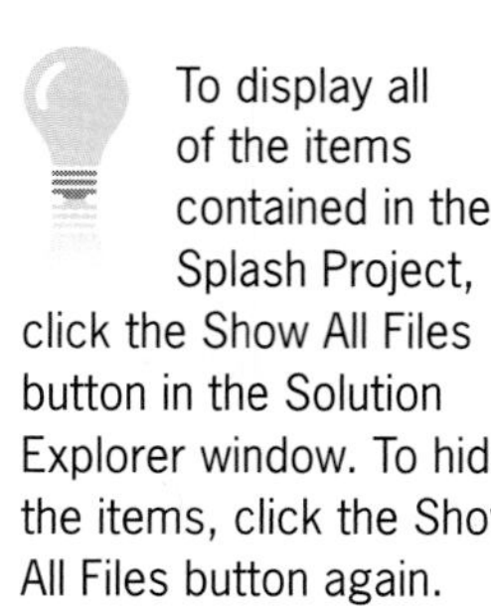

To display all of the items contained in the Splash Project, click the Show All Files button in the Solution Explorer window. To hide the items, click the Show All Files button again.

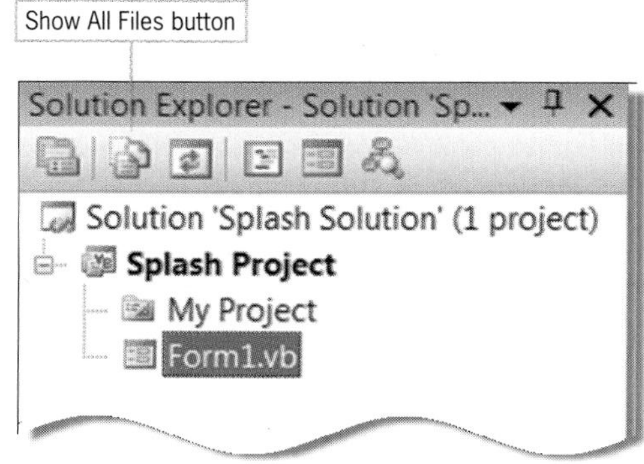

Figure 1-8 Solution Explorer window

The Form1.vb source file is referred to as a **form file**, because it contains the code associated with a form. The code associated with the first form included in a project is automatically stored in a form file named Form1.vb. The code associated with the second form in the same project is stored in a form file named Form2.vb, and so on. Because a project can contain many forms and, therefore, many form files, it is a good practice to give each form file a more meaningful name. Doing this will help you keep track of the various form files in the project. You can use the Properties window to change the filename.

The Properties Window

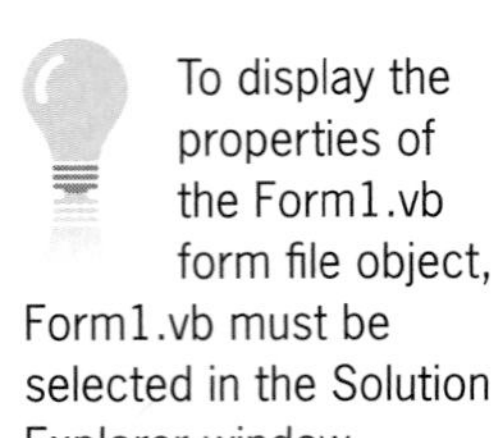

To display the properties of the Form1.vb form file object, Form1.vb must be selected in the Solution Explorer window.

As is everything in an object-oriented language, a file is an object. Each object has a set of attributes that determine its appearance and behavior. The attributes are called **properties** and are listed in the **Properties window**. When an object is created, a default value is assigned to each of its properties. The Properties window shown in Figure 1-9 lists the default values assigned to the properties of the Form1.vb file. (You do not need to widen your Properties window to match Figure 1-9.) As indicated in the figure, the Properties window includes an Object box and a Properties list. The Object box contains the name of the selected object; in this case, it contains Form1.vb, which is the name of the form file object. The Properties list has two columns. The left column displays the names of the selected object's properties. The names can be displayed either alphabetically or by category. However, it's usually easier to work with the Properties window when the property names are listed in alphabetical order. The right column in the Properties list is called the Settings box and displays the current value (or setting) of each of the properties. A brief description of the selected property appears in the Description pane.

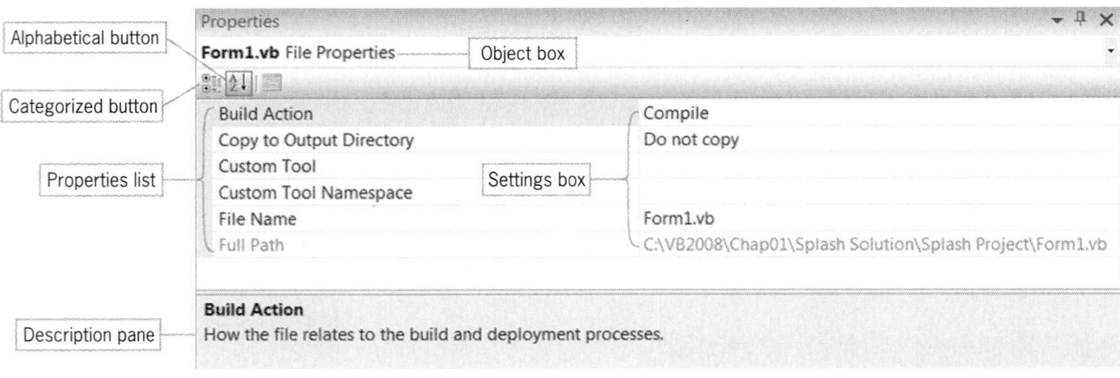

Figure 1-9 Properties window showing the properties of the Form1.vb file object

To use the Properties window to change the form file's name:

1. Form1.vb should be selected in the Solution Explorer window. Click **File Name** in the Properties list, then type **Splash Form.vb**. Be sure to include the .vb extension on the filename; otherwise, the computer will not recognize the file as a source file.

2. Press **Enter**. Splash Form.vb appears in the Solution Explorer and Properties windows and on the designer window's tab, as shown in Figure 1-10.

You also can change the File Name property by right-clicking Form1.vb in the Solution Explorer window and then clicking Rename on the context menu.

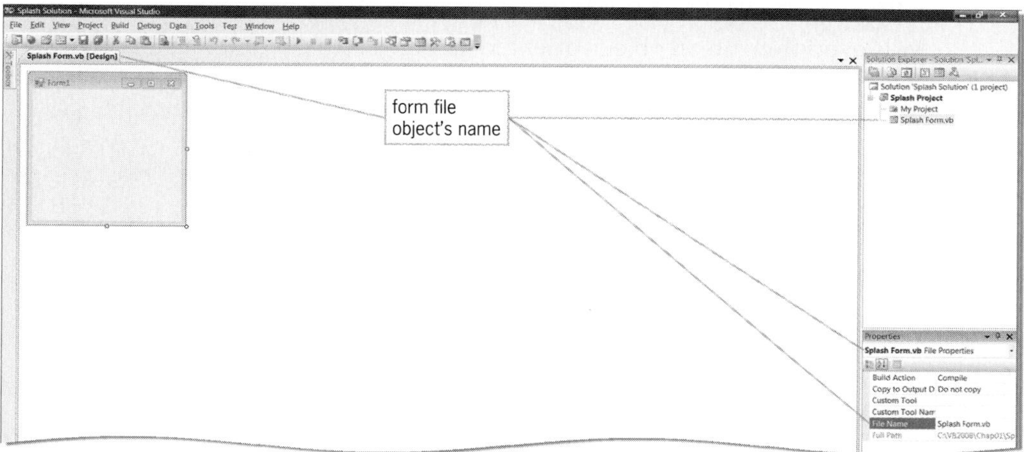

Figure 1-10 Form file's name shown in the designer, Solution Explorer, and Properties windows

Properties of a Windows Form

Like a form file, a Windows form also has a set of properties. The properties will appear in the Properties window when you select the form in the designer window.

To view the properties of the form:

1. Click the **form** in the designer window. The form's properties appear in the Properties window.

2. If the properties are not listed alphabetically, click the **Alphabetical** button. The Properties window in Figure 1-11 shows a partial listing of the properties of a form.

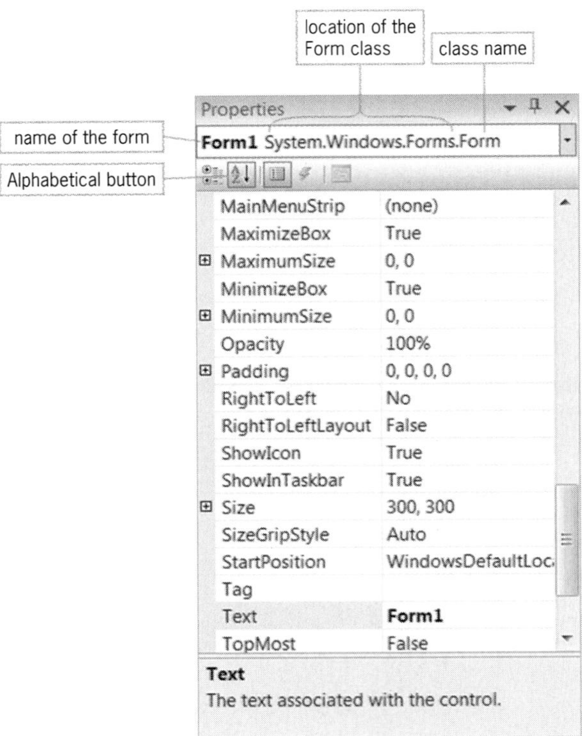

Figure 1-11 Properties window showing a partial listing of the form's properties

Notice that Form1 System.Windows.Forms.Form appears in the Object box in Figure 1-11. Form1 is the name of the form. The name is automatically assigned to the form when the form is instantiated (created). In System. Windows.Forms.Form, Form is the name of the class (pattern) used to instantiate the form. System.Windows.Forms is the namespace that contains the Form class definition. A **class definition** is a block of code that specifies (or defines) an object's appearance and behavior. All class definitions in Visual Basic 2008 are contained in namespaces, which you can picture as blocks of memory cells inside the computer. Each **namespace** contains the code that defines a group of related classes. The System.Windows.Forms namespace contains the definition of the Windows Form class. It also contains the class definitions for objects you add to a form, such as buttons and text boxes. The period that separates each word in System.Windows.Forms.Form is called the **dot member access operator**. Similar to the backslash (\) in a folder path, the dot member access operator indicates a hierarchy, but of namespaces rather than folders. In other words, the backslash in the path C:\VB2008\Chap01\Splash Solution\Splash Project\Splash Form.vb indicates that the Splash Form.vb file is contained in (or is a member of) the Splash Project folder, which is a member of the Splash Solution folder, which is a member of the Chap01 folder, which is a member of the VB2008 folder, which is a member of the C: drive. Likewise, the name System.Windows.Forms.Form indicates that the Form class is a member of the Forms namespace, which is a member of the Windows namespace, which is a member of the System namespace. The dot member access operator allows the computer to locate the Form class in the computer's internal memory, similar to the way the backslash (\) allows the computer to locate the Splash Form.vb file on your computer's disk.

The Name Property

Unlike a form file, a form has a Name property rather than a File Name property. The first form in a project is automatically assigned the name Form1; the second form is assigned Form2, and so on. The default names assigned to forms are not very descriptive, so most programmers change the names to more meaningful ones, keeping in mind that each form in the same project must be unique. A form's name must begin with a letter and can contain only letters, numbers, and the underscore character. The name cannot include punctuation characters or spaces. There are several conventions for naming objects in Visual Basic. In this book, you will use a naming convention called Hungarian notation. Names in Hungarian notation begin with a three (or more) character ID that represents the object's type, with the remaining characters in the name representing the object's purpose. For example, using Hungarian notation, you might assign the name frmSplash to the current form. The "frm" identifies the object as a form, and "Splash" reminds you of the form's purpose. Hungarian notation names are entered using **camel case**, which means you lowercase the ID characters and then uppercase the first letter of each word in the name. Camel case refers to the fact that the uppercase letters appear as "humps" in the name because they are taller than the lowercase letters.

To change the name of the form:

1. Drag the scroll box in the Properties window to the top of the vertical scroll bar. As you scroll, notice the various properties associated with a form. Also notice that the items within parentheses appear at the top of the Properties list.
2. Click (**Name**) in the Properties list, then type **frmSplash** and press **Enter**. An asterisk (*) appears after [Design] on the designer window's tab. The asterisk indicates that the form has been changed since the last time it was saved to the form file.

The Text Property

Programmers who create applications for the Windows environment need to be aware of the conventions used in Windows applications. One such convention is that the name of the application (for example, Microsoft Visual Studio or Microsoft Word) usually appears in the application window's title bar, as well as on the application's button on the taskbar while the application is running. Because the form will become your application's window when the application is started, its title bar and taskbar button should follow the same convention. The text displayed in a form's title bar, as well as on its taskbar button, is controlled by a form's Text property. Form1 is the default value assigned to the Text property of the first form in a project. In this case, "Country Charm Inn" would be a more descriptive value.

To set the Text property of the form:

1. Scroll down the Properties window until you see the Text property in the Properties list, then click **Text**.
2. Type **Country Charm Inn** and press **Enter**. The new text appears in the property's Settings box and also in the form's title bar.

A form's Name and Text properties always should be changed to more meaningful values. The programmer uses the Name property when coding the application, and the user reads the Text property while the application is running.

The StartPosition Property

When an application is started, the computer uses the form's StartPosition property to determine the form's initial position on the screen. The frm-Splash form represents a splash screen, which typically appears in the middle of the screen.

To center a form on the screen when the application is started:

1. Click **StartPosition** in the Properties list. The down arrow button in the Settings box indicates that the StartPosition property has pre-defined settings.
2. Click the **down arrow** button in the Settings box, then click **CenterScreen** in the list.

The Font Property

A form's Font property determines the type, style, and size of the font used to display the text on the form. A font is the general shape of the characters in the text. Segoe UI, Tahoma, and Microsoft Sans Serif are examples of font types. Font styles include regular, bold, and italic. The numbers 9, 12, and 18 are examples of font sizes, which typically are measured in points, with one point equaling 1/72 of an inch. For applications created for the Windows Vista environment, Microsoft recommends that you use the Segoe UI font, because it offers improved readability. Segoe is pronounced SEE-go, and UI stands for user interface. In most applications, you will use the 9-point size of the font.

To set the form's Font property:

1. Locate the Font property in the Properties list. Click **Font**, then click the **...** (ellipsis) button in the Settings box. The Font dialog box opens.
2. Locate the Segoe UI font in the Font box, then click **Segoe UI**. Click **9** in the Size box, then click the **OK** button. (Don't be concerned that the height of the form changed.)

The Size Property

As you can with any Windows object, you can size a form by selecting it and then dragging the sizing handles that appear around it. You also can size an object by selecting it and then pressing and holding down the Shift key as you press the up, down, right, or left arrow key on your keyboard. In addition, you can set the object's Size property.

To set the form's Size property:

1. Locate the Size property in the Properties list, then click **Size**. Notice that the Size property contains two numbers separated by a comma and a space. The first number represents the width of the form, measured in pixels. The second number represents the height, also measured in pixels. A pixel, which is short for "picture element," is one spot in a grid of thousands of such spots that form an image produced on the screen by a computer or printed on a page by a printer.
2. Type **825, 685** in the Size property's Settings box and press **Enter**. Click the **plus box** that appears next to the Size property to verify that the first number listed in the property represents the width and the second number represents the height, then click the property's **minus box**.

Setting and Restoring the Value of a Property

In the next set of steps, you will practice setting and then restoring a property's value. More specifically, you will set and then restore the value of the form's BackColor property, which determines the background color of the form.

To set and then restore the value of the form's BackColor property:

1. Locate the BackColor property in the Properties list, then click **BackColor**. Click the **down arrow** button in the Settings box. Click the **Custom** tab, then click a **red square**. The background color of the form changes to red.
2. Now restore the BackColor property to its default setting. Right-click **BackColor** in the Properties list, then click **Reset** on the context menu. The background color of the form returns to its default setting. Figure 1-12 shows the status of the form in the IDE.

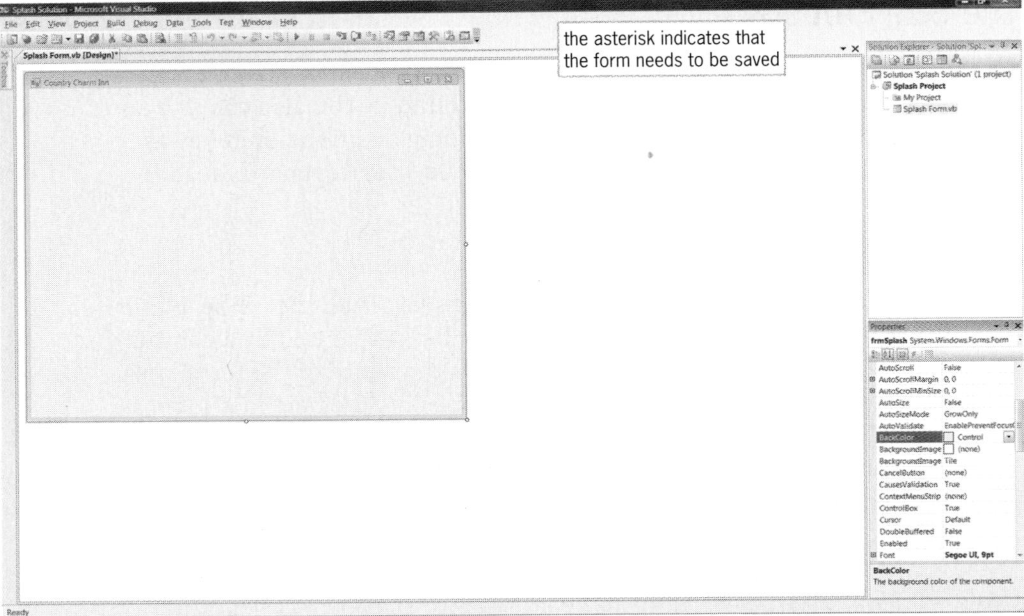

Figure 1-12 Status of the form in the IDE

Saving a Solution

The Save All button on the Standard toolbar looks like this: .

It is a good practice to save the current solution every 10 or 15 minutes so that you will not lose a lot of your work if the computer loses power. You can save the solution by clicking File on the menu bar and then clicking Save All. You also can click the Save All button on the Standard toolbar. When you save the solution, the computer saves any changes made to the files included in the solution. Saving the solution also removes the asterisk that appears on the designer window's tab.

To save the current solution:

1. Click **File** on the menu bar, then click **Save All**. No asterisk appears on the designer window's tab, indicating that all changes made to the form have been saved.

Closing the Current Solution

When you are finished working on a solution, you should close it. Closing a solution closes all projects and files contained in the solution.

To close the Splash Solution:

1. Click **File** on the menu bar. Notice that the menu contains a Close option and a Close Solution option. The Close option does not close the solution; instead, it merely closes the designer window in the IDE. Only the Close Solution option closes the solution.
2. Click **Close Solution**. The Solution Explorer window indicates that no solution is currently open in the IDE.

Opening an Existing Solution

You can use the File menu (or the Start Page) to open an existing solution. If a solution is already open in the IDE, it is closed before another solution is opened.

To open the Splash Solution:

1. Click **File** on the menu bar, then click **Open Project**. The Open Project dialog box opens.
2. Locate and then open the **VB2008\Chap01\Splash Solution** folder. Click **Splash Solution** (**Splash Solution.sln**) in the list of filenames, then click the **Open** button. (The ".sln" on the filename stands for "solution.")
3. The Solution Explorer window indicates that the solution is open. If the designer window is not open, right-click **Splash Form.vb** in the Solution Explorer window, then click **View Designer**.

Exiting Visual Studio 2008 or Visual Basic 2008 Express Edition

Finally, you learn how to exit Visual Studio 2008 or Visual Basic 2008 Express Edition. You will complete the splash screen in the remaining two lessons. You can exit Visual Studio or the Express Edition of Visual Basic using either the Close button on the title bar or the Exit option on the File menu.

To exit Visual Studio 2008 or Visual Basic 2008 Express Edition:

1. Click **File** on the menu bar and then click **Exit**.

Lesson A Summary

- **To start Visual Studio 2008 or Visual Basic 2008 Express Edition:**

  If you are using Visual Studio 2008, click the Start button, point to All Programs, click Microsoft Visual Studio 2008, then click Microsoft Visual Studio 2008. *If you are using Visual Basic 2008 Express Edition*, click the Start button, point to All Programs, then click Microsoft Visual Basic 2008 Express Edition.

- **To create a Visual Basic 2008 Windows application:**

  Start either Visual Studio 2008 or Visual Basic 2008 Express Edition. Click Tools and then click Options. Expand the Projects and Solutions node, if necessary, then click General. If necessary, select the Always show Error List if build finishes with errors, Always show solution, and Save new projects when created check boxes, and deselect the Show Output window when build starts check box. Click the OK button to close the Options dialog box. Click File and then click New Project. If you are using Visual Studio, expand the Visual Basic node, if necessary, then click Windows.

If necessary, click Windows Forms Application. Enter an appropriate name and location in the Name and Location boxes, respectively. If necessary, select the Create directory for solution check box. Enter an appropriate name in the Solution Name box. Click the OK button to close the New Project dialog box.

- **To reset the window layout in the IDE:**

  Click Window on the menu bar, then click Reset Window Layout, and then click the Yes button.

- **To close and open a window in the IDE:**

  Close the window by clicking the Close button on its title bar. Use the appropriate option on the View menu to open the window.

- **To auto-hide a window in the IDE:**

  Click the Auto Hide (vertical pushpin) button on the window's title bar.

- **To temporarily display an auto-hidden window in the IDE:**

  Place your mouse pointer on the window's tab.

- **To permanently display an auto-hidden window in the IDE:**

  Click the Auto Hide (horizontal pushpin) button on the window's title bar.

- **To set the value of a property:**

  Select the object whose property you want to set, then select the appropriate property in the Properties list. Type the new property value in the selected property's Settings box, or choose the value from the list, color palette, or dialog box.

- **To give a more meaningful name to an object:**

  Set the object's Name property.

- **To control the text appearing in the form's title bar and on the application's button on the taskbar when the application is running:**

  Set the form's Text property.

- **To specify the starting location of the form:**

  Set the form's StartPosition property.

- **To specify the type, style, and size of the font used to display text on the form:**

  Set the form's Font property.

- **To size a form:**

  Drag the form's sizing handles. You also can set the form's Size, Height, and Width values in the Properties window. In addition, you can select the form and then press and hold down the Shift key as you press the up, down, left, or right arrow key on your keyboard.

- **To change the background color of a form:**

  Set the form's BackColor property.

- **To restore a property to its default setting:**

  Right-click the property in the Properties list, then click Reset.

- **To save a solution:**

  Click File on the menu bar, then click Save All. You also can click the Save All button on the Standard toolbar.

- **To close a solution:**

  Click File on the menu bar, then click Close Solution.

- **To open an existing solution:**

  Click File on the menu bar, then click Open Project. Locate and then open the application's solution folder. Click the solution filename, which ends with .sln. Click the Open button. If the designer window is not open, right-click the form file's name in the Solution Explorer window, then click View Designer.

- **To exit Visual Studio 2008 or Visual Basic 2008 Express Edition:**

  Click the Close button on the Visual Studio 2008 or Visual Basic 2008 Express Edition title bar. You also can click File on the menu bar and then click Exit.

Lesson A Key Terms

Camel case—used when entering object names in Hungarian notation; refers to the fact that you lowercase the ID characters in the name and then uppercase the first letter of each word in the name

Class definition—a block of code that specifies (defines) an object's appearance and behavior

Code—program instructions

Dot member access operator—the period; used to indicate a hierarchy (such as a hierarchy of namespaces)

Form—the foundation for the user interface in a Windows application

Form file—a source file that contains the code associated with a form

GUI—graphical user interface

IDE—integrated development environment

Integrated development environment—an environment that contains all of the tools and features needed to create, run, and test programs

Namespace—a block of computer memory cells containing the code that defines a group of related classes

Properties—the attributes that determine an object's appearance and behavior

Properties window—the window that displays the properties of the selected object

Solution Explorer window—displays a list of the projects contained in a solution and the items contained in each project

Source file—a file that contains program instructions (code)

User interface—what the user sees and interacts with while an application is running

Windows Form Designer window—the window in which you create (design) an application's user interface

Windows Form object—the form in a Windows application

Lesson A Review Questions

1. You use the ______________________________ window to set the characteristics that control an object's appearance and behavior.
   a. Characteristics
   b. Object
   c. Properties
   d. Windows Form Designer

2. The ______________________________ window lists the projects and files included in a solution.
   a. Object
   b. Project
   c. Properties
   d. Solution Explorer

3. The names of solution files in Visual Basic 2008 end with ______________________________.
   a. .prg
   b. .sln
   c. .src
   d. .vb

4. Which of the following statements is true?
    a. You can auto-hide a window by clicking the Auto-Hide (vertical pushpin) button on its title bar.
    b. An auto-hidden window appears as a tab on the edge of the IDE.
    c. You temporarily display an auto-hidden window by placing your mouse pointer on its tab.
    d. All of the above.

5. The ______________________________ property controls the text displayed in a form's title bar.
    a. Caption
    b. Text
    c. Title
    d. TitleBar

6. You give an object a more meaningful name by setting the object's ______________________________ property.
    a. Application
    b. Caption
    c. Name
    d. Text

7. The ______________________________ property determines the initial position of a form when the application is started.
    a. InitialLocation
    b. Location
    c. StartLocation
    d. StartPosition

8. Explain the difference between a form's Text property and its Name property.

9. Explain the difference between a form file and a form.

10. What does the dot member access operator indicate in the text System.Windows.Forms.Label?

Lesson A Exercises

INTRODUCTORY

1. If necessary, start Visual Studio 2008 or Visual Basic 2008 Express Edition and permanently display the Solution Explorer window. Click File on the menu bar, then click Open Project. Open the Charities Solution (Charities Solution.sln) file, which is contained in the VB2008\Chap01\Charities Solution folder. If necessary, right-click the form file's name in the Solution Explorer window, then click View Designer. Change the form's Name property to frmMain. Change the form's BackColor property to a light blue. Change the form's Font property to Segoe UI, 9pt. Change the form's StartPosition property to CenterScreen and its Text property to Charities Unlimited. Click File on the menu bar, then click Save All to save the solution. Click File on the menu bar, then click Close Solution to close the solution.

INTERMEDIATE

2. If necessary, start Visual Studio 2008 or Visual Basic 2008 Express Edition and permanently display the Solution Explorer window. Create a Visual Basic Windows application. Name the solution, project, and form file Photo Solution, Photo Project, and Main Form.vb, respectively. Save the application in the VB2008\Chap01 folder. Change the form's name to frmMain. The form's title bar should say Photos Incorporated; set the appropriate property. The form should be centered on the screen when it first appears; set the appropriate property. Change the background color of the form to light blue. Any text on the form should appear in the Segoe UI, 9pt font; set the appropriate property. Save and then close the solution.

INTERMEDIATE

3. If necessary, start Visual Studio 2008 or Visual Basic 2008 Express Edition and permanently display the Solution Explorer window. Create a Visual Basic Windows application. Name the solution, project, and form file Yorktown Solution, Yorktown Project, and Main Form.vb. Save the solution in the VB2008\Chap01 folder. Change the form's name to frmMain. The form's title bar should say Yorktown Shopping Center; set the appropriate property, then widen the form. The form should be centered on the screen when it first appears; set the appropriate property. Any text on the form should appear in the Segoe UI, 9pt font; set the appropriate property. Save and then close the solution.

4. In this exercise, you learn about a form's ControlBox, MaximizeBox, and MinimizeBox properties. If necessary, start Visual Studio 2008 or Visual Basic 2008 Express Edition and permanently display the Solution Explorer window. Open the Greenwood Solution (Greenwood Solution.sln) file, which is contained in the VB2008\Chap01\Greenwood Solution folder. If necessary, open the designer window.

   a. Use the Properties window to view the properties of the form. Click the ControlBox property. What is the purpose of this property? (Refer to the Description pane in the Properties window.)

Set the ControlBox property to False. How does this setting affect the form? Set the ControlBox property to True.

b. Click the MaximizeBox property. What is the purpose of this property? Set the MaximizeBox property to False. How does this setting affect the form? Set the MaximizeBox property to True.

c. Click the MinimizeBox property. What is the purpose of this property? Set the MinimizeBox property to False. How does this setting affect the form? Set the MinimizeBox property to True. Close the solution without saving it.

Discovery

5. In this exercise, you research two properties of a form. If necessary, start Visual Studio 2008 or Visual Basic 2008 Express Edition and permanently display the Solution Explorer window. Open the Greenwood Solution (Greenwood Solution.sln) file, which is contained in the VB2008\Chap01\Greenwood Solution folder. If necessary, open the designer window. Use the Properties window to view the properties of the form. What property determines whether an icon is displayed in the form's title bar? What property determines whether the value stored in the form's Text property appears on the Windows taskbar when the application is running? Close the solution without saving it.

LESSON B

After studying Lesson B, you should be able to:

- Add a control to a form
- Set the properties of a label, picture box, and button control
- Select multiple controls
- Center controls on the form
- Open the Project Designer window
- Start and end an application
- Enter code in the Code Editor window
- Terminate an application using the `Me.Close()` instruction
- Run the project's executable file

The Toolbox Window

In Lesson A, you learned about the Windows Form Designer, Solution Explorer, and Properties windows. In this lesson, you will learn about the **Toolbox window**, referred to more simply as the toolbox. The **toolbox** contains the tools you use when creating your application's interface. Each tool represents a class. Recall that a class is a pattern from which one or more objects are instantiated. The tools allow you to instantiate objects such as text boxes, list boxes, and radio buttons. The objects, called **controls**, will appear on the form.

To open the Splash Solution from Lesson A and display the Toolbox window:

1. If necessary, start Visual Studio 2008 or Visual Basic 2008 Express Edition. Close the Start Page window. Open the **Splash Solution** (**Splash Solution.sln**) file, which is contained in the VB2008\Chap01\Splash Solution folder. If necessary, open the designer window.
2. If necessary, permanently display the Properties and Toolbox windows and auto-hide the Solution Explorer window.
3. The contents of the toolbox vary depending on the designer in use. The toolbox shown in Figure 1-13 appears when you are using the Windows Form Designer. Notice that both an icon and a name identify each tool in the toolbox. Rest your mouse pointer on the word ListBox in the toolbox. The tool's purpose appears in a box. See Figure 1-13.

Figure 1-13 Box describing the purpose of the ListBox tool

The Label Tool

You use the Label tool to instantiate a label control. The purpose of a **label control** is to display text that the user is not allowed to edit while the application is running. In this application, for example, you do not want the user to change the name of the inn or the welcome message. Therefore, you will display the information using two label controls.

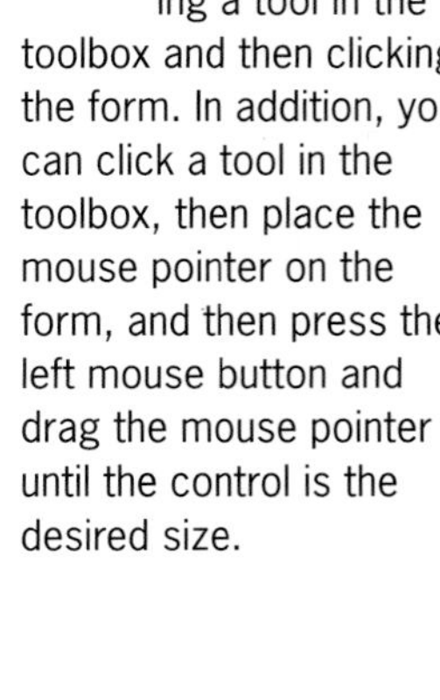

You also can add a control to the form by clicking a tool in the toolbox and then clicking the form. In addition, you can click a tool in the toolbox, then place the mouse pointer on the form, and then press the left mouse button and drag the mouse pointer until the control is the desired size.

To use the Label tool to instantiate a label control:

1. Click the **Label** tool in the toolbox, but do not release the mouse button. Hold down the mouse button as you drag the mouse pointer to the lower-left corner of the form. As you drag the mouse pointer, you will see a solid box, as well as an outline of a rectangle and a plus box, following the mouse pointer. The blue lines that appear between the form's left and bottom borders and the control's left and bottom borders are called margin lines, because their size is determined by the contents of the control's Margin property. The purpose of the margin lines is to assist you in spacing the controls properly on the form. See Figure 1-14.

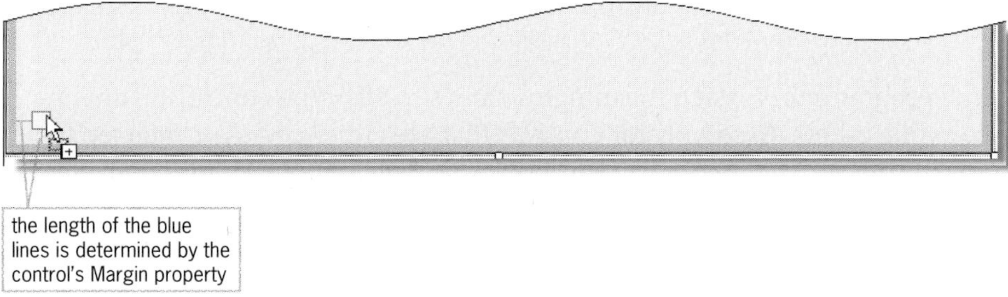

Figure 1-14 Label tool being dragged to the form

2. Release the mouse button. A label control appears on the form. See Figure 1-15. (If the wrong control appears on the form, right-click the control, click Delete, then repeat Steps 1 and 2.) Notice that Label1 System.Windows.Forms.Label appears in the Object box in the Properties window. (You may need to widen the Properties window to view the entire contents of the Object box.) Label1 is the default name assigned to the label control. System.Windows.Forms.Label indicates that the control is an instance of the Label class, which is defined in the System.Windows.Forms namespace.

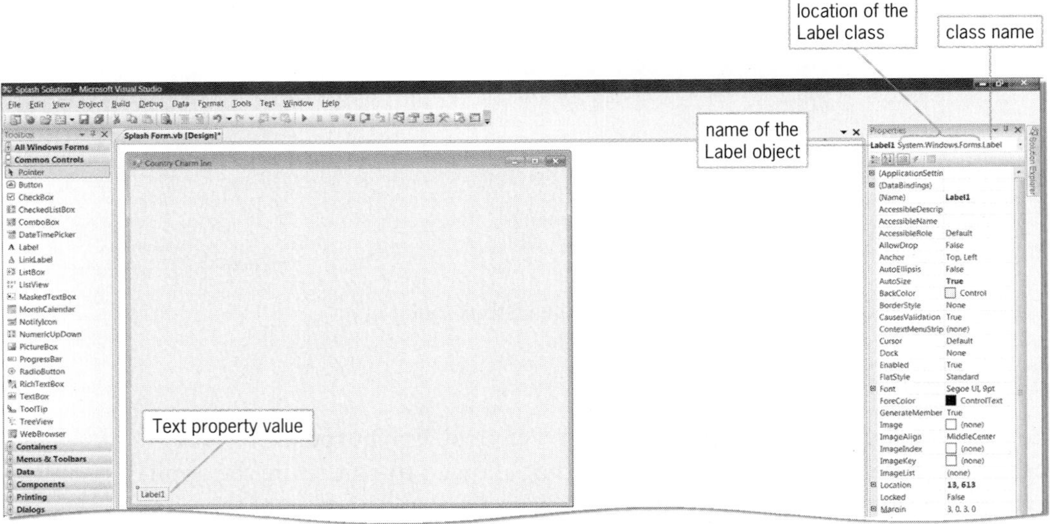

Figure 1-15 Label control added to the form

Recall from Lesson A that a default value is assigned to each of an object's properties when the object is created. Label1 is the default value assigned to the Text and Name properties of the first label control added to a form. The value of the Text property appears inside the label control, as indicated in Figure 1-15.

To add another label control to the form:

1. Click the **Label** tool in the toolbox, then drag the tool to the form, positioning it above the existing label control. (Do not worry about the exact location.)
2. Release the mouse button. Label2 is assigned to the control's Text and Name properties.

Some programmers assign meaningful names to all of the controls in an interface, while others do so only for controls that are either coded or referred to in code; in subsequent chapters in this book, you will follow the latter convention. In this chapter, however, you will assign a meaningful name to each control in the interface. The three-character ID used for naming labels is lbl.

To assign meaningful names to the label controls:

1. Click the **Label1** control on the form. This selects the control and displays its properties in the Properties window. Click **(Name)** in the Properties list. Type **lblName** in the Settings box and press **Enter**.
2. Click the **Label2** control on the form. Click **(Name)** in the Properties list, then type **lblWelcome** and press **Enter**.

Setting the Text Property

As you learned earlier, a label control's Text property determines the value that appears inside the control. In this application, you want the words "Country Charm Inn" to appear in the lblName control, and the words "Welcome to peace and quiet!" to appear in the lblWelcome control.

To set each label control's Text property:

1. Currently, the lblWelcome control is selected on the form. Click **Text** in the Properties list, then type **Welcome to peace and quiet!** and press **Enter**. The new text appears in the Text property's Settings box and in the lblWelcome control. Notice that the designer automatically sizes the lblWelcome control to fit its current contents; this is because the default setting of a Label control's AutoSize property is True. (You can verify that fact by viewing the AutoSize property in the Properties window.)
2. Click the **lblName** control on the form, then click **Text** in the Properties list. Type **Country Charm Inn** and press **Enter**. The lblName control stretches automatically to fit the contents of its Text property.

Setting the Location Property

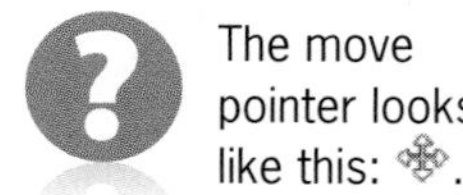

You can move a control to a different location on the form by placing your mouse pointer on the control until it becomes a move pointer, and then dragging the control to the desired location. You also can select the control and then press and hold down the Control (Ctrl) key as you press the up, down, left, or right arrow key on your keyboard. In addition, you can set the control's Location property, which specifies the position of the upper-left corner of the control.

To set each label control's Location property:

1. Click the **lblWelcome** control to select it. Click **Location** in the Properties list, then click the **plus box** next to the property's name. The X value specifies the number of pixels from the left border of the form to the left border of the control. The Y property specifies the number of pixels between the top border of the form and the top border of the control. In other words, the X value refers to the control's horizontal location on the form, whereas the Y value refers to its vertical location.
2. Type **150, 595** in the Location property and press **Enter**. The lblWelcome control moves to its new location. Click the **minus box** next to the Location property's name.
3. In addition to selecting a control by clicking it on the form, you also can select a control by clicking its entry (name and class) in the Object box in the Properties window. Click the **list arrow** button in the Properties window's Object box, and then click **lblName System.Windows.Forms.Label** in the list. Set the control's **Location** property to **150, 560**.

Changing the Property For More Than One Control At a Time

In Lesson A, you changed the form's Font property to Segoe UI, 9pt. When you add a control to the form, the control's Font property is set to the same value as the form's Font property. Using object-oriented programming terminology, the control "inherits" the Font attribute of the form. In this case, for example, the lblName and lblWelcome controls inherit the form's Font property setting: Segoe UI, 9pt. At times, you may want to use a different font type, style, or size for a control's text. One reason for doing this is to bring attention to a specific part of the screen. In the splash screen, for example, you can make the text in the two label controls more noticeable by increasing the size of the font used to display the text. You can change the font size for both controls at the same time by clicking one control and then pressing and holding down the Control key as you click the other control on the form. You can use the Control+click method to select as many controls as you want. To cancel the selection of one of the selected controls, press and hold down the Control key as you click the control. To cancel the selection of all of the selected controls, release the Control key, then click the form or an unselected control on the form. You also can select a group of controls on the form by placing the mouse pointer slightly above and to the left of the first control you want to select, then pressing the left mouse button and dragging. A dotted rectangle appears as you drag. When all of the controls you want to select are within (or at least touched by) the dotted rectangle, release the mouse button. All of the controls surrounded or touched by the dotted rectangle will be selected.

To select both label controls, and then set their Font property:

1. Verify that the lblName control is selected. Press and hold down the **Ctrl** (or Control) key as you click the **lblWelcome** control, then release the Ctrl key. Both controls are selected, as shown in Figure 1-16.

Figure 1-16 Label controls selected on the form

2. Click **Font** in the Properties list, then click the **...** (ellipsis) button in the Settings box. The Font dialog box opens. Click **16** in the Size box, then click the **OK** button. The Font dialog box closes, and the text in the two label controls appears in the new font size.

Using the Format Menu

> To experiment with the Align and Make Same Size options, complete Discovery Exercise 4 at the end of this lesson.

The Format menu provides options for manipulating the controls on the form. The Align option, for example, allows you to align two or more controls by their left, right, top, or bottom borders. You can use the Make Same Size option to make two or more controls the same width and/or height. Before you can use the Format menu to change the alignment or size of two or more controls, you first must select the controls. The first control you select should always be the one whose size and/or location you want to match. For example, to align the left border of the Label1 control with the left border of the Label2 control, you first select the Label2 control and then select the Label1 control. However, to align the left border of the Label2 control with the left border of the Label1 control, you must select the Label1 control before selecting the Label2 control. The first control you select is referred to as the **reference control**. The Format menu also has a Center in Form option that centers one or more controls either horizontally or vertically on the form. In the next set of steps, you will use the Center in Form option to center the two label controls on the form.

To center the label controls horizontally on the form:

1. Click the **form** to deselect the two label controls, then click the **lblName** control. Click **Format** on the menu bar. Point to **Center in Form**, then click **Horizontally**.
2. Click the **lblWelcome** control, then use the Format menu to center the control horizontally on the form.
3. Click **File** on the menu bar, then click **Save All** to save the solution.

The PictureBox Tool

The splash screen you previewed at the beginning of the chapter showed an image of a rural countryside. You can include an image on a form using a **picture box control**, which you instantiate using the PictureBox tool.

To add a picture box control to the form:

1. Click the **PictureBox** tool in the toolbox, then drag the mouse pointer to the upper-left corner of the form, and then release the mouse button. The picture box control's properties appear in the Properties list, and a box containing a triangle appears on the control. The box is referred to as the task box because, when you click it, it displays a list of the tasks associated with the control. Each task in the list is associated with one or more properties. You can set the properties using the task list or the Properties window.
2. Click the **task box** on the PictureBox1 control. See Figure 1-17.

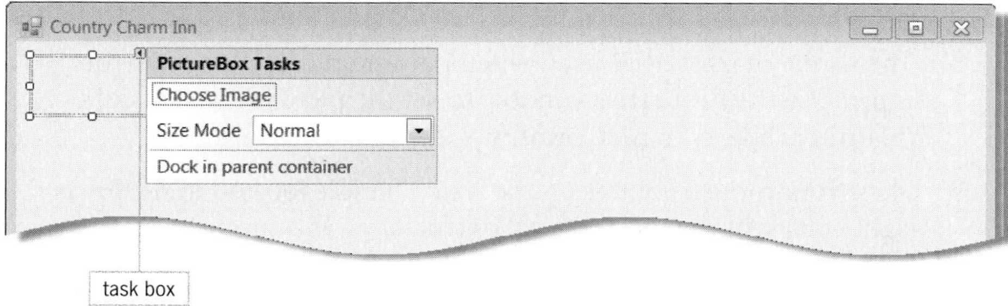

Figure 1-17 Task list for a picture box control

3. Click **Choose Image** to open the Select Resource dialog box. The Choose Image task is associated with the Image property in the Properties window.
4. To include the image file within the project itself, the Project resource file radio button must be selected in the Select Resource dialog box. Verify that the radio button is selected, then click the **Import** button. The Open dialog box opens.
5. The Country Charm image is stored in the Country Charm (Country Charm.jpg) file, which is contained in the VB2008\Chap01 folder. Open the VB2008\Chap01 folder, then click **Country Charm** (**Country Charm.jpg**) in the list of filenames. Click the **Open** button. See Figure 1-18.

Figure 1-18 Completed Select Resource dialog box

6. Click the **OK** button to close the Select Resource dialog box. A small portion of the image appears in the picture box control on the form, and Splash_Project.My.Resources.Resources.Country_Charm appears in the control's Image property in the Properties window.
7. Click the down arrow in the **Size Mode** box in the task list, and then click **StretchImage** in the list. Click the **picture box** control to close the task list.
8. The three-character ID used when naming picture box controls is pic. Use the Properties window to set the picture box control's **(Name)** property to **picCountry**.
9. Place your mouse pointer on the sizing handle located in the lower-right corner of the picture box control. Drag the control to the size shown in Figure 1-19, then release the mouse button. (Or, you can set the control's Size property to 780, 530.)

Figure 1-19 Image shown in the picture box control

The Button Tool

Every application should give the user a way to exit the program. Most Windows applications accomplish this task using either an Exit option on a File menu or an Exit button. In this lesson, the splash screen will provide a button for ending the application. In Windows applications, a **button control** is commonly used to perform an immediate action when clicked. Examples of button controls include the OK and Cancel buttons. You instantiate a button using the Button tool in the toolbox.

To add a button control to the form:

1. Click the **Button** tool in the toolbox. Drag the tool to the lower-right corner of the form, then release the mouse button.
2. The three-character ID used when naming button controls is btn. Set the button control's **(Name)** property to **btnExit**.
3. The button control's Text property determines the text that appears on the button's face. Set the button control's **Text** property to **Exit**.
4. Set the button control's **Size** property to **75, 30**. Set its **Location** property to **715, 600**.
5. Save the solution.

Starting and Ending an Application

Now that the user interface is complete, you can start the splash screen application to see how it will appear to the user. Before you start an application for the first time, you should open the Project Designer window and verify the name of the **startup form**, which is the form that the computer automatically displays each time the application is started. You can open the Project Designer window by right-clicking My Project in the Solution Explorer window, and then clicking Open on the context menu. Or, you can click Project on the menu bar, and then click <*project name*> Properties on the menu.

To verify the name of the startup form:

1. Auto-hide the Toolbox and Properties windows. Temporarily display the Solution Explorer window. Right-click **My Project** in the Solution Explorer window, then click **Open** to open the Project Designer.
2. If necessary, click the **Application** tab to display the Application pane, which is shown in Figure 1-20. If frmSplash does not appear in the Startup form list box, click the **Startup form** list arrow, then click **frmSplash** in the list.

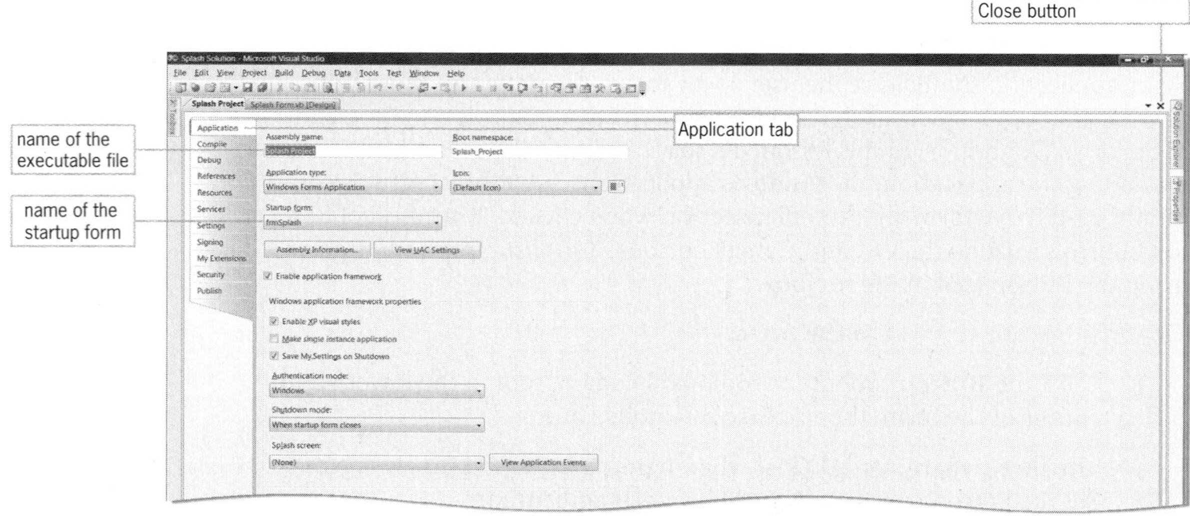

Figure 1-20 Application pane in the Project Designer window

You can start an application by clicking Debug on the menu bar and then clicking Start Debugging. You also can press the F5 key on your keyboard or click the Start Debugging button on the Standard toolbar. When you start a Visual Basic application, the computer automatically creates a file that can be run outside of the IDE (such as from the Run dialog box in Windows). The file is referred to as an **executable file**. The executable file's name is the same as the project's name, except it ends with .exe. The name of the executable file for the Splash Project, for example, is Splash Project.exe. The computer stores the executable file in the project's bin\Debug folder. In this case, the Splash Project.exe file is stored in the VB2008\Chap01\Splash Solution\Splash Project\bin\Debug folder. You can use the Project Designer window to change the name of the executable file.

In most cases, you give the user only the executable file, because it does not allow him or her to modify the application's code. To allow someone to modify the code, you need to provide the entire solution.

To change the name of the executable file, then save the solution and start and end the application:

1. The Project Designer window should still be open. Change the filename in the Assembly name box to **Splash**. Save the solution, then close the Project Designer window by clicking its **Close** button. (See Figure 1-20 for the location of the Close button.)
2. Click **Debug** on the menu bar, then click **Start Debugging** to start the application. See Figure 1-21. (Do not be concerned about any windows that appear at the bottom of the screen.)

Figure 1-21 Result of starting the splash screen application

3. Recall that the purpose of the Exit button is to allow the user to end the application. Click the **Exit** button on the splash screen. Currently, the button will not work as intended, because you have not yet entered the instructions that tell the button how to respond when clicked.
4. At this point, you can stop the application by clicking the Close button on the form's title bar. You also can click the designer window to make it the active window, then click Debug on the menu bar, and then click Stop Debugging. Click the **Close** button on the form's title bar. When the application ends, you are returned to the IDE.

Writing Visual Basic 2008 Code

After creating the interface, you can begin entering the Visual Basic instructions (code) that tell the controls how to respond to the user's actions. Those actions—such as clicking, double-clicking, or scrolling—

are called **events**. You tell an object how to respond to an event by writing an **event procedure**, which is a set of Visual Basic instructions that are processed when a specific event occurs. In this lesson, you will write a Click event procedure for the Exit button, which should end the application when it is clicked.

To open the Code Editor window:

1. Right-click the **form**, then click **View Code** on the context menu. The Code Editor window opens in the IDE, as shown in Figure 1-22. The Code Editor window contains the Visual Basic Class statement, which is used to create a class. In this case, the Class statement begins with the `Public Class frmSplash` clause and ends with the `End Class` clause. Within the Class statement you enter the code to tell the form and its objects how to react to the user's actions.

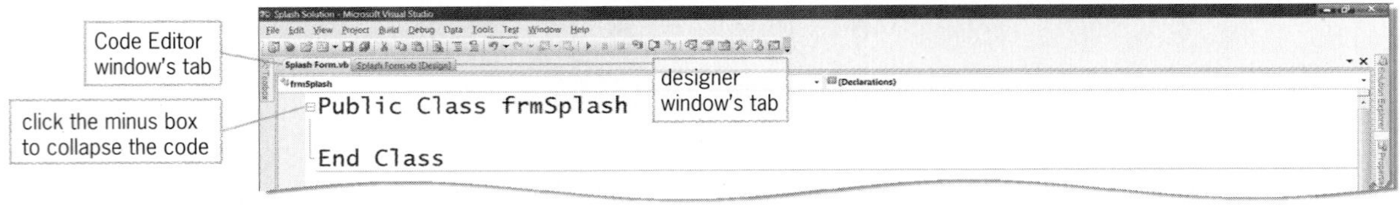

Figure 1-22 Code Editor window opened in the IDE

The `Public` keyword in the Class statement indicates that the class can be used by code defined outside of the class.

If the Code Editor window contains many lines of code, you might want to hide the sections of code that you are not presently working with or that you do not want to print. You hide a section (or region) of code by clicking the minus box that appears next to it. To unhide a region of code, you click the plus box that appears next to the code. Hiding and unhiding code is also referred to as collapsing and expanding the code, respectively.

To collapse and expand a region of code in the Code Editor window:

1. Click the **minus box** that appears next to the `Public Class frmSplash` clause in the Code Editor window. Doing this collapses the Class statement, as shown in Figure 1-23.

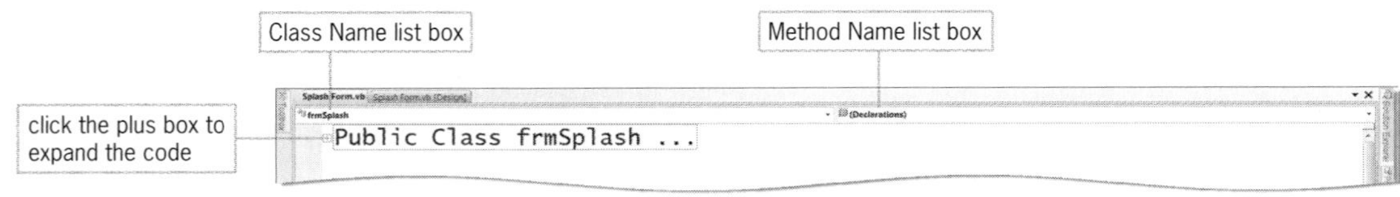

Figure 1-23 Code collapsed in the Code Editor window

2. Now click the **plus box** to expand the code.

As Figure 1-23 indicates, the Code Editor window contains a Class Name list box and a Method Name list box. The Class Name list box lists the names of the objects included in the user interface. The Method Name list box lists the events to which the selected object is capable of responding. In object-oriented programming (OOP), an event is considered a behavior of an object, because it represents an action to which the object can respond. In the context of OOP, the Code Editor window "exposes" an object's behaviors to the programmer. You use the Class Name and Method Name list boxes to select the object and event that you want to code. In this case, for example, you want the Exit button to end the application when the button is clicked. Therefore, you will select btnExit in the Class Name list box and Click in the Method Name list box.

To select the btnExit control's Click event:

1. Click the **Class Name** list arrow, then click **btnExit** in the list.
2. Click the **Method Name** list arrow, then click **Click** in the list. A code template for the btnExit control's Click event procedure appears in the Code Editor window. See Figure 1-24. (The font used to display the text in the Code Editor window shown in the figure was changed to 17-point Lucida Sans Typewriter. It is not necessary for you to change the font.)

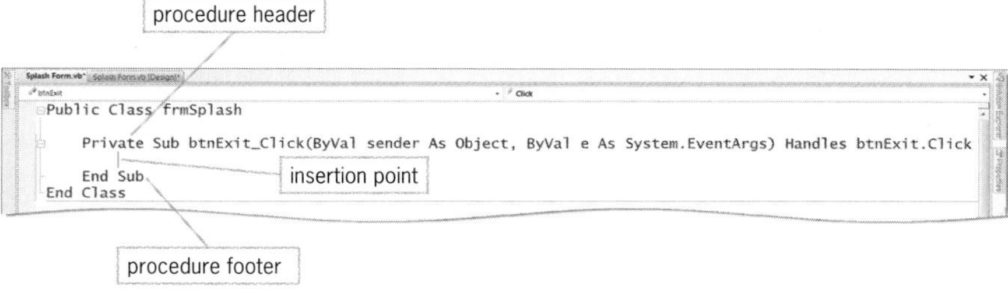

Figure 1-24 Code Editor window showing the btnExit control's Click event procedure

The Code Editor provides the code template to help you follow the rules of the Visual Basic language. The rules of a programming language are called the language's **syntax**. The first line in the code template is called the **procedure header**, and the last line is called the **procedure footer**. The procedure header begins with the two keywords `Private Sub`. A **keyword** is a word that has a special meaning in a programming language. Keywords appear in a different color from the rest of the code. The `Private` keyword indicates that the button's Click event procedure can be used only within the current Code Editor window. The `Sub` keyword is an abbreviation of the term **sub procedure**, which is a block of code that performs a specific task. Following the `Sub` keyword is the name of the object, an underscore, the name of the event, and parentheses containing some text. For now, you do not have to be concerned with the text that appears between the parentheses. After the closing parenthesis is `Handles btnExit.Click`. This part of the procedure header indicates that the procedure handles (or is associated with) the btnExit control's Click event. It tells the computer to process the procedure when the btnExit control is clicked. The code template ends with the procedure footer, which contains the keywords `End Sub`. You enter your Visual Basic instructions at the location of the insertion point, which appears between the Private Sub and End Sub lines in Figure 1-24. The Code Editor automatically indents the line between the procedure header and footer. Indenting the lines within a procedure makes the instructions easier to read and is a common programming practice. In this case, the instruction you enter will tell the btnExit control to end the application when it is clicked.

To change the font used to display text in the Code Editor window, click Tools, then click Options. Expand the Environment node in the Options dialog box, then click Fonts and Colors. Select Text Editor from the Show settings for list box. Select the font type and size, then click the OK button.

The Me.Close() Instruction

The `Me.Close()` instruction tells the computer to close the current form. If the current form is the only form in the application, closing it terminates the entire application. In the instruction, `Me` is a keyword that refers to the current form, and Close is one of the methods available in Visual Basic. A **method** is a predefined procedure that you can call (or invoke) when needed. For example, entering the `Me.Close()` instruction in the btnExit control's Click event procedure tells the computer to close the current form when the user clicks the Exit button. Notice the empty set of parentheses after the method's name in the instruction. The parentheses are required when calling some Visual Basic methods. However, depending on the method, the parentheses may or may not be empty.

> If the list of choices does not appear, click Tools on the menu bar, then click Options. Select the Show all settings check box. Expand the Text Editor node, then click Basic. Select the Auto list members check box, then click the OK button.

To code the btnExit control's Click event procedure:

1. You can type the `Me.Close()` instruction on your own; or you can use the IntelliSense feature that is built into the Code Editor. You will use the IntelliSense feature. Type **m** (but don't press Enter). The Code Editor's IntelliSense feature displays a list of properties, methods, and so on from which you can select. If necessary, click the **Common** tab. See Figure 1-25. The Common tab contains the most commonly used items, whereas the All tab contains all of the items.

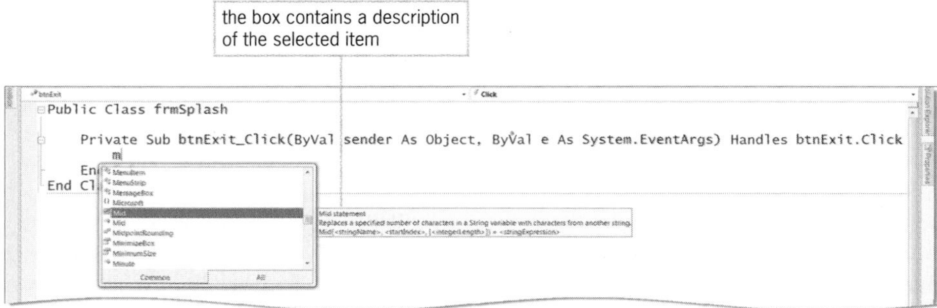

Figure 1-25 List displayed by the IntelliSense feature

2. Type **e.cl** to highlight the Close method in the list. Press **Tab** to include the Close method in the instruction, then press **Enter** to complete the instruction. The Code Editor enters the `Me.Close()` instruction in the procedure. Notice that the Code Editor automatically includes the parentheses after the method's name. See Figure 1-26.

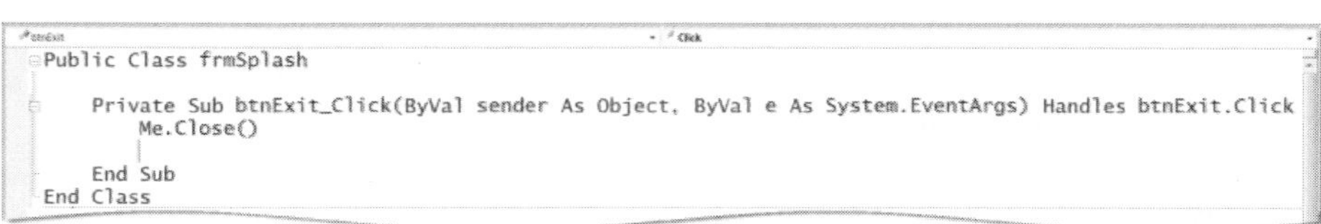

Figure 1-26 Completed Click event procedure for the btnExit control

It's a good programming practice to test a procedure after you have coded it. This way you'll know where to look if an error occurs. You can test the Exit button's Click event procedure by starting the application and then clicking the button. When the button is clicked, the computer will process the `Me.Close()` instruction contained in the procedure.

To test the btnExit control's Click event procedure, and also test the executable file:

1. Save the solution, then press the **F5** key to start the application. The splash screen appears.
2. Click the **Exit** button on the splash screen to end the application. Close the Code Editor window, then close the solution.
3. Press and hold down the **Windows logo** key on your keyboard as you tap the letter **r**, then release the logo key. The Run dialog box opens. Use the **Browse** button to locate and then open the VB2008\Chap01\Splash Solution\Splash Project\bin\Debug folder. Click **Splash** (**Splash.exe**), then click the **Open** button. Click the **OK** button in the Run dialog box. When the splash screen appears, click the **Exit** button.

Lesson B Summary

- **To add a control to a form:**

  Click a tool in the toolbox, but do not release the mouse button. Hold down the mouse button as you drag the tool to the form, then release the mouse button. You also can click a tool in the toolbox and then click the form. In addition, you can click a tool in the toolbox, then place the mouse pointer on the form, and then press the left mouse button and drag the mouse pointer until the control is the desired size.

- **To display text that the user cannot edit while the application is running:**

  Use the Label tool to instantiate a label control, then set the label control's Text property.

- **To move a control to a different location on the form:**

  Drag the control to the desired location. You also can set the control's Location property. In addition, you can select the control and then press and hold down the Control key as you press the up, down, right, or left arrow key on your keyboard.

- **To specify the type, style, and size of the font used to display text in a control:**

  Set the control's Font property.

- **To select multiple controls on a form:**

  Click the first control you want to select, then Ctrl+click each of the other controls you want to select. You also can select a group of controls on the form by placing the mouse pointer slightly above and to the left of the first control you want to select, then pressing the left mouse button and dragging. A dotted rectangle appears as you drag. When all of the controls you want to select are within (or at least touched by) the dotted rectangle, release the mouse button. All of the controls surrounded or touched by the dotted rectangle will be selected.

- **To cancel the selection of one or more controls:**

  You cancel the selection of one control by pressing and holding down the Control key as you click the control. You cancel the selection of all of the selected controls by releasing the Control key and then clicking the form or an unselected control on the form.

- **To center one or more controls on the form:**

  Select the controls you want to center. Click Format on the menu bar, point to Center in Form, and then click either Horizontally or Vertically.

- **To align the borders of two or more controls on the form:**

  Select the reference control, then select the other controls you want to align. Click Format on the menu bar, point to Align, and then click the appropriate option.

- **To make two or more controls on the form the same size:**

  Select the reference control, then select the other controls you want to size. Click Format on the menu bar, point to Make Same Size, and then click the appropriate option.

- **To display a graphic in a control in the user interface:**

  Use the PictureBox tool to instantiate a picture box control, then use the task box or Properties window to set the control's Image and SizeMode properties.

- **To display a standard button that performs an action when clicked:**

  Use the Button tool to instantiate a button control.

- **To verify or change the names of the startup form and/or executable file:**

  Use the Application pane in the Project Designer window. You can open the Project Designer window by right-clicking My Project in the Solution Explorer window, and then clicking Open on the context menu. Or, you can click Project on the menu bar, and then click <*project name*> Properties on the menu.

- **To start and stop an application:**

  You can start an application by clicking Debug on the menu bar, and then clicking Start Debugging. You also can press the F5 key on your keyboard or click the Start Debugging button on the Standard toolbar. You can stop an application by clicking the form's Close button. You also can first make the designer window the active window, and then click Debug on the menu bar and then click Stop Debugging.

- **To open the Code Editor window:**

  Right-click the form, then click View Code on the context menu.

- **To display an object's event procedure in the Code Editor window:**

  Open the Code Editor window. Use the Class Name list box to select the object's name, and then use the Method Name list box to select the event.

- **To allow the user to close the current form while an application is running:**

  Enter the `Me.Close()` instruction in an event procedure.

- **To run a project's executable file:**

  Open the Run dialog box in Windows. Use the Browse button to locate and then open the project's bin\Debug folder. Click the executable file's name, then click the Open button to close the Browse dialog box, and then click the OK button to close the Run dialog box.

Lesson B Key Terms

Button control—used in Windows applications to perform an immediate action when clicked

Controls—the objects added to a form

Event procedure—a set of Visual Basic instructions that tells an object how to respond when a specific event occurs

Events—actions (such as clicking and double clicking) to which an object can respond

Executable file—a file that can be run outside the IDE; created when you start a Visual Basic application

Keyword—a word that has a special meaning in a programming language

Label control—used to display text that the user is not allowed to edit while an application is running

Method—a predefined procedure that you can call (invoke) when needed

Picture box control—used to display an image on a form

Procedure footer—the last line in a procedure

Procedure header—the first line in a procedure

Reference control—the first control selected in a group of controls; this is the control whose size and/or location you want to match

Startup form—the form that appears automatically each time an application is started

Sub procedure—a block of code that performs a specific task

Syntax—the rules of a programming language

Toolbox—refers to the Toolbox window

Toolbox window—contains the tools used when creating a user interface

Lesson B Review Questions

1. The purpose of the ________________ control is to display text that the user is not allowed to edit while the application is running.
   a. Button
   b. DisplayBox
   c. Label
   d. PictureBox

2. The text displayed on a button's face is stored in the button's ________________ property.
   a. Caption
   b. Label
   c. Name
   d. Text

3. The Format menu contains options that allow you to ________________.
   a. align two or more controls
   b. center one or more controls horizontally on the form
   c. make two or more controls the same size
   d. All of the above.

4. You can use the ________________ instruction to terminate a running application.
   a. `Me.Close()`
   b. `Me.Done()`
   c. `Me.Finish()`
   d. `Me.Stop()`

5. Define the term "syntax."

Lesson B Exercises

INTRODUCTORY

1. Open the Mechanics Solution (Mechanics Solution.sln) file, which is contained in the VB2008\Chap01\Mechanics Solution folder. If necessary, open the designer window.
   a. Change the form file's name to Main Form.vb.
   b. Change the form's name to frmMain. Change its Font property to Segoe UI, 9pt. The form's title bar should say IMA; set the appropriate property. The form should be centered on the screen when it first appears; set the appropriate property.
   c. Add a label control to the form. The label control should contain the text "International Mechanics Association" (without the quotation marks); set the appropriate property. Display the label control's text in italics using the Segoe UI, 12pt font. The label control

should be located 16 pixels from the top of the form, and it should be centered horizontally on the form.

d. Add a button control to the form. Change the button control's name to btnExit. The button control should display the text "Exit" (without the quotation marks); set the appropriate property, then size the button. The button control should be located 200 pixels from the left border of the form, and 240 pixels from the top of the form.

e. Open the Code Editor window. Enter the `Me.Close()` instruction in the btnExit control's Click event procedure.

f. Display the Project Designer window. Verify that the name of the startup form is frmMain. Also use the Assembly name box to change the executable file's name to IMA. Close the Project Designer window.

g. Save the solution. Start the application, then use the Exit button to stop the application. Close the Code Editor window, then close the solution.

h. Use the Run dialog box to run the project's executable file.

INTERMEDIATE

2. Create a Visual Basic Windows application. Name the solution, project, and form file Costello Solution, Costello Project, and Main Form.vb, respectively. Save the application in the VB2008\Chap01 folder. Create the user interface shown in Figure 1-27. Change the form's Font property to Segoe UI, 9pt. You can use any font style and size for the label controls. The form should be centered on the screen when the application is started. Code the Exit button so that it closes the application when it is clicked. Use the Project Designer window to verify that the name of the startup form is correct, and to change the executable file's name to Costello Motors. Save the solution. Start the application, then use the Exit button to stop the application. Close the Code Editor window, then close the solution. Use the Run dialog box to run the project's executable file.

Figure 1-27 User interface for the Costello application

INTERMEDIATE

3. Create a Visual Basic Windows application. Name the solution, project, and form file Tabatha Solution, Tabatha Project, and Main Form.vb, respectively. Save the application in the VB2008\Chap01 folder. Create the user interface shown in Figure 1-28. Change the form's Font property to Segoe UI, 9pt. You can use any font style and size for the label control. The form should be centered on the screen when the application is started. Assign appropriate names to the form, label, and button. Code the Exit button so that it closes the application when it is clicked. Use the Project Designer window to verify that the name of the startup form is correct, and to change the executable file's name to Tabatha. Save the solution. Start the application, then use the Exit button to stop the application. Close the Code Editor window, then close the solution. Use the Run dialog box to run the project's executable file.

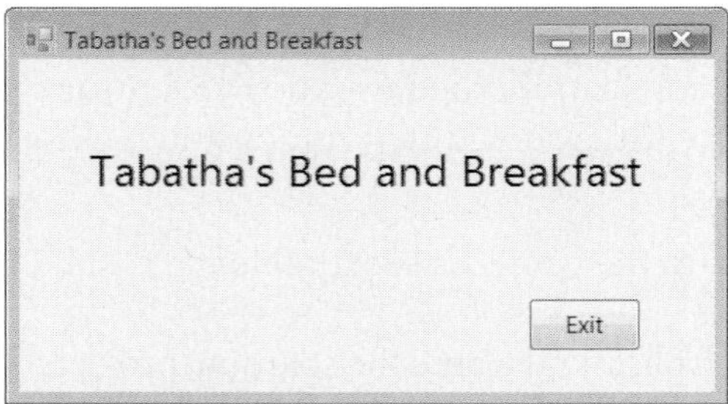

Figure 1-28 User interface for the Tabatha application

Discovery

4. In this exercise, you learn about the Format menu's Align and Make Same Size options. Open the Jerrods Solution (Jerrods Solution.sln) file, which is contained in the VB2008\Chap01\Jerrods Solution folder. If necessary, open the designer window.

   a. Click one of the button controls on the form, then press and hold down the Ctrl (or Control) key as you click the remaining two button controls. Release the Ctrl key. Notice that the sizing handles on the first button you selected are white, while the sizing handles on the other two buttons are black. The Align and Make Same Size options on the Format menu use the control with the white sizing handles as the reference control when aligning and sizing the selected controls. First, practice with the Align option by aligning the three buttons by their left borders. Click Format, point to Align, and then click Lefts. The left borders of the last two buttons you selected are aligned with the left border of the first button you selected.

   b. The Make Same Size option makes the selected objects the same height, width, or both. Here again, the first object you select determines the size. Click the form to deselect the three buttons. Click Button2, then Ctrl+click Button3, and then Ctrl+click Button1. Click Format, point to Make Same Size, and then click Both. The height and width of the last two controls you selected now match the height and width of the first control you selected.

   c. Click the form to deselect the buttons. Save and then close the solution.

LESSON C

After studying Lesson C, you should be able to:

- Set the properties of a timer control
- Delete a control from the form
- Delete code from the Code Editor window
- Code the timer control's Tick event procedure
- Remove and/or disable a form's Minimize, Maximize, and Close buttons
- Prevent the user from sizing a form
- Print the project's code

Using the Timer Tool

In Lesson B, you added an Exit button to the splash screen created for the Country Charm Inn. Splash screens usually do not contain an Exit button. Instead, they use a timer control to automatically remove themselves from the screen after a set period of time. In this lesson, you will remove the Exit button from the splash screen and replace it with a timer control.

To open the Splash Solution from Lesson B:

1. If necessary, start Visual Studio 2008 or Visual Basic 2008 Express Edition and close the Start Page window. Open the **Splash Solution** (**Splash Solution.sln**) file, which is contained in the VB2008\Chap01\Splash Solution folder. If necessary, open the designer window.
2. If necessary, permanently display the Toolbox and Properties windows, and auto-hide the Solution Explorer window.

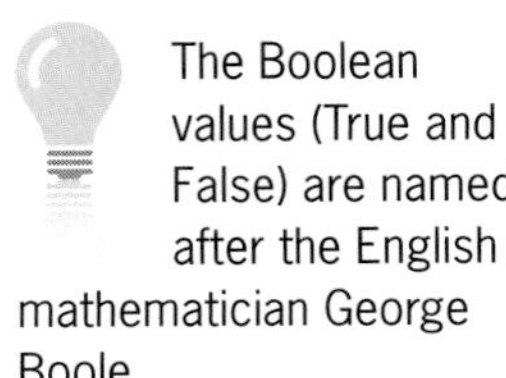

The Boolean values (True and False) are named after the English mathematician George Boole.

You instantiate a timer control using the Timer tool, which is located in the Components section of the toolbox. The purpose of a **timer control** is to process code at one or more regular intervals. The length of each interval is specified in milliseconds and entered in the timer's Interval property. A millisecond is 1/1000 of a second; in other words, there are 1000 milliseconds in a second. A timer's Enabled property, which can be set to either the Boolean value True or the Boolean value False, indicates the timer's state. When its Enabled property is set to True, the timer is running; when it is set to False, the timer is stopped. If the timer is running, its Tick event occurs each time an interval has elapsed. Therefore, you enter the code you want processed in the timer's Tick event procedure. If the timer is stopped, the Tick event does not occur and the code entered in the Tick event procedure is not processed.

When you instantiate a timer control, the control does not appear on the form in the designer window. Instead, it is placed in the component tray, which is a special area in the IDE. The **component tray** stores all controls that do not appear in the user interface when an application is running. In other words, the user will not see the timer when the form appears on the screen.

To add a timer control to the splash screen, and then change its properties:

1. If necessary, expand the Components node in the toolbox. Click the **Timer** tool in the Components section of the toolbox, and then drag the tool to the form. (Do not worry about the exact location.) When you release the mouse button, a timer control appears in the component tray, which is located at the bottom of the IDE.
2. The three-character ID used when naming timer controls is tmr. Set the timer control's **(Name)** property to **tmrExit**, and set its **Enabled** property to **True**.
3. You will have the timer control end the application after eight seconds, which are 8000 milliseconds. Set the timer control's **Interval** property to **8000**. See Figure 1-29.

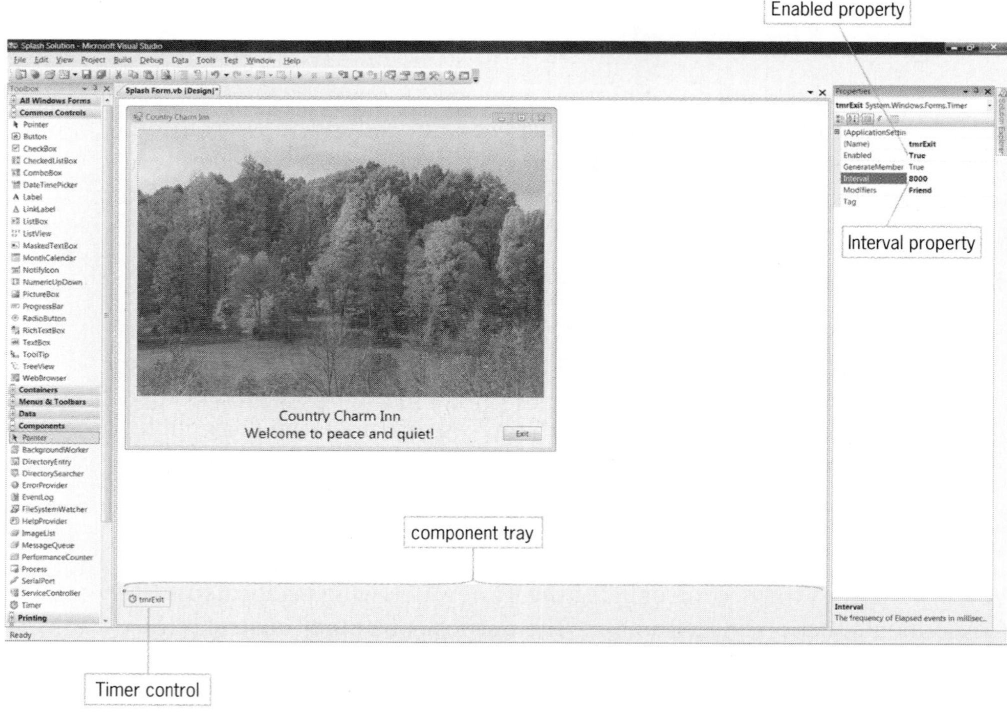

Figure 1-29 Timer control placed in the component tray

Now that you have a timer control on the form, you no longer need the Exit button; so you can delete it and its associated code. You then will enter the `Me.Close()` instruction in the timer's Tick event procedure.

To delete the Exit button and its code, and then code the tmrExit control:

1. Auto-hide the Toolbox and Properties windows. Click the **Exit** button to select it, then press **Delete** to delete the control from the form.
2. Deleting a control from the form does not delete the control's code, which remains in the Code Editor window. Open the Code Editor window by right-clicking the **form**, and then clicking **View Code**. Select (highlight) the entire Click event procedure for the btnExit control, as shown in Figure 1-30.

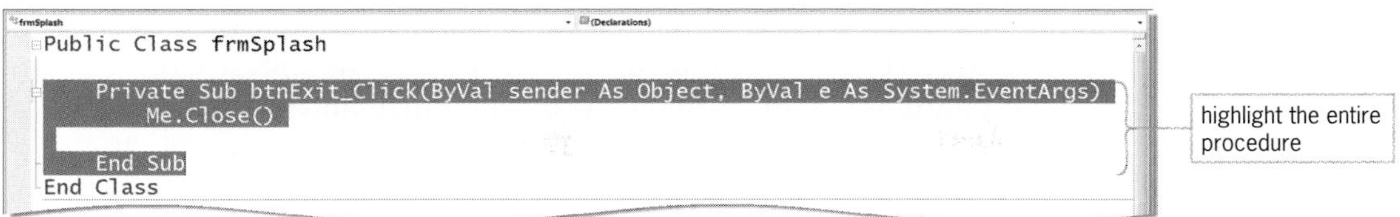

Figure 1-30 The Exit button's Click event procedure selected in the Code Editor window

3. Press **Delete** to delete the selected code from the Code Editor window.
4. Now enter the `Me.Close()` instruction in the timer's Tick event procedure. Click the **Class Name** list arrow, then click **tmrExit** in the list. Click the **Method Name** list arrow, then click **Tick** in the list. The tmrExit control's Tick event procedure appears in the Code Editor window. Type **me.close** and press **Enter**.
5. Click the **Save All** button to save the solution, then press the **F5** key on your keyboard to start the application. The splash screen appears on the screen.
6. Place your mouse pointer on the right border of the form until it becomes a sizing pointer, then drag the form's border to the left. Notice that you can size the form while the application is running. Typically, a user is not allowed to change the size of a splash screen. You can prevent the user from sizing the form by changing the form's FormBorderStyle property, which you will do in the next set of steps.

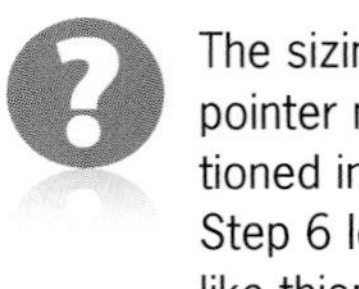

The sizing pointer mentioned in Step 6 looks like this: ⇔.

7. When eight seconds have elapsed, the application ends and the splash screen disappears. Click the **Splash Form.vb [Design]** tab to make the designer window the active window.

Setting the FormBorderStyle Property

A form's FormBorderStyle property determines the border style of the form. For most applications, you will leave the property at its default setting, Sizable. Doing this allows the user to change the form's size by dragging its borders while the application is running. When a form represents a splash screen, however, you typically set the FormBorderStyle property to either None or FixedSingle. The None setting removes the form's border, whereas the FixedSingle setting draws a fixed, thin line around the form.

To change the FormBorderStyle property, then save and start the application:

1. Click the **form's title bar** to select the form. Temporarily display the Properties window, then set the **FormBorderStyle** property to **FixedSingle**.
2. Save the solution, then start the application. Try to size the form by dragging one of its borders. You will notice that you cannot size the form using its border.

3. When eight seconds have elapsed, the application ends. Press the **F5** key to start the application again. Notice that the splash screen's title bar contains a Minimize button, a Maximize button, and a Close button. As a general rule, most splash screens do not contain these elements. You will learn how to remove the elements, as well as the title bar itself, in the next section. Here again, the application ends after eight seconds have elapsed.

The MinimizeBox, MaximizeBox, and ControlBox Properties

You can use a form's MinimizeBox property to disable the Minimize button that appears on the form's title bar. Similarly, you can use the MaximizeBox property to disable the Maximize button. You experiment with both properties in the next set of steps.

To experiment with the MinimizeBox and MaximizeBox properties:

1. If necessary, click the **form's title bar** to select the form. First, you will disable the Minimize button. Set the form's **MinimizeBox** property to **False**. Notice that the Minimize button appears dimmed (grayed-out) on the title bar. This indicates that the button is not available for use.
2. Now you will enable the Minimize button and disable the Maximize button. Set the **MinimizeBox** property to **True**, then set the **MaximizeBox** property to **False**. Now only the Maximize button appears dimmed (grayed-out) on the title bar.
3. Now observe what happens if both the MinimizeBox and MaximizeBox properties are set to False. Set the **MinimizeBox** property to **False**. (The MaximizeBox property is already set to False.) Notice that when both properties are set to False, the buttons are not disabled; instead, they are removed from the title bar.
4. Now return the buttons to their original state. Set the **MinimizeBox** and **MaximizeBox** properties to **True**.

Unlike most applications, splash screens typically do not contain a title bar. You can remove the title bar by setting the form's ControlBox property to False, and then removing the text from its Text property. You will try this next.

To remove the title bar from the splash screen:

1. Set the form's **ControlBox** property to **False**. This removes the title bar elements (icon and buttons) from the form; however, it does not remove the title bar itself. To remove the title bar, you must delete the contents of the form's Text property. Select the text in the Text property, then press the **Delete** key, and then press **Enter**.

2. Save the solution, then start the application. The splash screen appears without a title bar. See Figure 1-31. The application ends after eight seconds have elapsed.

Country Charm Inn
Welcome to peace and quiet!

Figure 1-31 Completed splash screen

Printing Your Code

You always should print a copy of your application's code, because the printout will help you understand and maintain the application in the future. To print the code, the Code Editor window must be the active (current) window.

To print the splash screen's code:

1. Click the **Splash Form.vb** tab to make the Code Editor window the active window. Click **File** on the menu bar, then click **Print**. The Print dialog box opens. See Figure 1-32. Notice that you can include line numbers in the printout. You also can choose to hide the collapsed regions of code. Currently, the Hide collapsed regions check box is grayed-out, indicating that no code is collapsed in the Code Editor window.

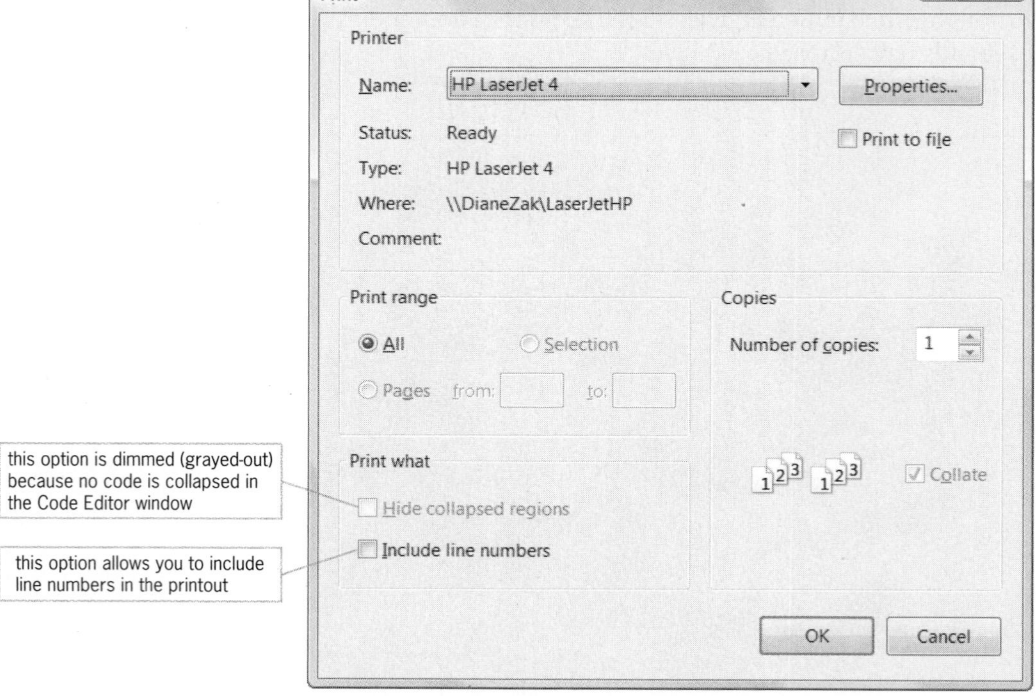

Figure 1-32 Print dialog box

2. If your computer is connected to a printer, click the **OK** button to begin printing; otherwise, click the **Cancel** button. If you clicked the OK button, your printer prints the code.
3. Close the Code Editor window, then close the solution and exit Visual Studio 2008 or Visual Basic 2008 Express Edition.

Lesson C Summary

- **To process code at specified intervals of time:**

  Use the Timer tool to instantiate a timer control. Set the timer's Interval property to the number of milliseconds for each interval. Set the timer's Enabled property to True to turn the timer on. Enter the code in the timer's Tick event procedure.

- **To delete a control:**

  Select the control you want to delete, then press Delete. If the control contains code, open the Code Editor window and delete the code contained in the control's event procedures.

- **To control the border style of the form:**

  Set the form's FormBorderStyle property.

- **To enable/disable the Minimize button on the form's title bar:**

  Set the form's MinimizeBox property.

- **To enable/disable the Maximize button on the form's title bar:**

  Set the form's MaximizeBox property.

- **To control whether the icon, as well as the Minimize, Maximize, and Close buttons, appear in the form's title bar:**

  Set the form's ControlBox property.

- **To print the Visual Basic code:**

  Open the Code Editor window. Collapse any code you do not want to print. Click File on the menu bar, and then click Print. If you don't want to print the collapsed code, select the Hide collapsed regions check box. If you want to print line numbers, select the Include line numbers check box. Click the OK button in the Print dialog box.

Lesson C Key Terms

Component tray—a special area in the IDE; stores controls that do not appear in the interface while an application is running

Timer control—used to process code at one or more regular intervals

Lesson C Review Questions

1. The code in a timer's ______________________________ event procedure is processed after each time interval has elapsed.
   a. Interval
   b. Tick
   c. Timed
   d. Timer

2. Which of the following is false?
   a. When you add a timer control to a form, the control appears in the component tray.
   b. The user can see a timer control while the application is running.
   c. You stop a timer by setting its Enabled property to False.
   d. The number entered in a timer control's Interval property represents the number of milliseconds for each interval.

3. To disable the Minimize button on a form's title bar, set the form's ______________________ property to False.
   a. ButtonMinimize
   b. Minimize
   c. MinimizeBox
   d. MinimizeButton

4. You can remove the Minimize, Maximize, and Close buttons from a form's title bar by setting the form's ______________________ property to False.
   a. ControlBox
   b. ControlButton
   c. TitleBar
   d. TitleBarElements

5. Explain how you delete a control that contains code.

Lesson C Exercises

INTRODUCTORY

1. In this exercise, you modify an existing form by replacing its Exit button control with a timer control. Open the Jefferson Solution (Jefferson Solution.sln) file, which is contained in the VB2008\Chap01\Jefferson Solution folder. If necessary, open the designer window.
   a. Delete the Exit button from the form, then delete the btnExit control's code from the Code Editor window.
   b. Return to the designer window. Add a timer control to the form. Change the timer control's name to tmrExit. Set the timer control's Enabled property to True. The timer control should end the application after 10 seconds have elapsed; set the appropriate property. Enter the `Me.Close()` instruction in the appropriate event procedure in the Code Editor window.
   c. Save the solution, then start the application. When 10 seconds have elapsed, the application ends.
   d. Remove the elements (icon and buttons) from the form's title bar. Delete the text that appears in the form's title bar. Set the form's FormBorderStyle property to FixedSingle.
   e. Save the solution, then start the application. After 10 seconds, the application ends. Close the Code Editor window, then close the solution.

INTERMEDIATE

2. In this exercise, you design your own user interface. Create a Visual Basic Windows application. Name the solution, project, and form file My Splash Solution, My Splash Project, and My Splash Form.vb. Save the application in the VB2008\Chap01 folder. Create your own splash

screen. Save the solution, then start the application. When the application ends, close the Code Editor window, then close the solution.

Discovery

3. In this exercise, you learn how to enter an assignment statement in an event procedure.

   a. Create a Visual Basic Windows application. Name the solution, project, and form file OnOff Solution, OnOff Project, and Main Form.vb. Save the application in the VB2008\Chap01 folder. Change the form's name to frmMain.

   b. Add a picture box control and three buttons to the form. (The location and size of the controls are not important.) Name the controls picIcon, btnOn, btnOff, and btnExit. Include any graphic in the picture box control; or, you can use the Logo.bmp file contained in the VB2008\Chap01 folder.

   c. The captions for the three buttons should be On, Off, and Exit. Change the appropriate property for each button.

   d. The Exit button should end the application when clicked. Enter the appropriate code in the Code Editor window.

   e. Display the btnOff control's Click event procedure in the Code Editor window. In the procedure, enter the instruction `picIcon.Visible = False`. This instruction is called an assignment statement, because it assigns a value to a container. In this case, the container is the Visible property of the picIcon control. When you click the btnOff control, the assignment statement will hide the picture box from view.

   f. Display the btnOn control's Click event procedure in the Code Editor window. In the procedure, enter an instruction that will display the picture box.

   g. Save the solution, then start the application. Use the Off button to hide the picture box, then use the On button to display the picture box. Finally, use the Exit button to end the application. Close the Code Editor window, then close the solution.

Discovery

4. In this exercise, you learn how to display a graphic on the face of a button control.

   a. Use Windows to make a copy of the OnOff Solution folder from Discovery Exercise 3. The folder is contained in the VB2008\Chap01 folder. Rename the folder Modified OnOff Solution.

   b. Open the OnOff Solution (OnOff Solution.sln) file contained in the VB2008\Chap01\Modified OnOff Solution folder. Open the designer window.

c. You use a button's Image property to specify the graphic you want displayed on the face of the button. You use a button's ImageAlign property to specify the graphic's alignment on the button. Click the On button. Set the Image property to any graphic file. Set the On button's ImageAlign property to TopLeft. (Hint: When you click the ImageAlign property's down arrow, nine buttons will appear in the list. Select the button in the top left corner.) Set the Image and ImageAlign properties of the Off and Exit buttons. (Use any small graphics for the Image properties.)

d. Save the solution, then start the application. Test each button, then close the solution.

Discovery

5. In this exercise, you learn how to display a tooltip. Open the ToolTip Solution (ToolTip Solution.sln) file, which is contained in the VB2008\Chap01\ToolTip Solution folder. If necessary, open the designer window. Click the ToolTip tool in the toolbox, then drag the tool to the form. Notice that a tooltip control appears in the component tray rather than on the form. Click the btnExit control to select it. Set the button's ToolTip on ToolTip1 property to "Ends the application." (without the quotation marks). Save the solution, then start the application. Hover your mouse pointer over the Exit button. The tooltip "Ends the application." appears in a tooltip box. Click the Exit button to end the application, then close the solution.

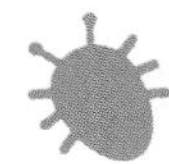

Swat The Bugs

6. Open the Debug Solution (Debug Solution.sln) file, which is contained in the VB2008\Chap01\Debug Solution folder. If necessary, open the designer window. Start the application. Click the Exit button. Notice that the Exit button does not end the application. Click the Close button on the form's title bar. Locate and then correct the error. Save the solution, then start the application. Click the Exit button, which should end the application. Close the Code Editor window, then close the solution.

CHAPTER 2

Designing Applications

Creating the Playtime Cellular Application

In this chapter, you create an application for Playtime Cellular, a small company that sells toy cell phones for children. The phones are priced at $25 each and are available in two colors: blue and pink. The application will allow the salespeople to enter the customer's name and address, as well as the number of blue and pink phones ordered. It then will calculate and display the total number of phones ordered and the total price of the order.

Previewing the Playtime Cellular Application

To open the Run dialog box, press and hold down the Windows logo key as you tap the letter r, then release the logo key.

To preview the completed Playtime Cellular application:

1. Open the Run dialog box. Use the **Browse** button to locate and then open the VB2008\Chap02 folder. Click **Playtime Cellular** (**Playtime Cellular.exe**) in the list of filenames, then click the **Open** button. Click the **OK** button in the Run dialog box. (If a Security Warning dialog box appears, click Run.) The interface shown in Figure 2-1 appears. In addition to the picture box, label, and button controls that you learned about in Chapter 1, the interface contains seven text boxes. A text box provides an area in the form for the user to enter data.

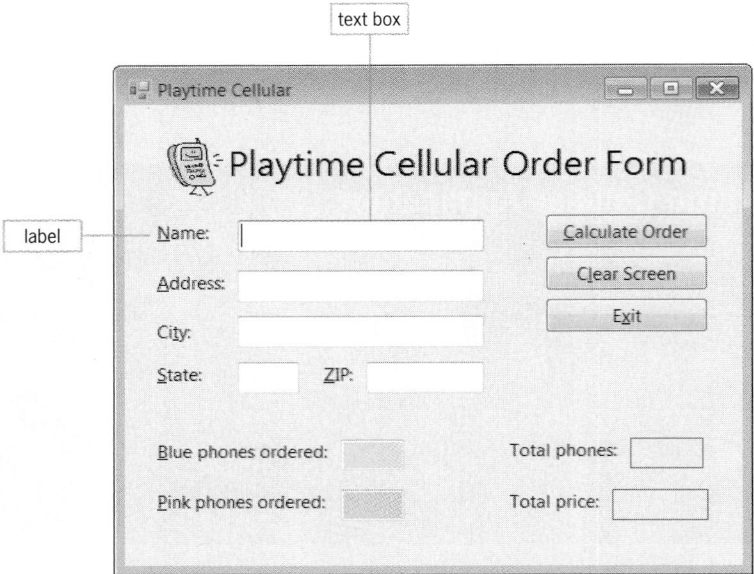

Figure 2-1 Order screen for Playtime Cellular

2. The insertion point is located in the first text box. The label control to the left of the text box identifies the information the user should enter. In this case, the user should enter the customer's name. Type **Ray's Toys** as the customer's name, then press **Tab** twice. The insertion point appears in the City text box.

3. Type **Chicago** as the city name, then press **Shift+Tab** (press and hold down the Shift key as you tap the Tab key) to move the insertion point to the Address text box. Type **2467 Grove Avenue** as the address, then press **Tab** twice. Type **IL** as the state, then press **Tab**. Type **60634** as the ZIP code, then press **Tab** to position the insertion point in the Blue phones ordered text box.

4. Type **10** as the number of blue phones ordered, then click the **Calculate Order** button. The Calculate Order button calculates and displays the total phones (10) and total price ($250.00).

5. Click the **Pink phones ordered** text box, type **20**, then click the **Calculate Order** button. The application recalculates the total phones (30) and total price ($750.00).

6. Change the number of blue phones ordered from 10 to **35**, then click the **Calculate Order** button. The application recalculates the total phones (55) and total price ($1,375.00). See Figure 2-2.

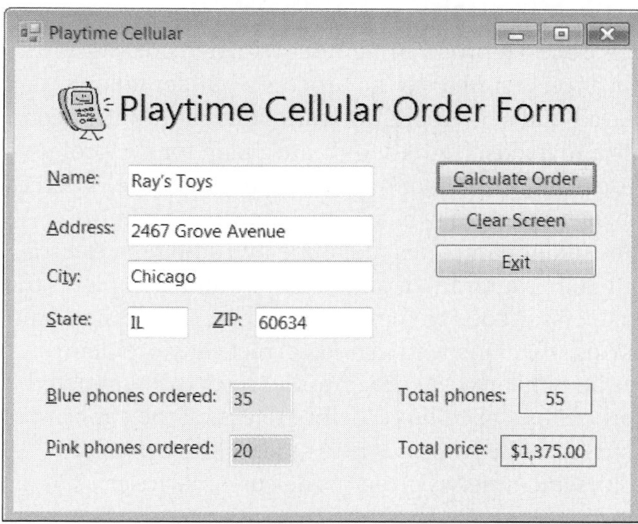

Figure 2-2 Completed order form

7. Click the **Clear Screen** button to remove the customer's information from the order form, then click the **Exit** button to end the application.

The Playtime Cellular application is an object-oriented program, because it uses objects (such as buttons and text boxes) to accomplish its goal. In Lesson A, you will learn how a programmer plans an object-oriented program. You will create the Playtime Cellular application in Lessons B and C. Be sure to complete each lesson in full and do all of the end-of-lesson questions and several exercises before moving on to the next lesson.

LESSON A

After studying Lesson A, you should be able to:

- Plan an object-oriented application in Visual Basic 2008
- Complete a TOE (Task, Object, Event) chart
- Follow the Windows standards regarding the layout and labeling of controls

Creating an Object-Oriented Application

As Figure 2-3 indicates, the process a programmer follows when creating an object-oriented (OO) application is similar to the process a builder follows when building a home. Like a builder, a programmer first meets with the client to discuss the client's wants and needs. Both then create a plan for the project. After the client approves the plan, the builder builds the home's frame, whereas the programmer builds the user interface, which is the application's frame. Once the frame is built, the builder completes the home by adding the electrical wiring, walls, and so on. The programmer, on the other hand, completes the application by adding the necessary code to the user interface. When the home is complete, the builder makes a final inspection and corrects any problems before the customer moves in. Similarly, the programmer tests the completed application and fixes any problems, called **bugs**, before releasing the application to the user. The final step in both processes is to assemble the project's documentation (paperwork), which then is given to the customer/user.

A builder's process	A programmer's process
1. Meet with the client	1. Meet with the client
2. Plan the home (blueprint)	2. Plan the application (TOE chart)
3. Build the frame	3. Build the user interface
4. Complete the home	4. Code the application
5. Inspect the home and fix any problems	5. Test and debug the application
6. Assemble the documentation	6. Assemble the documentation

Figure 2-3 Processes used by a builder and a programmer

You will learn how to plan an OO application in this lesson. Steps three through six of the process are covered in Lessons B and C.

Planning an Object-Oriented Application

As any builder will tell you, the most important aspect of a home is not its beauty. Rather, it is how closely the home matches the buyer's wants and needs. The same is true of an OO application. For an application to fulfill the wants and needs of the user, it is essential for the programmer to plan the application jointly with the user. It cannot be stressed enough that the only way to guarantee the success of an application is to actively involve the user in the planning phase. The steps for planning an OO application are listed in Figure 2-4.

1. Identify the tasks the application needs to perform.
2. Identify the objects to which you will assign the tasks.
3. Identify the events required to trigger an object into performing its assigned tasks.
4. Draw a sketch of the user interface.

Figure 2-4 Steps for planning an OO application

You can use a TOE (Task, Object, Event) chart to record the application's tasks, objects, and events, which are identified in the first three steps of the planning phase. In the next section, you begin completing a TOE chart for the Playtime Cellular application. The first step is to identify the application's tasks.

Identifying the Application's Tasks

Realizing that it is essential to involve the user when planning the application, you meet with the sales manager of Playtime Cellular, Ms. Garrison, to determine her requirements. You ask Ms. Garrison to bring the form the salespeople currently use to record the orders. Viewing the current forms and procedures will help you gain a better understanding of the application. You also can use the current form as a guide when designing the user interface. Figure 2-5 shows the current order form used by the company.

Playtime Cellular Order Form

Customer name: __________

Address: __________

City: __________ State: __________ ZIP: __________

Number of blue phones ordered	Number of pink phones ordered	Total number of phones ordered	Total price

Figure 2-5 Current order form used by Playtime Cellular

When identifying the tasks an application needs to perform, it is helpful to ask the following questions:

- What information will the application need to display on the screen and/or print on the printer?
- What information will the user need to enter into the interface to display and/or print the desired information?
- What information will the application need to calculate to display and/or print the desired information?

- How will the user end the application?
- Will previous information need to be cleared from the screen before new information is entered?

The answers to these questions will help you identify the application's major tasks. The answers for each question for the Playtime Cellular application are as follows.

What information will the application need to display on the screen and/or print on the printer? The Playtime Cellular application should display the customer's name, street address, city, state, ZIP code, number of blue phones ordered, number of pink phones ordered, total number of phones ordered, and total price of the order. In this case, the application does not need to print anything on the printer.

What information will the user need to enter into the interface to display and/or print the desired information? In the Playtime Cellular application, the salesperson (the user) must enter the customer's name, street address, city, state, ZIP code, and number of blue and pink phones ordered.

What information will the application need to calculate to display and/or print the desired information? The Playtime Cellular application needs to calculate the total number of phones ordered and the total price of the order.

How will the user end the application? In Chapter 1, you learned that all applications should provide a way for the user to end the application. The Playtime Cellular application will use an Exit button for this task.

Will previous information need to be cleared from the screen before new information is entered? After the salesperson enters and calculates an order, he or she will need to clear the customer's information from the screen before entering the next order.

Figure 2-6 shows the Playtime Cellular application's tasks listed in a TOE chart. The tasks do not need to be listed in any particular order. In this case, the data entry tasks are listed first, followed by the calculation tasks, display tasks, application ending task, and screen clearing task.

You can either draw a TOE chart by hand or use the table feature in a word processor (such as Microsoft Word).

Task	**Object**	**Event**
Get the following order information from the user:		
Customer's name		
Street address		
City		
State		
ZIP code		
Number of blue phones ordered		
Number of pink phones ordered		

Figure 2-6 Tasks entered in a TOE chart *(continues)*

(continued)

Task	Object	Event
Calculate total phones ordered and total price		
Display the following information:		
Customer's name		
Street address		
City		
State		
ZIP code		
Number of blue phones ordered		
Number of pink phones ordered		
Total phones ordered		
Total price		
End the application		
Clear screen for the next order		

Figure 2-6 Tasks entered in a TOE chart

Identifying the Objects

After completing the Task column of the TOE chart, you then assign each task to an object in the user interface. For this application, the only objects you will use besides the Windows form itself are the button, label, and text box controls. As you learned in Chapter 1, you use a label control to display information that you do not want the user to change while the application is running, and you use a button control to perform an action immediately after the user clicks it. You use a text box to give the user an area in which to enter data.

The first task listed in Figure 2-6 is to get the order information from the user. For each order, the salesperson will need to enter the customer's name, address, city, state, and ZIP code, as well as the number of blue phones ordered and the number of pink phones ordered. Because you need to provide the salesperson with areas in which to enter the information, you will assign the first task to seven text boxes—one for each item of information. The three-character ID used when naming text boxes is txt, so you will name the text boxes txtName, txtAddress, txtCity, txtState, txtZip, txtBlue, and txtPink.

The second task listed in the TOE chart is to calculate both the total number of phones ordered and the total price. So that the salesperson can calculate these amounts at any time, you will assign the task to a button named btnCalc.

The third task listed in the TOE chart is to display the order information, the total number of phones ordered, and the total price. The order information will be displayed automatically when the user enters that information in the seven text boxes. The total phones ordered and the total price, however, are not entered by the user. Rather, those amounts will be calculated by the btnCalc control. Because the user should not be allowed to change the calculated results, you will have the btnCalc control display the total phones ordered and the total price in two label controls named lblTotalPhones and lblTotalPrice. Notice that the task of displaying the total phones ordered involves two objects: btnCalc and lblTotalPhones. The task of displaying the total price also involves two objects: btnCalc and lblTotalPrice.

The last two tasks listed in the TOE chart are "End the application" and "Clear the screen for the next order." You will assign the tasks to buttons so that the user has control over when the tasks are performed. The buttons will be named btnExit and btnClear. Figure 2-7 shows the TOE chart with the Task and Object columns completed.

Task	**Object**	**Event**
Get the following order information from the user:		
Customer's name	txtName	
Street address	txtAddress	
City	txtCity	
State	txtState	
ZIP code	txtZip	
Number of blue phones ordered	txtBlue	
Number of pink phones ordered	txtPink	
Calculate total phones ordered and total price	btnCalc	
Display the following information:		
Customer's name	txtName	
Street address	txtAddress	
City	txtCity	
State	txtState	
ZIP code	txtZip	
Number of blue phones ordered	txtBlue	
Number of pink phones ordered	txtPink	
Total phones ordered	btnCalc, lblTotalPhones	
Total price	btnCalc, lblTotalPrice	
End the application	btnExit	
Clear screen for the next order	btnClear	

Figure 2-7 Tasks and objects entered in a TOE chart

Identifying the Events

After defining the application's tasks and assigning the tasks to objects in the interface, you then determine which event (if any) must occur for an object to do its assigned task. The seven text boxes listed in the TOE chart in Figure 2-7 are assigned the task of getting and displaying the order information. Text boxes accept and display information automatically, so no special event is necessary for them to do their assigned task. The two label controls listed in the TOE chart are assigned the task of displaying the total number of phones ordered and the total price of the order. Label controls automatically display their contents; so, here again, no special event needs to occur. (Recall that the two label controls will get their values from the btnCalc control.) The remaining objects listed in the TOE chart are the three buttons: btnCalc, btnClear, and btnExit. You will have the buttons perform their assigned tasks when the user clicks them. Figure 2-8 shows the completed TOE chart for the Playtime Cellular application.

Task	**Object**	**Event**
Get the following order information from the user:		
Customer's name	txtName	None
Street address	txtAddress	None
City	txtCity	None
State	txtState	None
ZIP code	txtZip	None
Number of blue phones ordered	txtBlue	None
Number of pink phones ordered	txtPink	None
Calculate total phones ordered and total price	btnCalc	Click
Display the following information:		
Customer's name	txtName	None
Street address	txtAddress	None
City	txtCity	None
State	txtState	None
ZIP code	txtZip	None
Number of blue phones ordered	txtBlue	None
Number of pink phones ordered	txtPink	None
Total phones ordered	btnCalc, lblTotalPhones	Click, None
Total price	btnCalc, lblTotalPrice	Click, None
End the application	btnExit	Click
Clear screen for the next order	btnClear	Click

Figure 2-8 Completed TOE chart ordered by task

If the application you are creating is small, as is the Playtime Cellular application, you can use the TOE chart in its current form to help you write the Visual Basic code. When the application you are creating is large, however, it is helpful to rearrange the TOE chart so that it is ordered by object rather than by task. To do so, you list all of the objects in the Object column, being sure to list each object only once. Then list each object's tasks in the Task column and its events in the Event column. Figure 2-9 shows the rearranged TOE chart, ordered by object rather than by task.

Task	Object	Event
1. Calculate total phones ordered and total price 2. Display total phones ordered and total price in lblTotalPhones and lblTotalPrice	btnCalc	Click
Clear screen for next order	btnClear	Click
End the application	btnExit	Click
Display total phones ordered (from btnCalc)	lblTotalPhones	None
Display total price (from btnCalc)	lblTotalPrice	None
Get and display the order information	txtName, txtAddress, txtCity, txtState, txtZip, txtBlue, txtPink	None

Figure 2-9 Completed TOE chart ordered by object

After completing the TOE chart, the next step is to draw a rough sketch of the user interface.

Drawing a Sketch of the User Interface

Although the TOE chart lists the objects to include in the interface, it does not tell you *where* to place those objects on the form. While the design of an interface is open to creativity, there are some guidelines to which you should adhere so that your application is consistent with the Windows standards. This consistency will make your application easier to both learn and use, because the user interface will have a familiar look to it. The guidelines are referred to as GUI guidelines, because they pertain to Graphical User Interfaces. The first GUI guideline covered in this book pertains to the organization of the controls in the interface. In Western countries, the user interface should be organized so that the information flows either vertically or horizontally, with the most important information always located in the upper-left corner of the screen. In a vertical arrangement, the information flows from top to bottom: the essential information is located in the first column of the screen, while secondary information is placed in subsequent columns. In a horizontal arrangement, on the other hand, the information flows from left to right: the essential information is placed in the first row of the screen, with secondary information placed in subsequent rows. Related controls should be grouped together using either white (empty) space or one of the tools located in the Containers section of the toolbox. Examples of tools found in the Containers section include the GroupBox, Panel, and TableLayoutPanel tools. The difference between a panel and a group box is that, unlike a group box, a panel can have scroll bars. However, unlike a panel, a group box has a Text property that you can use to indicate the contents of the control. Unlike the panel and group box controls, the table layout panel control provides a table structure in which you place other controls.

Figures 2-10 and 2-11 show two different sketches of the Playtime Cellular interface. In Figure 2-10 the information is arranged vertically, and white space is used to group the related controls together. In Figure 2-11 the information is arranged horizontally, with related controls grouped together using tools from the Containers section of the toolbox. Each text box and button in both figures is labeled so the user knows the control's purpose. The "Name:" label that identifies the txtName control tells the user the type of information to enter in the text box. Similarly, the "Calculate Order" caption on the btnCalc control indicates the action the button will perform when it is clicked.

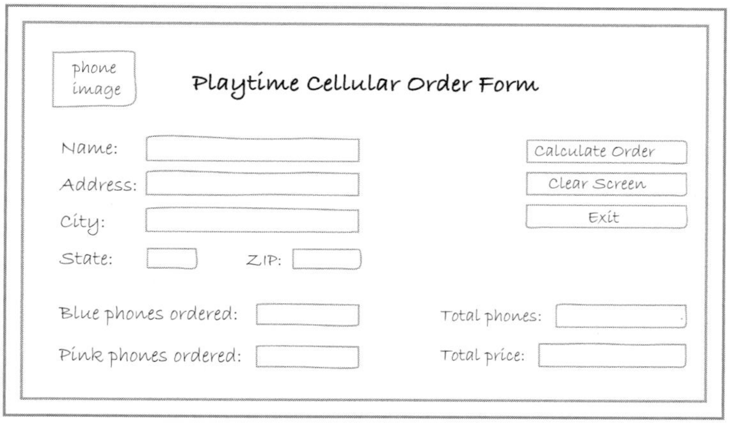

Figure 2-10 Vertical arrangement of the Playtime Cellular application

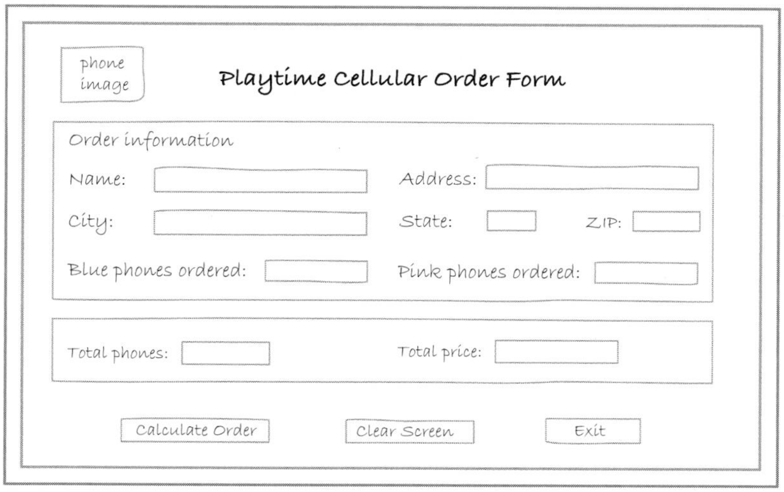

Figure 2-11 Horizontal arrangement of the Playtime Cellular application

Most times, program output (such as the result of calculations) is displayed in a label control in the interface. Label controls that display program output should be labeled to make their contents obvious to the user. In Figures 2-10 and 2-11, for example, the "Total phones:" and "Total price:" labels describe the contents of the lblTotalPhones and lblTotalPrice controls. The text contained in an identifying label should be meaningful and left-aligned within the label. An identifying label should be from one to three words only and appear on one line. In addition, the label should be positioned either above or to the left of the control it identifies. An identifying label should end with a colon (:), as shown in Figures 2-10 and 2-11. The colon distinguishes an identifying label from other text in the interface, such as the heading text "Playtime Cellular Order Form". Some assistive technologies, which are technologies that provide assistance to individuals with disabilities, rely on the colons to make the distinction. The Windows standard is to use sentence capitalization for identifying labels. **Sentence capitalization** means you capitalize only the first letter in the first word and in any words that are customarily capitalized.

As you learned in Chapter 1, a button is identified by the text that appears on its face. The text should be meaningful. In addition, it should be from one to three words only and appear on one line. A button's text should be entered using **book title capitalization**, which means you capitalize the first letter in each word, except for articles, conjunctions, and prepositions that do not occur at either the beginning or the end of the text. Always size the buttons in the interface relative to each other. When the buttons are positioned horizontally, as they are in Figure 2-11, all the buttons should be the same height; their widths, however, may vary if necessary. If the buttons are stacked vertically, as they are in Figure 2-10, all the buttons should be the same height and the same width. In a group of buttons, always place the most commonly used button first. If the buttons are positioned horizontally, the most commonly used button should be the leftmost button in the group, as shown in Figure 2-11. If the buttons are stacked vertically, the most commonly used button should be at the top of the button group, as shown in Figure 2-10.

Some companies have their own standards for interfaces used within the company. A company's standards supersede the Windows standards

When positioning the controls in the interface, be sure to maintain a consistent margin from the edges of the form. Related controls should be placed close to each other on the form. Typically, controls that are not part of any logical grouping are positioned farther away from other controls. Try to minimize the number of different margins used in the interface so that the user can more easily scan the information. You can do this by aligning the borders of the controls wherever possible. As you will observe in Lesson B, you can align the borders using the snap lines that appear as you are building the interface. Or, you can use the Format menu to align (and also size) the controls.

In this lesson you learned some basic guidelines to follow when sketching a GUI (Graphical User Interface). You will learn more GUI guidelines in the remaining lessons and in subsequent chapters. You can find a complete list of the GUI guidelines in Appendix A of this book.

GUI DESIGN TIP Layout and Organization of the User Interface

- Organize the user interface so that the information flows either vertically or horizontally, with the most important information always located in the upper-left corner of the screen. When positioning the controls, maintain a consistent margin from the edges of the form.
- Group related controls together using either white (empty) space or one of the tools contained in the Containers section of the toolbox.
- Use a label to identify each text box in the user interface. Also use a label to identify other label controls that display program output. The label text should be meaningful. It also should be from one to three words only and appear on one line. Left-align the text within the label, and position the label either above or to the left of the control it identifies. Follow the label text with a colon (:) and use sentence capitalization.
- Display meaningful text on the face of each button. Enter the text using book title capitalization. The text should indicate the action the button will perform when it is clicked. Place the text on one line and use from one to three words only.
- Size the buttons in a group of buttons relative to each other, and place the most commonly used button first in the group.
- Align the borders of the controls wherever possible to minimize the number of different margins used in the interface.

Lesson A Summary

- **To create an OO application:**
  1. Meet with the client
  2. Plan the application
  3. Build the user interface
  4. Code the application
  5. Test and debug the application
  6. Assemble the documentation

- **To plan an OO application in Visual Basic 2008:**
  1. Identify the tasks the application needs to perform.
  2. Identify the objects to which you will assign the tasks.
  3. Identify the events required to trigger an object into performing its assigned tasks.
  4. Draw a sketch of the user interface.
- **To assist you in identifying the tasks an application needs to perform, ask the following questions:**
  1. What information will the application need to display on the screen and/or print on the printer?
  2. What information will the user need to enter into the user interface to display and/or print the desired information?
  3. What information will the application need to calculate to display and/or print the desired information?
  4. How will the user end the application?
  5. Will prior information need to be cleared from the screen before new information is entered?

Lesson A Key Terms

Book title capitalization—the capitalization used for the text on a button's face; refers to capitalizing the first letter in each word, except for articles, conjunctions, and prepositions that do not occur at either the beginning or end of the text

Bugs—the errors in a program

Sentence capitalization—the capitalization used for identifying labels in the interface; refers to capitalizing only the first letter in the first word and in any words that are customarily capitalized

Lesson A Review Questions

1. When designing a user interface, the most important information should be placed in the ______________________________ corner of the screen.

   a. lower-left

   b. lower-right

   c. upper-left

   d. upper-right

2. The text on a button's face should be entered using ______________________________.

   a. book title capitalization

   b. sentence capitalization

   c. either book title capitalization or sentence capitalization

3. Which of the following statements is false?
   a. The text contained in identifying labels should be left-aligned within the label.
   b. An identifying label should be positioned either above or to the left of the control it identifies.
   c. Identifying labels should be entered using book title capitalization.
   d. Identifying labels should end with a colon (:).

4. Listed below are the four steps you should follow when planning an OO application. Put the steps in the proper order by placing a number (1 through 4) on the line to the left of the step.

   ______________ Identify the objects to which you will assign the tasks.

   ______________ Draw a sketch of the user interface.

   ______________ Identify the tasks the application needs to perform.

   ______________ Identify the events required to trigger an object into performing its assigned tasks.

5. Listed below are the six steps you should follow when creating an OO application. Put the steps in the proper order by placing a number (1 through 6) on the line to the left of the step.

   ______________ Test and debug the application

   ______________ Build the user interface

   ______________ Code the application

   ______________ Assemble the documentation

   ______________ Plan the application

   ______________ Meet with the client

Lesson A Exercises

INTRODUCTORY

1. Sarah Brimley is the accountant at Paper Products. The salespeople at Paper Products are paid a commission, which is a percentage of the sales they make. Sarah wants you to create an application that will compute the commission after she enters the salesperson's name, sales, and commission rate (expressed as a decimal number). In other words, if Sarah enters 2000 as the sales and .1 (the decimal equivalent of 10%) as the commission rate, the commission amount should be 200. Prepare a TOE chart ordered by task, then rearrange the TOE chart so that it is ordered by object. Draw a sketch of the user interface.

INTERMEDIATE

2. RM Sales divides its sales territory into four regions: North, South, East, and West. Robert Gonzales, the sales manager, wants an application that allows him to enter the current year's sales for each region and the projected increase (expressed as a decimal number) for each region. He wants the application to compute the following year's projected sales for each region. As an example, if Robert enters 10000 as the current sales for the South region, and then enters .05 (the decimal equivalent of 5%) as the projected increase, the application should display 10500 as the next year's projected sales. Prepare a TOE chart ordered by task, then rearrange the TOE chart so that it is ordered by object. Draw a sketch of the user interface.

INTERMEDIATE

3. Open the Time Solution (Time Solution.sln) file, which is contained in the VB2008\Chap02\Time Solution folder. If necessary, open the designer window. Lay out and organize the interface so it follows all of the GUI design guidelines you have learned so far. (Refer to Appendix A for a listing of the guidelines.) Code the Exit button's Click event procedure so it ends the application. Save the solution, then start the application. Click the Exit button to end the application, then close the solution.

LESSON B

After studying Lesson B, you should be able to:

- Build the user interface using your TOE chart and sketch
- Follow the Windows standards regarding the use of graphics, fonts, and color
- Set a control's BorderStyle property
- Add a text box to a form
- Lock the controls on the form
- Assign access keys to controls
- Set the TabIndex property

Building the User Interface

In Lesson A, you planned the Playtime Cellular application. Planning the application is the second of the six steps involved in creating an OO application. You now are ready to tackle the third step, which is to build the user interface. You use the TOE chart and sketch you created in the planning step as guides when building the interface, which involves placing the appropriate controls on the form and setting the applicable properties of the controls. Recall that an object's properties determine the appearance and behavior of the object, such as its font, size, and so on. Some programmers create the entire interface before setting the properties of the objects. Other programmers change the properties of each object as it is added to the form. Either way will work, so it's really just a matter of personal preference. To save you time, the VB2008\Chap02\Playtime Solution folder contains a partially completed application for Playtime Cellular. When you open the solution, you will find that most of the user interface has been created and most of the properties have been set. You will complete the interface in this lesson.

To open the partially completed application:

1. If necessary, start Visual Studio 2008 or Visual Basic 2008 Express Edition. Close the Start Page window.
2. Open the **Playtime Solution (Playtime Solution.sln)** file, which is contained in the VB2008\Chap02\Playtime Solution folder. If necessary, open the designer window. Figure 2-12 shows the partially completed interface, which resembles the sketch shown in Figure 2-10 in Lesson A.

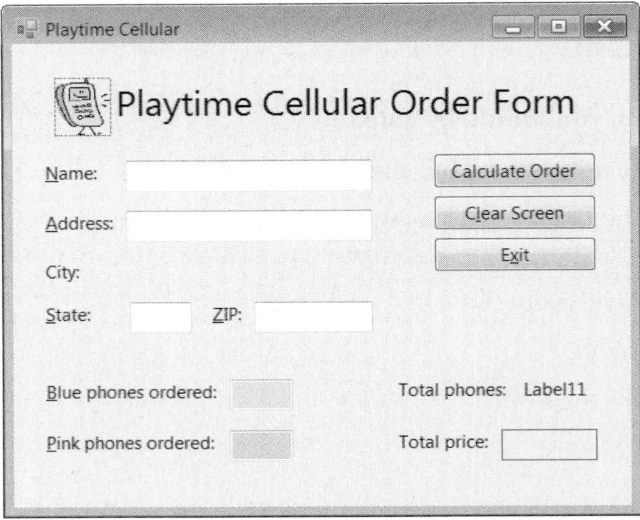

Figure 2-12 Partially completed interface for the Playtime Cellular application

The application's user interface follows the GUI guidelines covered in Lesson A. The information is arranged vertically, with the most important information located in the upper-left corner of the screen. A consistent margin is maintained from the edges of the form, and the controls are aligned wherever possible to minimize the number of different margins appearing in the interface. Each text box and button, as well as each label control that displays program output, is labeled so the user knows the control's purpose. The text contained in the identifying labels is entered using sentence capitalization. In addition, the text ends with a colon and is left-aligned within the label. The identifying labels are positioned to the left of the controls they identify. The text on each button's face is entered using book title capitalization. The button and label text appears on one line and does not exceed the three-word limit. Because the buttons are stacked in the interface, each button has the same height and width, and the most commonly used button (Calculate Order) is placed at the top of the button group.

When building the user interface, keep in mind that you want to create a screen that no one notices. Snazzy interfaces may get "oohs" and "aahs" during their initial use, but they become tiresome after a while. The most important point to remember is that the interface should not distract the user from doing his or her work. Unfortunately, it is difficult for some application developers to refrain from using the many different graphics, fonts, and colors available in Visual Basic. Actually, using these elements is not the problem; the problem is *overusing* them. So that you do not overload your user interfaces with too many graphics, too many fonts, and too much color, the next three sections provide some guidelines to follow regarding these elements.

Including Graphics in the Interface

The human eye is attracted to pictures before text, so include a graphic in an interface only if it is necessary to do so. Graphics typically are used to either emphasize or clarify a portion of the screen. You also can use a graphic for aesthetic purposes, as long as the graphic is small and placed in a location that does not distract the user. The small graphic in the Playtime Cellular interface is included for aesthetics only. The graphic is purposely located in the upper-left corner of the interface, which is where you want the user's eye to be drawn first anyway. The cell phone image adds a personal touch to the order form without being distracting to the user.

GUI DESIGN TIP Adding Graphics

Include a graphic in an interface only if it is necessary to do so. If the graphic is used solely for aesthetics, use a small graphic and place it in a location that will not distract the user.

Selecting Fonts for the Interface

As you learned in Chapter 1, you can use the Font property to change the type, style, and size of the font used to display the text in an interface. Recall that Segoe UI, Tahoma, and Microsoft Sans Serif are examples of font types. Font styles include regular, bold, and italic. The numbers 9, 12, and 18 are examples of font sizes. Some font types are serif, while others are sans serif. A serif is a light cross stroke that appears at the top or bottom of a character. The characters in a serif font have the light strokes, whereas the characters in a sans serif font do not. ("Sans" is a French word meaning "without.") Books use serif fonts, because serif fonts are easier to read on the printed page. User interfaces, on the other hand, use sans serif fonts, which are easier to read on the screen. You should use only one font type for all of the text in the interface, and use no more than two different font sizes. In addition, avoid using italics and underlining in an interface, because both font styles make text difficult to read. The use of bold text should be limited to titles, headings, and key items that you want to emphasize.

GUI DESIGN TIP Selecting Font Types, Styles, and Sizes

- Use only one font type for all of the text in the interface. Use a sans serif font, preferably the Segoe UI font.
- Use no more than two different font sizes in the interface.
- Avoid using italics and underlining, because these font styles make text difficult to read.
- Limit the use of bold text to titles, headings, and key items that you want to emphasize.

Adding Color to the Interface

Just as the human eye is attracted to graphics before text, it also is attracted to color before black and white; therefore, use color sparingly. It is a good practice to build the interface using black, white, and gray first, then add color only if you have a good reason to do so. Keep the following three points in mind when deciding whether to include color in an interface:

1. Many people have some form of either color-blindness or color confusion, so they will have trouble distinguishing colors.
2. Color is very subjective: a pretty color to you may be hideous to someone else.
3. A color may have a different meaning in a different culture.

You can change the background color of a text box by setting its BackColor property.

Usually, it is best to use black text on a white, off-white, or light gray background. This is because dark text on a light background is the easiest to read. You should never use a dark color for the background or a light color for the text, because a dark background is hard on the eyes, and light-colored text can appear blurry. If you are going to include color in an interface, limit the number of colors to three, not including white, black, and gray. Be sure that the colors you choose complement each other. Although color can be used to identify an important element in the interface, it should never be used as the only means of identification. In the Playtime Cellular application, for example, the blue and pink text boxes help the salesperson quickly identify where to enter the order for blue and pink phones, respectively. However, color is not the only means of identifying those areas in the interface: the labels to the left of the text boxes also tell the user where to enter the orders for blue and pink phones.

GUI DESIGN TIP Selecting Colors

- Build the interface using black, white, and gray first, then add color only if you have a good reason to do so.
- Use white, off-white, or light gray for the background and black for the text.
- Never use a dark color for the background or a light color for the text. A dark background is hard on the eyes, and light-colored text can appear blurry.
- Limit the number of colors in an interface to three, not including white, black, and gray. The colors you choose should complement each other.
- Never use color as the only means of identification for an element in the user interface.

The BorderStyle and AutoSize Properties

The BorderStyle property determines the style of a control's border and can be set to None, FixedSingle, or Fixed3D. Controls with a BorderStyle property set to None have no border. Setting the BorderStyle property to FixedSingle surrounds the control with a thin line, and setting it to Fixed3D gives the control a three-dimensional appearance. In most cases, a text box's BorderStyle property should be left at its default setting: Fixed3D. The BorderStyle property for each text box in the Playtime Cellular interface follows this convention. The appropriate BorderStyle property setting for a label control depends on the control's purpose. Label controls that identify other controls (such as those that identify text boxes) should have a BorderStyle property setting of None, which is the default setting. This is the setting for each identifying label in the Playtime Cellular interface. Label controls that display program output, such as those that display the result of a calculation, typically have a BorderStyle property setting of FixedSingle. The BorderStyle property of the lblTotalPrice control is set to FixedSingle.

A label control's AutoSize property determines whether the control automatically sizes to fit its current contents. The appropriate setting depends on the label's purpose. Label controls that identify other controls use the default setting, which is True. However, you typically set to False the AutoSize property of label controls that display program output. In the next set of steps, you will change the AutoSize and BorderStyle properties of the lblTotalPhones control.

To change the properties of the lblTotalPhones control, and then size the control:

1. Click the **lblTotalPhones** control, which contains the text Label11.
2. Set the control's **AutoSize** property to **False**, then set its **BorderStyle** property to **FixedSingle**.
3. Next, you will remove Label11 from the Text property. Click **Text** in the Properties list, then select (highlight) Label11. Press **Delete**, then press **Enter**.
4. Now tell the computer to center any text appearing in the control. Click **TextAlign** in the Properties list, then click the property's **down arrow**. Click the **center** button to change the property's setting to MiddleCenter.
5. Finally, make the lblTotalPhones control the same height as the lblTotalPrice control. As you learned in Chapter 1, to size (or align) two or more controls, you first select the reference control and then select the other controls. Recall that the reference control is the control whose size (or alignment) you want the other controls to match. Click the **lblTotalPrice** control, then press and hold down the **Ctrl** (or Control) key as you click the **lblTotalPhones** control. Click **Format** on the menu bar, point to **Make Same Size**, then click **Height**.
6. Click the **form** to deselect the two labels.

GUI DESIGN TIP Setting the BorderStyle Property of a Text Box or Label

- Keep the BorderStyle property of text boxes at the default value, Fixed3D.
- Keep the BorderStyle property of labels that identify other controls at the default value, None.
- Set to FixedSingle the BorderStyle property of labels that display program output, such as those that display the result of a calculation.
- In Windows applications, a control that contains data that the user is not allowed to edit does not usually appear three-dimensional. Therefore, you should avoid setting a label control's BorderStyle property to Fixed3D.

GUI DESIGN TIP Setting the AutoSize Property of a Label

- Keep the AutoSize property of identifying labels at the default value, True.
- In most cases, change to False the AutoSize property of label controls that display program output.

Adding a Text Box Control to the Form

Recall that each tool in the toolbox is a class, which is a pattern from which one or more objects are instantiated. A text box is an instance of the TextBox class.

As mentioned earlier, a **text box** provides an area in the form for the user to enter data. Missing from the Playtime Cellular interface is the text box for entering the city name. In the next set of steps, you will use the TextBox tool to add a text box to the form.

To add the missing text box to the form:

1. Click the **TextBox tool** in the toolbox, then drag the tool to the form, positioning it immediately below the Address text box. Release the mouse button. Click **(Name)** in the Properties list, then type **txtCity** and press **Enter**.
2. Now make the City text box the same size as the Address text box. Click the **txtAddress** control, then Ctrl+click the **txtCity** control. Click **Format** on the menu bar, point to **Make Same Size**, then click **Both**.
3. You can align the City text box using either the Format menu or the snap lines. You will use the snap lines. Click the **form** to deselect the City and Address text boxes. Place the mouse pointer on the City text box, then press and hold down the left mouse button as you drag the text box to the location shown in Figure 2-13. The blue snap lines help you align the City text box with the Address text box. The pink snap line allows you to align the text in both the City text box and its identifying label.

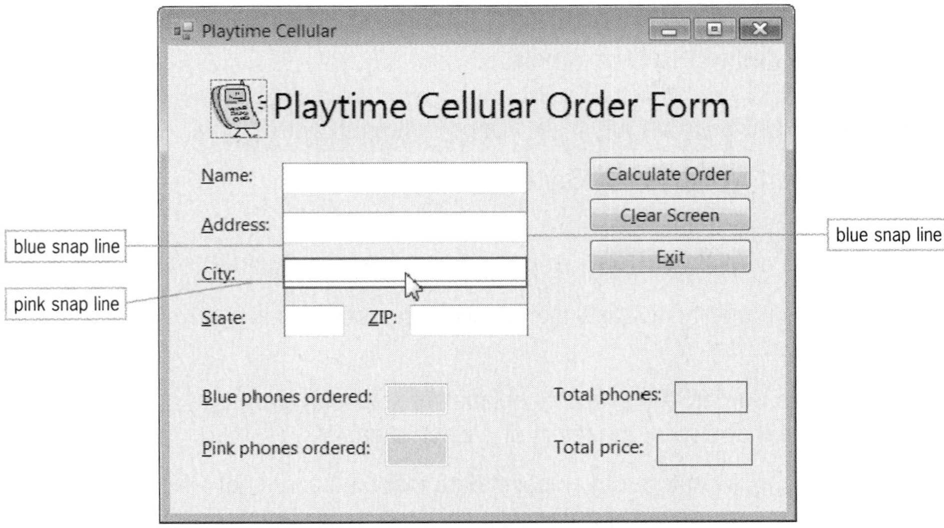

Figure 2-13 Snap lines shown in the interface

4. When the City text box is in the correct location, release the mouse button.

Locking the Controls on a Form

Once you have placed all of the controls in the desired locations on the form, it is a good idea to lock the controls in their current positions so you do not inadvertently move them. You can lock the controls by clicking the form (or any control on the form), then clicking Format on the menu bar, and then clicking Lock Controls; you can follow the same procedure to unlock the controls. You also can lock and unlock the controls by right-clicking the form (or any control on the form) and then clicking Lock Controls on the context menu. When a control is locked, a small lock appears in the upper-left corner of the control.

A locked control can be deleted. It also can be moved by setting its Location property.

To lock the controls on the form, then save the solution:

1. Right-click the **form**, then click **Lock Controls** on the context menu.
2. Save the solution. Try dragging one of the controls to a different location on the form. You will not be able to do so.

Assigning Access Keys

Looking closely at the Playtime Cellular interface in Figure 2-13, you will notice that the text in many of the controls contains an underlined letter, which is called an access key. An **access key** allows the user to select an object using the Alt key in combination with a letter or number. In Visual Studio, for example, you can select the File menu by pressing Alt+F, because the letter "F" is the File menu's access key. Access keys are not case sensitive; therefore, you can select the File menu by pressing either Alt+F or Alt+f. Similarly, you can select the Exit button in the Playtime Cellular interface by pressing either Alt+X or Alt+x. Depending on your system's settings, the access keys may or may not appear underlined while an application is running. If you do not see the underlined access keys, you can show them temporarily by pressing the Alt key. You can subsequently hide them by pressing the Alt key again. (To always display access keys, see the Summary section at the end of this lesson.) You should assign access keys to each of the controls that can accept user input. Examples of such controls include text boxes and buttons, because the user can enter information in a text box and he or she can click a button. The only exceptions to this rule are the OK and Cancel buttons, which typically do not have access keys in Windows applications. It is important to assign access keys for the following three reasons:

1. Access keys allow a user to work with the application even when the mouse becomes inoperative.
2. Access keys allow users who are fast typists to keep their hands on the keyboard.
3. Access keys allow people with disabilities, which may prevent them from working with a mouse, to use the application.

You assign an access key by including an ampersand (&) in the control's caption or identifying label. If the control is a button, you include the ampersand in the button's Text property, which is where a button's caption is stored. If the control is a text box, however, you include the ampersand in the Text property of its identifying label control. (As you will learn later in this lesson, you also must set the identifying label's TabIndex property to a value that is one number less than the value stored in the text box's TabIndex property.) You enter the ampersand to the immediate left of the character you want to designate as the access key. For example, to assign the letter C as the access key for the Calculate Order button, you enter &Calculate Order in the button's Text property. To assign the letter N as the access key for the txtName control, you enter &Name: in the Text property of its identifying label. Notice that the Total phones: and Total price: labels in Figure 2-13 do not have access keys. This is because the labels do not identify controls that accept user input; instead, they identify other label controls. Users cannot access label controls while an application is running, so it is inappropriate to assign an access key to the controls.

Each access key in an interface should be unique. The first choice for an access key is the first letter of the caption or identifying label, unless another letter provides a more meaningful association. For example, the letter "x" is the access key for an Exit button, because it provides a more meaningful association than does the letter "E". If you can't use the first letter (perhaps because it already is used as the access key for another control) and no other letter provides a more meaningful association, then use a distinctive consonant in the caption or label. The last choices for an access key are a vowel or a number.

To assign an access key to the btnCalc and txtCity controls:

1. Click the **Calculate Order** button, then click **Text** in the Properties list. Position the mouse pointer to the left of the C in Calculate, then click at that location. Type **&** (ampersand), then press **Enter**. The Text property now contains &Calculate Order, and the interface shows the letter "C" underlined on the button's face.
2. Click the **City:** label, which identifies the txtCity control. The letter "C" would be a good choice for an access key; however, the letter is already assigned to the Calculate Order button. (Recall that each access key in an interface must be unique.) Therefore, you will use the letter "t" instead. Change the label's Text property to **Ci&ty:** and press **Enter**. The interface shows the letter "t" underlined in the label.

GUI DESIGN TIP Assigning Access Keys

- Assign a unique access key to each control that can accept user input, such as text boxes and buttons.
- When assigning an access key to a control, use the first letter of the caption or identifying label, unless another letter provides a more meaningful association. If you can't use the first letter and no other letter provides a more meaningful association, then use a distinctive consonant. Lastly, use a vowel or a number.

Setting the TabIndex Property

Most controls have a TabIndex property. A control's TabIndex property contains a number that represents the order in which the control was added to the form. The first control added to a form has a TabIndex value of 0; the second control has a TabIndex value of 1, and so on. The TabIndex values determine the tab order, which is the order that each control receives the focus when the user either presses the Tab key or employs an access key while an application is running. A control having a TabIndex of 2 will receive the focus immediately after the control whose TabIndex is 1. Likewise, a control with a TabIndex of 18 will receive the focus immediately after the control whose TabIndex is 17. When a control has the **focus**, it can accept user input. Most times, you will need to reset the TabIndex values for an interface, because controls are rarely added to a form in the desired tab order. To determine the appropriate TabIndex values, you first make a list of the controls that can accept user input. The list should reflect the order in which the user will want to access the controls. In the Playtime Cellular interface, the user typically will want to access the txtName control first, followed by the txtAddress control, the txtCity control, and so on. If a control that accepts user input is identified by a label control, you also include the label control in the list. (A text box is an example of a control that accepts user input and is identified by a label control.) You place the name of the label control immediately above the name of the control it identifies in the list. In the Playtime Cellular interface, the Label2 control (which contains Name:) identifies the txtName control; therefore, Label2 should appear immediately above txtName in the list. The names of controls that do not accept user input, as well as those that do not identify controls that accept user input, should be listed at the bottom of the list; these names do not need to appear in any specific order. After listing the control names, you then assign each control in the list a TabIndex value, beginning with the number 0. If a control does not have a TabIndex property, you do not assign it a TabIndex value in the list. You can tell whether a control has a TabIndex property by viewing its Properties list.

Figure 2-14 shows the list of control names and TabIndex values for the Playtime Cellular interface. The first column in the list contains two sections. The first section is titled "Controls that accept user input, along with their identifying labels." This section contains the names of the seven text boxes and three buttons in the interface, because those controls can accept user input. Each text box in the list is associated with an identifying label control, whose name appears immediately above the text box name in the list. Notice that the TabIndex value assigned to each text box's identifying label is one number less than the value assigned to the text box itself. For example, the Label2 control has a TabIndex value of 0, and its corresponding text box (txtName) has a TabIndex value of 1. Likewise, the Label3 control and its corresponding text box have TabIndex values of 2 and 3, respectively. For a text box's access key (which is defined in the identifying label) to work appropriately, you must be sure to set the identifying label's TabIndex property to a value that is one number less than the value stored in the text box's TabIndex property. The second section in the list is titled "Other controls." In this section, you list the names of controls that neither accept user input nor identify controls that accept user input.

Controls that accept user input, along with their identifying labels	TabIndex value
Label2 (Name:)	0
txtName	1
Label3 (Address:)	2
txtAddress	3
Label4 (City:)	4
txtCity	5
Label5 (State:)	6
txtState	7
Label6 (ZIP:)	8
txtZip	9
Label7 (Blue phones ordered:)	10
txtBlue	11
Label8 (Pink phones ordered:)	12
txtPink	13
btnCalc	14
btnClear	15
btnExit	16
Other controls	
Label1 (Playtime Cellular Order Form)	17
Label9 (Total phones:)	18
Label10 (Total price:)	19
lblTotalPhones	20
lblTotalPrice	21
PictureBox1	N/A

Figure 2-14 List of control names and TabIndex values

You can set each control's TabIndex property using either the Properties window or the Tab Order option on the View menu. The Tab Order option is available only when the designer window is the active window.

To set the TabIndex values, then verify the tab order:

1. Click the **form** to make the designer window the active window. Click **View** on the menu bar, then click **Tab Order**. The current TabIndex value for each control (except the PictureBox1 control) appears in blue boxes on the form. The TabIndex values reflect the order in which each control was added to the form.

2. You begin specifying the desired tab order by placing the mouse pointer on the first control you want in the tab order. According to Figure 2-14, the first control in the tab order should be the Label2 control, which displays the Name: text. Place the mouse pointer on the blue box that contains the number 1, then click the **blue box**. (You also can place the mouse pointer directly on the Label2 control and then click the control.) The number 0 replaces the number 1 in the box, and the color of the box changes from blue to white to indicate that you have set the TabIndex value for that control.

3. The second control in the tab order should be the txtName control, which currently has a TabIndex value of 6. Click the **blue box that contains the number 6**. The number 1 replaces the number 6 in the box, and the color of the box changes from blue to white.

4. Use the information shown in Figure 2-15 to set the TabIndex property for the remaining controls, which have TabIndex values of 2 through 21. Be sure to set the values in numerical order. If you make a mistake, press the Esc key to remove the TabIndex boxes from the form, then repeat Steps 1 through 4. When you have finished setting all of the TabIndex values, the color of the boxes will automatically change from white to blue, as shown in Figure 2-15.

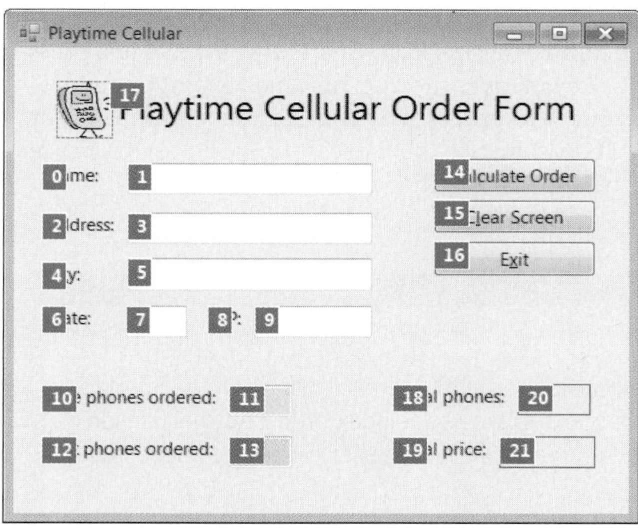

Figure 2-15 TabIndex boxes showing the correct TabIndex values

5. Press **Esc** to remove the TabIndex boxes from the form.

6. Save the solution, then start the application. When you start an application, the computer sends the focus to the control whose TabIndex is 0. In the Playtime Cellular interface, that control is the Label2 (Name:) control. However, because label controls cannot receive the focus, the computer sends the focus to the next control in the tab order sequence. In this case, it sends the focus to the txtName control. The blinking insertion point that appears in the txtName control indicates that the text box has the focus and is ready to receive input from you.

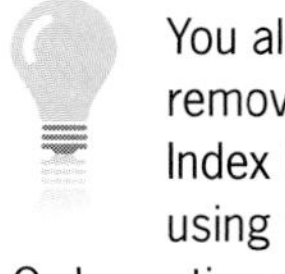

You also can remove the Tab-Index boxes using the Tab Order option on the View menu.

7. Type **Toys For All** in the txtName control. The information you entered is recorded in the text box's Text property.
8. In Windows applications, the Tab key moves the focus forward, and the Shift+Tab key combination moves the focus backward. Press **Tab** to move the focus to the txtAddress control, then press **Shift+Tab** to move the focus back to the txtName control.
9. Now use the Tab key to verify the tab order of the controls in the interface. Press **Tab**, slowly, nine times. The focus moves to the following controls: txtAddress, txtCity, txtState, txtZip, txtBlue, txtPink, btnCalc, btnClear, and btnExit.
10. When the focus moves to a button, the button's border is highlighted and a dotted rectangle appears around its caption. Pressing the Enter key when a button has the focus invokes the button's Click event and causes the computer to process any code contained in the event procedure. Press **Enter** to invoke the btnExit control's Click event procedure, which contains the `Me.Close()` statement. The application ends and you are returned to the designer window.
11. You also can move the focus using a text box's access key. Start the application. Press **Alt+b** to move the focus to the txtBlue control, then press **Alt+n** to move the focus to the txtName control. On your own, try the access keys for the remaining text boxes in the interface.
12. Unlike pressing a text box's access key, which moves the focus, pressing a button's access key invokes the button's Click event procedure and causes the computer to process any code contained in the event procedure. Press **Alt+x** to invoke the Exit button's Click event procedure, which ends the application, then close the solution.

GUI DESIGN TIP Using the TabIndex Property to Control the Focus

- Assign a TabIndex value (starting with 0) to each control in the interface, except for controls that do not have a TabIndex property. The TabIndex values should reflect the order in which the user will want to access the controls.
- To give users keyboard access to a text box, assign an access key to the text box's identifying label. Set the identifying label's TabIndex property to a value that is one number less than the value stored in the text box's TabIndex property.

Lesson B Summary

- **To specify a control's border:**

  Set the control's BorderStyle property.

- **To specify whether a label control should automatically size to fit its current contents:**

  Set the label control's AutoSize property.

- **To lock/unlock the controls on the form:**

  Right-click the form or any control on the form, then select Lock Controls on the context menu. You also can use the Lock Controls option on the Format menu.

- **To assign an access key to a control:**

  Type an ampersand (&) in the Text property of the control or identifying label. The ampersand should appear to the immediate left of either the letter or number that you want to designate as the access key.

- **To provide keyboard access to a text box:**

  Assign an access key to the text box's identifying label. Set the identifying label's TabIndex property to a value that is one number less than the text box's TabIndex value.

- **To employ an access key:**

  Press and hold down the Alt key as you press the access key.

- **To set the tab order:**

  Set each control's TabIndex property to a number (starting with 0) that represents the order in which the control should receive the focus. You can set the TabIndex property using either the Properties window or the Tab Order option on the View menu.

- **To always display access keys:**

  To always display access keys in Windows Vista, click Start on the Windows Vista taskbar, click Control Panel, then click Appearance and Personalization. In the Ease of Access Center section, click Underline keyboard shortcuts and access keys, then select the Underline keyboard shortcuts and access keys check box. (You may need to scroll down to view the check box.) Click the Save button, then close the Ease of Access Center dialog box.

  To always display access keys when using the Classic View in Windows Vista, click Start, click Control Panel, double-click Ease of Access Center, click Make the keyboard easier to use, select the Underline keyboard shortcuts and access keys check box, click the Save button, then close the dialog box.

To always display access keys when using the Category View in Windows XP, click Start, click Control Panel, click Appearance and Themes, click Display, click the Appearance tab, click the Effects button, deselect the Hide underlined letters for keyboard navigation until I press the Alt key check box, click OK, then click OK again.

To always display access keys when using the Classic View in Windows XP, click Start, click Control Panel, double-click Display, click the Appearance tab, click the Effects button, deselect the Hide underlined letters for keyboard navigation until I press the Alt key check box, click OK, then click OK again.

Lesson B Key Terms

Access key—the underlined character in an object's identifying label or caption; allows the user to select the object using the Alt key in combination with the underlined character

Focus—indicates that a control is ready to accept user input

Text box—a control that provides an area in the form for the user to enter data

Lesson B Review Questions

1. The ______________________________ property determines the order in which a control receives the focus when the user either presses the Tab key or employs an access key.
   a. SetOrder
   b. TabIndex
   c. TabNumber
   d. TabOrder

2. An Exit button's access key is always the letter ______________________________.
   a. E
   b. i
   c. t
   d. x

3. You assign an access key using a control's ______________________________ property.
   a. Access
   b. Caption
   c. Key
   d. Text

4. Which of the following specifies the letter D as the access key?
   a. &Display
   b. #Display
   c. ^Display
   d. D&isplay

5. Explain the method for providing keyboard access to a text box.

Lesson B Exercises

INTRODUCTORY

1. Open the Paper Solution (Paper Solution.sln) file, which is contained in the VB2008\Chap02\Paper Solution folder. If necessary, open the designer window. Figure 2-16 shows the completed interface. Finish building the interface by adding a text box named txtName to the form. Lock the controls on the form. Assign the access keys (shown in the figure) to the text boxes and buttons. Set the TabIndex values appropriately. Save the solution, then start the application. Verify that the tab order is correct. Also verify that the access keys work appropriately. Use the Exit button to end the application. (You will code the Calculate Commission and Clear Screen buttons in Lesson C's Exercise 1.) Close the solution.

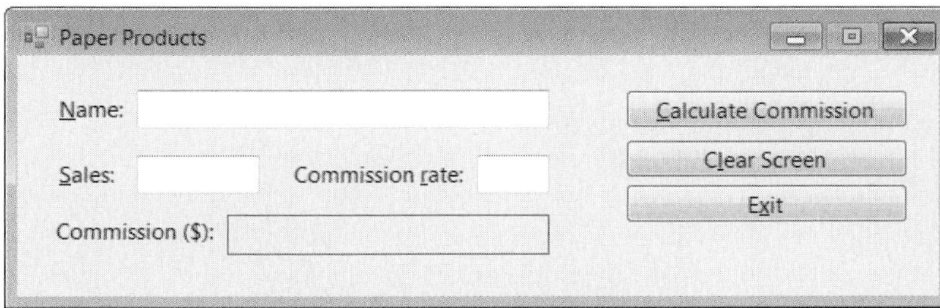

Figure 2-16 User interface for the Paper Products application

INTERMEDIATE

2. Open the RM Sales Solution (RM Sales Solution.sln) file, which is contained in the VB2008\Chap02\RM Sales Solution folder. If necessary, open the designer window. Figure 2-17 shows the completed interface. Finish building the interface by adding a label control named lblNorth to the form. Lock the controls on the form. Change the label's BorderStyle property to the appropriate setting. Set the tab order to allow the user to enter the North region's sales and increase percentage before entering the South region's sales and increase percentage, and so on. Save the solution, then start the application. Verify that the tab order is correct. Also verify that the access keys work appropriately. Use the Exit button to end the application. (You will code the Calculate Projected Sales and Clear Screen buttons in Lesson C's Exercise 2.) Close the solution.

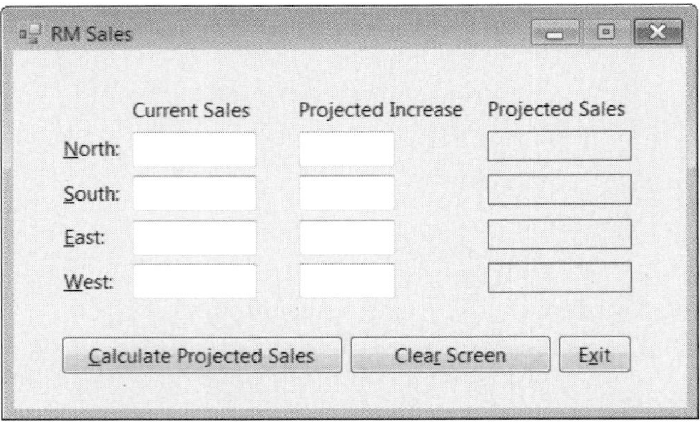

Figure 2-17 User interface for the RM Sales application

INTERMEDIATE

3. In this exercise, you modify the application from Lesson A's Exercise 3. Open the Time Solution (Time Solution.sln) file, which is contained in the VB2008\Chap02\Time Solution folder. If necessary, open the designer window. Lock the controls on the form. Assign access keys to the controls that can accept user input. Set each control's Tab-Index property. Save the solution, then start the application. Verify that the tab order is correct. Also verify that the access keys work appropriately. Click the Exit button to end the application, then close the solution.

LESSON C

After studying Lesson C, you should be able to:

- Code an application using its TOE chart
- Plan an object's code using pseudocode or a flowchart
- Write an assignment statement
- Send the focus to a control while an application is running
- Include internal documentation in the code
- Write arithmetic expressions
- Use the Val and Format functions

Coding the Application

In Lessons A and B, you created a TOE chart and user interface for the Playtime Cellular application. The user interface and TOE chart are shown in Figures 2-18 and 2-19, respectively. After planning an application and building its user interface, you then can begin coding the application. You code an application so that the objects in the interface perform their assigned tasks when the appropriate event occurs. The objects and events that need to be coded, as well as the tasks assigned to each object and event, are listed in the application's TOE chart. The TOE chart in Figure 2-19 indicates that only the three buttons require coding, as they are the only objects with an event listed in the third column of the chart.

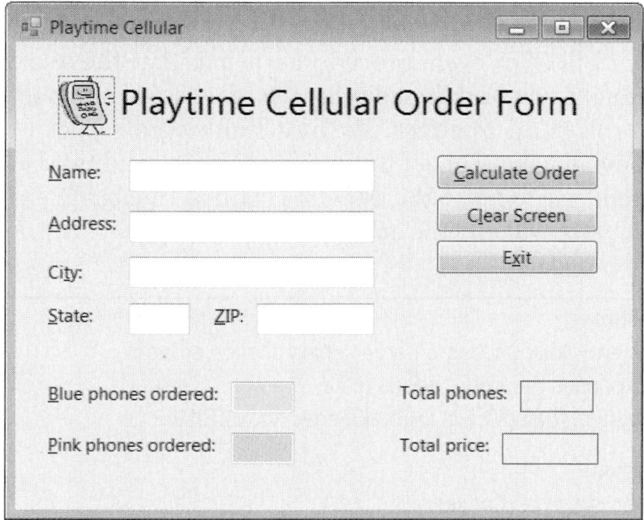

Figure 2-18 Playtime Cellular application's interface

Task	Object	Event
1. Calculate total phones ordered and total price 2. Display total phones ordered and total price in lblTotalPhones and lblTotalPrice	btnCalc	Click
Clear screen for next order	btnClear	Click
End the application	btnExit	Click
Display total phones ordered (from btnCalc)	lblTotalPhones	None
Display total price (from btnCalc)	lblTotalPrice	None
Get and display the order information	txtName, txtAddress, txtCity, txtState, txtZip, txtBlue, txtPink	None

Figure 2-19 Playtime Cellular application's TOE chart (ordered by object)

You should plan an object's event procedure before you begin coding it. Many programmers use planning tools such as pseudocode or flowcharts. You will learn about pseudocode first.

Planning a Procedure Using Pseudocode

Pseudocode uses short phrases to describe the steps a procedure must take to accomplish its goal. Even though the word *pseudocode* might be unfamiliar to you, you already have written pseudocode without even realizing it. Think about the last time you gave directions to someone. You wrote each direction down on paper, in your own words; your directions were a form of pseudocode. Figure 2-20 shows the pseudocode for the procedures that need to be coded in the Playtime Cellular application. As the pseudocode indicates, the btnCalc control's Click event procedure will calculate the total phones ordered and the total price, and then display the calculated results in the appropriate label controls in the interface. The btnClear control's Click event procedure will remove the contents of the seven text boxes and two label controls, and then send the focus to the txtName control. The btnExit control's Click event procedure will end the application.

btnCalc Click event procedure
1. calculate total phones ordered = blue phones ordered + pink phones ordered
2. calculate total price = total phones ordered * phone price
3. display total phones ordered and total price in lblTotalPhones and lblTotalPrice

btnClear Click event procedure
1. clear the Text property of the seven text boxes
2. clear the Text property of the lblTotalPhones and lblTotalPrice controls
3. send the focus to the txtName control so the user can begin entering the next order

btnExit Click event procedure
1. end the application

Figure 2-20 Pseudocode for the Playtime Cellular application

Planning a Procedure Using a Flowchart

Unlike pseudocode, which consists of short phrases, a **flowchart** uses standardized symbols to show the steps a procedure must follow to reach its goal. Figure 2-21 shows the flowcharts for the procedures that need to be coded in the Playtime Cellular application. The logic illustrated in the flowcharts is the same as the logic shown in the pseudocode in Figure 2-20. The flowcharts in Figure 2-21 contain three different symbols: an oval, a rectangle, and a parallelogram. The oval symbol is called the **start/stop symbol**. The start oval indicates the beginning of the flowchart, and the stop oval indicates the end of the flowchart. The rectangles that appear between the start and stop ovals are called **process symbols**. You use the process symbol to represent tasks such as making calculations. The parallelogram in a flowchart is called the **input/output symbol** and is used to represent input tasks (such as getting information from the user) and output tasks (such as displaying information). The parallelogram in Figure 2-21 represents an output task. The symbols in a flowchart are connected with lines, called flowlines.

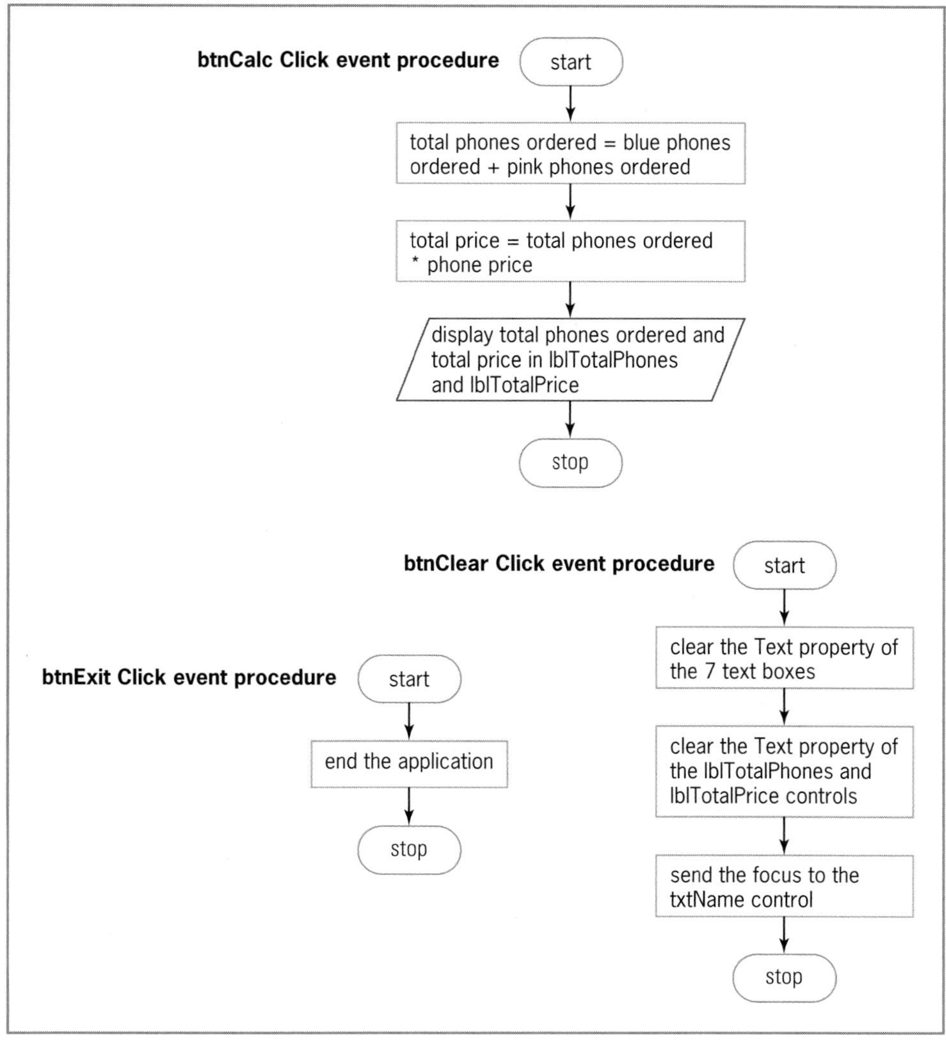

Figure 2-21 Flowcharts for the Playtime Cellular application

When planning a procedure, you do not need to create both a flowchart and pseudocode; you need to use only one of these planning tools. The tool you use is really a matter of personal preference. For simple procedures, pseudocode works just fine. When a procedure becomes more complex, however, the procedure's steps may be easier to understand in a flowchart. The programmer uses either the procedure's pseudocode or its flowchart as a guide when coding the procedure. In this lesson, you will use the pseudocode.

Coding the btnClear Control's Click Event Procedure

You also can use the Clear method to clear the contents of a text box. You learn about the Clear method in Discovery Exercise 12 at the end of this lesson.

According to the pseudocode shown in Figure 2-22, the btnClear control's Click event procedure should clear the Text property of the seven text boxes and two of the labels in the interface, and then send the focus to the txtName control. You can clear the Text property of an object by assigning a zero-length string to it. A **string** is a group of characters enclosed in quotation marks. The word "Jones" is a string. Likewise, "45" is a string, but 45 is not; 45 is a number. "Jones" is a string with a length of five, because there are five characters between the quotation marks. "45" is a string with a length of two, because there are two characters between the quotation marks. Following this logic, a **zero-length string**, also called an **empty string**, is a set of quotation marks with nothing between them, like this: "". Assigning a zero-length string to the Text property of an object while an application is running removes the contents of the object. You also can clear an object's Text property by assigning the value **String.Empty** to it while an application is running. When you do this, the computer assigns the empty string ("") to the Text property, thereby removing its contents.

btnClear Click event procedure
1. clear the Text property of the seven text boxes
2. clear the Text property of the lblTotalPhones and lblTotalPrice controls
3. send the focus to the txtName control so the user can begin entering the next order

Figure 2-22 Pseudocode for the btnClear control's Click event procedure

In Chapter 1, you learned how to use the Properties window to set an object's properties during design time, which is when you are building the interface. In the next section, you will learn how to set an object's properties while the application is running.

Assigning a Value to a Property During Run Time

You use an **assignment statement**, which is one of many different types of Visual Basic instructions, to assign a value to something (such as to the property of an object) while an application is running. The syntax of an assignment statement that assigns a value to an object's property is *object.property* = *expression*. In the syntax, *object* and *property* are the names of the object and property to which you want the value of the *expression* assigned. You use a period to separate the object name from the property name. As you learned in Chapter 1, the period is called the dot member access operator. In this case, the operator indicates that the *property* is a member of the *object*. You use an equal sign (=) between the *object.property* information and the *expression*. The equal sign in an assignment statement is called the **assignment operator**. When the computer processes an assignment statement, it assigns the value of the expression that appears on the right side of the assignment operator to the object and property that appears on the left side of the assignment operator. The assignment statement `txtName.Text = String.Empty`, for example, assigns the empty string to the txtName control's Text property. Similarly, the assignment statement `txtState.Text = "IL"` assigns the string "IL" to the Text property of the txtState control. You will use assignment statements to code the btnClear control's pseudocode.

To open the btnClear control's Click event procedure:

1. If necessary, start Visual Studio 2008 or Visual Basic 2008 Express Edition and close the Start Page window. Open the **Playtime Solution** (**Playtime Solution.sln**) file, which is contained in the VB2008\Chap02\Playtime Solution folder. If necessary, open the designer window.
2. Open the Code Editor window by right-clicking the **form**, and then clicking **View Code**. Notice that the btnExit control's Click event procedure, which is responsible for ending the application, has already been coded for you.
3. Click the **Class Name** list arrow in the Code Editor window, then click **btnClear** in the list. Click the **Method Name** list arrow, then click **Click** in the list. The code template for the btnClear control's Click event procedure opens in the Code Editor window. Press **Enter** to insert a blank line below the procedure header.

You also can open the Code Editor window by pressing the F7 key. Or, you can use the Code option on the View menu.

Step 1 in the procedure's pseudocode is to clear the Text property of the seven text boxes in the interface. You can do this using either the *textbox*`.Text = String.Empty` instruction or the *textbox*`.Text = ""` instruction, where *textbox* is the name of the appropriate text box. As you learned in Chapter 1, you can either type the Visual Basic instructions on your own or use the IntelliSense feature that is built into the Code Editor. In the next set of steps, you will use the IntelliSense feature.

To begin coding the btnClear control's Click event procedure:

1. First, you will enter the `txtName.Text = String.Empty` assignment statement. Type the two letters **tx**. The IntelliSense feature lists the names of the seven text boxes, as shown in Figure 2-23.

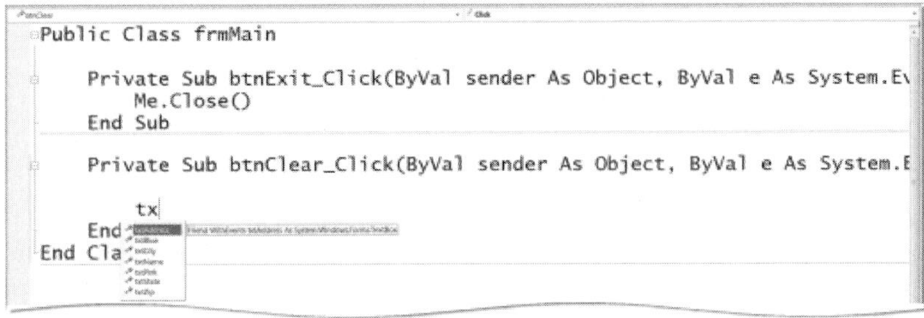

Figure 2-23 Listing of text box names

2. Type **tn** to highlight txtName in the list, then press **Tab** to enter txtName in the assignment statement. Now type **.** (a period) to display a listing of the properties and methods of the txtName control. If Text is not highlighted in the list, type **te**. At this point, you can either press the Tab key to enter the Text choice in the assignment statement, or you can simply type the assignment operator, which is the character that comes after Text in the statement. Type = to enter the Text choice in the statement.

3. Next, type **stri.e** and press **Enter**. The `txtName.Text = String.Empty` statement appears in the Code Editor window.

When entering code, you can type the names of commands, objects, and properties in lowercase letters. When you move to the next line, the Code Editor automatically changes your code to reflect the proper capitalization of those elements. This provides a quick way of verifying that you entered an object's name and property correctly, and that you entered the code using the correct syntax. If the capitalization does not change, it means that the Code Editor does not recognize the object, command, or property. In this book you always will be given the complete instruction to enter, including the appropriate capitalization. Keep in mind that you can type the instruction on your own, or you can use the IntelliSense feature to enter the instruction.

To continue coding the btnClear control's Click event procedure:

1. Enter the following six assignment statements:

   txtAddress.Text = String.Empty
   txtCity.Text = String.Empty
   txtState.Text = String.Empty
   txtZip.Text = String.Empty
   txtBlue.Text = String.Empty
   txtPink.Text = String.Empty

2. The second step in the procedure's pseudocode is to clear the Text property of the lblTotalPhones and lblTotalPrice controls. Enter the following two instructions. Press **Enter** twice after typing the last instruction.

   lblTotalPhones.Text = String.Empty
   lblTotalPrice.Text = String.Empty

The last step in the procedure's pseudocode is to send the focus to the txtName control. You can accomplish this task using the Focus method. As you learned in Chapter 1, a method is a predefined Visual Basic procedure that you can call (or invoke) when needed.

Using the Focus Method

You can use the **Focus method** to move the focus to a specified control while the application is running. As you learned in Lesson B, a control that has the focus can accept user input. The syntax of the Focus method is *object*.**Focus()**, where *object* is the name of the object to which you want the focus sent.

To enter the Focus method in the btnClear control's Click event procedure:

1. Type **txtName.Focus()** and press **Enter**.
2. Save the solution.

Internally Documenting the Program Code

It is a good practice to include comments, called internal documentation, as reminders in the Code Editor window. Programmers typically use comments to document a procedure's purpose, as well as to explain various sections of a procedure's code, because comments make the code more readable and easier to understand by anyone viewing it. You create a comment in Visual Basic by placing an apostrophe (') before the text that represents the comment. The computer ignores everything that appears after the apostrophe on that line. Although it is not required, some programmers use a space to separate the apostrophe from the comment text.

To add comments to the btnClear control's Click event procedure:

1. Click the **blank line** above the `txtName.Text = String.Empty` statement. Type **' prepare the screen for the next order** (be sure to type the apostrophe followed by a space) and press **Enter**. Notice that comments appear in a different color from the rest of the code.
2. Click the **blank line** above the `txtName.Focus()` statement. Type **' send the focus to the Name text box**. Figure 2-24 shows the completed Click event procedure for the btnClear control.

```
Private Sub btnClear_Click(ByVal sender As Object, ByVal e As System.E
    ' prepare the screen for the next order

    txtName.Text = String.Empty
    txtAddress.Text = String.Empty
    txtCity.Text = String.Empty
    txtState.Text = String.Empty
    txtZip.Text = String.Empty
    txtBlue.Text = String.Empty
    txtPink.Text = String.Empty
    lblTotalPhones.Text = String.Empty
    lblTotalPrice.Text = String.Empty
    ' send the focus to the Name text box
    txtName.Focus()
End Sub
```

Figure 2-24 Completed Click event procedure for the btnClear control

It is a good programming practice to write the code for one object at a time, and then test and debug that object's code before coding the next object. This way, if something is wrong with the program, you know exactly where to look for the error.

To test the btnClear control's Click event procedure:

1. Save the solution, then start the application. Enter your name and address information (including the city, state, and ZIP) in the appropriate text boxes, then enter **10** as the number of blue phones ordered and **10** as the number of pink phones ordered.

2. Click the **Clear Screen** button. Following the instructions you entered in the button's Click event procedure, the computer removes the contents of the seven text boxes, as well as the contents of the lblTotalPhones and lblTotalPrice controls. It also sends the focus to the Name text box. Click the **Exit** button to end the application. You are returned to the Code Editor window.

Many programmers also use comments to document the project's name and purpose, as well as to document the programmer's name and the date the code was either created or modified. Such comments are placed at the beginning of the application's code, above the Public Class statement. The area above the Public Class statement in the Code Editor window is called the General Declarations section.

To include comments in the General Declarations section:

1. Click **before the letter P** in the `Public Class frmMain` line, then press **Enter** to insert a blank line. Press the **up arrow** key on your keyboard to position the insertion point in the blank line.

2. Type the comments shown in Figure 2-25, replacing the <your name> and <current date> text with your name and the current date, then save the solution.

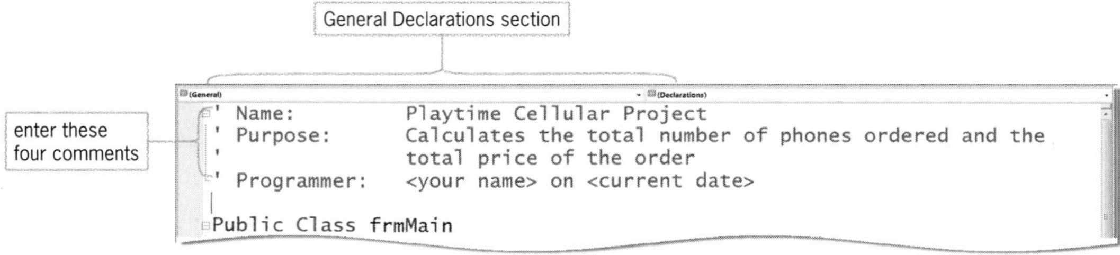

Figure 2-25 Comments entered in the General Declarations section

Before coding the btnCalc control's Click event procedure, you will learn how to write arithmetic expressions in Visual Basic.

Writing Arithmetic Expressions

Most applications require the computer to perform one or more calculations. You instruct the computer to perform a calculation by writing an arithmetic expression, which is an expression that contains one or more arithmetic operators. Figure 2-26 lists the most commonly used arithmetic operators available in Visual Basic, along with their precedence numbers. The precedence numbers indicate the order in which the computer performs the operation in an expression. Operations with a precedence number of 1 are performed before operations with a precedence number of 2, which are performed before operations with a precedence number of 3, and so on. However, you can use parentheses to override the order of precedence, because operations within parentheses always are performed before operations outside parentheses.

Operator	Operation	Precedence number
^	exponentiation (raises a number to a power)	1
–	negation	2
*, /	multiplication and division	3
\	integer division	4
Mod	modulus	5
+, –	addition and subtraction	6

Figure 2-26 Most commonly used arithmetic operators and their order of precedence

The difference between the negation and subtraction operators listed in Figure 2-26 is that the negation operator is unary, whereas the subtraction operator is binary. Unary and binary refer to the number of operands required by the operator. Unary operators require one operand, whereas binary operators require two operands. The expression -7, for example, uses the negation operator to turn the positive number 7 into a negative number. The expression 9 - 4, on the other hand, uses the subtraction operator to subtract the number 4 from the number 9.

Notice that some operators shown in Figure 2-26 have the same precedence number. For example, both the addition and subtraction operators have a precedence number of 6. If an expression contains more than one operator having the same priority, those operators are evaluated from left to right. In the expression 5 + 12 / 3 - 1, for instance, the division (/) is performed first, then the addition (+), and then the subtraction (-). In other words, the computer first divides 12 by 3, giving 4. It then adds the result of the division to 5, giving 9. Lastly, it subtracts 1 from the result of the addition, giving 8. You can use parentheses to change the order in which the operators in an expression are evaluated. For example, the expression 5 + 12 / (3 - 1) evaluates to 11, not 8. This is because the parentheses tell the computer to subtract 1 from 3 first, then divide the difference (2) into 12, and then add the quotient (6) to 5, giving 11.

Two of the arithmetic operators listed in Figure 2-26 might be less familiar to you: the integer division operator (\) and the modulus operator (Mod). You use the **integer division operator** (\) to divide two integers (whole numbers) and then return the result as an integer. For instance, the expression 211\4 results in 52, which is the integer result of dividing 211 by 4. (If you use the standard division operator [/] to divide 211 by 4, the result is 52.75 rather than 52.) You might use the integer division operator in a program that determines the number of quarters, dimes, and nickels to return as change to a customer. For example, if a customer should receive 53 cents in change, you could use the expression 53\25 to determine the number of quarters to return; the expression evaluates to 2. The modulus operator also is used to divide two numbers, but the numbers do not have to be integers. After dividing the numbers, the **modulus operator** returns the remainder of the division. For instance, 211 Mod 4 equals 3, which is the remainder of 211 divided by 4. You can use the modulus operator to determine whether a number is even or odd. If you divide a number by 2 and the remainder is 0, the number is even. If the remainder is 1, on the other hand, the number is odd.

When entering an arithmetic expression in code, you do not enter a comma or special characters, such as the dollar sign or percent sign. If you want to include a percentage in an arithmetic expression, you do so using its decimal equivalent; for example, you would enter .05 rather than 5%. Figure 2-27 shows examples of using arithmetic operators in expressions.

Expression	Result
2 ^ 3	8
4 * –3	–12
25 / 4	6.25
25 \ 4	6
25 Mod 4	1
80 * .05	4
7 + 6 * (5 – 2)	25

Figure 2-27 Expressions containing arithmetic operators

Coding the Calculate Order Button

According to the Playtime Cellular application's TOE chart (shown earlier in Figure 2-19), the btnCalc control is responsible for calculating both the total number of phones ordered and the total price of the order, and then displaying the calculated amounts in the lblTotalPhones and lblTotalPrice controls. The instructions to accomplish the button's tasks should be placed in the button's Click event procedure, because you want the instructions processed when the user clicks the button. The pseudocode shown in Figure 2-28 lists the steps the procedure must take to accomplish its tasks.

btnCalc Click event procedure

1. calculate total phones ordered = blue phones ordered + pink phones ordered
2. calculate total price = total phones ordered * phone price
3. display total phones ordered and total price in lblTotalPhones and lblTotalPrice

Figure 2-28 Pseudocode for the btnCalc control's Click event procedure

Step 1 in the pseudocode is to calculate the total number of phones ordered. This is accomplished by adding the number of blue phones ordered to the number of pink phones ordered. The number of blue phones ordered is recorded in the txtBlue control's Text property as the user enters that information in the interface. Likewise, the number of pink phones ordered is recorded in the txtPink control's Text property. You can use an assignment statement to add together the Text property of the two text boxes, and then assign the sum to the Text property of the lblTotalPhones control. The total phones ordered calculation is illustrated in Figure 2-29.

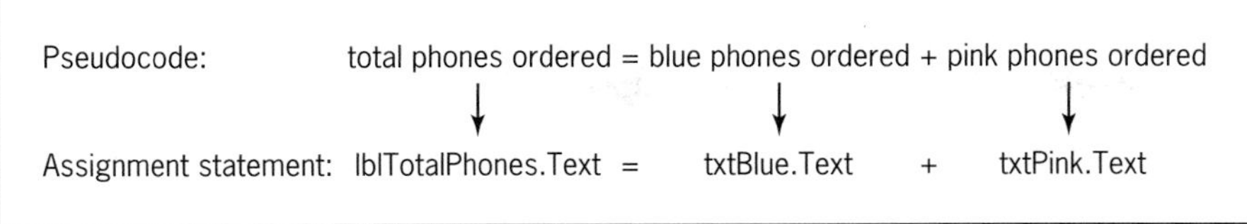

Figure 2-29 Illustration of the total phones ordered calculation

The next step shown in the procedure's pseudocode is to calculate the total price of the order. You can accomplish this task by multiplying the total number of phones ordered (which is recorded in the lblTotalPhones control) by the phone price ($25). The total price should be displayed in the lblTotalPrice control. The total price calculation is illustrated in Figure 2-30.

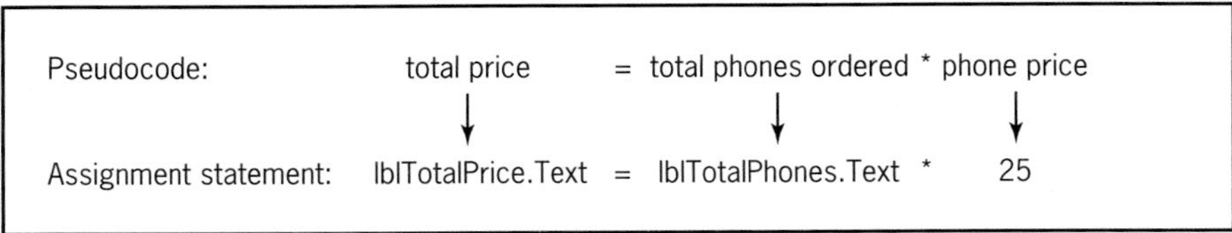

Figure 2-30 Illustration of the total price calculation

The last step in the procedure's pseudocode is to display the total phones ordered and total price in the lblTotalPhones and lblTotalPrice controls. The assignment statements shown in Figures 2-29 and 2-30 accomplish this task.

To code the btnCalc control's Click event procedure, and then test the procedure:

1. Open the code template for the btnCalc control's Click event procedure. Type **' calculates total number of phones ordered and total price** and press **Enter** twice.
2. Type **lblTotalPhones.Text = txtBlue.Text + txtPink.Text** and press **Enter**.
3. Type **lblTotalPrice.Text = lblTotalPhones.Text * 25** and press **Enter**.
4. Save the solution, then start the application. Press **Tab** five times to move the focus to the txtBlue control. Type **5** as the number of blue phones ordered, then press **Tab**. Type **10** as the number of pink phones ordered, then click the **Calculate Order** button. The btnCalc control's Click event procedure calculates the total number of phones ordered and the total price, displaying the results in the lblTotalPhones and lblTotalPrice controls. As Figure 2-31 indicates, the results are incorrect. Instead of mathematically adding the two order quantities together, giving 15, the second order quantity was appended to the first order quantity, giving 510. When the total phones ordered amount is incorrect, the total price also will be incorrect, because the total phones ordered amount is used in the total price calculation.

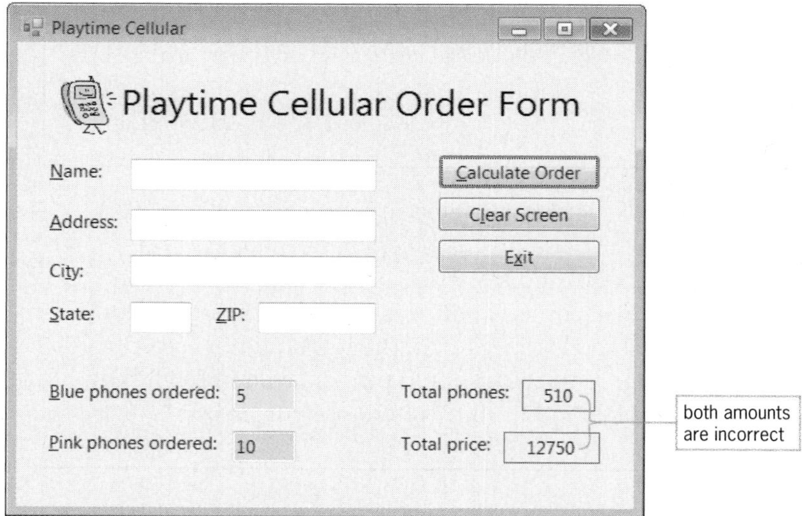

Figure 2-31 Interface showing the incorrect results of the calculations

5. Click the **Exit** button to end the application.

Even though you do not see the quotation marks around the value, a value stored in the Text property of an object is treated as a string rather than as a number. Adding strings together does not give you the same result as adding numbers together. As shown in the previous set of steps, adding the string "5" to the string "10" results in the string "510", whereas adding the number 5 to the number 10 results in the number 15. To add together the contents of two text boxes, you need to tell the computer to treat the contents as numbers rather than as strings. You can do this using either the Val function or the TryParse method. In this chapter (and only in this chapter), you will use the Val function, because it is the easiest to learn. However, keep in mind that most programmers now use the TryParse method, which you will learn about in Chapter 3.

The Val Function

A **function** is a predefined procedure that performs a specific task and then returns a value after completing the task. The **Val function**, for instance, temporarily converts a string to a number and then returns the number. The number is stored in the computer's memory only while the function is processing. The syntax of the Val function is **Val**(*string*), where *string* is the string you want treated as a number. Because the computer must be able to interpret the *string* as a numeric value, the *string* cannot include a letter, a comma, or a special character (such as the dollar sign or percent sign); it can, however, include a period or a space. When the computer encounters an invalid character in the Val function's *string*, it stops converting the *string* to a number at that point. Figure 2-32 shows some examples of how the Val function converts various strings.

Val function	Numeric result
Val("456")	456
Val("24,500")	24
Val("123X")	123
Val("25%")	25
Val(" 12 34 ")	1234
Val("$56.88")	0
Val("Abc")	0
Val("")	0

Figure 2-32 Examples of the Val function

To include the Val function in the btnCalc control's code:

1. Change the `lblTotalPhones.Text = txtBlue.Text + txtPink.Text` statement to **lblTotalPhones.Text = Val(txtBlue.Text) + Val(txtPink.Text)**. Be sure to watch the placement of the parentheses in the statement.
2. Change the `lblTotalPrice.Text = lblTotalPhones.Text * 25` statement to **lblTotalPrice.Text = Val(lblTotalPhones.Text) * 25**. See Figure 2-33.

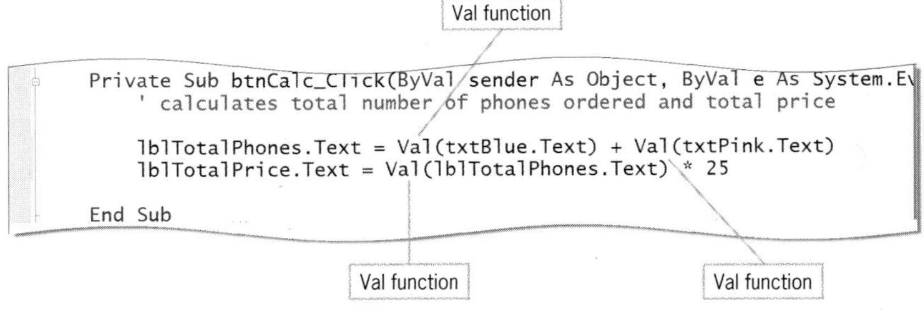

Figure 2-33 Val function entered in the assignment statements

3. Save the solution, then start the application. Click the **txtBlue** control, type **5** as the number of blue phones ordered, then press **Tab**. Type **10** as the number of pink phones ordered, then click the **Calculate Order** button. The application correctly calculates and displays the total number of phones ordered (15) and the total price of the order (375). In the next section, you will improve the appearance of the interface by including a dollar sign, a comma thousand separator, and two decimal places in the total price amount.
4. Click the **Clear Screen** button to clear the screen, then click the **Exit** button.

Using the Format Function to Format Numeric Output

You can use the **Format function** to improve the appearance of numbers in an interface. The syntax of the Format function is **Format**(*expression, style*). *Expression* specifies the number, date, time, or string whose appearance you want to format. *Style* is either the name of a predefined Visual Basic format style or, if you want more control over the appearance of the *expression*, a string containing special symbols that indicate how you want the *expression* displayed. (You can display the Help screen for the Format function to learn more about these special symbols.) In this case, you will use one of the predefined Visual Basic format styles, some of which are explained in Figure 2-34.

Format style	Description
Currency	Formats the number with a dollar sign, two decimal places, and (if appropriate) a thousand separator; negative numbers are enclosed in parentheses
Fixed	Formats the number with at least one digit to the left and two digits to the right of the decimal point
Standard	Formats the number with at least one digit to the left of the decimal point, two digits to the right of the decimal point, and (if appropriate) a thousand separator
Percent	Multiplies the number by 100 and formats the result with a percent sign and two digits to the right of the decimal point

Figure 2-34 Some of the predefined format styles in Visual Basic

To format the total price amount:

1. Click the **blank line** below the total price equation, then type **lblTotalPrice.Text = Format(lblTotalPrice.Text, "Currency")** and press **Enter**. Figure 2-35 shows the Format function entered in the btnCalc control's Click event procedure.

You also can include the Format function in the equation that calculates the total price, like this: `lblTotalPrice.Text = Format(Val(lblTotalPhones.Text) * 25, "Currency")`.

```
Private Sub btnCalc_Click(ByVal sender As Object, ByVal e As System.E
    ' calculates total number of phones ordered and total price

    lblTotalPhones.Text = Val(txtBlue.Text) + Val(txtPink.Text)
    lblTotalPrice.Text = Val(lblTotalPhones.Text) * 25
    lblTotalPrice.Text = Format(lblTotalPrice.Text, "Currency")

End Sub
```

Format function

Figure 2-35 Format function entered in the procedure

You have completed the first four of the six steps involved in creating an OO application: meeting with the client, planning the application, building the user interface, and coding the application. The fifth step is to test and debug the application.

Testing and Debugging the Application

You test an application by starting it and entering some sample data. You should use both valid and invalid data when testing an application. **Valid data** is data that the application is expecting the user to enter, whereas **invalid data** is data that the application is not expecting the user to enter. The Playtime Cellular application, for instance, expects the user to enter a numeric value in the txtBlue control; it does not expect the user to enter a letter. In most cases, invalid data is a result of a typing error made by the user. You should test an application as thoroughly as possible, because you don't want to give the user an application that ends abruptly when invalid data is entered.

Debugging refers to the process of locating and correcting the errors, called bugs, in a program. Program bugs typically are caused by either syntax errors or logic errors. As you learned in Chapter 1, the term "syntax" refers to the set of rules you must follow when using a programming language. A **syntax error** occurs when you break one of the language's rules. Most syntax errors are a result of typing errors that occur when entering instructions, such as typing `Me.Clse()` instead of `Me.Close()`. The Code Editor detects most syntax errors as you enter the instructions. An example of a much more difficult type of error to find, and one that the Code Editor cannot detect, is a logic error. A **logic error** can occur for a variety of reasons, such as forgetting to enter an instruction or entering the instructions in the wrong order. Some logic errors occur as a result of calculation statements that are correct syntactically, but incorrect mathematically. An example of this is the `lblSquared.Text = Val(txtNum1.Text) + Val(txtNum1.Text)` statement. The statement's syntax is correct, but it is incorrect mathematically: you square a value by multiplying it by itself, not by adding it to itself.

To test and debug the Playtime Cellular application:

1. Save the solution, then start the application. First, test the application by clicking the **Calculate Order** button without entering any data. The application displays 0 as the total number of phones ordered, and $0.00 as the total price. (Recall that the Val function converts the empty string to the number 0.)

2. Click the **Clear Screen** button to clear the calculated results from the label controls. Enter the letter **r** as the number of blue phones ordered and the letter **p** as the number of pink phones ordered. Click the **Calculate Order** button. The application displays 0 and $0.00 as the total number of phones ordered and total price, respectively. (Recall that the Val function converts a letter to the number 0.)

3. Click the **Clear Screen** button. Now enter the following correct order: **Toys For All**, **123 Main Street**, **Chicago**, **IL**, **60631**, **25** blue phones ordered, **20** pink phones ordered. Click the **Calculate Order** button. See Figure 2-36.

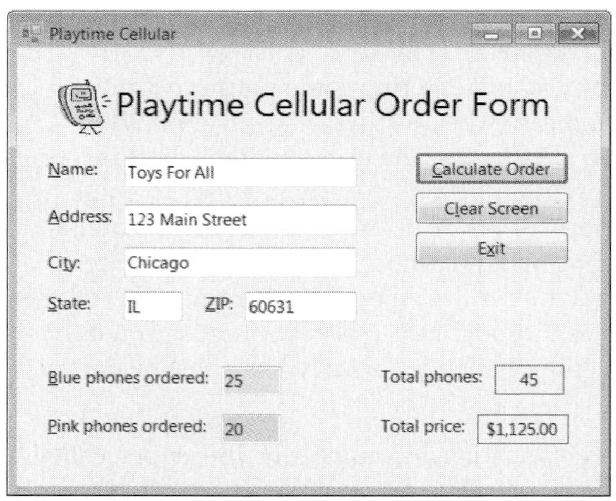

Figure 2-36 Result of calculating the Toys For All order

4. Click the **Clear Screen** button, then practice with other entries to see how the application responds. When you are finished testing the application, click the **Exit** button to end the application.

In the following set of steps, you will introduce two syntax errors in the application's code. You also will learn how to locate and correct the errors.

To introduce two syntax errors in the code, and also debug the code:

1. In the btnExit control's Click event procedure, change the `Me.Close()` statement to **Me.Clse()**, then click the **blank line** above the procedure header. The jagged blue line that appears below the statement indicates that the statement contains a syntax error. Position your mouse pointer on the `Me.Clse()` statement, as shown in Figure 2-37. The Code Editor displays an appropriate error message in a box. In this case, the message indicates that Clse is not a member of the form.

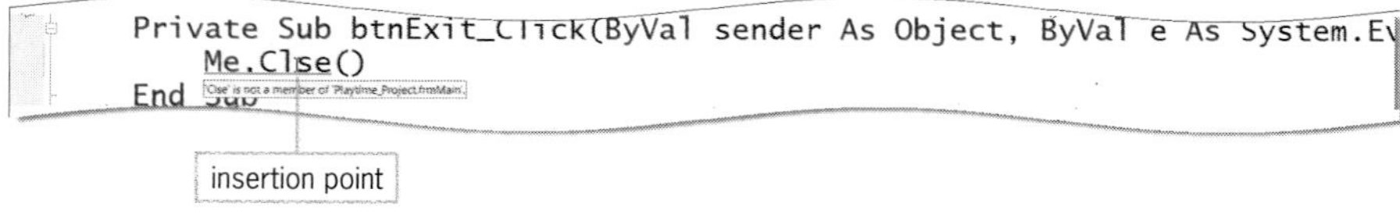

Figure 2-37 Jagged blue line and message indicate a syntax error

2. At this point, you usually would correct the error before starting the application. However, observe what happens when you start an application that contains a syntax error. Save the solution, then start the application. A message box similar to the one shown in Figure 2-38 appears.

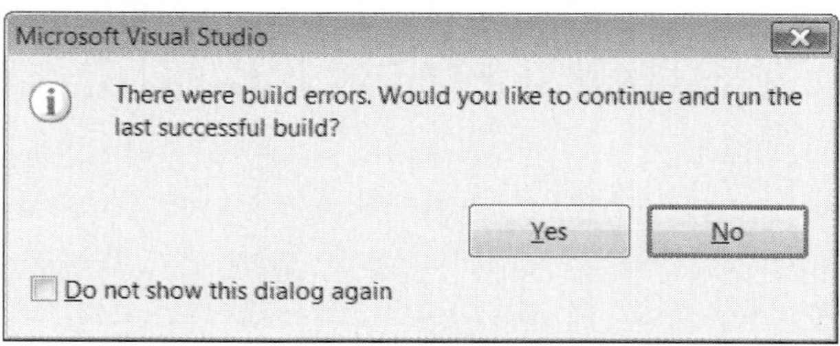

Figure 2-38 Message box indicates that the code contains errors

3. Click the **No** button. The Error List window shown in Figure 2-39 opens at the bottom of the IDE. The Error List window indicates that the code contains an error, and it provides a description and the location of the error.

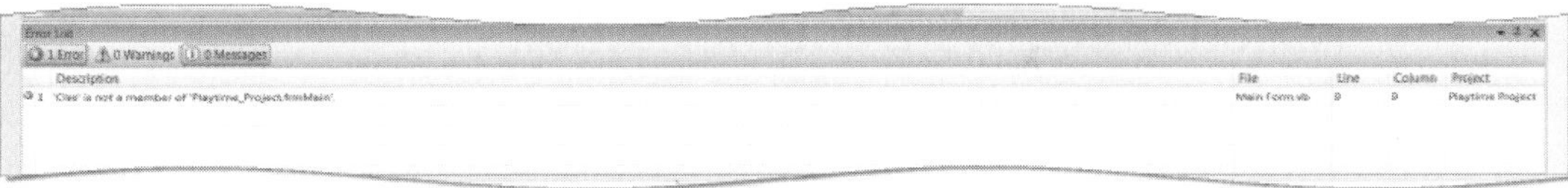

Figure 2-39 Error List window in the IDE

4. Double-click the **error's description** in the Error List window. The Code Editor highlights the error—in this case, the `Me.Clse` text. Change the `Me.Clse` text to **Me.Close**, then click the **blank line** above the procedure header. The jagged blue line disappears and the error is removed from the Error List window. Close the Error List window, then save the solution.

5. In the btnCalc control's Click event procedure, delete the ending parenthesis in the last assignment statement, then click the **blank line** below the statement. The thin red rectangle below the last character in the statement alerts you that the statement contains a syntax error. Position your mouse pointer on the rectangle, as shown in Figure 2-40. A box and an Error icon (a white exclamation point in a red circle) appear. The box contains a description of the syntax error.

```
lblTotalPrice.Text = Val(lblTotalPhones.Text) * 25
lblTotalPrice.Text = Format(lblTotalPrice.Text, "Currency"
```

Figure 2-40 Thin red rectangle, message, and Error icon indicate a syntax error

6. You can fix the syntax error yourself by simply typing the missing parenthesis at the end of the statement. Or, you can have the Code Editor correct the mistake for you. In this step, you'll put the Code Editor to work. Position your mouse pointer on the Error icon until a down arrow appears, then click the **down arrow** to open a window that contains one or more suggestions for fixing the error. In this case, the window, called the Error Correction window, contains only one suggestion, which is to insert the missing parenthesis. See Figure 2-41.

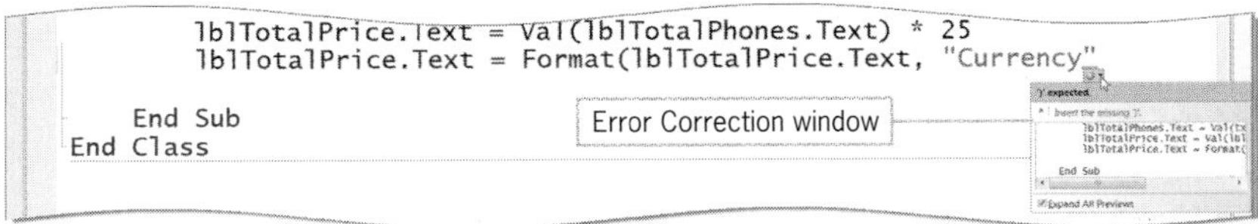

Figure 2-41 The Error Correction window displays a way to correct the syntax error

7. Move the scroll bar that appears at the bottom of the Error Correction window all the way to the right. The window indicates that the parenthesis will be inserted at the end of the assignment statement that contains the syntax error.

8. Click **Insert the missing ')'.** in the Error Correction window. Save the solution, then start the application. Test the application using your own sample data. When you are finished testing the application, click the **Exit** button to end the application.

Assembling the Documentation

After you have tested the application to verify that it is working correctly, you can move to the last step involved in creating an OO application: assemble the documentation. Assembling the documentation refers to putting your planning tools and a printout of the application's code and interface in a safe place, so you can refer to them if you need to change the application in the future. Your planning tools include the TOE chart, a sketch of the user interface, and either the flowcharts or pseudocode. In the next set of steps, you will learn how to print the application's code and interface.

To print the application's code and interface:

1. The Code Editor window should be open, which is necessary for printing the code. Click **File** on the menu bar, then click **Print**.
2. You can use the Include line numbers check box to print a line number next to each line in the printout. If necessary, click the **Include line numbers** check box to select it.
3. If your computer is connected to a printer, click the **OK** button to begin printing; otherwise, click the **Cancel** button. Figure 2-42 shows the application's code.

```
'Name:          Playtime Cellular Project
'Purpose:       Calculates the total number of phones ordered and the
'               total price of the order
'Programmer:    <your name> on <current date>

Public Class frmMain

    Private Sub btnExit_Click(ByVal sender As Object, _
        ByVal e As System.EventArgs) Handles btnExit.Click
        Me.Close()
    End Sub

    Private Sub btnClear_Click(ByVal sender As Object, _
        ByVal e As System.EventArgs) Handles btnClear.Click
        ' prepare the screen for the next order

        txtName.Text = String.Empty
        txtAddress.Text = String.Empty
        txtCity.Text = String.Empty
        txtState.Text = String.Empty
        txtZip.Text = String.Empty
        txtBlue.Text = String.Empty
        txtPink.Text = String.Empty
        lblTotalPhones.Text = String.Empty
        lblTotalPrice.Text = String.Empty
        ' send the focus to the Name text box
        txtName.Focus()

    End Sub

    Private Sub btnCalc_Click(ByVal sender As Object, _
        ByVal e As System.EventArgs) Handles btnCalc.Click
        ' calculates total number of phones ordered and total price

        lblTotalPhones.Text = Val(txtBlue.Text) + Val(txtPink.Text)
        lblTotalPrice.Text = Val(lblTotalPhones.Text) * 25
        lblTotalPrice.Text = Format(lblTotalPrice.Text, "Currency")

    End Sub
End Class
```

Figure 2-42 Playtime Cellular application's code

4. Close the Code Editor window. To print the interface, the designer window must be the active, or current, window. Click the **form**, then press **Alt+Print Screen** (Prnt Scrn) to place a picture of the interface on the Clipboard.

5. Start an application that can display a picture, such as the Microsoft Word application, and open a new document (if necessary). Press **Ctrl+v** to paste the contents of the Clipboard in the document.

6. Press **Ctrl+p** to open the Print dialog box. If your computer is connected to a printer, click the **OK** button; otherwise, click the **Cancel** button.

7. Close the Microsoft Word (or other) application without saving the changes, then close the solution.

Lesson C Summary

- **To plan an object's code:**

  Use pseudocode or a flowchart.

- **To clear the text property of an object while an application is running:**

  Assign the empty (or zero-length) string ("") or the `String.Empty` value to the object's Text property.

- **To assign a value to an object's property while an application is running:**

  Use an assignment statement that follows the syntax *object.property = expression*.

- **To move the focus to an object while an application is running:**

  Use the Focus method. The method's syntax is *object*.**Focus()**.

- **To create a comment in Visual Basic:**

  Begin the comment text with an apostrophe (').

- **To divide two integers and then return the result as an integer:**

  Use the integer division operator (\).

- **To divide two numbers and then return the remainder as an integer:**

  Use the modulus operator (Mod).

- **To temporarily convert a string to a number:**

  Use the Val function. The function's syntax is **Val**(*string*).

- **To improve the appearance of numbers in the user interface:**

  Use the Format function. The function's syntax is **Format**(*expression, style*).

- **To print an application's interface:**

  Make the designer window the active (current) window. Press Alt+Print Screen (Prnt Scrn). Start an application that can display a picture. If necessary, open a new document. Press Ctrl+v, then press Ctrl+p. Click the OK button.

Lesson C Key Terms

Assignment operator—the equal sign in an assignment statement

Assignment statement—an instruction that assigns a value to something, such as the property of an object

Debugging—the process of locating and correcting the bugs (errors) in a program

Empty string—also called a zero-length string; a set of quotation marks with nothing between them, like this: ""

Flowchart—a planning tool that uses standardized symbols to show the steps a procedure must follow to reach its goal

Focus method—the method used to move the focus to a specified control while an application is running

Format function—used to improve the appearance of numbers in an interface

Function—a predefined procedure that returns a value after completing its task

Input/output symbol—the parallelogram in a flowchart; used to represent input and output tasks

Integer division operator—the backslash (\); divides two integers and returns the result as an integer

Invalid data—data that an application is not expecting the user to enter

Logic error—an error that occurs when you enter an instruction that is syntactically correct, but does not give you the expected results, or when you neglect to enter an instruction or enter the instructions in the wrong order

Modulus operator—Mod; divides two numbers and returns the remainder

Process symbols—the rectangle symbol in a flowchart; used to represent tasks such as making calculations

Pseudocode—a planning tool that uses short phrases to describe the steps a procedure must take to accomplish its goal

Start/stop symbol—the oval symbol in a flowchart; used to indicate the beginning and end of the flowchart

String—a group of characters enclosed in quotation marks

String.Empty—a value that represents the empty string in Visual Basic

Syntax error—an error that occurs when an instruction violates a programming language's syntax

Val function—temporarily converts a string to a number and then returns the number

Valid data—data that an application is expecting the user to enter

Zero-length string—another term for the empty string

Lesson C Review Questions

1. Which of the following assignment statements will *not* calculate correctly?
   a. `lblTotal.Text = Val(txtSales1.Text) + Val(txtSales2.Text)`
   b. `lblTotal.Text = Val(txtSales1.Text + txtSales2.Text)`
   c. `lblTotal.Text = Val(txtQuantity.Text) * 2`
   d. `lblTotal.Text = Val(lblTotal.Text) * 1.1`
2. The ______________ function temporarily converts a string to a number.
   a. Format
   b. StringToNumber
   c. Val
   d. Value
3. Which symbol is used in a flowchart to represent a calculation task?
   a. circle
   b. oval
   c. parallelogram
   d. rectangle
4. What value is assigned to the lblNum control when the `lblNum.Text = 73 \ 25` instruction is processed by the computer?
5. What value is assigned to the lblNum control when the `lblNum.Text = 73 Mod 25` instruction is processed by the computer?

Lesson C Exercises

NOTE: In several of the exercises in this lesson, you perform the second through sixth steps involved in creating an OO application. Recall that the six steps are:

1. Meet with the client.
2. Plan the application. (Prepare a TOE chart that is ordered by object, then draw a sketch of the user interface.)
3. Build the user interface. (Refer to Appendix A for a listing of the GUI guidelines you have learned so far. To help you remember the names of the controls as you are coding, print the application's interface and then write the names next to each object.)
4. Code the application. (Write pseudocode for each of the objects that will be coded, and include appropriate comments in the code.)

5. Test and debug the application.

6. Assemble the documentation (your planning tools and a printout of the interface and code).

INTRODUCTORY

1. In this exercise, you complete the application saved in Lesson B's Exercise 1. Open the Paper Solution (Paper Solution.sln) file, which is contained in the VB2008\Chap02\Paper Solution folder. If necessary, open the designer window.

   a. Code the Calculate Commission button; be sure to use the Val function. Use the Format function to display the commission with a dollar sign, a comma thousand separator, and two decimal places. Use the Focus method to send the focus to the Clear Screen button.

   b. Code the Clear Screen button. Send the focus to the Name text box.

   c. Save the solution, then start the application. Test the application using valid and invalid data. Use the following information for the valid data: Pat Brown, 2000, and .1. Stop the application. Close the Code Editor window, then close the solution.

INTRODUCTORY

2. In this exercise, you complete the application saved in Lesson B's Exercise 2. Open the RM Sales Solution (RM Sales Solution.sln) file, which is contained in the VB2008\Chap02\RM Sales Solution folder. If necessary, open the designer window.

   a. Code the Calculate Projected Sales button; be sure to use the Val function. Use the Format function to display the projected sales using the Standard format.

   b. Code the Clear Screen button. Send the focus to the txtNorth-Sales control.

   c. Save the solution, then start the application. Test the application using valid and invalid data. Use the following information for the valid data:

North sales and percentage:	25000, .1
South sales and percentage:	10000, .05
East sales and percentage:	10000, .04
West sales and percentage:	15000, .11

   d. Stop the application. Close the Code Editor window, then close the solution.

INTRODUCTORY

3. In this exercise, you complete the application saved in Lesson B's Exercise 3. Open the Time Solution (Time Solution.sln) file, which is contained in the VB2008\Chap02\Time Solution folder. If necessary, open the designer window. Code the Calculate Hours button; be sure to use the Val function. Send the focus to the Monday text box. Save the solution, then start the application. Test the application using valid and invalid data. Stop the application. Close the Code Editor window, then close the solution.

4. John Lee wants an application in which he can enter the following three pieces of information: his cash balance at the beginning of the month, the amount of money he earned during the month, and the amount of money he spent during the month. He wants the application to display his ending balance.

INTRODUCTORY

   a. Create a Visual Basic Windows application. Name the solution, project, and form file JohnLee Solution, JohnLee Project, and Main Form.vb, respectively. Save the application in the VB2008\Chap02 folder.

   b. Assign the name frmMain to the form. Perform the steps involved in creating an OO application. (See the NOTE at the beginning of the Exercises section.)

   c. Test the application using the following valid and invalid data, then stop the application and close the Code Editor window and the solution.

Beginning cash balance: 5000	Earnings: 2500	Expenses: 3000
Beginning cash balance: xyz	Earnings: xyz	Expenses: xyz

5. In this exercise, you modify the Playtime Cellular application from the chapter.

INTERMEDIATE

   a. Use Windows to make a copy of the Playtime Solution folder, which is contained in the VB2008\Chap02 folder. Rename the folder Modified Playtime Solution.

   b. Open the Playtime Solution (Playtime Solution.sln) file contained in the VB2008\Chap02\Modified Playtime Solution folder. Open the designer window.

   c. Modify the interface so that it allows the user to enter the phone price. Also modify the application's code. Save the solution, then start and test the application. Stop the application, then close the Code Editor window and the solution.

6. Lana Jones wants an application that will display the average of any three numbers she enters.

INTERMEDIATE

   a. Create a Visual Basic Windows application. Name the solution, project, and form file LanaJones Solution, LanaJones Project, and Main Form.vb, respectively. Save the application in the VB2008\Chap02 folder.

   b. Assign the name frmMain to the form. Perform the steps involved in creating an OO application. (See the NOTE at the beginning of the Exercises section.)

   c. Test the application using the following valid and invalid data, then stop the application and close the Code Editor window and the solution.

First Number: 27	Second Number: 9	Third Number: 18
First Number: A	Second Number: B	Third Number: C

INTERMEDIATE

7. Martha Arenso, the manager of Bookworms Inc., needs an inventory application. Martha will enter the title of a book, the number of paperback versions of the book currently in inventory, the number of hardcover versions of the book currently in inventory, the cost of the paperback version, and the cost of the hardcover version. Martha wants the application to display the value of the paperback versions of the book, the value of the hardcover versions of the book, the total number of paperback and hardcover versions, and the total value of the paperback and hardcover versions.

   a. Create a Visual Basic Windows application. Name the solution, project, and form file Bookworms Solution, Bookworms Project, and Main Form.vb, respectively. Save the application in the VB2008\Chap02 folder.

   b. Assign the name frmMain to the form. Perform the steps involved in creating an OO application. (See the NOTE at the beginning of the Exercises section.) Format the calculated dollar amounts to show a dollar sign, comma thousand separator, and two decimal places.

   c. Test the application using the following valid and invalid data, then stop the application and close the Code Editor window and the solution.

      Book Title: An Introduction to Visual Basic 2008
      Paperback versions: 100 Paperback cost: 40
      Hardcover versions: 50 Hardcover cost: 75

      Book Title: Advanced Visual Basic 2008
      Paperback versions: A Paperback cost: B
      Hardcover versions: C Hardcover cost: D

INTERMEDIATE

8. Jackets Unlimited is having a 25% off sale. The store manager wants an application that allows the clerk to enter the original price of a jacket. The application should display the discount and new price.

   a. Create a Visual Basic Windows application. Name the solution, project, and form file Jackets Solution, Jackets Project, and Main Form.vb, respectively. Save the application in the VB2008\Chap02 folder.

   b. Assign the name frmMain to the form. Perform the steps involved in creating an OO application. (See the NOTE at the beginning of the Exercises section.) Format the discount and new price using the Standard format style. Test the application using valid and invalid data, then stop the application and close the Code Editor window and the solution.

INTERMEDIATE

9. Typing Salon charges $.10 per typed envelope and $.25 per typed page. The company accountant wants an application to help her prepare bills. She will enter the customer's name, the number of typed envelopes, and the number of typed pages. The application should calculate and display the customer's total bill.

   a. Create a Visual Basic Windows application. Name the solution, project, and form file TypingSalon Solution, TypingSalon Project, and Main Form.vb, respectively. Save the application in the VB2008\Chap02 folder.

   b. Assign the name frmMain to the form. Perform the steps involved in creating an OO application. (See the NOTE at the beginning of the Exercises section.) Format the total bill using the Currency format style.

   c. Test the application using the following valid and invalid data, then stop the application and close the Code Editor window and the solution.

      Customer's name: Alice Wong
      Number of typed envelopes: 250 Number of typed pages: 200

      Customer's name: Alice Wong
      Number of typed envelopes: $4 Number of typed pages: AB

ADVANCED

10. Suman Gadhari, the payroll clerk at Sun Projects, wants an application that displays the net pay for each of the company's employees. Suman will enter the employee's name, hours worked, and rate of pay. For this application, you do not have to worry about overtime, because this company does not allow anyone to work more than 40 hours. Suman wants the application to calculate and display the gross pay, the federal withholding tax (FWT), the Social Security tax (FICA), the state income tax, and the net pay. The FWT is 20% of the gross pay. The FICA tax is 8% of the gross pay. The state income tax is 2.5% of the gross pay.

    a. Create a Visual Basic Windows application. Name the solution, project, and form file Sun Solution, Sun Project, and Main Form.vb, respectively. Save the application in the VB2008\Chap02 folder.

    b. Assign the name frmMain to the form. Perform the steps involved in creating an OO application. (See the NOTE at the beginning of the Exercises section.) Format the calculated amounts using the Standard format style. Test the application using valid and invalid data. Stop the application, then close the Code Editor window and the solution.

ADVANCED

11. Colfax Industries needs an application that allows the shipping clerk to enter the quantity of an item in inventory and the number of the items that can be packed in a box for shipping. When the shipping clerk clicks a button, the application should compute and display the number of full boxes that can be packed and the number of items left over.

    a. Create a Visual Basic Windows application. Name the solution, project, and form file Colfax Solution, Colfax Project, and Main Form.vb, respectively. Save the application in the VB2008\Chap02 folder.

    b. Assign the name frmMain to the form. Perform the steps involved in creating an OO application. (See the NOTE at the beginning of the Exercises section.)

    c. Save the solution, then start the application. Colfax has 45 skateboards in inventory. If six skateboards can fit into a box for shipping, how many full boxes can the company ship and how many skateboards will remain in inventory? Stop the application, then close the Code Editor window and the solution.

Discovery

12. In this exercise, you learn about the TabStop property and the Clear method.

    a. Use Windows to make a copy of the Playtime Solution folder, which is contained in the VB2008\Chap02 folder. Rename the folder Discovery Playtime Solution.

    b. Open the Playtime Solution (Playtime Solution.sln) file contained in the VB2008\Chap02\Discovery Playtime Solution folder. Open the designer window.

    c. Most of Playtime Cellular's customers reside in Illinois. Use the Properties window to set the txtState control's Text property to IL.

    d. Because the txtState control already contains IL, there is no need for the user to tab into the control when entering data. You can use the control's TabStop property to bypass (or skip over) the control. If the user wants to change the State value, he can click the control or use the control's access key. Change the txtState control's TabStop property to False, then save the solution and start the application. Verify that the txtState control is bypassed when you tab through the controls in the interface.

    e. Click the Clear Screen button. Notice that the button removes the IL from the txtState control. Stop the application. Modify the btnClear control's Click event procedure to assign the string "IL" (rather than the `String.Empty` value) to the txtState control.

f. Save the solution, then start the application. Click the txtState control. Delete the IL, then type TX. Click the Clear Screen button. The button should assign the value IL to the txtState control. Stop the application.

g. You can use a text box control's Clear method to remove the contents of the control while an application is running. The method's syntax is *textbox*.**Clear()**. Use the Clear method in the btnClear control's Click event procedure to remove the contents of the text boxes (except the txtState text box). (You cannot use the Clear method to remove the contents of label controls.)

h. Save the solution, then start the application. Enter an order, then click the Calculate Order button. Click the Clear Screen button. Stop the application, then close the Code Editor window and the solution.

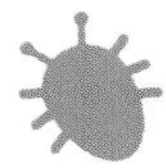

Swat The Bugs

13. Open the Debug Solution (Debug Solution.sln) file, which is contained in the VB2008\Chap02\Debug Solution folder. If necessary, open the designer window. Open the Code Editor window. Locate and then correct the syntax errors in the code. Save the solution, then start and test the application. Stop the application, then close the Code Editor window and the solution.

CHAPTER 3

Using Variables and Constants

Revising the Playtime Cellular Application

In this chapter, you modify the Playtime Cellular application created in Chapter 2. The modified application will calculate and display a 3% sales tax. It also will display the name of the salesperson who recorded the order.

Previewing the Playtime Cellular Application

To preview the completed Playtime Cellular application:

1. Open the Run dialog box. Use the **Browse** button to locate and then open the VB2008\Chap03 folder. Click **Playtime Cellular** (**Playtime Cellular.exe**) in the list of filenames, then click the **Open** button. Click the **OK** button in the Run dialog box. An order form similar to the one created in Chapter 2 appears on the screen.

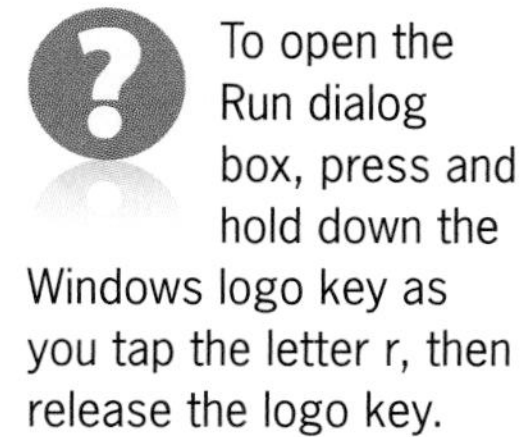

To open the Run dialog box, press and hold down the Windows logo key as you tap the letter r, then release the logo key.

If a Security Warning dialog box appears, click Run.

2. Enter the following customer information on the order form: **Johansen's, 3400 Esquire Drive, Chicago, IL, 60654**.
3. Enter **25** as the number of blue phones ordered, then enter **5** as the number of pink phones ordered.
4. Although the Calculate Order button does not have the focus, you can select it by pressing the Enter key. This is because the Calculate Order button is the default button in the user interface. You will learn how to designate a default button in Lesson B. Press **Enter** to calculate the order. A Name Entry dialog box appears and requests the salesperson's name, as shown in Figure 3-1.

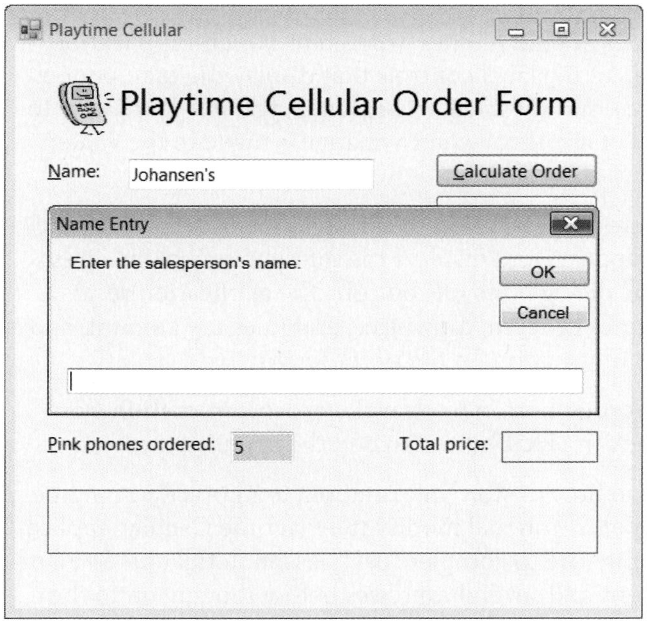

Figure 3-1 Name Entry dialog box

5. Type **Harriet Nozinski** as the salesperson's name and press **Enter**. The application calculates the order. The completed order form is shown in Figure 3-2. Notice that the sales tax amount and the salesperson's name appear on the order form. The application uses string concatenation, which you learn about in Lesson B, to display the information.

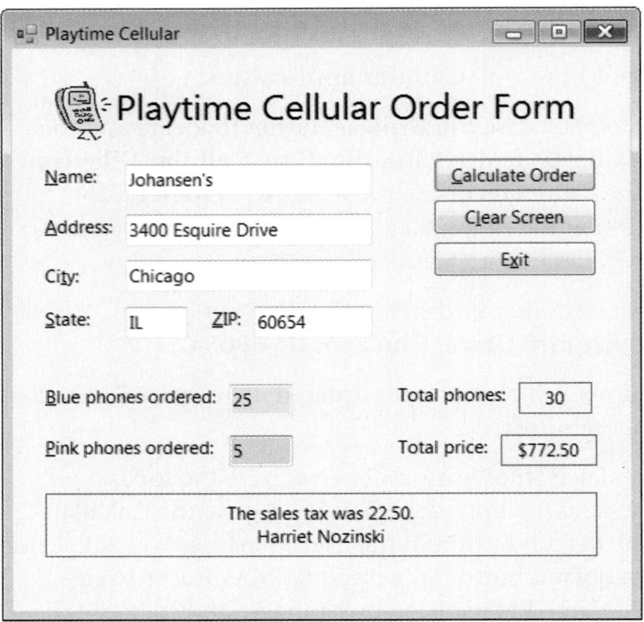

Figure 3-2 Completed order form

6. Change the number of pink phones ordered to **10**. The application clears the contents of the label controls that display the total phones ordered, total price, and message. In Lesson C, you will learn how to clear the contents of a control when a change is made to the value stored in a different control.

7. Click the **Calculate Order** button to calculate the order. The Name Entry dialog box appears and displays the salesperson's name. Press **Enter** to select the dialog box's OK button. The application recalculates the total phones ordered, total price, and sales tax amount, and then displays the information on the order form.

8. Click the **Clear Screen** button to clear the order information from the form, then click the **Exit** button to end the application.

In Lesson A, you will learn how to store information, temporarily, in memory locations inside the computer. You will modify the Playtime Cellular application in Lessons B and C. Be sure to complete each lesson in full and do all of the end-of-lesson questions and several exercises before moving on to the next lesson.

LESSON A

After studying Lesson A, you should be able to:

- Declare variables and named constants
- Assign data to an existing variable
- Convert string data to a numeric data type using the TryParse method
- Convert numeric data to a different data type using the Convert class methods
- Explain the scope and lifetime of variables and named constants
- Explain the purpose of Option Explicit, Option Infer, and Option Strict

Using Variables to Store Information

All of the order information in the Playtime Cellular application from Chapter 2 is temporarily stored in the properties of various controls on the order form. For example, the number of blue phones ordered is stored in the Text property of the txtBlue control, and the number of pink phones ordered is stored in the Text property of the txtPink control. The application uses the Text properties of the txtBlue and txtPink controls in the assignment statement that calculates the total phones ordered, like this: `lblTotalPhones.Text = Val(txtBlue.Text) + Val(txtPink.Text)`. The assignment statement assigns the calculated result to the Text property of the lblTotalPhones control. The application uses the lblTotalPhones control's Text property in the `lblTotalPrice.Text = Val(lblTotalPhones.Text) * 25` assignment statement, which calculates the total price of the order and assigns the result to the lblTotalPrice control.

Besides storing data in the properties of controls, a programmer also can store data, temporarily, in memory locations inside the computer. The memory locations are called **variables**, because the contents of the locations can change as the application is running. It may be helpful to picture a variable as a small box inside the computer. You can enter and store data in the box, but you cannot actually see the box. One use for a variable is to hold information that is not stored in a control on the form. For example, if you did not need to display the total number of phones ordered on the Playtime Cellular order form, you could eliminate the lblTotalPhones control from the form and store the total number of phones ordered in a variable instead. You then would use the value stored in the variable, rather than the value stored in the Text property of the lblTotalPhones control, in the total price equation. You also can use a variable to store the data contained in a control's property, such as the data contained in a control's Text property. Programmers typically do this when the data is a numeric amount that will be used in a calculation. As you will learn in the next section, assigning numeric data to a variable allows you to control the preciseness of the data. It also makes your code run more efficiently, because the computer can process data stored in a variable much faster than it can process data stored in the property of a control.

Every variable has a data type, name, scope, and lifetime. First, you will learn how to select an appropriate data type for a variable.

Selecting a Data Type for a Variable

Variables used in an application should be assigned a data type by the programmer. The **data type** determines the type of data the variable can store. Figure 3-3 describes most of the basic data types available in Visual Basic 2008. Each data type is a class, which means that each data type is a pattern from which one or more objects—in this case, variables—are instantiated (created). As the figure indicates, variables assigned the Integer, Long, or Short data type can store integers, which are whole numbers—positive or negative numbers without any decimal places. The differences among these three data types are in the range of integers each type can store and the amount of memory each type needs to store the integer. Decimal, Double, and Single variables, on the other hand, can store numbers containing a decimal place. Here again, the differences among these three data types are in the range of numbers each type can store and the amount of memory each type needs to store the numbers. However, calculations involving Decimal variables are not subject to the small rounding errors that may occur when using Double or Single variables. In most cases, the small rounding errors do not create any problems in an application. One exception to this is when the application contains complex equations dealing with money, where you need accuracy to the penny. In those cases, the Decimal data type is the best type to use.

Also listed in Figure 3-3 are the Char, String, Boolean, Date, and Object data types. The Char data type can store one Unicode character, while the String data type can store from zero to approximately two billion Unicode characters. **Unicode** is the universal coding scheme for characters. It assigns a unique numeric value to each character used in the written languages of the world. (For more information, see The Unicode Standard at *www.unicode.org*.) You use a Boolean variable to store a Boolean value (either True or False), and a Date variable to store date and time information. The Object data type can store any type of data. However, your application will pay a price for this flexibility: it will run more slowly, because the computer has to determine the type of data currently stored in an Object variable. It is best to avoid using the Object data type.

Data type	Stores	Memory required
Boolean	a logical value (True, False)	2 bytes
Char	one Unicode character	2 bytes
Date	date and time information Date range: January 1, 0001 to December 31, 9999 Time range: 0:00:00 (midnight) to 23:59:59	8 bytes
Decimal	a number with a decimal place Range with no decimal place: +/-79,228,162,514,264,337,593,543,950,335 Range with 28 decimal places: +/-7.9228162514264337593543950335	16 bytes
Double	a number with a decimal place Range: +/- 4.94065645841247 X 10^{-324} to +/-1.79769313486231 X 10^{308}	8 bytes

Figure 3-3 Basic data types in Visual Basic *(continues)*

(continued)

Data type	Stores	Memory required
Integer	integer Range: -2,147,483,648 to 2,147,483,647	4 bytes
Long	integer Range: -9,223,372,036,854,775,808 to 9,223,372,036,854,775,807	8 bytes
Object	data of any type	4 bytes
Short	integer Range: -32,768 to 32,767	2 bytes
Single	a number with a decimal place Range: +-1.401298 X 10^{-45} to +/-3.402823 X 10^{38}	4 bytes
String	text; 0 to approximately 2 billion characters	

Figure 3-3 Basic data types in Visual Basic

In this book, you will use the Integer data type for variables that will store integers used in calculations, even when the integers are small enough to fit into a Short variable. This is because a calculation containing Integer variables takes less time to process than the equivalent calculation containing Short variables. You will use either the Decimal data type or the Double data type for numbers that contain decimal places and are used in calculations. You will use the String data type for variables that contain text or numbers not used in calculations, and the Boolean data type to store Boolean values.

Selecting a Name For a Variable

In addition to assigning a data type to the variables used in an application, the programmer also must assign a name to each variable. The name, also called the identifier, should be descriptive in that it should help you remember the variable's purpose. In other words, it should describe the contents of the variable. A good variable name is one that is meaningful right after you finish a program, and also years later when you (or perhaps a co-worker) need to modify the program. There are several conventions for naming variables in Visual Basic. In this book, you will use Hungarian notation, which is the same naming convention used for controls. Variable names in Hungarian notation begin with a three character ID that represents the variable's data type. For example, the names of Integer variables begin with `int`, while the names of Decimal and Double variables begin with `dec` and `dbl`, respectively. The names of String variables begin with `str`, and the names of Boolean variables begin with `bln`. The remaining characters in a variable's name represent the variable's purpose. Using Hungarian notation, you might assign the name `intAge` to an Integer variable that stores a person's age, and the name `decGrossPay` to a Decimal variable that stores the amount of an employee's gross pay. Like control names, variable names are entered using camel case, which means you lowercase the ID and then uppercase the first letter of each word in the name. Figure 3-4 lists the rules for naming variables and includes examples of valid and invalid variable names.

Rules for naming variables

1. The name must begin with a letter or an underscore.
2. The name can contain only letters, numbers, and the underscore character. No punctuation marks, spaces, or other special characters (such as $ or %) are allowed in the name.
3. Although the name can contain thousands of characters, 32 characters is the recommended maximum number of characters to use.
4. The name cannot be a reserved word, such as `Sub` or `Double`.

Valid names

`intJanuary_Sales`, `decSales2011`, `dblWestRegion`, `strFirstName`, `blnIsValid`

Invalid names	Problem
`2ndQuarterSales`	the name must begin with a letter or an underscore
`dblWest Region`	the name cannot contain a space
`strFirst.Name`	the name cannot contain punctuation
`decSales$North`	the name cannot contain a special character

Figure 3-4 Variable naming rules and examples

Declaring a Variable

Dim comes from the word *dimension*, which is how programmers in the 1960s referred to the process of allocating the computer's memory. *Dimension* refers to the "size" of something.

Now that you know how to select an appropriate data type and name for a variable, you can learn how to declare a variable in code. Declaring a variable tells the computer to set aside a small section of its internal memory, and it allows you to refer to the section by the variable's name. The size of the section is determined by the variable's data type. You declare a variable using a declaration statement. Figure 3-5 shows the syntax of a declaration statement and includes several examples of declaring variables. The {`Dim` | `Private` | `Static`} portion of the syntax indicates that you can select only one of the keywords appearing within the braces. In most instances, you declare a variable using the `Dim` keyword. (You will learn about the `Private` and `Static` keywords later in this lesson.) *VariableName* and *dataType* are the variable's name and data type, respectively. As mentioned earlier, a variable is considered an object in Visual Basic and is an instance of the class specified in the *dataType* information. The `Dim dblHoursWorked As Double` statement, for example, creates an object named `dblHoursWorked`; the object is an instance of the Double class. *InitialValue* is the value you want stored in the variable when it is created in the computer's internal memory. The square brackets in the syntax indicate that the " = *initialValue*" part of a variable declaration statement is optional. If you do not assign an initial value to a variable when it is declared, the computer stores a default value in the variable; the default value depends on the variable's data type. A variable declared using one of the numeric data types is automatically initialized to—in other words, given a beginning value of—the number 0. The computer automatically initializes a Boolean variable using the keyword `False`, and a Date variable to 1/1/0001 12:00:00 AM. Object and String variables are automatically initialized using the keyword `Nothing`. Variables initialized to `Nothing` do not actually contain the word "Nothing"; rather, they contain no data at all.

Variable declaration statement

Syntax

{**Dim** | **Private** | **Static**} *variableName* **As** *dataType* [= *initialValue*]

Example 1

```
Dim dblHoursWorked As Double
```

declares a Double variable named `dblHoursWorked`; the variable is automatically initialized to 0

Example 2

```
Dim decPrice As Decimal
Dim decDiscount As Decimal
```

declares two Decimal variables named `decPrice` and `decDiscount`; the variables are automatically initialized to 0

Example 3

```
Dim blnIsValid As Boolean = True
```

declares a Boolean variable named `blnIsValid` and initializes it using the keyword `True`

Example 4

```
Dim strMessage As String = "Good morning"
```

declares a String variable named `strMessage` and initializes it using the string "Good morning"

Figure 3-5 Syntax and examples of a variable declaration statement

Assigning Data to an Existing Variable

In Chapter 2, you learned how to use an assignment statement to assign a value to a control's property while an application is running. An assignment statement also is used to assign a value to a variable while an application is running. The syntax for doing this is *variableName = expression*, where *expression* can contain items such as literal constants, properties of controls, variables, or arithmetic operators. A **literal constant** is an item of data whose value does not change while the application is running; examples include the string literal constant "Mary" and the numeric literal constant 500. When the computer processes an assignment statement, it assigns the value of the expression that appears on the right side of the assignment operator to the variable (memory location) whose name appears on the left side of the assignment operator. In other words, the computer evaluates the expression and then stores the result in the variable. The data type of the value assigned to a variable should be the same data type as the variable itself. Figure 3-6 shows examples of assigning values to variables having the same data type.

Recall that the equal sign in an assignment statement is called the assignment operator.

Assigning values to variables having the same data type

Example 1

```
intQuantity = 500
```

assigns the integer 500 to an Integer variable named `intQuantity`

Example 2

```
strFirstName = "Mary"
```

assigns the string "Mary" to a String variable named `strFirstName`

Example 3

```
strZipCode = txtZip.Text
```

assigns the string contained in the txtZip control's Text property to a String variable named `strZipCode`

Example 4

```
dblDiscountRate = .03
```

assigns the Double number .03 to a Double variable named `dblDiscountRate`

Example 5

```
decTaxRate = .05D
```

converts the Double number .05 to Decimal and then assigns the result to a Decimal variable named `decTaxRate`

Example 6

```
dblCommission = dblSales * .1
```

multiplies the contents of the `dblSales` variable by .1 and then assigns the result to a Double variable named `dblCommission`

Figure 3-6 Examples of assignment statements that assign values to variables having the same data type

In Example 1 in Figure 3-6, the `intQuantity = 500` assignment statement stores the numeric literal constant 500, an integer, in an Integer variable named `intQuantity`. Similarly, the `strFirstName = "Mary"` assignment statement in Example 2 stores the string literal constant "Mary" in a String variable named `strFirstName`. Notice that string literal constants are enclosed in quotation marks, but numeric literal constants and variable names are not. The quotation marks differentiate a string from both a number and a variable name. In other words, "500" is a string, but 500 is a number. Similarly, "Mary" is a string, but Mary (without the quotation marks) would be interpreted by the computer as the name of a variable. When the computer processes an assignment statement that assigns a string to a String variable, it assigns only the characters that appear between the quotation marks; the computer does not assign the quotation marks.

As you learned in Chapter 2, the value stored in the Text property of an object is always treated as a string.

The `strZipCode = txtZip.Text` statement in Example 3 in Figure 3-6 assigns the string contained in the txtZip control's Text property to a String variable named `strZipCode`. The `dblDiscountRate = .03` statement in Example 4 assigns the Double number .03 to a Double variable named `dblDiscountRate`. This is because a numeric literal constant that has a decimal place is automatically treated as a Double number in Visual Basic. The `decTaxRate = .05D` statement in Example 5 shows how you convert a numeric literal constant of the Double data type to the Decimal data type, and then assign the result to a Decimal variable. The D that follows the number .05 in the statement is one of the literal type characters in Visual Basic. A **literal type character** forces a literal constant to assume a data type other than the one its form indicates. In this case, the D forces the Double number .05 to assume the Decimal data type. The `dblCommission = dblSales * .1` statement in Example 6 multiplies the contents of the `dblSales` variable by the Double number .1 and then assigns the result to the `dblCommission` variable. When an assignment statement's *expression* contains the name of a variable, the computer uses the value stored inside the variable to evaluate the expression.

You will learn about another literal type character, the letter C, in Chapter 8.

Keep in mind that a variable can store only one value at any one time. When you use an assignment statement to assign another value to the variable, the new value replaces the existing value. To illustrate this point, assume that a button's Click event procedure contains the following two lines of code: `Dim intNumber As Integer = 500` and `intNumber = intNumber * 2`. When you start the application and click the button, the two lines of code are processed as follows:

1. The Dim statement creates the `intNumber` variable in memory and initializes it to the number 500.
2. The `intNumber = intNumber * 2` assignment statement first multiplies the contents of the `intNumber` variable by the number 2, giving 1000. The assignment statement then replaces the current contents of the `intNumber` variable (500) with 1000. Notice that the calculation appearing on the right side of the assignment operator is performed first, and then the result is assigned to the variable whose name appears on the left side of the assignment operator.

In all of the assignment statements in Figure 3-6, the data type of the value matched the data type of the variable to which it was assigned. At times, however, the value's data type might be different from the variable's data type. You can change the value's data type to match the variable's data type using either the TryParse method or one of the methods in the Convert class. You will learn about the TryParse method first.

The TryParse Method

Like the Val function, which you learned about in Chapter 2, the **TryParse method** converts a string to a number. However, for the following two reasons, most programmers prefer the TryParse method over the Val function. First, although the Val function has been a part of the Visual Basic language since its inception, Microsoft does not guarantee that it will always be a part of the language. Second, the Val function always returns a Double number, whereas the TryParse method allows you to specify the number's data type. Every numeric data type in Visual Basic has a TryParse method that converts a string to that particular data type. The basic syntax of the TryParse method is ***dataType*.TryParse(*string*, *variable*)**, where *dataType* is one of the numeric data types available in Visual Basic, such as Decimal, Double, or Integer. The items within the parentheses in the syntax are called arguments and represent information that is passed to the method while the method is processing. The *string* argument is the string you want converted to a

The dot member access operator in the TryParse method's syntax indicates that the method is a member of the *dataType* class.

You will learn more about the TryParse method in Chapter 4.

number of the *dataType* type and typically is either the Text property of a control or the name of a String variable. The *variable* argument is the name of a numeric variable where the TryParse method can store the number. The numeric variable must have the same data type as specified in the *dataType* portion of the syntax. In other words, when using the TryParse method to convert a string to a Double number, you need to provide the method with the name of a Double variable in which to store the number. The TryParse method parses the string, which means it looks at each character in the string, to determine whether the string can be converted to a number of the specified data type. If the string can be converted, the TryParse method converts the string to a number and stores the number in the variable specified in the *variable* argument. If the TryParse method determines that the string cannot be converted to the appropriate data type, it assigns the number 0 to the variable. Figure 3-7 shows the basic syntax of the TryParse method and includes examples of using the method.

Using the TryParse method

Basic syntax

dataType.**TryParse(***string*, *variable***)**

Example 1

```
Double.TryParse(txtSales.Text, dblSales)
```

If the string contained in the txtSales control can be converted to a Double number, the TryParse method converts the string and stores the result in the `dblSales` variable; otherwise, it stores the number 0 in the `dblSales` variable.

Example 2

```
Decimal.TryParse(txtGross.Text, decGross)
```

If the string contained in the txtGross control can be converted to a Decimal number, the TryParse method converts the string and stores the result in the `decGross` variable; otherwise, it stores the number 0 in the `decGross` variable.

Example 3

```
Integer.TryParse(strNumber, intNumber)
```

If the string contained in the `strNumber` variable can be converted to an Integer number, the TryParse method converts the string and stores the result in the `intNumber` variable; otherwise, it stores the number 0 in the `intNumber` variable.

Figure 3-7 Basic syntax and examples of the TryParse method

Figure 3-8 shows how the TryParse method of the Double, Decimal, and Integer data types would convert various strings. As the figure indicates, the three methods can convert a string that contains only numbers, as well as one that also contains a leading sign or leading or trailing spaces. In addition, the Double.TryParse and Decimal.TryParse methods can convert a string that contains a decimal point or a comma. However, none of the three methods can convert a string that contains a dollar sign, a percent sign, a letter, or a space within the string.

string	**Double.TryParse**	**Decimal.TryParse**	**Integer.TryParse**
"62"	62	62	62
-9	-9	-9	-9
"12.55"	12.55	12.55	0
"-4.23"	-4.23	-4.23	0
"1,457"	1457	1457	0
" 33 "	33	33	33
"$5"	0	0	0
"7%"	0	0	0
"122a"	0	0	0
"1 345"	0	0	0
empty string	0	0	0

Figure 3-8 Results of the TryParse method for the Double, Decimal, and Integer data types

The Convert Class

At times, you may need to convert a number (rather than a string) from one data type to another. Visual Basic provides several ways of accomplishing this task. One way is to use the Visual Basic conversion functions, which are listed in Appendix B in this book. You also can use one of the methods defined in the **Convert class**. In this book you will use the Convert class methods, because they have an advantage over the conversion functions: the methods can be used in any of the languages built into Visual Studio, whereas the conversion functions can be used only in the Visual Basic language. The more commonly used methods in the Convert class are the ToDecimal, ToDouble, ToInt32, and ToString methods. The methods convert a value to the Decimal, Double, Integer, and String data types, respectively. Figure 3-9 shows the syntax of the Convert class methods. In the syntax, *value* is the value you want converted to a different data type. In most cases, value will be a numeric value that you want converted either to the String data type or to a different numeric data type (for example, from Double to Decimal). Although you can use the Convert methods to convert a string to a numeric data type, the TryParse method is the recommended method to use for that task. This is because, unlike the Convert methods, the TryParse method does not produce an error when it tries to convert the empty string; instead, it assigns the number 0 to its *variable* argument. In addition to showing the syntax of the Convert class methods, Figure 3-9 also shows examples of using the methods. The statements in Examples 1 and 3 are equivalent to the `decTaxRate = .05D` and `decCommission = decSales * .1D` statements, respectively. However, many programmers would argue that using the Convert.ToDecimal method, rather than the literal type character (D), makes the code clearer.

The dot member access operator in the syntax shown in Figure 3-9 indicates that the *method* is a member of the Convert class.

Using the Convert class methods

Syntax

Convert.*method***(***value***)**

Example 1

```
decTaxRate = Convert.ToDecimal(.05)
```

converts the Double number .05 to Decimal and then assigns the result to the `decTaxRate` variable

Example 2

```
lblTotal.Text = Convert.ToString(intTotalScores)
```

converts the contents of the `intTotalScores` variable to String and then assigns the result to the lblTotal control's Text property

Example 3

```
decCommission = decSales * Convert.ToDecimal(.1)
```

converts the Double number .1 to Decimal, then multiplies the result by the contents of the `decSales` variable, and then assigns that result to the `decCommission` variable

Figure 3-9 Syntax and examples of the Convert class methods

The Scope and Lifetime of a Variable

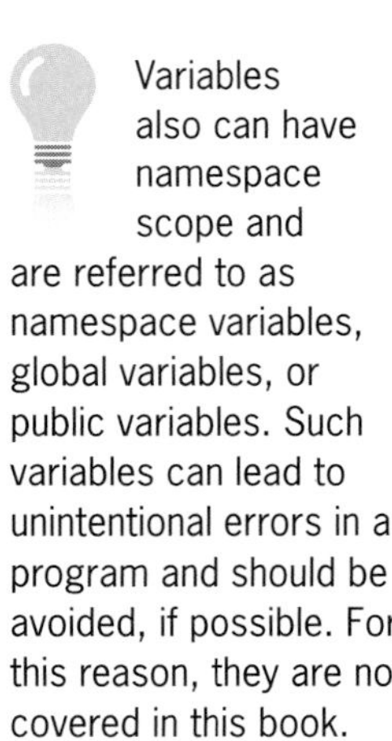

Variables also can have namespace scope and are referred to as namespace variables, global variables, or public variables. Such variables can lead to unintentional errors in a program and should be avoided, if possible. For this reason, they are not covered in this book.

Besides a name, data type, and initial value, every variable also has a scope and a lifetime. A variable's **scope** indicates where in the application's code the variable can be used, and its **lifetime** indicates how long the variable remains in the computer's internal memory. Variables can have module scope, procedure scope, or block scope. However, most of the variables used in an application will have procedure scope. This is because fewer unintentional errors occur in applications when the variables are declared using the minimum scope needed, which usually is procedure scope. A variable's scope and lifetime are determined by where you declare the variable—in other words, where you enter the variable's declaration statement. Typically, you enter the declaration statement either in a procedure, such as an event procedure, or in the Declarations section of a form. A form's Declarations section is not the same as the General Declarations section, which you learned about in Chapter 2. The General Declarations section is located above the Public Class line in the Code Editor window, whereas the form's Declarations section is located between the Public Class and End Class lines. Variables declared in a procedure have either procedure scope or block scope, depending on where in the procedure they are declared. Variables declared in a form's Declarations section have module scope. In the next two sections, you will learn about procedure scope variables and module scope variables. Variables having block scope are covered in Chapter 4.

Variables with Procedure Scope

Procedure-level variables are also called local variables, and their scope is sometimes referred to as local scope.

When you declare a variable in a procedure, the variable is called a **procedure-level variable** and it has **procedure scope**, because only that procedure can use the variable. For example, if you enter the `Dim intNumber As Integer` statement in the btnCalc control's Click event procedure, only the btnCalc control's Click event procedure can use the `intNumber` variable; no other procedures in the application are allowed to use the variable. As a matter of fact, no other procedures in the application will even be aware of the `intNumber` variable's existence. Procedure-level variables remain in the computer's internal memory only while the procedure in which they are declared is running; they are removed from memory when the procedure ends. In other words, a procedure-level variable has the same lifetime as the procedure that declares it. As mentioned earlier, most of the variables in your applications will be procedure-level variables.

As you will learn later in this lesson, you can use the `Static` keyword to declare a procedure-level variable that remains in the computer's memory even when the procedure in which it is declared ends.

The Sales Tax Calculator application that you view next illustrates the use of procedure-level variables. As the interface shown in Figure 3-10 indicates, the application allows the user to enter a sales amount. It then calculates and displays either a 2% sales tax or a 5% sales tax, depending on the button selected by the user.

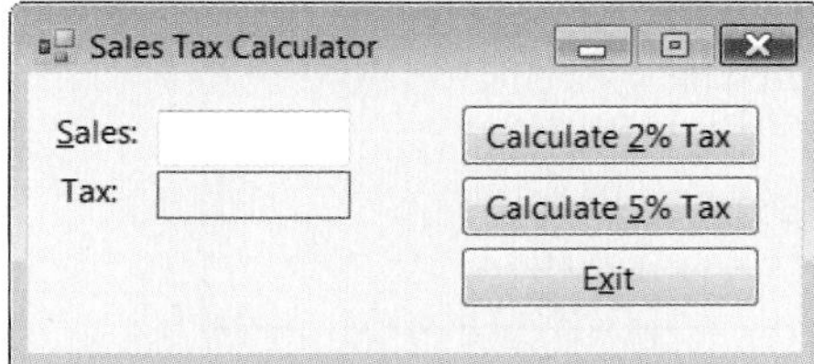

Figure 3-10 User interface for the Sales Tax Calculator application

Figure 3-11 shows the Click event procedures for the Calculate 2% Tax and Calculate 5% Tax buttons. Both procedures declare two procedure-level Double variables. It is customary to enter the declaration statements for procedure-level variables at the beginning of the procedure, as shown in the figure. When the user clicks the Calculate 2% Tax button, the button's Click event procedure creates and initializes the `dblSales` and `dblTax2` variables; the variables can be used only by that procedure. The TryParse method converts the sales amount entered in the txtSales control to Double and stores the result in the `dblSales` variable. The first assignment statement in the procedure multiplies the contents of the `dblSales` variable by the Double number .02 and stores the result in the `dblTax2` variable. The last assignment statement in the procedure converts the contents of the `dblTax2` variable to String and assigns the result to the lblTax control. When the procedure ends, the computer removes the `dblSales` and `dblTax2` procedure-level variables from memory. The variables will be created again the next time the user clicks the Calculate 2% Tax button. A similar process is followed when the user clicks the Calculate 5% Tax button, except the variable that stores the tax amount is named `dblTax5` and the tax is calculated using a rate of .05 rather than .02.

```
Private Sub btnCalcTax2_Click(ByVal sender As Object, _
     ByVal e As System.EventArgs) Handles btnCalcTax2.Click
     ' calculates a 2% sales tax

     ' declare variables
     Dim dblSales As Double      procedure-level variables in the
     Dim dblTax2 As Double       btnCalcTax2 Click event procedure

     ' calculate and display the sales tax
     Double.TryParse(txtSales.Text, dblSales)
     dblTax2 = dblSales * 0.02
     lblTax.Text = Convert.ToString(dblTax2)
End Sub

Private Sub btnCalcTax5_Click(ByVal sender As Object, _
     ByVal e As System.EventArgs) Handles btnCalcTax5.Click
     ' calculates a 5% sales tax

     ' declare variables
     Dim dblSales As Double      procedure-level variables in the
     Dim dblTax5 As Double       btnCalcTax5 Click event procedure

     ' calculate and display the sales tax
     Double.TryParse(txtSales.Text, dblSales)
     dblTax5 = dblSales * 0.05
     lblTax.Text = Convert.ToString(dblTax5)
End Sub
```

Figure 3-11 Click event procedures using procedure-level variables

You may have noticed that both procedures shown in Figure 3-11 declare a variable named `dblSales`. When you use the same name to declare a variable in more than one procedure, each procedure creates its own variable when the procedure is invoked. Each procedure also destroys its own variable when the procedure ends. In other words, although the `dblSales` variables in both procedures have the same name, they are not the same variable. Rather, each refers to a different section in memory, and each is created and destroyed independently from the other.

To code and then test the Sales Tax Calculator application:

1. If necessary, start Visual Studio 2008 or Visual Basic 2008 Express Edition. Close the Start Page window.
2. Open the **Sales Tax Solution** (**Sales Tax Solution.sln**) file, which is contained in the VB2008\Chap03\Sales Tax Solution-Procedure-level folder. If necessary, open the designer window. The user interface shown earlier in Figure 3-10 appears on the screen.
3. Open the Code Editor window. For now, do not be concerned about the three Option statements that appear in the window. You will learn about the Option statements later in this lesson. Replace the <your name> and <current date> text in the comments with your name and the current date.
4. Open the code template for the btnCalcTax2 control's Click event procedure. Also open the code template for the btnCalcTax5 control's Click event procedure. In the procedures, enter the comments and code shown in Figure 3-11.

5. Close the Code Editor window. Save the solution, then start the application.
6. Enter **1000** as the sales amount, then click the **Calculate 2% Tax** button. The button's Click event procedure calculates and displays a tax of 20. Click the **Calculate 5% Tax** button. The button's Click event procedure calculates and displays a tax of 50.
7. Change the sales amount from 1000 to the letter **a**, then click the **Calculate 2% Tax** button. The button's Click event procedure calculates and displays a tax of 0. Click the **Calculate 5% Tax** button. The button's Click event procedure calculates and displays a tax of 0.
8. Click the **Exit** button to end the application, then close the solution.

Variables with Module Scope

In addition to declaring a variable in a procedure, you also can declare a variable in the form's Declarations section, which begins with the Public Class line and ends with the End Class line. When you declare a variable in the form's Declarations section, the variable is called a **module-level variable** and it has **module scope**. You typically use a module-level variable when you need more than one procedure in the same form to use the same variable, because a module-level variable can be used by all of the procedures in the form, including the procedures associated with the controls contained on the form. Unlike a procedure-level variable, which you declare using the `Dim` keyword, you declare a module-level variable using the `Private` keyword. For example, to declare a module-level variable named `intNumber`, you enter the statement `Private intNumber As Integer` in the form's Declarations section. Because the variable has module scope, it can be used by every procedure in the form. Module-level variables retain their values and remain in the computer's internal memory until the application ends. In other words, a module-level variable has the same lifetime as the application itself. The Total Sales application that you view next illustrates the use of a module-level variable. As the interface shown in Figure 3-12 indicates, the application calculates the total of the sales amounts entered by the user.

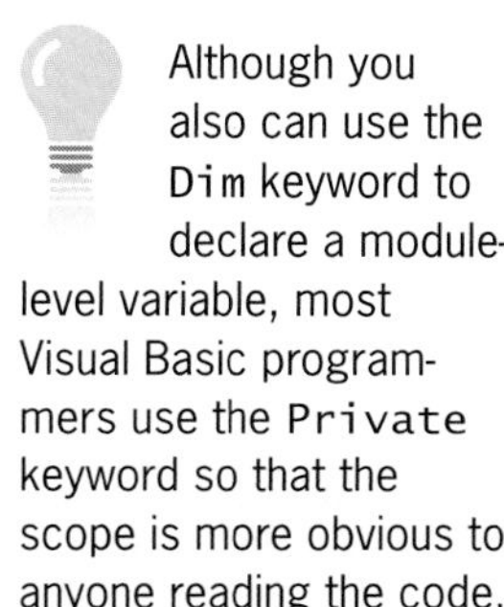

Although you also can use the `Dim` keyword to declare a module-level variable, most Visual Basic programmers use the `Private` keyword so that the scope is more obvious to anyone reading the code.

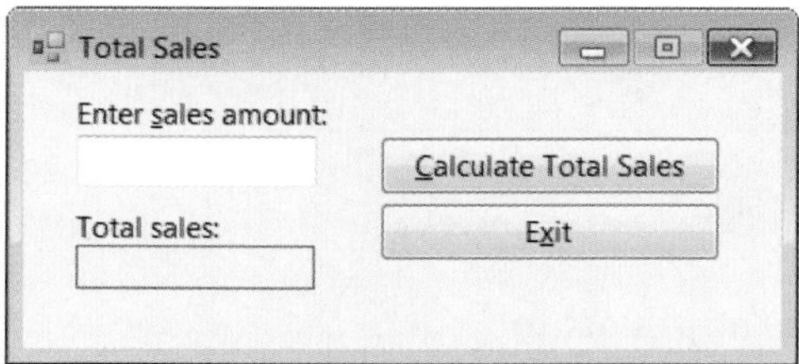

Figure 3-12 User interface for the Total Sales application

Figure 3-13 shows the code for the Total Sales application. The code uses a module-level variable named `decTotalSales` to accumulate (add together) the sales amounts entered by the user. You enter the declaration statement for a module-level variable after the Public Class line, but before the first Private Sub line, in the form's Declarations section. When the Total Sales application is started, the Private statement contained in the form's Declarations section is processed first. The statement creates a Decimal variable named decTotalSales and initializes it to the number 0. The variable is created and initialized only once, when the application is first started. It remains in the computer's internal memory until the application ends. Each time the user enters a sales amount in the interface and then clicks the Calculate Total Sales button, the button's Click event procedure creates a procedure-level variable named decSalesAmount and initializes it to the number 0. The TryParse method converts the sales amount entered by the user to Decimal and stores the result in the decSalesAmount variable. The first assignment statement in the procedure adds the contents of the procedure-level decSalesAmount variable to the contents of the module-level decTotalSales variable. At this point, the decTotalSales variable contains the sum of all of the sales amounts entered so far. The last assignment statement in the procedure converts the contents of the decTotalSales variable to String and assigns the result to the lblTotalSales control. The procedure then sends the focus to the txtSales control. When the procedure ends, the computer removes the procedure-level decSalesAmount variable from its memory; however, it does not remove the module-level decTotalSales variable. The decTotalSales variable is removed from the computer's memory only when the application ends.

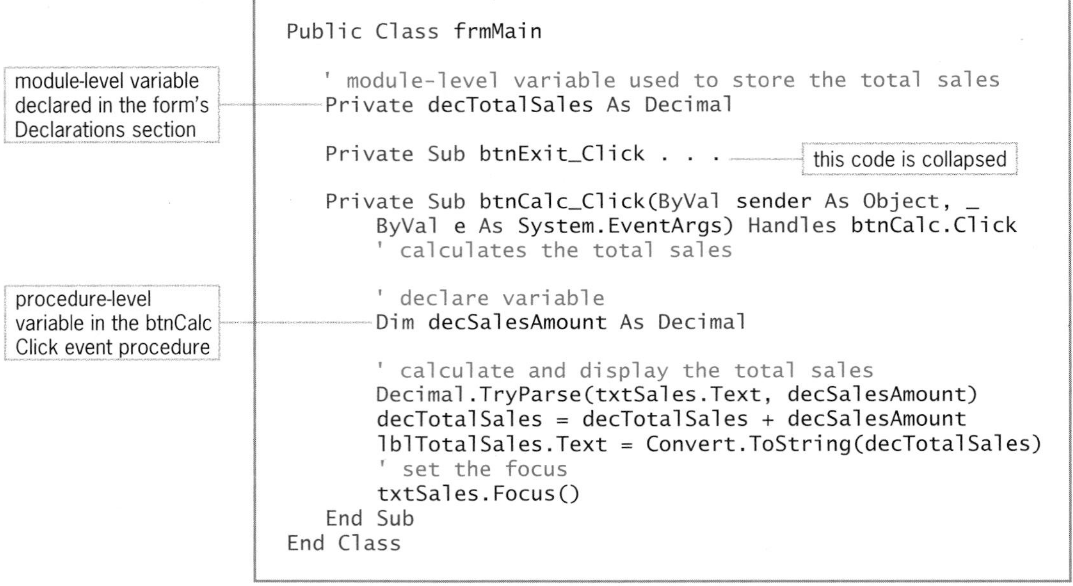

```
Public Class frmMain

    ' module-level variable used to store the total sales
    Private decTotalSales As Decimal

    Private Sub btnExit_Click . . .

    Private Sub btnCalc_Click(ByVal sender As Object, _
        ByVal e As System.EventArgs) Handles btnCalc.Click
        ' calculates the total sales

        ' declare variable
        Dim decSalesAmount As Decimal

        ' calculate and display the total sales
        Decimal.TryParse(txtSales.Text, decSalesAmount)
        decTotalSales = decTotalSales + decSalesAmount
        lblTotalSales.Text = Convert.ToString(decTotalSales)
        ' set the focus
        txtSales.Focus()
    End Sub
End Class
```


Figure 3-13 Code using a module-level variable

To code and then test the Total Sales application:

1. Open the **Total Sales Solution** (**Total Sales Solution.sln**) file, which is contained in the VB2008\Chap03\Total Sales Solution-Module-level folder. If necessary, open the designer window. The user interface shown earlier in Figure 3-12 appears on the screen.

2. Open the Code Editor window. Here again, do not be concerned about the three Option statements that appear in the window. You will learn about the Option statements later in this lesson. Replace the <your name> and <current date> text in the comments with your name and the current date.

3. First, declare the module-level `decTotalSales` variable in the form's Declarations section. Click the **blank line** below the `' module-level variable used to store the total sales` comment, then type **Private decTotalSales As Decimal** and press **Enter**.
4. Open the code template for the btnCalc control's Click event procedure. In the procedure, enter the comments and code shown in Figure 3-13.
5. Close the Code Editor window. Save the solution, then start the application.
6. Enter **2000** as the sales amount, then click the **Calculate Total Sales** button. The button's Click event procedure calculates and displays the total sales: 2000.
7. Change the sales amount from 2000 to **4000**, then click the **Calculate Total Sales** button. The number 6000 appears in the Total sales box.
8. Change the sales amount from 4000 to **500**, then click the **Calculate Total Sales** button. The number 6500 appears in the Total sales box.
9. Click the **Exit** button to end the application, then close the solution.

Static Variables

The `Static` keyword can be used only in a procedure.

As the syntax shown earlier in Figure 3-5 indicates, you can declare a variable using the `Dim`, `Private`, or `Static` keywords. You already know how to use the `Dim` keyword to declare a procedure-level variable, and how to use the `Private` keyword to declare a module-level variable. In this section, you will learn how to use the `Static` keyword to declare a special type of procedure-level variable, called a static variable. A **static variable** is a procedure-level variable that remains in memory and also retains its value even when the procedure in which it is declared ends. Similar to a module-level variable, a static variable is not removed from the computer's internal memory until the application ends. However, unlike a module-level variable, which can be used by all of the procedures in a form, a static variable can be used only by the procedure in which it is declared. In other words, a static variable has a narrower scope than does a module-level variable. As mentioned earlier, you can prevent many unintentional errors from occurring in an application by declaring the variables using the minimum scope needed.

In the previous section, you viewed the interface (Figure 3-12) and code (Figure 3-13) for the Total Sales application. Recall that the application uses a module-level variable to accumulate the sales amounts entered by the user. Rather than using a module-level variable for that purpose, you also can use a static variable. Figure 3-14 shows the Total Sales application's code using a static variable. The first time the user clicks the Calculate Total Sales button in the interface, the button's Click event procedure creates and initializes (to 0) a procedure-level variable named `decSalesAmount` and a static variable named `decTotalSales`. The TryParse method converts the sales amount entered by the user to Decimal, storing the result in the `decSalesAmount` variable. The first assignment statement adds the contents of the `decSalesAmount` variable to the contents of the `decTotalSales` variable. The last assignment statement in the procedure converts the contents of the `decTotalSales` variable to String and assigns the result to the lblTotalSales control. The procedure then sends the focus to the txtSales control. When the procedure ends, the computer removes from its internal memory the variable declared using the `Dim` keyword (`decSalesAmount`). But it does not remove the variable declared using the `Static` keyword (`decTotalSales`). Each subsequent time the user clicks the Calculate Total Sales button, the computer re-creates and re-initializes the `decSalesAmount` variable declared in the button's Click event procedure. However, it does not re-create or re-initialize the `decTotalSales` variable because that variable, as well as its current value, is still in the computer's memory. After re-creating and re-initializing the `decSalesAmount` variable, the computer processes the remaining instructions contained in the button's Click event procedure. Here again, each time the procedure ends, the `decSalesAmount` variable is removed from the computer's internal memory. The `decTotalSales` variable is removed only when the application ends.

```
Public Class frmMain

  Private Sub btnExit_Click . . .

  Private Sub btnCalc_Click(ByVal sender As Object, _
     ByVal e As System.EventArgs) Handles btnCalc.Click
     ' calculates the total sales

     ' declare variables
     Dim decSalesAmount As Decimal
     Static decTotalSales As Decimal

     ' calculate and display the total sales
     Decimal.TryParse(txtSales.Text, decSalesAmount)
     decTotalSales = decTotalSales + decSalesAmount
     lblTotalSales.Text = Convert.ToString(decTotalSales)
     ' set the focus
     txtSales.Focus()
  End Sub
End Class
```

static variable in the btnCalc Click event procedure

Figure 3-14 Code using a static variable

To use a static variable in the Total Sales application:

1. Use Windows to make a copy of the Total Sales Solution-Module-level folder contained in the VB2008\Chap03 folder. Rename the folder **Total Sales Solution-Static**.
2. Open the **Total Sales Solution** (**Total Sales Solution.sln**) file contained in the VB2008\Chap03\Total Sales Solution-Static folder. Open the designer window. The user interface shown earlier in Figure 3-12 appears on the screen.
3. Open the Code Editor window. Delete the `' module-level variable used to store the total sales` comment and the `Private decTotalSales As Decimal` statement.
4. Modify the btnCalc control's Click event procedure so that it uses a static variable rather than a module-level variable. Use the code shown in Figure 3-14 as a guide.

5. Close the Code Editor window. Save the solution, then start the application.
6. Enter **2000** as the sales amount, then click the **Calculate Total Sales** button. The number 2000 appears as the total sales. Change the sales amount from 2000 to **4000**, then click the **Calculate Total Sales** button. The number 6000 appears as the total sales. Change the sales amount from 4000 to **500**, then click the **Calculate Total Sales** button. The number 6500 appears as the total sales.
7. Click the **Exit** button to end the application, then close the solution.

Named Constants

In addition to using literal constants and variables in your code, you also can use named constants. Like a variable, a **named constant** is a memory location inside the computer. However, unlike a variable's value, a named constant's value cannot be changed while the application is running. You create a named constant using the **Const statement**. Figure 3-15 shows the syntax of the Const statement and includes examples of declaring named constants. To differentiate the name of a constant from the name of a variable, you can lowercase the three-character ID that represents the constant's data type and then uppercase the remaining characters in the name, as shown in the examples in the figure. The Const statement stores the value of the *expression* in the named constant. The *expression* can contain a literal constant, another named constant, or an arithmetic operator; however, it cannot contain a variable. The expression's value must have the same data type as the named constant. You can use the Const statements shown in the first two examples to create procedure-level named constants. To do this, you need simply to enter the statements in the appropriate procedure. You would use the Const statement shown in the last example in the figure to create a module-level named constant. When creating a module-level named constant, you precede the `Const` keyword with the `Private` keyword, and you enter the Const statement in the form's Declarations section.

Declaring a named constant

Syntax

Const *constantName* **As** *dataType* = *expression*

Example 1

```
Const dblPI As Double = 3.141593
```

declares `dblPI` as a Double named constant whose value is the Double number 3.141593

Example 2

```
Const intMAX_HOURS As Integer = 40
```

declares `intMAX_HOURS` as an Integer named constant whose value is the integer 40

Example 3

```
Private Const strCOMPANY As String = "ABC Company"
```

declares `strCOMPANY` as a String named constant whose value is the string "ABC Company"

Figure 3-15 Syntax and examples of the Const statement

Named constants make code more self-documenting and easier to modify, because they allow you to use meaningful words in place of values that are less clear. The named constant `dblPI`, for example, is much more meaningful than is the number 3.141593, which is the value of pi rounded to six decimal places. Once you create a named constant, you then can use the constant's name rather than its value in the application's code. Unlike the value stored in a variable, the value stored in a named constant cannot be inadvertently changed while the application is running. Using a named constant to represent a value has another advantage: if the value changes in the future, you will need to modify only the Const statement in the program, rather than all of the program statements that use the value. The Area Calculator application that you view next illustrates the use of a named constant. Figure 3-16 shows the application's user interface. As the interface indicates, the application allows the user to enter the radius of a circle. It then calculates and displays the area of the circle. The formula for calculating the area of a circle is πr^2, where π stands for pi (3.141593).

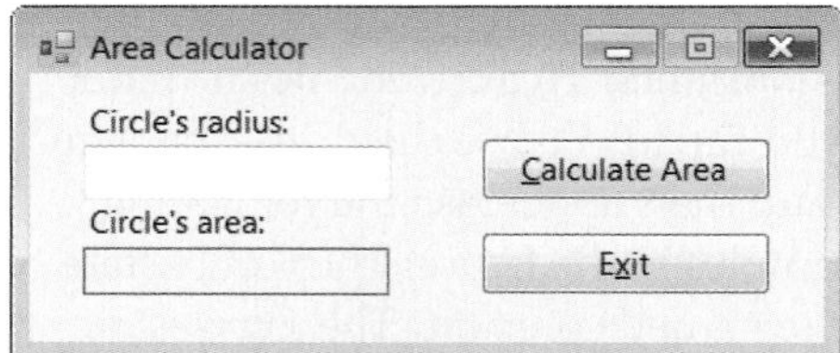

Figure 3-16 User interface for the Area Calculator application

Figure 3-17 shows the code for the Calculate Area button's Click event procedure. The procedure declares and initializes a named constant and two variables. The TryParse method converts (to Double) the radius value entered by the user, and it stores the result in the `dblRadius` variable. The `dblArea = dblPI * dblRadius * dblRadius` statement calculates the circle's area using the values stored in the `dblPI` named constant and `dblRadius` variable, and then assigns the result to the `dblArea` variable. Lastly, the procedure displays the contents of the `dblArea` variable (converted to String) in the lblArea control. When the procedure ends, the computer removes the named constant and two variables from its internal memory.

You also can calculate the area using the expression `dblPI * dblRadius ^ 2`.

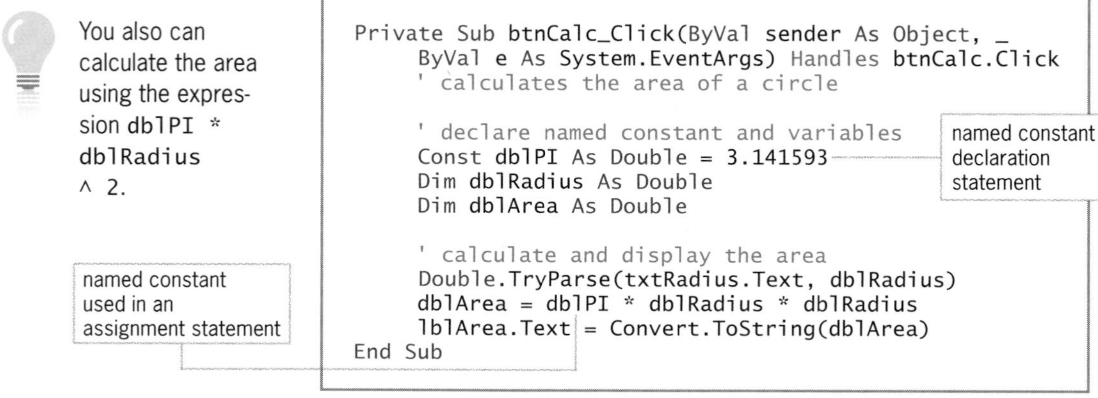

```
Private Sub btnCalc_Click(ByVal sender As Object, _
     ByVal e As System.EventArgs) Handles btnCalc.Click
     ' calculates the area of a circle

     ' declare named constant and variables
     Const dblPI As Double = 3.141593
     Dim dblRadius As Double
     Dim dblArea As Double

     ' calculate and display the area
     Double.TryParse(txtRadius.Text, dblRadius)
     dblArea = dblPI * dblRadius * dblRadius
     lblArea.Text = Convert.ToString(dblArea)
End Sub
```


Figure 3-17 Calculate Area button's Click event procedure

To code and then test the Area Calculator application:

1. Open the **Area Calculator Solution** (**Area Calculator Solution.sln**) file, which is contained in the VB2008\Chap03\Area Calculator Solution folder. If necessary, open the designer window. The user interface shown earlier in Figure 3-16 appears on the screen.
2. Open the Code Editor window. Replace the <your name> and <current date> text in the comments with your name and the current date.
3. Open the code template for the btnCalc control's Click event procedure, then enter the comments and code shown in Figure 3-17.
4. Close the Code Editor window. Save the solution, then start the application.
5. Type **10** as the radius, then click the **Calculate Area** button. The button's Click event procedure calculates and displays the area: 314.1593.
6. Click the **Exit** button to end the application, then close the solution.

Option Explicit, Option Infer, and Option Strict

It is important to declare the variables used in an application, because doing so allows you to control their data type. It also makes the application more self-documenting, which means it will be clearer and easier to understand by anyone reading your code. A word of caution: In Visual Basic you can create variables "on the fly," which means that if your code contains the name of an undeclared variable, Visual Basic creates the variable for you and assigns the Object data type to it. (An undeclared variable is a variable that does not appear in a declaration statement, such as a Dim statement.) Recall that the Object type is not a very efficient data type, and its use should be limited. Because it is so easy to forget to declare a variable—and so easy to misspell a variable's name while coding, thereby inadvertently creating an undeclared variable—Visual Basic provides a way that prevents you from using undeclared variables in your code. You simply enter the statement `Option Explicit On` in the General Declarations section of the Code Editor window. Then if your code contains the name of an undeclared variable, the Code Editor informs you of the error. When you also enter the `Option Infer Off` statement in the General Declarations section, the Code Editor ensures that every variable is declared with a data type. The statement tells Visual Basic not to "infer" a variable's data type based on the data assigned to the variable.

Recall that the General Declarations section is located above the Public Class line in the Code Editor window.

As you learned earlier, the data type of the value assigned to a memory location (variable or named constant) should be the same as the data type of the memory location itself. If the value's data type does not match the memory location's data type, the computer uses a process called **implicit type conversion** to convert the value to fit the memory location. For example, when processing the statement `Dim dblSales As Double = 9`, the computer converts the integer 9 to a Double number before storing the value in the variable. It does this by appending a decimal point and the number 0 to the end of the integer. In this case, the integer 9 will be converted to the Double number 9.0 before the number is assigned to the `dblSales` variable. When a value is converted from one data type to another data type that can store larger numbers, the value is said to be **promoted**. In this case, if the `dblSales` variable is used subsequently in a calculation, the results of the calculation will not be adversely affected by the implicit promotion of the number 9 to the number 9.0. However, if you inadvertently assign a Double number to a memory location that can store only integers—as does the statement `Dim intScore As Integer = 78.4`—the computer converts the Double number to an integer before storing the value in the memory location. It does this by rounding the number to the nearest whole number and then truncating (dropping off) the decimal portion of the number. In this case, the computer converts the Double number 78.4 to the integer 78, which then is assigned to the `intScore` variable. When a value is converted from one data type to another data type that can store only smaller numbers, the value is said to be **demoted**. If the `intScore` variable is used subsequently in a calculation, the results of the calculation probably will be adversely affected by the implicit demotion of the number 78.4 to the number 78. More than likely, the demotion will cause the calculated results to be incorrect.

With implicit type conversions, data loss can occur when a value is converted from one data type to a narrower data type, which is a data type with less precision or smaller capacity. You can eliminate the problems that occur as a result of implicit type conversions by entering the `Option Strict On` statement in the General Declarations section of the Code Editor window. When the `Option Strict On` statement appears in an application's code, the computer uses the type conversion rules listed in Figure 3-18. The figure also includes examples of these rules. According to the first rule, the computer will not implicitly convert a string to a number. As a result, the Code Editor will issue the warning "Option Strict On disallows implicit conversions from 'String' to 'Double'" when your code contains the statement `dblHours = txtHours.Text`, because the statement tells the computer to store a string in a Double variable. As you learned earlier, you can use the TryParse method to explicitly convert a string to the Double data type before assigning it to a Double variable. In this case, the appropriate statement to use is `Double.TryParse(txtHours.Text, dblHours)`. According to the second rule, the computer will not implicitly convert a number to a string. Therefore, the Code Editor will issue the warning "Option Strict On disallows implicit conversions from 'Decimal' to 'String'" when your code contains the statement `lblGross.Text = decGrossPay`, because the statement assigns a number to a string. Recall that you can use the Convert class methods to explicitly convert a number to the String data type. The appropriate statement to use here is `lblGross.Text = Convert.ToString(decGrossPay)`. The third rule states that wider data types will not be implicitly demoted to narrower data types. A data type is wider than another data type if it can store larger numbers, or store numbers with greater precision. Because of this rule, a Double number will not be implicitly demoted to the Decimal or Integer data types. If your code contains the statement `Dim decRate As Decimal = .05`, the Code Editor will issue the "Option Strict On disallows implicit conversions from 'Double' to 'Decimal'" warning, because the statement assigns a Double number to a Decimal variable. The correct statement to use in this case is either `Dim decRate As Decimal = .05D` or `Dim decRate As Decimal = Convert.ToDecimal(.05)`. According to the last rule listed in Figure 3-18, the computer will implicitly convert narrower data types to wider data types. For example, when processing the statement `dblAverage = dblTotal / intNum`, the computer will implicitly promote the contents of the `intNum` variable to Double before dividing it into the contents of the `dblTotal` variable. The result, a Double number, will be assigned to the `dblAverage` variable.

Type conversion rules

1. Strings will not be implicitly converted to numbers. The Code Editor will display a warning message when a statement attempts to use a string where a number is expected.

```
dblHours = txtHours.Text                          incorrect
Double.TryParse(txtHours.Text, dblHours)          correct
```

2. Numbers will not be implicitly converted to strings. The Code Editor will display a warning message when a statement attempts to use a number where a string is expected.

```
lblGross.Text = decGrossPay                       incorrect
lblGross.Text = Convert.ToString(decGrossPay)     correct
```

3. Wider data types will not be implicitly demoted to narrower data types. The Code Editor will display a warning message when a statement attempts to use a wider data type where a narrower data type is expected.

```
Dim decRate As Decimal = .05                      incorrect
Dim decRate As Decimal =.05D                      correct
Dim decRate As Decimal = Convert.ToDecimal(.05)   correct
```

4. Narrower data types will be implicitly promoted to wider data types.

```
dblAverage = dblTotal / intNum                    correct
```

Figure 3-18 Rules and examples of type conversions

Figure 3-19 shows the three Option statements entered in the General Declarations section of the Code Editor window for the Area Calculator application, which you viewed earlier in Figures 3-16 and 3-17. The statements typically are entered below the comments that document the project's name and purpose, the programmer's name, and the date the code was either created or modified. If a project contains more than one form, the statements must be entered in each form's Code Editor window.

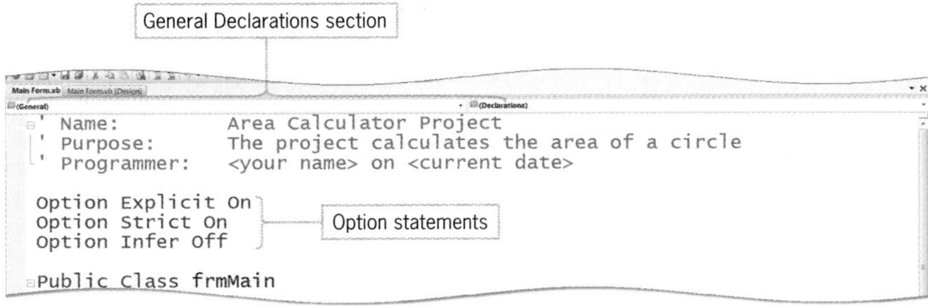

Figure 3-19 Option statements entered in the General Declarations section

Rather than entering the Option statements in the Code Editor window, you also can set the options using either the Project Designer window or the Options dialog box. However, it is strongly recommended that you enter the Option statements in the Code Editor window, because doing so ensures that the options are set appropriately; it also makes your code more self-documenting. The steps for setting the options in the Project Designer window and Options dialog box are listed in the Lesson A Summary section.

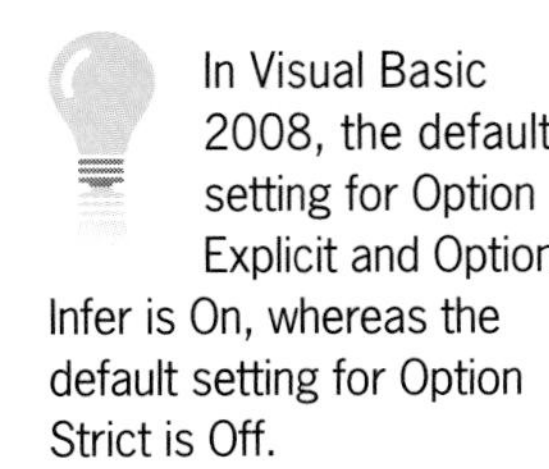

In Visual Basic 2008, the default setting for Option Explicit and Option Infer is On, whereas the default setting for Option Strict is Off.

Lesson A Summary

- **To declare a variable:**

  The syntax of a variable declaration statement is {**Dim** | **Private** | **Static**} *variableName* **As** *dataType* [= *initialValue*]. Use camel case for a variable's name.

- **To declare a procedure-level variable:**

  Enter the variable declaration statement in a procedure; use the `Dim` keyword.

- **To declare a module-level variable:**

  Enter the variable declaration statement in a form's Declarations section; use the `Private` keyword.

- **To declare a static variable:**

  Enter the variable declaration statement in a procedure; use the `Static` keyword.

- **To use an assignment statement to assign data to a variable:**

  Use the syntax *variableName = expression.*

- **To force a Double literal constant to assume the Decimal data type:**

  Append the letter D to the end of the Double literal constant.

- **To convert a string to a numeric data type:**

  Use the TryParse method, whose syntax is *dataType***.TryParse(***string***,** *variable***)**.

- **To convert a numeric value to a different data type:**

  Use one of the Convert methods, whose syntax is **Convert.***method***(***value***)**.

- **To create a named constant:**

  Use the Const statement, whose syntax is **Const** *constantName* **As** *dataType* = *expression*. Lowercase the three-character ID and then uppercase the remainder of the name.

- **To create a procedure-level named constant:**

  Enter the Const statement in a procedure.

- **To create a module-level named constant:**

  Enter the Const statement, preceded by the keyword `Private`, in a form's Declarations section.

- **To prevent the computer from creating an undeclared variable:**

  Enter the `Option Explicit On` statement in the General Declarations section of the Code Editor window.

- **To prevent the computer from inferring a variable's data type:**

  Enter the `Option Infer Off` statement in the General Declarations section of the Code Editor window.

- **To prevent the computer from making implicit type conversions that may result in a loss of data:**

  Enter the `Option Strict On` statement in the General Declarations section of the Code Editor window.

- **To use the Project Designer window to set Option Explicit, Option Infer, and Option Strict for an entire project:**

  Open the solution that contains the project, then right-click My Project in the Solution Explorer window. Click Open to open the Project Designer window, then click the Compile tab. Use the Option explicit, Option infer, and Option strict boxes to set the options. Save the solution, then close the Project Designer window.

- **To use the Options dialog box to set Option Explicit, Option Infer, and Option Strict for all of the projects you create:**

  Click Tools on the Visual Studio menu bar, then click Options. When the Options dialog box opens, expand the Projects and Solutions node, then click VB Defaults. Use the Option Explicit, Option Infer, and Option Strict boxes to set the options, then click the OK button to close the Options dialog box.

Lesson A Key Terms

Const statement—the statement used to create a named constant

Convert class—contains methods that return the result of converting a value to a specified data type

Data type—refers to the type of data a memory location can store

Demoted—the process of converting a value from one data type to another data type that can store only smaller numbers or numbers with less precision

Implicit type conversion—the process by which a value is automatically converted to fit the memory location to which it is assigned

Lifetime—indicates how long a variable or named constant remains in the computer's internal memory

Literal constant—an item of data whose value does not change while an application is running

Literal type character—a character (such as the letter D) appended to a literal constant for the purpose of forcing the literal constant to assume a different data type (such as Decimal)

Module scope—the scope of a module-level variable; refers to the fact that the variable can be used by any procedure in the form

Module-level variable—a variable that is declared in a form's Declarations section; the variable has module scope

Named constant—a computer memory location whose contents cannot be changed while the application is running; created using the Const statement

Procedure scope—the scope of a procedure-level variable; refers to the fact that the variable can be used only by the procedure in which it is declared

Procedure-level variable—a variable that is declared in a procedure; the variable has procedure scope

Promoted—the process of converting a value from one data type to another data type that can store larger numbers or numbers with greater precision

Scope—indicates where in the application's code a variable or named constant can be used

Static variable—a special type of procedure-level variable that remains in memory and retains its value even when the procedure ends

TryParse method—used to convert a string to a number of the specified data type

Unicode—the universal coding scheme that assigns a unique number to each character in the written languages of the world

Variables—computer memory locations where programmers can temporarily store data, as well as change the data, while an application is running

Lesson A Review Questions

1. ______________________________ are computer memory locations in which you store information, temporarily.
   a. Literal constants
   b. Named constants
   c. Variables
   d. Both b and c.

2. A ______________________________ is a data item whose value does not change while the application is running.
   a. literal constant
   b. literal variable
   c. named constant
   d. variable

3. If Option Explicit is off and you enter the statement `Dim intAge` in a procedure, Visual Basic 2008 assigns the ____________________ data type to the variable.
   a. Decimal
   b. Integer
   c. Object
   d. String

4. You use the ____________________ keyword to declare a module-level variable.
   a. `Dimension`
   b. `Global`
   c. `Private`
   d. `Module`

5. Which of the following statements declares a procedure-level variable that retains its value until the application ends?
   a. `Dim Static intScore As Integer`
   b. `Private Static intScore As Integer`
   c. `Static intScore As Integer`
   d. Both b and c.

6. Which of the following declares a procedure-level String variable?
   a. `Dim String strCity`
   b. `Dim strCity As String`
   c. `Private strCity As String`
   d. `String strCity`

7. Which of the following assigns the contents of the txtSales control to a Double variable named `dblSales`? (The application contains the `Option Strict On` statement.)
   a. `dblSales = txtSales.Text`
   b. `dblSales = txtSales.Text.Convert.ToDouble`
   c. `Double.TryParse(txtSales.Text, dblSales)`
   d. `TryParse.Double(txtSales.Text, dblSales)`

8. Which of the following declares a named constant having the Double data type?
   a. `Const dblRATE As Double = .09`
   b. `Const dblRATE As Double`
   c. `Constant dblRATE = .09`
   d. Both a and b.

9. Which of the following assigns the sum of two Integer variables to the Text property of the lblTotal control? (The application contains the `Option Strict On` statement.)
   a. `lblTotal.Text = Convert.ToInteger(intNum1 + intNum2)`
   b. `lblTotal.Text = Convert.ToInt32(intNum1 + intNum2)`
   c. `lblTotal.Text = Convert.ToString(intNum1) + Convert.ToString(intNum2)`
   d. None of the above.

10. The ______________________ statement prevents data loss due to implicit type conversions.
    a. `Option Explicit On`
    b. `Option Strict On`
    c. `Option Implicit Off`
    d. `Option Convert Off`

Lesson A Exercises

INTRODUCTORY

1. A procedure needs to store an item's name and price (which may have decimal places). Write the appropriate Dim statements to declare the necessary procedure-level variables.

INTRODUCTORY

2. A procedure needs to store the name of an item in inventory and its height and weight. The height may have a decimal place; the weight will be whole numbers only. Write the appropriate Dim statements to declare the necessary procedure-level variables.

INTRODUCTORY

3. A procedure needs to store the name of an inventory item, the number of units in stock at the beginning of the current month, the number of units purchased during the current month, the number of units sold during the current month, and the number of units in stock at the end of the current month. The number of units is always a whole number. Write the appropriate Dim statements to declare the necessary procedure-level variables.

4. Write an assignment statement that assigns Miami to an existing String variable named `strCity`. INTRODUCTORY

5. Write an assignment statement that assigns the word Desk to a String variable named `strItemName`. Also write an assignment statement that assigns the number 40 to an Integer variable named `intQuantityInStock`, and an assignment statement that assigns the number 20 to an Integer variable named `intQuantityOnOrder`. INTRODUCTORY

6. Write the statement to declare a procedure-level named constant named `decTAX_RATE` whose value is .05. INTRODUCTORY

7. Write the statement to assign the contents of the txtUnits control to an Integer variable named `intNumberOfUnits`. INTRODUCTORY

8. Write the statement to assign, to the lblUnits control, the contents of an Integer variable named `intNumberOfUnits`. INTRODUCTORY

9. An application needs to store the part number of an item and its cost (which may contain a decimal place). An example of a part number for this application is A103. Write the appropriate Private statements to declare the necessary module-level variables. INTRODUCTORY

10. Write an assignment statement that adds together the contents of the `dblNorthSales` and `dblSouthSales` variables, and then assigns the sum to the `dblTotalSales` variable. INTRODUCTORY

11. Write an assignment statement that multiplies the contents of the `decSalary` variable by the number 1.5, and then assigns the result to the `decSalary` variable. INTRODUCTORY

12. Write the statement to assign, to a String variable named `strTotalSales`, the sum of the values stored in the `decWestSales` and `decEastSales` variables. INTERMEDIATE

13. A form contains two buttons named btnSalary and btnBonus. Both buttons' Click event procedures need to use the same String variable: `strEmployeeName`. Write the appropriate statement to declare the variable. Also specify where you will need to enter the statement and whether the variable is a procedure-level or module-level variable. INTERMEDIATE

Discovery

14. In this exercise, you experiment with procedure-level and module-level variables. Open the Scope Solution (Scope Solution.sln) file, which is contained in the VB2008\Chap03\Scope Solution folder. The Scope application allows the user to calculate either a 5% or 10% commission on a sales amount. It displays the sales and commission amounts in the lblSales and lblCommission controls, respectively.

a. Open the Code Editor window, then open the code template for the btnSales control's Click event procedure. Code the procedure so that it declares a variable named `dblSales`. The procedure also should use an assignment statement to assign the number 500 to the variable. In addition, the procedure should display the contents of the variable in the lblSales control on the form.

b. Save the solution, then start the application. Click the Display Sales button. What does the button's Click event procedure display in the lblSales control? When the Click event procedure ends, what happens to the `dblSales` variable? Click the Exit button to end the application.

c. Open the code template for the btnComm5 control's Click event procedure. In the procedure, enter an assignment statement that multiplies a variable named `dblSales` by .05, and then assigns the result to the lblCommission control on the form. When you press the Enter key after typing the assignment statement, a jagged line appears below `dblSales` in the instruction. The jagged line indicates that there is something wrong with the code. To determine the problem, rest your mouse pointer on the variable name, `dblSales`. The message in the box indicates that the variable is not declared. In other words, the btnComm5 control's Click event procedure cannot locate the variable's declaration statement, which you previously entered in the btnSales control's Click event procedure. As you learned in Lesson A, only the procedure in which a variable is declared can use the variable. No other procedure is even aware that the variable exists.

d. Now observe what happens when you use the same name to declare a variable in more than one procedure. Insert a blank line above the assignment statement in the btnComm5 control's Click event procedure. In the blank line, type a statement that declares the `dblSales` variable, then click the assignment statement to move the insertion point away from the current line. Notice that the jagged line disappears from the assignment statement. Save the solution, then start the application. Click the Display Sales button. The contents of the `dblSales` variable declared in the btnSales control's Click event procedure (500) appears in the lblSales control. Click the 5% Commission button. Why does the number 0 appear in the lblCommission control? What happens to the `dblSales` variable declared in the btnComm5 control's Click event procedure when the procedure ends? Click the Exit button to end the application. As this example shows, when you use the same name to declare a variable in more than one procedure, each procedure creates its own procedure-level variable. Although the variables have the same name, each refers to a different location in memory.

e. Next, you use a module-level variable in the application. Click the blank line above the btnExit control's Click event procedure. The Class Name and Method Name boxes show frmMain and

(Declarations), respectively. Press Enter to insert a blank line. In the blank line, type a statement that declares a module-level variable named `dblSales`.

f. Delete the Dim statement from the btnSales control's Click event procedure. Also delete the Dim statement from the btnComm5 control's Click event procedure.

g. Open the code template for the btnComm10 control's Click event procedure. In the procedure, enter an assignment statement that multiplies the `dblSales` variable by .1, assigning the result to the lblCommission control.

h. Save the solution, then start the application. The variable declaration statement in the form's Declarations section creates the `dblSales` variable and initializes it to 0. Click the Display Sales button. The button's Click event procedure stores the number 500 in the `dblSales` variable and then displays the contents of the variable (500) in the lblSales control. Click the 5% Commission button. The button's Click event procedure multiplies the contents of the `dblSales` variable (500) by .05 and then displays the result (25) in the lblCommission control. Click the 10% Commission button. The button's Click event procedure multiplies the contents of the `dblSales` variable (500) by .1 and then displays the result (50) in the lblCommission control. As this example shows, any procedure in the form can use a module-level variable. Click the Exit button to end the application. What happens to the `dblSales` variable when the application ends? Close the Code Editor window, then close the solution.

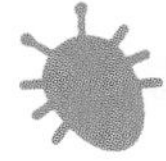

Swat The Bugs

15. Open the Debug Solution (Debug Solution.sln) file, which is contained in the VB2008\Chap03\Debug Solution-Lesson A folder. The application is supposed to display the number of times the Count button is pressed, but it is not working correctly.

    a. Start the application. Click the Count button. The message indicates that you have pressed the Count button once, which is correct. Click the Count button several more times. The message still displays the number 1. Click the Exit button to end the application.

    b. Open the Code Editor window and study the code. What are two ways that you can use to correct the code? Which way is the preferred way? Modify the code using the preferred way. Save the solution, then start the application. Click the Count button several times. Each time you click the Count button, the message should change to indicate the number of times the button was pressed. Click the Exit button to end the application. Close the Code Editor window, then close the solution.

LESSON B

After studying Lesson B, you should be able to:

- Include a procedure-level and module-level variable in an application
- Concatenate strings
- Get user input using the InputBox function
- Include the `ControlChars.NewLine` constant in code
- Designate the default button for a form
- Format numbers using the ToString method

Modifying the Playtime Cellular Application

Recall that your task in this chapter is to modify the Playtime Cellular application created in Chapter 2. The modified application will calculate and display a 3% sales tax. It also will display the name of the salesperson who recorded the order. Before making modifications to an application's existing code, you should review the application's documentation and revise the necessary documents. In this case, you need to revise the Playtime Cellular application's TOE chart and also the pseudocode for the Calculate Order button, which is responsible for making the application's calculations. The revised TOE chart is shown in Figure 3-20. Changes made to the original TOE chart, which is shown in Chapter 2's Figure 2-19, are shaded in the figure. (You will view the revised pseudocode for the Calculate Order button later in this lesson.) Notice that the btnCalc control's Click event procedure has two additional tasks to perform: it must calculate the sales tax and also display the sales tax and salesperson's name in the lblMessage control. Two additional objects (frmMain and lblMessage) also are included in the revised TOE chart. The frmMain Load event procedure, which occurs before the form is displayed the first time, is responsible for getting the salesperson's name when the application is started. The lblMessage control will show the sales tax and salesperson's name. As the revised TOE chart indicates, you need to change the code in the btnCalc control's Click event procedure, and you also need to code the form's Load event procedure. The lblMessage control, however, does not need to be coded.

Task	Object	Event
1. Calculate total phones ordered and total price 2. Display total phones ordered and total price in lblTotalPhones and lblTotalPrice 3. Calculate the sales tax 4. Display the sales tax and salesperson's name in lblMessage	btnCalc	Click

Figure 3-20 Revised TOE chart for the Playtime Cellular application (continues)

(continued)

Task	Object	Event
Clear screen for next order	btnClear	Click
End the application	btnExit	Click
Display total phones ordered (from btnCalc)	lblTotalPhones	None
Display total price (from btnCalc)	lblTotalPrice	None
Get and display the order information	txtName, txtAddress, txtCity, txtState, txtZip, txtBlue, txtPink	None
Get the salesperson's name	frmMain	Load
Show the sales tax and salesperson's name (from btnCalc)	lblMessage	None

Figure 3-20 Revised TOE chart for the Playtime Cellular application

To open the Playtime Cellular application:

1. If necessary, start Visual Studio 2008 or Visual Basic 2008 Express Edition. Close the Start Page window.
2. Open the **Playtime Solution** (**Playtime Solution.sln**) file, which is contained in the VB2008\Chap03\Playtime Solution folder. If necessary, open the designer window. Figure 3-21 shows the application's user interface.

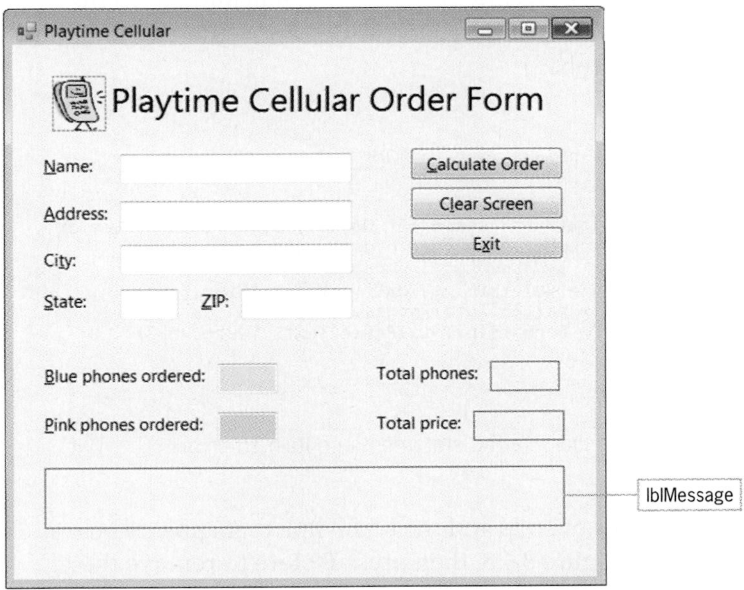

Figure 3-21 Playtime Cellular interface

Two modifications were made to the application that you created in Chapter 2: the lblMessage control was added to the interface and the statement `lblMessage.Text = String.Empty` was added to the btnClear control's Click event procedure. The statement will remove the contents of the lblMessage control when the user clicks the Clear Screen button.

Modifying the Calculate Order Button's Code

Currently, the Calculate Order button calculates the total phones ordered and total price using the Val function along with the Text properties of the txtBlue, txtPink, and lblTotalPhones controls. In this lesson, you will modify the button's code to use the TryParse method and variables. Because you will be using variables, you will enter the three Option statements in the Code Editor window.

To begin modifying the application's code:

1. Open the Code Editor window. Replace the <your name> and <current date> text with your name and the current date, respectively.
2. Click the **blank line** above the `Public Class frmMain` line, then press **Enter** to insert another blank line. Enter the following three statements:

   Option Explicit On
   Option Strict On
   Option Infer Off

3. Scroll down the Code Editor window until the entire btnCalc control's Click event procedure is visible. Notice that jagged blue lines appear below the expressions in the two calculations. The jagged lines indicate that the expressions contain an error.
4. Position your mouse pointer on the first jagged blue line, as shown in Figure 3-22. An explanation of the error appears in a box. The error message says "Option Strict On disallows implicit conversions from 'Double' to 'String'." You received this error message because the assignment statement is trying to assign a Double number to the Text property of a control. (As you learned in Lesson A, the Val function returns a Double number.)

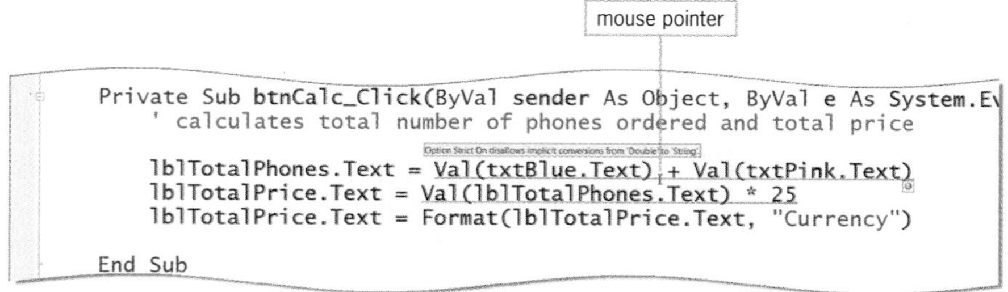

Figure 3-22 Jagged blue lines indicate the statements contain an error

5. Select the three lines of code and the blank line that appears below them, as shown in Figure 3-23, then press **Delete** to remove the selected lines from the procedure.

```
Private Sub btnCalc_Click(ByVal sender As Object, ByVal e As System.Ev
    ' calculates total number of phones ordered and total price

    lblTotalPhones.Text = Val(txtBlue.Text) + Val(txtPink.Text)
    lblTotalPrice.Text = Val(lblTotalPhones.Text) * 25
    lblTotalPrice.Text = Format(lblTotalPrice.Text, "Currency")

End Sub
```

Figure 3-23 Lines to delete from the procedure

If you inadvertently deleted the Private Sub and End Sub lines, click the Class Name list arrow, then click btnCalc in the list. Click the Method Name list arrow, then click Click in the list.

Figure 3-24 shows the revised pseudocode for the btnCalc control's Click event procedure. Changes made to the original pseudocode, which is shown in Chapter 2's Figure 2-28, are shaded in the figure. The Click event procedure includes two additional calculations: one for the subtotal and the other for the sales tax. The subtotal is computed by multiplying the total number of phones ordered by the phone price. The sales tax is computed by multiplying the subtotal by the sales tax rate. Notice that the total price equation has changed: it now adds the subtotal to the sales tax. Lastly, the Click event procedure displays the sales tax and the salesperson's name in the lblMessage control.

btnCalc Click event procedure

1. calculate total phones ordered = blue phones ordered + pink phones ordered
2. calculate subtotal = total phones ordered * phone price
3. calculate sales tax = subtotal * sales tax rate
4. calculate total price = subtotal + sales tax
5. display total phones ordered and total price in lblTotalPhones and lblTotalPrice
6. display the sales tax and salesperson's name in lblMessage

Figure 3-24 Revised pseudocode for the btnCalc control's Click event procedure

Before you begin coding a procedure, you first study the procedure's pseudocode to determine the variables and named constants (if any) the procedure will use. When determining the named constants, look for items whose value will be the same each time the procedure is invoked. In the btnCalc control's Click event procedure, the phone price and sales tax rate will always be $25 and .03 (the decimal equivalent of 3%), respectively; therefore, you will assign both values to Decimal constants named `decPHONE_PRICE` and `decTAX_RATE`. At this point, you may be wondering why the `decPHONE_PRICE` constant will be declared using the Decimal data type rather than the Integer data type. Although the phone price does not currently contain any decimal places, it is possible that the price may include a decimal place in the future. By using the Decimal data type now, you can change the constant's value to include a decimal place without having to remember to also change its data type.

When determining a procedure's variables, look in the pseudocode for items whose value probably will change each time the procedure is processed. In the btnCalc control's Click event procedure, the numbers of blue and pink phones ordered probably will be different each time the procedure is processed, and so will the total number of phones ordered, subtotal, sales tax, and total price. Therefore, you will assign those values to variables. Integer variables are a good choice for storing the numbers of blue and pink phones, as well as the total phones, because a customer can order only a whole number of phones. You will use Decimal variables to store the subtotal, sales tax, and total price, because these amounts may contain a decimal place. Figure 3-25 lists the names and data types of the two named constants and six variables you will use in the btnCalc control's Click event procedure.

Named constant/Variable	Data type
decPHONE_PRICE	Decimal
decTAX_RATE	Decimal
intBluePhones	Integer
intPinkPhones	Integer
intTotalPhones	Integer
decSubtotal	Decimal
decSalesTax	Decimal
decTotalPrice	Decimal

Figure 3-25 Named constants and variables for the btnCalc control's Click event procedure

To declare the named constants and variables:

1. The insertion point should be located in the blank line above the End Sub line. Press **Tab** twice, if necessary, to align the blinking insertion point with the apostrophe in the comment.
2. First, you will declare the decPHONE_PRICE constant. When declaring constants and variables, be sure to enter the name using the exact capitalization you want. Then, any time you want to refer to the named constant or variable in the code, you can enter its name using any case and the Code Editor will adjust the name to match the case used in the declaration statement. Type **const decPHONE_PRICE as decimal = 25d** and press **Enter**. For now, don't be concerned about the green jagged line that appears below the Const statement.
3. Type **const decTAX_RATE as decimal = .03d** and press **Enter**.
4. Enter the following six variable declaration statements. Press **Enter** twice after typing the last statement.

   dim intBluePhones as integer
   dim intPinkPhones as integer
   dim intTotalPhones as integer
   dim decSubtotal as decimal
   dim decSalesTax as decimal
   dim decTotalPrice as decimal

5. Notice the green jagged lines that appear below the Const and Dim statements. Place your mouse pointer on the last green jagged line. A box containing a message appears, as shown in Figure 3-26. The message indicates that, although the `decTotalPrice` variable has been declared, it has not been used yet. In other words, the variable name does not appear in any other statement in the code. The green jagged line will disappear when you include the variable name in another statement in the procedure.

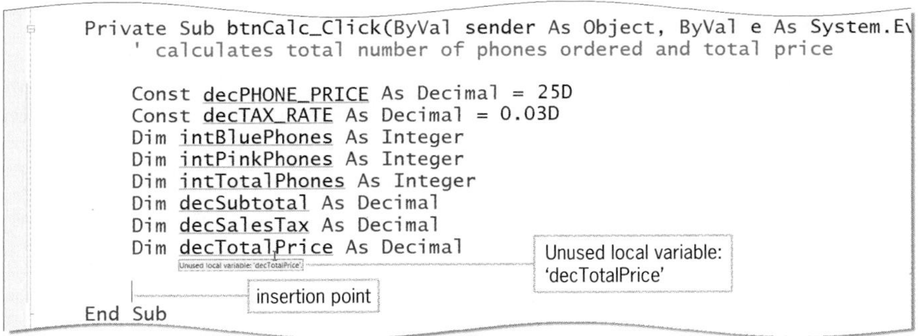

Figure 3-26 Const and Dim statements entered in the procedure

After declaring the named constants and variables, you can begin coding each step in the procedure's pseudocode (shown earlier in Figure 3-24). Keep in mind that some steps may require more than one line of code. The first step in the pseudocode is to calculate the total number of phones ordered. The calculation is made by adding the number of blue phones ordered (which is stored in the Text property of the txtBlue control) to the number of pink phones ordered (which is stored in the Text property of the txtPink control). You will use the TryParse method to convert the Text properties of both text boxes to integers, which you will store in the `intBluePhones` and `intPinkPhones` variables. You then will use an assignment statement to add together the contents of both variables, assigning the sum to the `intTotalPhones` variable.

To continue coding the btnCalc control's Click event procedure:

1. The insertion point should be positioned as shown earlier in Figure 3-26. Type **' calculate the total number of phones ordered** and press **Enter**.

2. Type **integer.tryparse(txtBlue.text, intBluePhones)** and press **Enter**. Notice that the green jagged line below the `Dim intBluePhones As Integer` statement disappears. (You can type control and variable names—in this case, txtBlue and intBluePhones—using all lowercase letters, like this: txtblue and intbluephones. However, to improve readability, the steps in this book will always use the exact capitalization.)

3. Type **integer.tryparse(txtPink.text, intPinkPhones)** and press **Enter**. Then type **intTotalPhones = intBluePhones + intPinkPhones** and press **Enter** twice. Notice that all of the variables in the assignment statement have the same data type: Integer.

4. The second step in the pseudocode is to calculate the subtotal by multiplying the total number of phones ordered (which is stored in the `intTotalPhones` variable) by the phone price (which is stored in the decPHONE_PRICE named constant). You will assign the subtotal to the `decSubtotal` variable. Type **' calculate the subtotal** and press **Enter**, then type **decSubtotal = intTotalPhones * decPHONE_PRICE** and press **Enter** twice. When processing the assignment statement, the computer will implicitly convert the integer stored in the `intTotalPhones` variable to Decimal before multiplying it by the decimal number stored in the `decPHONE_PRICE` constant. It then will assign the result to the `decSubtotal` variable.

5. The third step in the pseudocode is to calculate the sales tax by multiplying the subtotal by the sales tax rate. You will assign the sales tax to the `decSalesTax` variable. Type **' calculate the sales tax** and press **Enter**, then type **decSalesTax = decSubtotal * decTAX_RATE** and press **Enter** twice. Notice that the variables and named constant have the same data type: Decimal.

6. The fourth step in the pseudocode is to calculate the total price by adding together the subtotal and the sales tax. You will assign the result to the `decTotalPrice` variable. Type **' calculate the total price** and press **Enter**, then type **decTotalPrice = decSubtotal + decSalesTax** and press **Enter** twice. Notice that all of the variables in the assignment statement have the same data type: Decimal.

7. Step 5 in the pseudocode is to display the total phones ordered and the total price in the lblTotalPhones and lblTotalPrice controls. The total number of phones ordered is stored in the `intTotalPhones` variable, and the total price is stored in the `decTotalPrice` variable. Because both variables have a numeric data type, you will need to convert their contents to the String data type before assigning the contents to the label controls. You can use the ToString method of the Convert class to make the conversions. Type **' display total amounts** and press **Enter**. Type **lblTotalPhones.text = convert.tostring(intTotalPhones)** and press **Enter**, then type **lblTotalPrice.text = convert.tostring(decTotalPrice)** and press **Enter** twice.

8. The last step in the pseudocode is to display the sales tax and the salesperson's name in the lblMessage control. For now, you will display only the sales tax. Type **' display tax and salesperson's name** and press **Enter**, then type **lblMessage.text = convert.tostring (decSalesTax)** and press **Enter**. Figure 3-27 shows the code entered in the btnCalc control's Click event procedure.

```
Private Sub btnCalc_Click(ByVal sender As Object, _
   ByVal e As System.EventArgs) Handles btnCalc.Click
   ' calculates total number of phones ordered and total price

   Const decPHONE_PRICE As Decimal = 25D
   Const decTAX_RATE As Decimal = 0.03D
   Dim intBluePhones As Integer
   Dim intPinkPhones As Integer
   Dim intTotalPhones As Integer
   Dim decSubtotal As Decimal
   Dim decSalesTax As Decimal
   Dim decTotalPrice As Decimal

   ' calculate the total number of phones ordered
   Integer.TryParse(txtBlue.Text, intBluePhones)
   Integer.TryParse(txtPink.Text, intPinkPhones)
   intTotalPhones = intBluePhones + intPinkPhones

   ' calculate the subtotal
   decSubtotal = intTotalPhones * decPHONE_PRICE

   ' calculate the sales tax
   decSalesTax = decSubtotal * decTAX_RATE

   ' calculate the total price
   decTotalPrice = decSubtotal + decSalesTax

   ' display total amounts
   lblTotalPhones.Text = Convert.ToString(intTotalPhones)
   lblTotalPrice.Text = Convert.ToString(decTotalPrice)

   ' display tax and salesperson's name
   lblMessage.Text = Convert.ToString(decSalesTax)

End Sub
```

Figure 3-27 Code entered in the btnCalc control's Click event procedure

To save the solution, then start and test the application:

1. Save the solution, then start the application.
2. Enter **10** as the number of blue phones ordered, and enter **5** as the number of pink phones ordered. Click the **Calculate Order** button. The total number of phones ordered, total price, and sales tax appear in the interface, as shown in Figure 3-28. However, it's not obvious to the user that the 11.25 is the sales tax. You can fix this problem by displaying the message "The sales tax was" before the sales tax amount. Before you can accomplish this task, you need to learn how to concatenate (link together) strings. String concatenation is covered in the next section.

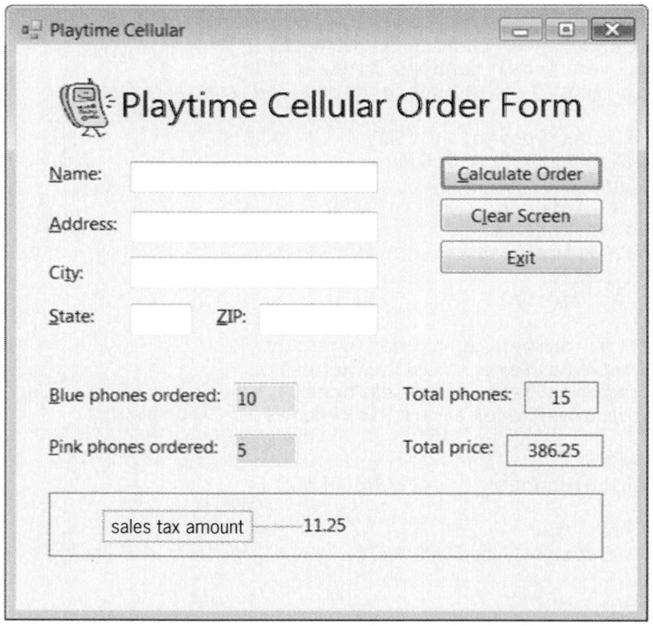

Figure 3-28 Calculated amounts shown in the interface

3. Click the **Clear Screen** button to clear the order form, then click the **Exit** button to end the application.

Concatenating Strings

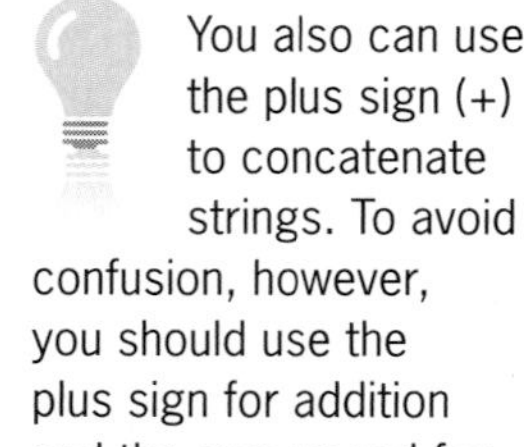

You also can use the plus sign (+) to concatenate strings. To avoid confusion, however, you should use the plus sign for addition and the ampersand for concatenation.

You use the **concatenation operator**, which is the ampersand (&), to concatenate (connect or link) strings together. When concatenating strings, you must be sure to include a space before and after the ampersand; otherwise, the Code Editor will not recognize the ampersand as the concatenation operator. Figure 3-29 shows some examples of string concatenation.

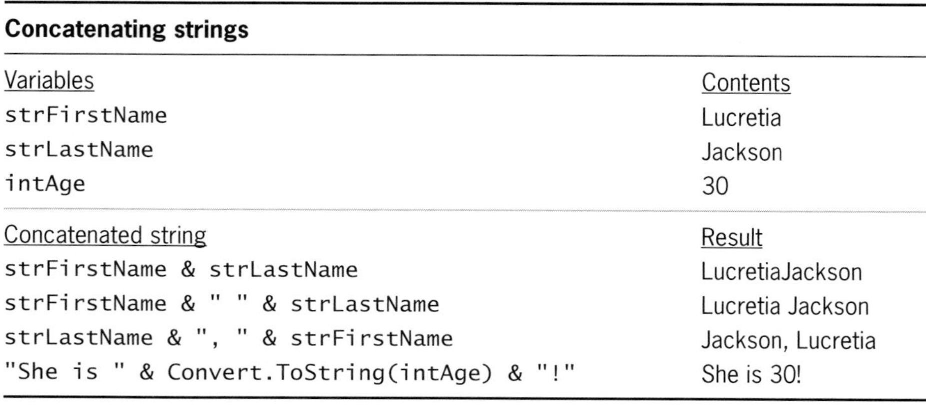

Concatenating strings

Variables	Contents
`strFirstName`	Lucretia
`strLastName`	Jackson
`intAge`	30
Concatenated string	**Result**
`strFirstName & strLastName`	LucretiaJackson
`strFirstName & " " & strLastName`	Lucretia Jackson
`strLastName & ", " & strFirstName`	Jackson, Lucretia
`"She is " & Convert.ToString(intAge) & "!"`	She is 30!

Figure 3-29 Examples of string concatenation

You will use the concatenation operator to link the following three strings into one sentence: the words "The sales tax was ", the contents of the `decSalesTax` variable after it has been converted to a string, and a period to mark the end of the sentence. Using the examples shown in Figure 3-29 as a guide, the correct assignment statement is `lblMessage.Text = "The sales tax was " & Convert.ToString(decSalesTax) & "."`.

To concatenate the strings, and then save the solution and start the application:

1. Change the `lblMessage.Text = Convert.ToString(decSalesTax)` statement as shown in Figure 3-30.

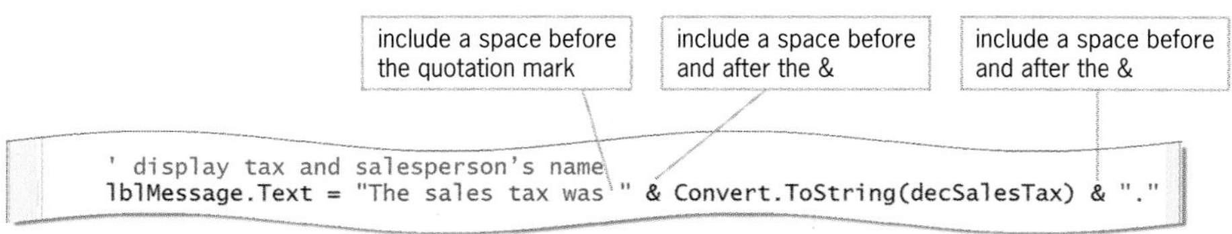

Figure 3-30 String concatenation included in the assignment statement

2. Save the solution, then start the application. Enter **10** as the number of blue phones ordered, and enter **5** as the number of pink phones ordered. Click the **Calculate Order** button. The lblMessage control contains the sentence "The sales tax was 11.25.", as shown in Figure 3-31.

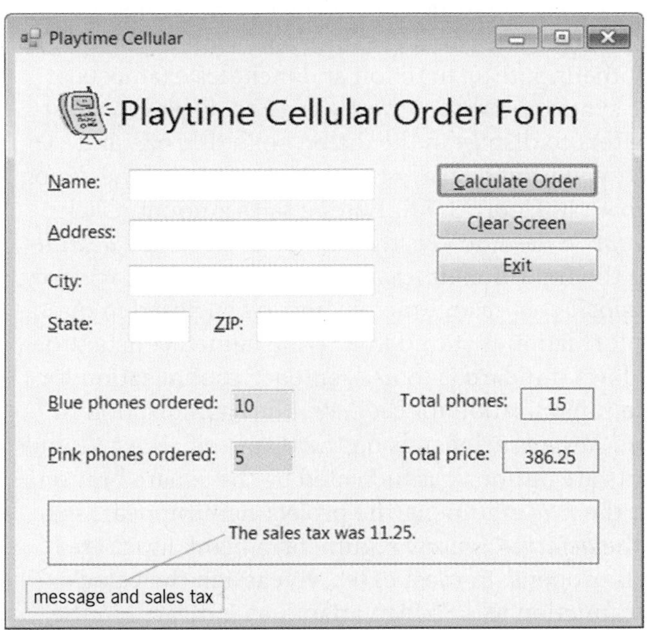

Figure 3-31 Order form showing the concatenated strings

3. Click the **Exit** button to end the application.

Recall that you also need to display the salesperson's name in the lblMessage control. You can use the InputBox function to obtain the name from the user.

The InputBox Function

The **InputBox function** displays one of the standard dialog boxes available in Visual Basic; an example is shown in Figure 3-32. The dialog box contains a message along with an OK button, a Cancel button, and an input area where the user can enter information. The value returned by the InputBox function depends on whether the user clicks the OK button, Cancel button, or Close button. If the user clicks the OK button, the InputBox function returns the value contained in the input area of the dialog box; this value is always treated as a string. If the user clicks either the Cancel button in the dialog box or the Close button on the dialog box's title bar, the InputBox function returns an empty string.

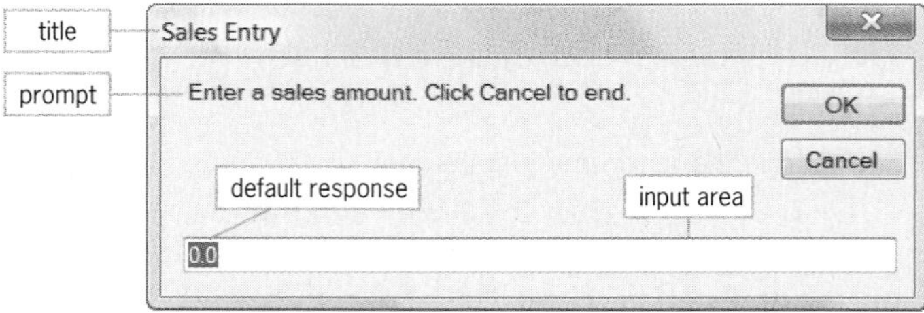

Figure 3-32 Example of a dialog box created by the InputBox function

The message in the dialog box should prompt the user to enter the appropriate information in the input area. The user then needs to click either the OK button or the Cancel button to continue working in the application. Figure 3-33 shows the basic syntax of the InputBox function and includes examples of using the function. In the syntax, *prompt* is the message to display inside the dialog box, *title* is the text to display in the dialog box's title bar, and *defaultResponse* is the text you want displayed in the input area of the dialog box. In the dialog box shown in Figure 3-32, "Enter a sales amount. Click Cancel to end." is the *prompt*, "Sales Entry" is the *title*, and "0.0" is the *defaultResponse.* When entering the InputBox function in the Code Editor window, the *prompt*, *title*, and *defaultResponse* arguments must be enclosed in quotation marks, unless that information is stored in a String named constant or String variable. The Windows standard is to use sentence capitalization for the *prompt*, but book title capitalization for the *title.* The capitalization (if any) you use for the *defaultResponse* depends on the text itself. The *title* and *defaultResponse* arguments are optional, as indicated by the square brackets in the syntax. If you omit the *title* argument, the project name appears in the title bar. If you omit the *defaultResponse* argument, a blank input area appears when the dialog box opens. In most cases, you assign the value returned by the InputBox function to a String variable, as indicated in the examples in Figure 3-33.

The InputBox function's syntax also includes optional *XPos* and *YPos* arguments for specifying the dialog box's horizontal and vertical positions. If omitted, the dialog box appears centered on the screen.

InputBox Function

Syntax

InputBox(*prompt*[, *title*][, *defaultResponse*]**)**

Example 1

```
strName = InputBox("Enter your first name:", "Name Entry")
```

Displays a dialog box that shows "Enter your first name:" as the message, "Name Entry" in the title bar, and an empty input area. Assigns the user's response to the `strName` variable.

Example 2

```
strState = InputBox("State name:", "State", "Alaska")
```

Displays a dialog box that shows "State name:" as the message, "State" in the title bar, and "Alaska" in the input area. Assigns the user's response to the `strState` variable.

Example 3

```
Const strPROMPT As String = "Enter the rate:"
Const strTITLE As String = "Rate"
strRate = InputBox(strPROMPT, strTITLE, ".00")
```

Displays a dialog box that shows the contents of the `strPROMPT` constant as the message, the contents of the `strTITLE` constant in the title bar, and ".00" in the input area. Assigns the user's response to the `strRate` variable.

Example 4

```
Integer.TryParse(InputBox("Enter the age", "Age"), intAge)
```

Displays a dialog box that prompts the user to enter an age, then converts the age to an integer and assigns the result to the `intAge` variable.

Figure 3-33 Basic syntax and examples of the InputBox function

GUI DESIGN TIP InputBox Function's Prompt and Title Capitalization

Use sentence capitalization for the *prompt*, but book title capitalization for the *title*.

You will use the InputBox function in the Playtime Cellular application to prompt the salesperson to enter his or her name. The InputBox function should be entered in the frmMain Load event procedure because, according to the revised TOE chart shown earlier in Figure 3-20, that is the procedure responsible for getting the salesperson's name. Recall that a form's Load event occurs before the form is displayed the first time. After the Load event procedure obtains the salesperson's name, you then will have the btnCalc control's Click event procedure concatenate the name to the message displayed in the lblMessage control.

Before entering the InputBox function in the Load event procedure, you must decide where to declare the String variable that will store the function's return value. In other words, should the variable have procedure scope or module scope? When deciding, consider the fact that the form's Load event procedure needs to assign the InputBox function's return value to the variable. The Calculate Order button's Click event procedure also needs to use the variable, because the procedure must concatenate the variable to the message displayed in the lblMessage control. Recall from Lesson A that when two procedures in the same form need to use the same variable, you declare the variable as a module-level variable. You do this by entering the variable declaration statement in the form's Declarations section.

To continue coding the Playtime Cellular application:

1. Scroll to the top of the Code Editor window, then click the **blank line** immediately below the `Public Class frmMain` line. When you do so, frmMain and (Declarations) appear in the Class Name and Method Name boxes, respectively, indicating that this is the form's Declarations section.

2. First, declare a module-level String variable named `strSalesPerson`. Press **Enter** to insert a blank line, then type **' declare module-level variable** and press **Enter**. Type **private strSalesPerson as string** and press **Enter**. See Figure 3-34.

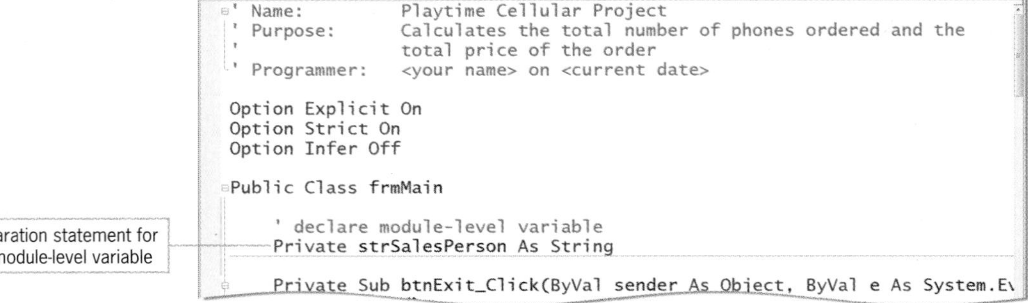

Figure 3-34 Module-level variable declared in the form's Declarations section

3. Now you will enter the InputBox function in the form's Load event procedure, so the function will be processed as soon as the salesperson starts the application. You access the form's procedures by selecting (frmMain Events) in the Class Name list box. Click the **Class Name** list arrow, then click **(frmMain Events)** in the list. Click the **Method Name** list arrow to view a list of the form's procedures. Scroll down the list until you see Load, then click **Load** in the list. The frmMain Load event procedure appears in the Code Editor window.

4. To make the assignment statement that contains the InputBox function shorter and easier to understand, you will create named constants for the function's *prompt* ("Enter the salesperson's name:") and *title* ("Name Entry") arguments, and then use the named constants rather than the longer strings in the function. You are using named constants rather than variables because the *prompt* and *title* arguments will not change as the application is running. Type the comments and code shown in Figure 3-35.

```
Private Sub frmMain_Load(ByVal sender As Object, ByVal e As System.Eve
    ' gets the salesperson's name

    Const strPROMPT As String = "Enter the salesperson's name:"
    Const strTITLE As String = "Name Entry"
    ' assign the name to the module-level variable
    strSalesPerson = InputBox(strPROMPT, strTITLE)

End Sub
```

enter these 2 comments and 3 lines of code

Figure 3-35 frmMain Load event procedure

5. Now concatenate the `strSalesPerson` variable to the message assigned to the lblMessage control. Locate the btnCalc control's Click event procedure. Click at the **end of the last assignment statement** in the procedure. Press the **spacebar**, then type **& strSalesPerson**. This changes the assignment statement to `lblMessage.Text = "The sales tax was " & Convert.ToString(decSalesTax) & "." & strSalesPerson`.

6. Save the solution, then start the application. The Name Entry dialog box created by the InputBox function appears first. See Figure 3-36.

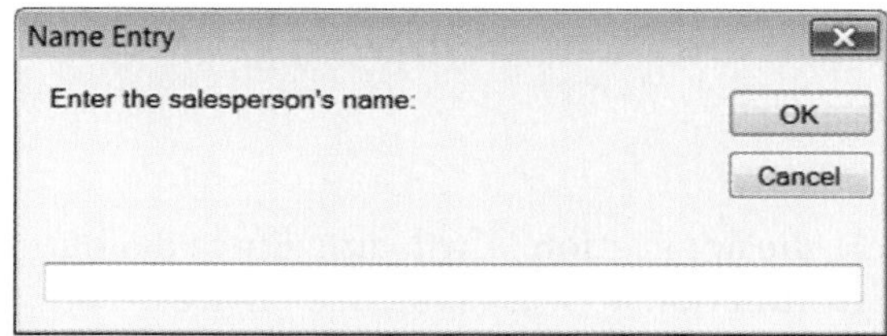

Figure 3-36 Dialog box created by the InputBox function

7. Type your name in the input area of the dialog box, then click the **OK** button. The order form appears. Enter **10** as the number of blue phones ordered, then click the **Calculate Order** button. Notice that your name appears much too close to the period in the lblMessage control. You can correct the spacing problem in the lblMessage control by replacing the period (".") in the assignment statement with a period and two spaces (". "). Or, you can use the `ControlChars.NewLine` constant to display the salesperson's name on the next line in the lblMessage control. Click the **Exit** button to end the application.

The ControlChars.Newline Constant

The **ControlChars.NewLine constant** instructs the computer to issue a carriage return followed by a line feed, which advances the insertion point to the next line in a control. (You also can use it to advance the insertion point in a file or on the printer.) Whenever you want to start a new line, you simply type the `ControlChars.NewLine` constant at the appropriate location in your code. In this case, you want to advance to a new line after displaying the period—in other words, before displaying the salesperson's name. The appropriate assignment statement is `lblMessage.Text = "The sales tax was " & Convert.ToString(decSalesTax) & "." &`

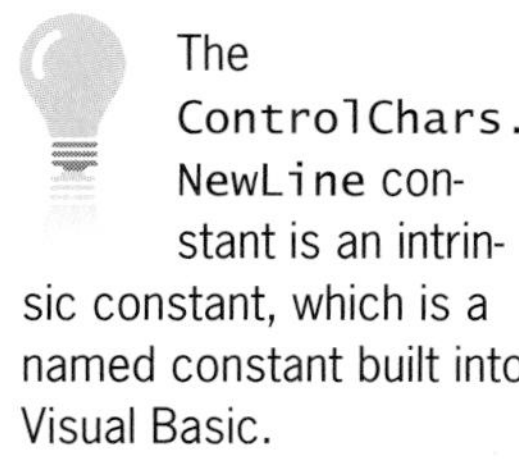

The `ControlChars.NewLine` constant is an intrinsic constant, which is a named constant built into Visual Basic.

`ControlChars.NewLine & strSalesPerson`. The assignment statement is rather long and, depending on the size of the font used in the Code Editor window, you may not be able to view the entire statement without scrolling the window. You can use the **line continuation character**, which is an underscore (_), to break up a long instruction into two or more physical lines in the Code Editor window. Breaking up an instruction in this manner makes the instruction easier to read and understand. The line continuation character must be immediately preceded by a space and appear at the end of a physical line of code.

To display the salesperson's name on a separate line in the lblMessage control:

1. In the btnCalc control's Click event procedure, modify the last assignment statement as indicated in Figure 3-37.

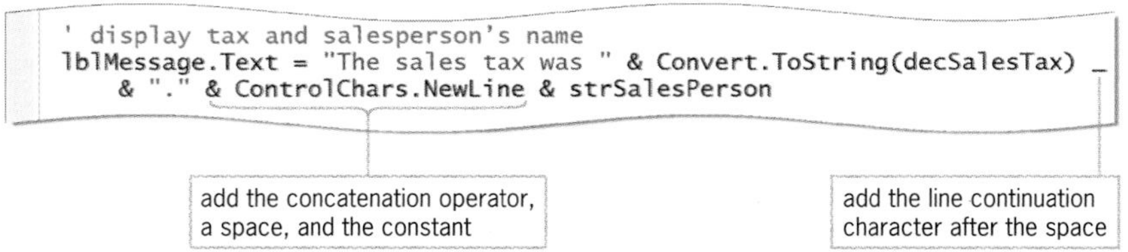

Figure 3-37 Modified assignment statement

2. Save the solution, then start the application. The Name Entry dialog box created by the InputBox function appears first. See Figure 3-38.

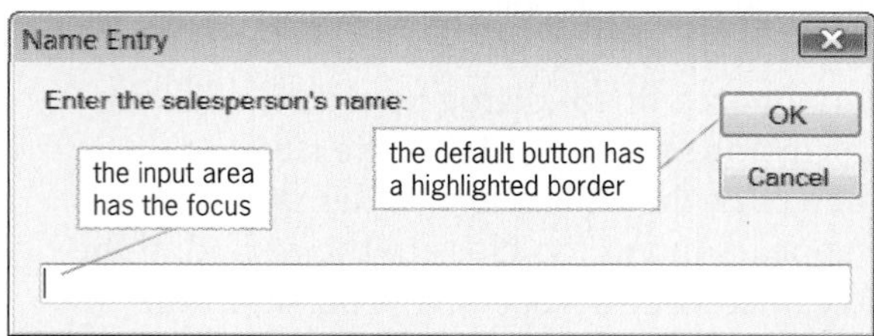

Figure 3-38 Focus and default button shown in the dialog box

3. Notice that the OK button in the dialog box has a highlighted border, even though it does not have the focus. The input area in the dialog box has the focus, as indicated by the position of the insertion point. In Windows terminology, a button that has a highlighted border when it does not have the focus is called the default button. You can select a default button by pressing Enter at any time. Type **Mary Jones** in the input area of the dialog box. Then, instead of clicking the OK button, simply press **Enter**. The order form appears.

4. Enter **5** as the number of blue phones ordered, then click the **Calculate Order** button. The salesperson's name now appears on a separate line in the lblMessage control, as shown in Figure 3-39. Click the **Exit** button to end the application.

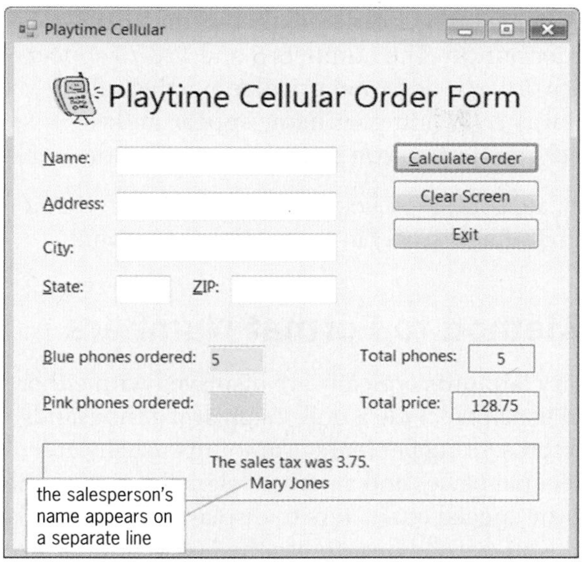

Figure 3-39 Order form showing the salesperson's name on a separate line

Designating a Default Button

As you already know from using Windows applications, you can select a button by clicking it or by pressing the Enter key when the button has the focus. If you make a button the **default button**, you also can select it by pressing the Enter key even when the button does not have the focus. When a button is selected, the computer processes the code contained in the button's Click event procedure. An interface does not have to have a default button. However, if one is used, it should be the button that is most often selected by the user, except in cases where the tasks performed by the button are both destructive and irreversible. For example, a button that deletes information should not be designated as the default button. If you assign a default button in an interface, it typically is the first button, which means that it is on the left when the buttons are positioned horizontally on the form, and on the top when the buttons are stacked vertically. A form can have only one default button. You specify the default button (if any) by setting the form's AcceptButton property to the name of the button.

A form's CancelButton property specifies the button whose Click event procedure is processed when the user presses the Esc key. A form can have only one cancel button.

GUI DESIGN TIP Assigning a Default Button

The default button should be the button that is most often selected by the user, except in cases where the tasks performed by the button are both destructive and irreversible. In most interfaces, the default button is the first button.

To make the Calculate Order button the default button:

1. Click the **Main Form.vb [Design]** tab to return to the designer window. Set the form's **AcceptButton** property to **btnCalc**. A highlighted border appears around the Calculate Order button.
2. Save the solution, then start the application. Type your name in the Name Entry dialog box and press **Enter**. The order form appears.

3. Enter **5** as the number of blue phones ordered, then press **Enter** to select the Calculate Order button. The numbers 5 and 128.75 appear as the number of phones ordered and total price, respectively. In addition, "The sales tax was 3.75." and your name appear in the lblMessage control. Click the **Exit** button to end the application.

Lastly, you will modify the btnCalc control's Click event procedure so that it displays a dollar sign and comma (if necessary) in the total price amount.

Using the ToString Method to Format Numbers

Numbers representing monetary amounts typically are displayed with either zero or two decimal places and usually include a dollar sign and a thousands separator. Similarly, numbers representing percentage amounts usually are displayed with zero or more decimal places and a percent sign. Specifying the number of decimal places and the special characters to display in a number is called **formatting**. In Chapter 2, you learned how to use the Format function to format a number for output as a string. Although you can still use the Format function in Visual Basic 2008, many programmers now use the ToString method, because the method can be used in any of the languages built into Visual Studio. The method's syntax is *variable***.ToString(***formatString***)**. In the syntax, *variable* is the name of a numeric variable and ToString is a method that can be used with any of the numeric data types. The **ToString method** formats the contents of the numeric variable and returns the result as a string. The *formatString* argument in the syntax is a string that specifies the format you want to use. The *formatString* argument must take the form "*Axx*", where *A* is an alphabetic character called the format specifier, and *xx* is a sequence of digits called the precision specifier. The format specifier must be one of the built-in format characters. The most commonly used format characters are listed in Figure 3-40. Notice that you can use either an uppercase letter or a lowercase letter as the format specifier. When used with one of the format characters listed in Figure 3-40, the precision specifier controls the number of digits that will appear after the decimal point in the formatted number. Also included in Figure 3-40 are several examples of using the ToString method.

Using the ToString method to format a number

Syntax
*variable***.ToString(***formatString***)**

Format specifier (Name)	Description
C or c (Currency)	displays the string with a dollar sign; if appropriate, includes a thousands separator; negative values are enclosed in parentheses
N or n (Number)	similar to the Currency format, but does not include a dollar sign and negative values are preceded by a minus sign

Figure 3-40 Syntax and examples of the ToString method *(continues)*

(continued)

Using the ToString method to format a number

Format specifier (Name)	Description
F or f (Fixed-point)	same as the Number format, but does not include a thousands separator
P or p (Percent)	multiplies the value by 100 and displays the result with a percent sign; negative values are preceded by a minus sign

Example 1

```
lblCommission.Text = intCommission.ToString("C2")
```

if the `intCommission` variable contains the number 1250, the statement assigns the string "$1,250.00" to the Text property of the lblCommission control

Example 2

```
lblTotal.Text = decTotal.ToString("N2")
```

if the `decTotal` variable contains the number 123.675, the statement assigns the string "123.68" to the Text property of the lblTotal control

Example 3

```
lblRate.Text = dblRate.ToString("P0")
```

if the `dblRate` variable contains the number .06, the statement assigns the string "6 %" to the Text property of the lblRate control

Figure 3-40 Syntax and examples of the ToString method

In the Playtime Cellular application, the btnCalc control's Click event procedure displays the total price of the order in the lblTotalPrice control. You can include a dollar sign, thousands separator, and two decimal places when displaying the total price by changing the `lblTotalPrice.Text = Convert.ToString(decTotalPrice)` statement in the procedure to `lblTotalPrice.Text = decTotalPrice.ToString("C2")`.

To format the total price:

1. Click the **Main Form.vb** tab to return to the Code Editor window. In the btnCalc control's Click event procedure, change the `lblTotalPrice.Text = Convert.ToString(decTotalPrice)` statement to **lblTotalPrice.Text = decTotalPrice.ToString("C2")**.
2. Close the Code Editor window. Save the solution, then start the application. Type **Perry Hormel** in the input area of the dialog box, then press **Enter**. The order form appears.
3. Enter **15** as the number of blue phones ordered, and enter **25** as the number of pink phones ordered. Click the **Calculate Order** button. The total price appears with a dollar sign, a thousands separator, and two decimal places. See Figure 3-41.

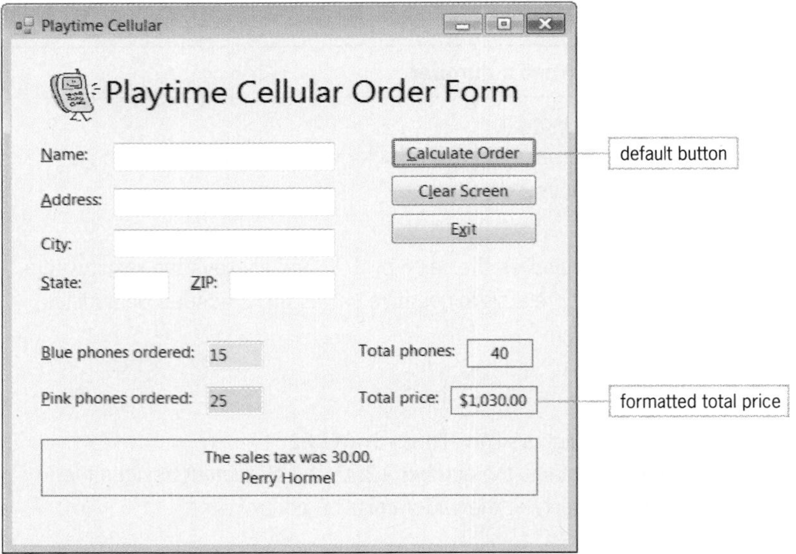

Figure 3-41 Order form showing the formatted total price

4. Click the **Exit** button to end the application. Close the Code Editor window, then close the solution. Figure 3-42 shows the application's code at the end of Lesson B.

```
' Name:          Playtime Cellular Project
' Purpose:       Calculates the total number of phones ordered and the
'                total price of the order
' Programmer:    <your name> on <current date>

Option Explicit On
Option Strict On
Option Infer Off


Public Class frmMain
   ' declare module-level variable
   Private strSalesPerson As String

   Private Sub btnExit_Click(ByVal sender As Object, _
      ByVal e As System.EventArgs) Handles btnExit.Click
      Me.Close()
   End Sub

   Private Sub btnClear_Click(ByVal sender As Object, _
      ByVal e As System.EventArgs) Handles btnClear.Click
      ' prepare the screen for the next order

      txtName.Text = String.Empty
      txtAddress.Text = String.Empty
      txtCity.Text = String.Empty
      txtState.Text = String.Empty
      txtZip.Text = String.Empty
      txtBlue.Text = String.Empty
      txtPink.Text = String.Empty
      lblTotalPhones.Text = String.Empty
```

Figure 3-42 Playtime Cellular application's code at the end of Lesson B *(continues)*

(continued)

```
        lblTotalPrice.Text = String.Empty
        lblMessage.Text = String.Empty
        ' send the focus to the Name text box
        txtName.Focus()

    End Sub

    Private Sub btnCalc_Click(ByVal sender As Object, _
        ByVal e As System.EventArgs) Handles btnCalc.Click
        ' calculates total number of phones ordered and total price

        Const decPHONE_PRICE As Decimal = 25D
        Const decTAX_RATE As Decimal = 0.03D
        Dim intBluePhones As Integer
        Dim intPinkPhones As Integer
        Dim intTotalPhones As Integer
        Dim decSubtotal As Decimal
        Dim decSalesTax As Decimal
        Dim decTotalPrice As Decimal

        ' calculate the total number of phones ordered
        Integer.TryParse(txtBlue.Text, intBluePhones)
        Integer.TryParse(txtPink.Text, intPinkPhones)
        intTotalPhones = intBluePhones + intPinkPhones

        ' calculate the subtotal
        decSubtotal = intTotalPhones * decPHONE_PRICE

        ' calculate the sales tax
        decSalesTax = decSubtotal * decTAX_RATE

        ' calculate the total price
        decTotalPrice = decSubtotal + decSalesTax

        ' display total amounts
        lblTotalPhones.Text = Convert.ToString(intTotalPhones)
        lblTotalPrice.Text = decTotalPrice.ToString("C2")

        ' display tax and salesperson's name
        lblMessage.Text = "The sales tax was " & Convert.ToString(decSalesTax) _
            & "." & ControlChars.NewLine & strSalesPerson

    End Sub

    Private Sub frmMain_Load(ByVal sender As Object, _
        ByVal e As System.EventArgs) Handles Me.Load
        ' gets the salesperson's name

        Const strPROMPT As String = "Enter the salesperson's name:"
        Const strTITLE As String = "Name Entry"
        ' assign the name to the module-level variable
        strSalesPerson = InputBox(strPROMPT, strTITLE)

    End Sub
End Class
```

Figure 3-42 Playtime Cellular application's code at the end of Lesson B

Lesson B Summary

- **To concatenate strings:**

  Use the concatenation operator, which is the ampersand (&). Be sure to include a space before and after the ampersand.

- **To display a dialog box containing a prompt, an input area, and OK and Cancel buttons:**

  Use the InputBox function, whose syntax is **InputBox(***prompt***[,** *title***] [,** *defaultResponse***])**. The *prompt*, *title*, and *defaultResponse* arguments must be enclosed in quotation marks, unless the information is stored in a String named constant or String variable. Use sentence capitalization for the *prompt*, but book title capitalization for the *title*.

  If the user clicks the OK button, the InputBox function returns the value contained in the input area of the dialog box; this value is always treated as a string. If the user clicks either the Cancel button in the dialog box or the Close button on the dialog box's title bar, the InputBox function returns an empty string.

- **To advance the insertion point to the next line:**

  Use the `ControlChars.NewLine` constant in code.

- **To break up a long instruction into two or more physical lines in the Code Editor window:**

  Use the line continuation character, which is an underscore (_); the line continuation character must be immediately preceded by a space and appear at the end of a physical line of code.

- **To make a button the default button:**

  Set the form's AcceptButton property to the name of the button.

- **To format a number for output as a string:**

  Use the ToString method, whose syntax is *variable***. ToString(***formatString***)**.

Lesson B Key Terms

Concatenation operator—the ampersand (&); used to concatenate strings; must be preceded and followed by a space character

ControlChars.NewLine constant—used to advance the insertion point to the next line in a control

Default button—the button that can be selected by pressing the Enter key even when it does not have the focus

Formatting—specifying the number of decimal places and the special characters to display in a number

InputBox function—displays one of the standard dialog boxes available in Visual Basic; the dialog box contains a message, OK and Cancel buttons, and an input area

Line continuation character—the underscore (_); used to break up a long instruction into two or more physical lines in the Code Editor window

ToString method—formats the contents of a numeric variable and returns the result as a string

Lesson B Review Questions

1. The InputBox function displays a dialog box containing which of the following?
   a. input area
   b. OK and Cancel buttons
   c. prompt
   d. All of the above.

2. Which of the following is the concatenation operator?
   a. @
   b. &
   c. $
   d. #

3. The `strRegion1` variable contains the string "North", and the `strRegion2` variable contains the string "West". Which of the following will display the string "NorthWest" (one word) in the lblRegion control?
   a. `lblRegion.Text = strRegion1 & strRegion2`
   b. `lblRegion.Text = "strRegion1" & "strRegion2"`
   c. `lblRegion.Text = strRegion1 @ strRegion2`
   d. `lblRegion.Text = strRegion1 # strRegion2`

4. The `strCityName` variable contains the string "Boston", and the `strStateName` variable contains the string "MA". Which of the following will display the string "Boston, MA" (the city, a comma, a space, and the state) in the lblAddress control?

   a. `lblAddress.Text = strCityName , & strStateName`

   b. `lblAddress.Text = "strCityName" & "," & "strStateName"`

   c. `lblAddress.Text = strCityName & ", " & strStateName`

   d. None of the above.

5. Which of the following Visual Basic constants advances the insertion point to the next line?

   a. `Advance`

   b. `ControlChars.Advance`

   c. `ControlChars.NewLine`

   d. `ControlChars.NextLine`

6. The form's ________________________ property allows the user to select a specific button by pressing the Enter key, even when the button does not have the focus.

   a. AcceptButton

   b. DefaultButton

   c. EnterButton

   d. FocusButton

7. Which of the following statements prompts the user for a number, and then correctly assigns the user's response to a Double variable named `dblNum`?

   a. `Double.TryParse(InputBox("Enter a number:", "Number") , dblNum)`

   b. `dblNum = Double.TryParse(InputBox("Enter a number:", "Number"))`

   c. `dblNum = InputBox("Enter a number:", "Number")`

   d. `TryParse.Double(InputBox("Enter a number:", "Number"), dblNum)`

8. Which of the following statements prompts the user for the name of a city, and then correctly assigns the user's response to a String variable named `strCity`?

   a. `String.TryParse(InputBox("Enter the city:", "City"), strCity)`

   b. `strCity = String(InputBox("Enter the city:", "City"))`

   c. `strCity = InputBox("Enter the city:", "City")`

   d. None of the above.

9. The InputBox function's *prompt* argument should be entered using ________________________.

   a. book title capitalization

   b. sentence capitalization

10. If the `decSales` variable contains the number 12345.89, which of the following statements displays the number as 12,345.89?

    a. `lblSales.Text = decSales.ToString("C2")`

    b. `lblSales.Text = decSales.ToString("N2")`

    c. `lblSales.Text = decSales.ToString("D2")`

    d. `lblSales.Text = decSales.ToString("F2")`

Lesson B Exercises

1. The `strCity` and `strState` variables contain the strings "Madison" and "WI", respectively. Write an assignment statement to display the string "Madison, WI" in the lblAddress control. INTRODUCTORY

2. The `strZip` variable contains the string "53711". Write an assignment statement to display the string "My ZIP code is 53711." in the lblMsg control. INTRODUCTORY

3. In this exercise, you modify the Playtime Cellular application that you coded in the lesson. Use Windows to make a copy of the Playtime Solution folder, which is contained in the VB2008\Chap03 folder. Rename the folder Modified Playtime Solution. Open the Playtime Solution (Playtime Solution.sln) file contained in the VB2008\Chap03\Modified Playtime Solution folder. Open the designer window. Modify the btnCalc control's Click event procedure so that it displays the sales tax amount with a dollar sign, two decimal places, and a thousands separator (if necessary). Save the solution, then start and test the application. Click the Exit button to end the application. Close the Code Editor window, then close the solution. INTRODUCTORY

INTRODUCTORY

4. Open the Commission Solution (Commission Solution.sln) file, which is contained in the VB2008\Chap03\Commission Solution folder. If necessary, open the designer window. The application calculates and displays a salesperson's commission, using a commission rate of 10%. Make the Calculate Commission button the default button. Open the Code Editor window and review the code in the Calculate Commission button's Click event procedure. Recode the procedure so that it uses variables. Also use a named constant for the commission rate. Be sure to enter the `Option Explicit On`, `Option Strict On`, and `Option Infer Off` statements in the General Declarations section. Use the ToString method to display the commission amount with a dollar sign, two decimal places, and a thousands separator (if necessary). Save the solution, then start the application. Test the application by calculating the commission for sales of 7500. The commission should be $750.00. Click the Exit button to end the application. Close the Code Editor window, then close the solution.

INTERMEDIATE

5. The `strCity` and `strState` variables contain the strings "Madison" and "WI", respectively. Write an assignment statement to display the string "The capital of WI is Madison." in the lblMsg control.

INTERMEDIATE

6. Open the Mingo Solution (Mingo Solution.sln) file, which is contained in the VB2008\Chap03\Mingo Solution folder. If necessary, open the designer window. The application allows the sales manager to enter the sales made in three states. It then calculates and displays both the total sales made and the total commission earned in the three states.

   a. Make the Calculate button the default button.

   b. Enter the appropriate Option statements in the Code Editor window.

   c. Code the Exit button so that it ends the application when it is clicked.

   d. Use the pseudocode shown in Figure 3-43 to code the Calculate button's Click event procedure. Be sure to use variables. The commission rate is 5%. Use the ToString method to display a thousands separator (if necessary) and two decimal places in the total sales and commission amounts.

btnCalc Click event procedure

1. calculate the total sales = New York sales + Maine sales + Florida sales
2. calculate the commission = total sales * commission rate
3. display the total sales and commission in lblTotalSales and lblCommission
4. send the focus to the New York sales text box

Figure 3-43 Pseudocode for the procedure in the Mingo Solution

e. Save the solution, then start the application. Test the application by calculating the total sales and commission for the following amounts: New York sales of 15000, Maine sales of 25000, and Florida sales of 10500.

f. Click the Exit button to end the application. Close the Code Editor window, then close the solution.

7. In this exercise, you modify the Mingo Sales application from Exercise 6. Use Windows to make a copy of the Mingo Solution folder, which is contained in the VB2008\Chap03 folder. Rename the folder Modified Mingo Solution. Open the Mingo Solution (Mingo Solution.sln) file contained in the VB2008\Chap03\Modified Mingo Solution folder. Open the designer window. Code the form's Load event procedure so that it uses the InputBox function to ask the user for the commission rate before the form appears. Modify the code in the btnCalc control's Click event procedure so that it uses the commission rate entered by the user. Save the solution, then start the application. When you are prompted to enter the commission rate, type .1 (the decimal equivalent of 10%) and then click the OK button. Test the application using 26000 as the New York sales, 34000 as the Maine sales, and 17000 as the Florida sales. Click the Exit button to end the application. Close the Code Editor window, then close the solution.

INTERMEDIATE

8. Open the IMY Solution (IMY Solution.sln) file, which is contained in the VB2008\Chap03\IMY Solution folder. If necessary, open the designer window. The application calculates the new hourly pay for each of three job codes, given the current hourly pay for each job code and the raise percentage (entered as a decimal number). The application should display the message "Raise percentage: *XX*" in a label control on the form. The *XX* in the message should be replaced by the actual raise percentage, formatted using the "P0" *formatString*.

INTERMEDIATE

a. Code the Exit button so that it ends the application when it is clicked.

b. Before the form appears, use the InputBox function to prompt the personnel clerk to enter the raise percentage. You will use the raise percentage to calculate the new hourly pay for each job code.

c. Use the pseudocode shown in Figure 3-44 to code the Calculate button's Click event procedure. Create a named constant for the "Raise percentage:" message. Format the new hourly pays using the "N2" *formatString*. Format the raise rate (in the message) using the "P0" *formatString*.

btnCalc Click event procedure

1. calculate each new hourly pay = current hourly pay * raise rate + current hourly pay
2. display the new hourly pays in the appropriate label controls
3. display the message and raise rate in the lblMessage control
4. send the focus to the Job Code 1 text box

Figure 3-44 Pseudocode for the event procedure in the IMY Solution

d. Save the solution, then start the application. When you are prompted to enter the raise percentage, type .05 (the decimal equivalent of 5%) and then click the OK button. Use the following information to calculate the new hourly pay for each job code:

Current hourly pay for job code 1: 5

Current hourly pay for job code 2: 6.5

Current hourly pay for job code 3: 8.75

e. Click the Exit button to end the application. Close the Code Editor window, then close the solution.

ADVANCED

9. In this exercise, you modify the IMY Industries application from Exercise 8. The modified application will allow the user to enter a separate raise percentage for each job code. Use Windows to make a copy of the IMY Solution folder, which is contained in the VB2008\Chap03 folder. Rename the folder Modified IMY Solution. Open the IMY Solution (IMY Solution.sln) file contained in the VB2008\Chap03\Modified IMY Solution folder. Open the designer window.

   a. Modify the application's code so that it asks the personnel clerk to enter the raise for each job code separately. Display the following information on separate lines in the lblMessage control. Be sure to replace the *XX* in each line with the appropriate raise percentage. (You will need to change the size of the form and lblMessage control.)

   Job Code 1: *XX* %

   Job Code 2: *XX* %

   Job Code 3: *XX* %

   b. Save the solution, then start the application. When you are prompted to enter the raise percentages for the job codes, use .03 for job code 1, .05 for job code 2, and .04 for job code 3. Use the following information to calculate the new hourly pay for each job code:

   Current hourly pay for job code 1: 5

   Current hourly pay for job code 2: 6.5

   Current hourly pay for job code 3: 8.75

   c. Click the Exit button to end the application. Close the Code Editor window, then close the solution.

Discovery

10. In this exercise, you learn about the CancelButton property of a Windows form. Open the Cancel Solution (Cancel Solution.sln) file, which is contained in the VB2008\Chap03\Cancel Solution folder.

    a. Open the Code Editor window and review the existing code. Start the application. Type your first name in the text box, then press Enter to select the Clear button, which is the form's default button. The Clear button removes your name from the text box. Click the Undo button. Your name reappears in the text box. Click the Exit button to end the application.

    b. Return to the designer window. Set the form's CancelButton property to btnUndo. This tells the computer to process the code in the Undo button's Click event procedure when the user presses the Esc key. Save the solution, then start the application. Type your first name in the text box, then press Enter to select the Clear button. Press Esc to select the Undo button. Your name reappears in the text box. Click the Exit button to end the application. Close the Code Editor window, then close the solution.

LESSON C

After studying Lesson C, you should be able to:

- Include a static variable in code
- Code the TextChanged event procedure
- Create a procedure that handles more than one event

Modifying the Load and Click Event Procedures

Currently, the Playtime Cellular application allows the user to enter the salesperson's name only once, when the application first starts. In this lesson you will modify the application's code so that it asks for the salesperson's name before each order is calculated. This way, while a salesperson is at lunch or on a break, another salesperson can use the same computer to take an order without having to start the application again. As you learned in Lesson B, you should review an application's documentation and revise the necessary documents before making modifications to the code. Figure 3-45 shows the revised TOE chart. Changes made to the TOE chart from Lesson B are shaded in the figure. (Lesson B's TOE chart is shown in Figure 3-20.) Notice that the Calculate Order button's Click event procedure, rather than the frmMain Load event procedure, is responsible for getting the salesperson's name.

Task	Object	Event
1. Get the salesperson's name 2. Calculate total phones ordered and total price 3. Display total phones ordered and total price in lblTotalPhones and lblTotalPrice 4. Calculate the sales tax 5. Display the sales tax and salesperson's name in lblMessage	btnCalc	Click
Clear screen for next order	btnClear	Click
End the application	btnExit	Click
Display total phones ordered (from btnCalc)	lblTotalPhones	None
Display total price (from btnCalc)	lblTotalPrice	None
Get and display the order information	txtName, txtAddress, txtCity, txtState, txtZip, txtBlue, txtPink	None
~~Get the salesperson's name~~	~~frmMain~~	~~Load~~
Show the sales tax and salesperson's name (from btnCalc)	lblMessage	None

Figure 3-45 Revised TOE chart

Figure 3-46 shows the revised pseudocode for the Calculate Order button's Click event procedure. Changes made to the pseudocode from Lesson B are shaded in the figure. (Lesson B's pseudocode is shown in Figure 3-24.)

btnCalc Click event procedure
1. get the salesperson's name
2. calculate total phones ordered = blue phones ordered + pink phones ordered
3. calculate subtotal = total phones ordered * phone price
4. calculate sales tax = subtotal * sales tax rate
5. calculate total price = subtotal + sales tax
6. display total phones ordered and total price in lblTotalPhones and lblTotalPrice
7. display the sales tax and salesperson's name in lblMessage

Figure 3-46 Revised pseudocode for the Calculate Order button

First, you will open the Playtime Cellular application from Lesson B. You then will move the code contained in the frmMain Load event procedure to the btnCalc control's Click event procedure.

To open the Playtime Cellular application and then move some of the code:

1. Start Visual Studio 2008 or Visual Basic 2008 Express Edition, if necessary. Close the Start Page window.
2. Open the **Playtime Solution** (**Playtime Solution.sln**) file, which is contained in the VB2008\Chap03\Playtime Solution folder. If necessary, open the designer window
3. Open the Code Editor window, then locate the frmMain Load event procedure. Highlight the two Const statements in the procedure. Press **Ctrl+x** to cut the two Const statements from the procedure.
4. Locate the btnCalc control's Click event procedure. Click the **blank line** above the first Const statement in the procedure, then press **Enter** to insert a new blank line. With the insertion point in the new blank line, press **Ctrl+v**. The two Const statements that you cut from the Load event procedure now appear in the Click event procedure.
5. Return to the frmMain Load event procedure. Highlight the second comment and the assignment statement. Press **Ctrl+x** to remove the comment and the assignment statement from the procedure.
6. Return to the btnCalc control's Click event procedure. Click the **blank line** below the last Dim statement, then press **Enter** to insert a new blank line. With the insertion point in the new blank line, press **Ctrl+v**. The comment and assignment statement that you cut from the Load event procedure now appear in the Click event procedure. Press **Enter** to insert a new blank line below the assignment statement, then remove the word `module-level` from the comment.
7. Return to the frmMain Load event procedure. Delete the remaining lines in the procedure, beginning with the Private Sub line and ending with the End Sub line.

Now that you have moved the InputBox function from the frmMain Load event procedure to the btnCalc control's Click event procedure, only one procedure—the btnCalc control's Click event procedure—needs to use the `strSalesPerson` variable. Therefore, you can move the statement that declares the variable from the form's Declarations section to the btnCalc control's Click event procedure. In addition, you will need to change the keyword in the declaration statement from `Private` to `Dim`. Recall that you use the `Private` keyword to declare module-level variables, but you use the `Dim` keyword to create procedure-level variables.

To move the declaration statement, then modify the statement:

1. Delete the `' declare module-level variable` comment from the form's Declarations section, then highlight the `Private strSalesPerson As String` statement. Press **Ctrl+x** to cut the statement from the Declarations section.
2. Locate the btnCalc control's Click event procedure. Click the **blank line** below the last Dim statement in the procedure, then press **Ctrl+v** to paste the Private statement in the procedure. Press **Enter** to insert a blank line below the statement.
3. The blue jagged line that appears below the `Private` keyword indicates that there is something wrong with the statement. You can determine the problem by resting your mouse pointer somewhere on the word (or words) immediately above the jagged line. Rest your mouse pointer on the `Private` keyword. The error message indicates that the `Private` keyword is not valid on a local variable declaration. Change `Private` in the variable declaration statement to **Dim**.
4. Save the solution, then start the application. The order form appears. Click the **Calculate Order** button. Type your name in the Name Entry dialog box, then press **Enter**. The message "The sales tax was 0.00." and your name appear in the lblMessage control.
5. Click the **Calculate Order** button again. Notice that the Name Entry dialog box requires the user to enter the salesperson's name again. It would be more efficient for the user if the salesperson's name appeared as the default response the second and subsequent times the Calculate Order button is clicked.
6. Click the **Cancel** button in the dialog box. No name appears in the lblMessage control, because the InputBox function returns an empty string when you click the Cancel button in the dialog box. Click the **Exit** button to end the application.

As you learned in Lesson B, the InputBox function allows you to specify a default response, which appears in the input area of the dialog box each time the dialog box appears. In the next set of steps, you will observe the effect of using the `strSalesPerson` variable as the *defaultResponse* argument in the InputBox function.

To modify the InputBox function:

1. Change the `strSalesPerson = InputBox (strPROMPT, strTITLE)` statement in the btnCalc control's Click event procedure to **strSalesPerson = InputBox(strPROMPT, strTITLE,**

strSalesPerson), then click the blank line below the statement. The green jagged line indicates that there is a problem with the `strSalesPerson` entry in the InputBox function.

2. Position your mouse pointer on the green jagged line. A message explaining the problem appears in a box, as shown in Figure 3-47. The message says "Variable 'strSalesPerson' is used before it has been assigned a value. A null reference exception could result at runtime."


```
' assign the name to the variable
strSalesPerson = InputBox(strPROMPT, strTITLE, strSalesPerson)
```

Figure 3-47 Message explaining the problem

In this case, the InputBox function is attempting to use the `strSalesPerson` variable before the variable has been assigned a value. (Recall that the computer processes the expression that appears on the right side of the assignment operator before assigning the result to the variable whose name appears on the left side of the assignment operator.) But, you might be wondering, doesn't the `Dim strSalesPerson As String` statement provide an initial value for the variable? As you learned in Lesson A, String variables are automatically initialized using the `Nothing` keyword. However, recall that variables initialized to `Nothing` do not actually contain the word "Nothing"; rather, they contain no data at all. You can fix the problem by assigning an initial value to the `strSalesPerson` variable. In this case, you will assign the empty string.

To fix the problem with the InputBox function:

1. Change the `Dim strSalesPerson As String` statement in the btnCalc control's Click event procedure to **Dim strSalesPerson As String = String.Empty**, then click a **different line** in the procedure. Notice that the green jagged line disappears.

2. Save the solution, then start the application. Click the **Calculate Order** button. Type your name in the Name Entry dialog box, then press **Enter**. The message "The sales tax was 0.00." and your name appear in the lblMessage control.

3. Click the **Calculate Order** button again. Notice that your name still does not appear in the input area of the dialog box. This is because the `strSalesPerson` variable is both created in and removed from the computer's internal memory each time you click the Calculate Order button. (Recall that the Dim statement creates the variable in memory, and the variable is removed from memory when the End Sub statement is processed.)

4. Click the **Cancel** button in the dialog box, then click the **Exit** button to end the application.

To display the salesperson's name in the dialog box when the Calculate Order button is clicked the second and subsequent times, you can declare the `strSalesPerson` variable as either a module-level variable or a static variable. In this case, a static variable is a better choice, because static variables have a lesser scope than module-level variables. Recall that a static variable is really just a special type of procedure-level variable. As you learned in Lesson A, fewer unintentional errors occur in applications when variables are declared using the minimum scope needed. In this case, for example, only the btnCalc control's Click event procedure needs to use the `strSalesPerson` variable, so a variable with procedure scope is a much better choice than one with module scope.

To declare the strSalesPerson variable as a static variable:

1. Change the `Dim` in the `Dim strSalesPerson As String = String.Empty` statement in the btnCalc control's Click event procedure to **Static**.
2. Save the solution, then start the application. Enter **5** as the number of blue phones ordered, and enter **10** as the number of pink phones ordered. Press **Enter** to calculate the order. Type your name in the Name Entry dialog box, then press **Enter**. The application calculates and displays the total phones ordered (15) and total price ($386.25). In addition, the message "The sales tax was 11.25." and your name appear in the lblMessage control.
3. Change the number of blue phones ordered to **20**. Notice that, at this point, the calculated amounts on the order form are incorrect, because they do not reflect the change in the order of blue phones. To display the correct amounts, you will need to recalculate the order by selecting the Calculate Order button.
4. Press **Enter** to recalculate the order. Your name appears highlighted in the input area of the Name Entry dialog box. Press **Enter** to select the OK button in the dialog box. The application calculates and displays the total phones ordered (30) and total price ($772.50). The message "The sales tax was 22.50." and your name appear in the lblMessage control. Click the **Exit** button to end the application.

Having the previously calculated amounts remain on the screen when a change is made to the interface could be misleading. A better approach is to clear the amounts when a change is made to either the number of blue phones ordered or the number of pink phones ordered.

Coding the TextChanged Event Procedure

A control's **TextChanged event** occurs when a change is made to the contents of the control's Text property. This can happen as a result of either the user entering data into the control or the application's code assigning data to the control's Text property. In the next set of steps, you will code the txtBlue control's TextChanged event procedure so that it clears the contents of the lblTotalPhones, lblTotalPrice, and lblMessage controls when the user changes the number of blue phones ordered.

To code the txtBlue control's TextChanged event procedure:

1. Open the code template for the txtBlue control's TextChanged event procedure. Type **' clears the total phones, total price, and message** and press **Enter** twice.

2. Enter the following three assignment statements:

   lblTotalPhones.Text = String.Empty
   lblTotalPrice.Text = String.Empty
   lblMessage.Text = String.Empty

3. Save the solution, then start the application. Enter **5** as the number of blue phones ordered, and enter **15** as the number of pink phones ordered. Press **Enter** to calculate the order.

4. Type your name in the Name Entry dialog box, then press **Enter**. The application calculates and displays the total phones ordered (20), total price ($515.00), and sales tax (15.00).

5. Change the number of blue phones ordered to **3**. When you make a change to the number of blue phones ordered, the txtBlue control's TextChanged event procedure clears the total phones ordered, total price, and message information from the form. Click the **Exit** button to end the application.

Recall that you also want to clear the calculated amounts when a change is made to the number of pink phones ordered. You could code the TextChanged event procedure for the txtPink control separately, as you did with the txtBlue control. However, an easier way is simply to create one procedure for the computer to process when the TextChanged event of either of the two controls occurs.

Associating a Procedure With Different Objects and Events

As you learned in Chapter 1, the `Handles` keyword appears in an event procedure's header and indicates the object and event associated with the procedure. The `Handles txtBlue.TextChanged` clause that appears at the end of the procedure header in Figure 3-48 indicates that the txtBlue_ TextChanged procedure will be processed when the txtBlue control's TextChanged event occurs.

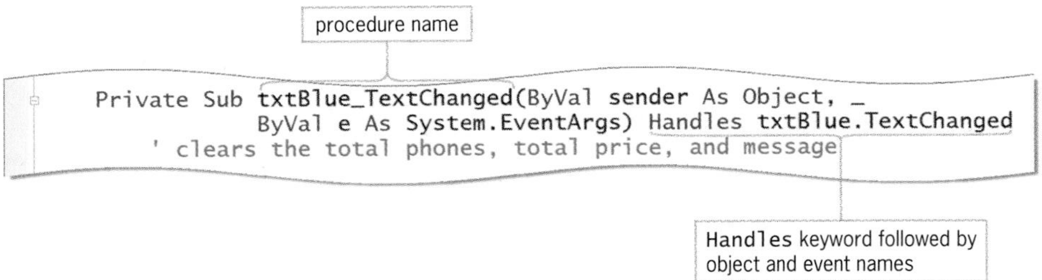

Figure 3-48 txtBlue control's TextChanged event procedure

Although the name of an event procedure includes both the object name and event name, both of which appear after the `Handles` keyword, that is not a requirement. You can change the name of an event procedure to almost anything you like, as long as the name follows the same rules for naming variables. Procedure names are entered using Pascal case, which means you capitalize the first letter in the name, as well as the first letter of each subsequent word in the name. For example, you can change the name txtBlue_TextChanged in Figure 3-48 to ClearLabels and the procedure will still work correctly. This is because the `Handles` clause, rather than the event procedure's name, determines when the procedure is invoked. You also can associate a procedure with more than one object and event, as long as each event contains the same parameters in its procedure header. To do so, you simply list each object and event, separated by commas, in the `Handles` section of the procedure header. In the Playtime Cellular application, you will change the name of the txtBlue_TextChanged procedure to ClearLabels. You then will associate the ClearLabels procedure with the txtBlue.TextChanged and txtPink.TextChanged events.

To change the procedure's name, and then associate the procedure with different objects and events:

1. Change txtBlue_TextChanged, which appears after Private Sub in the procedure header, to **ClearLabels**.
2. In the ClearLabels procedure header, click immediately before the letter H in the word `Handles`. Type _ (the underscore, which is the line continuation character). Be sure there is a space between the ending parentheses and the underscore.
3. Press **Enter** to move the `Handles` portion of the procedure header to the next line in the procedure, then press **Tab** to indent the line.
4. Click immediately after `Handles txtBlue.TextChanged`. The ClearLabels procedure is already associated with the txtBlue. TextChanged event. You just need to associate it with the txtPink. TextChanged event. Type **,** (a comma). Scroll the list of object names until you see txtPink. Click **txtPink** in the list, then press **Tab** to enter the object name in the procedure.
5. Type **.** (a period), then scroll the list of event names (if necessary) until you see TextChanged. Click **TextChanged**, then press **Tab**. Figure 3-49 shows the completed ClearLabels procedure.

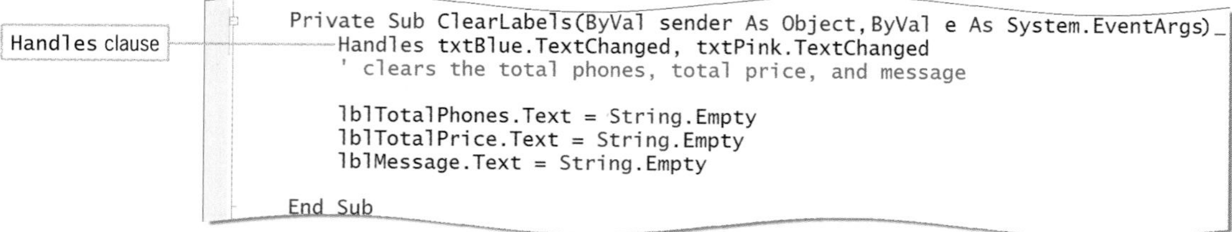


```
Private Sub ClearLabels(ByVal sender As Object, ByVal e As System.EventArgs) _
    Handles txtBlue.TextChanged, txtPink.TextChanged
    ' clears the total phones, total price, and message

    lblTotalPhones.Text = String.Empty
    lblTotalPrice.Text = String.Empty
    lblMessage.Text = String.Empty

End Sub
```

Figure 3-49 Completed ClearLabels procedure

6. Save the solution, then start the application. Enter **5** as the number of blue phones ordered, and enter **10** as the number of pink phones ordered. Press **Enter** to select the Calculate Order button.
7. Type your name in the Name Entry dialog box, then press **Enter**. The application calculates the total phones ordered (15), total price ($386.25), and sales tax (11.25).
8. Change the number of pink phones ordered to **4**. The ClearLabels procedure clears the total phones ordered, total price, and message information from the form.

9. Press **Enter** to select the Calculate Order button, then press **Enter** to select the OK button in the Name Entry dialog box. The application calculates the total phones ordered (9), total price ($231.75), and sales tax (6.75).

10. Change the number of blue phones ordered to **2**. The ClearLabels procedure clears the total phones ordered, total price, and message information from the form.

11. Click the **Exit** button to end the application. Close the Code Editor window, then close the solution.

Figure 3-50 shows the application's code.

```
' Name:         Playtime Cellular Project
' Purpose:      Calculates the total number of phones ordered and the
'               total price of the order
' Programmer:   <your name> on <current date>

Option Explicit On
Option Strict On
Option Infer Off

Public Class frmMain

    Private Sub btnExit_Click(ByVal sender As Object, _
       ByVal e As System.EventArgs) Handles btnExit.Click
       Me.Close()
    End Sub

    Private Sub btnClear_Click(ByVal sender As Object, _
       ByVal e As System.EventArgs) Handles btnClear.Click
       ' prepare the screen for the next order

       txtName.Text = String.Empty
       txtAddress.Text = String.Empty
       txtCity.Text = String.Empty
       txtState.Text = String.Empty
       txtZip.Text = String.Empty
       txtBlue.Text = String.Empty
       txtPink.Text = String.Empty
       lblTotalPhones.Text = String.Empty
       lblTotalPrice.Text = String.Empty
       lblMessage.Text = String.Empty
       ' send the focus to the Name text box
       txtName.Focus()

    End Sub

    Private Sub btnCalc_Click(ByVal sender As Object, _
       ByVal e As System.EventArgs) Handles btnCalc.Click
       ' calculates total number of phones ordered and total price

       Const strPROMPT As String = "Enter the salesperson's name:"
       Const strTITLE As String = "Name Entry"
       Const decPHONE_PRICE As Decimal = 25D
       Const decTAX_RATE As Decimal = 0.03D
       Dim intBluePhones As Integer
       Dim intPinkPhones As Integer
       Dim intTotalPhones As Integer
       Dim decSubtotal As Decimal
       Dim decSalesTax As Decimal
       Dim decTotalPrice As Decimal
       Static strSalesPerson As String = String.Empty

```

Figure 3-50 Playtime Cellular application's code at the end of Lesson C *(continues)*

(continued)

```
        ' assign the name to the variable
        strSalesPerson = InputBox(strPROMPT, strTITLE, strSalesPerson)

        ' calculate the total number of phones ordered
        Integer.TryParse(txtBlue.Text, intBluePhones)
        Integer.TryParse(txtPink.Text, intPinkPhones)
        intTotalPhones = intBluePhones + intPinkPhones

        ' calculate the subtotal
        decSubtotal = intTotalPhones * decPHONE_PRICE

        ' calculate the sales tax
        decSalesTax = decSubtotal * decTAX_RATE

        ' calculate the total price
        decTotalPrice = decSubtotal + decSalesTax

        ' display total amounts
        lblTotalPhones.Text = Convert.ToString(intTotalPhones)
        lblTotalPrice.Text = decTotalPrice.ToString("C2")

        ' display tax and salesperson's name
        lblMessage.Text = "The sales tax was " & Convert.ToString(decSalesTax) _
            & "." & ControlChars.NewLine & strSalesPerson

    End Sub

    Private Sub ClearLabels(ByVal sender As Object, _
        ByVal e As System.EventArgs) _
        Handles txtBlue.TextChanged, txtPink.TextChanged
        ' clears the total phones, total price, and message

        lblTotalPhones.Text = String.Empty
        lblTotalPrice.Text = String.Empty
        lblMessage.Text = String.Empty

    End Sub
End Class
```

Figure 3-50 Playtime Cellular application's code at the end of Lesson C

Lesson C Summary

- **To process code when a change is made to the contents of a control's Text property:**

  Enter the code in the control's TextChanged event procedure.

- **To create a procedure for more than one object or event:**

  List each object and event (using the syntax *object.event*) after the `Handles` keyword in the procedure header.

Lesson C Key Term

TextChanged event—occurs when a change is made to the contents of a control's Text property

Lesson C Review Questions

1. A ______________________ variable is a procedure-level variable that retains its value after the procedure in which it is declared ends.

   a. constant

   b. static

   c. stationary

   d. term

2. Which of the following statements declares a procedure-level variable that retains its value after the procedure in which it is declared ends?

   a. `Const intCounter As Integer`

   b. `Dim intCounter As Constant`

   c. `Dim intCounter As Integer`

   d. `Static intCounter As Integer`

3. The ______________________ event occurs when the contents of a text box have changed.

   a. Change

   b. Changed

   c. TextChanged

   d. TextChange

4. Which of the following Handles clauses indicates that a procedure should be processed when the user clicks either the txtNum1 or txtNum2 controls?

   a. `Handles txtNum1.Click, txtNum2.Click`

   b. `Handles txtNum1, txtNum2`

   c. `Handles txtNum1.Click And txtNum2.Click`

   d. None of the above.

Lesson C Exercises

INTRODUCTORY

1. Open the Name Solution (Name Solution.sln) file, which is contained in the VB2008\Chap03\Name Solution folder. Code the form's Load event procedure so that it uses two InputBox functions to prompt the user to enter his or her first name and last name. Assign the results of both functions to variables. Code the Display button's Click event procedure so that it displays the user's last name, a comma, a space, and the user's first name in the lblName control. Save the solution, then start the application. Test the application by entering your first and last names, and then clicking the Display button. Click the Exit button to end the application. Close the Code Editor window, then close the solution.

INTRODUCTORY

2. In this exercise, you create an application that converts American dollars to British pounds and Mexican pesos. Create a Visual Basic Windows application. Name the solution, project, and form file Currency Calculator Solution, Currency Calculator Project, and Main Form.vb, respectively. Save the application in the VB2008\Chap03 folder. Create the interface shown in Figure 3-51. Make the Calculate button the default button. Code the application appropriately. Calculate the number of pounds by multiplying the number of dollars by .56773. Calculate the number of pesos by multiplying the number of dollars by 10.4682. The number of pounds and pesos should be displayed with three decimal places. Clear the number of pounds and pesos when a change is made to the number of dollars. Save the solution, then start and test the application. Stop the application. Close the Code Editor window, then close the solution.

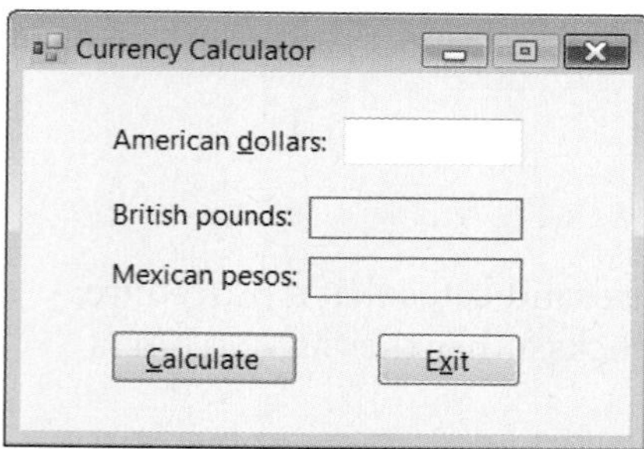

Figure 3-51 User interface for the Currency Calculator application

INTERMEDIATE

3. In this exercise, you create an application that allows the user to enter the number of pennies he has in a jar. The application should calculate the number of dollars, quarters, dimes, nickels, and pennies he will receive when he cashes in the pennies at a bank. Create a Visual Basic Windows application. Name the solution, project, and form file Pennies Solution, Pennies Project, and Main Form.vb, respectively. Save the application in the VB2008\Chap03 folder. Create the interface shown in Figure 3-52. Make the Calculate button the default button. Code the application appropriately. (It might be helpful to review the arithmetic operators listed in Figure 2-26 in Chapter 2.) Clear the calculated amounts when a change is made to the number of pennies

entered by the user. Save the solution, then start the application. Test the application twice, using the following data: 2311 pennies and 7333 pennies. Stop the application. Close the Code Editor window, then close the solution.

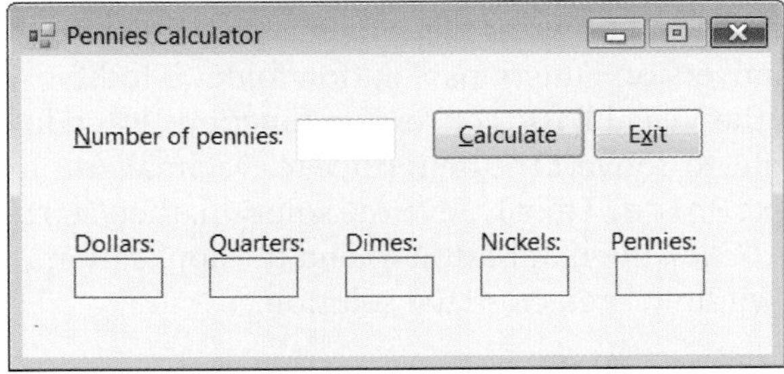

Figure 3-52 User interface for the Pennies Calculator application

ADVANCED

4. In this exercise, you create an application that can help students in grades 1 through 6 learn how to make change. The application should allow the student to enter the amount of money a customer owes and the amount of money the customer paid. It then should calculate the amount of change, as well as the number of dollars, quarters, dimes, nickels, and pennies to return to the customer. For now, you do not have to worry about the situation where the amount owed is greater than the amount paid. You can assume that the customer pays either the exact amount or more than the exact amount. Create a Visual Basic Windows application. Name the solution, project, and form file Change Solution, Change Project, and Main Form.vb, respectively. Save the application in the VB2008\Chap03 folder. Create the interface shown in Figure 3-53. Make the Calculate Change button the default button. Code the application appropriately. (It might be helpful to review the arithmetic operators listed in Figure 2-26 in Chapter 2.) Clear the calculated amounts when a change is made to either the amount owed or amount paid. Save the solution, then start the application. Test the application three times, using the following data: 75.33 as the amount owed and 80.00 as the amount paid, 39.67 as the amount owed and 50.00 as the amount paid, and 45.55 as the amount owed and 45.55 as the amount paid. Stop the application. Close the Code Editor window, then close the solution.

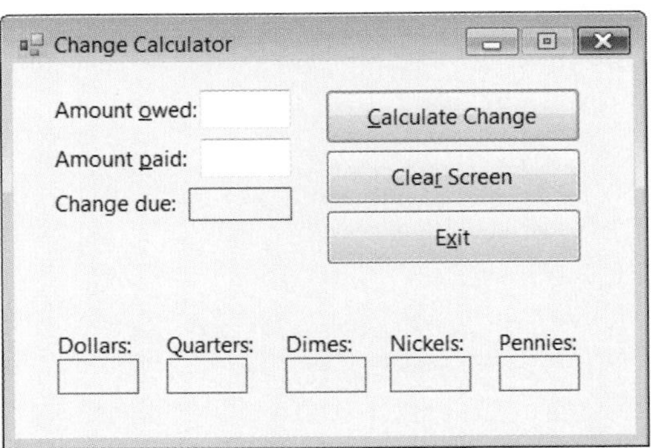

Figure 3-53 User interface for the Change Calculator application

Discovery

5. In this exercise, you experiment with the Visual Basic conversion functions listed in Appendix B. Open the Conversion Functions Solution (Conversion Functions Solution.sln) file, which is contained in the VB2008\Chap03\Conversion Functions Solution folder. Modify the code so that it uses the Visual Basic conversion functions listed in Appendix B. For example, to convert the item price to Decimal, use `decPrice = CDec(txtPrice.Text)`. Save the solution, then start and test the application. Click the Exit button to end the application. Close the Code Editor window, then close the solution.

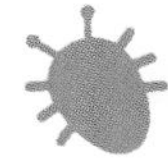

Swat The Bugs

6. Open the Debug Solution (Debug Solution.sln) file, which is contained in the VB2008\Chap03\Debug Solution-Lesson C folder. Start the application, then test the application. Locate and correct any errors. When the application is working correctly, close the Code Editor window, then close the solution.

CHAPTER 4

The Selection Structure

Creating the Monthly Payment Calculator Application

While shopping for her dream car, Jennifer Johnston has noticed that many auto dealers, in an effort to boost sales, are offering buyers a choice of either a large cash rebate or an extremely low financing rate, much lower than the rate Jennifer would pay by financing the car through her local credit union. Jennifer is not sure whether to take the lower financing rate from the dealer, or take the rebate and then finance the car through the credit union. In this chapter, you will create an application that Jennifer can use to calculate and display her monthly car payment using both scenarios.

Previewing the Monthly Payment Calculator Application

To open the Run dialog box, press and hold down the Windows logo key as you tap the letter r, then release the logo key.

To preview the completed Monthly Payment Calculator application:

1. Use the Run dialog box to run the **Monthly Payment** (**Monthly Payment.exe**) file, which is contained in the VB2008\Chap04 folder. The application's user interface appears on the screen.
2. First, calculate the monthly payment on a $9,000 loan at 5% interest for 3 years. Enter **9000** as the principal, then enter **5** as the rate. Click the **Calculate Monthly Payment** button. The message box shown in Figure 4-1 appears on the screen. You will learn how to create a message box in Lesson B.

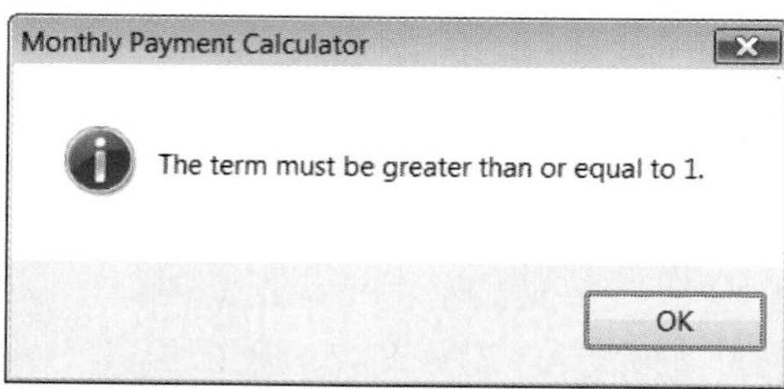

Figure 4-1 Message box

3. Click the **OK** button to close the message box. Enter **3** as the term, then click the **Calculate Monthly Payment** button. The application calculates and displays the monthly payment amount. See Figure 4-2.

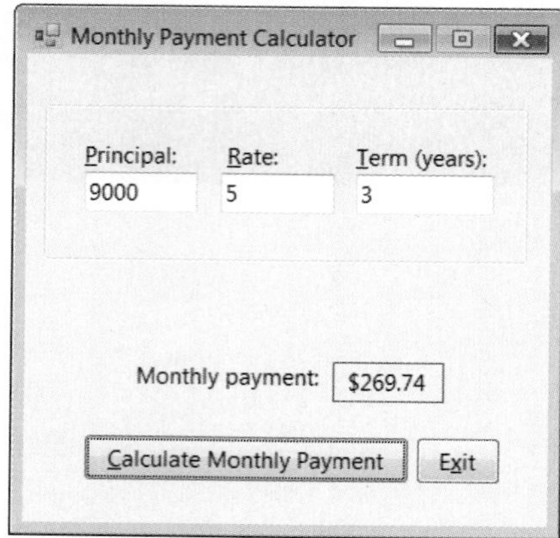

Figure 4-2 Monthly payment amount shown in the interface

4. Click the **Exit** button to end the application.

The Monthly Payment Calculator application uses the selection structure, which you will learn about in Lesson A. You will complete the application's interface in Lesson B, and also begin coding the application. You finish coding the application in Lesson C.

LESSON A

After studying Lesson A, you should be able to:

- Write pseudocode for the selection structure
- Create a flowchart to help you plan an application's code
- Write an If...Then...Else statement
- Write code that uses comparison operators and logical operators
- Change the case of a string
- Determine the success of the TryParse method

The Selection Structure

The applications from the previous three chapters use the sequence programming structure only. In those applications, a procedure's instructions are processed one after another in the order in which each appears in the procedure. In many applications, however, the next instruction processed depends on the result of a decision or comparison that the program must make. A payroll program, for example, typically compares the number of hours an employee worked with the number 40 to determine whether the employee should receive overtime pay in addition to regular pay. Based on the result of that comparison, the program then selects either an instruction that computes regular pay only or an instruction that computes regular pay plus overtime pay. You use the **selection structure**, also called the decision structure, when you want a program to make a decision or comparison and then select the appropriate path, depending on the result of that decision or comparison. Although the idea of using the selection structure in a program is new to you, you already are familiar with the concept of the selection structure because you use it each day to make hundreds of decisions. For example, every morning you have to decide whether you are hungry and, if you are, what you are going to eat. Figure 4-3 shows other examples of selection structures you might use today. The portion in italics is called the **condition** and specifies the decision you are making. The condition must be phrased so that it results in either a true or false answer only. In Example 1, either it is raining (true) or it is not raining (false). In Example 2, either you have a test tomorrow (true) or you do not have a test tomorrow (false). If the condition is true, you perform a specific set of tasks. If the condition is false, on the other hand, you might or might not need to perform a different set of tasks.

Example 1	Example 2
if *it is raining*	if *you have a test tomorrow*
wear a raincoat	study tonight
bring an umbrella	otherwise
	watch a movie

Figure 4-3 Selection structures you might use today

The selection structure is one of the three programming structures. The other two are sequence and repetition. You will learn about the repetition structure in Chapter 6.

Like you, the computer also can evaluate a condition and then select the appropriate tasks to perform based on that evaluation. When using the selection structure in a program, the programmer must be sure to phrase the condition so that it results in either a true or a false answer only. The programmer also must specify the tasks to be performed when the condition is true and, if necessary, the tasks to be performed when the condition is false. Visual Basic provides four forms of the selection structure: If, If/Else, If/ElseIf/Else, and Case. You will learn about the If and If/Else selection structures in this chapter. The If/ElseIf/Else and Case selection structures are covered in Chapter 5.

Writing Pseudocode for If and If/Else Selection Structures

An **If selection structure** contains only one set of instructions, which are processed when the condition is true. An **If/Else selection structure** contains two sets of instructions: one set is processed when the condition is true and the other when the condition is false. Figure 4-4 shows examples of the If and If/Else structures written in pseudocode. Although pseudocode is not standardized—every programmer has his or her own version—you will find some similarities among the various versions. For example, many programmers begin the selection structure with the word "if" and end the structure with the two words "end if." They also use the word "else" to designate the instructions to be performed when the condition is false.

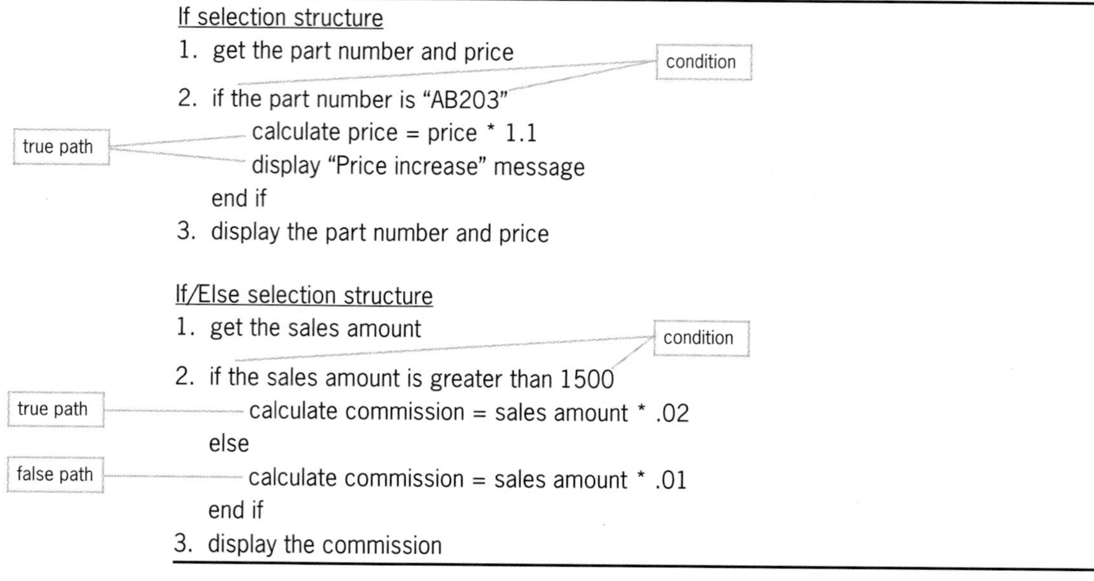

Figure 4-4 Examples of the If and If/Else selection structures written in pseudocode

Each example's condition results in either a true or false answer only. When the condition is true, the set of instructions following the condition is selected for processing. The instructions following the condition are referred to as the true path—the path you follow when the condition is true. The true path ends when you come to the "else" or, if there is no "else", when you come to the end of the selection structure (the "end if"). After the true path instructions are processed, the instruction following the "end if" is processed. In the examples shown in Figure 4-4, the display instructions are processed after the instructions in the true path.

The instructions processed when the condition is false depend on whether the selection structure contains an "else". When there is no "else", the selection structure ends when its condition is false, and processing continues with the instruction following the "end if". In the first example in Figure 4-4, the "display the part number and price" instruction is processed when the part number is not "AB203". In cases where the selection structure contains an "else", the instructions between the "else" and the "end if" are processed before the instruction after the "end if" is processed. In the second example, the "calculate commission = sales amount * .01" instruction is processed first, followed by the "display the commission" instruction. The instructions between the "else" and "end if" are referred to as the false path—the path you follow when the condition is false.

Flowcharting the If and If/Else Selection Structures

Rather than using pseudocode to plan a procedure's code, some programmers use flowcharts. Unlike pseudocode, which consists of short phrases, a flowchart uses standardized symbols to show the steps the computer must take to accomplish a task. Figure 4-5 shows Figure 4-4's examples in flowchart form. Recall that the oval in a flowchart is the start/stop symbol, the rectangle is the process symbol, and the parallelogram is the input/output symbol. The diamond in each flowchart is called the **decision symbol**, because it is used to represent the condition (decision) in both the selection and repetition structures. In Figure 4-5's flowcharts, each diamond represents the condition in a selection structure. (You will learn how to use the diamond to represent a repetition structure's condition in Chapter 6.) Inside each diamond is a comparison that evaluates to either true or false only. Each diamond has one flowline entering the symbol and two flowlines leaving the symbol. The two flowlines leading out of the diamond should be marked so that anyone reading the flowchart can distinguish the true path from the false path. You mark the flowline leading to the true path with a "T" (for true), and you mark the flowline leading to the false path with an "F" (for false). You also can mark the flowlines leading out of the diamond with a "Y" and an "N" (for yes and no).

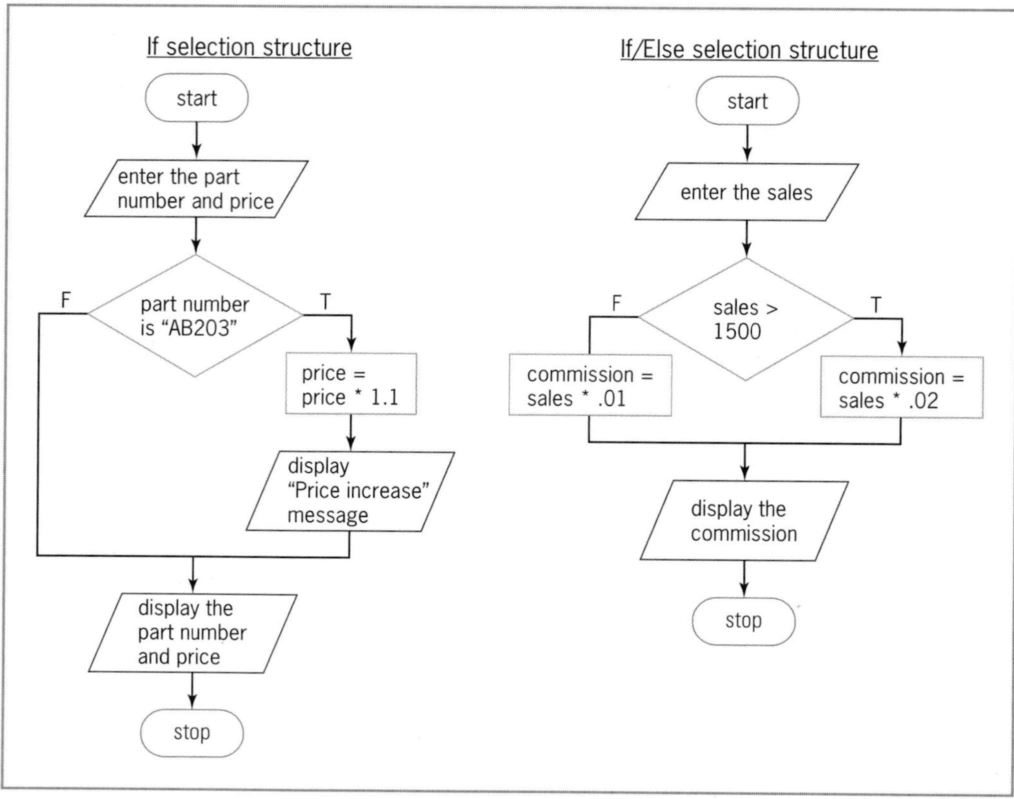

Figure 4-5 Examples of the If and If/Else selection structures drawn in flowchart form

Coding the If and If/Else Selection Structures

In Visual Basic, a statement block is a set of statements terminated by an Else, End If, Loop, or Next clause. You will learn about the Loop and Next clauses in Chapters 6 and 7.

You use the **If...Then...Else statement** to code the If and If/Else selection structures in Visual Basic. Figure 4-6 shows the statement's syntax. The items in square brackets in the syntax are optional. In other words, you do not always need to include the Else portion of the syntax, referred to as the Else clause, in an If...Then...Else statement. Items in boldface—such as the keywords `If`, `Then`, and `End If`—are essential components of the statement and must be included. The keyword `Else` is necessary only when the selection structure includes a false path. Italicized items indicate where the programmer must supply information pertaining to the current application. In the If...Then...Else statement, the programmer must supply the *condition* that the computer needs to evaluate before further processing can occur. The condition must be a Boolean expression, which is an expression that results in a Boolean value (True or False). Besides providing the condition, the programmer must provide the statements to be processed in the true path and, if used, the false path. The set of statements contained in the true path, as well as the set of statements contained in the false path, is referred to as a **statement block**. In addition to showing the If...Then...Else statement's syntax, Figure 4-6 also shows examples of using the statement.

If...Then...Else statement for coding the If and If/Else selection structures

Syntax

If *condition* **Then**

statement block to be processed when the condition is true

[Else

statement block to be processed when the condition is false]

End If

Example 1

```
If strPartNumber = "AB203" Then
   dblPrice = dblPrice * 1.1
   lblMsg.Text = "Price increase"
End If
```

If the `strPartNumber` variable contains the string "AB203", the computer processes the two instructions in the true path; otherwise, the instructions are skipped over.

Example 2

```
If dblSales > 1500 Then
   dblCommission = dblSales * .02
Else
   dblCommission = dblSales * .01
End If
```

If the `dblSales` variable contains a number that is greater than 1500, the instruction in the true path calculates a 2% commission; otherwise, the instruction in the false path calculates a 1% commission.

Figure 4-6 Syntax and examples of the If and If/Else statement for coding the If and If/Else selection structures

An If...Then...Else statement's condition can contain variables, literal constants, named constants, properties, functions, methods, arithmetic operators, comparison operators, and logical operators. You already know about variables, literal constants, named constants, properties, functions, methods, and arithmetic operators. You will learn about comparison and logical operators in the following sections.

Comparison Operators

Visual Basic provides nine **comparison operators**, also referred to as relational operators. Figure 4-7 lists the six most commonly used comparison operators and includes examples of using the operators in an If...Then...Else statement's condition. Notice that the expression contained in each example's condition evaluates to one of two Boolean values—either True or False. All expressions containing a comparison operator will result in an answer of either True or False only.

Comparison operator	Operation
=	equal to
>	greater than
>=	greater than or equal to
<	less than
<=	less than or equal to
<>	not equal to

Example 1

```
If decNorthSales = decSouthSales Then
```

The condition evaluates to True when both variables contain the same value; otherwise, it evaluates to False.

Example 2

```
If intAge >= 21 Then
```

The condition evaluates to True when the `intAge` variable's value is greater than or equal to 21; otherwise, it evaluates to False.

Example 3

```
If decPrice < 67.89D Then
```

The condition evaluates to True when the `decPrice` variable's value is less than 67.89; otherwise, it evaluates to False. You also can write the condition as `decPrice < Convert.ToDecimal(67.89)`.

Example 4

```
If strState <> "TN" Then
```

The condition evaluates to True when the `strState` variable does not contain the string "TN"; otherwise, it evaluates to False.

Figure 4-7 Listing and examples of commonly used comparison operators

Unlike arithmetic operators, comparison operators do not have an order of precedence. If an expression contains more than one comparison operator, the computer evaluates the comparison operators from left to right in the expression. Keep in mind, however, that comparison operators are evaluated after any arithmetic operators in the expression. In other words, in the expression $5 - 2 > 1 + 2$, the two arithmetic operators are evaluated before the comparison operator is evaluated. The result of the expression is the Boolean value False, as shown in Figure 4-8.

Evaluation steps	Result
Original expression	5 – 2 > 1 + 2
5 – 2 is evaluated first	3 > 1 + 2
1 + 2 is evaluated second	3 > 3
3 > 3 is evaluated last	False

Figure 4-8 Evaluation steps for an expression containing arithmetic and comparison operators

Next, you will view two examples of procedures that contain a comparison operator in an If...Then...Else statement's condition. The first procedure uses the If selection structure, and the second procedure uses the If/Else selection structure.

Using Comparison Operators—Swapping Numeric Values

Figure 4-9 shows a sample run of an application that displays the lowest and highest of two numbers entered by the user. Figures 4-10, 4-11, and 4-12 show the pseudocode, flowchart, and code for the Display button's Click event procedure.

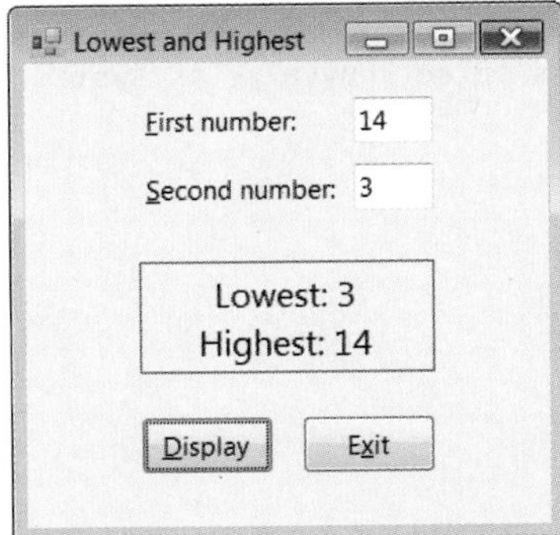

Figure 4-9 Sample run of the Lowest and Highest application

btnDisplay Click event procedure
1. store the text box values in two variables
2. if the number contained in the first variable is greater than the number contained in the second variable
       swap the numbers so that the first variable contains the smaller number
   end if
3. display the lowest and highest numbers

Figure 4-10 Display button's pseudocode showing the If selection structure

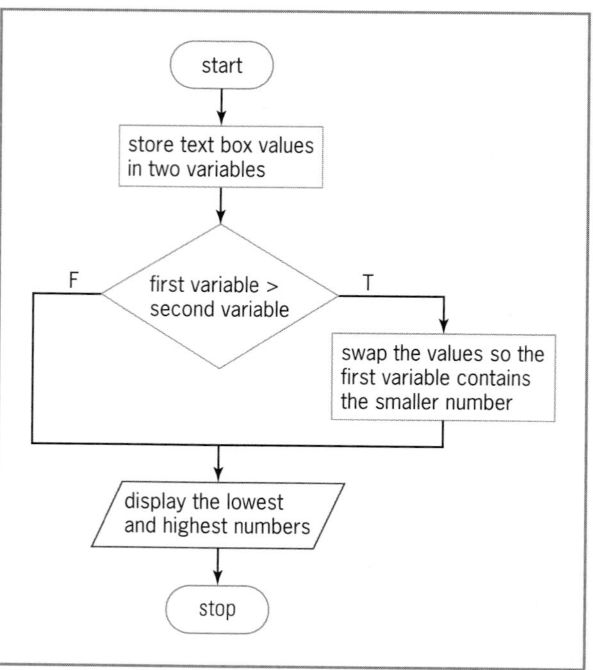

Figure 4-11 Display button's flowchart showing the If selection structure

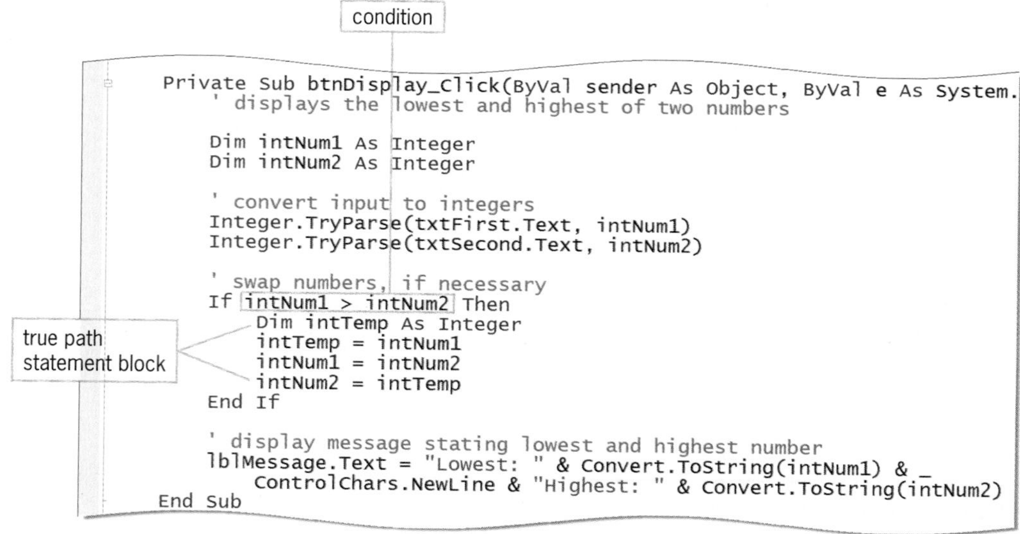


```
Private Sub btnDisplay_Click(ByVal sender As Object, ByVal e As System.
    ' displays the lowest and highest of two numbers

    Dim intNum1 As Integer
    Dim intNum2 As Integer

    ' convert input to integers
    Integer.TryParse(txtFirst.Text, intNum1)
    Integer.TryParse(txtSecond.Text, intNum2)

    ' swap numbers, if necessary
    If intNum1 > intNum2 Then
        Dim intTemp As Integer
        intTemp = intNum1
        intNum1 = intNum2
        intNum2 = intTemp
    End If

    ' display message stating lowest and highest number
    lblMessage.Text = "Lowest: " & Convert.ToString(intNum1) & _
        ControlChars.NewLine & "Highest: " & Convert.ToString(intNum2)
End Sub
```

Figure 4-12 Display button's Click event procedure showing the If selection structure

The first two Dim statements in Figure 4-12 declare procedure-level Integer variables named `intNum1` and `intNum2`. The TryParse method converts the contents of the two text boxes to integers and assigns the integers to the variables. The condition in the If...Then...Else statement then compares the contents of both variables. If the `intNum1` variable's value is greater than the `intNum2` variable's value, the condition evaluates to True and the four instructions in the statement's true path swap the values contained in those variables. Swapping the values places the smaller number in the `intNum1` variable, and places the larger number in the `intNum2` variable. If the condition evaluates to False, on the other hand, the true path instructions are skipped over. The instructions do not need to be processed because the `intNum1` variable already contains a number that is smaller than (or possibly equal to) the one stored in the `intNum2` variable. The last statement in the code displays a message that indicates the lowest number (which is contained in the `intNum1` variable) and the highest number (which is contained in the `intNum2` variable).

Study closely the instructions used to swap the values stored in the `intNum1` and `intNum2` variables. The first instruction is a Dim statement that declares a variable named `intTemp`. Like the variables declared at the beginning of a procedure, variables declared within a statement block remain in memory until the procedure ends. However, unlike variables declared at the beginning of a procedure, variables declared within a statement block have block scope rather than procedure scope. A variable that has procedure scope can be used anywhere within the procedure, whereas a variable that has **block scope** can be used only within the statement block in which it is declared. In this case, the `intNum1` and `intNum2` variables can be used anywhere within the btnDisplay control's Click event procedure, but the `intTemp` variable can be used only within the If...Then...Else statement's true path. You may be wondering why the `intTemp` variable was not declared at the beginning of the procedure, along with the other variables. Although there is nothing wrong with declaring all variables at the beginning of a procedure, the `intTemp` variable is not needed unless a swap is necessary, so there is no reason to create the variable until it is needed.

The second instruction in the If...Then...Else statement's true path assigns the value in the `intNum1` variable to the `intTemp` variable. The `intTemp` variable is necessary to store the contents of the `intNum1` variable temporarily so that the swap can be made. If you did not store the `intNum1` variable's value in the `intTemp` variable, the value would be lost when the computer processes the next statement, `intNum1 = intNum2`, which replaces the contents of the `intNum1` variable with the contents of the `intNum2` variable. Finally, the `intNum2 = intTemp` instruction assigns the `intTemp` variable's value to the `intNum2` variable. Figure 4-13 illustrates the concept of swapping, assuming the user enters the numbers 14 and 3 in the txtFirst and txtSecond controls, respectively.

	intNum1	intNum2	intTemp
values stored in the variables immediately before the `intTemp = intNum1` instruction is processed	14	3	0
result of the `intTemp = intNum1` instruction	14	3	14
result of the `intNum1 = intNum2` instruction	3	3	14
result of the `intNum2 = intTemp` instruction	3	14	14

values were swapped

Figure 4-13 Illustration of the swapping concept

To code and then test the Lowest and Highest application:

1. If necessary, start Visual Studio 2008 or Visual Basic 2008 Express Edition. Close the Start Page window.
2. Open the **Lowest and Highest Solution** (**Lowest and Highest Solution.sln**) file, which is contained in the VB2008\Chap04\Lowest and Highest Solution folder. If necessary, open the designer window.
3. Open the Code Editor window. Replace the <your name> and <current date> text in the comments with your name and the current date.
4. Open the code template for the btnDisplay control's Click event procedure, then enter the comments and code shown earlier in Figure 4-12.
5. Close the Code Editor window. Save the solution, then start the application.
6. Enter **14** as the first number, then enter **3** as the second number. Click the **Display** button. The button's Click event procedure displays the lowest and highest numbers, as shown earlier in Figure 4-9.
7. Click the **Exit** button to end the application, then close the solution.

Using Comparison Operators—Displaying the Sum or Difference

Figure 4-14 shows a sample run of an application that displays either the sum of or the difference between two numbers entered by the user. Figures 4-15, 4-16, and 4-17 show the pseudocode, flowchart, and code for the Calculate button's Click event procedure.

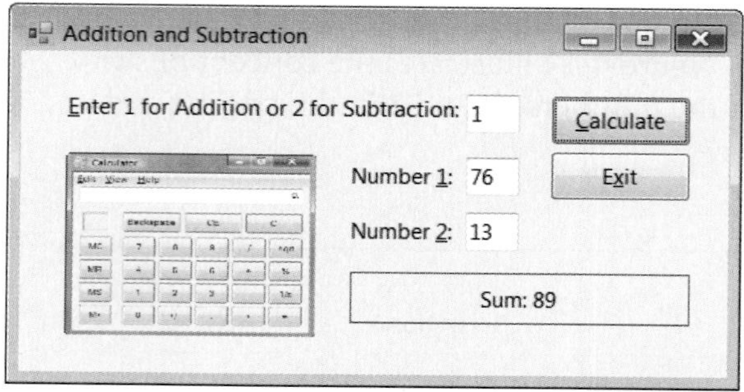

Figure 4-14 Sample run of the Addition and Subtraction application

btnCalc Click event procedure

1. store the text box values in three variables
2. if the user wants to perform addition
        calculate the sum by adding together the two numbers entered by the user
        display the message "Sum:" along with the sum
    else
        calculate the difference by subtracting the second number from the first number
        display the message "Difference:" along with the difference
    end if

Figure 4-15 Calculate button's pseudocode showing the If/Else selection structure

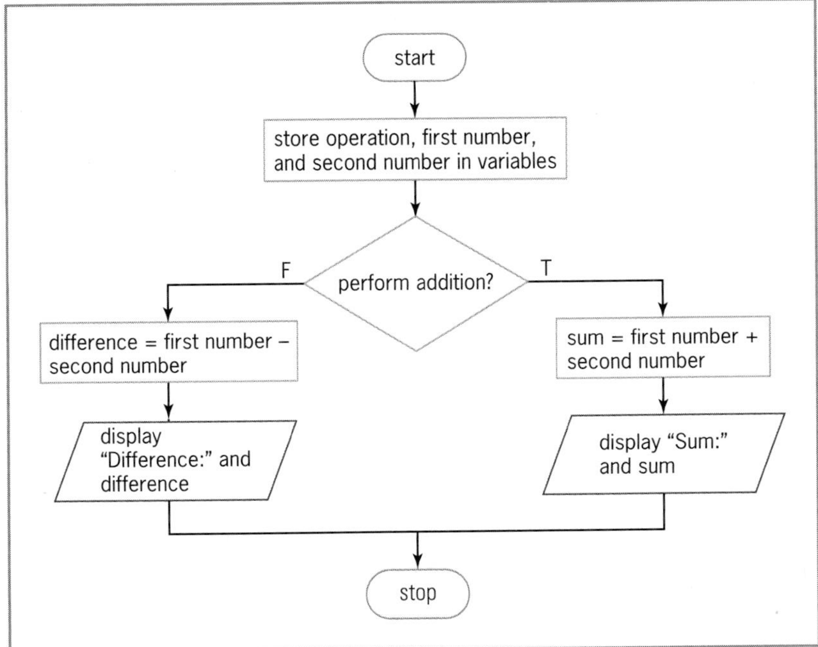

Figure 4-16 Calculate button's flowchart showing the If/Else selection structure

```
Private Sub btnCalc_Click(ByVal sender As Object, ByVal e As System.Eve
    ' calculates either a sum or a difference

    Dim strOperation As String
    Dim intNumber1 As Integer
    Dim intNumber2 As Integer
    Dim intAnswer As Integer

    ' store input in variables
    strOperation = txtOperation.Text
    Integer.TryParse(txtNumber1.Text, intNumber1)
    Integer.TryParse(txtNumber2.Text, intNumber2)

    ' calculate and display the sum or difference
    If strOperation = "1" Then
        intAnswer = intNumber1 + intNumber2
        lblAnswer.Text = "Sum: " & Convert.ToString(intAnswer)
    Else
        intAnswer = intNumber1 - intNumber2
        lblAnswer.Text = "Difference: " & Convert.ToString(intAnswer)
    End If
End Sub
```

Figure 4-17 Calculate button's Click event procedure showing the If/Else selection structure

The Dim statements in Figure 4-17 declare four procedure-level variables: a String variable and three Integer variables. The next three statements store the contents of the text boxes in the appropriate variables. The If...Then...Else statement's condition compares the contents of the `strOperation` variable with the string "1". If the condition evaluates to True, the instructions in the selection structure's true path calculate and display the sum of the two numbers entered by the user. If the condition evaluates to False, the instructions in the selection structure's false path calculate and display the difference between the two numbers.

To code and then test the Addition and Subtraction application:

1. Open the **Addition and Subtraction Solution** (**Addition and Subtraction Solution.sln**) file, which is contained in the VB2008\Chap04\Addition and Subtraction Solution folder. If necessary, open the designer window.
2. Open the Code Editor window. Replace the <your name> and <current date> text in the comments with your name and the current date.
3. Open the code template for the btnCalc control's Click event procedure, then enter the comments and code shown earlier in Figure 4-17.
4. Close the Code Editor window. Save the solution, then start the application.
5. Enter the number **1** as the operation, **76** as the first number, and **13** as the second number. Click the **Calculate** button. The button's Click event procedure displays the sum of both numbers, as shown earlier in Figure 4-14.
6. Change the 1 in the Enter 1 for Addition or 2 for Subtraction box to **2**, then click the **Calculate** button. The button's Click event procedure displays the difference between both numbers.
7. Click the **Exit** button to end the application, then close the solution.

Logical Operators

You also can use logical operators in an If...Then...Else statement's condition. **Logical operators**, sometimes referred to as **Boolean operators**, allow you to combine two or more conditions into one compound condition. Visual Basic provides six logical operators, which are listed along with their order of precedence in Figure 4-18. The figure also contains examples of using logical operators in the If...Then...Else statement's condition. Like expressions containing comparison operators, expressions containing logical operators always evaluate to a Boolean value.

Logical operator	Operation	Precedence number
Not	reverses the truth-value of the condition; True becomes False, and False becomes True	1
And	all conditions must be true for the compound condition to evaluate to True	2
AndAlso	same as the And operator, except performs short-circuit evaluation	2
Or	only one of the conditions must be true for the compound condition to evaluate to True	3
OrElse	same as the Or operator, except performs short-circuit evaluation	3
Xor	one and only one of the conditions can be true for the compound condition to evaluate to True	4

Example 1

```
If Not blnIsInsured Then
```

The condition evaluates to True when the `blnIsInsured` variable contains the Boolean value False; otherwise, it evaluates to False. The clause also could be written as `If Not blnIsInsured = True Then`; or, more clearly as `If blnIsInsured = False Then`.

Example 2

```
If dblHours > 0 AndAlso dblHours <= 40 Then
```

The compound condition evaluates to True when the `dblHours` variable contains a value that is greater than 0 but less than or equal to 40; otherwise, it evaluates to False.

Example 3

```
If strState = "TN" AndAlso decSales > 50000D Then
```

The compound condition evaluates to True when the `strState` variable contains the string "TN" and, at the same time, the `decSales` variable contains a value that is greater than 50000; otherwise, it evaluates to False.

Example 4

```
If strState = "TN" OrElse decSales > 50000D Then
```

The compound condition evaluates to True when the `strState` variable contains the string "TN" or when the `decSales` variable contains a value that is greater than 50000; otherwise, it evaluates to False.

Example 5

```
If strCoupon1 = "USE" Xor strCoupon2 = "USE" Then
```

The compound condition evaluates to True when only one of the variables contains the string "USE"; otherwise, it evaluates to False.

Figure 4-18 Listing and examples of logical operators

The tables shown in Figure 4-19, called **truth tables**, summarize how the computer evaluates the logical operators in an expression. As indicated in the figure, the Not operator reverses the truth-value of the *condition*. If the value of the *condition* is True, then the value of Not *condition* is False. Likewise, if the value of the *condition* is False, then the value of Not *condition* is True. When you use the And or AndAlso operators to combine two conditions, the resulting compound condition evaluates to True only when both conditions are true. If either condition is false or if both conditions are false, then the compound condition evaluates to False. The difference between the And and AndAlso operators is that the And operator always evaluates both conditions, while the AndAlso operator performs a **short-circuit evaluation**, which means it does not always evaluate *condition2*. Because both conditions combined with the AndAlso operator need to be true for the compound condition to evaluate to True, the AndAlso operator does not evaluate *condition2* when *condition1* is false; this makes the AndAlso operator more efficient than the And operator. When you combine conditions using the Or or OrElse operators, the compound condition evaluates to False only when both conditions are false. If either condition is true or if both conditions are true, then the compound condition evaluates to True. The difference between the Or and OrElse operators is that the Or operator always evaluates both conditions, while the OrElse operator performs a short-circuit evaluation. In this case, because only one of the conditions combined with the OrElse operator needs to be true for the compound condition to evaluate to True, the OrElse operator does not evaluate *condition2* when *condition1* is true. As a result, the OrElse operator is more efficient than the Or operator. Finally, when you combine conditions using the Xor operator, the compound condition evaluates to True only when one and only one condition is true. If both conditions are true or both conditions are false, then the compound condition evaluates to False.

Truth table for the Not operator

value of *condition*	value of `Not` *condition*
True	False
False	True

Truth table for the And operator

value of *condition1*	value of *condition2*	value of *condition1* `And` *condition2*
True	True	True
True	False	False
False	True	False
False	False	False

Figure 4-19 Truth tables for the logical operators *(continues)*

(continued)

Truth table for the AndAlso operator

value of *condition1*	value of *condition2*	value of *condition1* `AndAlso` *condition2*
True	True	True
True	False	False
False	(not evaluated)	False

Truth table for the Or operator

value of *condition1*	value of *condition2*	value of *condition1* `Or` *condition2*
True	True	True
True	False	True
False	True	True
False	False	False

Truth table for the OrElse operator

value of *condition1*	value of *condition2*	value of *condition1* `OrElse` *condition2*
True	(not evaluated)	True
False	True	True
False	False	False

Truth table for the Xor operator

value of *condition1*	value of *condition2*	value of *condition1* `Xor` *condition2*
True	True	False
True	False	True
False	True	True
False	False	False

Figure 4-19 Truth tables for the logical operators

Using the Truth Tables

A procedure needs to calculate a commission for each A-rated salesperson whose monthly sales total more than $50,000. The procedure uses the `strRating` and `dblSales` variables to store the salesperson's rating and sales amount, respectively. Therefore, you can phrase *condition1* as `strRating = "A"` and *condition2* as `dblSales > 50000`. Which logical operator should you use to combine both conditions into one compound condition? You can use the truth tables from Figure 4-19 to answer this question. For a salesperson to receive a commission, both *condition1* (`strRating = "A"`) and *condition2* (`dblSales > 50000`) must be true at the same time. If either condition is false or if both conditions are false, then the compound condition should be false and the salesperson should not receive a commission. According to the truth tables, the And, AndAlso, Or, and OrElse operators evaluate the compound condition as True when both conditions are true. However, only the And and AndAlso operators evaluate the compound condition as False when either one or both of the conditions are false. The Or and OrElse operators evaluate the compound condition as False only when both conditions are false. Therefore, the correct compound condition to use here is either `strRating = "A" And dblSales > 50000` or `strRating = "A" AndAlso dblSales > 50000`. However, remember that the AndAlso operator is more efficient than the And operator.

Now assume you want to send a letter to all A-rated salespeople and all B-rated salespeople. If the rating is stored in the `strRating` variable, you can phrase *condition1* as `strRating = "A"` and phrase *condition2* as `strRating = "B"`. Now which logical operator should you use to combine both conditions? At first it might appear that either the And or the AndAlso operator is the correct one to use, because the example says to send the letter to "all A-rated salespeople and all B-rated salespeople." In everyday conversations, you will find that people sometimes use the word *and* when what they really mean is *or*. Although both words do not mean the same thing, using *and* instead of *or* generally does not cause a problem, because we are able to infer what another person means. Computers, however, cannot infer anything; they simply process the directions you give them, word for word. In this case, you actually want to send a letter to all salespeople with either an A or a B rating (a salesperson can have only one rating), so you will need to use either the Or or the OrElse operator. As the truth tables indicate, the Or and OrElse operators are the only operators that evaluate the compound condition as True when one or more of the conditions is true. Therefore, the correct compound condition to use here is either `strRating = "A" Or strRating = "B"` or `strRating = "A" OrElse strRating = "B"`. However, the OrElse operator is more efficient than the Or operator.

Finally, assume that when placing an order, a customer is allowed to use only one of two coupons. If a procedure uses the variables `strCoupon1` and `strCoupon2` to keep track of the coupons, you can phrase *condition1* as `strCoupon1 = "USE"` and phrase *condition2* as `strCoupon2 = "USE"`. Now which operator should you use to combine both conditions? According to the truth tables, the Xor operator is the only operator that evaluates the compound condition as True when one and only one condition is true. Therefore, the correct compound condition to use here is `strCoupon1 = "USE" Xor strCoupon2 = "USE"`.

Figure 4-20 shows the order of precedence for the arithmetic, concatenation, comparison, and logical operators you have learned so far. Notice that logical operators are evaluated after any arithmetic operators or comparison operators in an expression. As a result, when the computer processes the expression 30 > 75 / 3 AndAlso 5 < 10 * 2, it evaluates the arithmetic operators first, followed by the comparison operators, followed by the logical operator. The expression evaluates to True, as shown in the example included in the figure.

Operator	Operation	Precedence number
^	exponentiation (raises a number to a power)	1
–	negation	2
*, /	multiplication and division	3
\	integer division	4
Mod	modulus	5
+, –	addition and subtraction	6
&	concatenation	7
=, >, >=, <, <=, <>	equal to, greater than, greater than or equal to, less than, less than or equal to, not equal to	8
Not	reverses the truth-value of the condition; True becomes False, and False becomes True	9
And, AndAlso	all conditions must be true for the compound condition to evaluate to True	10
Or, OrElse	only one of the conditions must be true for the compound condition to evaluate to True	11
Xor	one and only one of the conditions can be true for the compound condition to evaluate to True	12

Example

Evaluation steps	Result
Original expression	30 > 75 / 3 AndAlso 5 < 10 * 2
75 / 3 is evaluated first	30 > 25 AndAlso 5 < 10 * 2
10 * 2 is evaluated second	30 > 25 AndAlso 5 < 20
30 > 25 is evaluated third	True AndAlso 5 < 20
5 < 20 is evaluated fourth	True AndAlso True
True AndAlso True is evaluated last	True

Figure 4-20 Listing and an example of arithmetic, concatenation, comparison, and logical operators

Using Logical Operators: Calculating Gross Pay

A procedure needs to calculate and display an employee's gross pay. To keep this example simple, no one at the company works more than 40 hours per week and everyone earns the same hourly rate, $11.55. Before making the gross pay calculation, the program should verify that the number of hours entered by the user is greater than or equal to 0, but less than or equal to 40. Programmers refer to the process of verifying that the input data is within the expected range as **data validation**. In this case, if the number of hours is valid, the program should calculate and display the gross pay; otherwise, it should display an error message alerting the user that the input data is incorrect. Figure 4-21 shows two ways of writing the Visual Basic code for the procedure. The compound condition in Example 1 uses the AndAlso operator to determine whether the value stored in the `dblHoursWorked` variable is greater than or equal to the number 0 and, at the same time, less than or equal to the number 40. If the compound condition evaluates to True, the selection structure calculates and displays the gross pay; otherwise, it displays the "Error" message. The compound condition in Example 2 uses the OrElse operator to determine whether the value stored in the `dblHoursWorked` variable is less than the number 0 or greater than the number 40. If the compound condition evaluates to True, the selection structure displays the "Error" message; otherwise, it calculates and displays the gross pay. Both examples produce the same results and simply represent two different ways of performing the same task.

Example 1 – using the AndAlso operator

```
Const dblRATE As Double = 11.55
Dim dblHoursWorked As Double
Dim dblGrossPay As Double

Double.TryParse(txtHours.Text, dblHoursWorked)

If dblHoursWorked >= 0 AndAlso dblHoursWorked <= 40 Then
   ' calculate and display the gross pay
   dblGrossPay = dblHoursWorked * dblRATE
   lblGross.Text = dblGrossPay.ToString("C2")
Else
   ' display an error message
   lblGross.Text = "Error"
End If
```

Example 2 – using the OrElse operator

```
Const dblRATE As Double = 11.55
Dim dblHoursWorked As Double
Dim dblGrossPay As Double

Double.TryParse(txtHours.Text, dblHoursWorked)

If dblHoursWorked < 0 OrElse dblHoursWorked > 40 Then
   ' display an error message
   lblGross.Text = "Error"
Else
   ' calculate and display the gross pay
   dblGrossPay = dblHoursWorked * dblRATE
   lblGross.Text = dblGrossPay.ToString("C2")
End If
```

Figure 4-21 AndAlso and OrElse logical operators in the If..Then...Else statement's condition

To code and then test the Gross Pay application:

1. Open the **Gross Pay Solution** (**Gross Pay Solution.sln**) file, which is contained in the VB2008\Chap04\Gross Pay Solution folder. If necessary, open the designer window.
2. Open the Code Editor window. Replace the <your name> and <current date> text in the comments with your name and the current date.
3. Locate the code template for the btnCalc control's Click event procedure, then enter the comments and code shown in either of the two examples in Figure 4-21.
4. Close the Code Editor window. Save the solution, then start the application.
5. Type **20** in the Hours worked box, then press **Enter** to select the Calculate button. The button's Click event procedure calculates and displays the gross pay amount. See Figure 4-22.

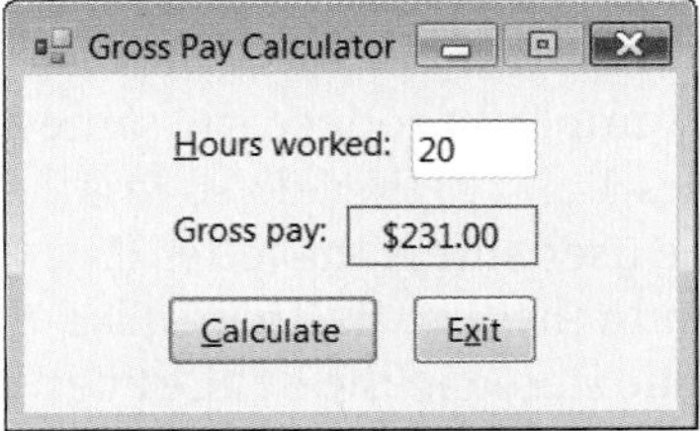

Figure 4-22 Gross pay amount shown in the interface

6. Change the number of hours worked to **52**, then press **Enter** to select the Calculate button. The button's Click event procedure displays the "Error" message in the lblGross control.
7. Click the **Exit** button to end the application, then close the solution.

In addition to comparing numeric values and numbers treated as strings, an If...Then...Else statement's condition also can compare letters or Boolean values. First, you will learn how to compare strings containing letters.

Comparing Strings Containing Letters

A procedure needs to display the word "Pass" when the user enters the letter P in the txtLetter control, and the word "Fail" when the user enters anything else. Figure 4-23 shows four ways of writing the Visual Basic code for the procedure. The `strLetter = "P" OrElse strLetter = "p"` compound condition in Example 1 determines whether the value stored in the `strLetter` variable is either the uppercase letter P or the lowercase letter p. When the variable contains one of those two letters, the compound condition evaluates to True and the selection structure displays the word "Pass" on the screen; otherwise, it displays the word "Fail". You may be wondering why you need to compare the contents of the `strLetter` variable with both the uppercase and lowercase version of the letter P. As is true in many programming languages, string comparisons in Visual Basic are case sensitive, which means that the uppercase version of a letter is not the same as its lowercase counterpart. So, although a human being recognizes P and p as being the same letter, a computer does not; to a computer, a P is different from a p. The reason for this differentiation is that each character on the computer keyboard is stored differently in the computer's internal memory. In this case, for example, the uppercase letter P is stored using a Unicode value of 50, whereas the lowercase letter p is stored using a Unicode value of 70. As you learned in Chapter 3, Unicode is the universal coding scheme for characters. In Example 2, the compound condition `strLetter <> "P" AndAlso strLetter <> "p"` determines whether the value stored in the `strLetter` variable is not equal to either the uppercase letter P or the lowercase letter p. When the variable does not contain either of those two letters, the compound condition evaluates to True and the selection structure displays the word "Fail" on the screen; otherwise, it displays the word "Pass". Rather than using one If...Then...Else statement with an Else clause, as in Examples 1 and 2, Example 3 uses two If...Then...Else statements with no Else clause in either one. Although the If...Then...Else statements in Example 3 produce the same results as the If...Then...Else statement in Examples 1 and 2, they do so less efficiently. To illustrate this point, assume that the user enters the letter P in the txtLetter control. The compound condition in the first If...Then...Else statement in Example 3 determines whether the value stored in the `strLetter` variable is equal to either P or p. In this case, the compound condition evaluates to True, because the variable contains the letter P. As a result, the first If...Then...Else statement's true path displays the word "Pass" before the statement ends. Although the appropriate word ("Pass") already appears in the interface, the procedure still evaluates the second If...Then...Else statement's compound condition to determine whether to display the "Fail" message. The second evaluation is unnecessary and makes Example 3's code less efficient than the code shown in Examples 1 and 2. Finally, the If...Then...Else statement in Example 4 also contains a string comparison in its condition, but notice that the condition does not use a logical operator; rather, it uses the ToUpper method. You learn about the ToUpper method next.

Example 1 – using the OrElse operator

```
Dim strLetter As String
strLetter = txtLetter.Text
If strLetter = "P" OrElse strLetter = "p" Then
   lblMessage.Text = "Pass"
Else
   lblMessage.Text = "Fail"
End If
```

Example 2 – using the AndAlso operator

```
Dim strLetter As String
strLetter = txtLetter.Text
If strLetter <> "P" AndAlso strLetter <> "p" Then
   lblMessage.Text = "Fail"
Else
   lblMessage.Text = "Pass"
End If
```

Figure 4-23 Visual Basic code showing string comparisons in the If...Then...Else statement's condition *(continues)*

(continued)

Example 3 – correct, but less efficient, solution

```
Dim strLetter As String
strLetter = txtLetter.Text
If strLetter = "P" OrElse strLetter = "p" Then
   lblMessage.Text = "Pass"
End If
If strLetter <> "P" AndAlso strLetter <> "p" Then
   lblMessage.Text = "Fail"
End If
```

Example 4 – using the ToUpper method

```
Dim strLetter As String
strLetter = txtLetter.Text
If strLetter.ToUpper = "P" Then
   lblMessage.Text = "Pass"
Else
   lblMessage.Text = "Fail"
End If
```

Figure 4-23 Visual Basic code showing string comparisons in the If...Then...Else statement's condition

Converting a String to Uppercase or Lowercase

You will use the CharacterCasing property in Discovery Exercise 18 at the end of this lesson.

As already mentioned, string comparisons in Visual Basic are case-sensitive, which means that the string "Yes" is not the same as either the string "YES" or the string "yes". A problem occurs when a comparison needs to include a string that is either entered by the user or read from a file, because you cannot always control the case of the string. Although you can change a text box's CharacterCasing property from its default value of Normal to either Upper (which converts the user's entry to uppercase) or Lower (which converts the user's entry to lowercase), you may not want to change the case of the user's entry as he or she is typing it. And it's entirely possible that you may not be aware of the case of strings that are read from a file. Before using a string in a comparison, you can convert it to either uppercase or lowercase and then use the converted string in the comparison. You use the **ToUpper method** to convert a string to uppercase, and the **ToLower method** to convert a string to lowercase. The ToUpper and ToLower methods affect only characters that represent letters of the alphabet, as these are the only characters that have uppercase and lowercase forms. Figure 4-24 shows the syntax of both methods and includes examples of using the methods. In each syntax, *string* typically is either the name of a String variable or the Text property of an object. Both methods temporarily convert the *string* to the specified case. When using the ToUpper method in a comparison, be sure that everything you are comparing is uppercase; otherwise, the comparison will not evaluate correctly. For example, the clause `If strLetter.ToUpper = "p" Then` is not correct: the condition will always evaluate to False, because the uppercase version of a letter will never be equal to its lowercase counterpart. Likewise, when using the ToLower method in a comparison, be sure that everything you are comparing is lowercase. You also can use the ToUpper and ToLower methods to permanently convert the contents of either a String variable or a control's Text property to uppercase or lowercase, respectively. You do this using an assignment statement, as shown in Example 5.

ToUpper and ToLower methods

Syntax
string.**ToUpper**
string.**ToLower**

Example 1
```
If strLetter.ToUpper = "P" Then
```
compares the uppercase version of the string stored in the `strLetter` variable with the uppercase letter P

Example 2
```
If strItem1.ToUpper = strItem2.ToUpper Then
```
compares the uppercase version of the string stored in the `strItem1` variable with the uppercase version of the string stored in the `strItem2` variable

Example 3
```
If "paris" = txtCity.Text.ToLower Then
```
compares the lowercase string "paris" to the lowercase version of the string stored in the txtCity control's Text property

Example 4
```
lblName.Text = strCustomer.ToUpper
```
assigns the uppercase version of the string stored in the `strCustomer` variable to the Text property of the lblName control

Example 5
```
strName = strName.ToUpper
txtState.Text = txtState.Text.ToLower
```
changes the contents of the `strName` variable to uppercase, and changes the contents of the txtState control's Text property to lowercase

Figure 4-24 Syntax and examples of the ToUpper and ToLower methods

Using the ToUpper and ToLower Methods: Displaying a Message

A procedure needs to display the message "We have a store in this state." when the user enters any of the following three state IDs: Il, In, Ky. When the user enters an ID other than these, the procedure should display the message "We do not have a store in this state." Figure 4-25 shows three ways of writing the Visual Basic code for this procedure. When the computer processes the compound condition in Example 1, it first temporarily converts the contents of the `strState` variable to uppercase, and then compares the result to the string "IL". If the comparison evaluates to False, the computer again temporarily converts the contents of the variable to uppercase, this time comparing the result to the string "IN". If the comparison evaluates to False, it again converts the contents of the variable to uppercase, and compares the result to the string "KY". Notice that, depending on the result of each condition, the computer might need to convert the contents of the `strState` variable to uppercase three times. Example 2 provides a more efficient way of writing Example 1's code. The `strState = txtState.Text.ToUpper` statement in Example 2 temporarily converts the contents of the txtState control's Text property to uppercase and assigns the result to the `strState` variable. The compound condition then compares the contents of the `strState` variable (which now contains uppercase letters) to the string "IL". If the comparison evaluates to False, the computer compares the variable's contents to the string "IN". If this comparison evaluates to False, the computer compares the variable's contents to the string "KY". Notice that the contents of the `strState` variable is converted to uppercase only once, rather than three times. However, keep in mind that, although the code shown in Example 2 is more efficient than the code shown in Example 1, there may be times when you will not want to change the case of the string stored in a variable. For example, you may need to display (on the screen or in a printed report) the variable's contents using the exact case entered by the user. The `strState = txtState.Text.ToLower` statement in Example 3 assigns the contents of the txtState control's Text property, in lowercase, to the `strState` variable. The compound condition in Example 3 is processed similarly to the compound condition in Example 2. However, the comparisons are made using lowercase letters rather than uppercase letters, and the comparisons test for inequality rather than equality. The three examples in Figure 4-25 produce the same results and simply represent different ways of performing the same task.

Example 1 – using the ToUpper method in the condition

```
Dim strState As String
strState = txtState.Text
If strState.ToUpper = "IL" OrElse strState.ToUpper = "IN" _
   OrElse strState.ToUpper = "KY" Then
   lblMsg.Text = "We have a store in this state."
Else
   lblMsg.Text = "We do not have a store in this state."
End If
```

Example 2 – using the ToUpper method in the assignment statement

```
Dim strState As String
strState = txtState.Text.ToUpper
If strState = "IL" OrElse strState = "IN" OrElse strState = "KY" Then
   lblMsg.Text = "We have a store in this state."
Else
   lblMsg.Text = "We do not have a store in this state."
End If
```

Example 3 – using the ToLower method

```
Dim strState As String
strState = txtState.Text.ToLower
If strState <> "il" AndAlso strState <> "in" _
   AndAlso strState <> "ky" Then
   lblMsg.Text = "We do not have a store in this state."
Else
   lblMsg.Text = "We have a store in this state."
End If
```

Figure 4-25 Examples of using the ToUpper and ToLower methods in a procedure

To code and then test the State application:

1. Open the **State Solution** (**State Solution.sln**) file, which is contained in the VB2008\Chap04\State Solution folder. If necessary, open the designer window.
2. Open the Code Editor window. Replace the <your name> and <current date> text in the comments with your name and the current date.
3. Open the btnToUpper1 control's Click event procedure, then enter the code shown in Example 1 in Figure 4-25.
4. Open the btnToUpper2 control's Click event procedure, then enter the code shown in Example 2 in Figure 4-25.
5. Open the btnToLower control's Click event procedure, then enter the code shown in Example 3 in Figure 4-25.
6. Close the Code Editor window. Save the solution, then start the application.
7. Type **ky** in the State ID box, then click the **ToUpper Example 1** button. The button's Click event procedure displays the appropriate message. See Figure 4-26.

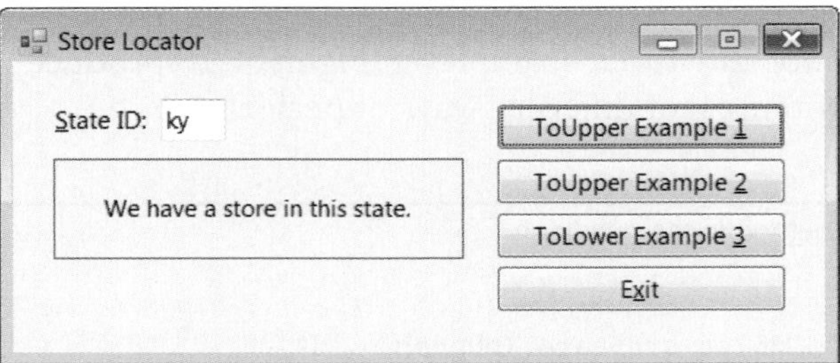

Figure 4-26 Message shown in the interface

8. Change the state ID to **tn**, then click the **ToUpper Example 1** button. The button's Click event procedure displays the "We do not have a store in this state." message.
9. On your own, test the code for the ToUpper Example 2 and ToLower Example 3 buttons. When you are finished, click the **Exit** button to end the application, then close the solution.

Comparing Boolean Values

You also can compare Boolean values in an If...Then...Else statement's condition, as shown in the examples in Figure 4-27. Each example uses a Boolean variable named `blnIsInsured`. As you learned in Chapter 3, a Boolean variable can store either the Boolean value True or the Boolean value False. The `blnIsInsured = True` condition in Example 1 and the `blnIsInsured` condition in Example 2 produce the same result: both conditions evaluate to True when the `blnIsInsured` variable contains the Boolean value True. In the last two examples, the `blnIsInsured = False` condition and the `Not blnIsInsured` condition also produce the same result. In this case, both conditions evaluate to True when the `blnIsInsured` variable contains the Boolean value False.

As you learned earlier in this lesson, the Not operator reverses the truth-value of the condition. Therefore, if the `blnIsInsured` variable contains False, then `Not blnIsInsured` evaluates to True.

Example 1

```
If blnIsInsured = True Then
```

The condition evaluates to True when the `blnIsInsured` variable contains the Boolean value True; otherwise, it evaluates to False.

Example 2

```
If blnIsInsured Then
```

Same as the previous example.

Example 3

```
If blnIsInsured = False Then
```

The condition evaluates to True when the `blnIsInsured` variable contains the Boolean value False; otherwise, it evaluates to True.

Example 4

```
If Not blnIsInsured Then
```

Same as the previous example.

Figure 4-27 Examples of comparing Boolean values in an If...Then...Else statement's condition

Comparing Boolean Values: Determining Whether a String Can Be Converted to a Number

In Chapter 3, you learned how to use the TryParse method to convert a string to a specific numeric data type. Recall that if the string can be converted, the TryParse method stores the number in the numeric variable specified in the method's *variable* argument. However, if the TryParse method determines that the string cannot be converted to the appropriate data type, the method assigns the number 0 to the numeric variable. In addition to assigning a value to the numeric variable, the TryParse method also returns a Boolean value that indicates whether the conversion was successful. It returns the Boolean value True when the string can be converted to the specified numeric data type, and returns the Boolean value False when it cannot be converted. You can assign the value returned by the TryParse method to a Boolean variable, as shown in the syntax and example in Figure 4-28. You then can use an If...Then...Else statement to determine the result of the conversion and take the appropriate action.

Using the Boolean value returned by the TryParse method

Syntax

booleanVariable = *dataType*.**TryParse(***string*, *variable***)**

Example

```
blnIsSalesOk = Double.TryParse(txtSales.Text, dblSales)
```

If the string contained in the txtSales control can be converted to a Double number, the TryParse method converts the string and stores the result in the `dblSales` variable. It also assigns the Boolean value True to the `blnIsSalesOk` variable. If the string cannot be converted to a Double number, the TryParse method stores the number 0 in the `dblSales` variable and also assigns the Boolean value False to the `blnIsSalesOk` variable.

Figure 4-28 Syntax and an example of using the Boolean value returned by the TryParse method

To use the TryParse method's Boolean value in a procedure:

1. Open the **New Pay Solution** (**New Pay Solution.sln**) file, which is contained in the VB2008\Chap04\New Pay Solution folder. If necessary, open the designer window.
2. Open the Code Editor window. Replace the <your name> and <current date> text in the comments with your name and the current date.
3. Locate the btnCalc control's Click event procedure. Notice that the code does not use the Boolean value returned by the TryParse method. Before modifying the code, you will observe how the procedure currently works. Start the application. Type **10** as the old pay, then click the **Calculate** button. Even though no raise rate was entered, the btnCalc control's Click event procedure displays a new pay amount in the lblNewPay control. In this case, it displays the old pay amount ($10.00) as the new pay amount. See Figure 4-29.

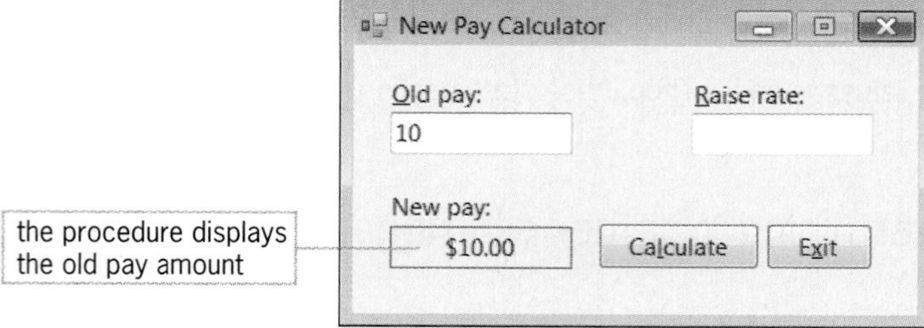

Figure 4-29 New pay displayed by the current procedure

4. Type **a** in the Raise rate box, then click the **Calculate** button. Here again, the procedure displays $10.00 as the new pay amount, even though the raise rate is invalid.
5. Change the raise rate to **.05**, then click the **Calculate** button. The procedure calculates and displays $10.50 as the new pay amount, which is correct. Click the **Exit** button to end the application.
6. Use the code shown in Figure 4-30 to modify the btnCalc control's Click event procedure. The modifications are shaded in the figure.

```
Private Sub btnCalc_Click(ByVal sender As Object, _
   ByVal e As System.EventArgs) Handles btnCalc.Click
   ' calculates and displays the new pay

   Dim dblOldPay As Double
   Dim dblRate As Double
   Dim dblNewPay As Double
   Dim blnIsOldOk As Boolean
   Dim blnIsRateOk As Boolean

   ' convert the input to numbers
   blnIsOldOk = Double.TryParse(txtOldPay.Text, dblOldPay)
   blnIsRateOk = Double.TryParse(txtRate.Text, dblRate)
```

Figure 4-30 Modified btnCalc control's Click event procedure *(continues)*

(continued)

```
    ' determine whether the conversions were successful
    If blnIsOldOk AndAlso blnIsRateOk Then
        ' calculate and display the new pay
        dblNewPay = dblOldPay + dblOldPay * dblRate
        lblNewPay.Text = dblNewPay.ToString("C2")
    Else
        lblNewPay.Text = "Invalid data"
    End If

    ' set the focus
    txtOldPay.Focus()
End Sub
```

Figure 4-30 Modified btnCalc control's Click event procedure

7. Close the Code Editor window. Save the solution, then start the application. Type **10** as the old pay, then click the **Calculate** button. Because no raise rate was entered, the procedure displays the "Invalid data" message in the lblNewPay control.
8. Type **.05** in the Raise rate box, then click the **Calculate** button. The procedure calculates and displays $10.50 as the new pay amount, which is correct.
9. Change the old pay to the letter **a**, then click the **Calculate** button. The procedure displays the "Invalid data" message, which is correct.
10. Click the **Exit** button to end the application, then close the solution.

Lesson A Summary

- **To evaluate an expression containing arithmetic, comparison, and logical operators:**

  Evaluate the arithmetic operators first, then evaluate the comparison operators, and then evaluate the logical operators. Figure 4-20 shows the order of precedence for the arithmetic, concatenation, comparison, and logical operators.

- **To code the If and If/Else forms of the selection structure:**

  Use the If...Then...Else statement, whose syntax is shown in Figure 4-6.

- **To compare two values:**

  Use the comparison operators listed in Figure 4-7.

- **To swap the values contained in two variables:**

  Assign the first variable's value to a temporary variable, then assign the second variable's value to the first variable, and then assign the temporary variable's value to the second variable.

- **To create a compound condition:**

  Use the logical operators listed in Figure 4-18. The truth tables for the logical operators are shown in Figure 4-19.

- **To convert the user's text box entry to either uppercase or lowercase as the user is typing the text:**

  Change the text box's CharacterCasing property from Normal to either Upper or Lower.

- **To temporarily convert a string to uppercase:**

  Use the ToUpper method, whose syntax is *string*.**ToUpper**.

- **To temporarily convert a string to lowercase:**

  Use the ToLower method, whose syntax is *string*.**ToLower**.

- **To determine whether the TryParse method converted a string to the specified numeric data type:**

  Use the syntax *booleanVariable* = *dataType*.**TryParse(***string***,** *variable***)**. The TryParse method returns the Boolean value True when the string can be converted to the numeric *dataType*; otherwise, it returns the Boolean value False.

Lesson A Key Terms

Block scope—the scope of a variable declared within a statement block; refers to the fact that the variable can be used only within the statement block

Boolean operators—another term for logical operators

Comparison operators—operators used to compare values in a selection structure's condition; also called relational operators

Condition—specifies the decision or comparison you are making and must be phrased so that it results in an answer of either true or false

Data validation—the process of verifying that a program's input data is within the expected range

Decision symbol—the diamond in a flowchart; used to represent the condition in either a selection or repetition structure

If selection structure—contains only one set of instructions, which are processed when the selection structure's condition evaluates to True

If/Else selection structure—contains two sets of instructions: one set is processed when the selection structure's condition evaluates to True, and the other is processed when the condition evaluates to False

If...Then...Else statement—used to code the If and If/Else forms of the selection structure in Visual Basic

Logical operators—operators used to combine two or more conditions into one compound condition; also called Boolean operators

Selection structure—one of the three programming structures; tells the computer to make a decision or comparison and then select the appropriate path based on the result; also called the decision structure

Short-circuit evaluation—refers to the fact that the AndAlso and OrElse operators do not always evaluate the second condition in a compound condition

Statement block—in a selection structure, the set of statements terminated by an Else or End If clause

ToLower method—temporarily converts a string to lowercase

ToUpper method—temporarily converts a string to uppercase

Truth tables—summarize how the computer evaluates the logical operators in an expression

Lesson A Review Questions

1. What is the scope of variables declared in an If...Then...Else statement's false path?
   a. the entire application
   b. the procedure in which the If...Then...Else statement appears
   c. the entire If...Then...Else statement
   d. only the false path in the If...Then...Else statement

2. Which of the following is a valid condition for an If...Then...Else statement?
   a. `dblSales > 500 AndAlso < 800`
   b. `dblCost > 100 AndAlso dblCost <= 1000`
   c. `strState.ToUpper = "Alaska" OrElse strState.ToUpper = "Hawaii"`
   d. None of the above.

3. Which of the following conditions should you use in an If...Then...Else statement to compare the string contained in the txtName control with the name Bob? (Be sure the condition will handle Bob, BOB, bob, and so on.)
   a. `txtName.Text = ToUpper("BOB")`
   b. `txtName.Text = ToUpper("Bob")`
   c. `ToUpper(txtName.Text) = "BOB"`
   d. `txtName.Text.ToUpper = "BOB"`

4. The six logical operators are listed below. Indicate their order of precedence by placing a number (1, 2, and so on) on the line to the left of the operator. (If two or more operators have the same precedence, assign the same number to each.)

    ______________ Xor

    ______________ And

    ______________ Not

    ______________ Or

    ______________ AndAlso

    ______________ OrElse

5. An expression can contain arithmetic, comparison, and logical operators. Indicate the order of precedence for the three types of operators by placing a number (1, 2, or 3) on the line to the left of the operator type.

    ______________ Arithmetic

    ______________ Logical

    ______________ Comparison

6. The expression `3 > 6 AndAlso 7 > 4` evaluates to ______________.

    a. True

    b. False

7. The expression `4 > 6 OrElse 10 < 2 * 6` evaluates to ______________.

    a. True

    b. False

8. The expression `7 >= 3 + 5 OrElse 6 < 4 AndAlso 2 < 5` evaluates to ______________.

    a. True

    b. False

9. The expression `5 * 2 > 5 * 3 AndAlso True` evaluates to ______________.

    a. True

    b. False

10. The expression `5 * 3 > 3 ^ 2` evaluates to ______________________________.

    a. True

    b. False

11. The expression `5 * 3 > 3 ^ 2 AndAlso True OrElse False` evaluates to ______________________________.

    a. True

    b. False

Use the following selection structure to answer Questions 12 and 13:

```
If intNumber <= 100 Then
   intNumber = intNumber * 2
Else
   intNumber = intNumber * 3
End If
```

12. The `intNumber` variable contains the number 90. What value will be in the variable after the above selection structure is processed?

    a. 0

    b. 90

    c. 180

    d. 270

13. The `intNumber` variable contains the number 1000. What value will be in the `intNumber` variable after the above selection structure is processed?

    a. 0

    b. 1000

    c. 2000

    d. 3000

14. If the txtPrice control contains the value 75, the `Decimal.TryParse(txtPrice.Text, decPrice)` method returns ______________________________.

    a. False

    b. True

    c. 75

    d. 75.00

Lesson A Exercises

INTRODUCTORY

1. Draw the flowchart that corresponds to the following pseudocode:

   if the hours are greater than 40
       display "Overtime pay"
   else
       display "Regular pay"
   end if

INTRODUCTORY

2. Write an If...Then...Else statement that displays the string "Pontiac" in the lblCarMake control when the txtCar control contains the string "Grand Am" (in any case).

INTRODUCTORY

3. Write an If...Then...Else statement that displays the string "Please enter your ZIP code" in the lblMsg control when the txtZip control does not contain any data.

INTRODUCTORY

4. Write an If...Then...Else statement that displays the string "Entry error" in the lblMsg control when the `intUnits` variable contains a number that is less than 0; otherwise, display the string "Valid Number".

INTRODUCTORY

5. Write an If...Then...Else statement that displays the string "Reorder" in the lblMsg control when the `intQuantity` variable contains a number that is less than 10; otherwise, display the string "OK".

INTRODUCTORY

6. Write an If...Then...Else statement that assigns the number 10 to the `intBonus` variable when the `dblSales` variable contains a number that is less than or equal to $250; otherwise, assign the number 15.

INTRODUCTORY

7. Write an If...Then...Else statement that displays the value 25 in the lblShipping control when the `strState` variable contains the string "Hawaii" (in any case); otherwise, display the value 50.

INTRODUCTORY

8. A procedure contains the `blnIsSalesOk = Double.TryParse(txtSales.Text, dblSales)` statement. Write an If...Then...Else statement that displays the string "Please enter a number" in the lblMsg control when the contents of the txtSales control cannot be converted to a Double number; otherwise, multiply the contents of the `dblSales` variable by 10% and display the result in the lblMsg control.

INTRODUCTORY

9. Write an If...Then...Else statement that displays the string "Dog" in the lblAnimal control when the `strAnimal` variable contains the letter "D" (in any case); otherwise, display the string "Cat". Also draw the flowchart.

INTRODUCTORY

10. A procedure should calculate a 3% sales tax when the `strState` variable contains the string "Colorado" (in any case); otherwise, it should calculate a 4% sales tax. The sales tax is calculated by multiplying the tax rate by the contents of the `dblSales` variable. Display the sales tax amount in the lblTax control. Draw the flowchart, then write the Visual Basic code.

11. A procedure should calculate an employee's gross pay. Employees working more than 40 hours receive time and one-half for the hours over 40. Use the variables `decHours`, `decHourRate`, and `decGross`. Display the contents of the `decGross` variable in the lblGross control. Write the pseudocode, then write the Visual Basic code. INTERMEDIATE

12. A procedure should calculate a 10% discount on desks sold to customers in Colorado. Use the variables `strItem`, `strState`, `dblSales`, and `dblDiscount`. Format the discount using the "C2" format and display it in the lblDiscount control. Write the Visual Basic code. INTERMEDIATE

13. A procedure should calculate a 2% price increase on all red shirts, but a 1% price increase on all other items. In addition to calculating the price increase, the procedure also should calculate the new price. You can use the variables `strItemColor`, `strItem`, `decOrigPrice`, `decIncrease`, and `decNewPrice`. Format the original price, price increase, and new price using the "N2" format. Display the original price, price increase, and new price in the lblOriginal, lblIncrease, and lblNewPrice controls, respectively. Write the Visual Basic code. INTERMEDIATE

14. Write the Visual Basic code that swaps the values stored in the `decLowSales` and `decHighSales` variables, but only if the value stored in the `decHighSales` variable is less than the value stored in the `decLowSales` variable. INTERMEDIATE

15. In this exercise, you modify the Addition and Subtraction application you coded in the lesson. Use Windows to make a copy of the Addition and Subtraction Solution folder, which is contained in the VB2008\Chap04 folder. Rename the folder Modified Addition and Subtraction Solution. Open the Addition and Subtraction Solution (Addition and Subtraction Solution.sln) file contained in the VB2008\Chap04\Modified Addition and Subtraction Solution folder. Open the designer window. Change the Label1's text from "Enter 1 for Addition or 2 for Subtraction" to "Enter A for Addition or S for Subtraction". Open the Code Editor window. Make the appropriate modifications to the btnCalc control's Click event procedure. (The user should be able to enter the operation letter in either uppercase or lowercase.) Save the solution, then start and test the application. Click the Exit button to end the application. Close the Code Editor window, then close the solution. INTERMEDIATE

16. Open the Bonus Solution (Bonus Solution.sln) file, which is contained in the VB2008\Chap04\Bonus Solution folder. If necessary, open the designer window. The btnCalc control's Click event procedure should calculate a 5% bonus and display the result (formatted using the "C2" format) in the lblBonus control. Calculate and display the bonus only when the TryParse method is successful; otherwise, display the message "Invalid sales" in the lblBonus control. Code the procedure. Save the solution, then start and test the application. Click the Exit button to end the application. Close the Code Editor window, then close the solution. INTERMEDIATE

INTERMEDIATE

17. Open the Sum Solution (Sum Solution.sln) file, which is contained in the VB2008\Chap04\Sum Solution folder. If necessary, open the designer window. The btnCalc control's Click event procedure should calculate the sum of the two values entered by the user, and then display the result in the lblSum control. Calculate and display the sum only when both values can be converted to the Integer data type; otherwise, display the message "Please enter two integers" in the lblSum control. Code the procedure. Save the solution, then start and test the application. Click the Exit button to end the application. Close the Code Editor window, then close the solution.

Discovery

18. In this exercise, you learn how to use a text box's CharacterCasing property. Open the CharCase Solution (CharCase Solution.sln) file, which is contained in the VB2008\Chap04\CharCase Solution folder. If necessary, open the designer window.

    a. Open the Code Editor window and study the code contained in the btnDisplay control's Click event procedure. The code compares the contents of the txtState control with the strings "IL", "IN", and "KY". However, it does not convert the contents of the text box to uppercase. Start the application. Enter ky as the state ID, then click the Display button. The button's Click event procedure displays the "We do not have a store in this state." message, which is incorrect. Click the Exit button.

    b. Use the Properties window to change the txtState control's CharacterCasing property to Upper. Save the solution, then start the application. Enter ky as the state ID. Notice that the letters appear in uppercase in the text box. Click the Display button. The button's Click event procedure displays the "We have a store in this state." message, which is correct. Click the Exit button to end the application. Close the Code Editor window, then close the solution.

LESSON B

After studying Lesson B, you should be able to:

- Group objects using a GroupBox control
- Calculate a periodic payment using the Financial.Pmt method
- Create a message box using the MessageBox.Show method
- Determine the value returned by a message box

Creating the Monthly Payment Calculator Application

Recall that your task in this chapter is to create an application that calculates and displays the monthly payment on a car loan. To make the calculation, the application must know the loan amount (principal), the annual percentage rate (APR) of interest, and the life of the loan (term) in years.

To open the partially completed Monthly Payment Calculator application:

1. If necessary, start Visual Studio 2008 or Visual Basic 2008 Express Edition. Close the Start Page window.
2. Open the **Payment Solution** (**Payment Solution.sln**) file, which is contained in the VB2008\Chap04\Payment Solution folder. If necessary, open the designer window. Missing from the interface is a group box control.

Adding a Group Box to the Form

You use the GroupBox tool to add a group box to the interface. The GroupBox tool is located in the Containers section of the toolbox, because a **group box** serves as a container for other controls. You can use a group box to visually separate related controls from other controls on the form. The group box in the Monthly Payment Calculator interface will visually separate the controls relating to the principal, rate, and term information from the rest of the controls. The group box and the controls contained in the group box are treated as one unit. When you move the group box, the controls inside the group box also move. Likewise, when you delete the group box, the controls inside the group box also are deleted. You can include an identifying label on a group box by setting the group box's Text property. Labeling a group box is optional; but if you do label it, the label should be entered using sentence capitalization.

GUI DESIGN TIP Labeling a Group Box

Use sentence capitalization for the optional identifying label, which is entered in the group box's Text property.

To add a group box to the interface, and then drag several of the existing controls into the group box:

1. If necessary, expand the Containers node in the toolbox. Click the **GroupBox** tool, then drag the mouse pointer to the form. You do not need to worry about the exact location. Release the mouse button. The GroupBox1 control appears on the form.

2. Position and size the group box as shown in Figure 4-31. (Or, you can set the group box's Location and Size properties to 12, 25 and 315, 115, respectively.)

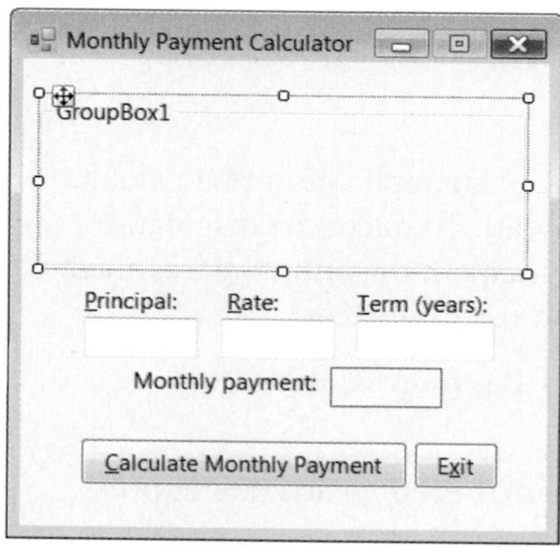

Figure 4-31 Interface showing the location and size of the group box

3. Delete the contents of the group box's Text property, because the group box will not need an identifying label in this interface.

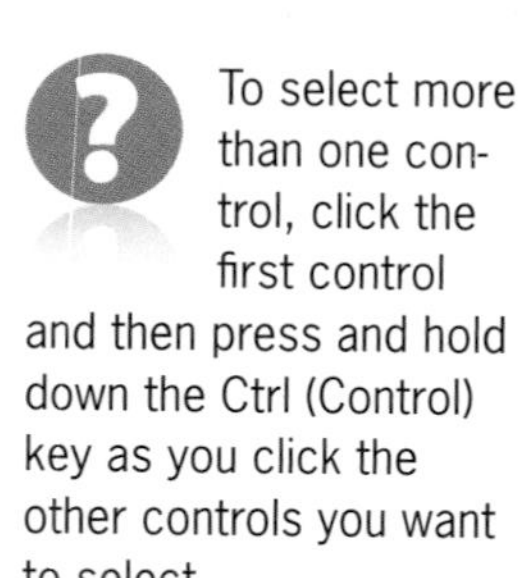

To select more than one control, click the first control and then press and hold down the Ctrl (Control) key as you click the other controls you want to select.

4. Next, you will drag the controls related to the principal, rate, and term into the group box, and then center the controls within the group box. Select the following six controls: Label1 (Principal:), txtPrincipal, Label2 (Rate:), txtRate, Label3 (Term (years):), and txtTerm. Place your mouse pointer on one of the selected controls. The mouse pointer turns into the move pointer. Press and hold down the left mouse button as you drag the selected controls into the group box, then release the mouse button.

5. Use the Format menu to center the selected controls both horizontally and vertically in the group box, then click the **form** to deselect the controls.

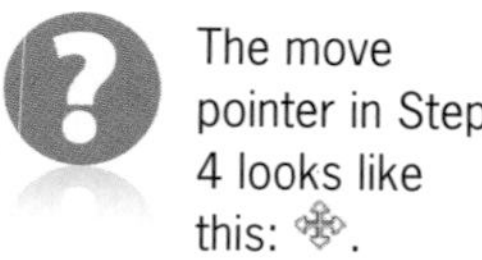

The move pointer in Step 4 looks like this: ✥.

6. Now you will lock the controls in place and set the tab order. Right-click the **form**, then click **Lock Controls**. Click **View** on the menu bar, then click **Tab Order**. The current TabIndex value for each control appears in blue boxes on the form. Notice that the TabIndex values of the controls contained within the group box begin with the number 10, which is the TabIndex value of the group box itself. The TabIndex value indicates that the controls belong to the group box rather than to the form. As mentioned earlier, if you move or delete the group box, the controls that belong to the group box also will be moved or deleted. The numbers that appear after the period in the TabIndex values indicate the order in which each control was added to the group box.

7. Use the information in Figure 4-32 to set each control's TabIndex value. When you are finished, press **Esc** to remove the TabIndex boxes, then save the solution.

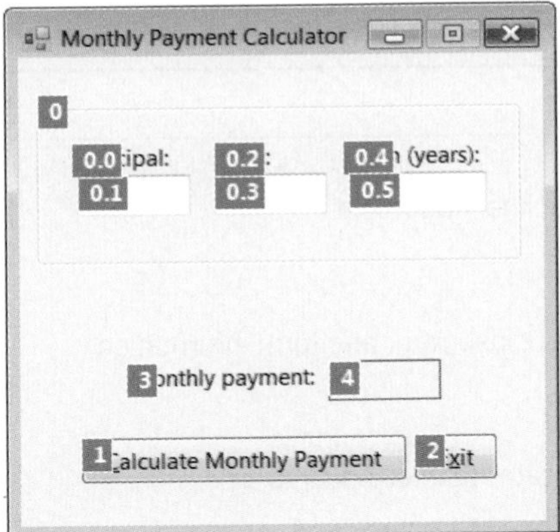

Figure 4-32 Correct TabIndex values for the completed user interface

Coding the Monthly Payment Calculator Application

According to the application's TOE chart, which is shown in Figure 4-33, the Click event procedures for the two buttons, as well as the TextChanged, KeyPress, and Enter events for the three text boxes, need to be coded. When you open the Code Editor window, you will notice that the btnExit control's Click event procedure and the TextChanged event procedures for the three text boxes have been coded for you. In this lesson, you will code the btnCalc control's Click event procedure. You will code the KeyPress and Enter event procedures in Lesson C.

Task	Object	Event
1. Calculate the monthly payment 2. Display the monthly payment in lblPayment	btnCalc	Click
End the application	btnExit	Click
Display the monthly payment (from btnCalc)	lblPayment	None
Get and display the principal, rate, and term	txtPrincipal, txtRate, txtTerm	None
Clear the contents of lblPayment		TextChanged
Allow the text box to accept only numbers, the period, and the Backspace key		KeyPress
Select the contents of the text box		Enter

Figure 4-33 TOE chart for the Monthly Payment Calculator application

Coding the btnCalc Control's Click Event Procedure

The btnCalc control's Click event procedure is responsible for calculating the monthly payment and then displaying the result in the lblPayment control. The procedure's pseudocode is shown in Figure 4-34.

btnCalc Click event procedure

```
1. if the interest rate >= 1
       divide the interest rate by 100 to get its decimal equivalent
   end if
2. if the term >= 1
       calculate the monthly payment using the principal, rate, and term information
       display the monthly payment
   else
       display the message "The term must be greater than or equal to 1."
   end if
```

Figure 4-34 Pseudocode for the btnCalc control's Click event procedure

To begin coding the btnCalc control's Click event procedure:

1. Open the Code Editor window. Replace the <your name> and <current date> text with your name and the current date.
2. Open the code template for the btnCalc control's Click event procedure. Type **' calculates and displays a monthly payment** and press **Enter** twice.

First, study the procedure's pseudocode to determine the variables and named constants (if any) the procedure will use. When determining the named constants, look for items whose value will be the same each time the procedure is invoked. In the btnCalc control's Click event procedure, the number 1 that appears in Steps 1 and 2, as well as the number 100 that appears in Step 1 and the message that appears in Step 2, will be the same each time the procedure is invoked. Although you could create named constants for the numbers 1 and 100, doing so is unnecessary because those values are already self-documenting and are unlikely to change. You will, however, create a named constant for the message. The named constant will make the code easier to understand. In addition, it will allow you (or another programmer) to quickly locate the message should it need to be changed in the future. When determining the procedure's variables, look in the pseudocode for items whose value probably will change each time the procedure is processed. In this case, the principal, rate, term, and monthly payment amounts probably will be different each time the Calculate Monthly Payment button is clicked; therefore, you will assign the values to variables.

To continue coding the btnCalc control's Click event procedure:

1. Enter the following Const and Dim statements. (Enter the entire Const statement on the same line.) Press **Enter** twice after typing the last Dim statement.

   Const strMSG As String = "The term must be greater than or equal to 1."
   Dim dblPrincipal As Double
   Dim dblRate As Double
   Dim dblTerm As Double
   Dim dblMonthlyPayment As Double

2. Now you will assign the principal, rate, and term information to the appropriate variables. Enter the following TryParse methods. Press **Enter** twice after typing the last TryParse method.

   Double.TryParse(txtPrincipal.Text, dblPrincipal)
   Double.TryParse(txtRate.Text, dblRate)
   Double.TryParse(txtTerm.Text, dblTerm)

3. Next, you will use a selection structure to handle Step 1 in the pseudocode. Step 1 determines whether the interest rate needs to be converted to its decimal equivalent. This is necessary because the user might enter the rate as either a whole number or a decimal number. For example, an interest rate of 5% might be entered as either 5 or .05. Type **' convert the rate to decimal form, if necessary** and press **Enter**. Type **If dblRate >= 1 Then** and press **Enter**. The Code Editor automatically enters the End If clause in the procedure. Type **dblRate = dblRate / 100** between the If and End If clauses.

4. Click **at the end of the End If clause**, then press **Enter** twice to insert two blank lines after the clause.

5. The second step in the pseudocode is to determine whether the term entered by the user is valid. To be valid, the term must be greater than or equal to one year. Type **' verify that the term is valid** and press **Enter**. Type **If dblTerm >= 1 Then** and press **Enter**. Figure 4-35 shows the code currently entered in the procedure.

Using a blank line to separate related blocks of code in the Code Editor window makes the code easier to read and understand.

```
Private Sub btnCalc_Click(ByVal sender As Object, ByVal e As System.EventAr
    ' calculates and displays a monthly payment

    Const strMSG As String = "The term must be greater than or equal to 1."
    Dim dblPrincipal As Double
    Dim dblRate As Double
    Dim dblTerm As Double
    Dim dblMonthlyPayment As Double

    Double.TryParse(txtPrincipal.Text, dblPrincipal)
    Double.TryParse(txtRate.Text, dblRate)
    Double.TryParse(txtTerm.Text, dblTerm)

    ' convert the rate to decimal form, if necessary
    If dblRate >= 1 Then
        dblRate = dblRate / 100
    End If

    ' verify that the term is valid
    If dblTerm >= 1 Then
        |                                        insertion point
    End If
End Sub
```

Figure 4-35 Partially completed Click event procedure

If the term is valid, the procedure should calculate the monthly payment and then display the result. You can calculate the monthly payment using the Financial.Pmt method.

Using the Financial.Pmt Method

The **Financial.Pmt method** calculates a periodic payment on either a loan or an investment. ("Pmt" stands for "Payment.") It returns the periodic payment as a Double type number. Figure 4-36 shows the method's basic syntax and lists the meaning of each argument. The *Rate* and *NPer* (number of periods) arguments must be expressed using the same units. If *Rate* is a monthly interest rate, then *NPer* must specify the number of monthly payments. Similarly, if *Rate* is an annual interest rate, then *NPer* must specify the number of annual payments. Figure 4-36 also includes examples of using the Financial.Pmt method. Example 1 calculates the annual payment for a loan of $9,000 for 3 years at 5% interest. As the example indicates, the annual payment rounded to the nearest cent is -3,304.88. This means that if you borrow $9,000 for 3 years at 5% interest, you will need to make three annual payments of $3,304.88 to pay off the loan. Notice that the Financial.Pmt method returns a negative number. To change the negative number to a positive number, you can precede the method with the negation operator, like this: `-Financial.Pmt(.05, 3, 9000)`. As you learned in Chapter 2, the purpose of the negation operator is to reverse the sign of a number. A negative number preceded by the negation operator becomes a positive number, and vice versa. The Financial.Pmt method in Example 2 calculates the monthly payment for a loan of $12,000 for 5 years at 6% interest. In this example, the *Rate* and *NPer* arguments are expressed in monthly terms rather than in annual terms. The monthly payment for this loan, rounded to the nearest cent and expressed as a positive number, is 231.99.

Exercise 3 at the end of this lesson uses the Financial.Pmt method to calculate the amount you need to save each period to accumulate a specific sum.

Financial.Pmt method

Syntax

Financial.Pmt(*Rate*, *NPer*, *PV***)**

Argument	Meaning
Rate	interest rate per period
NPer	total number of payment periods (the term)
PV	present value of the loan; in other words, the loan amount

Example 1

```
Financial.Pmt(.05, 3, 9000)
```

Calculates the annual payment for a loan of $9,000 for 3 years at 5% interest. *Rate* is .05, *NPer* is 3, and *PV* is 9000. The annual payment (rounded to the nearest cent) is -3,304.88.

Example 2

```
-Financial.Pmt(.06/12, 5 * 12, 12000)
```

Calculates the monthly payment for a loan of $12,000 for 5 years at 6% interest. *Rate* is .06/12, *NPer* is 5 * 12, and *PV* is 12000. The monthly payment (rounded to the nearest cent and expressed as a positive number) is 231.99.

Figure 4-36 Basic syntax and examples of the Financial.Pmt method

In the current application, you will use the Financial.Pmt method to calculate the monthly payment on a car loan. When entering the method, you must convert the annual interest rate entered by the user to a monthly rate. You do this by dividing the contents of the `dblRate` variable by 12. You also must convert the term of the loan, which is expressed in years and stored in the `dblTerm` variable, to months. To convert an annual term to a monthly term, you multiply the annual term by 12.

To continue coding the btnCalc control's Click event procedure:

1. The insertion point should be positioned in the blank line below the `If dblTerm >= 1 Then` clause, as shown earlier in Figure 4-35. Type **' calculate and display the monthly payment** and press **Enter**.
2. Type **dblMonthlyPayment =** _ and press **Enter**. (Be sure to include a space before the line continuation character.) Press **Tab**, then type **-Financial.Pmt(dblRate/12, dblTerm * 12, dblPrincipal)** and press **Enter**. (Be sure to enter the negation operator before the Financial.Pmt method so that a positive number is assigned to the dblMonthly-Payment variable.)
3. Next, you will format the monthly payment to show a dollar sign and two decimal places, and then display the formatted amount in the lblPayment control. Type **lblPayment.Text = dblMonthlyPayment.ToString("C2")** and press **Enter**.
4. Save the solution. Figure 4-37 shows the selection structure's true path coded in the procedure.

```
        ' verify that the term is valid
        If dblTerm >= 1 Then
            ' calculate and display the monthly payment
            dblMonthlyPayment = _
                -Financial.Pmt(dblRate / 12, dblTerm * 12, dblPrincipal)
            lblPayment.Text = dblMonthlyPayment.ToString("C2")

        End If
    End Sub
```

true path — insertion point

Figure 4-37 Selection structure's true path coded in the procedure

When the term entered by the user is not greater than or equal to 1, the btnCalc control's Click event procedure should display an appropriate message. In the next section, you will learn how to display the message in a message box.

The MessageBox.Show Method

The **MessageBox.Show method** displays a message box that contains text, one or more buttons, and an icon. The method allows an application to communicate with the user while the application is running. Figure 4-38 shows the method's syntax and lists the meaning of each argument. The figure also includes examples of using the method. Figure 4-39 and 4-40 show the message boxes created by the two examples.

MessageBox.Show method

Syntax

MessageBox.Show(*text*, *caption*, *buttons*, *icon*[, *defaultButton*]**)**

Argument	Meaning
text	text to display in the message box; use sentence capitalization
caption	text to display in the title bar of the message box; use book title capitalization

buttons	buttons to display in the message box; can be one of the following constants:
	`MessageBoxButtons.AbortRetryIgnore`
	`MessageBoxButtons.OK` (default setting)
	`MessageBoxButtons.OKCancel`
	`MessageBoxButtons.RetryCancel`
	`MessageBoxButtons.YesNo`
	`MessageBoxButtons.YesNoCancel`

icon	icon to display in the message box; typically, one of the following constants:
	`MessageBoxIcon.Exclamation`
	`MessageBoxIcon.Information`
	`MessageBoxIcon.Question`
	`MessageBoxIcon.Stop`

defaultButton	button automatically selected when the user presses Enter; can be one of the following constants:
	`MessageBoxDefaultButton.Button1` (default setting)
	`MessageBoxDefaultButton.Button2`
	`MessageBoxDefaultButton.Button3`

Figure 4-38 Syntax and examples of the MessageBox.Show method *(continues)*

(continued)

MessageBox.Show method

Example 1

```
MessageBox.Show("Record deleted.", "Payroll", _
   MessageBoxButtons.OK, MessageBoxIcon.Information)
```

displays an informational message box that contains the message "Record deleted."

Example 2

```
MessageBox.Show("Delete this record?", "Payroll", _
   MessageBoxButtons.YesNo, MessageBoxIcon.Exclamation, _
   MessageBoxDefaultButton.Button2)
```

displays a warning message box that contains the message "Delete this record?"

Figure 4-38 Syntax and examples of the MessageBox.Show method

Figure 4-39 Message box displayed by the code in Example 1 in Figure 4-38

Figure 4-40 Message box displayed by the code in Example 2 in Figure 4-38

GUI DESIGN TIP MessageBox.Show method

- Use sentence capitalization for the *text* argument, but book title capitalization for the *caption* argument.
- Display the Exclamation or Question icon to alert the user that he or she must make a decision before the application can continue. You can phrase the message as a question.
- Display the Information icon along with an OK button in a message box that displays an informational message.
- Display the Stop icon to alert the user of a serious problem that must be corrected before the application can continue.
- The default button in the dialog box should be the one that represents the user's most likely action, as long as that action is not destructive.

After displaying the message box, the MessageBox.Show method waits for the user to choose one of the buttons. It then closes the message box and returns an integer indicating the button chosen by the user. Sometimes you are not interested in the value returned by the MessageBox.Show method. This is the case when the message box is for informational purposes only, like the message box shown in Figure 4-39. Many times, however, the button selected by the user determines the next task performed by an application. Selecting the Yes button in the message box shown in Figure 4-40 tells the application to delete the record, whereas selecting the No button tells the application not to delete the record. Figure 4-41 lists the integer values returned by the MessageBox.Show method. Each value is associated with a button that can appear in a message box. The figure also lists the DialogResult values assigned to each integer, and the meaning of the integers and DialogResult values. As the figure indicates, the MessageBox.Show method returns the integer 6 when the user selects the Yes button. The integer 6 is represented by the DialogResult value, `Windows.Forms.DialogResult.Yes`. When referring to the method's return value in code, you should use the DialogResult values rather than the integers, because the values make the code more self-documenting and easier to understand. Figure 4-41 also contains two examples of using the value returned by the MessageBox.Show method. In the first example, the return value is assigned to a DialogResult variable named `dlgButton`. The selection structure in the example compares the contents of the `dlgButton` variable to the `Windows.Forms.DialogResult.Yes` value. In the second example, the method's return value is not stored in a variable. Instead, the method appears in the selection structure's condition, where its return value is compared to the `Windows.Forms.DialogResult.Yes` value. The selection structure shown in the second example performs one set of tasks when the user selects the Yes button in the message box, but a different set of tasks when the user selects the No button. It is a good programming practice to document the Else portion of the selection structure as shown in the figure, because it makes it clear that the Else portion is processed only when the user selects the No button.

MessageBox.Show method's return values

Number	DialogResult value	Meaning
1	`Windows.Forms.DialogResult.OK`	user chose the OK button
2	`Windows.Forms.DialogResult.Cancel`	user chose the Cancel button
3	`Windows.Forms.DialogResult.Abort`	user chose the Abort button
4	`Windows.Forms.DialogResult.Retry`	user chose the Retry button
5	`Windows.Forms.DialogResult.Ignore`	user chose the Ignore button
6	`Windows.Forms.DialogResult.Yes`	user chose the Yes button
7	`Windows.Forms.DialogResult.No`	user chose the No button

Figure 4-41 Values returned by the MessageBox.Show method *(continues)*

(continued)

Example 1

```
Dim dlgButton As DialogResult
dlgButton = MessageBox.Show("Delete this record?", "Payroll", _
        MessageBoxButtons.YesNo, MessageBoxIcon.Exclamation,
        MessageBoxDefaultButton.Button2)
If dlgButton = Windows.Forms.DialogResult.Yes Then
        instructions to delete the record
End If
```

Example 2

```
If MessageBox.Show("Play another game?", "Math Monster", _
        MessageBoxButtons.YesNo, MessageBoxIcon.Exclamation) = _
        Windows.Forms.DialogResult.Yes Then
        instructions to start another game
Else    ' No button
        instructions to close the game application
End If
```

Figure 4-41 Values returned by the MessageBox.Show method

In the current application, the btnCalc control's Click event procedure should display a message box when the term entered by the user is not greater than or equal to 1. The message box is for informational purposes only. Therefore, it should contain the Information icon and the OK button, and you do not need to be concerned with its return value. The message to display in the message box is stored in the strMSG constant.

To complete the btnCalc control's Click event procedure:

1. The insertion point should be positioned in the blank line above the End If clause, as shown earlier in Figure 4-37. Type **Else** and press **Enter**.
2. Type **MessageBox.Show(strMSG, "Monthly Payment Calculator",** _ and press **Enter**. (Be sure to include a space before the line continuation character.) Type **MessageBoxButtons.OK, MessageBoxIcon.Information)**. Figure 4-42 shows the completed procedure.

```
Private Sub btnCalc_Click(ByVal sender As Object, _
   ByVal e As System.EventArgs) Handles btnCalc.Click
   ' calculates and displays a monthly payment

   Const strMSG As String = "The term must be greater than or equal to 1."
   Dim dblPrincipal As Double
   Dim dblRate As Double
   Dim dblTerm As Double
   Dim dblMonthlyPayment As Double

   Double.TryParse(txtPrincipal.Text, dblPrincipal)
   Double.TryParse(txtRate.Text, dblRate)
   Double.TryParse(txtTerm.Text, dblTerm)
```

Figure 4-42 Completed btnCalc control's Click event procedure *(continues)*

(continued)

```
    ' convert the rate to decimal form, if necessary
    If dblRate >= 1 Then
        dblRate = dblRate / 100
    End If

    ' verify that the term is valid
    If dblTerm >= 1 Then
        ' calculate and display the monthly payment
        dblMonthlyPayment = _
           -Financial.Pmt(dblRate / 12, dblTerm * 12, dblPrincipal)
        lblPayment.Text = dblMonthlyPayment.ToString("C2")
    Else
        MessageBox.Show(strMSG, "Monthly Payment Calculator", _
           MessageBoxButtons.OK, MessageBoxIcon.Information)
    End If
End Sub
```

Figure 4-42 Completed btnCalc control's Click event procedure

To test the btnCalc control's Click event procedure:

1. Save the solution, then start the application. First, calculate the monthly payment for a loan of $12,000 for 5 years at 6% interest. Enter **12000** as the principal, **6** as the rate, and **5** as the term. Click the **Calculate Monthly Payment** button. The button's Click event procedure calculates and displays the monthly payment. See Figure 4-43.

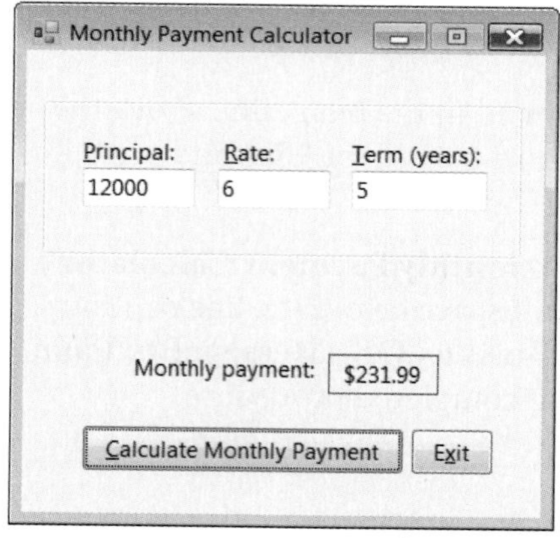

Figure 4-43 Interface showing the monthly payment

2. Next, verify that the application works correctly when the user enters an incorrect term. Change the term from 5 to **0**, then click the **Calculate Monthly Payment** button. The application displays the message box shown in Figure 4-44.

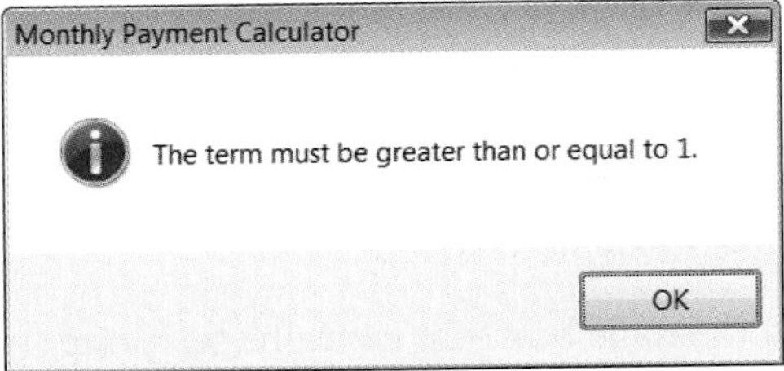

Figure 4-44 Message box created by the MessageBox.Show method

3. Click the **OK** button to close the message box.
4. Now verify that the application works correctly when the user enters the interest rate as a decimal number. Change the rate from 6 to **.06**, and change the term from 0 to **5**. Click the **Calculate Monthly Payment** button. The button's Click event procedure calculates and displays a monthly payment of $231.99, which is the same monthly payment shown in Figure 4-43.
5. Click the **Exit** button to end the application. Close the Code Editor window, then close the solution.

Lesson B Summary

- **To use a group box to group controls together:**

  Use the GroupBox tool to add a group box to the form. Drag controls from either the form or the toolbox into the group box. To include an optional identifying label on a group box, set the group box's Text property. The TabIndex value of a control contained within a group box is composed of two numbers separated by a period. The number to the left of the period is the TabIndex value of the group box itself. The number to the right of the period indicates the order in which the control was added to the group box.

- **To calculate a periodic payment on either a loan or an investment:**

  Use the Financial.Pmt method, whose basic syntax is **Financial.Pmt(***Rate, NPer, PV***)**. Refer to Figure 4-36 for a description of each argument and examples of using the method to calculate a periodic payment.

- **To display a message box that contains text, one or more buttons, and an icon:**

  Use the MessageBox.Show method, whose syntax is **MessageBox.Show(***text, caption, buttons, icon*[*, defaultButton*]**)**. Refer to Figure 4-38 for a description of each argument and examples of using the method to display a message box. Refer to Figure 4-41 for a listing and description of the values returned by the MessageBox.Show method.

Lesson B Key Terms

Financial.Pmt method—calculates a periodic payment on either a loan or an investment

Group box—used as a container for other controls

MessageBox.Show method—displays a message box that contains text, one or more buttons, and an icon; allows an application to communicate with the user while the application is running

Lesson B Review Questions

1. Which of the following statements is false?
   a. When you delete a group box, the controls contained within the group box remain on the form.
   b. Use sentence capitalization for the group box's identifying label.
   c. You can include an identifying label on a group box by setting the group box's Text property.
   d. You can drag a control from the form into a group box.

2. Assume that the TabIndex value of a group box is 5. If the txtName control was the first control added to the group box, its TabIndex value will be ________________________.
   a. 1
   b. 1.5
   c. 5.0
   d. 5.1

3. Which of the following calculates the monthly payment on a loan of $5,000 for 2 years at 4% interest? Payments should be expressed as a positive number.
   a. `-Financial.Pmt(.04/12, 2 * 12, 5000)`
   b. `-Financial.Pmt(24, .04/12, 5000)`
   c. `-Financial.Pmt(5000, .04/12, 2 * 12)`
   d. None of the above.

4. Which of the following calculates the quarterly payment on a loan of $6,000 for 3 years at 9% interest? Payments should be expressed as a negative number.
   a. `Financial.Pmt(.09/4, 3 * 12, 6000)`
   b. `Financial.Pmt(.09/4, 3 * 4, 6000)`
   c. `Financial.Pmt(.09/12, 3 * 12, 6000)`
   d. None of the above.

5. You use the ____________________ constant to include the Exclamation icon in a message box.
   a. `MessageBox.Exclamation`
   b. `MessageBox.IconExclamation`
   c. `MessageBoxIcon.Exclamation`
   d. `MessageBox.WarningIcon`

6. If a message is for informational purposes only and does not require the user to make a decision, the message box should display which of the following?
   a. an OK button and the Information icon
   b. an OK button and the Exclamation icon
   c. a Yes button and the Information icon
   d. any button and the Information icon

7. If the user clicks the OK button in a message box, the message box returns the number 1, which is equivalent to which constant?
   a. `Windows.Forms.DialogResult.OK`
   b. `Windows.Forms.DialogResult.OKButton`
   c. `MessageBox.OK`
   d. `MessageResult.OK`

Lesson B Exercises

INTRODUCTORY

1. In this exercise, you create an application that calculates and displays the quarterly payment on a loan. Create a Visual Basic Windows application. Name the solution, project, and form file Quarterly Payment Solution, Quarterly Payment Project, and Main Form.vb, respectively. Save the application in the VB2008\Chap04 folder. Create the interface shown in Figure 4-45. Code the application. Clear the quarterly payment when a change is made to any of the text boxes. Convert the interest rate to its decimal form, if necessary. Use the MessageBox.Show method to display an appropriate message when the term is less than one year. Save the solution, then start the application. Test the application using 10000 as the loan amount, 4 as the interest rate, and 3 as the term. The quarterly payment should be $888.49. Stop the application. Close the Code Editor window, then close the solution.

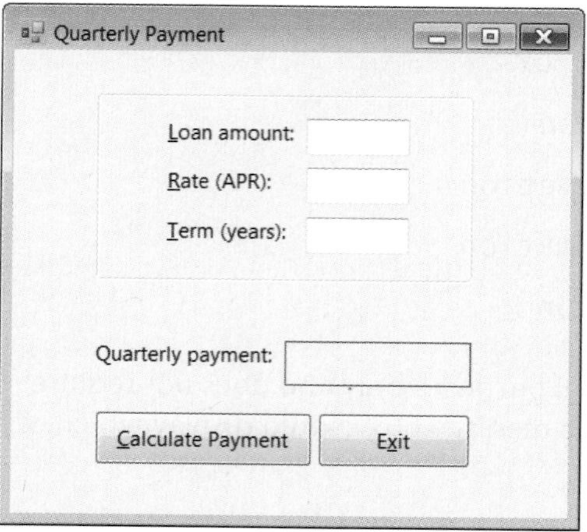

Figure 4-45 User interface for the Quarterly Payment application

INTRODUCTORY

2. In this exercise, you code an application that calculates the total amount a customer owes. Create a Visual Basic Windows application. Name the solution, project, and form file Mingo Solution, Mingo Project, and Main Form.vb, respectively. Save the application in the VB2008\Chap04 folder. Create the interface shown in Figure 4-46. The user will enter the quantity ordered and price per unit in the text boxes. Code the Calculate button's Click event procedure. The procedure should verify that the text boxes contain valid data. (Hint: Use the Boolean value returned by the TryParse method.) If both text boxes contain valid data, the procedure should calculate and display both a 10% discount and the total amount the customer owes; otherwise, it should display an appropriate message in a message box. Display the discount with two decimal places. Display the total due with a dollar sign and two decimal places. The discount and total due should be removed from the interface when a change is made to the contents of a text box. Save the solution, then start and test the application. Stop the application. Close the Code Editor window, then close the solution.

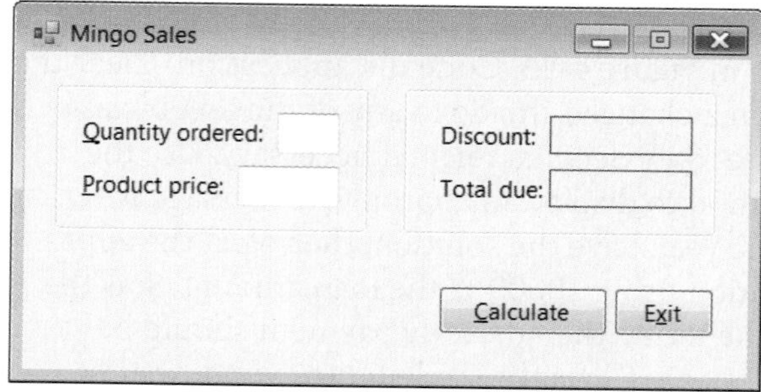

Figure 4-46 User interface for the Mingo Sales application

INTERMEDIATE

3. Open the Investment Solution (Investment Solution.sln) file, which is contained in the VB2008\Chap04\Investment Solution folder. If necessary, open the designer window. The application should calculate the amount you need to save each month to accumulate a specific amount, given the term and interest rate. You can calculate this amount using the Financial.Pmt method. However, you need to use the following syntax **Financial.Pmt(*Rate*, *NPer*, *PV*, *FV*)**. As you learned in this lesson, the *Rate* argument is the interest rate per period, and the *NPer* argument is the total number of payment periods. The *PV* argument is the present value of the investment, which is 0 (zero). The *FV* argument is the future value of the investment and represents the amount you want to accumulate. Code the Calculate button's Click event procedure. Display the monthly amount as a positive number. Save the solution, then start the application. Test the application by calculating the amount you need to save to accumulate $40,000 at the end of 20 years, assuming a 6% interest rate. The application should show that you need to save $86.57 per month. Stop the application. Close the Code Editor window, then close the solution.

ADVANCED

4. In this exercise, you modify the Mingo Sales application from Exercise 2. Use Windows to make a copy of the Mingo Solution folder, which is contained in the VB2008\Chap04 folder. Rename the folder Modified Mingo Solution. Open the Mingo Solution (Mingo Solution.sln) file contained in the VB2008\Chap04\Modified Mingo Solution folder. Open the designer window, then open the Code Editor window. Before calculating the discount and total due, the btnCalc control's Click event procedure should display the message "Are you a wholesaler?" in a message box. Only wholesalers receive the 10% discount. Modify the btnCalc control's Click event procedure. Save the solution, then start the application. Test the application by calculating the total due for a wholesaler ordering 4 units of product at $10 per unit. Then test the application by calculating the total due for a nonwholesaler ordering 2 units of product at $5 per unit. Stop the application. Close the Code Editor window, then close the solution.

LESSON C

After studying Lesson C, you should be able to:

- Prevent the entry of unwanted characters in a text box
- Select the existing text in a text box

Coding the KeyPress Event Procedures

To complete the Monthly Payment Calculator application, you need to code the KeyPress and Enter event procedures for the three text boxes. You will code the KeyPress event procedures first.

To open the Monthly Payment Calculator application from Lesson B:

1. If necessary, start Visual Studio 2008 or Visual Basic 2008 Express Edition. Close the Start Page window.
2. Open the **Payment Solution** (**Payment Solution.sln**) file, which is contained in the VB2008\Chap04\Payment Solution folder. If necessary, open the designer window.
3. Open the Code Editor window, then open the code template for the txtPrincipal control's KeyPress event procedure. See Figure 4-47.

Figure 4-47 Code template for the txtPrincipal control's KeyPress event procedure

A control's KeyDown event also occurs when the user presses a key while the control has the focus. The KeyDown event occurs before the KeyPress event. When the user releases the key, the control's KeyUp event occurs.

The items contained within parentheses in the procedure header are called **parameters** and represent information passed to the procedure when the KeyPress event occurs. A control's **KeyPress event** occurs each time the user presses a key while the control has the focus. When the KeyPress event occurs, a character corresponding to the pressed key is sent to the KeyPress event's `e` parameter. For example, when the user presses the period (.) while entering data into a text box, the text box's KeyPress event occurs and a period is sent to the event's `e` parameter. Similarly, when the Shift key along with a letter is pressed, the uppercase version of the letter is sent to the `e` parameter. To prevent a text box from accepting an inappropriate character, you first use the `e` parameter's **KeyChar property** to determine the pressed key. (KeyChar stands for "key character.") You then use the `e` parameter's **Handled property** to cancel the key if it is an inappropriate one. You cancel the key by setting the Handled property to True, like this: `e.Handled = True`. Figure 4-48 shows examples of using the KeyChar and Handled properties in the KeyPress event procedure. The selection structure in Example 1 prevents the txtSales control from accepting the dollar sign. It does this by first comparing the contents of the KeyChar property with a dollar sign. If the condition evaluates to True, the `e.Handled = True` instruction cancels the $ key before it is entered in the txtSales control. You can use the selection structure in Example 2 to allow the text box to accept only numbers and the Backspace key (which is used for editing). You refer to the Backspace key on your keyboard using Visual Basic's **ControlChars.Back constant**.

Controlling the characters accepted by a text box

Example 1

```
Private Sub txtSales_KeyPress(ByVal sender As Object, _
   ByVal e As System.Windows.Forms.KeyPressEventArgs) _
   Handles txtSales.KeyPress
   ' prevents the text box from accepting the dollar sign

   If e.KeyChar = "$" Then
      e.Handled = True
   End If
End Sub
```

Example 2

```
Private Sub txtAge_KeyPress(ByVal sender As Object, _
   ByVal e As System.Windows.Forms.KeyPressEventArgs) _
   Handles txtAge.KeyPress
   ' allows the text box to accept only numbers and the Backspace key

   If (e.KeyChar < "0" OrElse e.KeyChar > "9") _
      AndAlso e.KeyChar <> ControlChars.Back Then
      e.Handled = True
   End If
End Sub
```

Figure 4-48 Examples of using the KeyChar and Handled properties in the KeyPress event procedure

According to the application's TOE chart, each text box's KeyPress event procedure should allow the text box to accept only numbers, the period, and the Backspace key. All other keys should be canceled. (The TOE chart is shown in Figure 4-33 in Lesson B.)

To allow the three text boxes to accept numbers, the period, and the Backspace key:

1. Change `txtPrincipal_KeyPress` in the procedure header to **CancelKeys**.
2. Click immediately before the letter H in the keyword `Handles` in the procedure header. Type _ (the underscore, which is the line continuation character), and then press **Enter** to move the `Handles txtPrincipal.KeyPress` clause to the next line in the procedure. Press **Tab** to indent the clause.
3. Click at the end of the `Handles txtPrincipal.KeyPress` clause, then type **, txtRate.KeyPress, txtTerm.KeyPress** and press **Enter**. (Be sure to type the comma and the space after `txtPrincipal.KeyPress`.)
4. Type **' allows numbers, the period, and the Backspace key** and press **Enter** twice.
5. Type **if (e.KeyChar < "0" OrElse e.KeyChar > "9")** _ and press **Enter**. (Be sure to include a space before the line continuation character.)

6. Press **Tab** to indent the line. Type **AndAlso e.KeyChar <> "."** _ and press **Enter**, then type **AndAlso e.KeyChar <> ControlChars.Back Then** and press **Enter**.

7. Type **' cancel the key** and press **Enter**, then type **e.Handled = True**. Figure 4-49 shows the completed CancelKeys procedure, which is associated with each text box's KeyPress event.


```
Private Sub CancelKeys(ByVal sender As Object, ByVal e As System.Windo
    Handles txtPrincipal.KeyPress, txtRate.KeyPress, txtTerm.KeyPress
    ' allows numbers, the period, and the Backspace key

    If (e.KeyChar < "0" OrElse e.KeyChar > "9") _
        AndAlso e.KeyChar <> "." _
        AndAlso e.KeyChar <> ControlChars.Back Then
        ' cancel the key
        e.Handled = True
    End If
End Sub
```

Figure 4-49 Completed CancelKeys procedure

In the next set of steps, you will test the CancelKeys procedure to verify that it allows the text boxes to accept only numbers, the period, and the Backspace key.

To test the CancelKeys procedure:

1. Save the solution, then start the application. Try entering a letter in the Principal box, then try entering a dollar sign. Type **30000** in the Principal box, then press **Backspace** to delete the last zero. The text box now contains 3000.

2. Try entering a letter in the Rate text box, then try entering a percent sign. Type **.045** in the Rate text box, then press **Backspace** to delete the number 5. The text box now contains .04.

3. Try entering a letter in the Term text box, then try entering an ampersand. Type **20** in the Term text box, then press **Backspace** to delete the zero. The text box now contains 2.

4. Click the **Calculate Monthly Payment** button. The monthly payment is $130.27.

5. Press **Tab** twice to move the focus to the txtPrincipal control. Notice that the insertion point appears at the end of the number 3000. It is customary in Windows applications to have a text box's existing text selected (highlighted) when the text box receives the focus. You will learn how to select the existing text in the next section. Click the **Exit** button to end the application.

Coding the Enter Event Procedure

To complete the Monthly Payment Calculator application, you just need to code the Enter event procedures for the three text boxes. A text box's **Enter event** occurs when the text box receives the focus, which can happen as a result of the user tabbing to the control or using the control's access key. It also occurs when the Focus method is used in code to send the focus to the control. The Enter event procedure for each text box in the current application is responsible for selecting the contents of the text box. When the text is selected in a text box, the user can remove the text simply by pressing a key—for example, the letter "n" on the keyboard. The key that is pressed—in this case, the letter "n"—replaces the selected text. You use the **SelectAll method** to select all of the text contained in a text box. Figure 4-50 shows the method's syntax and includes an example of using the method. In the syntax, *textbox* is the name of the text box whose contents you want to select (highlight). For example, to select the contents of the txtName control, you use the statement `txtName.SelectAll()`. You will use the SelectAll method to select the contents of the text boxes in the Monthly Payment Calculator application. You will enter the method in each text box's Enter event procedure so that the method is processed when the text box receives the focus.

SelectAll method

Syntax

textbox.**SelectAll()**

Example

`txtName.SelectAll()`

selects the contents of the txtName control

Figure 4-50 Syntax and an example of the SelectAll method

To code each text box's Enter event procedure, then test the procedures:

1. Open the code template for the txtPrincipal control's Enter event procedure. Type **' selects the contents when the text box receives the focus** and press **Enter** twice. Type **txtPrincipal.SelectAll()**.
2. Open the code template for the txtRate control's Enter event procedure. Type **' selects the contents when the text box receives the focus** and press **Enter** twice. Type **txtRate.SelectAll()**.
3. Open the code template for the txtTerm control's Enter event procedure. Type **' selects the contents when the text box receives the focus** and press **Enter** twice. Type **txtTerm.SelectAll()**.
4. Save the solution, then start the application. Enter **10000** as the principal, **8** as the rate, and **5** as the term. Click the **Calculate Monthly Payment** button. A monthly payment amount of $202.76 appears in the interface.
5. Press **Tab** twice to move the focus to the txtPrincipal control. The control's Enter event procedure selects the contents of the text box, as shown in Figure 4-51.

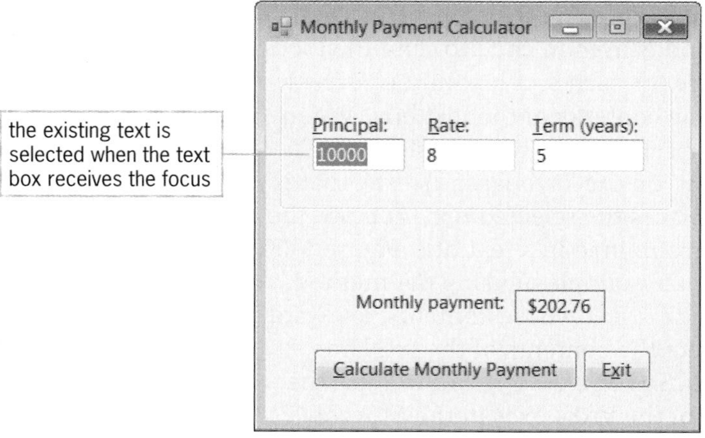

Figure 4-51 Existing text selected in the txtPrincipal control

6. Press **Tab** twice to move the focus to the txtRate and txtTerm controls. Each control's Enter event procedure selects the contents of its associated text box.

7. Click the **Exit** button to end the application. Close the Code Editor window, then close the solution. Figure 4-52 shows the Monthly Payment Calculator application's code.

```
' Name: Payment Project
' Purpose: Calculates the monthly payment on a loan
' Programmer: <your name> on <current date>

Option Explicit On
Option Strict On
Option Infer Off

Public Class frmMain

    Private Sub btnExit_Click(ByVal sender As Object, _
        ByVal e As System.EventArgs) Handles btnExit.Click
        Me.Close()
    End Sub

    Private Sub txtPrincipal_Enter(ByVal sender As Object, _
        ByVal e As System.EventArgs) Handles txtPrincipal.Enter
        ' selects the contents when the text box receives the focus

        txtPrincipal.SelectAll()
    End Sub

    Private Sub txtRate_Enter(ByVal sender As Object, _
        ByVal e As System.EventArgs) Handles txtRate.Enter
        ' selects the contents when the text box receives the focus

        txtRate.SelectAll()
    End Sub

    Private Sub txtTerm_Enter(ByVal sender As Object, _
        ByVal e As System.EventArgs) Handles txtTerm.Enter
        ' selects the contents when the text box receives the focus

        txtTerm.SelectAll()
    End Sub

```

Figure 4-52 Monthly Payment Calculator application's code at the end of Lesson C *(continues)*

(continued)

```
    Private Sub CancelKeys(ByVal sender As Object, _
       ByVal e As System.Windows.Forms.KeyPressEventArgs) _
       Handles txtPrincipal.KeyPress, txtRate.KeyPress, txtTerm.KeyPress
       ' allows numbers, the period, and the Backspace key

       If (e.KeyChar < "0" OrElse e.KeyChar > "9") _
          AndAlso e.KeyChar <> "." _
          AndAlso e.KeyChar <> ControlChars.Back Then
          ' cancel the key
          e.Handled = True
       End If
    End Sub

    Private Sub ClearPayment(ByVal sender As Object, _
       ByVal e As System.EventArgs) _
       Handles txtPrincipal.TextChanged, _
       txtRate.TextChanged, txtTerm.TextChanged
       ' clears the monthly payment

       lblPayment.Text = String.Empty
    End Sub

    Private Sub btnCalc_Click(ByVal sender As Object, _
       ByVal e As System.EventArgs) Handles btnCalc.Click
       ' calculates and displays a monthly payment

       Const strMSG As String = "The term must be greater than or equal to 1."
       Dim dblPrincipal As Double
       Dim dblRate As Double
       Dim dblTerm As Double
       Dim dblMonthlyPayment As Double

       Double.TryParse(txtPrincipal.Text, dblPrincipal)
       Double.TryParse(txtRate.Text, dblRate)
       Double.TryParse(txtTerm.Text, dblTerm)

       ' convert the rate to decimal form, if necessary
       If dblRate >= 1 Then
          dblRate = dblRate / 100
       End If

       ' verify that the term is valid
       If dblTerm >= 1 Then
          ' calculate and display the monthly payment
          dblMonthlyPayment = _
             -Financial.Pmt(dblRate / 12, dblTerm * 12, dblPrincipal)
          lblPayment.Text = dblMonthlyPayment.ToString("C2")
       Else
          MessageBox.Show(strMSG, "Monthly Payment Calculator", _
             MessageBoxButtons.OK, MessageBoxIcon.Information)
       End If
    End Sub
End Class
```

Figure 4-52 Monthly Payment Calculator application's code at the end of Lesson C

Lesson C Summary

- **To allow a text box to accept only certain keys:**

  Code the text box's KeyPress event procedure. The key the user pressed is stored in the e.KeyChar property. You use the `e.Handled = True` instruction to cancel the key pressed by the user.

- **To select the existing text in a text box:**

  Use the SelectAll method, whose syntax is *textbox*.**SelectAll()**.

- **To process code when a control receives the focus:**

  Enter the code in the control's Enter event procedure.

Lesson C Key Terms

ControlChars.Back constant—refers to the Backspace key on the keyboard

Enter event—occurs when a control receives the focus

Handled property—a property of the KeyPress event procedure's `e` parameter; when assigned the value `True`, it cancels the key pressed by the user

KeyChar property—a property of the KeyPress event procedure's `e` parameter; stores the character associated with the key pressed by the user

KeyPress event—occurs each time the user presses a key while a control has the focus

Parameters—the items contained within parentheses in a procedure header; represent information passed to the procedure when the procedure is invoked

SelectAll method—used to select all of the text contained in a text box

Lesson C Review Questions

1. A control's ______________________________ event occurs each time a user presses a key while the control has the focus.

   a. Key

   b. KeyPress

   c. Press

   d. PressKey

2. When entered in the appropriate event, which of the following statements cancels the key pressed by the user?

   a. `Cancel = True`

   b. `e.Cancel = True`

   c. `e.Handled = True`

   d. `Key = Null`

3. Which of the following If clauses determines whether the user pressed the Backspace key?

   a. `If ControlChars.Back = True Then`

   b. `If e.KeyChar = Backspace Then`

   c. `If e.KeyChar = ControlChars.Backspace Then`

   d. `If e.KeyChar = ControlChars.Back Then`

4. Which of the following If clauses determines whether the user pressed the $ key?

   a. `If ControlChars.DollarSign = True Then`

   b. `If e.KeyChar = "$" Then`

   c. `If e.KeyChar = Chars.DollarSign Then`

   d. `If KeyChar.ControlChars = "$" Then`

5. When a user tabs to a text box, the text box's ______________________ event occurs.

   a. Access

   b. Enter

   c. TabOrder

   d. TabbedTo

6. Which of the following highlights all of the text contained in the txtCity control?

   a. `txtCity.SelectAll()`

   b. `txtCity.HighlightAll()`

   c. `Highlight(txtCity)`

   d. `SelectAll(txtCity)`

Lesson C Exercises

INTRODUCTORY

1. Open the State ID Solution (State ID Solution.sln) file, which is contained in the VB2008\Chap04\State ID Solution folder. If necessary, open the designer window. Open the Code Editor window. The txtState control should accept only letters and the Backspace key; code the appropriate procedure. When the txtState control receives the focus, its existing text should be selected; code the appropriate procedure. Save the solution, then start the application. Test the application with both valid data (uppercase and lowercase letters and the Backspace key) and invalid data (numbers and special characters). Stop the application. Close the Code Editor window, then close the solution.

INTRODUCTORY

2. In this exercise, you modify the Playtime Cellular application from Chapter 3. Use Windows to make a copy of the Playtime Solution folder, which is contained in the VB2008\Chap04 folder. Rename the folder Playtime Solution-Introductory. Open the Playtime Solution (Playtime Solution.sln) file contained in the VB2008\Chap04\Playtime Solution-Introductory folder. Open the designer window, then open the Code Editor window. When a text box receives the focus, its existing text should be selected; code the appropriate procedures. The txtBlue and txtPink controls should accept only numbers and the Backspace key; code the appropriate procedures. Save the solution, then start and test the application. Stop the application. Close the Code Editor window, then close the solution.

INTRODUCTORY

3. Open the MessageBox Value Solution (MessageBox Value Solution.sln) file, which is contained in the VB2008\Chap04\MessageBox Value Solution folder. If necessary, open the designer window. Open the Code Editor window. The btnCalc control's Click event procedure should use the MessageBox.Show method to ask whether the user wants to include a dollar sign in the gross pay amount. Include Yes and No buttons in the message box. If the user clicks the Yes button, the procedure should display the gross pay amount using the "C2" format. If the user clicks the No button, the procedure should display the gross pay amount using the "N2" format. Modify the btnCalc control's code. In addition, when the text box receives the focus, its existing text should be selected; code the appropriate procedure. Save the solution, then start and test the application. Stop the application. Close the Code Editor window, then close the solution.

INTRODUCTORY

4. In this exercise, you create an application for Micro Seminars. The application displays the total amount a company owes for a seminar. The seminar charge is $80 per person. Create a Visual Basic Windows application. Name the solution, project, and form file Micro Solution, Micro Project, and Main Form.vb, respectively. Save the application in the VB2008\Chap04 folder. Create the interface shown in Figure 4-53. Code the application. Allow the text box to accept only numbers and the Backspace key. When a change is made to the number of registrants, clear the contents of the label control that displays the total owed. When the text box receives the focus, select its existing text.

The Calculate button's Click event procedure should display an appropriate message when the number of registrants is either less than 1 or greater than 50. It should display the total owed with a dollar sign and two decimal places. Save the solution, then start and test the application. Stop the application. Close the Code Editor window, then close the solution.

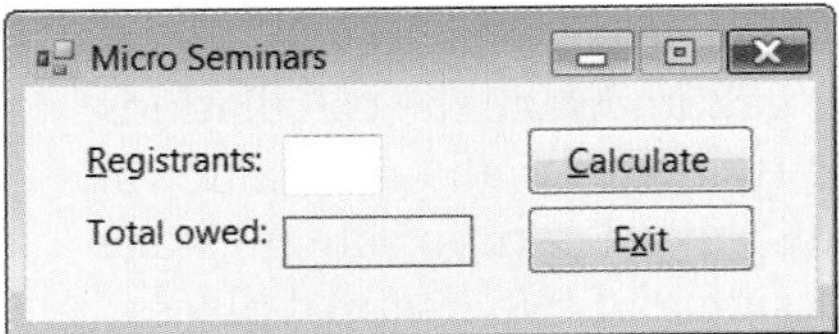

Figure 4-53 User interface for the Micro Seminars application

INTRODUCTORY

5. Open the Shipping Solution (Shipping Solution.sln) file, which is contained in the VB2008\Chap04\Shipping Solution folder. If necessary, open the designer window. Code the Display Shipping Charge button's Click event procedure. The procedure should display $32.00 as the shipping charge for the following ZIP codes: 60618, 60320, and 60544. All other ZIP codes are charged $37.75 for shipping. Save the solution, then start and test the application. Stop the application. Close the Code Editor window, then close the solution.

INTERMEDIATE

6. In this exercise, you create an application designed to teach the Spanish words for red, blue, and green. The Spanish words are rojo, azul, and verde. Create a Visual Basic Windows application. Name the solution, project, and form file Spanish Colors Solution, Spanish Colors Project, and Main Form.vb. Save the application in the VB2008\Chap04 folder. Create the interface shown in Figure 4-54. The interface contains three text boxes, five buttons, and one label. After entering the Spanish word corresponding to a button's color, the user should click the button to verify the entry. If the Spanish word is correct, the button's Click event procedure should change the color of the text box to match the button's color. (Hint: Assign the button's BackColor property to the text box's BackColor property.) Otherwise, it should display the appropriate Spanish word. The Clear button should change each text box's background color to white, using the Visual Basic constant `Color.White`, as well as clear the contents of each text box. Save the solution, then start and test the application. Stop the application. Close the Code Editor window, then close the solution.

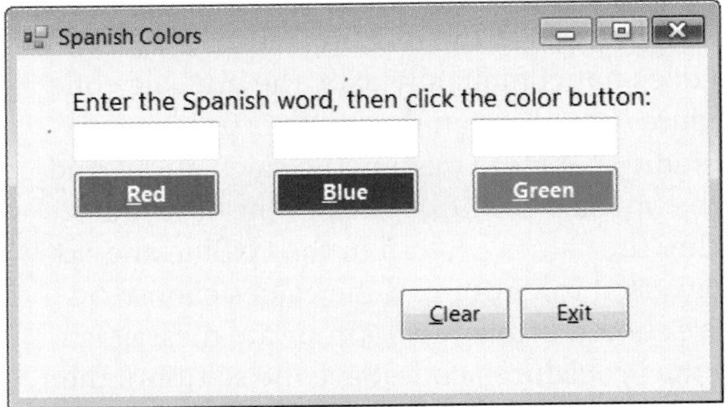

Figure 4-54 User interface for the Spanish Colors application

INTERMEDIATE

7. In this exercise, you code an application that calculates a customer's water bill. Create a Visual Basic Windows application. Name the solution, project, and form file Allenton Solution, Allenton Project, and Main Form.vb, respectively. Save the application in the VB2008\Chap04 folder. Create the interface shown in Figure 4-55. Code the application so that it calculates and displays the number of gallons of water used and the total charge for the water. The charge for water is $1.75 per 1000 gallons, or .00175 per gallon. Make the calculations only when the current meter reading is greater than or equal to the previous meter reading; otherwise, display an appropriate message. Display the total charge with a dollar sign and two decimal places. The text boxes should accept only numbers and the Backspace key. Clear the number of gallons used and the total charge when a change is made to the contents of a text box on the form. When a text box receives the focus, select its existing text. Save the solution, then start and test the application. Stop the application. Close the Code Editor window, then close the solution.

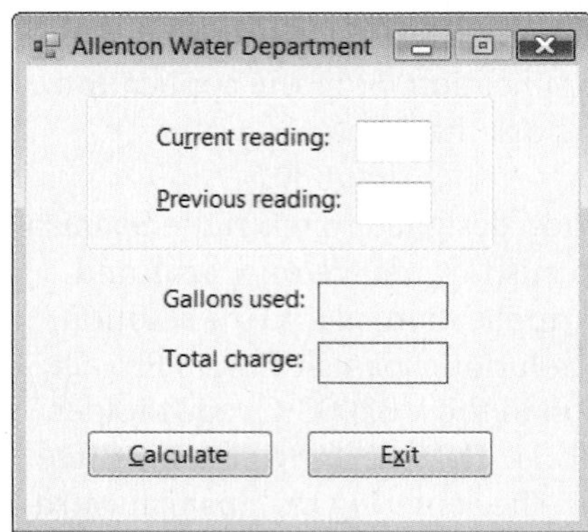

Figure 4-55 User interface for the Allenton Water Department

INTERMEDIATE

8. In this exercise, you modify the Playtime Cellular application from Exercise 2. Use Windows to make a copy of the Playtime Solution-Introductory folder, which is contained in the VB2008\Chap04 folder. Rename the folder Playtime Solution-Intermediate. Open the Playtime Solution (Playtime Solution.sln) file contained in the VB2008\Chap04\Playtime Solution-Intermediate folder. Open the designer window, then open the Code Editor window. If the txtBlue control does not contain any data, the btnCalc control's Click event procedure should assign the number 0 to the text box's Text property. Likewise, if the txtPink does not contain any data, the btnCalc control's Click event procedure should assign the number 0 to the text box's Text property. In addition, before making the calculations and displaying the results, the btnCalc control's Click event procedure should determine whether the values entered in the txtBlue and txtPink controls can be converted to integers. If the values cannot be converted, the procedure should display an appropriate message in a message box. Modify the procedure's code. Save the solution, then start and test the application. Stop the application. Close the Code Editor window, then close the solution.

INTERMEDIATE

9. Create a Visual Basic Windows application. Name the solution, project, and form file Marcy Solution, Marcy Project, and Main Form.vb, respectively. Save the application in the VB2008\Chap04 folder. Marcy's Department Store is having a BoGoHo (Buy One, Get One Half Off) sale. The application should allow the user to enter the prices of two items. It then should calculate and display the total owed. The half-off should always be taken on the item having the lowest price. For example, if one item costs $24.99 and the other costs $12.50, the half-off would be taken on the $12.50 item. The total owed would be $31.24 (24.99 + 6.25). Code the application. Save the solution, then start and test the application. Stop the application. Close the Code Editor window, then close the solution.

ADVANCED

10. Create a Visual Basic Windows application. Name the solution, project, and form file Novelty Solution, Novelty Project, and Main Form.vb, respectively. Save the application in the VB2008\Chap04 folder. Create the interface shown in Figure 4-56. When the user clicks the Calculate Total button, the button's Click event procedure should add the item price to the total of the prices already entered; this amount represents the subtotal owed by the customer. The procedure should display the subtotal on the form. It also should display a 3% sales tax, the shipping charge, and the grand total owed by the customer. The grand total is calculated by adding together the subtotal, the 3% sales tax, and a $15 shipping charge. For example, if the user enters 26.75 as the price and then clicks the Calculate Total button, the button's Click event procedure should display 26.75 as the subtotal, 0.80 as the sales tax, 15.00 as the shipping charge, and 42.55 as the grand total. If the user subsequently enters 30 as the price and then clicks the Calculate Total button, the button's Click event procedure should display 56.75 as the subtotal, 1.70 as the sales tax, 15.00 as the shipping charge, and 73.45 as the grand total. However, when the subtotal is at least $100, the shipping charge is 0.00. Code the application appropriately. Save the solution, then start and test the application. Stop the application. Close the Code Editor window, then close the solution.

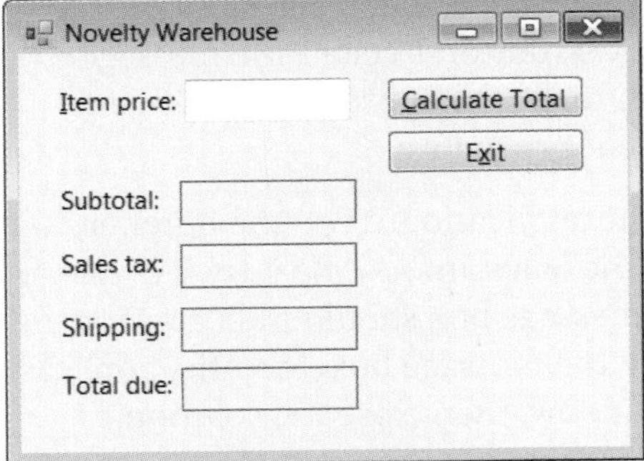

Figure 4-56 User interface for the Novelty Warehouse application

Discovery

11. In this exercise, you learn how to specify the maximum number of characters that can be entered in a text box. Open the Zip Solution (Zip Solution.sln) file, which is contained in the VB2008\Chap04\Zip Solution folder. If necessary, open the designer window. Click the txtZip control. Scan the Properties list, looking for a property that allows you to specify the maximum number of characters that can be entered in the text box. When you locate the property, set its value to 10. Save the solution, then start the application. Test the application by trying to enter more than 10 characters in the text box. Stop the application. Close the Code Editor window, then close the solution.

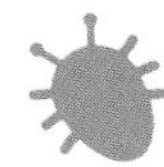

Swat The Bugs

12. Open the Debug Solution (Debug Solution.sln) file, which is contained in the VB2008\Chap04\Debug Solution-Lesson C folder. Open the Code Editor window and review the existing code. The btnCalc control's Click event procedure should calculate a 10% bonus when the code entered by the user is either 1 or 2 and, at the same time, the sales amount is greater than $10,000; otherwise, the bonus rate is 5%. Also, the CancelKeys procedure should allow the two text boxes to accept only numbers and the Backspace key.

    a. Start the application. Type the number 1 in the Code box, then press the Backspace key. Notice that the Backspace key is not working correctly. Stop the application, then make the appropriate change to the CancelKeys procedure.

    b. Save the solution, then start the application. Type the number 12 in the Code text box, then press the Backspace key to delete the 2. The Code text box now contains the number 1.

    c. Type 200 in the Sales amount box, then click the Calculate Bonus button. A message box appears and indicates that the bonus amount is $20.00 (10% of $200), which is incorrect; it should be $10.00 (5% of $200). Click the OK button to close the message box. Stop the application, then make the appropriate change to the btnCalc control's Click event procedure.

    d. Save the solution, then start the application. Type the number 1 in the Code box. Type 200 in the Sales amount box, then click the Calculate Bonus button. The message box should indicate that the bonus amount is $10.00. Close the message box. Stop the application. Close the Code Editor window, then close the solution.

CHAPTER 5

More on the Selection Structure

Creating a Math Practice Application

In this chapter, you create an application for Susan Chen, the principal of a local primary school. The application will be used by the first and second grade students to practice both adding and subtracting numbers. The application should display the math problem on the screen, and then allow the student to enter the answer and verify that the answer is correct. The application should give the student as many chances as necessary to answer the problem correctly. The math problems for first grade students should use numbers from 1 through 10 only, whereas the ones for second grade students should use numbers from 10 through 99. Because the first and second grade students have not learned about negative numbers yet, the subtraction problems should never ask them to subtract a larger number from a smaller one. Ms. Chen also wants the application to keep track of the number of correct and incorrect responses made by the student; this information will help her assess the student's math ability. Finally, she wants to be able to control the display of the assessment information to keep students from being distracted or pressured by the number of right and wrong answers.

Previewing the Math Practice Application

To preview the completed Math Practice application:

To open the Run dialog box, press and hold down the Windows logo key as you tap the letter r, then release the logo key.

1. Use the Run dialog box to run the **Math** (**Math.exe**) file, which is contained in the VB2008\Chap05 folder. The application's user interface appears on the screen. See Figure 5-1. Because the application displays random numbers, the numbers on your screen may not match the ones shown in the figure. You will learn how to display random numbers in Lesson B. You also will learn about the radio button and check box controls.

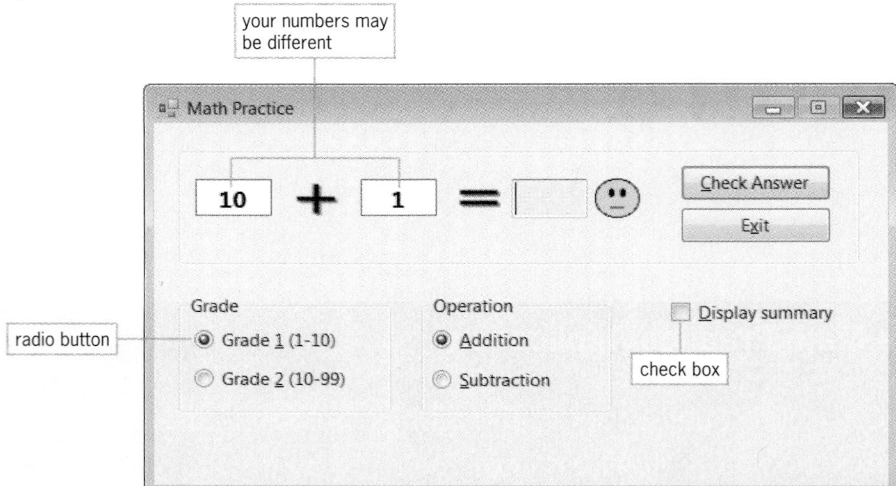

Figure 5-1 Math Practice application's user interface

2. Type the correct answer to the addition problem appearing in the interface, then press **Enter** to select the Check Answer button, which is the default button on the form. When you answer the math problem correctly, a happy face icon appears in the picture box located to the left of the Check Answer button, and a new problem appears in the interface.

3. Click the **Display summary** check box to select it. A check mark appears inside the check box, and a group box appears below the check box. The label controls contained in the group box display the number of correct and incorrect responses, as shown in Figure 5-2. In this case, you have made 1 correct response and 0 incorrect responses.

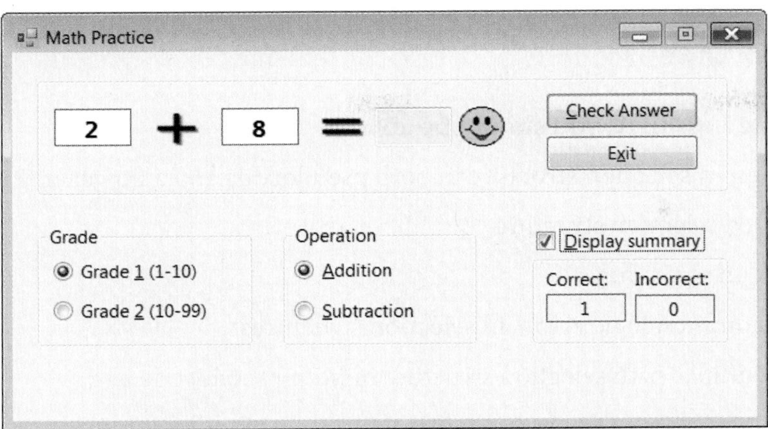

Figure 5-2 Number of correct and incorrect responses shown in the interface

4. Click the **Subtraction** radio button. A colored dot appears in the center of the Subtraction radio button to indicate that the radio button is selected, and the math problem changes to one involving subtraction.

5. Click the **text box** in which you enter the answer. Type an incorrect answer to the subtraction problem appearing on the screen, then press **Enter**. The application replaces the happy face icon in the picture box with an icon whose facial expression is neutral. It also displays the "Try again!" message in a message box.

6. Press **Enter** to close the message box. The application highlights the incorrect answer in the text box and gives you another chance to enter a correct response. The interface shows that you have made 1 correct response and 1 incorrect response.

7. Type the correct answer to the subtraction problem, then press **Enter**. The happy face icon reappears in the picture box, and the number of correct responses now says 2. In addition, a new math problem appears in the interface.

8. Click the **Display summary** check box to deselect it. The application removes the check mark from the check box and hides the group box that contains the summary information. Click the **Exit** button to end the application.

The Math Practice application uses a multiple-path selection structure, which you will learn about in Lesson A. You also will learn about nested selection structures. As mentioned earlier, random numbers and radio button and check box controls are covered in Lesson B. You will code the Math Practice application in Lessons B and C.

LESSON A

After studying Lesson A, you should be able to:

- Include a nested selection structure in both pseudocode and a flowchart
- Code a nested selection structure
- Desk-check an algorithm
- Recognize common logic errors in selection structures
- Include a multiple-path selection structure in both pseudocode and a flowchart
- Code a multiple-path selection structure using the If/ElseIf/Else and Case forms of the selection structure

Nested Selection Structures

As you learned in Chapter 4, you use the selection structure when you want a procedure to make a decision or comparison and then select the appropriate path, depending on the result of that decision or comparison. The paths in a selection structure can include instructions that declare variables, perform calculations, and so on. The paths also can include other selection structures. When either a selection structure's true path or its false path contains another selection structure, the inner selection structure is referred to as a **nested selection structure**, because it is contained (nested) within the outer selection structure. You use a nested selection structure when more than one decision must be made before the appropriate action can be taken. An example of this would be a selection structure that displays one of three messages based on a person's voter eligibility. The messages and criteria for displaying each message are shown in Figure 5-3. As the chart indicates, the person's age and voter registration status determine the appropriate message to display. If the person is younger than 18 years old, the procedure should display the message "You are too young to vote." However, if the person is at least 18 years old, the procedure should display one of two different messages. The correct message to display is determined by the person's voter registration status. If the person is registered, then the appropriate message is "You can vote."; otherwise, it is "You need to register before you can vote." Notice that determining the person's voter registration status is important only after his or her age is determined. You can think of the decision regarding the age as being the **primary decision**, and the decision regarding the registration status as being the **secondary decision**, because whether the registration decision needs to be made depends on the result of the age decision. The primary decision is always made by the outer selection structure, while the secondary decision is always made by the inner (nested) selection structure.

Message	Criteria
You are too young to vote.	younger than 18 years old
You can vote.	at least 18 years old and registered to vote
You need to register before you can vote.	at least 18 years old but not registered to vote

Figure 5-3 Messages and criteria

Figure 5-4 shows a sample run of the Voter Eligibility application. Figures 5-5, 5-6, and 5-7 show the pseudocode, flowchart, and code for the Display Message button's Click event procedure. In the figures, the outer selection structure determines the age (the primary decision), and the nested selection structure determines the voter registration status (the secondary decision). Notice that the nested selection structure appears in the outer selection structure's true path in the figures.

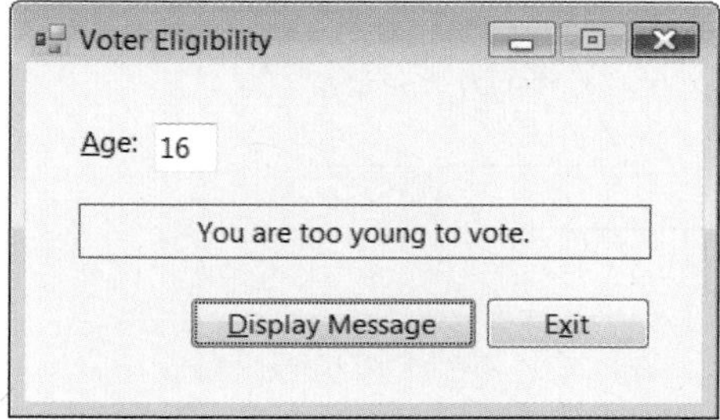

Figure 5-4 Sample run of the Voter Eligibility application

```
btnDisplay Click event procedure
1. store the age in a variable
2. if the age is greater than or equal to 18
       ask whether the person is registered
       if the person is registered
           display "You can vote."
       else
           display "You need to register before you can vote."
       end if
   else
       display "You are too young to vote."
   end if
```

Figure 5-5 Display Message button's pseudocode with the nested selection structure in the true path

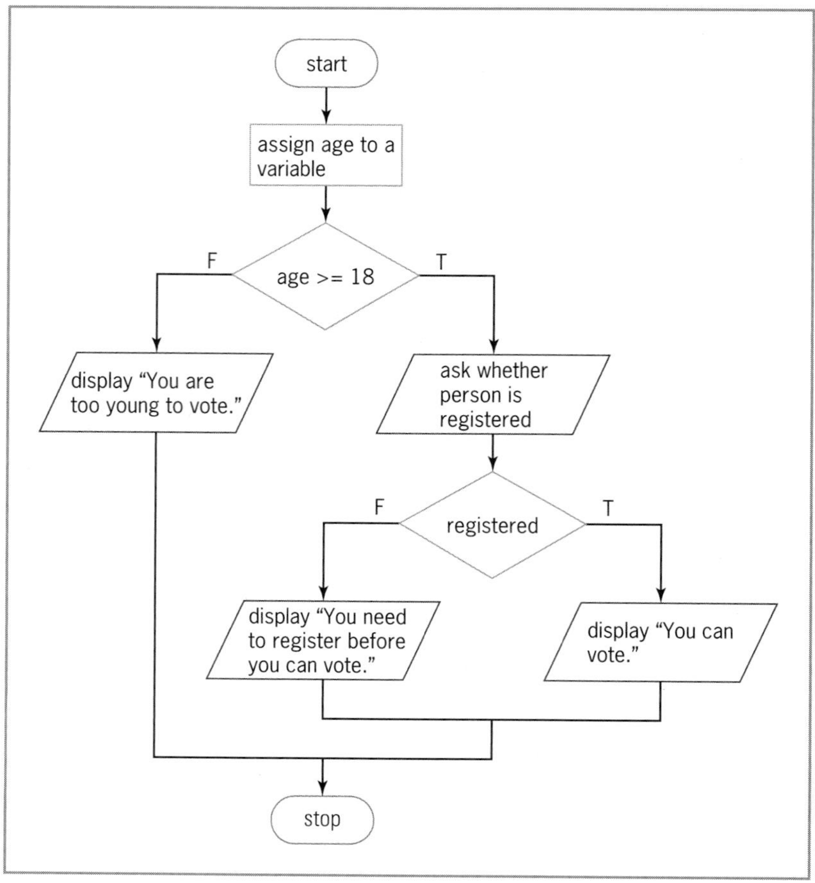

Figure 5-6 Display Message button's flowchart with the nested selection structure in the true path

```
Private Sub btnDisplay_Click(ByVal sender As Object, _
   ByVal e As System.EventArgs) Handles btnDisplay.Click
   ' displays a message

   Const strMSG1 As String = "You are too young to vote."
   Const strMSG2 As String = _
      "You need to register before you can vote."
   Const strMSG3 As String = "You can vote."
   Const strPROMPT As String = _
      "Are you registered to vote?"
   Dim intAge As Integer
   Dim dlgButton As DialogResult

   Integer.TryParse(txtAge.Text, intAge)
```

Figure 5-7 Display Message button's Click event procedure with the nested selection structure in the true path *(continues)*

(continued)

```
        If intAge >= 18 Then
            dlgButton = MessageBox.Show(strPROMPT, _
                        "Voter Eligibility", _
                        MessageBoxButtons.YesNo, _
                        MessageBoxIcon.Exclamation)
            If dlgButton = Windows.Forms.DialogResult.Yes Then
                lblMsg.Text = strMSG3
            Else
                lblMsg.Text = strMSG2
            End If
        Else
            lblMsg.Text = strMSG1
        End If
    End Sub
```

Figure 5-7 Display Message button's Click event procedure with the nested selection structure in the true path

The condition in the outer selection structure in Figure 5-7 determines whether the `intAge` variable's value is greater than or equal to 18. If the condition evaluates to False, it means that the person is not old enough to vote. In that case, only one message—the "You are too young to vote." message—is appropriate. After the message is displayed, both the outer selection structure and the procedure end. If the outer selection structure's condition evaluates to True, on the other hand, it means that the person *is* old enough to vote. In that case, the outer selection structure's true path displays a message box that asks whether the person is registered. Notice that the message box contains Yes and No buttons. A nested selection structure then is used to determine which of the message box buttons was chosen. If the Yes button was chosen, the instruction in the nested selection structure's true path displays the "You can vote." message. If the No button was chosen, the instruction in the nested selection structure's false path displays the "You need to register before you can vote." message. After the appropriate message is displayed, both selection structures and the procedure end. Notice that the nested selection structure in this procedure is processed only when the outer selection structure's condition evaluates to True.

Figures 5-8 and 5-9 show the pseudocode and flowchart for a different version of the voter eligibility procedure, and Figure 5-10 shows the corresponding Visual Basic code. As in the previous version, the outer selection structure in this version determines the age (the primary decision), and the nested selection structure determines the voter registration status (the secondary decision). In this version, however, the nested selection structure appears in the false path of the outer selection structure. Rather than checking whether the value stored in the `intAge` variable is greater than or equal to 18, the outer selection structure in this version checks whether the value is less than 18. If the condition evaluates to True, the instruction in the outer selection structure's true path displays the "You are too young to vote." message. If the condition evaluates to False, the outer selection structure's false path first displays a message box that asks whether the person is registered. A nested selection structure then is used to determine which of the message box buttons the user chose. If the user selected the Yes button, the instruction in the nested selection structure's true path displays the "You can vote." message. If the user selected the No button, the instruction in the nested selection structure's false path displays the "You need to register before you can vote." message. After the appropriate message is displayed, both selection structures and the procedure end. Unlike in the previous version of the procedure, the nested selection structure in this version is processed only when the outer selection structure's condition evaluates to False. Both versions of the procedure produce the same results. Neither version is better than the other; each simply represents a different way of solving the same problem.


```
btnDisplay Click event procedure
1. store the age in a variable
2. if the age is less than 18
       display "You are too young to vote."
   else
       ask the user if the person is registered
       if the person is registered
           display "You can vote."
       else
           display "You need to register before you can vote."
       end if
   end if
```

Figure 5-8 Display Message button's pseudocode with the nested selection structure in the false path

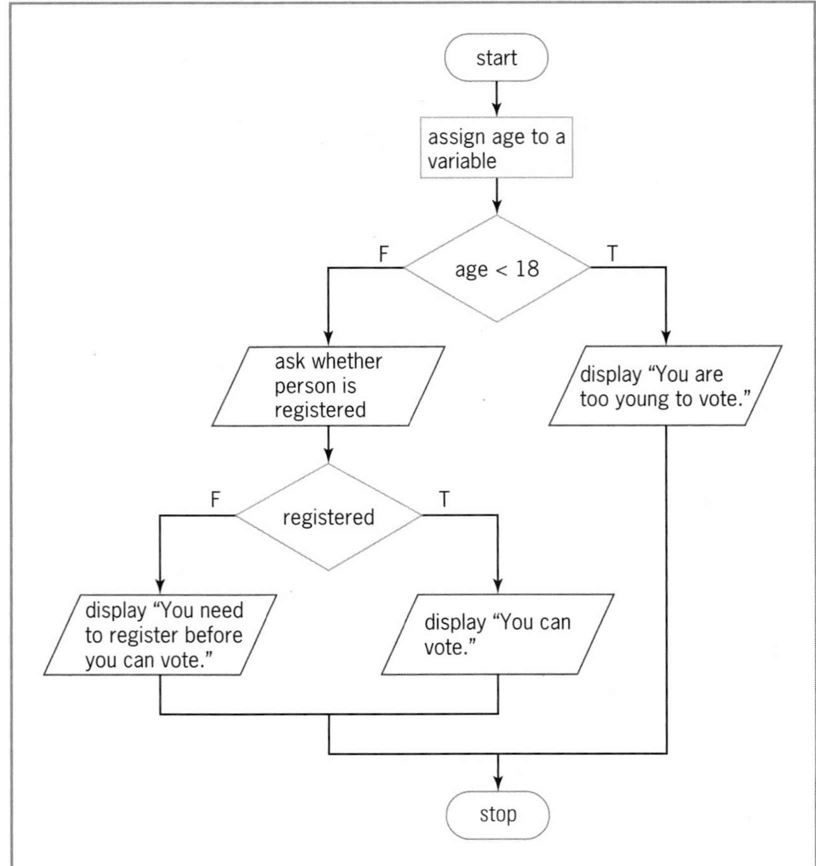

Figure 5-9 Display Message button's flowchart with the nested selection structure in the false path

```
Private Sub btnDisplay_Click(ByVal sender As Object, _
   ByVal e As System.EventArgs) Handles btnDisplay.Click
   ' displays a message

   Const strMSG1 As String = "You are too young to vote."
   Const strMSG2 As String = _
         "You need to register before you can vote."
   Const strMSG3 As String = "You can vote."
   Const strPROMPT As String = _
         "Are you registered to vote?"
   Dim intAge As Integer
   Dim dlgButton As DialogResult

   Integer.TryParse(txtAge.Text, intAge)

   If intAge < 18 Then
      lblMsg.Text = strMSG1
   Else
      dlgButton = MessageBox.Show(strPROMPT, _
                  "Voter Eligibility", _
                  MessageBoxButtons.YesNo, _
                  MessageBoxIcon.Exclamation)
      If dlgButton = Windows.Forms.DialogResult.Yes Then
         lblMsg.Text = strMSG3
      Else
         lblMsg.Text = strMSG2
      End If
   End If
End Sub
```

Figure 5-10 Display Message button's Click event procedure with the nested selection structure in the false path

To code and then test the Voter Eligibility application:

1. If necessary, start Visual Studio 2008 or Visual Basic 2008 Express Edition. Close the Start Page window.
2. Open the **Voter Solution** (**Voter Solution.sln**) file, which is contained in the VB2008\Chap05\Voter Solution folder. If necessary, open the designer window.
3. Open the Code Editor window. Replace the <your name> and <current date> text in the comments with your name and the current date.
4. Open the code template for the btnDisplay control's Click event procedure, then enter the comment and code shown in either Figure 5-7 or Figure 5-10.
5. Close the Code Editor window. Save the solution, then start the application. Enter **16** as the age, then press **Enter**. The button's Click event procedure displays the "You are too young to vote." message, as shown earlier in Figure 5-4.
6. Change the age to **25**, then press **Enter**. A message box opens and displays the "Are you registered to vote?" message. Press **Enter** to select the Yes button. The "You can vote." message appears in the interface.
7. Click the **Display Message** button, then click the **No** button in the message box. The "You need to register before you can vote." message appears in the interface. Click the **Exit** button to end the application, then close the solution.

Logic Errors in Selection Structures

In the next few sections, you will observe some of the common logic errors made when writing selection structures. Being aware of these errors will help prevent you from making them. In most cases, logic errors in selection structures are a result of one of the following three mistakes: using a compound condition rather than a nested selection structure; reversing the primary and secondary decisions; or using an unnecessary nested selection structure. The XYZ Company's bonus procedure will be used to demonstrate each of these logic errors. The company pays its salespeople an 8% bonus on their sales. However, salespeople having a sales code of X receive an additional $150 bonus when their sales are greater than or equal to $10,000; otherwise, they receive an additional $125 bonus. Notice that the salesperson's code is a factor in determining whether the salesperson is eligible for the additional bonus amount. If the salesperson is entitled to the additional bonus, then the amount of his or her sales determines the appropriate additional amount. In this case, the decision regarding the salesperson's code is the primary decision, and the decision regarding the sales amount is the secondary decision, because whether the sales amount decision needs to be made depends on the result of the code decision. The pseudocode shown in Figure 5-11 represents a correct algorithm for the bonus procedure. An **algorithm** is the set of step-by-step instructions for accomplishing a task.

You also can write the nested selection structure's condition as follows: if the sales are less than 10000. You then would reverse the instructions in the true and false paths.

Correct algorithm for the bonus procedure

```
1. calculate the bonus by multiplying the sales by .08
2. if the code is X
       if the sales are greater than or equal to 10000
           add 150 to the bonus
       else
           add 125 to the bonus
       end if
   end if
3. display the bonus
```

Figure 5-11 A correct algorithm for the bonus procedure

You can verify that the algorithm in Figure 5-11 works correctly by desk-checking it. The term **desk-checking** refers to the fact that the programmer reviews the algorithm while seated at his or her desk rather than in front of the computer. Desk-checking is also called **hand-tracing**, because the programmer uses a pencil and paper to follow each of the algorithm's instructions by hand. Programmers desk-check an algorithm to verify that it is not missing any steps, and that the existing steps are correct and in the proper order. If any errors are found in the algorithm, the errors are corrected before the programmer begins coding the algorithm. Before you begin the desk-check, you first choose a set of sample data for the input values, which you then use to manually compute the expected output values. You will desk-check the algorithm in Figure 5-11 three times. For the first desk-check, you will use X as the code and $15,000 as the sales amount. Using this test data, the algorithm should display a bonus amount of $1,350. For the second desk-check, you will use X as the code and $9,000 as the sales amount; in this case, the algorithm should display a bonus amount of $845. For the third desk-check, you will use A as the code and $13,000 as the sales amount. With this set of test data, the algorithm should display a bonus amount of $1,040.

Using the first set of test data (X and 15000), Step 1 in the algorithm multiplies the sales amount by .08, giving 1200. The outer selection structure's condition in Step 2 determines whether the salesperson's code is X; it is, so the nested selection structure's condition checks whether the sales amount is greater than or equal to 10000. The sales amount is greater than 10000, so the nested selection structure's true path adds 150 to the bonus amount, giving 1350, which is correct. After doing this, both selection structures end. Step 3 in the algorithm then displays the bonus amount of 1350. Using the second set of test data (X and 9000), Step 1 in the algorithm multiplies the sales amount by .08, giving 720. The outer selection structure's condition in Step 2 determines whether the salesperson's code is X; it is, so the nested selection structure's condition checks whether the sales amount is greater than or equal to 10000. The sales amount is not greater than or equal to 10000, so the nested selection structure's false path adds 125 to the bonus amount, giving 845, which is correct. After doing this, both selection structures end. Step 3 in the algorithm then displays the bonus amount of 845. Using the third set of test data (A and 13000), Step 1 in the algorithm multiplies the sales amount by .08, giving 1040. The outer selection structure's condition in Step 2 determines whether the salesperson's code is X. The code is not X, so the outer selection structure ends. Notice that the nested selection structure is not processed when the outer selection structure's condition is false. The algorithm then displays the bonus amount of 1040. Figure 5-12 shows the results of desk-checking the correct algorithm.

Desk-check		Result
First:	using X as the code and 15000 as the sales	1350
Second:	using X as the code and 9000 as the sales	845
Third:	using A as the code and 13000 as the sales	1040

Figure 5-12 Results of desk-checking the correct algorithm

Using a Compound Condition Rather Than a Nested Selection Structure

A common error made when writing selection structures is to use a compound condition in the outer selection structure's condition when a nested selection structure is needed. Figure 5-13 shows an example of this error in the bonus algorithm. The correct algorithm is included in the figure for comparison. Notice that the incorrect algorithm uses one selection structure rather than two selection structures, and the selection structure contains a compound condition. Consider why the selection structure in the incorrect algorithm cannot be used in place of the selection structures in the correct algorithm. In the correct algorithm, the outer and nested selection structures indicate that a hierarchy exists between the code and sales decisions: the code decision is always made first, followed by the sales decision (if necessary). In the incorrect algorithm, the compound condition indicates that no hierarchy exists between the code and sales decisions; each has equal weight and neither is dependent on the other, which is incorrect.

a logical operator is used rather than a nested selection structure

Correct algorithm	Incorrect algorithm

1. calculate the bonus by multiplying
the sales by .08
2. if the code is X
if the sales are greater than or equal
to 10000
add 150 to the bonus
else
add 125 to the bonus
end if
end if
3. display the bonus
	1. calculate the bonus by multiplying
	the sales by .08
	2. if the code is X and the sales are
	greater than or equal to 10000
	add 150 to the bonus
	else
	add 125 to the bonus
	end if
	3. display the bonus

Figure 5-13 Correct algorithm and an incorrect algorithm containing the first logic error

To better understand why the incorrect algorithm in Figure 5-13 will not work correctly, you will desk-check it using the same test data used to desk-check the correct algorithm. Using the first set of test data (X and 15000), Step 1 in the incorrect algorithm multiplies the sales amount by .08, giving 1200. The selection structure in Step 2 contains a compound condition that determines whether the salesperson's code is X and, at the same time, the sales amount is greater than or equal to 10000. In this case, the compound condition evaluates to True. Therefore, the selection structure's true path adds 150 to the bonus amount, giving 1350. Step 3 in the incorrect algorithm then displays the bonus amount of 1350. Even though the algorithm's selection structure is phrased incorrectly, notice that the incorrect algorithm produces the same result as the correct algorithm using the first set of test data. Using the second set of test data (X and 9000), Step 1 in the incorrect algorithm multiplies the sales amount by .08, giving 720. The compound condition in Step 2's selection structure determines whether the salesperson's code is X and, at the same time, the sales amount is greater than or equal to 10000. In this case, the compound condition evaluates to False, because the sales amount is not greater than or equal to 10000. Therefore, the selection structure's false path adds 125 to the bonus amount, giving 845. Step 3 in the incorrect algorithm then displays the bonus amount of 845. Here again, using the second set of test data, the incorrect algorithm produces the same result as the correct algorithm. Using the third set of test data (A and 13000), Step 1 in the incorrect algorithm multiplies the sales amount by .08, giving 1040. The compound condition in Step 2's selection structure determines whether the salesperson's code is X and, at the same time, the sales amount is greater than or equal to 10000. In this case, the compound condition evaluates to False, because the salesperson's code is not X. As a result, the selection structure's false path adds 125 to the bonus amount, giving 1165. Step 3 in the incorrect algorithm then displays the bonus amount of 1165. Notice that the incorrect algorithm produces erroneous results for the third set of test data; according to Figure 5-12, the algorithm should have displayed 1040 as the bonus. It is important to desk-check an algorithm several times using different test data. In this case, if you had used only the first two sets of data to desk-check the incorrect algorithm, you would not have discovered the error. Figure 5-14 shows the results of desk-checking the incorrect algorithm shown in Figure 5-13. As indicated in the figure, the results of the first and second desk-checks are correct, but the result of the third desk-check is not correct.

Desk-check		Result
First:	using X as the code and 15000 as the sales	1350 (correct)
Second:	using X as the code and 9000 as the sales	845 (correct)
Third:	using A as the code and 13000 as the sales	1165 (incorrect)

Figure 5-14 Results of desk-checking the incorrect algorithm shown in Figure 5-13

Reversing the Primary and Secondary Decisions

Another common error made when writing a selection structure that contains a nested selection structure is to reverse the primary and secondary decisions—in other words, put the secondary decision in the outer selection structure, and put the primary decision in the nested selection structure. Figure 5-15 shows an example of this error in the bonus algorithm. The correct algorithm is included in the figure for comparison. Unlike the selection structures in the correct algorithm, which determine the code before determining the sales amount, the selection structures in the incorrect algorithm determine the sales amount before determining the code. Consider how this difference changes the algorithm. In the correct algorithm, the selection structures indicate that only salespeople who have a code of X receive an additional bonus, which is correct. The selection structures in the incorrect algorithm, on the other hand, indicate that the additional bonus is given to all salespeople whose sales are greater than or equal to 10000, which is not correct.

Correct algorithm

```
1. calculate the bonus by multiplying
   the sales by .08
2. if the code is X
      if the sales are greater than or equal
      to 10000
         add 150 to the bonus
      else
         add 125 to the bonus
      end if
   end if
3. display the bonus
```

Incorrect algorithm

```
1. calculate the bonus by multiplying
   the sales by .08
2. if the sales are greater than or equal
   to 10000
      if the code is X
         add 150 to the bonus
      else
         add 125 to the bonus
      end if
   end if
3. display the bonus
```

primary and secondary decisions reversed

Figure 5-15 Correct algorithm and an incorrect algorithm containing the second logic error

Figure 5-16 shows the results of desk-checking the incorrect algorithm shown in Figure 5-15. As indicated in the figure, only the result of the first desk-check is correct.

Desk-check		Result
First:	using X as the code and 15000 as the sales	1350 (correct)
Second:	using X as the code and 9000 as the sales	720 (incorrect)
Third:	using A as the code and 13000 as the sales	1165 (incorrect)

Figure 5-16 Results of desk-checking the incorrect algorithm shown in Figure 5-15

Using an Unnecessary Nested Selection Structure

Another common error made when writing selection structures is to include an unnecessary nested selection structure. In most cases, a selection structure containing this error still will produce the correct results; however, it will do so less efficiently than selection structures that are properly structured. Figure 5-17 shows an example of this error in the bonus algorithm. The correct algorithm is included in the figure for comparison. Unlike the correct algorithm, which contains two selection structures, the inefficient algorithm contains three selection structures. Notice that the condition in the third selection structure determines whether the sales are less than 10000 and is processed only when the condition in the second selection structure is false. In other words, it is processed only when the sales are not greater than or equal to 10000. However, if the sales are not greater than or equal to 10000, then they would have to be less than 10000, so the third selection structure is unnecessary.

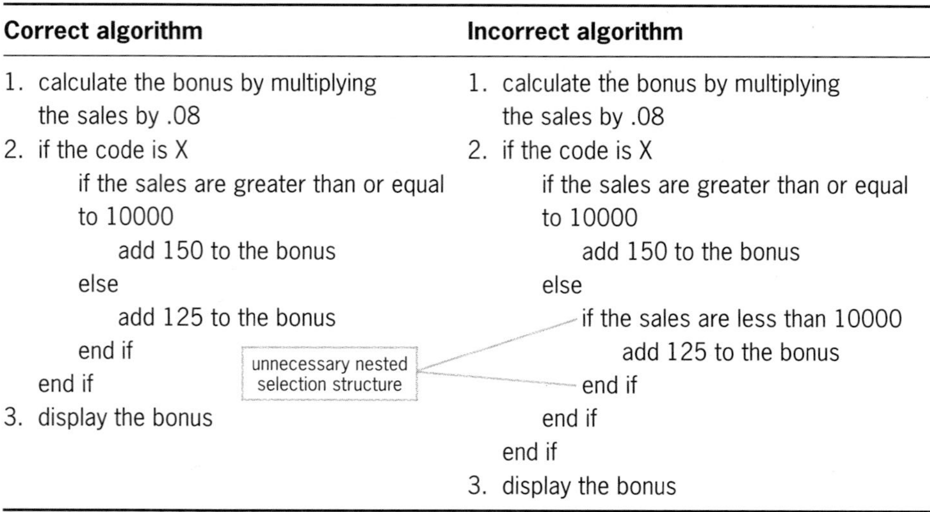

Correct algorithm

```
1. calculate the bonus by multiplying
   the sales by .08
2. if the code is X
      if the sales are greater than or equal
      to 10000
         add 150 to the bonus
      else
         add 125 to the bonus
      end if
   end if
3. display the bonus
```

Incorrect algorithm

```
1. calculate the bonus by multiplying
   the sales by .08
2. if the code is X
      if the sales are greater than or equal
      to 10000
         add 150 to the bonus
      else
         if the sales are less than 10000
            add 125 to the bonus
         end if
      end if
   end if
3. display the bonus
```


Figure 5-17 Correct algorithm and an incorrect algorithm containing the third logic error

Figure 5-18 shows the results of desk-checking the inefficient algorithm shown in Figure 5-17. As indicated in the figure, although the results of the three desk-checks are correct, the result of the second desk-check is obtained in a less efficient manner.

Desk-check		Result
First:	using X as the code and 15000 as the sales	1350 (correct)
Second:	using X as the code and 9000 as the sales	845 (correct)
Third:	using A as the code and 13000 as the sales	1040 (correct)

result obtained in a less efficient manner

Figure 5-18 Results of desk-checking the inefficient algorithm shown in Figure 5-17

Multiple-Path Selection Structures

At times, you may need to create a selection structure that can choose from several alternatives. Such selection structures are referred to as **multiple-path selection structures** or as **extended selection structures**. An example of this would be a selection structure that displays a message based on a letter grade entered by the user. The valid letter grades and their corresponding messages are shown in Figure 5-19. As the figure indicates, when the letter grade is an A, the selection structure should display the message "Excellent." When the letter grade is a B, the selection structure should display the message "Above Average," and so on.

Letter grade	Message
A	Excellent
B	Above Average
C	Average
D	Below Average
F	Below Average

Figure 5-19 Letter grades and messages

Figure 5-20 shows a multiple-path selection structure written in pseudocode and drawn in flowchart form. Unlike the condition in the selection structures from Chapter 4, the condition in a multiple-path selection structure does not require a true or false answer. Instead, it requires an expression whose value determines which path is chosen; in Figure 5-20, the expression is *grade*. As is true of all selection structures, the condition in a multiple-path selection structure is represented by a diamond in a flowchart. However, in a multiple-path selection structure, the diamond has one flowline leading into the symbol but several flowlines leading out of the symbol. Each flowline represents a possible path for the selection structure and must be marked appropriately, indicating which value or values are necessary for each path to be chosen.

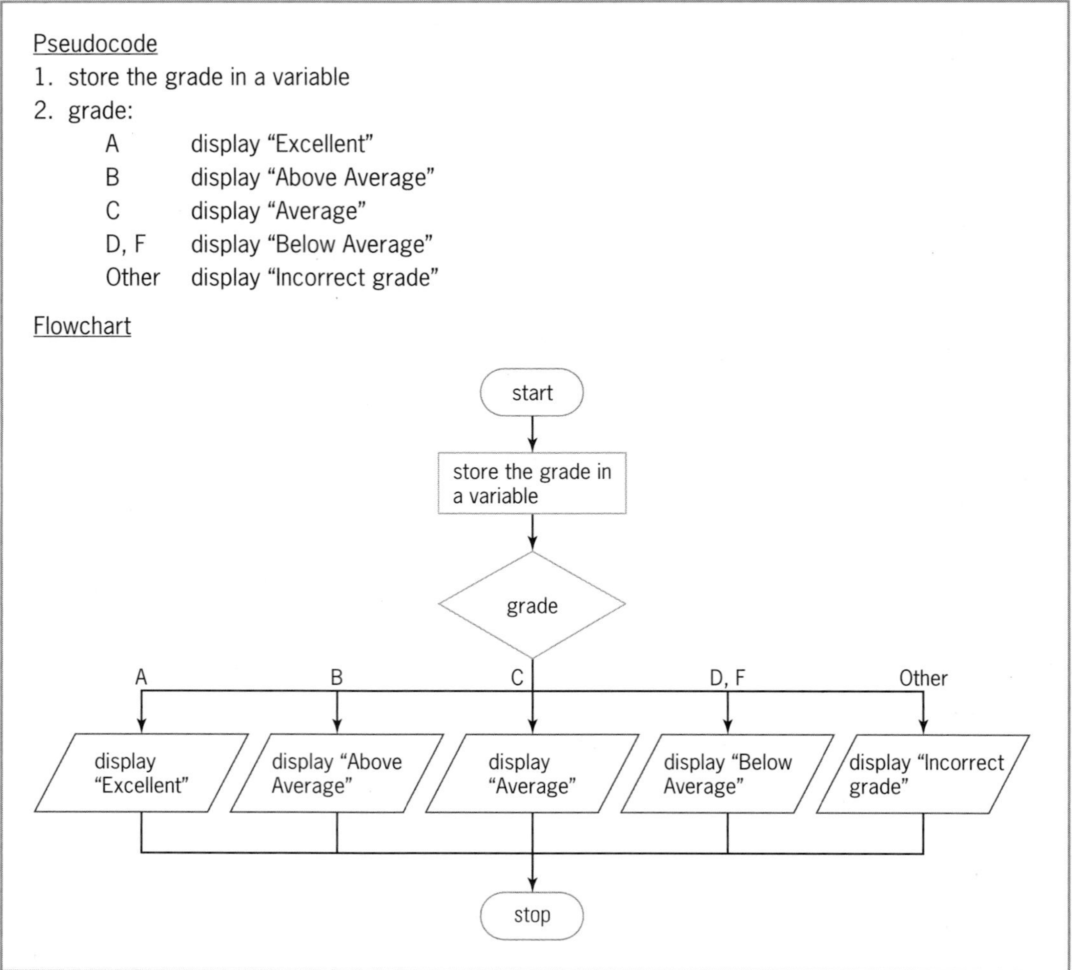

Figure 5-20 Pseudocode and flowchart showing a multiple-path selection structure

Recall that Visual Basic provides four forms of the selection structure: If, If/Else, If/ElseIf/Else, and Case. You learned about the If and If/Else forms in Chapter 4.

In most cases, you code a multiple-path selection structure using either the If/ElseIf/Else form of the selection structure or the Case form. You will learn about the If/ElseIf/Else form first.

The If/ElseIf/Else Form of the Selection Structure

Figure 5-21 shows two versions of the Visual Basic code for a multiple-path selection structure that displays a message based on a letter grade. The first version uses nested If/Else forms of the selection structure, while the second version uses the If/ElseIf/Else form. Although you can write the selection structure using either version of the code, the **If/ElseIf/Else selection structure** provides a much more convenient way of writing a multiple-path selection structure.

Version 1—using nested If/Else forms of the selection structure

```
If strGrade = "A" Then
   lblMsg.Text = "Excellent"
Else
   If strGrade = "B" Then
      lblMsg.Text = "Above Average"
   Else
      If strGrade = "C" Then
         lblMsg.Text = "Average"
      Else
         If strGrade = "D" OrElse strGrade = "F" Then
            lblMsg.Text = "Below Average"
         Else
            lblMsg.Text = "Incorrect grade"
         End If
      End If
   End If
End If
```

you need 4 End If clauses to mark the end of the entire If/Else selection structure

Version 2—using an If/ElseIf/Else form of the selection structure

```
If strGrade = "A" Then
   lblMsg.Text = "Excellent"
ElseIf strGrade = "B" Then
   lblMsg.Text = "Above Average"
ElseIf strGrade = "C" Then
   lblMsg.Text = "Average"
ElseIf strGrade = "D" OrElse strGrade = "F" Then
   lblMsg.Text = "Below Average"
Else
   lblMsg.Text = "Incorrect grade"
End If
```

you need only 1 End If clause to mark the end of the If/ElseIf/Else selection structure

Figure 5-21 Two versions of the code for the multiple-path selection structure

To code and then test the Grade application:

1. Open the **Grade Solution** (**Grade Solution.sln**) file, which is contained in the VB2008\Chap05\Grade Solution-If folder. If necessary, open the designer window.
2. Open the Code Editor window. Replace the <your name> and <current date> text in the comments with your name and the current date.
3. In the btnDisplay control's Click event procedure, enter the code shown in Version 2 in Figure 5-21.
4. Close the Code Editor window. Save the solution, then start the application. Type the letter **a**, then press **Enter** to select the Display button. The button's Click event procedure displays the "Excellent" message. See Figure 5-22.

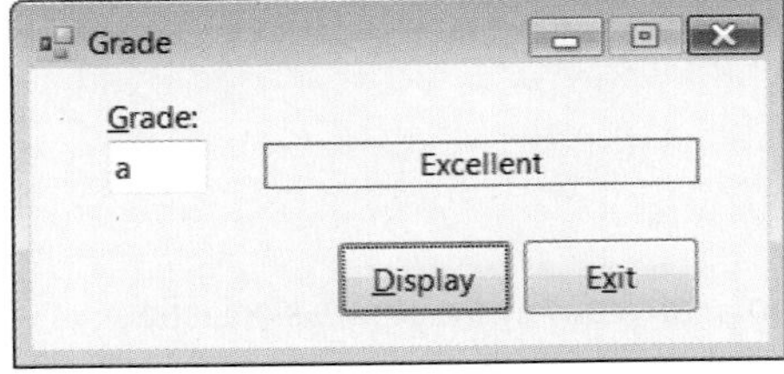

Figure 5-22 Excellent message shown in the interface

5. On your own, test the application using the following grades: **b**, **c**, **d**, **x**, and **f**. When you are finished testing, click the **Exit** button to end the application, then close the solution.

The Case Selection Structure

In situations where the selection structure has many paths from which to choose, it is often simpler and clearer to use the Case form of the selection structure rather than the If/ElseIf/Else form. You code the **Case selection structure** using the Select Case statement. Figure 5-23 shows the statement's syntax and includes an example of using the statement to display a message corresponding to a letter grade. The statement begins with the keywords `Select Case`, followed by a *selectorExpression*. The *selectorExpression* can contain any combination of variables, constants, functions, methods, operators, or properties. In the example in Figure 5-23, the *selectorExpression* is the `strGrade` variable. The Select Case statement ends with the End Select clause. Between the Select Case and End Select clauses are the individual Case clauses. Each Case clause represents a different path that the computer can follow. It is customary to indent each Case clause, as well as the instructions within each Case clause, as shown in the figure. You can have as many Case clauses as necessary in a Select Case statement. However, if the Select Case statement includes a Case Else clause, the Case Else clause must be the last clause in the statement. Each of the individual Case clauses, except the Case Else clause, must contain an *expressionList*, which can include one or more expressions. To include more than one expression in an *expressionList*, you separate each expression with a comma, as in the *expressionList* `Case "D", "F"`. The *selectorExpression* needs to match only one of the expressions listed in an *expressionList*. The data type of the expressions must be compatible with the data type of the *selectorExpression*. If the *selectorExpression* is numeric, the expressions in the Case clauses should be numeric. Likewise, if the *selectorExpression* is a string, the expressions should be strings. In the example in Figure 5-23, the *selectorExpression* (`strGrade`) is a string, and so are the expressions—"A", "B", "C", "D", and "F".

Select Case statement

Syntax

Select Case *selectorExpression*
  Case *expressionList1*
    instructions for the first Case
  [**Case** *expressionList2*
    instructions for the second Case]
  [**Case** *expressionListN*
    instructions for the Nth Case]
  [**Case Else**
    instructions for when the selectorExpression does not match any of the expressionLists]
End Select

Figure 5-23 Syntax and an example of the Select Case statement *(continues)*

(continued)

Select Case statement

Example

```
Select Case strGrade
   Case "A"
      lblMsg.Text = "Excellent"
   Case "B"
      lblMsg.Text = "Above Average"
   Case "C"
      lblMsg.Text = "Average"
   Case "D", "F"
      lblMsg.Text = "Below Average"
   Case Else
      lblMsg.Text = "Incorrect grade"
End Select
```

Figure 5-23 Syntax and an example of the Select Case statement

When processing the Select Case statement, the computer first compares the value of the *selectorExpression* with the values listed in *expressionList1*. If a match is found, the computer processes the instructions for the first Case, stopping when it reaches either another Case clause or the End Select clause; it then skips to the instruction following the End Select clause. For example, if the `strGrade` variable contains the letter A, the code in Figure 5-23 will assign the message "Excellent" to the lblMsg control before the Select Case statement ends. If a match is not found in *expressionList1*, the computer skips to the second Case clause, where it compares the *selectorExpression* with the values listed in *expressionList2*. If a match is found, the computer processes the instructions for the second Case clause and then skips to the instruction following the End Select clause. If a match is not found, the computer skips to the third Case clause, and so on. If a Case clause contains more than one value, as does the `Case "D", "F"` clause, the *selectorExpression* needs to match only one of the values. As a result, the code in Figure 5-23 will assign the message "Below Average" when the `strGrade` variable contains either the letter D or the letter F. If the *selectorExpression* does not match any of the values listed in any of the *expressionLists*, the computer processes the instructions listed in the Case Else clause (if there is one), and then skips to the instruction following the End Select clause. Keep in mind that if the *selectorExpression* matches a value in more than one Case clause, only the instructions in the first match are processed.

To code and then test the Grade application:

1. Open the **Grade Solution** (**Grade Solution.sln**) file, which is contained in the VB2008\Chap05\Grade Solution-Case folder. If necessary, open the designer window.
2. Open the Code Editor window. Replace the <your name> and <current date> text in the comments with your name and the current date.
3. In the btnDisplay control's Click event procedure, enter the code shown in Figure 5-23.
4. Close the Code Editor window. Save the solution, then start the application. Type the letter **a**, then press **Enter** to select the Display button. The button's Click event procedure displays the "Excellent" message, as shown earlier in Figure 5-22.

5. On your own, test the application using the following grades: **b**, **c**, **d**, **x**, and **f**. When you are finished testing, click the **Exit** button to end the application, then close the solution.

Specifying a Range of Values in an ExpressionList

If you neglect to type the `Is` keyword in an expression, the Code Editor types it in for you. In other words, if you enter `Case > 10`, the Code Editor will change the clause to `Case Is > 10`.

Be sure to always test your code thoroughly, because the computer will not display an error message when the value preceding `To` in a Case clause is greater than the value following `To`. Instead, the Select Case statement will not give the correct results.

You also can specify a range of values in an *expressionList*, such as the values 1 through 4 or values greater than 10. You do this using either the keyword `To` or the keyword `Is`. You use the `To` keyword when you know both the upper and lower bounds of the range, and you use the `Is` keyword when you know only one end of the range (either the upper or lower end). To illustrate this concept, the price of an item sold by ABC Corporation depends on the number of items ordered, as shown in Figure 5-24. The figure also shows the Select Case statement that will assign the appropriate price to the `intPrice` variable. According to the price chart, the price for 1 to 5 items is $25 each. Therefore, you could write the first Case clause as `Case 1, 2, 3, 4, 5`. However, the `To` keyword provides a more convenient way of writing that range of numbers, but you must follow this syntax: **Case** *smallest value in the range* **To** *largest value in the range*. In Figure 5-24's example, the expression `1 To 5` in the first Case clause specifies the range of numbers from 1 to 5, inclusive. The expression `6 To 10` in the second Case clause specifies the range of numbers from 6 to 10, inclusive. Notice that both Case clauses state both the lower (1 and 6) and upper (5 and 10) ends of each range. The third Case clause, `Case Is > 10`, contains the `Is` keyword rather than the `To` keyword. Recall that you use the `Is` keyword when you know only one end of the range of values. In this case you know only the lower end of the range, 10. You always use the `Is` keyword in combination with one of the following comparison operators: =, <, <=, >, >=, <>. The `Case Is > 10` clause specifies all numbers greater than the number 10. Because `intNumOrdered` is an Integer variable, you also can write this Case clause as `Case Is >= 11`. The Case Else clause in the example is processed only when the `intNumOrdered` variable contains a value that is not included in any of the previous Case clauses, such as the number 0.

ABC Corporation Price Chart

Number of items ordered	Price per item
1 – 5	$25
6 – 10	$23
More than 10	$20

Example

```
Select Case intNumOrdered
   Case 1 To 5
      intPrice = 25
   Case 6 To 10
      intPrice = 23
   Case Is > 10
      intPrice = 20
   Case Else
      intPrice = 0
End Select
```

Figure 5-24 Example of using the `To` and `Is` keywords in a Select Case statement

To code and then test the ABC Corporation application:

1. Open the **ABC Solution** (**ABC Solution.sln**) file, which is contained in the VB2008\Chap05\ABC Solution folder. If necessary, open the designer window.
2. Open the Code Editor window. Replace the <your name> and <current date> text in the comments with your name and the current date.
3. In the btnDisplay control's Click event procedure, enter the code shown in Figure 5-24.
4. Close the Code Editor window. Save the solution, then start the application. Enter **3** as the number ordered, then click the **Display Price** button. The button's Click event procedure displays $25.00 as the price per item, as shown in Figure 5-25.

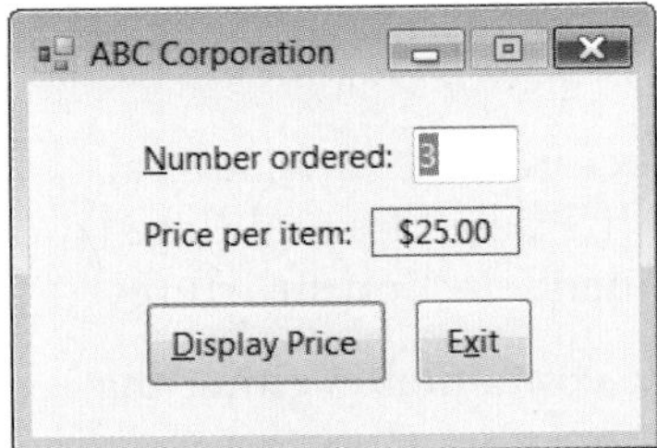

Figure 5-25 Price per item shown in the interface

5. On your own, test the application using 6, 11, and 0 as the number ordered. When you are finished, click the **Exit** button to end the application, then close the solution.

Lesson A Summary

- **To create a selection structure that evaluates both a primary and a secondary decision:**

  Place (or nest) the selection structure for the secondary decision within either the true path or false path of the selection structure for the primary decision.

- **To verify that an algorithm works correctly:**

  Desk-check (or hand-trace) the algorithm.

- **To code a multiple-path (or extended) selection structure:**

  Use either the If...Then...Else statement or the Select Case statement.

- **To specify a range of values in a Case clause contained in a Select Case statement:**

  Use the `To` keyword when you know both the upper and lower ends of the range. The syntax for using the `To` keyword is **Case** *smallest value in the range* **To** *largest value in the range*. Use the `Is` keyword when you know only one end of the range—either the upper end or the lower end. The `Is` keyword is used in combination with one of the following comparison operators: =, <, <=, >, >=, <>.

Lesson A Key Terms

Algorithm—a set of step-by-step instructions for accomplishing a task

Case selection structure—one of the four forms of the selection structure; provides a simple and clear way of writing a multiple-path selection structure

Desk-checking—the process of manually walking through each of the steps in an algorithm, using sample data; also called hand-tracing

Extended selection structures—another term for multiple-path selection structures

Hand-tracing—another term for desk-checking

If/ElseIf/Else selection structure—one of the four forms of the selection structure; provides a convenient way of writing a multiple-path selection structure

Multiple-path selection structures—selection structures that have several alternatives from which to choose; refers to the If/ElseIf/Else and Case forms of the selection structure; also called extended selection structures

Nested selection structure—a selection structure contained in either the true path or false path of another selection structure

Primary decision—when a selection structure is nested within another selection structure, the primary decision is made by the outer selection structure and determines whether the nested selection structure is processed

Secondary decision—when a selection structure is nested within another selection structure, the secondary decision is made by the inner selection structure

Lesson A Review Questions

Use the following code to answer Questions 1 through 3:

```
If intNumber <= 100 Then
   intNumber = intNumber * 2
ElseIf intNumber > 500 Then
   intNumber = intNumber * 3
End If
```

1. If the `intNumber` variable contains the number 90, what value will be in the `intNumber` variable after the preceding code is processed?
   a. 0
   b. 90
   c. 180
   d. 270

2. If the `intNumber` variable contains the number 1000, what value will be in the `intNumber` variable after the preceding code is processed?

   a. 0

   b. 1000

   c. 2000

   d. 3000

3. If the `intNumber` variable contains the number 200, what value will be in the `intNumber` variable after the preceding code is processed?

   a. 0

   b. 200

   c. 400

   d. 600

Use the following code to answer Questions 4 through 7:

```
If intId = 1 Then
   lblName.Text = "Janet"
ElseIf intId = 2 OrElse intId = 3 Then
   lblName.Text = "Mark"
ElseIf intId = 4 Then
   lblName.Text = "Jerry"
Else
   lblName.Text = "Sue"
End If
```

4. What will the preceding code display when the `intId` variable contains the number 2?

   a. Janet

   b. Jerry

   c. Mark

   d. Sue

5. What will the preceding code display when the `intId` variable contains the number 4?

   a. Janet

   b. Jerry

   c. Mark

   d. Sue

6. What will the preceding code display when the `intId` variable contains the number 3?
   a. Janet
   b. Jerry
   c. Mark
   d. Sue

7. What will the preceding code display when the `intId` variable contains the number 8?
   a. Janet
   b. Jerry
   c. Mark
   d. Sue

8. A nested selection structure can appear in ______________ of another selection structure.
   a. only the true path
   b. only the false path
   c. either the true path or false path

9. If the *selectorExpression* in a Select Case statement is a variable named `intCode`, which of the following Case clauses is valid?
   a. `Case Is > 7`
   b. `Case 3, 5`
   c. `Case 1 To 4`
   d. All of the above.

Use the following Select Case statement to answer Questions 10 through 12:

```
Select Case intId
   Case 1
      lblName.Text = "Janet"
   Case 2 To 4
      lblName.Text = "Mark"
   Case 5, 7
      lblName.Text = "Jerry"
   Case Else
      lblName.Text = "Sue"
End Select
```

10. What will the preceding Select Case statement display when the `intId` variable contains the number 2?

    a. Janet

    b. Mark

    c. Jerry

    d. Sue

11. What will the preceding Select Case statement display when the `intId` variable contains the number 3?

    a. Janet

    b. Mark

    c. Jerry

    d. Sue

12. What will the preceding Select Case statement display when the `intId` variable contains the number 6?

    a. Janet

    b. Mark

    c. Jerry

    d. Sue

13. A procedure needs to display the appropriate fee to charge a golfer. Club members are free. Non-members golfing on Monday through Thursday are charged $15. Non-members golfing on Friday through Sunday are charged $15. In this procedure, which is the primary decision and which is the secondary decision? Why?

14. List the three errors commonly made when writing selection structures. Which error makes the selection structure inefficient, but not incorrect?

15. Explain the meaning of the term "desk-checking."

Lesson A Exercises

INTRODUCTORY

1. Write the Visual Basic code for the algorithm shown in Figure 5-11 in this lesson. The salesperson's code and sales amount are entered in the txtCode and txtSales controls, respectively. Store the text box values and bonus amount in variables. Display the appropriate bonus amount in the lblMsg control.

INTRODUCTORY

2. Write the Visual Basic code that displays the message "Highest honors" when a student's test score is 90 or above. When the test score is 70 through 89, display the message "Good job". For all other test scores, display the message "Retake the test". Use the If/ElseIf/Else selection structure. The test score is stored in the `intScore` variable. Display the appropriate message in the lblMsg control.

INTRODUCTORY

3. Rewrite the code from Exercise 2 using the Select Case statement.

INTRODUCTORY

4. Write the Visual Basic code that compares the contents of the `intQuantity` variable with the number 10. When the variable contains a number that is equal to 10, display the string "Equal" in the lblMsg control. When the variable contains a number that is greater than 10, display the string "Over 10". When the variable contains a number that is less than 10, display the string "Not over 10". Use the If/ElseIf/Else selection structure.

INTRODUCTORY

5. Rewrite the code from Exercise 4 using the Select Case statement.

INTRODUCTORY

6. Write the Visual Basic code that corresponds to the flowchart shown in Figure 5-26. Store the salesperson's code, which is entered in the txtCode control, in the `intCode` variable. Store the sales amount, which is entered in the txtSales control, in the `decSales` variable. Display the result of the calculation, or the error message, in the lblMsg control. Use the Select Case statement.

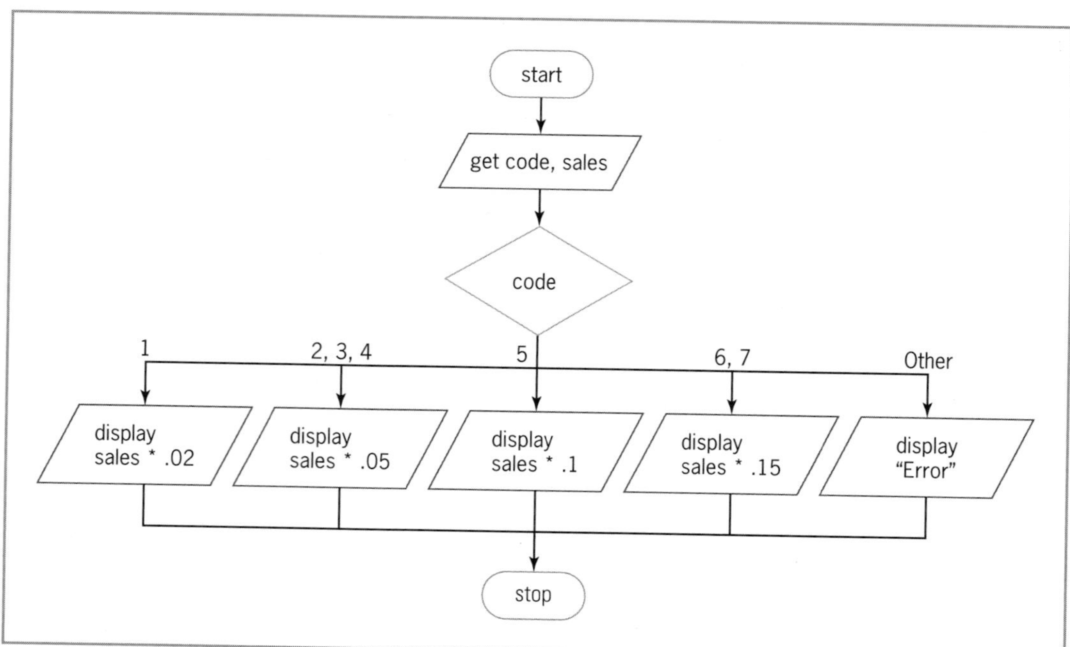

Figure 5-26 Flowchart for Exercises 6 and 7

INTRODUCTORY

7. Code the flowchart shown in Figure 5-26 using the If/ElseIf/Else form of the selection structure.

INTRODUCTORY

8. Open the Animal Solution (Animal Solution.sln) file, which is contained in the VB2008\Chap05\Animal Solution folder. Open the designer window, if necessary, then open the Code Editor window.

   a. Complete the If...Then...Else button's Click event procedure by writing an If...Then...Else statement that displays the string "Dog" when the `intAnimal` variable contains the number 1. Display the string "Cat" when the variable contains the number 2. Display the string "Bird" when the variable contains anything other than the number 1 or the number 2. Display the appropriate string in the lblMsg control.

   b. Save the solution, then start the application. Test the If...Then...Else button's code three times, using the numbers 1, 2, and 5. Stop the application.

   c. Complete the Select Case button's Click event procedure by writing a Select Case statement that displays the string "Dog" when the `strAnimal` variable contains either the letter "D" or the letter "d". Display the string "Cat" when the variable contains either the letter "C" or the letter "c". Display the string "Bird" when the variable contains anything other than the letters "D", "d", "C", or "c". Display the appropriate string in the lblMsg control.

   d. Save the solution, then start the application. Test the Select Case button's code three times, using the letters D, c, and x. Stop the application. Close the Code Editor window, then close the solution.

INTERMEDIATE

9. A procedure needs to display a shipping charge based on the state name stored in the `strState` variable. The state name is stored using uppercase letters. Write a Select Case statement that assigns the shipping charge to the `dblShipping` variable. The shipping charge for Hawaii is $25. The shipping charge for Oregon is $30. The shipping charge for California is $32.50. Display an appropriate message in the lblMsg control when the `strState` variable contains a value that is not one of these three states; also assign the number 0 to the `dblShipping` variable. Display the shipping charge in the lblShipping control.

INTERMEDIATE

10. Rewrite the code from Exercise 9 using an If...Then...Else statement.

INTERMEDIATE

11. The price of a concert ticket depends on the seat location stored in the `strSeat` variable. The seat location is stored using uppercase letters. Write a Select Case statement that displays the price in the lblPrice control. Box seats are $75. Pavilion seats are $30. Lawn seats are $21. Display an appropriate message in the lblPrice control when the `strSeat` variable contains a value that is not one of these three seat locations.

INTERMEDIATE

12. Rewrite the code from Exercise 11 using an If...Then...Else statement.

INTERMEDIATE

13. Open the Month Solution (Month Solution.sln) file, which is contained in the VB2008\Chap05\Month Solution folder. Open the designer window, if necessary, then open the Code Editor window.

    a. Complete the If...Then...Else button's Click event procedure by writing an If...Then...Else statement that displays the name of the month corresponding to the number entered by the user. For example, if the user enters the number 1, the procedure should display the string "January". If the user enters an invalid number (one that is not in the range 1 through 12), display an appropriate message. Display the appropriate month name or message in the lblMsg control.

    b. Save the solution, then start the application. Test the If...Then... Else button's code three times, using the numbers 3, 7, and 20. Stop the application.

    c. Now assume that the user will enter the first three characters of the month's name (rather than the month number) in the text box. Complete the Select Case button's Click event procedure by writing a Select Case statement that displays the name of the month corresponding to the characters entered by the user. For example, if the user enters the three characters "Jan" (in any case), the procedure should display the string "January". If the user enters "Jun", the procedure should display "June". If the three characters entered by the user do not match any of the expressions in the Case clauses, display an appropriate message. Display the appropriate month name or message in the lblMsg control.

    d. Save the solution, then start the application. Test the Select Case button's code three times, using the following data: jun, dec, xyz. Stop the application. Close the Code Editor window, then close the solution.

INTERMEDIATE

14. Open the Bonus Solution (Bonus Solution.sln) file, which is contained in the VB2008\Chap05\Bonus Solution folder. If necessary, open the designer window. Open the Code Editor window. Complete the Calculate button's Click event procedure by writing an If...Then...Else statement that assigns the number 25 to the `intBonus` variable when the user enters a sales amount that is greater than or equal to $100, but less than or equal to $250. When the user enters a sales amount that is greater than $250, assign the number 50 to the variable. When the user enters a sales amount that is less than $100, assign the number 0 as the bonus. Save the solution, then start the application. Test the Calculate button's code three times, using sales amounts of 100, 300, and 40. Stop the application. Close the Code Editor window, then close the solution.

ADVANCED

15. Open the Seminar Solution (Seminar Solution.sln) file, which is contained in the VB2008\Chap05\Seminar Solution folder. If necessary, open the designer window. Computer Workshop offers programming seminars to companies. The price per person depends on the number of people the company registers. The first 4 people registered are charged $100 per person. Registrants 5 through 10 are charged $80 per person. Registrants over 10 are charged $60 per person. For example, if the company registers 7 people, then the total amount owed is $640. The $640 is calculated by first multiplying 4 by 100, giving 400. You then multiply 3 by 80, giving 240. You then add the 400 to the 240, giving 640. Display the total amount owed in the lblTotal control. Use the Select Case statement to complete the Calculate button's Click event procedure. Save the solution, then start and test the application. Stop the application. Close the Code Editor window, then close the solution.

LESSON B

After studying Lesson B, you should be able to:

- Include a group of radio buttons in an interface
- Designate a default radio button
- Include a check box in an interface
- Create and call an independent Sub procedure
- Generate random numbers

Creating the Math Practice Application

Recall that Susan Chen, the principal of a local primary school, wants an application that the first and second grade students can use to practice both adding and subtracting numbers. The application should display the math problem on the screen, and then allow the student to enter the answer and verify that the answer is correct. The application should give the student as many chances as necessary to answer the problem correctly. The math problems for the first grade students should use numbers from 1 through 10 only. The math problems for the second grade students should use numbers from 10 through 99. Because the students have not learned about negative numbers yet, the subtraction problems should never ask them to subtract a larger number from a smaller one. Recall that Ms. Chen wants the application to keep track of the number of correct and incorrect responses made by the student, and she wants the ability to control the display of that information.

To open the partially completed Math Practice application:

1. If necessary, start Visual Studio 2008 or Visual Basic 2008 Express Edition. Close the Start Page window.
2. Open the **Math Solution** (**Math Solution.sln**) file, which is contained in the VB2008\Chap05\Math Solution folder. If necessary, open the designer window. The interface contains one text box, two buttons, three radio buttons, seven picture boxes, four group boxes, and various labels. Missing from the interface are the Subtraction radio button and the Display summary check box.

Adding a Radio Button to the Interface

A radio button is created using the RadioButton tool in the toolbox and it allows you to limit the user to only one choice in a group of two or more related but mutually exclusive choices. The radio buttons in the Math Practice application will limit the user to one grade level selection (either Grade 1 or Grade 2) and one mathematical operation selection (either Addition or Subtraction). Each radio button in an interface should be labeled so that the user knows its purpose. You enter the label using sentence capitalization in the radio button's Text property. Each radio button also should have a unique access key, which allows the user to select the button using the keyboard. In the next set of steps, you will add the missing Subtraction radio button to the interface.

To add a radio button to the interface:

1. Click the **RadioButton** tool in the toolbox, then drag the mouse pointer into the Operation group box, placing it below the Addition radio button. Release the mouse button. The RadioButton1 control appears in the group box.
2. The three-character ID for a radio button is rad. Change the RadioButton1 control's name to **radSubtraction**, then change its Text property to **&Subtraction**. Position the radio button as shown in Figure 5-27.

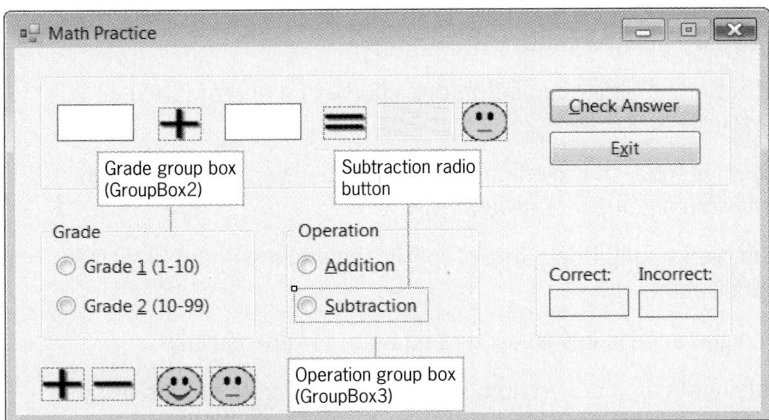

Figure 5-27 Subtraction radio button added to the Operation group box

Two groups of radio buttons appear in the Math Practice interface: one group contains the two grade radio buttons and the other contains the two operation radio buttons. To include two groups of radio buttons in an interface, at least one of the groups must be placed within a container, such as a group box. Otherwise, the radio buttons are considered to be in the same group and only one can be selected at any one time. In this case, the radio buttons pertaining to the grade choice are contained in the Grade group box, and the radio buttons pertaining to the operation choice are contained in the Operation group box. Placing each group of radio buttons in a separate group box allows the user to select one button from each group. Keep in mind that the minimum number of radio buttons in a group is two, because the only way to deselect a radio button is to select another radio button. The recommended maximum number of radio buttons in a group is seven. It is customary in Windows applications to have one of the radio buttons in each group already selected when the user interface first appears. The selected button is called the default radio button and is either the radio button that represents the user's most likely choice or the first radio button in the group. You designate the default radio button by setting the button's Checked property to the Boolean value True. In the Math Practice application, you will make the first radio button in each group the default radio button.

To designate a default radio button in each group:

1. Click the **Grade 1 (1-10)** radio button, then set its **Checked** property to **True**. When you set the Checked property to True in the Properties window, a colored dot appears inside the button's circle to indicate that the button is selected.

2. Click the **Addition** radio button, then set its **Checked** property to **True**. A colored dot appears inside the circle in the Addition radio button.

GUI DESIGN TIP Radio Button Standards

- Use radio buttons to limit the user to one choice in a group of related but mutually exclusive choices.
- The minimum number of radio buttons in a group is two and the recommended maximum number is seven.
- The label in the radio button's Text property should be entered using sentence capitalization.
- Assign a unique access key to each radio button in an interface.
- Use a container (such as a group box) to create separate groups of radio buttons. Only one button in each group can be selected at any one time.
- Designate a default radio button in each group of radio buttons.

Adding a Check Box to the Interface

You add a check box to an interface using the CheckBox tool in the toolbox. Like radio buttons, check boxes can be either selected or deselected. However, unlike radio buttons, check boxes allow the user to select any number of choices from a group of one or more independent and nonexclusive choices. In other words, whereas only one button in a group of radio buttons can be selected at any one time, any number of check boxes on a form can be selected at the same time. Each check box in an interface should be labeled to make its purpose obvious. You enter the label using sentence capitalization in the check box's Text property. Each check box also should have a unique access key.

To add a check box to the interface:

1. Click the **CheckBox** tool in the toolbox, then drag the mouse pointer onto the form, positioning it immediately above the grpSummary control. (See Figure 5-28 for the location of the grpSummary control.) Release the mouse button. The CheckBox1 control appears on the form.
2. The three-character ID for a check box is chk. Change the CheckBox1 control's name to **chkSummary**, then change its Text property to **&Display summary**. Position the check box as shown in Figure 5-28.

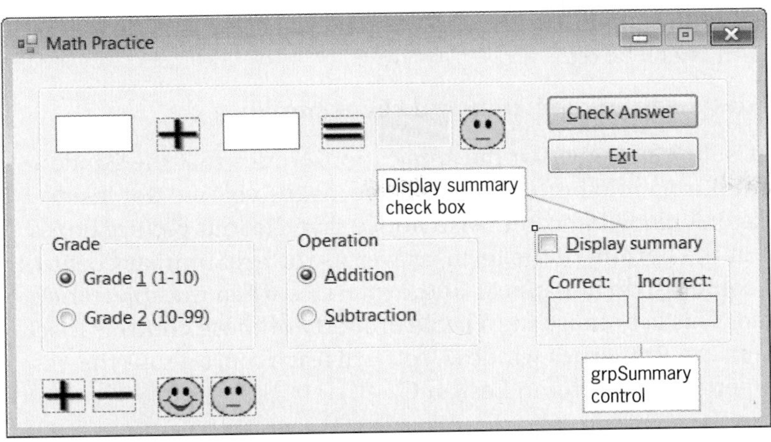

Figure 5-28 Display summary check box added to the interface

GUI DESIGN TIP Check Box Standards

- Use check boxes to allow the user to select any number of choices from a group of one or more independent and nonexclusive choices.
- The label in the check box's Text property should be entered using sentence capitalization.
- Assign a unique access key to each check box in an interface.

Now that you have completed the user interface, you can lock the controls in place and then set each control's TabIndex property.

To lock the controls and then set each control's TabIndex property:

1. Right-click the **form**, then click **Lock Controls** on the context menu.
2. Click **View** on the menu bar, then click **Tab Order**. Use Figure 5-29 to set the TabIndex values for the controls on the form. (As you learned in Chapter 2, picture boxes do not have a TabIndex property.) When you are finished, press **Esc** to remove the TabIndex boxes from the form.

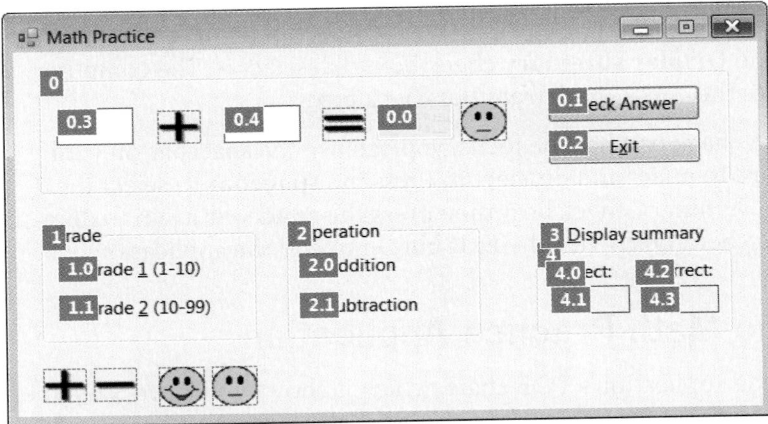

Figure 5-29 Correct TabIndex values

Next, you will start the application to observe how you select and deselect radio buttons and check boxes.

To select and deselect radio buttons and check boxes:

1. Save the solution, then start the application. Notice that the Grade 1 and Addition radio buttons are selected, as the colored dot inside each button's circle indicates. Also notice that the four picture boxes located at the bottom of the form, as well as the grpSummary control and its contents, do not appear in the interface when the application is started. This is because the Visible property of those controls is set to False in the Properties window. You will learn more about the Visible property of a control in Lesson C.
2. You can select a different radio button by clicking it. You can click either the circle or the text that appears inside the radio button. Click the **Subtraction** radio button. The computer selects the Subtraction radio button as it deselects the Addition radio button. This is because both radio buttons belong to the same group and only one radio button in a group can be selected at any one time.
3. Click the **Grade 2 (10-99)** radio button. The computer selects the Grade 2 (10-99) radio button as it deselects the Grade 1 (1-10) radio button. Here again, the Grade 1 (1-10) and Grade 2 (10-99) radio buttons belong to the same group, so selecting one deselects the other.
4. After selecting a radio button in a group, you then can use the ↑ and ↓ keys on your keyboard to select another radio button in the group. Press the ↑ key to select the Grade 1 (1-10) radio button, then press the ↓ key to select the Grade 2 (10-99) radio button.
5. Press **Tab**. Notice that the focus moves to the Subtraction radio button rather than to the Addition radio button. In a group of radio buttons, only the selected radio button receives the focus when the user tabs to the group.
6. You can select a check box by clicking either the square or the text that appears inside the control. Click the **Display summary** check box to select it. A check mark appears inside the check box to indicate that the check box is selected.
7. Click the **Display summary** check box to deselect it. The computer removes the check mark from the check box.
8. When a check box has the focus, you can use the spacebar on your keyboard to select and deselect it. Press the **spacebar** to select the Display summary check box, then press the **spacebar** again to deselect the check box. Click the **Exit** button to end the application.

Coding the Math Practice Application

According to the application's TOE chart, which is shown in Figure 5-30, the Click event procedures for seven of the controls, as well as the Load event procedure for the form, need to be coded. In this lesson, you code all but the

Click event procedures for the btnExit control (which already has been coded for you) and the btnCheckAnswer and chkSummary controls (which you code in Lesson C).

Task	Object	Event
End the application	btnExit	Click
Display an addition problem	frmMain	Load
1. Display the plus sign in picOperator 2. Generate and display two random integers in lblNum1 and lblNum2	radAddition	Click
1. Display the minus sign in picOperator 2. Generate and display two random integers in lblNum1 and lblNum2	radSubtraction	Click
Generate and display two random integers in lblNum1 and lblNum2	radGrade1, radGrade2	Click
Show or hide the grpSummary control	chkSummary	Click
1. Calculate the correct answer to the math problem 2. Compare the correct answer to the user's answer 3. Display either the happy face or neutral face in picFace 4. If the user's answer is correct, generate and display two random integers in lblNum1 and lblNum2 5. If the user's answer is incorrect, display the "Try Again!" message 6. Add 1 to the number of either correct or incorrect responses 7. Display the number of correct and incorrect responses in lblCorrect and lblIncorrect, respectively	btnCheckAnswer	Click
Display the number of correct responses (from btnCheckAnswer)	lblCorrect	None
Display the number of incorrect responses (from btnCheckAnswer)	lblIncorrect	None
Display two random integers (from radGrade1, radGrade2, radAddition, radSubtraction, btnCheckAnswer)	lblNum1, lblNum2	None
Display either the plus sign or the minus sign (from radAddition and radSubtraction)	picOperator	None
Display either the happy face or neutral face (from btnCheckAnswer)	picFace	None
Get and display the user's answer	txtAnswer	None

Figure 5-30 TOE chart for the Math Practice application

Notice that the task of generating and displaying two random integers in the lblNum1 and lblNum2 controls appears in the Task column for five of the controls. The task is listed as Step 2 for the radAddition and radSubtraction controls. It is listed as the only task for the radGrade1 and radGrade2 controls, and it also appears in Step 4 for the btnCheckAnswer control. Rather than entering the appropriate code in the Click event procedures for each of the five controls, you will enter the code in an independent Sub procedure. You then will have the five Click event procedures call (or invoke) the Sub procedure.

Creating an Independent Sub Procedure

There are two types of Sub procedures in Visual Basic: event procedures and independent Sub procedures. The procedures coded in previous chapters were event procedures. An event procedure is a Sub procedure that is associated with a specific object and event, such as a button's Click event or a text box's TextChanged event. Recall that the computer automatically processes an event procedure's code when the event occurs. An **independent Sub procedure**, on the other hand, is a procedure that is independent of any object and event. An independent Sub procedure is processed only when called (invoked) from code. Programmers use independent Sub procedures for two reasons. First, they allow the programmer to avoid duplicating code in different parts of a program. If different parts of a program need to perform the same task, it is more efficient to enter the appropriate code once, in a procedure, and then call the procedure to perform the task when needed. Second, procedures allow large and complex applications, which typically are written by a team of programmers, to be broken into small and manageable tasks. Each member of the team is assigned one or more tasks to code as a procedure. When each programmer completes his or her procedure, all of the procedures are gathered together into one application.

Using Pascal case, you capitalize the first letter in the procedure name and the first letter of each subsequent word in the name.

Figure 5-31 shows the syntax you use to create an independent Sub procedure, as well as the steps you follow to enter an independent Sub procedure in the Code Editor window. As do all procedures, independent Sub procedures have both a procedure header and procedure footer. In most cases, the procedure header begins with the `Private` keyword, which indicates that the procedure can be used only within the current Code Editor window. Following the `Private` keyword is the `Sub` keyword, which identifies the procedure as a Sub procedure. After the `Sub` keyword is the procedure name. The rules for naming an independent Sub procedure are the same as those for naming variables; however, procedure names typically are entered using Pascal case. You should select a descriptive name for the Sub procedure. The name should indicate the task the procedure performs. It is a common practice to begin the name with a verb. For example, a good name for a Sub procedure that generates and displays two random integers is GenerateAndDisplayIntegers. Following the procedure name in the procedure header is a set of parentheses that contains an optional *parameterList*. The *parameterList* lists the data type and name of one or more memory locations, called parameters. As you learned in Chapter 4, parameters store the information passed to the procedure when it is invoked. If the procedure does not require any information to be passed to it, an empty set of parentheses follows the procedure name in the procedure header. You will learn more about parameters in Chapter 7. The procedure footer for a Sub procedure is always End Sub. Between the procedure header and procedure footer, you enter the instructions to be processed when the procedure is invoked. Some programmers enter independent Sub procedures above the first event procedure in the Code Editor window, while others enter them below the last event procedure. Still others enter them either immediately above or below the procedure from which they are invoked.

Independent Sub procedure

Syntax
Private Sub *procedureName***(**[*parameterList*]**)**
  [*statements*]
End Sub

Steps
1. Click a blank line in the Code Editor window. The blank line can be anywhere between the Public Class and End Class lines. However, it must be outside any other Sub or Function procedure.
2. Type the Sub procedure header, then press Enter. The Code Editor automatically enters the End Sub line for you.

Figure 5-31 Syntax and steps for creating an independent Sub procedure

To create the GenerateAndDisplayIntegers procedure:

1. Open the Code Editor window. The Exit button's Click event procedure already contains the appropriate code. Replace the <your name> and <current date> text in the comments with your name and the current date.
2. Click the **blank line** above the End Class clause, then press **Enter** to insert another blank line. In the new blank line, type **Private Sub GenerateAndDisplayIntegers()** and press **Enter**.

Figure 5-32 shows the pseudocode for the GenerateAndDisplayIntegers procedure.

GenerateAndDisplayIntegers procedure
1. if the Grade 1 radio button is selected
      generate two random integers from 1 through 10
   else
      generate two random integers from 10 through 99
   end if
2. if the Subtraction radio button is selected and the first random integer is less than the second random integer
      swap the two random integers
   end if
3. display the random integers in the lblNum1 and lblNum2 controls

Figure 5-32 Pseudocode for the GenerateAndDisplayIntegers procedure

To begin coding the GenerateAndDisplayIntegers procedure:

1. Type **' generates and displays two random integers** and press **Enter** twice.
2. Recall that before you begin coding a procedure, you first study the procedure's pseudocode to determine the variables and named constants (if any) the procedure will use. In this case, the procedure will

not use any named constants. However, it will use two Integer variables to store the two random integers it generates. Enter the following two Dim statements. Press **Enter** twice after typing the second Dim statement.

Dim intRandom1 As Integer
Dim intRandom2 As Integer

You also can write the condition in Step 3 as `radGrade1.Checked = True`.

3. Step 1 in the pseudocode is to determine whether the Grade 1 radio button is selected in the interface. You can use the radio button's Checked property to make that determination. The Checked property will contain the Boolean value True when the radio button is selected; otherwise, it will contain the Boolean value False. Type **' generate random integers** and press **Enter**, then type **if radGrade1.Checked Then** and press **Enter**.

If the Grade 1 radio button is selected, then the GenerateAndDisplayIntegers procedure should generate two random integers from 1 through 10.

Generating Random Integers

In Exercise 5 at the end of this lesson, you learn how to use the Random.NextDouble method to generate a random number containing a decimal place.

Visual Basic provides a **pseudo-random number generator**, which is a device that produces a sequence of numbers that meet certain statistical requirements for randomness. Pseudo-random numbers are chosen with equal probability from a finite set of numbers. The chosen numbers are not completely random, because a definite mathematical algorithm is used to select them, but they are sufficiently random for practical purposes. Figure 5-33 shows the syntax you use to generate random integers, and it includes examples of using the syntax. As the figure indicates, you first create a Random object to represent the pseudo-random number generator. You create the Random object by declaring it in a Dim statement. You enter the Dim statement in the procedure that will use the number generator. After the Random object is created, you can use the object's Random.Next method to generate random integers. In the method's syntax, *randomObjectName* is the name of the Random object. The *minValue* and *maxValue* arguments in the syntax must be integers, and *minValue* must be less than *maxValue*. The **Random.Next method** returns an integer that is greater than or equal to *minValue*, but less than *maxValue*.

Generating random integers

Syntax
Dim *randomObjectName* **As New Random**
randomObjectName.**Next(***minValue*, *maxValue***)**

Example 1
```
Dim randomGenerator As New Random
intNumber = randomGenerator.Next(1, 51)
```
The Dim statement creates a Random object named `randomGenerator`. The assignment statement assigns (to the `intNumber` variable) a random integer that is greater than or equal to 1, but less than 51.

Figure 5-33 Syntax and examples of generating random integers *(continues)*

(continued)

Generating random integers

Example 2
```
Dim randomGenerator As New Random
intNumber = randomGenerator.Next(-10, 0)
```
The Dim statement creates a Random object named `randomGenerator`. The assignment statement assigns (to the `intNumber` variable) a random integer that is greater than or equal to –10, but less than 0.

Figure 5-33 Syntax and examples of generating random integers

To continue coding the GenerateAndDisplayIntegers procedure:

1. Click the **blank line** below the second Dim statement, then type **Dim randomGenerator As New Random** and press **Enter**.
2. If the Grade 1 radio button is selected, the GenerateAndDisplay-Integers procedure should generate two random integers from 1 through 10. To generate integers within that range, you use the number 1 as the *minValue* and the number 11 as the *maxValue.* Click the **blank line** above the End If clause, then enter the following two assignment statements.

   intRandom1 = randomGenerator.Next(1, 11)
   intRandom2 = randomGenerator.Next(1, 11)

3. If the Grade 1 radio button is not selected, then the Grade 2 radio button must be selected. In that case, the procedure should generate two integers from 10 through 99. Type **Else** and press **Enter**, then enter the additional code shown in Figure 5-34. Also position the insertion point as shown in the figure.

```
Private Sub GenerateAndDisplayIntegers()
    ' generates and displays two random integers

    Dim intRandom1 As Integer
    Dim intRandom2 As Integer
    Dim randomGenerator As New Random

    ' generate random integers
    If radGrade1.Checked Then
        intRandom1 = randomGenerator.Next(1, 11)
        intRandom2 = randomGenerator.Next(1, 11)
    Else
        intRandom1 = randomGenerator.Next(10, 100)
        intRandom2 = randomGenerator.Next(10, 100)
    End If

End Sub
```


Figure 5-34 Random number generation code entered in the procedure

4. Step 2 in the pseudocode is to determine whether the Subtraction radio button is selected and whether the first random integer is less than the second random integer. If both conditions are true, then the procedure should swap (interchange) the two random integers, because no subtraction problem should result in a negative number. Enter the additional code shown in Figure 5-35, then position the insertion point as shown in the figure.

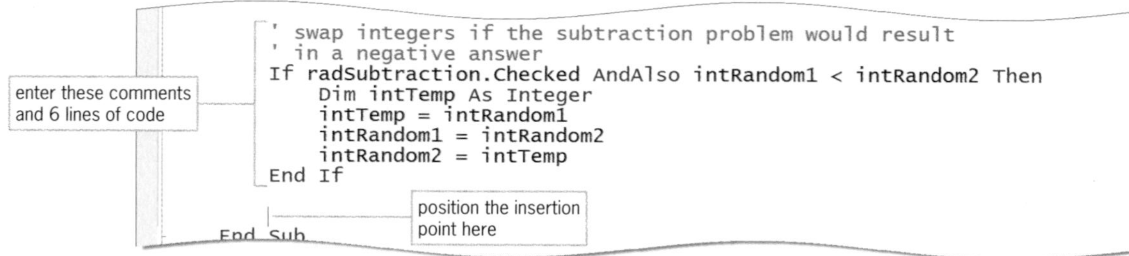

Figure 5-35 Additional code entered in the procedure

5. The last step in the pseudocode is to display the random integers in the lblNum1 and lblNum2 controls. Enter the following comment and assignment statements, then save the solution.

   ' display integers
   lblNum1.Text = Convert.ToString(intRandom1)
   lblNum2.Text = Convert.ToString(intRandom2)

Coding the Grade Radio Buttons' Click Event Procedures

According to the TOE chart shown earlier in Figure 5-30, the radGrade1 and radGrade2 controls should generate and display two random integers when clicked. The code to generate and display the random integers is entered in the GenerateAndDisplayIntegers procedure. The radio buttons can use the procedure's code by invoking the procedure. You can invoke an independent Sub procedure using the **Call statement**, whose syntax is **Call** *procedureName*([*argumentList*]). In the syntax, *procedureName* is the name of the procedure you are calling (invoking), and *argumentList* (which is optional) is a comma-separated list of arguments you want passed to the procedure. If you have no information to pass to the procedure that you are calling, as is the case in the GenerateAndDisplayIntegers procedure, you include an empty set of parentheses after the *procedureName* in the Call statement. (You will learn how to pass information to a procedure in Chapter 7.) Figure 5-36 shows two examples of including the `Call GenerateAndDisplayIntegers()` statement in the Click event procedures for the radGrade1 and radGrade2 controls. In Example 1, the Call statement is entered in both Click event procedures. In Example 2, the Call statement is entered in a procedure named ProcessGradeRadioButtons. According to its Handles section, the ProcessGradeRadioButtons procedure is processed when the Click event occurs for either the radGrade1 or radGrade2 control. In this case, neither example is better than the other; both simply represent different ways of performing the same task.

Examples of calling the GenerateAndDisplayIntegers procedure

Example 1
```
Private Sub radGrade1_Click(ByVal sender As Object, _
   ByVal e As System.EventArgs) Handles radGrade1.Click
   Call GenerateAndDisplayIntegers()
End Sub

Private Sub radGrade2_Click(ByVal sender As Object, _
   ByVal e As System.EventArgs) Handles radGrade2.Click
   Call GenerateAndDisplayIntegers()
End Sub
```

Example 2
```
Private Sub ProcessGradeRadioButtons(ByVal sender As Object, _
   ByVal e As System.EventArgs) _
      Handles radGrade1.Click, radGrade2.Click
   Call GenerateAndDisplayIntegers()
End Sub
```

Figure 5-36 Examples of including the Call statement in the Click event procedures for the Grade radio buttons

The word "Call" is optional when invoking a Sub procedure. You can call the GenerateAndDisplayIntegers procedure using either the statement `Call GenerateAndDisplayIntegers()` or the statement `GenerateAndDisplayIntegers()`.

To call the GenerateAndDisplayIntegers procedure when either Grade radio button is clicked, and then test the code:

1. Open the code template for the radGrade1 control's Click event procedure. Change `radGrade1_Click` in the procedure header to **ProcessGradeRadioButtons**.
2. Modify the procedure as shown in Figure 5-37. Be sure to include a space before each line continuation character.

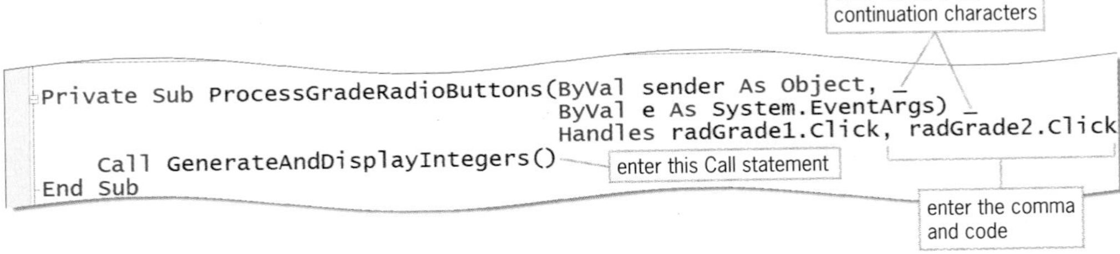

Figure 5-37 Completed ProcessGradeRadioButtons procedure

When the user clicks either Grade radio button, the computer processes the Call statement contained in the ProcessGradeRadioButtons procedure. When the Call statement is processed, the computer leaves the Process-GradeRadioButtons procedure, temporarily, to process the instructions contained in the GenerateAndDisplayIntegers procedure. When the Generate-AndDisplayIntegers procedure ends, the computer returns to the line below the Call statement in the ProcessGradeRadioButtons procedure; that line is the End Sub clause, which ends the ProcessGradeRadioButtons procedure. In the next set of steps, you will test the code you have entered so far to verify that it is working correctly.

To test the code:

1. Save the solution, then start the application. Click the **Grade 2 (10-99)** radio button. Two random integers from 10 through 99 appear in the interface, as shown in Figure 5-38. Your random integers might be different from the ones shown in the figure.

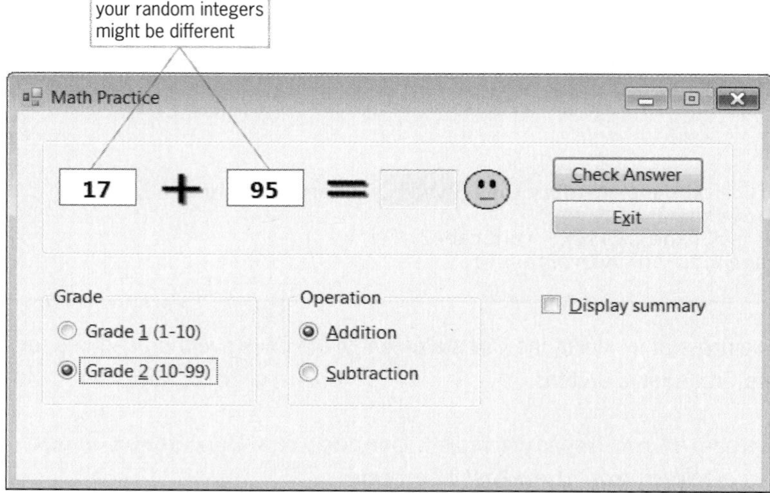

Figure 5-38 Random integers shown in the interface

2. Click the **Grade 1 (1-10)** radio button. Two random integers from 1 through 10 appear in the interface. Click the **Exit** button.

Coding the Operation Radio Buttons' Click Event Procedures

According to the TOE chart shown earlier in Figure 5-30, the Click event procedures for both Operation radio buttons should display the appropriate mathematical operator (either a plus sign or a minus sign) in the picOperator control. Both procedures also should generate and then display two random integers in the lblNum1 and lblNum2 controls.

To code the Click event procedures for the Operation radio buttons, then test the code:

1. Open the code template for the radAddition control's Click event procedure. Type **' display the plus sign, then display random numbers** and press **Enter** twice.

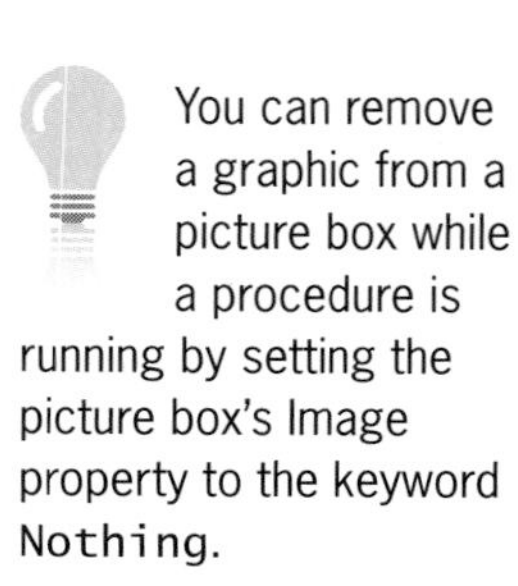

You can remove a graphic from a picture box while a procedure is running by setting the picture box's Image property to the keyword `Nothing`.

2. The plus sign appears in the picPlus control, which is located at the bottom of the form. You can display the plus sign in the picOperator control by assigning the value stored in the picPlus control's Image property to the picOperator control's Image property. Type **picOperator.Image = picPlus.Image** and press **Enter**.
3. Type **Call GenerateAndDisplayIntegers()** and press **Enter**.
4. Open the code template for the radSubtraction control's Click event procedure. Type **' display the minus sign, then display random numbers** and press **Enter** twice. The minus sign appears in the

picMinus control located at the bottom of the form. Type **picOperator.Image = picMinus.Image** and press **Enter**, then type **Call GenerateAndDisplayIntegers()** and press **Enter**.

5. Save the solution, then start the application. Notice that, even though the Grade 1 and Addition radio buttons are selected in the interface, an addition problem does not automatically appear in the interface. You will fix that problem in the next section.
6. Click the **Subtraction** radio button. A minus sign appears in the picOperator control, and two random integers from 1 through 10 appear in the interface.
7. Click the **Addition** radio button. A plus sign appears in the picOperator control, and two random integers from 1 through 10 appear in the interface.
8. Click the **Grade 2** radio button. Two random integers from 10 through 99 appear in the interface. Click the **Exit** button.

An addition problem should be displayed automatically when the Math Practice form first appears on the screen. You can accomplish this task in two ways: you can either use the Call statement to call the GenerateAndDisplayIntegers procedure or use the PerformClick method to invoke the radAddition control's Click event procedure. Whichever way you choose, the appropriate code must be entered in the form's Load event procedure, which is the last procedure you code in this lesson.

Coding the Form's Load Event Procedure

As you learned in Chapter 3, a form's Load event occurs when the application is started and the form is displayed the first time. The form does not appear on the screen until all of the instructions in its Load event procedure are processed. To automatically display an addition problem when the Math Practice form appears, you can enter either one of the following statements in the Load event procedure: `Call GenerateAndDisplayIntegers()` or `radAddition.PerformClick()`. The latter statement uses the **PerformClick method** to invoke the Addition radio button's Click event, which causes the computer to process the code contained in the Click event procedure. The PerformClick method's syntax is *object*.**PerformClick()**, where *object* is the name of the object whose Click event you want invoked.

To automatically display an addition problem when the Math Practice form first appears:

1. Click the **Class Name** arrow in the Code Editor window, then click **(frmMain Events)** in the list. Click the **Method Name** arrow, then click **Load** in the list. The template for the frmMain Load event procedure appears in the Code Editor window.
2. Type **' display an addition problem** and press **Enter** twice, then type **radAddition.PerformClick()** and press **Enter**.
3. Save the solution, then start the application. An addition problem appears in the interface, as shown in Figure 5-39.

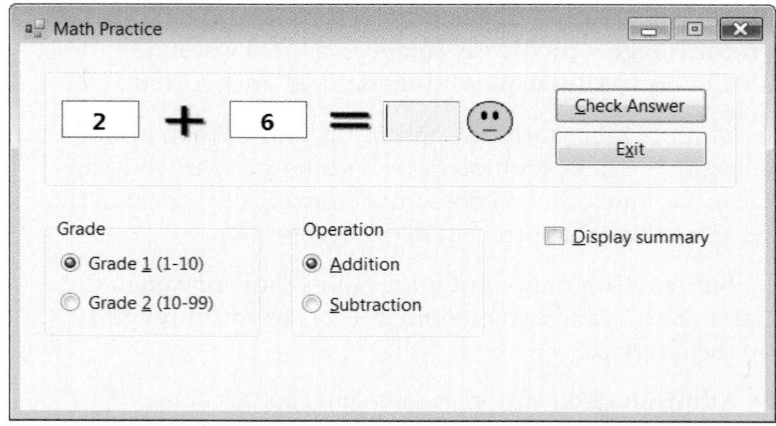

Figure 5-39 Addition problem appears automatically

4. Click the **Exit** button to end the application. Close the Code Editor window, then close the solution. Figure 5-40 shows the application's code at the end of Lesson B.

```
' Name:         Math Project
' Purpose:      Displays math problems involving addition and subtraction
' Programmer:   <your name> on <current date>

Option Explicit On
Option Strict On
Option Infer Off

Public Class frmMain

   Private Sub btnExit_Click(ByVal sender As Object, _
      ByVal e As System.EventArgs) Handles btnExit.Click
      Me.Close()
   End Sub

   Private Sub GenerateAndDisplayIntegers()
      ' generates and displays two random integers

      Dim intRandom1 As Integer
      Dim intRandom2 As Integer
      Dim randomGenerator As New Random

      ' generate random integers
      If radGrade1.Checked Then
         intRandom1 = randomGenerator.Next(1, 11)
         intRandom2 = randomGenerator.Next(1, 11)
      Else
         intRandom1 = randomGenerator.Next(10, 100)
         intRandom2 = randomGenerator.Next(10, 100)
      End If

      ' swap integers if the subtraction problem would result
      ' in a negative answer
      If radSubtraction.Checked AndAlso intRandom1 < intRandom2 Then
      Dim intTemp As Integer
         intTemp = intRandom1
         intRandom1 = intRandom2
         intRandom2 = intTemp
      End If

```

Figure 5-40 Math Practice application's code at the end of Lesson B *(continues)*

(continued)

```
            ' display integers
            lblNum1.Text = Convert.ToString(intRandom1)
            lblNum2.Text = Convert.ToString(intRandom2)
        End Sub

        Private Sub ProcessGradeRadioButtons(ByVal sender As Object, _
                    ByVal e As System.EventArgs) _
                    Handles radGrade1.Click, radGrade2.Click
            Call GenerateAndDisplayIntegers()
        End Sub

        Private Sub radAddition_Click(ByVal sender As Object, _
            ByVal e As System.EventArgs) Handles radAddition.Click
            ' display the plus sign, then display random numbers

            picOperator.Image = picPlus.Image
            Call GenerateAndDisplayIntegers()

        End Sub

        Private Sub radSubtraction_Click(ByVal sender As Object, _
            ByVal e As System.EventArgs) Handles radSubtraction.Click
            ' display the minus sign, then display random numbers

            picOperator.Image = picMinus.Image
            Call GenerateAndDisplayIntegers()

        End Sub

        Private Sub frmMain_Load(ByVal sender As Object, _
            ByVal e As System.EventArgs) Handles Me.Load
            ' display an addition problem

            radAddition.PerformClick()

        End Sub
    End Class
```

Figure 5-40 Math Practice application's code at the end of Lesson B

Lesson B Summary

- **To limit the user to only one choice in a group of two or more related but mutually exclusive choices:**

  Use the RadioButton tool to add a radio button control to the interface. To include two groups of radio buttons in an interface, at least one of the groups must be placed within a container, such as a group box.

- **To allow the user to select any number of choices from a group of one or more independent and nonexclusive choices:**

  Use the CheckBox tool to add a check box control to the interface.

- **To create a collection of code that can be invoked from one or more places in a program:**

  Create an independent Sub procedure. The Sub procedure's name should begin with a verb and indicate the task performed by the procedure. The name should be entered using Pascal case.

- **To generate random integers:**

  Create a Random object to represent the Visual Basic pseudo-random number generator. Typically, the syntax for creating a Random object is **Dim** *randomObjectName* **As New Random**. Use the Random.Next method to generate a random integer. The syntax of the Random.Next method is *randomObjectName***.Next(***minValue***,** *maxValue***)**, where *randomObjectName* is the name of the Random object, and *minValue* and *maxValue* are integers. The Random.Next method returns an integer that is greater than or equal to *minValue*, but less than *maxValue*.

- **To call (invoke) an independent Sub procedure:**

  Use the Call statement. The syntax of the Call statement is **Call** *procedureName* **(**[*argumentList*]**)**, where *procedureName* is the name of the procedure you want to call, and *argumentList* (which is optional) contains the information you want to send to the Sub procedure.

- **To invoke an object's click event from code:**

  Use the PerformClick method, whose syntax is *object***.PerformClick()**, where *object* is the name of the object whose Click event you want invoked.

Lesson B Key Terms

Call statement—used to call (invoke) an independent Sub procedure

Independent Sub procedure—a procedure that is not associated with any specific object or event and is processed only when invoked (called) from code

PerformClick method—used to invoke a control's Click event

Pseudo-random number generator—used to generate random numbers in Visual Basic

Random.Next method—used to generate a random integer that is greater than or equal to a minimum value, but less than a maximum value

Lesson B Review Questions

1. The minimum number of radio buttons in a group is ______________________.
   a. one
   b. two
   c. three
   d. There is no minimum number of radio buttons.

2. The text appearing in check boxes and radio buttons should be entered using ______________________.
   a. book title capitalization
   b. sentence capitalization
   c. either book title capitalization or sentence capitalization

3. It is customary in Windows applications to designate a default check box.
   a. True
   b. False

4. A form contains two group boxes. Each group box contains three radio buttons. How many of the radio buttons can be selected at the same time?
   a. one
   b. two
   c. three
   d. six

5. A form contains two group boxes. Each group box contains three check boxes. How many of the check boxes can be selected at the same time?
   a. one
   b. two
   c. three
   d. six

6. If a radio button is selected, its ______________________ property contains the Boolean value True.
   a. Checked
   b. On
   c. Selected
   d. Selection

7. Which of the following statements declares an object to represent the pseudo-random number generator in a procedure?
   a. `Dim randomGenerator As New RandomNumber`
   b. `Dim randomGenerator As New Generator`
   c. `Dim randomGenerator As New Random`
   d. `Dim randomGenerator As New RandomObject`

8. Which of the following statements generates a random integer from 1 to 25, inclusive?
    a. `intNum = randomGenerator.Next(1, 25)`
    b. `intNum = randomGenerator.Next(1, 26)`
    c. `intNum = randomGenerator(1, 25)`
    d. `intNum = randomGenerator.NextNumber(1, 26)`

9. You can use the ______________ statement to invoke an independent Sub procedure.
    a. Call
    b. Get
    c. Invoke
    d. ProcedureCall

10. Which of the following statements invokes the radAlaska control's Click event?
    a. `radAlaska.Click()`
    b. `radAlaska.ClickIt()`
    c. `radAlaska.PerformClick()`
    d. `PerformClick.radAlaska()`

Lesson B Exercises

INTRODUCTORY

1. Use Windows to make a copy of the Math Solution folder, which is contained in the VB2008\Chap05 folder. Rename the folder Math Solution-Call. Open the Math Solution (Math Solution.sln) file contained in the VB2008\Chap05\Math Solution-Call folder. Open the designer window, then open the Code Editor window. Replace the `radAddition.PerformClick()` statement in the form's Load event procedure with a Call statement that invokes the GenerateAndDisplayIntegers procedure. Save the solution, then start the application. An addition problem automatically appears in the interface. Stop the application. Close the Code Editor window, then close the solution.

INTRODUCTORY

2. In this exercise, you code an application that allows the user to select the name of a state and the name of a capital city. After making both selections, the user can click the Verify Answer button to verify that the selected city is the capital of the selected state. Open the Capitals Solution (Capitals Solution.sln) file, which is contained in the VB2008\Chap05\Capitals Solution folder. If necessary, open the designer window.

a. Designate the first radio button in each group as the default radio button for the group.

b. Enter the code to invoke the Click event for the two default radio buttons when the form first appears on the screen.

c. Declare two module-level String variables named `strCapital` and `strChoice`.

d. Code the state radio buttons' Click event procedures so that each assigns the appropriate capital to the `strCapital` variable, and each removes the contents of the lblMsg control.

e. Code the capital radio buttons' Click event procedures so that each assigns the selected capital to the `strChoice` variable, and each removes the contents of the lblMsg control.

f. Code the Verify Answer button's Click event procedure so that it compares the correct capital with the capital chosen by the user. Display the word "Correct" in the lblMsg control when both capitals match; otherwise, display the word "Incorrect".

g. Save the solution, then start the application. Test the application by selecting Illinois from the state group and Salem from the capital group. Click the Verify Answer button. The word "Incorrect" appears in the lblMsg control. Now select Wisconsin from the state group and Madison from the capital group. Click the Verify Answer button. The word "Correct" appears in the lblMsg control. Stop the application. Close the Code Editor window, then close the solution.

INTERMEDIATE

3. In this exercise, you code an application that displays a letter grade based on the average of three test scores entered by the user. Open the Juarez Solution (Juarez Solution.sln) file, which is contained in the VB2008\Chap05\Juarez Solution folder. If necessary, open the designer window.

   a. Code the Display Grade button's Click event procedure so that it displays the appropriate letter grade based on the average of three test scores. Each test is worth 100 points. Display an appropriate message if any of the test scores cannot be converted to the Double data type. Use the information shown in Figure 5-41 to display the appropriate grade.

Test average	**Grade**
90–100	A
80–89	B
70–79	C
60–69	D
below 60	F

Figure 5-41 Grade information

b. When the user makes a change to the contents of a text box, the application should remove the contents of the lblGrade control. Code the appropriate event procedures.

c. The application should select a text box's existing text when the text box receives the focus. Code the appropriate event procedures.

d. Save the solution, then start and test the application. For the first test, use scores of 90, 95, and 100. For the second test, use scores of 83, 72, and 65. For the third test, use scores of 40, 30, and 20. Next, test the application using letters, then test it using an empty text box. Stop the application. Close the Code Editor window, then close the solution.

INTERMEDIATE

4. In this exercise, you create an application that allows the user to enter the total number of calories and grams of fat contained in a specific food. The application should calculate and display two values: the food's fat calories (the number of calories attributed to fat) and its fat percentage (the ratio of the food's fat calories to its total calories). You calculate the number of fat calories in a food by multiplying the number of fat grams contained in the food by the number 9, because each gram of fat contains 9 calories. To calculate the fat percentage, you divide the food's fat calories by its total calories, and then multiply the result by 100. The application should display the message "This food is high in fat." when the fat percentage is over 30%; otherwise, it should display the message "This food is not high in fat." Create a Visual Basic Windows application. Name the solution, project, and form file Fat Calculator Solution, Fat Calculator Project, and Main Form.vb, respectively. Save the application in the VB2008\Chap05 folder. Create the interface shown in Figure 5-42. Code the application. Save the solution, then start and test the application. Stop the application. Close the Code Editor window, then close the solution.

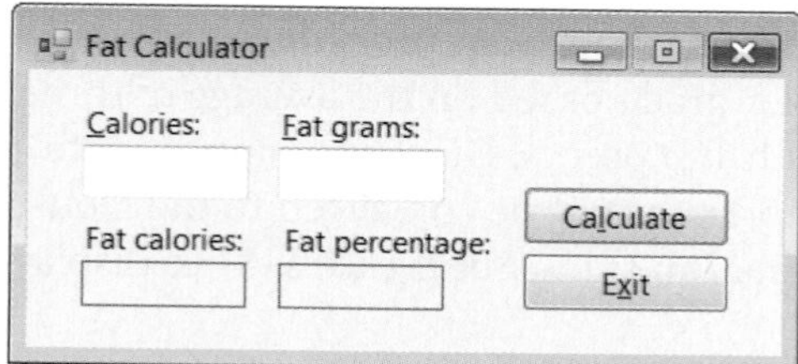

Figure 5-42 User interface for the Fat Calculator application

Discovery

5. In this exercise, you learn how to generate and display random numbers containing decimal places. Open the Random Double Solution (Random Double Solution.sln) file, which is contained in the VB2008\Chap05\Random Double Solution folder. If necessary, open the designer window.

   a. You can use the Random.NextDouble method to return a random number that is greater than or equal to 0.0, but less than 1.0. The syntax of the Random.NextDouble method is *randomObjectName* **.NextDouble**. Code the Display Random Number button's Click event procedure so that it displays a random number in the lblNumber control. Save the solution, then start the application. Click the Display Random Number button several times. Each time you click the button, a random number that is greater than or equal to 0.0, but less than 1.0, appears in the lblNumber control. Stop the application.

   b. You can use the following formula to generate random numbers within a specified range: (*maxValue* – *minValue* + **1**) * *randomObjectName*.**NextDouble** + *minValue*. For example, assuming the Random object's name is `randomGenerator`, the formula `(10 - 1 + 1) * randomGenerator.NextDouble + 1` generates random numbers that are greater than or equal to 1.0, but less than 11.0. Modify the Display Random Number button's Click event procedure so that it displays a random number that is greater than or equal to 25.0, but less than 51.0. Display two decimal places in the number. Save the solution, then start the application. Click the Display Random Number button several times. Each time you click the button, a random number that is greater than or equal to 25.0, but less than 51.0, appears in the lblNumber control. Stop the application. Close the Code Editor window, then close the solution.

LESSON C

After studying Lesson C, you should be able to:

- Code a check box's Click event procedure
- Show and hide a control

Coding the Check Answer Button's Click Event Procedure

To complete the Math Practice application, you still need to code the Click event procedures for the btnCheckAnswer and chkSummary controls. You will code the btnCheckAnswer control's Click event procedure first.

To open the Math Practice application from Lesson B:

1. If necessary, start Visual Studio 2008 or Visual Basic 2008 Express Edition. Close the Start Page window.
2. Open the **Math Solution** (**Math Solution.sln**) file, which is contained in the VB2008\Chap05\Math Solution folder. If necessary, open the designer window.

Figure 5-43 shows the pseudocode for the btnCheckAnswer control's Click event procedure.

```
btnCheckAnswer Click event procedure
1. if the Addition radio button is selected
         calculate the correct answer by adding the lblNum1 control's value to the lblNum2 control's value
   else
         calculate the correct answer by subtracting the lblNum2 control's value from the lblNum1 control's value
   end if
2. if the user's answer equals the correct answer
         display the happy face icon in the picFace control
         add 1 to the number of correct responses
         clear the contents of the txtAnswer control
         call the GenerateAndDisplayIntegers procedure to generate and display two random integers
   else
         display the neutral face icon in the picFace control
         add 1 to the number of incorrect responses
         display the "Try again!" message in a message box
         select the existing text in the txtAnswer control
   end if
3. send the focus to the txtAnswer control
4. display the number of correct and incorrect responses in lblCorrect and lblIncorrect
```

Figure 5-43 Pseudocode for the btnCheckAnswer control's Click event procedure

Study the procedure's pseudocode to determine the variables and named constants (if any) the procedure will use. In this case, the procedure will use a named constant for the "Try again!" message. It also will use the six Integer variables listed in Figure 5-44. Notice that the `intCorrectResponses` and `intIncorrectResponses` variables will be declared as static variables. As you learned in Chapter 3, a static variable is a local variable that retains its value even when the procedure in which it is declared ends. In this case, the two variables need to be static variables because they must keep a running tally of the number of correct and incorrect responses.

Name	Purpose
`intNum1`	store the random number contained in the lblNum1 control
`intNum2`	store the random number contained in the lblNum2 control
`intUserAnswer`	store the user's answer, which is contained in the txtAnswer control
`intCorrectAnswer`	store the correct answer
`intCorrectResponses`	store the number of correct responses made by the user; declare as a static variable
`intIncorrectResponses`	store the number of incorrect responses made by the user; declare as a static variable

Figure 5-44 Variables used by the btnCheckAnswer control's Click event procedure

To begin coding the btnCheckAnswer control's Click event procedure:

1. Open the Code Editor window, then open the code template for the btnCheckAnswer control's Click event procedure. Enter the following four comments. Press **Enter** twice after typing the last comment.

   ' calculates the correct answer and then compares
   ' the correct answer to the user's answer
   ' keeps track of the number of correct
   ' and incorrect responses

2. Type **Const strMSG As String = "Try again!"** and press **Enter**.

3. Enter the following six statements. Press **Enter** twice after typing the last statement.

   Dim intNum1 As Integer
   Dim intNum2 As Integer
   Dim intUserAnswer As Integer
   Dim intCorrectAnswer As Integer
   Static intCorrectResponses As Integer
   Static intIncorrectResponses As Integer

4. Now assign the two random numbers and the user's answer to the appropriate variables. Enter the following comment and three assignment statements. Press **Enter** twice after typing the last assignment statement.

   ' assign random numbers and user's answer
   Integer.TryParse(lblNum1.Text, intNum1)
   Integer.TryParse(lblNum2.Text, intNum2)
   Integer.TryParse(txtAnswer.Text, intUserAnswer)

5. Step 1 in the pseudocode (shown earlier in Figure 5-43) is to determine whether the Addition radio button is selected in the interface. If it is, the procedure should add the two random numbers together. Otherwise, it should subtract the second random number from the first random number. Enter the comments and selection structure shown in Figure 5-45, then position the insertion point as shown in the figure.

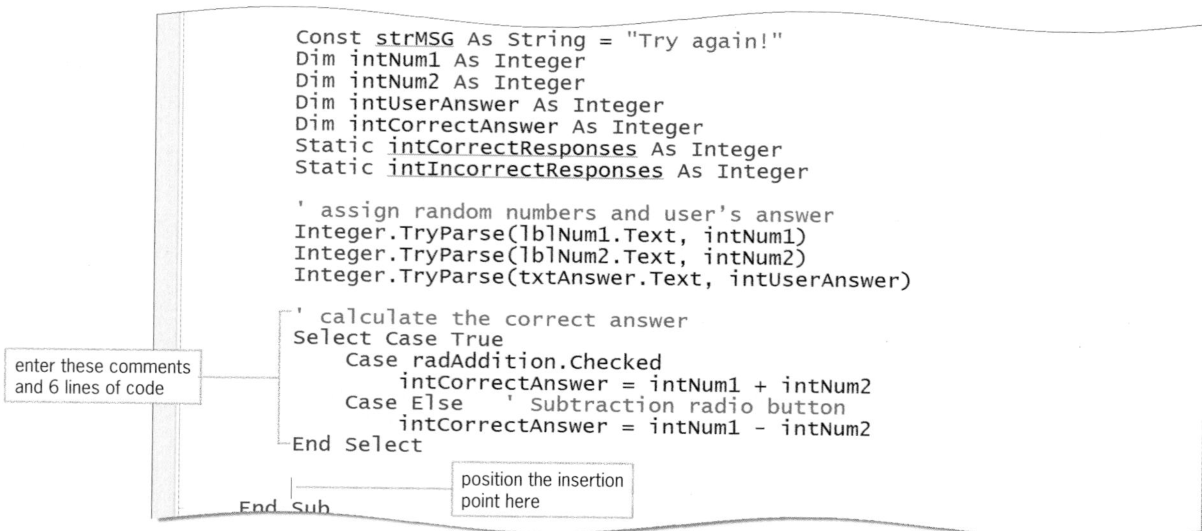

Figure 5-45 Comments and selection structure entered in the procedure

Step 2 in the procedure's pseudocode is to determine whether the user's answer is correct. You can do this by comparing the contents of the `intUserAnswer` variable with the contents of the `intCorrectAnswer` variable.

To continue coding the btnCheckAnswer control's Click event procedure:

1. Type **' determine whether the user's answer is correct** and press **Enter**, then type **If intUserAnswer = intCorrectAnswer Then** and press **Enter**.

2. If the user's answer is correct, the procedure should perform the following four tasks: display the happy face icon in the picFace control, add the number 1 to the number of correct responses, clear the contents of the txtAnswer control, and call the GenerateAndDisplayIntegers procedure to generate and display two random integers. Enter the additional code shown in Figure 5-46, then position the insertion point as shown in the figure.

```
        ' determine whether the user's answer is correct
        If intUserAnswer = intCorrectAnswer Then
            picFace.Image = picHappy.Image
            intCorrectResponses = intCorrectResponses + 1
            txtAnswer.Text = String.Empty
            Call GenerateAndDisplayIntegers()

        End If
    End Sub
```

enter these 4 lines of code

position the insertion point here

Figure 5-46 Additional code entered in the procedure

3. If the user's answer is not correct, the procedure should perform the following four tasks: display the neutral face icon in the picFace control, add the number 1 to the number of incorrect responses, display the "Try again!" message in a message box, and select the existing text in the txtAnswer control. Type **Else** and press **Enter**, then enter the additional code shown in Figure 5-47. Also position the insertion point as shown in the figure.

```
        Else
            picFace.Image = picNeutral.Image
            intIncorrectResponses = intIncorrectResponses + 1
            MessageBox.Show(strMSG, "Math Practice", _
                      MessageBoxButtons.OK, MessageBoxIcon.Information)
            txtAnswer.SelectAll()
        End If

    End Sub
```

enter these 5 lines of code

position the insertion point here

Figure 5-47 Code entered in the selection structure's false path

4. The last two steps in the procedure's pseudocode are to send the focus to the txtAnswer control and then display the number of correct and incorrect responses in the lblCorrect and lblIncorrect controls. Enter the following three lines of code, then save the solution.

   txtAnswer.Focus()
   lblCorrect.Text = Convert.ToString(intCorrectResponses)
   lblIncorrect.Text = Convert.ToString(intIncorrectResponses)

Coding the Display Summary Check Box's Click Event Procedure

Recall that the four picture boxes located at the bottom of the form do not appear in the interface when the application is running. This is because their **Visible property** is set to False in the Properties window. The Visible property of the grpSummary control also is set to False, which explains why you do not see the control and its contents when the form appears on the screen. As you learned in Chapter 4, a group box and its controls are treated as one unit. As a result, hiding the group box also hides the controls contained within the group box. According to the application's TOE chart, the chkSummary control's Click event procedure is responsible for both showing and hiding the grpSummary control. The procedure should show the group box when the user selects the check box, and it should hide the group box when the user deselects the check box. When a check box is selected, its Checked property contains the Boolean value True; otherwise, it contains the Boolean value False.

To code the chkSummary control's Click event procedure:

1. Open the code template for the chkSummary control's Click event procedure. Type **' shows/hides the grpSummary control** and press **Enter** twice.

You also can write the condition in Step 2 as `chkSummary.Checked = True`.

2. If the user selects the check box, the procedure should display the grpSummary control. This is accomplished by setting the grpSummary control's Visible property to the Boolean value True. Type **If chkSummary.Checked Then** and press **Enter**, then type **grpSummary.Visible = True** and press **Enter**.
3. If the user deselects the check box, the procedure should hide the grpSummary control. This is accomplished by setting the grpSummary control's Visible property to the Boolean value False. Type **Else** and press **Enter**, then type **grpSummary.Visible = False**.

When coded, the Click event procedure for a check box always will contain a selection structure that determines whether the check box was selected or deselected. The selection structure is not necessary in a radio button's Click event procedure, because clicking a radio button always selects the button; the user cannot deselect a radio button by clicking it.

To test the application's code:

1. Save the solution, then start the application. Type the correct answer to the addition problem, then press **Enter** to select the Check Answer button, which is the default button on the form. The happy face icon and a new addition problem appear in the interface.
2. Click the **Display summary** check box to select it. A check mark appears in the check box, and the grpSummary control and its contents appear in the interface. Notice that the label controls within the group box indicate that you have made 1 correct response and 0 incorrect responses.
3. Click the **text box** in which you enter the answer. Type an incorrect answer to the current addition problem, then press **Enter**. A neutral face icon appears in the interface, and a message box appears on the screen, as shown in Figure 5-48.

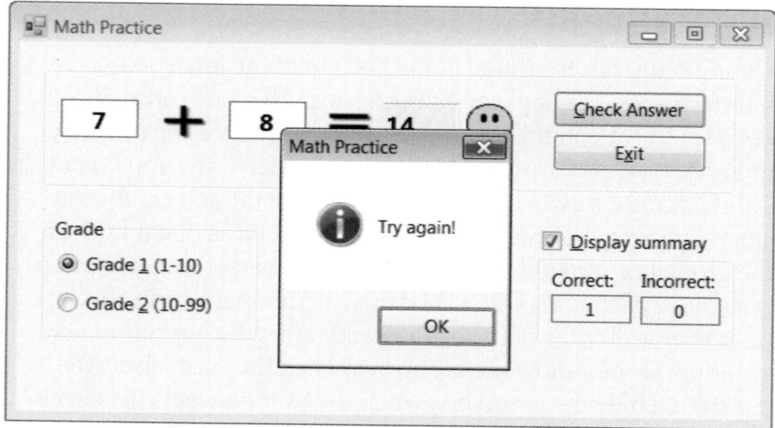

Figure 5-48 Result of entering an incorrect response to the addition problem

4. Press **Enter** to close the message box. The number of incorrect responses changes from 0 to 1, and the incorrect answer is selected in the txtAnswer control. Type the correct answer to the current addition problem, then press **Enter**. The number of correct responses changes from 1 to 2, and the happy face icon appears in the interface.

5. Click the **Display summary** check box to deselect it. The check mark is removed from the check box, and the grpSummary control and its contents are hidden.

6. Click the **Exit** button to end the application. Close the Code Editor window, then close the solution. Figure 5-49 shows the application's code.

```
' Name:        Math Project
' Purpose:     Displays math problems involving addition and subtraction
' Programmer:  <your name> on <current date>

Option Explicit On
Option Strict On
Option Infer Off

Public Class frmMain

    Private Sub btnExit_Click(ByVal sender As Object, _
        ByVal e As System.EventArgs) Handles btnExit.Click
        Me.Close()
    End Sub

    Private Sub GenerateAndDisplayIntegers()
        ' generates and displays two random integers

        Dim intRandom1 As Integer
        Dim intRandom2 As Integer
        Dim randomGenerator As New Random

        ' generate random integers
        If radGrade1.Checked Then
            intRandom1 = randomGenerator.Next(1, 11)
            intRandom2 = randomGenerator.Next(1, 11)
        Else
            intRandom1 = randomGenerator.Next(10, 100)
            intRandom2 = randomGenerator.Next(10, 100)
        End If

        ' swap integers if the subtraction problem would result
        ' in a negative answer
        If radSubtraction.Checked AndAlso intRandom1 < intRandom2 Then
            Dim intTemp As Integer
            intTemp = intRandom1
            intRandom1 = intRandom2
            intRandom2 = intTemp
        End If

        ' display integers
        lblNum1.Text = Convert.ToString(intRandom1)
        lblNum2.Text = Convert.ToString(intRandom2)
    End Sub

    Private Sub ProcessGradeRadioButtons(ByVal sender As Object, _
        ByVal e As System.EventArgs) _
        Handles radGrade1.Click, radGrade2.Click
        Call GenerateAndDisplayIntegers()
    End Sub

```

Figure 5-49 Math Practice application's code at the end of Lesson C *(continues)*

(continued)

```
    Private Sub radAddition_Click(ByVal sender As Object, _
       ByVal e As System.EventArgs) Handles radAddition.Click
       ' display the plus sign, then display random numbers

       picOperator.Image = picPlus.Image
       Call GenerateAndDisplayIntegers()

    End Sub

    Private Sub radSubtraction_Click(ByVal sender As Object, _
       ByVal e As System.EventArgs) Handles radSubtraction.Click
       ' display the minus sign, then display random numbers

       picOperator.Image = picMinus.Image
       Call GenerateAndDisplayIntegers()

    End Sub

    Private Sub frmMain_Load(ByVal sender As Object, _
       ByVal e As System.EventArgs) Handles Me.Load
       ' display an addition problem

       radAddition.PerformClick()

    End Sub

    Private Sub btnCheckAnswer_Click(ByVal sender As Object, _
       ByVal e As System.EventArgs) Handles btnCheckAnswer.Click
       ' calculates the correct answer and then compares
       ' the correct answer to the user's answer
       ' keeps track of the number of correct
       ' and incorrect responses

       Const strMSG As String = "Try again!"
       Dim intNum1 As Integer
       Dim intNum2 As Integer
       Dim intUserAnswer As Integer
       Dim intCorrectAnswer As Integer
       Static intCorrectResponses As Integer
       Static intIncorrectResponses As Integer

       ' assign random numbers and user's answer
       Integer.TryParse(lblNum1.Text, intNum1)
       Integer.TryParse(lblNum2.Text, intNum2)
       Integer.TryParse(txtAnswer.Text, intUserAnswer)

       ' calculate the correct answer
       Select Case True
         Case radAddition.Checked
               intCorrectAnswer = intNum1 + intNum2
         Case Else ' Subtraction radio button
               intCorrectAnswer = intNum1 - intNum2
       End Select

```

Figure 5-49 Math Practice application's code at the end of Lesson C *(continues)*

(continued)

```
        ' determine whether the user's answer is correct
        If intUserAnswer = intCorrectAnswer Then
          picFace.Image = picHappy.Image
          intCorrectResponses = intCorrectResponses + 1
          txtAnswer.Text = String.Empty
          Call GenerateAndDisplayIntegers()
        Else
          picFace.Image = picNeutral.Image
          intIncorrectResponses = intIncorrectResponses + 1
          MessageBox.Show(strMSG, "Math Practice", _
          MessageBoxButtons.OK, MessageBoxIcon.Information)
          txtAnswer.SelectAll()
        End If

        txtAnswer.Focus()
        lblCorrect.Text = Convert.ToString(intCorrectResponses)
        lblIncorrect.Text = Convert.ToString(intIncorrectResponses)

    End Sub

    Private Sub chkSummary_Click(ByVal sender As Object, _
        ByVal e As System.EventArgs) Handles chkSummary.Click
        ' shows/hides the grpSummary control

        If chkSummary.Checked Then
          grpSummary.Visible = True
        Else
          grpSummary.Visible = False
        End If
    End Sub
End Class
```

Figure 5-49 Math Practice application's code at the end of Lesson C

Lesson C Summary

- **To show or hide a control:**

  Set the control's Visible property to the Boolean value True to show the control. Set the control's Visible property to the Boolean value False to hide the control.

- **To code a check box's click event procedure:**

  Use a selection structure to determine whether the check box was either selected or deselected by the user.

Lesson C Key Term

Visible property—determines whether a control is visible in the interface while an application is running

Lesson C Review Questions

1. Which of the following statements hides the picDivision control?
   a. `picDivision.Hide`
   b. `picDivision.Hide = True`
   c. `Hide.picDivision = True`
   d. None of the above.

2. If a check box is deselected, its ______________________ property contains the Boolean value False.
   a. Checked
   b. Deselected
   c. On
   d. None of the above.

3. When coded, a check box's Click event procedure always will contain a selection structure that determines whether the check box is selected or deselected.
   a. True
   b. False

4. Like a check box, a radio button can be deselected by clicking it.
   a. True
   b. False

Lesson C Exercises

INTRODUCTORY

1. Use Windows to make a copy of the Math Solution folder, which is contained in the VB2008\Chap05 folder. Rename the folder Modified Math Solution. Open the Math Solution (Math Solution.sln) file contained in the VB2008\Chap05\Modified Math Solution folder. Open the designer window, then open the Code Editor window.
   a. Change the If...Then...Else statement in the chkSummary control's Click event procedure to a Select Case statement.
   b. Change the first selection structure in the btnCheckAnswer control's Click event procedure to an If...Then...Else statement.
   c. Change the second selection structure in the btnCheckAnswer control's Click event procedure to a Select Case statement.
   d. Save the solution, then start and test the application. Stop the application. Close the Code Editor window, then close the solution.

INTRODUCTORY

2. In this exercise, you code an application that displays a class rank based on a code entered by the user. The rank for code 1 is Freshman. The rank for code 2 is Sophomore. The rank for code 3 is Junior, and the rank for code 4 is Senior. Open the Washington Solution (Washington Solution.sln) file, which is contained in the VB2008\Chap05\Washington Solution folder. If necessary, open the designer window. Center the rank in the label control. Set the text box's MaxLength property to the number 1 so that the user can enter only one character in the text box. Open the Code Editor window. Code the application. Allow the text box to accept only the numeric keys 1, 2, 3, and 4 and the Backspace key. When a change is made to the code entered in the text box, clear the contents of the label control that displays the rank. Save the solution, then start and test the application. Stop the application. Close the Code Editor window, then close the solution.

INTRODUCTORY

3. Jacques Cousard has been playing the lottery for four years and has yet to win any money. He wants an application that will select the six lottery numbers for him. Each lottery number can range from 1 to 54 only. (An example of six lottery numbers would be: 4 8 35 15 20 3.) Create a Visual Basic Windows application. Name the solution, project, and form file Lottery Solution, Lottery Project, and Main Form.vb, respectively. Save the application in the VB2008\Chap05 folder. Create the interface shown in Figure 5-50, then code the application. For now, do not worry if the lottery numbers are not unique. You will learn how to display unique numbers in Chapter 9. Save the solution, then start and test the application. Stop the application. Close the Code Editor window, then close the solution.

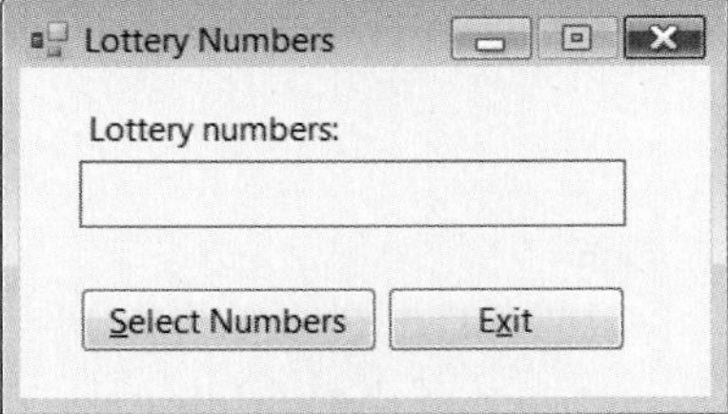

Figure 5-50 User interface for the Lottery Numbers application

INTRODUCTORY

4. Ferris Seminars offers computer seminars to various companies. The owner of Ferris Seminars wants an application that the registration clerks can use to calculate the registration fee for a company. The clerk will enter the number registered for the seminar, and then select either the Seminar 1 radio button or the Seminar 2 radio button. If a company is entitled to a 10% discount, the clerk will click the 10% discount check box. After the selections are made, the clerk will click the Calculate Total Due button to calculate the total registration fee. Seminar 1 is $100 per person, and Seminar 2 is $120 per person. Open the Ferris Solution (Ferris Solution.sln) file, which is contained in the VB2008\Chap05\Ferris Solution folder. If necessary, open the designer window. Code the application. Remove the total fee when a change is made to the number registered, the seminar, or the discount. The

text box should accept only numbers and the Backspace key. Save the solution, then start and test the application. Stop the application. Close the Code Editor window, then close the solution.

INTRODUCTORY

5. In this exercise, you modify the application created in Chapter 4. Use Windows to copy the Payment Solution folder from the VB2008\Chap04 folder to the VB2008\Chap05 folder. Open the designer window, then open the Code Editor window. Delete the ClearPayment procedure, then create an independent Sub procedure named ClearPayment. The independent Sub procedure should clear the contents of the lblPayment control. Call the independent Sub procedure when a change is made to any of the three text boxes. Save the solution, then start and test the application. Stop the application. Close the Code Editor window, then close the solution.

INTERMEDIATE

6. In this exercise, you create an application that displays a health club member's monthly dues. Create a Visual Basic Windows application. Name the solution, project, and form file Health Solution, Health Project, and Main Form.vb, respectively. Save the application in the VB2008\Chap05 folder. Create the interface shown in Figure 5-51.

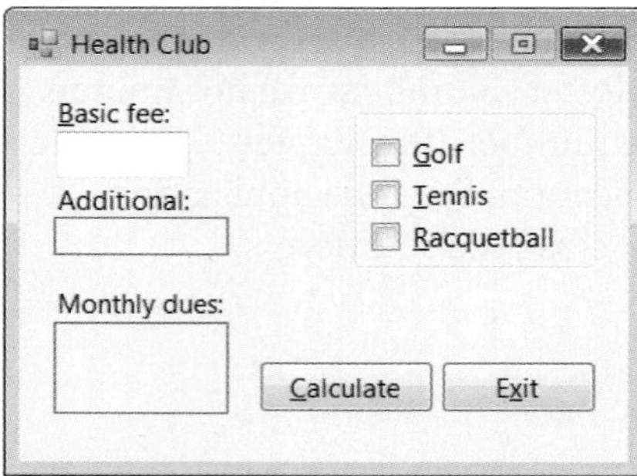

Figure 5-51 User interface for the Health Club application

a. Declare a module-level variable to keep track of the additional charges.

b. Code each check box's Click event procedure so that it adds the appropriate additional charge to the module-level variable when the check box is selected, and subtracts the additional charge from the variable when the check box is deselected. The additional charges are $30 per month for tennis, $25 per month for golf, and $20 per month for racquetball. Each check box's Click event procedure should display the contents of the module-level variable in the Additional box, and also clear the contents of the Monthly dues box.

c. Code the Calculate button's Click event procedure so that it calculates the monthly dues. The dues are calculated by adding the basic fee to the total additional charge. Display the total due with a dollar sign and two decimal places.

d. When the user makes a change to the Basic fee text box, the application should clear the contents of the Monthly dues box. Code the appropriate event procedure.

e. The Basic fee text box should accept only numbers and the Backspace key. Code the appropriate event procedure.

f. Save the solution, then start the application. Test the application by entering 80 as the basic fee and then selecting the Golf check box. The number 25 appears as the additional charge. Click the Calculate button. The monthly dues are $105.00.

g. Now select the Tennis and Racquetball check boxes and deselect the Golf check box. The number 50 appears as the additional charge. Click the Calculate button. The monthly dues are $130.00. Stop the application. Close the Code Editor window, then close the solution.

INTERMEDIATE

7. In this exercise, you create an application that displays a seminar fee. The fee is based on the membership status and age entered by the user. The fee for club members younger than 65 years old is $10. The fee for club members at least 65 years old is $5. The fee for non-members is $20. Create a Visual Basic Windows application. Name the solution, project, and form file Barren Solution, Barren Project, and Main Form.vb, respectively. Save the application in the VB2008\Chap05 folder. Create the interface shown in Figure 5-52, then code the application. When the user clicks a radio button, clear the contents of the label control that displays the fee. Save the solution, then start and test the application. Stop the application. Close the Code Editor window, then close the solution.

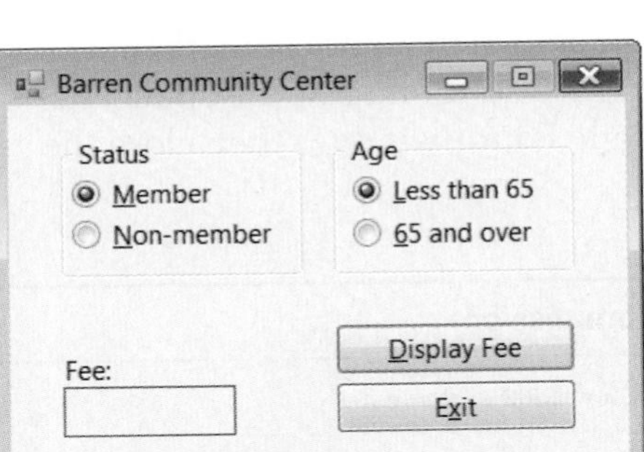

Figure 5-52 User interface for the Barren Community Center application

INTERMEDIATE

8. In this exercise, you create an application for Golf Pro. Each of Golf Pro's salespeople receives a commission based on the total of his or her domestic and international sales. The commission rates are shown in Figure 5-53. Create a Visual Basic Windows application. Name the solution, project, and form file Golf Pro Solution, Golf Pro Project, and Main Form.vb, respectively. Save the application in the VB2008\Chap05 folder. Create the interface shown in Figure 5-54, then code the application. The text boxes should accept only numbers and the Backspace key. Save the solution, then start and test the application. Stop the application. Close the Code Editor window, then close the solution.

Sales	Commission
1–100,000.99	2% * sales
100,001–400,000.99	2,000 + 5% * sales over 100,000
400,001 and over	17,000 + 10% * sales over 400,000

Figure 5-53 Commission rates for Golf Pro

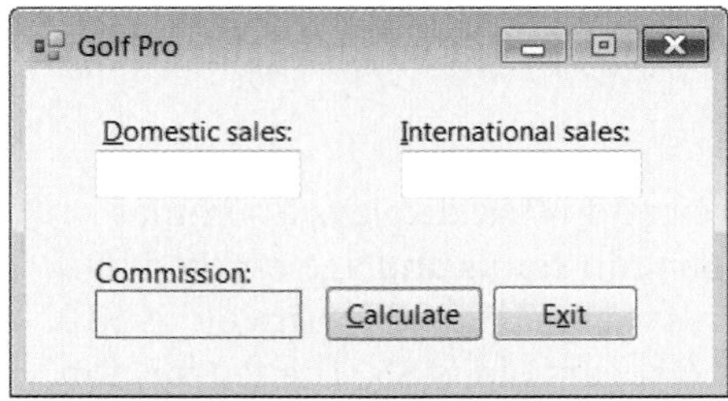

Figure 5-54 User interface for the Golf Pro application

INTERMEDIATE

9. In this exercise, you create an application for Marshall Sales Corporation. Each of the company's salespeople receives a commission based on the amount of his or her sales. The commission rates are shown in Figure 5-55. Create a Visual Basic Windows application. Name the solution, project, and form file Marshall Solution, Marshall Project, and Main Form.vb, respectively. Save the application in the VB2008\Chap05 folder. Create the interface shown in Figure 5-56, then code the application. Save the solution, then start and test the application. Stop the application. Close the Code Editor window, then close the solution.

Sales	Commission
1–100,000.99	2% * sales
100,001–200,000.99	4% * sales
200,001–300,000.99	6% * sales
300,001–400,000.99	8% * sales
400,001 and over	10% * sales

Figure 5-55 Commission rates for Marshall Sales Corporation

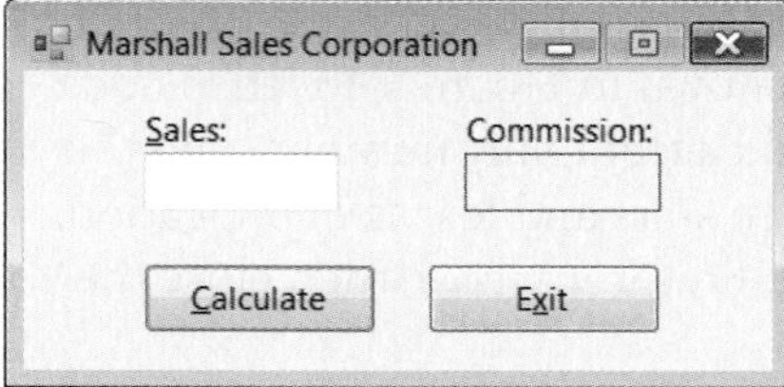

Figure 5-56 User interface for the Marshall Sales Corporation application

INTERMEDIATE

10. In this exercise, you create an application for Willow Health Club. The application calculates and displays the number of daily calories needed to maintain your current weight. Use the information shown in Figure 5-57 when coding the application. Create a Visual Basic Windows application. Name the solution, project, and form file Willow Solution, Willow Project, and Main Form.vb, respectively. Save the application in the VB2008\Chap05 folder. Create the interface shown in Figure 5-58, then code the application. Save the solution, then start and test the application. Stop the application. Close the Code Editor window, then close the solution.

Moderately active female	daily calories = weight * 12 calories per pound
Relatively inactive female	daily calories = weight * 10 calories per pound
Moderately active male	daily calories = weight * 15 calories per pound
Relatively inactive male	daily calories = weight * 13 calories per pound

Figure 5-57 Daily calories information

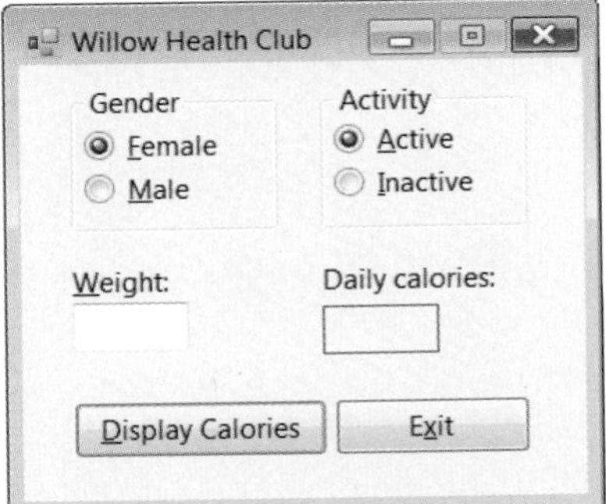

Figure 5-58 User interface for the Willow Health Club application

ADVANCED

11. In this exercise, you create an application for Johnson Products. The application calculates and displays the price of an order, based on the number of units ordered and the customer's status (either wholesaler or retailer). The price per unit is shown in Figure 5-59. Create a Visual Basic Windows application. Name the solution, project, and form file Johnson Solution, Johnson Project, and Main Form.vb, respectively. Save the application in the VB2008\Chap05 folder. Design an appropriate interface, using radio buttons to determine the customer's status. (Refer to Appendix A for a listing of the GUI guidelines you have learned so far.) Code the application. Save the solution, then start and test the application. Stop the application. Close the Code Editor window, then close the solution.

Wholesaler		**Retailer**	
Number of units	Price per unit ($)	Number of units	Price per unit ($)
1–4	10	1–3	15
5 and over	9	4–8	14
		9 and over	12

Figure 5-59 Pricing chart for Johnson Products

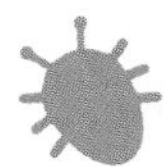

Swat The Bugs

12. The purpose of this exercise is to demonstrate the importance of testing an application thoroughly. Open the Debug Solution (Debug Solution.sln) file, which is contained in the VB2008\Chap05\Debug Solution-Lesson C folder. If necessary, open the designer window. The application displays a shipping charge, which is based on the total price entered by the user. If the total price is greater than or equal to $100 but less than $501, the shipping charge is $10. If the total price is greater than or equal to $501 but less than $1001, the shipping charge is $7. If the total price is greater than or equal to $1001, the shipping charge is $5. No shipping charge is due if the total price is less than $100. Start the application. Test the application using the following total prices: 100, 501, 1500, 500.75, 30, 1000.33. You will notice that the application does not display the correct shipping charge for some of these total prices. Stop the application. Correct the application's code, then save the solution. Start and then test the application again. Stop the application. Close the Code Editor window, then close the solution.

CHAPTER 6

The Repetition Structure

Creating the Shoppers Haven Application

In this chapter, you create an application that allows the user to enter an item's original price and its discount rate. The discount rates range from 10% through 30% in increments of 5%. The application will calculate and display the amount of the discount and also the discounted price.

Previewing the Shoppers Haven Application

To open the Run dialog box, press and hold down the Windows logo key as you tap the letter r, then release the logo key.

To preview the completed Shoppers Haven application:

1. Use the Run dialog box to run the **Shoppers** (**Shoppers.exe**) file, which is contained in the VB2008\Chap06 folder. The application's user interface appears on the screen. The interface contains a list box control, which you learn about in Lesson C.
2. Type **56.99** in the Original price box, then click **15** in the list of discount rates. Click the **Calculate** button. The item's discount and discounted price appear in the interface, as shown in Figure 6-1.

Figure 6-1 Discount and discounted price shown in the interface

3. Click the **Exit** button to end the application.

The Shoppers Haven application uses the repetition structure, which is covered in Lessons A and B. You will code the Shoppers Haven application in Lesson C.

LESSON A

After studying Lesson A, you should be able to:

- Code the repetition structure using the Do...Loop statement
- Include the repetition structure in pseudocode
- Include the repetition structure in a flowchart
- Initialize and update counters and accumulators
- Code the repetition structure using the For...Next statement

The Repetition Structure

As you learned in Chapter 1, the three programming structures are sequence, selection, and repetition. Every procedure in a Visual Basic program contains the sequence structure, where the procedure instructions are processed one after another in the order they appear in the procedure. Many procedures also contain the selection structure, which you learned about in Chapters 4 and 5. Programmers use the selection structure when they need the computer to make a decision and then take the appropriate action based on the result of the decision. In addition to including the sequence and selection structures, many procedures also include the repetition structure. Programmers use the **repetition structure**, referred to more simply as a **loop**, when they need the computer to repeatedly process one or more program instructions until some condition is met, at which time the repetition structure ends. As an example, you may want to process a set of instructions—such as the instructions to calculate net pay—for each employee in a company. Or, you may want to process a set of instructions until the user enters a negative sales amount, which indicates that he or she has no more sales amounts to enter. As with the sequence and selection structures, you already are familiar with the repetition structure. An example of a repetition structure can be found on most shampoo bottles. The bottles typically direct you to repeat the "apply shampoo to hair," "lather," and "rinse" steps until your hair is clean.

A repetition structure can be either a pretest loop or a posttest loop. In both types of loops, the condition is evaluated with each repetition, or iteration, of the loop. In a **pretest loop**, the evaluation occurs *before* the instructions within the loop are processed. In a **posttest loop**, the evaluation occurs *after* the instructions within the loop are processed. Depending on the result of the evaluation, the instructions in a pretest loop may never be processed. The instructions in a posttest loop, however, always will be processed at least once. Of the two types of loops, the pretest loop is the most commonly used. You code a loop (repetition structure) in Visual Basic using one of the following statements: Do...Loop, For...Next, or For Each...Next. You learn about the Do...Loop and For...Next statements in this lesson. The For Each...Next statement is covered in Chapter 9.

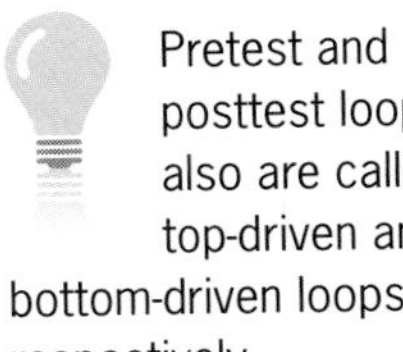

Pretest and posttest loops also are called top-driven and bottom-driven loops, respectively.

You can use the Exit Do statement to exit the Do...Loop statement prematurely, which means to exit it before the loop has finished processing. You may need to do this if the computer encounters an error when processing the loop instructions.

You can nest Do...Loop statements, which means you can place one Do...Loop statement within another Do...Loop statement.

The Do...Loop Statement

The **Do...Loop statement** can be used to code both a pretest loop and a posttest loop. Figure 6-2 shows two slightly different versions of the statement's syntax, along with an example of using each version to display the numbers 1, 2, and 3 in message boxes. You use Version 1 of the syntax to code a pretest loop, and Version 2 to code a posttest loop. In both versions of the syntax, the statement begins with the Do clause and ends with the Loop clause. Between both clauses, you enter the instructions you want the computer to repeat. The {**While** | **Until**} portion of each syntax indicates that you can select only one of the keywords appearing within the braces. You do not type the braces ({}) or the pipe symbol (|) when entering the Do...Loop statement. You follow the `While` or `Until` keyword with a *condition*, which can contain variables, constants, properties, functions, methods, and operators. Like the condition used in an If...Then...Else statement, the condition used in a Do...Loop statement must evaluate to a Boolean value—either True or False. The condition determines whether the computer processes the loop instructions. The keyword `While` indicates that the loop instructions should be processed *while* the condition is true. The keyword `Until`, on the other hand, indicates that the loop instructions should be processed *until* the condition becomes true. Notice that the keyword (either `While` or `Until`) and the condition appear in the Do clause in a pretest loop, but they appear in the Loop clause in a posttest loop.

Do...Loop statement

Syntax for a pretest loop

Do {**While** | **Until**} *condition*

[*instructions to be processed either while the condition is true or until the condition becomes true*]

Loop

Pretest loop example

```
Dim intNumber As Integer = 1
Do While intNumber <= 3
   MessageBox.Show(intNumber.ToString)
   intNumber = intNumber + 1
Loop
```

Syntax for a posttest loop

Do

[*instructions to be processed either while the condition is true or until the condition becomes true*]

Loop {**While** | **Until**} *condition*

Posttest loop example

```
Dim intNumber As Integer = 1
Do
   MessageBox.Show(intNumber.ToString)
   intNumber = intNumber + 1
Loop Until intNumber > 3
```

Figure 6-2 Syntax versions and examples of the Do...Loop statement

Figures 6-3 and 6-4 describe the way the computer processes the code shown in the examples in Figure 6-2.

Processing steps for the pretest loop example

1. The computer creates the `intNumber` variable and initializes it to 1.
2. The computer processes the Do clause, which checks whether the `intNumber` variable's value is less than or equal to 3. It is.
3. The MessageBox.Show method displays 1 (the contents of the `intNumber` variable).
4. The `intNumber = intNumber + 1` statement adds 1 to the contents of the `intNumber` variable, giving 2.
5. The computer processes the Loop clause, which returns processing to the Do clause (the beginning of the loop).
6. The computer processes the Do clause, which checks whether the `intNumber` variable's value is less than or equal to 3. It is.
7. The MessageBox.Show method displays 2 (the contents of the `intNumber` variable).
8. The `intNumber = intNumber + 1` statement adds 1 to the contents of the `intNumber` variable, giving 3.
9. The computer processes the Loop clause, which returns processing to the Do clause.
10. The computer processes the Do clause, which checks whether the `intNumber` variable's value is less than or equal to 3. It is.
11. The MessageBox.Show method displays 3 (the contents of the `intNumber` variable).
12. The `intNumber = intNumber + 1` statement adds 1 to the contents of the `intNumber` variable, giving 4.
13. The computer processes the Loop clause, which returns processing to the Do clause.
14. The computer processes the Do clause, which checks whether the `intNumber` variable's value is less than or equal to 3. It isn't, so the computer stops processing the Do...Loop statement. Processing continues with the statement following the Loop clause.

Figure 6-3 Processing steps for the pretest loop example from Figure 6-2

Processing steps for the posttest loop example

1. The computer creates the `intNumber` variable and initializes it to 1.
2. The computer processes the Do clause, which marks the beginning of the loop.
3. The MessageBox.Show method displays 1 (the contents of the `intNumber` variable).
4. The `intNumber = intNumber + 1` statement adds 1 to the contents of the `intNumber` variable, giving 2.
5. The computer processes the Loop clause, which checks whether the `intNumber` variable's value is greater than 3. It isn't, so processing returns to the Do clause (the beginning of the loop).
6. The MessageBox.Show method displays 2 (the contents of the `intNumber` variable).
7. The `intNumber = intNumber + 1` statement adds 1 to the contents of the `intNumber` variable, giving 3.
8. The computer processes the Loop clause, which checks whether the `intNumber` variable's value is greater than 3. It isn't, so processing returns to the Do clause.
9. The MessageBox.Show method displays 3 (the contents of the `intNumber` variable).
10. The `intNumber = intNumber + 1` statement adds 1 to the contents of the `intNumber` variable, giving 4.
11. The computer processes the Loop clause, which checks whether the `intNumber` variable's value is greater than 3. It is, so the computer stops processing the Do... Loop statement. Processing continues with the statement following the Loop clause.

Figure 6-4 Processing steps for the posttest loop example from Figure 6-2

Figure 6-5 shows the flowchart and pseudocode associated with the pretest loop example from Figure 6-2. Figure 6-6 shows the flowchart and pseudocode for the posttest loop example.

Pretest loop's pseudocode and flowchart

1. assign 1 to a variable
2. repeat while the variable's value is less than or equal to 3
   display the contents of the variable
   add 1 to the variable's value
   end repeat

start
assign 1 to a variable
variable's value <= 3
F
stop
T
display variable's value
add 1 to the variable's value

Figure 6-5 Pseudocode and flowchart for the pretest loop example from Figure 6-2

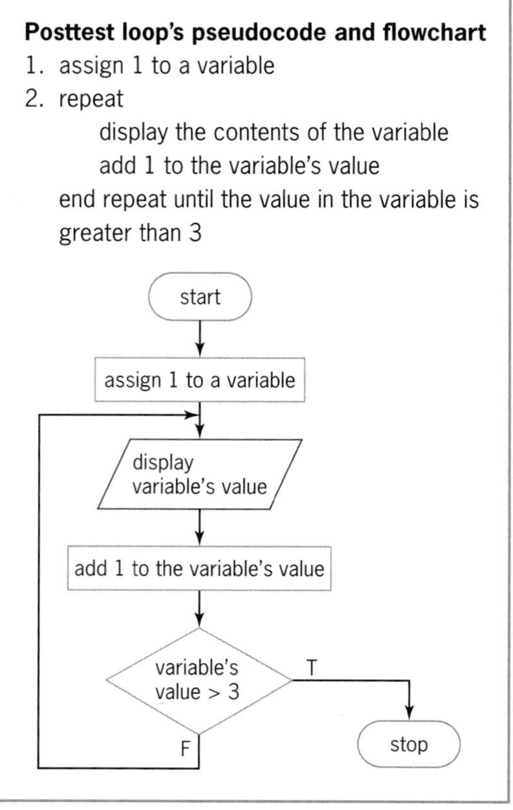

Figure 6-6 Pseudocode and flowchart for the posttest loop example from Figure 6-2

As shown in Figures 6-5 and 6-6, the loop condition in a flowchart is represented by the decision symbol, which is a diamond. Inside each diamond is a comparison that evaluates to either True or False only. The result of the comparison determines whether the computer processes the instructions within the loop. The diamonds in Figures 6-5 and 6-6 have one flowline entering the symbol and two flowlines leaving the symbol. The two flowlines leading out of the diamond should be marked so that anyone reading the flowchart can distinguish the true path from the false path. You mark the flowline leading to the true path with a "T" and the flowline leading to the false path with an "F". You also can mark the flowlines leading out of the diamond with a "Y" and an "N" (for yes and no). In the flowchart of the pretest loop in Figure 6-5, the flowline entering the diamond, as well as the symbols and flowlines within the True path, form a circle or loop. In the posttest loop's flowchart in Figure 6-6, the loop is formed by all of the symbols and flowlines in the False path. It is this loop, or circle, that distinguishes the repetition structure from the selection structure in a flowchart.

Although it appears that the pretest and posttest loops produce the same results—in this case, both examples in Figure 6-2 display the numbers 1 through 3—that will not always be the case. In other words, the two loops are not always interchangeable. To illustrate, if the `intNumber` variable in the pretest loop example in Figure 6-2 is initialized to 10 rather than to 1, the instructions in the pretest loop will not be processed because the `intNumber <= 3` condition (which is evaluated *before* the instructions are processed) evaluates to False. However, if the `intNumber` variable in the posttest loop example in Figure 6-2 is initialized to 10 rather than to 1, the instructions in the posttest loop will be processed one time because the `intNumber > 3` condition is evaluated *after* (rather than before) the loop instructions are processed.

Counters and Accumulators

Some applications require you to calculate a subtotal, a total, or an average. You make these calculations using a repetition structure that includes a counter, or an accumulator, or both. A **counter** is a numeric variable used for counting something, such as the number of employees paid in a week. An **accumulator** is a numeric variable used for accumulating (adding together) something, such as the total dollar amount of a week's payroll. Two tasks are associated with counters and accumulators: initializing and updating. **Initializing** means assigning a beginning value to the counter or accumulator. Typically, counters and accumulators are initialized to the number 0. However, they can be initialized to any number, depending on the value required by the application. The initialization task is performed before the loop is processed, because it needs to be performed only once. **Updating**, also called incrementing, means adding a number to the value stored in the counter or accumulator. The number can be either positive or negative, integer or non-integer. A counter is always incremented by a constant value—typically the number 1—whereas an accumulator is incremented by a value that varies. The assignment statement that updates a counter or an accumulator is placed within the loop in a procedure, because the update task must be performed each time the loop instructions are processed. The Sales Express application, which you view next, includes a counter and an accumulator, as well as a repetition structure.

The Sales Express Application

Sales Express wants an application that displays the average amount the company sold during the prior year. The sales manager will enter the amount of each salesperson's sales. The application will use a counter to keep track of the number of sales amounts entered, and an accumulator to total the sales amounts. When the sales manager has finished entering the sales amounts, the application will calculate the average sales amount by dividing the value stored in the accumulator by the value stored in the counter. It then will display the average sales amount on the screen. Figure 6-7 shows the pseudocode for the btnCalc control's Click event procedure, which is contained in the Sales Express application. Step 1 in the pseudocode is to get a sales amount from the user. Step 2 is a pretest loop whose instructions are processed as long as the user enters a sales amount. If a sales amount was entered, the first two instructions in the loop increment the counter variable by 1 and increment the accumulator variable by the sales amount. The next instruction in the loop requests another sales amount from the user. The loop then checks whether a sales amount was entered; this is necessary to determine whether the loop instructions should be processed again. When the user has finished entering sales amounts, the loop ends and processing continues with Step 3 in the pseudocode. Step 3 is a selection structure that checks whether the counter variable contains a value that is greater than zero. Before using a variable as the divisor in an expression, you always should verify that the variable does not contain the number 0 because, as in math, division by zero is not mathematically possible. Dividing by zero in a procedure will cause the application to end abruptly with an error. As Step 3 indicates, if the counter variable contains a value that is greater than zero, the average sales amount is calculated and then displayed; otherwise, the number 0 is displayed. Notice that "get a sales amount from the user" appears twice in the pseudocode: immediately above the loop and also within the loop. The "get a sales amount from the user" entry that appears above the loop is referred to as the **priming read**, because it is used to prime (prepare or set up) the loop. In this case, the priming read gets only the first salesperson's sales amount from the user. Because the loop in Figure 6-7 is a pretest loop, the first value determines whether the loop instructions are processed at all. The "get a sales amount from the user" entry that appears within the loop gets the sales amounts for the remaining salespeople (if any) from the user.

btnCalc Click event procedure

```
1. get a sales amount from the user          (priming read)
2. repeat while the user entered a sales amount
       add 1 to a counter variable
       add the sales amount to an accumulator variable
       get a sales amount from the user
   end repeat
3. if the counter variable's value is greater than 0
       average sales = accumulator variable / counter variable
       display the average sales
   else
       display the number 0
   end if
```

Figure 6-7 Pseudocode for the btnCalc control's Click event procedure

To open the Sales Express application:

1. If necessary, start Visual Studio 2008 or Visual Basic 2008 Express Edition. Close the Start Page window. Open the **Sales Express Solution** (**Sales Express Solution.sln**) file, which is contained in the VB2008\Chap06\Sales Express Solution folder. If necessary, open the designer window.

2. Open the Code Editor window. Replace the <your name> and <current date> text in the comments with your name and the current date.

3. Locate the btnCalc control's Click event procedure. The procedure declares two named constants and five variables. The named constants and `strInputSales` variable will be used, along with the InputBox function, to get a sales amount from the user. The `decSales` variable will store the sales amount after it has been converted to Decimal. The `intCounter` variable will keep track of the number of sales amounts entered, and the `decAccumulator` variable will accumulate the sales amounts. The `decAverage` variable will store the average sales amount after it has been calculated.

Recall that counters and accumulators must be initialized. Because the Dim statement automatically assigns the number 0 to Integer and Decimal variables when the variables are created, you do not need to enter any additional code to initialize the `intCounter` and `decAccumulator` variables. In cases where you need to initialize a counter or an accumulator to a value other than zero, you can do so either in the Dim statement that declares the variable or in an assignment statement. For example, to initialize the `intCounter` variable to the number 1, you could use either the declaration statement `Dim intCounter As Integer = 1` or the assignment statement `intCounter = 1` in your code. (To use the assignment statement, the variable must already be declared.)

To begin coding the btnCalc control's Click event procedure:

1. Click the **blank line** below the `' get first sales amount` comment in the btnCalc control's Click event procedure. Type **strInputSales = InputBox(strPROMPT, strTITLE, "0")** and press **Enter**.
2. Click the **blank line** below the `' repeat as long as the user enters a sales amount` comment, then enter the following loop.

```
Do While strInputSales <> String.Empty
    Decimal.TryParse(strInputSales, decSales)
    ' update the counter and accumulator
    intCounter = intCounter + 1
    decAccumulator = decAccumulator + decSales
    ' get the next sales amount
    strInputSales = InputBox(strPROMPT, strTITLE, "0")
Loop
```

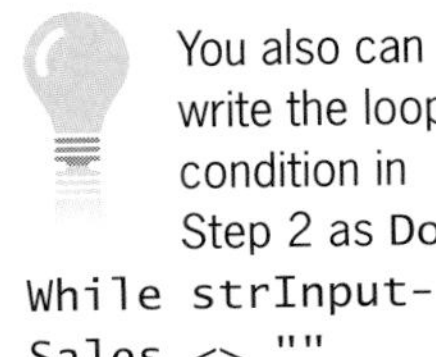
You also can write the loop condition in Step 2 as `Do While strInputSales <> ""`.

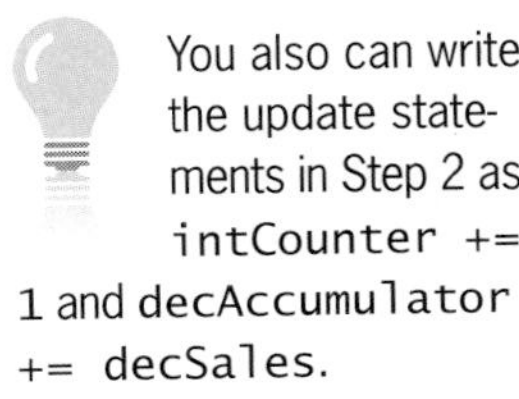
You also can write the update statements in Step 2 as `intCounter += 1` and `decAccumulator += decSales`.

The first statement in the loop converts the string returned by the InputBox function to the Decimal data type. The second statement, `intCounter = intCounter + 1`, updates the counter variable by adding a constant value of 1 to it. Notice that the counter variable appears on both sides of the assignment operator. The statement tells the computer to add 1 to the contents of the variable, and then place the result back in the variable. The `intCounter` variable's value will be incremented by 1 each time the loop is processed. The third statement in the loop, `decAccumulator = decAccumulator + decSales`, updates the accumulator variable by adding the current sales amount to it. Like the counter variable in the previous statement, the accumulator variable appears on both sides of the assignment operator. The statement tells the computer to add the contents of the `decSales` variable to the contents of the accumulator variable, and then place the result back in the accumulator variable. The `decAccumulator` variable's value will be incremented by a sales amount, which will vary, each time the loop is processed. The last statement in the loop prompts the user for another sales amount and then assigns the user's entry to the `strInputSales` variable. Notice that the statement appears twice in the code—before the Do...Loop statement and within the Do...Loop statement. As you learned earlier, the input instruction located above the loop is referred to as the priming read and its task is to get only the first sales amount from the user. The input instruction located within the loop gets each of the remaining sales amounts (if any). If you forget to enter the input instruction within the loop, you will create an endless or infinite loop. To stop an endless loop, click the form in the designer window, then click Debug on the menu bar, and then click Stop Debugging.

To complete the btnCalc control's Click event procedure:

1. Click the **blank line** below the `' display 0 as the average sales amount` comment, then enter the following code.

   ```
   If intCounter > 0 Then
      decAverage = _
         decAccumulator / Convert.ToDecimal(intCounter)
      lblAverage.Text = decAverage.ToString("C2")
   Else
      lblAverage.Text = "0"
   End If
   ```

2. Save the solution. Figure 6-8 shows the procedure's code.

```
Private Sub btnCalc_Click(ByVal sender As Object, _
   ByVal e As System.EventArgs) Handles btnCalc.Click
   ' calculates and displays the average sales amount

   Const strPROMPT As String = _
      "Enter a sales amount. Click Cancel to end."
   Const strTITLE As String = "Sales Entry"
   Dim strInputSales As String
   Dim decSales As Decimal
   Dim intCounter As Integer
   Dim decAccumulator As Decimal
   Dim decAverage As Decimal

   ' get first sales amount
   strInputSales = InputBox(strPROMPT, strTITLE, "0")

   ' repeat as long as the user enters a sales amount
   Do While strInputSales <> String.Empty
      Decimal.TryParse(strInputSales, decSales)
      ' update the counter and accumulator
      intCounter = intCounter + 1
      decAccumulator = decAccumulator + decSales
      ' get the next sales amount
      strInputSales = InputBox(strPROMPT, strTITLE, "0")
   Loop

   ' if counter is greater than 0, calculate
   ' and display the average sales amount; otherwise
   ' display 0 as the average sales amount
   If intCounter > 0 Then
      decAverage = _
         decAccumulator / Convert.ToDecimal(intCounter)
      lblAverage.Text = decAverage.ToString("C2")
   Else
      lblAverage.Text = "0"
   End If
End Sub
```

Figure 6-8 Code entered in the btnCalc control's Click event procedure

To test the btnCalc control's Click event procedure:

1. Start the application. Click the **Calculate** button. The Sales Entry dialog box opens. Type **84** in the input area of the dialog box, then press **Enter** to select the OK button. Type **78** in the dialog box, then press **Enter**. Click the **Cancel** button. The btnCalc Click event procedure calculates and displays the average sales amount, which is $81.00.

2. Click the **Exit** button to end the application. Close the Code Editor window, then close the solution.

The For...Next Statement

The **For...Next statement** provides a convenient way to code a loop whose instructions you want processed a precise number of times. The loop created by the For...Next statement is a pretest loop, because the loop's condition is evaluated *before* the instructions in the loop are processed. Figure 6-9 shows the syntax of the For...Next statement and includes examples of using the statement. Between the statement's For and Next clauses, you enter the instructions you want the loop to repeat. In the syntax, *counter* represents the name of a numeric variable that the computer can use to keep track of the number of times it processes the loop instructions. Notice that *counter* appears in both the For clause and the Next clause. Although, technically, you do not need to specify the name of the *counter* variable in the Next clause, doing so is highly recommended because it makes your code more self-documenting. You can use the `As` *dataType* portion of the For clause to declare the *counter* variable, as shown in the first two examples in Figure 6-9. When you declare a variable in the For clause, the variable has block scope and can be used only within the For...Next loop. Alternatively, you can declare the *counter* variable in a Dim statement, as shown in Example 3 in Figure 6-9. As you know, when a variable is declared in a Dim statement at the beginning of a procedure, it has procedure scope and can be used within the entire procedure. When deciding where to declare the *counter* variable, keep in mind that if the variable is needed only by the For...Next loop, then it is a better programming practice to declare the variable in the For clause. As mentioned in Chapter 3, fewer unintentional errors occur in applications when the variables are declared using the minimum scope needed. Block variables have the smallest scope, followed by procedure-level variables, followed by module-level variables. You should declare the *counter* variable in a Dim statement only when its value is required by statements outside the For...Next loop in the procedure.

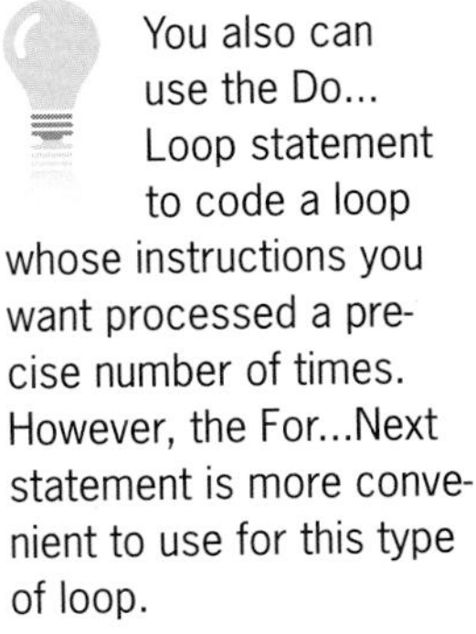

You also can use the Do...Loop statement to code a loop whose instructions you want processed a precise number of times. However, the For...Next statement is more convenient to use for this type of loop.

The *startValue*, *endValue*, and *stepValue* items in the For...Next statement's syntax control the number of times the loop instructions are processed. The *startValue* tells the computer where to begin counting, and the *endValue* tells the computer when to stop counting. The *stepValue* tells the computer how much to count by—in other words, how much to add to the *counter* variable each time the loop is processed. If you omit the *stepValue*, a *stepValue* of positive 1 is used. In Example 1 in Figure 6-9, the *startValue* is 10, the *endValue* is 13, and the *stepValue* (which is omitted) is 1. Those values tell the computer to start counting at 10 and, counting by 1s, stop at 13—in other words, count 10, 11, 12, and 13. The computer will process the instructions in Example 1's loop four times. The For clause's *startValue*, *endValue*, and *stepValue* must be numeric and can be either positive or negative, integer or non-integer. If the *stepValue* is positive, the *startValue* must be less than or equal to the *endValue* for the loop instructions to be processed. For instance, the instruction `For intPrice As Integer = 10 To 13` is correct, but the instruction `For intPrice As Integer = 13 To 10` is not correct because you cannot count from 13 (the *startValue*) to 10 (the *endValue*) by adding increments of 1 (the *stepValue*). If, on the other hand, the *stepValue* is negative, then the *startValue* must be greater than or equal to the *endValue* for the loop instructions to be processed. As a result, the instruction `For intPrice As Integer = 13 To 10 Step -1` is correct, but the instruction `For intPrice As Integer = 10 To 13 Step -1` is not

You can use the `Exit For` statement to exit the For...Next statement prematurely, which means to exit it before it has finished processing. You may need to do this if the computer encounters an error when processing the loop instructions.

Adding increments of a negative number is referred to as decrementing. In other words, adding increments of negative 1 is the same as decrementing by 1.

You can nest For...Next statements, which means you can place one For...Next statement within another For...Next statement.

correct because you cannot count from 10 to 13 by adding increments of negative 1. In addition to the syntax and examples of the For...Next statement, Figure 6-9 also shows the tasks performed by the computer when processing the statement.

For...Next statement

Syntax

For *counter* [**As** *dataType*] = *startValue* **To** *endValue* [**Step** *stepValue*]
[*statements*]
Next *counter*

Example 1

```
For intPrice As Integer = 10 To 13
   lblPrice.Text = lblPrice.Text & Convert.ToString(intPrice) _
      & ControlChars.NewLine
Next intPrice
```

displays the numbers 10, 11, 12, and 13 in the lblPrice control

Example 2

```
For intPrice As Integer = 13 To 10 Step -1
   lblPrice.Text = lblPrice.Text & intPrice.ToString _
      & ControlChars.NewLine
Next intPrice
```

displays the numbers 13, 12, 11, and 10 in the lblPrice control

Example 3

```
Dim decRate As Decimal
For decRate = .05D To .1D Step .01D
   lblRate.Text = lblRate.Text & decRate.ToString("P0") _
      & ControlChars.NewLine
Next decRate
```

displays the values 5 %, 6 %, 7 %, 8 %, 9 %, and 10 % in the lblRate control

Processing tasks

1. If the *counter* variable is declared in the For clause, the computer creates and then initializes the variable to the *startValue*; otherwise, it just performs the initialization task. This is done only once, at the beginning of the loop.
2. The computer evaluates the loop condition by comparing the value in the *counter* variable with the *endValue*. If the *stepValue* is a positive number, the comparison determines whether the *counter* variable's value is greater than the *endValue*. If the *stepValue* is a negative number, the comparison determines whether the *counter* variable's value is less than the *endValue*.
3. If the loop condition evaluates to True, the computer stops processing the loop; processing continues with the statement following the Next clause. If the loop condition evaluates to False, the computer processes the instructions within the loop and then task 4 is performed. Notice that the computer evaluates the loop condition before processing the instructions within the loop.
4. Task 4 is performed only when the loop condition evaluates to False. In this task, the computer adds the *stepValue* to the contents of the *counter* variable. It then repeats tasks 2, 3, and 4 until the loop condition evaluates to True.

Figure 6-9 Syntax, examples, and tasks associated with the For...Next statement

Figure 6-10 describes the way the computer processes the code shown in Example 1 in Figure 6-9. Notice that when the For...Next statement in the example ends, the value stored in the `intPrice` variable is 14.

Processing steps for Example 1

1. The computer creates the `intPrice` variable and initializes it to 10.
2. The computer checks whether the value in the `intPrice` variable is greater than 13. It's not, so the computer displays the number 10 on the first line in the lblPrice control and then adds 1 to the contents of the `intPrice` variable, giving 11.
3. The computer again checks whether the value in the `intPrice` variable is greater than 13. It's not, so the computer displays the number 11 on the second line in the lblPrice control and then adds 1 to the contents of the `intPrice` variable, giving 12.
4. The computer again checks whether the value in the `intPrice` variable is greater than 13. It's not, so the computer displays the number 12 on the third line in the lblPrice control and then adds 1 to the contents of the `intPrice` variable, giving 13.
5. The computer again checks whether the value in the `intPrice` variable is greater than 13. It's not, so the computer displays the number 13 on the fourth line in the lblPrice control and then adds 1 to the contents of the `intPrice` variable, giving 14.
6. The computer again checks whether the value in the `intPrice` variable is greater than 13. It is, so the computer stops processing the For...Next loop. Processing continues with the statement following the Next clause.

Figure 6-10 Processing steps for Example 1 in Figure 6-9

Figure 6-11 shows the pseudocode and flowchart corresponding to Example 1 in Figure 6-9. Many programmers use a hexagon, which is a six-sided figure, to represent the For clause in a flowchart. Four values are recorded inside the hexagon: the name of the *counter* variable, the *startValue*, the *stepValue*, and the *endValue*. Notice that a greater-than sign (>) precedes the *endValue* in the hexagon in Figure 6-11. The greater-than sign reminds you that the loop stops when the value in the *counter* variable is greater than the *endValue*. When the *stepValue* is a negative number, a less-than sign (<) should precede the *endValue* in the hexagon, because a loop with a negative *stepValue* stops when the value in the *counter* variable is less than the *endValue*.

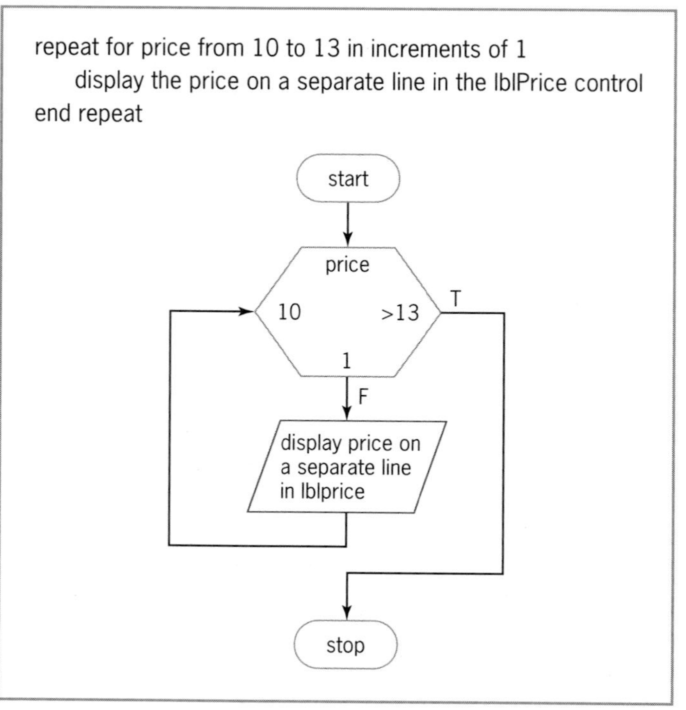

Figure 6-11 Pseudocode and flowchart for Example 1 in Figure 6-9

Next, you will view an application that uses the For...Next statement.

The Monthly Payment Calculator Application

The Monthly Payment Calculator application displays the monthly payments on a car loan, using a term of 5 years and annual interest rates of 5%, 6%, 7%, 8%, 9%, and 10%.

To open the Monthly Payment Calculator application:

1. Open the **Payment Calculator Solution** (**Payment Calculator Solution.sln**) file, which is contained in the VB2008\Chap06\Payment Calculator Solution folder. If necessary, open the designer window.
2. Open the Code Editor window. Replace the <your name> and <current date> text in the comments with your name and the current date, then locate the code template for the btnCalc control's Click event procedure.

The btnCalc control's Click event procedure declares and initializes an Integer named constant for the term. It also declares two Double variables to store the principal and payment amounts, and a Boolean variable to store the value returned by the TryParse method. Next, the procedure clears the contents of the lblPayments control. It then uses the TryParse method to convert the contents of the txtPrincipal control to a Double number. If the conversion is not successful, the statement in the selection structure's false path displays an appropriate message in a message box. However, if the conversion is successful, the statements in the selection structure's true path should calculate and display the monthly payments using interest rates from 5% to 10% in increments of 1%. You will complete the true path in the following steps. The last statements in the procedure send the focus to the txtPrincipal control and also select the control's existing text.

To complete and then test the btnCalc control's Click event procedure:

1. Click the **blank line** below the `' calculate and display payments` comment. Type **For dblRate As Double = .05 To .1 Step .01** and press **Enter**. The For clause tells the computer to repeat the instructions in the loop six times, using interest rates of .05, .06, .07, .08, .09, and .1.
2. Change the Next clause to **Next dblRate**.
3. Enter the additional lines of code indicated in Figure 6-12.

```
If blnIsConverted Then
    ' calculate and display payments
    For dblRate As Double = 0.05 To 0.1 Step 0.01
        dblPayment = _
            -Financial.Pmt(dblRate / 12, intTERM * 12, dblPrincipal)
        lblPayments.Text = lblPayments.Text & dblRate.ToString("P0") & " -> " _
            & dblPayment.ToString("C2") & ControlChars.NewLine
    Next dblRate
Else    ' principal cannot be converted to a number
    MessageBox.Show("Please re-enter the principal.", _
        "Payment Calculator", MessageBoxButtons.OK, _
        MessageBoxIcon.Information)
End If
```

enter these 4 lines of code

Figure 6-12 Additional code entered in the btnCalc control's Click event procedure

4. Close the Code Editor window. Save the solution, then start the application.
5. Enter **10000** as the principal, then press **Enter** to select the Calculate button. The button's Click event procedure displays the monthly payments. See Figure 6-13.

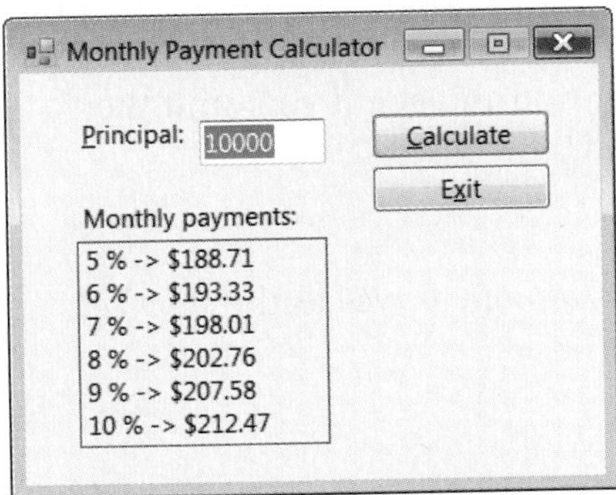

Figure 6-13 Monthly payments shown in the interface

6. Click the **Exit** button to end the application, then close the solution.

Lesson A Summary

- **To have the computer repeat a set of instructions either while a condition is true or until a condition becomes true:**

  Use a repetition structure (loop). You can code a repetition structure in Visual Basic using one of the following statements: For...Next, Do...Loop, and For Each...Next. (The For Each...Next statement is covered in Chapter 9.)

- **To use the Do...Loop statement to code a loop:**

  Refer to Figure 6-2 for the two versions of the Do...Loop statement's syntax. The Do...Loop statement can be used to code both pretest and posttest loops. In a pretest loop, the loop condition appears in the Do clause; it appears in the Loop clause in a posttest loop. The loop condition must evaluate to a Boolean value.

- **To use a counter:**

  Initialize the counter, if necessary. Update the counter using an assignment statement within a repetition structure. You update a counter by incrementing (or decrementing) its value by a constant amount, which can be either positive or negative, integer or non-integer.

- **To use an accumulator:**

  Initialize the accumulator, if necessary. Update the accumulator using an assignment statement within a repetition structure. You update an accumulator by incrementing (or decrementing) its value by an amount that varies. The amount can be either positive or negative, integer or non-integer.

- **To use the For...Next statement to code a loop:**

  Refer to Figure 6-9 for the syntax of the For...Next statement. The For...Next statement can be used to code pretest loops only. In the syntax, *counter* is the name of the numeric variable that keeps track of the number of times the loop instructions are processed. The *startValue, endValue,* and *stepValue* items control the number of times the loop instructions are processed. The *startValue, endValue,* and *stepValue* items must be numeric and can be positive or negative, integer or non-integer. If you omit the *stepValue*, a *stepValue* of positive 1 is used.

- **To flowchart a For...Next loop:**

  Use a hexagon that shows the name of the *counter*, as well as the *startValue, stepValue,* and *endValue.*

Lesson A Key Terms

Accumulator—a numeric variable used for accumulating (adding together) something

Counter—a numeric variable used for counting something

Do...Loop statement—a Visual Basic statement that can be used to code either a pretest loop or a posttest loop

For...Next statement—a Visual Basic statement that provides a convenient way of coding a pretest loop whose instructions you want processed a precise number of times

Initializing—assigning a beginning value to a variable, such as a counter or accumulator variable

Loop—another term for the repetition structure

Posttest loop—a loop whose condition is evaluated *after* the instructions within the loop are processed

Pretest loop—a loop whose condition is evaluated *before* the instructions within the loop are processed

Priming read—the input instruction that appears above the loop it controls; determines whether the loop instructions will be processed the first time

Repetition structure—one of the three programming structures; used to repeatedly process one or more program instructions until some condition is met, at which time the repetition structure ends; also called a loop

Updating—adding a number to the value stored in a counter or accumulator variable

Lesson A Review Questions

1. You can use the ______________________ statement to code a loop whose instructions you want processed 10 times.
   a. Do...Loop
   b. For...Next
   c. either a or b

2. The instructions in a ______________________ loop are always processed at least once, whereas the instructions in a ______________________ loop might not be processed at all.
   a. posttest, pretest
   b. pretest, posttest

3. Which of the following clauses stops the loop when the value in the `intAge` variable is less than the number 0?
   a. `Do While intAge >= 0`
   b. `Do Until intAge < 0`
   c. `Loop While intAge >= 0`
   d. All of the above.

4. How many times will the MessageBox.Show method in the following code be processed?

```
Dim intCounter As Integer
Do While intCounter > 3
   MessageBox.Show("Hello")
   intCounter = intCounter + 1
Loop
```

   a. 0
   b. 1
   c. 3
   d. 4

5. How many times will the MessageBox.Show method in the following code be processed?

```
Dim intCounter As Integer
Do
   MessageBox.Show("Hello")
   intCounter = intCounter + 1
Loop While intCounter > 3
```

   a. 0
   b. 1
   c. 3
   d. 4

6. How many times will the MessageBox.Show method in the following code be processed?

```
For intCounter As Integer = 4 To 11 Step 2
   MessageBox.Show("Hello")
Next intCounter
```

   a. 3
   b. 4
   c. 5
   d. 8

7. What is the value stored in the `intCounter` variable when the loop in Question 6 ends?

   a. 10
   b. 11
   c. 12
   d. 13

8. A procedure allows the user to enter one or more values. The first input instruction will get the first value only and is referred to as the ____________________ read.

   a. entering

   b. initializer

   c. priming

   d. starter

Refer to Figure 6-14 to answer Questions 9 through 12.

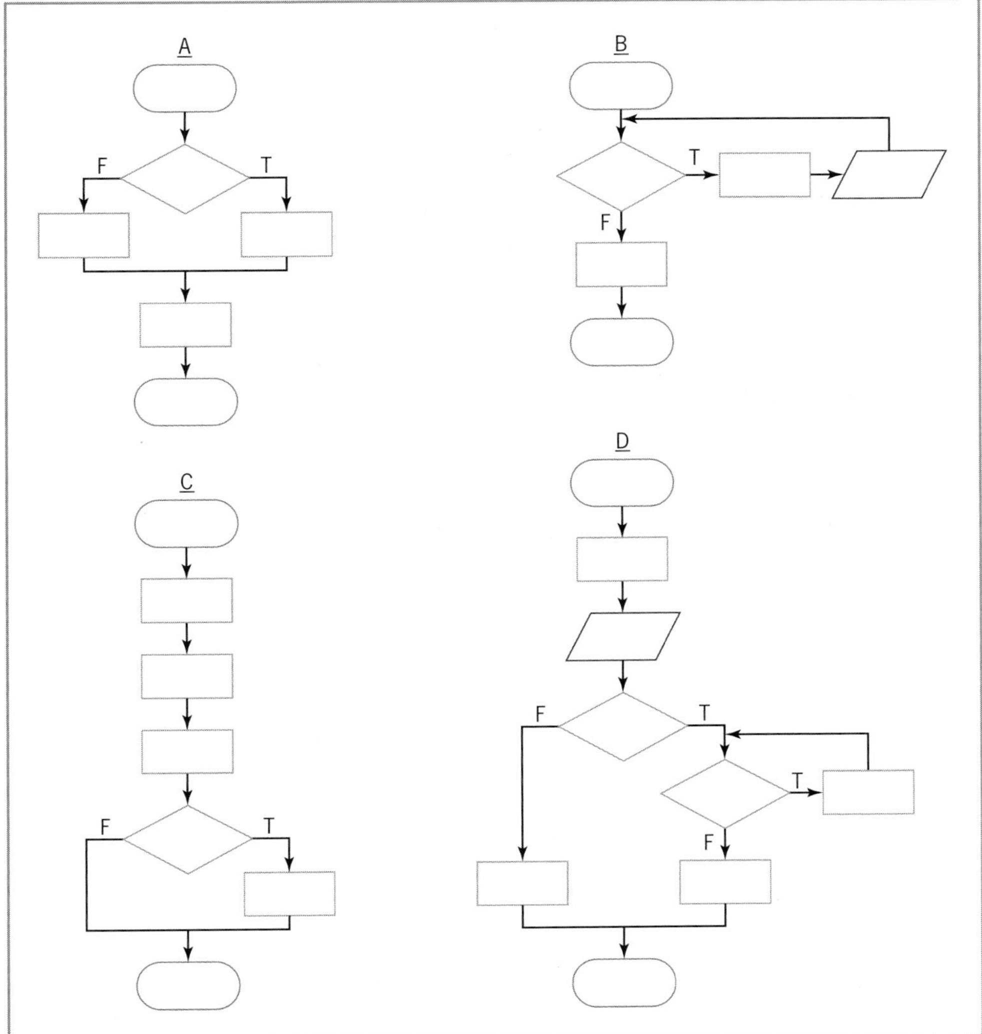

Figure 6-14 Flowcharts for Questions 9 through 12

9. Which of the following programming structures are used in flowchart A in Figure 6-14? (Select all that apply.)

   a. sequence

   b. selection

   c. repetition

10. Which of the following programming structures are used in flowchart B in Figure 6-14? (Select all that apply.)
    a. sequence
    b. selection
    c. repetition

11. Which of the following programming structures are used in flowchart C in Figure 6-14? (Select all that apply.)
    a. sequence
    b. selection
    c. repetition

12. Which of the following programming structures are used in flowchart D in Figure 6-14? (Select all that apply.)
    a. sequence
    b. selection
    c. repetition

Lesson A Exercises

INTRODUCTORY

1. Write a Visual Basic Do clause that processes the loop instructions as long as the value in the intQuantity variable is greater than the number 0. Use the `While` keyword.

INTRODUCTORY

2. Rewrite the Do clause from Exercise 1 using the `Until` keyword.

INTRODUCTORY

3. Write a Visual Basic Do clause that stops the loop when the value in the `intInStock` variable is less than or equal to the value in the `intReorder` variable. Use the `Until` keyword.

INTRODUCTORY

4. Rewrite the Do clause from Exercise 3 using the `While` keyword.

INTRODUCTORY

5. Write a Visual Basic Loop clause that processes the loop instructions as long as the value in the `strLetter` variable is either Y or y. Use the `While` keyword.

INTRODUCTORY

6. Rewrite the Loop clause from Exercise 5 using the `Until` keyword.

INTRODUCTORY

7. Write a Visual Basic Do clause that processes the loop instructions as long as the value in the `strEmpName` variable is not "Done" (in any case). Use the `While` keyword.

8. Rewrite the Do clause from Exercise 7 using the `Until` keyword. INTRODUCTORY

9. What will the following code display in message boxes? INTRODUCTORY

```
Dim intX As Integer
Do While intX < 5
   MessageBox.Show(Convert.ToString(intX))
   intX = intX + 1
Loop
```

10. What will the following code display in message boxes? INTRODUCTORY

```
Dim intX As Integer
Do
   MessageBox.Show(Convert.ToString(intX))
   intX = intX + 1
Loop Until intX > 5
```

11. Write a Visual Basic assignment statement that updates the `intQuantity` counter variable by 2. INTRODUCTORY

12. Write a Visual Basic assignment statement that updates the `decTotal` accumulator variable by the value stored in the `decPurchase` variable. INTRODUCTORY

13. Write a Visual Basic assignment statement that updates the `intTotal` counter variable by -3. INTERMEDIATE

14. Write a Visual Basic assignment statement that subtracts the contents of the `decReturns` variable from the `decSales` accumulator variable. INTERMEDIATE

15. Write the Visual Basic code for a pretest loop that uses an Integer variable named `intEvenNum` to display the even integers from 2 through 10 in the lblNumbers control. Use the For...Next statement. Display each number on a separate line in the control. INTERMEDIATE

16. Rewrite the pretest loop from Exercise 15 using the Do...Loop statement. INTERMEDIATE

17. Change the pretest loop from Exercise 16 to a posttest loop. INTERMEDIATE

18. Write the Visual Basic code that corresponds to the flowchart shown in Figure 6-15. Display the calculated results on separate lines in the lblCount control. INTERMEDIATE

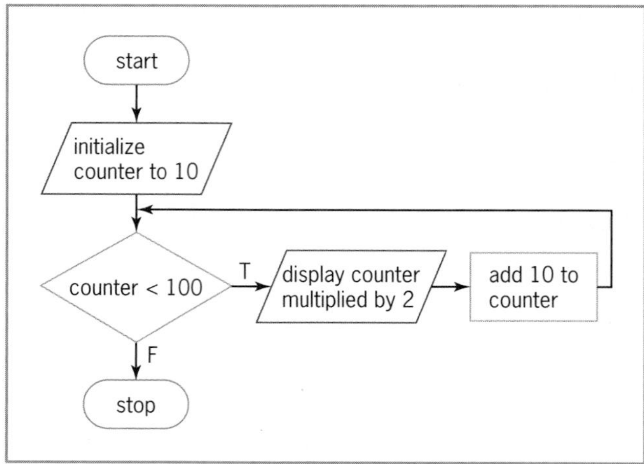

Figure 6-15 Flowchart for Exercise 18

INTERMEDIATE

19. Write a For...Next statement that displays the numbers from 0 through 117, in increments of 9, in the lblNumbers control. Display each number on a separate line in the control.

INTERMEDIATE

20. Write a For...Next statement that calculates and displays the squares of the even numbers from 2 through 12. Display the results in the lblNumbers control. Display each number on a separate line in the control.

INTERMEDIATE

21. An instruction is missing from the following code. What is the missing instruction and where does it belong in the code?

```
Dim intNumber As Integer = 1
Do While intNumber < 5
   MessageBox.Show(intNumber.ToString)
Loop
```

INTERMEDIATE

22. An instruction is missing from the following code. What is the missing instruction and where does it belong in the code?

```
Dim intNumber As Integer = 10
Do
   MessageBox.Show(intNumber.ToString)
Loop Until intNumber = 0
```

INTERMEDIATE

23. What will the following code display?

```
Dim intTotal As Integer
Do While intTotal <= 5
   MessageBox.Show(intTotal.ToString)
   intTotal = intTotal + 2
Loop
```

INTERMEDIATE

24. What will the following code display?

```
Dim intTotal As Integer = 1
Do
   MessageBox.Show(intTotal.ToString)
   intTotal = intTotal + 2
Loop Until intTotal >= 3
```

INTERMEDIATE

25. Use Windows to make a copy of the Payment Calculator Solution folder, which is contained in the VB2008\Chap06 folder. Rename the folder Modified Payment Calculator Solution. Open the Payment Calculator Solution (Payment Calculator Solution.sln) file contained in the VB2008\Chap06\Modified Payment Calculator Solution folder. Open the designer window, then open the Code Editor window. Change the For...Next statement in the btnCalc control's Click event procedure to a Do...Loop statement. Save the solution, then start and test the application. Stop the application. Close the Code Editor window, then close the solution.

ADVANCED

26. Use Windows to make a copy of the Sales Express Solution folder, which is contained in the VB2008\Chap06 folder. Rename the folder Modified Sales Express Solution. Open the Sales Express Solution (Sales Express Solution.sln) file contained in the VB2008\Chap06\Modified Sales Express Solution folder. Open the designer window, then open the Code Editor window. Each time the application is started, the user will enter five sales amounts. Change the Do...Loop statement in the btnCalc control's Click event procedure to a For...Next statement. If a sales amount cannot be converted to a number, use the `Exit For` statement to exit the loop. Calculate the average only when the user enters five valid sales amounts; otherwise, display an appropriate message in a message box and the number 0 in the lblAverage control. Save the solution, then start and test the application. Stop the application. Close the Code Editor window, then close the solution.

Swat The Bugs

27. The following code should display a 10% bonus for each sales amount that is entered. The code is not working properly, because an instruction is missing. What is the missing instruction and where does it belong in the code?

```
Dim strInput As String
Dim dblSales As Double
Dim dblBonus As Double
strInput = InputBox("Sales amount:", "Sales")
Do While strInput <> String.Empty
   Double.TryParse(strInput, dblSales)
   dblBonus = dblSales * .1
   MessageBox.Show(dblBonus.ToString("C2"))
Loop
```

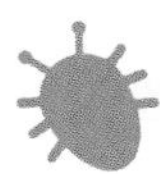

Swat The Bugs

28. The following code should display a 10% bonus for each sales amount that is entered. The code is not working properly. What is wrong with the code and how can you fix it?

```
Dim strInput As String
Dim dblSales As Double
Dim dblBonus As Double
strInput = InputBox("Sales amount:", "Sales")
Double.TryParse(strInput, dblSales)
Do
   strInput = InputBox("Sales amount:", "Sales")
   Double.TryParse(strInput, dblSales)
   dblBonus = dblSales * .1
   MessageBox.Show(dblBonus.ToString("C2"))
Loop Until dblSales <= 0
```

LESSON B

After studying Lesson B, you should be able to:

- Nest repetition structures
- Refresh the screen
- Delay program execution

Nested Repetition Structures

Like selection structures, repetition structures can be nested. In other words, you can place one repetition structure (called the nested or inner repetition structure) within another repetition structure (called the outer repetition structure). Both repetition structures can be either pretest loops or posttest loops. Or, one can be a pretest loop and the other a posttest loop. Although the idea of nested loops may sound confusing, you already are familiar with the concept. A clock uses nested loops to keep track of the time. For example, consider a clock's hour and minute hands only. The minute hand is controlled by the inner (nested) loop, whereas the hour hand is controlled by the outer loop. The minute hand on a clock moves one position, clockwise, for every minute that has elapsed. After the minute hand moves 60 positions, the hour hand moves one position, also clockwise. The minute hand then begins its journey around the clock again. Figure 6-16 shows the logic used by a clock's hour and minute hands. Notice that the entire nested loop is contained within the outer loop; this must be true for the loop to be nested and for it to work correctly.

```
repeat for hours from 0 through 23 in increments of 1
    repeat for minutes from 0 through 59 in increments of 1
        move minute hand 1 position, clockwise
    end repeat
    move hour hand 1 position, clockwise
end repeat
```

Figure 6-16 Logic used by a clock's hour and minute hands

To code and then test the Clock application:

1. If necessary, start Visual Studio 2008 or Visual Basic 2008 Express Edition. Close the Start Page window.
2. Open the **Clock Solution** (**Clock Solution.sln**) file, which is contained in the VB2008\Chap06\Clock Solution folder. If necessary, open the designer window. See Figure 6-17. (The clock image is from the Microsoft Office Clip Art collection, which is available at *http://office.microsoft.com*.)

Figure 6-17 Clock application's user interface

3. Open the Code Editor window. Replace the <your name> and <current date> text in the comments with your name and the current date.

4. Open the code template for the btnStart control's Click event procedure. Type **' displays hours and minutes** and press **Enter** twice.

5. You will use an outer loop to display the number of hours, and a nested loop to display the number of minutes. For simplicity in watching the hours and minutes tick away, you will display hour values from 0 through 3 (rather than from 0 through 23) and minute values from 0 through 9 (rather than from 0 through 59). Enter the following code.

```
For intHours As Integer = 0 To 3
    lblHours.Text = intHours.ToString
    For intMinutes As Integer = 0 To 9
        lblMinutes.Text = intMinutes.ToString
    Next intMinutes
Next intHours
```

6. Save the solution, then start the application. Click the **Start** button. The computer processes the code entered in the button's Click event procedure. However, it processes it so quickly that you don't get a chance to see each of the values assigned to the label controls. Rather, only the final values (3 and 9) appear in the label controls. You can fix this problem by refreshing the interface and then delaying program execution each time the contents of the lblMinutes control changes.

The Refresh and Sleep Methods

You use the Refresh method to refresh (or redraw) the interface. The **Refresh method** ensures that any code appearing before it that affects the interface's appearance is processed. The Refresh method's syntax is **Me.Refresh()**, where Me refers to the current form. You can delay program execution using the **Sleep method** in the following syntax: **System.Threading.Thread.Sleep(*milliseconds*)**. The *milliseconds* argument is the number of milliseconds to suspend the program. A millisecond is 1/1000 of a second, which means there are 1000 milliseconds in a second. In the Clock application, you will delay program execution for a half of a second, which is 500 milliseconds.

To include the Refresh and Sleep methods in the procedure, and then test the code:

1. Enter the additional comment and two lines of code indicated in Figure 6-18.

```
Private Sub btnStart_Click(ByVal sender As Object, ByVal e As System.Even
    ' displays hours and minutes

    For intHours As Integer = 0 To 3
        lblHours.Text = intHours.ToString
        For intMinutes As Integer = 0 To 9
            lblMinutes.Text = intMinutes.ToString
            ' refresh interface, then pause execution
            Me.Refresh()
            System.Threading.Thread.Sleep(500)
        Next intMinutes
    Next intHours
End Sub
```

enter this comment and 2 lines of code

Figure 6-18 Refresh and Sleep methods added to the procedure

2. Save the solution, then start the application. Click the **Start** button. The number 0 appears in the lblHours control, and the numbers 0 through 9 appear (one at a time) in the lblMinutes control. Notice that the number of hours is increased by 1 when the number of minutes changes from 9 to 0. (On a real digital clock, the hour value is updated when the number of minutes changes from 59 to 0.) When the procedure ends, the lblHours and lblMinutes controls contain the numbers 3 and 9, respectively. (If you want to end the procedure prematurely, click the form in the designer window, then click Debug on the menu bar, and then click Stop Debugging.)

3. Click the **Exit** button. Close the Code Editor window, then close the solution.

Monthly Payment Calculator Application—Nested For...Next Statements

In this section, you view a different version of the Monthly Payment Calculator application from Lesson A. This version uses two For...Next statements, one nested within the other, to calculate and display the monthly car payments. The outer For...Next statement will control the interest rates, which range from 5% to 10% in increments of 1%. The inner For...Next statement will control the terms, which are 3 years, 4 years, and 5 years.

To code and then test the Nested Payment application:

1. Open the **Nested Payment Solution** (**Nested Payment Solution.sln**) file, which is contained in the VB2008\Chap06\Nested Payment Solution folder. If necessary, open the designer window.

2. Open the Code Editor window. Replace the <your name> and <current date> text in the comments with your name and the current date.

3. Locate the code template for the btnCalc control's Click event procedure. Click the **blank line** below the `' calculate and display payments`

comment. First, enter the loop that controls the interest rates. Type **For dblRate As Double = .05 To .1 Step .01** and press **Enter**, then change the Next clause to **Next dblRate**.

4. Click the **blank line** below the For clause. You will display the current rate (formatted as a percentage) in the lblPayments control. Type **lblPayments.Text = lblPayments.Text _** (be sure to include a space before the line continuation character) and press **Enter**. Press **Tab**, then type **& dblRate.ToString("P0") & "   "** (include 4 spaces between the second set of quotation marks) and press **Enter** twice.

5. Now enter the loop that controls the term. Type **For intTerm As Integer = 3 To 5** and press **Enter**, then change the Next clause to **Next intTerm**.

6. Click the **blank line** below the inner For clause. Now you will enter the code to calculate and display the monthly payments. Type the following lines of code. Include 4 spaces between the second set of quotation marks in the last line.

```
dblPayment = _
    -Financial.Pmt(dblRate / 12, _
                   intTerm * 12, dblPrincipal)
lblPayments.Text = lblPayments.Text _
    & dblPayment.ToString("N2") & "    "
```

7. Finally, display a blank line after each rate in the lblPayments control. Click **immediately after the letter m** in the `Next intTerm` line, then press **Enter** twice. Enter the additional line of code indicated in Figure 6-19.

```
' calculate and display payments
For dblRate As Double = 0.05 To 0.1 Step 0.01
    lblPayments.Text = lblPayments.Text _
        & dblRate.ToString("P0") & "    "

    For intTerm As Integer = 3 To 5
        dblPayment = _
            -Financial.Pmt(dblRate / 12, _
                           intTerm * 12, dblPrincipal)
        lblPayments.Text = lblPayments.Text _
            & dblPayment.ToString("N2") & "    "
    Next intTerm

    lblPayments.Text = lblPayments.Text & ControlChars.NewLine
Next dblRate
```

enter this line of code

Figure 6-19 Outer and inner (nested) loops entered in the procedure

Although both loops in Figure 6-19 are pretest loops, you also can use two posttest loops or a combination of a pretest and a posttest loop.

8. Save the solution, then start the application. Type **10000** in the Principal box, then press **Enter** to select the Calculate button. Figure 6-20 shows the monthly payments.

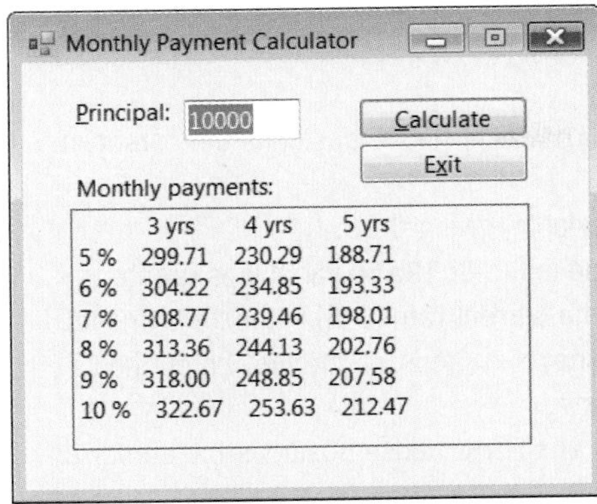

Figure 6-20 Monthly payments shown in the interface

9. Click the **Exit** button. Close the Code Editor window, then close the solution.

Figure 6-21 describes the way the computer processes the loops shown in Figure 6-19. Notice that when the inner loop ends, the value stored in the `intTerm` variable is 6. When the outer loop ends, the value stored in the `dblRate` variable is .11.

Processing steps for Figure 6-19's loops

1. The computer creates the `dblRate` variable and initializes it to 0.05.
2. The computer checks whether the value in the `dblRate` variable is greater than 0.1. It's not, so the computer displays the current rate (5 %) in the lblPayments control and then processes the inner loop as follows:
   a. The computer creates the `intTerm` variable and initializes it to 3.
   b. The computer checks whether the value in the `intTerm` variable is greater than 5. It's not, so the computer calculates the monthly car payment using 0.05 as the rate and 3 as the term, and then displays the result in the lblPayments control.
   c. The computer adds 1 to the `intTerm` variable, giving 4.
   d. The computer again checks whether the value in the `intTerm` variable is greater than 5. It's not, so the computer calculates the monthly car payment using 0.05 as the rate and 4 as the term, and then displays the result in the lblPayments control.
   e. The computer adds 1 to the `intTerm` variable, giving 5.
   f. The computer again checks whether the value in the `intTerm` variable is greater than 5. It's not, so the computer calculates the monthly car payment using 0.05 as the rate and 5 as the term, and then displays the result in the lblPayments control.
   g. The computer adds 1 to the `intTerm` variable, giving 6.
   h. The computer again checks whether the value in the `intTerm` variable is greater than 5. It is, so the computer removes the `intTerm` variable from memory and then stops processing the inner loop. Processing continues with the statement immediately below the `Next intTerm` clause.

Figure 6-21 Processing steps for the loops shown in Figure 6-19 *(continues)*

(continued)

Processing steps for Figure 6-19's loops

3. The statement immediately below the `Next intTerm` clause positions the cursor on the next line in the lblPayments control.
4. The computer adds 0.01 to the `dblRate` variable, giving 0.06.
5. The computer again checks whether the value in the `dblRate` variable is greater than 0.1. It's not, so the computer displays the current rate (6 %) in the lblPayments control. It then processes the inner loop as shown in Steps 2a through 2h on the previous page; this time using 0.06 as the rate.
6. The statement immediately below the `Next intTerm` clause positions the cursor on the next line in the lblPayments control.
7. The computer adds 0.01 to the `dblRate` variable, giving 0.07.
8. The computer again checks whether the value in the `dblRate` variable is greater than 0.1. It's not, so the computer displays the current rate (7 %) in the lblPayments control. It then processes the inner loop as shown in Steps 2a through 2h on the previous page; this time using 0.07 as the rate.
9. The statement immediately below the `Next intTerm` clause positions the cursor on the next line in the lblPayments control.
10. The computer adds 0.01 to the `dblRate` variable, giving 0.08.
11. The computer again checks whether the value in the `dblRate` variable is greater than 0.1. It's not, so the computer displays the current rate (8 %) in the lblPayments control. It then processes the inner loop as shown in Steps 2a through 2h on the previous page; this time using 0.08 as the rate.
12. The statement immediately below the `Next intTerm` clause positions the cursor on the next line in the lblPayments control.
13. The computer adds 0.01 to the `dblRate` variable, giving 0.09.
14. The computer again checks whether the value in the `dblRate` variable is greater than 0.1. It's not, so the computer displays the current rate (9 %) in the lblPayments control. It then processes the inner loop as shown in Steps 2a through 2h on the previous page; this time using 0.09 as the rate.
15. The statement immediately below the `Next intTerm` clause positions the cursor on the next line in the lblPayments control.
16. The computer adds 0.01 to the `dblRate` variable, giving 0.1.
17. The computer again checks whether the value in the `dblRate` variable is greater than 0.1. It's not, so the computer displays the current rate (10 %) in the lblPayments control. It then processes the inner loop as shown in Steps 2a through 2h on the previous page; this time using 0.1 as the rate.
18. The statement immediately below the `Next intTerm` clause positions the cursor on the next line in the lblPayments control.
19. The computer adds 0.01 to the `dblRate` variable, giving 0.11.
20. The computer again checks whether the value in the `dblRate` variable is greater than 0.1. It is, so the computer removes the `dblRate` variable from memory and then stops processing the outer loop. Processing continues with the statement immediately below the `Next dblRate` clause.

Figure 6-21 Processing steps for the loops shown in Figure 6-19

Lesson B Summary

- **To nest a repetition structure:**

  Place the entire inner loop within the outer loop.

- **To refresh the interface:**

  Use the Refresh method. The method's syntax is **Me.Refresh()**.

- **To pause program execution:**

  Use the Sleep method, whose syntax is **System.Threading.Thread. Sleep(*milliseconds*)**.

Lesson B Key Terms

Refresh method—used to refresh (redraw) the interface

Sleep method—used to delay program execution

Lesson B Review Questions

1. What will appear in the lblAsterisks control after the computer processes the following code?

```
For intX As Integer = 1 To 2
   For intY As Integer = 1 To 3
      lblAsterisks.Text = lblAsterisks.Text & "*"
   Next intY
   lblAsterisks.Text = lblAsterisks.Text & _
      ControlChars.NewLine
Next intX
```

a. ***
   ***

b. ***
   ***
   ***

c. **
   **
   **

d. ***
   ***
   ***
   ***

2. What number will appear in the lblSum control after the computer processes the following code?

```
Dim intSum As Integer
Dim intY As Integer
Do While intY < 3
   For intX As Integer = 1 To 4
      intSum = intSum + intX
   Next intX
   intY = intY + 1
Loop
lblSum.Text = Convert.ToString(intSum)
```

a. 5

b. 8

c. 15

d. 30

3. Which of the following statements will pause program execution for 1 second?

a. `System.Threading.Thread.Pause(1000)`

b. `System.Threading.Thread.Pause(1)`

c. `System.Threading.Thread.Sleep(1000)`

d. `System.Threading.Thread.Sleep(100)`

Lesson B Exercises

INTRODUCTORY

1. Use Windows to make a copy of the Clock Solution folder, which is contained in the VB2008\Chap06 folder. Rename the folder Clock Solution-Introductory1. Open the Clock Solution (Clock Solution.sln) file contained in the VB2008\Chap06\Clock Solution-Introductory1 folder. Open the designer window, then open the Code Editor window. Change the outer For...Next statement to a Do...Loop statement. Save the solution, then start and test the application. Stop the application. Close the Code Editor window, then close the solution.

INTRODUCTORY

2. Use Windows to make a copy of the Clock Solution folder, which is contained in the VB2008\Chap06 folder. Rename the folder Clock Solution-Introductory2. Open the Clock Solution (Clock Solution.sln) file contained in the VB2008\Chap06\Clock Solution-Introductory2 folder. Open the designer window, then open the Code Editor window. Change the inner For...Next statement to a Do...Loop statement. (Hint: You will need to reset the minutes in the outer loop.) Save the solution, then start and test the application. Stop the application. Close the Code Editor window, then close the solution.

INTRODUCTORY

3. Use Windows to make a copy of the Nested Payment Solution folder, which is contained in the VB2008\Chap06 folder. Rename the folder Nested Payment Solution-Introductory. Open the Nested Payment Solution (Nested Payment Solution.sln) file contained in the VB2008\Chap06\Nested Payment Solution-Introductory folder. Open the designer window, then open the Code Editor window. Change the For...Next statement that controls the term to a Do...Loop statement. Save the solution, then start and test the application. Stop the application. Close the Code Editor window, then close the solution.

INTERMEDIATE

4. Use Windows to make a copy of the Nested Payment Solution folder, which is contained in the VB2008\Chap06 folder. Rename the folder Nested Payment Solution-Intermediate. Open the Nested Payment Solution (Nested Payment Solution.sln) file contained in the VB2008\Chap06\Nested Payment Solution-Intermediate folder. Open the designer window, then open the Code Editor window. Change both For...Next statements to Do...Loop statements. Save the solution, then start and test the application. Stop the application. Close the Code Editor window, then close the solution.

INTERMEDIATE

5. Professor Arkins needs an application that allows him to assign a grade to any number of students. Each student's grade is based on three test scores, with each test worth 100 points. The application should total the test scores and then assign the appropriate grade using the information shown in Figure 6-22. Open the Grade Calculator Solution (Grade Calculator Solution.sln) file, which is contained in the VB2008\Chap06\Grade Calculator Solution folder. Open the designer window, then open the Code Editor window. Code the application. Save the solution, then start and test the application. Stop the application. Close the Code Editor window, then close the solution.

Total points earned	**Grade**
270–300	A
240–269	B
210–239	C
180–209	D
below 180	F

Figure 6-22 Grade information

ADVANCED

6. Open the Car Solution (Car Solution.sln) file, which is contained in the VB2008\Chap06\Car Solution folder. When the Click Me button is clicked, the "I WANT THIS CAR!" message should blink 10 times. In other words, it should disappear and then reappear, disappear and then reappear, and so on. Use the For...Next statement. Save the solution, then start and test the application. Stop the application. Close the Code Editor window, then close the solution.

LESSON C

After studying Lesson C, you should be able to:

- Include a list box in an interface
- Select a list box item from code
- Determine the selected item in a list box

Coding the Shoppers Haven Application

Recall that your task is to create an application that allows the user to enter an item's original price and its discount rate. The discount rates range from 10% through 30% in increments of 5%. The application will calculate and display the amount of the discount and also the discounted price. Figure 6-23 shows the application's TOE chart.

Task	Object	Event
End the application	btnExit	Click
1. Calculate the discount and discounted price 2. Display the discount and discounted price in lblDiscount and lblDiscountPrice	btnCalc	Click
Get and display the original price	txtOrigPrice	None
Select the existing text		Enter
Clear the lblDiscount and lblDiscountPrice controls		TextChanged
1. Fill the lstRate control with values 2. Select a default value in the lstRate control	frmMain	Load
Display the discount (from btnCalc)	lblDiscount	None
Display the discounted price (from btnCalc)	lblDiscountPrice	None
Get and display the discount rates	lstRate	None
Clear the lblDiscount and lblDiscountPrice controls		SelectedValueChanged

Figure 6-23 TOE chart for the Shoppers Haven application

To open the Shoppers Haven application:

1. If necessary, start Visual Studio 2008 or Visual Basic 2008 Express Edition. Close the Start Page window.
2. Open the **Shoppers Haven Solution** (**Shoppers Haven Solution.sln**) file, which is contained in the VB2008\Chap06\Shoppers Haven Solution folder. If necessary, open the designer window. Figure 6-24 shows the partially completed user interface. Only the list box control is missing from the interface.

Figure 6-24 Partially completed user interface for the Shoppers Haven application

Including a List Box in an Interface

You add a list box to an interface using the ListBox tool in the toolbox. A **list box** displays a list of choices from which the user can select zero choices, one choice, or more than one choice. The number of choices the user can select is controlled by the list box's SelectionMode property. The default value for the property is One, which allows the user to select only one choice at a time. You can make a list box any size you want. However, the Windows standard for list boxes is to display a minimum of three choices and a maximum of eight choices at a time. If you have more items than fit into the list box, the control automatically displays a scroll bar that you can use to view the complete list of items. You should use a label control to provide keyboard access to the list box. For the access key to work correctly, you must set the label's TabIndex property to a value that is one less than the list box's TabIndex value.

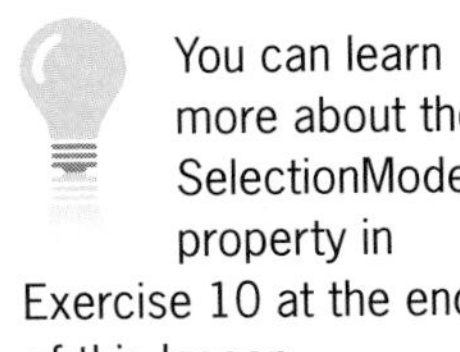

You can learn more about the SelectionMode property in Exercise 10 at the end of this lesson.

If you have only two choices to offer the user, you should use two radio buttons rather than a list box.

To add a list box control to the form, then lock the controls and set the TabIndex values:

1. Click the **ListBox** tool in the toolbox, then drag the mouse pointer to the form. Position the mouse pointer below the Discount rate label, then release the mouse button.
2. The three-character ID used for naming list boxes is lst. Change the list box's name to **lstRate**. Do not be concerned that the list box's name appears inside the control. The name will not appear when the application is started.
3. Set the list box's **Size** property to **66, 64**.
4. Lock the controls on the form, then use the information in Figure 6-25 to set the TabIndex values.

Figure 6-25 Correct TabIndex values

5. Press **Esc** to remove the TabIndex boxes from the form, then save the solution.

Adding Items to a List Box

The items in a list box belong to a collection called the **Items collection**. A **collection** is a group of individual objects treated as one unit. The first item in the Items collection appears as the first item in the list box, the second item in the collection appears as the second item in the list box, and so on. A unique number called an index identifies each item in the Items collection. The first item in the collection (which also is the first item in the list box) has an index of 0. The second item has an index of 1, and so on. You specify each item to display in a list box using the Items collection's Add method. The Add method's syntax is shown in Figure 6-26. In the syntax, *object* is the name of the control to which you want the item added, and *item* is the text you want displayed in the control. Figure 6-26 also includes two examples of using the Add method to add items to a list box. In Example 1, the Add methods add the strings "Dog", "Cat", and "Horse" to the lstAnimal control. In Example 2, the Add method displays numbers from 100 through 105 in the lstCode control. Notice that the ToString method is used to convert each number to the String data type before adding it to the list box. (You also could use the Convert.ToString method to convert the numbers to strings.) In most cases, you enter the Add methods in the form's Load event procedure, because you typically want the list box to display its values when the interface first appears on the screen.

To learn about the Items collection's Insert, Remove, RemoveAt, and Clear methods, as well as its Count property, complete Exercise 11 at the end of this lesson.

To learn how to use the String Collection Editor dialog box to add items to a list box, complete Exercise 12 at the end of this lesson.

Add method

Syntax
object.**Items.Add(***item***)**

Example 1
```
lstAnimal.Items.Add("Dog")
lstAnimal.Items.Add("Cat")
lstAnimal.Items.Add("Horse")
```

Example 2
```
For intCode As Integer = 100 To 105
      lstCode.Items.Add(intCode.ToString)
Next intCode
```

Figure 6-26 Syntax and examples of the Add method

Figure 6-27 shows the lstAnimal and lstCode controls after the computer processes the code shown in Figure 6-26.

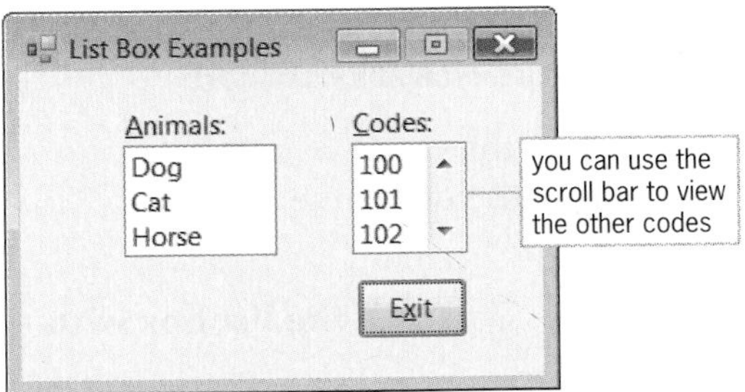

Figure 6-27 Result of processing the code shown in Figure 6-26

The position of an item in the list depends on the value stored in the list box's Sorted property. When the Sorted property is set to False (the default value), the item is added at the end of the list. The Sorted property of both list boxes in Figure 6-27 is set to False. When the Sorted property is set to True, the item is sorted along with the existing items and then placed in its proper position in the list. The items in the lstAnimal control will appear in the following order when the list box's Sorted property is set to True: Cat, Dog, Horse. Visual Basic sorts the list box items in dictionary order, which means numbers are sorted before letters, and a lowercase letter is sorted before its uppercase equivalent. The items in a list box are sorted based on the leftmost characters in each item. As a result, the items "Personnel", "Inventory", and "Payroll" will appear in the following order when the list box's Sorted property is set to True: Inventory, Payroll, Personnel. Likewise, the items 1, 2, 3, and 10 will appear in the following order: 1, 10, 2, 3. The application determines whether you display the list box items in either sorted order or the order in which they are added to the list box. If several list items are selected much more frequently than other items, you typically leave the list box's Sorted property set to False, and then add the frequently used items first so that the items appear at the beginning of the list. However, if the list box items are selected fairly equally, you typically set the list box's Sorted property to True, because it is easier to locate items when they appear in a sorted order.

GUI DESIGN TIP List Box Standards

- A list box should contain a minimum of three items.
- A list box should display a minimum of three choices and a maximum of eight choices at a time.
- Use a label control to provide keyboard access to the list box. Set the label's TabIndex property to a value that is one less than the list box's TabIndex value.
- List box items are either arranged by use, with the most used entries appearing first in the list, or sorted in ascending order.

You will use the Add method to add the discount rates to the lstRate control in the Shoppers Haven interface. You will enter the appropriate code in the form's Load event procedure, because you want the list box to display its values when the interface first appears on the screen.

To specify the discount rates to display in the lstRate control:

1. Open the Code Editor window. Replace the <your name> and <current date> text in the comments with your name and the current date.

2. Open the form's Load event procedure. Type **' fill the list box with values** and press **Enter** twice.

> To open the form's Load event procedure, click the Class Name arrow, then click (frmMain events). Click the Method Name arrow, then click Load.

3. Type the For...Next loop shown in Figure 6-28, then position the insertion point as shown in the figure. (Be sure to change the Next clause to `Next dblRates`.)

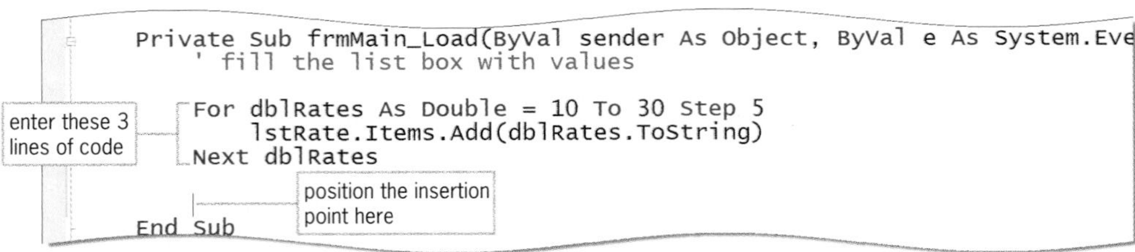

Figure 6-28 For...Next loop entered in the Load event procedure

4. Save the solution, then start the application. The numbers 10, 15, and 20 appear in the list box. (Depending on your screen's resolution, the number 25 also may appear in the list box.) Scroll down the list box to verify that it also contains the numbers 25 and 30. Scroll to the top of the list box, then click **15** in the list. See Figure 6-29. When you select an item in a list box, the item appears highlighted in the list. In addition, the item's value (in this case, the string "15") is stored in the list box's SelectedItem property, and the item's index (in this case, the number 1) is stored in the list box's SelectedIndex property. You will learn more about the SelectedItem and SelectedIndex properties in the next section.

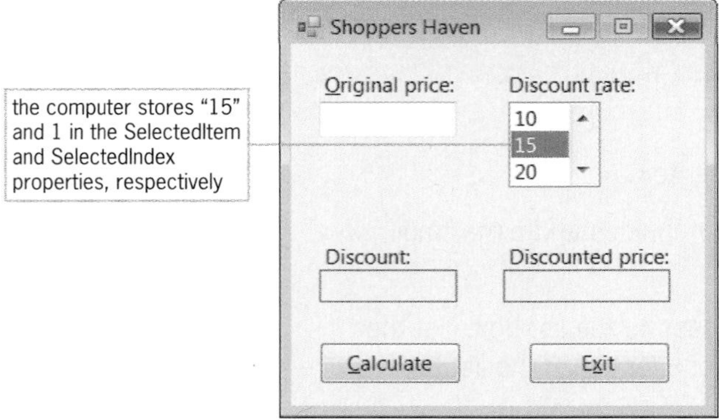

Figure 6-29 Second item selected in the list box

5. Click the **Exit** button to end the application.

The SelectedItem and SelectedIndex Properties

You can use either the SelectedItem or SelectedIndex property to determine whether an item is selected in a list box. When no item is selected, the SelectedItem property contains the empty string, while the SelectedIndex property contains the number -1 (negative 1). Otherwise, the SelectedItem and SelectedIndex properties contain the value of the selected item and the item's index, respectively. If a list box allows the user to make only one selection, it is customary in Windows applications to have one of the list box items already selected when the interface appears. The selected item, called the **default list box item**, should be either the item selected most frequently or, if all of the items are selected fairly equally, the first item in the list. You can use either the SelectedItem property or the SelectedIndex property to select the default list box item from code, as shown in the examples in Figure 6-30. (The examples refer to the list boxes shown earlier in Figure 6-27.)

SelectedItem and SelectedIndex properties

Example 1 (SelectedItem property)

```
lstAnimal.SelectedItem = "Cat"
```

selects the Cat item in the lstAnimal control

Example 2 (SelectedItem property)

```
lstCode.SelectedItem = "101"
```

selects the 101 item in the lstCode control

Example 3 (SelectedIndex property)

```
lstCode.SelectedIndex = 2
```

selects the third item in the lstCode control

Figure 6-30 Examples of the SelectedItem and SelectedIndex properties

To select a default item in the lstRate control:

1. The insertion point should be positioned two lines below the `Next dblRates` line in the form's Load event procedure. Type **lstRate.SelectedIndex = 0** and press **Enter**.

2. Save the solution, then start the application. A default item—in this case, the first item—is selected in the list box. See Figure 6-31.

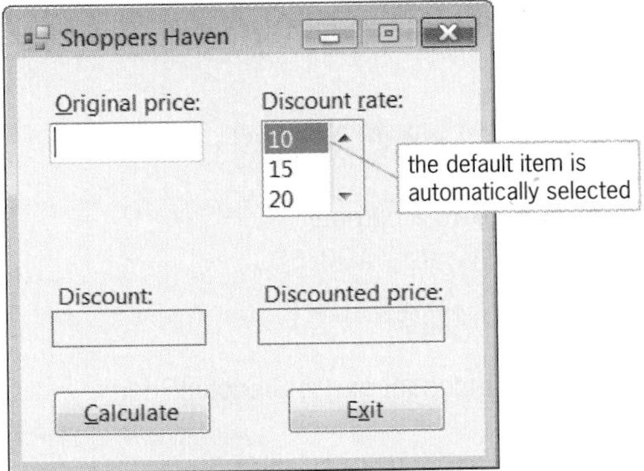

Figure 6-31 Default item selected in the list box

3. Click the **Exit** button to end the application.

GUI DESIGN TIP Default List Box Item

If a list box allows the user to make only one selection, a default item should be selected when the interface first appears. The default item should be either the item selected most frequently or the first item in the list. However, if a list box allows more than one selection at a time, you do not select a default item.

The SelectedValueChanged and SelectedIndexChanged Events

Each time either the user or a statement selects an item in a list box, the list box's SelectedValueChanged and SelectedIndexChanged events occur. You can use the procedures associated with these events to perform one or more tasks when the selected item has changed. In the Shoppers Haven application, you will code the lstRate control's SelectedValueChanged procedure so that it clears both the discount and discounted price amounts whenever a change is made to the discount rate.

To code the list box's SelectedValueChanged event procedure:

1. Open the code template for the lstRate control's SelectedValue-Changed event. Type **' clear the calculated results** and press **Enter** twice.
2. Enter the following lines of code.

   lblDiscount.Text = String.Empty
   lblDiscountPrice.Text = String.Empty

3. Save the solution.

Coding the btnCalc Control's Click Event Procedure

To complete the Shoppers Haven application, you need to code the btnCalc control's Click event procedure. Figure 6-32 shows the procedure's pseudocode.

```
btnCalc Click event procedure
1. convert the original price, which is entered in the text box, to a number
2. if the original price can be converted to a number
       convert the discount rate selected in the list box to a number
       calculate the discount = original price * discount rate / 100
       calculate the discounted price = original price – discount
   end if
3. display the discount and discounted price in the lblDiscount and lblDiscountPrice
   controls
```

Figure 6-32 Pseudocode for the btnCalc control's Click event procedure

To code the btnCalc control's Click event procedure, then test the application's code:

1. Open the code template for the btnCalc control's Click event procedure. Type **' calculate the discount and discounted price** and press **Enter** twice. Recall that before you begin coding a procedure, you first study the procedure's pseudocode to determine the variables and named constants (if any) the procedure will use. In this case, the procedure will not use any named constants; however, it will use five variables.
2. Type **Dim dblOriginalPrice As Double** and press **Enter**. The procedure will use this variable to store the original price entered in the txtOrigPrice control.
3. Type **Dim dblRate As Double** and press **Enter**. The procedure will use this variable to store the discount rate selected in the lstRate control.
4. Type **Dim dblDiscount As Double** and press **Enter**, then type **Dim dblDiscountPrice As Double** and press **Enter**. The procedure will use these variables to store the calculated amounts.
5. Type **Dim blnIsPriceOk As Boolean** and press **Enter** twice. The `blnIsPriceOk` variable will store the value returned by the TryParse method when it attempts to convert the contents of the txtOrigPrice control to a Double number.
6. The first step in the pseudocode is to convert the original price to a number. Enter the following lines of code. (Be sure to include a space before the line continuation character.)

   blnIsPriceOk = _
   Double.TryParse(txtOrigPrice.Text, dblOriginalPrice)

7. Next is a selection structure that determines whether the TryParse method succeeded in converting the original price to a number. Type **If blnIsPriceOk Then** and press **Enter**.
8. If the TryParse method was successful, the first instruction in the selection structure's true path should convert the rate selected in the list box to a number. Type **dblRate = Convert.ToDouble(lstRate.SelectedItem)**.

You also could write the statement in Step 8 as `Double.TryParse(lstRate.SelectedItem.ToString, dblRate)`.

9. The next instruction in the true path should calculate the discount amount. Type **dblDiscount = dblOriginalPrice * dblRate / 100** and press **Enter**.
10. The last instruction in the true path should calculate the discounted price. Type **dblDiscountPrice = dblOriginalPrice – dblDiscount**.
11. Step 3 in the pseudocode is to display the discount and discounted price in the appropriate label controls. Click **after the letter f** in the End If clause, then press **Enter** twice. Type **lblDiscount.Text = dblDiscount.ToString("C2")** and press **Enter**. Then type **lblDiscountPrice.Text = dblDiscountPrice.ToString("C2")** and press **Enter**.

12. Save the solution, then start the application. Type **100** in the Original price box, then click **20** in the list of discount rates. Click the **Calculate** button. The button's Click event procedure displays the discount and discounted price. See Figure 6-33.

Figure 6-33 Discount and discounted price shown in the interface

13. Click **10** in the Discount rate list box. The list box's SelectedValueChanged procedure removes the discount and discounted price from the label controls.

14. Click the **Calculate** button. The button's Click event procedure displays $10.00 and $90.00 as the discount and discounted price, respectively. Click the **Exit** button to end the application. Close the Code Editor window, then close the solution. Figure 6-34 shows the application's code.

```
' Name:         Shoppers Haven Project
' Purpose:      Displays the discount and discounted price
' Programmer:   <your name> on <current date>

Option Explicit On
Option Strict On
Option Infer Off

Public Class frmMain

    Private Sub btnExit_Click(ByVal sender As Object, _
        ByVal e As System.EventArgs) Handles btnExit.Click
        Me.Close()
    End Sub

    Private Sub txtOrigPrice_Enter(ByVal sender As Object, _
        ByVal e As System.EventArgs) Handles txtOrigPrice.Enter
        ' select the existing text

        txtOrigPrice.SelectAll()
    End Sub

    Private Sub txtOrigPrice_TextChanged(ByVal sender As Object, _
        ByVal e As System.EventArgs) Handles txtOrigPrice.TextChanged
        ' clear the calculated results

```

Figure 6-34 Shoppers Haven application's code *(continues)*

(continued)

```
        lblDiscount.Text = String.Empty
        lblDiscountPrice.Text = String.Empty
    End Sub

    Private Sub frmMain_Load(ByVal sender As Object, _
        ByVal e As System.EventArgs) Handles Me.Load
        ' fill the list box with values

        For dblRates As Double = 10 To 30 Step 5
            lstRate.Items.Add(dblRates.ToString)
        Next dblRates

        lstRate.SelectedIndex = 0

    End Sub

    Private Sub lstRate_SelectedValueChanged(ByVal sender As Object, _
        ByVal e As System.EventArgs) Handles lstRate.SelectedValueChanged
        ' clear the calculated results

        lblDiscount.Text = String.Empty
        lblDiscountPrice.Text = String.Empty

    End Sub

    Private Sub btnCalc_Click(ByVal sender As Object, _
        ByVal e As System.EventArgs) Handles btnCalc.Click
        ' calculate the discount and discounted price

        Dim dblOriginalPrice As Double
        Dim dblRate As Double
        Dim dblDiscount As Double
        Dim dblDiscountPrice As Double
        Dim blnIsPriceOk As Boolean

        blnIsPriceOk = _
            Double.TryParse(txtOrigPrice.Text, dblOriginalPrice)
        If blnIsPriceOk Then
            dblRate = Convert.ToDouble(lstRate.SelectedItem)
            dblDiscount = dblOriginalPrice * dblRate / 100
            dblDiscountPrice = dblOriginalPrice - dblDiscount
        End If

        lblDiscount.Text = dblDiscount.ToString("C2")
        lblDiscountPrice.Text = dblDiscountPrice.ToString("C2")

    End Sub
End Class
```

Figure 6-34 Shoppers Haven application's code

Lesson C Summary

- **To add a list box control to a form:**

  Use the ListBox tool in the toolbox.

- **To specify whether the user can select zero choices, one choice, or more than one choice in a list box:**

  Set the list box's SelectionMode property.

- **To add items to a list box:**

  Use the Items collection's Add method, whose syntax is *object*.**Items.Add(***item***)**. In the syntax, *object* is the name of the control to which you want the item added, and *item* is the text you want displayed in the control.

- **To automatically sort the items in a list box:**

  Set the list box's Sorted property to True.

- **To determine the item selected in a list box, or to select a list box item from code:**

  Use either the list box's SelectedItem property or its SelectedIndex property.

- **To perform tasks when a different item is selected in a list box:**

  Enter the code in either the SelectedValueChanged or SelectedIndexChanged procedure.

Lesson C Key Terms

Collection—a group of individual objects treated as one unit

Default list box item—the item automatically selected in a list box

Items collection—the collection composed of the items in a list box

List box—a control used to display a list of choices from which the user can select zero choices, one choice, or more than one choice

Lesson C Review Questions

1. You use the ______________________ method to add items to a list box.

   a. Add b. AddList

   c. Item d. ItemAdd

2. The items in a list box belong to the ______________________ collection.

   a. Items b. List

   c. ListItems d. Values

3. The ______________________________ property stores the index of the item selected in a list box.

   a. Index
   b. SelectedIndex
   c. Selection
   d. SelectionIndex

4. Which of the following statements selects the "Horse" item, which appears third in the lstAnimal control?

   a. `lstAnimal.SelectedIndex = 2`
   b. `lstAnimal.SelectedIndex = 3`
   c. `lstAnimal.SelectedItem = 2`
   d. `lstAnimal.SelectedItem = 3`

5. The ______________________________ event occurs when the user selects a different item in a list box.

   a. SelectionChanged
   b. SelectedItemChanged
   c. SelectedValueChanged
   d. None of the above.

Lesson C Exercises

INTRODUCTORY

1. Use Windows to make a copy of the Shoppers Haven Solution folder, which is contained in the VB2008\Chap06 folder. Rename the folder Modified Shoppers Haven Solution. Open the Shoppers Haven Solution (Shoppers Haven Solution.sln) file contained in the VB2008\Chap06\Modified Shoppers Haven Solution folder. Open the designer window, then open the Code Editor window. Change the For...Next statement in the form's Load event procedure to a Do...Loop statement. Save the solution, then start and test the application. Stop the application. Close the Code Editor window, then close the solution.

INTRODUCTORY

2. In this exercise, you create an application that displays the telephone extension corresponding to the name selected in a list box. The names and extensions are shown in Figure 6-35. Create a Visual Basic Windows application. Name the solution, project, and form file Phone Solution, Phone Project, and Main Form.vb, respectively. Save the application in the VB2008\Chap06 folder. Create the interface shown in Figure 6-36. The items in the list box should be sorted; set the appropriate property. Code the application. The form's Load event procedure should add the names shown in Figure 6-35 to the list box and then select the first name in the list. The list box's SelectedValueChanged event procedure should assign the item selected in the list box to a variable. It then should use the Select Case statement to display the telephone extension corresponding to the name. Save the solution, then start and test the application. Stop the application. Close the Code Editor window, then close the solution.

Smith, Joe	3388
Jones, Mary	3356
Adkari, Joel	2487
Lin, Sue	1111
Li, Vicky	2222

Figure 6-35 Names and telephone extensions

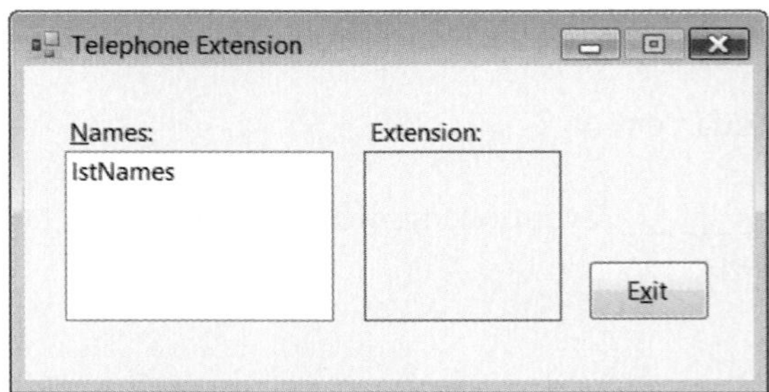

Figure 6-36 Interface for the Telephone Extension application

INTRODUCTORY

3. In this exercise, you modify the application from Exercise 2. Use Windows to make a copy of the Phone Solution folder, which is contained in the VB2008\Chap06 folder. Change the name of the folder to Modified Phone Solution. Open the Phone Solution (Phone Solution.sln) file contained in the VB2008\Chap06\Modified Phone Solution folder. Open the designer window, then open the Code Editor window. Modify the list box's SelectedValueChanged event procedure so that it assigns the index of the item selected in the list box to a variable. Modify the Select Case statement so that it displays the telephone extension corresponding to the index stored in the variable. Save the solution, then start and test the application. Stop the application. Close the Code Editor window, then close the solution.

INTRODUCTORY

4. In this exercise, you create an application that displays a multiplication table similar to the one shown in Figure 6-37. Open the Multiplication Solution (Multiplication Solution.sln) file, which is contained in the VB2008\Chap06\Multiplication Solution folder. Code the application. Save the solution, then start and test the application. Stop the application. Close the Code Editor window, then close the solution.

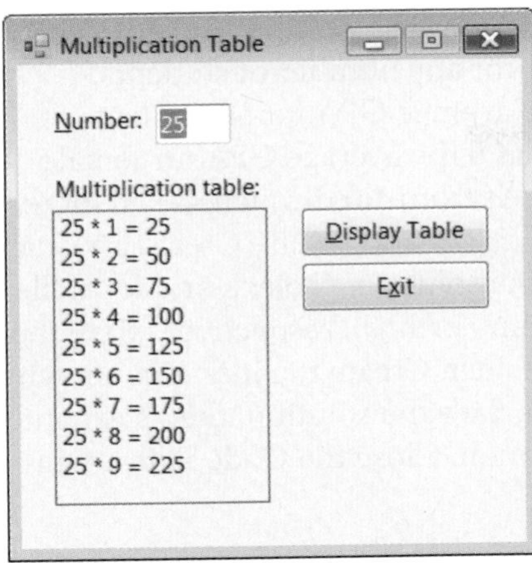

Figure 6-37 Sample run of the Multiplication Table application

INTERMEDIATE

5. Powder Skating Rink holds a weekly ice-skating competition. Competing skaters must perform a two-minute program in front of a panel of judges. The number of judges varies from week to week. At the end of a skater's program, each judge assigns a score of 0 through 10 to the skater. The manager of the ice rink wants an application that calculates and displays a skater's average score. The application also should display the skater's total score and the number of scores entered. Create a Visual Basic Windows application. Name the solution, project, and form file Powder Solution, Powder Project, and Main Form.vb, respectively. Save the application in the VB2008\Chap06 folder. Create the interface shown in Figure 6-38. Code the application. Save the solution, then start and test the application. Stop the application. Close the Code Editor window, then close the solution.

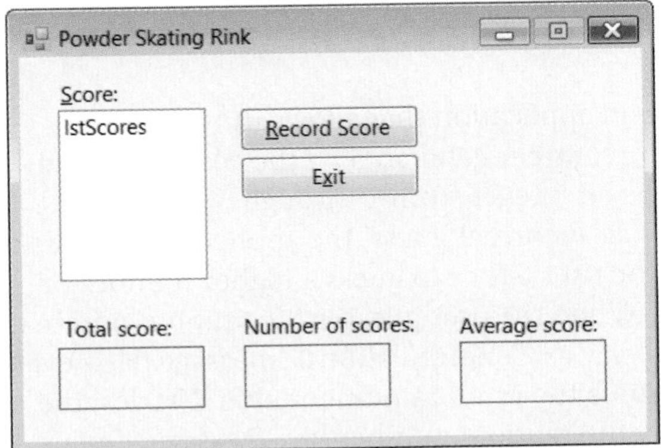

Figure 6-38 Interface for the Powder Skating Rink application

INTERMEDIATE

6. In this exercise, you create an application that allows the user to enter the gender (either F or M) and GPA for any number of students. The application should calculate the average GPA for all students, the average GPA for male students, and the average GPA for female students. The list box should list GPAs from 1.0 through 4.0, in increments of .1. (For example, 1.0, 1.1, 1.2, 1.3, and so on.) Create a Visual Basic Windows application. Name the solution, project, and form file GPA Solution, GPA Project, and Main Form.vb, respectively. Save the application in the VB2008\Chap06 folder. Create the interface shown in Figure 6-39. Code the application. Save the solution, then start and test the application. Stop the application. Close the Code Editor window, then close the solution.

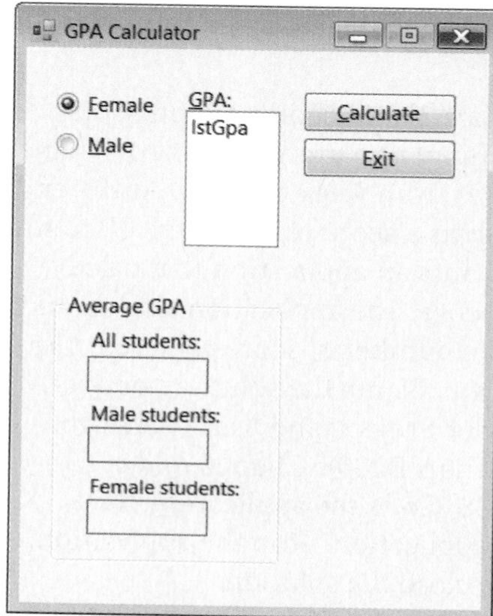

Figure 6-39 Interface for the GPA Calculator application

ADVANCED

7. In this exercise, you code an application that allows the user 10 chances to guess a random number generated by the computer. The random number should be an integer from 1 through 50, inclusive. Each time the user makes an incorrect guess, the application will display a message that tells the user either to guess a higher number or to guess a lower number. When the user guesses the random number, the application should display a "Congratulations!" message. However, if the user is not able to guess the random number after 10 tries, the application should display the random number in a message. Open the Random Solution (Random Solution.sln) file, which is contained in the VB2008\Chap06\Random Solution folder. If necessary, open the designer window. Code the application. Save the solution, then start and test the application. Stop the application. Close the Code Editor window, then close the solution.

ADVANCED

8. In this exercise, you code an application that displays the first 10 Fibonacci numbers: 1, 1, 2, 3, 5, 8, 13, 21, 34, and 55. Notice that, beginning with the third number in the series, each Fibonacci number is the sum of the prior two numbers. In other words, 2 is the sum of

1 plus 1, 3 is the sum of 1 plus 2, 5 is the sum of 2 plus 3, and so on. Open the Fibonacci Solution (Fibonacci Solution.sln) file, which is contained in the VB2008\Chap06\Fibonacci Solution folder. If necessary, open the designer window. Code the application. Display the numbers in the lblNumbers control. Save the solution, then start and test the application. Stop the application. Close the Code Editor window, then close the solution.

ADVANCED

9. The accountant at Sonheim Manufacturing Company wants an application that calculates an asset's annual depreciation. The accountant will enter the asset's cost, useful life (in years), and salvage value (which is the value of the asset at the end of its useful life). Use a list box to display the useful life, which should range from 3 through 20 years. The application should use the double-declining balance method to calculate the annual depreciation amounts, and then display the amounts in the interface. You can use the Financial.DDB method to calculate the depreciation. The method's syntax is **Financial.DDB(*cost, salvage, life, period*)**. In the syntax, the *cost, salvage*, and *life* arguments are the asset's cost, salvage value, and useful life, respectively. The *period* argument is the period for which you want the depreciation amount calculated. The method returns the depreciation amount as a Double number. Figure 6-40 shows a sample depreciation schedule for an asset with a cost of $1,000, a useful life of 4 years, and a salvage value of $100. Create a Visual Basic Windows application. Name the solution, project, and form file Sonheim Solution, Sonheim Project, and Main Form.vb, respectively. Save the application in the VB2008\Chap06 folder. Create the interface shown in Figure 6-40. Set the txtSchedule control's Multiline and ReadOnly properties to True, and set its ScrollBars property to Vertical. Code the application. Save the solution, then start and test the application. Stop the application. Close the Code Editor window, then close the solution.

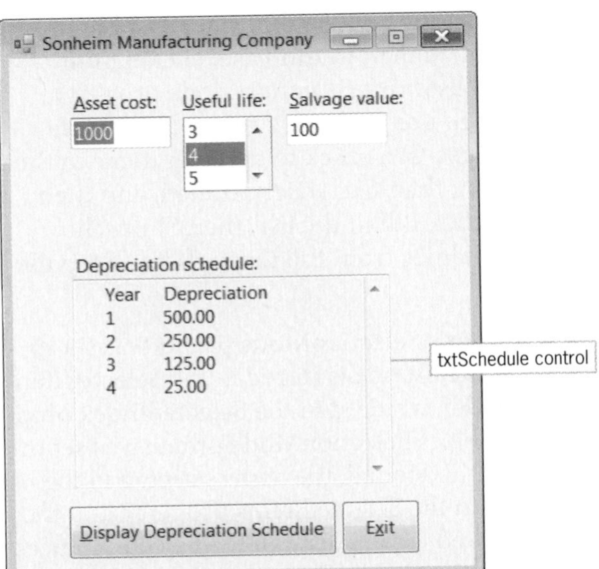

Figure 6-40 Sample run of the Sonheim Manufacturing Company application

Discovery

10. In this exercise, you learn how to create a list box that allows the user to select more than one item at a time. Open the Multi Solution (Multi Solution.sln) file, which is contained in the VB2008\Chap06\Multi Solution folder. If necessary, open the designer window. The interface contains a list box named lstNames. The list box's Sorted property is set to True, and its SelectionMode property is set to One.

    a. Open the Code Editor window. The form's Load event procedure adds five names to the list box. Code the btnSingle control's Click event procedure so that it displays, in the lblResult control, the item selected in the lstNames control. For example, if the user clicks Debbie in the list box and then clicks the Single Selection button, the name Debbie should appear in the lblResult control.

    b. Save the solution, then start the application. Click Debbie in the list box, then click Ahmad, and then click Bill. When the list box's SelectionMode property is set to One, you can select only one item at a time in the list. Click the Single Selection button. The name "Bill" appears in the lblResult control. Stop the application.

    c. Change the list box's SelectionMode property to MultiSimple. Save the solution, then start the application. Click Debbie in the list box, then click Ahmad, then click Bill, and then click Ahmad. When the list box's SelectionMode property is set to MultiSimple, you can select more than one item at a time in the list. Notice that you click to both select and deselect an item. You also can use Ctrl+click or Shift+click, as well as press the Spacebar, to select and deselect items when the list box's SelectionMode property is set to MultiSimple. Stop the application.

    d. Change the list box's SelectionMode property to MultiExtended. Save the solution, then start the application. Click Debbie in the list, then click Jim. Notice that, in this case, clicking Jim deselects Debbie. When a list box's SelectionMode property is set to MultiExtended, you use Ctrl+click to select multiple items in the list. You also use Ctrl+click to deselect items in the list. Click Debbie in the list, then Ctrl+click Ahmad, and then Ctrl+click Debbie. Next, click Bill in the list, then Shift+click Jim; this selects all of the names from Bill through Jim. Stop the application.

    e. As you know, when a list box's SelectionMode property is set to One, the item selected in the list box is stored in the SelectedItem property, and the item's index is stored in the SelectedIndex property. However, when a list box's SelectionMode property is set to either MultiSimple or MultiExtended, the items selected in the list box are stored (as strings) in the SelectedItems property, and the indices of the items are stored (as integers) in the SelectedIndices property. Code the btnMulti control's Click event procedure so that it first clears the contents of the lblResult control. The procedure then should display the selected names (which are stored in the SelectedItems property) on separate lines in the lblResult control.

f. Save the solution, then start the application. Click Ahmad in the list box, then Shift+click Jim. Click the Multi-Selection button. The five names should appear on separate lines in the lblResult control. Stop the application. Close the Code Editor window, then close the solution.

Discovery

11. In this exercise, you learn how to use the Items collection's Insert, Remove, RemoveAt, and Clear methods. You also learn how to use the Items collection's Count property. Open the Items Solution (Items Solution.sln) file, which is contained in the VB2008\Chap06\Items Solution folder. If necessary, open the designer window.

    a. You can use the Items collection's Insert method to add an item at a desired position in a list box while an application is running. The Insert method's syntax is ***object*.Items.Insert(*position*, *item*)**, where *position* is the index of the *item*. Open the Code Editor window. Code the Insert button's Click event procedure so it adds your name as the fourth item in the list box.

    b. You can use the Items collection's Remove method to remove an item from a list box while an application is running. The Remove method's syntax is ***object*.Items.Remove(*item*)**, where *item* is the item's value. Code the Remove button's Click event procedure so it removes your name from the list box.

    c. Like the Remove method, the Items collection's RemoveAt method also allows you to remove an item from a list box while an application is running. However, in the RemoveAt method you specify the item's index rather than its value. The RemoveAt method's syntax is ***object*.Items.RemoveAt(*index*)**, where *index* is the item's index. Code the Remove At button's Click event procedure so it removes the second name from the list box.

    d. You can use the Items collection's Clear method to remove (or clear) all items from a list box while an application is running. The Clear method's syntax is ***object*.Items.Clear()**. Code the Clear button's Click event procedure so it clears the items from the list box.

    e. The Items collection's Count property stores the number of items contained in a list box. Code the Count button's Click event procedure so it displays the number of items contained in the lstNames control.

    f. Save the solution, then start and test the application. Stop the application. Close the Code Editor window, then close the solution.

Discovery

12. In this exercise, you learn how to use the String Collection Editor dialog box to fill a list box with values. Open the ListBox Solution (ListBox Solution.sln) file, which is contained in the VB2008\Chap06\ListBox Solution folder. If necessary, open the designer window. Open the Code Editor window. Remove the Add methods and the For...Next statement from the form's Load event procedure. Close the Code Editor window. Click the lstAnimal control on the form. Click the Items property in the Properties list, then click the ellipsis (...) button in the Settings box. The String Collection Editor dialog box opens. Type Dog and press Enter. Type Cat and press Enter, then type Horse and press Enter. Click the OK button to close the dialog box. Use the String Collection Editor dialog box to enter the following codes in the lstCode control: 101, 102, 103, 104, and 105. Save the solution, then start the application. Stop the application, then close the solution.

Swat The Bugs

13. Open the Debug Solution (Debug Solution.sln) file, which is contained in the VB2008\Chap06\Debug Solution-Lesson C folder. If necessary, open the designer window. Open the Code Editor window and review the existing code. Start and then test the application. Be sure to include non-integers in your test data. Stop the application. (To stop an endless loop, click the designer window, then click Debug, and then click Stop Debugging.) Correct any errors in the code. Save the solution, then start and test the application again. Stop the application. Close the Code Editor window, then close the solution.

CHAPTER 7

Sub and Function Procedures

Creating the Harvey Industries Application

Jefferson Williams, the payroll manager at Harvey Industries, manually calculates each employee's weekly gross pay, federal withholding tax (FWT), Social Security and Medicare (FICA) tax, and net pay—a very time-consuming process and one that is prone to mathematical errors. Mr. Williams has asked you to create an application that he can use to perform the payroll calculations both efficiently and accurately.

Previewing the Harvey Industries Application

To open the Run dialog box, press and hold down the Windows logo key as you tap the letter r, then release the logo key.

To preview the completed Harvey Industries application:

1. Use the Run dialog box to run the **Harvey** (**Harvey.exe**) file, which is contained in the VB2008\Chap07 folder. The application's user interface appears on the screen.
2. Type **Kent Montara** in the Name box, then click the **Married** radio button.
3. Scroll down the Hours list box until you see the number 41.0, then click **41.0** in the list.
4. Scroll down the Rate list box until you see the number 10.50, then click **10.50** in the list.
5. The interface contains a combo box that allows you to either type the number of withholding allowances or select the number from a list. Click the **list arrow** button in the Allowances combo box, then click **3** in the list.
6. Click the **Calculate** button. The gross pay, federal withholding tax (FWT), Social Security and Medicare (FICA) tax, and net pay appear in the interface, as shown in Figure 7-1.

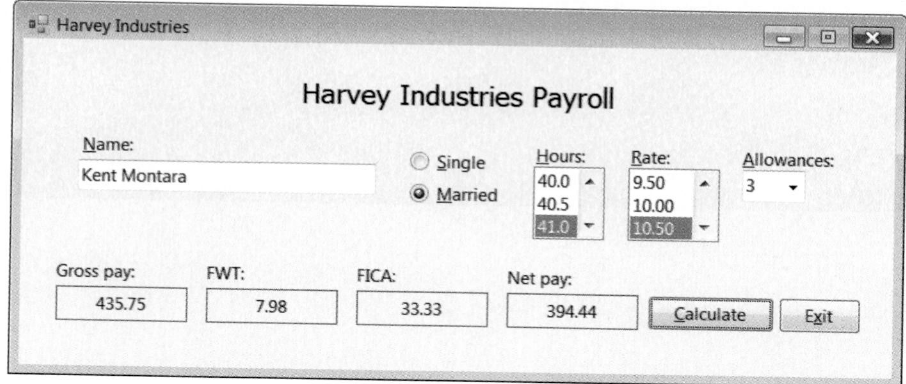

Figure 7-1 Payroll calculations shown in the interface

7. Click the **Exit** button. The "Do you want to exit?" message appears in a message box. Click the **No** button. Notice that the form remains on the screen. In Lesson C, you will learn how to prevent the computer from closing a form.
8. Click the **Exit** button, then click the **Yes** button in the message box. The application ends.

The Harvey Industries application uses a combo box and a Function procedure. Function procedures are covered in Lesson A, and combo boxes are covered in Lesson B. You will code the Harvey Industries application in Lesson C.

LESSON A

After studying Lesson A, you should be able to:

- Explain the difference between a Sub procedure and a Function procedure
- Create a procedure that receives information passed to it
- Explain the difference between passing data *by value* and passing data *by reference*
- Create a Function procedure

Procedures

As you already know, a procedure is a block of program code that performs a specific task. Most procedures in Visual Basic are either Sub procedures or Function procedures. The difference between both types of procedures is that a **Function procedure** returns a value after performing its assigned task, whereas a **Sub procedure** does not return a value. Although you have been using Sub procedures since Chapter 1, this lesson provides a more in-depth look into their creation and use. After exploring the topic of Sub procedures, you then will learn how to create and use Function procedures.

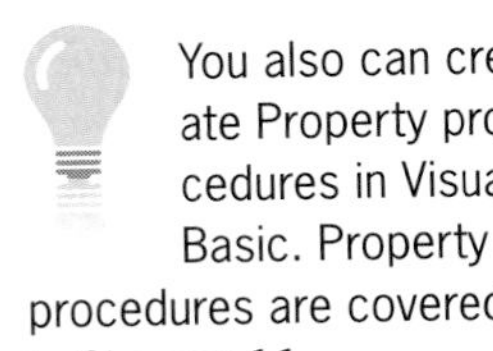

You also can create Property procedures in Visual Basic. Property procedures are covered in Chapter 11.

Sub Procedures

As you learned in Chapter 5, there are two types of Sub procedures in Visual Basic: event procedures and independent Sub procedures. An event procedure is a Sub procedure that is associated with a specific object and event, such as a button's Click event or a text box's TextChanged event. The computer automatically processes an event procedure when the event occurs. An independent Sub procedure, on the other hand, is a procedure that is independent of any object and event. An independent Sub procedure is processed only when called (invoked) from code. You learned how to create an independent Sub procedure in Chapter 5. You also learned how to use the Call statement to invoke a procedure. Figure 7-2 shows the syntax of an independent Sub procedure, as well as the syntax of the Call statement. Following the procedure name in the procedure header is a set of parentheses that contains an optional *parameterList*. The *parameterList* lists the data type and name of one or more memory locations, called **parameters**. The parameters store the information passed to the procedure when the procedure is invoked. If the procedure does not require any information to be passed to it, an empty set of parentheses follows the procedure name in the procedure header. In the Call statement's syntax, the optional *argumentList* is a comma-separated list of arguments you want passed to the procedure. The number of arguments listed in the Call statement's *argumentList* should agree with the number of parameters listed in the *parameterList* in the procedure header. If the *parameterList* contains one parameter, then the Call statement should have one argument in its *argumentList*. Similarly, a procedure that contains three

When you enter a procedure below the last event procedure, be sure to enter it above the End Class clause.

Visual Basic allows you to specify that an argument in the Call statement is optional. To learn more about optional arguments, complete Exercise 15 at the end of this lesson.

parameters requires three arguments in the Call statement. If a procedure does not contain any parameters, you include an empty set of parentheses in the Call statement. In addition to having the same number of arguments as parameters, the data type and position of each argument should agree with the data type and position of its corresponding parameter. For example, if the first parameter has a data type of String and the second a data type of Decimal, then the first argument in the Call statement should have the String data type and the second should have the Decimal data type. Some programmers enter independent Sub procedures above the first event procedure in the Code Editor window, while others enter them below the last event procedure. Still others enter them either immediately above or below the procedure from which they are invoked. In this book, you usually will enter the independent Sub procedures above the first event procedure.

Independent Sub procedure and Call statement

Syntax of an independent Sub procedure
Private Sub *procedureName*(*[parameterList]*)
    [statements]
End Sub

Syntax of the Call statement
Call *procedureName*(*[argumentList]*)

Figure 7-2 Syntax of an independent Sub procedure and the Call statement

You can pass a literal constant, named constant, keyword, or variable to an independent Sub procedure. In most cases, you will pass a variable.

Passing Variables

The internal memory of a computer is similar to a large post office. Like each post office box, each memory cell has a unique address.

Every variable has both a value and a unique address that represents its location in the computer's internal memory. Visual Basic allows you to pass either the variable's value or its address to the receiving procedure. Passing a variable's value is referred to as **passing by value**. Passing a variable's address is referred to as **passing by reference**. The method you choose—*by value* or *by reference*—depends on whether you want the receiving procedure to have access to the variable in memory. In other words, it depends on whether you want to allow the receiving procedure to change the contents of the variable. Although the idea of passing information *by value* and *by reference* may sound confusing at first, it is a concept with which you already are familiar. To illustrate, assume you have a savings account at a local bank. During a conversation with your friend Melissa, you mention the amount of money you have in the account. Sharing this information with Melissa is similar to passing a variable *by value*. Knowing the balance in your account does not give Melissa access to your bank account. It merely provides information that she can use to compare to the amount of money she has saved. The savings account example also provides an illustration of passing information *by reference*. To deposit money to or withdraw money from your account, you must provide the bank teller with your account number. The account number represents the location of your account at the bank and allows the teller to change the account balance. Giving the teller your bank account number is similar to passing a variable *by reference*. The account number allows the teller to change the contents of your bank account, similar to the way the variable's address allows the receiving procedure to change the contents of the variable passed to the procedure.

Passing a Variable by Value

To pass a variable *by value* in Visual Basic, you include the keyword `ByVal` (which stands for "by value") before the variable's corresponding parameter in the receiving procedure's *parameterList*. When you pass a variable *by value*, the computer passes only the contents of the variable to the receiving procedure. When only the contents are passed, the receiving procedure is not given access to the variable in memory; therefore, it cannot change the value stored inside the variable. You pass a variable *by value* when the receiving procedure needs to *know* the variable's contents, but the receiving procedure does not need to *change* the contents. Unless specified otherwise, variables are passed *by value* in Visual Basic. In the next set of steps, you will finish coding the Pet Information application, which passes two variables *by value* to an independent Sub procedure.

To complete the Pet Information application:

1. If necessary, start Visual Studio 2008 or Visual Basic 2008 Express Edition. Close the Start Page window.
2. Open the **Pet Information Solution** (**Pet Information Solution.sln**) file, which is contained in the VB2008\Chap07\Pet Information Solution folder. If necessary, open the designer window.
3. Open the Code Editor window. Replace the <your name> and <current date> text in the comments with your name and the current date.
4. Locate the btnDisplay control's Click event procedure. The procedure declares two String variables and an Integer variable. The `strInputName` and `strInputAge` variables are used by the InputBox functions to get the name and current age of a pet. Next, the TryParse method converts the contents of the `strInputAge` variable to the Integer data type and stores the result in the `intCurrentAge` variable. Before the event procedure ends, it will call an independent Sub procedure named ShowMsg to calculate the pet's age on his or her next birthday, and then display the pet's name and next age in the lblMsg control. The event procedure will need to pass the pet's name and current age to the ShowMsg procedure. The name and age are stored in the `strInputName` and `intCurrentAge` variables. The ShowMsg procedure will not need to change the values stored in the variables, so you will pass the variables *by value*. Click the **blank line** above the `End Sub` clause in the btnDisplay control's Click event procedure, then type **Call ShowMsg(strInputName, intCurrentAge)** and press **Enter**.

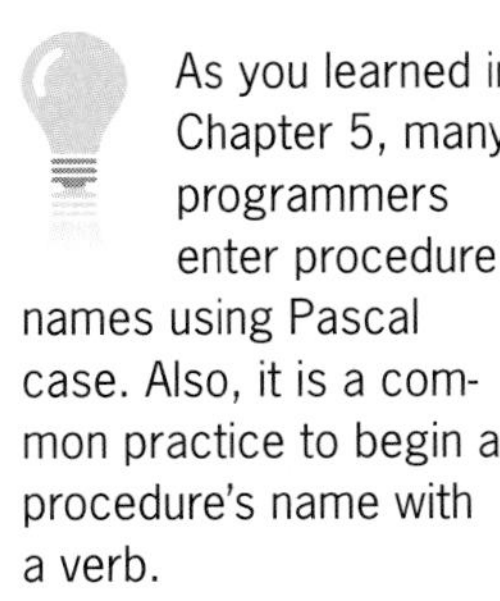

As you learned in Chapter 5, many programmers enter procedure names using Pascal case. Also, it is a common practice to begin a procedure's name with a verb.

5. Now you will create the ShowMsg procedure. The procedure will need to receive the values stored in the `strInputName` and `intCurrentAge` variables. You will use `strName` and `intAge`

for the names of the parameters. Click the **blank line** below the `Public Class frmMain` clause, then press **Enter**. Type **Private Sub ShowMsg(ByVal strName As String, ByVal intAge As Integer)** and press **Enter**.

6. Type **' calculates the age on the next birthday, then** and press **Enter**, then type **' displays a message containing the name and next age** and press **Enter** twice.
7. First, declare a variable that the procedure can use to calculate the age on the pet's next birthday. Type **Dim intNextAge As Integer** and press **Enter**.
8. Now perform the calculation. Type **intNextAge = intAge + 1** and press **Enter**.
9. Finally, display the name and next age in the lblMsg control. Enter the additional lines of code indicated in Figure 7-3.

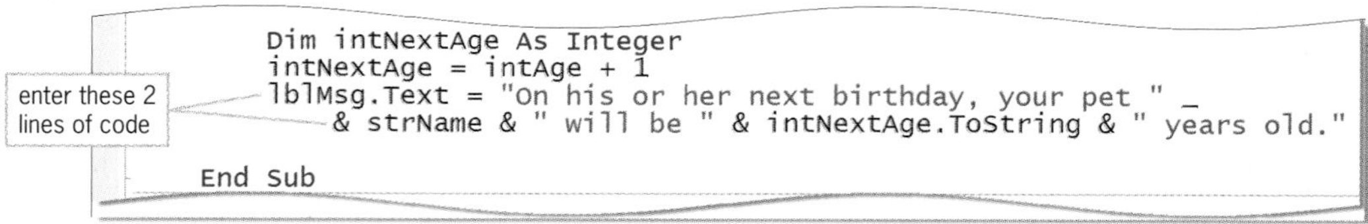

Figure 7-3 Additional lines of code entered in the ShowMsg procedure

10. Save the solution, then start the application. Click the **Display Message** button. Type **Chester** in the Name Entry dialog box, then press **Enter**. Type **6** in the Age Entry dialog box, then press **Enter**. The message shown in Figure 7-4 appears in the lblMsg control.

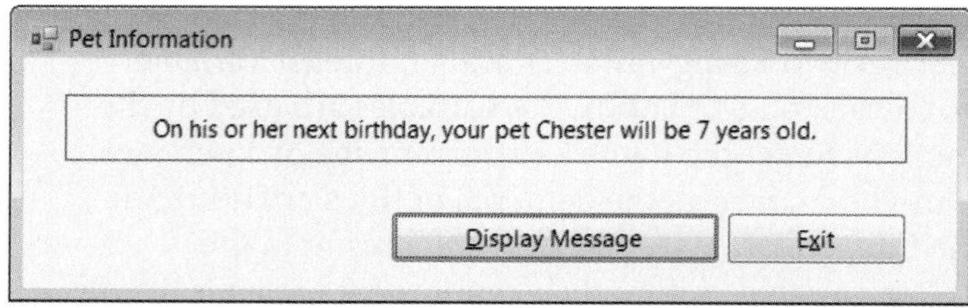

Figure 7-4 Message displayed in the interface

11. Click the **Exit** button to end the application. Close the Code Editor window, then close the solution.

Figure 7-5 shows the code entered in both the ShowMsg procedure and btnDisplay control's Click event procedure. Notice that the number, data type, and sequence of the arguments in the Call statement match the number, data type, and sequence of the corresponding parameters in the procedure header. Also notice that the names of the parameters do not need to be identical to the names of the corresponding arguments. In fact, to avoid confusion, it usually is better to use different names for the arguments and parameters. The variables that appear in a procedure header have procedure scope, which means they can be used only by the procedure in which they are declared.

parameterList

```
Private Sub ShowMsg(ByVal strName As String, ByVal intAge As Integer)
    ' calculates the age on the next birthday, then
    ' displays a message containing the name and next age

    Dim intNextAge As Integer
    intNextAge = intAge + 1
    lblMsg.Text = "On his or her next birthday, your pet " _
        & strName & " will be " & intNextAge.ToString & " years old."

End Sub

Private Sub btnDisplay_Click(ByVal sender As Object, _
    ByVal e As System.EventArgs) Handles btnDisplay.Click
    ' gets the pet information, then calls a procedure to
    ' display the information

    Dim strInputName As String
    Dim strInputAge As String
    Dim intCurrentAge As Integer

    strInputName = InputBox("Pet's name:", "Name Entry")
    strInputAge = InputBox("Pet's current age (years):", "Age Entry")
    Integer.TryParse(strInputAge, intCurrentAge)

    Call ShowMsg(strInputName, intCurrentAge)

End Sub
```

argumentList

Figure 7-5 ShowMsg procedure and btnDisplay Click event procedure

You cannot determine by looking at the Call statement whether a variable is being passed *by value* or *by reference*. You must look at the procedure header to make the determination.

Passing a Variable by Reference

In addition to passing a variable's value to a procedure, you also can pass a variable's address—in other words, its location in the computer's internal memory. As you learned earlier, passing a variable's address is referred to as passing *by reference*, and it gives the receiving procedure access to the variable being passed. You pass a variable *by reference* when you want the receiving procedure to change the contents of the variable. To pass a variable *by reference* in Visual Basic, you include the keyword `ByRef` (which stands for "by reference") before the variable's corresponding parameter in the receiving procedure's header. The `ByRef` keyword tells the computer to pass the variable's address rather than its contents. In the next set of steps, you will finish coding the Gross Pay Calculator application, which passes three variables to an independent Sub procedure: two *by value* and one *by reference*.

To complete the Gross Pay Calculator application:

1. Open the **Gross Pay Solution** (**Gross Pay Solution.sln**) file, which is contained in the VB2008\Chap07\Gross Pay Solution-Sub folder. If necessary, open the designer window. The application will calculate and display an employee's gross pay, which is based on the hours worked and pay rate entered by the user.
2. Open the Code Editor window. Replace the <your name> and <current date> text in the comments with your name and the current date.

3. Locate the btnCalc control's Click event procedure. The procedure declares three Double variables. Next, the TryParse methods convert the items selected in the list boxes to the Double data type, storing the results in the `dblHoursWkd` and `dblRateOfPay` variables. Before displaying the gross pay, the procedure will call an independent Sub procedure named CalcGrossPay to calculate the gross pay. For the CalcGrossPay procedure to perform this task, it needs to know the number of hours worked and the pay rate. Those values are stored in the `dblHoursWkd` and `dblRateOfPay` variables. The CalcGrossPay procedure will not need to change the values stored in the variables, so you will pass the variables *by value*. The CalcGrossPay procedure also needs to know where to store the gross pay after it has been calculated. To have the procedure store the gross pay in the `dblGrossPay` variable, you will need to pass it the variable's address. In other words, you will need to pass the variable *by reference*. Click the **blank line** below the `' use a Sub procedure to calculate the gross pay` comment in the btnCalc control's Click event procedure, then type **Call CalcGrossPay(dblHoursWkd, dblRateOfPay, dblGrossPay)** and press **Enter**.

4. Now you will create the CalcGrossPay procedure. The procedure will need to receive the values stored in the `dblHoursWkd` and `dblRateOfPay` variables, as well as the address of the `dblGrossPay` variable. You will use `dblHours`, `dblRate`, and `dblGross` for the names of the parameters. Click the **blank line** below the `Public Class frmMain` clause, then press **Enter**. Enter the following procedure header. Be sure to include a space before each line continuation character.

   Private Sub CalcGrossPay(ByVal dblHours As Double, _
   ByVal dblRate As Double, _
   ByRef dblGross As Double)

5. Type **' calculates the gross pay** and press **Enter** twice.

6. The gross pay is calculated by multiplying the hours worked by the pay rate. Type **dblGross = dblHours * dblRate** and press **Enter**. However, if the hours worked are over 40, the employee should receive overtime pay, which is an additional half-time for the hours worked over 40. Enter the comment and selection structure shown in Figure 7-6.

enter this comment and lines of code

```
dblGross = dblHours * dblRate
' add overtime, if necessary
If dblHours > 40 Then
    dblGross = dblGross + (dblHours - 40) * dblRate / 2
End If
```

Figure 7-6 Comment and selection structure entered in the CalcGrossPay procedure

7. Save the solution, then start the application. Locate and then click **43.0** in the Hours list box, then click **7.75** in the Rate list box. Click the **Calculate** button. See Figure 7-7.

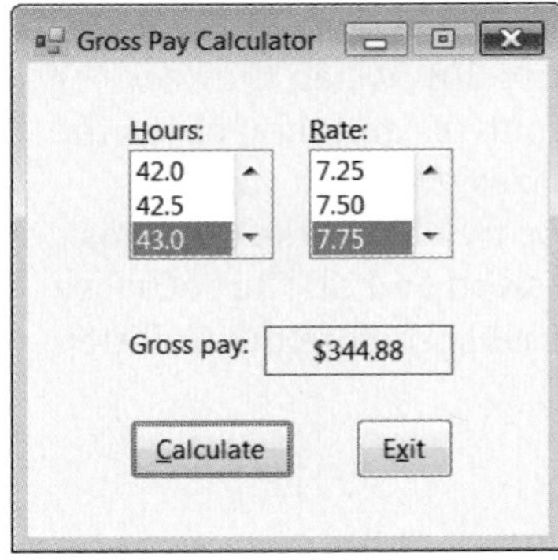

Figure 7-7 Gross pay displayed in the interface

8. Click the **Exit** button to end the application. Close the Code Editor window, then close the solution.

Figure 7-8 shows the code entered in both the CalcGrossPay procedure and btnCalc control's Click event procedure. Here again, notice that the number, data type, and sequence of the arguments in the Call statement match the number, data type, and sequence of the corresponding parameters in the procedure header. The *parameterList* indicates that the first two variables in the *argumentList* are passed *by value*, and the third variable is passed *by reference*.

```
Private Sub CalcGrossPay(ByVal dblHours As Double, _
                         ByVal dblRate As Double, _
                         ByRef dblGross As Double)
    ' calculates the gross pay

    dblGross = dblHours * dblRate
    ' add overtime, if necessary
    If dblHours > 40 Then
        dblGross = dblGross + (dblHours - 40) * dblRate / 2
    End If
End Sub


Private Sub btnCalc_Click(ByVal sender As Object, _
    ByVal e As System.EventArgs) Handles btnCalc.Click
    ' calculates and displays a gross pay amount

    Dim dblHoursWkd As Double
    Dim dblRateOfPay As Double
    Dim dblGrossPay As Double

    Double.TryParse(lstHours.SelectedItem.ToString, dblHoursWkd)
    Double.TryParse(lstRate.SelectedItem.ToString, dblRateOfPay)

    ' use a Sub procedure to calculate the gross pay
    Call CalcGrossPay(dblHoursWkd, dblRateOfPay, dblGrossPay)

    lblGross.Text = dblGrossPay.ToString("C2")
End Sub
```

parameterList

argumentList

Figure 7-8 CalcGrossPay procedure and btnCalc control's Click event procedure

To illustrate the difference between passing *by value* and passing *by reference*, you will desk-check the procedures shown in Figure 7-8. When the user selects 43.0 and 7.75 in the lstHours and lstRate controls and then clicks the Calculate button, the computer creates and initializes the three variables declared in the button's Click event procedure. The two TryParse methods then store the hours and pay rate in the `dblHoursWkd` and `dblRateOfPay` variables. Figure 7-9 shows the contents of the variables before the Call statement is processed.

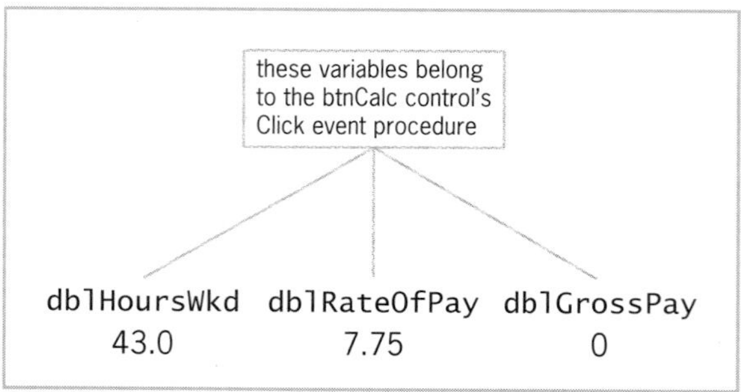

Figure 7-9 Desk-check table before the computer processes the Call statement

Next, the computer processes the `Call CalcGrossPay(dblHoursWkd, dblRateOfPay, dblGrossPay)` statement. At this point, the computer temporarily leaves the Click event procedure to process the code contained in the CalcGrossPay procedure; the procedure header is processed first. The `ByVal` keyword indicates that the first two parameters are receiving a value from the Call statement; as a result, the computer creates the `dblHours` and `dblRate` variables to store the values. In this case, the computer stores the value 43.0 in the `dblHours` variable and the number 7.75 in the `dblRate` variable. The `ByRef` keyword indicates that the third parameter is receiving the address of a variable. When you pass a variable's address to a procedure, the computer uses the address to locate the variable in its internal memory. It then assigns the parameter name to the memory location. In this case, the computer locates the `dblGrossPay` variable in memory and assigns the name `dblGross` to it. At this point, the memory location has two names: one assigned by the btnCalc control's Click event procedure and the other assigned by the CalcGrossPay procedure, as indicated in Figure 7-10. Notice that two variables in the table belong strictly to the Click event procedure, and two belong strictly to the CalcGrossPay procedure. One memory location, however, belongs to both procedures. Although both procedures can access the memory location, each procedure uses a different name to do so. The Click event procedure uses the name `dblGrossPay`, whereas the CalcGrossPay procedure uses the name `dblGross`.

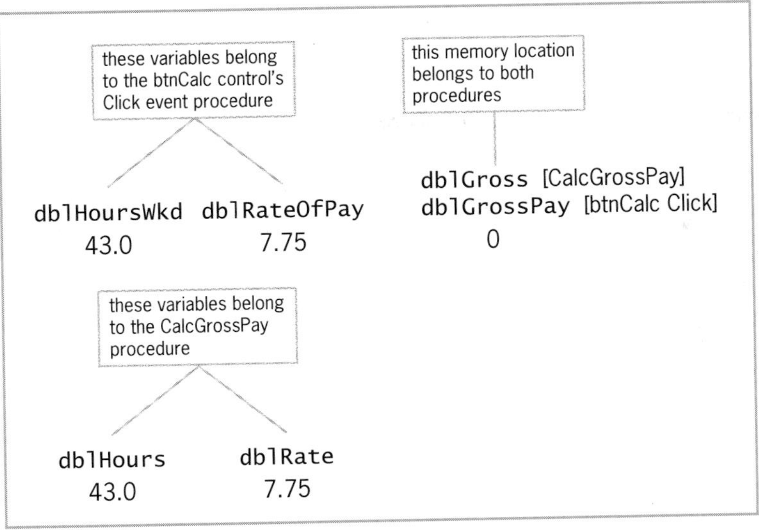

Figure 7-10 Desk-check table after the computer processes the Call statement and the CalcGrossPay procedure header

After processing the CalcGrossPay procedure header, the computer processes the code contained in the procedure. The first statement calculates the gross pay by multiplying the contents of the `dblHours` variable (43.0) by the contents of the `dblRate` variable (7.75), and then assigns the result (333.25) to the `dblGross` variable. Figure 7-11 shows the desk-check table after the statement is processed. Notice that when the contents of the `dblGross` variable changes, the contents of the `dblGrossPay` variable also changes. This happens because the names `dblGross` and `dblGrossPay` refer to the same location in the computer's internal memory.

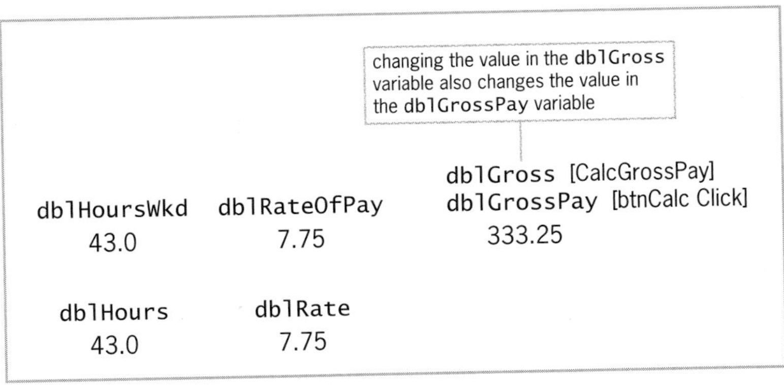

Figure 7-11 Desk-check table after the computer processes the first statement in the CalcGrossPay procedure

The `dblHours` variable contains a value that is greater than 40, so the statement in the selection structure's true path calculates the overtime pay (11.63) and adds it to the regular pay (333.25). It assigns the result (344.88) to the `dblGross` variable. Figure 7-12 shows the desk-check table after the statement is processed.

dblHoursWkd	dblRateOfPay	dblGross [CalcGrossPay] dblGrossPay [btnCalc Click]
43.0	7.75	344.88
dblHours	dblRate	
43.0	7.75	

Figure 7-12 Desk-check table after the computer processes the statement in the selection structure's true path

Next, the computer processes the CalcGrossPay procedure's `End Sub` clause, which marks the end of the procedure. At this point, the computer removes the `dblHours` and `dblRate` variables from memory. It also removes the `dblGross` name from the appropriate location in memory, as illustrated in Figure 7-13.

dblHoursWkd	dblRateOfPay	~~dblGross [CalcGrossPay]~~ dblGrossPay [btnCalc Click]
43.0	7.75	344.88
~~dblHours~~	~~dblRate~~	
~~43.0~~	~~7.75~~	

Figure 7-13 Desk-check table after the CalcGrossPay procedure ends

After the CalcGrossPay procedure ends, the computer returns to the line of code below the Call statement in the btnCalc control's Click event procedure. In this case, it returns to the `lblGross.Text = dblGrossPay.ToString("C2")` statement, which formats the contents of the `dblGrossPay` variable and displays the result ($344.88), as shown earlier in Figure 7-7. Finally, the computer processes the Click event procedure's `End Sub` clause. When the Click event procedure ends, the computer removes the procedure's variables from memory.

Function Procedures

In addition to creating Sub procedures, you also can create Function procedures. The difference between both types of procedures is that a Function procedure returns a value after performing its assigned task, whereas a Sub procedure does not return a value. Function procedures are referred to more simply as **functions**. Figure 7-14 shows the syntax for creating a function in Visual Basic. The header and footer in a function are almost identical to the header and footer in a Sub procedure, except the function's header and footer contain the `Function` keyword rather than the `Sub` keyword. Also different from a Sub procedure header, a function's header includes the `As` *dataType* section, which specifies the data type of the value returned by the function. As is true with a Sub procedure, a function can receive information either *by value* or *by reference*. The information it receives is listed in the *parameterList* in the header. Between the function's header and footer, you enter the instructions you want the computer to process when the function is invoked. In most cases, the last statement within a function is `Return` *expression*, where *expression* represents the one and only value that will be returned to the statement invoking the function. The data type of the *expression* in the Return statement must agree with the data type specified in the As *dataType* section of the header. In addition to the syntax, Figure 7-14 also includes an example of a function, as well as the steps you follow to enter a function in the Code Editor window. As with Sub procedures, you can enter your functions above the first event procedure, below the last event procedure, or immediately above or below the procedure from which they are invoked. In this book, you usually will enter the functions above the first event procedure. Like Sub procedure names, function names are entered using Pascal case and typically begin with a verb. The name should indicate the task the function performs. For example, a good name for a function that returns a new price is GetNewPrice.

Using Pascal case, you capitalize the first letter in the procedure name and the first letter of each subsequent word in the name.

Function procedure

Syntax

Private Function *procedureName*(*[parameterList]*) **As** *dataType*
    [statements]
    Return *expression*
End Function

Example

```
Private Function GetNewPrice(ByVal dblOld As Double) As Double
    ' increases the current price by 5% and returns the new price

    Dim dblNew As Double

    dblNew = dblOld * 1.05
    Return dblNew
End Function
```

Steps

1. Click a blank line in the Code Editor window. The blank line can be anywhere between the Public Class and End Class lines. However, it must be outside any other Sub or Function procedure.
2. Type the Function procedure header, then press Enter. The Code Editor automatically enters the End Function line for you.

Figure 7-14 Syntax, example, and steps for creating a function

After creating a function, you can invoke it from one or more places in an application's code. You invoke a function that you create in exactly the same way as you invoke one of Visual Basic's built-in functions, such as the InputBox function. You do this by including the function's name, along with any arguments, in a statement. The number, data type, and position of the arguments should agree with the number, data type, and position of the function's parameters. Usually the statement that invokes a function will assign the function's return value to a variable. However, it also may use the return value in a calculation or simply display the return value. Figure 7-15 shows examples of invoking the GetNewPrice function from Figure 7-14. The `GetNewPrice(dblCurrentPrice)` entry in each example invokes the function, passing it the value stored in the `dblCurrentPrice` variable. In Example 1, the function's return value is assigned to a variable. Example 2 shows how you can use the return value in a calculation, and Example 3 shows how you can display the return value in a label control.

Invoking a function

Example 1 – assigning the return value to a variable

```
dblNewPrice = GetNewPrice(dblCurrentPrice)
```

Example 2 – using the return value in a calculation

```
dblTotalDue = intQuantity * GetNewPrice(dblCurrentPrice)
```

Example 3 – displaying the return value

```
lblNewPrice.Text = GetNewPrice(dblCurrentPrice).ToString
```

Figure 7-15 Examples of invoking the GetNewPrice function

In the next set of steps, you will modify the Gross Pay Calculator application that you completed in the previous section. The modified application will use a function (rather than a Sub procedure) to calculate and return the gross pay.

To modify the Gross Pay Calculator application to use a function:

1. Use Windows to make a copy of the Gross Pay Solution-Sub folder, which is contained in the VB2008\Chap07 folder. Rename the folder Gross Pay Solution-Function.
2. Open the **Gross Pay Solution** (**Gross Pay Solution.sln**) file contained in the VB2008\Chap07\Gross Pay Solution-Function folder. Open the designer window, then open the Code Editor window. If necessary, replace the <your name> and <current date> text in the comments with your name and the current date.
3. Locate the btnCalc control's Click event procedure. Change the comment above the Call statement to `' use a function to calculate the gross pay`.
4. The Call statement will need to be replaced with a statement that invokes the CalcGrossPay function (rather than the CalcGrossPay Sub procedure). The statement will assign the function's return value, which is the gross pay, to the `dblGrossPay` variable. Like the Sub procedure, the function will need the statement to pass the values stored in the `dblHoursWkd` and `dblRateOfPay` variables, because those values are needed to calculate the gross pay. However, the function will not need the statement to pass the address of the `dblGrossPay` variable, because the statement itself will store the gross pay in the variable. Change the Call statement to **dblGrossPay = CalcGrossPay(dblHoursWkd, dblRateOfPay)**, then click the **blank line** below the statement. (Don't be concerned about the jagged line that appears below a portion of the statement. The jagged line will disappear after you complete Step 7 in this set of steps.)
5. Now you will change the CalcGrossPay Sub procedure to a function. Locate the CalcGrossPay Sub procedure in the Code Editor window. First, change the `Sub` keyword in the procedure header to **Function**, then click the **blank line** above the procedure. The Code Editor automatically changes the procedure's footer to `End Function`. (Here again, don't be concerned about the jagged line that appears in both the function header and footer.)

6. Next, delete the third line of the function header. The third line contains `ByRef dblGross As Double)`. Then replace `, _` (the comma, space, and underscore) in the second line of the header with `)`.

7. Recall that the data type of the function's return value—in this case, Double—is specified at the end of the function header. The insertion point should be located after the `)` in the function header. Press the **Spacebar**, then type **As Double**, and then click the **blank line** below the first comment in the procedure.

8. Now that the function header no longer contains `ByRef dblGross As Double`, which creates the `dblGross` variable, a jagged line appears below each occurrence of `dblGross` in the function. The jagged line indicates that the variable has not been declared. In order to use the `dblGross` variable, the function will need to declare it in a Dim statement. The insertion point should be located below the `' calculates the gross pay` comment. Press **Enter** to insert another blank line, then type **Dim dblGross As Double** and press **Enter**.

9. Finally, you need to tell the function to return the gross pay to the statement that invoked the function. Click **after the letter f** in the `End If` clause, then press **Enter**. Type **Return dblGross** and press **Enter**. Figure 7-16 shows the code entered in the CalcGrossPay function and btnCalc control's Click event procedure. The modified lines of code are shaded in the figure.

```
Private Function CalcGrossPay(ByVal dblHours As Double, _
                              ByVal dblRate As Double) As Double
    ' calculates the gross pay

    Dim dblGross As Double

    dblGross = dblHours * dblRate
    ' add overtime, if necessary
    If dblHours > 40 Then
        dblGross = dblGross + (dblHours - 40) * dblRate / 2
    End If
    Return dblGross

End Function


Private Sub btnCalc_Click(ByVal sender As Object, _
    ByVal e As System.EventArgs) Handles btnCalc.Click
    ' calculates and displays a gross pay amount

    Dim dblHoursWkd As Double
    Dim dblRateOfPay As Double
    Dim dblGrossPay As Double

    Double.TryParse(lstHours.SelectedItem.ToString, dblHoursWkd)
    Double.TryParse(lstRate.SelectedItem.ToString, dblRateOfPay)

    ' use a function to calculate the gross pay
    dblGrossPay = CalcGrossPay(dblHoursWkd, dblRateOfPay)

    lblGross.Text = dblGrossPay.ToString("C2")
End Sub
```

invokes the function and assigns its return value to a variable

Figure 7-16 CalcGrossPay function and btnCalc control's Click event procedure

To test the application's code:

1. Close the Code Editor window. Save the solution, then start the application.
2. Locate and then click **43.0** in the Hours list box, then click **7.75** in the Rate list box. Click the **Calculate** button. The gross pay is $344.88, as shown earlier in Figure 7-7.
3. Click the **Exit** button to end the application, then close the solution.

Lesson A Summary

- **To create an independent Sub procedure:**

  Refer to the syntax shown in Figure 7-2.

- **To call an independent sub procedure:**

  Use the syntax **Call** *procedureName*([*argumentList*])

- **To pass information to a Sub or Function procedure:**

  Include the information in the Call statement's *argumentList*. In the *parameterList* in the procedure header, include the names of memory locations that will store the information. The number, data type, and sequence of the arguments in the *argumentList* should agree with the number, data type, and sequence of the parameters in the *parameterList*.

- **To pass a variable *by value* to a procedure:**

  Include the `ByVal` keyword before the parameter name in the procedure header's *parameterList*. Because only the value stored in the variable is passed, the receiving procedure cannot access the variable.

- **To pass a variable *by reference*:**

  Include the `ByRef` keyword before the parameter name in the procedure header's *parameterList*. Because the address of the variable is passed, the receiving procedure can change the contents of the variable.

- **To create a Function procedure:**

  Refer to the syntax and steps shown in Figure 7-14.

Lesson A Key Terms

Function procedure—a procedure that returns a value after performing its assigned task

Functions—another term for Function procedures

Parameters—the memory locations listed in a procedure header

Passing by reference—the process of passing a variable's address to a procedure so that the value of the variable can be changed

Passing by value—the process of passing a variable's contents to a procedure

Sub procedure—a procedure that does not return a value after performing its assigned task

Lesson A Review Questions

1. Which of the following is false?
   a. A function can return one or more values to the statement that invoked it.
   b. A procedure can accept one or more items of data passed to it.
   c. The *parameterList* in a procedure header is optional.
   d. At times, a memory location inside the computer's internal memory may have more than one name.

2. The items listed in the Call statement are referred to as ________________.
   a. arguments
   b. parameters
   c. passers
   d. None of the above.

3. Each memory location listed in the *parameterList* in the procedure header is referred to as ________________.
   a. an address
   b. a constraint
   c. a parameter
   d. a value

4. To determine whether a variable is being passed to a procedure *by value* or *by reference*, you will need to examine ________________.
   a. the Call statement
   b. the procedure header
   c. the statements entered in the procedure
   d. Either a or b.

5. Which of the following statements invokes the GetArea Sub procedure, passing it two variables *by value*?
   a. `Call GetArea(dblLength, dblWidth)`
   b. `Call GetArea(ByVal dblLength, ByVal dblWidth)`
   c. `Invoke GetArea(dblLength, dblWidth)`
   d. `GetArea(dblLength, dblWidth) As Double`

6. Which of the following procedure headers receives only the contents of a String variable?
   a. `Private Sub DisplayName(ByContents strName As String)`
   b. `Private Sub DisplayName(ByValue strName As String)`
   c. `Private Sub DisplayName ByVal(strName As String)`
   d. None of the above.

7. Which of the following is a valid header for a procedure that receives an integer followed by a number with a decimal place?
   a. `Private Sub GetFee(intBase As Integer, decRate As Decimal)`
   b. `Private Sub GetFee(ByRef intBase As Integer, ByRef decRate As Decimal)`
   c. `Private Sub GetFee(ByVal intBase As Integer, ByVal decRate As Decimal)`
   d. None of the above.

8. Which of the following is false?
   a. The sequence of the arguments listed in the Call statement should agree with the sequence of the parameters listed in the receiving procedure's header.
   b. The data type of each argument in the Call statement should match the data type of its corresponding parameter in the procedure header.
   c. The name of each argument in the Call statement should be identical to the name of its corresponding parameter in the procedure header.
   d. When you pass information to a procedure *by value*, the procedure stores the value of each item it receives in a separate memory location.

9. Which of the following instructs a function to return the contents of the `decStateTax` variable?

    a. `Return decStateTax`

    b. `Return ByVal decStateTax`

    c. `Send decStateTax`

    d. `SendBack decStateTax`

10. Which of the following is a valid header for a procedure that receives the value stored in an Integer variable first, and the address of a Decimal variable second?

    a. `Private Sub GetFee(ByVal intBase As Integer, ByAdd decRate As Decimal)`

    b. `Private Sub GetFee(intBase As Integer, decRate As Decimal)`

    c. `Private Sub GetFee(ByVal intBase As Integer, ByRef decRate As Decimal)`

    d. None of the above.

11. Which of the following is a valid header for a procedure that is passed the number 15?

    a. `Private Function GetTax(ByVal intRate As Integer) As Decimal`

    b. `Private Function GetTax(ByAdd intRate As Integer) As Decimal`

    c. `Private Sub CalcTax(ByVal intRate As Integer)`

    d. Both a and c.

12. If the statement `Call CalcNet(decNetPay)` passes the variable's address, the variable is said to be passed ______________________.

    a. *by address*

    b. *by content*

    c. *by reference*

    d. *by value*

13. Which of the following is false?

    a. When you pass a variable *by reference*, the receiving procedure can change its contents.

    b. To pass a variable *by reference* in Visual Basic, you include the `ByRef` keyword before the variable's name in the Call statement.

    c. When you pass a variable *by value*, the receiving procedure creates a procedure-level variable that it uses to store the value passed to it.

    d. Unless specified otherwise, all variables in Visual Basic are passed *by value*.

14. A Sub procedure named GetEndingInventory is passed four Integer variables named `intBegin`, `intSales`, `intPurchases`, and `intEnding`. The procedure should calculate the ending inventory using the beginning inventory, sales, and purchase amounts passed to the procedure. The result should be stored in the `intEnding` variable. Which of the following procedure headers is correct?

    a. `Private Sub GetEndingInventory(ByVal intB As Integer, ByVal intS As Integer, ByVal intP As Integer, ByRef intFinal As Integer)`

    b. `Private Sub GetEndingInventory(ByVal intB As Integer, ByVal intS As Integer, ByVal intP As Integer, ByVal intFinal As Integer)`

    c. `Private Sub GetEndingInventory(ByRef intB As Integer, ByRef intS As Integer, ByRef intP As Integer, ByVal intFinal As Integer)`

    d. `Private Sub GetEndingInventory(ByRef intB As Integer, ByRef intS As Integer, ByRef intP As Integer, ByRef intFinal As Integer)`

15. Which of the following statements should you use to call the GetEndingInventory procedure described in Question 14?

    a. `Call GetEndingInventory(intBegin, intSales, intPurchases, intEnding)`

    b. `Call GetEndingInventory(ByVal intBegin, ByVal intSales, ByVal intPurchases, ByRef intEnding)`

    c. `Call GetEndingInventory(ByRef intBegin, ByRef intSales, ByRef intPurchases, ByRef intEnding)`

    d. `Call GetEndingInventory(ByVal intBegin, ByVal intSales, ByVal intPurchases, ByVal intEnding)`

16. The memory locations listed in the *parameterList* in a procedure header have procedure scope and are removed from the computer's internal memory when the procedure ends.

    a. True

    b. False

17. Which of the following statements invokes the GetDiscount function, passing it the contents of two Decimal variables named `decSales` and `decDiscountRate`? The statement should assign the function's return value to the `decDiscount` variable.

    a. `decDiscount = Call GetDiscount(decSales, decDiscountRate)`

    b. `Call GetDiscount(decSales, decDiscountRate, decDiscount)`

    c. `decDiscount = GetDiscount(decSales, decDiscountRate)`

    d. None of the above.

18. Explain the difference between a Sub procedure and a Function procedure.

19. Explain the difference between passing a variable *by value* and passing it *by reference.*

20. Explain the difference between invoking a Sub procedure and invoking a function.

Lesson A Exercises

INTRODUCTORY

1. Write the Visual Basic code for a Sub procedure that receives an integer passed to it. The procedure should divide the integer by 2 and then display the result in the lblNum control. Name the procedure DivideByTwo. Then write a statement to invoke the procedure, passing it the number 87.

INTRODUCTORY

2. Write the Visual Basic code for a Sub procedure that prompts the user to enter the name of a city, and then stores the user's response in the String variable whose address is passed to the procedure. Name the procedure GetCity. Then write a statement to invoke the procedure, passing it the `strCity` variable.

INTRODUCTORY

3. Write the Visual Basic code for a function that prompts the user to enter the name of a state, and then returns the user's response. Name the function GetState. Then write a statement to invoke the GetState function. Display the function's return value in a message box.

INTRODUCTORY

4. Write the Visual Basic code for a Sub procedure that receives three Double variables: the first two *by value* and the last one *by reference.* The procedure should divide the first variable by the second variable, and then store the result in the third variable. Name the procedure CalcQuotient.

INTRODUCTORY

5. Write the Visual Basic code for a function that receives the value stored in an Integer variable. The function should divide the value by 2 and then return the result, which may contain a decimal place. Name the function GetQuotient. Then write an appropriate statement to invoke the function, passing it the `intNumber` variable. Assign the function's return value to the `dblAnswer` variable.

INTRODUCTORY

6. In this exercise, you experiment with passing variables *by value* and *by reference.* Open the Passing Solution (Passing Solution.sln) file, which is contained in the VB2008\Chap07\Passing Solution folder. If necessary, open the designer window.

   a. Open the Code Editor window and review the existing code. Notice that the `strMyName` variable is passed *by value* to the GetName procedure. Start the application. Click the Display Name button. When prompted to enter a name, type your name and press Enter. Explain why the btnDisplay control's Click event procedure does not display your name in the lblName control. Stop the application.

   b. Modify the application's code so that it passes the `strMyName` variable *by reference* to the GetName procedure. Save the solution, then start the application. Click the Display Name button. When prompted to enter a name, type your name and press Enter. This time, your name appears in the lblName control. Explain why the btnDisplay control's Click event procedure now works correctly. Stop the application. Close the Code Editor window, then close the solution.

INTERMEDIATE

7. Write the Visual Basic code for a function that receives the contents of four Integer variables. The function should calculate the average of the four integers and then return the result, which may contain a decimal place. Name the function CalcAverage. Then write a statement to invoke the function, passing it the `intNum1`, `intNum2`, `intNum3`, and `intNum4` variables. Assign the function's return value to the `dblAverage` variable.

INTERMEDIATE

8. Write the Visual Basic code for a Sub procedure that receives four Integer variables: the first two *by value* and the last two *by reference.* The procedure should calculate the sum of and the difference between the two variables passed *by value,* and then store the results in the variables passed *by reference.* When calculating the difference, subtract the contents of the second variable from the contents of the first variable. Name the procedure GetSumAndDiff. Then write an appropriate statement to invoke the procedure, passing it the `intFirst`, `intSecond`, `intSum`, and `intDifference` variables.

INTERMEDIATE

9. Open the Temperature Solution (Temperature Solution.sln) file, which is contained in the VB2008\Chap07\Temperature Solution folder. If necessary, open the designer window. Open the Code Editor window. Code the application so that it uses two independent Sub procedures: one to convert a temperature from Fahrenheit to Celsius, and the other to convert a temperature from Celsius to Fahrenheit. Save the solution, then start and test the application. Stop the application. Close the Code Editor window, then close the solution.

INTERMEDIATE

10. In this exercise, you modify the application from Exercise 9. Use Windows to make a copy of the Temperature Solution folder, which is contained in the VB2008\Chap07 folder. Rename the folder Modified Temperature Solution. Open the Temperature Solution (Temperature Solution.sln) file contained in the VB2008\Chap07\Modified Temperature Solution folder. Open the designer window, then open the Code Editor window. Modify the code to use two functions, rather than two Sub procedures, to convert the temperatures. Save the solution, then start and test the application. Stop the application. Close the Code Editor window, then close the solution.

INTERMEDIATE

11. The owner of Pine Lodge wants an application that calculates an employee's new hourly pay, given the employee's current hourly pay and raise rate. Create a Visual Basic Windows application. Name the solution, project, and form file Pine Lodge Solution, Pine Lodge Project, and Main Form.vb, respectively. Save the application in the VB2008\Chap07 folder. Create the interface shown in Figure 7-17. Code the application. Display pay amounts from 7.00 through 12.00 in increments of .50 in the lstPay control. Display rates from 2 through 11 in increments of 1 in the lstRate control. Clear the new pay when a change is made to either list box. Use a function to calculate and return the new pay. Save the solution, then start the application. Calculate the new pay based on a current pay of 8.00 and a raise rate of 5. The answer should be $8.40. Stop the application. Close the Code Editor window, then close the solution.

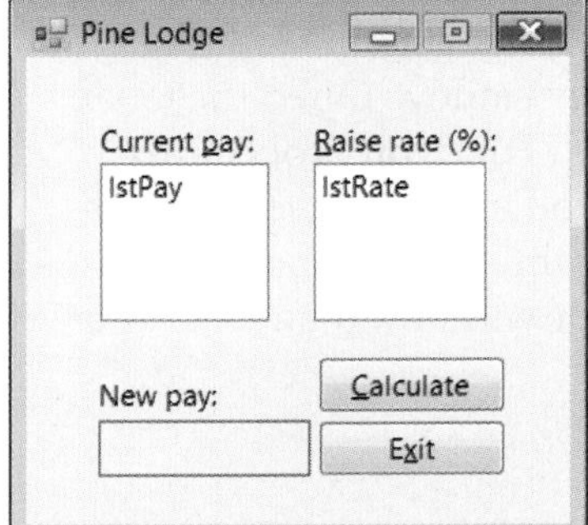

Figure 7-17 Interface for the Pine Lodge application

INTERMEDIATE

12. In this exercise, you modify the application from Exercise 11. Use Windows to make a copy of the Pine Lodge Solution folder, which is contained in the VB2008\Chap07 folder. Rename the folder Modified Pine Lodge Solution. Open the Pine Lodge Solution (Pine Lodge Solution.sln) file contained in the VB2008\Chap07\Modified Pine Lodge Solution folder. Open the designer window, then open the Code Editor window. Modify the code to use a Sub procedure, rather than a function, to calculate the new pay amount. Save the solution, then start and test the application. Stop the application. Close the Code Editor window, then close the solution.

ADVANCED

13. Create a Visual Basic Windows application. Name the solution, project, and form file Rainfall Solution, Rainfall Project, and Main Form.vb, respectively. Save the application in the VB2008\Chap07 folder. Create the interface shown in Figure 7-18. The user will enter a monthly rainfall amount and then click the Calculate button. The button's Click event procedure should calculate and display both the total and average of the rainfall amounts entered so far. Code the application. Use a Sub procedure named CalcTotalAndAverage to make the necessary calculations. Save the solution, then start and test the application. Stop the application. Close the Code Editor window, then close the solution.

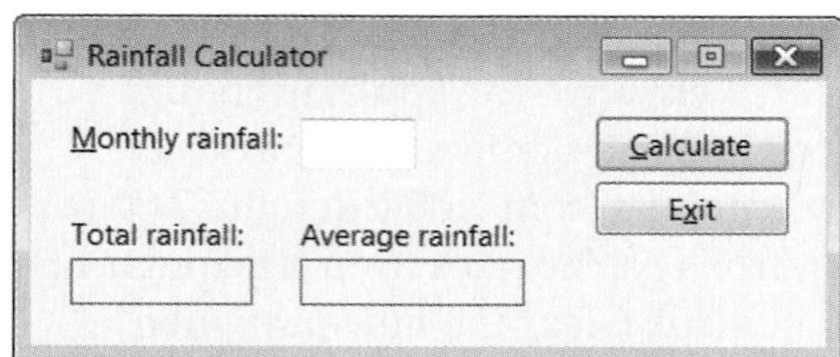

Figure 7-18 Interface for the Rainfall Calculator application

ADVANCED

14. In this exercise, you modify the Rainfall Calculator application from Exercise 13. Use Windows to make a copy of the Rainfall Solution folder, which is contained in the VB2008\Chap07 folder. Rename the folder Modified Rainfall Solution. Open the Rainfall Solution (Rainfall Solution.sln) file contained in the VB2008\Chap07\Modified Rainfall Solution folder. Open the designer window. Open the Code Editor window. Modify the code to use two Function procedures, rather than a Sub procedure, to calculate the total and average rainfall amounts. Save the solution, then start and test the application. Stop the application. Close the Code Editor window, then close the solution.

Discovery

15. In this exercise, you learn how to specify that one or more arguments are optional in a Call statement. Open the Optional Solution (Optional Solution.sln) file, which is contained in the VB2008\Chap07\Optional Solution folder. If necessary, open the designer window.

a. Open the Code Editor window and review the existing code. Notice that the btnCalc control's Click event procedure contains two Call statements. The first Call statement passes three variables to the CalcBonus procedure. The second call statement, however, passes only two variables to the procedure. (Do not be concerned about the jagged line that appears below the second Call statement.) Notice that the `dblRate` variable is omitted from the second Call statement. You indicate that the `dblRate` variable is optional in the Call statement by including the keyword `Optional` before the variable's corresponding parameter in the procedure header; you enter the `Optional` keyword before the `ByVal` keyword. You also assign a default value that the procedure will use for the missing argument when the procedure is called. You assign the default value by entering the assignment operator, followed by the default value, after the corresponding parameter in the procedure header. In this case, you will assign the number .1 as the default value for the `dblRate` variable. (Optional parameters must be listed at the end of the procedure header.)

b. Change the `ByVal dblBonusRate As Double` in the procedure header appropriately. Save the solution, then start the application. Calculate the bonus for a salesperson with an "a" code, $1000 in sales, and a rate of .05. The `Call CalcBonus(dblSales, dblBonus, dblRate)` statement calls the CalcBonus procedure, passing it the number 1000, the address of the `dblBonus` variable, and the number .05. The CalcBonus procedure stores the number 1000 in the `dblTotalSales` variable. It also assigns the name `dblBonusAmount` to the `dblBonus` variable, and stores the number .05 in the `dblBonusRate` variable. The procedure then multiplies the contents of the `dblTotalSales` variable (1000) by the contents of the `dblBonusRate` variable (.05), assigning the result (50) to the `dblBonusAmount` variable. The `lblBonus.Text = dblBonus.ToString("C2")` statement then displays $50.00 in the lblBonus control.

c. Now calculate the bonus for a salesperson with a code of "b" and a sales amount of $2000. The `Call CalcBonus(dblSales, dblBonus)` statement calls the CalcBonus procedure, passing it the number 2000 and the address of the `dblBonus` variable. The CalcBonus procedure stores the number 2000 in the `dblTotalSales` variable, and assigns the name `dblBonusAmount` to the `dblBonus` variable. Because the Call statement did not supply a value for the `dblBonusRate` parameter, the default value (.1) is assigned to the variable. The procedure then multiplies the contents of the `dblTotalSales` variable (2000) by the contents of the `dblBonusRate` variable (.1), assigning the result (200) to the `dblBonusAmount` variable. The `lblBonus.Text = dblBonus.ToString("C2")` statement then displays $200.00 in the lblBonus control. Stop the application. Close the Code Editor window, then close the solution.

LESSON B

After studying Lesson B, you should be able to:

- Include a combo box in an interface
- Add items to a combo box
- Select a combo box item from code
- Determine the item either selected or entered in a combo box
- Code a combo box's TextChanged event procedure

Including a Combo Box in an Interface

In many interfaces, combo boxes are used in place of list boxes. You use the ComboBox tool in the toolbox to add a combo box to an interface. A **combo box** is similar to a list box in that it allows the user to select from a list of choices. However, unlike a list box, the full list of choices in a combo box can be hidden, allowing you to save space on the form. Also unlike a list box, a combo box contains a text field. Depending on the style of the combo box, the text field may or may not be editable by the user. Three styles of combo boxes are available in Visual Basic. The style is controlled by the combo box's DropDownStyle property, which can be set to Simple, DropDown (the default), or DropDownList. Each style of combo box contains a text portion and a list portion. When the DropDownStyle property is set to either Simple or DropDown, the text portion of the combo box is editable. However, in a Simple combo box the list portion is always displayed, while in a DropDown combo box the list portion appears only when the user clicks the combo box's list arrow. When the DropDownStyle property is set to the third style, DropDownList, the text portion of the combo box is not editable and the user must click the combo box's list arrow to display the list of choices. Figure 7-19 shows an example of each combo box style. You should use a label control to provide keyboard access to the combo box, as shown in the figure. For the access key to work correctly, you must set the label's TabIndex property to a value that is one less than the combo box's TabIndex value. Like the items in a list box, the items in the list portion of a combo box are either arranged by use, with the most used entries listed first, or sorted in ascending order. To sort the items in the list portion of a combo box, you use the combo box's Sorted property.

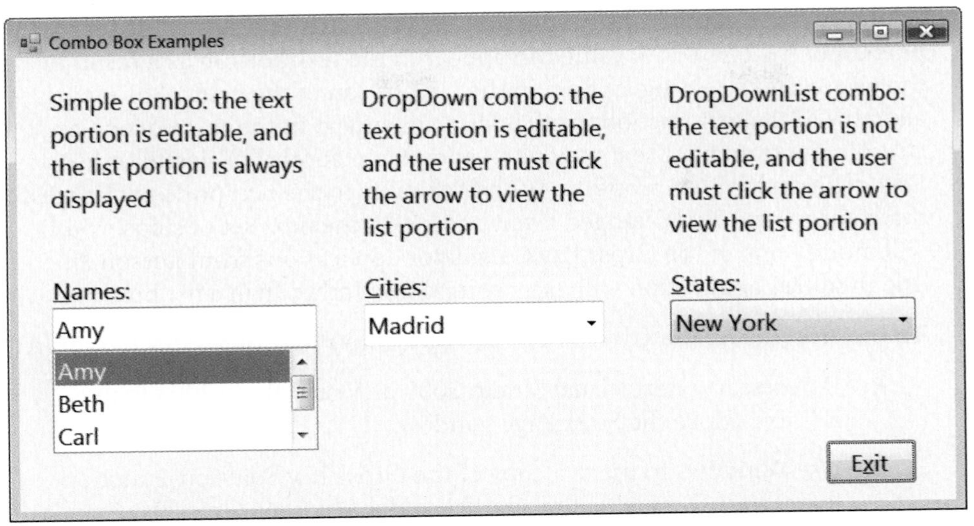

Figure 7-19 Examples of the combo box styles

Figure 7-20 shows the code used to fill the combo boxes in Figure 7-19 with values. As you do with a list box, you use the Items collection's Add method to add an item to a combo box. To select a default item, which will appear in the text portion of the combo box, you can use the SelectedIndex, SelectedItem, or Text property. If no item is selected, the SelectedItem and Text properties contain the empty string, and the SelectedIndex property contains -1.

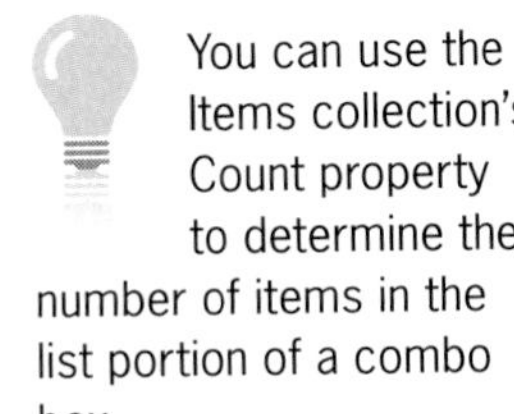

You can use the Items collection's Count property to determine the number of items in the list portion of a combo box.

Like the first item in a list box, the first item in a combo box has an index of 0.

```
Private Sub frmMain_Load(ByVal sender As Object, ByVal e As System.Even
    ' fills the combo boxes with values

    cboName.Items.Add("Amy")
    cboName.Items.Add("Beth")
    cboName.Items.Add("Carl")
    cboName.Items.Add("Dan")
    cboName.SelectedIndex = 0

    cboCity.Items.Add("London")
    cboCity.Items.Add("Madrid")
    cboCity.Items.Add("Paris")
    cboCity.SelectedItem = "Madrid"

    cboState.Items.Add("Alabama")
    cboState.Items.Add("Maine")
    cboState.Items.Add("New York")
    cboState.Items.Add("South Dakota")
    cboState.Text = "New York"
End Sub
```

you can use any of these 3 properties to select the default item in a combo box

Figure 7-20 Code used to add items to the combo boxes and also select a default item

GUI DESIGN TIP Combo Box Standards

- Use a label control to provide keyboard access to the combo box. Set the label's TabIndex property to a value that is one less than the combo box's TabIndex value.
- Combo box items are either arranged by use, with the most used entries appearing first in the list, or sorted in ascending order.

A combo box's Text property contains the value that appears in the text portion of the control. A value can appear in the text portion as a result of the user either selecting an item in the list portion of the control or typing an entry in the text portion itself. It also can appear in the text portion as a result of a statement that assigns a value to the control's SelectedIndex, SelectedItem, or Text property. When the value in the text portion changes, the combo box's TextChanged event occurs. In the next set of steps, you will modify one of the Gross Pay Calculator applications from Lesson A. The modified application will use a combo box rather than a list box.

To modify one of the Gross Pay Calculator applications from Lesson A:

1. If necessary, start Visual Studio 2008 or Visual Basic 2008 Express Edition. Close the Start Page window.

2. Use Windows to make a copy of the Gross Pay Solution-Function folder from Lesson A. Rename the folder Modified Gross Pay Solution-Function. Open the **Gross Pay Solution** (**Gross Pay Solution.sln**) file, which is contained in the VB2008\Chap07\Modified Gross Pay Solution-Function folder. Open the designer window.

3. First, you will replace the Rate list box with a DropDownList combo box. Unlock the controls on the form. Click the **lstRate** control, then press **Delete**. Click the **ComboBox** tool in the toolbox, then drag the mouse pointer to the form. Position the mouse pointer below the Rate label, then release the mouse button. Change the combo box's **DropDownStyle** property to **DropDownList**.

4. The three-character ID used for naming combo boxes is cbo. Change the combo box's name to **cboRate**, then size the control to match Figure 7-21. (Or, change its Size property to 81, 28.)

5. Lock the controls on the form, then use the information shown in Figure 7-21 to set the TabIndex values.

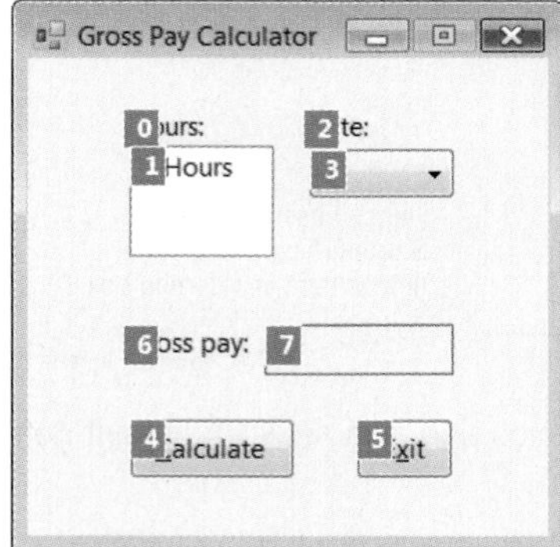

Figure 7-21 Correct TabIndex values

6. Press **Esc** to remove the TabIndex boxes from the form, then save the solution.

7. Open the Code Editor window. Locate the form's Load event procedure. Change `lstRate` in the second For...Next loop, as well as in the `lstRate.SelectedIndex = 0` statement, to **cboRate**. Also change `list boxes` in the first comment to **a list box and combo box**.

8. Locate the btnCalc control's Click event procedure. Replace `lstRate.SelectedItem.ToString` in the second TryParse method with **cboRate.Text**.

9. Locate the lstRate_SelectedValueChanged procedure, then delete the entire procedure from the Code Editor window. Open the code template for the cboRate control's TextChanged event procedure, then type **lblGross.Text = String.Empty**.

10. Save the solution, then start the application. Click the **arrow** in the Rate combo box, then click **9.00** in the list. Click the **Calculate** button. The gross pay is $360.00, as shown in Figure 7-22.

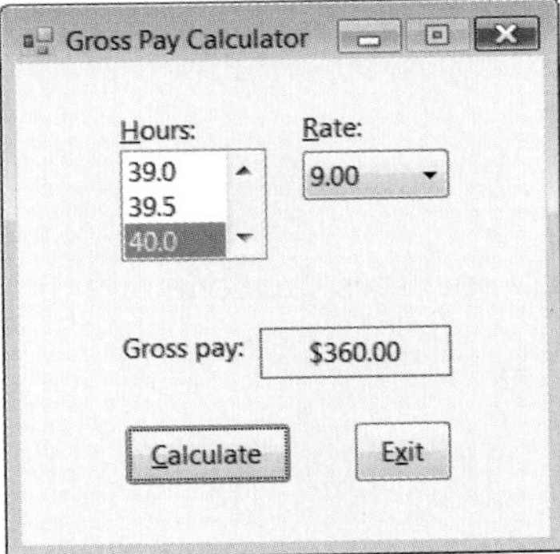

Figure 7-22 Interface showing the gross pay

11. Click the **Exit** button to end the application. Close the Code Editor window, then close the solution.

Lesson B Summary

- **To add a combo box to a form:**

  Use the ComboBox tool in the toolbox.

- **To specify the style of a combo box:**

  Set the combo box's DropDownStyle property.

- **To add items to a combo box:**

  Use the Items collection's Add method, whose syntax is *object*.**Items.Add(***item***)**. In the syntax, *object* is the name of the control to which you want the item added, and *item* is the text you want displayed in the control.

- **To automatically sort the items in the list portion of a combo box:**

  Set the combo box's Sorted property to True.

- **To select a combo box item from code:**

  Use the combo box's SelectedIndex, SelectedItem, or Text property.

- **To determine the item selected in the list portion of a combo box or entered in the text portion:**

  Use the combo box's Text property. However, if the combo box is a DropDownList style, you also can use the SelectedIndex or SelectedItem property.

- **To process code when the value in a combo box's Text property changes:**

  Enter the code in the combo box's TextChanged event procedure.

Lesson B Key Term

Combo box—a control used to display a list of choices; also contains a text field that may or may not be editable

Lesson B Review Questions

1. The ______________________________ property specifies the style of a combo box.
   a. ComboBoxStyle
   b. DropDownStyle
   c. DropStyle
   d. Style

2. The items in a combo box belong to the ______________________________ collection.
   a. Items
   b. List
   c. ListBox
   d. Values

3. Which of the following selects the "Cat" item, which appears third in the cboAnimal control?
   a. `cboAnimal.SelectedIndex = 2`
   b. `cboAnimal.SelectedItem = "Cat"`
   c. `cboAnimal.Text = "Cat"`
   d. All of the above.

4. The ________________________ property stores the item that appears in the text portion of a combo box.

   a. SelectedText

   b. SelectedValue

   c. Text

   d. TextItem

5. The ________________________ event occurs when the user either types a value in the text portion of a combo box or selects a different item in the list portion.

   a. ChangedItem

   b. ChangedValue

   c. SelectedItemChanged

   d. TextChanged

Lesson B Exercises

1. In this exercise, you modify one of the Gross Pay Calculator applications from Lesson A. Use Windows to make a copy of the Gross Pay Solution-Sub folder, which is contained in the VB2008\Chap07 folder. Rename the folder Modified Gross Pay Solution-Sub. Open the Gross Pay Solution (Gross Pay Solution.sln) file contained in the VB2008\Chap07\Modified Gross Pay Solution-Sub folder. Open the designer window. Replace the Hours list box with a DropDownList combo box. Open the Code Editor window and make the necessary modifications to the code. Save the solution, then start and test the application. Stop the application. Close the Code Editor window, then close the solution.

   INTRODUCTORY

2. In this exercise, you modify the Shoppers Haven application that you created in Chapter 6's Lesson C. Use Windows to make a copy of the Shoppers Haven Solution folder, which is contained in the VB2008\Chap06 folder. Save the copy in the VB2008\Chap07 folder. Open the Shoppers Haven Solution (Shoppers Haven Solution.sln) file contained in the VB2008\Chap07\Shoppers Haven Solution folder. Open the designer window. Replace the Discount rate list box with a DropDown combo box. Open the Code Editor window and make the necessary modifications to the code. Save the solution, then start and test the application. Stop the application. Close the Code Editor window, then close the solution.

   INTRODUCTORY

INTERMEDIATE

3. Create a Visual Basic Windows application. Name the solution, project, and form file Car Shoppers Solution, Car Shoppers Project, and Main Form.vb, respectively. Save the application in the VB2008\Chap07 folder. Create the interface shown in Figure 7-23. The Interest rate combo box should have the DropDown style and contain rates from .02 through .1 in increments of .01. The Term combo box should have the DropDownList style and contain terms of 2, 3, 4, and 5 years. Open the Code Editor window. The application should calculate and display the monthly payment on a car loan. Code the application. Create a function that calculates and returns the monthly payment. (Hint: Use the Financial.Pmt method, which you learned about in Chapter 4, to calculate the monthly payment.) Create a Sub procedure that clears the Monthly payment box when a change is made to any of the text boxes or combo boxes. Save the solution, then start and test the application. Stop the application. Close the Code Editor window, then close the solution.

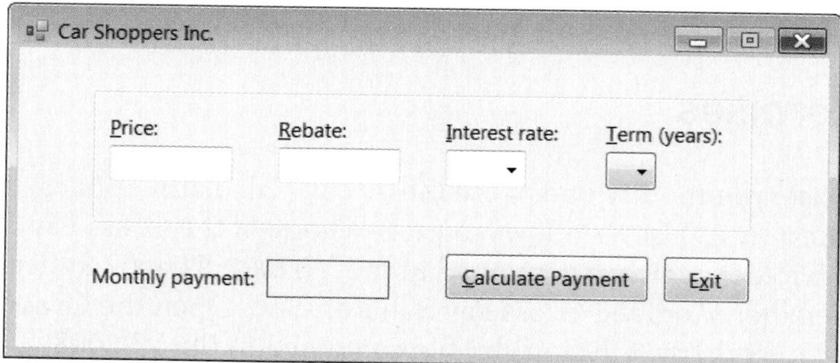

Figure 7-23 Interface for the Car Shoppers application

LESSON C

After studying Lesson C, you should be able to:

- Prevent a form from closing
- Round a number

Coding the Harvey Industries Application

Recall that your task is to create an application that calculates an employee's weekly gross pay, federal withholding tax (FWT), Social Security and Medicare (FICA) tax, and net pay. Figure 7-24 shows the application's TOE chart.

Task	Object	Event
End the application	btnExit	Click
1. Calculate the gross pay, FWT, FICA, and net pay 2. Display the calculated amounts in the appropriate labels	btnCalc	Click
Display the calculated amounts (from btnCalc)	lblGross, lblFwt, lblFica, lblNet	None
Clear lblGross, lblFwt, lblFica, and lblNet	txtName, cboAllowances	TextChanged
	lstHours, lstRate	SelectedValueChanged
	radMarried, radSingle	Click
Select the existing text	txtName	Enter
Allow only numbers and the Backspace key	cboAllowances	KeyPress
Get and display the name, hours worked, pay rate, marital status, and withholding allowances	txtName, lstHours, lstRate, radMarried, radSingle, cboAllowances	None
Fill lstHours, lstRate, and cboAllowances with values, then select a default item	frmMain	Load
Verify that the user wants to close the application, then take the appropriate action based on the user's response		FormClosing

Figure 7-24 TOE chart for the Harvey Industries application

To open the Harvey Industries application:

1. If necessary, start Visual Studio 2008 or Visual Basic 2008 Express Edition. Close the Start Page window.
2. Open the **Harvey Industries Solution** (**Harvey Industries Solution.sln**) file, which is contained in the VB2008\Chap07\Harvey Industries Solution folder. If necessary, open the designer window. See Figure 7-25. The interface provides a text box for entering the employee's name, and radio buttons for entering his or her marital status. It also provides list boxes for specifying the hours worked and rate of pay. The combo box in the interface allows the user to either select the number of withholding allowances from the list portion of the control or type a number in the text portion.

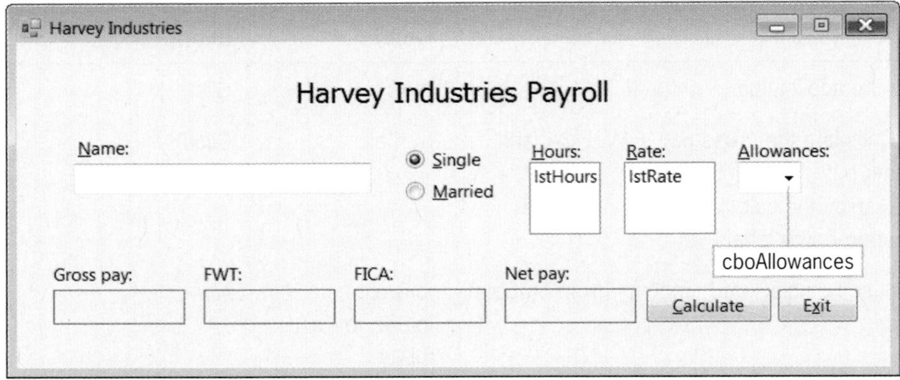

Figure 7-25 User interface for the Harvey Industries application

3. Open the Code Editor window and review the existing code.

To complete the Harvey Industries application, you will need to code the btnCalc control's Click event procedure and the form's FormClosing event procedure.

Coding the FormClosing Event Procedure

A form's **FormClosing event** occurs when a form is about to be closed. In most cases, this happens when the computer processes the `Me.Close()` statement in the form's code. However, it also occurs when the user clicks the Close button on the form's title bar. According to the TOE chart, the FormClosing event procedure is responsible for verifying that the user wants to close the application, and then taking the appropriate action based on the user's response. Figure 7-26 shows the procedure's pseudocode.

frmMain FormClosing event procedure

```
1. use a message box to ask the user whether he or she wants to exit the application
2. if the user does not want to exit the application
       prevent the form from closing
   end if
```

Figure 7-26 Pseudocode for the FormClosing event procedure

To begin coding the FormClosing event procedure:

1. Click the **Class Name** arrow, then click **(frmMain Events)** in the list. Click the **Method Name** arrow, then click **FormClosing** in the list. The code template for the FormClosing event procedure appears above the Load event procedure in the Code Editor window.
2. Type **' verify that the user wants to exit the application** and press **Enter** twice.
3. The procedure will use the MessageBox.Show method to display the appropriate message in a message box. The method's return value will be assigned to a variable named `dlgButton`. Type **Dim dlgButton As DialogResult** and press **Enter**.
4. The message box will contain the "Do you want to exit?" message, as well as Yes and No buttons and the Exclamation icon. The Yes button will be designated as the default button. Type **dlgButton = MessageBox.Show("Do you want to exit?", _** (be sure to include a space before the line continuation character) and press **Enter**. Type **"Harvey Industries", MessageBoxButtons.YesNo, _** and press **Enter**. Type **MessageBoxIcon.Exclamation, _** and press **Enter**, then type **MessageBoxDefaultButton.Button1)** and press **Enter** twice.

If the user selects the No button in the message box, the FormClosing procedure should stop the computer from closing the form. You prevent the computer from closing a form by setting the **Cancel property** of the FormClosing procedure's e parameter to True.

To complete the FormClosing event procedure, then test the procedure:

1. Type **' if the No button was selected, don't close the form** and press **Enter**. Type **If dlgButton = Windows.Forms.DialogResult.No Then** and press **Enter**, then type **e.Cancel = True**.
2. Save the solution, then start the application. Click the **Close** button on the form's title bar. Doing this invokes the FormClosing event procedure, which displays the message box shown in Figure 7-27.

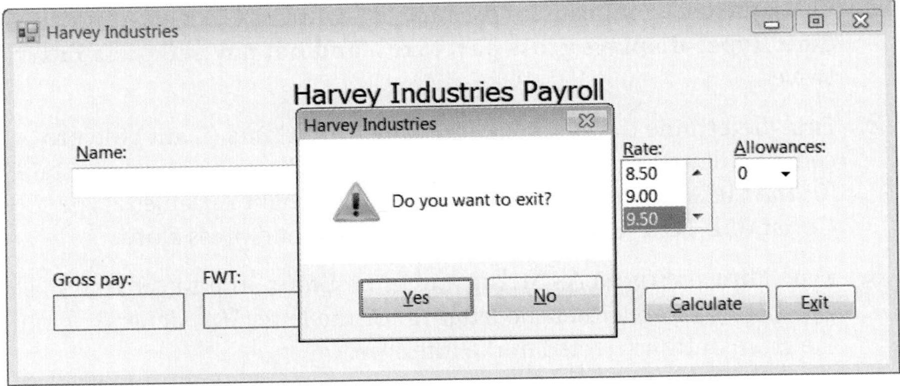

Figure 7-27 Message box displayed by the FormClosing event procedure

3. Click the **No** button in the message box. Notice that the form remains on the screen.

4. Click the **Exit** button. This time, click the **Yes** button in the message box. The application ends.

Coding the btnCalc Control's Click Event Procedure

According to the application's TOE chart, the btnCalc control's Click event procedure is responsible for calculating and displaying the gross pay, FWT (federal withholding tax), FICA tax, and net pay. Figure 7-28 shows the procedure's pseudocode.

```
btnCalc Click event procedure
1. convert the hours, pay rate, and allowances to numbers
2. if the Single radio button is selected
        assign "S" as the marital status
   else
        assign "M" as the marital status
   end if

3. if the number of hours is less than or equal to 40
        calculate the gross pay = hours * pay rate
   else
        calculate the gross pay = 40 * pay rate + (hours – 40) * pay rate * 1.5
   end if

4. call a function to calculate and return the FWT
5. calculate the FICA tax = gross pay * 7.65%
6. round the gross pay, FWT, and FICA tax to two decimal places
7. calculate the net pay = gross pay – FWT – FICA tax
8. display the gross pay, FWT, FICA tax, and net pay in the appropriate labels
```

Figure 7-28 Pseudocode for the btnCalc control's Click event procedure

To begin coding the btnCalc control's Click event procedure:

1. Open the code template for the btnCalc control's Click event procedure. Type **' displays gross pay, taxes, and net pay** and press **Enter** twice.

2. First, determine the variables and named constants (if any) the procedure will use. In this case, the procedure will use a named constant for the FICA tax rate (7.65%). It also will use eight variables. Type **Const dblFICA_RATE As Double = .0765** and press **Enter**.

3. Type **Dim strStatus As String** and press **Enter**. The `strStatus` variable will store either the letter "S" or the letter "M", depending on the radio button selected in the interface.

4. Type **Dim dblHours As Double** and press **Enter**. The `dblHours` variable will store the number of hours worked, which is selected in the lstHours control.

5. Type **Dim dblPayRate As Double** and press **Enter**. The `dblPayRate` variable will store the pay rate selected in the lstRate control.

6. Type **Dim intAllowances As Integer** and press **Enter**. The `intAllowances` variable will store the number of withholding allowances, which is either selected or entered in the cboAllowances control.

7. Now declare variables to store the calculated amounts, which are the gross pay, FWT, FICA, and net pay. Enter the following declaration statements. Press **Enter** twice after typing the last declaration statement.

   Dim dblGross As Double
   Dim dblFwt As Double
   Dim dblFica As Double
   Dim dblNet As Double

8. Step 1 in the procedure's pseudocode is to convert the hours, pay rate, and allowances to numbers. Enter the following statements. Press **Enter** twice after typing the last statement.

   dblHours = Convert.ToDouble(lstHours.SelectedItem.ToString)
   dblPayRate = Convert.ToDouble(lstRate.SelectedItem.ToString)
   intAllowances = Convert.ToInt32(cboAllowances.Text)

9. Step 2 in the pseudocode is a selection structure that determines the employee's marital status. Type the selection structure shown in Figure 7-29, then position the insertion point as shown in the figure.

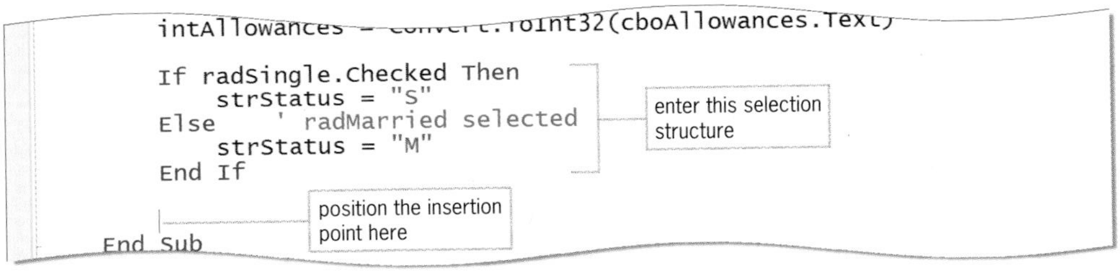

```
        intAllowances = Convert.ToInt32(cboAllowances.Text)

        If radSingle.Checked Then
            strStatus = "S"
        Else     ' radMarried selected
            strStatus = "M"
        End If

        |
    End Sub
```

enter this selection structure

position the insertion point here

Figure 7-29 Selection structure entered in the procedure

10. The next step is a selection structure that compares the number of hours worked with the number 40, and then calculates the gross pay based on the result. Type **' calculate gross pay** and press **Enter**, then type **If dblHours <= 40 Then** and press **Enter**.

11. If the number of hours worked is less than or equal to 40, the selection structure's true path should calculate the gross pay by multiplying the number of hours worked by the pay rate. Type **dblGross = dblHours * dblPayRate** and press **Enter**.

12. If the number of hours worked is greater than 40, the employee is entitled to his or her regular pay rate for the hours worked up to and including 40, and then time and one-half for the hours worked over 40. Type **Else** and press **Enter**, then type **dblGross = 40 * dblPayRate + (dblHours - 40) * dblPayRate * 1.5**.

13. Save the solution.

Step 4 in the procedure's pseudocode is to call a function to calculate and return the FWT (federal withholding tax). Before entering the appropriate instruction, you will create the function.

Coding the GetFwt Function

The amount of federal withholding tax (FWT) to deduct from an employee's weekly gross pay is based on the employee's weekly taxable wages and his or her filing status, which is either single (including head of household) or married. You calculate the weekly taxable wages by first multiplying the number of withholding allowances by $67.31, which is the value of one withholding allowance in 2008; you then subtract the result from the weekly gross pay. For example, if your weekly gross pay is $400 and you have two withholding allowances, your weekly taxable wages are $265.38. The $265.38 is calculated by multiplying 67.31 by 2, and then subtracting the result (134.62) from 400. You use the weekly taxable wages, along with the filing status and the weekly Federal Withholding Tax tables, to determine the amount of tax to withhold. Figure 7-30 shows the weekly FWT tables for the year 2008.

FWT Tables – Weekly Payroll Period

Single person (including head of household)

If the taxable wages are:	The amount of income tax to withhold is:			
Over	**But not over**	**Base amount**	**Percentage**	**Of excess over**
	$ 51	0		
$ 51	$ 198	0	10%	$ 51
$ 198	$ 653	$ 14.70 plus	15%	$ 198
$ 653	$1,533	$ 82.95 plus	25%	$ 653
$1,533	$3,202	$ 302.95 plus	28%	$1,533
$3,202	$6,916	$ 770.27 plus	33%	$3,202
$6,916		$1,995.89 plus	35%	$6,916

Married person

If the taxable wages are:	The amount of income tax to withhold is:			
Over	**But not over**	**Base amount**	**Percentage**	**Of excess over**
	$ 154	0		
$ 154	$ 453	0	10%	$ 154
$ 453	$1,388	$ 29.90 plus	15%	$ 453
$1,388	$2,651	$ 170.15 plus	25%	$1,388
$2,651	$3,994	$ 485.90 plus	28%	$2,651
$3,994	$7,021	$ 861.94 plus	33%	$3,994
$7,021		$1,860.85 plus	35%	$7,021

Figure 7-30 Weekly FWT tables

Both tables in Figure 7-30 contain five columns of information. The first two columns list various ranges, also called brackets, of taxable wage amounts. The first column (Over) lists the amount that a taxable wage in that range must be over, and the second column (But not over) lists the maximum amount included in the range. The remaining three columns (Base amount, Percentage, and Of excess over) tell you how to calculate the tax for each range. For example, assume that you are married and your weekly taxable wages are $288.46. Before you can calculate the amount of your tax, you need to locate your taxable wages in the first two columns of the Married table. Taxable wages of $288.46 fall within the $154 through $453 range. After locating the range that contains your taxable wages, you then use the remaining three columns in the table to calculate your tax. In this case, you calculate the tax by first subtracting 154 (the amount shown in the Of excess over column) from your taxable wages of 288.46, giving 134.46. You then multiply 134.46 by 10% (the amount shown in the Percentage column), giving 13.45. You add the amount shown in the Base amount column—in this case, 0—to that result, giving $13.45 as your tax. The calculations are shown in Figure 7-31.

Taxable wages	$288.46
Of excess over	–154.00
	134.46
Percentage	* .10
	13.45
Base amount	+ 0.00
Tax	$ 13.45

Figure 7-31 FWT calculation for a married taxpayer with taxable wages of $288.46

Now calculate the tax for a single taxpayer with a weekly taxable wage of $600. Figure 7-32 shows how the tax amount is calculated.

Taxable wages	$600.00
Of excess over	– 198.00
	402.00
Percentage	* .15
	60.30
Base amount	+ 14.70
Tax	$ 75.00

Figure 7-32 FWT calculation for a single taxpayer with taxable wages of $600.00

To calculate the federal withholding tax, the GetFwt function needs to know the employee's gross pay amount, as well as the number of his or her withholding allowances and his or her marital status. The gross pay amount and number of withholding allowances are necessary to calculate the taxable wages, and the marital status indicates the appropriate FWT table to use when calculating the tax. The function will receive the necessary information from the btnCalc control's Click event procedure, which will pass the information when it calls the function. Recall that the information is stored in the procedure's `dblGross`, `intAllowances`, and `strStatus` variables. Figure 7-33 shows the function's pseudocode.

```
1. calculate the taxable wages = gross pay – number of withholding allowances * 67.31
2. if the marital status is Single
       calculate the FWT using the Single FWT table
   else
       calculate the FWT using the Married FWT table
   end if
3. return the FWT
```

Figure 7-33 Pseudocode for the GetFwt function

To code the GetFwt function:

1. Scroll to the top of the Code Editor window. Click the **blank line** below the `Public Class frmMain` clause, then press **Enter** to insert a blank line.

2. When it calls the GetFwt function, the btnCalc control's Click event procedure will need to pass the values stored in its `strStatus`, `intAllowances`, and `dblGross` variables. In this case, it is appropriate to pass each variable's value rather than its address, because you do not want the GetFwt function to change the contents of the variables. You will store the values passed to the function in three parameters named `strMarital`, `intNumAllow`, and `dblWeekPay`. The GetFwt function will use the information it receives to calculate and return the FWT as a Double number. Type the code and comment shown in Figure 7-34, then position the insertion point as shown in the figure. (Notice that the Code Editor automatically enters the procedure footer for you.)

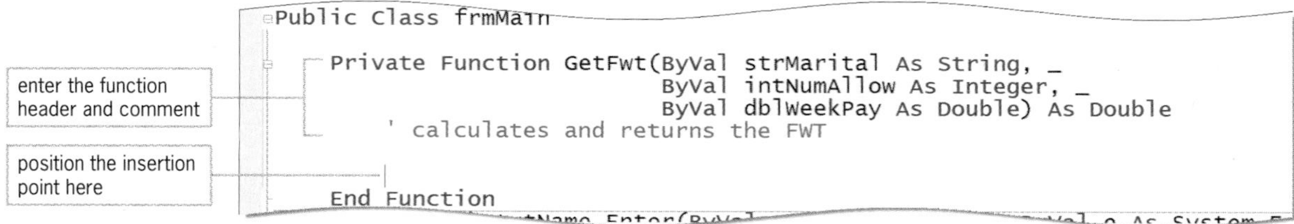

Figure 7-34 GetFwt function header and footer

3. The function will use a named constant for the withholding allowance amount (67.31). Type **Const dblONE_ALLOW As Double = 67.31** and press **Enter**.

4. The function also will use two additional variables: one to store the taxable wages and the other to store the FWT. Type **Dim dblTaxableWages As Double** and press **Enter**, then type **Dim dblTax As Double** and press **Enter** twice.

5. Step 1 in the function's pseudocode is to calculate the taxable wages. Type **' calculate taxable wages** and press **Enter**, then type **dblTaxableWages = dblWeekPay – intNumAllow * dblONE_ALLOW** and press **Enter** twice.

6. Step 2 in the function's pseudocode is a selection structure that determines the marital status and then calculates the appropriate tax. Type **' determine marital status, then calculate FWT** and press **Enter**, then type **If strMarital = "S" Then** and press **Enter**.

7. If the `strMarital` variable contains the letter "S", the selection structure's true path should calculate the federal withholding tax using the information from the Single tax table. You will find the appropriate code in the Single.txt file. Click **File** on the menu bar, then click **Open File**. If necessary, open the Harvey Industries Project folder. Click **Single.txt** in the list of filenames, then click the **Open** button. Click **Edit**, then click **Select All**. Press **Ctrl+c** to copy the selected text to the Windows clipboard. Close the Single.txt window.

8. The insertion point should be in the blank line below the If clause in the GetFwt function. Press **Ctrl+v** to paste the copied text into the selection structure's true path.

9. If the `strMarital` variable does not contain the letter "S", the selection structure's false path should calculate the federal withholding tax using the information from the Married tax table. You will find the appropriate code in the Married.txt file. Click **File**, then click **Open File**. Click **Married.txt** in the list of filenames, then click the **Open** button. Click **Edit**, then click **Select All**. Press **Ctrl+c** to copy the selected text to the Windows clipboard. Close the Married.txt window.

10. The insertion point should be in the blank line below the `End Select` clause. Type **Else** and press **Tab**, then type **' strMarital = "M"** and press **Enter**. Press **Ctrl+v** to paste the copied text into the selection structure's false path.

11. The last step in the function's pseudocode is to return the federal withholding tax amount to the statement that invoked the function. The tax amount is stored in the `dblTax` variable. Click **immediately after the letter f** in the `End If` clause, then press **Enter** twice. Type **Return dblTax**, then save the solution. (You can look ahead to Figure 7-36 to view the function's code.)

Recall that you still need to complete the btnCalc control's Click event procedure.

Completing the btnCalc Control's Click Event Procedure

Now that you have created the GetFwt function, you can call the function from the btnCalc control's Click event procedure. Calling the GetFwt function is one of the steps listed in the event procedure's pseudocode (shown earlier in Figure 7-28).

To continue coding the btnCalc control's Click event procedure:

1. Locate the btnCalc control's Click event procedure. Click **immediately after the letter f** in the second `End If` clause, then press **Enter** twice.
2. Recall that the procedure needs to pass three values to the GetFwt function: the value stored in the `strStatus` variable, the value stored in the `intAllowances` variable, and the value stored in the `dblGross` variable. The value returned by the function will be assigned to the `dblFwt` variable. Type **' call a function to calculate the FWT** and press **Enter**, then type **dblFwt = GetFwt(strStatus, intAllowances, dblGross)** and press **Enter** twice.
3. The next step in the procedure's pseudocode is to calculate the FICA tax by multiplying the gross pay amount by the FICA rate. Type **' calculate FICA tax** and press **Enter**, then type **dblFica = dblGross * dblFICA_RATE** and press **Enter** twice.
4. Save the solution.

Next, the procedure should round the gross pay, FWT, and FICA tax amounts to two decimal places. Rounding these amounts before making the net pay calculation will prevent the "penny off" error from occurring. (You can observe the "penny off" error by completing Exercise 1 at the end of this lesson.) You can use the **Math.Round function** to return a number rounded to a specific number of decimal places. The syntax of the Math.Round function is **Math.Round(***value*[**,** *digits*]**)**. In the syntax, *value* is a numeric expression and *digits* (which is optional) is an integer indicating how many places to the right of the decimal point are included in the rounding. The Math.Round function rounds up a number when the number to its right is at least 5; otherwise the function truncates the excess digits. For example, `Math.Round(3.235, 2)` returns the number 3.24, but `Math.Round(3.234, 2)` returns the number 3.23. If the *digits* argument is omitted, the Math.Round function returns an integer.

To complete the btnCalc control's Click event procedure, then test the application:

1. Enter the following comment and assignment statements. Press **Enter** twice after typing the last assignment statement.

   ' round gross pay, FWT, and FICA tax
   dblGross = Math.Round(dblGross, 2)
   dblFwt = Math.Round(dblFwt, 2)
   dblFica = Math.Round(dblFica, 2)

2. Next, the procedure should calculate the net pay by subtracting the two tax amounts from the gross pay amount. Enter the following comment and assignment statement. Press **Enter** twice after typing the assignment statement.

   ' calculate net pay
   dblNet = dblGross - dblFwt - dblFica

3. The last step in the pseudocode is to display the calculated amounts in the appropriate label controls. Enter the following comment and assignment statements.

   ‘ display calculated amounts
   lblGross.Text = dblGross.ToString(“N2”)
   lblFwt.Text = dblFwt.ToString(“N2”)
   lblFica.Text = dblFica.ToString(“N2”)
   lblNet.Text = dblNet.ToString(“N2”)

4. Save the solution, then start the application. First, calculate the weekly gross pay, taxes, and net pay for Kate Kaufman. Last week, Kate worked 40 hours. She earns $10 per hour and her marital status is Single. She claims one withholding allowance. Type **Kate Kaufman** in the Name box. Locate and then click **10.00** in the Rate list box. Click the **list arrow** button in the Allowances combo box, then click **1** in the list. Click the **Calculate** button. See Figure 7-35.

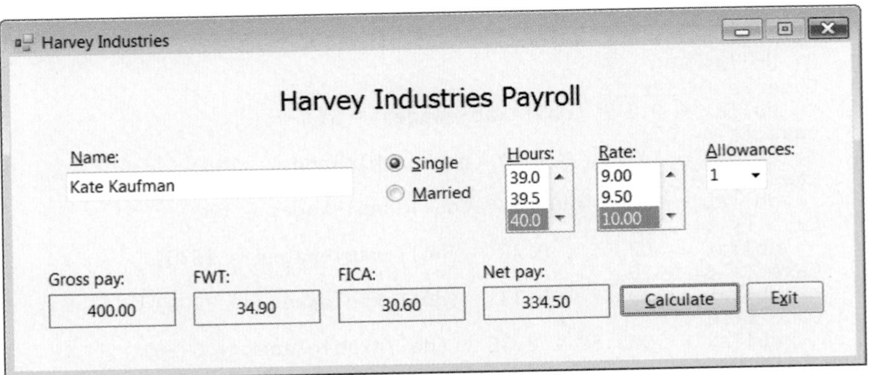

Figure 7-35 Payroll calculations displayed in the interface

5. Now calculate the weekly gross pay, taxes, and net pay for Carl Schmidt. Last week, Carl worked 39.5 hours. He earns $7.50 per hour and his marital status is Married. He claims two withholding allowances. Change the name entered in the Name box to **Carl Schmidt**, then click the **Married** radio button. Click **39.5** in the Hours list box, then locate and click **7.50** in the Rate list box. Press **Tab** to move the focus to the Allowances combo box. In addition to selecting the number of allowances in the list portion of the combo box, the user also can type the number in the text portion. Type **2**, then click the **Calculate** button. The application displays 296.25, 0.76, 22.66, and 272.83 as Carl's gross pay, FWT, FICA tax, and net pay amounts, respectively.

6. Click the **Exit** button, then click the **Yes** button to end the application. Close the Code Editor window, then close the solution. Figure 7-36 shows the application's code.

```
' Name: Harvey Industries Project
' Purpose: Displays an employee's gross pay, taxes, and net pay
' Programmer: <your name> on <current date>

Option Explicit On
Option Strict On
Option Infer Off

Public Class frmMain

   Private Function GetFwt(ByVal strMarital As String, _
      ByVal intNumAllow As Integer, _
      ByVal dblWeekPay As Double) As Double
      ' calculates and returns the FWT

      Const dblONE_ALLOW As Double = 67.31
      Dim dblTaxableWages As Double
      Dim dblTax As Double

      ' calculate taxable wages
      dblTaxableWages = dblWeekPay - intNumAllow * dblONE_ALLOW

      ' determine marital status, then calculate FWT
      If strMarital = "S" Then
         Select Case dblTaxableWages
            Case Is <= 51
               dblTax = 0
            Case Is <= 198
               dblTax = 0.1 * (dblTaxableWages - 51)
            Case Is <= 653
               dblTax = 14.7 + 0.15 * (dblTaxableWages - 198)
            Case Is <= 1533
               dblTax = 82.95 + 0.25 * (dblTaxableWages - 653)
            Case Is <= 3202
               dblTax = 302.95 + 0.28 * (dblTaxableWages - 1533)
            Case Is <= 6916
               dblTax = 770.27 + 0.33 * (dblTaxableWages - 3202)
            Case Else
               dblTax = 1995.89 + 0.35 * (dblTaxableWages - 6916)
         End Select
      Else ' strMarital = "M"
         Select Case dblTaxableWages
            Case Is <= 154
               dblTax = 0
            Case Is <= 453
               dblTax = 0.1 * (dblTaxableWages - 154)
            Case Is <= 1388
               dblTax = 29.9 + 0.15 * (dblTaxableWages - 453)
            Case Is <= 2651
               dblTax = 170.15 + 0.25 * (dblTaxableWages - 1388)
            Case Is <= 3994
               dblTax = 485.9 + 0.28 * (dblTaxableWages - 2651)
            Case Is <= 7021
               dblTax = 861.94 + 0.33 * (dblTaxableWages - 3994)
            Case Else
               dblTax = 1860.85 + 0.35 * (dblTaxableWages - 7021)
         End Select
      End If

      Return dblTax
   End Function
```

Figure 7-36 Harvey Industries application's code *(continues)*

(continued)

```
Private Sub txtName_Enter(ByVal sender As Object, _
   ByVal e As System.EventArgs) Handles txtName.Enter
   ' select the existing text

   txtName.SelectAll()
End Sub

Private Sub cboAllowances_KeyPress(ByVal sender As Object,_
   ByVal e As System.Windows.Forms.KeyPressEventArgs) _
   Handles cboAllowances.KeyPress
   ' allow only numbers and the Backspace key

   If (e.KeyChar < "0" OrElse e.KeyChar > "9") AndAlso _
       e.KeyChar <> ControlChars.Back Then
       e.Handled = True
   End If
End Sub


Private Sub ClearLabels(ByVal sender As Object, _
   ByVal e As System.EventArgs) _
   Handles lstHours.SelectedValueChanged, _
   lstRate.SelectedValueChanged, _
   radSingle.Click, radMarried.Click, txtName.TextChanged, _
   cboAllowances.TextChanged

   lblGross.Text = String.Empty
   lblFwt.Text = String.Empty
   lblFica.Text = String.Empty
   lblNet.Text = String.Empty
End Sub

Private Sub frmMain_FormClosing(ByVal sender As Object, _
   ByVal e As System.Windows.Forms.FormClosingEventArgs) _
   Handles Me.FormClosing
   ' verify that the user wants to exit the application

   Dim dlgButton As DialogResult
   dlgButton = MessageBox.Show("Do you want to exit?", _
      "Harvey Industries", MessageBoxButtons.YesNo, _
      MessageBoxIcon.Exclamation, _
      MessageBoxDefaultButton.Button1)

   ' if the No button was selected, don't close the form
   If dlgButton = Windows.Forms.DialogResult.No Then
       e.Cancel = True
   End If
End Sub

Private Sub frmMain_Load(ByVal sender As Object, _
   ByVal e As System.EventArgs) Handles Me.Load
   ' fills the list boxes with values, then selects a default value

   For dblHours As Double = 0 To 55 Step 0.5
      lstHours.Items.Add(dblHours.ToString("N1"))
   Next dblHours

   For dblRates As Double = 7.5 To 15.5 Step 0.5
      lstRate.Items.Add(dblRates.ToString("N2"))
   Next dblRates

```

Figure 7-36 Harvey Industries application's code *(continues)*

(continued)

```
        For intAllow As Integer = 0 To 10
            cboAllowances.Items.Add(intAllow.ToString)
        Next intAllow

        lstHours.SelectedItem = "40.0"
        lstRate.SelectedItem = "9.50"
        cboAllowances.SelectedIndex = 0
    End Sub

    Private Sub btnExit_Click(ByVal sender As Object, _
        ByVal e As System.EventArgs) Handles btnExit.Click
        Me.Close()
    End Sub

    Private Sub btnCalc_Click(ByVal sender As Object, _
        ByVal e As System.EventArgs) Handles btnCalc.Click
        ' displays gross pay, taxes, and net pay

        Const dblFICA_RATE As Double = 0.0765
        Dim strStatus As String
        Dim dblHours As Double
        Dim dblPayRate As Double
        Dim intAllowances As Integer
        Dim dblGross As Double
        Dim dblFwt As Double
        Dim dblFica As Double
        Dim dblNet As Double

        dblHours = Convert.ToDouble(lstHours.SelectedItem.ToString)
        dblPayRate = Convert.ToDouble(lstRate.SelectedItem.ToString)
        intAllowances = Convert.ToInt32(cboAllowances.Text)

        If radSingle.Checked Then
            strStatus = "S"
        Else ' radMarried selected
            strStatus = "M"
        End If

        ' calculate gross pay
        If dblHours <= 40 Then
            dblGross = dblHours * dblPayRate
        Else
            dblGross = 40 * dblPayRate + (dblHours - 40) * dblPayRate * 1.5
        End If

        ' call a function to calculate the FWT
        dblFwt = GetFwt(strStatus, intAllowances, dblGross)

        ' calculate FICA tax
        dblFica = dblGross * dblFICA_RATE

        ' round gross pay, FWT, and FICA tax
        dblGross = Math.Round(dblGross, 2)
        dblFwt = Math.Round(dblFwt, 2)
        dblFica = Math.Round(dblFica, 2)

        ' calculate net pay
        dblNet = dblGross - dblFwt - dblFica

        ' display calculated amounts
        lblGross.Text = dblGross.ToString("N2")
        lblFwt.Text = dblFwt.ToString("N2")
        lblFica.Text = dblFica.ToString("N2")
        lblNet.Text = dblNet.ToString("N2")
    End Sub
End Class
```

Figure 7-36 Harvey Industries application's code

Lesson C Summary

- **To process code when a form is about to be closed:**

  Enter the code in the form's FormClosing event procedure, which occurs when the user clicks the Close button on a form's title bar or when the computer processes the `Me.Close()` statement.

- **To prevent a form from being closed:**

  Set the Cancel property of the FormClosing event procedure's `e` parameter to True.

- **To round a number to a specific number of decimal places:**

  Use the Math.Round function. The function's syntax is **Math. Round(*value*[, *digits*])**, where *value* is a numeric expression and *digits* (which is optional) is an integer indicating how many places to the right of the decimal point are included in the rounding. If the *digits* argument is omitted, the Math.Round function returns an integer.

Lesson C Key Terms

Cancel property—a property of the `e` parameter in the FormClosing event procedure; when set to True, it prevents the form from closing

FormClosing event—occurs when a form is about to be closed, which can happen as a result of the computer processing the `Me.Close()` statement or the user clicking the Close button on the form's title bar

Math.Round function—used to round a number

Lesson C Review Questions

1. The form's ______________________ event is triggered when you click the Close button on its title bar.

   a. Close

   b. Closing

   c. FormClose

   d. FormClosing

2. The form's ______________________ event is triggered when the computer processes the `Me.Close()` statement.

   a. Close

   b. Closing

   c. FormClose

   d. FormClosing

3. Which of the following statements prevents a form from being closed?
   a. `e.Cancel = False`
   b. `e.Cancel = True`
   c. `e.Close = False`
   d. `sender.Close = False`

4. Which of the following rounds the contents of the `intNum` variable to three decimal places?
   a. `Math.Round(3, intNum)`
   b. `Math.Round(intNum, 3)`
   c. `Round.Math(intNum, 3)`
   d. None of the above.

Lesson C Exercises

INTRODUCTORY

1. In this exercise, you remove the Math.Round function from the payroll application created in the lesson. Doing this will allow you to observe the "penny off" error. Use Windows to make a copy of the Harvey Industries Solution folder, which is contained in the VB2008\Chap07 folder. Rename the folder No Rounding Harvey Industries Solution. Open the Harvey Industries Solution (Harvey Industries Solution.sln) file contained in the VB2008\Chap07\No Rounding Harvey Industries Solution folder. Open the designer window, then open the Code Editor window. The Math.Round function appears in three statements in the btnCalc control's Click event procedure. Type an apostrophe at the beginning of each of the three statements, making them comments. Save the solution, then start the application. Test the application by entering Carl Schmidt in the Name box. Click the Married radio button, then click 39.5 in the Hours list box. Click 7.50 in the Rate list box, then click 2 in the Allowances combo box. Click the Calculate button. What is wrong with the calculated amounts? Stop the application. Close the Code Editor window, then close the solution.

INTRODUCTORY

2. In this exercise, you modify one of the Gross Pay applications completed in Lesson A. Use Windows to make a copy of the Gross Pay Solution-Sub folder, which is contained in the VB2008\Chap07 folder. Rename the folder FormClosing Gross Pay Solution-Sub. Open the Gross Pay Solution (Gross Pay Solution.sln) file contained in the VB2008\Chap07\FormClosing Gross Pay Solution-Sub folder. Open the designer window, then open the Code Editor window. Code the form's FormClosing event procedure so that it asks the user whether he or she wants to exit the application. Take the appropriate action based on the user's response. Save the solution, then start and test the application. Stop the application. Close the Code Editor window, then close the solution.

INTERMEDIATE

3. Use Windows to make a copy of the Harvey Industries Solution folder, which is contained in the VB2008\Chap07 folder. Rename the folder Harvey Industries Solution-Sub. Open the Harvey Industries Solution (Harvey Industries Solution.sln) file contained in the VB2008\Chap07\Harvey Industries Solution-Sub folder. Open the designer window, then open the Code Editor window. Change the GetFwt function to an independent Sub procedure, then modify the statement that calls the procedure. Save the solution, then start and test the application. Click the Exit button, then click the Yes button. Close the Code Editor window, then close the solution.

INTERMEDIATE

4. Use Windows to make a copy of the Harvey Industries Solution folder, which is contained in the VB2008\Chap07 folder. Rename the folder Modified Harvey Industries Solution. Open the Harvey Industries Solution (Harvey Industries Solution.sln) file contained in the VB2008\Chap07\Modified Harvey Industries Solution folder. Open the designer window, then open the Code Editor window. Modify the code so that the GetFwt function, rather than btnCalc control's Click event procedure, determines the selected radio button. Save the solution, then start and test the application. Click the Exit button, then click the Yes button to end the application. Close the Code Editor window, then close the solution.

ADVANCED

5. Create a Visual Basic Windows application. Name the solution, project, and form file Cable Direct Solution, Cable Direct Project, and Main Form.vb, respectively. Save the application in the VB2008\Chap07 folder. Create the interface shown in Figure 7-37. Code the application. The application should calculate and display a customer's cable bill. The cable rates are shown in Figure 7-38. Business customers must have at least one connection. Verify that the user wants to close the application. Save the solution, then start and test the application. Stop the application. Close the Code Editor window, then close the solution.

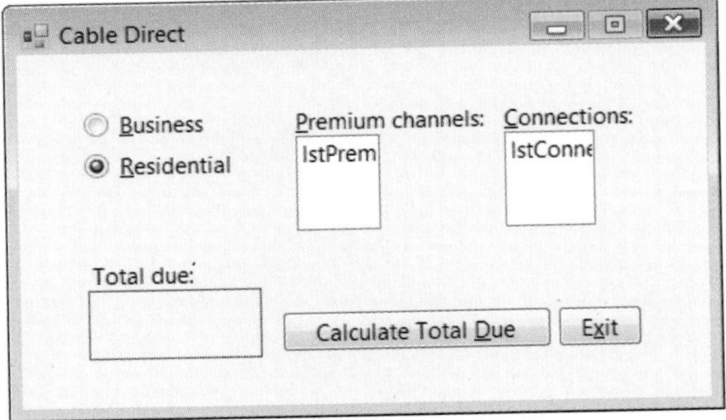

Figure 7-37 User interface for the Cable Direct application

Residential customers:	
Processing fee:	$4.50
Basic service fee:	$30
Premium channels:	$5 per channel
Business customers:	
Processing fee:	$16.50
Basic service fee:	$80 for the first 10 connections; $4 for each additional connection
Premium channels:	$50 per channel for any number of connections

Figure 7-38 Rates for the Cable Direct application

Swat The Bugs

6. The purpose of this exercise is to demonstrate a common error made when using functions. Open the Debug Solution (Debug Solution.sln) file, which is contained in the VB2008\Chap07\Debug Solution-Lesson C folder. If necessary, open the designer window. Open the Code Editor window and review the existing code. Start the application. Click 20 in the Length list box, then click 30 in the Width list box. Click the Calculate Area button, which should display the area of a rectangle having a length of 20 feet and a width of 30 feet. Notice that the application is not working properly. Stop the application. Correct the application's code, then save the solution and start and test the application again. Stop the application. Close the Code Editor window, then close the solution.

CHAPTER 8

String Manipulation

Creating a Hangman Game Application

Mr. Mitchell teaches second grade at Hinsbrook School. On days when the weather is bad and the students cannot go outside to play, he spends recess time playing a simplified version of the Hangman game with his class. The game requires two people to play. Currently, Mr. Mitchell thinks of a word that has five letters. He then draws five dashes on the chalkboard—one for each letter in the word. One student then is chosen to guess the word, letter by letter. When the student guesses a correct letter, Mr. Mitchell replaces the appropriate dash or dashes with the letter. For example, if the original word is moose and the student guesses the letter o, Mr. Mitchell changes the five dashes on the chalkboard to -oo--. If the student's letter does not appear in the word, Mr. Mitchell begins drawing the Hangman image, which contains nine lines and one circle. The game is over when the student either guesses all of the letters in the word or makes 10 incorrect guesses, whichever comes first.

Previewing the Hangman Game Application

To open the Run dialog box, press and hold down the Windows logo key as you tap the letter r, then release the logo key.

To preview the completed Hangman Game application:

1. Use the Run dialog box to run the **Hangman** (**Hangman.exe**) file, which is contained in the VB2008\Chap08 folder. The application's user interface appears on the screen. As indicated in Figure 8-1, the interface contains a File menu. You will learn how to include a menu in an interface in Lesson B.

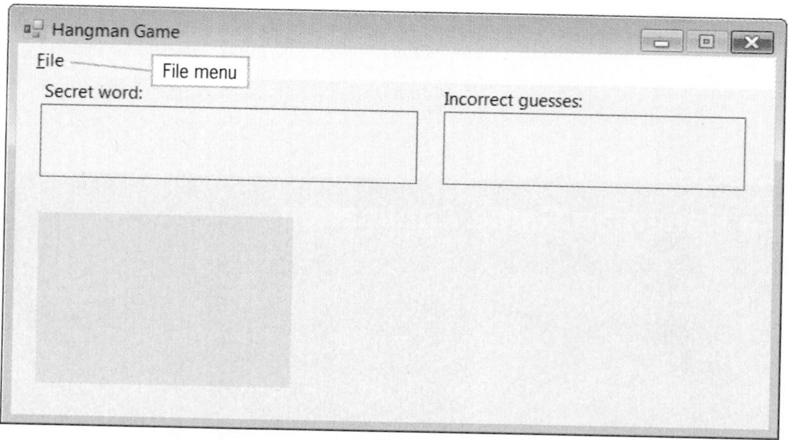

Figure 8-1 Hangman Game application's interface

2. Click **File** on the menu bar, then click **New Game**. The Hangman Game dialog box opens and prompts you to enter a 5-letter word.
3. Type **puppy** and press **Enter** to select the OK button. Five dashes (hyphens)—one for each letter in the word "puppy"—appear in the application's interface. In addition, the Letter dialog box opens and prompts you to enter a letter.
4. You will guess the letter y first. Type **y** and press **Enter** to select the OK button. The application replaces the last dash in the Secret word box with the letter Y. This indicates that the letter Y is the last letter in the word.
5. Now you will guess the letter x. Type **x** and press **Enter**. The letter x does not appear in the word "puppy", so the application displays the letter X in the Incorrect guesses box. It also displays the bottom line of the Hangman image. Recall that the image contains nine lines and one circle.
6. Next, you will guess the letter a. Type **a** and press **Enter**. The letter a does not appear in the word "puppy", so the application displays the letter A in the Incorrect guesses box. It also displays another line in the Hangman image.

7. Now you will guess the letter u. Type **u** and press **Enter**. The application replaces the second dash in the Secret word box with the letter U.

8. Next, you will guess the letters d, g, and b. Type **d** and press **Enter**, then type **g** and press **Enter**, and then type **b** and press **Enter**. The letters you entered do not appear in the word "puppy", so the application displays the letters in the Incorrect guesses box. It also displays two additional lines and a circle in the Hangman image.

9. Now you will guess the letter p. Type **p** and press **Enter**. The application replaces the remaining dashes in the Secret word box with the letter P. It then displays the "Great guessing!" message in a message box. See Figure 8-2.

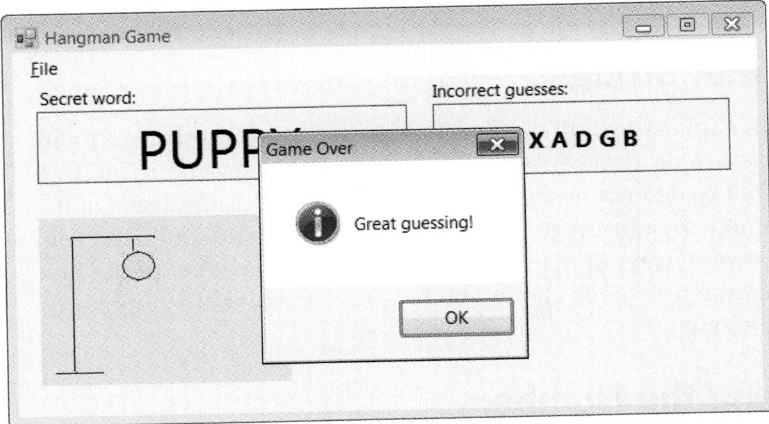

Figure 8-2 Result of guessing the word

10. Press **Enter** to close the message box. Click **File** on the menu bar, then click **Exit** to end the application.

Before you can begin coding the Hangman Game application, you need to learn how to manipulate strings in Visual Basic and how to create a menu. You learn about string manipulation in Lesson A and about the MenuStrip tool in Lesson B. You complete the Hangman Game application's interface in Lesson B, and code the application in Lessons B and C.

LESSON A

After studying Lesson A, you should be able to:

- Determine the number of characters in a string
- Remove spaces from the beginning and end of a string
- Replace characters in a string
- Insert characters in a string
- Search a string
- Access characters in a string
- Compare strings using pattern-matching

Working with Strings

Many times, an application will need to manipulate (process) string data in some way. For example, it may need to look at the first character in an inventory part number to determine the part's location in the warehouse. Or, it may need to search an address to determine the street name. In this lesson, you will learn several ways of manipulating strings in Visual Basic. The first string manipulation technique shows you how to determine the number of characters in a string.

Determining the Number of Characters in a String

If an application expects the user to enter a seven-digit phone number or a five-digit ZIP code, the application's code should verify that the user entered the required number of characters. The number of characters in a string is stored as an integer in the string's **Length property**. Figure 8-3 shows the syntax of the Length property and includes examples of using the property.

Length property

Syntax	Purpose
string.**Length**	stores the number of characters contained in a string

Example 1

```
strName = "Veronica Yardley"
intNumCharacters = strName.Length
```

assigns the number 16 to the `intNumCharacters` variable

Example 2

```
Do
   strPhone = InputBox("7-digit phone number (no dashes)", "Phone")
Loop Until strPhone.Length = 7
```

gets a phone number from the user until the phone number contains exactly seven characters

Figure 8-3 Syntax, purpose, and examples of the Length property

Removing Spaces from the Beginning and End of a String

When entering data in either a text box or input box, it's not unusual for a user to inadvertently press the spacebar after typing the data, thereby including an extraneous space character at the end of the data. You can use the **Trim method** to remove (trim) any spaces from both the beginning and end of a string. Figure 8-4 shows the method's syntax and includes an example of using the method. When processing the Trim method, the computer first makes a temporary copy of the *string* in memory. It then performs the necessary trimming on the copy only. In other words, the Trim method does not remove any characters from the original string. The Trim method returns a string that excludes any leading or trailing spaces.

Trim method

Syntax	Purpose
string.**Trim**	removes any spaces from both the beginning and end of a string

Example

```
strCity = txtCity.Text.Trim
```

assigns the contents of the txtCity control, excluding any leading and trailing spaces, to the `strCity` variable

Figure 8-4 Syntax, purpose, and an example of the Trim method

You will use the Length property and the Trim method in the Product ID application, which you code in the next section.

The Product ID Application

The Product ID application displays (in a label control) a listing of the product IDs entered by the user. Each product ID must contain exactly five characters.

To code and then test the Product ID application:

1. If necessary, start Visual Studio 2008 or Visual Basic 2008 Express Edition. Close the Start Page window.
2. Open the **Product Solution** (**Product Solution.sln**) file, which is contained in the VB2008\Chap08\Product Solution folder. If necessary, open the designer window. The user interface provides a text box for entering the product ID.
3. Open the Code Editor window. Replace the <your name> and <current date> text in the comments with your name and the current date.
4. Locate the btnAdd control's Click event procedure. Before verifying the product ID's length, you will remove any leading and trailing spaces from the ID. Click the **blank line** below the `' remove any leading and trailing spaces` comment. Type **strId = txtId.Text.Trim** and press **Enter**.

5. Now determine whether the ID contains exactly five characters. Click the **blank line** below the `' verify length` comment. Type **If strId.Length = 5 Then** and press **Enter**.

6. If the ID contains exactly five characters, the procedure should display the ID in the lblListing control; otherwise, it should display an appropriate message. Type the lines of code indicated in Figure 8-5.

```
Private Sub btnAdd_Click(ByVal sender As Object, ByVal e As System.Even
    ' add product ID to listing

    Dim strId As String

    ' remove any leading and trailing spaces
    strId = txtId.Text.Trim

    ' verify length
    If strId.Length = 5 Then
        lblListing.Text = lblListing.Text & strId.ToUpper _
            & ControlChars.NewLine
    Else
        MessageBox.Show("The product ID must contain 5 characters.", _
                        "Product ID", MessageBoxButtons.OK, _
                        MessageBoxIcon.Information)
    End If

    txtId.Focus()
End Sub
```

enter these six lines of code

Figure 8-5 Completed Click event procedure for the btnAdd control

7. Save the solution, then start the application. First, enter an ID that contains four characters. Type **abc2** as the product ID, then click the **Add to List** button. A message box opens and displays the message "The product ID must contain 5 characters." Close the message box.

8. Now include two trailing spaces after the ID. Change the product ID to **abc23**, then press the **Spacebar** twice. Click the **Add to List** button. ABC23 appears in the listing of product IDs.

9. On your own, test the application using an ID that contains nine characters. Also test it using an ID that contains both leading and trailing spaces. When you are finished testing the application, click the **Exit** button. Close the Code Editor window, then close the solution.

Replacing Characters in a String

Visual Basic provides the **Replace method** for replacing a sequence of characters in a string with another sequence of characters, such as replacing area code "(800)" with area code "(877)" in a phone number. Figure 8-6 shows the syntax of the Replace method and includes examples of using the method. In the syntax, *oldValue* is the sequence of characters that you want to replace in the *string*, and *newValue* is the replacement characters. When processing the Replace method, the computer makes a temporary copy of the *string* in memory, and then replaces the characters in the copy only. The Replace method returns a string with *all* occurrences of *oldValue* replaced with *newValue*.

Replace method

Syntax
string.**Replace(***oldValue*, *newValue***)**

Purpose
replaces every occurrence of *oldValue* with *newValue*

Example 1

```
strPhone = "(800) 111-2222"
strPhone = strPhone.Replace("(800)", "(877)")
```

assigns the string "(877) 111-2222" to the `strPhone` variable

Example 2

```
strWord = "latter"
strWord = strWord.Replace("t", "d")
```

assigns the string "ladder" to the `strWord` variable

Example 3

```
strName = "James Jameston"
strName = strName.Replace("James", "Smith")
```

assigns the string "Smith Smithton" to the `strName` variable

Figure 8-6 Syntax, purpose, and examples of the Replace method

The Mid Statement

At times, you may need to replace only a specific portion of a string with another string; for this, you use the Mid statement rather than the Replace method. The **Mid statement** replaces a specified number of characters in a string with characters from another string. Figure 8-7 shows the syntax of the Mid statement and includes examples of using the statement. In the syntax, *targetString* is the string in which you want characters replaced, and *replacementString* contains the replacement characters. *Start* is the character position of the first character you want replaced in the *targetString*. The first character in the *targetString* is in character position 1; the second is in character position 2, and so on. The optional *count* argument specifies the number of characters to replace in the *targetString*. If *count* is omitted, the Mid statement replaces the lesser of either the number of characters in the *replacementString* or the number of characters in the *targetString* from position *start* through the end of the *targetString*. For instance, in Example 2 in the figure, the number of characters in the *replacementString* is 4, whereas the number of characters in the *targetString* from position *start* through the end of the *targetString* is 7. Therefore, the Mid statement replaces 4 characters. In Example 3, the number of characters in the *replacementString* is 9, whereas the number of characters in the *targetString* from position *start* through the end of the *targetString* is 3. Therefore, the Mid statement replaces 3 characters.

Mid statement

Syntax	Purpose
Mid(*targetString*, *start* [, *count*]**) =** *replacementString*	replaces a specific number of characters in a string with characters from another string

Example 1

```
strName = "Rob Smith"
Mid(strName, 7, 1) = "y"
```

changes the contents of the `strName` variable to "Rob Smyth"

Example 2

```
strName = "Carl Carlson"
Mid(strName, 6) = "John"
```

changes the contents of the `strName` variable to "Carl Johnson"

Example 3

```
strName = "Denzel Cho"
Mid(strName, 8) = "Liverpool"
```

changes the contents of the `strName` variable to "Denzel Liv"

Figure 8-7 Syntax, purpose, and examples of the Mid statement

You will use the Replace method and Mid statement in the Phone Number application, which you code in the next section.

The Phone Number Application

The Phone Number application allows the user to enter a phone number in the following format: 999-999-9999. It then displays the phone number either without the hyphens or with the area code changed to 800.

To code the Phone Number application:

1. Open the **Phone Number Solution** (**Phone Number Solution.sln**) file, which is contained in the VB2008\Chap08\Phone Number Solution folder. If necessary, open the designer window. The user interface provides a text box for entering the phone number.

2. Open the Code Editor window. Replace the <your name> and <current date> text in the comments with your name and the current date.

3. Locate the btnReplace control's Click event procedure. The procedure should remove the hyphens from the phone number entered by the user, and then display the result in the interface. You can remove the hyphens by replacing them with the empty string. You can perform this task using the Replace method. Click the **blank line** below the `' replace the hyphens with the empty string` comment. Type **strPhone = strPhone.Replace("-", String.Empty)** and press **Enter**. The statement tells the computer to replace any hyphen in the `strPhone` variable with the empty string, and then assign the result to the `strPhone` variable. If the `strPhone` variable contains the string "111-222-3333", the statement will assign the string "1112223333" to the variable.

4. Locate the btnMid control's Click event procedure. The procedure should change the area code entered by the user to 800. You can accomplish this task using the Mid statement. Click the **blank line** below the `' change the first three characters to 800` comment. Type **Mid(strPhone, 1, 3) = "800"** and press **Enter**. The statement tells the computer to replace 3 characters in the `strPhone` variable, beginning with the character located in character position 1, with the string "800". Figure 8-8 shows the code entered in the Click event procedures for the btnReplace and btnMid controls.

```
Private Sub btnReplace_Click(ByVal sender As Object, _
    ByVal e As System.EventArgs) Handles btnReplace.Click
    ' removes all hyphens

    Dim strPhone As String
    strPhone = txtOriginal.Text.Trim

    ' replace the hyphens with the empty string
    strPhone = strPhone.Replace("-", String.Empty)

    If strPhone.Length = 10 Then
        lblNoHyphens.Text = strPhone
    Else
        lblNoHyphens.Text = "Please re-enter the phone number."
    End If
    txtOriginal.Focus()
End Sub

Private Sub btnMid_Click(ByVal sender As Object, _
    ByVal e As System.EventArgs) Handles btnMid.Click
    ' changes the area code to 800

    Dim strPhone As String
    strPhone = txtOriginal.Text.Trim

    If strPhone.Length = 12 Then
        ' change the first three characters to 800
        Mid(strPhone, 1, 3) = "800"

        lblChangedAreaCode.Text = strPhone
    Else
        lblChangedAreaCode.Text = "Please re-enter the phone number."
    End If
    txtOriginal.Focus()
End Sub
```

statement containing the Replace method

Mid statement

Figure 8-8 Click event procedures for the btnReplace and btnMid controls

To test the Phone Number application's code:

1. Save the solution, then start the application. Type **111-222-3333** as the phone number, then click the **Remove Hyphens-Replace** button. The button's Click event procedure displays 1112223333 in the interface. Now click the **Change Area Code-Mid** button. The procedure displays 800-222-3333 in the interface. See Figure 8-9.

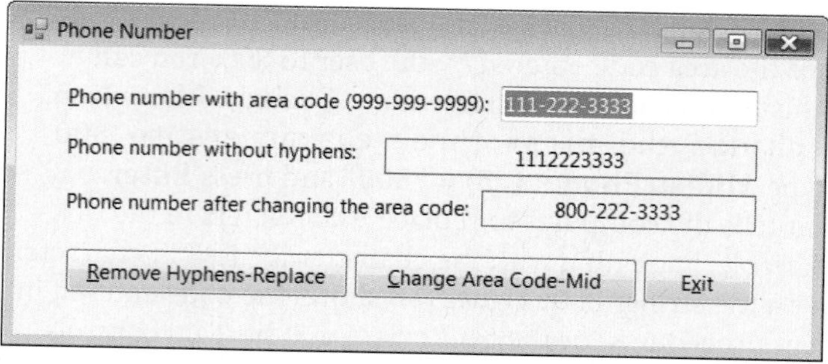

Figure 8-9 Modified phone numbers displayed in the interface

2. Click the **Exit** button. Close the Code Editor window, then close the solution.

Inserting Characters in a String

The letter D (or d) is also a literal type character. Recall that you use the letter D to force a number to assume the Decimal data type.

Visual Basic's PadLeft and PadRight methods allow you to insert characters at the beginning or end of a string. Both methods pad the string with a character until the string is a specified length; then they return the padded string. The **PadLeft method** pads the string on the left. In other words, it inserts the padded characters at the beginning of the string, which right-aligns the characters within the string. The **PadRight method**, on the other hand, pads the string on the right. Doing this inserts the padded characters at the end of the string and left-aligns the characters within the string. Figure 8-10 shows the syntax of the PadLeft and PadRight methods. In each syntax, *length* is an integer that represents the desired length of the *string*. In other words, *length* represents the total number of characters you want the *string* to contain. The *character* argument is the character that each method uses to pad the *string* until it reaches the desired *length*. The *character* argument is optional in each syntax; if omitted, the default *character* is the space character. When processing the PadLeft and PadRight methods, the computer makes a temporary copy of the *string* in memory, and then inserts the characters in the copy only. Examples of using the methods are shown in Figure 8-10. Notice that two methods appear in the expression in Example 3: ToString and PadLeft. When an expression contains more than one method, the computer processes the methods from left to right. In this case, the computer will process the ToString method before processing the PadLeft method. Also notice the letter c that appears after the string in Example 3's *character* argument. The letter c is one of the literal type characters in Visual Basic. As you learned in Chapter 3, a literal type character forces a literal constant to assume a data type other than the one its form indicates. In this case, the letter c forces the "*" string to assume the Char (character) data type.

PadLeft and PadRight methods

Syntax	Purpose
string.**PadLeft(***length*[, *character*]**)**	pads the beginning of a string with a character until the string is a specified length
string.**PadRight(***length*[, *character*]**)**	pads the end of a string with a character until the string is a specified length

Example 1

```
strOutputNumber = "42"
strOutputNumber = strOutputNumber.PadLeft(5)
```

assigns "   42" (three spaces followed by 42) to the `strOutputNumber` variable

Example 2

```
strFirstName = "Sue"
strFirstName = strFirstName.PadRight(10)
```

assigns "Sue   " (the string "Sue" followed by seven spaces) to the `strFirstName` variable

Example 3

```
dblNetPay = 767.89
strFormattedNetPay = dblNetPay.ToString("C2").PadLeft(15, "*"c)
```

assigns "********$767.89" to the `strFormattedNetPay` variable (Many companies use this type of formatted net pay on their employee paychecks, because it makes it difficult for someone to change the amount.)

Figure 8-10 Syntax, purpose, and examples of the PadLeft and PadRight methods

Insert Method

The PadLeft and PadRight methods can be used to insert characters only at the beginning and end, respectively, of a string. To insert characters within a string, you use the **Insert method**. Possible uses for the method include inserting an employee's middle initial within his or her name, or inserting parentheses around the area code in a phone number. Figure 8-11 shows the Insert method's syntax and includes an example of using the method. In the syntax, *startIndex* specifies where in the string you want the *value* inserted. The *startIndex* argument is an integer that represents the character's index—in other words, its position in the string. The first character in a string has an index of 0; the second character has an index of 1, and so on. To insert the *value* beginning with the fifth character in the string, you use a *startIndex* of 4, as shown in the example in the figure. When processing the Insert method, the computer makes a temporary copy of the *string* in memory, and then inserts the characters in the copy only. The Insert method returns a string with the appropriate characters inserted.

Insert method

Syntax	Purpose
string.**Insert(***startIndex*, *value***)**	inserts characters in a string

Example

```
strName     = "Rob Smith"
strFullName = strName.Insert(4, "T. ")
```

assigns the string "Rob T. Smith" to the `strFullName` variable

Figure 8-11 Syntax, purpose, and an example of the Insert method

You will use the PadLeft and Insert methods in the Net Pay application, which you code in the next section.

The Net Pay Application

The Net Pay application allows the user to enter the amount of an employee's net pay. It then displays the net pay with a leading dollar sign, asterisks, and two decimal places. For example, if the net pay is 500, the application will display the net pay as $***500.00.

To code the Net Pay application:

1. Open the **Net Pay Solution** (**Net Pay Solution.sln**) file, which is contained in the VB2008\Chap08\Net Pay Solution folder. If necessary, open the designer window. The user interface provides a text box for entering the net pay.
2. Open the Code Editor window. Replace the <your name> and <current date> text in the comments with your name and the current date.
3. Locate the btnFormat control's Click event procedure. First, the procedure should include two decimal places in the net pay. Click the **blank line** below the `' format the net pay with two decimal places` comment. Type **strFormatted = decNet.ToString("N2")** and press **Enter**.
4. Next, the procedure should pad the net pay with asterisks until it contains 10 characters. You can use the PadLeft method to include the asterisks before the net pay. Click the **blank line** below the `' pad the net pay with asterisks until its length is 10` comment. Type **strFormatted = strFormatted.PadLeft(10, "*"c)** and press **Enter**.
5. Finally, the procedure should insert a dollar sign at the beginning of the formatted net pay. Click the **blank line** below the `' insert a dollar sign as the first character` comment. Type **strFormatted = strFormatted.Insert(0, "$")** and press **Enter**. Figure 8-12 shows the code entered in the btnFormat control's Click event procedure.

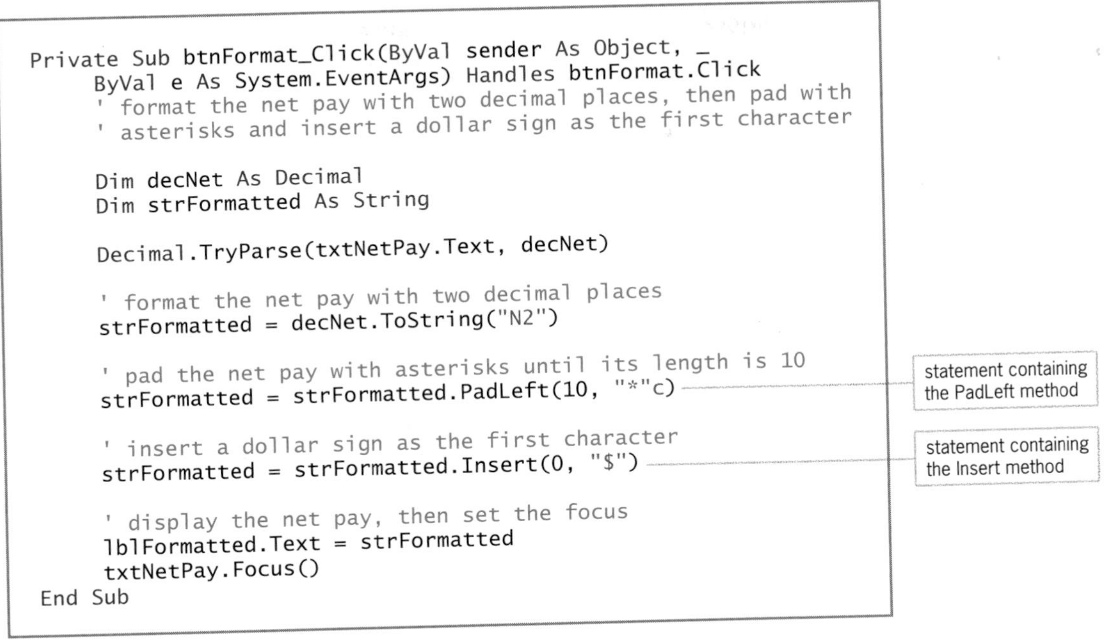

```
Private Sub btnFormat_Click(ByVal sender As Object, _
     ByVal e As System.EventArgs) Handles btnFormat.Click
     ' format the net pay with two decimal places, then pad with
     ' asterisks and insert a dollar sign as the first character

     Dim decNet As Decimal
     Dim strFormatted As String

     Decimal.TryParse(txtNetPay.Text, decNet)

     ' format the net pay with two decimal places
     strFormatted = decNet.ToString("N2")

     ' pad the net pay with asterisks until its length is 10
     strFormatted = strFormatted.PadLeft(10, "*"c)

     ' insert a dollar sign as the first character
     strFormatted = strFormatted.Insert(0, "$")

     ' display the net pay, then set the focus
     lblFormatted.Text = strFormatted
     txtNetPay.Focus()
End Sub
```


Figure 8-12 btnFormat control's Click event procedure

To test the Net Pay application's code:

1. Save the solution, then start the application. Type **1256** as the net pay, then click the **Format** button. The button's Click event procedure displays $**1,256.00 in the interface. See Figure 8-13.

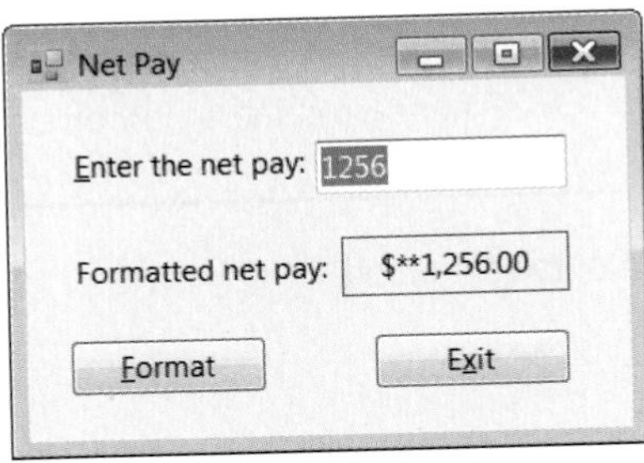

Figure 8-13 Formatted net pay displayed in the interface

2. Click the **Exit** button. Close the Code Editor window, then close the solution.

Searching a String

You can use the **Contains method** to search a string to determine whether it contains a specific sequence of characters. Possible uses for the method include determining whether a particular area code appears in a phone number or whether a certain street name appears in an address. Figure 8-14 shows the syntax of the Contains method and includes examples of using the method. In the syntax, *subString* represents the sequence of characters for which you are searching within the *string*. The Contains method returns the Boolean value True when the *subString* is contained anywhere within the *string*; otherwise, it returns the Boolean value False. The Contains method performs a case-sensitive search, which means that the case of the *subString* must match the case of the *string* for the method to return the True value.

Contains method

Syntax	Purpose
string.**Contains(***subString***)**	searches a string to determine whether it contains a specific sequence of characters, and then returns a Boolean value that indicates whether the characters appear in the string

Example 1

```
strCity = "Nashville, TN"
blnIsContained = strCity.Contains("Tn")
```

assigns the Boolean value False to the `blnIsContained` variable, because "Tn" does not appear in the `strCity` variable

Example 2

```
strAddress = "345 Main Street, Glendale, CA"
blnIsContained = strAddress.ToUpper.Contains("MAIN STREET")
```

assigns the Boolean value True to the `blnIsContained` variable, because "MAIN STREET" appears in the `strAddress` variable when the variable's contents are temporarily converted to uppercase

Example 3

```
strPhone = "(312) 999-9999"
If strPhone.Contains("(312)") Then
```

The *condition* in the If clause evaluates to True, because "(312)" appears in the `strPhone` variable

Figure 8-14 Syntax, purpose, and examples of the Contains method

The IndexOf Method

In addition to using the Contains method to search for a *subString* anywhere within a *string*, you also can use the IndexOf method. Unlike the Contains method, which returns a Boolean value that indicates whether the *string* contains the *subString*, the **IndexOf method** returns an integer that represents the location of the *subString* within the *string*. Figure 8-15 shows the syntax of the IndexOf method and includes examples of using the method. In the syntax, *subString* is the sequence of characters for which you are searching in the *string*, and *startIndex* is the index of the character at which the search should begin. In other words, *startIndex* specifies the starting position for the search. Recall that the first character in a string has an index of 0; the second character has an index of 1, and so on. The *startIndex* argument is optional in the IndexOf method's syntax. If the *startIndex* argument is omitted, the method begins the search with the first character in the *string*. The IndexOf method searches for the *subString* within the *string*, beginning with the character whose index is *startIndex*. If the IndexOf method does not find the *subString*, it returns the number -1. Otherwise, it returns the index of the starting position of the *subString* within the *string*. Like the Contains method, the IndexOf method performs a case-sensitive search.

IndexOf method

Syntax	Purpose
string.**IndexOf(***subString*[, *startIndex*]**)**	searches a string to determine whether it contains a specific sequence of characters, and then returns an integer that indicates the starting position of the characters within the string

Example 1

```
strMessage = "The IndexOf method returns an integer."
intIndexNum = strMessage.IndexOf("Method")
```

assigns the number -1 to the `intIndexNum` variable, because the string "Method" does not appear in the `strMessage` variable

Example 2

index 12

```
strMessage = "The IndexOf method returns an integer."
intIndexNum = strMessage.ToUpper.IndexOf("METHOD")
```

assigns the number 12 to the `intIndexNum` variable, because the string "METHOD" appears in the `strMessage` variable when the variable's contents are temporarily converted to uppercase

Example 3

```
strMessage = "The IndexOf method returns an integer."
intIndexNum = strMessage.IndexOf("x", 10)
```

assigns the number -1 to the `intIndexNum` variable, because the string "x" does not appear in the `strMessage` variable when the search starts with the character whose index is 10 (the letter f)

Figure 8-15 Syntax, purpose, and examples of the IndexOf method

You will use the IndexOf method in the City and State application, which you code in the next section.

The City and State Application

The City and State application allows the user to enter a string composed of a city name, followed by a comma, a space, and a state name. It then displays the index of the comma contained in the string.

To code the City and State application:

1. Open the **City State Solution** (**City State Solution.sln**) file, which is contained in the VB2008\Chap08\City State Solution folder. If necessary, open the designer window. The user interface provides a text box for entering the string.
2. Open the Code Editor window. Replace the <your name> and <current date> text in the comments with your name and the current date.

3. Locate the btnLocate control's Click event procedure. Click the **blank line** below the `' determine the comma's index` comment. To begin the search with the first character in the string, you can use either `strCityState.IndexOf(",", 0)` or `strCityState.IndexOf(",")`. You will assign the IndexOf method's return value to the `intCommaIndex` variable. Type **intCommaIndex = strCityState.IndexOf(",")** and press **Enter**. Figure 8-16 shows the code entered in the btnLocate control's Click event procedure.

```
Private Sub btnLocate_Click(ByVal sender As Object, _
     ByVal e As System.EventArgs) Handles btnLocate.Click
     ' locates the comma in a string and then
     ' displays its index

     Dim strCityState As String
     Dim intCommaIndex As Integer

     strCityState = txtCityState.Text

     ' determine the comma's index
     intCommaIndex = strCityState.IndexOf(",")

     lblCommaIndex.Text = intCommaIndex.ToString
     txtCityState.Focus()
End Sub
```

statement containing the IndexOf method

Figure 8-16 btnLocate control's Click event procedure

To test the City and State application's code:

1. Save the solution, then start the application. Type **Nashville, TN** in the text box, then click the **Locate the Comma** button. As Figure 8-17 shows, the comma's index is 9.

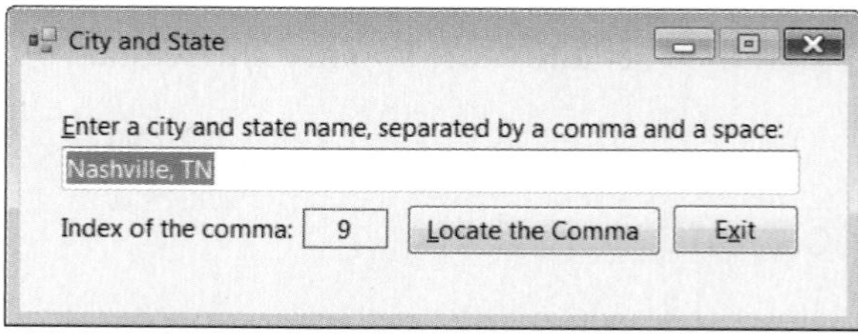

Figure 8-17 Comma's index shown in the interface

2. Click the **Exit** button. Close the Code Editor window, then close the solution.

Accessing Characters Contained in a String

In some applications, it is necessary to access one or more characters contained in a string. For instance, you may need to display only the string's first five characters, which identify an item's location in the warehouse. Visual Basic provides the **Substring method** for accessing any number of characters contained in a string. Figure 8-18 shows the method's syntax, which contains two arguments: *startIndex* and *count*. *StartIndex* is the index of the first character you want to access in the *string*. As you already know, the first character in a string has an index of 0. The optional *count* argument specifies the number of characters you want to access. The Substring method returns a string that contains *count* number of characters, beginning with the character whose index is *startIndex*. If you omit the *count* argument, the Substring method returns all characters from the *startIndex* position through the end of the string. Figure 8-18 also includes examples of using the Substring method.

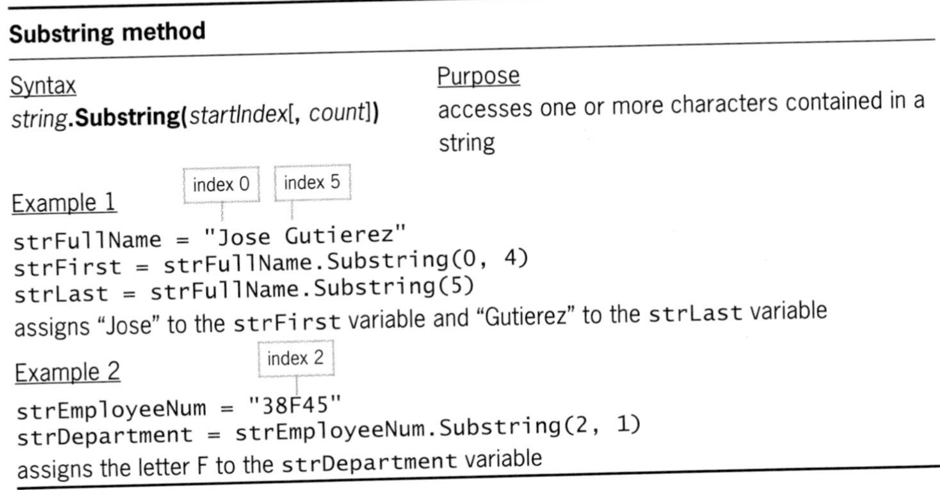

Substring method

Syntax	Purpose
string.**Substring(***startIndex*[, *count*]**)**	accesses one or more characters contained in a string

Example 1


```
strFullName = "Jose Gutierez"
strFirst = strFullName.Substring(0, 4)
strLast = strFullName.Substring(5)
```

assigns "Jose" to the `strFirst` variable and "Gutierez" to the `strLast` variable

Example 2


```
strEmployeeNum = "38F45"
strDepartment = strEmployeeNum.Substring(2, 1)
```

assigns the letter F to the `strDepartment` variable

Figure 8-18 Syntax, purpose, and examples of the Substring method

You will use the Substring method in the Rearrange Name application, which you code in the next section.

The Rearrange Name Application

The Rearrange Name application's user interface provides a text box for entering a person's first name followed by a space and the person's last name. The application rearranges the name so that the last name comes first, followed by a comma, a space, and the first name.

To code the Rearrange Name application:

1. Open the **Rearrange Name Solution** (**Rearrange Solution.sln**) file, which is contained in the VB2008\Chap08\Rearrange Name Solution folder. If necessary, open the designer window.
2. Open the Code Editor window. Replace the <your name> and <current date> text in the comments with your name and the current date.
3. Locate the btnRearrange control's Click event procedure. The procedure assigns the name entered by the user, excluding any leading or trailing spaces, to the `strName` variable.
4. Before you can rearrange the name stored in the `strName` variable, you need to separate the first name from the last name. To do this, you first search for the space character that appears between the names.

Click the **blank line** below the `' search for the space in the name` comment. Type **intIndex = strName.IndexOf(" ")** (be sure to include a space character between the quotation marks) and press **Enter**. If the `strName` variable contains a space character, the statement assigns the character's index to the `intIndex` variable; otherwise, it assigns the number -1 to the `intIndex` variable.

5. If the value in the `intIndex` variable is greater than -1, the procedure should continue rearranging the name; otherwise, it should display the "Invalid name format" message. Change the If clause in the procedure to **If intIndex > -1 Then**. The statement to display the "Invalid name format" message is already entered in the selection structure's false path.

6. Now use the value stored in the `intIndex` variable to separate the first name from the last name. Click the **blank line** below the `' separate the first and last names` comment. All of the characters to the left of the space character represent the first name. Type **strFirstName = strName.Substring(0, intIndex)** and press **Enter**. All of the characters to the right of the space character represent the last name. Type **strLastName = strName.Substring(intIndex + 1)** and press **Enter**.

7. Finally, display the rearranged name in the interface. Click the **blank line** above the Else clause. Type **lblRearrangedName.Text = strLastName & ", " & strFirstName** and press **Enter**. (Be sure to include a space character after the comma.) Figure 8-19 shows the code entered in the btnRearrange control's Click event procedure.

```
Private Sub btnRearrange_Click(ByVal sender As Object, _
     ByVal e As System.EventArgs) Handles btnRearrange.Click
     ' rearranges and then displays a name

     Dim strName As String
     Dim strFirstName As String
     Dim strLastName As String
     Dim intIndex As Integer

     ' assign the input to a variable
     strName = txtName.Text.Trim

     ' search for the space in the name
     intIndex = strName.IndexOf(" ")

     ' if the input contains a space
     If intIndex > -1 Then
         ' separate the first and last names
         strFirstName = strName.Substring(0, intIndex)
         strLastName = strName.Substring(intIndex + 1)

         ' display last name, comma, space, and first name
         lblRearrangedName.Text = strLastName & ", " & strFirstName
     Else   'processed when the name does not contain a space
         MessageBox.Show("Invalid name format", "Rearrange Name", _
                         MessageBoxButtons.OK, _
                         MessageBoxIcon.Information)
     End If
     txtName.Focus()
End Sub
```

statements containing the Substring method

be sure to include a space after the comma

Figure 8-19 btnRearrange control's Click event procedure

To test the Rearrange Name application's code:

1. Save the solution, then start the application. Type **Suman Patel** as the name, then click the **Rearrange Name** button. The rearranged name appears in the interface. See Figure 8-20.

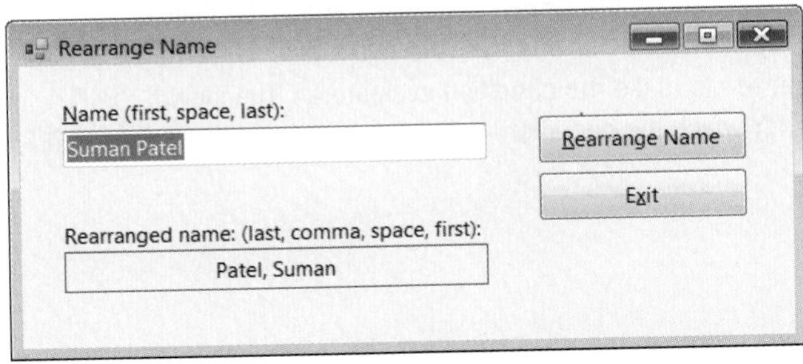

Figure 8-20 Rearranged name shown in the interface

2. Click the **Exit** button. Close the Code Editor window, then close the solution.

Using Pattern-Matching to Compare Strings

The **Like operator** allows you to use pattern-matching characters to determine whether one string is equal to another string. Figure 8-21 shows the Like operator's syntax and includes examples of using the operator. In the syntax, both *string* and *pattern* must be String expressions. However, *pattern* can contain one or more of the pattern-matching characters listed in the figure. The last two pattern-matching characters contain a *charList*, which stands for *character list* and is simply a listing of characters. "[A9M]" is a *charList* that contains three characters: A, 9, and M. You also can include a range of values in a *charList*. You do this using a hyphen to separate the lowest value in the range from the highest value in the range. For example, to include all lowercase letters in a *charList*, you use "[a-z]". To include both lowercase and uppercase letters, you use "[a-zA-Z]" as the *charList*. The Like operator evaluates to True when the *string* matches the *pattern*; otherwise it evaluates to False.

Like operator

Syntax	Purpose
string **Like** *pattern*	compares two strings using pattern-matching characters

Pattern-matching characters	Matches in *string*
?	any single character
*	zero or more characters
#	any single digit (0-9)
[*charList*]	any single character in the *charList* (for example, "[AMT]" matches A, M, or T, whereas "[a-z]" matches any lowercase letter)
[!*charList*]	any single character not in the *charList* (for example, "[!a-z]" matches any character that is not a lowercase letter)

Figure 8-21 Syntax, purpose, and examples of the Like operator *(continues)*

(continued)

Like operator

Example 1

```
If strFirstName.ToUpper Like "B?LL" Then
```

The condition evaluates to True when the string stored in the `strFirstName` variable (converted to uppercase) begins with the letter B followed by one character and then the two letters LL; otherwise, it evaluates to False. Examples of strings that would make the condition evaluate to True include "Bill", "Ball", "bell", and "bull". Examples of strings for which the condition would evaluate to False include "BPL", "BLL", and "billy".

Example 2

```
If strState Like "K*" Then
```

The condition evaluates to True when the string stored in the `strState` variable begins with the letter K followed by zero or more characters; otherwise, it evaluates to False. Examples of strings that would make the condition evaluate to True include "KANSAS", "Ky", and "Kentucky". Examples of strings for which the condition would evaluate to False include "kansas" and "ky".

Example 3

```
Do While strId Like "###*"
```

The condition evaluates to True when the string stored in the `strId` variable begins with three digits followed by zero or more characters; otherwise, it evaluates to False. Examples of strings that would make the condition evaluate to True include "178" and "983Ab". Examples of strings for which the condition would evaluate to False include "X34" and "34Z5".

Example 4

```
If strFirstName.ToUpper Like "T[OI]M" Then
```

The condition evaluates to True when the string stored in the `strFirstName` variable (converted to uppercase) is either "TOM" or "TIM". When the variable does not contain "TOM" or "TIM"—for example, when it contains "Tam" or "Tommy"—the condition evaluates to False.

Example 5

```
If strLetter Like "[a-z]" Then
```

The condition evaluates to True when the string stored in the `strLetter` variable is a lowercase letter; otherwise, it evaluates to False.

Example 6

```
For intIndex As Integer = 0 to strUserEntry.Length - 1
   If strUserEntry.Substring(intIndex, 1) Like "[!a-zA-Z]" Then
      intNonLetter = intNonLetter + 1
   End If
Next intIndex
```

Compares each character contained in the `strUserEntry` variable with the lowercase and uppercase letters of the alphabet, and counts the number of characters that are not letters.

Figure 8-21 Syntax, purpose, and examples of the Like operator

Modifying the Product ID Application

Earlier in the chapter, you coded the Product ID application, which displayed a listing of the product IDs entered by the user. As you may remember, each product ID contained exactly five characters. In the following set of steps, you will modify the application to ensure that the five characters are three letters followed by two numbers.

To modify and then test the Product ID application:

1. Use Windows to make a copy of the Product Solution folder. Save the copy in the VB2008\Chap08 folder. Rename the copy Modified Product Solution.
2. Open the **Product Solution (Product Solution.sln)** file contained in the VB2008\Chap08\Modified Product Solution folder. Open the designer window.
3. Open the Code Editor window and locate the btnAdd control's Click event procedure. Change the `' remove any leading and trailing spaces` comment to **' remove any leading and trailing spaces, then convert to uppercase**. Also change the `strId = txtId.Text.Trim` statement to **strId = txtId.Text.Trim.ToUpper**.
4. Change the `' verify length` comment to **' verify that the ID contains 3 letters followed by 2 numbers**. Also change the If clause to **If strId Like "[A-Z][A-Z][A-Z]##" Then**.
5. In the statement below the If clause, change `strId.ToUpper` to **strId**. Finally, change the message in the MessageBox.Show method to **"Invalid product ID"**. Figure 8-22 shows the modified Click event procedure. The modified comments and code are shaded in the figure.

```
Private Sub btnAdd_Click(ByVal sender As Object, ByVal e As System.EventA
    ' add product ID to listing

    Dim strId As String

    ' remove any leading and trailing spaces, then convert to uppercase
    strId = txtId.Text.Trim.ToUpper

    ' verify that the ID contains 3 letters followed by 2 numbers
    If strId Like "[A-Z][A-Z][A-Z]##" Then
        lblListing.Text = lblListing.Text & strId _
            & ControlChars.NewLine
    Else
        MessageBox.Show("Invalid product ID", _
                        "Product ID", MessageBoxButtons.OK, _
                        MessageBoxIcon.Information)
    End If

    txtId.Focus()
End Sub
```

Figure 8-22 Modified btnAdd Click event procedure

6. Save the solution, then start the application. First, enter an invalid ID. Type **abc2f** as the product ID, then click the **Add to List** button. A message box opens and displays the "Invalid product ID" message. Close the message box.
7. Now enter a valid ID. Change the product ID to **abc23**, then click the **Add to List** button. ABC23 appears in the listing of product IDs.
8. On your own, test the application using different valid and invalid IDs. When you are finished testing the application, click the **Exit** button. Close the Code Editor window, then close the solution.

Lesson A Summary

- **To manipulate strings in Visual Basic:**

  Use one of the techniques listed in Figure 8-23.

Technique	Syntax	Purpose
Length property	*string*.**Length**	stores the number of characters contained in a string
Trim method	*string*.**Trim**	removes any spaces from both the beginning and end of a string
Replace method	*string*.**Replace(***oldValue*, *newValue***)**	replaces every occurrence of *oldValue* with *newValue*
Mid statement	**Mid(***targetString*, *start* [, *count*]**)** = *replacementString*	replaces a specific number of characters in a string with characters from another string
PadLeft method	*string*.**PadLeft(***length* [, *character*]**)**	pads the beginning of a string with a character until the string is a specified length
PadRight method	*string*.**PadRight(***length* [, *character*]**)**	pads the end of a string with a character until the string is a specified length
Insert method	*string*.**Insert(***startIndex*, *value***)**	inserts characters in a string
Contains method	*string*.**Contains(***subString***)**	searches a string to determine whether it contains a specific sequence of characters, and then returns a Boolean value that indicates whether the characters appear in the string
IndexOf method	*string*.**IndexOf(***subString* [, *startIndex*]**)**	searches a string to determine whether it contains a specific sequence of characters, and then returns an integer that indicates the starting position of the characters in the string
Substring method	*string*.**Substring(***startIndex* [, *count*]**)**	accesses one or more characters contained in a string
Like operator	*string* **Like** *pattern*	compares two strings using pattern-matching characters

Figure 8-23 String manipulation techniques covered in Lesson A

Lesson A Key Terms

Contains method—searches a string to determine whether it contains a specific sequence of characters; returns a Boolean value

IndexOf method— searches a string to determine whether it contains a specific sequence of characters; returns an integer

Insert method—inserts characters within a string

Length property—stores the number of characters contained in a string

Like operator—uses pattern-matching characters to determine whether one string is equal to another string

Mid statement—replaces a specified number of characters in a string with characters from another string

PadLeft method—inserts characters at the beginning of a string

PadRight method—inserts characters at the end of a string

Replace method—replaces a sequence of characters in a string with another sequence of characters

Substring method—used to access any number of characters contained in a string

Trim method—removes spaces from both the beginning and end of a string

Lesson A Review Questions

1. The `strState` variable contains the string "MI   " (the letters M and I followed by three spaces). Which of the following statements removes the three spaces from the variable's contents?
   a. `strState = strState.Trim`
   b. `strState = Trim(strState)`
   c. `strState = Trim(strState, String.Empty)`
   d. None of the above.

2. Which of the following statements assigns the first three characters in the `strPartNum` variable to the `strCode` variable?
   a. `strCode = strPartNum.Assign(0, 3)`
   b. `strCode = strPartNum.Sub(0, 3)`
   c. `strCode = strPartNum.Substring(0, 3)`
   d. `strCode = strPartNum.Assign(3, 1)`

3. The `strWord` variable contains the string "Bells". Which of the following statements changes the contents of the variable to "Bell"?

   a. `strWord = strWord.Replace("s", String.Empty)`

   b. `Mid(strWord, 5, 1) = String.Empty`

   c. `Mid(strWord, 5, 1) = ""`

   d. All of the above.

4. Which of the following statements changes the contents of the `strZip` variable from "60121" to "60323"?

   a. `Replace(strZip, "1", "3")`

   b. `strZip.Replace("1", "3")`

   c. `strZip = strZip.Replace("1", "3")`

   d. `strZip = strZip.Replace("3", "1")`

5. Which of the following methods can be used to determine whether the `strAmount` variable contains the dollar sign?

   a `blnResult = strAmount.Contains("$")`

   b. `intResult = strAmount.IndexOf("$")`

   c. `intResult = strAmount.IndexOf("$", 0)`

   d. All of the above.

6. Which of the following statements changes the contents of the `strZip` variable from "60537" to "60536"?

   a. `Mid(strZip, "7", "6")`

   b. `Mid(strZip, 4, "6")`

   c. `strZip = Mid(strZip, 5, "6")`

   d. None of the above.

7. Which of the following statements changes the contents of the `strWord` variable from "men" to "mean"?

   a. `strWord = strWord.AddTo(2, "a")`

   b. `strWord = strWord.Insert(2, "a")`

   c. `strWord = strWord.Insert(3, "a")`

   d. `strWord = strWord.Replace(2, "a")`

8. If the `strMsg` variable contains the string "Happy holidays", what value will the `strMsg.IndexOf("day")` method return?

   a. –1

   b. 0

   c. 10

   d. 11

9. Which of the following statements assigns the fifth character in the `strWord` variable, which contains the word "window", to the `strLetter` variable?

   a. `strLetter = strWord.Substring(4)`

   b. `strLetter = strWord.Substring(4, 1)`

   c. `strLetter = strWord(5).Substring`

   d. None of the above.

10. Which of the following changes the string stored in the `strName` variable from "Mary Smyth" to "Mark Smyth"?

    a. `strName = strName.Change("y", "k")`

    b. `strName = strName.Replace("y", "k")`

    c. `strName = strName.Replace(3, "k")`

    d. None of the above.

11. Which of the following expressions evaluates to True when the `strPart` variable contains the string "123X45"?

    a. `strPart Like "999[A-Z]99"`

    b. `strPart Like "######"`

    c. `strPart Like "###[A-Z]##"`

    d. None of the above.

12. Which of the following changes the contents of the `strCityState` variable from "Boise Idaho" to "Boise, Idaho"?

    a. `strCityState = strCityState.Insert(5, ",")`

    b. `strCityState = strCityState.Insert(6, ",")`

    c. `strCityState = strCityState.Insert(7, ",")`

    d. None of the above.

13. If the `strMsg` variable contains the string "Today is Monday", which of the following assigns the number 9 to the `intNum` variable?

    a. `intNum = strMsg.Substring(0, "M")`

    b. `intNum = strMsg.Contains("M")`

    c. `intNum = strMsg.IndexOf("M")`

    d. `intNum = strMsg.IndexOf(0, "M")`

14. If the `strName` variable contains the string "John Jones", which of the following changes the contents of the variable to "John K. Jones"?

    a. `strName = strName.Replace(" ", " K. ")`

    b. `strName = strName.Insert(5, "K. ")`

    c. `strName= strName.Insert(4, " K.")`

    d. All of the above.

15. The `strAmount` variable contains the string "76.89". Which of the following statements changes the contents of the variable to "76.89!!!!"?
    a. `strAmount = strAmount.PadRight(4, "!"c)`
    b. `strAmount = strAmount.PadRight(9, "!"c)`
    c. `strAmount= strAmount.PadLeft(4, "!"c)`
    d. None of the above.

16. If the `strAddress` variable contains the string "34 Elm Street", the `strAddress.IndexOf("Elm")` method returns ______________________.
    a. −1
    b. 3
    c. 4
    d. True

17. If the `strAddress` variable contains the string "34 Elm Street", the `strAddress.IndexOf("Elm", 4)` method returns ______________________.
    a. −1
    b. 3
    c. 4
    d. False

Lesson A Exercises

INTRODUCTORY

1. Write a Visual Basic statement that removes the leading and trailing spaces from the `txtAddress` control.

INTRODUCTORY

2. Write a Visual Basic statement that uses the Insert method to change the contents of the `strWord` variable from "men" to "women".

INTRODUCTORY

3. Write a Visual Basic statement that uses the Replace method to change the contents of the `strWord` variable from "dog" to "frog".

INTRODUCTORY

4. The `strPartNum` variable contains the string "ABCD34G". Write a Visual Basic statement that assigns the string "CD34" from the `strPartNum` variable to the `strCode` variable.

INTRODUCTORY

5. Write the Visual Basic statements to accomplish the following tasks.
    a. Display in the lblSize control the number of characters contained in the `strMsg` variable.
    b. Remove the leading and trailing spaces from the `strCity` variable.

c. Use the Mid statement to change the contents of the `strWord` variable from "mouse" to "mouth".

d. Use the Insert method to change the contents of the `strWord` variable from "mend" to "amend".

e. Change the contents of the `strPay` variable from "235.67" to "****235.67".

6. The `strAmount` variable contains the string "3,123,560". Write the Visual Basic statement to change the contents of the variable to "3123560"; use the Replace method.

INTRODUCTORY

7. Write the Visual Basic statement that uses the Contains method to determine whether the `strAddress` variable contains the street name "Maple Street" (entered in uppercase, lowercase, or a combination of uppercase and lowercase). Assign the method's return value to a Boolean variable named `blnIsContained`.

INTRODUCTORY

8. Open the City Names Solution (City Names Solution.sln) file, which is contained in the VB2008\Chap08\City Names Solution folder. If necessary, open the designer window. The interface allows the user to enter a city name. Code the Add Name button's Click event procedure so that it removes any leading and/or trailing spaces from the city name before adding the name to the combo box. It then should send the focus to the combo box. Save the solution, then start the application. Test the application by entering spaces before and after the following city names: New York and Miami. Stop the application. Close the Code Editor window, then close the solution.

INTRODUCTORY

9. Open the Social Security Solution (Social Security Solution.sln) file, which is contained in the VB2008\Chap08\Social Security Solution-Replace folder. If necessary, open the designer window. The interface allows the user to enter a Social Security number. Code the Remove Dashes button's Click event procedure so that it first verifies that the Social Security number contains exactly 11 characters. It then should remove the dashes from the Social Security number before displaying the number in the lblNumber control. Use the Replace method to remove the dashes. Save the solution, then start the application. Test the application using the following data: 123-45 and 123-45-6789. Stop the application. Close the Code Editor window, then close the solution.

INTRODUCTORY

10. Open the Area Code Solution (Area Code Solution.sln) file, which is contained in the VB2008\Chap08\Area Code Solution folder. If necessary, open the designer window. The interface allows the user to enter a phone number, including the area code. Code the Change Area Code button's Click event procedure so that it uses the Mid statement to change the area code to 800 before displaying the phone number in the lblNew control. Save the solution, then start and test the application. Stop the application. Close the Code Editor window, then close the solution.

INTRODUCTORY

INTRODUCTORY

11. Open the Item Prices Solution (Item Prices Solution.sln) file, which is contained in the VB2008\Chap08\Item Prices Solution folder. If necessary, open the designer window. Open the Code Editor window. Modify the form's Load event procedure so that it right-aligns the prices listed in the cboRight control. Save the solution, then start the application. (The prices listed in the cboLeft control should still be left-aligned.) Stop the application. Close the Code Editor window, then close the solution.

INTRODUCTORY

12. Open the Date Solution (Date Solution.sln) file, which is contained in the VB2008\Chap08\Date Solution folder. If necessary, open the designer window. The interface allows the user to enter a date. Code the Change Date button's Click event procedure so that it uses the Insert method to change the year number from *yy* to *20yy* before displaying the year number in the lblDate control. Save the solution, then start and test the application. Stop the application. Close the Code Editor window, then close the solution.

INTERMEDIATE

13. The `strAmount` variable contains the string "3123560". Write the Visual Basic statements to change the variable's contents to "$3,123,560".

INTERMEDIATE

14. Open the Sales Tax Solution (Sales Tax Solution.sln) file, which is contained in the VB2008\Chap08\Sales Tax Solution folder. If necessary, open the designer window. The interface allows the user to enter a sales amount and a tax rate. Open the Code Editor window. The btnCalc control's Click event procedure should determine whether the tax rate ends with a percent sign. If it does, the procedure should remove the percent sign from the rate. Make the appropriate modifications to the code. Save the solution, then start the application. Test the application using the following data: a sales amount of 1000 and a tax rate of 5%, and then a sales amount of 5000 and a tax rate of 7%. Stop the application. Close the Code Editor window, then close the solution.

INTERMEDIATE

15. Open the Zip Solution (Zip Solution.sln) file, which is contained in the VB2008\Chap08\Zip Solution folder. If necessary, open the designer window. The Display Shipping Charge button's Click event procedure should display the appropriate shipping charge based on the ZIP code entered by the user. To be valid, the ZIP code must contain exactly five digits, and the first three digits must be either "605" or "606". The shipping charge for "605" ZIP codes is $25. The shipping charge for "606" ZIP codes is $30. Display an appropriate message if the ZIP code is invalid. Code the procedure. Save the solution, then start the application. Test the application using the following ZIP codes: 60677, 60511, 60344, and 7130. Stop the application. Close the Code Editor window, then close the solution.

LESSON B

After studying Lesson B, you should be able to:

- Include a MenuStrip control on a form
- Add elements to a menu
- Assign access keys to menu elements
- Assign shortcut keys to commonly used menu items
- Code a menu item's Click event procedure

Adding a Menu to a Form

In Visual Basic 2008, you use a **MenuStrip control** to include one or more menus in an application. You instantiate a MenuStrip control using the MenuStrip tool, which is located in the Menus & Toolbars section of the toolbox. Each menu in an application contains a menu title, which appears on the menu bar at the top of a Windows form. When you click a menu title, its corresponding menu opens and displays a list of options, called menu items. The menu items can be commands (such as Open or Exit), separator bars, or submenu titles. As in all Windows applications, clicking a command on a menu executes the command, and clicking a submenu title opens an additional menu of options. Each of the options on a submenu is referred to as a submenu item. The purpose of a separator bar is to visually group together the related items on a menu or submenu. Figure 8-24 identifies the location of these menu elements. Although you can create many levels of submenus, it is best to use only one level in your application, because too many layers of submenus can be confusing to the user.

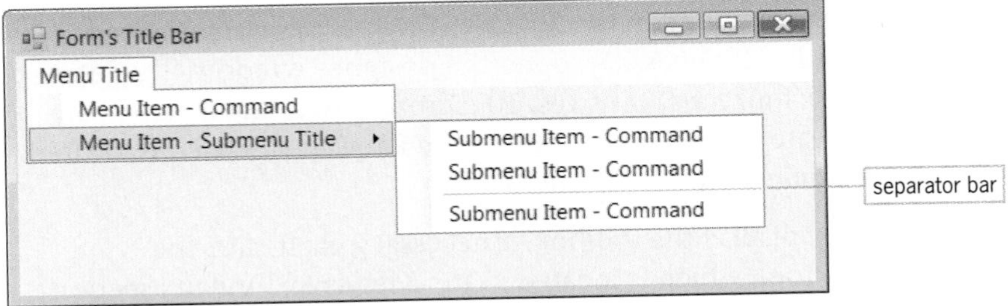

Figure 8-24 Location of menu elements

Each menu element is considered an object and has a set of properties associated with it. The most commonly used properties for a menu element are the Name and Text properties. The programmer uses the Name property to refer to the menu element in code. The Text property stores the menu element's caption, which is the text that the user sees when he or she is working with the menu. The caption indicates the purpose of the menu element. Examples of familiar captions for menu elements include Edit, Save As, Copy, and Exit. Menu title captions should be one word only, with the first letter capitalized. Each menu title should have a unique access key. The access key allows the user to open the menu by pressing the Alt key in combination with the access key. Unlike the captions for menu titles, the captions for menu items can be from one to three words. Use book title capitalization for the menu item captions, and assign each menu item a unique access key. The access key allows the user to select the item simply by pressing the access key when the menu is open. If a menu item requires additional information from the user, the Windows standard is to place an ellipsis (...) at the end of the caption. The ellipsis alerts the user that the menu item requires more information before it can perform its task.

The menus included in your application should follow the standard Windows conventions. For example, if your application uses a File menu, it should be the first menu on the menu bar. File menus typically contain commands for opening, saving, and printing files, as well as exiting the application. If your application requires Cut, Copy, and Paste commands, the commands should be placed on an Edit menu, which typically is the second menu on the menu bar.

Recall that your task in this chapter is to create an application that simulates the Hangman game. Most of the application's interface has been created for you. You will complete the interface in this lesson by adding a menu to it. You also will begin coding the application. You will finish coding the application in Lesson C.

To complete the Hangman Game interface:

1. If necessary, start Visual Studio 2008 or Visual Basic 2008 Express Edition. Close the Start Page window.
2. Open the **Hangman Game Solution** (**Hangman Game Solution.sln**) file, which is contained in the VB2008\Chap08\Hangman Game Solution folder. If necessary, open the designer window. The interface contains four label controls, 10 picture boxes, and a panel control. You create a panel control using the Panel tool, which is located in the Containers section of the toolbox.
3. Permanently display the toolbox, if necessary, then click the **MenuStrip** tool, which is located in the Menus & Toolbars section of the toolbox. Drag the mouse pointer to the form, then release the mouse button. A MenuStrip control named MenuStrip1 appears in the component tray, and the words "Type Here" appear in a box on the form's title bar. See Figure 8-25.

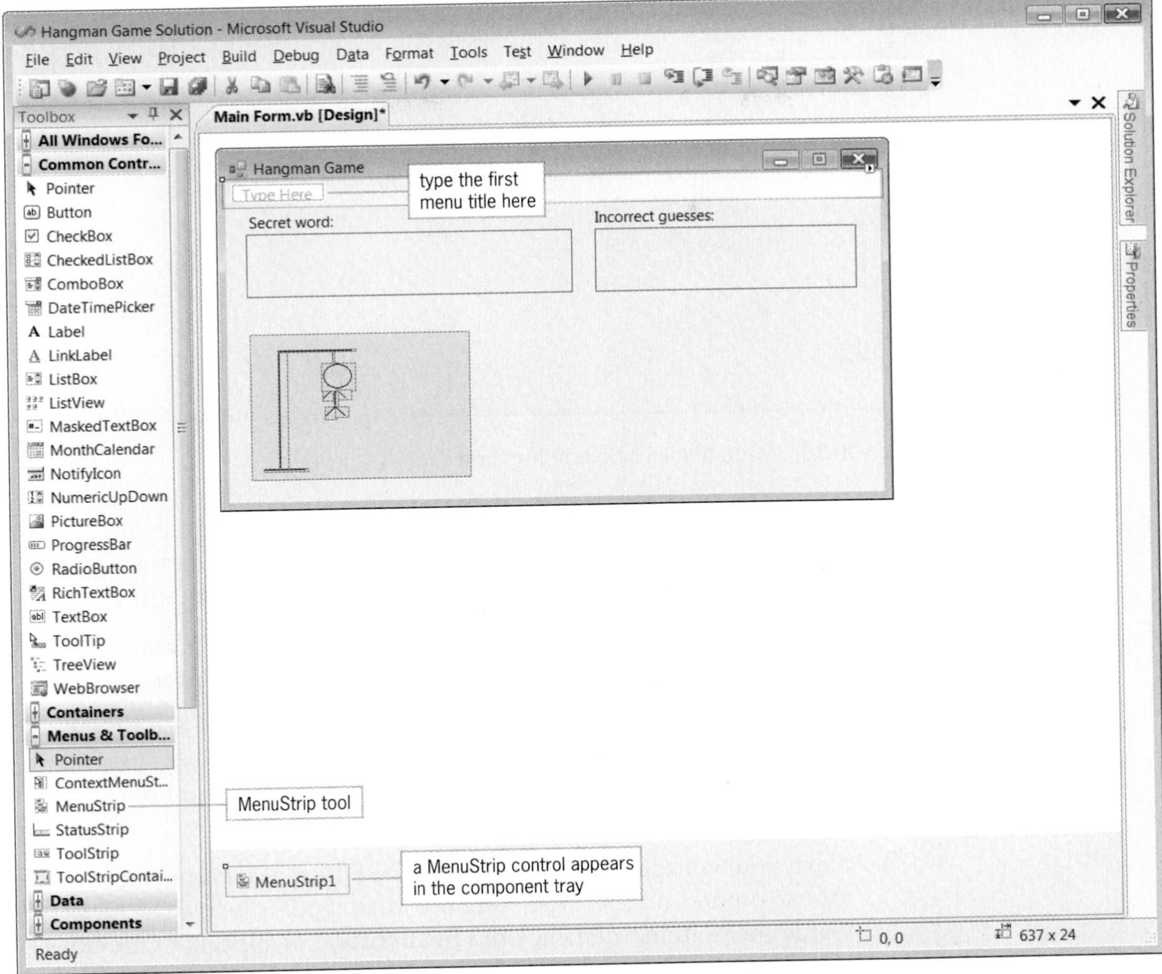

Figure 8-25 MenuStrip control added to the form

4. Auto-hide the toolbox.

You will include only a File menu title on the form's menu bar. The File menu will contain three menu items: a New Game command, a separator bar, and an Exit command.

To add the File menu title and three menu items:

1. Click the **Type Here** box on the menu bar, then type **&File**. See Figure 8-26. The Type Here box that appears below the menu title allows you to add a menu item to the File menu. The Type Here box that appears to the right of the menu title allows you to add another menu title to the menu bar.

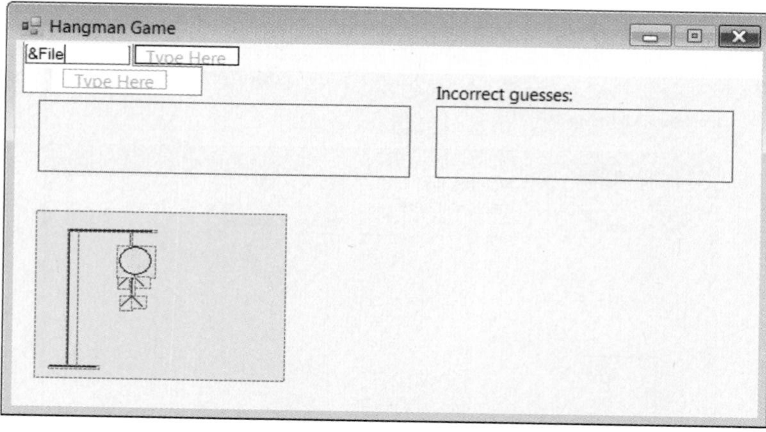

Figure 8-26 Menu title included on the form

2. Press **Enter**, then click the **File** menu title. Temporarily display the Properties window. Scroll the Properties window, if necessary, until you see the Text property. Notice that the property contains &File.
3. Scroll to the top of the Properties window, then click **(Name)**. Change the menu title's name to **mnuFile** and press **Enter**.
4. Click the **Type Here** box that appears below the File menu title, then type **&New Game** and press **Enter**. Click the **New Game** menu item. Change the menu item's name to **mnuFileNew** and press **Enter**.
5. Next, you will add a separator bar to the File menu. Place your mouse pointer on the Type Here box that appears below the New Game menu item, then click the **list arrow** that appears in the box. See Figure 8-27.

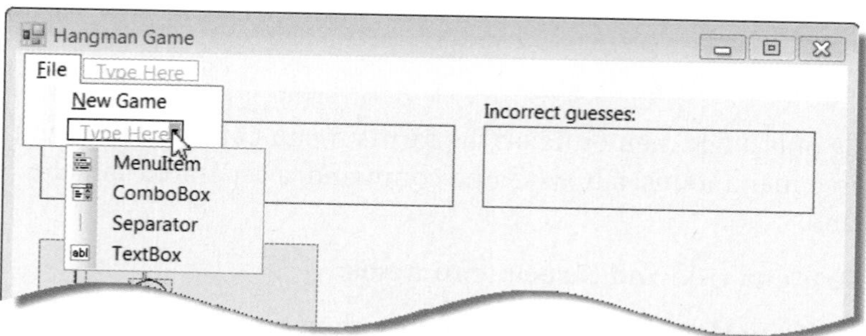

Figure 8-27 Drop-down list

6. Click **Separator** in the list. A separator bar, which is a horizontal line, appears below the New Game menu item. Click the **separator bar**, then change its name to **mnuFileSeparator** and press **Enter**.
7. Click the **Type Here** box that appears below the separator bar, then type **E&xit** and press **Enter**. Click the **Exit** menu item. Change the menu item's name to **mnuFileExit** and press **Enter**.
8. Save the solution, then start the application. Click **File** on the form's menu bar. The File menu opens and displays the New Game and Exit options, which are separated by a separator bar. See Figure 8-28.

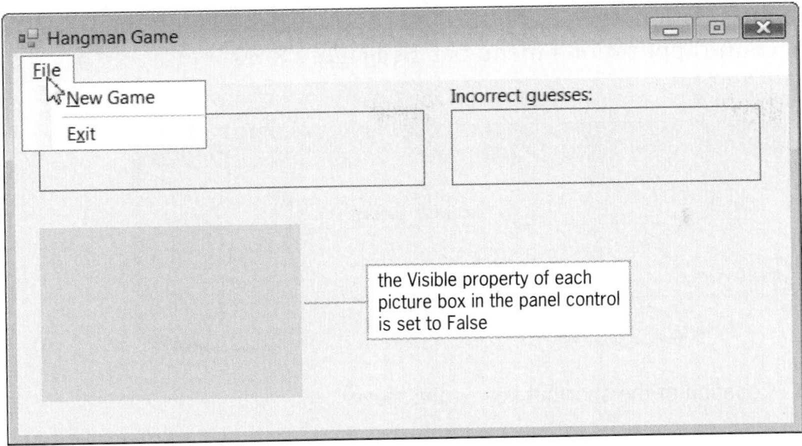

Figure 8-28 Open File menu

9. Click the **Close** button on the form's title bar to close the application.

Assigning Shortcut Keys to Menu Items

Shortcut keys appear to the right of a menu item and allow you to select an item without opening the menu. For example, in Windows applications you can select the Save command when the File menu is closed by pressing Ctrl+s. You should assign shortcut keys only to commonly used menu items. In the Hangman Game application, you will assign a shortcut key to the New Game option on the File menu.

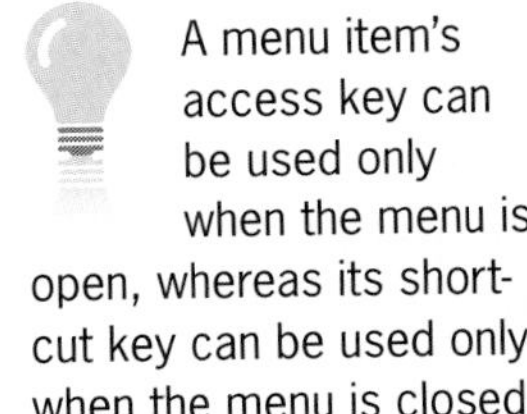

A menu item's access key can be used only when the menu is open, whereas its shortcut key can be used only when the menu is closed.

To assign a shortcut key to the New Game menu item:

1. Click the **New Game** menu item on the File menu. Click **ShortcutKeys** in the Properties window, then click the **list arrow** in the Settings box. A box opens and allows you to specify the shortcut key's modifiers and key. To assign Ctrl+n as the shortcut key, you specify Ctrl as the modifier and N as the key. Click the **Ctrl** check box to select it. Click the **list arrow** that appears in the Key section. A drop-down list opens. Scroll the list until you see the letter N, then click **N** in the list. See Figure 8-29.

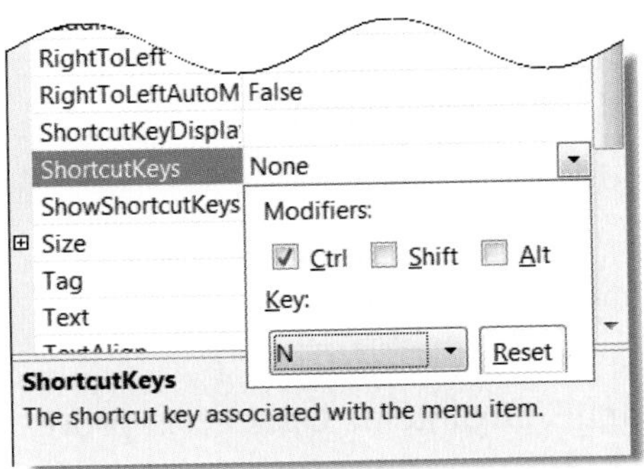

Figure 8-29 Shortcut key specified in the ShortcutKeys box

2. Press **Enter**. Ctrl+N appears in the ShortcutKeys property in the Properties window. It also appears to the right of the New Game menu item on the File menu.

3. Save the solution, then start the application. Click **File** on the Hangman Game application's menu bar. See Figure 8-30.

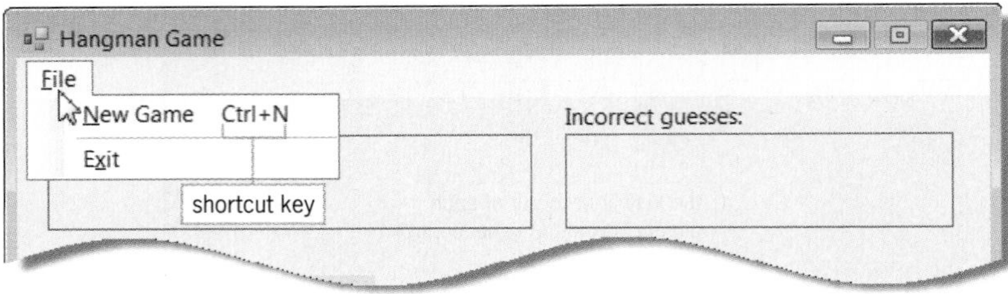

Figure 8-30 Location of the shortcut key on the menu

4. Click the **Close** button on the form's title bar to close the application.

GUI DESIGN TIP Menu Standards

- Menu title captions should be one word only, with the first letter capitalized. Each menu title should have a unique access key.
- Menu item captions can be from one to three words. Use book title capitalization and assign a unique access key to each menu item on the same menu.
- Assign unique shortcut keys to commonly used menu items.
- If a menu item requires additional information from the user, place an ellipsis (...) at the end of the item's caption, which is entered in the item's Text property.
- Follow the Windows standards for the placement of menu titles and items.
- Use a separator bar to separate groups of related menu items.

Coding the Exit Menu Item

When the user clicks the Exit option on the File menu, the option's Click event procedure should end the Hangman Game application.

To code the Exit menu item, then test the code:

1. Open the Code Editor window. Replace the <your name> and <current date> text in the comments with your name and the current date.
2. Open the code template for the mnuFileExit item's Click event procedure. Type **Me.Close()** and press **Enter**.
3. Save the solution, then start the application. Click **File** on the Hangman Game application's menu bar, and then click **Exit** to end the application. Close the Code Editor window, then close the solution.

Lesson B Summary

- **To add a MenuStrip control to a form:**

  Use the MenuStrip tool, which is located in the Menus & Toolbars section of the toolbox.

- **To create a menu:**

  Replace the words "Type Here" with the menu element's caption. Assign a meaningful name to each menu element. Assign a unique access key to each menu element, except separator bars.

- **To include a separator bar on a menu:**

  Place your mouse pointer on a Type Here box, then click the list arrow that appears in the box. Click Separator on the list.

- **To assign a shortcut key to a menu item:**

  Set the menu item's ShortcutKeys property.

Lesson B Key Terms

MenuStrip control—a control used to include one or more menus in an application

Shortcut keys—allow you to select a menu item without opening the menu; appear to the right of the menu item

Lesson B Review Questions

1. The horizontal line in a menu is called ______________________________.
   a. a menu bar
   b. a separator bar
   c. an item separator
   d. None of the above.

2. The underlined letter in a menu element's caption is called ______________________________.
   a. an access key
   b. a menu key
   c. a shortcut key
   d. None of the above.

3. ______________________ allows you to access a menu item without opening the menu.
   a. An access key
   b. A menu key
   c. A shortcut key
   d. None of the above.

4. Which of the following is false?
   a. Menu titles should be one word only.
   b. Each menu title should have a unique access key.
   c. You should assign a shortcut key to commonly used menu titles.
   d. Menu items should be entered using book title capitalization.

5. Explain the difference between a menu item's access key and its shortcut key.

Lesson B Exercises

INTRODUCTORY

1. Open the Bonus Solution (Bonus Solution.sln) file, which is contained in the VB2008\Chap08\Bonus Solution folder. If necessary, open the designer window. Add a File menu to the form. The File menu should contain an Exit menu item that ends the application when it is clicked. Enter the appropriate code in the menu item's Click event procedure. Save the solution, then start and test the application. Use the Exit option on the File menu to end the application. Close the Code Editor window, then close the solution.

INTERMEDIATE

2. Open the Commission Solution (Commission Solution.sln) file, which is contained in the VB2008\Chap08\Commission Solution folder. If necessary, open the designer window. Add a File menu and a Calculate menu to the form. Include an Exit menu item on the File menu. Include two menu items on the Calculate menu: 2% Commission and 5% Commission. Assign shortcut keys to the Calculate menu's items. When the user clicks the Exit menu item, the application should end. When the user clicks the 2% menu item, the application should calculate and display a 2% commission on the sales entered by the user. When the user clicks the 5% menu item, the application should calculate and display a 5% commission on the sales entered by the user. Enter the appropriate code in each menu item's Click event procedure. Save the solution, then start and test the application. Stop the application. Close the Code Editor window, then close the solution.

LESSON C

After studying Lesson C, you should be able to:

- Include the Length property in a procedure
- Include the Substring method in a procedure
- Include the Like operator in a procedure
- Include the Mid statement in a procedure
- Include the Contains method in a procedure

Completing the Hangman Game Application

Figure 8-31 shows the Hangman Game application's TOE chart. You coded the mnuFileExit object's Click event procedure in Lesson B. In this lesson, you will complete the application by coding the mnuFileNew object's Click event procedure.

Task	Object	Event
1. Hide the 10 picture boxes 2. Get a 5-letter word from player 1 3. Determine whether the word contains exactly 5 letters 4. Display 5 dashes in lblWord 5. Clear lblIncorrect 6. Get a letter from player 2 7. Search the word for the letter 8. If the letter is contained in the word, replace the appropriate dashes 9. If the letter is not contained in the word, display the letter in lblIncorrect, add 1 to the number of incorrect guesses, and show the appropriate picture box 10. If all of the dashes have been replaced, the game is over, so display the message "Great guessing!" in a message box 11. If the user makes 10 incorrect guesses, the game is over, so display an appropriate message and the word in a message box	mnuFileNew	Click
End the application	mnuFileExit	Click
Display the Hangman images	picBottom, picPost, picTop, picRope, picHead, picBody, picRightArm, picLeftArm, picRightLeg, picLeftLeg	None
Display dashes and letters (from mnuFileNew)	lblWord	None
Display the incorrect letters (from mnuFileNew)	lblIncorrect	None

Figure 8-31 TOE chart for the Hangman Game application

To open the Hangman Game application from Lesson B:

1. If necessary, start Visual Studio 2008 or Visual Basic 2008 Express Edition. Close the Start Page window.
2. Open the **Hangman Game Solution** (**Hangman Game Solution.sln**) file, which is contained in the VB2008\Chap08\Hangman Game Solution folder. If necessary, open the designer window. See Figure 8-32.

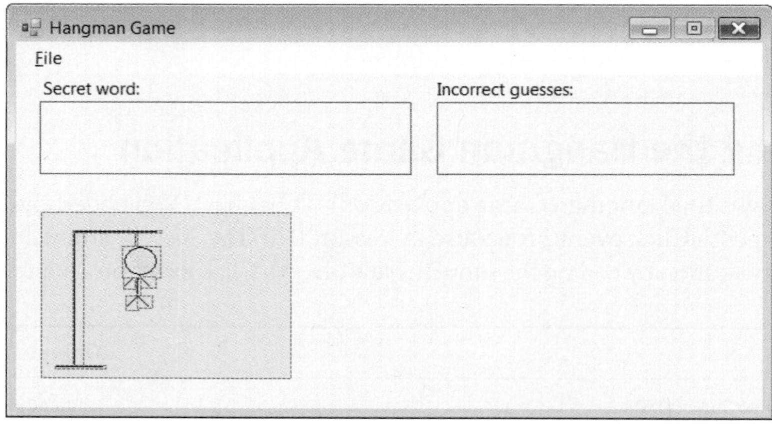

Figure 8-32 User interface for the Hangman Game application from Lesson B

Coding the mnuFileNew Object's Click Event Procedure

The mnuFileNew object's Click event procedure is invoked when the user clicks the New Game option on the Hangman Game application's File menu. The procedure should allow player 1 to enter a five-letter word and then allow player 2 to guess the word, letter by letter. The game is over when player 2 either guesses all of the letters in the word or makes 10 incorrect guesses, whichever comes first. The procedure's pseudocode is shown in Figure 8-33.

mnuFileNew Click event procedure

```
1. hide the 10 picture boxes
2. get a 5-letter word from player 1 and convert it to uppercase
3. if the word does not contain exactly 5 characters
         assign False to blnValidWord variable
   else
         if the word does not contain only letters
               assign False to blnValidWord variable
         end if
   end if
```

Figure 8-33 Pseudocode for the mnuFileNew object's Click event procedure *(continues)*

(continued)

```
mnuFileNew Click event procedure
4. if the blnValidWord variable contains False
        display an appropriate message
   else
        display 5 dashes in lblWord
        clear lblIncorrect

        get a letter from player 2 and convert it to uppercase
        repeat while the user entered a letter and the game is not over
              repeat for each letter in the word
                   if the current letter is the same as the letter entered by player 2
                        replace the appropriate dash in lblWord
                        assign True to blnDashReplaced variable
                   end if
              end repeat

              if the blnDashReplaced variable contains True
                   if lblWord does not contain any dashes
                        assign True to the blnGameOver variable
                        display the "Great guessing!" message
                   else
                        assign False to the blnDashReplaced variable
                   end if
              else
                   display the incorrect letter in lblIncorrect
                   add 1 to the number of incorrect guesses counter

                   value of the number of incorrect guesses counter:
                        1  show picBottom
                        2  show picPost
                        3  show picTop
                        4  show picRope
                        5  show picHead
                        6  show picBody
                        7  show picRightArm
                        8  show picLeftArm
                        9  show picRightLeg
                        10 show picLeftLeg
                             assign True to the blnGameOver variable
                             display the "Sorry, the word is" message and the word
              end if

              if the blnGameOver variable contains False
                   get another letter from the user
              end if
        end repeat
   end if
```

Figure 8-33 Pseudocode for the mnuFileNew object's Click event procedure

To code the mnuFileNew object's Click event procedure:

1. Open the Code Editor window, then open the code template for the mnuFileNew object's Click event procedure. Type **' simulates the Hangman game** and press **Enter** twice.

2. The procedure will use six variables: two String variables, three Boolean variables, and one Integer variable. The `strWord` and `strLetter` variables will store the word entered by player 1 and the letter entered by player 2, respectively. The `blnValidWord` variable will store a Boolean value that indicates whether the word entered by player 1 is valid. To be valid, the word must contain exactly five letters. The `blnDashReplaced` variable will keep track of whether a dash was replaced in the word, and the `blnGameOver` variable will indicate whether the game is over. The `intIncorrect` variable will keep track of the number of incorrect guesses made by player 2. Enter the following Dim statements. Press **Enter** twice after typing the last Dim statement.

```
Dim strWord As String
Dim strLetter As String
Dim blnValidWord As Boolean
Dim blnDashReplaced As Boolean
Dim blnGameOver As Boolean
Dim intIncorrect As Integer
```

3. The first step in the pseudocode is to hide the 10 picture boxes. Enter the following comment and assignment statements. Press **Enter** twice after typing the last assignment statement.

```
' hide the picture boxes
picBottom.Visible = False
picPost.Visible = False
picTop.Visible = False
picRope.Visible = False
picHead.Visible = False
picBody.Visible = False
picRightArm.Visible = False
picLeftArm.Visible = False
picRightLeg.Visible = False
picLeftLeg.Visible = False
```

4. The next step is to get a 5-letter word from player 1 and convert it to uppercase. Enter the following comment and lines of code. Be sure to include a space before the line continuation character. Press **Enter** twice after typing the last line.

```
' get a 5-letter word from player 1, convert to uppercase
strWord = InputBox("Enter a 5-letter word:", _
                   "Hangman Game").ToUpper
```

5. Now you need to verify that the word contains exactly 5 letters. Enter the comments and code indicated in Figure 8-34, then position the insertion point as shown in the figure. Be sure to include the exclamation point in the "[!A-Z]" *charList*.

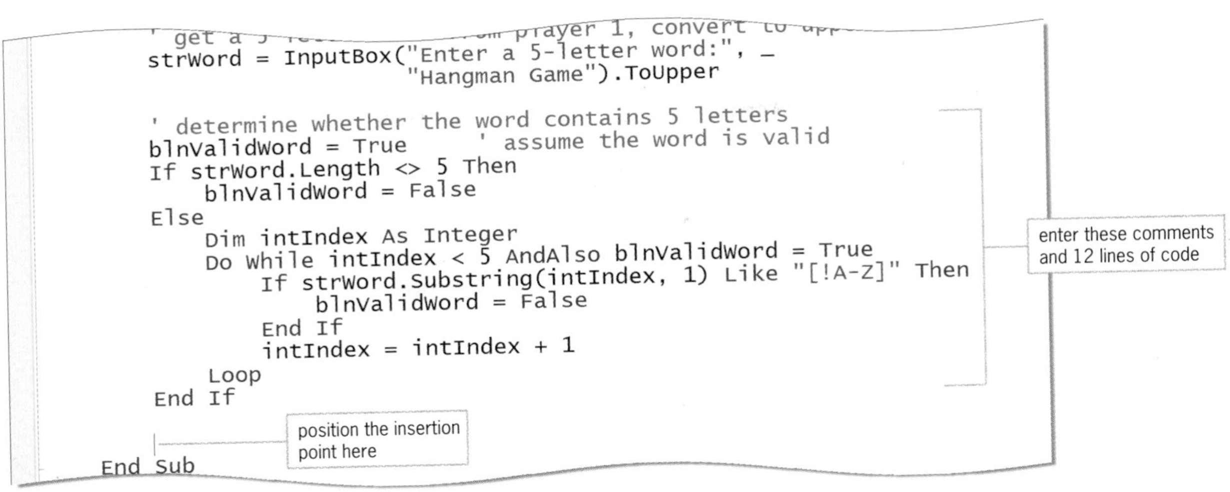

Figure 8-34 Additional comments and code entered in the procedure

6. If the word does not have exactly 5 letters, the `blnValidWord` variable will contain False. In that case, you should display an appropriate message. Enter the comment and code indicated in Figure 8-35, then position the insertion point as shown in the figure.

Figure 8-35 Comment and selection structure's true path

7. However, if the word has exactly 5 letters, you should display 5 dashes in the lblWord control and then clear the lblIncorrect control. Type **Else** and press **Enter**, then enter the following comment and assignment statements. (The first assignment statement assigns 5 hyphens to the lblWord control's Text property.) Press **Enter** twice after typing the last assignment statement.

' display five dashes in lblWord and clear lblIncorrect
lblWord.Text = "-----"
lblIncorrect.Text = String.Empty

8. Save the solution. Now get a letter from player 2 and convert it to uppercase. Enter the following comment and lines of code. Press **Enter** twice after typing the last line.

' get a letter from player 2, convert to uppercase
strLetter = InputBox("Enter a letter:", _
"Letter", "", 820, 590).ToUpper

9. The next task in the pseudocode is a pretest loop that repeats its instructions as long as both of the following conditions are true: player 2 entered a letter and the game is not over. Enter the following comments and Do clause. Be sure to include a space before the line continuation character.

' verify that player 2 entered a letter
' and that the game is not over
Do While strLetter <> String.Empty _
AndAlso blnGameOver = False

10. If the user entered a letter and the game is not over, you need to determine whether the letter appears in the word. You can accomplish this using a For loop that compares the letter with each character in the word, character by character. Enter the following comment and For clause, then change the Next clause to **Next intIndex**.

' search the word for the letter
For intIndex As Integer = 0 To 4

11. According to the pseudocode, the loop should use a selection structure to compare the current letter in the word with the letter entered by player 2. If both letters are the same, the selection structure's true path should replace the appropriate dash in the lblWord control. It also should assign the Boolean value True to the `blnDashReplaced` variable to indicate that a dash was replaced in the label control. Enter the comments and selection structure shown in Figure 8-36, then position the insertion point as shown in the figure.

```
        ' verify that player 2 entered a letter
        '  and that the game is not over
        Do While strLetter <> String.Empty _
            AndAlso blnGameOver = False
            ' search the word for the letter
            For intIndex As Integer = 0 To 4
                ' if the letter appears in the word, then
                ' replace the dash in lblWord and
                ' indicate that a replacement was made
                If strWord.Substring(intIndex, 1) = strLetter Then
                    Mid(lblWord.Text, intIndex + 1) = strLetter
                    blnDashReplaced = True
                End If
            Next intIndex

        Loop
    End If
```

enter these comments and 4 lines of code

position the insertion point here

Figure 8-36 Comments and selection structure entered in the procedure

12. If a dash was replaced in the lblWord control, you need to determine whether the control contains any more dashes. If there are no more dashes in the control, it means that the user has guessed the word and the game is over. In that case, you should assign True to the `blnGameOver` variable and display the "Great guessing!" message. However, if the lblWord control contains at least one dash, you should reset the `blnDashReplaced` variable's value to False. Enter the comments and selection structures shown in Figure 8-37, then position the insertion point as shown in the figure.

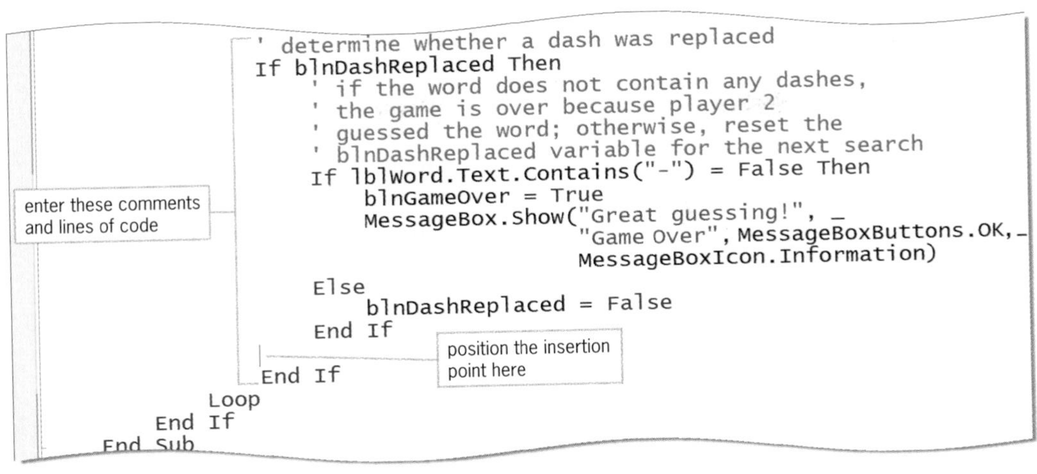

Figure 8-37 Additional comments and selection structures entered in the procedure

13. On the other hand, if no dash was replaced, it means that player 2's letter does not appear in the word. Therefore, you should display the incorrect letter in the lblIncorrect control, then update the `intIncorrect` variable by 1, and then use the variable's value to display the appropriate picture box. Type the following comments and lines of code. (Include a space between the quotation marks in the statement that assigns a value to the lblIncorrect control's Text property.)

```
Else    ' processed when no dash was replaced
    ' display the incorrect letter, then update
    ' the intIncorrect variable, then show
    ' the appropriate picture box
    lblIncorrect.Text = _
        lblIncorrect.Text & " " & strLetter
    intIncorrect = intIncorrect + 1
    Select Case intIncorrect
        Case 1
            picBottom.Visible = True
        Case 2
            picPost.Visible = True
        Case 3
            picTop.Visible = True
        Case 4
            picRope.Visible = True
        Case 5
            picHead.Visible = True
        Case 6
            picBody.Visible = True
        Case 7
            picRightArm.Visible = True
        Case 8
            picLeftArm.Visible = True
        Case 9
            picRightLeg.Visible = True
```

```
            Case 10
                picLeftLeg.Visible = True
                blnGameOver = True
                MessageBox.Show("Sorry, the word is " _
                                & strWord & ".", "Game Over", _
                                MessageBoxButtons.OK, _
                                MessageBoxIcon.Information)
        End Select
```

14. Save the solution. As the pseudocode shown earlier in Figure 8-33 indicates, the last task determines whether you need to get another letter from the user. Another letter is necessary only when the game is not over. Insert two blank lines above the Loop clause, then enter the comment and selection structure shown in Figure 8-38.

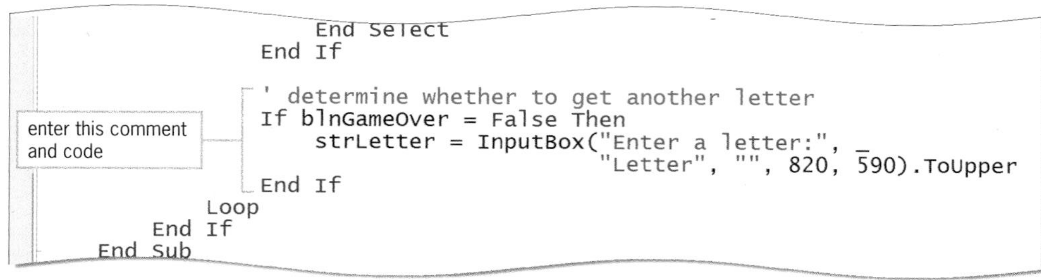

Figure 8-38 Final comment and selection structure entered in the procedure

To test the application's code:

1. Save the solution, then start the application. Click **File** on the application's menu bar, then click **New Game**. The Hangman Game dialog box opens and prompts you to enter a 5-letter word. Type **cat** in the dialog box, then press **Enter** to select the OK button. A message box opens and informs you that 5 letters are required. Press **Enter** to close the message box.

2. Press **Ctrl+n**, which is the New Game option's shortcut key. Type **cats4** in the dialog box and press **Enter**. A message box opens and informs you that 5 letters are required. Close the message box.

3. Click **File**, then click **New Game**. Type **puppy** and press **Enter**. The Letter dialog box opens and prompts you to enter a letter. Type **p** in the dialog box and press **Enter**. Three of the dashes in the lblWord control are replaced with the letter P. See Figure 8-39.

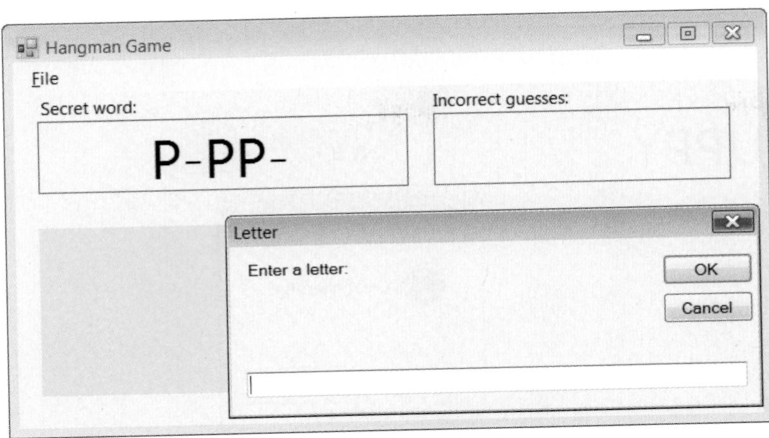

Figure 8-39 Dashes replaced with the letter P

4. Type **a** in the Letter dialog box and press **Enter**. The mnuFileNew object's Click event procedure displays the letter A in the lblIncorrect control and also makes the picBottom control visible. See Figure 8-40.

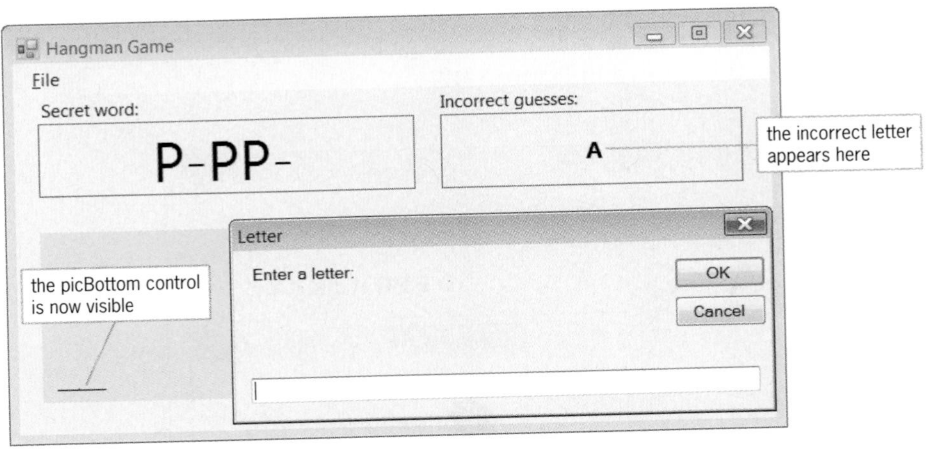

Figure 8-40 Result of entering the first incorrect letter

5. Type **b** in the Letter dialog box and press **Enter**. The letter B is appended to the contents of the lblIncorrect control and the picPost control is now visible.

6. Type **u** in the Letter dialog box and press **Enter**, then type **y** in the dialog box and press **Enter**. The "Great guessing!" message appears in a message box. Drag the message box down and to the right until you can see the entire contents of the lblWord and lblIncorrect controls. See Figure 8-41.

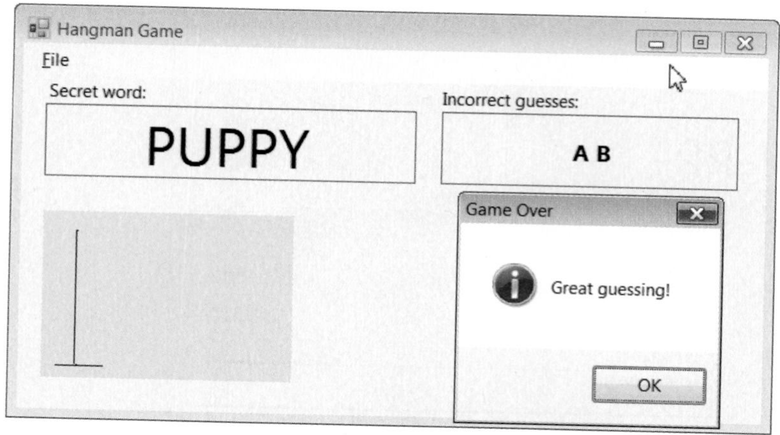

Figure 8-41 Result of guessing the word

7. Close the message box. Now you will observe what happens when you make 10 incorrect guesses. Press **Ctrl+n**, then type **basic** and press **Enter**. Now type the following 12 letters, pressing **Enter** after typing each letter: **d**, **c**, **e**, **f**, **g**, **h**, **a**, **j**, **k**, **x**, **y**, **z**. The mnuFileNew object's Click event procedure displays the 10 incorrect letters and 10 picture boxes, as well as a message box. Drag the message box to the location shown in Figure 8-42.

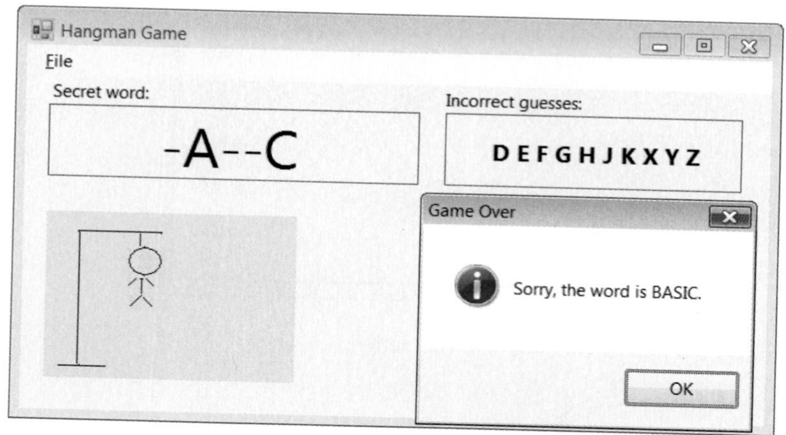

Figure 8-42 Result of making 10 incorrect guesses

8. Close the message box. Click **File** on the application's menu bar, then click **Exit**. Close the Code Editor window, then close the solution. Figure 8-43 shows the application's code.

```
' Name: Hangman Game Project
' Purpose: Simulates the Hangman game
' Programmer: <your name> on <current date>

Option Explicit On
Option Strict On
Option Infer Off

Public Class frmMain

    Private Sub mnuFileExit_Click(ByVal sender As Object, _
        ByVal e As System.EventArgs) Handles mnuFileExit.Click
        Me.Close()

    End Sub

    Private Sub mnuFileNew_Click(ByVal sender As Object, _
        ByVal e As System.EventArgs) Handles mnuFileNew.Click
        ' simulates the Hangman game

        Dim strWord As String
        Dim strLetter As String
        Dim blnValidWord As Boolean
        Dim blnDashReplaced As Boolean
        Dim blnGameOver As Boolean
        Dim intIncorrect As Integer

        ' hide the picture boxes
        picBottom.Visible = False
        picPost.Visible = False
        picTop.Visible = False
        picRope.Visible = False
        picHead.Visible = False
        picBody.Visible = False
        picRightArm.Visible = False
        picLeftArm.Visible = False
        picRightLeg.Visible = False
        picLeftLeg.Visible = False

        ' get a 5-letter word from player 1, convert to uppercase
        strWord = InputBox("Enter a 5-letter word:", _
                           "Hangman Game").ToUpper

        ' determine whether the word contains 5 letters
        blnValidWord = True ' assume the word is valid
        If strWord.Length <> 5 Then
            blnValidWord = False
        Else
            Dim intIndex As Integer
            Do While intIndex < 5 AndAlso blnValidWord = True
                If strWord.Substring(intIndex, 1) Like "[!A-Z]" Then
                    blnValidWord = False
                End If
                intIndex = intIndex + 1
            Loop
        End If

        ' if the word is not valid, display a message
        If blnValidWord = False Then
            MessageBox.Show("5 letters are required.", _
                           "Hangman Game", MessageBoxButtons.OK, _
                           MessageBoxIcon.Information)

```

Figure 8-43 Hangman Game application's code *(continues)*

(continued)

```
      Else
         ' display five dashes in lblWord and clear lblIncorrect
         lblWord.Text = "-----"
         lblIncorrect.Text = String.Empty

         ' get a letter from player 2, convert to uppercase
         strLetter = InputBox("Enter a letter:", _
                              "Letter", "", 820, 590).ToUpper

         ' verify that player 2 entered a letter
         ' and that the game is not over
         Do While strLetter <> String.Empty _
                       AndAlso blnGameOver = False
            ' search the word for the letter
            For intIndex As Integer = 0 To 4
               ' if the letter appears in the word, then
               ' replace the dash in lblWord and
               ' indicate that a replacement was made
               If strWord.Substring(intIndex, 1) = strLetter Then
                  Mid(lblWord.Text, intIndex + 1) = strLetter
                  blnDashReplaced = True
               End If
            Next intIndex

            ' determine whether a dash was replaced
            If blnDashReplaced Then
               ' if the word does not contain any dashes,
               ' the game is over because player 2
               ' guessed the word; otherwise, reset the
               ' blnDashReplaced variable for the next search
               If lblWord.Text.Contains("-") = False Then
                  blnGameOver = True
                  MessageBox.Show("Great guessing!", _
                      "Game Over", MessageBoxButtons.OK, _
                      MessageBoxIcon.Information)
               Else
                  blnDashReplaced = False
               End If
            Else   ' processed when no dash was replaced
               ' display the incorrect letter, then update
               ' the intIncorrect variable, then show
               ' the appropriate picture box
               lblIncorrect.Text = _
                    lblIncorrect.Text & " " & strLetter
               intIncorrect = intIncorrect + 1
               Select Case intIncorrect
                  Case 1
                      picBottom.Visible = True
                  Case 2
                      picPost.Visible = True
                  Case 3
                      picTop.Visible = True
                  Case 4
                      picRope.Visible = True
                  Case 5
                      picHead.Visible = True
                  Case 6
                      picBody.Visible = True
                  Case 7
                      picRightArm.Visible = True
                  Case 8
                      picLeftArm.Visible = True
                  Case 9
                      picRightLeg.Visible = True
```

Figure 8-43 Hangman Game application's code *(continues)*

(continued)

```
                  Case 10
                     picLeftLeg.Visible = True
                     blnGameOver = True
                     MessageBox.Show("Sorry, the word is " _
                                     & strWord & ".", "Game Over", _
                                     MessageBoxButtons.OK, _
                                     MessageBoxIcon.Information)
               End Select
            End If

            ' determine whether to get another letter
            If blnGameOver = False Then
               strLetter = InputBox("Enter a letter:", _
                  "Letter", "", 820, 590).ToUpper
            End If
         Loop
      End If
   End Sub
End Class
```

Figure 8-43 Hangman Game application's code

Lesson C Summary

- **To determine the length of a string:**

  Use the string's Length property.

- **To access each character in a string:**

  Use the Substring method.

- **To use pattern-matching to compare two strings:**

  Use the Like operator.

- **To replace a specific number of characters in a string with characters from another string:**

  Use the Mid statement.

- **To determine whether a specific character is contained in a string:**

  Use the Contains method.

Lesson C Key Terms

There are no key terms in Lesson C.

Lesson C Review Questions

1. Which of the following For clauses will access each character contained in the `strName` variable, character by character? The variable contains 10 characters.

   a. `For intIndex As Integer = 0 To 10`

   b. `For intIndex As Integer = 0 To strName.Length - 1`

   c. `For intIndex As Integer = 1 To 10`

   d. `For intIndex As Integer = 1 To strName.Length - 1`

2. Which of the following changes the first letter in the `strName` variable from "K" to "C"?

   a. `Mid(strName, 0, "C")`

   b. `Mid(strName, 0) = "C"`

   c. `Mid(strName, 1, "C")`

   d. `Mid(strName, 1) = "C"`

3. If the `strWord` variable contains the string "Irene Turner", the `strWord.Contains("r")` method returns ______________________.

   a. True

   b. False

   c. 1

   d. 2

4. Which of the following determines whether the `strItem` variable contains either the word "shirt" or the word "skirt"? The variable contains uppercase letters only.

   a. `If strItem = "SHIRT" AndAlso strItem = "SKIRT" Then`

   b. `If strItem = "S[HK]IRT" Then`

   c. `If strItem Like "S[HK]IRT" Then`

   d. `If strItem Like "S[H-K]IRT" Then`

5. Which of the following returns the Boolean value True when the `strPetName` variable contains the string "Micki"?

   a. `strPetName.Contains("k")`

   b. `strPetName Like "M*"`

   c. `strPetName.Substring(2, 1) = "c"`

   d. All of the above.

Lesson C Exercises

1. Open the Item Number Solution (Item Number Solution.sln) file, which is contained in the VB2008\Chap08\Item Number Solution folder. If necessary, open the designer window. Open the Code Editor window. The btnVerify control's Click event procedure should determine whether the user entered the item number in the required format: three digits, a hyphen, a letter, a hyphen, and two digits. Display an appropriate message if the format is not correct. Code the procedure. Save the solution, then start and test the application. Stop the application, then close the solution.

INTRODUCTORY

2. Open the Color Solution (Color Solution.sln) file, which is contained in the VB2008\Chap08\Color Solution folder. If necessary, open the designer window. The Display Color button's Click event procedure should display the color of the item whose item number is entered by the user. All item numbers contain exactly seven characters. All items are available in four colors: blue, green, red, and white. The fourth character in the item number indicates the item's color, as follows: a B or b indicates Blue, a G or g indicates Green, an R or r indicates Red, and a W or w indicates White. If the item number does not contain exactly seven characters, of if the fourth character is not one of the valid color characters, the procedure should display an appropriate message. Code the procedure. Save the solution, then start and test the application. Stop the application, then close the solution.

INTRODUCTORY

3. In this exercise, you modify the Hangman Game application completed in Lesson C. Use Windows to make a copy of the Hangman Game Solution folder, which is contained in the VB2008\Chap08 folder. Rename the copy Modified Hangman Game Solution. Open the Hangman Game Solution (Hangman Game Solution.sln) file contained in the VB2008\Chap08\Modified Hangman Game Solution folder. Open the designer window, then open the Code Editor window. Modify the code to allow player 1 to enter a word that contains any number of letters, up to a maximum of 10 letters. Also verify that the character entered by player 2 is a letter of the alphabet. Save the solution, then start and test the application. Stop the application. Close the Code Editor window, then close the solution.

INTERMEDIATE

4. Open the Reverse Letters Solution (Reverse Letters Solution.sln) file, which is contained in the VB2008\Chap08\Reverse Letters Solution folder. If necessary, open the designer window. The interface provides a text box for the user to enter a word. The Reverse Letters button's Click event procedure should display the letters in reverse order. In other words, if the user enters the word "Programming", the procedure should display "gnimmargorP". Code the procedure. Save the solution, then start and test the application. Stop the application. Close the Code Editor window, then close the solution.

INTERMEDIATE

INTERMEDIATE

5. Open the Proper Case Solution (Proper Case Solution.sln) file, which is contained in the Proper Case Solution folder. If necessary, open the designer window. The interface provides a text box for the user to enter a person's first and last names. The Proper Case button's Click event procedure should display the first and last names in the proper case. In other words, the first and last names should begin with an uppercase letter and the remaining letters should be lowercase. Code the procedure. Save the solution, then start and test the application. Stop the application. Close the Code Editor window, then close the solution.

INTERMEDIATE

6. In this exercise, you complete an application that selects the appropriate delivery method from a list box. Open the Part Number Solution (Part Number Solution.sln) file, which is contained in the VB2008\Chap08\Part Number Solution folder. If necessary, open the designer window. The interface allows the user to enter a part number, which will consist of two numbers followed by either one or two letters. The letter or letters represent the delivery method, as follows: "MS" represents "Mail – Standard", "MP" represents "Mail – Priority", "FS" represents "FedEx – Standard", "FO" represents "FedEx – Overnight", and "U" represents "UPS". Code the Select Delivery button's Click event procedure so that it uses the Like operator to select the appropriate delivery method in the list box. Display an appropriate message when the part number does not contain two numbers followed by one or two letters, or when the letters do not represent a valid delivery method. Save the solution, then start the application. Test the application using the following data: 73mp, 34fs, 12u, 78h, 9FO, and 34ms. Stop the application. Close the Code Editor window, then close the solution.

INTERMEDIATE

7. Open the Jacobson Solution (Jacobson Solution.sln) file, which is contained in the VB2008\Chap08\Jacobson Solution folder. If necessary, open the designer window. The interface provides a text box for entering a password. The password can contain five, six, or seven characters. The Display New Password button should create and display a new password using the following three rules. First, replace all vowels (A, E, I, O, and U) with the letter X. Second, replace all numbers with the letter Z. Third, reverse the characters in the password. Code the procedure. Save the solution, then start and test the application. Stop the application. Close the Code Editor window, then close the solution.

ADVANCED

8. Each salesperson at BobCat Motors is assigned an ID number that consists of four characters. The first character is either the letter F or the letter P. The letter F indicates that the salesperson is a full-time employee. The letter P indicates that he or she is a part-time employee. The middle two characters are the salesperson's initials, and the last character is either a 1 or a 2. A 1 indicates that the salesperson sells new cars, and a 2 indicates that the salesperson sells used cars. Create a Visual Basic Windows application that allows the sales manager to enter a salesperson's ID and the number of cars the salesperson sold during the month. The application should allow the sales manager to enter this information for as many salespeople as needed. The application should calculate and display the total number of cars sold by each of the following four categories of employees: full-time employees,

part-time employees, employees selling new cars, and employees selling used cars. Name the solution, project, and form file BobCat Motors Solution, BobCat Motors Project, and Main Form.vb, respectively. Save the solution in the VB2008\Chap08 folder. You can either create your own interface or create the one shown in Figure 8-44. Code the application. Save the solution, then start and test the application. Stop the application. Close the Code Editor window, then close the solution.

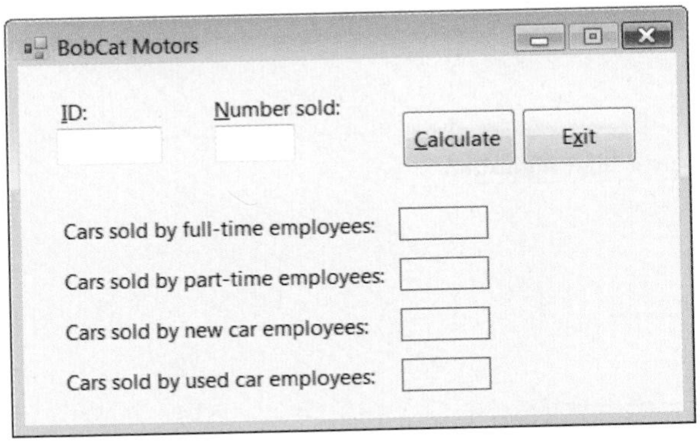

Figure 8-44 Sample interface for BobCat Motors

ADVANCED

9. Create a Visual Basic Windows application that allows the user to enter a word. The application should display the word in pig latin form. The rules for converting a word into pig latin form are shown in Figure 8-45. Name the solution, project, and form file Pig Latin Solution, Pig Latin Project, and Main Form.vb, respectively. Save the solution in the VB2008\Chap08 folder. Code the application. Save the solution, then start and test the application. Stop the application. Close the Code Editor window, then close the solution.

1. If the word begins with a vowel (A, E, I, O, or U), then add the string "-way" (a dash followed by the letters w, a, and y) to the end of the word. For example, the pig latin form of the word "ant" is "ant-way".
2. If the word does not begin with a vowel, first add a dash to the end of the word. Then continue moving the first character in the word to the end of the word until the first character is the letter A, E, I, O, U, or Y. Then add the string "ay" to the end of the word. For example, the pig latin form of the word "Chair" is "air-Chay".
3. If the word does not contain the letter A, E, I, O, U, or Y, then add the string "-way" to the end of the word. For example, the pig latin form of "56" is "56-way".

Figure 8-45 Pig latin rules

ADVANCED

10. Credit card companies typically assign a special digit, called a check digit, to the end of each customer's credit card number. Many methods for creating the check digit have been developed. One simple method is to multiply every other digit in the credit card number by two, then add the products to the remaining digits to get the total. You then take the last digit in the total and append it to the end of the credit card number, as illustrated in Figure 8-46. Create a Visual Basic Windows application that allows the user to enter a five-digit credit

card number, with the fifth digit being the check digit. The application should use the method illustrated in Figure 8-46 to verify that the credit card number is valid. Display appropriate messages indicating whether the credit card number is valid or invalid. Name the solution, project, and form file Georgetown Solution, Georgetown Project, and Main Form.vb, respectively. Save the solution in the VB2008\Chap08 folder. You can either create your own interface or create the one shown in Figure 8-47. Code the application. Save the solution, then start and test the application. Stop the application. Close the Code Editor window, then close the solution.

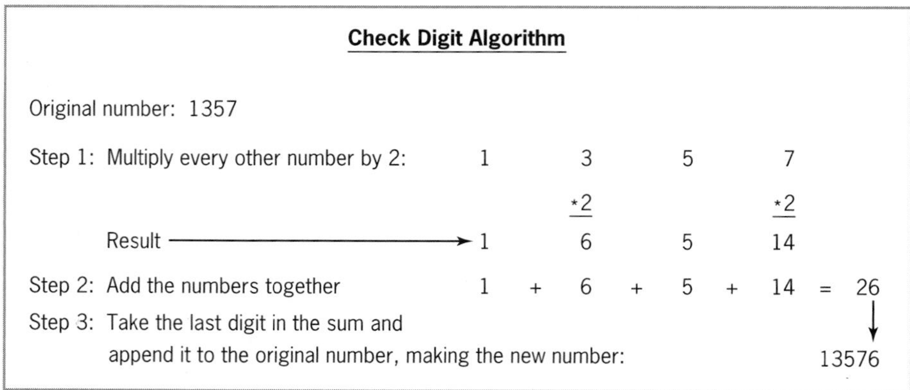

Figure 8-46 Illustration of a check digit algorithm

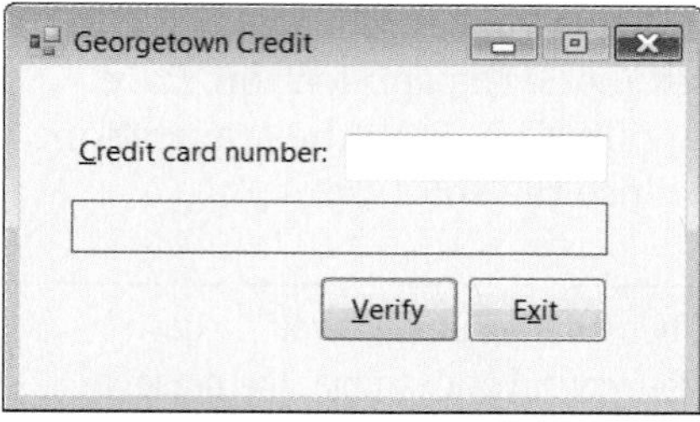

Figure 8-47 Sample interface for Georgetown Credit

ADVANCED

11. In this exercise, you code an application that determines the number of times a sequence of characters appears in a string. Open the Count Solution (Count Solution.sln) file, which is contained in the VB2008\Chap08\Count Solution folder. If necessary, open the designer window. The interface allows the user to enter a string. Code the Search button's Click event procedure so that it prompts the user to enter the sequence of characters for which he or she wants to search. The procedure should determine the number of times the sequence of characters appears in the string. Use the IndexOf method to search the string for the sequence of characters. Save the solution, then start the application. Enter the string "The weather is beautiful!" (without the quotes), then click the Search button. Search for the two characters "ea" (without the quotes). The two characters appear twice in the string. On your own, test the application using other data, then stop the application. Close the Code Editor window, then close the solution.

Discovery

12. Visual Basic provides the StartsWith and EndsWith methods for determining whether a specific sequence of characters occurs at the beginning or end, respectively, of a string. The StartsWith method's syntax is *string*.**StartsWith(***subString***)**, and the EndsWith method's syntax is *string*.**EndsWith(***subString***)**. Open the City Solution (City Solution.sln) file, which is contained in the VB2008\Chap08\City Solution folder. If necessary, open the designer window. The interface provides a text box for the user to enter the name of a city. The Add to List button's Click event procedure should add the city name to the list box, but only if the city name begins with either the letter L or the letters Ch. Code the procedure. Save the solution, then start and test the application. Stop the application. Close the Code Editor window, then close the solution.

Discovery

13. Visual Basic provides the Remove method for removing characters from anywhere in a string. The method's syntax is *string*.**Remove(***startIndex***,** *count***)**. When processing the Remove method, the computer makes a temporary copy of the *string* in memory, and then removes the characters from the copy only. Open the Social Security Solution (Social Security Solution.sln) file, which is contained in the VB2008\Chap08\Social Security Solution-Remove folder. If necessary, open the designer window. The interface allows the user to enter a Social Security number. Code the Remove Dashes button's Click event procedure so that it first verifies that the Social Security number contains three numbers followed by a hyphen, two numbers, a hyphen, and four numbers. It then should remove the dashes from the Social Security number before displaying the number in the lblNumber control. Use the Remove method to remove the dashes. Save the solution, then start and test the application. Stop the application. Close the Code Editor window, then close the solution.

Discovery

14. Visual Basic provides the TrimStart and TrimEnd methods for removing one or more characters from the beginning or end, respectively, of a string. The TrimStart method's syntax is *string*.**TrimStart**[(*trimChars*)], and the TrimEnd method's syntax is *string*.**TrimEnd**[(*trimChars*)]. The optional *trimChars* argument is a comma-separated list of characters that you want removed (trimmed). For example, if the txtSales control contains the string "$56.80", you can remove the dollar sign from the control's Text property using the statement `txtSales.Text = txtSales.Text.TrimStart("$"c)`. The default value for the *trimChars* argument

is the space character (" "c). When processing the TrimStart and TrimEnd methods, the computer makes a temporary copy of the *string* in memory, and then removes the characters from the copy only. Open the Tax Calculator Solution (Tax Calculator Solution.sln) file, which is contained in the VB2008\Chap08\Tax Calculator Solution folder. If necessary, open the designer window. The Calculate button's Click event procedure should calculate and display the sales tax, using the amount entered in the text box and the rate selected in the list box. Code the procedure. Save the solution, then start and test the application. Stop the application. Close the Code Editor window, then close the solution.

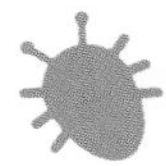

Swat The Bugs

15. Open the Debug Solution (Debug Solution.sln) file, which is contained in the VB2008\Chap08\Debug Solution-Lesson C folder. If necessary, open the designer window. Open the Code Editor window and review the existing code. Start and then test the application. Notice that the application is not working correctly. Stop the application. Locate and correct any errors in the code. Save the solution, then start and test the application again. Stop the application. Close the Code Editor window, then close the solution.

CHAPTER 9

Arrays

Creating the Treasures Gift Shop Application

In this chapter, you will create an application for Takoda Tapahe, the owner of a small gift shop named Treasures. The application will allow Takoda to enter a product ID. It then will display the product's price. Figure 9-1 shows a portion of the gift shop's price list.

Product ID	Price
BX35	13
CR20	10
FE15	12
KW10	24
MM67	4

Figure 9-1 Partial price list

Previewing the Treasures Gift Shop Application

To open the Run dialog box, press and hold down the Windows logo key as you tap the letter r, then release the logo key.

To preview the completed Treasures Gift Shop application:

1. Use the Run dialog box to run the **Treasures** (**Treasures.exe**) file, which is contained in the VB2008\Chap09 folder. The application's user interface appears on the screen.
2. Type **bx35** in the Product ID box. Because the text box's CharacterCasing property is set to Upper, the letters you enter appear in uppercase. Click the **Display Price** button. The product's price appears in the interface. See Figure 9-2.

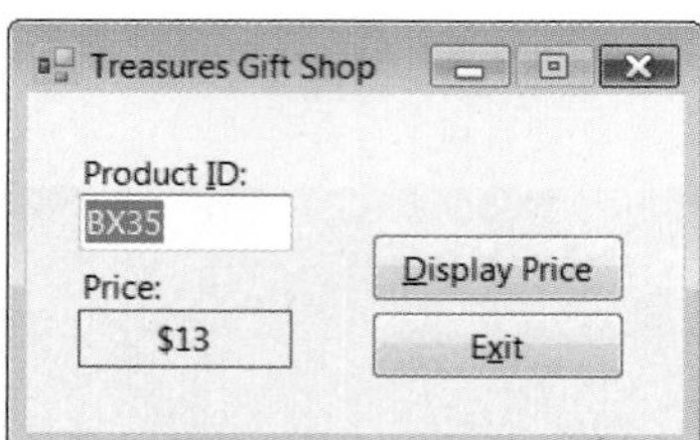

Figure 9-2 Interface showing the product's price

3. Try typing **tr678** in the Product ID box. Notice that the text box accepts only the first four characters (in this case, tr67); this is because its MaxLength property is set to 4. Click the **Display Price** button. TR67 is not a valid ID, so the application displays the message "Invalid ID" in a message box.
4. Close the message box, then click the **Exit** button.

Before you can begin coding the Treasures Gift Shop application, you need to learn about arrays. One-dimensional arrays are covered in Lesson A. Parallel and two-dimensional arrays are covered in Lesson B. You will code the Treasures Gift Shop application in Lesson B. In Lesson C, you will learn how to create a smart device application for Treasures Gift Shop.

LESSON A

After studying Lesson A, you should be able to:

- Declare and initialize a one-dimensional array
- Store data in a one-dimensional array
- Display the contents of a one-dimensional array
- Code a loop using the For Each...Next statement
- Access an element in a one-dimensional array
- Search a one-dimensional array
- Compute the average of a one-dimensional array's contents
- Find the highest entry in a one-dimensional array
- Update the contents of a one-dimensional array
- Sort a one-dimensional array

Using Arrays

All of the variables you have used so far have been simple variables. A simple variable, also called a scalar variable, is one that is unrelated to any other variable in memory. In many applications, however, you may need to reserve a block of variables, referred to as an array. An **array** is a group of variables that have the same name and data type and are related in some way. Each variable in the array might contain an inventory quantity, a state name, or an employee record (name, Social Security number, pay rate, and so on). It may be helpful to picture an array as a group of small, adjacent boxes inside the computer's memory. You can write information to the boxes and you can read information from the boxes; you just cannot *see* the boxes. Programmers use arrays to temporarily store related data in the internal memory of the computer. Examples of data stored in an array would include the federal withholding tax tables in a payroll application and a price list in an order entry application. Storing data in an array increases the efficiency of your code, because data can be both written to and read from internal memory much faster than it can be written to and read from a file on a disk. In addition, the data can be used as many times as desired while the application is running. A payroll application, for example, can use the federal withholding tax tables stored in an array to calculate the amount of each employee's federal withholding tax. The most commonly used arrays are one-dimensional and two-dimensional. One-dimensional arrays are covered in Lesson A. Parallel one-dimensional arrays and two-dimensional arrays are covered in Lesson B.

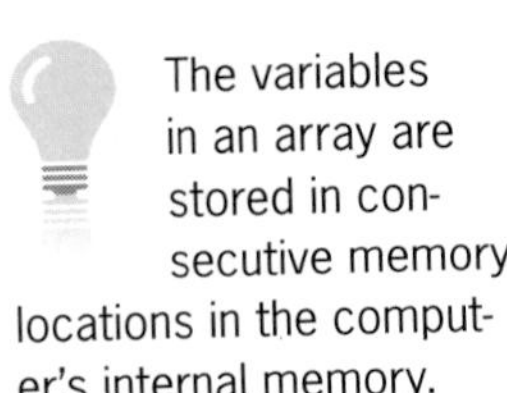
The variables in an array are stored in consecutive memory locations in the computer's internal memory.

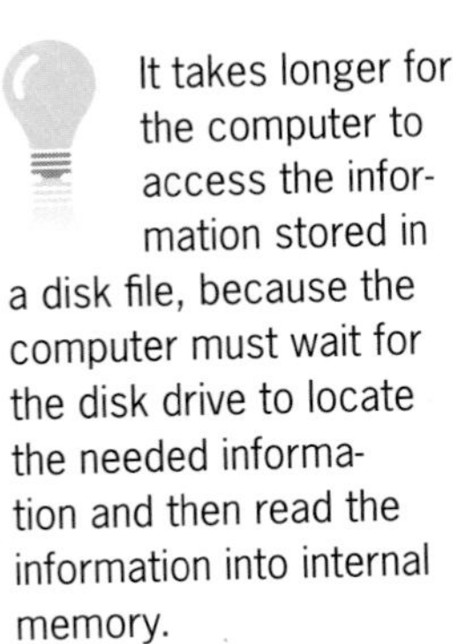
It takes longer for the computer to access the information stored in a disk file, because the computer must wait for the disk drive to locate the needed information and then read the information into internal memory.

One-Dimensional Arrays

A subscript is also called an index.

You can visualize a **one-dimensional array** as a column of variables. A unique number called a **subscript** identifies each variable in a one-dimensional array. The computer assigns the subscripts to the array variables when the array is created. The subscript indicates the variable's position in the array. The first variable in a one-dimensional array is assigned a subscript of 0, the second a subscript of 1, and so on. You refer to each variable in an array by the array's name and the variable's subscript, which is specified in a set of parentheses immediately following the array name. For example, to refer to the first variable in a one-dimensional array named `strCities`, you use `strCities(0)`—read "`strCities` sub zero." Similarly, to refer to the third variable in the `strCities` array, you use `strCities(2)`. Figure 9-3 illustrates this naming convention.

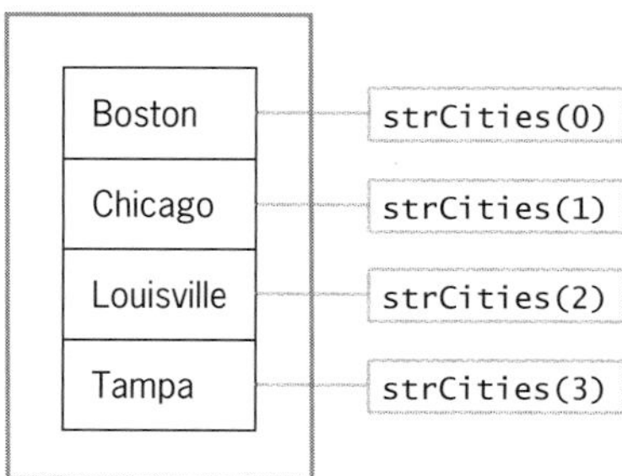

Figure 9-3 Names of the variables in the one-dimensional `strCities` array

Before you can use an array, you first must declare (create) it. Figure 9-4 shows two versions of the syntax you use to declare a one-dimensional array in Visual Basic. The {`Dim` | `Private`} portion in each version indicates that you can select only one of the keywords appearing within the braces. The appropriate keyword depends on whether you are creating a procedure-level array (`Dim`) or a module-level array (`Private`). *ArrayName* is the name of the array, and *dataType* is the type of data the array variables, referred to as elements, will store. In Version 1 of the syntax, *highestSubscript* is an integer that specifies the highest subscript in the array. When the array is created, it will contain one element more than the number specified in the *highestSubscript* argument; this is because the first element in a one-dimensional array has a subscript of 0. Also included in Figure 9-4 are examples of using both versions of the syntax.

Like module-level variables, module-level arrays are declared in the form's Declarations section, which begins with the Public Class line and ends with the End Class line.

Declaring a one-dimensional array

Syntax – Version 1
{**Dim** | **Private**} *arrayName*(*highestSubscript*) **As** *dataType*

Syntax – Version 2
{**Dim** | **Private**} *arrayName*() **As** *dataType* = {*initialValues*}

Figure 9-4 Syntax versions and examples of declaring a one-dimensional array *(continues)*

(continued)

Declaring a one-dimensional array

Example 1

```
Dim strCities(3) As String
```

declares a 4-element procedure-level array named `strCities`; each element is automatically initialized using the keyword `Nothing`

Example 2

```
Private intNumbers(5) As Integer
```

declares a 6-element module-level array named `intNumbers`; each element is automatically initialized to the number 0

Example 3

```
Dim decSales() As Decimal = {75.33D, 9.65D, 23.55D, 6.89D}
```

declares and initializes a 4-element procedure-level array named `decSales`

Figure 9-4 Syntax versions and examples of declaring a one-dimensional array

When you use Version 1 of the syntax, the computer automatically initializes each element in the array when the array is created. If the array's data type is String, each element in the array is initialized using the keyword `Nothing`. As you learned in Chapter 3, variables initialized to `Nothing` do not actually contain the word "Nothing"; rather, they contain no data at all. Elements in a numeric array are initialized to the number 0, and elements in a Boolean array are initialized using the Boolean keyword `False`. Date array elements are initialized to 12:00 AM January 1, 0001.

Rather than having the computer use a default value to initialize each array element, you can use Version 2 of the syntax to specify each element's initial value when the array is declared. Assigning initial values to an array is often referred to as **populating the array**. You list the initial values in the *initialValues* section of the syntax, using commas to separate the values, and you enclose the list of values in braces ({}). Notice that Version 2's syntax does not include the *highestSubscript* argument; instead, an empty set of parentheses follows the array name. The computer automatically calculates the highest subscript based on the number of values listed in the *initialValues* section. Because the first subscript in a one-dimensional array is the number 0, the highest subscript is always one number less than the number of values listed in the *initialValues* section. The `Dim decSales() As Decimal = {75.33D, 9.65D, 23.55D, 6.89D}` statement in Example 3 in Figure 9-4, for instance, creates a four-element array with subscripts of 0, 1, 2, and 3. The computer assigns the number 75.33 to the `decSales(0)` element, 9.65 to the `decSales(1)` element, 23.55 to the `decSales(2)` element, and 6.89 to the `decSales(3)` element.

After an array is declared, you can use another statement (such as an assignment statement or a statement that contains the TryParse method) to store a different value in an array element. Figure 9-5 shows examples of such statements.

Storing data in a one-dimensional array

Example 1

```
strCities(0) = "Madrid"
```

assigns the string "Madrid" to the first element in the `strCities` array

Example 2

```
For intX As Integer = 1 To 6
   intNumbers(intX - 1) = intX * intX
Next intX
```

assigns the squares of the numbers from 1 through 6 to the `intNumbers` array

Example 3

```
Decimal.TryParse(txtSales.Text, decSales(2))
```

assigns either the value entered in the txtSales control (converted to Decimal) or the number 0 to the third element in the `decSales` array

Figure 9-5 Examples of statements used to store data in a one-dimensional array

Manipulating One-Dimensional Arrays

The variables (elements) in an array can be used just like any other variables. You can assign values to them, use them in calculations, display their contents, and so on. In the next several sections, you will code applications that perform the following tasks using a one-dimensional array:

1. Display the contents of an array.
2. Access an array element using its subscript.
3. Search an array.
4. Calculate the average of the data stored in a numeric array.
5. Find the highest value stored in an array.
6. Update the array elements.
7. Sort the array elements.

In most applications, the values stored in an array come from a file on the computer's disk and are assigned to the array after it is declared. However, so that you can follow the code and its results more easily, most of the applications you view in this lesson use the Dim statement to store the appropriate values in the array.

Displaying the Contents of a One-Dimensional Array

The Months application uses a one-dimensional array to store the names of the 12 months in a year. It then displays the array's contents in a list box. When the user selects an item in the list box, the application displays the item in a label control.

To code and then test the Months application:

1. If necessary, start Visual Studio 2008 or Visual Basic 2008 Express Edition. Close the Start Page window.
2. Open the **Months Solution** (**Months Solution.sln**) file, which is contained in the VB2008\Chap09\Months Solution folder. If necessary, open the designer window.
3. Open the Code Editor window. Replace the <your name> and <current date> text in the comments with your name and the current date.
4. Click the **blank line** above the End Sub clause in the form's Load event procedure. First, declare and initialize a 12-element, one-dimensional String array named `strMonths`. Enter the following lines of code. Be sure to include a space before each line continuation character. Press **Enter** twice after typing the last line.

```
Dim strMonths() As String = {"JAN", "FEB", "MAR", _
                             "APR", "MAY", "JUN", _
                             "JUL", "AUG", "SEP", _
                             "OCT", "NOV", "DEC"}
```

5. Now use a For...Next statement to add each array element to the lstMonths control, then select the first item in the control. Enter the following lines of code.

```
For intSubscript As Integer = 0 To 11
    lstMonths.Items.Add(strMonths(intSubscript))
Next intSubscript
lstMonths.SelectedIndex = 0
```

As you learned in Chapter 6, you can code a loop using the For... Next, Do...Loop, or For Each...Next statement.

6. Locate the lstMonths control's SelectedValueChanged procedure. The procedure should display the selected item in the lblSelectedItem control. Click the **blank line** above the End Sub clause. Type **lblSelectedItem.Text = lstMonths.SelectedItem.ToString**.
7. Close the Code Editor window. Save the solution, then start the application. See Figure 9-6. When the application is started, the computer processes the form's Load event procedure, which creates and initializes the `strMonths` array. The procedure's loop is processed next. The first time the loop is processed, the `intSubscript` variable contains the number 0 and the Add method adds the contents of the `strMonths(0)` element—JAN—to the list box. The computer then updates the `intSubscript` variable by 1, giving 1. When the loop is processed the second time, the Add method adds the contents of the `strMonths(1)` variable—FEB—to the list box, and so on.

The computer repeats the loop instructions for each element in the `strMonths` array, beginning with the element whose subscript is 0 (JAN) and ending with the element whose subscript is 11 (DEC). The computer stops processing the loop when the `intSubscript` variable's value is 12, which is one number more than the highest subscript in the array.

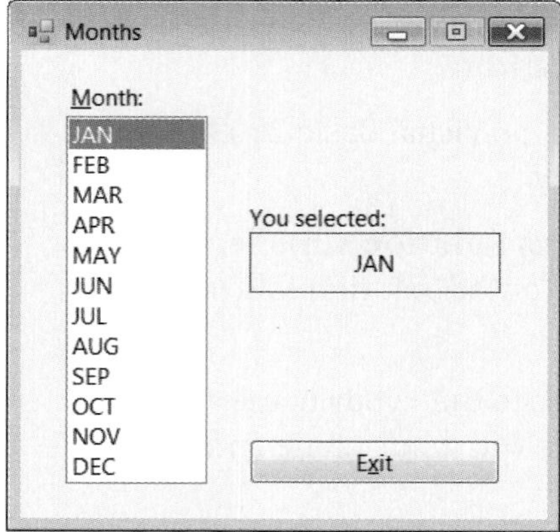

Figure 9-6 Result of starting the Months application

8. Click **AUG** in the list box. AUG appears in the You selected box. Click the **Exit** button, then close the solution.

In the Months application, the form's Load event procedure uses the For...Next statement to add each array element to the list box. You also could use the Do...Loop statement (which you learned about in Chapter 6) or the For Each...Next statement (which you learn about next).

The For Each...Next Statement

You can use the **For Each...Next statement** to code a loop whose instructions you want processed for each element in a group, such as for each variable in an array. Figure 9-7 shows the statement's syntax. Between the For Each and Next clauses, you enter the instructions you want the loop to repeat for each *element* in the *group*. When using the For Each...Next statement to process an array, *element* is the name of a variable that the computer can use to keep track of each array element, and *group* is the name of the array. You can use the `As` *dataType* portion of the For Each clause to declare the *element* variable, as shown in Example 1 in Figure 9-7. When you declare a variable in the For Each clause, the variable has block scope and can be used only by instructions within the For Each...Next loop. Alternatively, you can declare the *element* variable in a Dim statement, as shown in Example 2 in Figure 9-7. When a variable is declared in a Dim statement at the beginning of a procedure, it has procedure scope and can be used by the entire procedure. The data type of the *element* variable must match the data type of the *group*. If the *group* is an Integer array, then the *element*'s data type must be Integer. Likewise, if the *group* is a String array, then the *element*'s data type must be String. In the examples shown in Figure 9-7, *group* is a String array named `strMonths`, and *element* is a String variable named `strMonthName`. The `lstMonths.Items.Add(strMonthName)` statement in both examples adds the current array element to the lstMonths control and will be processed for each element in the `strMonths` array.

For Each...Next Statement

Syntax

For Each *element* [**As** *dataType*] **In** *group*
    [*statements*]
Next *element*

Example 1

```
For Each strMonthName As String In strMonths
   lstMonths.Items.Add(strMonthName)
Next strMonthName
```

displays the contents of the `strMonths` array in the lstMonths control

Example 2

```
Dim strMonthName As String
For Each strMonthName In strMonths
   lstMonths.Items.Add(strMonthName)
Next strMonthName
```

same as Example 1

Figure 9-7 Syntax and examples of the For Each...Next statement

You can use the `Exit For` statement to exit the For Each...Next statement prematurely, which means to exit it before it has finished processing. You may need to do this if the computer encounters an error when processing the loop instructions.

You can nest For Each...Next statements.

To modify and then test the Months application:

1. Use Windows to make a copy of the Months Solution folder, which is contained in the VB2008\Chap09 folder. Rename the folder **Months Solution-ForEach**.

2. Open the **Months Solution** (**Months Solution.sln**) file contained in the VB2008\Chap09\Months Solution-ForEach folder. Open the designer window.

3. Open the Code Editor window. Replace the For...Next statement in the form's Load event procedure with the For Each...Next statement shown in Example 1 in Figure 9-7.

4. Close the Code Editor window. Save the solution, then start the application. When the application is started, the computer processes the form's Load event procedure, which creates and initializes the `strMonths` array. The procedure's loop is processed next. The first time the loop is processed, the `strMonthName` variable contains JAN; as a result, the Add method adds JAN to the list box. When the loop is processed the second time, the `strMonthName` variable contains FEB and the Add method adds FEB to the list box, and so on. The computer repeats the loop instructions for each element in the `strMonths` group, beginning with the first element (JAN) and ending with the last element (DEC). The computer stops processing the loop when there are no more elements in the group. Notice that the interface appears as shown earlier in Figure 9-6.

5. Click **AUG** in the list box. AUG appears in the You selected box. On your own, test the application by clicking each of the remaining months in the list box. When you are finished testing the application, click the **Exit** button, then close the solution.

Using the Subscript to Access an Element in a One-Dimensional Array

The Salary Code application uses a one-dimensional array to store six salary amounts. Each salary amount is associated with a code, as shown in Figure 9-8. The application allows the user to select the code from a list box. It then displays the associated salary in a label control.

Code	Salary
101	25,000
102	35,000
103	55,000
104	75,000
105	80,200
106	90,500

Figure 9-8 Codes and salary amounts

To code and then test the Salary Code application:

1. Open the **Salary Code Solution** (**Salary Code Solution.sln**) file, which is contained in the VB2008\Chap09\Salary Code Solution folder. If necessary, open the designer window.
2. Open the Code Editor window. Replace the <your name> and <current date> text in the comments with your name and the current date.
3. Click the **blank line** above the End Sub clause in the form's Load event procedure. The procedure should fill the lstCodes control with the six codes, and then select the first code in the list. Enter the following lines of code.

```
For intCode As Integer = 101 To 106
    lstCodes.Items.Add(intCode.ToString)
Next intCode
lstCodes.SelectedIndex = 0
```

4. Click the **blank line** above the End Sub clause in the lstCodes control's SelectedValueChanged event procedure. First, you will declare and initialize a 6-element, one-dimensional Integer array named `intSalaries`. You will initialize the elements using the salary amounts from Figure 9-8. Enter the following lines of code. Be sure to include a space before the line continuation character.

```
Dim intSalaries() As Integer = {25000, 35000, 55000, _
                                75000, 80200, 90500}
```

5. Next, you will declare an Integer variable to store the index of the item selected in the list box. The index determines the appropriate salary in the array. For example, the first code in the list box (101)

has an index of 0 and is associated with the first salary in the array (25000), which has a subscript of 0. Similarly, the second code (102) and its associated salary (35000) have an index and subscript, respectively, of 1. The same relationship between the index and subscript holds true for the remaining codes and salaries. Therefore, you can use the code's index to access the appropriate salary in the array. Type **Dim intIndex As Integer** and press **Enter** twice.

6. Now you will assign the selected item's index to the `intIndex` variable. Type the following comment and assignment statement. Press **Enter** twice after typing the assignment statement.

   ' assign selected item's index to a variable
   intIndex = lstCodes.SelectedIndex

7. Finally, use the `intIndex` variable to display the appropriate salary from the array. Type the following comment and assignment statement.

   ' display salary
   lblSalary.Text = intSalaries(intIndex).ToString("C0")

8. Close the Code Editor window. Save the solution, then start the application. Because code 1 is automatically selected in the list box, the number $25,000 appears in the Salary amount box, as shown in Figure 9-9.

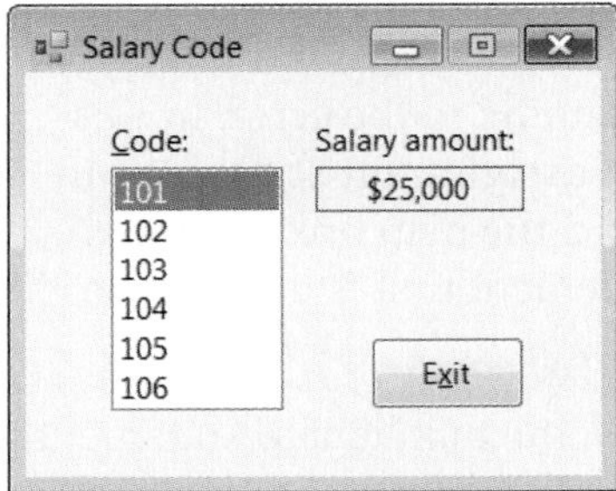

Figure 9-9 Salary amount shown in the Salary amount box

9. Click code **102**. The number $35,000 appears in the Salary amount box. On your own, test the application by clicking the remaining codes. When you are finished testing the application, click the **Exit** button, then close the solution.

Determining the Length of an Array

Before accessing an array element, a procedure always should verify that the subscript is valid for the array. In other words, it should verify that the subscript is at least 0 but not more than the highest subscript in the array. Using an invalid subscript will result in a **runtime error**, which is an error that occurs while an application is running. When a runtime error occurs, the computer displays an error message and the application ends abruptly. One way to determine the highest subscript in a one-dimensional array is to subtract the number 1 from the number of array elements, which is stored in the array's **Length property**. You need to subtract the number 1 from the number of elements, because the highest array subscript in a one-dimensional array is always one number less than the number of array elements; this is because the first array subscript is 0. In other words, if a one-dimensional array contains 5 elements, its Length property contains the number 5 but its highest subscript is 4. The Length property's syntax is *arrayName*.**Length**.

To modify and then test the Salary Code application:

1. Use Windows to make a copy of the Salary Code Solution folder, which is contained in the VB2008\Chap09 folder. Rename the folder **Salary Code Solution-Length**.
2. Open the **Salary Code Solution** (**Salary Code Solution.sln**) file contained in the VB2008\Chap09\Salary Code Solution-Length folder. Open the designer window.
3. Open the Code Editor window. First, observe the result of using an invalid array subscript. Locate the list box's SelectedValue-Changed event procedure, then delete the **, 90500** from the array declaration.
4. Save the solution, then start the application. The number $25,000 appears in the Salary amount box. The 90500 salary deleted from the array in the previous step is associated with code 106. Click **106** in the Code list box. Because this code does not have a corresponding salary in the array, a runtime error occurs. The Code Editor highlights the statement where the error was encountered, and it displays a help box that provides information pertaining to the error. In this case, the Code Editor highlights the last assignment statement in the SelectedValueChanged procedure, and the help box indicates that the statement is trying to access an element that is outside the bounds of the array.
5. Place your mouse pointer on `intIndex` in the highlighted statement, as shown in Figure 9-10. The variable contains the number 5, which is not a valid subscript. The valid subscripts for the array are 0 through 4.

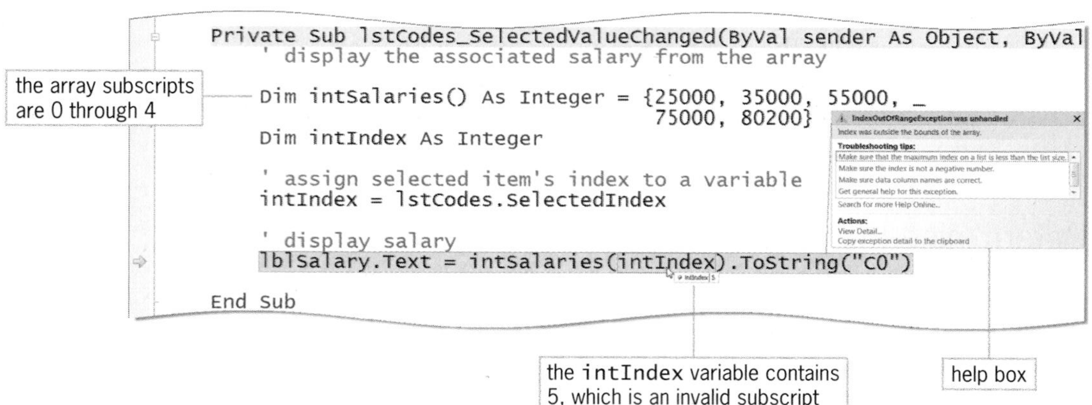

Figure 9-10 Result of the runtime error caused by an invalid subscript

6. Click **Debug** on the menu bar, then click **Stop Debugging**.

7. Modify the SelectedValueChanged procedure by adding the selection structure shown in Figure 9-11. Be sure to move the `' display salary` comment and `lblSalary.Text = intSalaries(intIndex).ToString("C0")` statement into the selection structure's true path.

```
' assign selected item's index to a variable
intIndex = lstCodes.SelectedIndex

If intIndex <= intSalaries.Length - 1 Then
    ' display salary
    lblSalary.Text = intSalaries(intIndex).ToString("C0")
Else
    MessageBox.Show("No salary available.", "Salary Code", _
                    MessageBoxButtons.OK, MessageBoxIcon.Information)
    lblSalary.Text = String.Empty
End If

End Sub
```

add this selection structure

Figure 9-11 Modified SelectedValueChanged procedure

8. Save the solution, then start the application. Click **106** in the Code list box. This time, the message "No salary available." appears in a message box. Close the message box, then click the **Exit** button.

9. Click **immediately after the 80200** in the array declaration statement, then type **, 90500**. Save the solution, then start the application. Click **106** in the Code list box. The number $90,500 appears in the Salary amount box. Click the **Exit** button. Close the Code Editor window, then close the solution.

Searching a One-Dimensional Array

The Sales application that you code next can be used to determine the number of salespeople selling above an amount provided by the user. To accomplish this task, the application will search a 5-element, one-dimensional array that contains the amount sold by each of five salespeople. The application will look for array values that are greater than the user's entry.

To code the Sales application:

1. Open the **Sales Solution** (**Sales Solution.sln**) file, which is contained in the VB2008\Chap09\Sales Solution folder. If necessary, open the designer window.

2. Open the Code Editor window. Replace the <your name> and <current date> text in the comments with your name and the current date.

3. Review the existing code. Notice that the text box's KeyPress event procedure allows the text box to accept only numbers and the Backspace key.

4. Locate the btnSearch control's Click event procedure. The procedure declares and initializes a 5-element, one-dimensional Integer array named `intSales`. Click the **blank line** below the Dim statement. First, declare an Integer variable to store the sales amount entered by the user. The procedure will search the array for all values that are greater than this amount. Type **Dim intSearchAmount As Integer** and press **Enter**.

5. The procedure will use a counter to keep track of the number of values greater than the user's entry. Type **Dim intCounter As Integer** and press **Enter** twice.

6. Now convert the user's entry to the Integer data type. Enter the following statement.

   Integer.TryParse(txtSales.Text, intSearchAmount)

7. Next, you will use a loop to search the array from beginning to end. You can use the Do...Loop, For...Next, or For Each...Next statement to code the loop. In this case, you will use the For...Next statement. Click the **blank line** below the `' value is greater than intSearchAmount value` comment. Enter the following For clause, then change the Next clause to **Next intSubscript**.

   For intSubscript As Integer = 0 To intSales.Length – 1

8. The loop should use a selection structure to compare the value stored in the current array element with the value stored in the `intSearchAmount` variable. If the array element's value is greater than the variable's value, the selection structure's true path should update the `intCounter` variable by 1. Click the **blank line** below the For clause, then enter the following selection structure.

   If intSales(intSubscript) > intSearchAmount Then
   intCounter = intCounter + 1
   End If

9. Finally, display the `intCounter` variable's value in the interface. Click the **blank line** below the `' display the result` comment. Type **lblCount.Text = intCounter.ToString** and press **Enter**. Figure 9-12 shows the btnSearch control's Click event procedure.

```
Private Sub btnSearch_Click(ByVal sender As Object, _
   ByVal e As System.EventArgs) Handles btnSearch.Click
   ' searches the array, looking for values that are
   ' greater than the value entered by the user

   Dim intSales() As Integer = {5000, 4500, 2000, 6000, 3000}
   Dim intSearchAmount As Integer
   Dim intCounter As Integer

   Integer.TryParse(txtSales.Text, intSearchAmount)

   ' search the array, update intCounter when array
   ' value is greater than intSearchAmount value
   For intSubscript As Integer = 0 To intSales.Length - 1
      If intSales(intSubscript) > intSearchAmount Then
         intCounter = intCounter + 1
      End If
   Next intSubscript

   ' display the result
   lblCount.Text = intCounter.ToString

   txtSales.Focus()
End Sub
```

Figure 9-12 btnSearch control's Click event procedure

To test the Sales application:

1. Save the solution, then start the application. Type **4000** in the Sales over box, then click the **Search** button. The number 3 appears in the Number of salespeople box. See Figure 9-13.

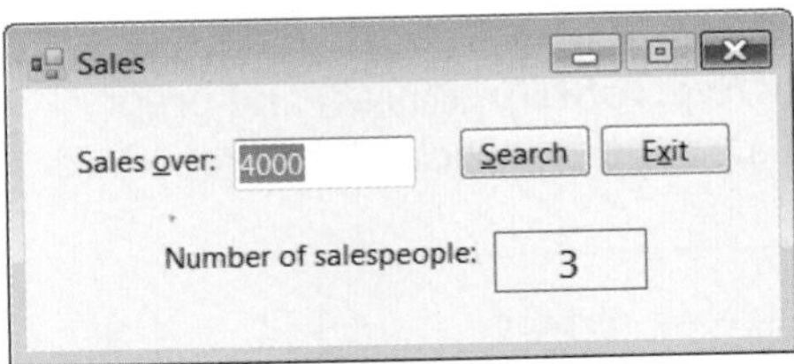

Figure 9-13 Interface showing the number of salespeople selling over $4000

2. On your own, test the application using different sales amounts. When you are finished testing the application, click the **Exit** button. Close the Code Editor window, then close the solution.

Calculating the Average Amount Stored in a One-Dimensional Numeric Array

The Average application calculates and displays the average test score stored in a 4-element, one-dimensional Integer array. It calculates the average by first adding together the array values, and then dividing the sum by the number of array elements.

To code the Average application:

1. Open the **Average Solution** (**Average Solution.sln**) file, which is contained in the VB2008\Chap09\Average Solution folder. If necessary, open the designer window.

2. Open the Code Editor window. Replace the <your name> and <current date> text in the comments with your name and the current date.

3. Locate the btnCalc control's Click event procedure. The procedure declares and initializes a 4-element, one-dimensional Integer array named `intScores`. Click the **blank line** below the Dim statement. First, declare an Integer variable that the procedure can use to accumulate the test scores. Type **Dim intTotal As Integer** and press **Tab** twice, then type **' accumulator** and press **Enter**.

4. Now declare a Double variable to store the average test score. Type **Dim dblAvg As Double** and press **Enter**.

5. Next, you will use a loop to access each array element. You can use the Do...Loop, For...Next, or For Each...Next statement to code the loop. In this case, you will use the For Each...Next statement. Click the **blank line** below the `' accumulate scores` comment. Enter the following For Each clause, then change the Next clause to **Next intTestScore**.

   For Each intTestScore As Integer In intScores

In the For Each clause in Step 5, the `intTestScore` variable is the *element* and the `intScores` array is the *group*. Each time the loop is processed, the computer assigns the current array element's value to the `intTestScore` variable.

6. The loop should contain an instruction that adds the current element's value to the accumulator variable. Click the **blank line** below the For Each clause, then type **intTotal = intTotal + intTestScore**.

7. Finally, calculate and display the average test score. Click the **blank line** below the `' calculate and display the average score` comment. Type **dblAvg = intTotal / intScores.Length** and press **Enter**, then type **lblAvg.Text = dblAvg.ToString("N1")** and press **Enter**. Figure 9-14 shows the btnCalc control's Click event procedure.

```
Private Sub btnCalc_Click(ByVal sender As Object, _
   ByVal e As System.EventArgs) Handles btnCalc.Click
   ' calculates and displays the average test score

   Dim intScores() As Integer = {98, 82, 66, 75}
   Dim intTotal As Integer      ' accumulator
   Dim dblAvg As Double

   ' accumulate scores
   For Each intTestScore As Integer In intScores
      intTotal = intTotal + intTestScore
   Next intTestScore

   ' calculate and display the average score
   dblAvg = intTotal / intScores.Length
   lblAvg.Text = dblAvg.ToString("N1")

End Sub
```

Figure 9-14 btnCalc control's Click event procedure

To test the Average application:

1. Save the solution, then start the application. Click the **Calculate Average** button. The average test score appears in the interface. See Figure 9-15.

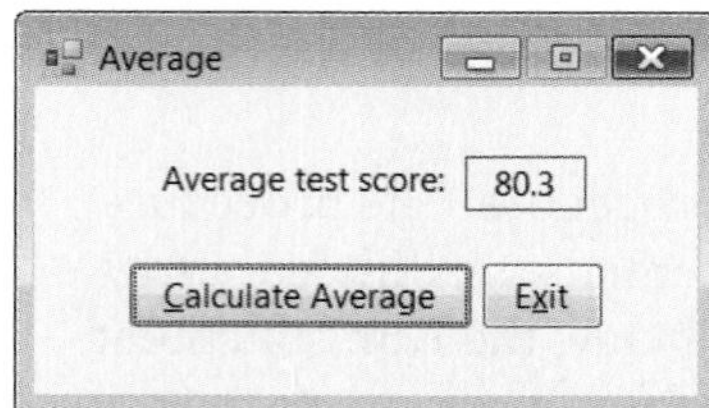

Figure 9-15 Interface showing the average test score

2. Click the **Exit** button. Close the Code Editor window, then close the solution.

Determining the Highest Value Stored in a One-Dimensional Array

The Highest Number application displays the highest number stored in a 10-element, one-dimensional Double array. Similar to the Sales application (shown earlier in Figures 9-12 and 9-13), the Highest Number application will need to search the array. However, rather than searching for numbers greater than a certain amount, the Highest Number application will look for the highest number in the array.

To code the Highest Number application:

1. Open the **Highest Number Solution** (**Highest Number Solution.sln**) file, which is contained in the VB2008\Chap09\Highest Number Solution folder. If necessary, open the designer window.

2. Open the Code Editor window. Replace the <your name> and <current date> text in the comments with your name and the current date.

3. Locate the btnDisplay control's Click event procedure. The procedure declares and initializes a 10-element, one-dimensional Double array named `dblNumbers`. It also declares a Double variable named `dblHighest` and an Integer variable named `intSub`. The procedure will use the `dblHighest` variable to keep track of the highest number in the array. It will use the `intSub` variable to keep track of the array subscripts as it searches the array.

4. First, you will assign the value stored in the first array element to the `dblHighest` variable. Click the **blank line** below the `' store the first array value in dblHighest` comment. Type **dblHighest = dblNumbers(0)** and press **Enter**.

5. Because the `dblHighest` variable already contains the value stored in the first array element, you can begin searching the array with the second element. Recall that the second element in an array has an index of 1. Click the **blank line** below the `' search the array, beginning with the second element` comment. Type **intSub = 1** and press **Enter**.

6. You will need a loop to search the array. In the previous applications in this lesson, you coded the loops using either the For...Next or For Each...Next statement. In this application, you will use the Do...Loop statement. Enter the following Do clause.

   Do While intSub < dblNumbers.Length

7. The loop should contain a selection structure that compares the value stored in the current array element with the value stored in the `dblHighest` variable. If the element's value is greater than the variable's value, the selection structure's true path should assign the element's value to the variable. For example, if the array element contains the number 30.25 and the `dblHighest` variable contains the number 25.6, the true path should assign the number 30.25 to the variable. Enter the following selection structure.

   ```
   If dblNumbers(intSub) > dblHighest Then
       ' store the higher value in dblHighest
       dblHighest = dblNumbers(intSub)
   End If
   ```

8. Next, you need to update the `intSub` variable, which keeps track of the array subscripts. Click **immediately after the letter f** in the End If clause. Press **Enter**, then type **intSub = intSub + 1**.

9. Finally, display the highest number in the interface. Click the **blank line** below the `' display the highest number` comment. Type **lblHighest.Text = dblHighest.ToString("N2")** and press **Enter**. Figure 9-16 shows the btnDisplay control's Click event procedure.

```
Private Sub btnDisplay_Click(ByVal sender As Object, _
   ByVal e As System.EventArgs) Handles btnDisplay.Click
   ' display the highest number stored in the array

   Dim dblNumbers() As Double = {25.6, 30.25, 50, _
                                  20, 25.45, 75.67, _
                                  5.23, 32.45, 8, 4.5}
   Dim dblHighest As Double
   Dim intSub As Integer

   ' store the first array value in dblHighest
   dblHighest = dblNumbers(0)

   ' search the array, beginning with the second element
   intSub = 1
   Do While intSub < dblNumbers.Length
      If dblNumbers(intSub) > dblHighest Then
         ' store the higher value in dblHighest
         dblHighest = dblNumbers(intSub)
      End If
      intSub = intSub + 1
   Loop

   ' display the highest number
   lblHighest.Text = dblHighest.ToString("N2")

End Sub
```

Figure 9-16 btnDisplay control's Click event procedure

To test the Highest Number application:

1. Save the solution, then start the application. Click the **Display Highest** button. The highest number in the array appears in the interface. See Figure 9-17.

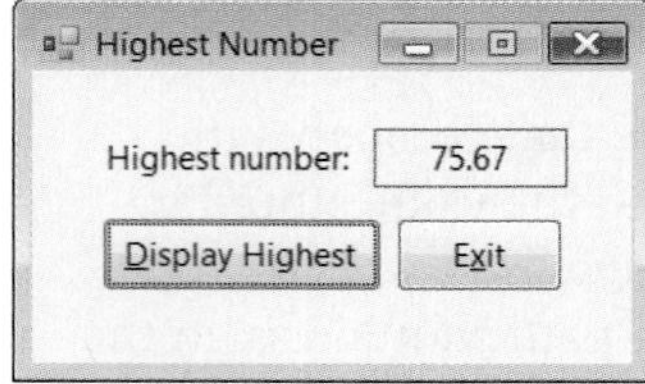

Figure 9-17 Interface showing the highest number in the array

2. Click the **Exit** button. Close the Code Editor window, then close the solution.

Updating the Values Stored in a One-Dimensional Array

The Price Increase application stores the prices of four items in a 4-element, one-dimensional Decimal array. It then increases each price by an amount entered by the user. The application displays both the old and new prices in list boxes.

To code the Price Increase application:

1. Open the **Price Increase Solution (Price Increase Solution.sln)** file, which is contained in the VB2008\Chap09\Price Increase Solution folder. If necessary, open the designer window.

2. Open the Code Editor window. Replace the <your name> and <current date> text in the comments with your name and the current date.

3. Review the existing code. Notice that the text box's KeyPress event procedure allows the text box to accept only numbers, the period, and the Backspace key.

4. Locate the btnDisplay control's Click event procedure. The procedure declares and initializes a 4-element, one-dimensional Decimal array named `decPrices`. It also declares a Decimal variable named `decIncrease`. The procedure will use the `decIncrease` variable to store the increase amount entered by the user. Each element in the array must be increased by this amount.

5. You will need a loop to access each element in the `decPrices` array. In this application, you will code the loop using the For...Next statement. Click the **blank line** below the `' update and display prices` comment. Enter the following For clause, then change the Next clause to **Next intSub**.

   For intSub As Integer = 0 To decPrices.Length - 1

6. First, display the old price in the lstOld control. Click the **blank line** below the For clause, then enter the following comment and statement.

   ' display old price
   lstOld.Items.Add(decPrices(intSub).ToString("N2"))

7. Now update the old price by adding the increase amount to it. Enter the following comment and statement.

   ' update old price
   decPrices(intSub) = decPrices(intSub) + decIncrease

8. Finally, display the new price in the lstNew control. Enter the following comment and statement, but do not press Enter after typing the statement.

   ' display new price
   lstNew.Items.Add(decPrices(intSub).ToString("N2"))

9. Save the solution. Figure 9-18 shows the btnDisplay control's Click event procedure.

```
Private Sub btnDisplay_Click(ByVal sender As Object, _
   ByVal e As System.EventArgs) Handles btnDisplay.Click
   ' updates the prices stored in an array
   ' displays the old and new prices

   Dim decPrices() As Decimal = {150.35D, 35.6D, 74.75D, 23.3D}
   Dim decIncrease As Decimal

   Decimal.TryParse(txtIncrease.Text, decIncrease)

   ' update and display prices
   For intSub As Integer = 0 To decPrices.Length - 1
      ' display old price
      lstOld.Items.Add(decPrices(intSub).ToString("N2"))
      ' update old price
      decPrices(intSub) = decPrices(intSub) + decIncrease
      ' display new price
      lstNew.Items.Add(decPrices(intSub).ToString("N2"))
   Next intSub

   txtIncrease.Focus()
End Sub
```

Figure 9-18 Click event procedure for the btnDisplay control

To test the Price Increase application:

1. Save the solution, if necessary, then start the application. Type **5** as the increase amount, then click the **Display Prices** button. The old and new prices appear in the interface. As Figure 9-19 shows, each new price is $5 more than its corresponding old price. (The SelectionMode property of each list box is set to None. Therefore, you cannot select an item in either list box.)

Figure 9-19 Interface showing the old and new prices

2. On your own, test the application using different increase amounts. When you are finished testing the application, click the **Exit** button. Close the Code Editor window, then close the solution.

Sorting the Data Stored in a One-Dimensional Array

In some applications, you might need to arrange the contents of an array in either ascending or descending order. Arranging data in a specific order is called **sorting**. When an array is sorted in ascending order, the first element in the array contains the smallest value and the last element contains the largest value. When an array is sorted in descending order, on the other hand, the first element contains the largest value and the last element contains the smallest value. You can use the **Array.Sort method** to sort the elements in a one-dimensional array in ascending order. The method's syntax is **Array.Sort(*arrayName*)**, where *arrayName* is the name of the one-dimensional array to be sorted. To sort a one-dimensional array in descending order, you first use the Array.Sort method to sort the array in ascending order, and then use the **Array.Reverse method** to reverse the array elements. The syntax of the Array.Reverse method is **Array.Reverse(*arrayName*)**, where *arrayName* is the name of the one-dimensional array whose elements you want reversed. The State application, which is the last application you code in this lesson, uses both the Array.Sort and Array.Reverse methods. The application allows the user to enter the names of five states. It stores the state names in a 5-element, one-dimensional String array named `strStates`. After entering the state names, the user can choose to display the names in either ascending or descending order.

To code the State application:

1. Open the **State Solution** (**State Solution.sln**) file, which is contained in the VB2008\Chap09\State Solution folder. If necessary, open the designer window.
2. Open the Code Editor window. Replace the <your name> and <current date> text in the comments with your name and the current date.
3. First, you will declare the `strStates` array. Unlike the arrays used in the previous applications in this lesson, the array in this application needs to be accessed by more than one procedure. More specifically, it needs to be accessed by the Click event procedures for the btnEnter, btnAscending, and btnDescending controls. For the array to be available to the three procedures, it will need to have module scope. Recall that you declare module-level memory locations in the form's Declarations section. Click the **blank line** below the `' module-level array` comment in the form's Declarations section. Type **Private strStates(4) As String** and press **Enter**.
4. Next, locate the btnEnter control's Click event procedure. Click the **blank line** below the `lstStates.Items.Clear()` statement, which clears the contents of the list box in the interface. You will use a loop and the InputBox function to get five state names from the user, storing each state name in an array element. Press **Enter**, then enter the following lines of code. Be sure to include a space before the line continuation character.

For intSub As Integer = 0 To strStates.Length – 1
strStates(intSub) = _
InputBox("State name", "State Names")
Next intSub

5. Now locate the btnAscending control's Click event procedure. Click the **blank line** below the `lstStates.Items.Clear()` statement, then press **Enter**. The procedure should sort the array values in ascending order and then display the values in the lstStates control. Enter the following lines of code.

Array.Sort(strStates)
For Each strName As String In strStates
lstStates.Items.Add(strName)
Next strName

6. Finally, locate the btnDescending control's Click event procedure. Click the **blank line** below the `lstStates.Items.Clear()` statement, then press **Enter**. The procedure should sort the array values in descending order and then display the values in the lstStates control. Enter the following lines of code.

Array.Sort(strStates)
Array.Reverse(strStates)
For Each strName As String In strStates
lstStates.Items.Add(strName)
Next strName

7. Save the solution. Figure 9-20 shows most of the application's code.

```
Public Class frmMain

    ' module-level array
    Private strStates(4) As String

    Private Sub btnExit_Click...

    Private Sub btnEnter_Click(ByVal sender As Object, _
        ByVal e As System.EventArgs) Handles btnEnter.Click
        ' allows the user to enter five state names
        ' stores the state names in the module-level
        ' strStates array

        lstStates.Items.Clear()

        For intSub As Integer = 0 To strStates.Length - 1
            strStates(intSub) = _
                InputBox("State name", "State Names")
        Next intSub
    End Sub

    Private Sub btnAscending_Click(ByVal sender As Object, _
        ByVal e As System.EventArgs) Handles btnAscending.Click
        ' sorts the array values in ascending order, then
        ' displays them in the lstStates control

        lstStates.Items.Clear()
```

Figure 9-20 Most of the State application's code *(continues)*

(continued)

```
        Array.Sort(strStates)
        For Each strName As String In strStates
            lstStates.Items.Add(strName)
        Next strName
    End Sub

    Private Sub btnDescending_Click(ByVal sender As Object, _
        ByVal e As System.EventArgs) Handles btnDescending.Click
        ' sorts the array values in descending order, then
        ' displays them in the lstStates control

        lstStates.Items.Clear()

        Array.Sort(strStates)
        Array.Reverse(strStates)
        For Each strName As String In strStates
            lstStates.Items.Add(strName)
        Next strName
    End Sub
End Class
```

Figure 9-20 Most of the State application's code

To test the State application:

1. Save the solution, if necessary, then start the application. Click the **Enter State Names** button. Type the following state names in the State Names dialog box, pressing **Enter** after typing each name: **Kentucky**, **Tennessee**, **Alaska**, **New York**, and **Idaho**.
2. Click the **Ascending Sort** button. The application displays the state names in ascending order. See Figure 9-21.

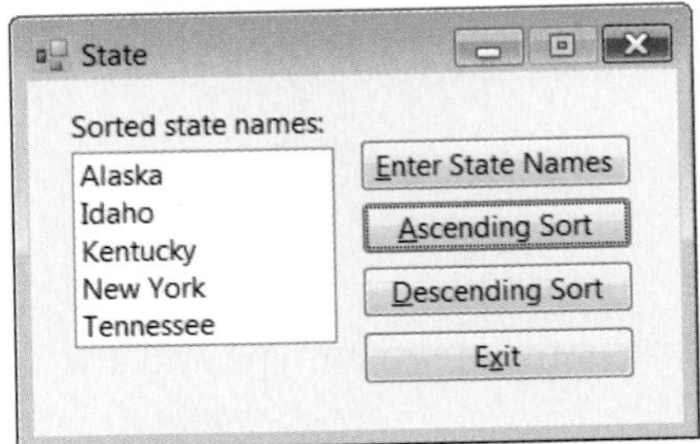

Figure 9-21 Interface showing the state names in ascending order

3. Click the **Descending Sort** button. The application displays the state names in descending order. Click the **Exit** button. Close the Code Editor window, then close the solution.

Lesson A Summary

- **To declare a one-dimensional array:**

  Use either of the following versions of the syntax. The *highestSubscript* argument in Version 1 is an integer that specifies the highest subscript in the array. Using Version 1's syntax, the computer automatically initializes the array elements. The *initialValues* section in Version 2 is a list of values separated by commas and enclosed in braces. The values are used to initialize each element in the array.

  Version 1: {**Dim** | **Private**} *arrayName*(*highestSubscript*) **As** *dataType*
  Version 2: {**Dim** | **Private**} *arrayName*() **As** *dataType* = {*initialValues*}

- **To process instructions for each element in a group:**

  Use the For Each...Next statement. The statement's syntax is shown in Figure 9-7.

- **To refer to an element in an array:**

  Use the array's name followed by the element's subscript, which is enclosed in a set of parentheses following the array name.

- **To determine the number of elements in a one-dimensional array:**

  Use the array's Length property in the following syntax: *arrayName*.**Length**.

- **To sort the elements in a one-dimensional array in ascending order:**

  Use the Array.Sort method. The method's syntax is **Array.Sort(***arrayName***)**.

- **To reverse the order of the elements in a one-dimensional array:**

  Use the Array.Reverse method. The method's syntax is **Array.Reverse(***arrayName***)**.

Lesson A Key Terms

Array—a group of variables that have the same name and data type and are related in some way

Array.Reverse method—reverses the order of the elements in a one-dimensional array

Array.Sort method—sorts the elements in a one-dimensional array in ascending order

For Each...Next statement—the Visual Basic statement used to code a loop whose instructions you want processed for each element in a group

Length property—stores the number of elements contained in an array

One-dimensional array—an array whose elements are identified by a unique number (subscript)

Populating the array—refers to the process of assigning the initial values to an array

Runtime error—an error that occurs while an application is running

Sorting—the process of arranging data in a specific order

Subscript—an integer that indicates the position of an element in an array

Lesson A Review Questions

1. Which of the following declares a 5-element, one-dimensional array?

   a. `Dim dblAmounts(4) As Double`

   b. `Dim dblAmounts(5) As Double`

   c. `Dim dblAmounts(4) As Double = {3.55, 6.70, 8, 4, 2.34}`

   d. Both a and c.

2. The `strItems` array is declared using the `Dim strItems(20) As String` statement. The `intSub` variable keeps track of the array subscripts and is initialized to 0. Which of the following Do clauses will process the loop instructions for each element in the array?

   a. `Do While intSub > 20`

   b. `Do While intSub < 20`

   c. `Do While intSub >= 20`

   d. `Do While intSub <= 20`

3. The `intSales` array was declared as follows: `Dim intSales() As Integer = {10000, 12000, 900, 500, 20000}`. The statement `intSales(3) = intSales(3) + 10` will ________________________.

   a. replace the 500 amount with 10

   b. replace the 500 amount with 510

   c. replace the 900 amount with 10

   d. replace the 900 amount with 910

4. The `intSales` array was declared as follows: `Dim intSales() As Integer = {10000, 12000, 900, 500, 20000}`. Which of the following If clauses can be used to determine whether the `intSub` variable contains a valid subscript for the array?

   a. `If intSales(intSub) >= 0 AndAlso intSales(intSub) < 4 Then`

   b. `If intSales(intSub) >= 0 AndAlso intSales(intSub) <= 4 Then`

   c. `If intSub >= 0 AndAlso intSub < 4 Then`

   d. `If intSub >= 0 AndAlso intSub <= 4 Then`

5. The `intSales` array was declared as follows: `Dim intSales() As Integer = {10000, 12000, 900, 500, 20000}`. Which of the following loops will correctly add 100 to each array element? The `intSub` variable contains the number 0 before the loops are processed.

   a.
   ```
   Do While intSub <= 4
       intSub = intSub + 100
   Loop
   ```

   b.
   ```
   Do While intSub <= 4
       intSales = intSales + 100
   Loop
   ```

   c.
   ```
   Do While intSub < 5
       intSales(intSub) = intSales(intSub) + 100
   Loop
   ```

   d. None of the above.

6. The `intNums` array was declared as follows: `Dim intNums() As Integer = {10, 5, 7, 2}`. Which of the following blocks of code will correctly calculate the average value stored in the array? The `intTotal`, `intSub`, and `dblAvg` variables contain the number 0 before the loops are processed.

   a.
   ```
   Do While intSub < 4
       intNums(intSub) = intTotal + intTotal
       intSub = intSub + 1
   Loop
   dblAvg = intTotal / intSub
   ```

   b.
   ```
   Do While intSub < 4
       intTotal = intTotal + intNums(intSub)
       intSub = intSub + 1
   Loop
   dblAvg = intTotal / intSub
   ```

   c.
   ```
   Do While intSub < 4
       intTotal = intTotal + intNums(intSub)
       intSub = intSub + 1
   Loop
   dblAvg = intTotal / intSub - 1
   ```

   d.
   ```
   Do While intSub < 4
       intTotal = intTotal + intNums(intSub)
       intSub = intSub + 1
   Loop
   dblAvg = intTotal / (intSub - 1)
   ```

7. The code in Question 6's answer a will assign ____________________ to the `dblAvg` variable.

   a. 0
   b. 5
   c. 6
   d. 8

8. The code in Question 6's answer b will assign ____________________________ to the `dblAvg` variable.

   a. 0 b. 5
   c. 6 d. 8

9. The code in Question 6's answer c will assign ____________________________ to the `dblAvg` variable.

   a. 0 b. 5
   c. 6 d. 8

10. The code in Question 6's answer d will assign ____________________________ to the `dblAvg` variable.

    a. 0 b. 5
    c. 6 d. 8

11. Which of the following statements sorts the `intQuantities` array in ascending order?
    a. `Array.Sort(intQuantities)`
    b. `intQuantities.Sort`
    c. `Sort(intQuantities)`
    d. `SortArray(intQuantities)`

12. Which of the following statements assigns to the `intElements` variable the number of elements contained in the `intNums` array?
    a. `intElements = Len(intNums)`
    b. `intElements = Length(intNums)`
    c. `intElements = intNums.Len`
    d. `intElements = intNums.Length`

13. Which of the following assigns the string "Rover" to the fifth element in a one-dimensional array named `strPetNames`?
    a. `strPetNames(4) = "Rover"`
    b. `strPetNames[4] = "Rover"`
    c. `strPetNames(5) = "Rover"`
    d. `strPetNames.Items.Add(5) = "Rover"`

Lesson A Exercises

INTRODUCTORY

1. Write the statement to declare a procedure-level one-dimensional array named `intNumbers`. The array should be able to store 20 integers. Then write the statement to store the number 7 in the second element.

INTRODUCTORY

2. Write the statement to declare a module-level one-dimensional array named `strProducts`. The array should be able to store 10 strings. Then write the statement to store the string "Paper" in the third element.

INTRODUCTORY

3. Write the statement to declare and initialize a procedure-level one-dimensional array named `dblRates`. Use the following numbers to initialize the array: 6.5, 8.3, 4, 2, 10.5.

INTRODUCTORY

4. Write the code to display the contents of the `dblRates` array from Exercise 3 in the lstRates control. Use the For...Next statement.

INTRODUCTORY

5. Rewrite the code from Exercise 4 using the Do...Loop statement.

INTRODUCTORY

6. Rewrite the code from Exercise 4 using the For Each...Next statement.

INTRODUCTORY

7. Write the statement to sort the `dblRates` array in ascending order.

INTRODUCTORY

8. Write the statement to reverse the contents of the `dblRates` array.

INTRODUCTORY

9. In this exercise, you modify one of the Months applications coded in the lesson. Use Windows to make a copy of the Months Solution folder, which is contained in the VB2008\Chap09 folder. Rename the folder Months Solution-DoLoop. Open the Months Solution (Months Solution.sln) file contained in the VB2008\Chap09\Months Solution-DoLoop folder. Open the designer window, then open the Code Editor window. Replace the For...Next statement in the form's Load event procedure with a Do...Loop statement. Save the solution, then start and test the application. Stop the application. Close the Code Editor window, then close the solution.

INTRODUCTORY

10. In this exercise, you modify the Salary Code application coded in the lesson. Use Windows to make a copy of the Salary Code Solution folder, which is contained in the VB2008\Chap09 folder. Rename the folder Modified Salary Code Solution. Open the Salary Code Solution (Salary Code Solution.sln) file contained in the VB2008\Chap09\Modified Salary Code Solution folder. Open the designer window, then open the Code Editor window. Change the salary for code 6 to 82,000. In addition, add a new code 7, which is associated with a salary of 90,500. Modify the code to accommodate these changes. Save the solution, then start and test the application. Stop the application. Close the Code Editor window, then close the solution.

INTRODUCTORY

11. In this exercise, you modify the Sales application coded in the lesson. Use Windows to make a copy of the Sales Solution folder, which is contained in the VB2008\Chap09 folder. Rename the folder Sales Solution-ForEach. Open the Sales Solution (Sales Solution.sln) file contained in the VB2008\Chap09\Sales Solution-ForEach folder. Open the designer window, then open the Code Editor window. Replace the For...Next statement in the btnSearch control's Click event procedure with a For Each...Next statement. Save the solution, then start and test the application. Stop the application. Close the Code Editor window, then close the solution.

INTERMEDIATE

12. Write the code to multiply by 3 the number stored in the first element of a one-dimensional array named `intNumbers`. Store the result in the `intTripleNum` variable.

INTERMEDIATE

13. Write the code to add together the numbers stored in the first and second elements of a one-dimensional array named `intNumbers`. Display the sum in the lblSum control.

INTERMEDIATE

14. Write two versions of the code to subtract the number 1 from each element in a 5-element, one-dimensional Integer array named `intQuantities`. First use the Do...Loop statement, then rewrite the code using the For...Next statement.

INTERMEDIATE

15. In this exercise, you modify the Average application coded in the lesson. Use Windows to make a copy of the Average Solution folder, which is contained in the VB2008\Chap09 folder. Rename the folder Modified Average Solution. Open the Average Solution (Average Solution.sln) file contained in the VB2008\Chap09\Modified Average Solution folder. Open the designer window, then open the Code Editor window.

    a. Type an apostrophe at the beginning of the array declaration line in the btnCalc control's Click event procedure; this makes the line a comment. Click the blank line above the comment, then type `Dim intScores() As Integer = {}`. Save the solution, then start and test the application. What appears in the lblAvg control when the array does not contain any values? Stop the application.

    b. Modify the code so that it displays 0 as the average, and also displays the "There are no test scores." message in a message box, when the array is empty. Save the solution, then start and test the application. Stop the application.

    c. Delete the `Dim intScores() As Integer = {}` line from the btnCalc control's Click event procedure, then delete the apostrophe from the array declaration line. Save the solution, then start and test the application. Stop the application. Close the Code Editor window, then close the solution.

INTERMEDIATE

16. Open the Lowest Solution (Lowest Solution.sln) file, which is contained in the VB2008\Chap09\Lowest Solution-ForNext folder. If necessary, open the designer window. Open the Code Editor window. Locate the btnDisplay control's Click event procedure. The procedure declares and initializes a 20-element, one-dimensional Integer array named `intScores`. Code the procedure to display the lowest score contained in the array. Use the For...Next statement. Save the solution, then start and test the application. Stop the application. Close the Code Editor window, then close the solution.

INTERMEDIATE

17. In this exercise, you modify the application from Exercise 16. Use Windows to make a copy of the Lowest Solution-ForNext folder, which is contained in the VB2008\Chap09 folder. Rename the folder Lowest Solution-ForEachNext. Open the Lowest Solution (Lowest Solution.sln) file contained in the VB2008\Chap09\Lowest Solution-ForEachNext folder. Open the designer window, then open the Code Editor window. Replace the For...Next statement in the btnDisplay control's Click event procedure with a For Each...Next statement. Save the solution, then start and test the application. Stop the application. Close the Code Editor window, then close the solution.

INTERMEDIATE

18. In this exercise, you modify the application from Exercise 16. Use Windows to make a copy of the Lowest Solution-ForNext folder, which is contained in the VB2008\Chap09 folder. Rename the folder Lowest Solution-DoLoop. Open the Lowest Solution (Lowest Solution.sln) file contained in the VB2008\Chap09\Lowest Solution-DoLoop folder. Open the designer window, then open the Code Editor window. Replace the For...Next statement in the btnDisplay control's Click event procedure with a Do...Loop statement. Save the solution, then start and test the application. Stop the application. Close the Code Editor window, then close the solution.

INTERMEDIATE

19. Open the Update Prices Solution (Update Prices Solution.sln) file, which is contained in the VB2008\Chap09\Update Prices Solution folder. If necessary, open the designer window. Open the Code Editor window, then open the code template for the btnIncrease control's Click event procedure. Declare a one-dimensional Double array named `dblPrices`. Initialize the array using the following 10 prices: 6.75, 12.50, 33.50, 10, 9.50, 25.50, 7.65, 8.35, 9.75, and 3.50. The procedure should ask the user for a percentage amount by which each price should be increased. It then should increase each price by that amount, and then display the increased prices in the list box. (Hint: You can clear the contents of a list box using the Items collection's Clear method.) Save the solution, then start the application. Click the Increase button. Increase each price by 5%. Stop the application. Close the Code Editor window, then close the solution.

20. In this exercise, you modify the application from Exercise 19. The modified application allows the user to update a specific price. Use Windows to make a copy of the Update Prices Solution folder, which is contained in the VB2008\Chap09 folder. Rename the folder Modified Update Prices Solution. Open the Update Prices Solution (Update Prices Solution.sln) file contained in the VB2008\Chap09\Modified Update Prices Solution folder. Open the designer window, then open the Code Editor window. Modify the btnIncrease control's Click event procedure so it also asks the user to enter a number from 1 through 10. If the user enters the number 1, the procedure should update the first price in the array. If the user enters the number 2, the procedure should update the second price in the array, and so on. Save the solution, then start the application. Click the Increase button. Increase the second price by 10%. Click the Increase button again. This time, increase the tenth price by 5%. (The second price in the list box should still reflect the 10% increase.) Stop the application. Close the Code Editor window, then close the solution. ADVANCED

21. In this exercise, you code an application that displays the number of students earning a specific score. Open the Scores Solution (Scores Solution.sln) file, which is contained in the VB2008\Chap09\Scores Solution folder. If necessary, open the designer window. Open the Code Editor window, then open the code template for the btnDisplay control's Click event procedure. Declare a 20-element, one-dimensional Integer array named `intScores`. Assign the following 20 numbers to the array: 88, 72, 99, 20, 66, 95, 99, 100, 72, 88, 78, 45, 57, 89, 85, 78, 75, 88, 72, and 88. Code the procedure so that it prompts the user to enter a score from 0 through 100. The procedure then should display (in a message box) the number of students who earned that score. Save the solution, then start the application. Use the application to answer the following questions: How many students earned a score of 72? How many students earned a score of 88? How many students earned a score of 20? How many students earned a score of 99? Stop the application. Close the Code Editor window, then close the solution. ADVANCED

22. In this exercise, you modify the application from Exercise 21. The modified application allows the user to display the number of students earning a score within a specific range. Use Windows to make a copy of the Scores Solution folder, which is contained in the VB2008\Chap09 folder. Rename the folder Modified Scores Solution. Open the Scores Solution (Scores Solution.sln) file contained in the VB2008\Chap09\Modified Scores Solution folder. Open the designer window, then open the Code Editor window. Modify the btnDisplay control's Click event procedure to prompt the user to enter both a minimum score and a maximum score. The procedure then should display (in a message box) the number of students who earned a score within that range. Save the solution, then start the application. Use the application to answer the following questions. How many students earned a score from 70 through 79? How many students earned a score from 65 through 85? How many students earned a score from 0 through 50? Stop the application. Close the Code Editor window, then close the solution. ADVANCED

ADVANCED

23. In this exercise, you code an application that generates and displays six unique random numbers for a lottery game. Each lottery number can range from 1 through 54 only. Open the Lottery Game Solution (Lottery Game Solution.sln) file, which is contained in the VB2008\Chap09\Lottery Game Solution folder. If necessary, open the designer window. Open the Code Editor window, then open the code template for the btnDisplay control's Click event procedure. Code the procedure so that it displays six unique random numbers in the interface. (Hint: Store the numbers in a one-dimensional array.) Save the solution, then start the application. Click the Display Lottery Numbers button several times. Each time you click the button, six unique random numbers between 1 and 54 (inclusive) should appear in the interface. Stop the application. Close the Code Editor window, then close the solution.

Discovery

24. Research the Visual Basic ReDim statement. What is the purpose of the statement? What is the purpose of the `Preserve` keyword? Open the ReDim Solution (ReDim Solution.sln) file, which is contained in the VB2008\Chap09\ReDim Solution folder. If necessary, open the designer window. Open the Code Editor window. Review the code contained in the btnGetDisplay control's Click event procedure. Modify the procedure to store any number of sales amounts in the `intSales` array. (Hint: Declare the array using empty sets of parentheses and braces. Use the ReDim statement to add an element to the array.) Save the solution, then start the application. Click the Get/Display Sales button, then enter the following sales amounts (one at a time): 700, 550, and 800. Click the Cancel button. The btnGetDisplay control's Click event procedure should display each sales amount in the list box. Click the Get/Display Sales button again, then enter the following sales amounts: 5, 9, 45, 67, 8, and 0. Click the Cancel button. The btnGetDisplay control's Click event procedure should display each sales amount in the list box. Stop the application. Close the Code Editor window, then close the solution.

LESSON B

After studying Lesson B, you should be able to:

- Create and manipulate parallel one-dimensional arrays
- Locate information in two parallel one-dimensional arrays
- Declare and initialize a two-dimensional array
- Store data in a two-dimensional array
- Search a two-dimensional array
- Determine the highest subscript in a two-dimensional array

Parallel One-Dimensional Arrays

Recall that your task in this chapter is to create an application for Takoda Tapahe, the owner of a small gift shop named Treasures. The application should allow Takoda to enter a product ID. It then should display the product's price. Figure 9-22 shows a portion of the gift shop's price list.

Product ID	Price
BX35	13
CR20	10
FE15	12
KW10	24
MM67	4

Figure 9-22 A portion of the gift shop's price list

Recall that all of the variables in an array have the same data type. So how can you store a price list, which includes a string (the product ID) and a number (the price), in an array? One solution is to use two one-dimensional arrays: a String array to store the product IDs and an Integer array to store the prices. Both arrays, referred to as parallel arrays, are illustrated in Figure 9-23. **Parallel arrays** are two or more arrays whose elements are related by their position in the arrays; in other words, they are related by their subscript. The `strIds` and `intPrices` arrays are parallel because each element in the `strIds` array corresponds to the element located in the same position in the `intPrices` array. For example, the item whose product ID is BX35 [`strIds(0)`] has a price of $13 [`intPrices(0)`]. Likewise, the item whose product ID is CR20 [`strIds(1)`] has a price of $10 [`intPrices(1)`]. The same relationship is true for the remaining elements in both arrays. To determine an item's price, you locate the item's ID in the `strIds` array and then view its corresponding element in the `intPrices` array.

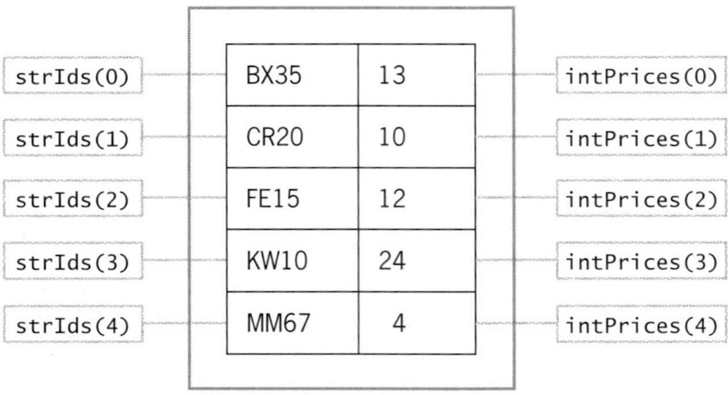

Figure 9-23 Illustration of a price list stored in two parallel one-dimensional arrays

To code the Price List application:

1. If necessary, start Visual Studio 2008 or Visual Basic 2008 Express Edition. Close the Start Page window.

2. Open the **Price List Solution** (**Price List Solution.sln**) file, which is contained in the VB2008\Chap09\Price List Solution-Parallel folder. If necessary, open the designer window. The text box's CharacterCasing and MaxLength properties are set to Upper and 4, respectively. Recall from Chapter 4 that when a text box's CharacterCasing property is set to Upper, any letters the user types will appear in uppercase. When a text box's MaxLength property is set to 4, the user can enter a maximum of four characters in the text box.

3. Open the Code Editor window. Replace the <your name> and <current date> text in the comments with your name and the current date.

4. Locate the btnDisplay control's Click event procedure. First, declare and initialize the two parallel one-dimensional arrays. Click the **blank line** above the `' assign the ID to a variable` comment, then enter the following declaration statements. Be sure to include a space before the line continuation character.

   Dim strIds() As String = _
   {"BX35", "CR20", "FE15", "KW10", "MM67"}
   Dim intPrices() As Integer = {13, 10, 12, 24, 4}

5. The procedure will use a String variable to store the product ID entered by the user. It also will use an Integer variable to keep track of the array subscripts while the array is being searched. Enter the following two declaration statements.

   Dim strSearchForId As String
   Dim intSubscript As Integer

6. Now assign the product ID entered by the user to the `strSearchForId` variable. Click the **blank line** below the `' assign the ID to a variable` comment, then type **strSearchForId = txtId.Text** and press **Enter**.

7. Next, you will use a loop to search each element in the `strIds` array, stopping either when the end of the array is reached or when the ID

is located in the array. Click the **blank line** below the `' the array or the ID is found` comment. Type the following lines of code. Be sure to include a space before the line continuation character.

```
Do Until intSubscript = strIds.Length _
    OrElse strSearchForId = strIds(intSubscript)
    intSubscript = intSubscript + 1
Loop
```

8. Now determine why the loop ended. You can do this using a selection structure whose condition compares the value stored in the `intSubscript` variable with the value stored in the `strIds` array's Length property. If the variable's value is less than the number of array elements, the loop ended because the ID was located in the array. In that case, the selection structure's true path should display the price located in the same position in the `intPrices` array. On the other hand, if the variable's value is not less than the number of array elements, the loop ended because it reached the end of the array without finding the ID. In that case, the selection structure's false path should display the "Invalid ID" message in a message box. Click the **blank line** below the `' determine whether the ID was found` comment, then enter the following lines of code. Be sure to include a space before each line continuation character.

```
If intSubscript < strIds.Length Then
    lblPrice.Text = intPrices(intSubscript).ToString("C0")
Else
    MessageBox.Show("Invalid ID", _
                    "Treasures Gift Shop", _
                    MessageBoxButtons.OK, _
                    MessageBoxIcon.Information)
End If
```

9. Save the solution. Figure 9-24 shows the btnDisplay control's Click event procedure.

```
Private Sub btnDisplay_Click(ByVal sender As Object, _
     ByVal e As System.EventArgs) Handles btnDisplay.Click
     ' displays the price associated with an ID

     Dim strIds() As String = _
         {"BX35", "CR20", "FE15", "KW10", "MM67"}
     Dim intPrices() As Integer = {13, 10, 12, 24, 4}
     Dim strSearchForId As String
     Dim intSubscript As Integer

     ' assign the ID to a variable
     strSearchForId = txtId.Text

     ' search the strIds array for the ID
     ' continue searching until the end of
     ' the array or the ID is found
     Do Until intSubscript = strIds.Length _
         OrElse strSearchForId = strIds(intSubscript)
         intSubscript = intSubscript + 1
     Loop
```

parallel one-dimensional array declarations

searches for the ID in the `strIds` array

Figure 9-24 btnDisplay control's Click event procedure using parallel one-dimensional arrays *(continues)*

(continued)

```
        ' determine whether the ID was found
        If intSubscript < strIds.Length Then
            lblPrice.Text = intPrices(intSubscript).ToString("C0")
        Else
            MessageBox.Show("Invalid ID", _
                            "Treasures Gift Shop", _
                            MessageBoxButtons.OK, _
                            MessageBoxIcon.Information)
        End If

        txtId.Focus()
    End Sub
```

displays the corresponding price from the intPrices array

Figure 9-24 btnDisplay control's Click event procedure using parallel one-dimensional arrays

To test the Price List application:

1. Save the solution, if necessary, then start the application. Type **cr20** in the Product ID box, then click the **Display Price** button. A price of $10 appears in the Price box. See Figure 9-25.

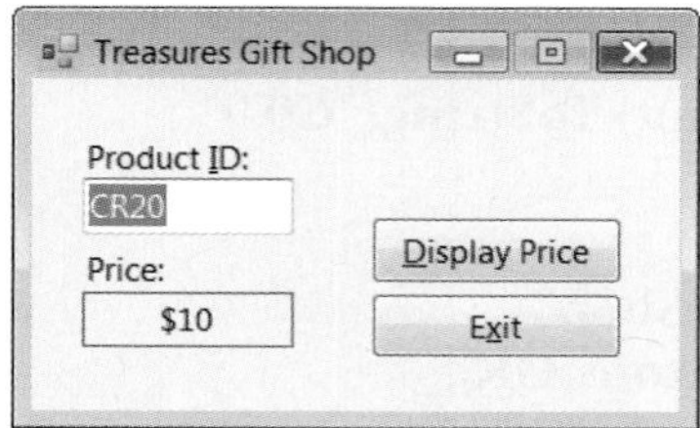

Figure 9-25 Interface showing the price for product ID CR20

2. Type **xx44** in the Product ID box, then click the **Display Price** button. The "Invalid ID" message appears in a message box. Close the message box.

3. On your own, test the application using other valid and invalid IDs. When you are finished testing the application, click the **Exit** button. Close the Code Editor window, then close the solution.

Two-Dimensional Arrays

Unlike a one-dimensional array, which you can visualize as a column of variables, a **two-dimensional array** resembles a table in that the variables (elements) are in rows and columns. Each element in a two-dimensional array is identified by a unique combination of two subscripts that the computer assigns to the element when the array is created. The subscripts specify the element's row and column position in the array. Elements located in the first row in a two-dimensional array are assigned a row subscript of 0. Elements in the second row are assigned a row subscript of 1, and so on. Similarly, elements located in the first column in a two-dimensional array are assigned a column subscript of 0. Elements in the second column are assigned a column subscript of 1, and so on. You refer to each element in a two-dimensional array by the array's name and the element's row and column subscripts, which are separated by a comma and specified in a set of parentheses immediately following the array name. To refer to the element located in the first row, first column in a two-dimensional array named `strProducts`, you use `strProducts(0, 0)`—read "strProducts sub zero comma zero." You use `strProducts(1, 2)` to refer to the element located in the second row, third column in the array. Figure 9-26 illustrates this naming convention. Notice that the row subscript is listed first within the parentheses.

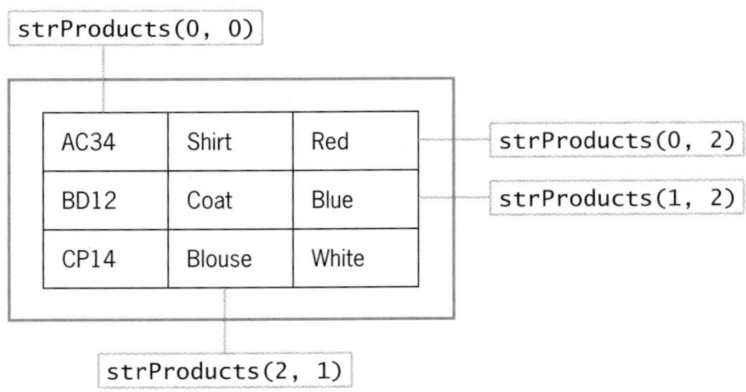

Figure 9-26 Names of some of the elements in the `strProducts` array

Figure 9-27 shows two versions of the syntax for declaring a two-dimensional array in Visual Basic. In each version, *arrayName* is the name of the array and *dataType* is the type of data the array variables will store. In Version 1's syntax, *highestRowSubscript* and *highestColumnSubscript* are integers that specify the highest row and column subscripts in the array. When the array is created, it will contain one row more than the number specified in the *highestRowSubscript* argument and one column more than the number specified in the *highestColumnSubscript* argument. This is because the first row subscript in a two-dimensional array is 0, and so is the first column subscript. When you declare a two-dimensional array using the syntax shown in Version 1, the computer automatically initializes each element in the array when the array is created. Compare Version 1's syntax with Version 2's syntax. Notice that a comma appears within the parentheses that follow the array name in Version 2. The comma indicates that the array is a two-dimensional array. (Recall that a comma is used to separate the row subscript from the column subscript in a two-dimensional array.) You can use Version 2's syntax to specify each variable's initial value when the array is created. You do this by including a separate *initialValues* section, enclosed in braces, for each row in the array. If the array has two rows, then the statement that declares and initializes the array should have two *initialValues* sections. If the array has five rows, then the declaration statement should have five *initialValues* sections. Within the individual *initialValues* sections, you enter one or more values separated by commas. The number of values to enter corresponds to the number of columns in the array. If the array contains 10 columns, then each individual *initialValues* section should contain 10 values. In addition to the set of braces enclosing each individual *initialValues* section, Version 2's syntax also requires all of the *initialValues* sections to be enclosed in a set of braces. Also included in Figure 9-27 are examples of using both syntax versions.

Declaring a two-dimensional array

Syntax - Version 1
{**Dim** | **Private**} *arrayName*(*highestRowSubscript*, *highestColumnSubscript*) **As** *dataType*

Syntax - Version 2
{**Dim** | **Private**} *arrayName*(,) **As** *dataType* = {{*initialValues*},...{*initialValues*}}

Example 1
```
Dim strCities(5, 3) As String
```
declares a 6-row, 4-column array named `strCities`; each element is automatically initialized using the keyword `Nothing`

Example 2
```
Dim intScores(,) As Integer = {{75, 90}, {9, 25}, {23, 56}, {6, 12}}
```
declares and initializes a 4-row, 2-column array named `intScores`; initializes `intScores(0, 0)` to 75, `intScores(0, 1)` to 90, `intScores(1, 0)` to 9, `intScores(1, 1)` to 25, `intScores(2, 0)` to 23, `intScores(2, 1)` to 56, `intScores(3, 0)` to 6, and `intScores(3, 1)` to 12

Figure 9-27 Syntax and examples of declaring a two-dimensional array

After a two-dimensional array is declared, you can use another statement (such as an assignment statement or a statement that contains the TryParse method) to store a different value in an array element. Figure 9-28 shows examples of such statements.

Storing data in a two-dimensional array

Example 1
```
strCities(0, 1) = "Paris"
```
assigns the string "Paris" to the element located in the first row, second column in the `strCities` array

Example 2
```
For intRow As Integer = 0 To 3
   For intColumn As Integer = 0 To 1
      intScores(intRow, intColumn) = 0
   Next intColumn
Next intRow
```
assigns the number 0 to each element in the `intScores` array

Figure 9-28 Examples of statements used to store data in a two-dimensional array

Searching a Two-Dimensional Array

Earlier in this lesson, you coded an application created for the Treasures gift shop. The application stores the gift shop's price list in two parallel one-dimensional arrays: a String array for the product IDs and an Integer array for the prices. It then searches the String array for the ID entered by the user. If the ID is in the array, the application displays its corresponding price from the Integer array; otherwise, it displays an appropriate message in a message box. Instead of using two parallel one-dimensional arrays for the price list, you can use a two-dimensional array. To do this, you store the product IDs in the first column of the array, and store the prices in the second column. However, you will need to treat the prices as strings, because all of the data in a two-dimensional array must have the same data type.

To use a two-dimensional array in the Price List application:

1. Use Windows to make a copy of the Price List Solution-Parallel folder, which is contained in the VB2008\Chap09 folder. Rename the folder Price List Solution-TwoDimensional.
2. Open the **Price List Solution** (**Price List Solution.sln**) file contained in the VB2008\Chap09\Price List Solution-TwoDimensional folder. Open the designer window.
3. Open the Code Editor window, then locate the btnDisplay control's Click event procedure. First, you will replace the two one-dimensional arrays with a two-dimensional array. Delete the two statements that declare the one-dimensional arrays, then enter the two-dimensional array declaration statement shown in Figure 9-29.

```
Private Sub btnDisplay_Click(ByVal sender As Object, ByVal e As System
    ' displays the price associated with an ID

    Dim strProducts(,) As String = {{"BX35", "13"}, _
                                    {"CR20", "10"}, _
                                    {"FE15", "12"}, _
                                    {"KW10", "24"}, _
                                    {"MM67", "4"}}
    Dim strSearchForId As String
    Dim intSubscript As Integer
```

replace the first two Dim statements with this Dim statement

Figure 9-29 Two-dimensional array declaration statement entered in the procedure

4. Now change the `Dim intSubscript As Integer` statement in the procedure to **Dim intRowSubscript As Integer**.
5. Click **Edit** on the menu bar, then click **Quick Replace** to open the Find and Replace dialog box. Type **intSubscript** in the Find what box, then type **intRowSubscript** in the Replace with box. Click the **Replace All** button. If the message "6 occurrence(s) replaced." appears in a message box, click the **OK** button to close the message box. Close the Find and Replace dialog box.
6. Change the `' search the strIds array for the ID` comment to **' search the strProducts array for the ID**, then save the solution.

Now you need to modify the Do clause to search the first column in the `strProducts` array, rather than the `strIds` array. However, because the Length property of a two-dimensional array stores the total number of elements in the array, you will need to use the GetUpperBound method to determine the number of rows in the first column of the array.

The GetUpperBound Method

An array's **GetUpperBound method** returns an integer that indicates the highest subscript in the specified dimension in the array. Figure 9-30 shows the method's syntax and includes examples of using the method. In the syntax, *arrayName* is the name of the array, and *dimension* is an integer that specifies the dimension whose upper or lower bound you want to retrieve. In a one-dimensional array, the *dimension* argument will always be 0. In a two-dimensional array, however, the *dimension* argument will be either 0 or 1. The 0 represents the row dimension, and the 1 represents the column dimension.

GetUpperBound method

Syntax
arrayName.**GetUpperBound(***dimension***)**

Example 1
```
Dim strCities(5, 3) As String
intHighestRowSubscript = strCities.GetUpperBound(0)
intHighestColumnSubscript = strCities.GetUpperBound(1)
```
assigns the number 5 to the `intHighestRowSubscript` variable, and assigns the number 3 to the `intHighestColumnSubscript`

Example 2
```
Dim intScores(,) As Integer = {{75, 90}, {9, 25}, {23, 56}, {6, 12}}
intHighestRowSubscript = intScores.GetUpperBound(0)
intHighestColumnSubscript = intScores.GetUpperBound(1)
```
assigns the number 3 to the `intHighestRowSubscript` variable, and assigns the number 1 to the `intHighestColumnSubscript`

Example 3
```
Dim dblSales() As Double = {4.5, 6.3, 10.2}
intHighestSubscript = dblSales.GetUpperBound(0)
```
assigns the number 2 to the `intHighestSubscript` variable

Figure 9-30 Syntax and examples of the GetUpperBound method

To continue modifying the btnDisplay control's Click event procedure:

1. First, make the necessary modifications to the loop's Do clause. Change = `strIds.Length` in the Do clause to **> strProducts.GetUpperBound(0)**. (Be sure to replace the = with >.) Also change `strIds(intRowSubscript)` in the Do clause to **strProducts(intRowSubscript, 0)**. This change tells the computer to search for the ID in the first column of the `strProducts` array.
2. Now modify the selection structure's If clause. Change < `strIds.Length` in the If clause to **<= strProducts.GetUpperBound(0)**.
3. Finally, replace the `lblPrice.Text = intPrices(intRowSubscript).ToString("C0")` statement in the selection structure's true path with the following three lines of code. The TryParse method in the code will assign to the `intPrice` variable the value stored in the second column of the current row in the array. You are assigning the value to a numeric variable so that you can use the ToString method to format the value with a dollar sign and no decimal places. (Recall that the ToString method is used with numeric variables.)

   Dim intPrice As Integer
   Integer.TryParse(strProducts(intRowSubscript, 1), intPrice)
   lblPrice.Text = intPrice.ToString("C0")

4. Save the solution. Figure 9-31 shows the code entered in the btnDisplay control's Click event procedure. The modifications you made to the original code (shown earlier in Figure 9-24) are shaded in the figure.

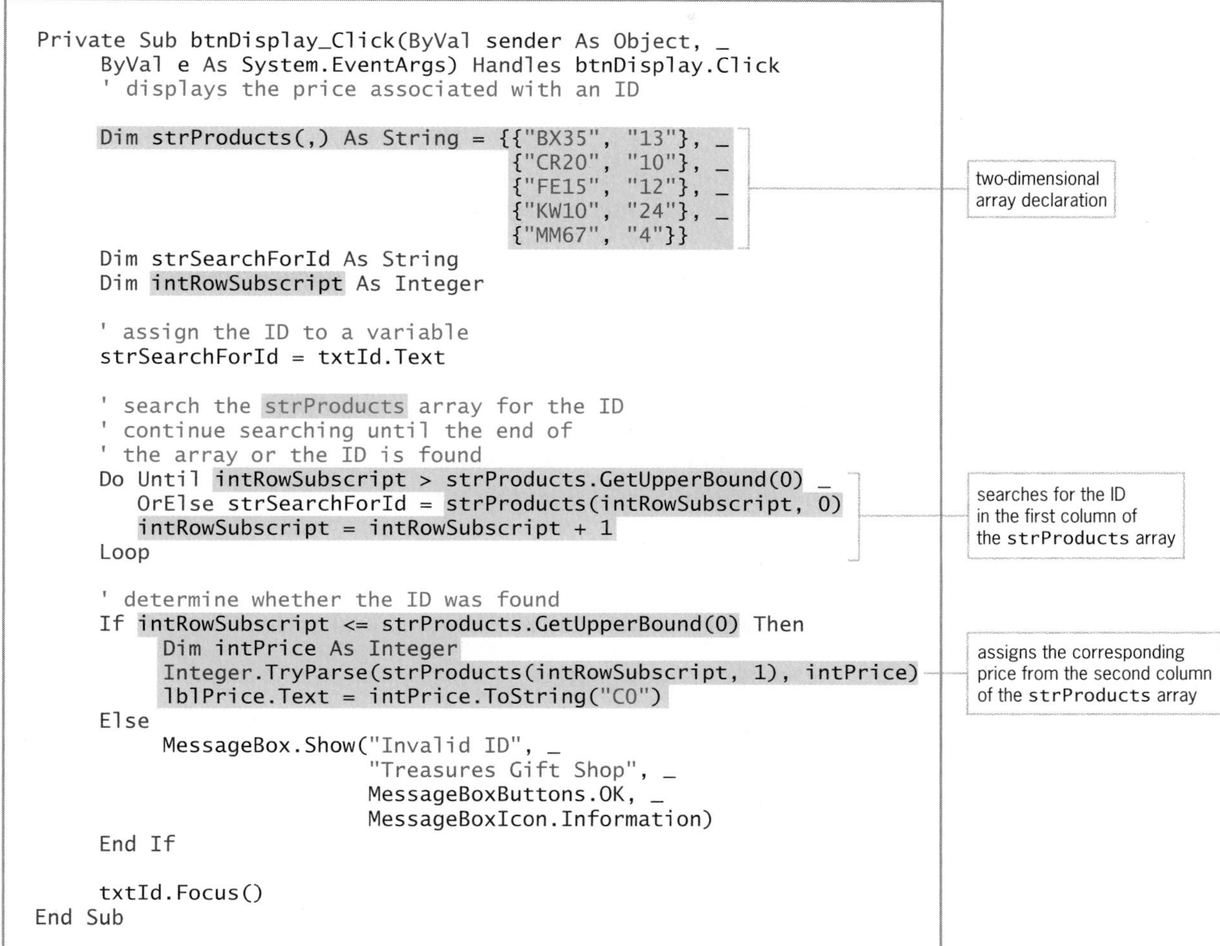

```
Private Sub btnDisplay_Click(ByVal sender As Object, _
     ByVal e As System.EventArgs) Handles btnDisplay.Click
     ' displays the price associated with an ID

     Dim strProducts(,) As String = {{"BX35", "13"}, _
                                      {"CR20", "10"}, _
                                      {"FE15", "12"}, _
                                      {"KW10", "24"}, _
                                      {"MM67", "4"}}
     Dim strSearchForId As String
     Dim intRowSubscript As Integer

     ' assign the ID to a variable
     strSearchForId = txtId.Text

     ' search the strProducts array for the ID
     ' continue searching until the end of
     ' the array or the ID is found
     Do Until intRowSubscript > strProducts.GetUpperBound(0) _
        OrElse strSearchForId = strProducts(intRowSubscript, 0)
        intRowSubscript = intRowSubscript + 1
     Loop

     ' determine whether the ID was found
     If intRowSubscript <= strProducts.GetUpperBound(0) Then
          Dim intPrice As Integer
          Integer.TryParse(strProducts(intRowSubscript, 1), intPrice)
          lblPrice.Text = intPrice.ToString("C0")
     Else
          MessageBox.Show("Invalid ID", _
                          "Treasures Gift Shop", _
                          MessageBoxButtons.OK, _
                          MessageBoxIcon.Information)
     End If

     txtId.Focus()
End Sub
```


Figure 9-31 btnDisplay control's Click event procedure using a two-dimensional array

To test the modified Price List application:

1. Save the solution, if necessary, then start the application. Type **cr20** in the Product ID box, then click the **Display Price** button. A price of $10 appears in the Price box, as shown earlier in Figure 9-25.
2. Type **xx44** in the Product ID box, then click the **Display Price** button. The "Invalid ID" message appears in a message box. Close the message box.
3. On your own, test the application using other valid and invalid IDs. When you are finished testing the application, click the **Exit** button. Close the Code Editor window, then close the solution.

Lesson B Summary

- **To create two parallel one-dimensional arrays:**

  Create two one-dimensional arrays. When assigning values to both arrays, be sure that the value stored in each element in the first array corresponds to the value stored in the same element in the second array.

- **To declare a two-dimensional array:**

  Use either of the following two syntax versions. The *highestRowSubscript* and *highestColumnSubscript* arguments in Version 1 are integers that specify the highest row and column subscripts, respectively, in the array. Using Version 1's syntax, the computer automatically initializes the array elements. The *initialValues* section in Version 2 is a list of values separated by commas and enclosed in braces. You include a separate *initialValues* section for each row in the array. Each *initialValues* section should contain the same number of values as there are columns in the array.

  Version 1: {**Dim** | **Private**} *arrayName*(*highestRowSubscript*, *highestColumnSubscript*) **As** *dataType*

  Version 2: {**Dim** | **Private**} *arrayName*(,) **As** *dataType* = {{*initialValues*},...{*initialValues*}}

- **To refer to an element in a two-dimensional array:**

  Use the syntax *arrayName*(*rowSubscript*, *columnSubscript*).

- **To determine the highest subscript in a specified dimension of an array:**

  Use the GetUpperBound method, whose syntax is *arrayName*.**GetUpperBound** (*dimension*).

Lesson B Key Terms

GetUpperBound method—returns an integer that represents the highest subscript in the specified dimension of the array

Parallel arrays—two or more arrays whose elements are related by their subscript (position) in the arrays

Two-dimensional array—an array whose elements are identified by a unique combination of two numbers: a row subscript and a column subscript

Lesson B Review Questions

1. If the elements in two arrays are related by their subscripts, the arrays are called ______________________ arrays.

   a. associated

   b. coupled

   c. matching

   d. parallel

2. The `strState` and `strCapital` arrays are parallel arrays. If Illinois is stored in the second element in the `strState` array, then Springfield is stored in the ______________________ element.

   a. `strCapital(1)`

   b. `strCapital(2)`

3. Which of the following creates a 3-row, 4-column two-dimensional array?

   a. `Dim decNums(2, 3) As Decimal`

   b. `Dim decNums(3, 4) As Decimal`

   c. `Dim decNums(3, 2) As Decimal`

   d. `Dim decNums(4, 3) As Decimal`

4. The `intSales` array was declared as follows: `Dim intSales(,) As Integer = {{1000, 1200, 900, 500, 2000}, {350, 600, 700, 800, 100}}`. The `intSales(1, 3) = intSales (1, 3) + 10` statement will ______________________.

   a. replace the 900 amount with 910

   b. replace the 500 amount with 510

   c. replace the 700 amount with 710

   d. replace the 800 amount with 810

5. The `intSales` array was declared as follows: `Dim intSales(,) As Integer = {{1000, 1200, 900, 500, 2000}, {350, 600, 700, 800, 100}}`. The `intSales(0, 4) = intSales (0, 4 - 2)` statement will ______________________.

   a. replace the 500 amount with 1200

   b. replace the 2000 amount with 900

   c. replace the 2000 amount with 1998

   d. result in an error

6. The `intSales` array was declared as follows: `Dim intSales(,) As Integer = {{1000, 1200, 900, 500, 2000}, {350, 600, 700, 800, 100}}`. Which of the following If clauses can be used to determine whether the `intRow` and `intCol` variables contain valid row and column subscripts, respectively, for the array?

   a. `If intSales(intRow, intCol) >= 0 AndAlso intSales(intRow, intCol) < 5 Then`

   b. `If intSales(intRow, intCol) >= 0 AndAlso intSales(intRow, intCol) <= 5 Then`

   c. `If intRow >= 0 AndAlso intRow < 3 AndAlso intCol >= 0 AndAlso intCol < 6 Then`

   d. `If intRow >= 0 AndAlso intRow < 2 AndAlso intCol >= 0 AndAlso intCol < 5 Then`

7. Which of the following statements assigns the string "California" to the element located in the third column, fifth row of the two-dimensional `strStates` array?

   a. `strStates(3, 5) = "California"`

   b. `strStates(5, 3) = "California"`

   c. `strStates(4, 2) = "California"`

   d. `strStates(2, 4) = "California"`

8. Which of the following assigns the number 1 to each element in a 5-element, one-dimensional Integer array named `intCounters`?

   a.
   ```
   For intSub As Integer = 0 To 4
      intCounters(intSub) = 1
   Next intSub
   ```

   b.
   ```
   Dim intSub As Integer
   Do While intSub < 5
      intCounters(intSub) = 1
      intSub = intSub + 1
   Loop
   ```

   c.
   ```
   For intSub As Integer = 1 To 5
      intCounters(intSub - 1) = 1
   Next intSub
   ```

   d. All of the above.

9. Which of the following assigns the number 0 to each element in a 2-row, 4-column Integer array named `intSums`?

   a.
   ```
   For intRow As Integer = 0 To 1
      For intCol As Integer = 0 To 3
         intSums(intRow, intCol) = 0
      Next intCol
   Next intRow
   ```

   b.
   ```
   Dim intRow As Integer
   Dim intCol As Integer
   Do While intRow < 2
      intCol = 0
      Do While intCol < 4
         intSums(intRow, intCol) = 0
         intCol = intCol + 1
      Loop
      intRow = intRow + 1
   Loop
   ```

   c.
   ```
   For intX As Integer = 1 To 2
      For intY As Integer = 1 To 4
         intSums(intX - 1, intY - 1) = 0
      Next intY
   Next intX
   ```

   d. All of the above.

10. . Which of the following returns the highest column subscript in a two-dimensional array named `decPays`?

    a. `decPays.GetUpperBound(1)`

    b. `decPays.GetUpperBound(0)`

    c. `decPays.GetUpperSubscript(0)`

    d. `decPays.GetHighestColumn(0)`

Lesson B Exercises

1. Write the statement to declare a procedure-level two-dimensional array named `intBalances`. The array should have four rows and six columns. Then write the statement to store the number 100 in the element located in the second row, fourth column. INTRODUCTORY

2. Write a loop that stores the number 10 in each element in the `intBalances` array from Exercise 1. Use the For...Next statement. INTRODUCTORY

3. Rewrite the code from Exercise 2 using a Do...Loop statement. INTRODUCTORY

4. Write the statement to assign the Boolean value True to the variable located in the third row, first column of a two-dimensional Boolean array named `blnAnswers`. INTRODUCTORY

5. In this exercise, you code an application that allows Professor Carver to display a grade based on the number of points he enters. The grading scale is shown in Figure 9-32. Open the Carver Solution (Carver Solution.sln) file, which is contained in the VB2008\Chap09\Carver Solution-Parallel folder. Open the designer window, if necessary, then open the Code Editor window. Open the code template for the btnDisplay control's Click event procedure. Store the minimum points in a 5-element, one-dimensional Integer array named `intPoints`. Store the grades in a 5-element, one-dimensional String array named `strGrades`. The arrays should be parallel arrays. The procedure should search the `intPoints` array for the number of points entered by the user, and then display the corresponding grade from the `strGrades` array. Save the solution, then start and test the application. Stop the application. Close the Code Editor window, then close the solution. INTERMEDIATE

Minimum points	Maximum points	Grade
0	299	F
300	349	D
350	399	C
400	449	B
450	500	A

Figure 9-32 Grading scale for Professor Carver's class

INTERMEDIATE

6. In this exercise, you modify the application from Exercise 5. The modified application allows the user to change the grading scale when the application is started. Use Windows to make a copy of the Carver Solution-Parallel folder, which is contained in the VB2008\Chap09 folder. Rename the folder Modified Carver Solution-Parallel. Open the Carver Solution (Carver Solution.sln) file contained in the VB2008\Chap09\Modified Carver Solution-Parallel folder. Open the designer window, then open the Code Editor window.

   a. When the form is loaded into the computer's memory, the application should use the InputBox function to prompt the user to enter the total number of possible points—in other words, the total number of points a student can earn in the course. Modify the application's code to perform this task.

   b. Modify the application's code to use the grading scale shown in Figure 9-33. For example, if the user enters the number 500 in response to the InputBox function, the code should enter 450 (90% of 500) as the minimum number of points for an A. If the user enters the number 300, the code should enter 270 (90% of 300) as the minimum number of points for an A.

   c. Save the solution, then start the application. Enter 300 as the number of possible points, then enter 185 in the Points text box. Click the Display Grade button. A grade of D appears in the interface. Stop the application.

   d. Start the application again. Enter 500 as the number of possible points, then enter 363 in the Points text box. Click the Display Grade button. A grade of C appears in the interface. Stop the application. Close the Code Editor window, then close the solution.

Minimum points	Grade
0	F
60% of the possible points	D
70% of the possible points	C
80% of the possible points	B
90% of the possible points	A

Figure 9-33 Modified grading scale for Professor Carver's class

INTERMEDIATE

7. In this exercise, you code an application that allows Ms. Laury to display a shipping charge based on the number of items ordered by a customer. The shipping charges are shown in Figure 9-34. Open the Laury Solution (Laury Solution.sln) file, which is contained in the VB2008\Chap09\Laury Solution-Parallel folder. If necessary, open the designer window. Open the Code Editor window, then open the code template for the btnDisplay control's Click event procedure. Store the minimum order amounts and shipping charges in parallel arrays.

The procedure should display the appropriate shipping charge with a dollar sign and two decimal places. Save the solution, then start and test the application. Stop the application. Close the Code Editor window, then close the solution.

Minimum order	Maximum order	Shipping
1	10	15
11	50	10
51	100	5
101	No maximum	0

Figure 9-34 Shipping charges for the Laury application

8. In this exercise, you modify the application from Exercise 5. The modified application will use a two-dimensional array rather than parallel arrays. Use Windows to make a copy of the Carver Solution-Parallel folder, which is contained in the VB2008\Chap09 folder. Rename the folder Carver Solution-TwoDimensional. Open the Carver Solution (Carver Solution.sln) file contained in the VB2008\Chap09\Carver Solution-TwoDimensional folder. Open the designer window, then open the Code Editor window. Make the necessary modifications to the code. Save the solution, then start and test the application. Stop the application. Close the Code Editor window, then close the solution.

ADVANCED

9. In this exercise, you modify the application from Exercise 7. The modified application will use a two-dimensional array rather than parallel arrays. Use Windows to make a copy of the Laury Solution-Parallel folder, which is contained in the VB2008\Chap09 folder. Rename the folder Laury Solution-TwoDimensional. Open the Laury Solution (Laury Solution.sln) file contained in the VB2008\Chap09\Laury Solution-TwoDimensional folder. Open the designer window, then open the Code Editor window. Make the necessary modifications to the code. Save the solution, then start and test the application. Stop the application. Close the Code Editor window, then close the solution.

ADVANCED

10. The sales manager at Conway Enterprises wants an application that she can use to display the total domestic, total international, and total company sales made during a six-month period. The sales amounts are shown in Figure 9-35. Create a Visual Basic Windows application. Name the solution, project, and form file Conway Solution, Conway Project, and Main Form.vb, respectively. Save the application in the VB2008\Chap09 folder. Create the interface shown in Figure 9-36. Open the Code Editor window. Code the application. Store the sales amounts in a two-dimensional array. Save the solution, then start and test the application. Stop the application. Close the Code Editor window, then close the solution.

ADVANCED

Month	Domestic	International
1	100,000	150,000
2	90,000	120,000
3	75,000	210,000
4	88,000	50,000
5	125,000	220,000
6	63,000	80,000

Figure 9-35 Sales amounts

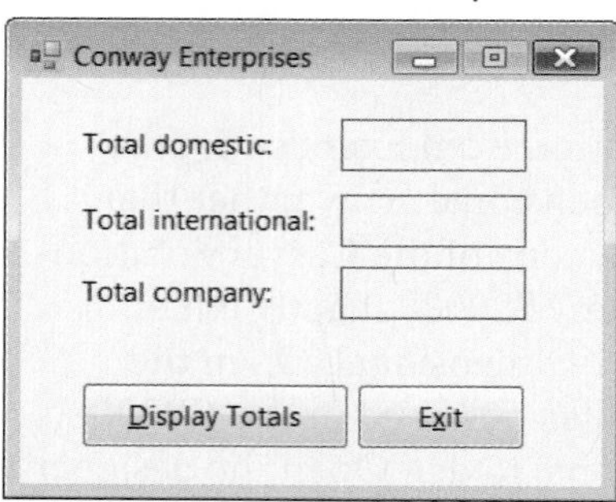

Figure 9-36 User interface for Conway Enterprises

ADVANCED

11. In this exercise, you code an application that displays the number of times a value appears in a two-dimensional array. Open the Count Solution (Count Solution.sln) file, which is contained in the VB2008\Chap09\Count Solution folder. If necessary, open the designer window. Code the Display button's Click event procedure so that it displays the number of times each of the numbers from one through nine appears in the `intNumbers` array. (Hint: Store the counts in a one-dimensional array.) Save the solution, then start the application. Click the Display button to display the nine counts. Stop the application. Close the Code Editor window, then close the solution.

Swat The Bugs

12. Open the Debug Solution (Debug Solution.sln) file, which is contained in the VB2008\Chap09\Debug Solution-Lesson B folder. If necessary, open the designer window. Open the Code Editor window and review the existing code. The first column in the `strNames` array contains first names, and the second column contains last names. The btnDisplay control's Click event procedure should display the first and last names in the lstFirst and lstLast controls, respectively. Correct the code to remove the jagged lines. Save the solution, then start the application. Click the Display button. If a runtime error occurs, click Debug on the menu bar, then click Stop Debugging. Correct the errors in the application's code. Save the solution, then start and test the application. Stop the application. Close the Code Editor window, then close the solution.

LESSON C

After studying Lesson C, you should be able to:

- Create a simple smart device application

Creating a Smart Device Application

You can use Visual Basic (except for the Express Edition) to create **Smart Device applications** that run on smart devices, such as Pocket PCs and Smartphones. In this lesson, you will learn how to create a simple Smart Device application for Treasures Gift Shop. Please note that you will not be able to complete this lesson using the Express Edition of Visual Basic 2008.

To begin creating the Smart Device application:

1. If necessary, start Visual Studio 2008. Close the Start Page window.
2. Click **File** on the menu bar, then click **New Project**. If necessary, expand the Visual Basic node, then click **Smart Device** in the Project types list. If necessary, click **Smart Device Project** in the list of Visual Studio installed templates. If necessary, use the Browse button to open the VB2008\Chap09 folder. Change the name in the Name box to **Price Finder Smart Project**, then change the name in the Solution Name box to **Price Finder Smart Solution**. See Figure 9-37.

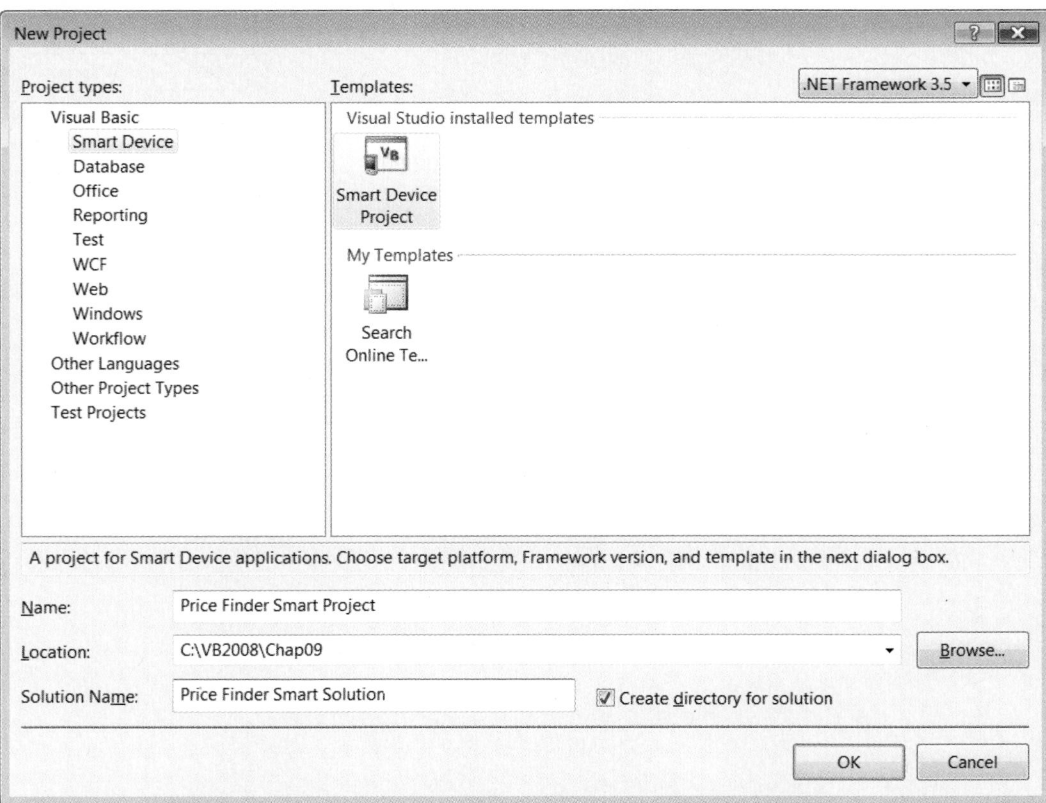

Figure 9-37 New Project dialog box

3. Click the **OK** button to close the New Project dialog box. The Add New Smart Device Project dialog box opens. If necessary, click **Windows Mobile 5.0 Pocket PC SDK** in the Target platform box. If necessary, click **Device Application** in the list of templates. See Figure 9-38.

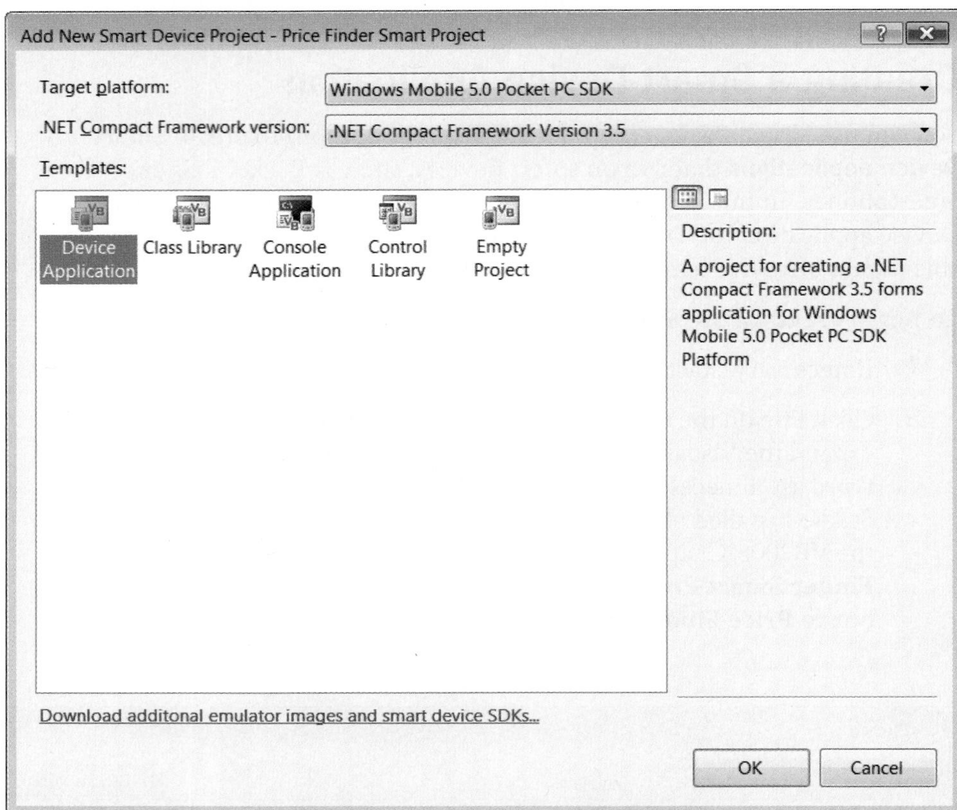

Figure 9-38 Add New Smart Device Project dialog box

4. Click the **OK** button to close the dialog box. The Pocket PC emulator form opens in the designer window. See Figure 9-39.

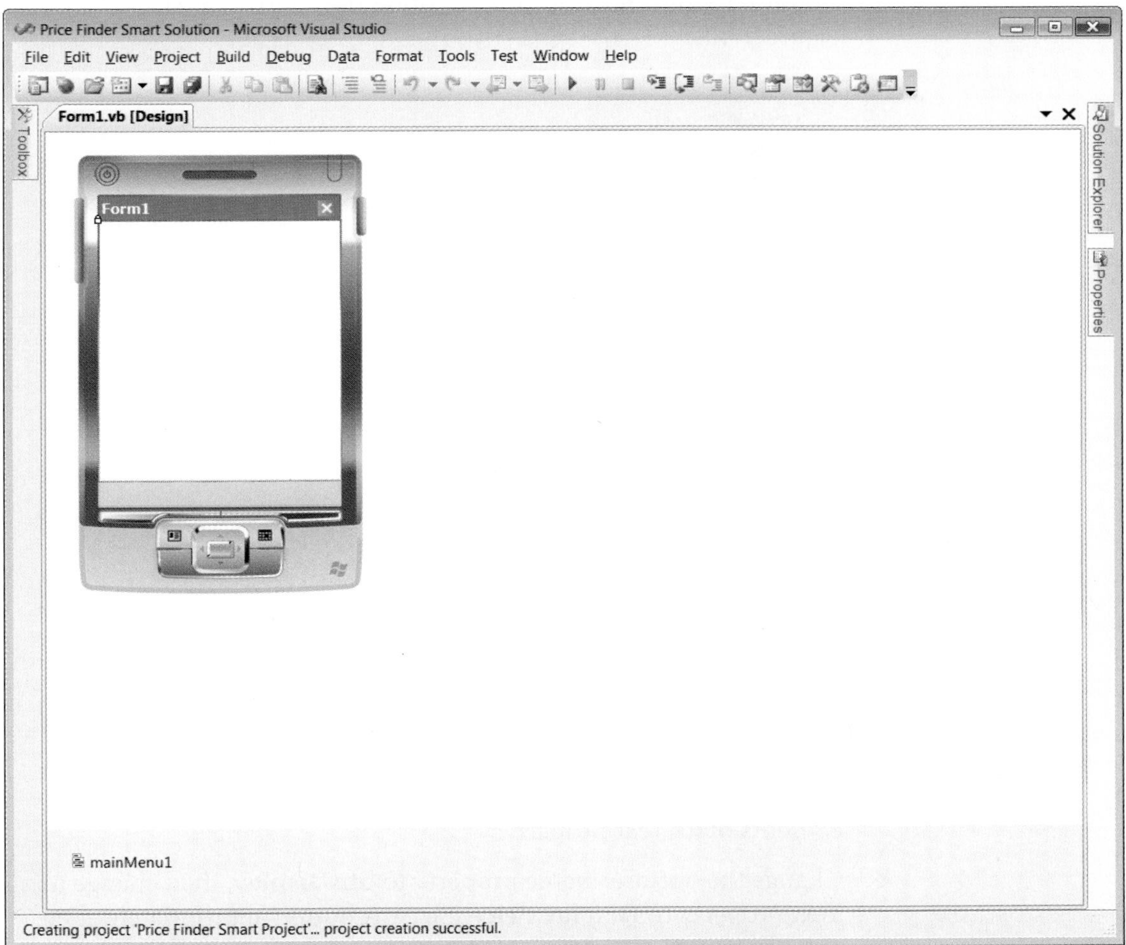

Figure 9-39 Pocket PC emulator form

5. Click the **form**, then change the form's Text property to **Treasures**.

6. Just as you can with the Windows forms you used in previous applications, you can use the tools in the toolbox to add objects to the emulator form. Use the toolbox to add three labels, one text box, and a button to the emulator form. Position the controls as shown in Figure 9-40.

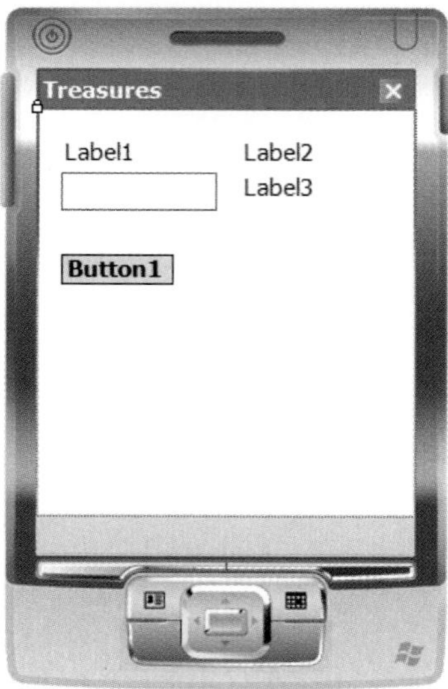

Figure 9-40 Controls added to the emulator form

7. Change Label1's Text property to **Product ID:**, then change Label2's Text property to **Price:**. Change the text box's Name property to **txtId**. Change Label3's Name property to **lblPrice**, then delete the contents of its Text property.
8. Change the button's Name property to **btnDisplay**, then change its Text property to **Display Price**. Size the button appropriately, then save the solution. Figure 9-41 shows the form after all of the changes have been made.

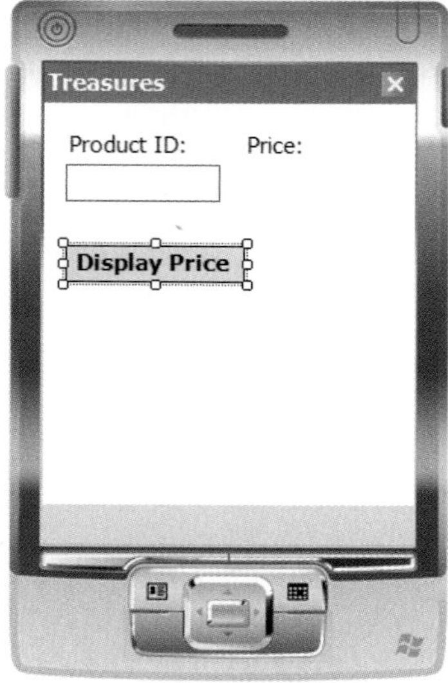

Figure 9-41 Emulator form after the changes are made

9. Right-click the **form**, then click **View Code**. Open the code template for the btnDisplay control's Click event procedure, then enter the code shown in Figure 9-42.

```
' displays the price associated with an ID

Dim strIds() As String = _
        {"BX35", "CR20", "FE15", "KW10", "MM67"}
Dim intPrices() As Integer = {13, 10, 12, 24, 4}
Dim strSearchForId As String
Dim intSubscript As Integer

' assign the ID to a variable
strSearchForId = txtId.Text.ToUpper

' search the strIds array for the ID
' continue searching until the end of
' the array or the ID is found
Do Until intSubscript = strIds.Length _
   OrElse strSearchForId = strIds(intSubscript)
   intSubscript = intSubscript + 1
Loop

' determine whether the ID was found
If intSubscript < strIds.Length Then
   lblPrice.Text = intPrices(intSubscript).ToString("C0")
Else
   lblPrice.Text = "Invalid ID"
End If
```

Figure 9-42 Code you need to enter in the btnDisplay control's Click event procedure

10. Save the solution, then close the Code Editor window. Click **Debug** on the menu bar, then click **Start Debugging**. The project's Deploy dialog box opens. See Figure 9-43.

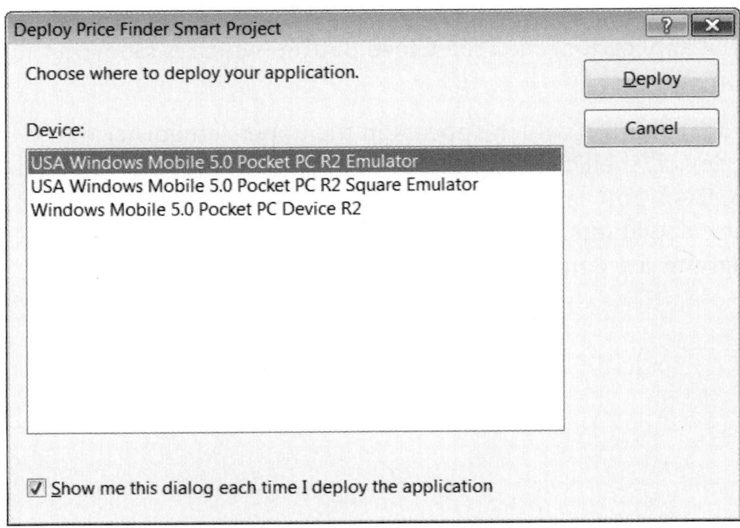

Figure 9-43 Project's Deploy dialog box

11. If necessary, click **USA Windows Mobile 5.0 Pocket PC R2 Emulator**, then click the **Deploy** button. After a short wait, the Pocket PC emulator opens. The Visual Studio status bar, which appears at the bottom of the IDE, indicates that the application is deploying.

12. After a short time, the application appears on the emulator device. Type **CR20** in the text box, then click the **Display Price** button. The application displays the price, which is $10. See Figure 9-44.

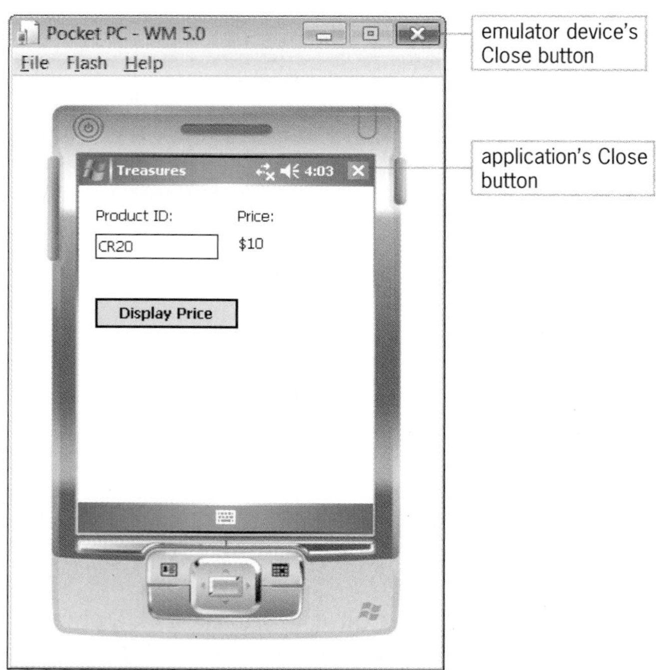

Figure 9-44 Price displayed on the emulator device

13. To close the application, click the **Close** button (which is blue) on the application's title bar.

14. Click the **Start** button, which appears in the upper-left corner of the emulator device, then click **Programs** to open the Programs folder. See Figure 9-45. You can use the Calculator program to perform arithmetic calculations. You also can play games on the emulator. The game programs are contained in the Games folder.

Figure 9-45 Items in the Programs folder

15. To close the emulator, click its **Close** button (which is red). The Device Emulator dialog box opens. See Figure 9-46.

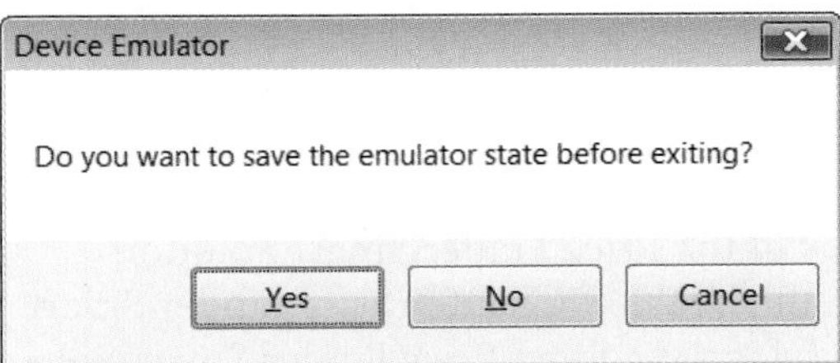

Figure 9-46 Device Emulator dialog box

16. You *must* click the No button in this dialog box. If you click the Yes button, any changes you make to the application will not be sent to the emulator the next time you run the application. Clicking the No button resets the device and ensures that the application is resent to the emulator the next time it is run. Click the **No** button.

17. If the dialog box shown in Figure 9-47 appears, click the **OK** button.

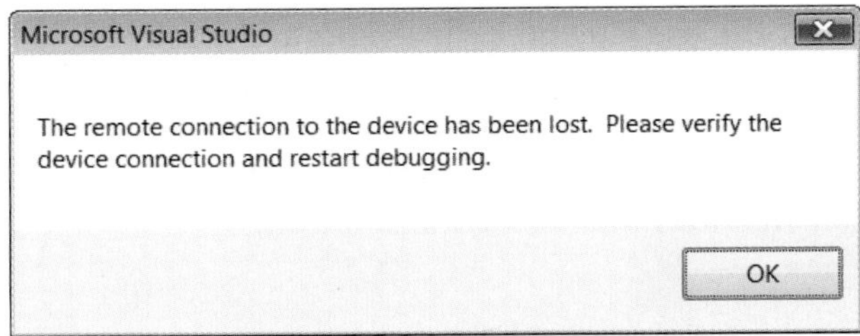

Figure 9-47 Remote connection dialog box

18. Close the solution.

Lesson C Summary

- **To be able to run an application on a Smart Device:**

  Create a Smart Device application.

Lesson C Key Term

Smart Device applications—applications that run on smart devices, such as Pocket PCs and Smartphones.

Lesson C Review Question

1. The Device Emulator dialog box contains the message "Do you want to save the emulator state before exiting?" You should click the ______________________________ button in this dialog box.

   a. No

   b. Yes

   c. Cancel

   d. Don't Save

Lesson C Exercises

INTRODUCTORY

1. Use Windows to make a copy of the Price Finder Smart Solution folder, which is contained in the VB2008\Chap09\Price Finder Smart Solution folder. Rename the folder Modified Price Finder Smart Solution. Open the Price Finder Smart Solution (Price Finder Smart Solution.sln) file contained in the VB2008\Chap09\Modified Price Finder Smart Solution folder. Modify the code to use a two-dimensional array rather than parallel one-dimensional arrays. Save the solution, then start and test the application. Close the emulator, then close the solution.

INTERMEDIATE

2. Create a Visual Basic Smart Device application. Name the solution and project Area Smart Device Solution and Area Smart Device Project, respectively. Save the application in the VB2008\Chap09 folder. The application should allow the user to enter the length and width of a rectangle, in feet. It then should calculate and display the rectangle's area. Code the application. Code each text box's TextChanged and KeyPress event procedures. Save the solution, then start and test the application. Close the emulator, then close the solution.

CHAPTER 10

Structures and Sequential Access Files

Creating the CD Collection Application

In this chapter, you code an application that keeps track of a person's CD collection. More specifically, the application saves each CD's name, as well as the artist's name and the CD price, in a sequential access file named CDs.txt. When the application is started, it displays the contents of the file in a list box. The application allows the user to add CD information to the file, as well as remove CD information from the file.

Previewing the CD Collection Application

To preview the completed CD Collection application:

To open the Run dialog box, press and hold down the Windows logo key as you tap the letter r, then release the logo key.

1. Use the Run dialog box to run the **CD** (**CD.exe**) file, which is contained in the VB2008\Chap10 folder. The application's user interface appears on the screen, with the contents of the CDs.txt file displayed in the list box. Notice that the list box contains three columns. You will learn how to align columnar information in Lesson C.

2. First, add a new CD to the list box. Click the **Add** button. Type **Breakout** as the CD name, then press **Enter**. Type **Miley Cyrus** as the artist name, then press **Enter**. Type **9** as the price and press **Enter**. The information you entered appears in the list box. See Figure 10-1.

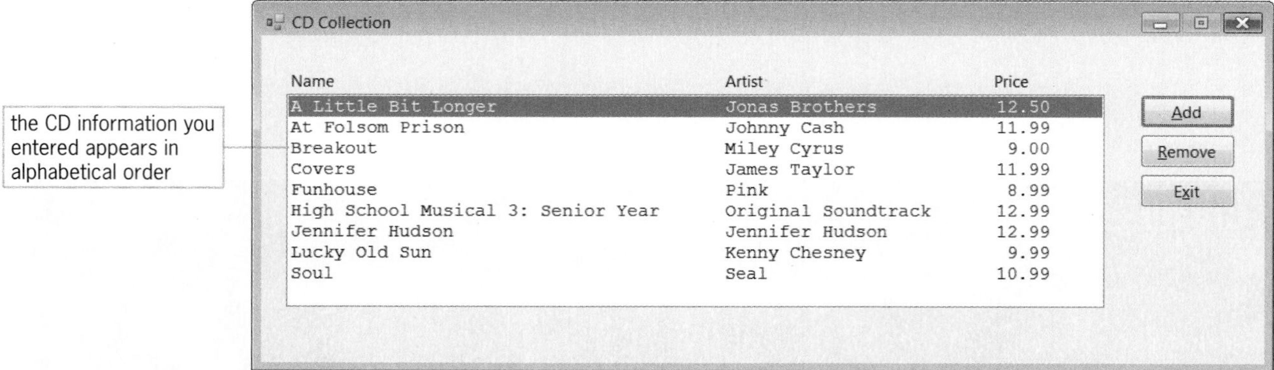

Figure 10-1 CD information added to the list box

3. Now remove the Covers CD from the list box. Click **Covers** in the list box, then click the **Remove** button. The information pertaining to the Covers CD is removed from the list box.

4. Click the **Exit** button to end the application. The application saves the contents of the list box in the CDs.txt sequential access file. You will learn about sequential access files in Lesson B.

5. Use Windows to open the VB2008\Chap10 folder. Right-click **CDs.txt** in the list of filenames. Point to **Open With** and then click **Notepad**. The contents of the CDs.txt file appears in a window. See Figure 10-2.

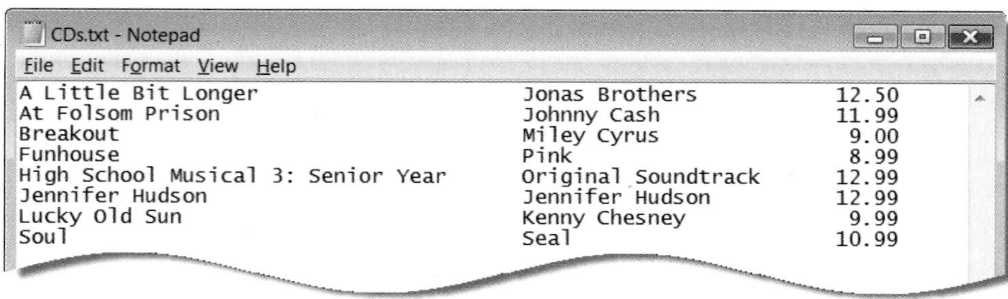

Figure 10-2 Contents of the CDs.txt file

6. Close the CDs.txt window by clicking its **Close** button. Start the application again. The list box displays the current contents of the CDs.txt file, which includes the Breakout CD information added in Step 2, but does not include the Covers CD information removed in Step 3.

7. Click the **Exit** button to end the application.

In Lesson A, you will learn how to create a structure in Visual Basic. Lesson B covers sequential access files. You will code the CD Collection application in Lesson C.

LESSON A

After studying Lesson A, you should be able to:

- Create a structure
- Declare a structure variable
- Pass a structure variable to a procedure
- Create and manipulate a one-dimensional array of structures

Creating a Structure

Most programmers use the Class statement (rather than the Structure statement) to create data types that contain procedures. You will learn about the Class statement in Chapter 12.

Recall that Pascal case means you capitalize the first letter in the name, as well as the first letter of each subsequent word in the name.

The data types used in previous chapters, such as the Integer and Double types, are built into the Visual Basic language. You also can create your own data types in Visual Basic using the **Structure statement**. Data types created using the Structure statement are referred to as **user-defined data types** or **structures**. Figure 10-3 shows the syntax of the Structure statement. Most programmers enter the structure's name using Pascal case. Between the Structure and End Structure clauses, you define the members included in the structure. The members can be variables, constants, or procedures. However, in most cases the members will be variables; such variables are referred to as **member variables**. Each member variable's definition contains the keyword `Public` followed by the name of the variable, the keyword `As`, and the variable's *dataType*. The *dataType* identifies the type of data the member variable will store and can be any of the standard data types available in Visual Basic; it also can be another structure (user-defined data type). The Employee structure shown in the example in Figure 10-3 contains four member variables: three String variables and one Double variable. In most applications, you enter the Structure statement in the form's Declarations section, which begins with the Public Class clause and ends with the End Class clause in the Code Editor window.

You also can include an array in a structure. This topic is explored in Exercises 9 and 10 at the end of this lesson.

Structure statement

Syntax
Structure *structureName*
  Public *memberVariableName1* **As** *dataType*
  [**Public** *memberVariableNameN* **As** *dataType*]
End Structure

Example
```
Structure Employee
   Public strId As String
   Public strFirstName As String
   Public strLastName As String
   Public dblPay As Double
End Structure
```

Figure 10-3 Syntax and an example of the Structure statement

The Structure statement allows the programmer to group related items into one unit: a structure. However, keep in mind that the Structure statement merely defines the members included in the structure; it does not reserve any memory locations inside the computer. You reserve memory locations by declaring a structure variable.

Declaring and Using a Structure Variable

The dot member access operator indicates that `strId`, `strFirstName`, `strLastName`, and `dblPay` are members of the `hourly` and `salaried` variables.

After entering the Structure statement in the Code Editor window, you then can use the structure to declare a variable. Variables declared using a structure are often referred to as **structure variables**. The syntax for creating a structure variable is shown in Figure 10-4. The figure also includes examples of declaring structure variables using the Employee structure from Figure 10-3. Similar to the way the `Dim intAge As Integer` instruction declares an Integer variable named `intAge`, the `Dim hourly As Employee` instruction in Example 1 declares an Employee variable named `hourly`. However, unlike the `intAge` variable, the `hourly` variable contains four member variables. In code, you refer to the entire structure variable by its name—in this case, `hourly`. You refer to a member variable by preceding its name with the name of the structure variable in which it is defined. You use the dot member access operator (a period) to separate the structure variable's name from the member variable's name. For instance, to refer to the member variables within the `hourly` structure variable, you use `hourly.strId`, `hourly.strFirstName`, `hourly.strLastName`, and `hourly.dblPay`. The `Private salaried As Employee` instruction in Example 2 declares a module-level Employee variable named `salaried`. The names of the member variables within the `salaried` variable are `salaried.strId`, `salaried.strFirstName`, `salaried.strLastName`, and `salaried.dblPay`.

Structure variable declaration statement

Syntax
{**Dim** | **Private**} *structureVariableName* **As** *structureName*

Example 1
```
Dim hourly As Employee
```
declares a procedure-level Employee structure variable named `hourly`

Example 2
```
Private salaried As Employee
```
declares a module-level Employee structure variable named `salaried`

Figure 10-4 Syntax and examples of declaring a structure variable

The member variables in a structure variable can be used just like any other variables. You can assign values to them, use them in calculations, display their contents, and so on. Figure 10-5 shows various ways of using the member variables created by the statements in Figure 10-4.

Using a member variable

Example 1

```
hourly.strLastName = "Yardley"
```

assigns the string "Yardley" to the `hourly.strLastName` member variable

Example 2

```
hourly.dblPay = hourly.dblPay * 1.05
```

multiplies the contents of the `hourly.dblPay` member variable by 1.05 and then assigns the result to the member variable

Example 3

```
lblSalary.Text = salaried.dblPay.ToString("C2")
```

formats the value contained in the `salaried.dblPay` member variable and then displays the result in the lblSalary control

Figure 10-5 Examples of using a member variable

Programmers use structure variables when they need to pass a group of related items to a procedure for further processing, because it's easier to pass one structure variable rather than many individual variables. Programmers also use structure variables to store related items in an array, even when the items have different data types. Rather than using parallel one-dimensional arrays—one array for each item—you can use one one-dimensional array that contains structure variables. In the next two sections, you will learn how to pass a structure variable to a procedure and also store a structure variable in an array.

Passing a Structure Variable to a Procedure

The sales manager at Willow Pools wants an application that determines the amount of water required to fill a rectangular pool. To perform this task, the application will need to calculate the volume of the pool. You calculate the volume by first multiplying the pool's length by its width, and then multiplying the result by the pool's depth. Assuming the length, width, and depth are measured in feet, this gives you the volume in cubic feet. To determine the number of gallons of water, you multiply the number of cubic feet by 7.48, because there are 7.48 gallons in one cubic foot.

To open and then test the Willow Pools application:

1. If necessary, start Visual Studio 2008 or Visual Basic 2008 Express Edition. Close the Start Page window.
2. Open the **Pool Solution** (**Pool Solution.sln**) file, which is contained in the VB2008\Chap10\Pool Solution folder. If necessary, open the designer window.
3. Start the application. Type **100** in the Length box, **30** in the Width box, and **4** in the Depth box. Click the **Calculate** button. The required number of gallons of water appears in the interface. See Figure 10-6.

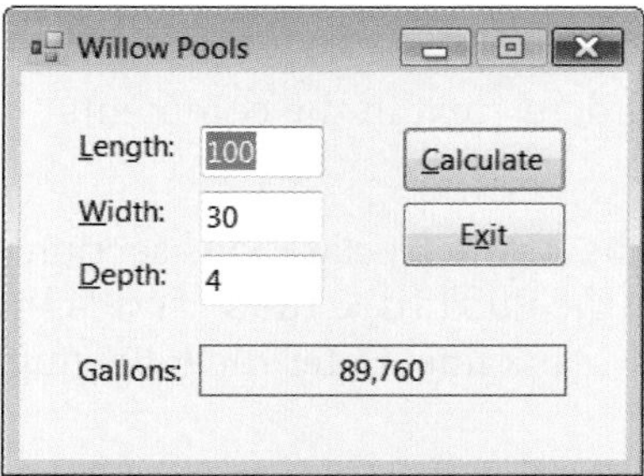

Figure 10-6 Interface showing the required number of gallons of water

4. Click the **Exit** button to end the application, then open the Code Editor window. Figure 10-7 shows the GetGallons function and btnCalc control's Click event procedure. The event procedure passes three variables *by value* to the function, which uses the values to calculate the number of gallons of water required to fill the pool. The function returns the number of gallons as a Double number to the event procedure, which assigns the value to the `dblGallons` variable.

```
Private Function GetGallons(ByVal dblLen As Double, _
                            ByVal dblWid As Double, _
                            ByVal dblDep As Double) As Double
    ' calculates and returns the number of gallons

    Const dblGAL_PER_CUBIC_FOOT As Double = 7.48

    Return dblLen * dblWid * dblDep * dblGAL_PER_CUBIC_FOOT
End Function

Private Sub btnCalc_Click(ByVal sender As Object, _
                          ByVal e As System.EventArgs) Handles btnCalc.Click
    ' displays the number of gallons

    Dim dblPoolLength As Double
    Dim dblPoolWidth As Double
    Dim dblPoolDepth As Double
    Dim dblGallons As Double


    Double.TryParse(txtLength.Text, dblPoolLength)
    Double.TryParse(txtWidth.Text, dblPoolWidth)
    Double.TryParse(txtDepth.Text, dblPoolDepth)

    dblGallons = _
       GetGallons(dblPoolLength, dblPoolWidth, dblPoolDepth)
    lblGallons.Text = dblGallons.ToString("N0")

    txtLength.Focus()
End Sub
```


Figure 10-7 Code for the Willow Pools application (without a structure)

A more convenient way of coding the Willow Pools application is to use a structure to group together the input items: length, width, and depth. It's logical to group the three items because they are related; each represents one of the three dimensions of a rectangular pool. A descriptive name for the structure would be Dimensions.

To modify the code to use a structure:

1. Replace the <your name> and <current date> text in the comments with your name and the current date.

2. First, you will declare the structure in the form's Declarations section. Click the **blank line** immediately below the `Public Class frmMain` line, then press **Enter** to insert another blank line. Enter the following Structure statement.

   Structure Dimensions
   Public dblLength As Double
   Public dblWidth As Double
   Public dblDepth As Double
   End Structure

3. Locate the btnCalc control's Click event procedure. The procedure will use a structure variable (rather than three separate variables) to store the input items. Replace the three Dim statements that declare the `dblPoolLength`, `dblPoolWidth`, and `dblPoolDepth` variables with the following Dim statement.

   Dim poolSize As Dimensions

4. Now store each input item in its corresponding member in the structure variable. In the first TryParse method, change `dblPoolLength` to **poolSize.dblLength**. In the second TryParse method, change `dblPoolWidth` to **poolSize.dblWidth**. In the third TryParse method, change `dblPoolDepth` to **poolSize.dblDepth**.

5. Next, consider the changes you will need to make to the statement that invokes the GetGallons function. Instead of sending three separate variables to the function, you now need to send only one variable: the structure variable. When you pass a structure variable to a procedure, all of its members are passed automatically. Although passing one structure variable rather than three separate variables may not seem like a huge advantage, consider the convenience of passing one structure variable rather than 10 separate variables! Change the statement that invokes the GetGallons function to **dblGallons = GetGallons(poolSize)**. Don't be concerned about the jagged line that appears below `GetGallons(poolSize)` in the statement. It will disappear when you modify the GetGallons function in the next step.

6. Locate the GetGallons function in the Code Editor window. The function will now receive a Dimensions structure variable rather than three Double variables. Like the Double variables, the structure variable will be passed *by value*, because the function does not need to change any member's value. Change the function's header to **Public Function GetGallons(ByVal pool As Dimensions) As Double**.

7. Now use the members of the structure variable to calculate the number of gallons. Replace `dblLen`, `dblWid`, and `dblDep` in the Return statement with **pool.dblLength**, **pool.dblWidth**, **pool.dblDepth**, respectively. Figure 10-8 shows the modified code, which uses a structure.

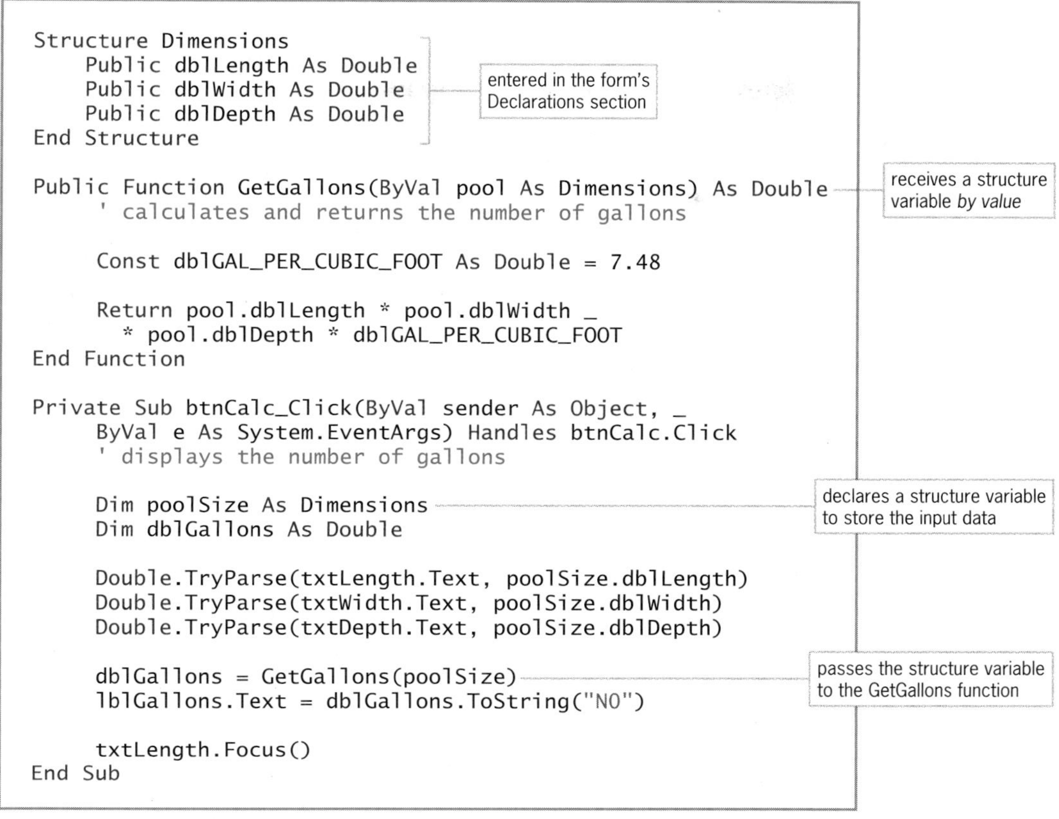

```
Structure Dimensions
    Public dblLength As Double
    Public dblWidth As Double
    Public dblDepth As Double
End Structure

Public Function GetGallons(ByVal pool As Dimensions) As Double
     ' calculates and returns the number of gallons

     Const dblGAL_PER_CUBIC_FOOT As Double = 7.48

     Return pool.dblLength * pool.dblWidth _
       * pool.dblDepth * dblGAL_PER_CUBIC_FOOT
End Function

Private Sub btnCalc_Click(ByVal sender As Object, _
     ByVal e As System.EventArgs) Handles btnCalc.Click
     ' displays the number of gallons

     Dim poolSize As Dimensions
     Dim dblGallons As Double

     Double.TryParse(txtLength.Text, poolSize.dblLength)
     Double.TryParse(txtWidth.Text, poolSize.dblWidth)
     Double.TryParse(txtDepth.Text, poolSize.dblDepth)

     dblGallons = GetGallons(poolSize)
     lblGallons.Text = dblGallons.ToString("N0")

     txtLength.Focus()
End Sub
```


Figure 10-8 Code for the Willow Pools application (with a structure)

To test the modified code:

1. Save the solution, then start the application. Type **100** in the Length box, **30** in the Width box, and **4** in the Depth box. Press **Enter** to select the Calculate button. The required number of gallons of water appears in the interface, as shown earlier in Figure 10-6.
2. Click the **Exit** button. Close the Code Editor window, then close the solution.

As mentioned earlier, the ability to pass a structure variable and its members as one unit is not the only advantage of using a structure. Another advantage of using a structure is that a structure variable can be stored in an array, even when its members have different data types.

Creating an Array of Structure Variables

In Chapter 9, you learned how to use two parallel one-dimensional arrays to store a price list for the Treasures gift shop. You stored each product's ID in a String array and its price in an Integer array. You also learned how to store the IDs and prices in a two-dimensional String array. Rather than using parallel one-dimensional arrays or a two-dimensional array, you also can use a one-dimensional array of structure variables. Each structure variable will contain two member variables: a String variable for the ID and an Integer variable for the price. (Notice that there are many different ways of solving the same problem.)

To open the Price List application:

1. Open the **Price List Solution** (**Price List Solution.sln**) file, which is contained in the VB2008\Chap10\Price List Solution-Structure folder. If necessary, open the designer window. The text box's CharacterCasing and MaxLength properties are set to Upper and 4, respectively.
2. Open the Code Editor window. Figure 10-9 shows the code entered in the btnDisplay control's Click event procedure. The code does not use a structure.

parallel one-dimensional arrays

```
Private Sub btnDisplay_Click(ByVal sender As Object, _
     ByVal e As System.EventArgs) Handles btnDisplay.Click
     ' displays the price associated with an ID

     Dim strIds() As String = _
               {"BX35", "CR20", "FE15", "KW10", "MM67"}
     Dim intPrices() As Integer = {13, 10, 12, 24, 4}
     Dim strSearchForId As String
     Dim intSubscript As Integer

     ' assign the ID to a variable
     strSearchForId = txtId.Text

     ' search the strIds array for the ID
     ' continue searching until the end of
     ' the array or the ID is found
     Do Until intSubscript = strIds.Length _
         OrElse strSearchForId = strIds(intSubscript)
         intSubscript = intSubscript + 1
     Loop

     ' determine whether the ID was found
     If intSubscript < strIds.Length Then
           lblPrice.Text = intPrices(intSubscript).ToString("C0")
     Else
           MessageBox.Show("Invalid ID", _
                           "Treasures Gift Shop", _
                           MessageBoxButtons.OK, _
                           MessageBoxIcon.Information)
     End If

     txtId.Focus()
End Sub
```

Figure 10-9 Code for the Treasures Gift Shop application (without a structure)

To begin modifying the code to use a structure:

1. Replace the <your name> and <current date> text in the comments with your name and the current date.
2. First, declare the structure in the form's Declarations section. A descriptive name for the structure would be ProductInfo. Click the **blank line** immediately below the `Public Class frmMain` line, then press **Enter** to insert another blank line. Enter the following Structure statement.

   Structure ProductInfo
       Public strId As String
       Public intPrice As Integer
   End Structure

3. Locate the btnDisplay control's Click event procedure. The procedure will use a one-dimensional array of ProductInfo structure variables (rather than two parallel one-dimensional arrays) to store the price list. Replace the two Dim statements that declare the `strIds` and `intPrices` arrays with the following Dim statement.

   Dim priceList(4) As ProductInfo

Next, you need to store the five product IDs and prices in the `priceList` array. Keep in mind that each element in the array is a structure variable, and each structure variable contains two member variables: `strId` and `intPrice`. To access a member of a structure variable in an array, you use the syntax *arrayName*(*subscript*)*.memberName*. For example, `priceList(0).strId` refers to the `strId` member contained in the first array element. Likewise, `priceList(4).intPrice` refers to the `intPrice` member contained in the last array element. Figure 10-10 illustrates this naming convention.

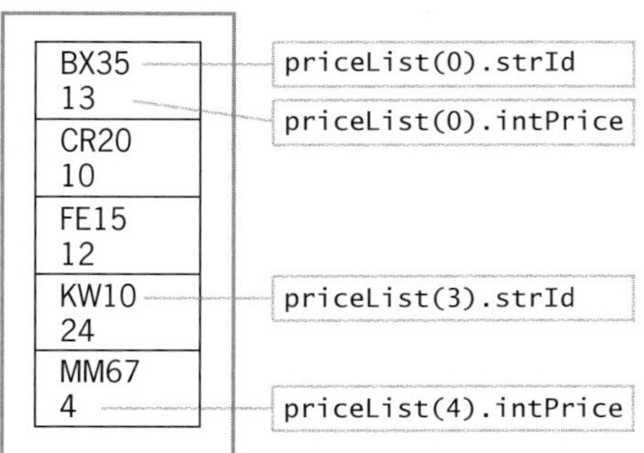

Figure 10-10 Names of some of the member variables in the `priceList` array

To continue modifying the code to use a structure:

1. Click the **blank line** below the `Dim intSubscript As Integer` instruction, then press **Enter** to insert another blank line. Enter the following 10 assignment statements.

   priceList(0).strId = "BX35"
   priceList(0).intPrice = 13
   priceList(1).strId = "CR20"
   priceList(1).intPrice = 10
   priceList(2).strId = "FE15"
   priceList(2).intPrice = 12
   priceList(3).strId = "KW10"
   priceList(3).intPrice = 24
   priceList(4).strId = "MM67"
   priceList(4).intPrice = 4

2. The procedure's loop now needs to search the `priceList` array (rather than the `strIds` array). Change `strIds` in the `' search the strIds array for the ID` comment to **priceList**.

3. The loop should search each element in the `priceList` array, comparing the value in the current element's `strId` member with the value in the `strSearchForId` variable. The loop should stop searching either when the end of the array is reached or when the ID is found. Change `strIds.Length` in the Do clause to **priceList.Length**, then change `strIds(intSubscript)` in the Do clause to **priceList(intSubscript).strId**.

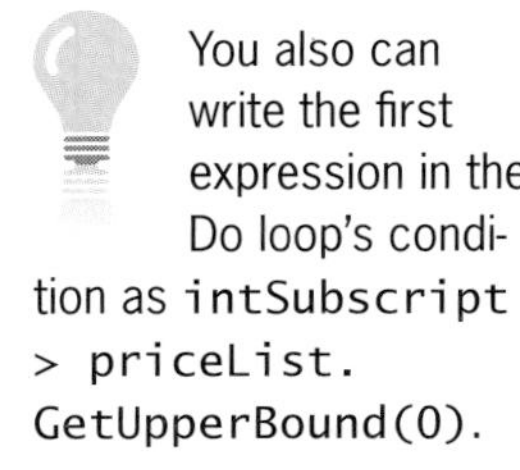

You also can write the first expression in the Do loop's condition as `intSubscript > priceList.GetUpperBound(0)`.

4. The selection structure in the procedure determines why the loop ended. If the `intSubscript` variable's value is less than the number of array elements, the loop ended because the ID was located in the array; in that case, the selection structure's true path should display the corresponding price. On the other hand, if the variable's value is not less than the number of array elements, the loop ended because it reached the end of the array without finding the ID. In that case, the selection structure's false path should display the "Invalid ID" message in a message box. Change `strIds.Length` in the If clause to **priceList.Length**, then change `intPrices(intSubscript)` in the assignment statement below the If clause to **priceList(intSubscript).intPrice**. Figure 10-11 shows the modified code, which uses a structure.

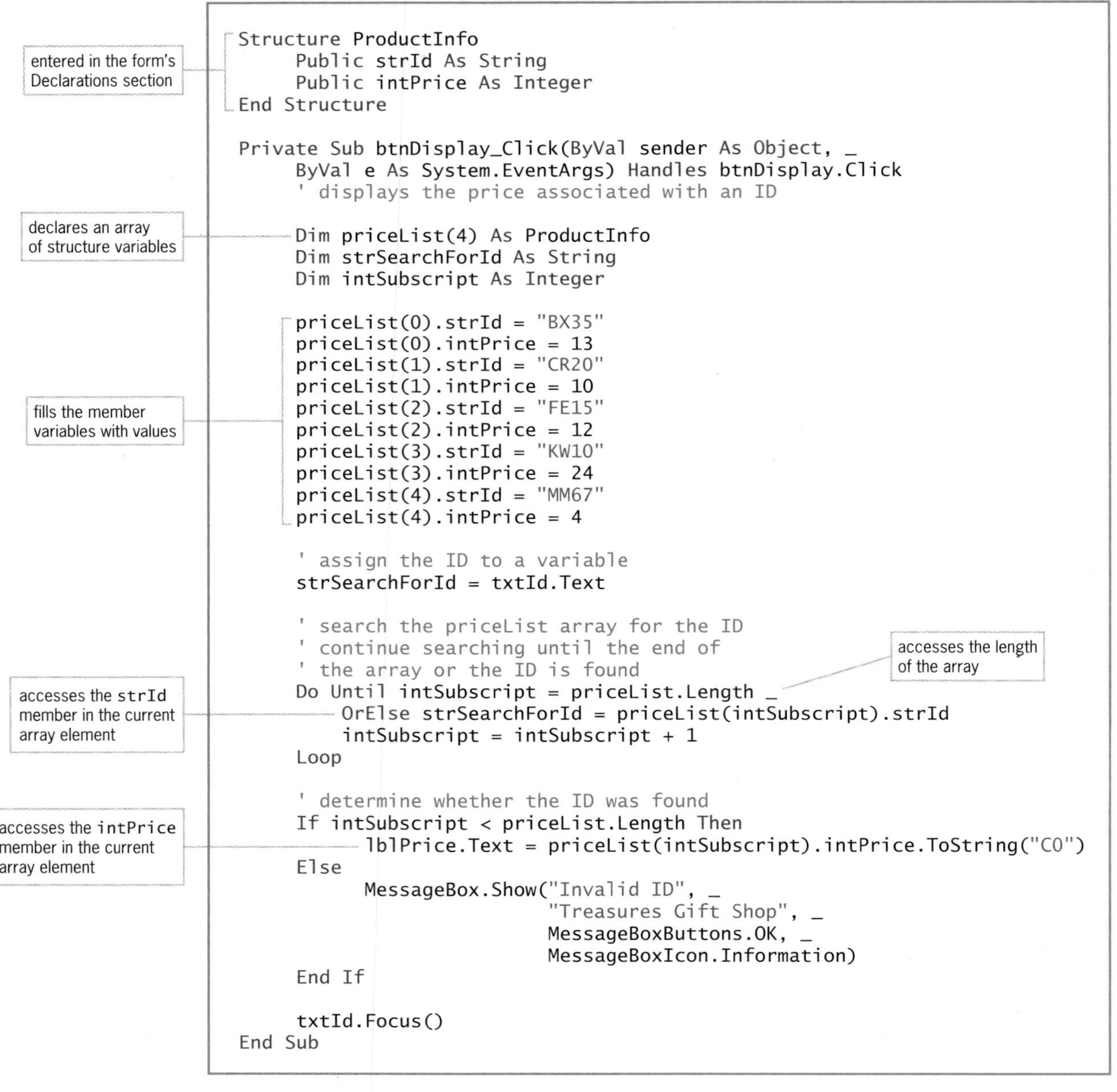


```
Structure ProductInfo
     Public strId As String
     Public intPrice As Integer
End Structure

Private Sub btnDisplay_Click(ByVal sender As Object, _
     ByVal e As System.EventArgs) Handles btnDisplay.Click
     ' displays the price associated with an ID

     Dim priceList(4) As ProductInfo
     Dim strSearchForId As String
     Dim intSubscript As Integer

     priceList(0).strId = "BX35"
     priceList(0).intPrice = 13
     priceList(1).strId = "CR20"
     priceList(1).intPrice = 10
     priceList(2).strId = "FE15"
     priceList(2).intPrice = 12
     priceList(3).strId = "KW10"
     priceList(3).intPrice = 24
     priceList(4).strId = "MM67"
     priceList(4).intPrice = 4

     ' assign the ID to a variable
     strSearchForId = txtId.Text

     ' search the priceList array for the ID
     ' continue searching until the end of
     ' the array or the ID is found
     Do Until intSubscript = priceList.Length _
         OrElse strSearchForId = priceList(intSubscript).strId
         intSubscript = intSubscript + 1
     Loop

     ' determine whether the ID was found
     If intSubscript < priceList.Length Then
           lblPrice.Text = priceList(intSubscript).intPrice.ToString("C0")
     Else
           MessageBox.Show("Invalid ID", _
                           "Treasures Gift Shop", _
                           MessageBoxButtons.OK, _
                           MessageBoxIcon.Information)
     End If

     txtId.Focus()
End Sub
```

Figure 10-11 Code for the Treasures Gift Shop application (with a structure)

To test the application's code:

1. Save the solution, then start the application. Type **cr20** in the Product ID box, then click the **Display Price** button. The product's price appears in the interface. See Figure 10-12.

Figure 10-12 Price shown in the interface

2. Click the **Exit** button. Close the Code Editor window, then close the solution.

Lesson A Summary

- **To create a structure (user-defined data type):**

  Use the Structure statement, whose syntax is shown in Figure 10-3. In most applications, you enter the Structure statement in the form's Declarations section.

- **To declare a structure variable:**

  Use the following syntax: {**Dim** | **Private**} *structureVariableName* **As** *structureName*.

- **To refer to a member within a structure variable:**

  Use the syntax *structureVariableName***.***memberName*.

- **To create an array of structure variables:**

  Declare the array using the structure as the data type.

- **To refer to a member within a structure variable stored in an array:**

  Use the syntax *arrayName***(***subscript***).***memberName*.

Lesson A Key Terms

Member variables—the variables contained in a structure

Structure statement—used to create user-defined data types (structures)

Structure variables—variables declared using a structure as the data type

Structures— data types created using the Structure statement; allow the programmer to group related items into one unit

User-defined data types—data types created using the Structure statement; also called structures

Lesson A Review Questions

1. You use the ________________________ statement to create a user-defined data type.
   a. Declare
   b. Define
   c. Structure
   d. UserType

2. In most applications, the code to define a user-defined data type is entered in the form's ________________________.
   a. Declarations section
   b. Definition section
   c. Load event procedure
   d. User-defined section

3. Which of the following statements assigns the string "Maple" to the `strStreet` member variable within a structure variable named `address`?
   a. `address&strStreet = "Maple"`
   b. `address.strStreet = "Maple"`
   c. `strStreet.address = "Maple"`
   d. None of the above.

4. An array is declared using the statement `Dim inventory(4) As Product`. Which of the following statements assigns the number 100 to the `intQuantity` member variable contained in the last array element?
   a. `inventory.intQuantity(4) = 100`
   b. `inventory(4).Product.intQuantity = 100`
   c. `inventory(3).intQuantity = 100`
   d. None of the above.

5. An application uses a structure named Employee. Which of the following statements creates a 5-element one-dimensional array of Employee structure variables?
   a. `Dim workers(4) As Employee`
   b. `Dim workers(5) As Employee`
   c. `Dim workers As Employee(4)`
   d. `Dim workers As Employee(5)`

Lesson A Exercises

1. Write a Structure statement that defines a structure named Book. The structure contains three member variables named `strTitle`, `strAuthor`, and `decPrice`. Then write a Dim statement that declares a Book variable named `fiction`. INTRODUCTORY

2. Write a Structure statement that defines a structure named Tape. The structure contains four member variables named `strName`, `strArtist`, `strSongLength`, and `intSongNum`. Then write a Private statement that declares a Tape variable named `blues`. INTRODUCTORY

3. An application contains the following Structure statement: INTRODUCTORY

```
Structure Computer
   Public strModel As String
   Public dblCost As Double
End Structure
```

   a. Write a Dim statement that declares a Computer variable named `homeUse`.

   b. Write an assignment statement that assigns the string "IB-50" to the `strModel` member.

   c. Write an assignment statement that assigns the number 2400 to the `dblCost` member.

4. An application contains the following Structure statement: INTRODUCTORY

```
Structure MyFriend
   Public strLast As String
   Public strFirst As String
End Structure
```

   a. Write a Dim statement that declares a MyFriend variable named `school`.

   b. Write an assignment statement that assigns the value in the txtFirst control to the `strFirst` member.

   c. Write an assignment statement that assigns the value in the txtLast control to the `strLast` member.

   d. Write an assignment statement that assigns the value in the `strLast` member to the lblLast control.

   e. Write an assignment statement that assigns the value in the `strFirst` member to the lblFirst control.

INTERMEDIATE

5. An application contains the following Structure statement:

```
Structure Computer
   Public strId As String
   Public decCost As Decimal
End Structure
```

   a. Write a Private statement that declares a 10-element one-dimensional array of Computer variables. Name the array `business`.

   b. Write an assignment statement that assigns the string "HPP405" to the first array element's `strId` member.

   c. Write an assignment statement that assigns the number 3600 to the first array element's `decCost` member.

INTERMEDIATE

6. An application contains the following Structure statement:

```
Structure MyFriend
   Public strName As String
   Public strBirthday As String
End Structure
```

   a. Write a Dim statement that declares a 5-element one-dimensional array of MyFriend variables. Name the array `home`.

   b. Write an assignment statement that assigns the value in the txtName control to the last array element's `strName` member.

   c. Write an assignment statement that assigns the value in the txtBirthday control to the last array element's `strBirthday` member.

INTERMEDIATE

7. In this exercise, you modify the Price List application completed in the lesson. Use Windows to make a copy of the Price List Solution-Structure folder, which is contained in the VB2008\Chap10 folder. Rename the folder Modified Price List Solution-Structure. Open the Price List Solution (Price List Solution.sln) file contained in the VB2008\Chap10\Modified Price List Solution-Structure folder. Open the designer window. Modify the application to display both the name and price corresponding to the product ID entered by the user. You will need to modify the interface and the code (including the Structure statement). The names of the products are shown in Figure 10-13. Save the solution, then start and test the application. Stop the application. Close the Code Editor window, then close the solution.

Product ID	Name
BX35	Necklace
CR20	Bracelet
FE15	Jewelry box
KW10	Doll
MM67	Ring

Figure 10-13 Product IDs and names

INTERMEDIATE

8. Open the Carver Solution (Carver Solution.sln) file, which is contained in the VB2008\Chap10\Carver Solution folder. If necessary, open the designer window. The application should display a grade based on the number of points entered by the user. The grading scale is shown in Figure 10-14. Open the Code Editor window. Create a structure that contains two members: an Integer variable for the minimum points and a String variable for the grades. Use the structure to declare a 5-element one-dimensional array. Store the minimum points and grades in the array. The application should search the array for the number of points earned and then display the appropriate grade from the array. Code the application. Save the solution, then start and test the application. Stop the application. Close the Code Editor window, then close the solution.

Minimum points	Maximum points	Grade
0	299	F
300	349	D
350	399	C
400	449	B
450	500	A

Figure 10-14 Grading scale

Discovery

9. Open the Average Solution (Average Solution.sln) file, which is contained in the VB2008\Chap10\Average Solution folder. If necessary, open the designer window. The application should display a student's name and the average of five test scores entered by the user.

   a. Open the Code Editor window. Create a structure named StudentInfo. The structure should contain two members: a String variable for the student's name and a Double array for the test scores. An array contained in a structure cannot be assigned an initial size, so you will need to include an empty set of parentheses after the array name, like this: `Dim dblScores() As Double`.

   b. Now code the btnCalc control's Click event procedure. First, use the StudentInfo structure to declare a structure variable. Next, research the Visual Basic ReDim statement, then use the ReDim statement to declare the array's size. The array should have five elements.

   c. The btnCalc control's Click event procedure should use the InputBox function to get the student's name. It also should use a repetition structure and the InputBox function to get the five test scores from the user, storing each in the array. The procedure should display the student's name and average test score in the lblAverage control.

   d. Save the solution, then start and test the application. Stop the application. Close the Code Editor window, then close the solution.

Discovery

10. In this exercise, you modify the application from Exercise 9. Use Windows to make a copy of the Average Solution folder, which is contained in the VB2008\Chap10 folder. Rename the folder Modified Average Solution. Open the Average Solution (Average Solution.sln) file contained in the VB2008\Chap10\Modified Average Solution folder. Open the designer window. Change the lblAverage control's Font property to Courier New, 9pt. Change its TextAlign property to TopLeft. Open the Code Editor window. Modify the application to calculate the average of five test scores for each of four students. (Hint: You will need to use an array of structure variables.) Display each student's name and average test score in the lblAverage control. Save the solution, then start and test the application. Stop the application. Close the Code Editor window, then close the solution.

LESSON B

After studying Lesson B, you should be able to:

- Open and close a sequential access file
- Write data to a sequential access file
- Read data from a sequential access file
- Determine whether a sequential access file exists
- Test for the end of a sequential access file

Sequential Access Files

In addition to getting data from the keyboard and sending data to the computer screen, an application also can get data from and send data to a file on a disk. Getting data from a file is referred to as "reading from the file," and sending data to a file is referred to as "writing to the file." Files to which data is written are called **output files**, because the files store the output produced by an application. Files that are read by the computer are called **input files**, because an application uses the data in the files as input. Most input and output files are composed of lines of text that are both read and written sequentially. In other words, they are read and written in consecutive order, one line at a time, beginning with the first line in the file and ending with the last line in the file. Such files are referred to as **sequential access files**, because of the manner in which the lines of text are accessed. Examples of text stored in sequential access files include an employee list, a memo, or a sales report.

Writing Data to a Sequential Access File

An item of data—such as the string "Jacob"—is viewed differently by a human being and a computer. To a human being, the string represents a person's name; to a computer, it is merely a sequence of characters. Programmers refer to a sequence of characters as a **stream of characters**. In Visual Basic, you use a **StreamWriter object** to write a stream of characters to a sequential access file. Before you create the StreamWriter object, you first declare a variable to store the object in the computer's internal memory. Figure 10-15 shows the syntax and an example of declaring a StreamWriter variable. The `IO` in the syntax stands for "Input/Output."

Declaring a StreamWriter variable

Syntax
{**Dim** | **Private**} *streamWriterVariableName* **As IO.StreamWriter**

Example
```
Dim outFile As IO.StreamWriter
```
declares a StreamWriter variable named `outFile`

Figure 10-15 Syntax and an example of declaring a StreamWriter variable

You will use a StreamWriter variable in the Game Show Contestants application, which you code in this lesson. The application will write the names of contestants to a sequential access file. It also will subsequently read the names and display them in a list box.

To open the Game Show Contestants application, and then begin coding the application:

1. If necessary, start Visual Studio 2008 or Visual Basic 2008 Express Edition. Close the Start Page window.
2. Open the **Contestant Solution** (**Contestant Solution.sln**) file, which is contained in the VB2008\Chap10\Contestant Solution folder. If necessary, open the designer window. See Figure 10-16.

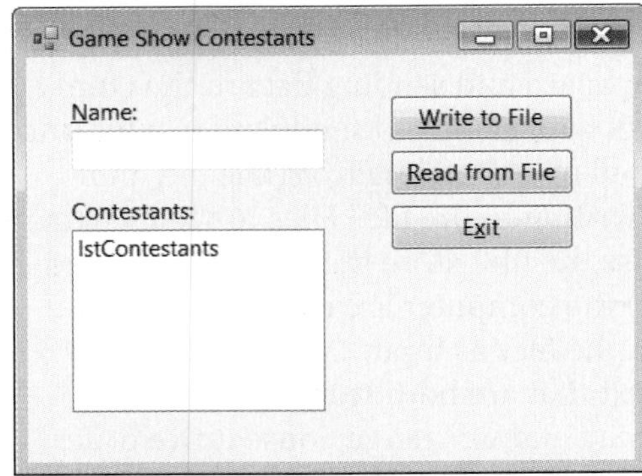

Figure 10-16 User interface for the Game Show Contestants application

3. Open the Code Editor window. Replace the <your name> and <current date> text in the comments with your name and the current date.
4. Locate the code template for the btnWrite control's Click event procedure. Click the **blank line** below the `' declare a StreamWriter variable` comment. Type **Dim outFile As IO.StreamWriter** and press **Enter**.

After declaring a StreamWriter variable, you can use the syntax shown in Figure 10-17 to create a StreamWriter object. As the figure indicates, creating a StreamWriter object involves opening a sequential access file using one of two methods: CreateText or AppendText. You use the **CreateText method** to open a sequential access file for output. When you open a file for output, the computer creates a new, empty file to which data can be written. If the file already exists, the computer erases the contents of the file before writing any data to it. You use the **AppendText method** to open a sequential access file for append. When a file is opened for append, new data is written after any existing data in the file. If the file does not exist, the computer creates the file for you. In addition to opening the file, both methods automatically create a StreamWriter object to represent the file in the application. You assign the StreamWriter object to a StreamWriter variable, which you use to refer to the file in code. Also included in Figure 10-17 are examples of using the CreateText and AppendText methods. When processing the statement in Example 1, the computer searches for the employee.txt file in the VB2008\Chap10 folder on the F drive. If the file exists, its contents are erased and the file is opened for output; otherwise, a new, empty file is created and opened for output. The statement creates a StreamWriter object and assigns it to the `outFile` variable. Unlike the *fileName* argument in Example 1, the *fileName* argument in Example 2 does not contain a folder path. Therefore, the computer will search for the file in the default folder, which is the current project's bin\Debug folder. In this case, if the computer locates the report.txt file in the default folder, it opens the file for append. If it does not find the file, it creates a new, empty file and then opens the file for append. Like the statement in Example 1, the statement in Example 2 creates a StreamWriter object and assigns it to the `outFile` variable.

Creating a StreamWriter object by opening a sequential access file

Syntax

IO.File.*method*(*fileName*)

method	Description
CreateText	opens a sequential access file for output
AppendText	opens a sequential access file for append

Example 1

```
outFile = IO.File.CreateText("F:\VB2008\Chap10\employee.txt")
```

opens the employee.txt file for output; creates a StreamWriter object and assigns it to the `outFile` variable

Example 2

```
outFile = IO.File.AppendText("report.txt")
```

opens the report.txt file for append; creates a StreamWriter object and assigns it to the `outFile` variable

Figure 10-17 Syntax and examples of creating a StreamWriter object by opening a file

Only specify the folder path in the *fileName* argument when you are sure that the folder path will not change. Keep in mind that a USB drive may have a different letter designation on another computer.

When the user clicks the Write to File button in the Game Show Contestants interface, the name entered in the Name box should be added to the end of the existing names in the file. Therefore, you will need to open the sequential access file for append. A descriptive name for a file that stores the names of contestants is contestants.txt. Although it is not a requirement, the "txt" (short for "text") filename extension is commonly used when naming sequential access files; this is because the files contain text.

To continue coding the btnWrite control's Click event procedure:

1. Click the **blank line** below the `' open the file for append` comment.
2. Type **outFile = IO.File.AppendText("contestants.txt")** and press **Enter**.

After opening a file for either output or append, you can begin writing data to it. You can do this using either the **Write method** or the **WriteLine method**; however, in most cases you will use the WriteLine method. The difference between both methods is that the WriteLine method writes a newline character after the data. Figure 10-18 shows the syntax and an example of both methods. As the figure indicates, when using the Write method, the next character written to the file will appear immediately after the letter o in the string "Hello". When using the WriteLine method, however, the next character written to the file will appear on the line immediately below the string. Notice that you do not need to include the file's name in either method's syntax. This is because the data will be written to the file associated with the StreamWriter variable.

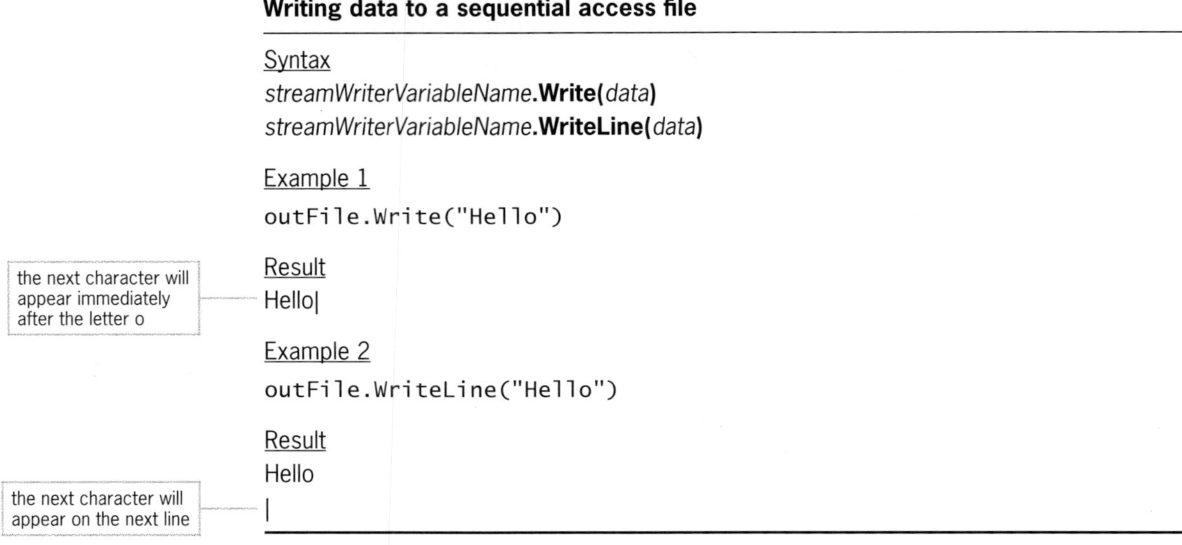

Writing data to a sequential access file

Syntax
streamWriterVariableName.**Write(***data***)**
streamWriterVariableName.**WriteLine(***data***)**

Example 1
```
outFile.Write("Hello")
```

Result
Hello|

the next character will appear immediately after the letter o

Example 2
```
outFile.WriteLine("Hello")
```

Result
Hello
|

the next character will appear on the next line

Figure 10-18 Syntax and examples of writing data to a sequential access file

Each contestant's name should appear on a separate line in the file, so you will use the WriteLine method to write each name to the file.

To continue coding the btnWrite control's Click event procedure:

1. Click the **blank line** below the `' write the name on a separate line in the file` comment.
2. Type **outFile.WriteLine(txtName.Text)** and press **Enter**.

You should use the **Close method** to close a sequential access file as soon as you are finished using it. This ensures that the data is saved and it makes the file available for use elsewhere in the application. The syntax to close a sequential access file associated with a StreamWriter object is *streamWriter-VariableName*.**Close()**. Here again, notice that you use the StreamWriter variable to refer to the file in code.

To finish coding the btnWrite control's Click event procedure, and then test the code:

1. Click the **blank line** below the `' close the file` comment, type **outFile.Close()** and press **Enter**.
2. Save the solution, then start the application. Type **Inez Harrison** in the Name box, then click the **Write to File** button. Use the application to write the following four names to the file:

   Clark Smith
   Khalid Shaw
   Joe Mendez
   Sue Chang

3. Click the **Exit** button. Now open the contestants.txt file to verify its contents. Click **File** on the menu bar, then click **Open File**. Open the project's bin\Debug folder. Click **contestants.txt** in the list of filenames, then click the **Open** button. The contestants.txt window opens and shows the five names contained in the file. See Figure 10-19.

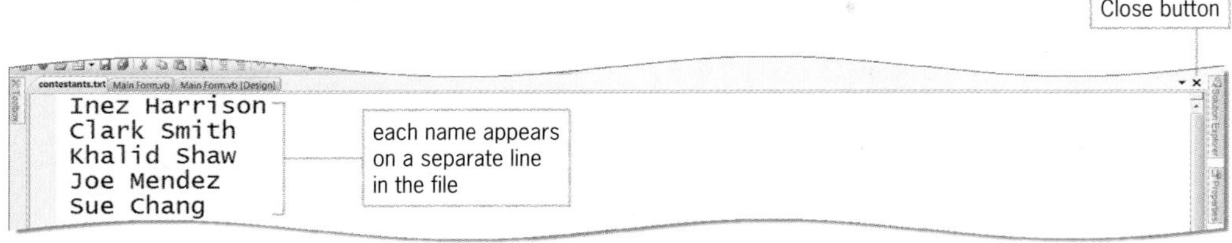

Figure 10-19 Names contained in the contestants.txt file

4. Close the contestants.txt window by clicking its **Close** button.

Reading Data From a Sequential Access File

Next, you will code the Read from File button. In Visual Basic, you use a **StreamReader object** to read data from a sequential access file. Before creating the StreamReader object, you first declare a variable to store the object in the computer's internal memory. Figure 10-20 shows the syntax and an example of declaring a StreamReader variable. As mentioned earlier, the `IO` in the syntax stands for "Input/Output."

Declaring a StreamReader variable

Syntax
{**Dim** | **Private**} *streamReaderVariableName* **As IO.StreamReader**

Example
```
Dim inFile As IO.StreamReader
```
declares a StreamReader variable named `inFile`

Figure 10-20 Syntax and an example of declaring a StreamReader variable

To begin coding the Read from File button's Click event procedure:

1. Locate the code template for the btnRead control's Click event procedure.

2. Click the **blank line** below the `' declare variables` comment. Type **Dim inFile As IO.StreamReader** and press **Enter**.

After declaring a StreamReader variable, you can use the **OpenText method** to open a sequential access file for input; doing this automatically creates a StreamReader object. When a file is opened for input, the computer can read the lines of text stored in the file. Figure 10-21 shows the OpenText method's syntax along with an example of using the method. The *fileName* argument in the example does not include a folder path, so the computer will search for the report.txt file in the current project's bin\Debug folder. If the computer finds the file, it opens the file for input; otherwise, a runtime error occurs, causing the application to end abruptly. You assign the StreamReader object created by the OpenText method to a StreamReader variable, which you use to refer to the file in code.

Creating a StreamReader object by opening a sequential access file

Syntax
IO.File.OpenText(*fileName***)**

Example
`inFile = IO.File.OpenText("report.txt")`
opens the report.txt file for input; creates a StreamReader object and assigns it to the `inFile` variable

Figure 10-21 Syntax and an example of creating a StreamReader object by opening a file

You can use the Exists method to avoid the runtime error that occurs when the computer cannot locate the file you want opened for input. Figure 10-22 shows the method's syntax and includes an example of using the method. Here too, if the *fileName* argument does not include a folder path, the computer searches for the file in the current project's bin\Debug folder. The **Exists method** returns the Boolean value True if the file exists; otherwise, it returns the Boolean value False.

Determining whether a sequential access file exists

Syntax
IO.File.Exists(*fileName***)**

Example
`If IO.File.Exists("report.txt") Then`
determines whether the report.txt file exists in the current project's bin\Debug folder; you also can write the If clause as `If IO.File.Exists("report.txt") = True Then`

Figure 10-22 Syntax and an example of the Exists method

To continue coding the btnRead control's Click event procedure:

1. Click the **blank line** below the `' determine whether the file exists` comment. Type **If IO.File.Exists("contestants.txt") Then** and press **Enter**.
2. If the file exists, you will use the OpenText method to open the file. Type **' open the file for input** and press **Enter**, then type **inFile = IO.File.OpenText("contestants.txt")** and press **Enter** twice.
3. If the file does not exist, you will display an appropriate message. Type **else** and press **Enter**, then type the additional lines of code shown in Figure 10-23.

```
        ' determine whether the file exists
        If IO.File.Exists("contestants.txt") Then
            ' open the file for input
            inFile = IO.File.OpenText("contestants.txt")

        Else
            MessageBox.Show("Can't find the contestants.txt file", _
                            "Game Show Contestants", MessageBoxButtons.OK, _
                            MessageBoxIcon.Information)
        End If
    End Sub
```

enter these 3 lines of code

Figure 10-23 Code entered in the selection structure's false path

After opening a file for input, you can use the **ReadLine method** to read the file's contents, one line at a time. A **line** is defined as a sequence (stream) of characters followed by the newline character. The ReadLine method returns a string that contains only the sequence of characters in the current line; the string does not include the newline character at the end of the line. In most cases, you assign the string returned by the ReadLine method to a String variable. Figure 10-24 shows the ReadLine method's syntax. The method does not require you to provide the file's name, because it uses the file associated with the StreamReader variable. Figure 10-24 also includes examples of using the ReadLine method to read a line of text from a sequential access file. The statement in Example 1 reads a line of text from the file associated with the `inFile` variable. It assigns the line, excluding the newline character, to a String variable named `strMessage`. In most cases, an application will need to read each line of text contained in a sequential access file, one line at a time. You can do this using a repetition structure along with the Peek method, as shown in Example 2 in Figure 10-24. The syntax of the Peek method is *streamReaderVariableName*.**Peek**. The **Peek method** "peeks" into the file to determine whether the file contains another character to read. If the file contains another character, the Peek method returns the character; otherwise, it returns the number -1. The `Do Until inFile.Peek = -1` clause in Example 2 tells the computer to process the loop instructions until the Peek method returns the number -1, which indicates that there are no more characters to read. In other words, the Do clause tells the computer to process the loop instructions until the end of the file is reached.

Reading data from a sequential access file

Syntax
streamReaderVariableName.**ReadLine**

Example 1

```
strMessage = inFile.ReadLine
```

reads a line from a sequential access file and assigns the line (excluding the newline character) to the `strMessage` variable

Example 2

```
Do Until inFile.Peek = -1
   strLine = inFile.ReadLine
   MessageBox.Show(strLine)
Loop
```

reads the lines in a sequential access file, line by line, assigning the line (excluding the newline character) to the `strLine` variable and then displaying the line in a message box

Figure 10-24 Syntax and examples of reading data from a sequential access file

To finish coding the btnRead control's Click event procedure:

1. First, declare a variable to store the string returned by the ReadLine method. Click the **blank line** below the `Dim inFile As IO.StreamReader` instruction. Each line in the contestants.txt file represents a name, so you will call the variable `strName`. Type **Dim strName As String** and press **Enter**.
2. Click the **blank line** below the `inFile = IO.File.OpenText ("contestants.txt")` statement. Enter the following comment and Do clause. Be sure to type the minus sign before the number 1.

   ' process loop instructions until end of file
   Do Until inFile.Peek = **–1**
3. Now read a line of text and assign it (excluding the newline character) to the `strName` variable. Type **' read a name** and press **Enter**, then type **strName** = **inFile.ReadLine** and press **Enter**.
4. Now add the name to the Contestants list box. Type **' add name to list box** and press **Enter**, then type **lstContestants.Items.Add(strName)**.
5. Finally, close the file. Click **after the letter p** in the Loop clause, then press **Enter** to insert a blank line. Type **' close the file** and press **Enter**, then type **inFile.Close()**.
6. Save the solution. Figure 10-25 shows the code entered in the Click event procedures for the btnWrite and btnRead controls.

```
Private Sub btnWrite_Click(ByVal sender As Object, _
    ByVal e As System.EventArgs) Handles btnWrite.Click
    ' writes a name to a sequential access file

    ' declare a StreamWriter variable
    Dim outFile As IO.StreamWriter

    ' open the file for append
    outFile = IO.File.AppendText("contestants.txt")

    ' write the name on a separate line in the file
    outFile.WriteLine(txtName.Text)

    ' close the file
    outFile.Close()

    ' clear the list box, then set the focus
    lstContestants.Items.Clear()
    txtName.Focus()
End Sub

Private Sub btnRead_Click(ByVal sender As Object, _
    ByVal e As System.EventArgs) Handles btnRead.Click
    ' reads names from a sequential access file
    ' and displays them in the interface
```

Figure 10-25 Code entered in the btnWrite and btnRead controls' Click event procedures *(continues)*

(continued)

```
    ' declare variables
    Dim inFile As IO.StreamReader
    Dim strName As String

    ' clear previous names from the list box
    lstContestants.Items.Clear()

    ' determine whether the file exists
    If IO.File.Exists("contestants.txt") Then
       ' open the file for input
       inFile = IO.File.OpenText("contestants.txt")
       ' process loop instructions until end of file
       Do Until inFile.Peek = -1
          ' read a name
          strName = inFile.ReadLine
          ' add name to list box
          lstContestants.Items.Add(strName)
       Loop
       ' close the file
       inFile.Close()
    Else
       MessageBox.Show("Can't find the contestants.txt file", _
                       "Game Show Contestants", MessageBoxButtons.OK, _
                       MessageBoxIcon.Information)
    End If
End Sub
```

Figure 10-25 Code entered in the btnWrite and btnRead controls' Click event procedures

To test the application's code:

1. Save the solution, if necessary, then start the application. Click the **Read from File** button. The five names contained in the contestants.txt file appear in the Contestants box. See Figure 10-26.

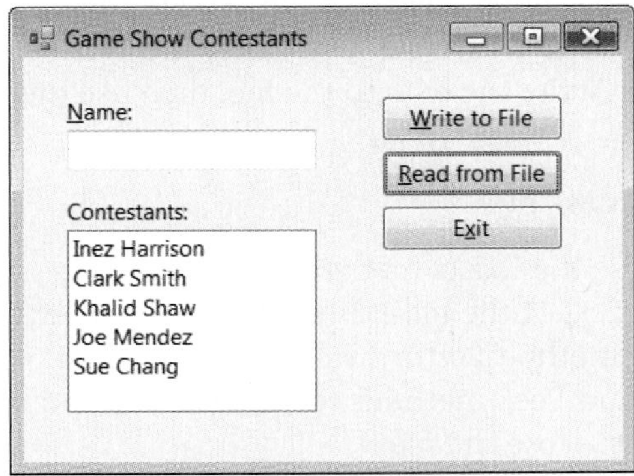

Figure 10-26 Contestant names appear in the Contestants box

2. On your own, use the Write to File button to add the following three names to the file.

   Opal Jones
   Willow Smith
   Hank Padito

3. Now use the Read from File button to display the eight names in the list box, then click the **Exit** button.

4. Next, you will modify the If clause in the btnRead control's Click event procedure to make the Exists method return the Boolean value False. This will allow you to test the code entered in the selection structure's false path. Change "contestants.txt" in the If clause to **"contestant.txt"**. Save the solution, then start the application. Click the **Read from File** button. The "Can't find the contestants.txt file" message appears in a message box. Click the **OK** button to close the message box, then click the **Exit** button.

5. Change "contestant.txt" in the If clause to **"contestants.txt"**. Save the solution, then start the application. Click the **Read from File** button, which displays the eight names in the list box. Click the **Exit** button. Close the Code Editor window, then close the solution.

Lesson B Summary

- **To write data to a sequential access file:**

  Declare a StreamWriter variable, then use either the CreateText method or the AppendText method to open a sequential access file. Assign the method's return value to the StreamWriter variable. Use either the Write method or the WriteLine method to write the data to the file, then use the Close method to close the file.

- **To read data from a sequential access file:**

  Declare a StreamReader variable. Use the Exists method to determine whether the sequential access file exists. If the file exists, use the OpenText method to open the file. Assign the method's return value to the StreamReader variable. Use the ReadLine and Peek methods to read the data from the file, then use the Close method to close the file.

- **To determine whether a sequential access file exists:**

  Use the Exists method in the following syntax: **IO.File.Exists(*fileName*)**. The method returns the Boolean value True if the file exists; otherwise, it returns the Boolean value False.

- **To determine whether the end of a sequential access file has been reached:**

  Use the Peek method in the following syntax: *streamReaderVariableName*.**Peek**. The method returns the number -1 when the end of the file has been reached; otherwise, it returns the next character in the file.

Lesson B Key Terms

AppendText method—used with a StreamWriter variable to open a sequential access file for append

Close method—used with either a StreamWriter variable or a StreamReader variable to close a sequential access file

CreateText method—used with a StreamWriter variable to open a sequential access file for output

Exists method—used with a StreamReader variable to determine whether a file exists

Input files—files from which an application reads data

Line—a sequence (stream) of characters followed by the newline character

OpenText method—used with a StreamReader variable to open a sequential access file for input

Output files—files to which an application writes data

Peek method—used with a StreamReader variable to determine whether a file contains another character to read

ReadLine method—used with a StreamReader variable to read a line of text from a sequential access file

Sequential access files—files composed of lines of text that are both read and written sequentially

Stream of characters—a sequence of characters

StreamReader object—used to read a sequence (stream) of characters from a sequential access file

StreamWriter object—used to write a sequence (stream) of characters to a sequential access file

Write method—used with a StreamWriter variable to write data to a sequential access file; differs from the WriteLine method in that it does not write a newline character after the data

WriteLine method—used with a StreamWriter variable to write data to a sequential access file; differs from the Write method in that it writes a newline character after the data

Lesson B Review Questions

1. Which of the following opens the states.txt file and allows the computer to write new data to the end of the existing data in the file?
   a. `outFile = IO.File.AddText("states.txt")`
   b. `outFile = IO.File.AppendText("states.txt")`
   c. `outFile = IO.File.InsertText("states.txt")`
   d. `outFile = IO.File.OpenText("states.txt")`

2. If the file to be opened exists, the ______________________ method erases the file's contents.

   a. AppendText

   b. CreateText

   c. InsertText

   d. OpenText

3. Which of the following reads a line of text from a sequential access file and assigns the line (excluding the newline character) to the `strText` variable?

   a. `inFile.Read(strText)`

   b. `inFile.ReadLine(strText)`

   c. `strText = inFile.ReadLine`

   d. `strText = inFile.Read(line)`

4. The Peek method returns ______________________ when the end of the file is reached.

   a. -1

   b. 0

   c. the last character in the file

   d. the newline character

5. Which of the following can be used to determine whether the employ.txt file exists?

   a. `If IO.File.Exists("employ.txt") Then`

   b. `If IO.File("employ.txt").Exists Then`

   c. `If IO.Exists("employ.txt") = True Then`

   d. `If IO.Exists.File("employ.txt") = True Then`

6. The OpenText method creates a ______________________ object.

   a. File

   b. SequenceReader

   c. StreamWriter

   d. None of the above.

7. The AppendText method creates a ______________________ object.

   a. File

   b. SequenceReader

   c. StreamWriter

   d. None of the above.

Lesson B Exercises

1. Write the code to declare a variable named `outFile` that can be used to write data to a sequential access file. Then write the statement to open a sequential access file named sales.txt for output. INTRODUCTORY

2. Write the code to declare a variable named `inFile` that can be used to read data from a sequential access file. Then write the statement to open a sequential access file named sales.txt for input. INTRODUCTORY

3. Write the code to close the sequential access file associated with a StreamWriter variable named `outFile`. INTRODUCTORY

4. Write an If clause that determines whether a sequential access file exists. The file's name is sales.txt. INTRODUCTORY

5. Write a Do clause that determines whether the end of a sequential access file has been reached. The file is associated with a StreamReader variable named `inFile`. INTRODUCTORY

6. Open the Gross Pay Solution (Gross Pay Solution.sln) file, which is contained in the VB2008\Chap10\Gross Pay Solution folder. If necessary, open the designer window. The interface provides a text box for entering a gross pay amount. The Save button should write the gross pay amount to a sequential access file named gross.txt. Save the file in the project's bin\Debug folder. The Display button should read the gross pay amounts from the gross.txt file and display each (formatted with a dollar sign and two decimal places) in the list box. Open the Code Editor window. Code the Click event procedures for the btnSave and btnDisplay controls. Save the solution, then start the application. Write the following 10 gross pay amounts to the file: 600, 1250, 750.67, 350.75, 2000, 450, 125.89, 560, 1400, and 555.78. Click the Display button to display the gross pay amounts in the interface. Stop the application. Close the Code Editor window, then close the solution. INTRODUCTORY

7. Open the Name Solution (Name Solution.sln) file, which is contained in the VB2008\Chap10\Name Solution folder. If necessary, open the designer window. Open the Code Editor window. Open the names.txt file contained in the project's bin\Debug folder. The sequential access file contains five names. Close the names.txt window. The btnDisplay control's Click event procedure should read the five names contained in the names.txt file, storing each in a 5-element one-dimensional array. The procedure should sort the array in descending order, and then display the contents of the array in the list box. Code the procedure. Save the solution, then start and test the application. Stop the application. Close the Code Editor window, then close the solution. (If you need to recreate the names.txt file, open the file in a window in the IDE. Delete the contents of the file, if necessary, then type the following five names, pressing Enter after typing each name: Joanne, Zelda, Abby, Ben, and Linda.) INTERMEDIATE

INTERMEDIATE

8. Open the Salary Solution (Salary Solution.sln) file, which is contained in the VB2008\Chap10\Salary Solution folder. If necessary, open the designer window. Open the Code Editor window and study the existing code. The btnDisplay control's Click event procedure stores six salary amounts in a one-dimensional array named `intSalaries`. Each salary amount corresponds to a salary code from 1 through 6. Code 1's salary is stored in the `intSalaries(0)` element in the array. Code 2's salary is stored in the `intSalaries(1)` element, and so on. After storing the salary amounts in the array, the procedure prompts the user to enter a salary code. It then displays the amount associated with the code. Currently, the Dim statement assigns the six salary amounts to the array. Modify the procedure so that it reads the salary amounts from the salary.txt file, which is contained in the project's bin\Debug folder, and stores each in the array. Save the solution, then start and test the application. Stop the application, then close the solution.

INTERMEDIATE

9. Open the Test Scores Solution (Test Scores Solution.sln) file, which is contained in the VB2008\Chap10\Test Scores Solution folder. If necessary, open the designer window. Open the Code Editor window. The btnSave control's Click event procedure should allow the user to enter an unknown number of test scores, saving each score in a sequential access file. The btnCount control's Click event procedure should display (in a message box) the number of scores stored in the file. Code both procedures. Save the solution, then start and test the application. Stop the application, then close the solution.

INTERMEDIATE

10. In this exercise, you code an application that reads five numbers from a sequential access file and stores the numbers in a one-dimensional array. The application then increases each number by 1 and writes the numbers to the file. The application also displays the current contents of the sequential access file. Open the Numbers Solution (Numbers Solution.sln) file, which is contained in the VB2008\Chap10\Numbers Solution folder. If necessary, open the designer window. Open the Code Editor window. Code the btnDisplay control's Click event procedure so it reads the five numbers stored in the numbers.txt file and displays the numbers in the list box. The numbers.txt file is contained in the project's bin\Debug folder. Currently, the file contains the numbers 1 through 5. Code the btnUpdate control's Click event procedure so it reads the five numbers from the numbers.txt file and stores the numbers in an array. It then should increase each number in the array by 1 and write the array contents to an empty numbers.txt file. Save the solution, then start the application. Click the Display button. The numbers 1 through 5 appear in the interface. Click the Update button, then click the Display button. The numbers 2 through 6 appear in the interface. Stop the application, then close the solution. (If you need to recreate the numbers.txt file, open the file in a window in the IDE. Delete the contents of the file, if necessary, then type the numbers 1 through 5, pressing Enter after typing each number.)

11. During July and August of each year, the Political Awareness Organization (PAO) sends a questionnaire to the voters in their district. The questionnaire asks the voter for his or her political party (Democratic, Republican, or Independent) and age. From the returned questionnaires, the organization's secretary tabulates the number of Democrats, Republicans, and Independents in the district. The secretary wants an application that she can use to save each respondent's information (political party and age) to a sequential access file. The application also should calculate and display the number of voters in each political party. Create a new Visual Basic Windows application. Name the solution, project, and form file PAO Solution, PAO Project, and Main Form.vb, respectively. Save the application in the VB2008\Chap10 folder. Create the interface shown in Figure 10-27. The Party list box should contain three items: Democratic, Republican, and Independent. The Age text box should accept only numbers and the Backspace key. Code the Click event procedures for the Write to File and Display Totals buttons. Save the solution, then start and test the application. Stop the application. Close the Code Editor window, then close the solution. ADVANCED

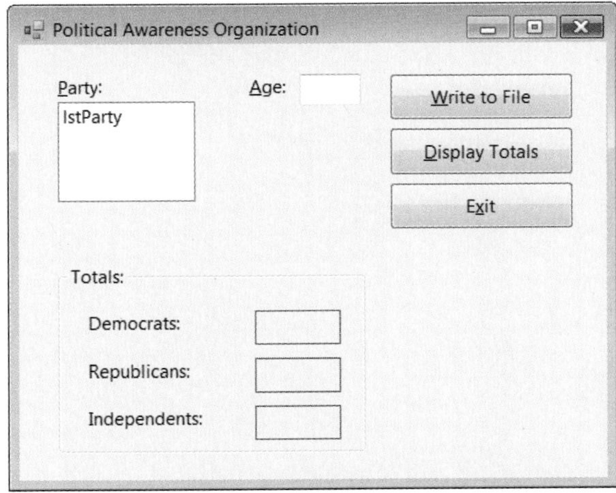

Figure 10-27 User interface for the PAO application

12. In this exercise, you modify the application from Exercise 11. Use Windows to make a copy of the PAO Solution folder, which is contained in the VB2008\Chap10 folder. Rename the folder Modified PAO Solution. Open the PAO Solution (PAO Solution.sln) file contained in the VB2008\Chap10\Modified PAO Solution folder. Open the designer window, then open the Code Editor window. Modify the code to use a structure. Save the solution, then start and test the application. Stop the application. Close the Code Editor window, then close the solution. ADVANCED

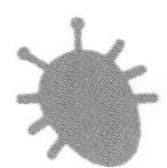

Swat The Bugs

13. Open the Debug Solution (Debug Solution.sln) file, which is contained in the VB2008\Chap10\Debug Solution-Lesson B folder. Open the Code Editor window and study the existing code. Start the application, then test it using Sue and 1000, and then using Pete and 5000. A runtime error occurs. Read the error message. Click Debug, then click Stop Debugging. Open the bonus.txt file, which is contained in the project's bin\Debug folder. Notice that the file is empty. Close the bonus.txt window. Locate and correct any errors in the code. Save the solution, then start and test the application again. Stop the application. Close the Code Editor window, then close the solution.

LESSON C

After studying Lesson C, you should be able to:

- Fill a list box with values stored in a sequential access file
- Add an item to a list box while an application is running
- Align columns of information
- Remove an item from a list box while an application is running
- Save list box items in a sequential access file

Coding the CD Collection Application

As you may remember, your task in this chapter is to create an application that uses a sequential access file to keep track of a person's CD collection. The application's user interface is shown in Figure 10-28, and its TOE chart is shown in Figure 10-29.

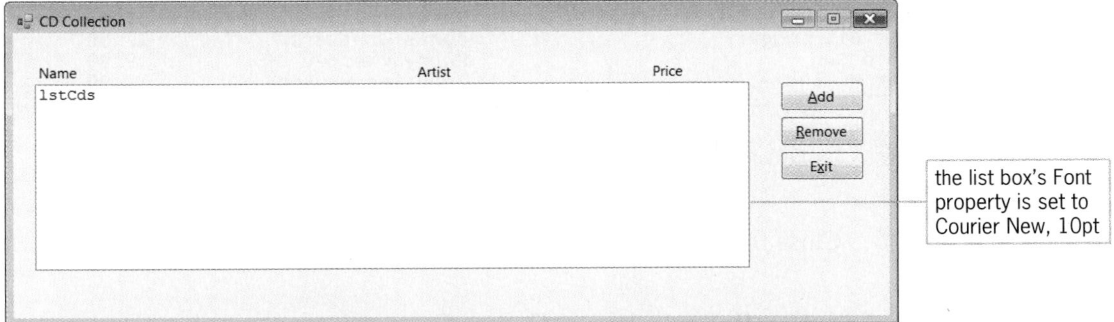

the list box's Font property is set to Courier New, 10pt

Figure 10-28 User interface for the CD Collection application

Task	**Object**	**Event**
Read the CDs.txt file and assign its contents to lstCds	frmMain	Load
Save the contents of lstCds in the CDs.txt file		FormClosing
End the application	btnExit	Click
1. Get CD name, artist name, and price 2. Add CD name, artist name, and price to lstCds	btnAdd	Click
Remove the selected line from lstCds	btnRemove	Click
Display the CD name, artist name, and price	lstCds	None

Figure 10-29 TOE chart for the CD Collection application

To open the CD Collection application, and then view the CDs.txt file:

1. If necessary, start Visual Studio 2008 or Visual Basic 2008 Express Edition. Close the Start Page window.
2. Open the **CD Collection Solution** (**CD Collection Solution.sln**) file, which is contained in the VB2008\Chap10\CD Collection Solution folder. If necessary, open the designer window.
3. Open the Code Editor window. Replace the <your name> and <current date> text with your name and the current date.
4. Click **File** on the menu bar, then click **Open File**. Open the project's bin\Debug folder. Click **CDs.txt** in the list of filenames, then click the **Open** button. The CDs.txt window shows the information contained in the file. See Figure 10-30.

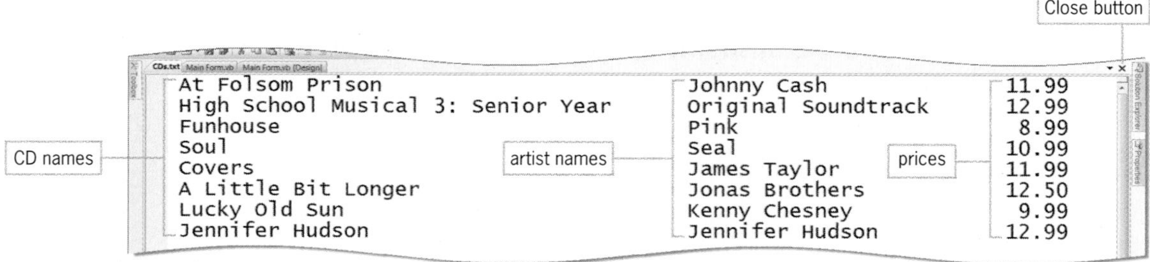

Figure 10-30 CDs.txt window showing the contents of the sequential access file

5. Close the CDs.txt window.

Coding the Form's Load Event Procedure

You will code the form's Load event procedure first. Figure 10-31 shows the procedure's pseudocode.

---

frmMain Load event procedure

1. if the CDs.txt sequential access file exists
   - open the file for input
   - repeat until the end of the file
     - read a line from the file
     - add the line to the lstCds control
   - end repeat
   - close the file
   - select the first line in the lstCds control

   else
   - display the "Can't find the CDs.txt file" message

   end if

Figure 10-31 Pseudocode for the form's Load event procedure

To code the form's Load event procedure, then test the procedure:

1. Locate the form's Load event procedure, then click the **blank line** below the `' declare variables` comment. As you learned in Lesson B, you use a StreamReader object to read data from a sequential access file. Before creating the StreamReader object, you first declare a variable to store the object in the computer's internal memory. Type **Dim inFile As IO.StreamReader** and press **Enter**.
2. The procedure also will need a variable to store the string returned by the ReadLine method when reading the file. Type **Dim strInfo As String** and press **Enter** twice.
3. Step 1 in the pseudocode begins by verifying that the CDs.txt file exists. If the file does not exist, the procedure should display an appropriate message. Enter the additional comment and lines of code indicated in Figure 10-32, then position the insertion point as shown in the figure.

position the insertion point here

```
        ' declare variables
        Dim inFile As IO.StreamReader
        Dim strInfo As String

        ' verify that the file exists
        If IO.File.Exists("CDs.txt") Then

        Else
            MessageBox.Show("Can't find the CDs.txt file", _
                            "CD Collection", MessageBoxButtons.OK, _
                            MessageBoxIcon.Information)
        End If
    End Sub
```

enter this comment and these lines of code

Figure 10-32 Additional comment and code entered in the form's Load event procedure

4. If the file exists, the procedure should open the file for input. Enter the following comment and assignment statement.

   ‘ open the file for input
   inFile = IO.File.OpenText(“CDs.txt”)

5. Now use a loop to read each line from the file, adding each to the list box. Enter the following comments and lines of code.

   ‘ process loop instructions until end of file
   Do Until inFile.Peek = -1
       ‘ read a line from the file
       strInfo = inFile.ReadLine
       ‘ add the line to the list box
       lstCds.Items.Add(strInfo)
   Loop

6. Now close the file. Click **after the letter p** in the Loop clause, then press **Enter** twice to insert two blank lines. Enter the following comment and line of code.

   ‘ close the file
   inFile.Close()

7. The last task in the selection structure's true path is to select the first item in the list box. Enter the following comment and line of code.

   ' select the first item in the list box
   lstCds.SelectedIndex = 0

8. Save the solution, then start the application. The information contained in the CDs.txt file appears in the list box. See Figure 10-33.

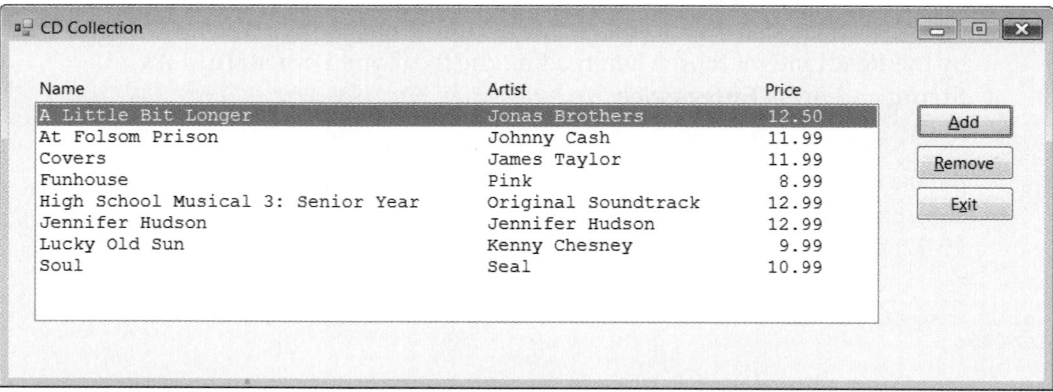

Figure 10-33 The contents of the CDs.txt file appears in the list box

9. Click the **Exit** button.

Coding the btnAdd Control's Click Event Procedure

According to the application's TOE chart, the btnAdd control's Click event procedure should get a CD name, artist name, and price from the user, and then display that information in the list box. Figure 10-34 shows the procedure's pseudocode.

btnAdd Click event procedure
1. use the InputBox function to get the CD name, artist name, and price
2. concatenate the CD name, artist name, and price, and then add the concatenated string to the lstCds control

Figure 10-34 Pseudocode for the btnAdd control's Click event procedure

To begin coding the btnAdd control's Click event procedure:

1. Locate the btnAdd control's Click event procedure, then click the **blank line** below the `' declare variables` comment. The procedure will use four String variables: three to store the input items (CD name, artist name, and price) and one to store the concatenated string. It also will use a Double variable to store the numeric equivalent of the price. Enter the following five Dim statements.

   Dim strName As String
   Dim strArtist As String
   Dim strPrice As String
   Dim strConcatenatedInfo As String
   Dim dblPrice As Double

2. Now use the InputBox function to get the CD name, artist name, and price from the user. Click the **blank line** below the `' get the CD information` comment, then enter the following lines of code.

```
strName = InputBox("CD name:", "CD Collection")
strArtist = InputBox("Artist:", "CD Collection")
strPrice = InputBox("Price:", "CD Collection")
```

Step 2 in the procedure's pseudocode is to concatenate the input items (CD name, artist name, and price) and then add the concatenated string to the list box. Notice that each input item appears in a separate column in the list box shown in Figure 10-33. The CD names and artist names in the first two columns are left-aligned within their respective column. The prices in the third column, however, are right-aligned within the column. In the next section, you will learn how to align columns of information.

Aligning Columns of Information

In Chapter 8, you learned how to use the PadLeft and PadRight methods to pad a string with a character until the string is a specified length. Recall that the syntax of the PadLeft method is *string*.**PadLeft(***length*[**,** *character*]**)**, and the syntax of the PadRight method is *string*.**PadRight(***length*[**,** *character*]**)**. In each syntax, *length* is an integer that represents the total number of characters you want the *string* to contain. The optional *character* argument is the character that each method uses to pad the *string* until it reaches the desired *length*. If the *character* argument is omitted, the default *character* is the space character. Figure 10-35 shows examples of using the PadLeft and PadRight methods to align columns of information added to a list box or written to a sequential access file. Example 1 aligns a column of numbers by the decimal point. Notice that you first format each number in the column to ensure that each has the same number of digits to the right of the decimal point. You then use the PadLeft method to insert spaces at the beginning of the number (if necessary); this right-aligns the number within the column. Because each number has the same number of digits to the right of the decimal point, aligning each number on the right will align each by its decimal point. Example 2 shows how you can align the second column of information when the first column contains strings with varying lengths. First, you use either the PadRight or PadLeft method to ensure that each string in the first column contains the same number of characters. You then concatenate the padded string to the information in the second column. The code in Example 2, for instance, uses the PadRight method to ensure that each name in the first column contains exactly 15 characters. It then concatenates the 15 characters with the string stored in the `strCity` variable, and then writes the concatenated string to the file. Because each name has 15 characters, each city entry will automatically appear beginning in character position 16 in the file. Example 2 also shows how you can use the **Strings.Space method** to include a specific number of space characters in a string. The method's syntax is **Strings.Space(***number***)**, where *number* is an integer representing the number of spaces to include.

In Example 1, you will also need to set the lstPrices control's Font property to a fixed-spaced font, such as Courier New. A fixed-spaced font uses the same amount of space to display each character.

Aligning columns of information

Example 1

```
Dim strFormatPrice As String
For dblPrice As Double = 9 To 11 Step 0.5
   strFormatPrice = dblPrice.ToString("N2")
   lstPrices.Items.Add(strFormatPrice.PadLeft(5))
Next dblPrice
```

Result

```
 9.00
 9.50
10.00
10.50
11.00
```

Example 2

```
Dim inFile As IO.StreamWriter
Dim strHeading As String = "Name" & Strings.Space(11) & "City"
Dim strName As String
Dim strCity As String

inFile = IO.File.CreateText("test.txt")
inFile.WriteLine(strHeading)

strName = InputBox("Enter name:", "Name")
Do While strName <> String.Empty
   strCity = InputBox("Enter city:", "City")
   inFile.WriteLine(strName.PadRight(15) & strCity)
   strName = InputBox("Enter name:", "Name")
Loop
inFile.Close()
```

Result (when the user enters the following: Janice, Paris, Sue, Rome)

```
Name      City
Janice    Paris
Sue       Rome
```

Figure 10-35 Examples of aligning columns of information

To complete the btnAdd control's Click event procedure, then test the procedure:

1. Click the **blank line** below the `' and 5 spaces for the price` comment. First, format the price to ensure that each contains two decimal places. Enter the following lines of code.

   Double.TryParse(strPrice, dblPrice)
   strPrice = dblPrice.ToString("N2")

2. Now concatenate the three input items, reserving 40 characters for the CD name, 25 characters for the artist name, and 5 characters for the price. Left-align the first two columns, but right-align the last column. Enter the following lines of code. Be sure to include a space before the line continuation character.

   strConcatenatedInfo = strName.PadRight(40) & _
   strArtist.PadRight(25) & strPrice.PadLeft(5)

3. Now add the concatenated string to the list box. Click the **blank line** below the `' add the information to the list box` comment. Enter the following line of code.

   lstCds.Items.Add(strConcatenatedInfo)

4. Save the solution, then start the application. Click the **Add** button. Type **Breakout** as the CD name, then press **Enter**. Type **Miley Cyrus** as the artist name, then press **Enter**. Type **8** as the price, then press **Enter**. The Add button's Click event procedure adds the CD information to the list box. The list box's Sorted property is set to True, so the information you entered appears in the third line of the list box. See Figure 10-36.

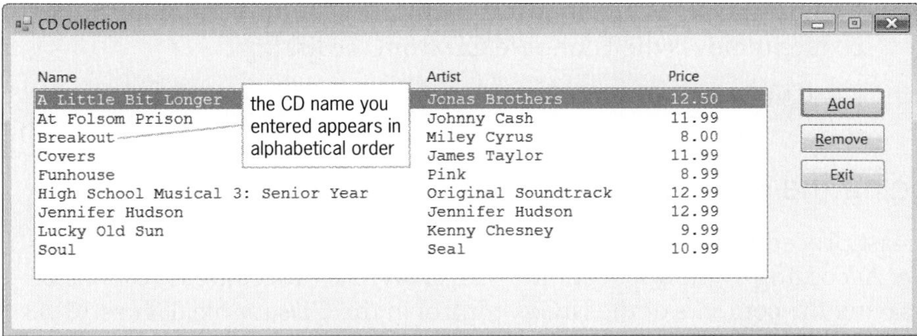

Figure 10-36 CD information added to the list box

5. Click the **Exit** button.

Coding the btnRemove Control's Click Event Procedure

According to the application's TOE chart, the btnRemove control's Click event procedure should remove the selected line from the lstCds control. Figure 10-37 shows the procedure's pseudocode.

btnRemove Click event procedure
1. if a line is selected in the lstCds control
        remove the line from the control
   end if

Figure 10-37 Pseudocode for the btnRemove control's Click event procedure

To begin coding the btnRemove control's Click event procedure:

1. Locate the btnRemove control's Click event procedure, then click the **blank line** below the `' if a line is selected, remove the line` comment.

2. If a line is selected in the list box, the list box's SelectedIndex property will contain the line's index; otherwise, it will contain the number -1. Enter the following If clause.

   If lstCds.SelectedIndex <> -1 Then

As you learned in Chapter 6, a list box has an Items collection. In addition to the Add method, which you use to add an item to a list box, the Items collection also has a RemoveAt method. The **RemoveAt method** allows you to specify the index of the item you want removed from the list box. The RemoveAt method's syntax is ***object*.Items.RemoveAt(*index*)**.

To complete the btnRemove control's Click event procedure, then test the procedure:

1. In the blank line below the If clause, type the following line of code, but don't press Enter.

   lstCds.Items.RemoveAt(lstCds.SelectedIndex)

2. Save the solution, then start the application. Click **Funhouse** in the list box, then click the **Remove** button. The button's Click event procedure removes the Funhouse CD from the list box.
3. Click the **Exit** button.

Coding the Form's FormClosing Event Procedure

You learned about the FormClosing event in Chapter 7's Lesson C.

The last procedure you need to code is the form's FormClosing event procedure. According to the application's TOE chart, the procedure is responsible for saving the contents of the lstCds control in the CDs.txt file. Figure 10-38 shows the procedure's pseudocode.

```
frmMain FormClosing event procedure
1. open the CDs.txt file for output
   repeat for each line in the list box
       write the line to the file
   end repeat
   close the file
```

Figure 10-38 Pseudocode for the form's FormClosing event procedure

To code the form's FormClosing event procedure, then test the application's code:

1. Locate the form's FormClosing event procedure, then click the **blank line** below the `' declare a StreamWriter variable` comment. As you learned in Lesson B, you use a StreamWriter object to write data to a sequential access file. Before creating the StreamWriter object, you first declare a variable to store the object in the computer's internal memory. Type **Dim outFile As IO.StreamWriter** and press **Enter**.
2. Step 1 in the pseudocode is to open the CDs.txt file for output. Click the **blank line** below the `' open the file for output` comment, then enter the following line of code.

   outFile = IO.File.CreateText("CDs.txt")

3. Now use a loop to write each line from the list box to the file. Click the **blank line** below the `' write each line in the list box` comment, then enter the following lines of code.

   ```
   For intIndex As Integer = 0 To lstCds.Items.Count - 1
       outFile.WriteLine(lstCds.Items(intIndex))
   Next intIndex
   ```

4. Finally, close the file. Click the **blank line** below the `' close the file` comment, then type **outFile.Close()**.

5. Save the solution, then start the application. Click the **Add** button. Type **Breakout** and press **Enter**. Type **Miley Cyrus** and press **Enter**, then type **8** and press **Enter**. The Add button's Click event procedure adds the CD information to the list box.

6. Click the **Exit** button. The computer processes the `Me.Close()` statement in the Exit button's Click event procedure; doing this invokes the form's FormClosing event. The FormClosing event procedure saves the contents of the list box to the CDs.txt file.

7. Now verify that the CD information you entered was saved to the CDs.txt file. Click **File** on the menu bar, then click **Open File**. Open the project's bin\Debug folder. Click **CDs.txt** in the list of filenames, then click the **Open** button. The CD information you entered appears in the third line in the file. Close the CDs.txt window by clicking its **Close** button.

8. Start the application. Click **Breakout** in the list box, then click the **Remove** button. The button's Click event procedure removes the CD information from the list box.

9. Click the **Exit** button. Now verify that the CDs.txt file does not contain the CD information you removed from the list box. Click **File** on the menu bar, then click **Open File**. Open the project's bin\Debug folder. Click **CDs.txt** in the list of filenames, then click the **Open** button. Notice that the Breakout CD's information does not appear in the file. Close the CDs.txt window.

10. Close the Code Editor window, then close the solution. Figure 10-39 shows the application's code.

```
' Name: CD Collection Project
' Purpose: Allows the user to add and delete list box entries
'          Reads CD information from a sequential access file
'          Writes CD information to a sequential access file
' Programmer: <your name> on <current date>

Option Explicit On
Option Strict On
Option Infer Off

Public Class frmMain

   Private Sub btnExit_Click(ByVal sender As Object, _
      ByVal e As System.EventArgs) Handles btnExit.Click
      Me.Close()
   End Sub

   Private Sub frmMain_FormClosing(ByVal sender As Object, _
      ByVal e As System.Windows.Forms.FormClosingEventArgs) _
      Handles Me.FormClosing
      ' save the list box information

      ' declare a StreamWriter variable
      Dim outFile As IO.StreamWriter

      ' open the file for output
      outFile = IO.File.CreateText("CDs.txt")

      ' write each line in the list box
      For intIndex As Integer = 0 To lstCds.Items.Count - 1
         outFile.WriteLine(lstCds.Items(intIndex))
      Next intIndex

      ' close the file
      outFile.Close()
   End Sub

   Private Sub frmMain_Load(ByVal sender As Object, _
      ByVal e As System.EventArgs) Handles Me.Load
      ' fills the list box with data
      ' stored in a sequential access file

      ' declare variables
      Dim inFile As IO.StreamReader
      Dim strInfo As String

      ' verify that the file exists
      If IO.File.Exists("CDs.txt") Then
         ' open the file for input
         inFile = IO.File.OpenText("CDs.txt")
         ' process loop instructions until end of file
         Do Until inFile.Peek = -1
            ' read a line from the file
            strInfo = inFile.ReadLine
            ' add the line to the list box
            lstCds.Items.Add(strInfo)
         Loop

```

Figure 10-39 CD Collection application's code *(continues)*

(continued)

```
            ' close the file
            inFile.Close()
            ' select the first item in the list box
            lstCds.SelectedIndex = 0

        Else
            MessageBox.Show("Can't find the CDs.txt file", _
                             "CD Collection", MessageBoxButtons.OK, _
                            MessageBoxIcon.Information)
        End If
    End Sub

    Private Sub btnAdd_Click(ByVal sender As Object, _
        ByVal e As System.EventArgs) Handles btnAdd.Click
        ' adds CD information to the list box

        ' declare variables
        Dim strName As String
        Dim strArtist As String
        Dim strPrice As String
        Dim strConcatenatedInfo As String
        Dim dblPrice As Double

        ' get the CD information
        strName = InputBox("CD name:", "CD Collection")
        strArtist = InputBox("Artist:", "CD Collection")
        strPrice = InputBox("Price:", "CD Collection")

        ' format the price, then concatenate the
        ' input items, using 40 spaces for the
        ' CD name, 25 spaces for the artist name,
        ' and 5 spaces for the price
        Double.TryParse(strPrice, dblPrice)
        strPrice = dblPrice.ToString("N2")
        strConcatenatedInfo = strName.PadRight(40) & _
            strArtist.PadRight(25) & strPrice.PadLeft(5)

        ' add the information to the list box
        lstCds.Items.Add(strConcatenatedInfo)

    End Sub

    Private Sub btnRemove_Click(ByVal sender As Object, _
        ByVal e As System.EventArgs) Handles btnRemove.Click
        ' removes the selected line from the list box

        ' if a line is selected, remove the line
        If lstCds.SelectedIndex <> -1 Then
            lstCds.Items.RemoveAt(lstCds.SelectedIndex)
        End If
    End Sub
End Class
```

Figure 10-39 CD Collection application's code

Lesson C Summary

- **To add items to a list box while an application is running:**

  Use the Add method of the list box's Items collection.

- **To right-align a string:**

  Use the PadLeft method, whose syntax is *string*.**PadLeft(***length*[, *character*]).

- **To left-align a string:**

  Use the PadRight method, whose syntax is *string*.**PadRight(***length*[, *character*]).

- **To align a column of numbers by the decimal point:**

  First, format each number in the column to ensure that each has the same number of digits to the right of the decimal point. Then use the PadLeft method to right-align the numbers.

- **To include a specific number of spaces in a string:**

  Use the Strings.Space method, whose syntax is **Strings.Space(***number***)**, where *number* is an integer representing the number of spaces to include.

- **To remove an item from a list box:**

  Use the RemoveAt method. The method's syntax is *object*.**Items.RemoveAt(***index***)**, where *index* is the index of the item you want removed.

Lesson C Key Terms

RemoveAt method—can be used to remove an item from a list box; allows you to specify the index of the item you want removed

Strings.Space method—can be used to include a specific number of spaces in a string

Lesson C Review Questions

1. Which of the following opens a sequential access file named "MyFriends.txt" for input?

   a. `inFile = IO.File.Input("MyFriends.txt")`

   b. `inFile = IO.InputFile("MyFriends.txt")`

   c. `inFile = IO.File.InputText("MyFriends.txt")`

   d. `inFile = IO.File.OpenText("MyFriends.txt")`

2. Which of the following right-aligns the contents of the `strNumbers` variable?
   a. `strNumbers = strNumbers.PadLeft(10)`
   b. `strNumbers = strNumbers.PadRight(10)`
   c. `strNumbers = strNumbers.AlignLeft(10)`
   d. `strNumbers = strNumbers.RightAlign(10)`
3. Which of the following removes the fourth item from the lstFriends control?
   a. `lstFriends.Items.Remove(4)`
   b. `lstFriends.Items.RemoveAt(4)`
   c. `lstFriends.Items.RemoveIndex(3)`
   d. None of the above.
4. Which of the following determines whether an item is selected in the lstFriends control?
   a. `If lstFriends.SelectedIndex >= 0`
   b. `If lstFriends.SelectedItem <> -1`
   c. `If lstFriends.IndexSelected = -1`
   d. None of the above.
5. The lstFriends control contains 5 items. Which of the following writes the last item to the file associated with the `outFile` variable?
   a. `outFile.WriteLine(lstFriends.Items(5))`
   b. `outFile.WriteLine(lstFriends.Items(4))`
   c. `outFile.WriteLine(lstFriends.Index(4))`
   d. None of the above.

Lesson C Exercises

INTRODUCTORY

1. In this exercise, you modify the CD Collection application coded in the lesson. Use Windows to make a copy of the CD Collection Solution folder, which is contained in the VB2008\Chap10 folder. Rename the folder CD Collection Solution-Verify Save. Open the CD Collection Solution (CD Collection Solution.sln) file contained in the VB2008\Chap10\CD Collection Solution-Verify Save folder. Open the designer window, then open the Code Editor window. Modify the FormClosing event procedure so it verifies that the user wants to save the changes made to the list box. The procedure should take the appropriate action based on the user's response. Save the solution, then start and test the application. Stop the application, then close the solution.

INTERMEDIATE

2. In this exercise, you modify the CD Collection application coded in the lesson. Use Windows to make a copy of the CD Collection Solution folder, which is contained in the VB2008\Chap10 folder. Rename the folder CD Collection Solution-Verify Remove. Open the CD Collection Solution (CD Collection Solution.sln) file contained in the VB2008\Chap10\CD Collection Solution-Verify Remove folder. Open the designer window, then open the Code Editor window. Modify the btnRemove control's Click event procedure so it verifies that the user wants to remove the selected CD information from the list box. Use the message "Do you want to remove the *x* CD?", where *x* is the name of the CD. The procedure should take the appropriate action based on the user's response. Save the solution, then start and test the application. Stop the application, then close the solution.

INTERMEDIATE

3. Open the Friends Solution (Friends Solution.sln) file, which is contained in the VB2008\Chap10\Friends Solution folder. If necessary, open the designer window. The Add button should add the name entered in the text portion of the combo box to the list portion, but only if the name is not already in the list. The Remove button should remove (from the list portion of the combo box) the name either entered in the text portion or selected in the list portion. (Hint: Use the Items collection's Remove method.) The form's FormClosing event procedure should save the combo box items in a sequential access file named MyFriends.txt. The form's Load event procedure should read the names from the MyFriends.txt file and add each to the combo box. Open the Code Editor window, and code the application. Save the solution, then start and test the application. Stop the application, then close the solution.

INTERMEDIATE

4. In this exercise, you modify the CD Collection application coded in the lesson. Use Windows to make a copy of the CD Collection Solution folder, which is contained in the VB2008\Chap10 folder. Rename the folder CD Collection Solution-No Duplicate. Open the CD Collection Solution (CD Collection Solution.sln) file contained in the VB2008\Chap10\CD Collection Solution-No Duplicate folder. Open the designer window, then open the Code Editor window. Before getting the artist name and price, the btnAdd control's Click event procedure should determine whether the CD name is already included in the list box. If the list box contains the CD name, the procedure should display an appropriate message, and then not add the CD to the list. Save the solution, then start and test the application. Stop the application, then close the solution.

INTERMEDIATE

5. In this exercise, you modify the CD Collection application coded in the lesson. Use Windows to make a copy of the CD Collection Solution folder, which is contained in the VB2008\Chap10 folder. Rename the folder CD Collection Solution-Undo. Open the CD Collection Solution (CD Collection Solution.sln) file contained in the VB2008\Chap10\CD Collection Solution-Undo folder. Open the designer window. Add an Undo Remove button to the form. The Undo Remove button's Click event procedure should restore the last line removed by the Remove button. Open the Code Editor window and make the necessary modifications to the code. Save the solution, then start and test the application. Stop the application, then close the solution.

INTERMEDIATE

6. In this exercise, you modify the CD Collection application coded in the lesson. Use Windows to make a copy of the CD Collection Solution folder, which is contained in the VB2008\Chap10 folder. Rename the folder CD Collection Solution-Structure. Open the CD Collection Solution (CD Collection Solution.sln) file contained in the VB2008\Chap10\CD Collection Solution-Structure folder. Open the designer window, then open the Code Editor window. Create a structure, then use the structure in the btnAdd control's Click event procedure. Save the solution, then start and test the application. Stop the application, then close the solution.

INTERMEDIATE

7. Glovers Industries stores the item numbers and prices of the items it sells in a sequential access file named ItemInfo.txt. The company's sales manager wants an application that displays the price corresponding to the item selected in a list box.
   a. Open the Glovers Solution (Glovers Solution.sln) file, which is contained in the VB2008\Chap10\Glovers Solution folder. If necessary, open the designer window.
   b. Open the Code Editor window, then open the ItemInfo.txt file, which is contained in the project's bin\Debug folder. Notice that the item number and price appear on separate lines in the file. Close the ItemInfo.txt window.
   c. Define a structure named Product. The structure should contain two member variables: a String variable to store the item number and a Double variable to store the price.
   d. Declare a module-level array that contains five Product structure variables.
   e. The form's Load event procedure should read the item numbers and prices from the ItemInfo.txt file, and store them in the module-level array. It also should add the item numbers to the list box. Code the procedure.
   f. When the user selects an item in the list box, the item's price should appear in the lblPrice control. Code the appropriate procedure.
   g. Save the solution, then start and test the application. Stop the application. Close the Code Editor window, then close the solution.

ADVANCED

8. Each year, WKRK-Radio polls its audience to determine the best Super Bowl commercial. The choices are as follows: Budweiser, FedEx, E*Trade, and Pepsi. The station manager wants an application that allows him to enter a caller's choice. The choice should be saved in a sequential access file. The application also should display the number of votes for each commercial. Create a Visual Basic Windows application. Name the solution, project, and form file WKRK Solution, WKRK Project, and Main Form.vb, respectively. Create the interface shown in Figure 10-40. Open the Code Editor window, then code the application. Save the solution, then start and test the application. Stop the application. Close the Code Editor window, then close the solution.

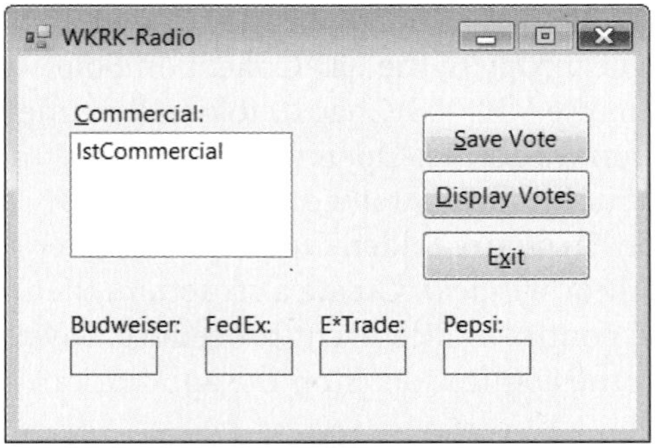

Figure 10-40 User interface for the WKRK-Radio application

ADVANCED

9. Carlton Industries stores the item numbers and prices of the items it sells in a sequential access file named ItemInfo.txt. The company's sales manager wants an application that displays the price corresponding to the item selected in a list box.

    a. Create a Visual Basic Windows application. Name the solution, project, and form file Carlton Solution, Carlton Project, and Main Form.vb, respectively. Create the interface shown in Figure 10-41.

    b. Use Windows to copy the ItemInfo.txt file from the VB2008\Chap10 folder to the project's bin\Debug folder. Open the Code Editor window, then open the ItemInfo.txt file contained in the project's bin\Debug folder. Each line contains an item's number followed by a comma and the price. Close the ItemInfo.txt window.

    c. Define a structure named Item. The structure should contain two member variables: a String variable to store the item number and a Decimal variable to store the price.

    d. Declare a module-level array that contains five Item structure variables.

    e. Code the form's Load event procedure so that it reads the item numbers and prices from the ItemInfo.txt file. The procedure should store the item numbers and prices in the module-level array. It also should add the item numbers to the list box.

    f. When the user selects an item in the list box, the item's price should appear in the lblPrice control. Code the appropriate procedure.

    g. Save the solution, then start and test the application. Stop the application. Close the Code Editor window, then close the solution.

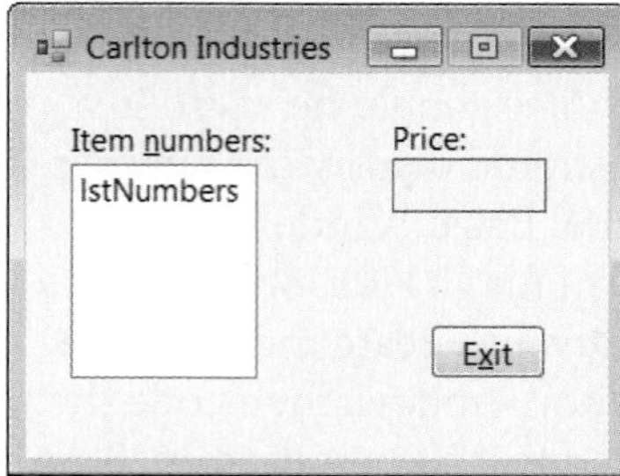

Figure 10-41 User interface for the Carlton Industries application

CHAPTER 11

Classes and Objects

Creating the ABC Company Application

In this chapter, you code an application that calculates and displays the gross pay for salaried and hourly employees. Salaried employees are paid twice per month. Therefore, each salaried employee's gross pay is calculated by dividing his or her annual salary by 24. Hourly employees are paid weekly. The gross pay for an hourly employee is calculated by multiplying the number of hours the employee worked during the week by his or her hourly pay rate.

Previewing the ABC Company Application

To preview the completed ABC Company application:

To open the Run dialog box, press and hold down the Windows logo key as you tap the letter r, then release the logo key.

1. Use the Run dialog box to run the **ABC** (**ABC.exe**) file, which is contained in the VB2008\Chap11 folder. The application's user interface appears on the screen.
2. First, calculate the gross pay for Sarah Lopez, who worked 38 hours and earns $9 per hour. Sarah's employee number is 1234. Type **1234** in the Number box, then press **Tab**. Type **Sarah Lopez** in the Name box. Click **38.0** in the Hours list box, then click **9.00** in the Rate list box. Click the **Calculate** button. See Figure 11-1.

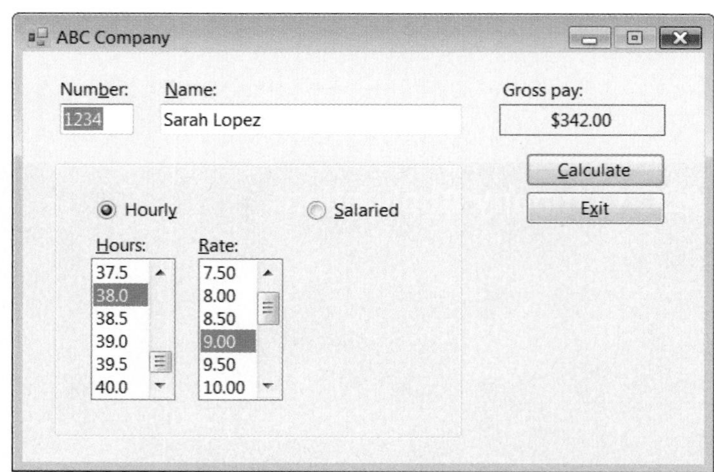

Figure 11-1 Interface showing the gross pay for an hourly employee

3. Now calculate the gross pay for a salaried employee earning $30,000 per year. Click the **Salaried** radio button. Scroll the Annual salary list box, then click **30000** in the list. Click the **Calculate** button. The Gross pay box indicates that the gross pay is $1,250.00
4. Click the **Exit** button to end the application.

In Lesson A, you will learn about object-oriented programming (OOP). More specifically, you will learn how to define a class and how to use the class to instantiate an object. You also will learn how to utilize the instantiated object in an application. You will code the ABC Company application in Lesson B. Lesson C covers an advanced OOP topic: inheritance.

LESSON A

After studying Lesson A, you should be able to:

- Define a class
- Instantiate an object from a class that you define
- Add Property procedures to a class
- Include data validation in a class
- Create a default constructor
- Include methods in a class

Object-Oriented Programming Terminology

As you learned in the Overview, Visual Basic 2008 is an object-oriented programming language, which is a language that allows the programmer to use objects to accomplish a program's goal. Recall that an object is anything that can be seen, touched, or used; in other words, an object is nearly any *thing*. The objects used in an object-oriented program can take on many different forms. The text boxes, list boxes, and buttons included in most Windows programs are objects. An object also can represent something found in real life, such as a wristwatch or a car. Every object is created from a **class**, which is a pattern or blueprint that the computer follows when creating the object. Using object-oriented programming (**OOP**) terminology, objects are **instantiated** (created) from a class, and each object is referred to as an **instance** of the class. A button control, for example, is an instance of the Button class, which is the class from which a button is instantiated. A text box, on the other hand, is an instance of the TextBox class. Keep in mind that the class itself is not an object. Only an instance of a class is an object.

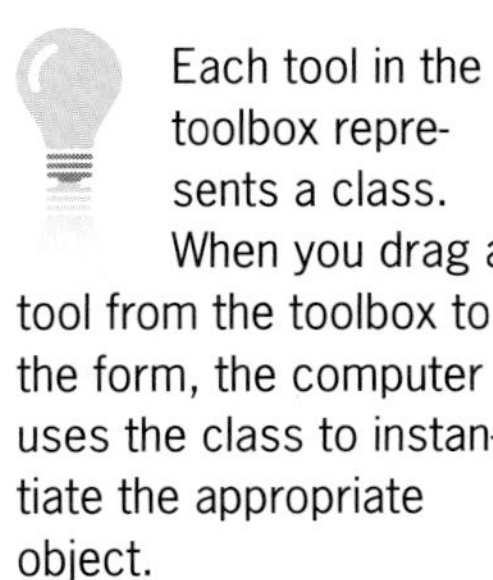

Each tool in the toolbox represents a class. When you drag a tool from the toolbox to the form, the computer uses the class to instantiate the appropriate object.

Every object has **attributes**, which are the characteristics that describe the object. Attributes are also called properties. Included in the attributes of buttons and text boxes are the Name and Text properties. List boxes have a Name property as well as a Sorted property. In addition to attributes, every object also has behaviors. An object's **behaviors** include methods and events. **Methods** are the operations (actions) that the object is capable of performing. For example, a button control can use its Focus method to send the focus to itself. **Events** are the actions to which an object can respond. A button control's Click event, for instance, allows it to respond to a mouse click. A class contains—or, in OOP terms, it **encapsulates**—all of the attributes and behaviors of the object it instantiates.

The term "encapsulate" means "to enclose in a capsule." In the context of OOP, the "capsule" is a class.

Creating a Class

In previous chapters, you instantiated objects using classes that are built into Visual Basic, such as the TextBox and Label classes. You used the instantiated objects in a variety of ways in many different applications. In some applications, you used a text box to enter a name, while in other applications you used it to enter a sales tax rate. Similarly, you used label controls to identify

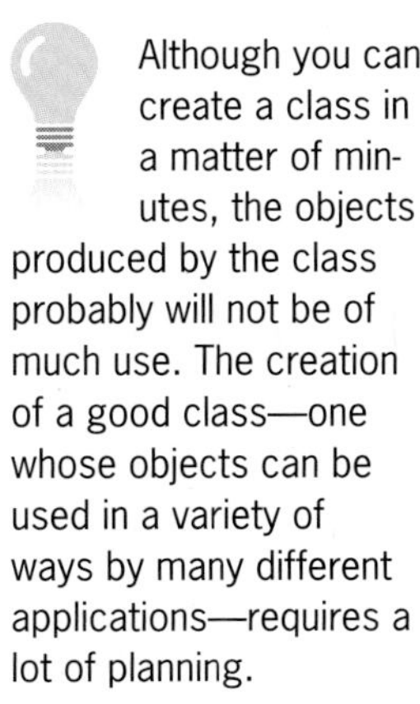

Although you can create a class in a matter of minutes, the objects produced by the class probably will not be of much use. The creation of a good class—one whose objects can be used in a variety of ways by many different applications—requires a lot of planning.

You also can include Event procedures in a Class statement. However, that topic is beyond the scope of this book.

text boxes and also to display the result of calculations. The ability to use an object for more than one purpose saves programming time and money—an advantage that contributes to the popularity of object-oriented programming. You also can define your own classes in Visual Basic and then create instances (objects) from those classes. The classes you define can represent something encountered in real life, such as a credit card receipt, a check, or an employee. Like the Visual Basic classes, your classes must specify the attributes and behaviors of the objects they create. You define the class using the **Class statement**. You enter the Class statement in a class file. Figure 11-2 shows the statement's syntax and lists the steps for adding a class file to an open project. Although it is not a requirement, the convention is to use Pascal case for the class name. The names of Visual Basic classes (for example, Integer and TextBox) also follow this naming convention. Within the Class statement, you define the attributes and behaviors of the objects the class will create. The attributes are represented by variables and Property procedures. You will learn about Property procedures later in this lesson. The behaviors are represented by Sub and Function procedures, more commonly referred to as methods. Also included in Figure 11-2 is an example of using the Class statement.

Class statement

Syntax

Public Class *className*
   attributes section
   behaviors section
End Class

Adding a class file to an open project

1. Click Project on the menu bar, then click Add Class. The Add New Item dialog box opens with Class selected in the Visual Studio installed templates section.
2. Type the name of the class followed by a period and the letters vb in the Name box, then click the Add button.

Example

```
Public Class TimeCard
    variables and Property procedures appear in the attributes section

    Sub and Function procedures appear in the behaviors section
End Class
```

Figure 11-2 Syntax and an example of the Class statement

After you define a class, it then can be used to instantiate one or more objects. Figure 11-3 shows two versions of the syntax that instantiates an object from a class. In both versions, *class* is the name of the class and *variableName* is the name of a variable that will represent the object. The difference between both versions relates to when the object is actually created. The computer creates the object only when it processes the statement containing the `New` keyword. (You will learn more about the `New` keyword later in this lesson.) Also included in Figure 11-3 is an example of using each version of the syntax. In Example 1, the `Private hoursInfo As TimeCard` instruction creates a module-level variable that can represent a TimeCard object;

however, it does not create the object. The object isn't created until the computer processes the `hoursInfo = New TimeCard` statement, which uses the TimeCard class to instantiate a TimeCard object. The statement assigns the object to the `hoursInfo` variable. In Example 2, the `Dim hoursInfo As New TimeCard` instruction creates a procedure-level variable named `hoursInfo`. It also instantiates a TimeCard object and assigns it to the variable.

Instantiating an object from a class

Syntax - Version 1
{**Dim** | **Private**} *variableName* **As** *class*
variableName = **New** *class*

Syntax - Version 2
{**Dim** | **Private**} *variableName* **As New** *class*

Example 1 (syntax version 1)

```
Private hoursInfo As TimeCard
hoursInfo = New TimeCard
```

the Private instruction creates a TimeCard variable named `hoursInfo`; the assignment statement instantiates a TimeCard object and assigns it to the `hoursInfo` variable

Example 2 (syntax version 2)

```
Dim hoursInfo As New TimeCard
```

the Dim instruction creates a TimeCard variable named `hoursInfo` and also instantiates a TimeCard object; it assigns the object to the `hoursInfo` variable

Figure 11-3 Syntax and examples of instantiating an object from a class

In the remainder of this lesson, you will view examples of class definitions, as well as examples of code in which objects are instantiated and used. The first example is a class that contains attributes only, with each attribute represented by a Public variable.

Example 1—Using a Class that Contains Public Variables Only

In its simplest form, the Class statement can be used in place of the Structure statement, which you learned about in Chapter 10. Like the Structure statement, the Class statement groups related items into one unit. However, the unit is called a class rather than a structure. In the following set of steps, you will modify the Willow Pools application from Chapter 10 to use a class instead of a structure.

To open the Willow Pools application:

1. If necessary, start Visual Studio 2008 or Visual Basic 2008 Express Edition. Close the Start Page window.

2. Open the **Pool Solution** (**Pool Solution.sln**) file, which is contained in the VB2008\Chap11\Pool Solution folder. If necessary, open the designer window.

3. Open the Code Editor window. Figure 11-4 shows the Structure statement, as well as the code entered in the GetGallons function and btnCalc control's Click event procedure. The Structure statement groups together the three dimensions of a rectangular pool: length, width, and depth. The event procedure declares a structure variable and then fills the variable's members with values. It then passes the structure variable to the GetGallons function, which calculates and returns the number of gallons required to fill the pool. The event procedure displays the returned value in the lblGallons control.

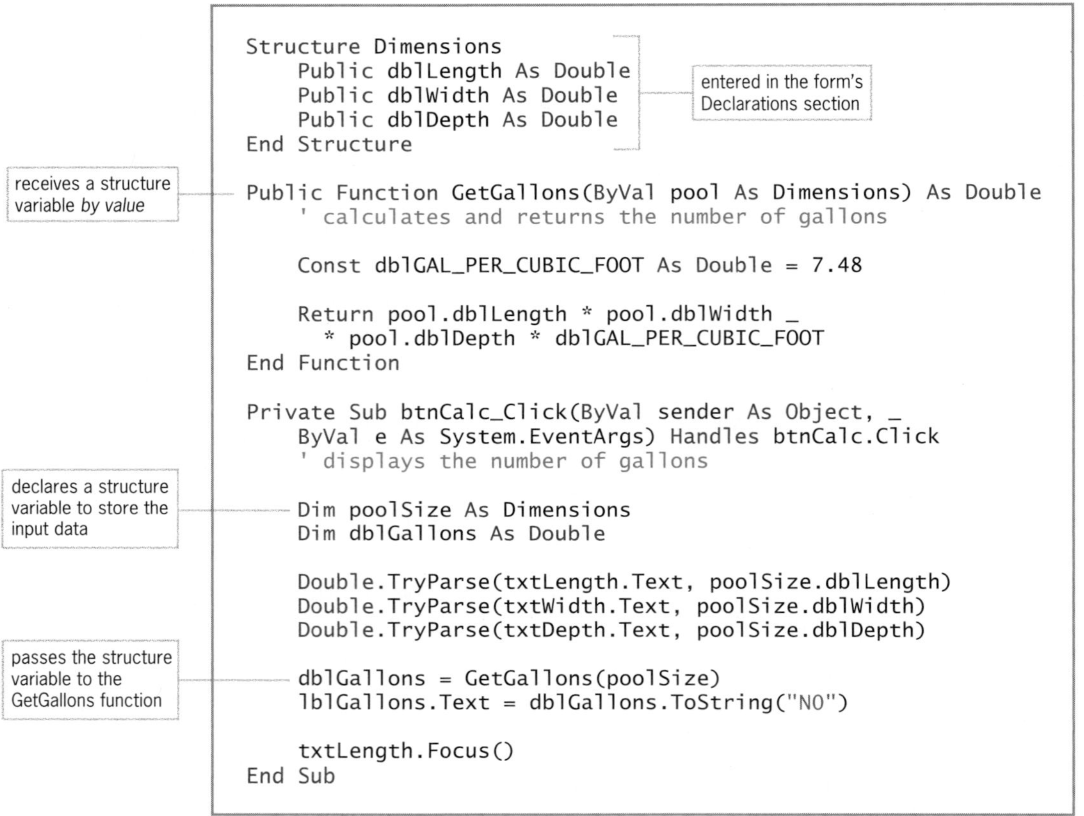


```
Structure Dimensions
    Public dblLength As Double
    Public dblWidth As Double
    Public dblDepth As Double
End Structure

Public Function GetGallons(ByVal pool As Dimensions) As Double
    ' calculates and returns the number of gallons

    Const dblGAL_PER_CUBIC_FOOT As Double = 7.48

    Return pool.dblLength * pool.dblWidth _
      * pool.dblDepth * dblGAL_PER_CUBIC_FOOT
End Function

Private Sub btnCalc_Click(ByVal sender As Object, _
    ByVal e As System.EventArgs) Handles btnCalc.Click
    ' displays the number of gallons

    Dim poolSize As Dimensions
    Dim dblGallons As Double

    Double.TryParse(txtLength.Text, poolSize.dblLength)
    Double.TryParse(txtWidth.Text, poolSize.dblWidth)
    Double.TryParse(txtDepth.Text, poolSize.dblDepth)

    dblGallons = GetGallons(poolSize)
    lblGallons.Text = dblGallons.ToString("N0")

    txtLength.Focus()
End Sub
```

Figure 11-4 Code for the Willow Pools application (with a structure)

To add a class file to the project:

1. Click **Project** on the menu bar, then click **Add Class**. The Add New Item dialog box opens with Class selected in the Visual Studio installed templates section. Type **RectangularPool.vb** in the Name box. As you learned in Chapter 1, the .vb on a filename indicates that the file contains Visual Basic code. See Figure 11-5. (If you are using Visual Basic 2008 Express Edition, you will not see the Categories list in the Add New Item dialog box.)

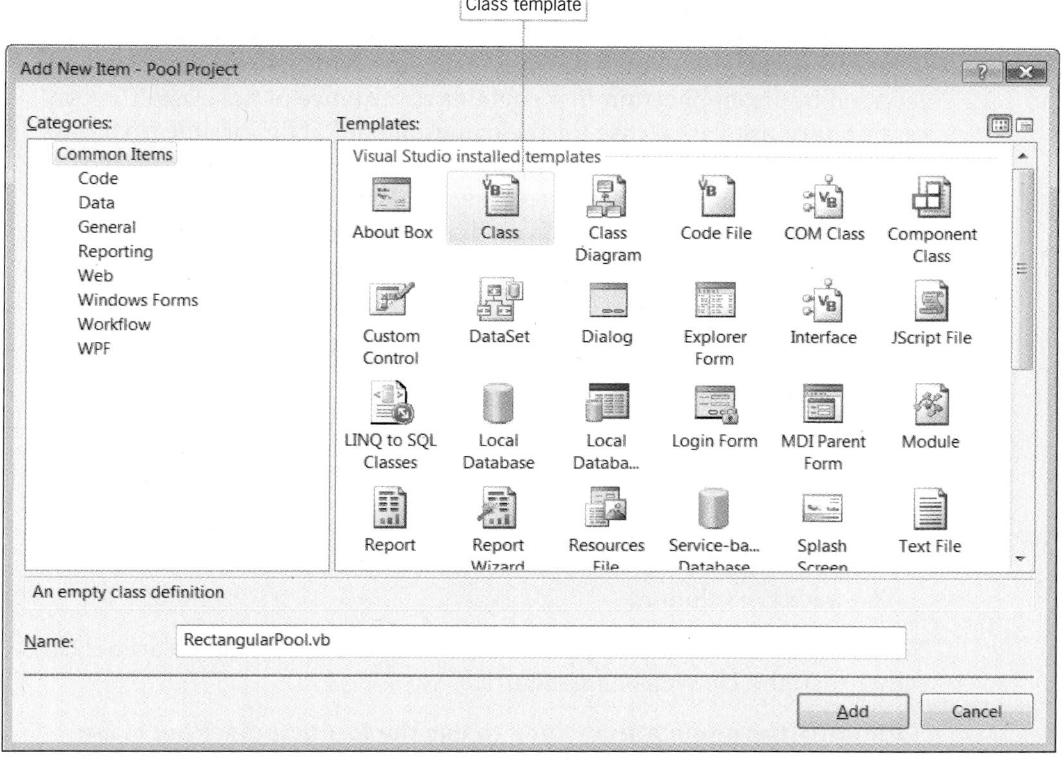

Figure 11-5 Add New Item dialog box

2. Click the **Add** button. The computer adds the RectangularPool.vb file to the project and opens the file, which contains the Class statement, in the Code Editor window. Temporarily display the Solution Explorer window, if necessary, to verify that the class file's name appears in the window.

3. Insert a blank line above the Class statement, then enter the comments and Option statements shown in Figure 11-6. (Replace the <your name> and <current date> text in the comments with your name and the current date.) Also position the insertion point as shown in the figure.

The Option statements have the same meaning in a class file as they have in a form file.

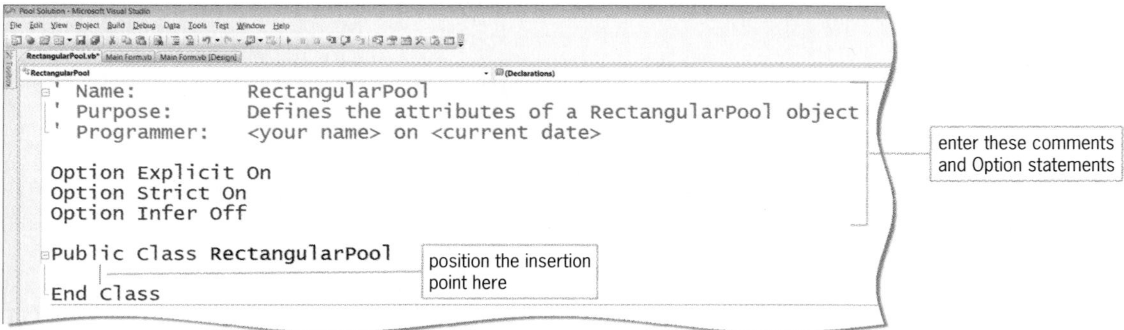

Figure 11-6 Comments and Option statements entered in the RectangularPool.vb file

A RectangularPool object has three attributes: length, width, and depth. In the Class statement, each attribute will be represented by a Public variable. When a variable in a class is declared using the `Public` keyword, it can be accessed by any application that contains an instance of the class. The convention is to use Pascal case for the names of the Public variables in a class, and to omit the three-character ID that indicates the variable's data type. This is because Public variables represent properties that will be seen by anyone using an object created from the class. The properties of Visual Basic objects—such as the Text and StartPosition properties—also follow this naming convention.

To enter the Public variables in the class definition:

1. Enter the following three instructions below the `Public Class RectangularPool` clause.

   Public Length As Double
   Public Width As Double
   Public Depth As Double

2. Save the solution.

Now you will modify the application's code to use the RectangularPool class rather than the Dimensions structure.

To modify the application's code to use the RectangularPool class:

1. Click the **Main Form.vb** tab to return to the form's Code Editor window. Replace the <your name> and <current date> text in the comments with your name and the current date.
2. First, delete the Structure statement from the form's Declarations section.
3. Next, locate the btnCalc control's Click event procedure. The procedure will instantiate a RectangularPool object. Replace the `Dim poolSize As Dimensions` instruction with **Dim customerPool As New RectangularPool**.
4. Now modify the three TryParse methods to use the object's Public variables. Highlight `poolSize.dblLength` in the first TryParse method. Type **customerPool.** and then click the **Common** tab (if necessary). Notice that the Public variables appear in the IntelliSense list. See Figure 11-7.

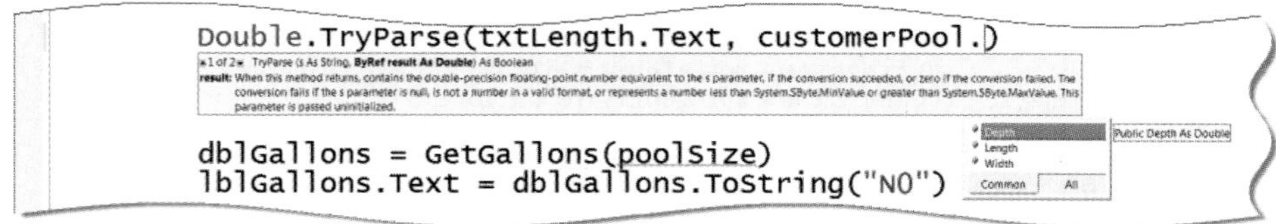

Figure 11-7 Public variables included in the IntelliSense list

5. Click **Length**, then press **Tab**. Now change `poolSize.dblWidth` and `poolSize.dblDepth` in the remaining TryParse methods to **customerPool.Width** and **customerPool.Depth**, respectively.

6. The procedure needs to pass the customerPool object, rather than the poolSize structure, to the GetGallons function. Change `poolSize` in the `dblGallons = GetGallons(poolSize)` statement to **customerPool**.

7. Locate the GetGallons function. The function will need to receive a RectangularPool object rather than a Dimensions structure. Change `Dimensions` in the function header to **RectangularPool**.

8. Finally, change `dblLength`, `dblWidth`, and `dblDepth` in the Return statement to **Length**, **Width**, and **Depth**, respectively.

9. Save the solution. Figure 11-8 shows the RectangularPool class definition, which is contained in the RectangularPool.vb file. It also shows the code entered in the GetGallons function and btnCalc control's Click event procedure in the Main Form.vb file. The changes made to the original code in the function and Click event procedure are shaded in the figure.

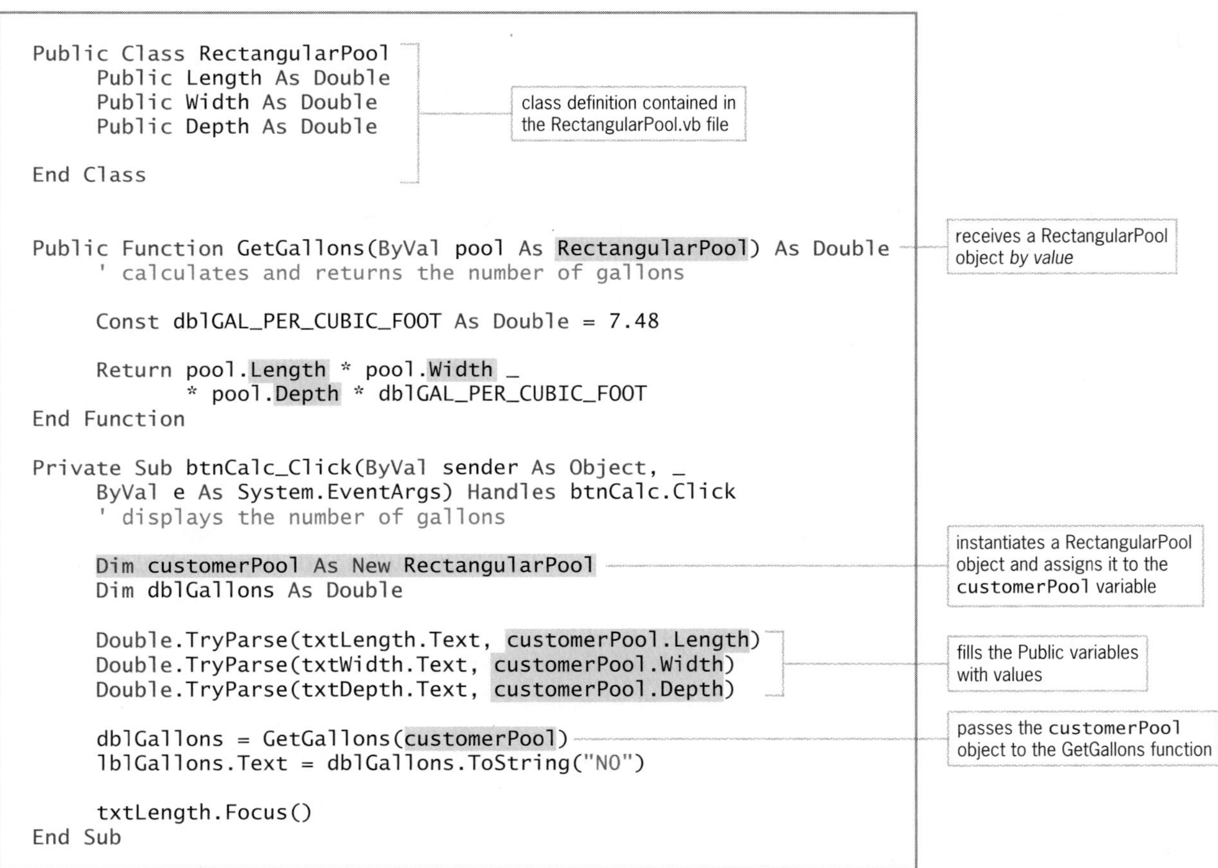

```
Public Class RectangularPool
     Public Length As Double
     Public Width As Double
     Public Depth As Double

End Class


Public Function GetGallons(ByVal pool As RectangularPool) As Double
     ' calculates and returns the number of gallons

     Const dblGAL_PER_CUBIC_FOOT As Double = 7.48

     Return pool.Length * pool.Width _
          * pool.Depth * dblGAL_PER_CUBIC_FOOT
End Function

Private Sub btnCalc_Click(ByVal sender As Object, _
     ByVal e As System.EventArgs) Handles btnCalc.Click
     ' displays the number of gallons

     Dim customerPool As New RectangularPool
     Dim dblGallons As Double

     Double.TryParse(txtLength.Text, customerPool.Length)
     Double.TryParse(txtWidth.Text, customerPool.Width)
     Double.TryParse(txtDepth.Text, customerPool.Depth)

     dblGallons = GetGallons(customerPool)
     lblGallons.Text = dblGallons.ToString("N0")

     txtLength.Focus()
End Sub
```


Figure 11-8 Class definition, GetGallons function, and btnCalc Click event procedure

To test the modified code:

1. Start the application. Type **60** in the Length box, **30** in the Width box, and **5** in the Depth box. Click the **Calculate** button to display the required number of gallons of water. See Figure 11-9.

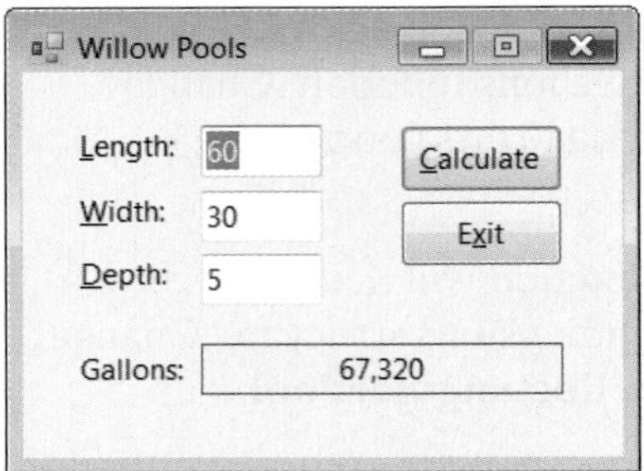

Figure 11-9 Interface showing the required number of gallons of water

2. Click the **Exit** button. Close the Main Form.vb and Rectangular-Pool.vb windows, then close the solution.

Example 2—Using a Class that Contains a Private Variable, a Property Procedure, and Two Methods

Although you can define a class that contains only attributes represented by Public variables—like the RectangularPool class shown in Figure 11-8—that is rarely done. The disadvantage of using Public variables in a class is that a class cannot control the values assigned to its Public variables. As a result, the class cannot validate the values to ensure they are appropriate for the variables. Furthermore, most classes contain not only attributes, but behaviors as well. This is because the purpose of a class in OOP is to encapsulate the properties that describe an object, the methods that allow the object to perform tasks, and the events that allow the object to respond to actions. In this section, you will create a class that contains data validation code and methods. (Including events in a class is beyond the scope of this book.) The class will be used in the Carpet Haven application, which calculates and displays the number of square yards of carpeting required to carpet a rectangular floor. It also calculates and displays the cost of the carpet.

To open the Carpet Haven application, and then add a class file to the application:

1. Open the **Carpet Calculator Solution** (**Carpet Calculator Solution.sln**) file, which is contained in the VB2008\Chap11\Carpet Calculator Solution folder. If necessary, open the designer window. See Figure 11-10. The interface allows the user to enter the length and width (in feet) of a room's floor and the price of a square yard of carpet. It displays the required number of square yards of carpet and the cost of the carpet.

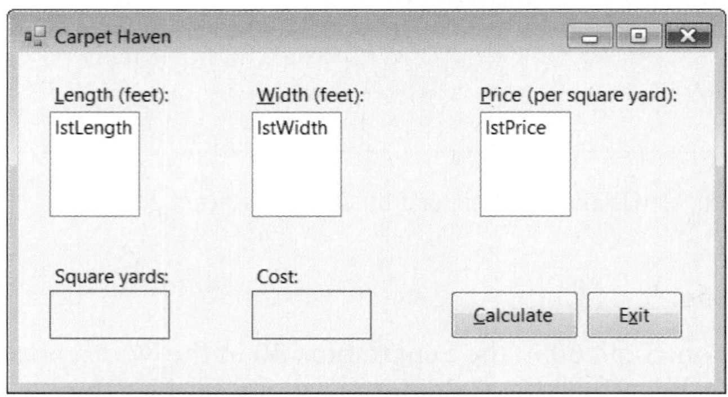

Figure 11-10 Interface for the Carpet Haven application

2. A room's floor is an object. More specifically, it is a rectangular object that has two attributes: length and width. For this application, you will create a class that can be used to create a rectangular object to represent the floor. Click **Project** on the menu bar, then click **Add Class**. Type **Rectangle.vb** in the Name box, then click the **Add** button. Insert a blank line above the Class statement, then enter the comments and Option statements shown in Figure 11-11. (Replace the <your name> and <current date> text in the comments with your name and the current date.) Also position the insertion point as shown in the figure.

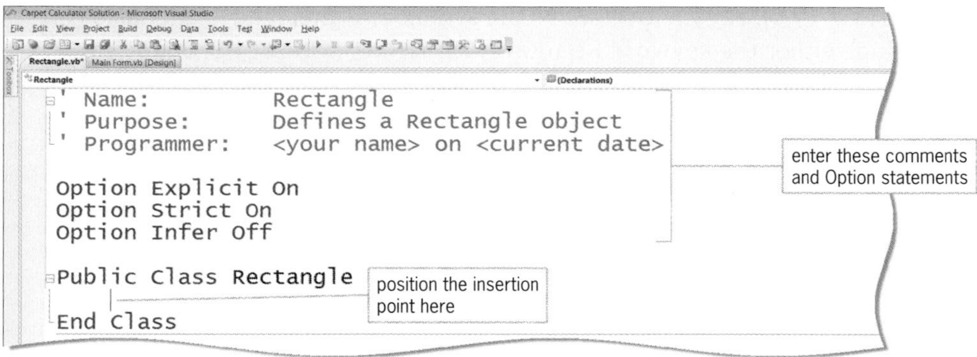

Figure 11-11 Comments and Option statements entered in the Rectangle.vb file

As already mentioned, a Rectangle object has two attributes: length and width. Rather than using Public variables to represent both attributes, the Rectangle class will use Private variables and Property procedures.

Private Variables and Property Procedures

When a variable in a class is declared using the `Private` keyword, it can be used only within the class. Unlike a class's Public variables, the Private variables in a class will not be visible to applications that contain an instance of the class. In other words, the names of the Private variables in a class will not appear in the IntelliSense list. When naming the Private variables in a class, many programmers use the underscore as the first character and then camel case for the remainder of the name. You will use the names `_dblLength` and `_dblWidth` for the Private variables in the Rectangle class.

To enter the Private variables in the Rectangle class:

1. Enter the following two instructions below the `Public Class Rectangle` clause. Press **Enter** twice after typing the last instruction.

   Private _dblLength As Double
   Private _dblWidth As Double

2. Save the solution.

When an application instantiates an object, only the Public members of the object's class are visible to the application; the application cannot access the Private members of the class. Using OOP terminology, the Public members are exposed to the application, whereas the Private members are hidden from the application. For an application to assign data to or retrieve data from a Private variable in a class, it must use a Public property. In other words, an application cannot directly refer to a Private variable in a class. Rather, it must refer to the variable indirectly, through the use of a Public property. You create a Public property using a **Property procedure**. Figure 11-12 shows the syntax of a Property procedure and includes examples of Property procedures. In most cases, a Property procedure header begins with the keywords `Public Property`. However, as the syntax indicates, the header also can include either the keyword `ReadOnly` or the keyword `WriteOnly`. The `ReadOnly` keyword indicates that the property's value can be retrieved (read) by an application, but the application cannot set (write to) the property. The property would get its value from the class itself rather than from the application. The `WriteOnly` keyword indicates that an application can set the property's value, but it cannot retrieve the value. In this case, the value would be set by the application for use within the class. Following the `Property` keyword in the header is the name of the property. You should use nouns and adjectives to name a property and enter the name using Pascal case, as in Side, Bonus, and AnnualSale. Following the property name is a set of parentheses, the keyword `As`, and the property's *dataType*. The *dataType* must match the data type of the Private variable associated with the Property procedure. Between a Property procedure's header and footer, you include a Get block of code, a Set block of code, or both Get and Set blocks of code. The appropriate block or blocks of code to include depends on the keywords contained in the procedure header. If the header contains the `ReadOnly` keyword, you include only a Get block of code in the Property procedure. The code contained in the **Get block** allows an application to retrieve the contents of the Private variable associated with the property. In the Property procedure shown in Example 2 in Figure 11-12, the `ReadOnly` keyword indicates that an application can retrieve the contents of the Bonus property, but it cannot set the property's value. If the header contains the `WriteOnly` keyword, you include only a Set block of code in the procedure. The code in the **Set block** allows an application to assign a value to the Private variable associated with the property. In the Property procedure shown in Example 3 in Figure 11-12, the `WriteOnly` keyword indicates that an application can assign a value to the AnnualSale property, but it cannot retrieve the property's contents. If the Property procedure header does not contain the `ReadOnly` or `WriteOnly` keywords, you include both a Get block of code and a Set block of code in the procedure, as shown in Example 1 in Figure 11-12. In this case, an application can both retrieve and set the Side property's value. A Public Property procedure creates a property that is visible to any application that contains an instance of the class.

A one-dimensional array's Length property, which you learned about in Chapter 9, is an example of a ReadOnly property.

Property procedure

Syntax

Public [**ReadOnly** | **WriteOnly**] **Property** *propertyName***()** **As** *dataType*
  Get
    [*instructions*]
    Return *privateVariable*
  End Get
  Set(ByVal value As *dataType***)**
    [*instructions*]
    privateVariable = {**value** | *defaultValue*}
  End Set
End Property

Example 1–an application can both retrieve and set the Side property's value

```
Public Property Side() As Integer
   Get
      Return _intSide
   End Get
   Set(ByVal value As Integer)
      If value > 0 Then
         _intSide = value
      Else
         _intSide = 0
      End If
   End Set
End Property
```

Example 2–an application can retrieve, but not set, the Bonus property's value

```
Public ReadOnly Property Bonus() As Decimal
   Get
      Return _decBonus
   End Get
End Property
```

Example 3–an application can set, but not retrieve, the AnnualSale property's value

```
Public WriteOnly Property AnnualSale() As Integer
   Set(ByVal value As Integer)
      _intAnnualSale = value
   End Set
End Property
```

Figure 11-12 Syntax and examples of a Property procedure

The Get block contains the **Get statement**, which begins with the keyword `Get` and ends with the keywords `End Get`. Most times, you will enter only the `Return` *privateVariable* instruction within the Get statement. The instruction directs the computer to return the contents of the Private variable associated with the property. In Example 1 in Figure 11-12, the `Return _intSide` statement tells the computer to return the contents of the `_intSide` variable, which is the Private variable associated with the Side property. Similarly, the `Return _decBonus` statement in Example 2 tells the computer to return the contents of the `_decBonus` variable, which is the Private variable associated with the Bonus property. Example 3 does not contain a Get statement, because the AnnualSale property is designated as a `WriteOnly` property.

The Set block contains the **Set statement**, which begins with the keyword `Set` and ends with the keywords `End Set`. The `Set` keyword is followed by a parameter enclosed in parentheses. The parameter begins with the keywords `ByVal value As`. The keywords are followed by a *dataType*, which must match the data type of the Private variable associated with the Property procedure. The `value` parameter temporarily stores the value that is passed to the property by the application. You can enter one or more instructions within the Set statement. One of the instructions should assign the contents of the `value` parameter to the Private variable associated with the property. In Example 3 in Figure 11-12, the `_intAnnualSale = value` statement assigns the contents of the procedure's `value` parameter to the Private `_intAnnualSale` variable. In the Set statement, you often will include instructions to validate the value received from the application before assigning it to the Private variable. The Set statement in Example 1 includes a selection structure that determines whether the side measurement received from the application is valid. In this case, a valid side measurement is an integer that is greater than zero. If the side measurement is valid, the `_intSide = value` instruction assigns the integer stored in the `value` parameter to the Private `_intSide` variable; otherwise, the `_intSide = 0` instruction assigns a default value (in this case, 0) to the variable. The Property procedure in Example 2 does not contain a Set statement, because the Bonus property is designated as a `ReadOnly` property.

To enter a Property procedure for each Private variable in the Rectangle class:

1. The insertion point should be positioned immediately above the End Class clause. Type **Public Property Length As Double** and press **Enter**. The Code Editor inserts parentheses after the property name. It also enters the Get and Set statements in the Property procedure, and positions the insertion point within the Get statement.

2. Recall that, in most cases, the Get statement simply returns the contents of the Private variable associated with the Property procedure. Type **Return _dblLength**.

3. The Set statement should assign either the contents of the procedure's `value` parameter or a default value to the Private variable associated with the Property procedure. In this case, you will assign the integer stored in the `value` parameter only when the integer is greater than 0; otherwise, you will assign the number 0. Click the **blank line** below the `Set(ByVal value As Double)` clause, then type the following selection structure.

   ```
   If value > 0 Then
       _dblLength = value
   Else
       _dblLength = 0
   End If
   ```

4. Save the solution. Figure 11-13 shows the completed Property procedure for the Length property.

```
Public Class Rectangle
    Private _dblLength As Double
    Private _dblWidth As Double

    Public Property Length() As Double
        Get
            Return _dblLength
        End Get
        Set(ByVal value As Double)
            If value > 0 Then
                _dblLength = value
            Else
                _dblLength = 0
            End If
        End Set
    End Property
End Class
```

Private `_dblLength` variable

Public Length Property procedure associated with the `_dblLength` variable

Figure 11-13 Completed Length Property procedure

5. Now enter a Property procedure for the Private `_dblWidth` variable. Click **immediately after the letter y** in the End Property clause, then press **Enter** twice. Type **Public Property Width As Double** and press **Enter**.
6. Type **Return _dblWidth** in the Get statement.
7. Click the **blank line** below the `Set(ByVal value As Double)` clause, then type the following selection structure.

   If value > 0 Then
   _dblWidth = value
   Else
   _dblWidth = 0
   End If

You have finished entering the class's Private variables and Property procedures. The class's methods are next. The first method you will learn about is a constructor.

Constructors

Every class should contain at least one constructor. A **constructor** is a class method whose sole purpose is to initialize the class's Private variables. As Figure 11-14 shows, a constructor's syntax begins with the keywords `Public Sub New` followed by a set of parentheses that contains an optional *parameterList*; it ends with the keywords `End Sub`. Between the constructor's header and footer, you enter instructions that assign beginning values to the class's Private variables. The instructions are automatically processed each time an object is instantiated from the class. Examples of statements that will instantiate a Rectangle object, thereby invoking the constructor, include `Dim myRectangle As New Rectangle` and `myRectangle = New Rectangle`. A class can have more than one constructor. Each constructor will have the same name, New, but its parameters (if any) must be

Constructors never return a value, so they are always Sub procedures (rather than Function procedures).

As you learned in Chapter 5, the syntax for creating a random object and assigning the object to a variable is **Dim** *randomObjectName* **As New Random**. The syntax uses the New keyword to invoke the Random class's default constructor.

different from any other constructor in the class. A constructor that has no parameters is called the **default constructor**. A class can have only one default constructor.

Constructor

Syntax
Public Sub New([*parameterList*]**)**
instructions to initialize the class's Private variables
End Sub

Example
```
Public Sub New()      ' default constructor
   _dblLength = 0
   _dblWidth = 0
End Sub
```

Figure 11-14 Syntax and an example of a constructor

To enter the Rectangle class's default constructor:

1. Click **immediately after the letter y** in the second End Property clause, then press **Enter** twice. Enter the following default constructor.

   Public Sub New()
   _dblLength = 0
   _dblWidth = 0
   End Sub

2. Save the solution.

Methods Other Than Constructors

A class also can contain methods other than constructors. Except for constructors, which must be Sub procedures, the methods included in a class can be either Sub procedures or Function procedures. Recall from Chapter 7 that the difference between both types of procedures is that a Function procedure returns a value after performing its assigned task, whereas a Sub procedure does not return a value. In the Rectangle class, you will include a method that allows a Rectangle object to calculate and return its area.

Figure 11-15 shows the syntax of a method that is not a constructor. The {`Sub` | `Function`} in the syntax indicates that you can select only one of the keywords appearing within the braces. Like property names, method names should be entered using Pascal case. However, unlike property names, the first word in a method name should be a verb, and any subsequent words should be nouns and adjectives. Figure 11-15 also includes the GetArea method you will include in the Rectangle class. The method is represented by a Function procedure. The `Return _dblLength * _dblWidth` statement within the procedure uses the class's Private variables to calculate the rectangle's area. The statement returns the area to the application that invoked the procedure.

Method that is not a constructor

Syntax

Public {**Sub** | **Function**} *methodName*(**[***parameterList***]**) **[As** *dataType***]**
instructions
End {**Sub** | **Function**}

Example

```
Public Function GetArea() As Double
   Return _dblLength * _dblWidth
End Function
```

Figure 11-15 Syntax and an example of a method that is not a constructor

To enter the GetArea method in the Rectangle class:

1. Click **immediately after the letter b** in the End Sub clause, then press **Enter** twice. Enter the following method.

   Public Function GetArea() As Double
   Return _dblLength * _dblWidth
   End Function

2. Save the solution, then close the Rectangle.vb window.

The code entered in the Rectangle class is shown in Figure 11-17.

Coding the Carpet Haven Application

The Calculate button's Click event procedure is the only procedure you need to code in the Carpet Haven application. Figure 11-16 shows the procedure's pseudocode.

btnCalc Click event procedure

1. instantiate a Rectangle object to represent the floor
2. declare variables to store the price per square yard, required number of square yards, and carpet cost
3. assign the input data to the appropriate properties and variable
4. calculate the required number of square yards by dividing the floor's area by 9
5. calculate the carpet cost by multiplying the price per square yard by the required number of square yards
6. display the required number of square yards and the carpet cost

Figure 11-16 Pseudocode for the Calculate button's Click event procedure

To code the Calculate button's Click event procedure:

1. Open the Code Editor window. Replace the <your name> and <current date> text in the comments with your name and the current date.

2. Open the code template for the btnCalc control's Click event procedure. Type **' displays number of square yards and cost of carpet** and press **Enter** twice.

3. First, instantiate a Rectangle object to represent the room's floor. Enter the following Dim statement.

   Dim floor As New Rectangle

4. Now declare variables to store the price of a square yard of carpet, the number of square yards needed, and the cost of the carpet. You won't need variables to store the floor's length and width, because the procedure will assign those values to the Rectangle object's Length and Width properties. Enter the following three Dim statements. Press **Enter** twice after typing the last Dim statement.

   Dim dblPriceSqYd As Double
   Dim dblSqYards As Double
   Dim dblCost As Double

5. Now assign the length and width entries to the Rectangle object's Length and Width properties, and assign the price entry to the `dblPriceSqYd` variable. Enter the following three lines of code. Press **Enter** twice after typing the last line. Notice that when you type `floor.`, the object's Length and Width properties appear in the IntelliSense list.

   Double.TryParse(lstLength.SelectedItem.ToString.Trim, floor.Length)
   Double.TryParse(lstWidth.SelectedItem.ToString.Trim, floor.Width)
   Double.TryParse(lstPrice.SelectedItem.ToString.Trim, dblPriceSqYd)

6. Step 4 in the pseudocode is to calculate the required number of square yards by dividing the floor's area (which is in square feet) by the number 9. You need to divide by 9 because there are 9 square feet in a square yard. You can use the Rectangle object's GetArea method to calculate and return the area of the floor. Enter the following comment and assignment statement. Here again, notice that when you type `floor.`, the object's GetArea method appears in the IntelliSense list.

   ' calculate the required number of square yards of carpet
   dblSqYards = floor.GetArea / 9

7. The next step is to calculate the cost of the carpet by multiplying the price per square yard by the required number of square yards. Enter the following comment and assignment statement. Press **Enter** twice after typing the assignment statement.

   ' calculate the carpet cost
   dblCost = dblPriceSqYd * dblSqYards

8. Finally, display the required number of square yards and the carpet cost in the appropriate label controls. Enter the following comment and assignment statements.

   ' display required number of square yards and carpet cost
   lblSquareYards.Text = dblSqYards.ToString("N1")
   lblCost.Text = dblCost.ToString("C2")

9. Save the solution. Figure 11-17 shows the Rectangle class definition, which is contained in the Rectangle.vb file. It also shows the code entered in the btnCalc control's Click event procedure in the Main Form.vb file.

```
Public Class Rectangle
     Private _dblLength As Double
     Private _dblWidth As Double

     Public Property Length() As Double
        Get
           Return _dblLength
        End Get
        Set(ByVal value As Double)
           If value > 0 Then
              _dblLength = value
           Else
              _dblLength = 0
           End If
        End Set
     End Property

     Public Property Width() As Double
        Get
           Return _dblWidth
        End Get
        Set(ByVal value As Double)
           If value > 0 Then
              _dblWidth = value
           Else
              _dblWidth = 0
           End If
        End Set
     End Property

     Public Sub New()
        _dblLength = 0
        _dblWidth = 0
     End Sub

     Public Function GetArea() As Double
        Return _dblLength * _dblWidth
     End Function
End Class

Private Sub btnCalc_Click(ByVal sender As Object, _
     ByVal e As System.EventArgs) Handles btnCalc.Click
     ' displays number of square yards and cost of carpet

     Dim floor As New Rectangle
     Dim dblPriceSqYd As Double
     Dim dblSqYards As Double
     Dim dblCost As Double

     Double.TryParse(lstLength.SelectedItem.ToString.Trim, floor.Length)
     Double.TryParse(lstWidth.SelectedItem.ToString.Trim, floor.Width)
     Double.TryParse(lstPrice.SelectedItem.ToString.Trim, dblPriceSqYd)

     ' calculate the required number of square yards of carpet
     dblSqYards = floor.GetArea / 9
     ' calculate the carpet cost
     dblCost = dblPriceSqYd * dblSqYards

     ' display required number of square yards and carpet cost
     lblSquareYards.Text = dblSqYards.ToString("N1")
     lblCost.Text = dblCost.ToString("C2")

End Sub
```

class definition contained in the Rectangle.vb file

instantiates a Rectangle object

assigns values to the object's Length and Width properties

invokes the object's GetArea method

Figure 11-17 Rectangle class definition and btnCalc Click event procedure

To test the application's code:

1. Save the solution, if necessary, then start the application. Click **9.0** in the Width (feet) list box, then click **8.00** in the Price (per square yard) list box. Click the **Calculate** button. The `Dim floor As New Rectangle` instruction in the button's Click event procedure instantiates a Rectangle object. At this point, the computer processes the class's default constructor, which initializes the object's Private `_dblLength` and `_dblWidth` variables to the number 0. The next three Dim statements in the procedure create and initialize the `dblPriceSqYd`, `dblSqYards`, and `dblCost` variables. The TryParse methods assign the appropriate values to the Rectangle object's Public Length and Width properties, as well as to the `dblPriceSqYd` variable. The procedure then calculates the required number of square yards of carpet, using the Rectangle object's GetArea method to calculate and return the area of the floor. Finally, the procedure calculates the cost of the carpet and then displays the required number of square yards and cost. See Figure 11-18.

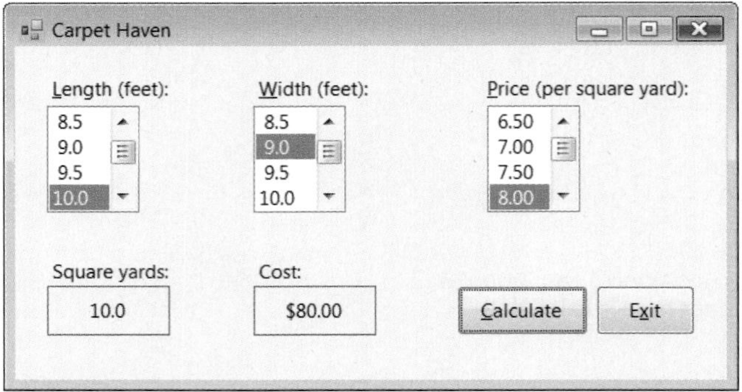

Figure 11-18 Interface showing the required number of square yards and cost

2. On your own, test the application using different lengths, widths, and prices. When you are finished, click the **Exit** button.
3. Close the Code Editor window, then close the solution.

Example 3—Reusing a Class

In Example 2, you used the Rectangle class to create an object that represented the floor in a room. In this example, you will use the Rectangle class to represent a square pizza. A square is simply a rectangle that has four equal sides. As mentioned earlier, the ability to use an object—in this case, a Rectangle object—for more than one purpose saves programming time and money—an advantage that contributes to the popularity of object-oriented programming.

To open the Pizza Roma application, and then add the Rectangle.vb file to the application:

1. Open the **Pizza Roma Solution** (**Pizza Roma Solution.sln**) file, which is contained in the VB2008\Chap11\Pizza Roma Solution folder. If necessary, open the designer window. The application provides text boxes for entering the side measurement of the entire pizza, as well as the side measurement of a slice of pizza. Using both side measurements, the application calculates and displays the number of pizza slices that can be cut from the entire pizza.
2. First, you will copy the Rectangle.vb class file from the Carpet Haven application to the Pizza Roma application. Use Windows to copy the Rectangle.vb file from the VB2008\Chap11\Carpet Calculator Solution\Carpet Calculator Project folder to the VB2008\Chap11\Pizza Roma Solution\Pizza Roma Project folder.
3. Now add the Rectangle.vb file to the project. Click **Project** on the menu bar, then click **Add Existing Item**. Open the Pizza Roma Project folder, if necessary, then click **Rectangle.vb**. Click the **Add** button. Temporarily display the Solution Explorer window, if necessary, to verify that the Rectangle.vb file was added to the project.
4. Open the Code Editor window. Replace the <your name> and <current date> text in the comments with your name and the current date.
5. Open the code template for the btnCalc control's Click event procedure, then enter the following two comments. Press **Enter** twice after typing the last comment.

   ' displays the number of square pizza slices
   ' that can be cut from a square pizza

Figure 11-19 shows the pseudocode for the btnCalc control's Click event procedure.

---

btnCalc Click event procedure

1. instantiate a Rectangle object to represent the entire square pizza
2. instantiate a Rectangle object to represent a square pizza slice
3. declare variables to store the area of the entire pizza, the area of a pizza slice, and the number of slices
4. assign the input data to the appropriate object's properties
5. calculate the area of the entire pizza
6. calculate the area of a pizza slice
7. calculate the number of pizza slices by dividing the area of the entire pizza by the area of a pizza slice
8. display the number of pizza slices

Figure 11-19 Pseudocode for the btnCalc control's Click event procedure

To code the btnCalc control's Click event procedure:

1. First, instantiate two Rectangle objects to represent the entire pizza and a pizza slice. Enter the following Dim statements.

   Dim entirePizza As New Rectangle
   Dim pizzaSlice As New Rectangle

2. Now declare variables to store the area of the entire pizza, the area of a pizza slice, and the number of slices. You won't need variables to store the side measurements of the entire pizza and slice of pizza, because the procedure will assign those values to each Rectangle object's Length and Width properties. Enter the following three Dim statements. Press **Enter** twice after typing the last Dim statement.

   Dim dblEntireArea As Double
   Dim dblSliceArea As Double
   Dim dblSlices As Double

3. Now assign the side measurements to the appropriate Rectangle object's Length and Width properties. Enter the following four lines of code. Press **Enter** twice after typing the last line. Notice that when you press the period after typing either `entirePizza` or `pizzaSlice`, the object's Length and Width properties appear in the IntelliSense list.

   Double.TryParse(txtEntirePizza.Text, entirePizza.Length)
   Double.TryParse(txtEntirePizza.Text, entirePizza.Width)
   Double.TryParse(txtPizzaSlice.Text, pizzaSlice.Length)
   Double.TryParse(txtPizzaSlice.Text, pizzaSlice.Width)

4. Steps 5 and 6 in the pseudocode are to calculate the area of the entire pizza and the area of a slice of pizza, respectively. You can accomplish both tasks using the Rectangle object's GetArea method. Because the method already contains the code needed to calculate the area of a rectangle, you do not need to waste time planning and then reentering the code. Enter the following comment and assignment statements.

   ' calculate area of entire pizza and pizza slice
   dblEntireArea = entirePizza.GetArea
   dblSliceArea = pizzaSlice.GetArea

5. The next step is to calculate the number of pizza slices by dividing the area of the entire pizza by the area of a pizza slice. Enter the following comment and assignment statement. Press **Enter** twice after typing the assignment statement.

   ' calculate number of slices
   dblSlices = dblEntireArea / dblSliceArea

6. Finally, display the number of pizza slices in the lblSlices control. Enter the following comment and assignment statement.

   ' display the number of slices
   lblSlices.Text = dblSlices.ToString("N1")

7. Save the solution. Figure 11-20 shows the code entered in the btnCalc control's Click event procedure.

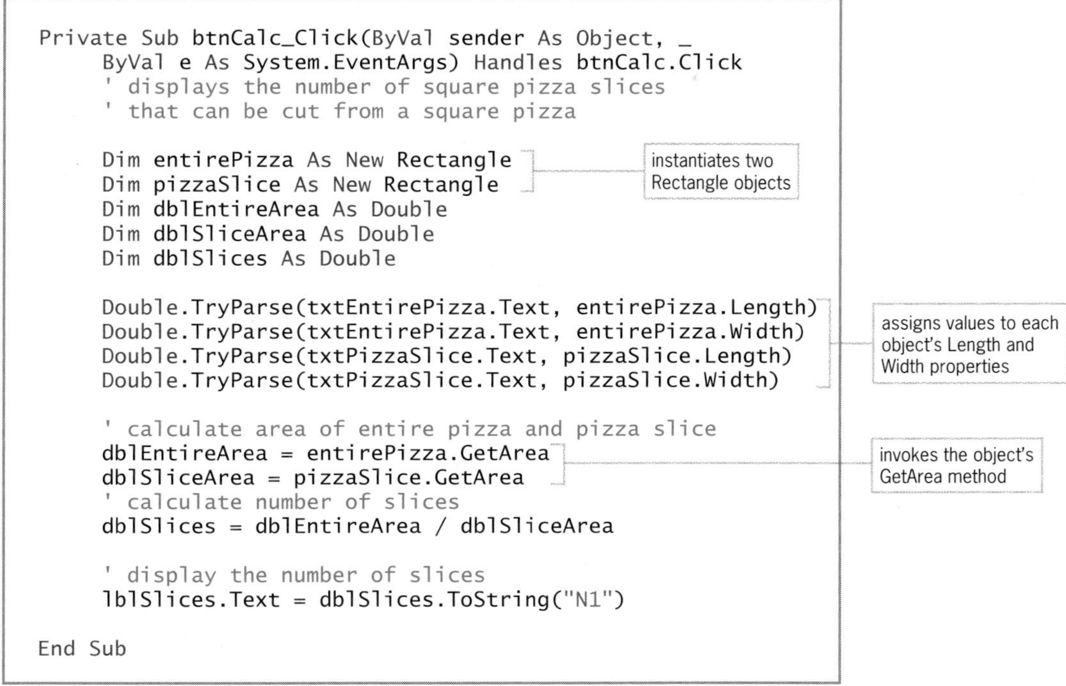

```
Private Sub btnCalc_Click(ByVal sender As Object, _
     ByVal e As System.EventArgs) Handles btnCalc.Click
     ' displays the number of square pizza slices
     ' that can be cut from a square pizza

     Dim entirePizza As New Rectangle
     Dim pizzaSlice As New Rectangle
     Dim dblEntireArea As Double
     Dim dblSliceArea As Double
     Dim dblSlices As Double

     Double.TryParse(txtEntirePizza.Text, entirePizza.Length)
     Double.TryParse(txtEntirePizza.Text, entirePizza.Width)
     Double.TryParse(txtPizzaSlice.Text, pizzaSlice.Length)
     Double.TryParse(txtPizzaSlice.Text, pizzaSlice.Width)

     ' calculate area of entire pizza and pizza slice
     dblEntireArea = entirePizza.GetArea
     dblSliceArea = pizzaSlice.GetArea
     ' calculate number of slices
     dblSlices = dblEntireArea / dblSliceArea

     ' display the number of slices
     lblSlices.Text = dblSlices.ToString("N1")

End Sub
```


Figure 11-20 Code entered in the btnCalc control's Click event procedure

To test the application's code:

1. Save the solution, if necessary, then start the application. First, determine the number of 4-inch slices that can be cut from a 12-inch pizza. Type **12** in the Entire square pizza box, then type **4** in the Square pizza slice box. Click the **Calculate** button. As indicated in Figure 11-21, 9 4-inch square pizza slices can be cut from a 12-inch square pizza.

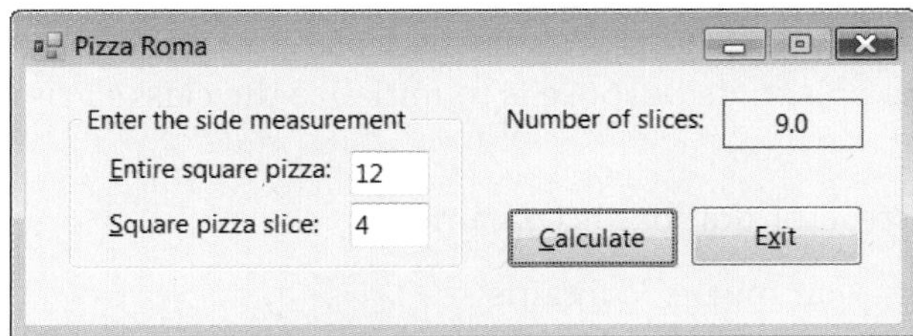

Figure 11-21 Number of pizza slices shown in the interface

2. On your own, test the application using different side measurements. When you are finished, click the **Exit** button. Close the Code Editor window, then close the solution.

Lesson A Summary

- **To define a class:**

  Use the Class statement, whose syntax is shown in Figure 11-2.

- **To add a class file to a project:**

  Click Project on the menu bar, then click Add Class. In the Name box, type the name of the class followed by .vb, then click the Add button.

- **To instantiate (create) an object from a class:**

  Use either of the syntax versions shown in Figure 11-3.

- **To create a Property procedure:**

  Use the syntax shown in Figure 11-12. The Get block allows an application to retrieve the contents of the Private variable associated with the Property procedure. The Set block allows an application to assign a value to the Private variable associated with the Property procedure.

- **To create a constructor:**

  Use the syntax shown in Figure 11-14. A constructor that has no parameters is called the default constructor.

- **To create a method other than a constructor:**

  Use the syntax shown in Figure 11-15.

Lesson A Key Terms

Attributes—the characteristics that describe an object

Behaviors—includes an object's methods and events

Class—a pattern (or blueprint) that the computer follows when creating (instantiating) an object

Class statement—the statement used to define a class in Visual Basic

Constructor—a method whose instructions are automatically processed each time the class instantiates an object; its purpose is to initialize the class's Private variables

Default constructor—a constructor that has no parameters

Encapsulates—an OOP term that means "contains"

Events—the actions to which an object can respond

Get block—the section of a Property procedure that contains the Get statement

Get statement—appears in a Get block in a Property procedure; contains the code that allows an application to retrieve the contents of the Private variable associated with the property

Instance—an object created from a class

Instantiated—the process of creating an object from a class

Methods—the actions that an object is capable of performing

OOP—an acronym for object-oriented programming

Property procedure—creates a Public property that can be used to access a Private variable in a class

Set block—the section of a Property procedure that contains the Set statement

Set statement—appears in a Set block in a Property procedure; contains the code that allows an application to assign a value to the Private variable associated with the property

Lesson A Review Questions

1. In Visual Basic, you enter the Class statement in a class file whose filename ends with ______________________.
   a. .cla
   b. .cls
   c. .vb
   d. None of the above.

2. A constructor is ______________________.
   a. a Function procedure
   b. a Property procedure
   c. a Sub procedure
   d. either a Function procedure or a Sub procedure

3. The Product class contains a Private variable named `_intPrice`. The Private variable is associated with a Public property named Price. An application instantiates a Product object and assigns it to a variable named `item`. Which of the following statements can the application use to assign the number 45 to the `_intPrice` variable?
   a. `_intPrice = 45`
   b. `Price = 45`
   c. `item._intPrice = 45`
   d. `item.Price = 45`

4. The Product class in Review Question 3 also contains a Public method named GetNewPrice. The method is a Function procedure. Which of the following statements can be used by the application in Review Question 3 to invoke the GetNewPrice method?

   a. `intNewPrice = Call GetNewPrice`

   b. `intNewPrice = Price.GetNewPrice`

   c. `intNewPrice = item.GetNewPrice`

   d. `intNewPrice = item.GetNewPrice(_intPrice)`

5. Which of the following statements is false?

   a. An example of an attribute is the `_intMinutes` variable in a Time class.

   b. An example of a behavior is the SetTime method in a Time class.

   c. An object created from a class is referred to as an instance of the class.

   d. A class is considered an object.

6. A Private variable in a class can be accessed directly by a Public method in the same class.

   a. True

   b. False

7. An application can access the Private variables in a class ______________________________.

   a. directly

   b. using properties created by Property procedures

   c. through Private procedures contained in the class

   d. None of the above.

8. To expose a variable or method contained in a class, you declare the variable or method using the keyword ______________________________.

   a. `Exposed`

   b. `Private`

   c. `Public`

   d. `Viewable`

9. The name of the default constructor for a class named Animal is ______________________.

   a. Animal

   b. AnimalConstructor

   c. Default

   d. None of the above.

10. Which of the following creates an Animal object and assigns it to the `dog` variable?

    a. `Dim dog As Animal`

    b. `Dim dog As New Animal`

    c. `Dim dog As Animal`

       `dog = New Animal`

    d. Both b and c.

11. If you need to validate a value before assigning it to a Private variable, you enter the validation code in the ______________________ block in a Property procedure.

    a. Assign

    b. Get

    c. Set

    d. Validate

12. The Return statement is entered in the ______________________ statement in a Property procedure.

    a. Get

    b. Set

Lesson A Exercises

INTRODUCTORY

1. Write a Class statement that defines a class named Book. The class contains three Public variables named `Title`, `Author`, and `Cost`. The `Title` and `Author` variables are String variables. The `Cost` variable is a Decimal variable. Then use the syntax shown in Version 1 in Figure 11-3 to declare a variable that can store a Book object; name the variable `fiction`. Also write a statement that creates the Book object and assigns it to the `fiction` variable.

INTRODUCTORY

2. Rewrite the Class statement from Exercise 1 so it uses three Private variables rather than three Public variables. Be sure to include the appropriate Property procedures and default constructor.

INTRODUCTORY

3. Write a Class statement that defines a class named Tape. The class contains four Private String variables named `_strName`, `_strArtist`, `_strSongNumber`, and `_strLength`. Name the corresponding properties TapeName, Artist, SongNumber, and Length. Then use the syntax shown in Version 2 in Figure 11-3 to create a Tape object, assigning it to a variable named `blues`.

INTRODUCTORY

4. An application contains the class definition shown in Figure 11-22.

   a. Write a Dim statement that creates a Computer object and assigns the object to a variable named `homeUse`.

   b. Using the Computer object from Step a, write an assignment statement that assigns the string "IB-50" to the Model property.

   c. Using the Computer object from Step a, write an assignment statement that assigns the number 2400 to the Cost property.

   d. Using the Computer object from Step a, write an assignment statement that invokes the GetNewPrice function. Assign the function's return value to a variable named `dblNewPrice`.

```
Public Class Computer
   Private _strModel As String
   Private _dblCost As Double

   Public Property Model() As String
      Get
         Return _strModel
      End Get
      Set(ByVal value As String)
         _strModel = value
      End Set
   End Property

   Public Property Cost() As Double
      Get
         Return _dblCost
      End Get
      Set(ByVal value As Double)
         _dblCost = value
      End Set
   End Property

   Public Sub New()
      _strModel = String.Empty
      _dblCost = 0
   End Sub

   Public Function GetNewPrice() As Double
      Return _dblCost * 1.2
   End Function
End Class
```

Figure 11-22 Computer class definition

INTRODUCTORY

5. In this exercise, you modify the Willow Pools application completed in the lesson. Use Windows to make a copy of the Pool Solution folder, which is contained in the VB2008\Chap11 folder. Rename the folder Modified Pool Solution-Introductory. Open the Pool Solution (Pool Solution.sln) file contained in the VB2008\Chap11\Modified Pool Solution-Introductory folder. Open the designer window, then open the RectangularPool.vb file. Modify the RectangularPool class so that it uses Private variables and Public Property procedures rather than Public variables. Include the default constructor. Save the solution, then start and test the application. Stop the application. Close the Code Editor window, then close the solution.

INTERMEDIATE

6. In this exercise, you modify the Willow Pools application from Exercise 5. Use Windows to make a copy of the Modified Pool Solution-Introductory folder, which is contained in the VB2008\Chap11 folder. Rename the folder Modified Pool Solution-Intermediate. Open the Pool Solution (Pool Solution.sln) file contained in the VB2008\Chap11\Modified Pool Solution-Intermediate folder.

   a. Open the designer window. Add two label controls to the form. Position the label controls as shown in Figure 11-23. Change the lblCost control's TextAlign property to MiddleCenter.

   b. Open the RectangularPool.vb file. Add a method that calculates and returns the volume of a pool. Name the method GetVolume. The formula for calculating the volume is *length * width * depth*. Save the solution, then close the RectangularPool.vb window.

   c. Open the form's Code Editor window. The btnCalc control's Click event procedure should use the RectangularPool object's GetVolume method to determine the pool's volume. It then should pass the pool's volume to the GetGallons function. The Click event procedure also should calculate and display the cost of filling the pool with water. The charge for water is $1.75 per 1000 gallons, or .00175 per gallon. Make the necessary modifications to the code. Save the solution, then start and test the application. Stop the application. Close the Code Editor window, then close the solution.

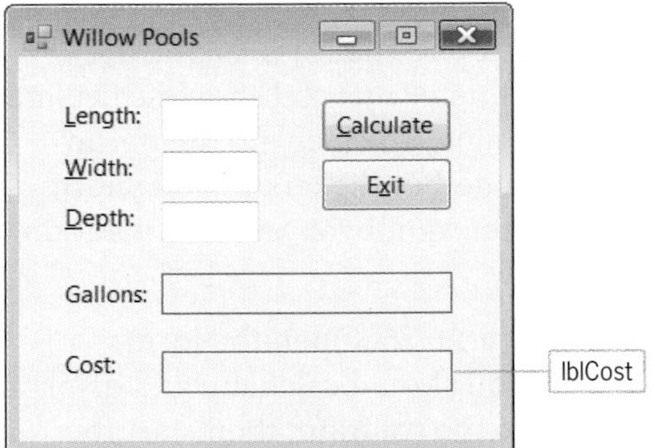

Figure 11-23 Willow Pools interface showing the location of the additional label controls

INTERMEDIATE

7. In this exercise, you create an application that can be used to estimate the cost of laying sod on a rectangular piece of property. Create a Visual Basic Windows application. Name the solution, project, and form file Kessler Solution, Kessler Project, and Main Form.vb, respectively. Save the application in the VB2008\Chap11 folder. Use Windows to copy the Rectangle.vb file from the VB2008\Chap11\Carpet Calculator Solution\Carpet Calculator Project folder to the VB2008\Chap11\Kessler Solution\Kessler Project folder. Use the Project menu to add the Rectangle.vb class file to the project. Create the interface shown in Figure 11-24. Open the form's Code Editor window, then code the application. Save the solution, then start and test the application. Stop the application. Close the Code Editor window, then close the solution.

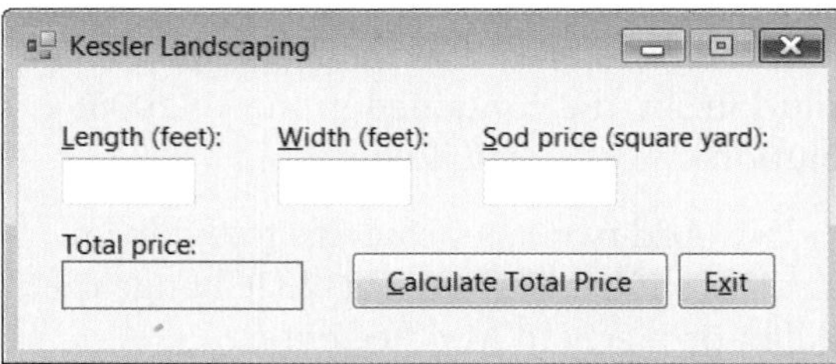

Figure 11-24 User interface for the Kessler Landscaping application

INTERMEDIATE

8. In this exercise, you create an application that can be used to calculate the cost of installing a fence around a rectangular area. Create a Visual Basic Windows application. Name the solution, project, and form file Fence Solution, Fence Project, and Main Form.vb, respectively. Save the application in the VB2008\Chap11 folder.

   a. Use Windows to copy the Rectangle.vb file from the VB2008\Chap11\Carpet Calculator Solution\Carpet Calculator Project folder to the VB2008\Chap11\Fence Solution\Fence Project folder. Use the Project menu to add the Rectangle.vb class file to the project.

   b. Right-click Rectangle.vb in the Solution Explorer window, then click View Code. Add another method to the class. Name the method GetPerimeter. The GetPerimeter method should calculate and return the perimeter of a rectangle. To calculate the perimeter, the method will need to add together the length and width measurements, and then multiply the sum by 2. Save the solution, then close the Rectangle.vb window.

   c. Create the interface shown in Figure 11-25. Open the form's Code Editor window. The application should calculate and display the cost of installing the fence. Save the solution, then start the application. Test the application using 120 feet as the length, 75 feet as the width, and 10 as the cost per linear foot of fencing. The installation cost should be $3,900.00. Stop the application. Close the Code Editor window, then close the solution.

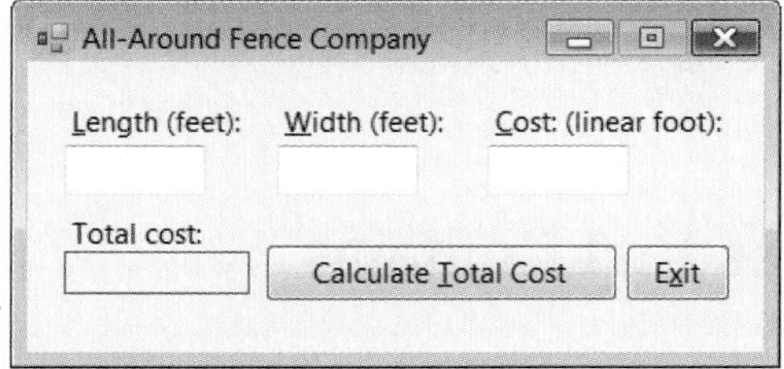

Figure 11-25 User interface for the All-Around Fence Company application

9. In this exercise, you define a Triangle class. You also create an application that allows the user to display either a Triangle object's area or its perimeter. The formula for calculating the area of a triangle is 1/2 * *base* * *height*. The formula for calculating the perimeter of a triangle is *a* + *b* + *c*, where *a*, *b*, and *c* are the lengths of the sides. Create a Visual Basic Windows application. Name the solution, project, and form file Math Solution, Math Project, and Main Form.vb, respectively. Save the application in the VB2008\Chap11 folder. ADVANCED

   a. Create the interface shown in Figure 11-26.

   b. Add a class file to the project. Name the class file Triangle.vb. The Triangle class should verify that the dimensions are greater than zero before assigning the values to the Private variables. The class also should include a method to calculate the area of a triangle and a method to calculate the perimeter of a triangle. Save the solution, then close the Triangle.vb window.

   c. Open the form's Code Editor window. Use the InputBox function to get the appropriate data from the user. Save the solution, then start and test the application. Stop the application. Close the Code Editor window, then close the solution.

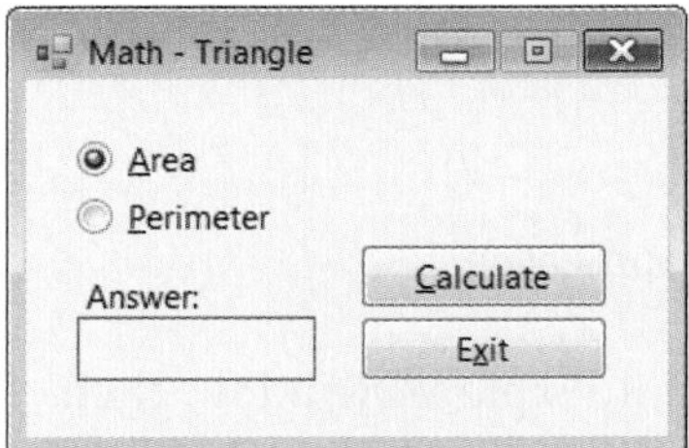

Figure 11-26 User interface for the Math – Triangle application

LESSON B

After studying Lesson B, you should be able to:

- Include a ReadOnly property in a class
- Include a parameterized method in a class
- Overload a method in a class

Example 4—Using a Class that Contains a ReadOnly Property

In Lesson A, you learned that a Property procedure's header can include the keyword `ReadOnly`. As you may remember, the `ReadOnly` keyword indicates that the property's value can be retrieved (read) by an application, but the application cannot set (write to) the property. A ReadOnly property gets its value from the class itself rather than from the application. In the next set of steps, you will include a ReadOnly property in a class named CourseGrade. You then will use the ReadOnly property in the Grade Calculator application, which you will finish coding later in this lesson. The application displays a grade based on two test scores entered by the user.

To open the Grade Calculator application, and then complete the CourseGrade class:

1. If necessary, start Visual Studio 2008 or Visual Basic 2008 Express Edition. Close the Start Page window.
2. Open the **Grade Solution** (**Grade Solution.sln**) file, which is contained in the VB2008\Chap11\Grade Solution folder. If necessary, open the designer window. The interface provides list boxes for entering the two test scores, which can range from 0 to 100 points each. See Figure 11-27.

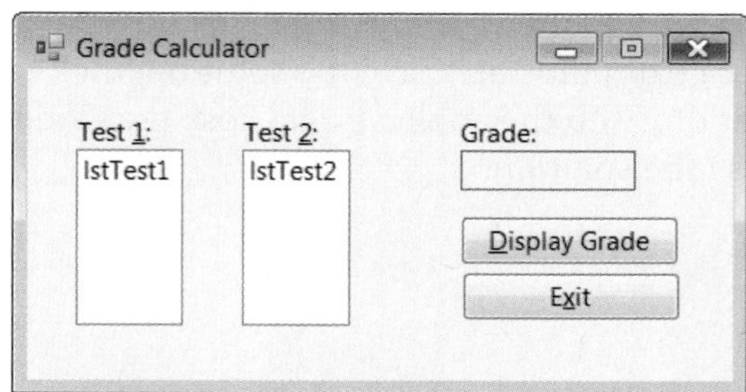

Figure 11-27 User interface for the Grade Calculator application

3. Right-click **CourseGrade.vb** in the Solution Explorer window, then click **View Code**. Replace the <your name> and <current date> text in the comments with your name and the current date.
4. The CourseGrade class should contain three attributes: two test scores and a letter grade. The Private variable for the letter grade is missing from the code. Click the **blank line** above the Score1 Property procedure's header, then enter the following line of code.

   Private _strLetterGrade As String

5. Now create a Public property for the Private `_strLetterGrade` variable. You will make the property ReadOnly so that the class (rather than the Grade Calculator application) determines the appropriate grade. By making the property ReadOnly, the application will be able to retrieve the grade, but it will not be able to change the grade. Click the **blank line** immediately above the End Class clause. Enter the property procedure shown in Figure 11-28, then position the insertion point as shown in the figure. (Notice that when you include the `ReadOnly` keyword in a Property procedure's header, the Code Editor includes only the Get block in the procedure.)

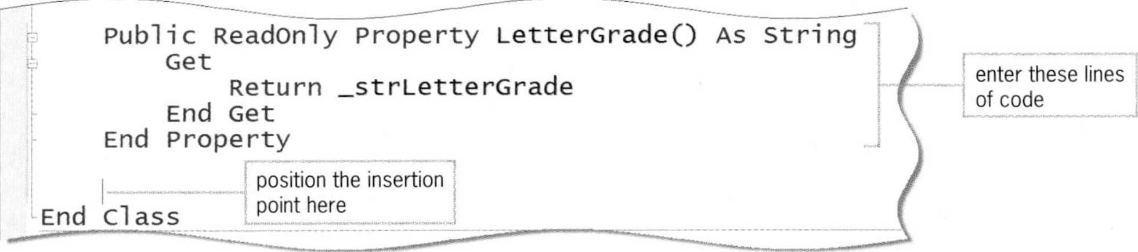

```
Public ReadOnly Property LetterGrade() As String
    Get
        Return _strLetterGrade
    End Get
End Property

End Class
```


Figure 11-28 Property procedure for the ReadOnly LetterGrade property

6. Next, create the default constructor, which will initialize the Private variables when a CourseGrade object is instantiated. Enter the following lines of code.

Public Sub New()
_intScore1 = 0
_intScore2 = 0
_strLetterGrade = String.Empty
End Sub

7. Finally, create the DetermineGrade method, which will assign the appropriate letter grade to the `_strLetterGrade` variable. The method will be a Sub procedure, because it will not need to return a value to the application that calls it. Click **immediately after the letter b** in the constructor's End Sub clause, then press **Enter** twice. Enter the DetermineGrade method shown in Figure 11-29.

The code entered in the CourseGrade class is shown in Figure 11-31.

```
    Public Sub DetermineGrade()
        Dim intTotal As Integer
        intTotal = _intScore1 + _intScore2

        Select Case intTotal
            Case Is >= 180
                _strLetterGrade = "A"
            Case Is >= 160
                _strLetterGrade = "B"
            Case Is >= 140
                _strLetterGrade = "C"
            Case Is >= 120
                _strLetterGrade = "D"
            Case Else
                _strLetterGrade = "F"
        End Select
    End Sub
End Class
```

enter the DetermineGrade method's code

Figure 11-29 DetermineGrade method entered in the class definition

8. Save the solution, then close the CourseGrade.vb window.

Now that you have finished defining the class, you can use the class to instantiate a CourseGrade object in the Grade Calculator application.

To finish coding the Grade Calculator application, and then test the code:

1. Open the form's Code Editor window. Replace the <your name> and <current date> text in the comments with your name and the current date.

2. Locate the btnDisplay control's Click event procedure. First, instantiate a CourseGrade object. Click the **blank line** above the `' assign test scores to object's properties` comment, then enter the following Dim statement.

   Dim grade As New CourseGrade

3. Now assign the test scores selected in the list boxes to the object's properties. Click the **blank line** below the `' assign test scores to object's properties` comment, then enter the following TryParse methods.

   Integer.TryParse(lstTest1.SelectedItem.ToString, grade.Score1)
   Integer.TryParse(lstTest2.SelectedItem.ToString, grade.Score2)

4. Now use the object's DetermineGrade method to determine the appropriate grade. Click the **blank line** below the `' calculate the grade using the object's DetermineGrade method` comment, then enter the following Call statement.

   Call grade.DetermineGrade()

5. Finally, display the grade, which is stored in the object's ReadOnly LetterGrade property. Click the **blank line** below the `' display the grade stored in the object's ReadOnly property` comment. Type **lblGrade.Text = grade.**, then click **LetterGrade** in the IntelliSense list. If necessary, click the **Common** tab. See Figure 11-30. The message that appears next to the IntelliSense list indicates that the LetterGrade property is ReadOnly.

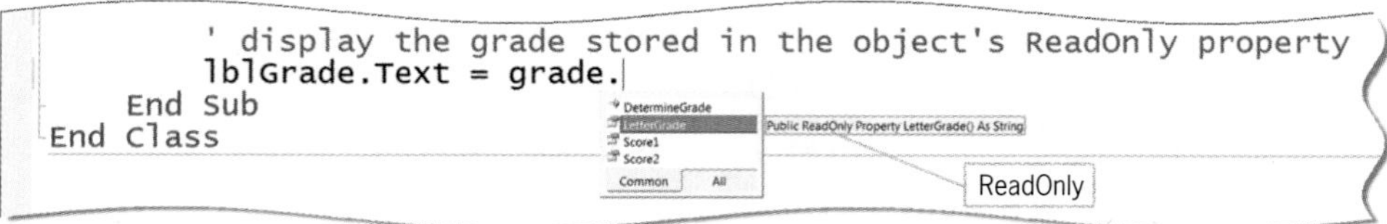

Figure 11-30 The message indicates that the property is ReadOnly

6. Press **Tab** to include the LetterGrade property in the assignment statement. Save the solution, then start the application. Scroll the Test 1 list box, then click **86** in the list. Scroll the Test 2 list box, then click **95** in the list. Click the **Display Grade** button. The letter A appears in the Grade box.

7. On your own, test the application using different test scores. When you are finished, click the **Exit** button. Close the Code Editor window, then close the solution. Figure 11-31 shows the CourseGrade class definition and the code entered in the btnDisplay control's Click event procedure.

```
Public Class CourseGrade
    Private _intScore1 As Integer
    Private _intScore2 As Integer
    Private _strLetterGrade As String

    Public Property Score1() As Integer
      Get
         Return _intScore1
      End Get
      Set(ByVal value As Integer)
        _intScore1 = value
      End Set
    End Property

    Public Property Score2() As Integer
      Get
        Return _intScore2
      End Get
      Set(ByVal value As Integer)
        _intScore2 = value
      End Set
    End Property

    Public ReadOnly Property LetterGrade() As String
      Get
        Return _strLetterGrade
      End Get
    End Property

    Public Sub New()
      _intScore1 = 0
      _intScore2 = 0
      _strLetterGrade = String.Empty
    End Sub

    Public Sub DetermineGrade()
      Dim intTotal As Integer
      intTotal = _intScore1 + _intScore2

      Select Case intTotal
        Case Is >= 180
          _strLetterGrade = "A"
        Case Is >= 160
          _strLetterGrade = "B"
        Case Is >= 140
          _strLetterGrade = "C"
        Case Is >= 120
          _strLetterGrade = "D"
        Case Else
          _strLetterGrade = "F"
      End Select
    End Sub
End Class

Private Sub btnDisplay_Click(ByVal sender As Object, _
     ByVal e As System.EventArgs) Handles btnDisplay.Click
     ' calculates and displays a letter grade

     Dim grade As New CourseGrade

     ' assign test scores to object's properties
     Integer.TryParse(lstTest1.SelectedItem.ToString, grade.Score1)
     Integer.TryParse(lstTest2.SelectedItem.ToString, grade.Score2)

     ' calculate the grade using the object's DetermineGrade method
     Call grade.DetermineGrade()

     ' display the grade stored in the object's ReadOnly property
     lblGrade.Text = grade.LetterGrade
End Sub
```

the class definition begins here

the btnDisplay Click event procedure begins here

Figure 11-31 CourseGrade class definition and btnDisplay Click event procedure

Example 5—Using a Class that Contains Two Constructors

As mentioned in Lesson A, a class can have more than one constructor, although only one can be the default constructor. The FormattedDate class in Figure 11-32 contains two constructors. The first constructor is the default constructor, because it does not have any parameters. The second constructor allows you to specify the initial values for a FormattedDate object when the object is created. In this case, the initial values must have the String data type, because the constructor's *parameterList* contains two String variables. You include the initial values, enclosed in a set of parentheses, in the statement that instantiates the object, like this: `Dim payDate As New FormattedDate(strNumMonth, strNumDay)`. Recall that the `New` keyword invokes a constructor in the class. The computer determines which class constructor to use by matching the number, data type, and position of the arguments in the statement that instantiates the object with the number, data type, and position of the parameters listed in each constructor's *parameterList*. For instance, when processing either the `Dim payDate As New FormattedDate` statement or the `payDate = New FormattedDate` statement, the computer will use the class's default constructor to initialize the object's variables; this is because neither statement contains any arguments. However, the computer will use the second constructor when processing the `Dim payDate As New FormattedDate(strNumMonth, strNumDay)` statement, because the statement contains two String variables in its *parameterList*. Constructors that contain parameters are called **parameterized constructors**. The method name combined with its optional *parameterList* is called the method's **signature**.

```
Public Class FormattedDate
   Private _strMonth As String
   Private _strDay As String

   Public Property Month() As String
     Get
        Return _strMonth
     End Get
     Set(ByVal value As String)
         Dim intMonth As Integer
         Integer.TryParse(value, intMonth)
         If intMonth < 1 OrElse intMonth > 12 Then
               _strMonth = String.Empty
         Else
               _strMonth = value
         End If
     End Set
   End Property

   Public Property Day() As String
     Get
         Return _strDay
     End Get
     Set(ByVal value As String)
         _strDay = value
     End Set
   End Property
```

Figure 11-32 FormattedDate class definition *(continues)*

(continued)

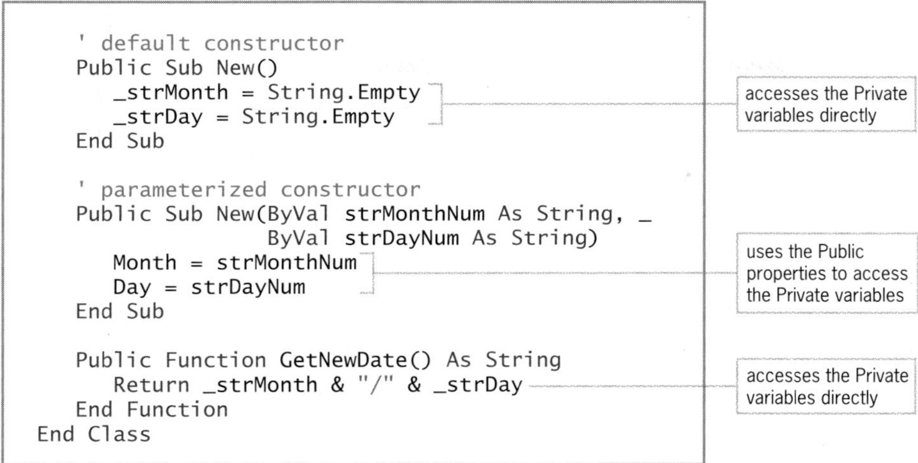
```
      ' default constructor
      Public Sub New()
         _strMonth = String.Empty
         _strDay = String.Empty
      End Sub

      ' parameterized constructor
      Public Sub New(ByVal strMonthNum As String, _
                     ByVal strDayNum As String)
         Month = strMonthNum
         Day = strDayNum
      End Sub

      Public Function GetNewDate() As String
         Return _strMonth & "/" & _strDay
      End Function
   End Class
```


Figure 11-32 FormattedDate class definition

In addition to the two constructors, the FormattedDate class in Figure 11-32 contains a method named GetNewDate. The GetNewDate method is a function procedure that returns the month and day numbers, separated by a slash. The month and day numbers are stored in the class's Private variables. The methods in a class can access the class's Private variables either directly (by name) or indirectly (through the Public properties). In the FormattedDate class, both the default constructor and the GetNewDate method use the names of the Private variables to access the variables directly. The default constructor assigns values to the Private variables, and the GetNewDate method retrieves the values stored in the Private variables. The parameterized constructor, on the other hand, uses the Public properties to access the Private variables indirectly. This is because the values passed to the parameterized constructor come from the application rather than from the class itself. Values that originate outside of the class should always be assigned to the Private variables indirectly, through the Public properties. Doing this ensures that the Property procedure's Set block, which typically contains validation code, is processed. Currently, only the Month Property procedure validates its incoming data. The Day Property procedure does not contain any data validation code. However, if validation code is added to the Day Property procedure at a later date, the code in the parameterized constructor will not need to be modified. The FormattedDate class is used in the Hire Date application, which you will finish coding in the following set of steps.

To finish coding the Hire Date application:

1. Open the **Hire Date Solution** (**Hire Date Solution.sln**) file, which is contained in the VB2008\Chap11\Hire Date Solution folder. If necessary, open the designer window. The interface provides list boxes for entering the month and day numbers.

2. Right-click **FormattedDate.vb** in the Solution Explorer window, then click **View Code**. The class definition from Figure 11-32 appears in the FormattedDate.vb window. Replace the <your name> and <current date> text in the comments with your name and the current date. Save the solution, then close the FormattedDate.vb window.

3. Open the form's Code Editor window. Replace the <your name> and <current date> text in the comments with your name and the current date.

4. You need to code the Click event procedures for the btnDefault and btnParameterized controls. Locate the btnDefault control's Click event procedure. First, instantiate a FormattedDate object, using the default constructor to initialize the object's variables. Click the **blank line** above the End Sub clause, then enter the following Dim statement.

   Dim hireDate As New FormattedDate

5. Next, assign the month and day numbers to the object's properties. Enter the following two assignment statements.

   hireDate.Month = lstMonth.SelectedItem.ToString
   hireDate.Day = lstDay.SelectedItem.ToString

6. Now use the object's GetNewDate method to get the formatted date. Assign the formatted date to the lblHireDate control. Enter the following assignment statement.

   lblHireDate.Text = hireDate.GetNewDate

7. Locate the btnParameterized control's Click event procedure. This time you will instantiate a FormattedDate object using the parameterized constructor to initialize the object's variables. Click the **blank line** above the End Sub clause, then enter the following Dim statement. Be sure to include a space before the line continuation character.

   Dim hireDate As New FormattedDate(lstMonth.SelectedItem.ToString, _
   lstDay.SelectedItem.ToString)

8. Finally, use the object's GetNewDate method to get the formatted date. Assign the formatted date to the lblHireDate control. Enter the following assignment statement.

   lblHireDate.Text = hireDate.GetNewDate

9. Save the solution. Figure 11-33 shows the code entered in the Click event procedures for the btnDefault and btnParameterized controls.

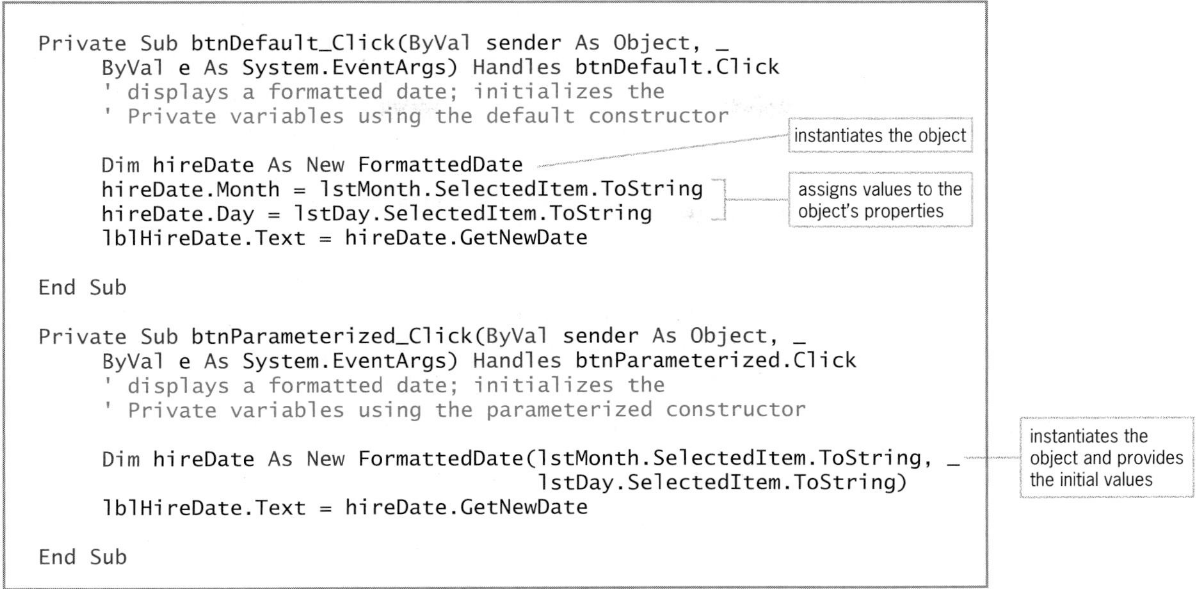

```
Private Sub btnDefault_Click(ByVal sender As Object, _
     ByVal e As System.EventArgs) Handles btnDefault.Click
     ' displays a formatted date; initializes the
     ' Private variables using the default constructor

     Dim hireDate As New FormattedDate
     hireDate.Month = lstMonth.SelectedItem.ToString
     hireDate.Day = lstDay.SelectedItem.ToString
     lblHireDate.Text = hireDate.GetNewDate

End Sub

Private Sub btnParameterized_Click(ByVal sender As Object, _
     ByVal e As System.EventArgs) Handles btnParameterized.Click
     ' displays a formatted date; initializes the
     ' Private variables using the parameterized constructor

     Dim hireDate As New FormattedDate(lstMonth.SelectedItem.ToString, _
                                       lstDay.SelectedItem.ToString)
     lblHireDate.Text = hireDate.GetNewDate

End Sub
```


Figure 11-33 Click event procedures for the btnDefault and btnParameterized controls

Study the code contained in the btnParameterized control's Click event procedure. The Dim statement instantiates a FormattedDate object and assigns it to the `hireDate` variable. The computer will use the parameterized constructor (shown earlier in Figure 11-32) to initialize the object's Private variables. To do this, the computer passes the two String arguments (*by value*) to the constructor. The constructor receives the values and stores them in its `strMonthNum` and `strDayNum` parameters. The `Month = strMonthNum` instruction in the constructor assigns the value stored in the `strMonthNum` parameter to the Public Month property. When you assign a value to a property, the computer passes the value to the property's Set statement, where it is stored in the Set statement's `value` parameter. In this case, the selection structure in the Set statement determines whether the `value` parameter contains a valid value. If the value is not valid, the selection structure's true path assigns the empty string to the Private `_strMonth` variable; otherwise, it assigns the `value` parameter's value to the variable. Next, the `Day = strDayNum` instruction in the constructor assigns the value stored in the `strDayNum` parameter to the Public Day property. The computer passes the value to the Day property's Set statement, where it is stored in the statement's `value` parameter. The `_strDay = value` instruction in the Set statement assigns the contents of the `value` parameter to the Private `_strDay` variable. Finally, the `lblHireDate.Text = hireDate.GetNewDate` statement in the Click event procedure uses the FormattedDate object's GetNewDate method to return the month and day numbers, separated by a slash. The statement displays the formatted date in the lblHireDate control.

Compare the code contained in the btnParameterized control's Click event procedure with the code contained in the btnDefault control's Click event procedure. Rather than using one Dim statement to both instantiate the FormattedDate object and assign the list box values to the object's properties, the btnDefault control's Click event procedure uses three statements: a Dim statement and two assignment statements.

To test the Hire Date application's code:

1. Save the solution, if necessary, then start the application. Click **3** in the Month list box, then click **2** in the Day list box. Click the **Display Hire Date - Default** button. See Figure 11-34.

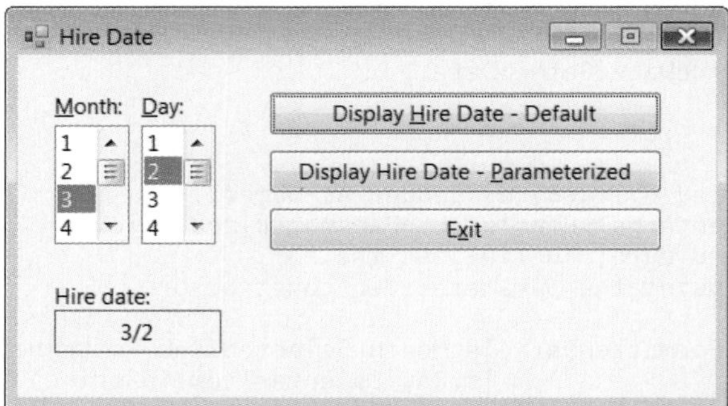

Figure 11-34 Interface showing the formatted date

2. Scroll the Month list box, then click **6** in the list. Click **4** in the Day list box, then click the **Display Hire Date - Parameterized** button. The button's Click event procedure displays 6/4 as the hire date.
3. Click the **Exit** button. Close the Code Editor window, then close the solution.

Example 6—Using a Class that Contains Overloaded Methods

In this example, you will use a class named Employee to instantiate an object. Employee objects have two attributes: an employee number and an employee name. Employee objects also have the following four behaviors:

1. They can initialize their attributes using values provided by the class.
2. They can initialize their attributes using values provided by the application in which they are instantiated.
3. They can calculate and return the gross pay for salaried employees. The gross pay is calculated by dividing the salaried employee's annual salary by 24, because the salaried employees are paid twice per month.
4. They can calculate and return the gross pay for hourly employees. The gross pay is calculated by multiplying the number of hours the employee worked during the week by his or her pay rate.

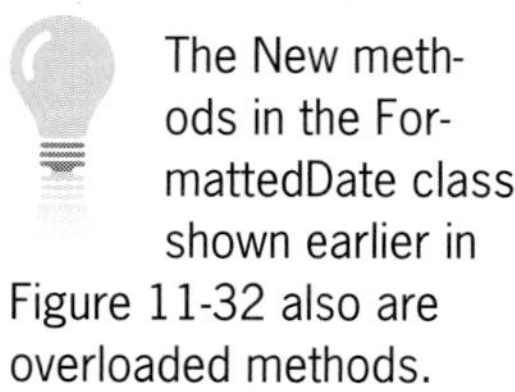

The New methods in the FormattedDate class shown earlier in Figure 11-32 also are overloaded methods.

Figure 11-35 shows the Employee class defined in the Employee.vb file. The class contains two Private variables named `_strNumber` and `_strEmpName`, along with their associated Number and EmpName Property procedures. It also contains four methods. The two New methods are the class's constructors. The first New method is the default constructor and the second is a parameterized constructor. When two or more methods have the same name but different parameters, the methods are referred to as **overloaded methods**.

The two constructors are overloaded methods, because each is named New and each has a different *parameterList*. You can overload any of the methods contained in a class, not just constructors. The two GetGross methods in the Employee class also are overloaded methods, because they have the same name but a different *parameterList*. If the methods being overloaded are not constructors, you must use the `Overloads` keyword in the procedure header, as shown in both GetGross methods in Figure 11-35. The `Overloads` keyword is not used when overloading constructors.

```
Public Class Employee
  Private _strNumber As String
  Private _strEmpName As String

  Public Property Number() As String
    Get
      Return _strNumber
    End Get
    Set(ByVal value As String)
      _strNumber = value
    End Set
  End Property

  Public Property EmpName() As String
    Get
      Return _strEmpName
    End Get
    Set(ByVal value As String)
      _strEmpName = value
    End Set
  End Property

  Public Sub New()
    _strNumber = String.Empty
    _strEmpName = String.Empty
  End Sub

  Public Sub New(ByVal strNum As String, ByVal strName As String)
    Number = strNum
    EmpName = strName
  End Sub

  Public Overloads Function GetGross(ByVal dblSalary As Double) As Double
    ' calculates the gross pay for salaried
    ' employees, who are paid twice per month

    Return dblSalary / 24
  End Function

  Public Overloads Function GetGross(ByVal dblHours As Double, _
                                     ByVal dblRate As Double) As Double
    ' calculates the weekly gross pay for hourly employees

    Return dblHours * dblRate
  End Function
End Class
```


Figure 11-35 Employee class definition

You already are familiar with overloaded methods, as you have used several of the overloaded methods built into Visual Basic. Examples of such methods include ToString, TryParse, Convert.ToDecimal, and MessageBox.Show. The IntelliSense feature in the Code Editor window displays a box that allows you to view a method's signatures, one signature at a time. The box shown in Figure 11-36 displays the second of the ToString method's four signatures. You use the up and down arrows in the box to display the other signatures. The IntelliSense feature also will display the signatures of the overloaded methods contained in the classes you create.

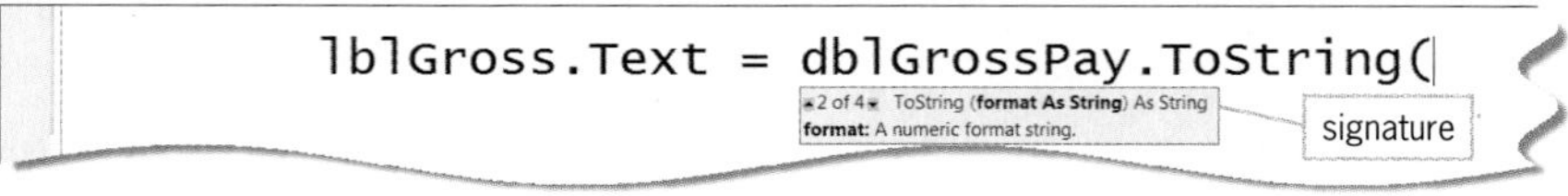

Figure 11-36 Box displaying one of the signatures of the ToString method

Overloading is useful when two or more methods require different parameters to perform essentially the same task. Both overloaded constructors in the Employee class initialize the class's Private variables. However, the default constructor does not need to be passed any information to perform the task, while the parameterized constructor requires two items of information (the employee number and name). Similarly, both GetGross methods in the Employee class calculate and return a gross pay amount. However, the first GetGross method performs its task for salaried employees and requires an application to pass it one item of information: the employee's annual salary. The second GetGross method performs its task for hourly employees and requires two items of information: the number of hours the employee worked and his or her rate of pay. Rather than using two overloaded GetGross methods, you could have used two methods having different names, such as GetSalariedGross and GetHourlyGross. However, by overloading the GetGross method, you need to remember the name of only one method. The ABC Company application, which you will finish coding in this section, uses the Employee class to instantiate an object.

To open the ABC Company application, and then view the class file:

1. Open the **ABC Solution** (**ABC Solution.sln**) file, which is contained in the VB2008\Chap11\ABC Solution-Overloads folder. If necessary, open the designer window. See Figure 11-37.

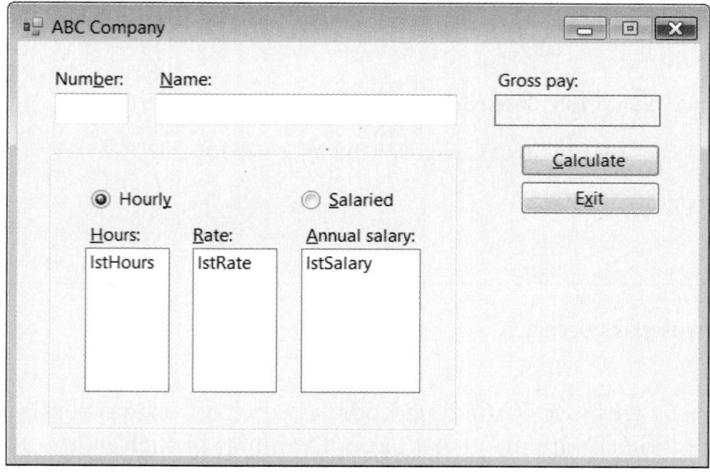

Figure 11-37 Interface for the ABC Company application

2. Right-click **Employee.vb** in the Solution Explorer window, then click **View Code**. The class definition from Figure 11-35 appears in the Employee.vb window. Replace the <your name> and <current date> text in the comments with your name and the current date. Save the solution, then close the Employee.vb window.

You will need to code only the Calculate button's Click event procedure. The procedure's pseudocode is shown in Figure 11-38.

btnCalc Click event procedure

```
1. declare variables to store an Employee object, the annual salary, hours worked, hourly
   pay rate, and gross pay
2. instantiate an Employee object to represent an employee; initialize the object's vari-
   ables using the number and name entered in the text boxes
3. if the Hourly radio button is selected
        assign the hours worked and hourly pay rate to the appropriate variables
        use the Employee object's GetGross method to calculate the gross pay for an
        hourly employee
   else
        assign the annual salary to the appropriate variable
        use the Employee object's GetGross method to calculate the gross pay for a sala-
        ried employee
   end if
4. display the gross pay
5. send the focus to the txtNum control
```

Figure 11-38 Pseudocode for the Calculate button's Click event procedure

To finish coding the ABC Company application, and then test the code:

1. Open the form's Code Editor window. Replace the <your name> and <current date> text in the comments with your name and the current date.

2. Locate the btnCalc control's Click event procedure. First, declare the necessary variables. Click the **blank line** above the `' create an Employee object and assign the` comment, then enter the following Dim statements.

   Dim abcEmployee As Employee
   Dim dblAnnualSalary As Double
   Dim dblHours As Double
   Dim dblHourRate As Double
   Dim dblGross As Double

3. Now instantiate an Employee object, using the text box values to initialize the object's variables. Click the **blank line** below the `' employee number and name to the object` comment, then enter the following assignment statement. Be sure to include a space before the line continuation character.

   abcEmployee = _
   New Employee(txtNum.Text, txtName.Text)

4. Step 3 in the pseudocode is to determine the selected radio button and then take the appropriate action. Click the **blank line** below the

`' determine the selected radio button` comment, then enter the following If clause.

If radHourly.Checked Then

5. If the Hourly radio button is selected, the selection structure's true path should use the Employee object's GetGross method to calculate the gross pay for an hourly employee. Enter the following comment and lines of code.

   ' calculate the gross pay for an hourly employee
   Double.TryParse(lstHours.SelectedItem.ToString, dblHours)
   Double.TryParse(lstRate.SelectedItem.ToString, dblHourRate)
   dblGross = abcEmployee.GetGross(dblHours, dblHourRate)

6. If the Salaried radio button is selected, the selection structure's false path should use the Employee object's GetGross method to calculate the gross pay for a salaried employee. Type **Else** and press **Enter**, then enter the additional comment and lines of code indicated in Figure 11-39.

enter this comment and these lines of code

```
        dblGross = abcEmployee.GetGross(dblHours, dblHourRate)
    Else
        ' calculate the gross pay for a salaried employee
        Double.TryParse(lstSalary.SelectedItem.ToString, _
                        dblAnnualSalary)
        dblGross = abcEmployee.GetGross(dblAnnualSalary)
    End If

    ' display the gross pay, then set the focus
```

Figure 11-39 Code entered in the selection structure's false path

7. The last two steps in the pseudocode are to display the gross pay and send the focus to the txtNum control. Click the **blank line** below the `' display the gross pay, then set the focus` comment, then enter the following two statements.

   lblGross.Text = dblGross.ToString("C2")
   txtNum.Focus()

8. Save the solution, then start the application. Type **120** in the Number box. Press **Tab**, then type **Peggy Milas** in the Name box. Click **8.00** in the Rate list box, then click the **Calculate** button. See Figure 11-40.

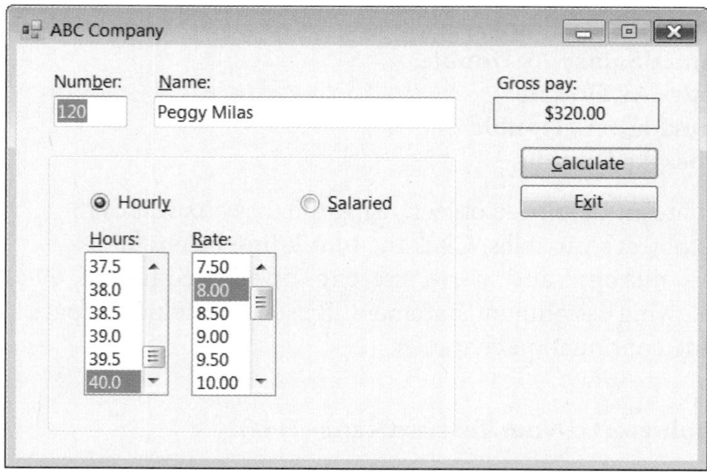

Figure 11-40 Gross pay amount shown in the interface

9. Type **9336** in the Number box. Press **Tab**, then type **Jackie Smith** in the Name box. Click the **Salaried** radio button. Scroll the Annual salary list box, then click **27000** in the list. Click the **Calculate** button. The button's Click event procedure displays the gross pay amount ($1,125.00) in the Gross pay box.

10. On your own, test the application using different hours, rates, and salaries. When you are finished, click the **Exit** button to end the application. Close the Code Editor window, then close the solution. Figure 11-41 shows the code entered in the btnCalc control's Click event procedure.

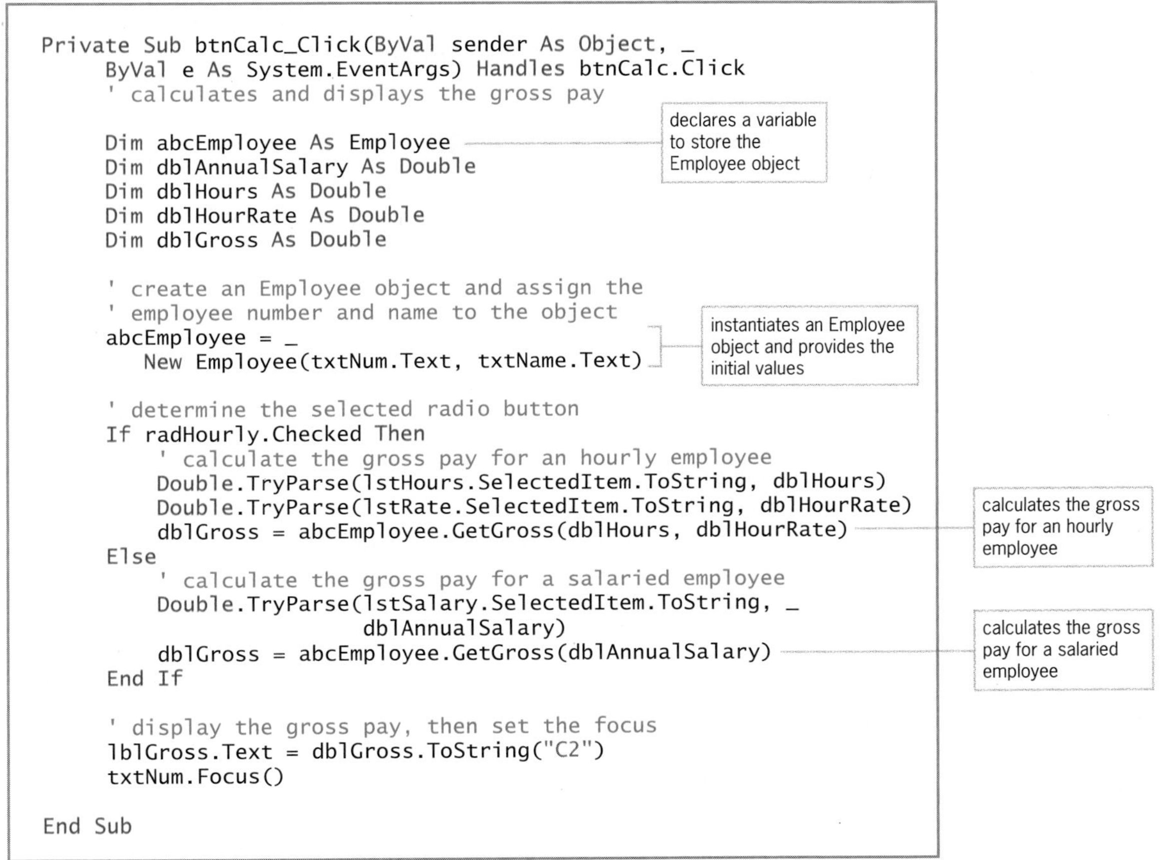

```
Private Sub btnCalc_Click(ByVal sender As Object, _
     ByVal e As System.EventArgs) Handles btnCalc.Click
     ' calculates and displays the gross pay

     Dim abcEmployee As Employee
     Dim dblAnnualSalary As Double
     Dim dblHours As Double
     Dim dblHourRate As Double
     Dim dblGross As Double

     ' create an Employee object and assign the
     ' employee number and name to the object
     abcEmployee = _
        New Employee(txtNum.Text, txtName.Text)

     ' determine the selected radio button
     If radHourly.Checked Then
         ' calculate the gross pay for an hourly employee
         Double.TryParse(lstHours.SelectedItem.ToString, dblHours)
         Double.TryParse(lstRate.SelectedItem.ToString, dblHourRate)
         dblGross = abcEmployee.GetGross(dblHours, dblHourRate)
     Else
         ' calculate the gross pay for a salaried employee
         Double.TryParse(lstSalary.SelectedItem.ToString, _
                         dblAnnualSalary)
         dblGross = abcEmployee.GetGross(dblAnnualSalary)
     End If

     ' display the gross pay, then set the focus
     lblGross.Text = dblGross.ToString("C2")
     txtNum.Focus()

End Sub
```


Figure 11-41 Code entered in the btnCalc control's Click event procedure

Lesson B Summary

- **To create a property whose value can be retrieved, but not set, by an application:**

  Include the `ReadOnly` keyword in the Property procedure's header.

- **To include a parameterized method in a class:**

  Enter the parameters between the parentheses that follow the method's name.

- **To create two or more methods that perform the same task but require different parameters:**

  Overload the methods by giving them the same name but different *parameterLists*. If the methods are not constructors, include the `Overloads` keyword in their procedure header.

Lesson B Key Terms

Overloaded methods—two or more class methods that have the same name but different *parameterLists*

Parameterized constructors—constructors that contain parameters

Signature—a method name combined with its optional *parameterList*

Lesson B Review Questions

1. When two methods have the same name but different *parameterLists*, the methods are referred to as ______________________ methods.

   a. loaded

   b. overloaded

   c. parallel

   d. None of the above.

2. The method name combined with the method's optional *parameterList* is called the method's ______________________.

   a. autograph

   b. inscription

   c. signature

   d. None of the above.

3. A class contains a Private variable named `_strLocation`. The variable is associated with a Public property named Location. Which of the following is the correct way for the default constructor to assign the value "Unknown" to the variable?

   a. `_strLocation = "Unknown"`

   b. `_strLocation.Location = "Unknown"`

   c. `Location._strLocation = "Unknown"`

   d. None of the above.

4. A class contains a Private variable named `_strCapital`. The variable is associated with a Public property named Capital. Which of the following is the best way for a parameterized constructor to assign the value stored in its `strCapName` parameter to the variable?

   a. `_strCapital = strCapName`

   b. `Capital = strCapName`

   c. `_strCapital.Capital = strCapName`

   d. None of the above.

5. A class can contain only one constructor.

   a. True
   b. False

6. An overloaded method that is not a constructor must contain the keyword ____________________ in its procedure header.

   a. Loaded

   b. Overload

   c. Overloaded

   d. None of the above.

7. An application instantiates a MyDate object and assigns it to the `payDate` variable. The MyDate class contains a Public Month property that is associated with a Private variable named `_strMonth`. Which of the following can the application use to assign the number 12 to the Month property?

   a. `payDate.Month = "12"`

   b. `payDate.Month._strMonth = "12"`

   c. `payDate._strMonth = "12"`

   d. `MyDate.Month = "12"`

8. The Salesperson class contains a ReadOnly property named Bonus. The property is associated with a Private variable named `_dblBonus`. A button's Click event procedure instantiates a Salesperson object and assigns it to the `ourSalesperson` variable. Which of the following statements is valid in the Click event procedure?

   a. `lblBonus.Text = ourSalesperson.Bonus.ToString("C2")`

   b. `ourSalesperson.Bonus = dblSales * .1`

   c. `ourSalesperson._dblBonus = 500`

   d. None of the above.

9. If a class contains more than one constructor, how does the computer determine the appropriate one to use?

10. What are overloaded methods and why are they used?

Lesson B Exercises

INTRODUCTORY

1. An application contains the Computer class definition shown in Figure 11-22 in Lesson A. Write a parameterized constructor for the class. Then write a Dim statement that creates a Computer object and initializes it using the parameterized constructor. Assign the object to a variable named `companyUse`. Use the following values to initialize the object: "IBM" and 1236.99.

INTRODUCTORY

2. Write the Property procedure for a ReadOnly property named BonusRate. The property is associated with the `_decBonusRate` variable.

INTRODUCTORY

3. Write the class definition for a class named Worker. The class should include Private variables and Property procedures for a Worker object's name and salary. The salary may contain a decimal place. The class also should contain two constructors: the default constructor and a parameterized constructor.

INTRODUCTORY

4. Add a method named GetNewSalary to the Worker class from Exercise 3. The method should calculate a Worker object's new salary, which is based on a raise percentage provided by the application using the object. Before calculating the new salary, the method should verify that the raise percentage is greater than or equal to zero. If the raise percentage is less than zero, the method should assign the number 0 as the new salary.

INTERMEDIATE

5. In this exercise, you modify the Pizza Roma application and Rectangle class from Lesson A. Use Windows to make a copy of the Pizza Roma Solution folder, which is contained in the VB2008\Chap11 folder. Rename the folder Modified Pizza Roma Solution. Open the Pizza Roma Solution (Pizza Roma Solution.sln) file contained in the VB2008\Chap11\Modified Pizza Roma Solution folder. Open the designer window, then open the Rectangle.vb file. Include a parameterized constructor in the class. Save the solution, then close the Rectangle.vb window. Open the form's Code Editor window. Modify the btnCalc control's Click event procedure to use the parameterized constructor. Save the solution, then start and test the application. Stop the application. Close the Code Editor window, then close the solution.

INTERMEDIATE

6. In this exercise, you use the Worker class completed in Exercise 4. Open the Salary Solution (Salary Solution.sln) file, which is contained in the VB2008\Chap11\Salary Solution folder. If necessary, open the designer window. Open the Worker.vb class file, then enter the class definition

completed in Exercise 4. Save the solution, then close the Worker.vb window. Open the form's Code Editor window, then use the comments in the btnCalc control's Click event procedure to enter the missing instructions. Save the solution, then start the application. Test the application by entering your name, a current salary amount of 54000, and a raise percentage of 10 (for 10%). The new salary should be $59,400. Stop the application. Close the Code Editor window, then close the solution.

INTERMEDIATE

7. In this exercise, you modify the Grade Calculator application coded in the lesson. Use Windows to make a copy of the Grade Solution folder, which is contained in the VB2008\Grade Solution folder. Rename the folder Modified Grade Solution. Open the Grade Solution (Grade Solution.sln) file contained in the VB2008\Chap11\Modified Grade Solution folder. Open the designer window.

   a. Open the CourseGrade.vb file. Modify the DetermineGrade method so that it accepts the maximum number of points that can be earned on both tests. (Currently, the maximum number of points is 200: 100 points per test.) For an A grade, the student must earn at least 90% of the total number of points. For a B, the student must earn at least 80%. For a C, the student must earn at least 70%. For a D, the student must earn at least 60%. If the student earns less than 60% of the total points, the grade is F. Make the appropriate modifications to the code, then save the solution and close the CourseGrade.vb window.

   b. Add a label control and text box to the form. Change the label control's Text property to "Maximum points".

   c. Open the form's Code Editor window and make the necessary modifications to the code. Each list box should display numbers from 0 through 200. The maximum number allowed in the text box should be 400. Save the solution, then start and test the application. Stop the application. Close the Code Editor window, then close the solution.

ADVANCED

8. Each member of Glasgow Health Club must pay monthly dues that consist of a basic fee and one or more optional charges. The basic monthly fee for a single membership is $50; for a family membership, it is $90. If the member has a single membership, the additional monthly charges are $30 for tennis, $25 for golf, and $20 for racquetball. If the member has a family membership, the additional monthly charges are $50 for tennis, $35 for golf, and $30 for racquetball. The application should display the member's basic fee, additional charges, and monthly dues. Create a Visual Basic Windows application. Name the solution, project, and form file

Glasgow Health Solution, Glasgow Health Project, and Main Form.vb, respectively. Save the application in the VB2008\Chap11 folder. Be sure to use a class in the application. You can either create your own interface or create the one shown in Figure 11-42.

Figure 11-42 Sample interface for Glasgow Health Club

ADVANCED

9. Jeremiah Carter, the manager of the Accounts Payable department at Franklin Calendars, wants an application that keeps track of the checks written by his department. More specifically, he wants to record (in a sequential access file) the check number, date, payee, and amount of each check. Create a Visual Basic Windows application. Name the solution, project, and form file Franklin Calendars Solution, Franklin Calendars Project, and Main Form.vb, respectively. Save the application in the VB2008\Chap11 folder. Be sure to use a class in the application. You can either create your own interface or create the one shown in Figure 11-43.

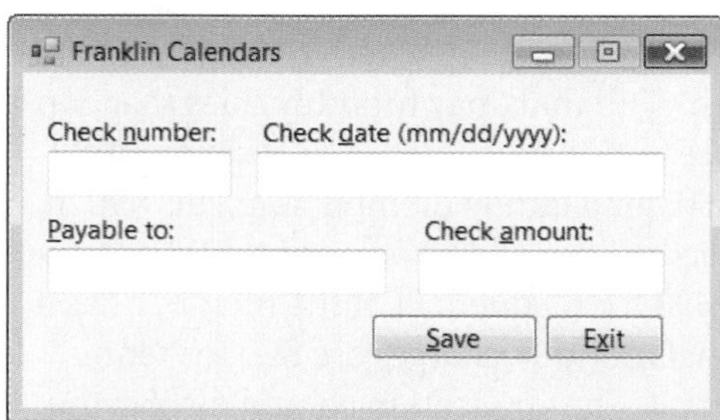

Figure 11-43 Sample interface for Franklin Calendars

LESSON C

After studying Lesson C, you should be able to:

- Create a derived class using inheritance
- Override a method in the base class
- Refer to the base class using the `MyBase` keyword

Example 7—Using a Base Class and a Derived Class

You can create one class from another class. In OOP, this is referred to as **inheritance**. The new class is called the **derived class** and it inherits the attributes and behaviors of the original class, called the **base class**. You indicate that a class is a derived class by including the Inherits clause in the derived class's Class statement. The syntax of the Inherits clause is **Inherits** *base*, where *base* is the name of the base class whose attributes and behaviors the derived class will inherit. You enter the Inherits clause immediately below the Public Class clause in the derived class. Figure 11-44 shows the code for a base class named Employee and a derived class named Salaried. Both class definitions are contained in the Employee.vb class file. (In Exercise 1 at the end of this lesson, you will add a derived class named Hourly to the file.) The Employee class definition in Figure 11-44 is almost identical to the Employee class definition shown in Figure 11-35 in Lesson B; only the GetGross method in both class definitions differs. In Figure 11-35, the GetGross method is an overloaded method that can calculate the gross pay for either a salaried employee or an hourly employee. The GetGross method in Figure 11-44, on the other hand, does not perform any calculations; it doesn't even contain any code. In addition, its procedure header contains the **Overridable** keyword. The keyword indicates that the method can be overridden by any class that is derived from the Employee class. In other words, classes derived from the Employee class will provide their own GetGross method.

```
' Name:       Employee (base class)
' Purpose:    Defines an Employee object
' Programmer: <your name> on <current date>

Option Explicit On
Option Strict On
Option Infer Off

Public Class Employee
  Private _strNumber As String
  Private _strEmpName As String

  Public Property Number() As String
    Get
      Return _strNumber
    End Get
    Set(ByVal value As String)
      _strNumber = value
    End Set
  End Property
```

the base Employee class starts here

Figure 11-44 Code for the Employee base class and Salaried derived class *(continues)*

(continued)

```
    Public Property EmpName() As String
      Get
        Return _strEmpName
      End Get
      Set(ByVal value As String)
        _strEmpName = value
      End Set
    End Property

    Public Sub New()
        _strNumber = String.Empty
        _strEmpName = String.Empty
    End Sub

    Public Sub New(ByVal strNum As String, ByVal strName As String)
        Number = strNum
        EmpName = strName
    End Sub

    Public Overridable Function GetGross() As Double
        ' will be overridden in the derived class
    End Function
End Class

' Name:       Salaried (derived class)
' Purpose:    Derived from the Employee class
' Programmer: <your name> on <current date>

Public Class Salaried
    Inherits Employee

    Private _dblSalary As Double

    Public Property Salary() As Double
      Get
        Return _dblSalary
      End Get
      Set(ByVal value As Double)
        _dblSalary = value
      End Set
    End Property

    Public Sub New()
      MyBase.New()
      _dblSalary = 0
    End Sub

    Public Sub New(ByVal strNum As String, _
             ByVal strName As String, _
             ByVal dblAnnualSalary As Double)
      MyBase.New(strNum, strName)
      Salary = dblAnnualSalary
    End Sub

    Public Overrides Function GetGross() As Double
      Return _dblSalary / 24
    End Function
End Class
```

indicates that the method can be overridden in the derived class

the derived Salaried class starts here

the derived class inherits the base class's attributes and behaviors

calls the base class's default constructor

calls the base class's parameterized constructor

indicates that the method overrides the one in the base class

Figure 11-44 Code for the Employee base class and Salaried derived class

Study the Salaried class's code. The `Inherits Employee` clause that appears below the `Public Class Salaried` line indicates that the Salaried class is derived from the Employee class. This means that the Salaried class includes all of the attributes and behaviors of the Employee class. The Salaried class also contains an attribute of its own: salary. The salary attribute is represented by the Private `_dblSalary` variable and the Public Salary property. The salary attribute belongs to the Salaried class only. Both constructors in the Salaried class contain the statement `MyBase.New ([`*parameterList*`])`. The statement tells the computer to process the code contained in the appropriate constructor in the base class. You refer to the base class using the **MyBase** keyword. The `MyBase.New()` statement in the default constructor tells the computer to process the code contained in the base class's default constructor. The `MyBase.New(strNum, strName)` statement in the parameterized constructor indicates that the code in the base class's parameterized constructor should be processed. The GetGross method in the Salaried class calculates the gross pay for a salaried employee. The method's header contains the **Overrides** keyword, which indicates that the method overrides (replaces) the GetGross method contained in the base Employee class.

To open the XYZ Corporation application, and then complete the Employee class definition:

1. If necessary, start Visual Studio 2008 or Visual Basic 2008 Express Edition. Close the Start Page window.
2. Open the **XYZ Corporation Solution** (**XYZ Corporation Solution.sln**) file, which is contained in the VB2008\Chap11\XYZ Corporation Solution-Inheritance folder. Open the designer window. See Figure 11-45.

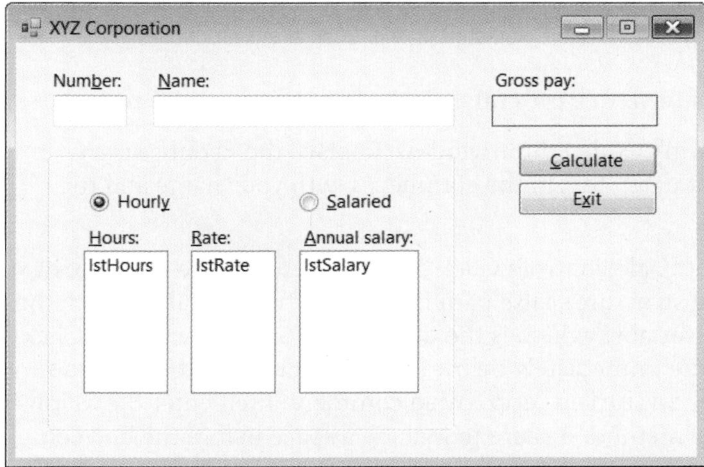

Figure 11-45 Interface for the XYZ Corporation application

3. Right-click **Employee.vb** in the Solution Explorer window, then click **View Code**. Replace the <your name> and <current date> text in the comments with your name and the current date.

4. Use the code shown earlier in Figure 11-44 to complete the class definitions. You will need to enter the GetGross function in the Employee class. You also will need to enter the entire Salaried class definition.

5. Save the solution, then close the Employee.vb window.

Now you can code the Calculate button's Click event procedure. The procedure's pseudocode is shown in Figure 11-46. Most of the procedure's code has already been entered in the Code Editor window for you. You need to code only the selection structure's true and false paths. In the next set of steps, you will code the false path. You will code the true path in Exercise 1 at the end of this lesson.

---

btnCalc Click event procedure

1. declare variables
2. if the Hourly radio button is selected
   - assign the hours worked and hourly pay rate to the appropriate variables
   - instantiate an Hourly object to represent an hourly employee; initialize the object's variables using the number and name entered in the text boxes, as well as the hours worked and hourly pay rate stored in the variables
   - use the Hourly object's GetGross method to calculate the gross pay

   else
   - assign the annual salary to the appropriate variable
   - instantiate a Salaried object to represent a salaried employee; initialize the object's variables using the number and name entered in the text boxes, as well as the annual salary stored in the variable
   - use the Salaried object's GetGross method to calculate the gross pay

   end if
3. display the gross pay
4. send the focus to the txtNum control

Figure 11-46 Pseudocode for the Calculate button's Click event procedure

To code the selection structure's false path, and then test the code:

1. Open the form's Code Editor window. Replace the <your name> and <current date> text in the comments with your name and the current date.

2. Locate the btnCalc control's Click event procedure. The first task in the selection structure's false path is to assign the annual salary to the appropriate variable, which is the `dblAnnualSalary` variable. Click the **blank line** immediately below the `' calculate the gross pay for a salaried employee` comment, then enter the following TryParse method. Be sure to include a space before the line continuation character.

   Double.TryParse(lstSalary.SelectedItem.ToString, _
   dblAnnualSalary)

3. Next, instantiate a Salaried object and initialize its Private variables. Assign the object to the `salariedEmployee` variable. Enter the following assignment statement. Be sure to include a space before the line continuation character.

   ```
   salariedEmployee = New Salaried(txtNum.Text, txtName.Text, _
                                   dblAnnualSalary)
   ```

4. Finally, use the Salaried object's GetGross method to calculate and return the gross pay. Assign the return value to the `dblGross` variable. Type the following assignment statement, but don't press Enter.

   ```
   dblGross = salariedEmployee.GetGross
   ```

5. Save the solution, then start the application. Click the **Salaried** radio button. Scroll the Annual salary list box, then click **24000** in the list. Click the **Calculate** button. The value $1,000 appears in the Gross pay box. (Recall that salaried employees are paid twice per month, which is 24 times per year.)

6. On your own, test the application using different annual salary amounts. When you are finished, click the **Exit** button. Close the Code Editor window, then close the solution.

Lesson C Summary

- **To allow a derived class to inherit the attributes and behaviors of a base class:**

  Enter the `Inherits` *base* clause, where *base* is the name of the base class, immediately below the Public Class clause in the derived class.

- **To indicate that a method in the base class can be overridden (replaced) in the derived class:**

  Use the `Overridable` keyword in the method's header.

- **To indicate that a method in the derived class overrides (replaces) a method in the base class:**

  Use the `Overrides` keyword in the method's header.

Lesson C Key Terms

Base class—the original class from which another class is derived

Derived class—a class that inherits the attributes and behaviors of a base class

Inheritance—the ability to create one class from another class

MyBase—a keyword used in a derived class to refer to the base class

Overridable—a keyword that appears in a method's header in a base class; indicates that the method can be overridden by any class that is derived from the base class

Overrides—a keyword that appears in a method's header in a derived class; indicates that the method overrides the method with the same name in the base class

Lesson C Review Questions

1. Which of the following clauses allows a derived class named Dog to have the same attributes and behaviors as its base class, which is named Animal?
   a. `Inherits Animal`
   b. `Inherits Dog`
   c. `Overloads Dog`
   d. `Overrides Animal`

2. A base class contains a method named GetBonus. Which of the following procedure headers can be used in the base class to indicate that a derived class can provide its own code for the method?
   a. `Public Inherits Sub GetBonus()`
   b. `Public Overloads Sub GetBonus()`
   c. `Public Overridable Sub GetBonus()`
   d. `Public Overrides Sub GetBonus()`

3. A base class contains a method named GetBonus. Which of the following procedure headers can be used in the derived class to indicate that it is providing its own code for the method?
   a. `Public Inherits Sub GetBonus()`
   b. `Public Overloads Sub GetBonus()`
   c. `Public Overridable Sub GetBonus()`
   d. `Public Overrides Sub GetBonus()`

Lesson C Exercises

INTERMEDIATE

1. In this exercise, you modify the XYZ Corporation application coded in the lesson. Use Windows to make a copy of the XYZ Corporation Solution-Inheritance folder, which is contained in the VB2008\Chap11 folder. Rename the folder Modified XYZ Corporation Solution-Inheritance. Open the XYZ Corporation Solution (XYZ Corporation Solution.sln) file contained in the VB2008\Chap11\Modified XYZ Corporation Solution-Inheritance folder.

   a. Open the Employee.vb file. Include another derived class definition in the file. Name the derived class Hourly. The Hourly class should contain a GetGross method that calculates the gross pay for an hourly employee. Calculate the gross pay by multiplying the hours worked by the pay rate. Save the solution, then close the Employee.vb window.

   b. Open the form's Code Editor window, then complete the selection structure's true path in the btnCalc control's Click event procedure. Use the pseudocode shown in Figure 11-46 as a guide. You also will need to declare variables to store the number of hours and hourly rate, as well as an Hourly object.

   c. Save the solution, then start and test the application. Stop the application. Close the Code Editor window, then close the solution.

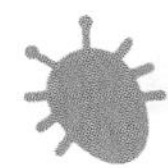

Swat The Bugs

2. Open the Debug Solution (Debug Solution.sln) file, which is contained in the VB2008\Chap11\Debug Solution-Lesson C folder. If necessary, open the designer window. Open the Code Editor windows for the form and class file. Review the existing code. Correct the code to remove the jagged lines in the Shape and Circle class definitions. Save the solution, then start and test the application. Notice that the application is not working correctly. Stop the application. Locate and correct any errors in the code. Save the solution, then start and test the application again. Stop the application. Close the Code Editor windows, then close the solution.

CHAPTER 12

Web Applications

Creating the DJ Tom Application

In this chapter, you will create a Web application for DJ (disc jockey) Tom. Although DJ Tom can be hired for any event, his specialty is weddings. Therefore, he has requested a Web page that allows the user to enter the names of the bride and groom, as well as the wedding date, an e-mail address, and the name of the first song to be danced by the newly married couple. The Web page will provide a Submit button that, when clicked, displays a message on the page. The message will contain the information entered by the user.

Previewing the DJ Tom Application

To preview the completed DJ Tom application:

1. If necessary, start Visual Studio 2008 or Visual Web Developer 2008 Express Edition. Close the Start Page window.
2. Click **File** on the menu bar, then click **Open Web Site**. The Open Web Site dialog box appears. If necessary, click the **File System** button. Click the **DJTom-Preview** folder, which is contained in the VB2008\Chap12 folder, then click the **Open** button. If the Default.aspx Web page does not appear in the Document window, right-click **Default.aspx** in the Solution Explorer window, then click **View Designer**.
3. Press **F5** to start the application. If the Debugging Not Enabled dialog box appears, select the **Modify the Web.config file to enable debugging.** radio button (if necessary) and then click the **OK** button. If the Script Debugging Disabled dialog box appears, click the **Yes** button. The Web page appears in a browser window.
4. Click the **box that appears to the right of the Bride: text**, then type **Melinda**. Press **Tab**, then type **Pierre** as the groom's name.
5. Click **any date** in the calendar. Type **anyEmail@domain.com** in the E-mail box. Click the **down arrow** in the First song box, then click **The Way You Look Tonight**.
6. Click the **Submit** button. A message appears in a purple box on the Web page. See Figure 12-1. (The top of your browser window may look slightly different from the one shown in Figure 12-1.)

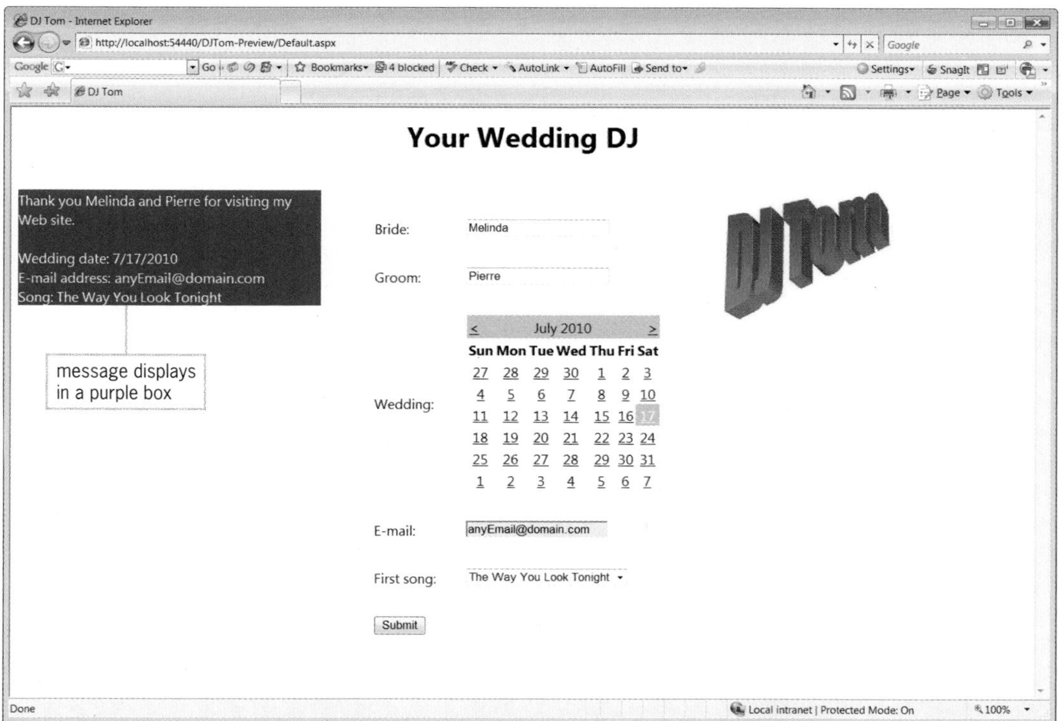

Figure 12-1 Result of clicking the Submit button

7. Close the browser window, then close the solution. If you are asked whether you want to save the changes to the DJTom-Preview.sln file, click the **No** button.

In Lesson A, you will learn how to create static Web pages. Lessons B and C cover dynamic Web pages. You will code the DJ Tom application in Lesson C.

LESSON A

After studying Lesson A, you should be able to:

- Create a Web application
- View a Web page in a browser window
- Add static text to a Web page
- View a Web page in full screen view
- Close and open a Web application
- Add an image to a Web page
- Move a control on a Web page

Web Applications

The Internet is the world's largest computer network, connecting millions of computers located all around the world. One of the most popular features of the Internet is the World Wide Web, often referred to simply as the Web. The Web consists of documents called **Web pages** that are stored on Web servers. A **Web server** is a computer that contains special software that "serves up" Web pages in response to requests from client computers. A **client computer** is a computer that requests information from a Web server. The information is requested and subsequently viewed through the use of a program called a Web browser or, more simply, a **browser**. Currently, the two most popular browsers are Microsoft Internet Explorer and Mozilla Firefox.

Many Web pages are static. A **static Web page** is a document whose purpose is merely to display information to the viewer. Figure 12-2 shows an example of a static Web page created for the Greenview Toy Store. Displayed on the Web page are the store's name, address, telephone number, and business hours.

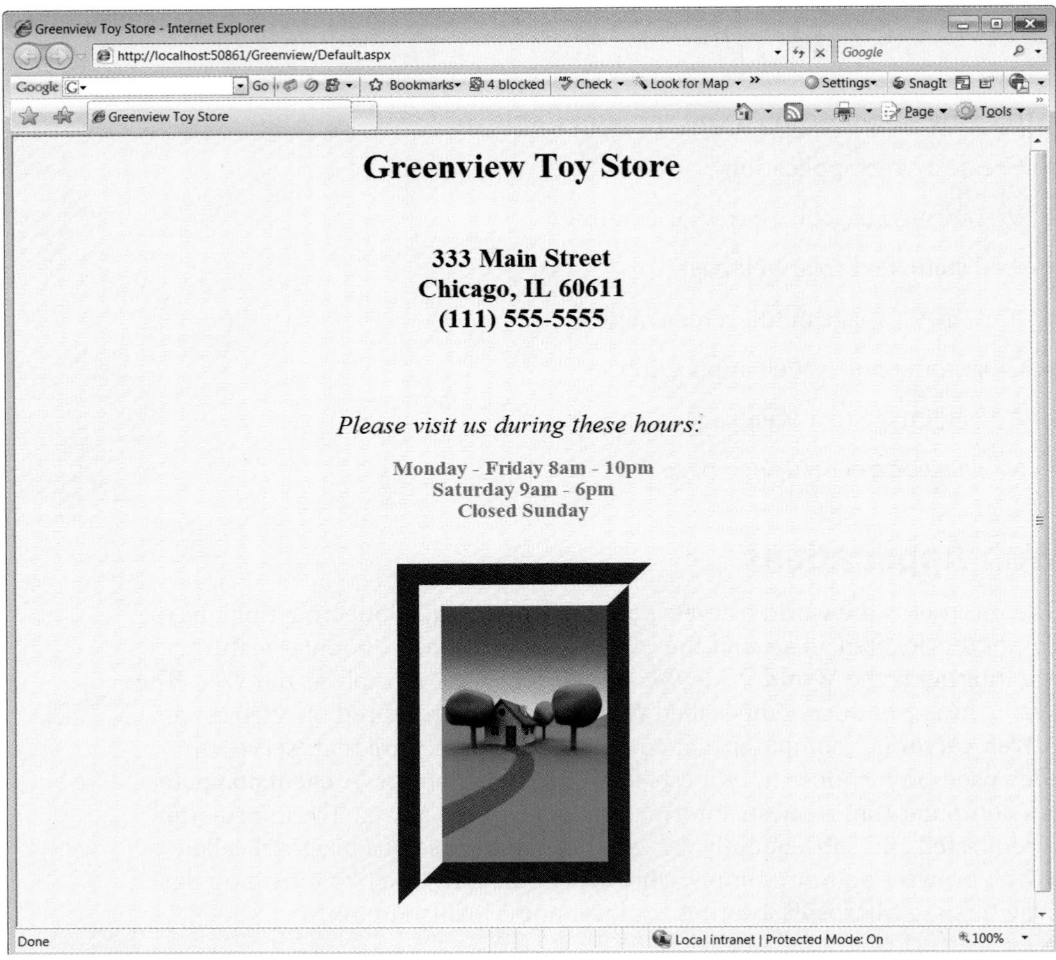

Figure 12-2 Example of a static Web page

One drawback of static Web pages is that they are not interactive. The only interaction that can occur between static Web pages and the user is through links that allow the user to "jump" from one Web page to another. Although static Web pages provide a means for a store to list its location and hours, a company wanting to do business on the Web must be able to do more than just list information: It must be able to interact with customers through its Web site. The Web site should allow customers to submit inquiries, select items for purchase, provide shipping information, and submit payment information. It also should allow the company to track customer inquiries and process customer orders. Tasks such as these can be accomplished using dynamic Web pages. Unlike a static Web page, a **dynamic Web page** is interactive; it can accept information from the user and also retrieve information for the user. Examples of dynamic Web pages that you might have already used include forms for purchasing merchandise online and for submitting online resumes. Figure 12-3 shows an example of a dynamic Web page that converts American dollars to British pounds. To use the Web page, you enter the number of American dollars in the American dollars box and then click the Submit button. The button's Click event procedure displays the corresponding number of British pounds on the Web page.

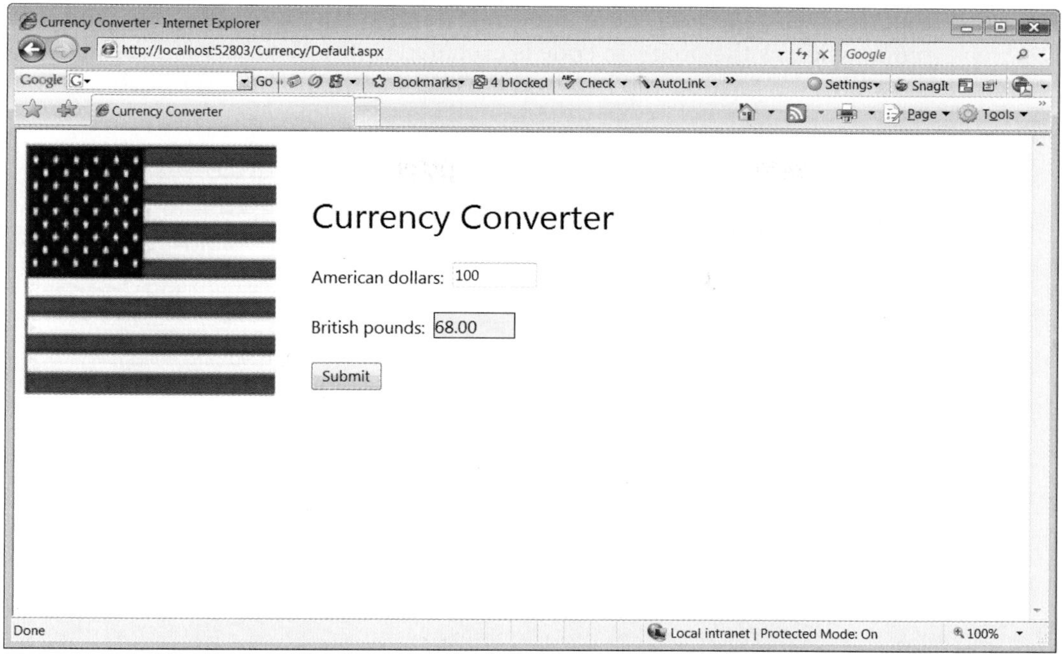

Figure 12-3 Example of a dynamic Web page

The Web applications you will create in this chapter use a technology called ASP.NET 3.5. **ASP** stands for "active server page" and refers to the type of Web page created by the ASP technology. All ASP pages contain HTML (Hypertext Markup Language) tags that tell the client's browser how to render the page on the computer screen. For example, the instruction `<h1>Hello</h1>` uses the opening <h1> tag and its closing </h1> tag to display the word "Hello" as a heading on the Web page. Many ASP pages also contain ASP tags that specify the controls to include on the Web page. In addition to the HTML and ASP tags, dynamic ASP pages contain code that tells the objects on the Web page how to respond to the user's actions. In this chapter, you will write the appropriate code using the Visual Basic programming language.

When a client computer's browser sends a request for an ASP page, the Web server locates the page and then sends the appropriate HTML instructions to the client. The client's browser uses the instructions to render the Web page on the computer screen. If the Web page is a dynamic one, like the Currency Converter page shown in Figure 12-3, the user can interact with the page by entering data. In most cases, the user then clicks a button on the Web page to submit the data to the server for processing. When the server receives the data, it executes the Visual Basic code associated with the Web page. It then sends back the appropriate HTML, which now includes the result of processing the code and data, to the client for rendering in the browser window. Using the Currency Converter Web page as an example, the user first enters the number of American dollars and then clicks the Submit button, which submits the user's entry to the Web server. The server executes the Visual Basic code to convert the American dollars to British pounds, and then sends back the HTML, which now includes the number of British pounds. Notice that the Web page's HTML is interpreted and executed by the client computer, whereas the program code is executed by the Web server. Figure 12-4 illustrates the relationship between the client computer and the Web server.

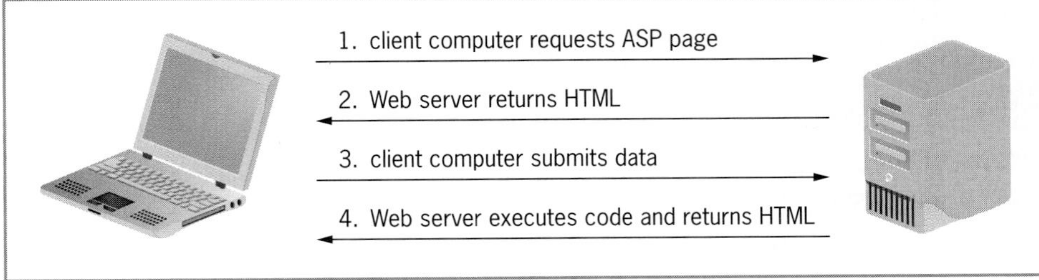

Figure 12-4 Illustration of the relationship between a client computer and a Web server

In this lesson, you will create a Web application that contains a static Web page. Web applications containing dynamic Web pages are covered in Lessons B and C.

Creating a Web Application

You create a Web application using Visual Web Developer 2008, which is available as a stand-alone product (called Visual Web Developer 2008 Express Edition) or as part of Visual Studio 2008. (You can download a copy of Visual Web Developer 2008 Express Edition from Microsoft's Web site. At the time of this writing, the address is *http://msdn.microsoft.com/express/vwd*.)

To create a Web application:

1. If necessary, start Visual Studio 2008 or Visual Web Developer 2008 Express Edition. Close the Start Page window. If necessary, permanently display the Solution Explorer window and auto-hide the Toolbox window.
2. Click **File** on the menu bar, then click **New Web Site**. The New Web Site dialog box opens with ASP.NET Web Site selected in the Visual Studio installed templates section.
3. If necessary, select **File System** in the Location box. The File System selection allows you to store your Web application in any folder on either your computer or a network drive.
4. In this chapter, you will be instructed to store your Web applications in the F:\VB2008\Chap12 folder; however, you can use any location. In the box that appears next to the Location box, replace the existing text with **F:\VB2008\Chap12\Greenview**.

5. If necessary, select **Visual Basic** in the Language box. Figure 12-5 shows the completed New Web Site dialog box. (Your New Web Site dialog box will look slightly different if you are using Visual Web Developer 2008 Express Edition.)

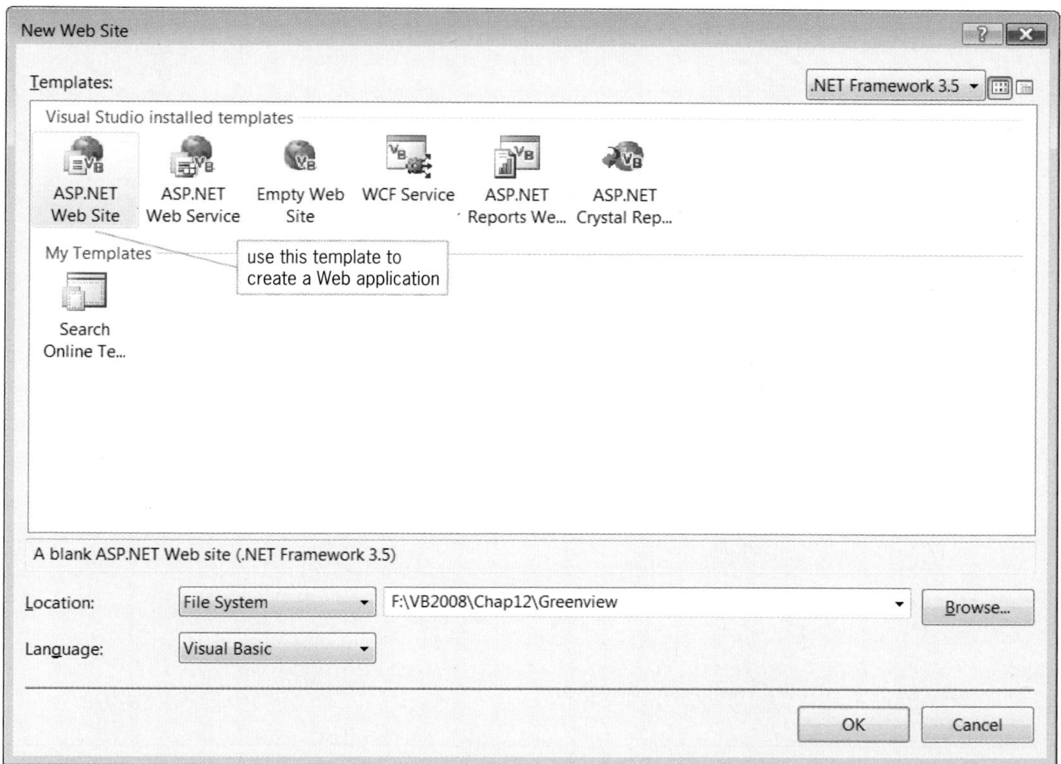

Figure 12-5 Completed New Web Site dialog box

6. Click the **OK** button to close the dialog box. Visual Web Developer creates the Greenview application and displays a Web page named Default.aspx in the Document window. If necessary, auto-hide the Properties window. Click the **Design** tab that appears at the bottom of the IDE. When the Design tab is selected, the Web page appears in Design view in the Document window. You can use Design view to add text and controls to the Web page. See Figure 12-6. (If you are using Visual Web Developer 2008 Express Edition, your screen will look slightly different from the one shown in Figure 12-6.)

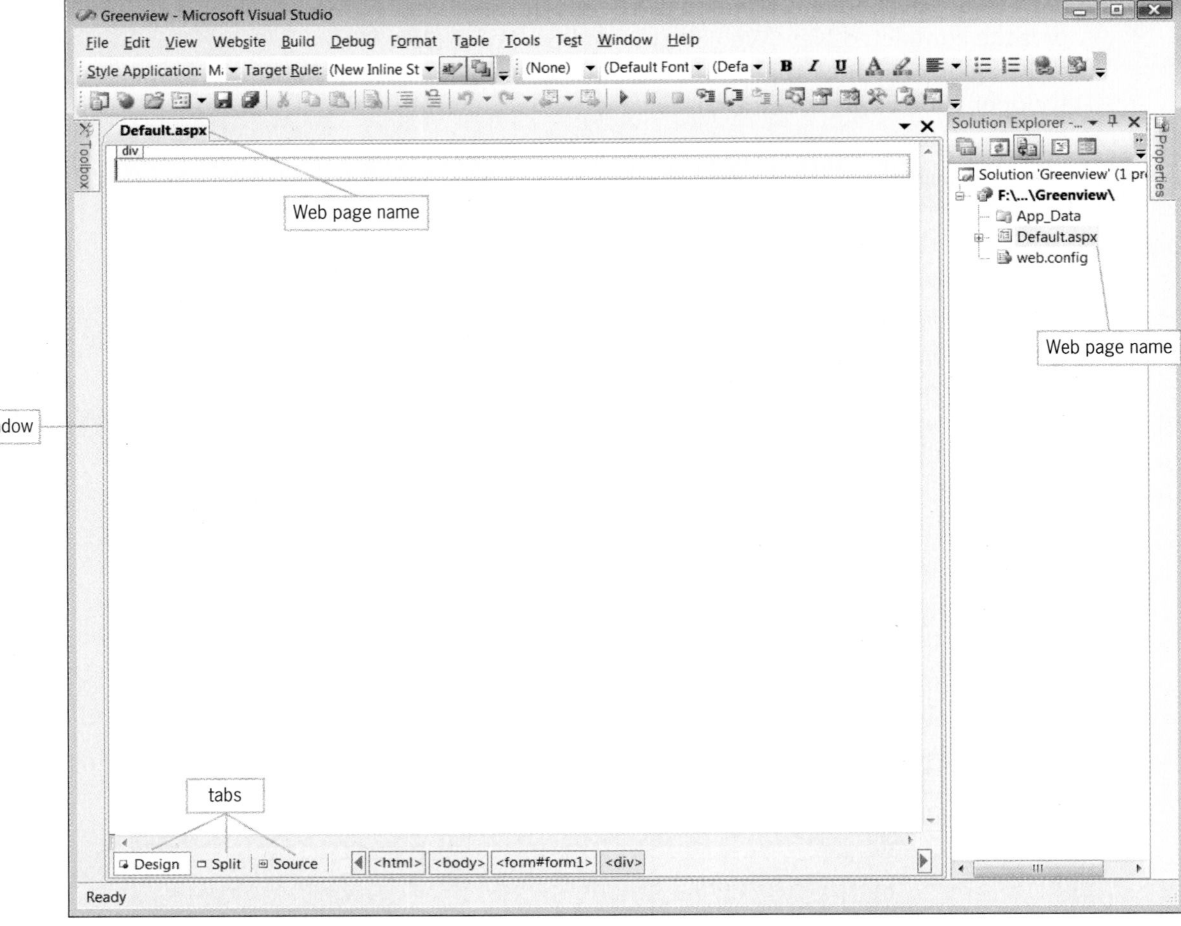

Figure 12-6 Default.aspx Web page

7. Click the **Source** tab to display the Web page in Source view. This view shows the HTML and ASP tags that tell a browser how to render the Web page. The tags are automatically generated for you as you are creating the Web page in Design view. Currently, the Web page contains only HTML tags.

8. Click the **Split** tab to split the Document window into two parts. The upper half displays the Web page in Source view, and the lower half displays it in Design view.

9. Click the **Design** tab to return to Design view, then auto-hide the Solution Explorer window and permanently display the Properties window.

10. If necessary, maximize the Visual Studio (or Visual Web Developer Express Edition) window.

11. Click **View** on the menu bar, then point to **Visual Aids**. Verify that the options shown in Figure 12-7 are selected on the Visual Aids submenu.

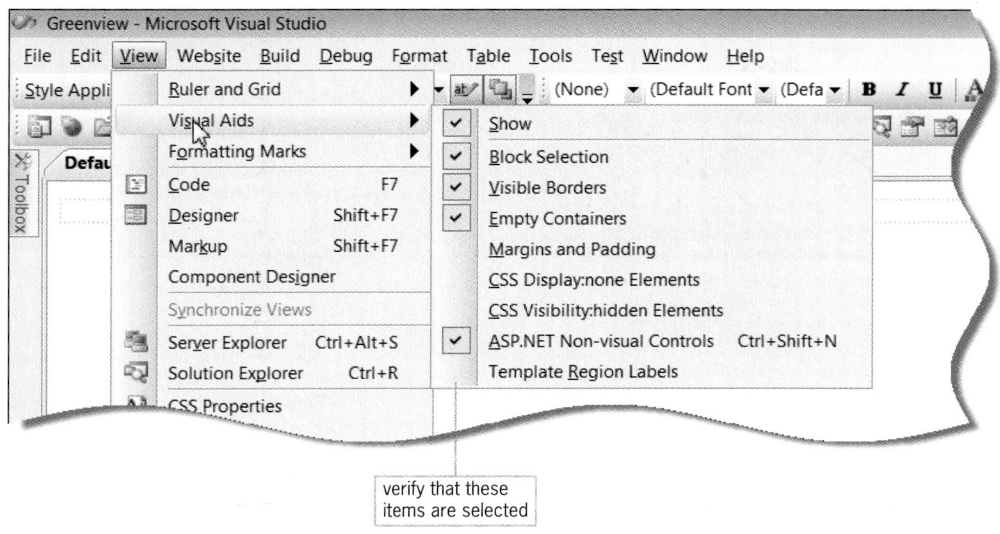

Figure 12-7 Visual Aids submenu

12. If necessary, click **View** again to open the View menu. This time, point to Toolbars. If the Formatting option is not selected, click **Formatting** to select it. If necessary, close the View menu.

Adding a Title to the Web Page

When a Web page is displayed in a browser, the value stored in its Title property appears in the browser's title bar. It also appears on the page's tab in the browser window. In the following set of steps, you will change the Web page's Title property to Greenview Toy Store. You then will start the application to display the page in a browser. When you start a Web application in Visual Studio 2008 (or in Visual Web Developer 2008 Express Edition), Visual Studio creates a temporary Web server on your computer. The temporary Web server allows you to view your Web page in a browser. Keep in mind, however, that your Web page will need to be placed on an actual Web server for others to view it.

To change the Title property and then display the page in a browser:

1. Click the **down arrow** button in the Properties window's Object box, then click **DOCUMENT** in the list. Click **Title**, then type **Greenview Toy Store** and press **Enter**.

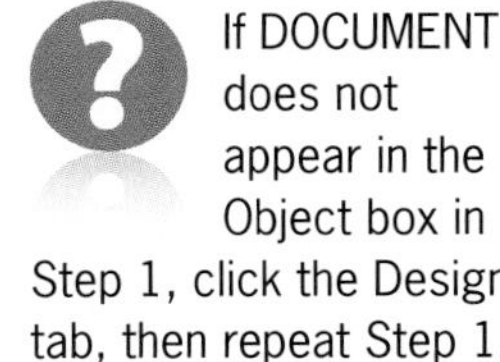

If DOCUMENT does not appear in the Object box in Step 1, click the Design tab, then repeat Step 1.

2. Save the solution either by clicking the **Save All** button or by clicking the **Save All** option on the File menu.

3. Start the Web application by pressing the **F5** key. (You also can click the Start Debugging option on the Debug menu.) If the Debugging Not Enabled dialog box appears, select the **Modify the Web.config file to enable debugging.** radio button (if necessary) and then click the **OK** button. If the Script Debugging Disabled dialog box appears, click the **Yes** button. The Web page appears in a browser window. Notice that the page's title appears in the browser's title bar and on the page's tab in the browser window. See Figure 12-8.

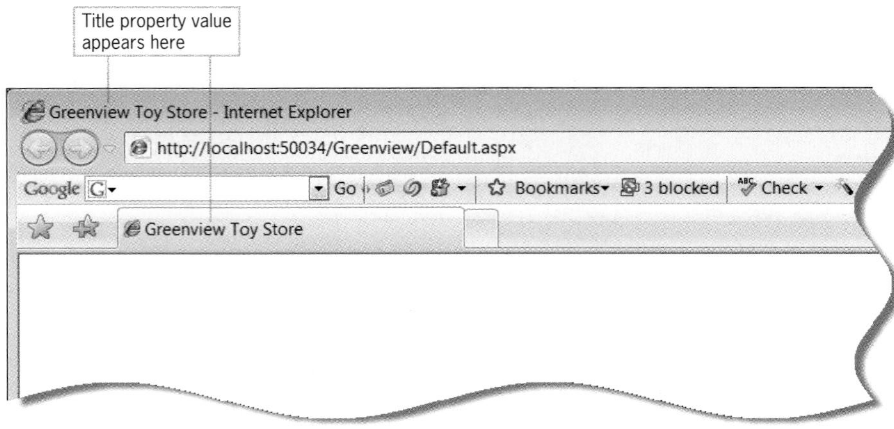

Figure 12-8 Browser window showing the Title property

4. Close the browser window by clicking the **Close** button on its title bar.

Changing the Background Color of a Web Page

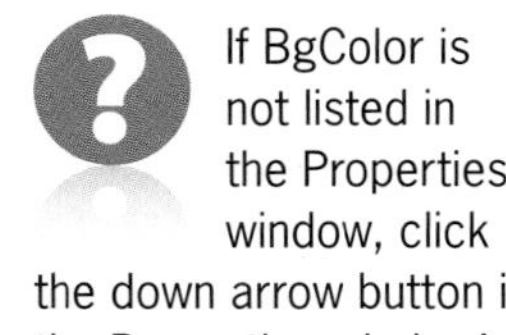

If BgColor is not listed in the Properties window, click the down arrow button in the Properties window's Object box, then click DOCUMENT in the list.

The background color of a Web page is controlled by the DOCUMENT object's BgColor property. BgColor stands for "background color."

To change the BgColor property:

1. Click **BgColor** in the Properties window, then click the **...** (ellipsis) button in the Settings box. The More Colors dialog box opens. Click the **hexagon** indicated in Figure 12-9.

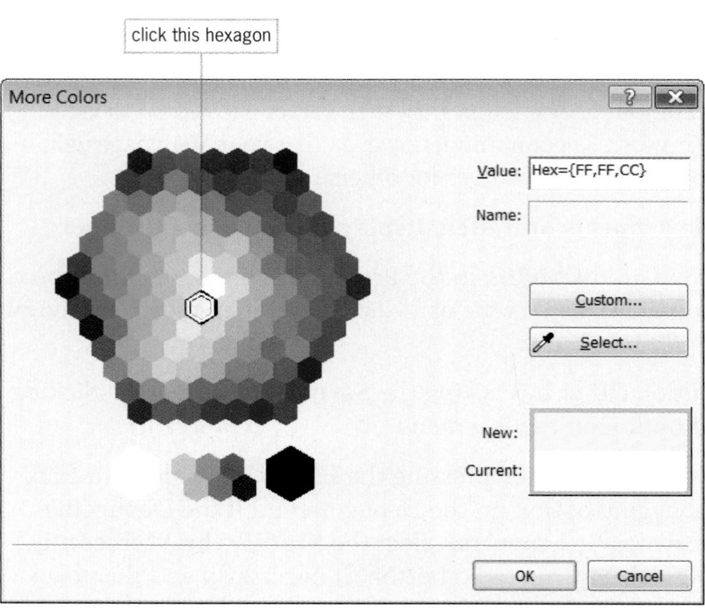

Figure 12-9 More Colors dialog box

2. Click the **OK** button. The page's background color changes from white to a pale yellow. Auto-hide the Properties window.

Adding Static Text to a Web Page

All Web pages contain some text that the user is not allowed to edit, such as a company name or the caption that identifies a text box. Text that cannot be changed by the user is referred to as **static text**. You can add static text to a Web page using a label control; or, you can simply type the text on the page itself. In this lesson, you will type the static text on the Web page.

To add static text to the Web page:

1. Click **inside the rectangle** that appears below the div tag at the top of the Document window. The div tag defines a division in a Web page. Type **Greenview Toy Store** and press **Enter** twice.

2. Enter the following three lines of text. Press **Enter** three times after typing the last line.

   333 Main Street
   Chicago, IL 60611
   (111) 555-5555

3. Type **Please visit us during these hours**: and press **Enter** twice.

4. Enter the following two lines of text.

   Monday – Friday 8am – 10pm
   Saturday 9am – 6pm

5. Type **Closed Sunday** and press **Enter**. See Figure 12-10.

If the div tag does not appear in the Document window, place your mouse pointer on the <div> button at the bottom of the IDE. Click the button's down arrow, then click Select Tag.

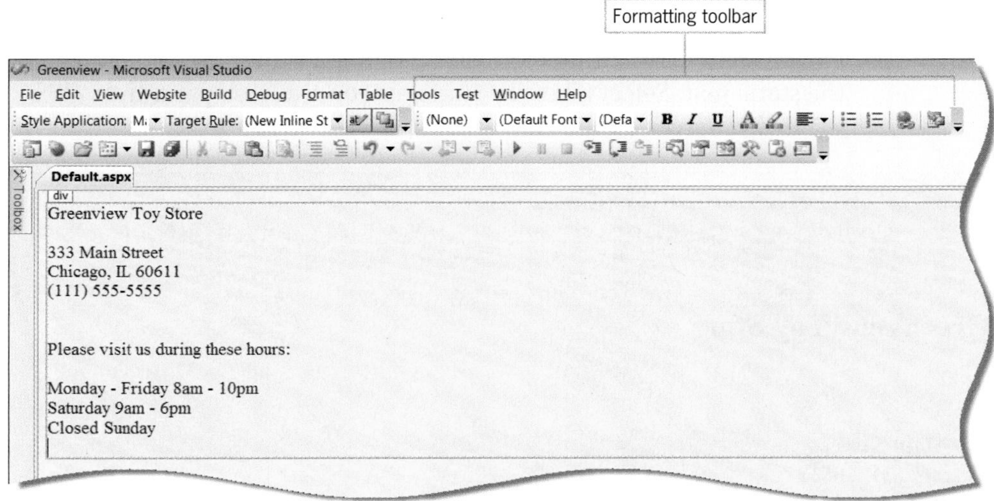

Figure 12-10 Static text entered on the Web page

6. Save the solution.

You can use either the Format menu or the Formatting toolbar to format the static text. Figure 12-11 indicates some of the tools available on the Formatting toolbar.

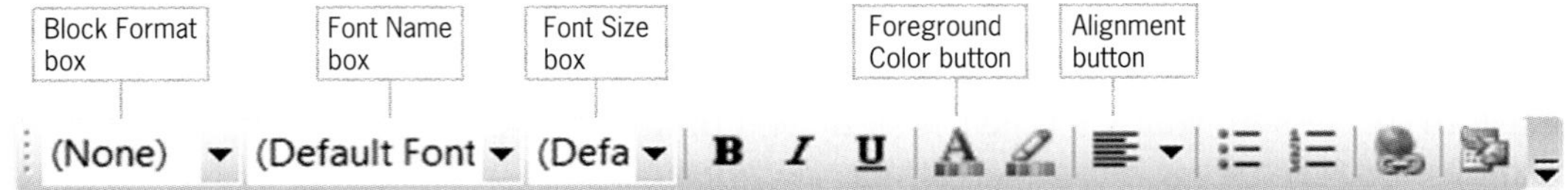

Figure 12-11 Formatting toolbar

To format the static text on the Web page:

1. Select (highlight) the Greenview Toy Store text on the Web page. Click the **down arrow** in the Block Format box, which currently contains (None), then click **Heading 1 <h1>**.
2. Select the address and phone number text. Click the **down arrow** in the Block Format box, then click **Heading 2 <h2>**.
3. Select the Please visit us during these hours: text. Click the **down arrow** in the Font Size box, then click **x-large (24pt)**. Also click the ***I*** (Italic) button on the Formatting toolbar.
4. Select the three lines of text that contain the store hours. Click the **down arrow** in the Font Size box, then click **large (18pt)**. Click the **B** (Bold) button on the Formatting toolbar. Now change the color of the selected text. Click the **Foreground Color** button on the Formatting toolbar to open the More Colors dialog box. Click any **dark green hexagon**, then click the **OK** button.
5. Now use the Formatting toolbar's Alignment button to center all of the static text. Select all of the static text on the Web page, then click the **down arrow** on the Alignment button. See Figure 12-12.

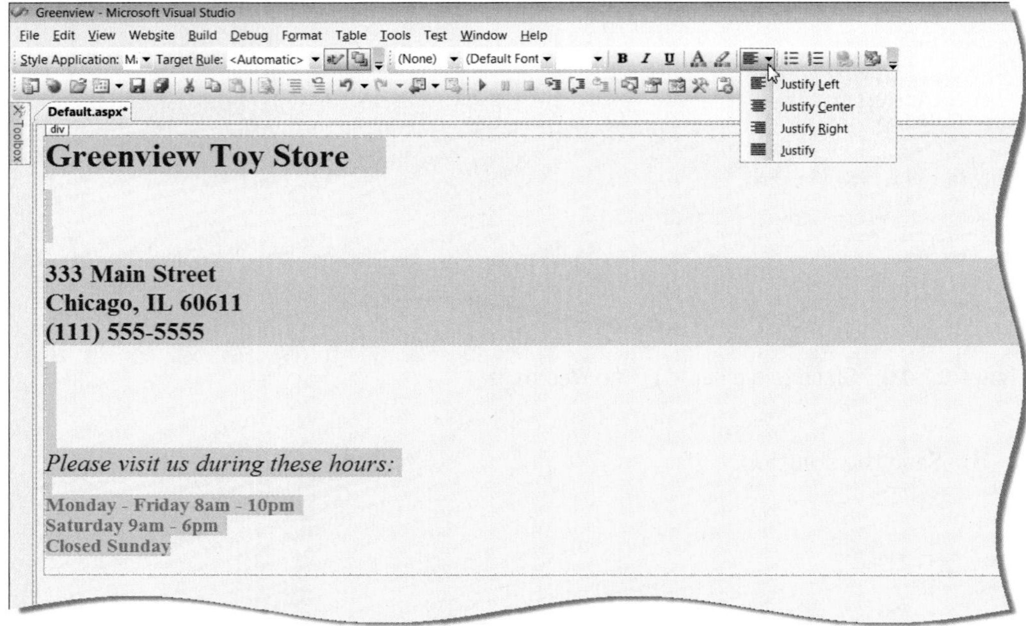

Figure 12-12 Selected text and alignment choices

6. Click **Justify Center**. The selected text appears centered, horizontally, on the Web page. Click **anywhere below the store hours** to deselect the selected text, then save the solution.

Viewing a Web Page in Full Screen View

While you are designing a Web page, you should periodically view the page either in a browser window or in full screen view to determine how it will appear to the user. As you learned earlier, you view a Web page in a browser by starting the Web application. To view a Web page in full screen view, you use the Full Screen option on the View menu.

To view the Web page using the Full Screen option:

1. Click **View** on the menu bar, then click **Full Screen**. See Figure 12-13. Although not identical to viewing in a browser window, full screen view provides a quick and easy way to verify the placement of controls and text on the Web page.

Figure 12-13 Web page displayed in full screen view

2. Click the **Full Screen** button to return to the standard view.

If you mistakenly clicked the window's Close button in Step 2, click the Full Screen button, then right-click Default.aspx in the Solution Explorer window and then click View Designer.

Closing and Opening an Existing Web Application

You can use the File menu to close and also open an existing Web application.

To close and then open the Greenview application:

1. *If you are using Visual Studio 2008*, click **File** on the menu bar, then click **Close Solution**. *If you are using Visual Web Developer 2008 Express Edition*, click **File** on the menu bar, then click **Close Project**.
2. Now open the application. Click **File** on the menu bar, then click **Open Web Site**. The Open Web Site dialog box appears. If necessary, click the **File System** button. Click the **Greenview** folder, which is contained in the VB2008\Chap12 folder, then click the **Open** button. If the Default.aspx Web page does not appear in the Document window, right-click **Default.aspx** in the Solution Explorer window, then click **View Designer**.

Adding an Image to a Web Page

In the next set of steps, you will add an image to the Greenview Toy Store Web page. The image is stored in the Small_house.jpg file, which is contained in the VB2008\Chap12 folder. The image file was downloaded from the Stock.XCHNG site and was generously contributed by photographer Gerrit Schneider. (You can browse and optionally download other free images at *www.sxc.hu*.) You can add an image to a Web page using the Image tool in the toolbox.

To add an image to the Web page:

1. First, you need to add the image file to the application. Click **Website** on the menu bar, then click **Add Existing Item**. Open the VB2008\Chap12 folder. Click **Small_house.jpg** in the list of filenames, then click the **Add** button.
2. Click **immediately after the letter y** in the Closed Sunday text on the Web page, then press **Enter** four times.
3. Now add an image control to the Web page. Temporarily display the Toolbox window, then click the **Image** tool. Drag your mouse pointer to the location shown in Figure 12-14, then release the mouse button.

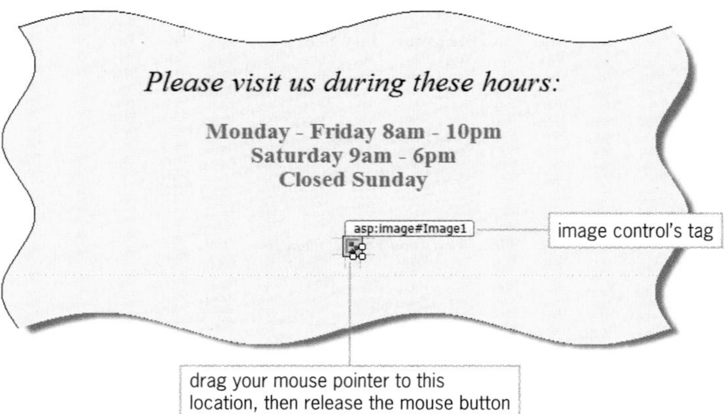

Figure 12-14 Image control added to the Web page

4. Now display the image in the image control. Temporarily display the Properties window, then click **ImageUrl**. Click the **...** (ellipsis) button in the Settings box. The Select Image dialog box opens. Click **Small_house.jpg** in the Contents of folder section, then click the **OK** button.
5. Next, you will put a colored border around the image control. Click **BorderStyle** in the Properties window. Click the **down arrow** in the Settings box, then click **Groove**.
6. Now make the border 50 pixels wide. Click **BorderWidth** in the Properties window, then type **50** and press **Enter**.
7. Next, change the border's color to match the Web page's color. Click **BorderColor** in the Properties window, then click the **...** (ellipsis) button. When the More Colors dialog box opens, click the same **hexagon** as you did for the DOCUMENT's BgColor. (If necessary, refer back to Figure 12-9.) Click the **OK** button, then click **an empty area** of the Web page.

8. Save the solution, then press **F5** to start the application. If the Script Debugging Disabled dialog box appears, click the **Yes** button. Your browser requests the Default.aspx page from the server. The server locates the page and then sends the appropriate HTML instructions back to your browser for rendering on the screen. Maximize the browser window, if necessary. See Figure 12-15.

Figure 12-15 Completed Web page displayed in a browser window

9. Restore the browser window. Place your mouse pointer on the window's right border, then drag the border to the left to make the window narrower. Notice that the text and image remain centered in the visible portion of the window. Now drag the right border to the right to make the window wider. Here again, the text and image remain centered in the visible portion of the window.
10. Close the browser window, then close the solution.

Repositioning a Control on a Web Page

At times, you may want to reposition a control on a Web page. In this section, you will move the Small_house.jpg image to a different location on the Greenview Toy Store's Web page. First, however, you will create a new Web application and then copy the Greenview files to the application.

To create a new Web application, and then copy the Greenview files to the application:

1. Use the New Web Site option on the File menu to create a new Web application named **Greenview2**. Save the application in the VB2008\Chap12 folder.
2. Close the Greenview2 solution.

3. Use Windows to open the Greenview2 folder. Select the folder's contents, which includes the App_Data folder and the Default.aspx, Default.aspx.vb, and web.config files. Delete the selected folder and files.
4. Use Windows to open the Greenview folder, which is contained in the VB2008\Chap12 folder. Select the folder's contents, which includes the App_Data folder and the Default.aspx, Default.aspx.vb, Small_house.jpg, and web.config files. Copy the selected contents to the Greenview2 folder.

Now you will open the Greenview2 application and move the image control to different locations on the Web page.

To open the Greenview2 application and move the image control:

1. Click **File** on the Visual Studio (or Visual Web Developer) menu bar, then click **Open Web Site**. Click the **File System** button, if necessary, in the Open Web Site dialog box. Click the **Greenview2** folder, which is contained in the VB2008\Chap12 folder, then click the **Open** button. If necessary, right-click **Default.aspx** in the Solution Explorer window, then click **View Designer**.
2. First, you will move the image control from the bottom of the Web page to the top of the Web page. If necessary, click **immediately before the letter G** in the Greenview Toy Store heading. Press **Enter** to insert a blank line above the heading.
3. Click the **image control** on the Web page, then press the left mouse button as you drag the image control to the blank line immediately above the heading. Release the mouse button. See Figure 12-16.

Figure 12-16 Image control dragged above the heading

4. Next, you will move the image control to the empty area below the phone number. Drag the image control to the empty area below the phone number, then release the mouse button.

5. Save the solution, then press **F5** to start the application. If the Script Debugging Disabled dialog box appears, click the **Yes** button. See Figure 12-17.

Figure 12-17 Modified Web page displayed in a browser window

6. Close the browser window, then close the Greenview2 solution.

Lesson A Summary

- **To create a Web application:**

  Click File on the menu bar, then click New Web Site. If necessary, select File System in the Location box. Enter an appropriate name and location for the application. If necessary, select Visual Basic in the Language box. Click the OK button.

- **To add a title to a Web page:**

  Set the DOCUMENT's Title property.

- **To display a Web page in a browser window:**

  Start the Web application by pressing F5 or by using the Start Debugging option on the Debug menu. If the Debugging Not Enabled dialog box appears, select the "Modify the Web.config file to enable debugging." radio button and then click the OK button. If the Script Debugging Disabled dialog box appears, click the Yes button.

- **To change the background color of a Web page:**

  Set the DOCUMENT's BgColor property.

- **To add static text to a Web page:**

  Type the text on the Web page; or use a label control.

- **To format the static text on a Web page:**

  Use either the Format menu or the Formatting toolbar.

- **To display a Web page in full screen view:**

  Click View on the menu bar, then click Full Screen.

- **To close a Web application:**

  Click File on the menu bar, then click either Close Solution (Visual Studio 2008) or Close Project (Visual Web Developer 2008 Express Edition).

- **To open an existing Web application:**

  Click File on the menu bar, then click Open Web Site.

- **To add an image file to an application:**

  Click Website on the menu bar, then click Add Existing Item. Open the appropriate folder, then click the image filename. Click the Add button.

- **To display an image on a Web page:**

  Use the Image tool to add an image control to the page. Set the image control's ImageUrl property.

- **To reposition a control on a Web page:**

  Drag the control to the new location.

Lesson A Key Terms

ASP—stands for "active server page"

Browser—a program that allows a client computer to request and view Web pages

Client computer—a computer that requests information from a Web server

Dynamic Web page—an interactive document that can accept information from the user and also retrieve information for the user

Static text—text that the user is not allowed to edit

Static Web page—a non-interactive document whose purpose is merely to display information to the user

Web pages—the documents stored on Web servers

Web server—a computer that contains special software that "serves up" Web pages in response to requests from client computers

Lesson A Review Questions

1. A computer that requests an ASP page from a Web server is called a ________________________ computer.
   a. browser
   b. client
   c. requesting
   d. None of the above.

2. A ________________________ is a program that uses HTML to render a Web page on the computer screen.
   a. browser
   b. client
   c. server
   d. None of the above.

3. An online form used to purchase a product is an example of a ________________________ Web page.
   a. dynamic
   b. static

4. The Web page in a new Web application is automatically assigned the name ________________________.
   a. Default.aps
   b. Default1.vb
   c. WebForm1.aspx
   d. None of the above.

5. The HTML instructions in a Web page are processed by the ________________________.
   a. client computer
   b. Web server

6. The background color of a Web page is determined by the ________________________ property.
   a. BackColor
   b. BackgroundColor
   c. BgColor
   d. None of the above.

Lesson A Exercises

INTRODUCTORY

1. Create a Web application named Johansen. Save the application in the VB2008\Chap12 folder. Click the down arrow in the Properties window's Object box, then click DOCUMENT. Change the DOCUMENT's Title property to Johansen Pet Supplies. Save the Web application. Create a Web page similar to the one shown in Figure 12-18. The static text should be centered, horizontally, on the page. Save and then start the application. If the Debugging Not Enabled dialog box appears, select the "Modify the Web.config file to enable debugging." radio button and then click the OK button. If the Script Debugging Disabled dialog box appears, click the Yes button. Close the browser window, then close the solution.

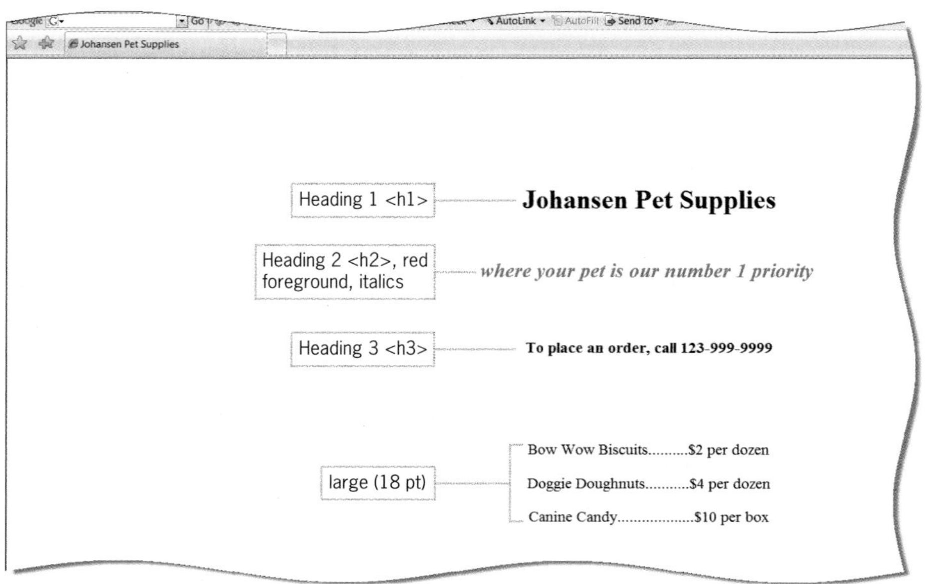

Figure 12-18 Web page for Johansen Pet Supplies

INTERMEDIATE

2. Create a Web application named Gutierrez. Save the application in the VB2008\Chap12 folder. Change the DOCUMENT's Title property to Gutierrez Heating and Cooling. Save the Web application. Create a Web page similar to the one shown in Figure 12-19. As you are creating the Web page, periodically view the page in full screen view, then switch back to standard view. Save and then start the application. Close the browser window, then close the solution.

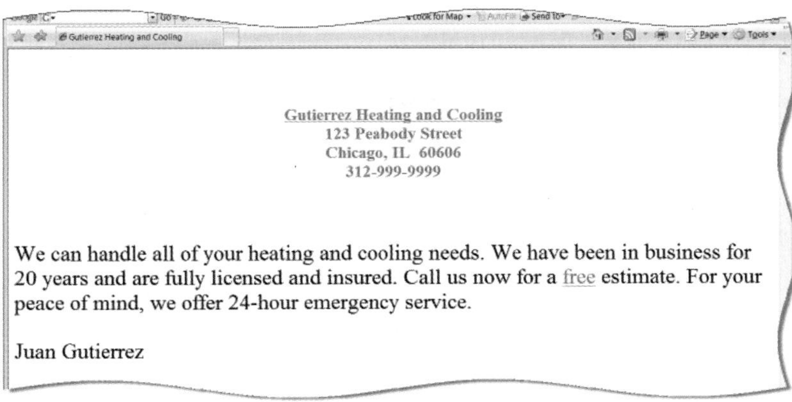

Figure 12-19 Web page for Gutierrez Heating and Cooling

INTERMEDIATE

3. Create a Web application named Winterland. Save the application in the VB2008\Chap12 folder. Change the DOCUMENT's Title property to Winterland Farms. Change the DOCUMENT's BgColor property to a light blue. Save the Web application. Create a Web page similar to the one shown in Figure 12-20. The winterland.jpg file is contained in the VB2008\Chap12 folder. Save and then start the application. Close the browser window, then close the solution.

Figure 12-20 Web page for Winterland Farms

LESSON B

After studying Lesson B, you should be able to:

- Add a text box, label, and button to a Web page
- Code a control on a Web page
- Include a RequiredFieldValidator control on a Web page

Dynamic Web Pages

A dynamic Web page contains controls with which the user can interact. It also contains code that tells the controls how to respond to the user's actions. In this lesson, you will create a dynamic Web page that allows the user to enter the number of American dollars. When the user clicks the page's Submit button, the button's Click event procedure will convert the dollars to British pounds and then display the result.

To create the Currency Converter Web application:

1. If necessary, start Visual Studio 2008 or Visual Web Developer 2008 Express Edition. Close the Start Page window. If necessary, permanently display the Solution Explorer window.
2. Use the New Web Site option on the File menu to create a new Web application named **Currency**. Save the application in the VB2008\Chap12 folder.
3. Change the DOCUMENT's Title property to **Currency Converter**.

Before you add any text or controls to a Web page, you should plan the page's layout. Figure 12-21 shows a sketch of the Web page for the Currency Converter application. The Web page will contain static text, as well as an image control, text box, label, and button.

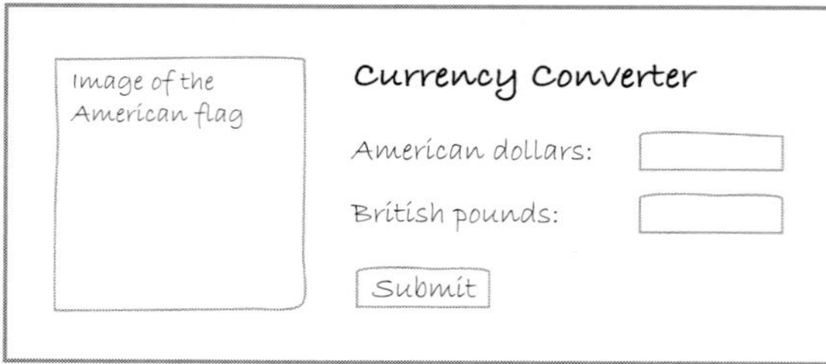

Figure 12-21 Sketch of the Currency Converter application's Web page

To begin creating the Web page:

1. Permanently display the Toolbox window.
2. Click **inside the rectangle** that appears below the div tag at the top of the Document window. Recall that the div tag defines a division in a Web page. All of the text in this division will use the Segoe UI font. If necessary, use the View menu to display the Formatting toolbar. Click the **down arrow** in the Font Name box, then scroll the list until you see Segoe UI. Click **Segoe UI** in the list.

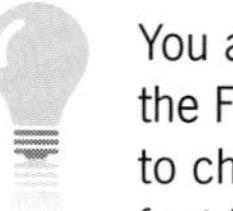

You also can use the Format menu to change the font in Step 2.

3. Before dragging an image control to the Web page, you will add the American flag image file to the application. Click **Website** on the menu bar, then click **Add Existing Item**. Open the VB2008\Chap12 folder. Click **USflag.jpg** in the list of filenames, then click the **Add** button.

4. Now drag an image control into the rectangle that appears below the div tag, then release the mouse button. Temporarily display the Properties window, if necessary, then click **ImageUrl**. Click the **...** (ellipsis) button in the Settings box. The Select Image dialog box opens. Click **USflag.jpg** in the Contents of folder section, then click the **OK** button.

5. Click an **empty area** to the right of the flag to deselect the image control, then press **Enter** twice.

6. Now enter the Web page's static text. Press **Tab** twice, then type **Currency Converter** and press **Enter** twice.

7. Press **Tab** twice. Type **American dollars:** and press the **Spacebar** twice, then press **Enter** twice.

8. Press **Tab** twice. Type **British pounds**: and press the **Spacebar** twice, then press **Enter** twice.

9. Press **Tab** twice. Figure 12-22 shows the image control and static text on the Web page.

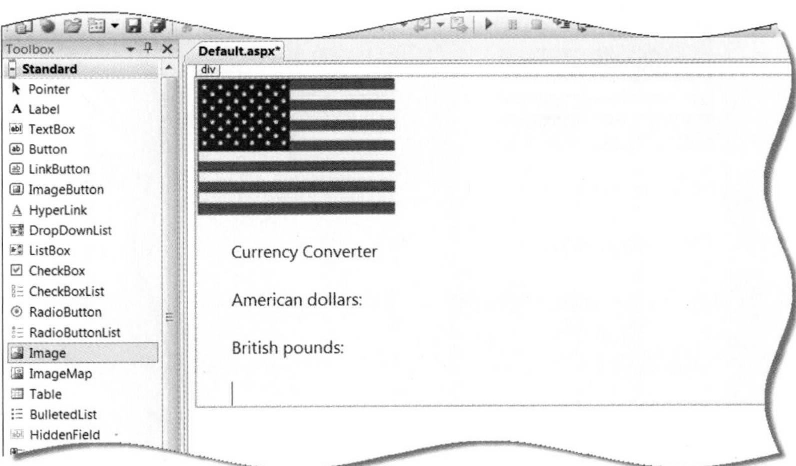

Figure 12-22 Image control and static text on the Web page

In addition to the image control and static text, the Web page will contain a text box, a label, and a button. You will add those controls next.

To add a text box, label, and button to the page:

1. Drag a text box control to the Web page. Position the control to the right of the two spaces in the "American dollars: " text, then release the mouse button.

2. Unlike Windows controls, Web controls have an ID property rather than a Name property. Use the Properties window to set the TextBox1 control's ID property to **txtDollars**. Also set its Width property to **90px**.

3. If necessary, click the **plus box** that appears next to Font in the Properties window. Click **Name**, then click the **down arrow** in the Settings box. Locate and then click **Segoe UI**.

4. Drag a label control to the Web page. Position the control to the right of the two spaces in the "British pounds: " text, then release the mouse button. Set the following properties for the Label1 control.

ID	**lblPounds**
BorderStyle	**Solid**
BorderWidth	**1px**
Width	**90px**

5. Change the label control's BackColor property to a light yellow. Also delete the contents of its Text property.

6. Finally, drag a button control to the Web page. Position the control two blank lines below the letter B in the "British pounds: " text, then release the mouse button. Set the button's ID property to **btnSubmit**, and set its Text property to **Submit**. If necessary, click the **plus box** that appears next to Font in the Properties window. Click **Name**, then click the **down arrow** in the Settings box. Locate and then click **Segoe UI**. See Figure 12-23.

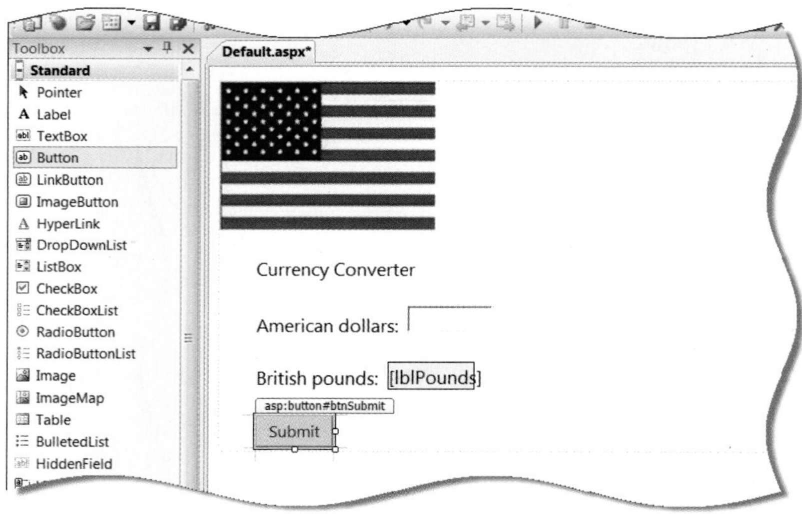

Figure 12-23 Additional controls added to the Web page

7. Auto-hide the Toolbox window, then save the solution.

Looking back at the sketch shown earlier in Figure 12-21, you will notice that the heading text, Currency Converter, is larger than the other text on the page. Also, the image control is positioned to the left of the static text and controls.

To complete the Web page's interface:

1. Select (highlight) the Currency Converter text. Click the **down arrow** in the Font Size box, then click **xx-large (36pt)**.

2. Click the **image control**. Click **Format** on the menu bar, then click **Position**. The Position dialog box opens. See Figure 12-24.

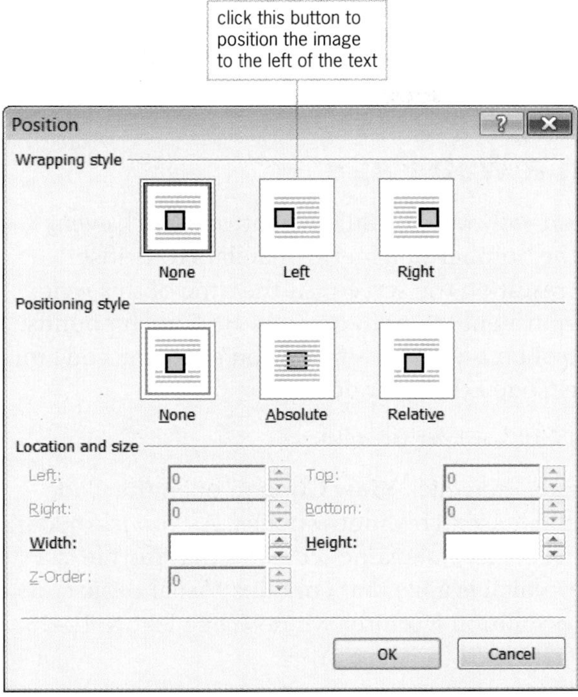

Figure 12-24 Position dialog box

3. You want the image control to appear on the left side of the text. Click **Left** in the Wrapping style section, then click the **OK** button.
4. Position your mouse pointer on the image control's lower right sizing handle, as shown in Figure 12-25, then drag the control until it is approximately the size shown in the figure. (The number of pixels may be different on your screen. Just be sure that all of the static text and controls appear to the right of the image control.)

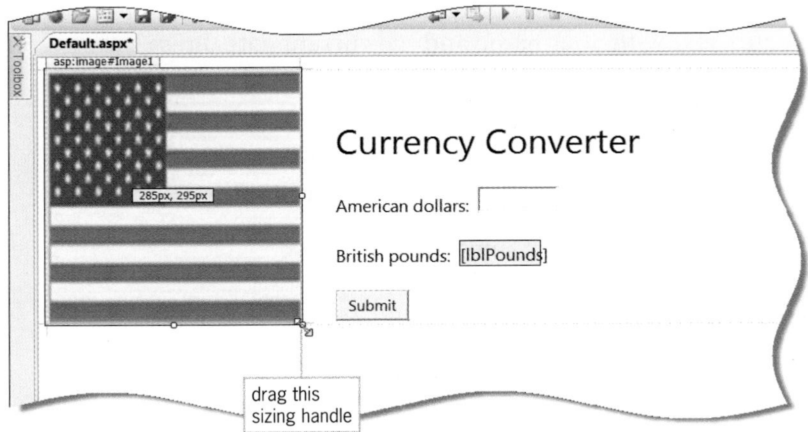

Figure 12-25 Size and position of the image control

5. Click an **empty area** on the Web page to deselect the image control. Save the solution, then press **F5** to start the application. If the Debugging Not Enabled dialog box appears, select the **Modify the Web.config file to enable debugging.** radio button (if necessary) and

then click the **OK** button. If the Script Debugging Disabled dialog box appears, click the **Yes** button. The Web page appears in a browser window. Close the browser window.

Coding a Control on a Web Page

In the following set of steps, you will code the Submit button's Click event procedure so that it converts the number of American dollars to British pounds, and then displays the result on the screen. At the time of this writing, an American dollar was equivalent to approximately .68 British pounds. As you do when coding a control on a Windows form, you enter the code for a control on a Web page in the Code Editor window.

To code the Submit button's Click event procedure:

1. Right-click the **Web page**, then click **View Code** to open the Code Editor window. The Default.aspx.vb window opens. As you learned in Chapter 1, the .vb extension on a filename indicates that the file is a Visual Basic source file, which is a file that contains Visual Basic code. Temporarily display the Solution Explorer window. See Figure 12-26.

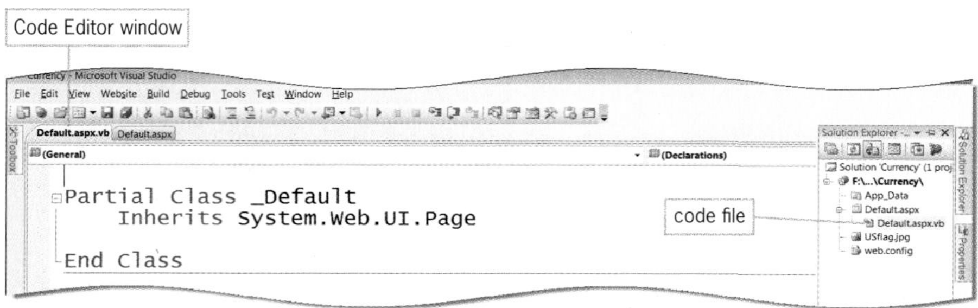

Figure 12-26 Code Editor and Solution Explorer windows

2. Enter the following comments, replacing the <your name> and <current date> text with your name and the current date. Press **Enter** twice after typing the last comment.

   ' Name: Currency
   ' Purpose: Convert dollars to pounds
   ' Programmer: <your name> on <current date>

3. Enter the following Option statements.

   Option Explicit On
   Option Strict On
   Option Infer Off

4. Open the btnSubmit control's Click event procedure. Type **' converts dollars to pounds** and press **Enter** twice.

5. First, declare a named constant to store the conversion rate of .68. Enter the following Const statement.

   Const dblPOUND_RATE As Double = .68

6. Now declare variables to store the number of American dollars and the number of British pounds. Enter the following Dim statements. Press **Enter** twice after typing the last statement.

   Dim dblDollars As Double
   Dim dblPounds As Double

7. Next, store the user's entry in the `dblDollars` variable. Enter the following TryParse method.

   Double.TryParse(txtDollars.Text, dblDollars)

8. Now convert the dollars to pounds and store the result in the `dblPounds` variable. Enter the following assignment statement.

   dblPounds = dblDollars * dblPOUND_RATE

9. Finally, display the number of pounds in the lblPounds control. Enter the following line of code.

   lblPounds.Text = dblPounds.ToString("N2")

10. Save the solution. Figure 12-27 shows the code entered in the btnSubmit control's Click event procedure.

```
Protected Sub btnSubmit_Click(ByVal sender As Object, ByVal e As Syste
    ' converts dollars to pounds

    Const dblPOUND_RATE As Double = 0.68
    Dim dblDollars As Double
    Dim dblPounds As Double

    Double.TryParse(txtDollars.Text, dblDollars)
    dblPounds = dblDollars * dblPOUND_RATE
    lblPounds.Text = dblPounds.ToString("N2")

End Sub
```

Figure 12-27 btnSubmit control's Click event procedure

Now test the Currency Converter application to verify that it is working correctly.

To test the Currency Converter application:

1. Start the application. If the Script Debugging Disabled dialog box appears, click the **Yes** button. Your browser requests the Default.aspx page from the server. The server locates the page and then sends the appropriate HTML instructions to your browser for rendering on the screen.

2. Click the **txtDollars** control to place the insertion point inside the American dollars box. Type **10**, then click the **Submit** button. Clicking the Submit button submits your entry to the server, along with a request for additional services. The server processes the code contained in the button's Click event procedure and then sends the appropriate HTML to the browser for rendering on the screen. See Figure 12-28.

Figure 12-28 Result of entering data and clicking the Submit button

3. Close the browser window, then close the Code Editor window.

Validating User Input

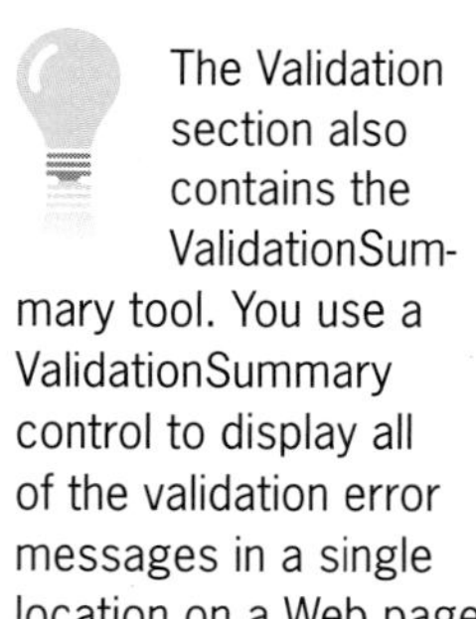

The Validation section also contains the ValidationSummary tool. You use a ValidationSummary control to display all of the validation error messages in a single location on a Web page.

The Validation section of the toolbox provides several tools for validating user input. The tools are referred to as **validator tools**. The name of each validator tool is listed in Figure 12-29 along with its purpose and important properties.

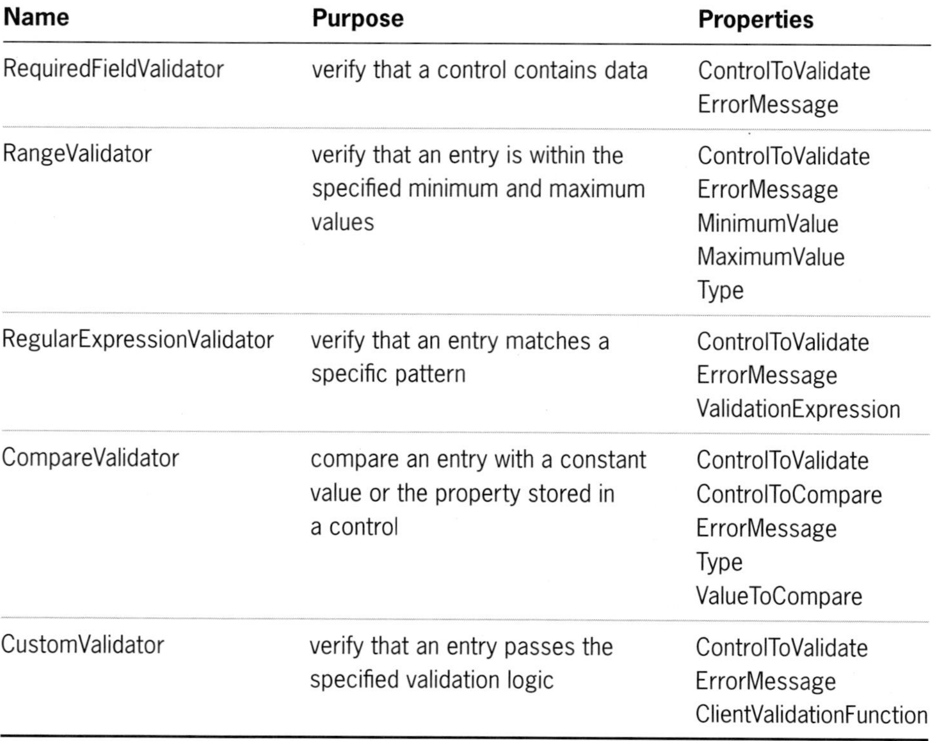

Name	Purpose	Properties
RequiredFieldValidator	verify that a control contains data	ControlToValidate ErrorMessage
RangeValidator	verify that an entry is within the specified minimum and maximum values	ControlToValidate ErrorMessage MinimumValue MaximumValue Type
RegularExpressionValidator	verify that an entry matches a specific pattern	ControlToValidate ErrorMessage ValidationExpression
CompareValidator	compare an entry with a constant value or the property stored in a control	ControlToValidate ControlToCompare ErrorMessage Type ValueToCompare
CustomValidator	verify that an entry passes the specified validation logic	ControlToValidate ErrorMessage ClientValidationFunction

Figure 12-29 Listing of validator tools

In the Currency Converter application, you will use a RequiredFieldValidator control to verify that the user entered the number of American dollars.

To verify that the user entered the number of American dollars:

1. If necessary, click the **plus box** that appears next to Validation in the toolbox, then click the **RequiredFieldValidator** tool. Drag a RequiredFieldValidator control to the Web page. Position the control to the right of the txtDollars control, then release the mouse button.
2. Use the Properties window to set the RequiredFieldValidator control's ControlToValidate property to **txtDollars**. Then set its ErrorMessage property to **Please enter the number of American dollars.** and press **Enter**.
3. Save the solution, then start the application. If the Script Debugging Disabled dialog box appears, click the **Yes** button. Click the **Submit** button without entering a value in the txtDollars control. The Required-FieldValidator control displays the "Please enter the number of American dollars." message. See Figure 12-30.

Figure 12-30 Result of clicking the Submit button before entering any data

4. Click the **txtDollars** control, then type **20** and click the **Submit** button. The error message is removed from the Web page and the number 13.60 appears in the lblPounds control.
5. Close the browser window, then close the solution.

Lesson B Summary

- **To wrap text around an image control:**

  Click the image control. Click Format on the menu bar, then click Position. Click the Left button in the Wrapping style section to place the image control on the left side of the text. Click the Right button to place the image control on the right side of the text.

- **To code a control on a Web page:**

  Enter the code in the Code Editor window.

- **To validate user input on a Web page:**

  Use one or more of the validator tools contained in the Validation section of the toolbox.

Lesson B Key Term

Validator tools—the tools contained in the Validation section of the toolbox; used to validate user input on a Web page

Lesson B Review Questions

1. In code, you refer to a control on a Web page using the control's ______________________________ property.
   a. Caption
   b. ID
   c. Name
   d. Text

2. If you want text to appear to the left of the selected image control on a Web form, you would need to click the ______________________________ button in the Position dialog box.
   a. Align
   b. AlignLeft
   c. Left
   d. Right

3. The Visual Basic code in a Web page is processed by the ______________________________.
   a. client computer
   b. Web server

4. You can use a ______________________________ control to verify that a control on a Web page contains data.
   a. RequiredFieldValidator
   b. RequiredField
   c. RequiredValidator
   d. None of the above.

5. You can use a ________________ control to verify that an entry on a Web page is within a minimum and maximum value.
   a. MinMaxValidation
   b. MaxMinValidation
   c. EntryValidator
   d. RangeValidator

Lesson B Exercises

1. In this exercise, you modify the Currency Converter application created in the lesson. INTRODUCTORY
   a. Create a new Web application named **CurrencyIntro**. Save the application in the VB2008\Chap12 folder. Close the CurrencyIntro solution.
   b. Use Windows to open the CurrencyIntro folder. Select the folder's contents, which includes the App_Data folder and the Default.aspx, Default.aspx.vb, and web.config files. Delete the selected folder and files.
   c. Use Windows to open the Currency folder, which is contained in the VB2008\Chap12 folder. Select the folder's contents, which includes the App_Data folder and the Default.aspx, Default.aspx.vb, USflag.jpg, and web.config files. Copy the selected contents to the CurrencyIntro folder.
   d. Open the CurrencyIntro folder in Visual Studio (or Visual Web Developer). If necessary, right-click Default.aspx in the Solution Explorer window, then click View Designer.
   e. Add a RangeValidator control to the Web page. Change the control's Type property to Double. The control should display an appropriate message if the number of American dollars is less than 1 or greater than 100,000.
   f. Save the solution, then start the application. If the Script Debugging Disabled dialog box appears, click the Yes button. Test the application. Close the browser window, then close the solution.

2. Create a Web application named Multiplication. Save the application in the VB2008\Chap12 folder. Click the down arrow in the Properties window's Object box, then click DOCUMENT. Change the DOCUMENT's Title property to Product Calculator. INTRODUCTORY
   a. Create a Web page similar to the one shown in Figure 12-31. Use the Segoe UI font for the static text and controls. The X image is contained in the VB2008\Chap12\Times.jpg file. Use RequiredFieldValidator controls to verify that both text boxes contain data.
   b. Open the Code Editor window. Enter comments for the project's name and purpose, as well as for your name and the current date. Also enter the appropriate Option statements. Code the Submit

button's Click event procedure so it multiplies the first number by the second number, and then displays the result in the lblProduct control.

c. Save the solution, then start the application. If the Debugging Not Enabled dialog box appears, select the "Modify the Web.config file to enable debugging." radio button and then click the OK button. If the Script Debugging Disabled dialog box appears, click the Yes button. Test the application. Close the browser window, then close the Code Editor window and the solution.

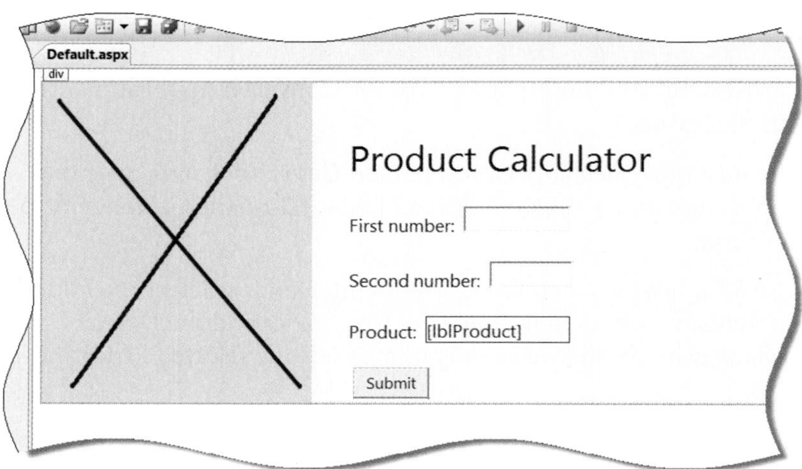

Figure 12-31 Web page for the Product Calculator application

INTRODUCTORY

3. Create a Web application named PoundsToDollars. Save the application in the VB2008\Chap12 folder. Change the DOCUMENT's Title property to Pounds to Dollars. The application should display the result of converting British pounds to American dollars. Create a Web page similar to the Currency Converter page from the lesson; however, display the BritishFlag.jpg image file in the image control. Open the Code Editor window. Enter comments for the project's name and purpose, as well as for your name and the current date. Also enter the appropriate Option statements. Code the Submit button's Click event procedure. Use 1.48 as the number of American dollars for each British pound. Save the solution, then start the application. If the Debugging Not Enabled dialog box appears, select the "Modify the Web.config file to enable debugging." radio button and then click the OK button. If the Script Debugging Disabled dialog box appears, click the Yes button. Test the application. Close the browser window, then close the Code Editor window and the solution.

INTERMEDIATE

4. Create a Web application named ZipCode. Save the application in the VB2008\Chap12 folder. Change the DOCUMENT's Title property to ZIP Code Verifier. Create a Web page similar to the one shown in Figure 12-32. Use the Segoe UI font for the static text and controls. Verify that the user entered the ZIP code, and that the ZIP code is in the appropriate format. (Hint: Use the RegularExpressionValidator control to verify the format.) Open the Code Editor window. If the ZIP code is valid, the Submit button should display the message

"Your ZIP code is *zip*.", where *zip* is the ZIP code entered by the user. Save the solution, then start the application. Test the application by clicking the Submit button without entering the ZIP code. Then test it using the following ZIP codes: 60611, 606123, 60611-3456, and 60611-5. Close the browser window, then close the Code Editor window and the solution.

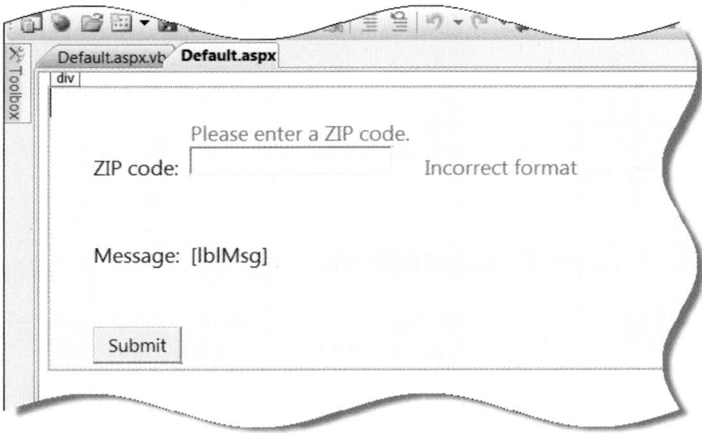

Figure 12-32 Web page for the ZIP Code Verifier application

5. In this exercise, you modify the Currency Converter application created in the lesson. INTERMEDIATE
   a. Create a new Web application named **CurrencyIntermediate**. Save the application in the VB2008\Chap12 folder. Close the CurrencyIntermediate solution.
   b. Use Windows to open the CurrencyIntermediate folder. Delete the folder's contents.
   c. Use Windows to open the Currency folder, which is contained in the VB2008\Chap12 folder. Copy the folder's contents to the CurrencyIntermediate folder.
   d. Open the CurrencyIntermediate folder in Visual Studio (or Visual Web Developer). If necessary, open the designer window.
   e. The Web page also should display the result of converting the number of American dollars to Mexican pesos. Make the appropriate modifications to the Web page and its code. Use 13.58 as the number of pesos for each American dollar.
   f. Save the solution, then start and test the application. Close the browser window, then close the Code Editor window and the solution.

LESSON C

After studying Lesson C, you should be able to:

- Make changes to the Web page in Source view
- Create columns using the <div> tag
- Utilize an ASP table in a Web page
- Add a calendar to a Web page
- Add a drop-down list box to a Web page
- Create a new line using the <br /> tag

Creating the DJ Tom Application

As you may remember, your task in this chapter is to create a Web application for DJ (disc jockey) Tom. The application's Web page should allow the user to enter the names of the bride and groom, the wedding date, an e-mail address, and the name of the first song to be danced by the newly married couple. The Web page should provide a Submit button that, when clicked, displays a message on the page. The message should contain the names of the bride and groom, the wedding date, the e-mail address, and the name of the first song. A sketch of the Web page is shown in Figure 12-33.

Figure 12-33 Sketch of the DJ Tom application's Web page

To begin creating the DJ Tom application:

1. If necessary, start Visual Studio 2008 or Visual Web Developer 2008 Express Edition. Close the Start Page window.
2. Use the New Web Site option on the File menu to create a new Web application named **DJTom**. Save the application in the VB2008\Chap12 folder.
3. Change the DOCUMENT's Title property to **DJ Tom**.

First, you will set the font for the text in the Web page. You can do this by switching to Source view and then setting one of the style attribute's properties in the <body> tag. More specifically, you set the style attribute's **font-family property**.

To set the font for the text, and then continue creating the Web page:

1. Click the **Source** button at the bottom of the IDE, then locate the <body> tag.
2. You can use the style attribute's font-family property to specify one or more fonts to use for the Web page's text. For example, the `style="font-family:Segoe UI, Arial, Sans-Serif"` attribute tells the browser to use the Segoe UI font when displaying text. However, if the Segoe UI font is not available, the browser should use the Arial font. If neither of those two fonts is available, the browser should use an available sans serif font. Modify the <body> tag as shown in Figure 12-34.

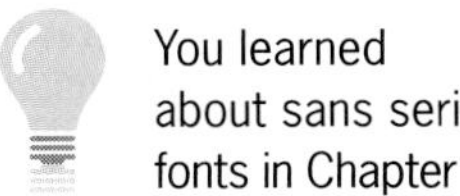
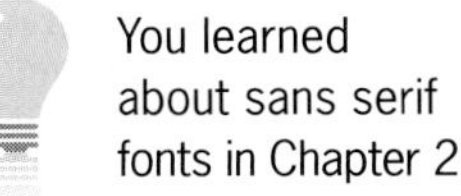

You learned about sans serif fonts in Chapter 2.

Figure 12-34 Modified <body> tag

3. Click the **Design** tab at the bottom of the IDE. If necessary, click **inside the rectangle** that appears below the div tag at the top of the Document window. Type **Your Wedding DJ** and press **Enter**.
4. If necessary, display the Formatting toolbar. Select (highlight) the Your Wedding DJ text.
5. Click the **down arrow** in the Block Format box, then click **Heading 1 <h1>** in the list. Click the **Alignment** button on the Formatting toolbar, then click **Justify Center**. Click an **empty area** of the Web page to deselect the text.

If the div tag does not appear in Step 3, click the <div> button at the bottom of the IDE.

Creating a Columnar Layout

The content in many Web pages is laid out in a columnar format, similar to a newspaper. The sketch of DJ Tom's Web page (shown earlier in Figure 12-33) indicates that the page contains three columns. The first column displays a message. The second column displays the data entry controls, and the third column displays DJ Tom's logo. You can divide a Web page into columns using the **<div> tag**.

To divide DJ Tom's Web page into three columns:

1. Click the **Source** tab, then click the **blank line** below the `<br />` tag. If necessary, press **Tab** to align the insertion point with the tag.
2. The first column, which you will name "MessageColumn", will occupy 30% of the page. You will change the column's background color to purple, and specify that the column should appear on the left side of the page. Type **<div>**. The Source view editor automatically enters the closing </div> tag for you. Click **immediately after the letter v** in

the <div> tag, then press the **Spacebar**. Complete the tag as shown in Figure 12-35, then position the insertion point as shown in the figure.

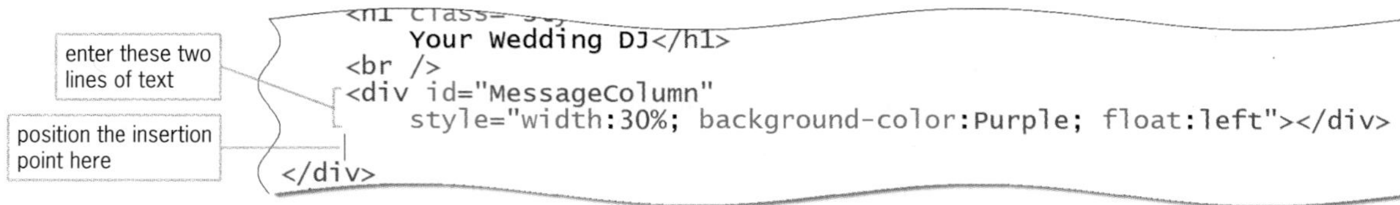

Figure 12-35 <div> tag for the first column

3. Now use another <div> tag to create the second column. The column will occupy 39% of the Web page, and it should appear next to the first column. Type the following <div> tag.

   <div id="ContentColumn" style="width:39%; float:left"></div>

4. Click **immediately after the </div> tag** from Step 3, then press **Enter**. The third column will occupy 30% of the Web page, and it should appear on the right side of the page. Type the following <div> tag.

   <div id="LogoColumn" style="width:30%; float:right"></div>

5. Click the **Design** tab. Three columns appear in the Web page. See Figure 12-36.

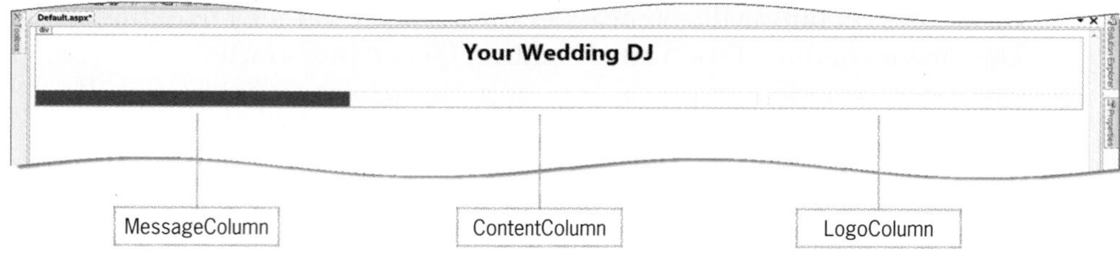

Figure 12-36 Web page showing the three columns

6. Permanently display the Toolbox and Properties windows, if necessary. Drag a label control into the MessageColumn. Set the control's ID property to **lblMsg**, and set its ForeColor property to **White**. Also remove the contents of its Text property.

7. Before dragging an image control to the Web page, you will add the DJ Tom image file to the application. Click **Website** on the menu bar, then click **Add Existing Item**. Open the VB2008\Chap12 folder. Click **DJ.jpg** in the list of filenames, then click the **Add** button.

8. Now drag an image control into the LogoColumn. Set the control's ImageUrl property to **DJ.jpg**. Click an **empty area** on the Web page to deselect the control.

Using an ASP Table

The Table tool in the Standard section of the toolbox creates an **ASP table control**. The control displays information in a row and column format, similar to a spreadsheet, and is often used to align the information on a Web page.

The ASP table control you will use in DJ Tom's Web page will have six rows and two columns. The intersection of a row and a column is called a **cell**.

To add an ASP table to the Web page:

1. Click the **Table** tool located in the Standard section of the toolbox, then drag a table control to the ContentColumn. (The HTML section of the toolbox also has a Table tool. Be sure to use the Table tool listed in the Standard section.) See Figure 12-37.

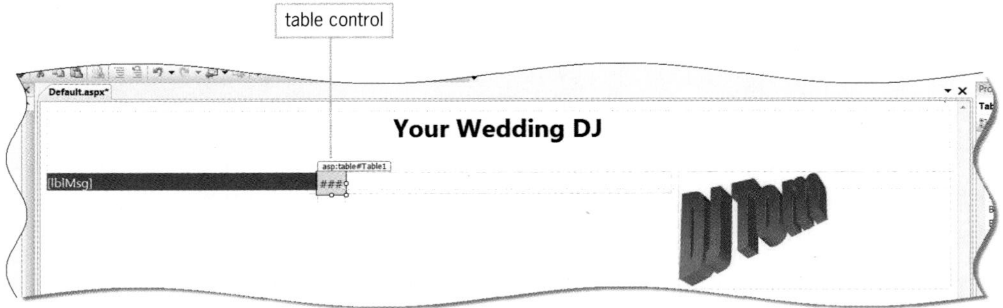

Figure 12-37 ASP table control added to the ContentColumn

2. Set the table control's CellSpacing property to **40**. The CellSpacing property controls the spacing between the table cells. Set the table control's HorizontalAlign property to **Center**.
3. Now you will begin defining the table rows. Click **Rows** in the Properties window, then click the **...** (ellipsis) button in the Settings box. The TableRow Collection Editor dialog box opens. Click the **Add** button, then click **(ID)** in the list of TableRow properties. Type **tblRow1** and press **Enter**. See Figure 12-38.

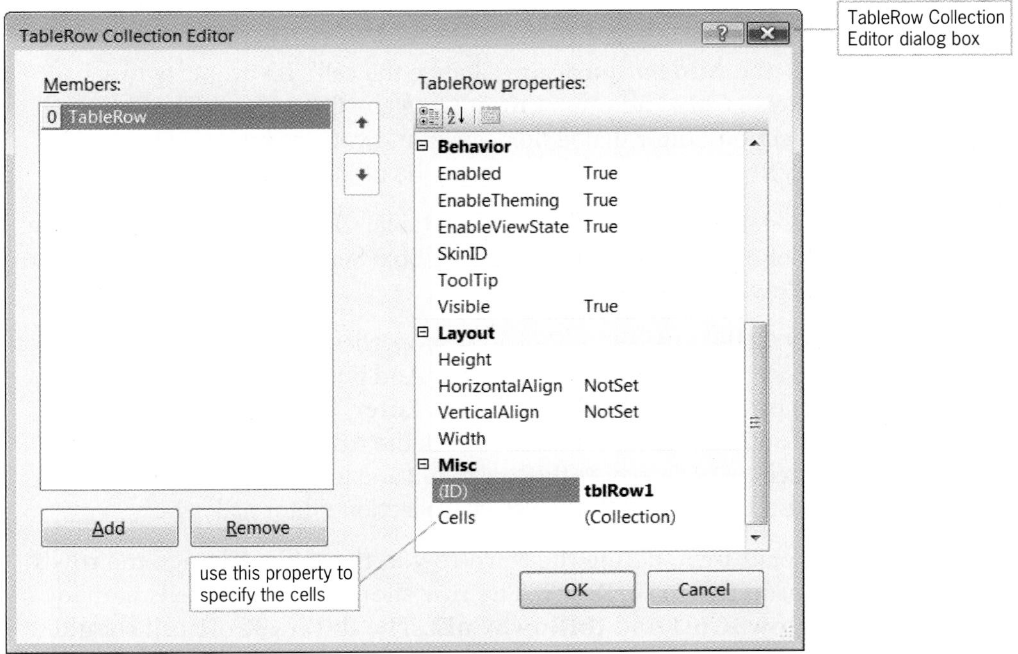

Figure 12-38 TableRow Collection Editor dialog box

4. The row will have two cells: one will contain the text "Bride:" and the other will contain a text box for entering the bride's name. Click **Cells** in the list of TableRow properties, then click the **...** (ellipsis) button in the Settings box. The TableCell Collection Editor dialog box opens. See Figure 12-39.

TableCell Collection Editor dialog box

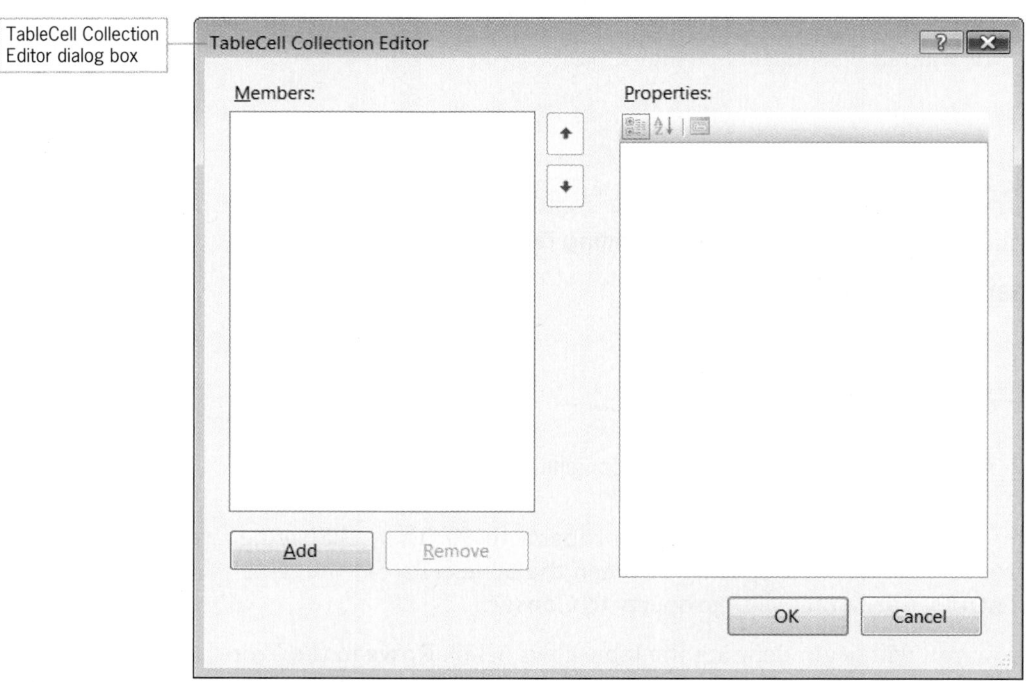

Figure 12-39 TableCell Collection Editor dialog box

When the properties are listed by category, the (ID) property is listed at the end of the properties list.

5. Click the **Add** button. Change the cell's Text property to **Bride:** and press **Enter**. Change its ID property to **tblRow1Col1** and press **Enter**.

6. Click the **Add** button again. Change the cell's ID property to **tblRow1Col2** and press **Enter**. Click the **OK** button. The TableCell Collection Editor dialog box closes and you are returned to the TableRow Collection Editor dialog box.

7. Now define the second row in the table. Click the **Add** button in the TableRow Collection Editor dialog box. Set the row's ID property to **tblRow2** and press **Enter**.

8. Click **Cells** in the list of TableRow properties, then click the **...** (ellipsis) button in the Settings box. Click the **Add** button. Change the cell's Text property to **Groom:** and press **Enter**. Change its ID property to **tblRow2Col1** and press **Enter**. Click the **Add** button again. Change the cell's ID property to **tblRow2Col2** and press **Enter**. Click the **OK** button to close the TableCell Collection Editor dialog box.

9. On your own, define the third row in the table. Change the row's ID property to **tblRow3**. The row should have two cells named **tblRow3Col1** and **tblRow3Col2**. The tblRow3Col1 cell should contain the text **Wedding:**. Close the TableCell Collection Editor dialog box.

10. On your own, define the fourth row in the table. Change the row's ID property to **tblRow4**. The row should have two cells named **tblRow4Col1** and **tblRow4Col2**. The tblRow4Col1 cell should contain the text **E-mail:**. Close the TableCell Collection Editor dialog box.
11. On your own, define the fifth row in the table. Change the row's ID property to **tblRow5**. The row should have two cells named **tblRow5Col1** and **tblRow5Col2**. The tblRow5Col1 cell should contain the text **First song:**. Close the TableCell Collection Editor dialog box.
12. Finally, define the last row in the table. Change the row's ID property to **tblRow6**. The row should have one cell named **tblRow6Col1**.
13. Click the **OK** button to close the TableCell Collection Editor dialog box, then click the **OK** button to close the TableRow Collection Editor dialog box. Save the solution. See Figure 12-40.

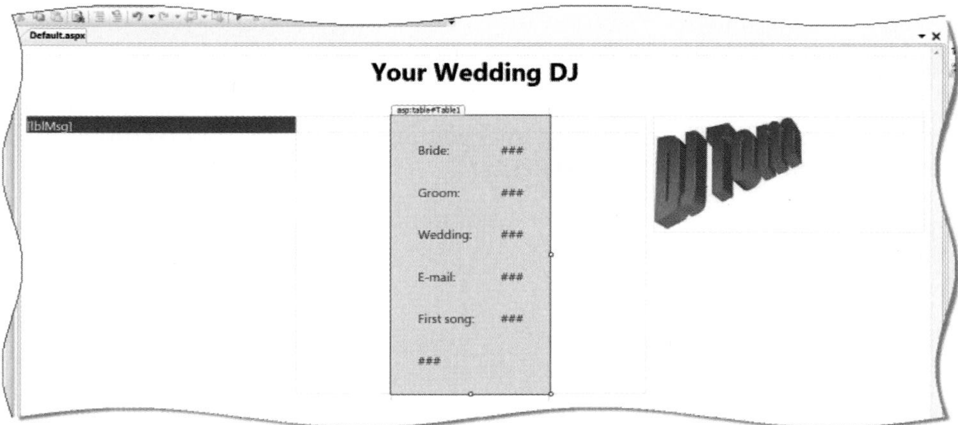

Figure 12-40 Table containing six rows and two columns

Dragging Controls in Source View

In the next set of steps, you will open the Web page in Source view. You then will drag the controls to the appropriate cells in the table.

To drag controls to the table in Source view:

1. Auto-hide the Properties window. Click an **empty area** of the Web page to deselect the table control, then click the **Source** tab at the bottom of the IDE.
2. First, you will drag a text box into the cell located next to the Bride: text. That cell is located in the second column of the first row in the table. Locate the `<asp:TableCell ID="tblRow1Col2" runat="server"></asp:TableCell>` tag. Click immediately before the `</asp:TableCell>` closing tag, then press **Enter**. Click the **TextBox** tool in the toolbox. Press and hold down the left mouse button as you drag your mouse pointer to the location shown in Figure 12-41.

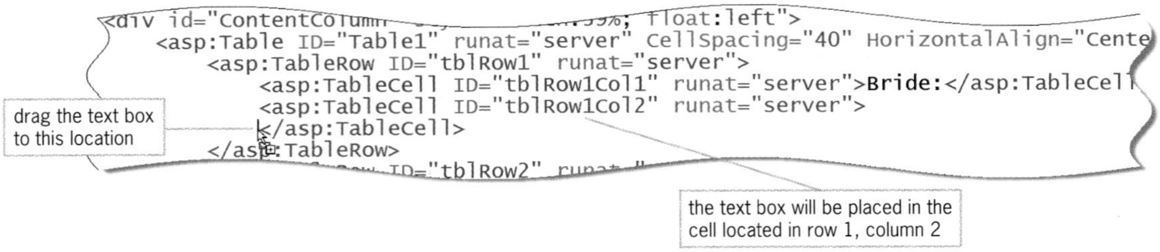

```
<div id="ContentColumn" ... float:left">
    <asp:Table ID="Table1" runat="server" CellSpacing="40" HorizontalAlign="Cente
        <asp:TableRow ID="tblRow1" runat="server">
            <asp:TableCell ID="tblRow1Col1" runat="server">Bride:</asp:TableCel
            <asp:TableCell ID="tblRow1Col2" runat="server">
            </asp:TableCell>
        </asp:TableRow>
```

drag the text box to this location

the text box will be placed in the cell located in row 1, column 2

Figure 12-41 Text box control being dragged in Source view

3. Release the mouse button. See Figure 12-42.

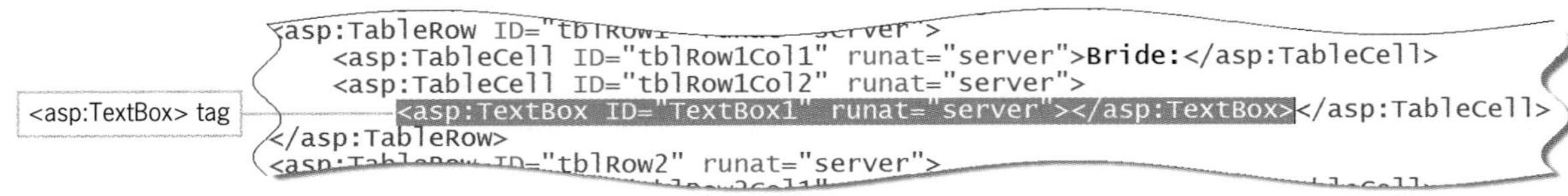

Figure 12-42 <asp:TextBox> tag added to the table instructions

4. In the <asp:TextBox> tag, change the text box control's ID property from "TextBox1" to **"txtBride"**.
5. Click the **Design** tab. A text box control appears in the second cell in row 1. See Figure 12-43.

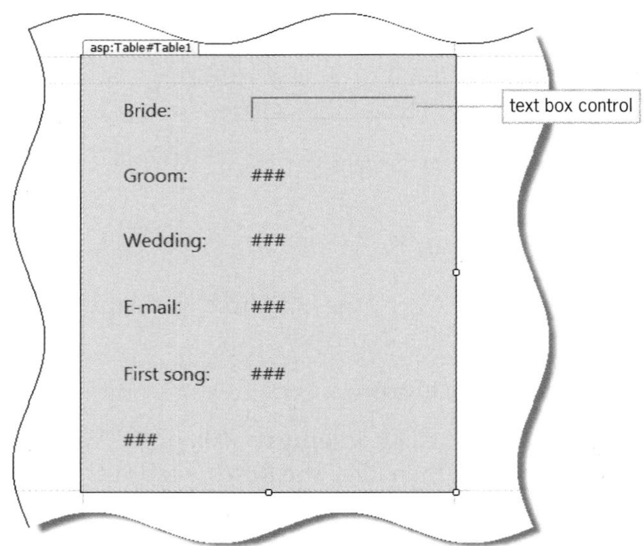

Figure 12-43 Text box control shown in the table

6. Click an **empty area** of the Web page to deselect the table control, then click the **Source** tab.

7. Now you will place a text box in the cell located in the second row, second column in the table. Locate the `<asp:TableCell ID="tblRow2Col2" runat="server"></asp:TableCell>` tag. Click immediately before the `</asp:TableCell>` closing tag, then press **Enter**. Drag a text box control to the immediate left of the `</asp:TableCell>` closing tag, then release the mouse button. Change the text box control's ID property to **"txtGroom"**.

8. Next, you will add a calendar control to the cell located in the second column of the table's third row. Locate the `<asp:TableCell ID="tblRow3Col2" runat="server"></asp:TableCell>` tag. Click immediately before the `</asp:TableCell>` closing tag, then press **Enter**. Click the **Calendar** tool in the toolbox. Drag a calendar control to the immediate left of the `</asp:TableCell>` closing tag, then release the mouse button. Change the calendar control's ID property to **"calWedding"**.

9. Now add a text box to the cell located in the second column of the fourth row. Locate the `<asp:TableCell ID="tblRow4Col2" runat="server"></asp:TableCell>` tag. Click immediately before the `</asp:TableCell>` closing tag, then press **Enter**. Drag a text box control to the immediate left of the `</asp:TableCell>` closing tag, then release the mouse button. Change the text box control's ID property to **"txtEmail"**.

10. Next, place a drop-down list control in the cell located in the second column of the fifth row. Locate the `<asp:TableCell ID="tblRow5Col2" runat="server"></asp:TableCell>` tag. Click immediately before the `</asp:TableCell>` closing tag, then press **Enter**. Click the **DropDownList** tool in the toolbox. Drag a drop-down list control to the immediate left of the `</asp:TableCell>` closing tag, then release the mouse button. Change the drop-down list control's ID property to **"ddlSongs"**.

11. Finally, add a button to the last row in the table. Locate the `<asp:TableCell ID="tblRow6Col1" runat="server"></asp:TableCell>` tag. Click immediately before the `</asp:TableCell>` closing tag, then press **Enter**. Drag a button control to the immediate left of the `</asp:TableCell>` closing tag, then release the mouse button.

12. In the `</asp:Button>` tag, change the ID property's value to **"btnSubmit"** and change the Text property's value to **"Submit"**.

13. Save the solution, then click the **Design** tab. See Figure 12-44.

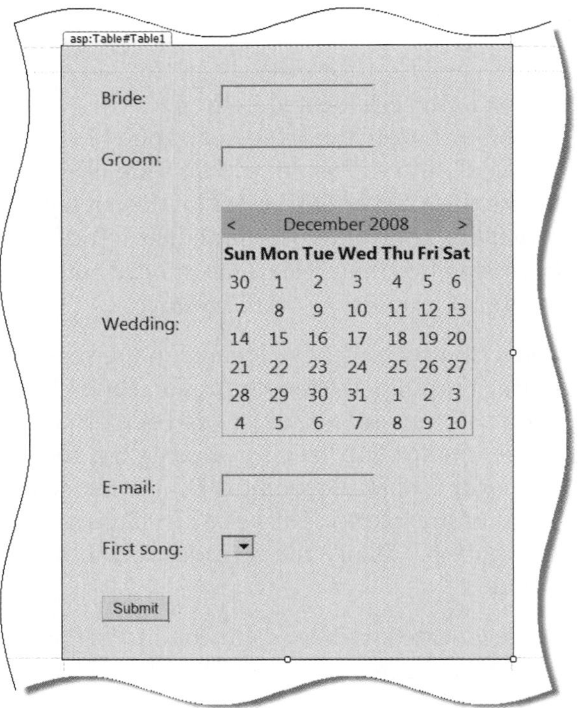

Figure 12-44 Controls added to the table

Adding Items to a DropDownList Control

Currently, the drop-down list control on DJ Tom's Web page does not contain any items. You add items to a drop-down list control using the **<asp:ListItem> tag**. In the next set of steps, you will add the following four song titles to the drop-down list control: From This Moment On, At Last, Because You Loved Me, and The Way You Look Tonight.

To add items to the drop-down list control:

1. Click an **empty area** of the Web page to deselect the table control, then click the **Source** tab.
2. Locate the `<asp:DropDownList ID="ddlSongs" runat="server">` tag. Click **immediately after the** > in the tag, then press **Enter**.

3. Press **Tab** to indent the line, then type **<asp:ListItem Text="From This Moment On">**. When you type the > symbol, the Source view editor automatically enters the closing `</asp:ListItem>` tag for you. See Figure 12-45.

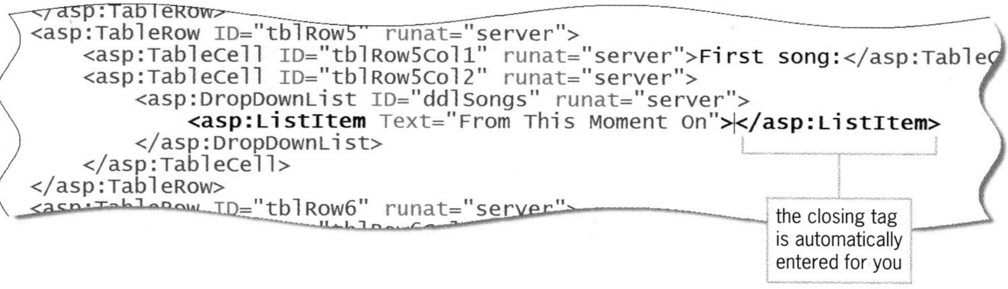

Figure 12-45 First song title added to the drop-down list control

4. Click **after the >** in the closing tag, then press **Enter**. Enter the three additional <asp:ListItem> tags indicated in Figure 12-46.

```
<asp:TableCell ID=...               runat="server">
    <asp:DropDownList ID="ddlSongs" runat="server">
        <asp:ListItem Text="From This Moment On"></asp:ListItem>
        <asp:ListItem Text="At Last"></asp:ListItem>
        <asp:ListItem Text="Because You Loved Me"></asp:ListItem>
        <asp:ListItem Text="The Way You Look Tonight"></asp:ListItem>
    </asp:DropDownList>
```

enter these three <asp:ListItem> tags

Figure 12-46 Remaining song titles added to the drop-down list control

5. Auto-hide the Toolbox window. Save the solution, then click the **Design** tab.

6. Press **F5** to start the application. If the Debugging Not Enabled dialog box appears, select the **Modify the Web.config file to enable debugging.** radio button (if necessary) and then click the **OK** button. If the Script Debugging Disabled dialog box appears, click the **Yes** button. Click the **down arrow** in the drop-down list control. See Figure 12-47.

Figure 12-47 Web page shown in a browser window

7. Close the browser window.

Coding DJ Tom's Web Page

Now that the interface is complete, you can code the Web page's Submit button. The button's Click event procedure will display a message in the lblMsg control. Recall that the control is contained in the MessageColumn on the Web page.

To code the Submit button's Click event procedure:

1. Right-click the **Web page**, then click **View Code** to open the Code Editor window. Enter the following comments. Replace the <your name> and <current date> text with your name and the current date. Press **Enter** twice after typing the last comment.

   ' Name: **DJTom**
   ' Purpose: **Display a message**
   ' Programmer: **<your name> on <current date>**

2. Now enter the following Option statements.

   Option Explicit On
   Option Strict On
   Option Infer Off

3. Open the code template for the btnSubmit control's Click event procedure. Type **' displays the user's input in a message** and press **Enter** twice.

4. First, declare variables to store the five input items. Enter the following Dim statements. Press **Enter** twice after typing the last statement.

   Dim strBride As String
   Dim strGroom As String
   Dim strWedDate As String
   Dim strEmail As String
   Dim strSong As String

5. Now assign the names of the bride and groom to the appropriate variables. Enter the following assignment statements.

   strBride = txtBride.Text.Trim
   strGroom = txtGroom.Text.Trim

6. Next, assign the date selected in the Calendar control to the `strWedDate` variable. The selected date is stored in the control's SelectedDate property. You can use the ToShortDateString method to convert the date to the String data type and, at the same time, format it as follows: mm/dd/yyyy. Enter the following assignment statement.

   strWedDate = calWedding.SelectedDate.ToShortDateString

The Calendar control also has a ToLongDateString method that formats the date as follows: day of the week, month name, day number, year number.

7. Now assign the e-mail address to the `strEmail` variable. Enter the following assignment statement.

   strEmail = txtEmail.Text.Trim

8. Next, assign the item selected in the drop-down list control to the `strSong` variable. The selected item is stored in the control's SelectedItem property. Type the following assignment statement, then press **Enter** twice.

   strSong = ddlSongs.SelectedItem.ToString

9. Finally, display the user's input in the lblMsg control. Enter the following lines of code. Be sure to include a space before each line continuation character.

```
lblMsg.Text = "Thank you " & strBride & " and " & strGroom _
      & " for visiting my Web site." _
      & "Wedding date: " & strWedDate _
      & "E-mail address: " & strEmail _
      & "Song: " & strSong
```

Now test the Submit button's Click event procedure to verify that its code is working correctly.

To test the Submit button's Click event procedure:

1. Save the solution, then start the application. If the Script Debugging Disabled dialog box appears, click the **Yes** button.

2. Click the **txtBride** control, then type **Pam**. Press **Tab**, then type **Nathan** in the txtGroom control.

3. Click **any date** in the Calendar control. Click the **txtEmail** control, then type **anyEmail@domain.com**. Click the **down arrow** in the drop-down list control, then click **Because You Loved Me** in the list.

4. Click the **Submit** button. The button's Click event procedure displays the message in the lblMsg control. See Figure 12-48. Notice that the message is difficult to read. It would be better if the "thank you" message, as well as the wedding date, e-mail address, and song title appeared on separate lines in the control. You will learn how to accomplish this in the next section.

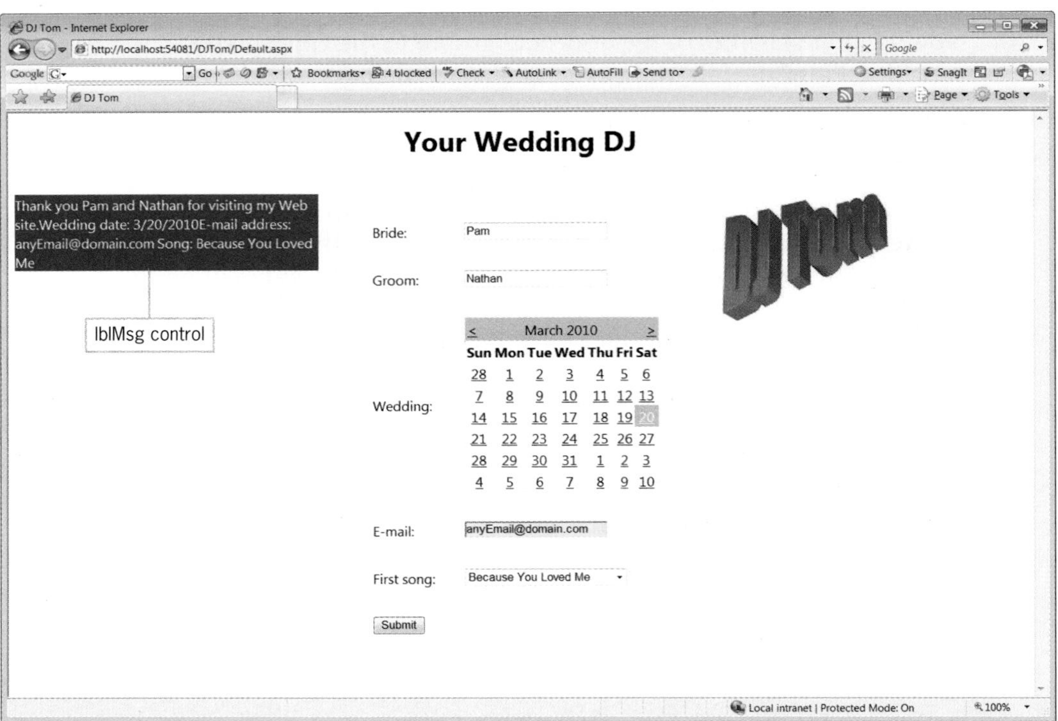

Figure 12-48 Message displayed in the lblMsg control

5. Close the browser window.

Using the
 Tag

At times, you may need to break the text on a Web page in a specific location. You can do this using the <br /> tag. The "br" in the tag stands for "break." The **
 tag** in a Web page is similar to the `ControlChars.NewLine` constant in a Windows form: both are used to create a new line. In DJ Tom's Web page, you will use the <br /> tag to separate the wedding date information from the "thank you" message. You also will use it to display the e-mail information and song information on separate lines in the lblMsg control.

To use the <br /> tag to separate the text in the lblMsg control, and then test the code:

1. Modify the btnSubmit control's Click event procedure as shown in Figure 12-49. The modifications are shaded in the figure.

```
Protected Sub btnSubmit_Click(ByVal sender As Object, _
     ByVal e As System.EventArgs) Handles btnSubmit.Click
     ' displays the user's input in a message

     Dim strBride As String
     Dim strGroom As String
     Dim strWedDate As String
     Dim strEmail As String
     Dim strSong As String

     strBride = txtBride.Text.Trim
     strGroom = txtGroom.Text.Trim
     strWedDate = calWedding.SelectedDate.ToShortDateString
     strEmail = txtEmail.Text.Trim
     strSong = ddlSongs.SelectedItem.ToString

     lblMsg.Text = "Thank you " & strBride & " and " & strGroom _
         & " for visiting my Web site." _
         & "<br /><br />Wedding date: " & strWedDate _
         & "<br />E-mail address: " & strEmail _
         & "<br />Song: " & strSong

End Sub
```

be sure to enter the <br /> tags after the quotation mark

Figure 12-49 Modified Click event procedure for the btnSubmit control

2. Save the solution, then start the application. If the Script Debugging Disabled dialog box appears, click the **Yes** button.

3. Type **Pam** as the bride's name, then type **Nathan** as the groom's name. Click **any date** in the Calendar control. Click the **txtE-mail** control, then type **anyEmail@domain.com**. Click the **down arrow** in the drop-down list control, then click **Because You Loved Me** in the list.

4. Click the **Submit** button. The button's Click event procedure displays the message in the lblMsg control. See Figure 12-50.

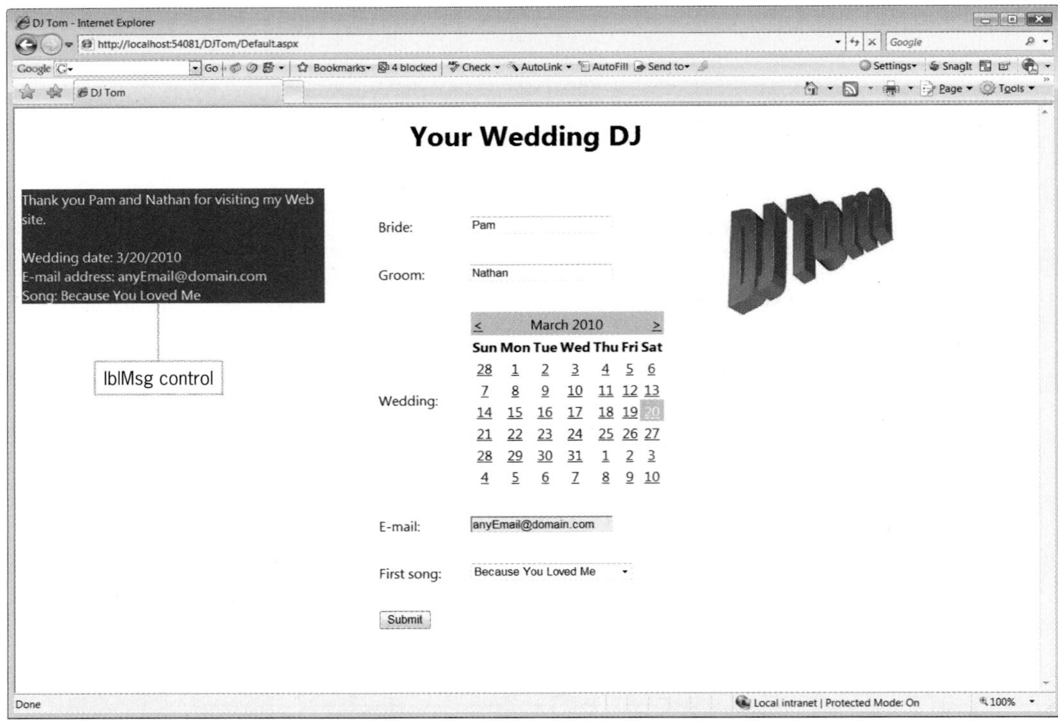

Figure 12-50 Message displayed on separate lines in the lblMsg control

5. Close the browser window. Close the Code Editor window, then close the solution.

Lesson C Summary

- **To set the font for the text on a Web page:**

  Assign one or more fonts to the style attribute's font-family property in the <body> tag.

- **To divide a Web page into columns:**

  Use the <div> tag. Assign a name to the column using the id attribute. Assign a percentage to the style attribute's width property. Assign either left or right to the style attribute's float property.

- **To use an ASP table:**

  Drag a table control from the Standard section of the toolbox. The table's CellSpacing property controls the spacing between the table cells. Its HorizontalAlign property controls its alignment on the Web page. Use the Rows property to add rows and columns (cells) to the table. It's helpful to set the ID property for each row and each cell.

- **To place a control in an ASP table:**

  Open the Web page in Source view. Drag the control to a location immediately before the desired cell's closing tag.

- **To add items to a drop-down list control:**

  Use a separate <asp:ListItem> tag for each item. In each tag, set the item's Text property. Place the tags between the opening <asp:DropDownList> and closing </asp:DropDownList> tags.

- **To determine the date selected in a Calendar control:**

  Use the control's SelectedDate property.

- **To format the date selected in a Calendar control:**

  Use the control's ToShortDateString method to format the date as follows: mm/dd/yyyy. Use the control's ToLongDateString method to format the date as follows: day of the week, month name, day number, year number.

- **To determine the item selected in a drop-down list control:**

  Use the control's SelectedItem property.

- **To create a new line on a Web page from code:**

  Use the <br /> tag.

Lesson C Key Terms

<asp:ListItem> tag—used to add items to a drop-down list control

**
 tag**—used to create a new line on a Web page or in a control

<div> tag—create a division on a Web page; can be used to divide a Web page into columns

ASP table control—displays information in a row and column format; can be used to align information on a Web page

Cell—the intersection of a row and column in a table

font-family property—a property of the style attribute; used to assign one or more fonts to be used for text

Lesson C Review Questions

1. Which of the following specifies the fonts to use for the text on a Web page?
   a. `style="font-family:Segoe UI, Arial, Sans-Serif"`
   b. `style="fonts:Segoe UI, Arial, Sans-Serif"`
   c. `style:"font-family=Segoe UI, Arial, Sans-Serif"`
   d. `style:"fonts=Segoe UI, Arial, Sans-Serif"`

2. Which of the following specifies that Col1 should occupy 15% of the Web page and be positioned on the right?
   a. <div id="Col1" "width:15%; position:right">
   b. <div id="Col1" style="width:15%; float:right">
   c. <div id="Col1" "position:right; column:15%">
   d. <div id="Col1" style="width:15%; position:right">

3. Which of the following adds the word "Dog" to a drop-down list control?
   a. <asp:ListItem Caption="Dog">
   b. <asp:ListItem Item="Dog">
   c. <asp:Item Text="Dog">
   d. None of the above.

4. The item selected in a drop-down list control is stored in the control's ______________________ property.
   a. Item
   b. Selected
   c. SelectedItem
   d. None of the above.

5. The date selected in a Calendar control is stored in the control's ______________________ property.
   a. Date
   b. SelectedDate
   c. DateSelection
   d. None of the above.

6. You can use the ______________________ tag to display text on the next line in a control.
   a.
   b. <break>
   c. <newline>
   d. None of the above.

Lesson C Exercises

1. In this exercise, you modify the DJ Tom application created in the lesson. INTRODUCTORY

   a. Create a new Web application named **DJTomIntro1**. Save the application in the VB2008\Chap12 folder. Close the DJTomIntro1 solution.

   b. Use Windows to open the DJTomIntro1 folder. Delete the folder's contents.

   c. Use Windows to open the DJTom folder, which is contained in the VB2008\Chap12 folder. Copy the folder's contents to the DJTom-Intro1 folder.

   d. Open the DJTomIntro1 folder in Visual Studio (or Visual Web Developer). If necessary, right-click Default.aspx in the Solution Explorer window, then click View Designer.

   e. Drag a RegularExpressionValidator control to the Web page. Don't be concerned about the control's location. The control will verify the format of the e-mail address entered by the user. Change the ErrorMessage, ValidationExpression, and ControlToValidate properties to " Invalid", Internet e-mail address, and "txtEmail", respectively. Click the Source tab. Cut the control's asp tag, then paste the tag before the txtEmail control's </asp:TableCell> tag. Click the Design tab.

   f. Save the solution, then start the application. If the Script Debugging Disabled dialog box appears, click the Yes button. Test the application. Close the browser window, then close the solution.

2. In this exercise, you modify the DJ Tom application created in the lesson. INTRODUCTORY

   a. Create a new Web application named **DJTomIntro2**. Save the application in the VB2008\Chap12 folder. Close the DJTomIntro2 solution.

   b. Use Windows to open the DJTomIntro2 folder. Delete the folder's contents.

   c. Use Windows to open the DJTom folder, which is contained in the VB2008\Chap12 folder. Copy the folder's contents to the DJTom-Intro2 folder.

   d. Open the DJTomIntro2 folder in Visual Studio (or Visual Web Developer). If necessary, right-click Default.aspx in the Solution Explorer window, then click View Designer.

e. Open the Web page in Source view. Add the titles of any four additional songs to the drop-down list control.

f. Save the solution, then start the application. If the Script Debugging Disabled dialog box appears, click the Yes button. Test the application. Close the browser window, then close the solution.

INTERMEDIATE

3. In this exercise, you modify the DJ Tom application created in the lesson.

   a. Create a new Web application named **DJTomIntermediate**. Save the application in the VB2008\Chap12 folder. Close the DJTom-Intermediate solution.

   b. Use Windows to open the DJTomIntermediate folder. Delete the folder's contents.

   c. Use Windows to open the DJTom folder, which is contained in the VB2008\Chap12 folder. Copy the folder's contents to the DJTom-Intermediate folder.

   d. Open the DJTomIntermediate folder in Visual Studio (or Visual Web Developer). If necessary, right-click Default.aspx in the Solution Explorer window, then click View Designer.

   e. Open the Web page in Source view. Locate the asp tag for the last table row. Change tblRow6 and tblRow6Col1 to tblRow8 and tblRow8Col1, respectively. Add two rows to the table. The rows should be added above the last row in the table. Both rows should contain two cells. In the first new row, enter the text "Father/Daughter:" (without the quotes) in the first column, and place a drop-down list control in the second column. In the second new row, enter the text "Mother/Son:" (without the quotes) in the first column, and place a drop-down list control in the second column. Add the titles of any four songs to the drop-down list control in the first new row. Add the titles of any three songs to the drop-down list control in the second new row.

   f. Save the solution, then switch to Design view. Open the Code Editor window and modify the code to display the additional user input in the lblMsg control.

   g. Save the solution, then start the application. If the Script Debugging Disabled dialog box appears, click the Yes button. Test the application. Close the browser window, then close the Code Editor window and solution.

INTERMEDIATE

4. Create a Web application named MarketFoods. Save the application in the VB2008\Chap12 folder. Change the DOCUMENT's Title property to Market Foods. Create a Web page similar to the sketch shown in Figure 12-51. The DropDownList control should contain the store numbers listed in Figure 12-52. When the user clicks the Submit button, the button's Click event procedure should display the names of the manager and assistant manager on the Web page. Open the Code Editor window. Enter the appropriate comments and Option statements. Code the button's Click event procedure. Save the solution, then start and test the application. Close the browser window, then close the Code Editor window and solution.

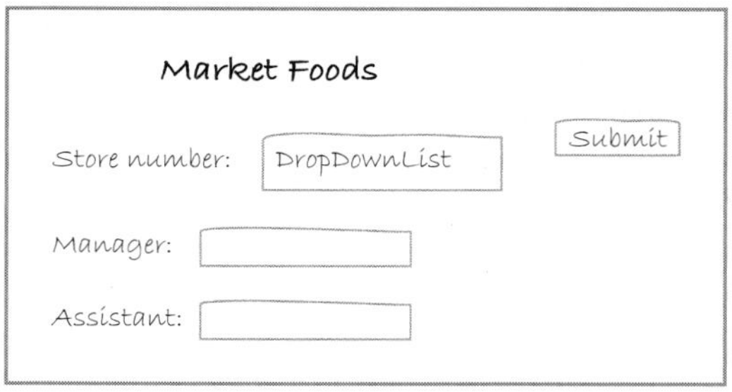

Figure 12-51 Sketch for the Market Foods application

Store number	Manager	Assistant manager
1001	Jeffrey Jefferson	Paula Hendricks
1002	Barbara Millerton	Sung Lee
1003	Inez Baily	Homer Gomez
1004	Lou Chan	Jake Johansen
1005	Henry Abernathy	Ingrid Nadkarni

Figure 12-52 Store information for the Market Foods application

INTERMEDIATE

5. Create a Web application named SalesTax. Save the application in the VB2008\Chap12 folder. Change the DOCUMENT's Title property to Sales Tax Calculator. Create a Web page similar to the sketch shown in Figure 12-53. The application should allow the user to enter the sales. When the user clicks the Calculate button, the button's Click event procedure should calculate both a 5% sales tax and a 6% sales tax, and then display both amounts on the Web page. Save the solution, then start and test the application. Close the browser window, then close the solution.

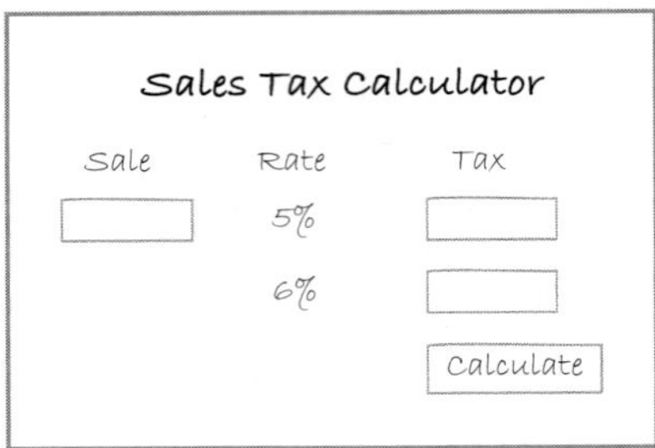

Figure 12-53 Sketch for the Sales Tax Calculator application

ADVANCED

6. Create a Web application named SkateAway. Save the application in the VB2008\Chap12 folder. Change the DOCUMENT's Title property to Skate-Away Sales. The Skate-Away Sales company sells skateboards by phone. The skateboards are priced at $100 each and are available in two colors: yellow and blue. The application should allow the salesperson to enter the customer's name and the number of blue and yellow skateboards ordered. It should calculate the total number of skateboards ordered and the total price of the order, including a 5% sales tax. Create an appropriate Web page. Save the solution, then start and test the application. Close the browser window, then close the Code Editor window and solution.

CHAPTER 13

Working with Access Databases and LINQ

Creating the Paradise Bookstore Application

In this chapter, you will create an application for the Paradise Bookstore. The application will display the records contained in a Microsoft Access 2007 database named Books. The application will allow the store manager to enter an author's name (or part of a name), and then display only the books written by the author. In addition, the application will allow the store manager to display the total value of the books in the store.

Previewing the Paradise Bookstore Application

To open the Run dialog box, press and hold down the Windows logo key as you tap the letter r, then release the logo key.

To preview the completed Paradise Bookstore application:

1. Use the Run dialog box to run the **Paradise** (**Paradise.exe**) file, which is contained in the VB2008\Chap13 folder. The application's user interface appears on the screen, with 11 records shown in a DataGridView control.
2. Display only the books written by Carol Smith. Click the **Author** text box, then type **Smith, C** (be sure to include a space after the comma). Click the **Go** button. See Figure 13-1.

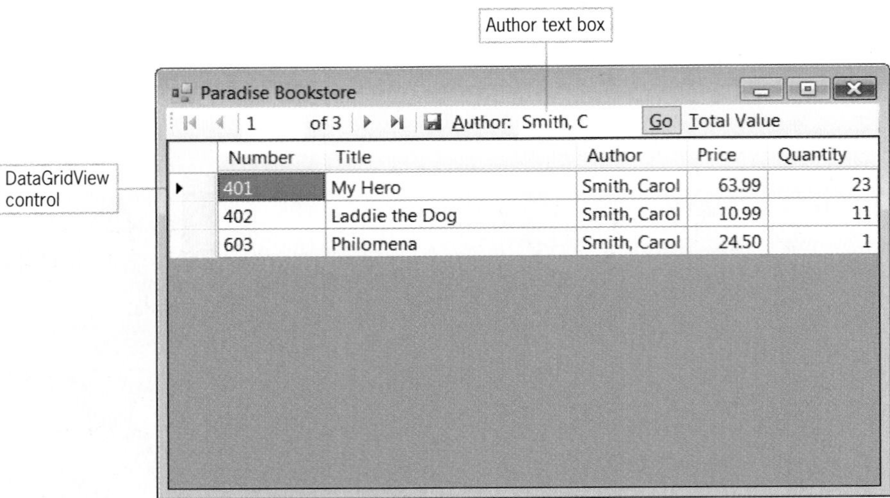

Figure 13-1 Books written by Carol Smith

3. Now display all of the records. Remove the Smith, C text from the Author text box, then click the **Go** button. The 11 records appear in the DataGridView control.
4. Finally, display the total value of the books in the store. Click the **Total Value** button. The number $3,921.72 appears in a message box.
5. Click the **OK** button to close the message box, then click the **Close** button on the form's title bar to stop the application.

In Lesson A, you will learn how to connect an application to a Microsoft Access database. Lesson B will show you how to query a database using LINQ, which stands for Language Integrated Query. You will complete the Paradise Bookstore application in Lesson C.

LESSON A

After studying Lesson A, you should be able to:

- Define the terms used when talking about databases
- Connect an application to a Microsoft Access database
- Bind table and field objects to controls
- Explain the purpose of the DataSet, BindingSource, TableAdapter, TableAdapterManager, and BindingNavigator objects
- Customize a DataGridView control
- Handle errors using the Try...Catch statement
- Position the record pointer in a dataset

Database Terminology

In order to maintain accurate records, most businesses store information about their employees, customers, and inventory in computer databases. A **computer database** is an electronic file that contains an organized collection of related information. Many products exist for creating computer databases; such products are called database management systems (or DBMS). Some of the most popular database management systems are Microsoft Access, Microsoft SQL Server, and Oracle. You can use Visual Basic to access the data stored in databases created by these database management systems. This allows a company to create a standard interface in Visual Basic that employees can use to access information stored in a variety of database formats. Instead of learning each DBMS's user interface, the employee needs to know only one interface. The actual format of the database is unimportant and will be transparent to the user.

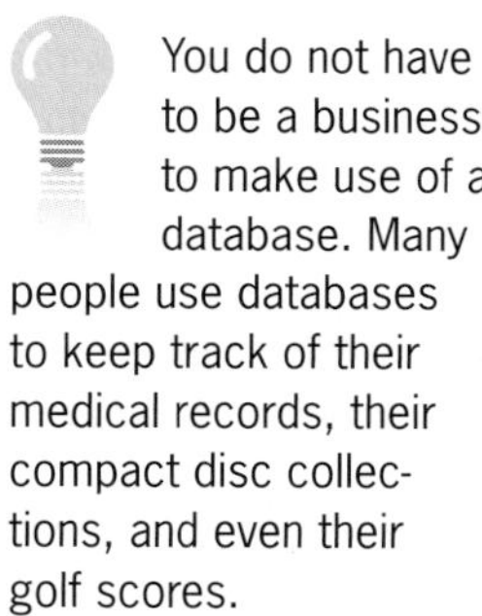

You do not have to be a business to make use of a database. Many people use databases to keep track of their medical records, their compact disc collections, and even their golf scores.

In this chapter, you will learn how to access the data stored in Microsoft Access databases. Databases created using Microsoft Access are relational databases. A **relational database** is one that stores information in tables composed of columns and rows, similar to the format used in a spreadsheet. Each column in a table represents a field and each row represents a record. A **field** is a single item of information about a person, place, or thing—such as a name, a salary amount, a Social Security number, or a price. A **record** is a group of related fields that contain all of the necessary data about a specific person, place, or thing. The college you are attending keeps a student record on you. Examples of fields contained in your student record include your Social Security number, name, address, phone number, credits earned, and grades earned. The place where you are employed also keeps a record on you. Your employee record contains your Social Security number, name, address, phone number, starting date, salary or hourly wage, and so on. A group of related records is called a **table**. Each record in a table pertains to the same topic, and each contains the same type of information. In other words, each record in a table contains the same fields.

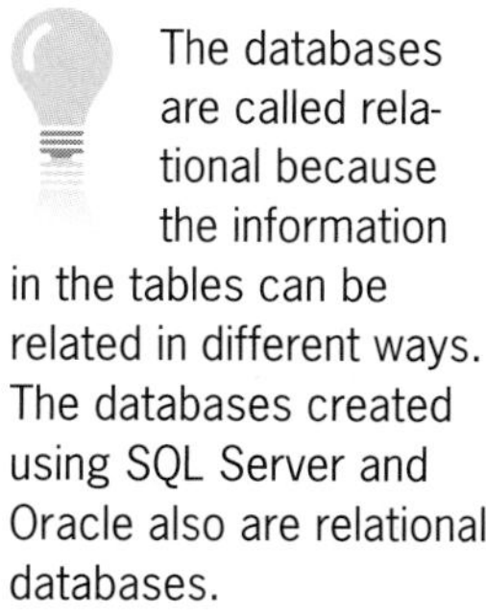

The databases are called relational because the information in the tables can be related in different ways. The databases created using SQL Server and Oracle also are relational databases.

A relational database can contain one or more tables. A one-table database would be a good choice for storing information about the college courses you have taken. An example of such a table is shown in Figure 13-2. Each record in the table contains four fields: an ID field that indicates the department name and course number, a course title field, a number of credit hours field, and a grade field. In most tables, one of the fields uniquely identifies each record and is called the **primary key**. In the table shown in Figure 13-2, you could use either the ID field or the Title field as the primary key, because the data in those fields will be unique for each record.

ID	Title	Hours	Grade
CIS100	Intro to Computers	3	A
ENG100	English Composition	3	B
PHIL105	Philosophy Seminar	2	C
CIS201	Visual Basic 2008	3	A

Figure 13-2 Example of a one-table relational database

Parent and child tables also are referred to as master and detail tables, respectively.

You might use a two-table database to store information about a CD (compact disc) collection. You would store the general information about each CD (such as the CD's name and the artist's name) in one table, and store the information about the songs on each CD (such as their title and track number) in the other table. You then would use a common field—for example, a CD number—to relate the records contained in both tables. Figure 13-3 shows an example of a two-table database that stores CD information. The first table is referred to as the **parent table**, and the second table is referred to as the **child table**. The CD_Number field is the primary key in the parent table, because it uniquely identifies each record in the table. The CD_Number field in the child table is used solely to link the song title and track information to the appropriate CD in the parent table. In the child table, the CD_Number field is called the **foreign key**.

CD_Number	Name	Artist
01	Western Way	Dolly Draton
02	Midnight Blue	Paul Elliot

the two tables are related by the CD_Number field

CD_Number	Song_Title	Track
01	Country	1
01	Night on the Road	2
01	Old Times	3
02	Lovely Nights	1
02	Colors	2
02	Heavens	3

Figure 13-3 Example of a two-table relational database

Storing data in a relational database offers many advantages. The computer can retrieve data stored in a relational format both quickly and easily, and the data can be displayed in any order. The information in the CD database, for example, can be arranged by artist name, song title, and so on. You also can control the amount of information you want to view from a relational database. You can view all of the information in the CD database, or you can view only the information pertaining to a certain artist, or only the names of the songs contained on a specific CD.

Connecting an Application to a Microsoft Access Database

In this lesson, you will use a Microsoft Access database named Employees. The Employees database is stored in the Employees.accdb file, which is located in the VB2008\Chap13\Access Databases folder. The .accdb filename extension stands for Access Database and indicates that the database was created using Microsoft Access 2007. The Employees database contains one table, which is named tblEmploy. Figure 13-4 shows the table data displayed in a window in the IDE. The table contains seven fields and 12 records. The Emp_Number field is the primary key, because it uniquely identifies each record in the table. The Status field contains the employment status, which is either the letter F (for full-time) or the letter P (for part-time). The Code field identifies the employee's department: 1 for Accounting, 2 for Advertising, 3 for Personnel, and 4 for Inventory.

To open a database table in the IDE, first connect the database to an application, then right-click the table's name in the Server Explorer (Database Explorer if you are using Visual Basic 2008 Express Edition) window, and then click Retrieve Data.

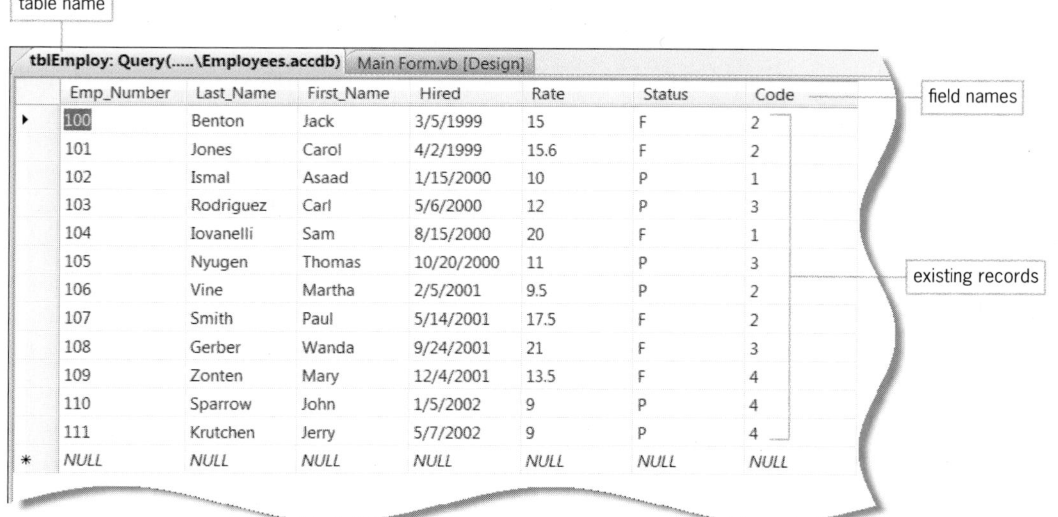

	Emp_Number	Last_Name	First_Name	Hired	Rate	Status	Code
▸	100	Benton	Jack	3/5/1999	15	F	2
	101	Jones	Carol	4/2/1999	15.6	F	2
	102	Ismal	Asaad	1/15/2000	10	P	1
	103	Rodriguez	Carl	5/6/2000	12	P	3
	104	Iovanelli	Sam	8/15/2000	20	F	1
	105	Nyugen	Thomas	10/20/2000	11	P	3
	106	Vine	Martha	2/5/2001	9.5	P	2
	107	Smith	Paul	5/14/2001	17.5	F	2
	108	Gerber	Wanda	9/24/2001	21	F	3
	109	Zonten	Mary	12/4/2001	13.5	F	4
	110	Sparrow	John	1/5/2002	9	P	4
	111	Krutchen	Jerry	5/7/2002	9	P	4
*	NULL	NULL	NULL	NULL	NULL	NULL	NULL

Figure 13-4 Data contained in the tblEmploy table

Before an application can access the data stored in a database, you need to connect the application to the database. You also need to specify the data you want to access from the database. The computer makes a copy of the data and stores it in its internal memory. The copy of the data you want to access is called a **dataset**. You can connect an application to a database using the Data Source Configuration Wizard. In the following set of steps, you will connect the Morgan Industries application to the Employees database.

To open the Morgan Industries application, then connect the application to the database:

1. If necessary, start Visual Studio 2008 or Visual Basic 2008 Express Edition. Close the Start Page window. If necessary, permanently display the Solution Explorer window.

2. Open the **Morgan Industries Solution** (**Morgan Industries Solution.sln**) file, which is contained in the VB2008\Chap13\Morgan Industries Solution-DataGridView folder. Open the designer window.

In Visual Basic 2008 Express Edition, the Server Explorer window is called the Database Explorer window.

3. Click **View** on the menu bar, then click **Server (Database) Explorer** to open the Server (Database) Explorer window, which lists the available connections.

4. Click **Data** on the menu bar, then click **Show Data Sources** to open the Data Sources window.

5. Click **Add New Data Source** in the Data Sources window to start the Data Source Configuration Wizard, which displays the Choose a Data Source Type screen. If necessary, click **Database**. See Figure 13-5.

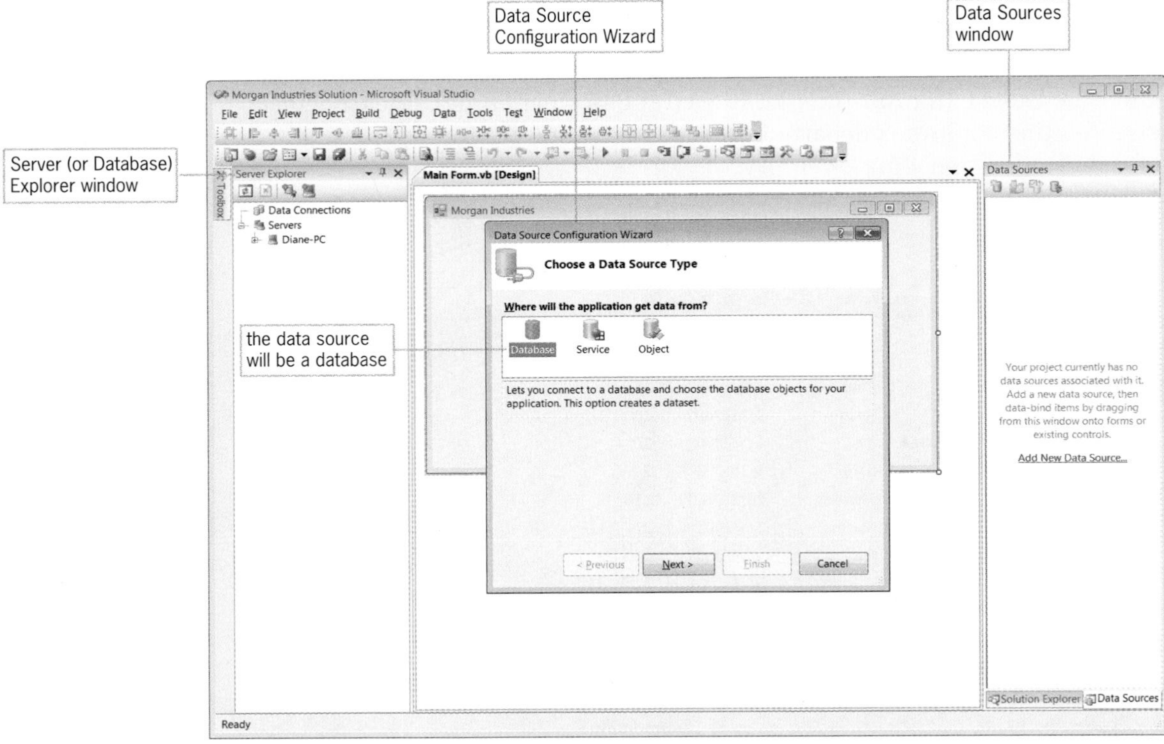

Figure 13-5 Data Source Configuration Wizard dialog box

6. Click the **Next** button to display the Choose Your Data Connection screen. Click the **New Connection** button to display the Add Connection dialog box. (If the Choose Data Source dialog box opens instead, click Microsoft Access Database File, then click the Continue button to open the Add Connection dialog box.) If Microsoft Access Database File (OLE DB) does not appear in the Data source box, click the **Change** button to open the Change Data Source dialog box, then click **Microsoft Access Database File**, and then click the **OK** button to return to the Add Connection dialog box.

7. Click the **Browse** button in the Add Connection dialog box. Open the VB2008\Chap13\Access Databases folder, then click **Employees.accdb** in the list of filenames. Click the **Open** button. Figure 13-6 shows the completed Add Connection dialog box. The dialog box in the figure has been widened to show the entire entry in the Database file name box. It is not necessary for you to widen the dialog box.

Figure 13-6 Completed Add Connection dialog box

8. Click the **Test Connection** button in the Add Connection dialog box. The "Test connection succeeded." message appears in a message box. Click the **OK** button to close the message box.

9. Click the **OK** button to close the Add Connection dialog box. Employees.accdb appears in the Choose Your Data Connection screen. Click the **Next** button. A message similar to the one shown in Figure 13-7 appears in a message box. The message asks whether you want to include the database file in the current project. By including the file in the current project, you can more easily copy the application and its database to another computer.

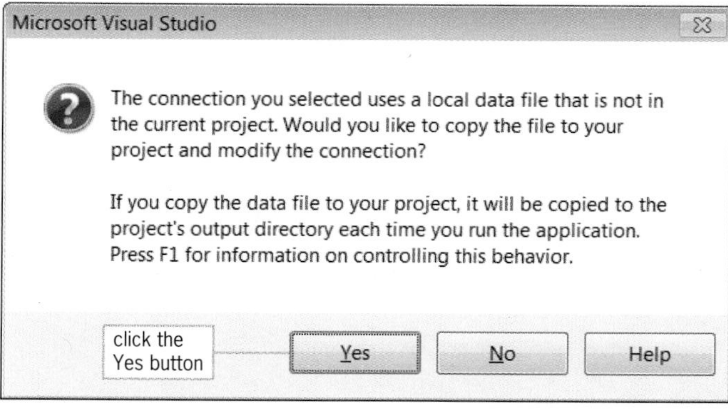

Figure 13-7 Message regarding copying the database file

10. Click the **Yes** button to add the Employees.accdb file to the current project. The file is added to the application's project folder. The Save the Connection String to the Application Configuration File screen appears next. The name of the connection string, EmployeesConnectionString, appears on the screen. See Figure 13-8. If necessary, select the **Yes, save the connection as** check box.

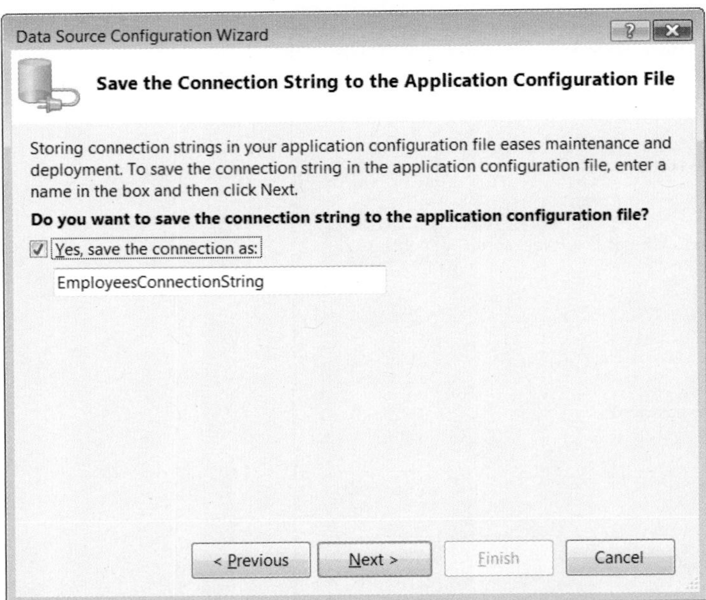

Figure 13-8 Save the Connection String to the Application Configuration File screen

11. Click the **Next** button to display the Choose Your Database Objects screen. Click the **plus box** next to Tables, then click the **plus box** next to tblEmploy. You can use this screen to select the table or field objects to include in the dataset, which is automatically named EmployeesDataSet.

12. In this application, you need to include all of the fields in the dataset. Click the **empty box** next to tblEmploy. Doing this selects the table and field check boxes. See Figure 13-9.

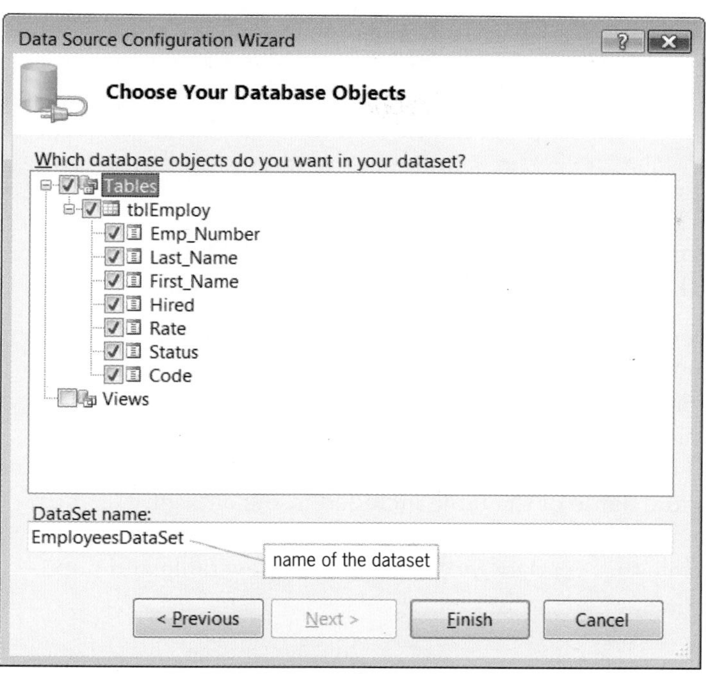

Figure 13-9 Objects selected in the Choose Your Database Objects screen

13. Click the **Finish** button. After connecting the application to the database, the Data Source Configuration Wizard adds several files to the project; the filenames appear in the Solution Explorer window. Click the **Solution Explorer** tab to view the names of the additional files. The Wizard also lists a connection to the database file in the Server (Database) Explorer window and adds a dataset's name to the Data Sources window. Click the **Data Sources** tab, then click the **plus box** next to tblEmploy in the Data Sources window. Also click the **plus box** next to Employees.accdb in the Server (Database) Explorer window, then click the **plus box** next to Tables, and then click the **plus box** next to tblEmploy. See Figure 13-10. The dataset contains one table and seven field objects.

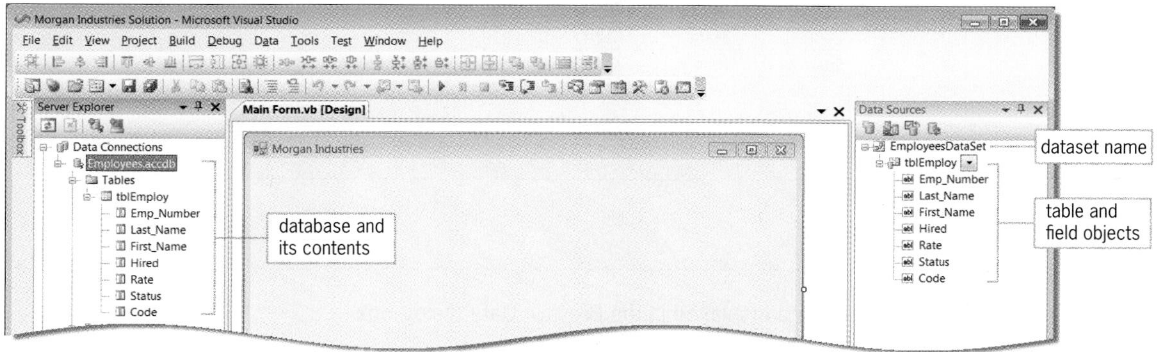

Figure 13-10 Result of running the Data Source Configuration Wizard

Previewing the Contents of a Dataset

After an application has been connected to a database, you can use the Preview Data option on the Data menu to view the fields and records in the dataset.

To view the contents of the EmployeesDataSet:

1. Click the **form** to make it the active window. Click **Data** on the menu bar, then click **Preview Data**. The Preview Data dialog box opens.
2. Click the **Preview** button. As Figure 13-11 shows, the Employees-DataSet contains 12 records (rows), each having 7 fields (columns). Notice that `EmployeesDataSet.tblEmploy.Fill, GetData()` appears in the Select an object to preview box in the figure. EmployeesDataSet is the name of the dataset in the application, and tblEmploy is the name of the table included in the dataset. Fill and GetData are methods. The Fill method populates an existing table with data, while the GetData method creates a new table and populates it with data.

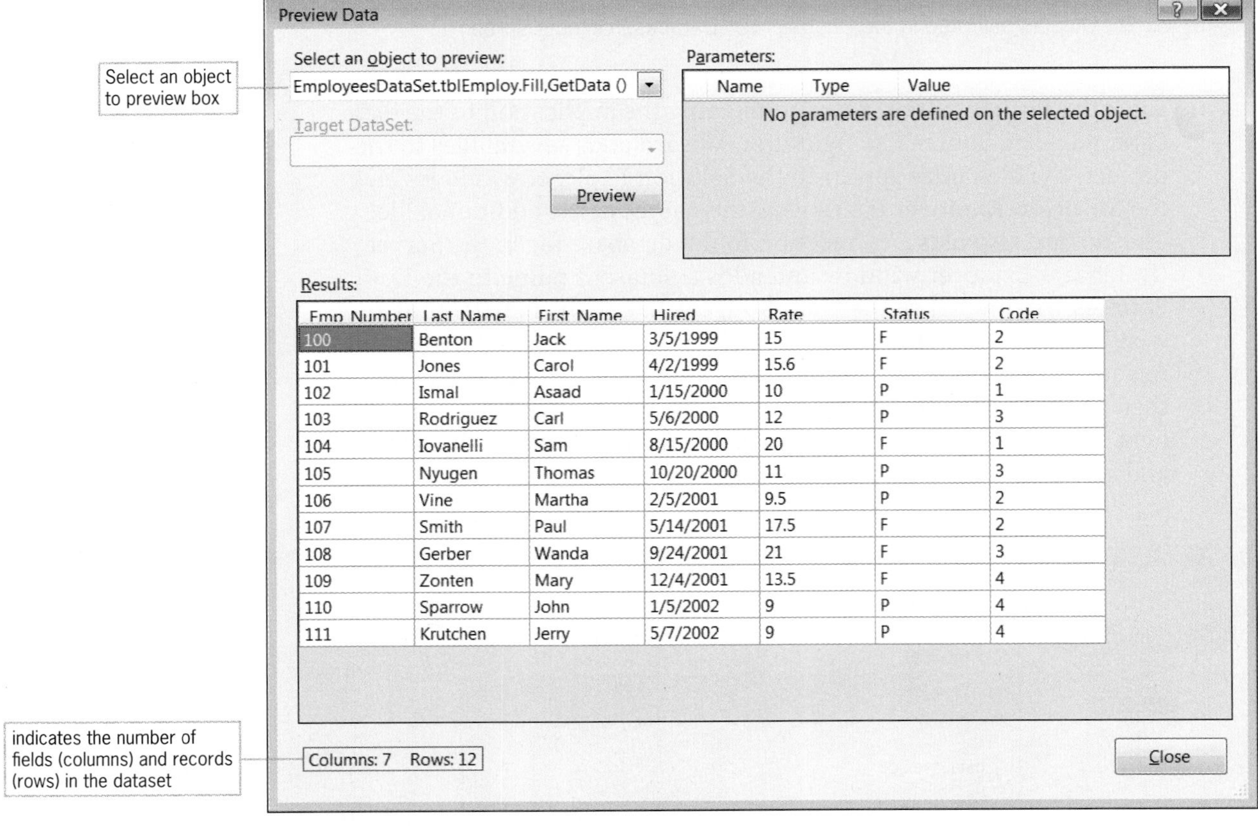

Emp Number	Last Name	First Name	Hired	Rate	Status	Code
100	Benton	Jack	3/5/1999	15	F	2
101	Jones	Carol	4/2/1999	15.6	F	2
102	Ismal	Asaad	1/15/2000	10	P	1
103	Rodriguez	Carl	5/6/2000	12	P	3
104	Iovanelli	Sam	8/15/2000	20	F	1
105	Nyugen	Thomas	10/20/2000	11	P	3
106	Vine	Martha	2/5/2001	9.5	P	2
107	Smith	Paul	5/14/2001	17.5	F	2
108	Gerber	Wanda	9/24/2001	21	F	3
109	Zonten	Mary	12/4/2001	13.5	F	4
110	Sparrow	John	1/5/2002	9	P	4
111	Krutchen	Jerry	5/7/2002	9	P	4

Figure 13-11 Data displayed in the Preview Data dialog box

3. Click the **Close** button to close the Preview Data dialog box.
4. Close the Server (Database) Explorer window, then save the solution.

Binding the Objects in a Dataset

For the user to view the contents of a dataset while an application is running, you need to connect one or more objects in the dataset to one or more controls in the interface. Connecting an object to a control is called **binding**, and the connected controls are called **bound controls**. Figure 13-12 shows various ways of binding an object in a dataset. You can bind the object to a control that the computer creates for you; or, you can bind it to an existing control in the interface. In the next section, you will learn how to have the computer create a bound control. You will learn how to bind to an existing control later in this lesson.

Bound controls also are referred to as data-aware controls.

Binding an object in a dataset

To have the computer create a control and then bind an object to it:
In the Data Sources window, click the object you want to bind. If necessary, use the object's list arrow to change the control type. Drag the object to an empty area on the form, then release the mouse button.

To bind an object to an existing control:
In the Data Sources window, click the object you want to bind. Drag the object to the control on the form, then release the mouse button. Alternatively, you can click the control on the form and then use the Properties window to set the appropriate property or properties. (Refer to the *Binding to an Existing Control* section in this lesson.)

Figure 13-12 Ways to bind an object in a dataset

Having the Computer Create a Bound Control

As indicated in Figure 13-12, when you drag an object from a dataset to an empty area on the form, the computer creates a control and automatically binds the object to it. The icon that appears before the object's name in the Data Sources window indicates the type of control the computer will create. The icon in Figure 13-13 indicates that a DataGridView control will be created when you drag the tblEmploy table object to the form. A **DataGridView control** displays the table data in a row and columnar format, similar to a spreadsheet. Each row in the control represents a record, and each column represents a field. You will learn more about the DataGridView control in the next section. The abl icon, also shown in Figure 13-13, indicates that the computer will create a text box when you drag a field object to the form.

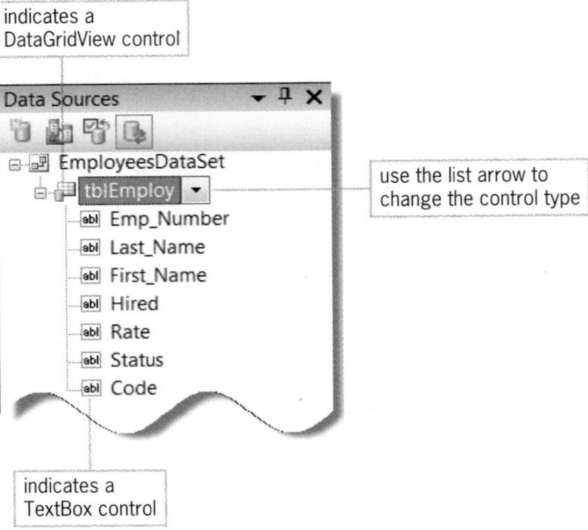

Figure 13-13 Icons in the Data Sources window

You can use the list arrow that appears next to an object's name to change the type of control the computer creates. To display the tblEmploy data in separate text boxes rather than in a DataGridView control, you click tblEmploy in the Data Sources window, then click the tblEmploy list arrow. See Figure 13-14. Clicking the Details option tells the computer to create a separate control for each field in the table.

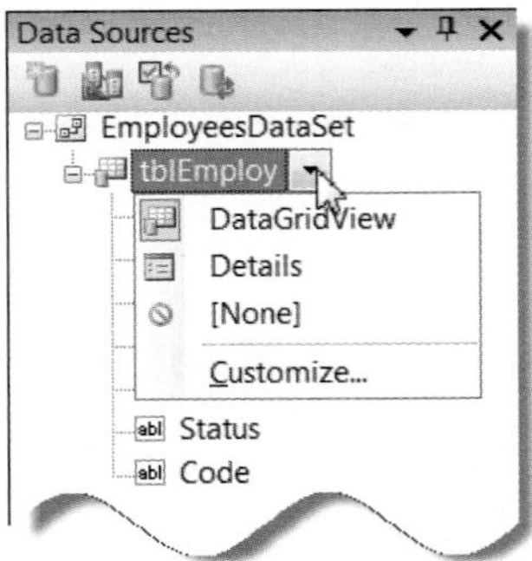

Figure 13-14 Result of clicking the tblEmploy object's list arrow

Similarly, to display the Last_Name field data in a label control rather than in a text box, you first click Last_Name in the Data Sources window. You then click the field's list arrow, as shown in Figure 13-15, and then click Label in the list.

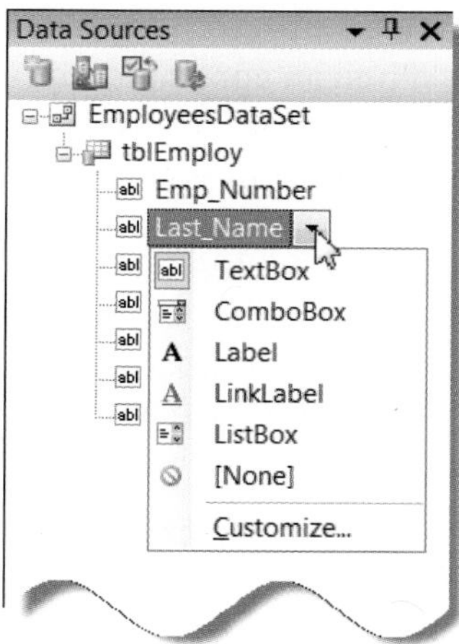

Figure 13-15 Result of clicking the Last_Name object's list arrow

In the following set of steps, you will drag the tblEmploy object from the Data Sources window to the form, using the default control type for a table.

To bind the tblEmploy object to a DataGridView control:

1. If necessary, click **tblEmploy** in the Data Sources window to select the tblEmploy object.
2. Drag the tblEmploy object from the Data Sources window to the form, then release the mouse button. The computer adds a DataGridView control to the form, and it binds the tblEmploy object to the control. See Figure 13-16.

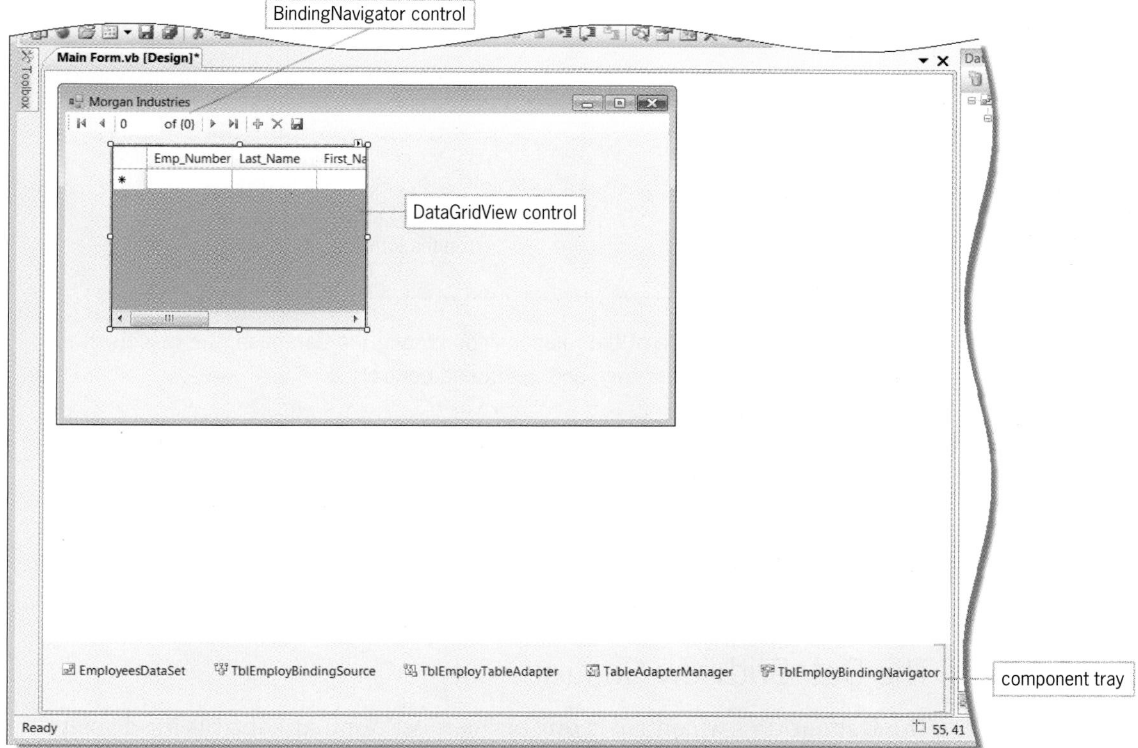

Figure 13-16 Result of dragging the table object to the form

As Figure 13-16 shows, besides adding a DataGridView control to the form, the computer also adds a BindingNavigator control. When an application is running, you can use the **BindingNavigator control** to move from one record to the next in the dataset, as well as to add or delete a record and save any changes made to the dataset. The computer also places five objects in the component tray: a DataSet, BindingSource, TableAdapter, TableAdapter-Manager, and BindingNavigator. As you learned in Chapter 1, the component tray stores objects that do not appear in the user interface while an application is running. An exception to this is the BindingNavigator object, which appears as the BindingNavigator control during both design time and run time.

The **TableAdapter object** connects the database to the **DataSet object**, which stores the information you want to access from the database. The TableAdapter is responsible for retrieving the appropriate information from the database and storing it in the DataSet. It also can be used to save to the database any changes made to the data contained in the DataSet. However, in most cases, you will use the **TableAdapterManager object** to save the changes, because it can handle saving data to multiple tables in the DataSet. The **BindingSource object** provides the connection between the DataSet and the bound controls on the form. The TblEmployBindingSource in Figure 13-16 connects the Employees-DataSet to two bound controls: a DataGridView control and a BindingNaviga-tor control. The TblEmployBindingSource allows the DataGridView control to display the data contained in the EmployeesDataSet. It also allows the Bind-ingNavigator control to access the records stored in the EmployeesDataSet. Figure 13-17 illustrates the relationships among the database, the objects in the component tray, and the bound controls on the form.

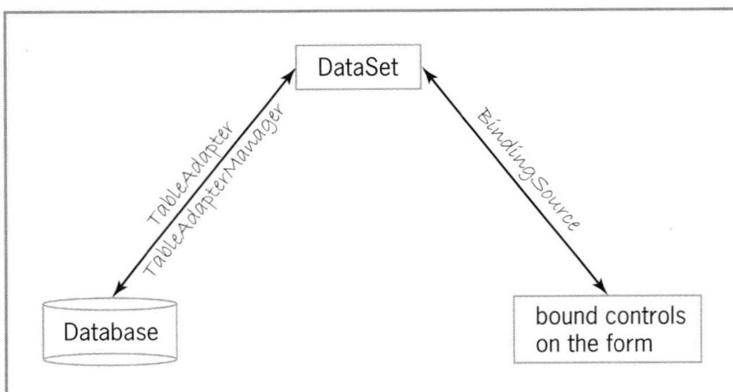

Figure 13-17 Illustration of the relationships among the database, the objects in the component tray, and the bound controls

If a table object's control type is changed from DataGridView to Details, the computer automatically provides the appropriate controls (such as text boxes, labels, and so on) when you drag the table object to the form. It also adds the BindingNavigator control to the form, and adds the five objects to the component tray. The appropriate controls and objects are also automati-cally included when you drag a field object to an empty area on the form.

The DataGridView Control

The DataGridView control is one of the most popular controls for display-ing table data, because it allows you to view a great deal of information at the same time. The control displays the data in a row and columnar format, similar to a spreadsheet. Each row represents a record, and each column represents a field. The intersection of a row and column in a DataGridView control is called a **cell**. Like the PictureBox control, which you learned about in Chapter 1, the DataGridView control has a task list. The task list is shown in Figure 13-18.

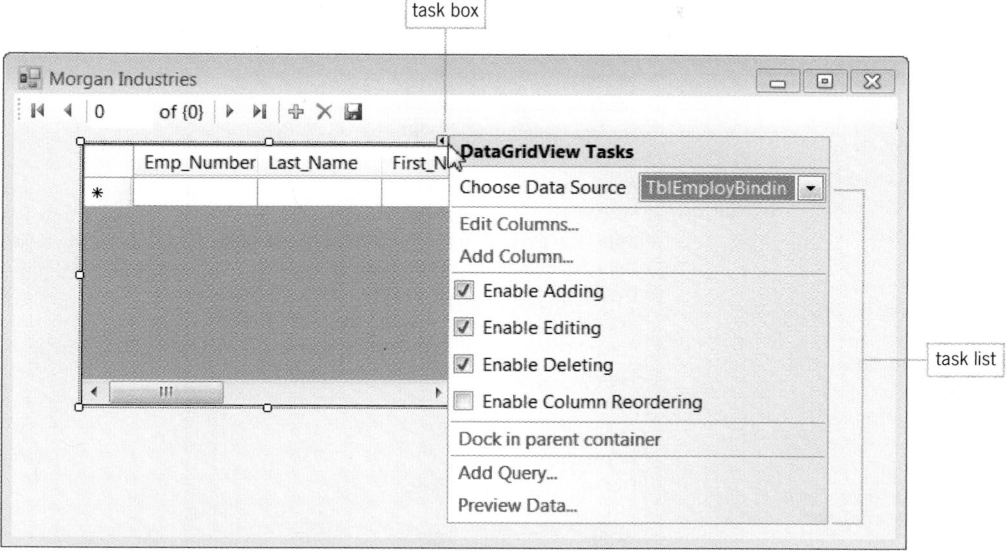

Figure 13-18 Task list for a DataGridView control

Figure 13-19 explains the purpose of each task in the DataGridView's task list, and Figure 13-20 shows the Edit Columns dialog box. The dialog box allows you to add and remove columns from the DataGridView control, as well as reorder the columns. You also can use the dialog box to set the properties of the bound columns. The DefaultCellStyle property, for example, allows you to format a column's data, as well as change the column's width and alignment. You can use the HeaderText property to change a column's heading.

Task	Purpose
Choose Data Source	select a data source
Edit Columns	open the Edit Columns dialog box (See Figure 13-20)
Add Column	add a new column
Enable Adding	allow/disallow the user to add data
Enable Editing	allow/disallow the user to edit data
Enable Deleting	allow/disallow the user to delete data
Enable Column Reordering	allow/disallow the user to reorder the columns
Dock in parent container	bind the borders of the control to the form
Add Query	filter data from a dataset
Preview Data	view the data bound to the control

Figure 13-19 Purpose of each task in the DataGridView's task list

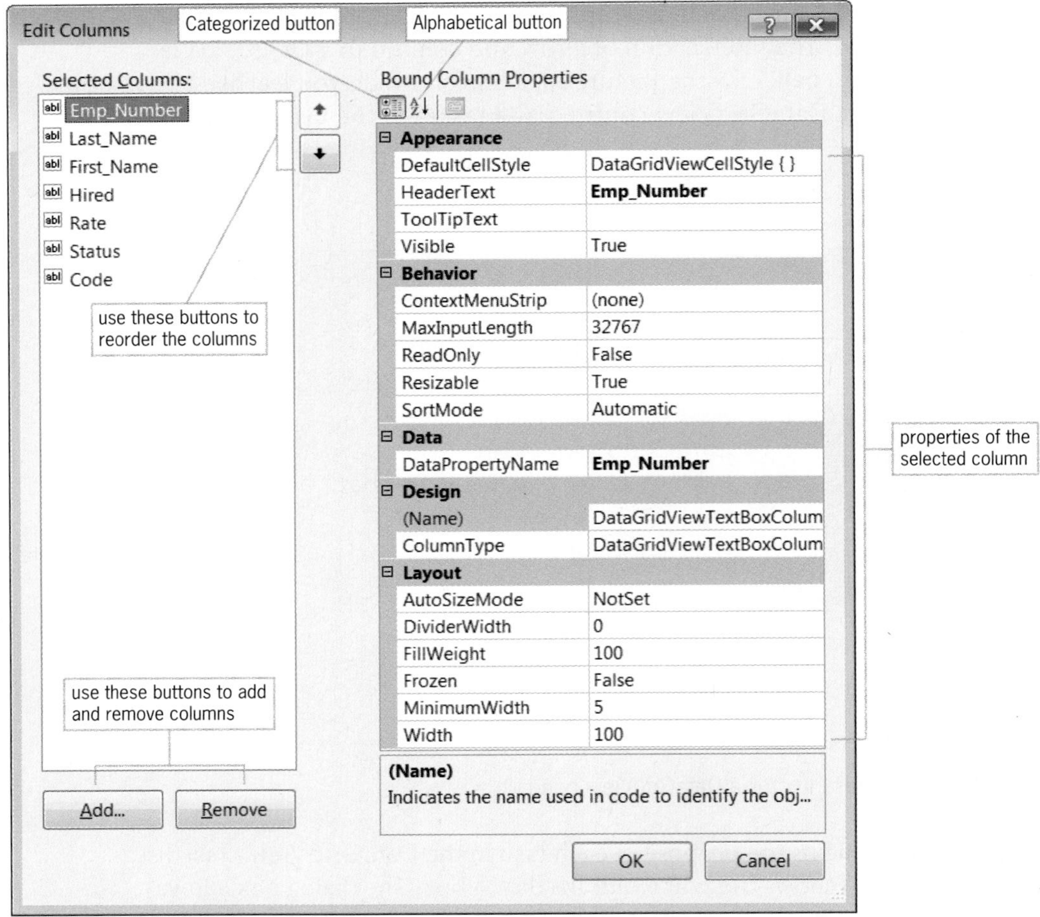

Figure 13-20 Edit Columns dialog box

Many properties of a DataGridView control are listed only in the Properties window. One such property is AutoSizeColumnsMode. The AutoSizeColumnsMode property has seven different settings that control the way the column widths are sized in the DataGridView control. The Fill setting, for example, automatically adjusts the column widths so that all of the columns exactly fill the display area of the control. The ColumnHeader setting, on the other hand, automatically adjusts the column widths based on the header text.

To improve the appearance of the DataGridView control in the application:

1. Permanently display the Properties window, if necessary, then click **AutoSizeColumnsMode** in the Properties list. Click the **down arrow** in the Settings box, then click **Fill**.
2. Click the TblEmployDataGridView control's **task box**, then click **Dock in parent container** in the task list. The DataGridView control expands to the size of the form. This is because the Dock in parent container option anchors the control's borders to the form's borders.

3. Next, you will change the header text on several of the columns. Click **Edit Columns** in the task list. Click the **Alphabetical** button (see Figure 13-20) to display the property names in alphabetical order. Emp_Number is currently selected in the Selected Columns list. Click **HeaderText** in the Bound Column Properties list, then type **Employee Number** and press **Enter**.

4. Click **Last_Name** in the Selected Columns list, then change the HeaderText property to **Last Name**. On your own, change the First_Name column's HeaderText property to **First Name**. Also change the Rate column's HeaderText property to **Pay Rate**.

5. Now you will have the DataGridView control format the pay rates to show two decimal places. With Pay Rate selected in the Selected Columns list, click **DefaultCellStyle**, then click the **...** (ellipsis) button to open the CellStyle Builder dialog box. Click **Format**, then click the **...** (ellipsis) button to open the Format String Dialog box. Click **Numeric** in the Format type list, then verify that the number 2 appears in the Decimal places box. Click the **OK** button to close the Format String Dialog box. You are returned to the CellStyle Builder dialog box.

6. Next, you will have the DataGridView control align the pay rates in the Pay Rate column. Click **Alignment**, then click the **down arrow** in the Settings box, and then click **MiddleRight**. Figure 13-21 shows the completed CellStyle Builder dialog box.

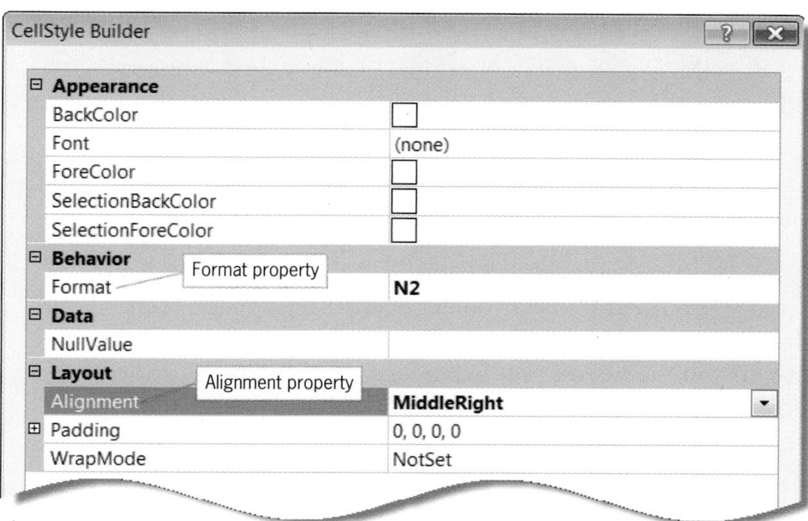

Figure 13-21 Completed CellStyle Builder dialog box

7. Click the **OK** button to close the CellStyle Builder dialog box, then click the **OK** button to close the Edit Columns dialog box.

8. Click the **DataGridView** control to close its task list, then save the application. Figure 13-22 shows the control after setting some of its properties. (You won't see the effect of the formatting and aligning until the application is started.)

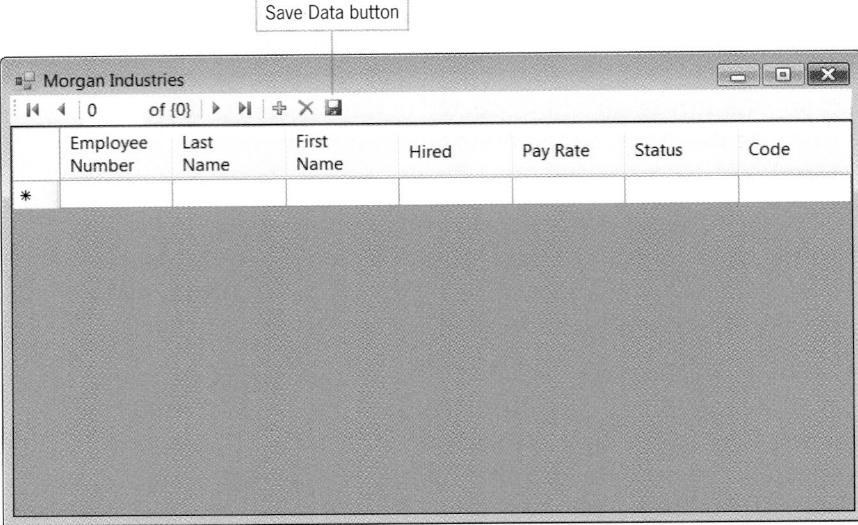

Figure 13-22 DataGridView control after setting some of its properties

Visual Basic Code

As you learned earlier, when a table or field object is dragged to the form, the computer adds the appropriate controls and objects to the application. It also enters some code in the Code Editor window.

To view the code automatically entered in the Code Editor window:

1. Auto-hide the Data Sources, Solution Explorer, and Properties windows.
2. Open the Code Editor window. Replace the <your name> and <current date> text in the comments with your name and the current date.
3. The two procedures shown in Figure 13-23 were automatically entered when the tblEmploy object was dragged to the form. (Your code will not contain the line continuation characters, and the comments in the Load event will appear on one line.) The form's Load event procedure uses the TableAdapter object's Fill method to retrieve the data from the database and store it in the DataSet object; in most applications, the code to fill a dataset belongs in this procedure. However, as the comments in the Load event procedure indicate, you can either move or delete the code. The TblEmployBindingNavigatorSaveItem_Click procedure is processed when you click the Save Data button on the BindingNavigator control. (See Figure 13-22.) The procedure's code validates the changes made to the data before saving the data to the database. Two methods are involved in the save operation: the BindingSource object's EndEdit method and the TableAdapterManager's UpdateAll method. The EndEdit method applies any pending changes (such as new records, deleted records, or changed records) to the dataset. The UpdateAll method commits the dataset changes to the database.

As you learned in Chapter 1, the keyword Me refers to the current form.

```
Private Sub TblEmployBindingNavigatorSaveItem_Click _
    (ByVal sender As System.Object, ByVal e As System.EventArgs) _
    Handles TblEmployBindingNavigatorSaveItem.Click
    Me.Validate()
    Me.TblEmployBindingSource.EndEdit()
    Me.TableAdapterManager.UpdateAll(Me.EmployeesDataSet)

End Sub

Private Sub frmMain_Load(ByVal sender As System.Object, _
    ByVal e As System.EventArgs) Handles MyBase.Load
    'TODO: This line of code loads data into
    'the() 'EmployeesDataSet.tblEmploy' table. You can move,
    'or remove it, as needed.
    Me.TblEmployTableAdapter.Fill(Me.EmployeesDataSet.tblEmploy)

End Sub
```

Figure 13-23 Code automatically entered in the Code Editor window

Because it is possible for an error to occur when saving data to a database, it is a good programming practice to add error handling code to the Save Data button's Click event procedure.

Handling Errors in the Code

An error that occurs while an application is running is called an **exception**. If you do not take deliberate steps in your code to handle the exceptions, Visual Basic "handles" them for you. Typically, it does this by displaying an error message and then abruptly terminating the application. You can prevent your application from behaving in such an unfriendly manner by taking control of the exception handling in your code; you can do this using the **Try...Catch statement**. Figure 13-24 shows the statement's basic syntax and includes examples of using the syntax. The basic syntax contains a Try block and a Catch block. Within the Try block you place the code that could possibly generate an exception. When an exception occurs in the Try block's code, the computer processes the code contained in the Catch block. It then skips to the code following the End Try clause. A description of the exception that occurred is stored in the Message property of the Catch block's `ex` parameter. You can access the description using the code `ex.Message`, as shown in Example 2 in the figure.

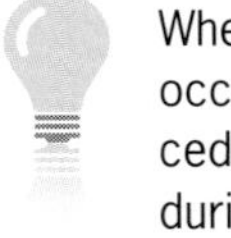

When an error occurs in a procedure's code during run time, programmers say that the procedure "threw an exception."

The Try...Catch statement also has a Finally block. The code in the Finally block is processed whether or not an exception is thrown within the Try block.

Try...Catch statement

Basic syntax

Try

one or more statements that might generate an exception

Catch ex As Exception

one or more statements to execute when an exception occurs

End Try

Figure 13-24 Syntax and examples of the Try...Catch statement *(continues)*

(continued)

Try...Catch statement

Example 1

```
Private Sub btnDisplay_Click(ByVal sender As System.Object, _
   ByVal e As System.EventArgs) Handles btnDisplay.Click

   Try
      inFile = IO.File.OpenText("report.txt")
   Catch ex As Exception
      MessageBox.Show("Can't find the report.txt file.", "File Error", _
         MessageBoxButtons.OK, MessageBoxIcon.Information)
   End Try
End Sub
```

if an exception occurs when processing the OpenText method, the code in the Catch block displays an appropriate message before the procedure ends

Example 2

```
Private Sub TblBooksBindingNavigatorSaveItem_Click _
   (ByVal sender As System.Object, ByVal e As System.EventArgs) _
   Handles TblBooksBindingNavigatorSaveItem.Click

   Try
      Me.Validate()
      Me.TblBooksBindingSource.EndEdit()
      Me.TableAdapterManager.UpdateAll(Me.BooksDataSet)
   Catch ex As Exception
      MessageBox.Show(ex.Message, "Book Sellers", _
         MessageBoxButtons.OK, MessageBoxIcon.Information)
   End Try
End Sub
```

if an exception occurs when processing the code in the Try block, the code in the Catch block displays a description of the exception before the procedure ends

Figure 13-24 Syntax and examples of the Try...Catch statement

To include a Try...Catch statement in the Save Data button's Click event procedure, then start the application:

1. Click **immediately before the letter M** in the `Me.Validate()` statement, then press **Enter** twice.
2. In the blank line above the `Me.Validate()` statement, type **Try** and press **Enter**. The Code Editor automatically enters the `Catch ex As Exception` and `End Try` clauses for you.
3. Select (highlight) the three statements that appear below the `End Try` clause, as well as the blank line below the statements. Press **Ctrl+x** to place the selected lines on the Clipboard. Click the **blank line** below the `Try` clause, then press **Ctrl+v**.
4. If the three statements in the Try block do not produce (throw) an exception, the Try block should display the "Changes saved" message; otherwise, the Catch block should display a description of the exception. Enter the two MessageBox.Show methods indicated in Figure 13-25.

```
Private Sub TblEmployBindingNavigatorSaveItem_Click _
    (ByVal sender As System.Object, ByVal e As System.EventArgs) _
    Handles TblEmployBindingNavigatorSaveItem.Click

    Try
        Me.Validate()
        Me.TblEmployBindingSource.EndEdit()
        Me.TableAdapterManager.UpdateAll(Me.EmployeesDataSet)
        MessageBox.Show("Changes saved", "Morgan Industries", _
                        MessageBoxButtons.OK, MessageBoxIcon.Information)
    Catch ex As Exception
        MessageBox.Show(ex.Message, "Morgan Industries", _
                        MessageBoxButtons.OK, MessageBoxIcon.Information)
    End Try

End Sub
```

enter these two lines of code

enter these two lines of code

Figure 13-25 Try...Catch statement entered in the Save Data button's Click event procedure

5. Save the solution, then start the application. The statement in the form's Load event procedure (shown earlier in Figure 13-23) retrieves the appropriate data from the Employees database and loads the data into the EmployeesDataSet. The data is displayed in the DataGridView control, which is bound to the tblEmploy table contained in the dataset. See Figure 13-26.

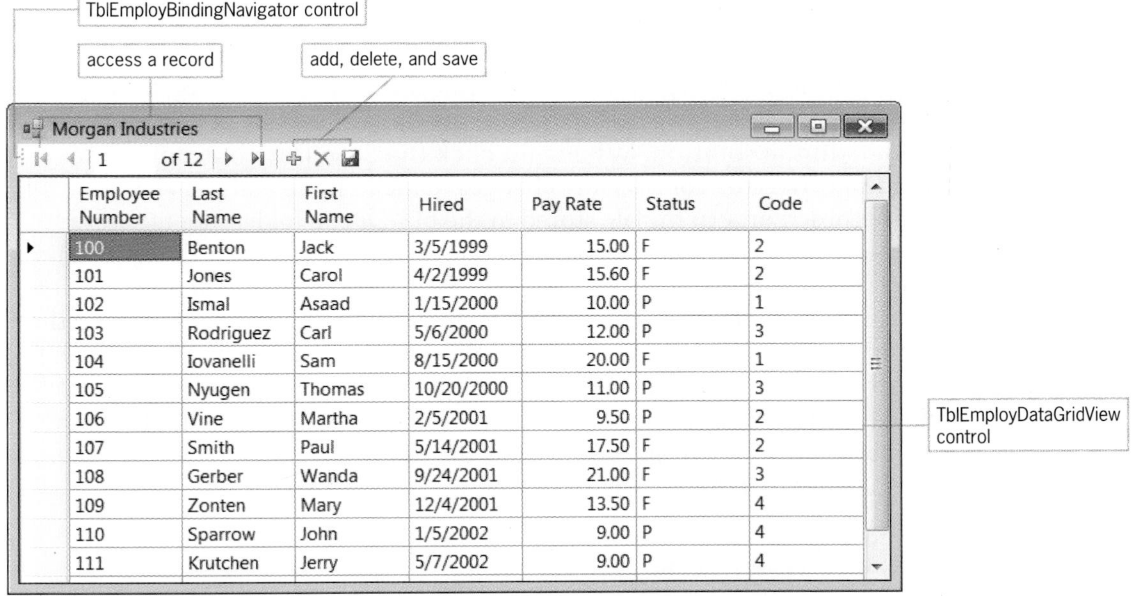

Employee Number	Last Name	First Name	Hired	Pay Rate	Status	Code
100	Benton	Jack	3/5/1999	15.00	F	2
101	Jones	Carol	4/2/1999	15.60	F	2
102	Ismal	Asaad	1/15/2000	10.00	P	1
103	Rodriguez	Carl	5/6/2000	12.00	P	3
104	Iovanelli	Sam	8/15/2000	20.00	F	1
105	Nyugen	Thomas	10/20/2000	11.00	P	3
106	Vine	Martha	2/5/2001	9.50	P	2
107	Smith	Paul	5/14/2001	17.50	F	2
108	Gerber	Wanda	9/24/2001	21.00	F	3
109	Zonten	Mary	12/4/2001	13.50	F	4
110	Sparrow	John	1/5/2002	9.00	P	4
111	Krutchen	Jerry	5/7/2002	9.00	P	4

Figure 13-26 Data displayed in the DataGridView control

6. You can use the arrow keys on your keyboard to move the highlight to a different cell in the DataGridView control. Press the ↓ key to move the highlight to the next record, then press the → key to move it to the next field.

7. The BindingNavigator control provides buttons for accessing the previous and next record in the dataset, as well as accessing the first and last record. Click the **Move next** button ▶ to move the highlight to the next record. Click the **Move last** button ▶| to move the highlight to the last record, then click the **Move first** button |◀ to move the highlight to the first record.

8. You also can use the BindingNavigator control to access a record by its record number. The first record in a dataset has a record number of 1; the second has a record number of 2, and so on. Click the **Current position** box, which contains the number 1. Replace the 1 with a **6** and press **Enter**. The highlight moves to the sixth record.

9. Click the **Close** button on the form's title bar to stop the application.

The BindingNavigator control also provides buttons for adding a record to the dataset, deleting a record from the dataset, and saving the changes made to the dataset. The way changes are saved to a database is controlled by the database file's Copy to Output Directory property.

The Copy to Output Directory Property

When the Data Source Configuration Wizard connected the Morgan Industries application to the Employees database, it added the database file (Employees.accdb) to the application's project folder. (You can verify this in the Solution Explorer window.) A database file contained in a project is referred to as a local database file. The way Visual Basic saves changes to a local database file is determined by the file's **Copy to Output Directory property**. When the property is set to its default setting, Copy always, the file is copied from the project folder to the project folder's bin\Debug folder each time you start the application. In this case, the Employees.accdb file is copied from the Morgan Industries Project folder to the Morgan Industries Project\bin\Debug folder. As a result, the file will appear in two different folders in the solution. When you click the Save Data button on the BindingNavigator control, any changes made in the DataGridView control are recorded only in the file stored in the bin\Debug folder; the file stored in the project folder is not changed. The next time you start the application, the file in the project folder is copied to the bin\Debug folder, overwriting the file that contains the changes. One way to fix this problem is to set the database file's Copy to Output Directory property to "Copy if newer." The "Copy if newer" setting tells the computer to compare the dates on both files to determine which file has the newer (more current) date. If the database file in the project folder has the newer date, then copy it to the bin\Debug folder; otherwise, don't copy it.

To change the Employees.accdb file's Copy to Output Directory property, then test the application:

1. Temporarily display the Solution Explorer window, if necessary. Right-click **Employees.accdb**, then click **Properties**. Change the Employees.accdb file's Copy to Output Directory property to **Copy if newer**.
2. Save the solution, then start the application.
3. Click the **Add new** button ✚ to add a new record to the end of the DataGridView control. Type **112** as the employee number, then press **Tab** and type **Jacobs** as the last name. Press **Tab**, then type **Susan** as the first name. On your own, enter **8/9/2008**, **10**, **P**, and **3** in the Hired, Pay Rate, Status, and Code fields, respectively. Press **Enter** after typing the number 3.

4. Click the **Move first** button to move the highlight to the Code field in the first record. When a cell is highlighted, you can modify its existing data by simply typing the new data. Type **3** and press **Enter** to change the entry in Jack Benton's Code field.
5. Click the **Save Data** button. The Changes saved message appears in a message box. Click the **OK** button to close the message box.
6. Click the **Close** button on the form's title bar to stop the application, then start the application again. The DataGridView control now contains the record you added, as well as the change you made to Jack Benton's Code field. (You will need to scroll down the DataGridView control to see the new record.)
7. Change Jack Benton's Code field from 3 to **2**. Click the **Move last** button to move the highlight to the last record, then click the **Delete** button ✕ to delete the record. Click the **Save Data** button. The Changes saved message appears in a message box. Click the **OK** button to close the message box.
8. Stop the application. Start the application again to verify that your changes were saved, then stop the application.
9. Close the Code Editor window, then close the solution.

Binding to an Existing Control

As indicated earlier in Figure 13-12, you can bind an object in a dataset to an existing control on the form. The easiest way to do this is by dragging the object from the Data Sources window to the control. However, you also can click the control and then set one or more properties in the Properties window. The appropriate property (or properties) to set depends on the control you are binding. For example, you use the DataSource property to bind a DataGridView control. However, you use the DataSource and DisplayMember properties to bind a ListBox control. To bind label and text box controls, you use the DataBindings/Text property.

When you drag an object from the Data Sources window to an existing control, the computer does not create a new control; rather, it merely binds the object to the existing control. Because a new control does not need to be created, the computer ignores the control type specified for the object in the Data Sources window. Therefore, it is not necessary to change the control type in the Data Sources window to match the existing control's type. In other words, you can drag an object that is associated with a text box in the Data Sources window to a label control on the form. The computer will bind the object to the label, but it will not change the label to a text box.

In the following set of steps, you will open a different version of the Morgan Industries application. You then will connect the application to the Employees database, and then bind objects from the dataset to existing label controls in the interface. In this version of the application, you will not need to change the database file's Copy to Output Directory property to Copy if newer, because the user will not be adding, deleting, or editing the records in the dataset.

To bind controls using a different version of the Morgan Industries application:

1. Open the **Morgan Industries Solution** (**Morgan Industries Solution.sln**) file, which is contained in the VB2008\Chap13\Morgan Industries Solution-Labels folder. Open the designer window. See Figure 13-27.

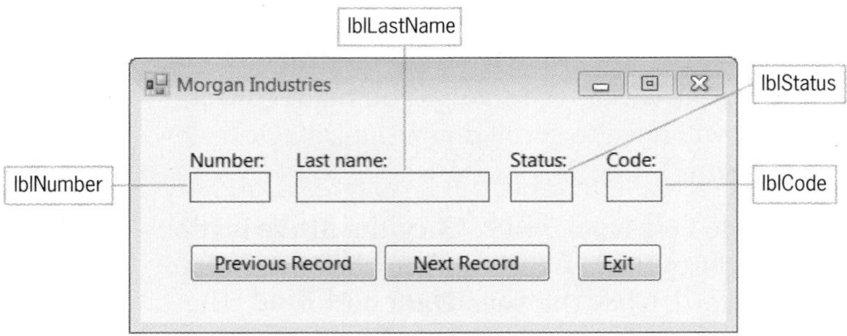

Figure 13-27 A different version of the Morgan Industries application

2. Temporarily display the Data Sources window, then click **Add New Data Source** to start the Data Source Configuration Wizard. If necessary, click **Database**.
3. Click the **Next** button to display the Choose Your Data Connection screen. Click the **New Connection** button to display the Add Connection dialog box. If necessary, click the **Change** button to open the Change Data Source dialog box, then click **Microsoft Access Database File**. Click the **OK** button to return to the Add Connection dialog box.
4. Click the **Browse** button in the Add Connection dialog box. Open the VB2008\Chap13\Access Databases folder, then click **Employees.accdb** in the list of filenames. Click the **Open** button. Click the **Test Connection** button in the Add Connection dialog box. The "Test connection succeeded." message appears in a message box. Click the **OK** button to close the message box.
5. Click the **OK** button to close the Add Connection dialog box. Click the **Next** button on the Choose Your Data Connection screen, then click the **Yes** button to add the Employees.accdb file to the application's project folder.
6. If necessary, select the **Yes, save the connection as** check box on the Save the Connection String to the Application Configuration File screen, then click the **Next** button to display the Choose Your Database Objects screen.
7. Click the **plus box** next to Tables in the Choose Your Database Objects screen, then click the **plus box** next to tblEmploy. In this application, you will include only four fields in the dataset. Click the **empty box** that appears next to each of the following four field names: Emp_Number, Last_Name, Status, and Code. Click the **Finish** button. The Wizard adds the EmployeesDataSet to the Data Sources window.
8. Permanently display the Data Sources window, then click the **plus box** next to tblEmploy. See Figure 13-28. The dataset contains one table and four field objects.

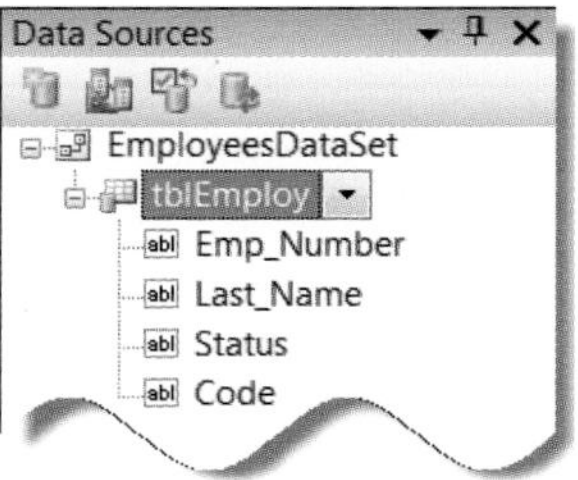

Figure 13-28 Dataset in this version of the Morgan Industries application

9. Click **Emp_Number** in the Data Sources window, then drag the field object to the lblNumber control. Release the mouse button. The computer binds the control and adds the EmployeesDataSet, TblEmployBindingSource, TblEmployTableAdapter, and TableAdapterManager objects to the component tray. However, notice that it does not add the BindingNavigator object and BindingNavigator control. When you drag an object from the Data Sources window to an existing control, the computer enters (in the Code Editor window) the Load event procedure shown earlier in Figure 13-23. Recall that the procedure uses the TableAdapter object's Fill method to retrieve the data from the database and store it in the DataSet object.
10. On your own, drag the Last_Name, Status, and Code field objects to the lblLastName, lblStatus, and lblCode controls, respectively.
11. Auto-hide the Data Sources window. Save the solution, then start the application. Only the first record in the dataset appears in the interface. Because the form does not contain a BindingNavigator control, which would allow you to move from one record to the next, you will need to code the Next Record and Previous Record buttons to view the remaining records. Click the **Exit** button to stop the application.

You can use the BindingNavigator tool to add a BindingNavigator control and object to the application. You then would set the control's DataSource property to the name of the BindingSource object—in this case, TblEmployBindingSource.

Coding the Next Record and Previous Record Buttons

The BindingSource object uses an invisible record pointer to keep track of the current record in the dataset. It stores the position of the record pointer in its **Position property**. The first record is in position 0; the second is in position 1, and so on. Figure 13-29 shows the Position property's syntax and includes examples of using the property.

BindingSource object's Position property

Syntax
bindingSourceName.**Position**

Example 1
```
intRecordNum = TblEmployBindingSource.Position
```
assigns the current record's position to the `intRecordNum` variable

Figure 13-29 Syntax and examples of the BindingSource object's Position property *(continues)*

(continued)

BindingSource object's Position property

Example 2

```
TblEmployBindingSource.Position = 4
```

moves the record pointer to the fifth record in the dataset

Example 3

```
TblEmployBindingSource.Position = _
   TblEmployBindingSource.Position + 1
```

moves the record pointer to the next record in the dataset

Figure 13-29 Syntax and examples of the BindingSource object's Position property

Rather than using the Position property to position the record pointer in a dataset, you also can use the BindingSource object's Move methods. The **Move methods** move the record pointer to the first, last, next, or previous record in the dataset. Figure 13-30 shows each Move method's syntax and includes examples of using two of the methods.

BindingSource object's Move methods

Syntax

bindingSourceName.**MoveFirst()**
bindingSourceName.**MoveLast()**
bindingSourceName.**MoveNext()**
bindingSourceName.**MovePrevious()**

Example 1

```
TblEmployBindingSource.MoveFirst()
```

moves the record pointer to the first record in the dataset

Example 2

```
TblEmployBindingSource.MoveNext()
```

moves the record pointer to the next record in the dataset

Figure 13-30 Syntax and examples of the BindingSource object's Move methods

To code the Next Record and Previous Record buttons, then test the code:

1. Open the Code Editor window. Replace the <your name> and <current date> text in the comments with your name and the current date.
2. When the user clicks the Next Record button, the button's Click event procedure should move the record pointer to the next record in the dataset. Open the code template for the btnNext control's Click event procedure. Type **' moves the record pointer to the next record** and press **Enter** twice, then enter the following line of code.

   TblEmployBindingSource.MoveNext()
3. Similarly, when the user clicks the Previous Record button, its Click event procedure should move the record pointer to the previous

record in the dataset. Open the code template for the btnPrevious control's Click event procedure. Type **' moves the record pointer to the previous record** and press **Enter** twice, then enter the following line of code.

TblEmployBindingSource.MovePrevious()

4. Save the solution. Figure 13-31 shows the code entered in each button's Click event procedure.

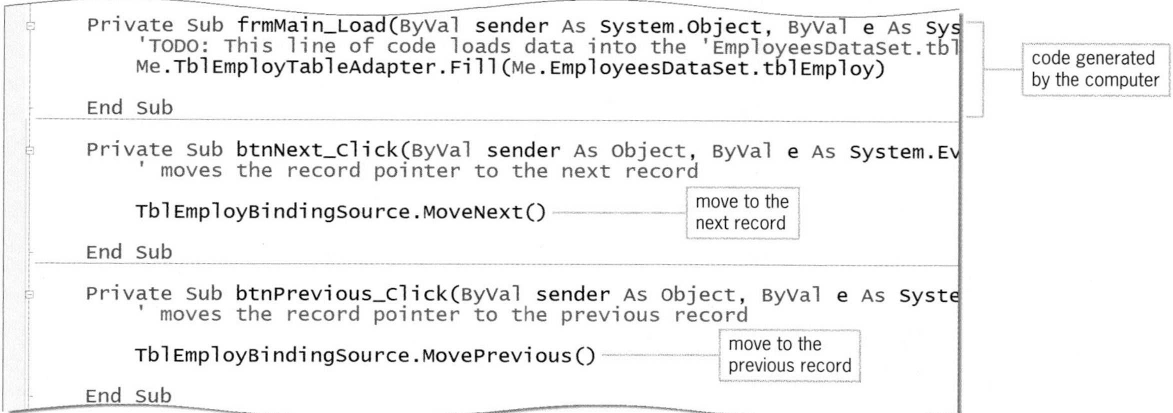

Figure 13-31 Code entered in each button's Click event procedure

5. Start the application. Click the **Next Record** button to display the second record, then continue clicking the **Next Record** button until the last record appears in the interface.
6. Click the **Previous Record** button until the first record appears in the interface, then click the **Exit** button.
7. Close the Code Editor window, then close the solution.

Lesson A Summary

- **To connect an application to a database:**

  Use the Configuration Wizard. To start the wizard, click Data on the menu bar, then click Show Data Sources, and then click Add New Data Source in the Data Sources window.

- **To preview the data contained in a dataset:**

  Click the form to make it the active window. Click Data on the menu bar, then click Preview Data. Click the Preview button in the Preview Data dialog box.

- **To bind an object in a dataset:**

  Use either of the ways shown in Figure 13-12.

- **To have the columns exactly fill the display area in a DataGridView control:**

  Set the DataGridView control's AutoSizeColumnsMode property to Fill.

- **To anchor the DataGridView control to the borders of the form:**

  Click Dock in parent container from the DataGridView control's task list; or, set the DataGridView control's Dock property in the Properties window.

- **To move the record pointer while an application is running:**

  You can use a BindingNavigator control. You also can use either the BindingSource object's Position property or one of its Move methods (MoveFirst, MoveLast, MoveNext, or MovePrevious).

Lesson A Key Terms

Binding—the process of connecting an object in a dataset to a control on a form

BindingNavigator control—can be used to move the record pointer from one record to another in a dataset, as well as to add, delete, and save records

BindingSource object—connects a DataSet object to the bound controls on a form

Bound controls—the controls connected to an object in a dataset

Cell—the intersection of a row and column in a DataGridView control

Child table—a table linked to a parent table

Computer database—an electronic file that contains an organized collection of related information

Copy to Output Directory property—a property of a database file; determines when and if the file is copied from the project folder to the project folder's bin\Debug folder

DataGridView control—displays data in a row and columnar format

Dataset—a copy of the data (database fields and records) that can be accessed by an application

DataSet object—stores the information you want to access from a database

Exception—an error that occurs while an application is running

Field—a single item of information about a person, place, or thing

Foreign key—the field used to link a child table to a parent table

Move methods—methods of a BindingSource object; used to move the record pointer to the first, last, next, or previous record in a dataset

Parent table—a table linked to a child table

Position property—a property of a BindingSource object; stores the position of the record pointer

Primary key—the field that uniquely identifies each record in a table

Record—a group of related fields that contain all of the necessary data about a specific person, place, or thing

Relational database—a database that stores information in tables composed of columns (fields) and rows (records)

Table—a group of related records

TableAdapter object—connects a database to a DataSet object

TableAdapterManager object—handles saving data to multiple tables in a dataset

Try...Catch statement—used for exception handling in a procedure

Lesson A Review Questions

1. The ______________________________ object connects a database to a DataSet object.
   a. BindingSource
   b. DataBase
   c. DataGridView
   d. TableAdapter

2. The ______________________________ property stores an integer that represents the location of the record pointer in a dataset.
   a. BindingNavigator object's Position
   b. BindingSource object's Position
   c. TableAdapter object's Position
   d. None of the above.

3. If the record pointer is positioned on record number 5 in a dataset, which of the following will move the record pointer to record number 4?
   a. `TblBooksBindingSource.GoPrevious`
   b. `TblBooksBindingSource.Move(4)`
   c. `TblBooksBindingSource.MovePrevious()`
   d. `TblBooksBindingSource.PositionPrevious`

4. A ______________________________ is an organized collection of related information stored in a computer file.
   a. database
   b. dataset
   c. field
   d. record

5. A ______________________ database stores information in tables.
   a. columnar
   b. relational
   c. sorted
   d. tabular

6. The ______________________ object provides the connection between a DataSet object and a control on a form.
   a. Bound
   b. Binding
   c. BindingSource
   d. Connecting

7. An application contains DataSet, BindingSource, TableAdapter, TableAdapterManager, and BindingNavigator objects named FriendsDataSet, TblNamesBindingSource, TblNamesTableAdapter, TableAdapterManager, and TblNamesBindingNavigator, respectively. Which of the following statements retrieves data from the Friends database and stores it in the FriendsDataSet?
   a. `Me.FriendsDataSet.Fill(Friends.accdb)`
   b. `Me.TblNamesBindingSource.Fill(Me.FriendsDataSet)`
   c. `Me.TblNamesBindingNavigator.Fill(Me.FriendsDataSet.tblNames)`
   d. `Me.TblNamesTableAdapter.Fill(Me.FriendsDataSet.tblNames)`

8. If an application contains the `Catch ex As Exception` clause, you can use ______________________ to access the exception's description.
   a. `ex.Description`
   b. `ex.Exception`
   c. `ex.Message`
   d. `Exception.Description`

9. If the current record is the second record in the dataset, which of the following statements will position the record pointer on the first record?
   a. `Me.TblEmployBindingSource.Position = 0`
   b.
   ```
   Me.TblEmployBindingSource.Position = _
          Me.TblEmployBindingSource.Position - 1
   ```
   c. `Me.TblEmployBindingSource.MoveFirst()`
   d. All of the above.

10. The field that links a child table to a parent table is called the ________________.
    a. foreign key in the child table
    b. foreign key in the parent table
    c. link key in the parent table
    d. primary key in the child table

11. The process of connecting a control to an object in a dataset is called ________________.
    a. assigning
    b. binding
    c. joining
    d. None of the above.

12. Which of the following statements is true about a relational database?
    a. Data stored in a relational database can be retrieved both quickly and easily by the computer.
    b. Data stored in a relational database can be displayed in any order.
    c. A relational database stores data in a column and row format.
    d. All of the above are true.

Lesson A Exercises

INTRODUCTORY

1. In this exercise, you learn how to open a database table in a window in the IDE. You also modify one of the Morgan Industries applications from the lesson.
    a. Use Windows to make a copy of the Morgan Industries Solution-Labels folder, which is contained in the VB2008\Chap13 folder. Rename the copy Modified Morgan Industries Solution-Labels. Open the Morgan Industries Solution (Morgan Industries Solution.sln) file contained in the VB2008\Chap13\Modified Morgan Industries Solution-Labels folder. Open the designer window.
    b. Click the plus box that appears next to Employees.accdb in the Server (Database) Explorer window, then click the plus box that appears next to Tables. Right-click tblEmploy, then click Retrieve Data. The table data appears in a window in the IDE, as shown earlier in Figure 13-4. Close the window that contains the table data.
    c. Open the Code Editor window. Modify the code in the Click event procedures for the btnNext and btnPrevious controls. Rather than using the MoveNext and MovePrevious methods, use the Position property to move the record pointer. Save the solution, then start and test the application. Stop the application. Close the Code Editor window, then close the solution.

INTRODUCTORY

2. The sales manager at Cartwright Industries records the item number, name, and price of each product the company sells in a database named Items. The Items database is stored in the Items.accdb file, which is contained in the VB2008\Chap13\Access Databases folder. The database contains a table named tblItems. The table contains 10 records, each composed of 3 fields. The ItemNum and ItemName fields contain text; the Price field contains numbers. The application should display the contents of the database in a DataGridView control. Open the Cartwright Solution (Cartwright Solution.sln) file, which is contained in the VB2008\Chap13\Cartwright Solution-DataGridView folder. If necessary, open the designer window. Connect the application to the Items database. Bind the table to a DataGridView control. Make the necessary modifications to the DataGridView control. Open the Code Editor window and enter the Try...Catch statement in the Save Data button's Click event procedure. Include appropriate messages. Save the solution, then start and test the application. Stop the application. Close the Code Editor window, then close the solution.

INTRODUCTORY

3. The sales manager at Cartwright Industries records the item number, name, and price of each product the company sells in a database named Items. The Items database is stored in the Items.accdb file, which is contained in the VB2008\Chap13\Access Databases folder. The database contains a table named tblItems. The table contains 10 records, each composed of 3 fields. The ItemNum and ItemName fields contain text; the Price field contains numbers. The application should display the contents of the database in label controls. Open the Cartwright Solution (Cartwright Solution.sln) file, which is contained in the VB2008\Chap13\Cartwright Solution-Labels folder. If necessary, open the designer window. Connect the application to the Items database. Bind the appropriate objects to the existing label controls. Open the Code Editor window. Code the Click event procedures for the Next Record, Previous Record, and Exit buttons. Save the solution, then start and test the application. Stop the application. Close the Code Editor window, then close the solution.

INTERMEDIATE

4. In this exercise, you modify one of the Morgan Industries applications from the lesson.

   a. Use Windows to make a copy of the Morgan Industries Solution-Labels folder, which is contained in the VB2008\Chap13 folder. Rename the copy Morgan Industries Solution-ListBox. Open the Morgan Industries Solution (Morgan Industries Solution.sln) file contained in the VB2008\Chap13\Morgan Industries Solution-ListBox folder. Open the designer window.

   b. Unlock the controls, then delete the lblNumber control from the form. Add a list box to the form. Name the list box lstNumber. Modify the interface to make room for the list box. Lock the controls, then set the tab order appropriately.

   c. Set the lstNumber control's DataSource property to TblEmployBindingSource, and set its DisplayMember property to Emp_Number. Save the solution, then start and test the application. Stop the application, then close the solution.

LESSON B

After studying Lesson B, you should be able to:

- Query a dataset using LINQ
- Add an item to a BindingNavigator control
- Use the LINQ aggregate operators

Creating a Query

You can arrange the records stored in a dataset in any order. The records in the EmployeesDataSet, for example, can be arranged by employee number, pay rate, status, and so on. You also can control the number of records you want to view at any one time. For example, you can view all of the records in the EmployeesDataSet; or you can choose to view only the records for the part-time employees. You use a **query** to specify both the records to select in a dataset and the order in which to arrange the records. You can create a query in Visual Basic 2008 using a new language feature called **Language Integrated Query** or, more simply, **LINQ**. Figure 13-32 shows the basic syntax of LINQ when used to select and arrange records in a dataset. The figure also includes examples of using the syntax. In the syntax, *variable* and *element* can be any names you choose, as long as the name follows the naming rules for variables. In other words, there is nothing special about the `records` and `employee` names used in the examples. The Where and Order By clauses are optional parts of the syntax. You use the **Where clause**, which contains a *condition*, to limit the records you want to view. Similar to the *condition* in If...Then...Else and Do...Loop statements, the Where clause *condition* specifies a requirement that must be met for a record to be selected. The **Order By clause** is used to arrange the records in either ascending (the default) or descending order by one or more fields. Notice that the LINQ syntax does not require you to specify the *variable*'s data type. Instead, the syntax allows the computer to infer the data type from the value being assigned to the *variable*. However, for this inference to take place, you must set Option Infer to On (rather than to Off, as you have been doing). You can do this by entering the `Option Infer On` statement in the General Declarations section of the Code Editor window.

When used to query a dataset, LINQ is referred to more specifically as LINQ to Datasets.

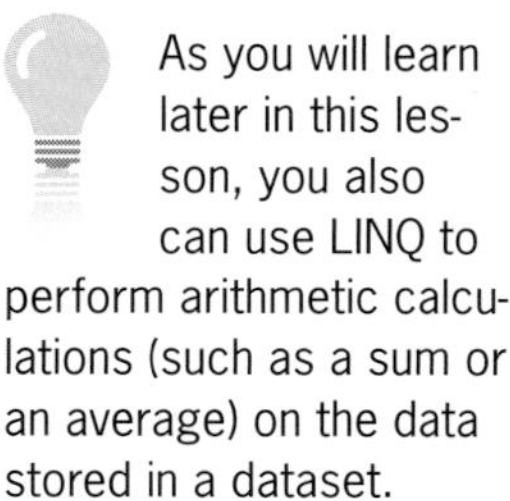

As you will learn later in this lesson, you also can use LINQ to perform arithmetic calculations (such as a sum or an average) on the data stored in a dataset.

Using LINQ to select and arrange records in a dataset

Basic syntax

Dim *variable* = **From** *element* **In** *dataset.table*
[**Where** *condition*]
[**Order By** *element.field1* [**Ascending**|**Descending**]
[, *element.fieldN* [**Ascending**|**Descending**]]
Select *element*

Figure 13-32 Basic LINQ syntax and examples for selecting and arranging records in a dataset *(continues)*

(continued)

Using LINQ to select and arrange records in a dataset

Example 1

```
Dim records = From employee In EmployeesDataSet.tblEmploy _
              Select employee
```

selects all the records contained in the dataset

Example 2

```
Dim records = From employee In EmployeesDataSet.tblEmploy _
              Order By employee.Code _
              Select employee
```

selects all the records contained in the dataset, and arranges the records in ascending order by the Code field

Example 3

```
Dim records = From employee In EmployeesDataSet.tblEmploy _
              Where employee.Status.ToUpper = "P" _
              Select employee
```

selects only the part-time employee records

Example 4

```
Dim records = From employee In EmployeesDataSet.tblEmploy _
              Where employee.Status.ToUpper = "P" _
              Order By employee.Code Descending _
              Select employee
```

selects only the part-time employee records, and arranges the records in descending order by the Code field

Figure 13-32 Basic LINQ syntax and examples for selecting and arranging records in a dataset

The syntax and examples in Figure 13-32 merely select and/or arrange the appropriate records. To actually view the records, you assign the *variable*'s contents to the DataSource property of a BindingSource control, using the syntax *bindingSource*.**DataSource** = *variable*.**AsDataView**. For instance, to view the records selected by Example 1's code, you use `TblEmployBindingSource.DataSource = records.AsDataView`. In the following set of steps, you will use LINQ to select specific records from a dataset.

To open the Morgan Industries Solution file, then use LINQ to select specific records:

1. If necessary, start Visual Studio 2008 or Visual Basic 2008 Express Edition. Close the Start Page window. Open the **Morgan Industries Solution** (**Morgan Industries Solution.sln**) file, which is contained in the VB2008\Chap13\Morgan Industries Solution-LINQ folder. Open the designer window. The Find Last Name button in the interface will display records whose Last_Name field begins with one or more characters entered by the user.
2. Open the Code Editor window. Replace the <your name> and <current date> text in the comments with your name and the current date.

3. The btnFind control's Click event procedure will use LINQ to select the appropriate records. Therefore, you will change the Option Infer setting from Off to On. Locate the `Option Infer Off` statement, then change `Off` to **On**. Press the **Tab** key, then type **' using LINQ**.

4. Locate the btnFind control's Click event procedure. The procedure uses the InputBox function to prompt the user to either enter one or more characters or leave the input area empty. The user's response is converted to uppercase and assigned to the `strFind` variable. First, you will enter the LINQ statement to select the appropriate records. Click the **blank line** below the `' select records matching the last name` comment, then enter the following lines of code. Notice that the Where clause's *condition* uses the Like operator and the asterisk pattern-matching character. The Where clause compares the uppercase contents of each record's Last_Name field with the user's entry followed by zero or more characters. You learned about the Like operator and the pattern-matching characters in Chapter 8.

   Dim records = From employee In EmployeesDataSet.tblEmploy _
   Where employee.Last_Name.ToUpper Like strFind & "*" _
   Select employee

5. Now you will display the contents of the `records` variable in the DataGridView control. You do this by assigning the variable to the TblEmployBindingSource control's DataSource property, like this: `TblEmployBindingSource.DataSource = records.AsDataView`. Press **Enter**, then enter the following assignment statement.

   TblEmployBindingSource.DataSource = records.AsDataView

6. Save the solution. The code entered in the General Declarations section and btnFind control's Click event procedure is shown in Figure 13-33.

```
Option Explicit On
Option Strict On
Option Infer On ' using LINQ

Private Sub btnFind_Click(ByVal sender As Object, _
     ByVal e As System.EventArgs) Handles btnFind.Click
     ' selects records from a dataset

     Const strPROMPT As String = _
         "One or more letters (leave empty to retrieve all records):"

     ' get the last name
     Dim strFind As String = _
         InputBox(strPROMPT, "Find Last Name").ToUpper.Trim
```

set Option Infer to On in the General Declarations section

Figure 13-33 Code entered in the Declarations section and btnFind Click event procedure *(continues)*

(continued)

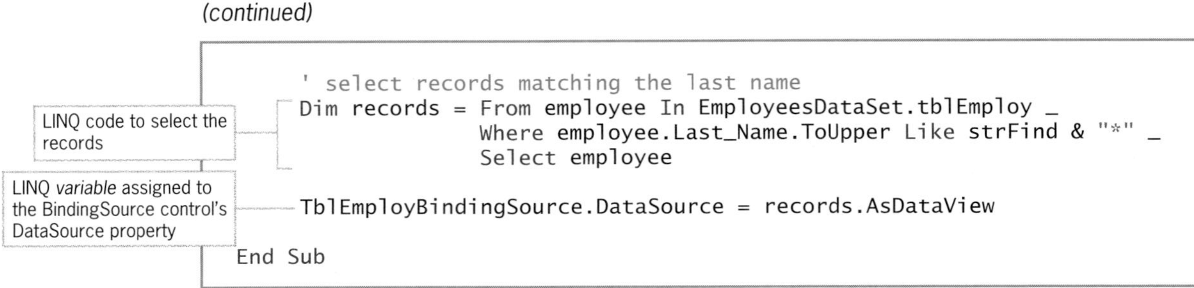


```
        ' select records matching the last name
        Dim records = From employee In EmployeesDataSet.tblEmploy _
                      Where employee.Last_Name.ToUpper Like strFind & "*" _
                      Select employee

        TblEmployBindingSource.DataSource = records.AsDataView
    End Sub
```

Figure 13-33 Code entered in the Declarations section and btnFind Click event procedure

To test the btnFind control's code:

1. Start the application. The 12 records in the dataset appear in the DataGridView control.
2. Click the **Find Last Name** button. First, find the record whose Last_Name field contains Vine. Type **vine** and press **Enter**. See Figure 13-34.

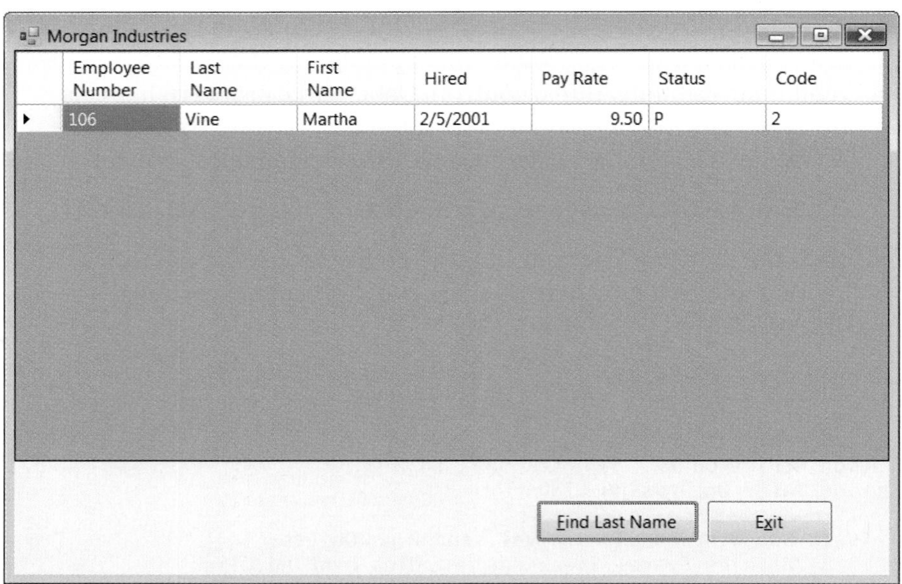

Figure 13-34 Vine record shown in the DataGridView control

3. Now display records whose last name begins with the letter i. Click the **Find Last Name** button. Type **i** and press **Enter**. Two records appear in the DataGridView control.
4. Now display all of the records. Click the **Find Last Name** button, then press **Enter**.

5. You can click a column header to sort the entries in the column. Click **Code** to sort the employee codes in ascending order, then click **Code** again to sort them in descending order.

6. Click the **Exit** button to stop the application. Close the Code Editor window, then close the solution.

Personalizing a BindingNavigator Control

As shown in Lesson A's Figure 13-26, the BindingNavigator control contains buttons that allow you to move to a different record in the dataset, as well as to add or delete a record and save any changes made to the dataset. At times, you may want to include additional items—such as another button, a text box, or a drop down button—on the BindingNavigator control. The steps for adding an item to a BindingNavigator control are shown in Figure 13-35.

Adding an item to a BindingNavigator control

1. Click an empty area on the BindingNavigator control, then click the control's task box.
2. Click Edit Items in the task list to open the Items Collection Editor dialog box.
3. Select the type of item to add, then click the Add button.
4. Make any needed modifications to the item's properties. For example, you may want to set an item's Name, DisplayStyle, Image, or Text property. If the item is a Drop-DownButton, which displays a menu of options, you will need to set its DropDownItems property.
5. Click the OK button.

Figure 13-35 Steps for adding an item to a BindingNavigator control

In the following set of steps, you will add a DropDownButton to the Binding-Navigator control in the Morgan Industries application. The DropDownButton will display a menu that contains three options: All Employees, Part-time Employees, and Full-time Employees. The All Employees option will display the average pay rate for all employees. The Part-time Employees and Full-time Employees options will display the average pay rate for part-time and full-time employees, respectively.

To add a DropDownButton to the BindingNavigator control:

1. Open the **Morgan Industries Solution** (**Morgan Industries Solution.sln**) file, which is contained in the VB2008\Chap13\Morgan Industries Solution-Aggregate folder. Open the designer window.

2. Click an **empty area** on the TblEmployBindingNavigator control, then click the control's **task box**.

3. Click **Edit Items** in the task list to open the Items Collection Editor dialog box. Click the **down arrow** in the "Select item and add to list below" box, then click **DropDownButton** in the list. Click the **Add** button. See Figure 13-36.

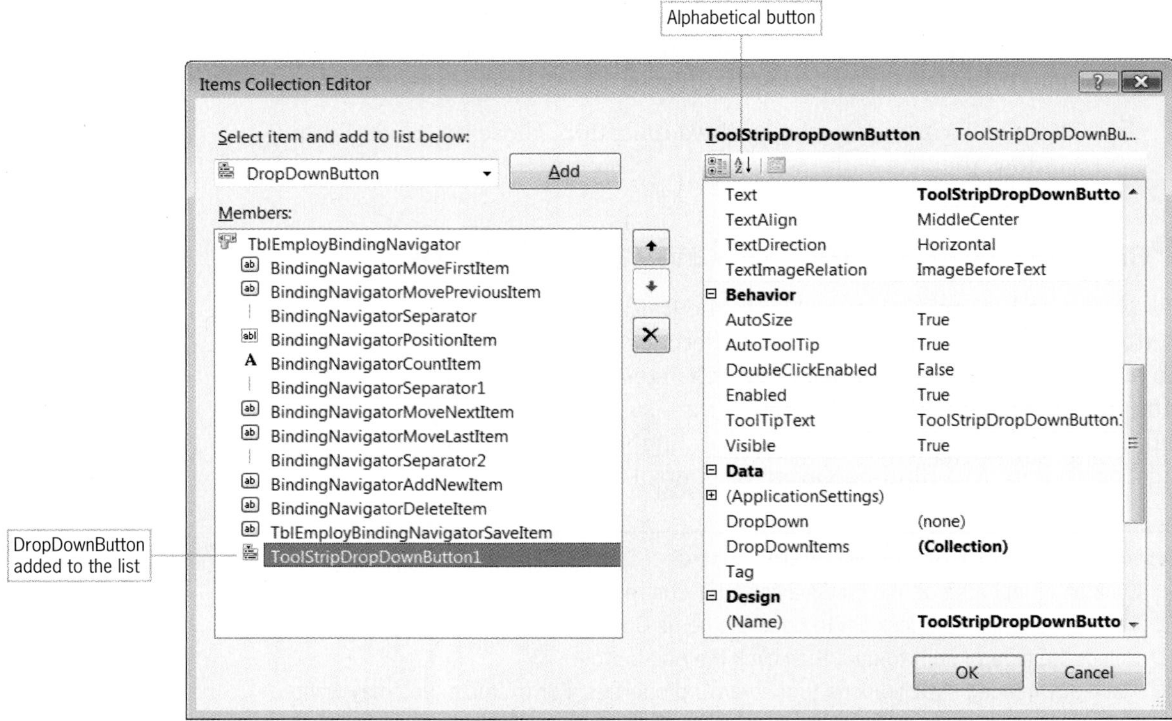

Figure 13-36 Items Collection Editor dialog box

4. Click the **Alphabetical** button to display the property names in alphabetical order. Click **(Name)** in the properties list, then type **ddbAverage** and press **Enter**. Change the DisplayStyle property to **Text**, then change the Text property to **Average Pay Rate**.

5. Click **DropDownItems**, then click the **...** (ellipsis) button. Click the **Add** button to add a menu item to the DropDownButton. Click the **Alphabetical** button to display the property names in alphabetical order. Click **(Name)** in the properties list, then type **mnuAverageAll** and press **Enter**. Change the DisplayStyle property to **Text**, then change the Text property to **All Employees**.

6. Click the **Add** button to add another menu item to the DropDown-Button. Change the menu item's Name, DisplayStyle, and Text properties to **mnuAveragePart**, **Text**, and **Part-time Employees**, respectively.

7. Click the **Add** button to add another menu item to the DropDown-Button. Change the menu item's Name, DisplayStyle, and Text properties to **mnuAverageFull**, **Text**, and **Full-time Employees**, respectively.

8. Click the **OK** button to close the Items Collection Editor (ddbAverage.DropDownItems) dialog box, then click the **OK** button to close the Items Collection Editor dialog box.

9. Save the solution. Click the **down arrow** on the Average Pay Rate button. See Figure 13-37.

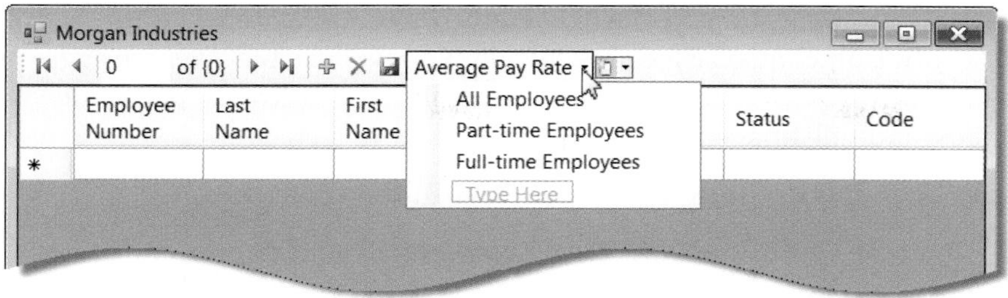

Figure 13-37 DropDownButton added to the TblEmployBindingNavigator control

Using the LINQ Aggregate Operators

LINQ provides several aggregate operators—namely, Average, Count, Max, Min, and Sum—that you can use when querying a dataset. An **aggregate operator** returns a single value from a group of values. The Sum operator, for example, returns the sum of the values in the group, whereas the Min operator returns the smallest value in the group. You include an aggregate operator in a LINQ statement using the syntax shown in Figure 13-38. The figure also includes examples of using the syntax.

LINQ aggregate operators

Syntax

Dim *variable* [**As** *dataType*] = **Aggregate** *element* **In** *dataset.table*
[**Where** *condition*]
Select *element.field*
Into *aggregateOperator*()

Example 1

```
Dim dblAvgRate As Double = _
   Aggregate employee In EmployeesDataSet.tblEmploy _
   Select employee.Rate _
   Into Average()
```

calculates the average of the pay rates in the dataset and assigns the result to the `dblAvgRate` variable

Example 2

```
Dim dblMaxRate As Double = _
   Aggregate employee In EmployeesDataSet.tblEmploy _
   Where employee.Status.ToUpper = "P" _
   Select employee.Rate _
   Into Max()
```

finds the highest pay rate for a part-time employee and assigns the result to the `dblMaxRate` variable

Example 3

```
Dim intCounter As Integer = _
   Aggregate employee In EmployeesDataSet.tblEmploy _
   Where employee.Code = 2 _
   Select employee.Emp_Number _
   Into Count()
```

counts the number of employees whose department code is 2 and assigns the result to the `intCounter` variable

Figure 13-38 Syntax and examples of the LINQ aggregate operators

In the following set of steps, you will code the three menu items on the DropDownButton control. More specifically, you will use the Average aggregate operator to calculate the average pay rate for all employees, part-time employees, and full-time employees.

To code the menu items on the DropDownButton control:

1. Open the Code Editor window. Replace the <your name> and <current date> text in the comments with your name and the current date.
2. Open the code template for the mnuAverageAll item's Click event procedure. Type **' displays the average pay rate for all employees** and press **Enter** twice.
3. Enter the following three lines of code. Be sure to include a space before each line continuation character. Press **Enter** twice after typing the last line.

```
Dim dblAverage As Double = _
    Aggregate employee In EmployeesDataSet.tblEmploy _
    Select employee.Rate Into Average()
```

4. Now enter the following four lines of code. Here again, be sure to include a space before each line continuation character.

```
MessageBox.Show("Average pay rate for all employees: " _
                & dblAverage.ToString("C2"), _
                "Morgan Industries", MessageBoxButtons.OK, _
                MessageBoxIcon.Information)
```

5. Open the code template for the mnuAveragePart item's Click event procedure. Type **' displays the average pay rate for part-time employees** and press **Enter** twice.
6. Enter the following four lines of code. Be sure to include a space before each line continuation character. Press **Enter** twice after typing the last line.

```
Dim dblAverage As Double = _
    Aggregate employee In EmployeesDataSet.tblEmploy _
    Where employee.Status.ToUpper = "P" _
    Select employee.Rate Into Average()
```

7. Now enter the following four lines of code. Here again, be sure to include a space before each line continuation character.

```
MessageBox.Show("Average pay rate for part-time employees: " _
                & dblAverage.ToString("C2"), _
                "Morgan Industries", MessageBoxButtons.OK, _
                MessageBoxIcon.Information)
```

8. Open the code template for the mnuAverageFull item's Click event procedure. Type **' displays the average pay rate for full-time employees** and press **Enter** twice.
9. On your own, enter the appropriate LINQ statement and MessageBox.Show method.

10. Save the solution. Figure 13-39 shows the code entered in each menu item's Click event procedure.

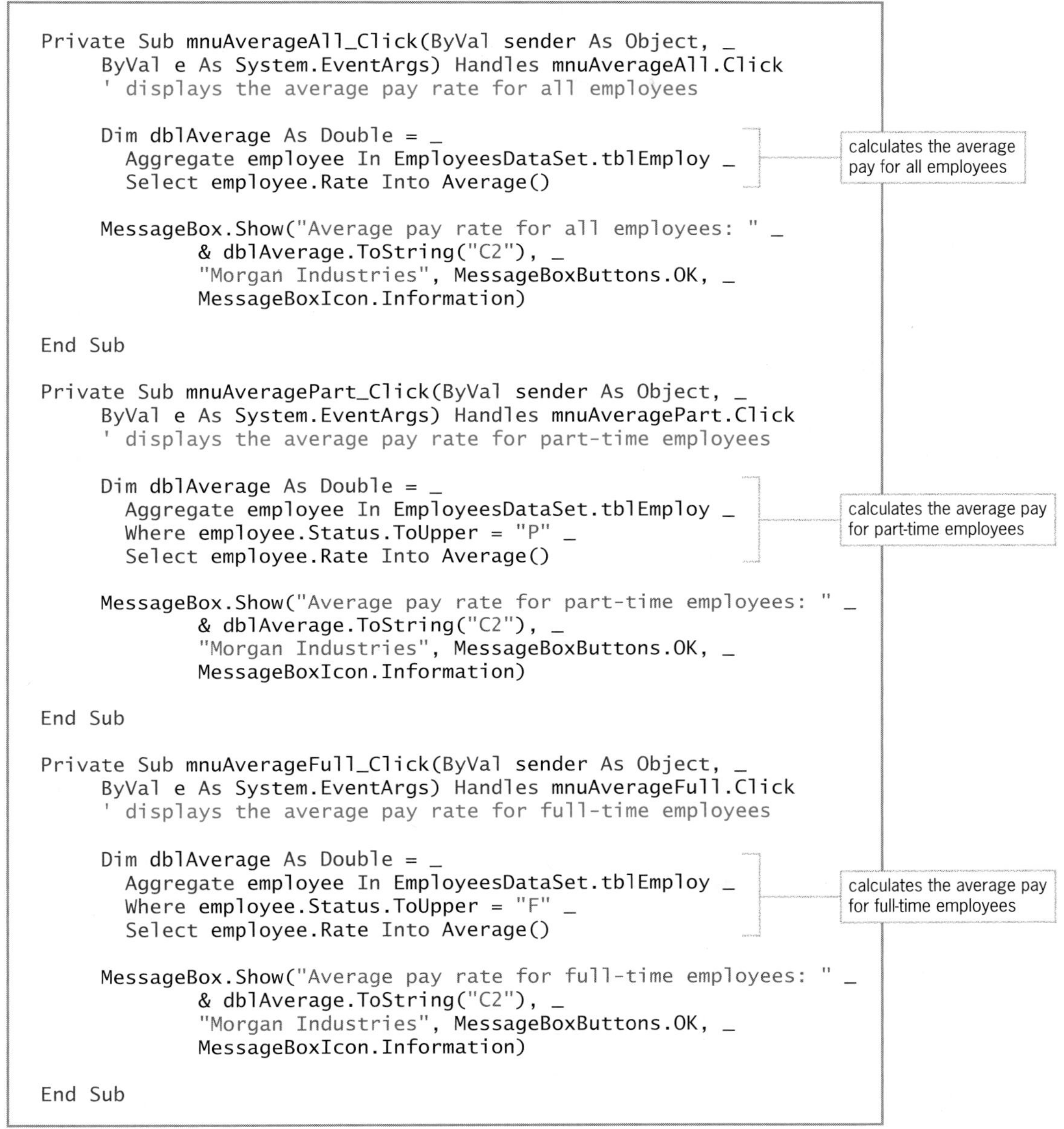

```
Private Sub mnuAverageAll_Click(ByVal sender As Object, _
     ByVal e As System.EventArgs) Handles mnuAverageAll.Click
     ' displays the average pay rate for all employees

     Dim dblAverage As Double = _
       Aggregate employee In EmployeesDataSet.tblEmploy _
       Select employee.Rate Into Average()

     MessageBox.Show("Average pay rate for all employees: " _
             & dblAverage.ToString("C2"), _
             "Morgan Industries", MessageBoxButtons.OK, _
             MessageBoxIcon.Information)

End Sub

Private Sub mnuAveragePart_Click(ByVal sender As Object, _
     ByVal e As System.EventArgs) Handles mnuAveragePart.Click
     ' displays the average pay rate for part-time employees

     Dim dblAverage As Double = _
       Aggregate employee In EmployeesDataSet.tblEmploy _
       Where employee.Status.ToUpper = "P" _
       Select employee.Rate Into Average()

     MessageBox.Show("Average pay rate for part-time employees: " _
             & dblAverage.ToString("C2"), _
             "Morgan Industries", MessageBoxButtons.OK, _
             MessageBoxIcon.Information)

End Sub

Private Sub mnuAverageFull_Click(ByVal sender As Object, _
     ByVal e As System.EventArgs) Handles mnuAverageFull.Click
     ' displays the average pay rate for full-time employees

     Dim dblAverage As Double = _
       Aggregate employee In EmployeesDataSet.tblEmploy _
       Where employee.Status.ToUpper = "F" _
       Select employee.Rate Into Average()

     MessageBox.Show("Average pay rate for full-time employees: " _
             & dblAverage.ToString("C2"), _
             "Morgan Industries", MessageBoxButtons.OK, _
             MessageBoxIcon.Information)

End Sub
```


Figure 13-39 Code entered in each menu item's Click event procedure

To test the code in each menu item's Click event procedure:

1. Save the solution, if necessary, then start the application. Click the **down arrow** on the Average Pay Rate button, then click **All Employees**. See Figure 13-40.

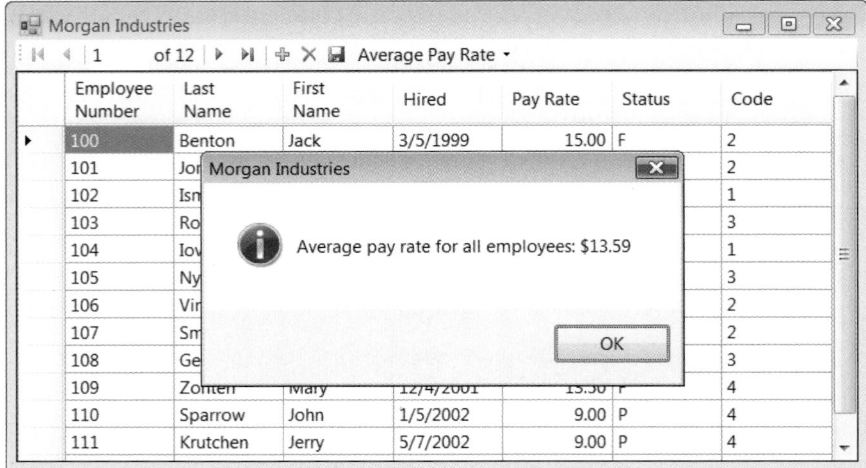

Figure 13-40 Message box showing the average pay rate for all employees

2. Click the **OK** button to close the message box. Click the **down arrow** on the Average Pay Rate button, then click **Part-time Employees**. The message indicates that the average pay rate for part-time employees is $10.08.

3. Click the **OK** button to close the message box. Click the **down arrow** on the Average Pay Rate button, then click **Full-time Employees**. The message indicates that the average pay rate for full-time employees is $17.10.

4. Click the **OK** button to close the message box, then click the **Close** button on the form's title bar to stop the application. Close the Code Editor window, then close the solution.

Lesson B Summary

- **To use LINQ to select and arrange records in a dataset:**

  Use the syntax shown in Figure 13-32.

- **To add items to a BindingNavigator control:**

  Follow the steps listed in Figure 13-35.

- **To use the LINQ aggregate operators:**

  Use the syntax shown in Figure 13-38.

Lesson B Key Terms

Aggregate operator—an operator that returns a single value from a group of values; LINQ provides the Average, Count, Max, Min, and Sum aggregate operators

Language Integrated Query—LINQ; the new query language in Visual Basic 2008

LINQ—an acronym for Language Integrated Query

Order By clause—used to arrange the records in a dataset

Query—specifies the records to select in a dataset, as well as the order in which to arrange the records

Where clause—used to limit the records you want to view in a dataset

Lesson B Review Questions

1. Which of the following will select only records whose LastName field begins with an uppercase letter A?

   a.
   ```
   Dim records = From name In NamesDataSet.tblNames _
                 Where name.LastName Like "A*" _
                 Select name
   ```
   b.
   ```
   Dim records = From NamesDataSet.tblNames _
                 Select LastName Like "A*"
   ```
   c.
   ```
   Dim records = From tblNames _
                 Where tblName.LastName Like "A*" _
                 Select name
   ```
   d.
   ```
   Dim records = From name In NamesDataSet.tblNames _
                 Where tblName.LastName Like "A* _"
                 Select name
   ```

2. Which of the following calculates the sum of the values stored in a numeric field named JulySales?

   a.
   ```
   Dim dblTotal As Double = _
       From sales In SalesDataSet.tblSales _
       Select sales.JulySales _
       Into Sum()
   ```
   b.
   ```
   Dim dblTotal As Double = _
       Aggregate sales In SalesDataSet.tblSales _
       Select sales.JulySales _
       Into Sum()
   ```
   c.
   ```
   Dim dblTotal As Double = _
       From sales In SalesDataSet.tblSales _
       Aggregate sales.JulySales _
       Into Sum()
   ```
   d.
   ```
   Dim dblTotal As Double = _
       From sales In SalesDataSet.tblSales _
       Sum sales.JulySales
   ```

3. Which of the following statements selects all of the records in the tblStates table?

a.
```
Dim records = _
    From state In StatesDataSet.tblStates _
    Select All state
```

b.
```
Dim records = _
    From state In StatesDataSet.tblStates _
    Select state
```

c.
```
Dim records = _
    Select state From StatesDataSet.tblStates
```

d.
```
Dim records = From StatesDataSet.tblStates _
    Select tblStates.state
```

4. The tblCities table contains a numeric field named Population. Which of the following statements selects all cities having a population that exceeds 15,000?

a.
```
Dim records = _
    From city In CitiesDataSet.tblCities _
    Where Population > 15000 _
    Select city
```

b.
```
Dim records = _
    From city In CitiesDataSet.tblCities _
    Select city.Population > 15000
```

c.
```
Dim records = _
    From city In CitiesDataSet.tblCities _
    Where city.Population > 15000 _
    Select city
```

d.
```
Dim records = Select city.Population > 15000 _
    From tblCities
```

5. The tblCities table contains a numeric field named Population. Which of the following statements calculates the total population of all the cities in the table?

a.
```
Dim intTotal As Integer = _
    Aggregate city In CitiesDataSet.tblCities _
    Select city.Population _
    Into Sum()
```

b.
```
Dim intTotal As Integer = _
    Sum city In CitiesDataSet.tblCities _
    Select city.Population _
    Into Total()
```

c.
```
Dim intTotal As Integer = _
    Aggregate CitiesDataSet.tblCities.city _
    Select city.Population _
    Into Sum()
```

d.
```
Dim intTotal As Integer = _
    Sum city In CitiesDataSet.tblCities.Population
```

6. In a LINQ statement, the ________________________ clause limits the records that will be selected.

   a. Limit b. Order By

   c. Select d. Where

Lesson B Exercises

INTRODUCTORY

1. The tblMagInfo table contains three fields. The Code and Cost fields are numeric. The Magazine field contains text. The dataset's name is MagsDataSet.

   a. Write a LINQ statement that arranges the records in descending order by the Cost field.

   b. Write a LINQ statement that selects records having a code of 9.

   c. Write a LINQ statement that selects records having a cost of $3 or more.

   d. Write a LINQ statement that selects the Daily Food Guide magazine.

   e. Write a LINQ statement that selects magazines whose name begins with the letter G (in either uppercase or lowercase).

   f. Write a LINQ statement that calculates the average cost of a magazine.

INTRODUCTORY

2. In this exercise, you modify one of the Morgan Industries applications from the lesson. Use Windows to make a copy of the Morgan Industries Solution-Aggregate folder, which is contained in the VB2008\Chap13 folder. Rename the copy Modified Morgan Industries Solution-Aggregate. Open the Morgan Industries Solution (Morgan Industries Solution.sln) file contained in the VB2008\Chap13\Modified Morgan Industries Solution-Aggregate folder. Open the designer window.

   a. Click an empty area on the TblEmployBindingNavigator control, then click the control's task box. Click Edit Items in the task list to open the Items Collection Editor dialog box. Add a DropDown-Button to the control. Change the DropDownButton's name to ddbDepartment. Change its DisplayStyle and Text properties to Text and Department, respectively.

   b. Use the DropDownItems property to add four menu items to the DropDownButton: Accounting, Advertising, Personnel, and Inventory. Be sure to change each menu item's name, as well as its DisplayStyle and Text properties.

   c. Each menu item should display (in a message box) the number of employees in the department. Code 1 is Accounting, Code 2 is Advertising, Code 3 is Personnel, and Code 4 is Inventory. Open the Code Editor window and code each menu item's Click event procedure.

   d. Save the solution, then start the application. Test each menu item. Stop the application, then close the Code Editor window and solution.

INTRODUCTORY

3. Open the Magazine Solution (Magazine Solution.sln) file, which is contained in the VB2008\Chap13\Magazine Solution-Introductory folder. If necessary, open the designer window. The application is connected to the Magazines database. The database is stored in the Magazines.accdb file, which is located in the VB2008\Chap13\Access Databases folder. The database contains a table named tblMagazine; the table has three fields. The Cost field is numeric. The Code and MagName fields contain text. Start the application to view the records contained in the dataset, then stop the application. Open the Code Editor window. Code the btnDisplayCode control's Click event procedure so that it displays the record whose Code field contains PG24. Code the btnDisplayName control's Click event procedure so that it displays only the Java record. Code the btnDisplayAll control's Click event procedure so that it displays all of the records. Save the solution, then start and test the application. Stop the application, then close the Code Editor window and solution.

INTERMEDIATE

4. Open the Magazine Solution (Magazine Solution.sln) file, which is contained in the VB2008\Chap13\Magazine Solution-Intermediate folder. If necessary, open the designer window. The application is connected to the Magazines database. The database is stored in the Magazines.accdb file, which is located in the VB2008\Chap13\Access Databases folder. The database contains a table named tblMagazine; the table has three fields. The Cost field is numeric. The Code and MagName fields contain text. Start the application to view the records contained in the dataset, then stop the application. Open the Code Editor window. Code the btnDisplayAll control's Click event procedure so that it displays all of the records. Code the btnDisplayCost control's Click event procedure so that it displays records having a cost of $4 or more. Code the btnDisplayName control's Click event procedure so that it displays only magazines whose name begins with the letter C (in either uppercase or lowercase). Code the btnDisplayAverage control's Click event procedure so that it displays the average cost of a magazine. Display the average in a message box. Save the solution, then start and test the application. Stop the application, then close the Code Editor window and solution.

LESSON C

After studying Lesson C, you should be able to:

- Prevent the user from adding and deleting records
- Remove buttons from a BindingNavigator control
- Add a label, text box, and button to a BindingNavigator control

Completing the Paradise Bookstore Application

As you may remember, your task in this chapter is to create an application for the Paradise Bookstore. The application should display the records contained in a Microsoft Access 2007 database named Books. The application should allow the store manager to enter an author's name (or part of a name), and then display only the books written by the author. You will accomplish this task using a label, text box, and button, which you will add to the application's BindingNavigator control. In addition, the application should allow the store manager to display the total value of the books in the store. You will provide a button on the BindingNavigator control for this purpose. The Books database is contained in the Books.accdb file, which is located in the VB2008\Chap13\Access Databases folder. The database contains one table, named tblBooks. The table has five fields and 11 records. The BookNumber, Price, and QuantityInStock fields are numeric. The Title and Author fields contain text. The fields and records contained in the tblBooks table are shown in Figure 13-41.

BookNumber	Title	Author	Price	QuantityInStock
101	Garden of Eden	Smith, Leona	35.99	15
146	Rosebud	Smith, Leona	24.5	20
224	Cycle World	Russel, John	15.99	5
233	Motorcycle Mania	Russel, John	12.99	2
322	Truthfully Yours	Staven, Harriet	45.5	20
367	Romance and You	Staven, Harriet	10.99	15
401	My Hero	Smith, Carol	63.99	23
402	Laddie the Dog	Smith, Carol	10.99	11
561	That Was the Day	Handel, Pat	15.99	4
581	Rusty the Robot	Handel, Pat	9.99	3
603	Philomena	Smith, Carol	24.5	1

Figure 13-41 tblBooks table in the Books database

To open the Paradise Bookstore application, and then modify the DataGridView and BindingNavigator controls:

1. If necessary, start Visual Studio 2008 or Visual Basic 2008 Express Edition. Close the Start Page window.
2. Open the **Paradise Bookstore** (**Paradise Bookstore.sln**) file, which is contained in the VB2008\Chap13 folder. If necessary, open the designer window.

3. In this application, the user will not be allowed to add or delete records. Click the **TblBooksDataGridView** control. (Be sure to click the TblBooksDataGridView control rather than the TblBooksBindingNavigator control.) Click the control's **task box** to open its task list. Click the **Enable Adding** and **Enable Deleting** check boxes to deselect both check boxes. Click the **form's title bar** to close the task list.
4. Click the **TblBooksBindingNavigator** control, then click its **task box**. Click **Edit Items** on the task list. Click **BindingNavigatorAddNewItem** in the Members list, then click the ***X*** button to remove the item from the list. This also removes the Add new button ✚ from the TblBooksBindingNavigator control.
5. Click **BindingNavigatorDeleteItem** in the Members list, then click the ***X*** button to remove the item from the list. This also removes the Delete button ✕ from the TblBooksBindingNavigator control.
6. Now add a label, text box, and button for entering the author's name. Click the **down arrow** in the "Select item and add to list below" box, then click **Label** in the list. Click the **Add** button. Click the **Alphabetical** button to display the property names in alphabetical order. Click **Text** in the properties list, then type **&Author:** and press **Enter**.
7. Click the **down arrow** in the "Select item and add to list below" box, then click **TextBox** in the list. Click the **Add** button. Click **(Name)** in the properties list, then type **txtAuthor** and press **Enter**.
8. Click the **down arrow** in the "Select item and add to list below" box, then click **Button** in the list. Click the **Add** button. Change the button's name to **btnGo**. Also change its DisplayStyle property to **Text**, and change its Text property to **&Go**.
9. Finally, add a button for displaying the total value of the books. Click the **Add** button again to add another button to the BindingNavigator control. Change the button's name to **btnTotal**. Also change its DisplayStyle property to Text, and change its Text property to **&Total Value**. Click the **OK** button to close the dialog box.
10. Save the solution, then click the **form's title bar**. See Figure 13-42.

Figure 13-42 Completed TblBooksBindingNavigator control

Coding the Paradise Bookstore Application

The Go button's Click event procedure should display only records whose Author field begins with the one or more characters entered in the txtAuthor control. If the text box is empty, the Go button should display all of the records.

To code the Go button's Click event procedure, then test the procedure:

1. Open the Code Editor window. Replace the <your name> and <current date> text in the comments with your name and the current date.
2. Open the code template for the btnGo control's Click event procedure. Type **' display records for a specific author** and press **Enter** twice.
3. You can use LINQ to select the appropriate records. Enter the following lines of code. Be sure to include a space before each line continuation character. Press **Enter** twice after typing the last line.

```
Dim records = From book In BooksDataSet.tblBooks _
              Where book.Author.ToUpper Like _
              txtAuthor.Text.ToUpper & "*" _
              Select book
```

4. Now display the records in the DataGridView control. As you learned in Lesson B, you do this by assigning the `records` variable to the BindingSource control's DataSource property. Enter the following line of code.

```
TblBooksBindingSource.DataSource = records.AsDataView
```

5. Save the solution, then start the application. Click the **Author** text box (or press Alt+a), then type the letter **s**. Click the **Go** button (or press Alt+g). The DataGridView control shows only the books written by authors whose name begins with the letter s. See Figure 13-43.

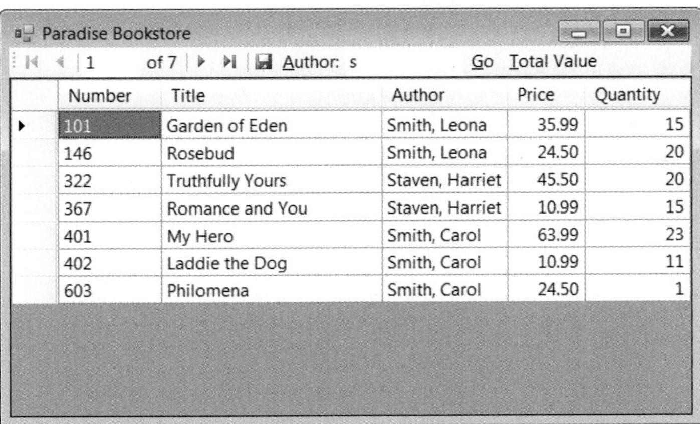

Number	Title	Author	Price	Quantity
101	Garden of Eden	Smith, Leona	35.99	15
146	Rosebud	Smith, Leona	24.50	20
322	Truthfully Yours	Staven, Harriet	45.50	20
367	Romance and You	Staven, Harriet	10.99	15
401	My Hero	Smith, Carol	63.99	23
402	Laddie the Dog	Smith, Carol	10.99	11
603	Philomena	Smith, Carol	24.50	1

Figure 13-43 Books written by authors whose name begins with s

6. Remove the letter s from the Author text box, then click the **Go** button. All of the records appear in the DataGridView control.
7. Click the **Close** button on the form's title bar to stop the application.

The Total Value button's Click event procedure should display the total value of the books in the store. The total value is calculated by multiplying the quantity of each book by its price, and then adding together the results.

To code the Total Value button's Click event procedure, then test the procedure:

1. Open the code template for the btnTotal control's Click event procedure. Type **' display the total value of the inventory** and press **Enter** twice.

2. You can use the Sum aggregate operator to accumulate the results of multiplying each book's quantity by its price. The quantity is stored in the QuantityInStock field, and the price is stored in the Price field. Enter the following lines of code. Be sure to include a space before each line continuation character. Press **Enter** twice after typing the last line.

```
Dim dblTotal As Double = _
    Aggregate book In BooksDataSet.tblBooks _
    Select book.QuantityInStock * book.Price _
    Into Sum()
```

3. Now display the total value in a message box. Enter the following lines of code. Here again, be sure to include a space before each line continuation character.

```
MessageBox.Show("Total value: " _
                & dblTotal.ToString("C2"), _
                "Paradise Bookstore", MessageBoxButtons.OK, _
                MessageBoxIcon.Information)
```

4. Save the solution, then start the application. Click the **Total Value** button (or press Alt+t). The total value of the inventory appears in a message box. See Figure 13-44.

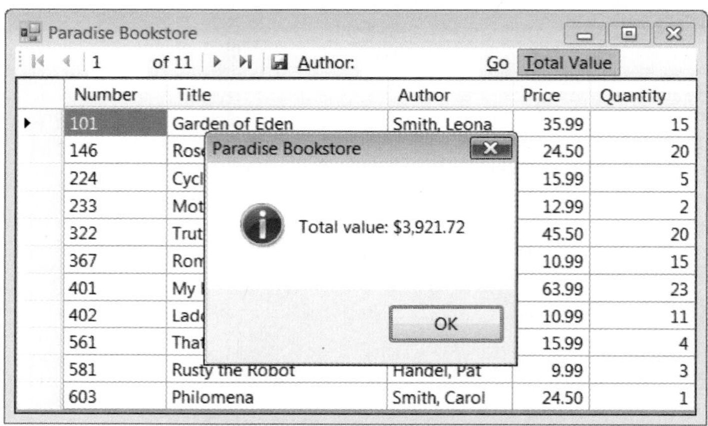

Figure 13-44 Message box showing the total value of the inventory

5. Click the **OK** button to close the message box, then click the **Close** button on the form's title bar to stop the application.

6. Close the Code Editor window, then close the solution. Figure 13-45 shows the code entered in the btnGo and btnTotal Click event procedures.

```
Private Sub btnGo_Click(ByVal sender As Object, _
   ByVal e As System.EventArgs) Handles btnGo.Click
   ' display records for a specific author

   Dim records = From book In BooksDataSet.tblBooks _
                 Where book.Author.ToUpper Like _
                 txtAuthor.Text.ToUpper & "*" _
                 Select book

   TblBooksBindingSource.DataSource = records.AsDataView

End Sub

Private Sub btnTotal_Click(ByVal sender As Object, _
   ByVal e As System.EventArgs) Handles btnTotal.Click
   ' display the total value of the inventory

   Dim dblTotal As Double = _
      Aggregate book In BooksDataSet.tblBooks _
      Select book.QuantityInStock * book.Price _
      Into Sum()

      MessageBox.Show("Total value: " _
                      & dblTotal.ToString("C2"), _
                      "Paradise Bookstore", MessageBoxButtons.OK, _
                      MessageBoxIcon.Information)

End Sub
```

Figure 13-45 Click event procedures for the btnGo and btnTotal controls

Lesson C Summary

- **To prevent the user from adding or deleting records in a DataGrid-View control:**

  Click the DataGridView control's task box, then deselect the Enable Adding and Enable Deleting check boxes.

- **To delete items from a BindingNavigator control:**

  Click the BindingNavigator control's task box, then click Edit Items. In the Members list, click the item you want to remove, then click the *X* button.

- **To add a label, text box, or button to a BindingNavigator control:**

  Click the BindingNavigator control's task box, then click Edit Items. Use the Members list and Add button to add the appropriate control.

Lesson C Key Terms

There are no key terms in Lesson C.

Lesson C Review Questions

1. The Enable Adding check box in a ______________________ control's task list determines whether a record can be added to the control.

   a. BindingNavigator

   b. DataGridView

   c. BindingSource

   d. DataBindingNavigator

2. Using the Books database from the lesson, which of the following will select book number 224? The BookNumber field is numeric.

   a.
   ```
   Dim records = From book In BooksDataSet.tblBooks _
          Where book.BookNumber = 224 _
          Select book
   ```

   b.
   ```
   Dim records = From book In BooksDataSet.tblBooks _
          Select book.BookNumber = 224
   ```

   c.
   ```
   Dim records = From book In BooksDataSet.tblBooks _
          Where book.BookNumber = "224" _
          Select book
   ```

   d. None of the above.

3. Using the Books database from the lesson, which of the following determines the number of records in the tblBooks table?

   a.
   ```
   Dim intNum As Integer = _
         Aggregate book In BooksDataSet.tblBooks _
         In Count()
   ```

   b.
   ```
   Dim intNum As Integer = _
         Aggregate book In BooksDataSet.tblBooks _
         Into Count()
   ```

   c.
   ```
   Dim intNum As Integer = _
         Aggregate book In BooksDataSet.tblBooks _
         Into Sum()
   ```

   d. None of the above.

Lesson C Exercises

INTRODUCTORY

1. Open the Addison Playhouse Solution (Addison Playhouse Solution.sln) file, which is contained in the VB2008\Chap13\Addison Playhouse Solution folder. If necessary, open the designer window. The application should display the contents of the Play database in a DataGridView control. The database is stored in the Play.accdb file, which is located in the VB2008\Chap13\Access Databases folder. The

Play database contains one table named tblReservations. The table contains 20 records, each having three fields: a numeric field named Seat and two text fields named Patron and Phone. The DataGridView control should allow the user to add, edit, delete, and save records. Create the interface, then open the Code Editor window and include a Try...Catch statement in the Save Data button's Click event procedure. Save the solution, then start and test the application. Stop the application. Close the Code Editor window, then close the solution.

INTRODUCTORY

2. Open the Sports Action Solution (Sports Action Solution.sln) file, which is contained in the VB2008\Chap13\Sports Action Solution folder. Open the designer window. The application should display each record contained in the Sports database, one at a time, in label controls. The database is stored in the Sports.accdb file, which is located in the VB2008\Chap13\Access Databases folder. The database contains one table named tblScores. The table contains 10 records, each having five fields that store the following information: a unique number that identifies the game, the name of the opposing team, the date of the game, the home team's score, and the opposing team's score. The user should not be allowed to add, delete, edit, or save records. Create the interface. Include a button on a BindingNavigator control to allow the user to display the average of the home team's scores. Open the Code Editor window and code the application. Save the solution, then start and test the application. Stop the application. Close the Code Editor window, then close the solution.

INTERMEDIATE

3. Carl Simons, the sales manager at JW Industries, records the item number, name, and price of each product the company sells in a database named Items. The Items database is stored in the Items.accdb file, which is contained in the VB2008\Chap13\Access Databases folder. The database contains one table, named tblItems. The table contains 10 records, each composed of three fields. The ItemNum and ItemName fields contain text, and the Price field contains numbers. Mr. Simons wants an application that displays the records in a DataGridView control, but does not allow him to add or delete records. The application should allow him to display records whose item number matches one or more characters he enters. In addition, the application should allow him to display the average price.

   a. Create a Visual Basic Windows application. Name the solution, project, and form file JW Solution, JW Project, and Main Form.vb, respectively. Save the application in the VB2008\Chap13 folder.

   b. Connect the application to the Items database, then drag the tblItems object to the form. Make the appropriate modifications to the DataGridView and BindingNavigator controls.

   c. Open the Code Editor window and code the application. Save the solution, then start and test the application. Stop the application. Close the Code Editor window, then close the solution.

INTERMEDIATE

4. In this exercise, you use a Microsoft Access 2007 database named Courses. The database is contained in the Courses.accdb file, which is located in the VB2008\Chap13\Access Databases folder. The database contains one table named tblCourses. The table has 10 records, each having four fields: ID, Title, CreditHours, and Grade. The CreditHours field is numeric; the other fields contain text.

   a. Open the College Courses Solution (College Courses Solution.sln) file, which is contained in the VB2008\Chap13\College Courses Solution folder. If necessary, open the designer window. Connect the application to the Courses database. Drag the table into the group box control, then dock the DataGridView control in its parent container. (In this case, the parent container is the group box control.) Use the task list to disable Adding, Editing, and Deleting. Change the DataGridView control's AutoSizeColumnsMode property to Fill. Change its RowHeadersVisible property to False.

   b. Remove the BindingNavigator control from the form by deleting the BindingNavigator object from the component tray.

   c. Open the Code Editor window. Delete the Save Data button's Click event procedure. Code the Next Record and Previous Record buttons. Code the Grade Display button so it allows the user to display either all the records or only the records matching a specific grade.

   d. Save the solution, then start and test the application. Stop the application, then close the Code Editor window and solution.

ADVANCED

5. In this exercise, you modify the College Courses application from Exercise 4. Use Windows to make a copy of the College Courses Solution folder, which is contained in the VB2008\Chap13 folder. Rename the folder Modified College Courses Solution. Open the College Courses Solution (College Courses Solution.sln) file contained in the VB2008\Chap13\Modified College Courses Solution folder. Open the designer window. Add a Calculate GPA button to the form. Open the Code Editor window. Code the Calculate GPA button's Click event procedure so it displays the student's GPA. (An A grade is worth 4 points, a B is worth 3 points, and so on.) Save the solution, then start and test the application. Stop the application, then close the Code Editor window and solution.

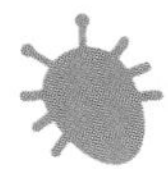

Swat The Bugs

6. Open the Debug Solution (Debug Solution.sln) file, which is contained in the VB2008\Chap13\Debug Solution-Lesson C folder. Open the Code Editor window and review the existing code. Correct the code to remove the jagged line that appears below one of the lines of code. Save the solution, then start and test the application. Notice that the application is not working correctly. Stop the application. Correct the errors in the application's code. Save the solution, then start and test the application again. Stop the application. Close the Code Editor window, then close the solution.

APPENDIX A

GUI Design Guidelines

Chapter 1—Lesson C

FormBorderStyle, ControlBox, MaximizeBox, MinimizeBox, and StartPosition properties:

- A splash screen should not have Minimize, Maximize, or Close buttons, and its borders should not be sizable. In most cases, a splash screen's FormBorderStyle property is set to either None or FixedSingle. Its StartPosition property is set to CenterScreen.
- A form that is not a splash screen should always have a Minimize button and a Close button, but you can choose to disable the Maximize button. Typically, the FormBorderStyle property is set to Sizable; however, it also can be set to FixedSingle. Most times, the form's StartPosition property is set to CenterScreen.

Chapter 2—Lesson A

Layout and Organization of the User Interface

- Organize the user interface so that the information flows either vertically or horizontally, with the most important information always located in the upper-left corner of the screen. When positioning the controls, maintain a consistent margin from the edge of the form.
- Group related controls together using either white (empty) space or one of the tools contained in the Containers section of the toolbox.
- Use a label to identify each text box in the user interface. Also use a label to identify other label controls that display program output. The label text should be meaningful. It also should be from one to three words only and appear on one line. Left-align the text within the label, and position the label either above or to the left of the control it identifies. Follow the label text with a colon (:) and use sentence capitalization.

- Display meaningful text on the face of each button. Enter the text using book title capitalization. The text should indicate the action the button will perform when it is clicked. Place the text on one line and use from one to three words only.
- Size the buttons in a group of buttons relative to each other, and place the most commonly used button first in the group.
- Align the borders of the controls wherever possible to minimize the number of different margins used in the interface.

Chapter 2—Lesson B

Adding Graphics

- Include a graphic in an interface only if it is necessary to do so. If the graphic is used solely for aesthetics, use a small graphic and place it in a location that will not distract the user.

Selecting Font Types, Styles, and Sizes

- Use only one font type for all of the text in the interface. Use a sans serif font, preferably the Segoe UI font.
- Use no more than two different font sizes in the interface.
- Avoid using italics and underlining, because these font styles make text difficult to read.
- Limit the use of bold text to titles, headings, and key items that you want to emphasize.

Selecting Colors

- Build the interface using black, white, and gray first, then add color only if you have a good reason to do so.
- Use white, off-white, or light gray for the background and black for the text.
- Never use a dark color for the background or a light color for the text. A dark background is hard on the eyes, and light-colored text can appear blurry.
- Limit the number of colors in an interface to three, not including white, black, and gray. The colors you choose should complement each other.
- Never use color as the only means of identification for an element in the user interface.

Setting the BorderStyle Property of a Text Box or Label

- Leave the BorderStyle property of text boxes at the default value, Fixed3D.
- Keep the BorderStyle property of labels that identify other controls at the default value, None.
- Set to FixedSingle the BorderStyle property of labels that display program output, such as those that display the result of a calculation.
- In Windows applications, a control that contains data that the user is not allowed to edit does not usually appear three-dimensional. Therefore, you should avoid setting a label control's BorderStyle property to Fixed3D.

Setting the AutoSize Property of a Label

- Keep the AutoSize property of identifying labels at the default value, True.
- In most cases, change to False the AutoSize property of label controls that display program output.

Assigning Access Keys

- Assign a unique access key to each control that can accept user input, such as text boxes and buttons.
- When assigning an access key to a control, use the first letter of the caption or identifying label, unless another letter provides a more meaningful association. If you can't use the first letter and no other letter provides a more meaningful association, then use a distinctive consonant. Lastly, use a vowel or a number.

Using the TabIndex Property to Control the Focus

- Assign a TabIndex value (starting with 0) to each control in the interface, except for controls that do not have a TabIndex property. The TabIndex values should reflect the order in which the user will want to access the controls.
- To give users keyboard access to a text box, assign an access key to the text box's identifying label. Set the identifying label's TabIndex property to a value that is one number less than the value stored in the text box's TabIndex property.

Chapter 3—Lesson B

InputBox Function's Prompt and Title Capitalization

- Use sentence capitalization for the *prompt*, but book title capitalization for the *title*.

Assigning a Default Button

- The default button should be the button that is most often selected by the user, except in cases where the tasks performed by the button are both destructive and irreversible. In most interfaces, the default button typically is the first button.

Chapter 4—Lesson B

Labeling a Group Box

- Use sentence capitalization for the optional identifying label, which is entered in the group box's Text property.

MessageBox.Show Method

- Use sentence capitalization for the *text* argument, but book title capitalization for the *caption* argument.
- Display the Exclamation or Question icon to alert the user that he or she must make a decision before the application can continue. You can phrase the message as a question.

- Display the Information icon along with an OK button in a message box that displays an informational message.
- Display the Stop icon to alert the user of a serious problem that must be corrected before the application can continue.
- The default button in the dialog box should be the one that represents the user's most likely action, as long as that action is not destructive.

Chapter 5—Lesson B

Radio Button Standards

- Use radio buttons to limit the user to one choice in a group of related but mutually exclusive choices.
- The minimum number of radio buttons in a group is two, and the recommended maximum number is seven.
- The label in the radio button's Text property should be entered using sentence capitalization.
- Assign a unique access key to each radio button in an interface.
- Use a container (such as a group box) to create separate groups of radio buttons. Only one button in each group can be selected at any one time.
- Designate a default radio button in each group of radio buttons.

Check Box Standards

- Use check boxes to allow the user to select any number of choices from a group of one or more independent and nonexclusive choices.
- The label in the check box's Text property should be entered using sentence capitalization.
- Assign a unique access key to each check box in an interface.

Chapter 6—Lesson C

List Box Standards

- A list box should contain a minimum of three items.
- A list box should display a minimum of three choices and a maximum of eight choices at a time.
- Use a label control to provide keyboard access to the list box. Set the label's TabIndex property to a value that is one less than the list box's TabIndex value.
- List box items are either arranged by use, with the most used entries appearing first in the list, or sorted in ascending order.

Default List Box Item

- If a list box allows the user to make only one selection, a default item should be selected when the interface first appears. The default item should be either the item selected most frequently or the first item in the list. However, if a list box allows more than one selection at a time, you do not select a default item.

Chapter 7—Lesson B

Combo Box Standards

- Use a label control to provide keyboard access to the combo box. Set the label's TabIndex property to a value that is one less than the combo box's TabIndex value.
- Combo box items are either arranged by use, with the most used entries appearing first in the list, or sorted in ascending order.

Chapter 8—Lesson B

Designing Menus

- Menu title captions should be one word only, with the first letter capitalized. Each menu title should have a unique access key.
- Menu item captions can be from one to three words. Use book title capitalization and assign a unique access key to each menu item on the same menu.
- Assign unique shortcut keys to commonly used menu items.
- If a menu item requires additional information from the user, place an ellipsis (...) at the end of the item's caption, which is entered in the item's Text property.
- Follow the Windows standards for the placement of menu titles and items.
- Use a separator bar to separate groups of related menu items.

APPENDIX B

Visual Basic Conversion Functions

Figure B-1 lists the Visual Basic conversion functions. As you learned in Chapter 3, you can use the conversion functions (rather than the Convert methods) to convert an expression from one data type to another.

Syntax	**Return data type**	**Range for *expression***
CBool(*expression*)	Boolean	Any valid String or numeric expression
CByte(*expression*)	Byte	0 through 255 (unsigned)
CChar(*expression*)	Char	Any valid String expression; value can be 0 through 65535 (unsigned); only first character is converted
CDate(*expression*)	Date	Any valid representation of a date and time
CDbl(*expression*)	Double	–1.79769313486231570E+308 through –4.94065645841246544E-324 for negative values; 4.94065645841246544E-324 through 1.79769313486231570E+308 for positive values
CDec(*expression*)	Decimal	+/–79,228,162,514,264,337,593,543,950,335 for zero-scaled numbers (numbers with no decimal places). For numbers with 28 decimal places, the range is +/–7.9228162514264337593543950335. The smallest possible non-zero number is 0.0000000000000000000000000001 (+/–1E-28)

Figure B-1 Visual Basic conversion functions *(continues)*

(continued)

Syntax	**Return data type**	**Range for *expression***
CInt(*expression*)	Integer	–2,147,483,648 through 2,147,483,647; fractional parts are rounded
CLng(*expression*)	Long	–9,223,372,036,854,775,808 through 9,223,372,036,854,775,807; fractional parts are rounded
CObj(*expression*)	Object	Any valid expression
CSByte(*expression*)	SByte	–128 through 127; fractional parts are rounded
CShort(*expression*)	Short	–32,768 through 32,767; fractional parts are rounded
CSng(*expression*)	Single	–3.402823E+38 through –1.401298E-45 for negative values; 1.401298E-45 through 3.402823E+38 for positive values
CStr(*expression*)	String	Depends on the *expression*
CUInt(*expression*)	UInt	0 through 4,294,967,295 (unsigned)
CULng(*expression*)	ULng	0 through 18,446,744,073,709,551,615 (unsigned)
CUShort(*expression*)	UShort	0 through 65,535 (unsigned)

Figure B-1 Visual Basic conversion functions

APPENDIX C

Locating Syntax and Logic Errors

Finding Syntax Errors

As you learned in Chapter 2, a syntax error occurs when you break one of a programming language's rules. Most syntax errors are a result of typing errors that occur when entering instructions, such as typing `Me.Clse()` instead of `Me.Close()`. The Code Editor detects most syntax errors as you enter the instructions. However, if you are not paying close attention to your computer screen, you may not notice the errors. In the following set of steps, you will observe what happens when you try to start an application that contains a syntax error.

To debug the Total Sales application:

1. Start Visual Studio 2008 or Visual Basic 2008 Express Edition. Close the Start Page window. Open the **Total Sales Solution** (**Total Sales Solution.sln**) file, which is contained in the VB2008\AppC\Total Sales Solution folder. If necessary, open the designer window. The application calculates and displays the total of the sales amounts entered by the user.

2. Open the Code Editor window. Replace the <your name> and <current date> text in the comments with your name and the current date. Figure C-1 shows the code entered in the btnCalc control's Click event procedure. The thin red boxes alert you that three lines of code contain a syntax error. However, you may fail to notice them if you are not paying really close attention to the code.

```
Private Sub btnCalc_Click(ByVal sender As Object, ByVal e
    ' calculates and displays the total sales

    ' declare variables
    Dim intNorth As Integer
    Dim intSouth As Integer
    Dim intEast As Integer
    Dim intWest As Integer
    Dim intTotal As Intger

    ' assign input to variables
    Integer.TryParse(txtNorth.Text, intNorth
    Integer.TryParse(txtSouth.Text, intSouth)
    Integer.TryParse(txtEast.Text, intEast)
    Integer.TryParse(txtWest.Text, intWest)

    ' calculate total sales
    intTota = intNorth + intSouth + intEast + intWest

    ' display total sales
    lblTotal.Text = intTotal.ToString("C0")
End Sub
```

syntax error

syntax error

syntax error

Figure C-1 btnCalc control's Click event procedure

3. Start the application. If the dialog box shown in Figure C-2 appears, click the **No** button.

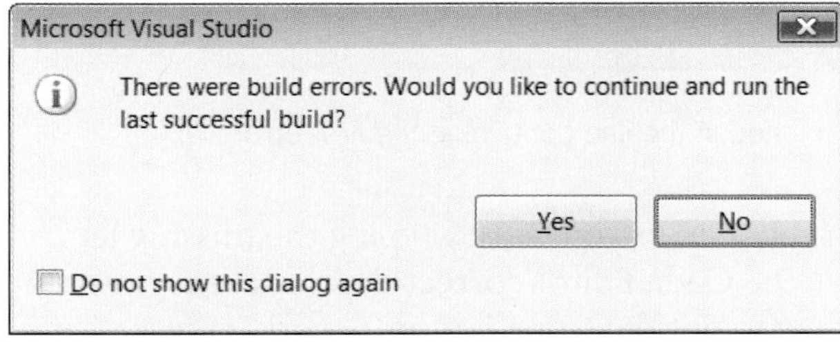

Figure C-2 Dialog box

4. The Error List window shown in Figure C-3 opens at the bottom of the IDE. The Error List window indicates that the code contains three errors. The window provides a description of each error and the location of each error in the code. If you want to change the size of the Error List window, position your mouse pointer on the window's top border until the mouse pointer becomes a sizing pointer, which has two horizontal lines with an up arrow and a down arrow. Then press and hold down the left mouse button while you drag the border either up or down.

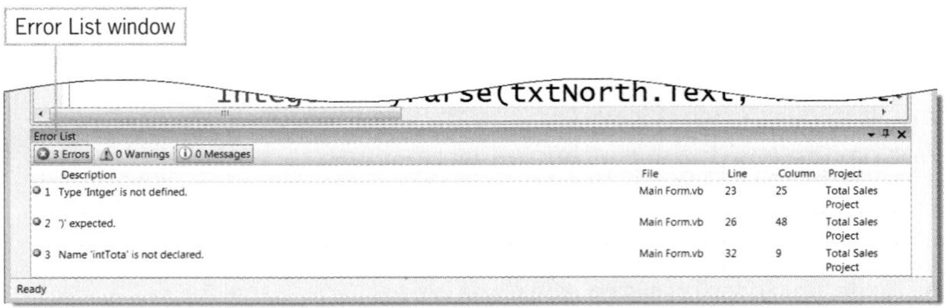

Figure C-3 Error List window in the IDE

5. Double-click **Type 'Intger' is not defined.** in the Error List window. The Code Editor places the insertion point in the line where the error was encountered. See Figure C-4. The first error is nothing more than a typing error: the programmer meant to type Integer.

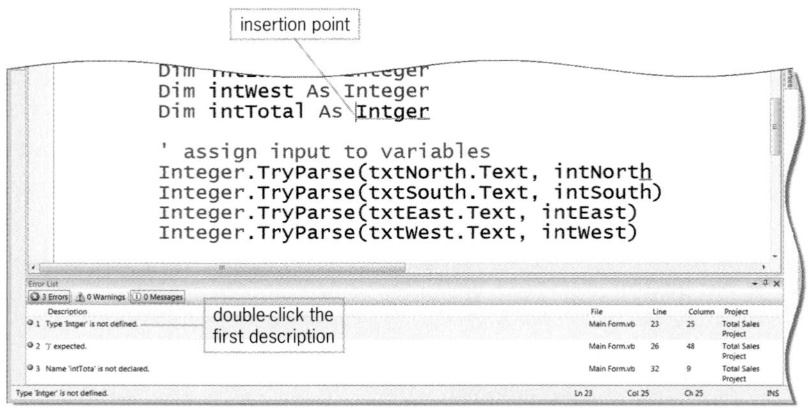

Figure C-4 Insertion point positioned in the line containing the first error

6. You can fix the first syntax error yourself by typing the missing letter e; or, you can have the Code Editor correct the mistake for you. In this step, you'll see how to put the Code Editor to work. Hover your mouse pointer over the thin red box that appears below the letter r. An Error icon (a white exclamation point in a red circle) appears along with a down arrow. (If you don't see the down arrow, hover your mouse pointer on the Error icon until the down arrow appears.) Click the **down arrow** to display a list of suggestions for fixing the error. See Figure C-5.

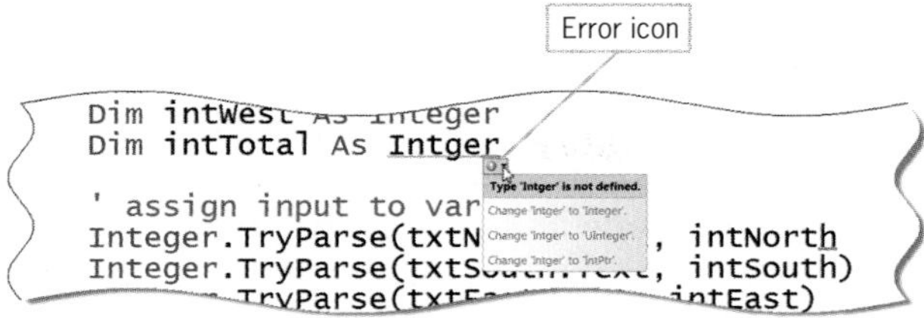

Figure C-5 List of possible solutions

7. Click **Change 'Intger' to 'Integer'.** in the list. The Code Editor changes `Intger` to `Integer` in the Dim statement and removes the error from the Error List window.

8. Double-click **')' expected.** in the Error List window. The Code Editor places the insertion point in the line containing the first TryParse method, because the ending parenthesis is missing from the statement. Hover your mouse pointer over the thin red box that appears below the letter h. When the Error icon and down arrow appear, click the **down arrow**. Click **Insert the missing ')'.** in the list. The Code Editor inserts the missing parenthesis and removes the error message from the Error List window.

9. Double-click **Name 'intTota' is not declared.** in the Error List window. The Code Editor places the insertion point at the beginning of the statement that calculates the total sales. Hover your mouse pointer over the thin red box that appears below the letter a. When the Error icon and down arrow appear, click the **down arrow**. As the message indicates, the Code Editor cannot offer any suggestions for correcting the error. See Figure C-6.

```
        ' calculate total sales
        intTota = intNorth + intSouth + intEast + intWest

        ' display total sales
        lblTotal.Text = intTotal.ToString("C0")
    End Sub
End Class
```

Figure C-6 Message that appears when no correction suggestions are available

10. The error's description (Name 'intTota' is not declared.) indicates that the Code Editor does not recognize the name `intTota`. The unrecognized name appears on the left side of an assignment statement, so it belongs to something that can store information: either a control or a variable. It doesn't refer to the Text property, so it's probably the name of a variable. Looking at the variable declarations at the beginning of the procedure, you will notice that the procedure declares a variable named `intTotal`. Obviously, the programmer mistyped the variable's name. Change `intTota` to **intTotal** in the assignment statement, then move the insertion point to another line in the Code Editor window. When you move the insertion point, the Code Editor removes the error message from the Error List window.

11. Close the Error List window. Save the solution, then start the application. Test the application using **2000** as the North sales, **3000** as the South sales, **1200** as the East sales, and **1800** as the West sales. Click the **Calculate** button. The total sales are $8,000. Click the **Exit** button to end the application. Close the Code Editor window, then close the solution.

Locating Logic Errors

As you observed in the previous section, the Code Editor makes syntax errors easy to find and correct. A much more difficult type of error to locate, and one that the Code Editor cannot detect, is a logic error. A logic error can occur for a variety of reasons, such as forgetting to enter an instruction or entering the instructions in the wrong order. Some logic errors occur as a result of calculation statements that are correct syntactically, but incorrect mathematically. An example of this is the `dblRadiusSquared = dblRadius + dblRadius` statement. The statement's syntax is correct, but it is incorrect mathematically: you square a value by multiplying it by itself, not by adding it to itself. In the remainder of this appendix, you will debug two applications that contain logic errors.

To debug the Discount application:

1. Open the **Discount Solution** (**Discount Solution.sln**) file, which is contained in the VB2008\AppC\Discount Solution folder. If necessary, open the designer window. The application calculates and displays three discount amounts, which are based on the price entered by the user.

2. Open the Code Editor window. Replace the <your name> and <current date> text in the comments with your name and the current date. Figure C-7 shows the code entered in the btnCalc control's Click event procedure.

```
Private Sub btnCalc_Click(ByVal sender As Object, ByVa
    ' calculates and displays a 10%, 20%, and
    ' 30% discount on an item's price

    ' declare variables
    Dim dblPrice As Double
    Dim dblDiscount10 As Double
    Dim dblDiscount20 As Double
    Dim dblDiscount30 As Double

    ' calculate dblDiscounts
    dblDiscount10 = dblPrice * 0.1
    dblDiscount20 = dblPrice * 0.2
    dblDiscount30 = dblPrice * 0.3

    ' display dblDiscounts
    lblDisc10.Text = dblDiscount10.ToString("N2")
    lblDisc20.Text = dblDiscount20.ToString("N2")
    lblDisc30.Text = dblDiscount30.ToString("N2")
End Sub
```

Figure C-7 Code entered in the btnCalc control's Click event procedure

3. Start the application. Type **100** in the Price text box, then click the **Calculate** button. The interface shows that each discount is 0.00, which is incorrect. Click the **Exit** button to stop the application.

4. You'll use the Debug menu to run the Visual Basic debugger, which is a tool that helps you locate the logic errors in your code. Click **Debug** on the menu bar. The menu's Step Into option will start your application and allow you to step through your code. It does this by executing the code one statement at a time, pausing immediately before each statement is executed. Click **Step Into**. Type **100** in the Price text box, then click the **Calculate** button. The debugger highlights the first instruction to be executed. In this case, it highlights the btnCalc_Click procedure header. In addition, an arrow points to the instruction, as shown in Figure C-8, and the code's execution is paused. (If the interface still appears on the screen, click the Code Editor window's title bar.)

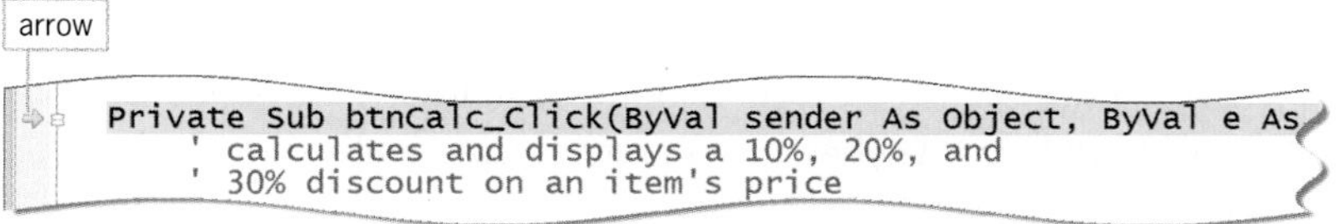

Figure C-8 Procedure header highlighted

5. To execute the highlighted instruction, you can use either the Debug menu's Step Into option or the F8 key on your keyboard. Press the **F8** key. After the computer processes the procedure header, the debugger highlights the next statement to be processed—in this case, the `dblDiscount10 = dblPrice * 0.1` statement—and then pauses execution of the code. (The Dim statements are skipped over because they are not considered executable by the debugger.)

6. While the execution of a procedure's code is paused, you can view the contents of controls and variables that appear in the highlighted statement, as well as in the statements above it in the procedure. Before you view the contents of a control or variable, however, you should consider the value you expect to find. Before the `dblDiscount10 = dblPrice * 0.1` statement is processed, the `dblDiscount10` variable should contain its initial value, 0. (Recall that the Dim statement initializes numeric variables to 0.) Place your mouse pointer on `dblDiscount10` in the highlighted statement. The variable's name and current value appear in a small box, as shown in Figure C-9. (The .0 indicates that the value's data type is Double.) At this point, the `dblDiscount10` variable's value is correct.

```
' declare variables
Dim dblPrice As Double
Dim dblDiscount10 As Double
Dim dblDiscount20 As Double
Dim dblDiscount30 As Double

' calculate dblDiscounts
dblDiscount10 = dblPrice * 0.1
dblDiscount20 = dblPrice * 0.2
dblDiscount30 = dblPrice * 0.3
```

variable's name and value

Figure C-9 Value stored in the `dblDiscount10` variable before the highlighted statement is executed

7. Now consider the value you expect the `dblPrice` variable to contain. Before the highlighted statement is processed, the `dblPrice` variable should contain the number 100, which is the value you entered in the Price text box. Place your mouse pointer on `dblPrice` in the highlighted statement. As Figure C-10 shows, the `dblPrice` variable contains 0.0, which is its initial value. Consider why the variable's value is incorrect. In this case, the value is incorrect because no statement above the highlighted statement assigns the text box's value to the `dblPrice` variable. In other words, a statement is missing from the procedure.

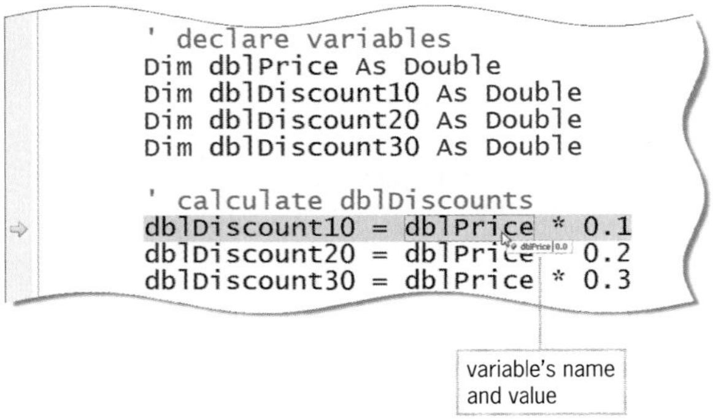

```
' declare variables
Dim dblPrice As Double
Dim dblDiscount10 As Double
Dim dblDiscount20 As Double
Dim dblDiscount30 As Double

' calculate dblDiscounts
dblDiscount10 = dblPrice * 0.1
dblDiscount20 = dblPrice * 0.2
dblDiscount30 = dblPrice * 0.3
```

variable's name and value

Figure C-10 Value stored in the `dblPrice` variable before the highlighted statement is executed

8. Click **Debug** on the menu bar, then click **Stop Debugging** to stop the debugger. Click the **blank line** below the last Dim statement, then press **Enter** to insert another blank line. Enter the following comment and TryParse method.

   ' assign price to a variable
   Double.TryParse(txtPrice.Text, dblPrice)

9. Save the solution. Click **Debug** on the menu bar, then click **Step Into**. Type **100** in the Price text box, then click the **Calculate** button. (If the interface still appears on the screen, click the Code Editor window's title bar.) Press **F8** to process the procedure header. The debugger highlights the `Double.TryParse(txtPrice.Text, dblPrice)` statement and pauses execution of the code.

10. Before the highlighted statement is processed, the txtPrice control's Text property should contain 100, which is the value you entered in the control. Place your mouse pointer on `txtPrice.Text` in the highlighted statement. The box shows that the Text property contains the expected value. The 100 is enclosed in quotation marks because it is considered a string.

11. The `dblPrice` variable should contain its initial value, 0.0. Place your mouse pointer on `dblPrice` in the highlighted statement. The box shows that the variable contains the expected value.

12. Press **F8** to process the TryParse method. The debugger highlights the `dblDiscount10 = dblPrice * 0.1` statement before pausing execution of the code. Place your mouse pointer on `dblPrice` in the TryParse method, as shown in Figure C-11. Notice that after the method is processed by the computer, the `dblPrice` variable contains the number 100.0.

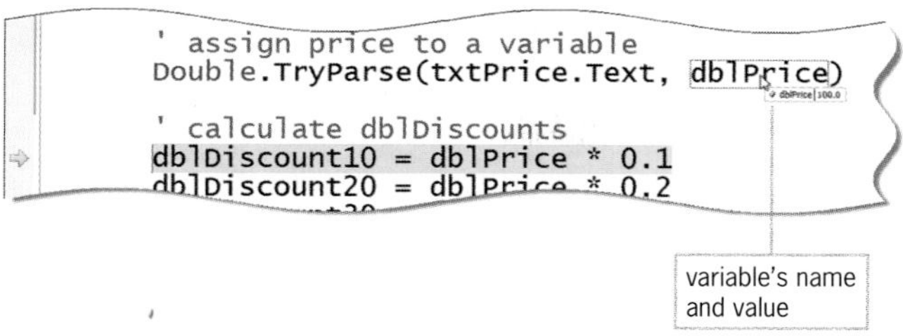

Figure C-11 Value stored in the `dblPrice` variable after the TryParse method is executed

13. Before the highlighted statement is executed, the `dblDiscount10` variable should contain its initial value, and the `dblPrice` variable should contain the value assigned to it by the TryParse method. Place your mouse pointer on `dblDiscount10` in the highlighted statement. The box shows that the variable contains 0.0, which is correct. Place your mouse pointer on `dblPrice` in the highlighted statement. The box shows that the variable contains 100.0, which also is correct.

14. After the highlighted statement is processed, the `dblPrice` variable should still contain 100.0. However, the `dblDiscount10` variable should contain 10.0, which is 10% of 100. Press **F8** to execute the `dblDiscount10 = dblPrice * 0.1` statement, then place your mouse pointer on `dblDiscount10` in the statement. The box shows that the variable contains the expected value. On your own, verify that the `dblPrice` variable in the statement contains the appropriate value.

15. To continue program execution without the debugger, click **Debug** on the menu bar, then click **Continue**. This time, the correct discount amounts (10.00, 20.00, and 30.00) appear in the interface. Click the **Exit** button to end the application. Close the Code Editor window, then close the solution.

Setting Breakpoints

Stepping through code one line at a time is not the only way to search for logic errors. You also can use a breakpoint to pause execution at a specific line in the code. You will learn how to set a breakpoint in the following set of steps.

To debug the Hours Worked application:

1. Open the **Hours Worked Solution** (**Hours Worked Solution.sln**) file, which is contained in the VB2008\AppC\Hours Worked Solution folder. If necessary, open the designer window. The application calculates and displays the total number of hours worked during four weeks.

2. Open the Code Editor window. Replace the <your name> and <current date> text in the comments with your name and the

current date. Figure C-12 shows the code entered in the btnCalc control's Click event procedure.

```
Private Sub btnCalc_Click(ByVal sender As Object, ByVal e A
    ' displays total number of hours worked during 4 weeks

    Dim decWeek1 As Decimal
    Dim decWeek2 As Decimal
    Dim decWeek3 As Decimal
    Dim decWeek4 As Decimal
    Dim decTotal As Decimal

    ' assign input to variables
    Decimal.TryParse(txtWeek1.Text, decWeek1)
    Decimal.TryParse(txtWeek2.Text, decWeek2)
    Decimal.TryParse(txtWeek3.Text, decWeek2)
    Decimal.TryParse(txtWeek4.Text, decWeek4)

    ' calculate total hours worked
    decTotal = decWeek1 + decWeek2 + decWeek3 + decWeek4

    ' display total hours worked
    lblTotal.Text = decTotal.ToString
End Sub
```

Figure C-12 Click event procedure for the btnCalc control

3. Start the application. Type the number **1** in each of the four text boxes, then click the **Calculate** button. The interface shows that the total number of hours is 3, which is incorrect; it should be 4. Click the **Exit** button to stop the application.

4. Obviously, something is wrong with the statement that calculates the total number of hours worked. Rather than having the computer pause before processing each line of code in the procedure, you will have it pause only before processing the calculation statement. You do this by setting a breakpoint on the statement. Right-click the **calculation statement**, point to **Breakpoint**, then click **Insert Breakpoint**. (You also can set a breakpoint by clicking the statement, and then using the Toggle Breakpoint option on the Debug menu.) The debugger highlights the statement and places a circle next to it, as shown in Figure C-13.

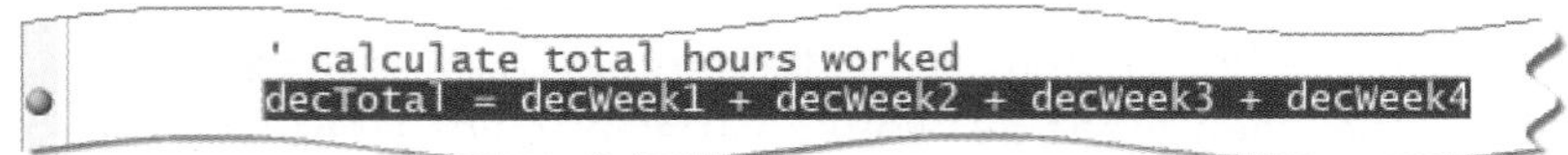

Figure C-13 Breakpoint set in the procedure

5. Start the application. Type the number **1** in each of the four text boxes, then click the **Calculate** button. The computer begins processing the code contained in the button's Click event procedure. It stops processing when it reaches the calculation statement, which it highlights. The highlighting indicates that the statement is the next one to be processed. See Figure C-14.

```
Private Sub btnCalc_Click(ByVal sender As Object, ByVal e A
    ' displays total number of hours worked during 4 weeks

    Dim decWeek1 As Decimal
    Dim decWeek2 As Decimal
    Dim decWeek3 As Decimal
    Dim decWeek4 As Decimal
    Dim decTotal As Decimal

    ' assign input to variables
    Decimal.TryParse(txtWeek1.Text, decWeek1)
    Decimal.TryParse(txtWeek2.Text, decWeek2)
    Decimal.TryParse(txtWeek3.Text, decWeek2)
    Decimal.TryParse(txtWeek4.Text, decWeek4)

    ' calculate total hours worked
    decTotal = decWeek1 + decWeek2 + decWeek3 + decWeek4
```

Figure C-14 Result of the computer reaching the breakpoint

6. Here too, before viewing the values contained in each variable in the highlighted statement, consider the values you expect to find. Before the calculation statement is processed, the `decTotal` variable should contain its initial value (0). The other four variables should contain the number 1, which is the value you entered in each text box. Place your mouse pointer on `decTotal` in the highlighted statement. The box shows that the variable's value is 0D, which is correct. (You can verify the variable's initial value by placing your mouse pointer on `decTotal` in its declaration statement.) Don't be concerned that 0D appears rather than 0. As you learned in Chapter 3, the letter D is one of the literal type characters in Visual Basic; it indicates that the value's data type is Decimal.

7. On your own, view the values contained in the `decWeek1`, `decWeek2`, `decWeek3`, and `decWeek4` variables. Notice that three of the variables contain 1D, which is correct. However, the `decWeek3` variable contains its initial value (0D), which is incorrect.

8. One of the TryParse methods is responsible for assigning a new value to the `decWeek3` variable. Looking closely at the four TryParse methods in the procedure, you will notice that the third one is incorrect. After converting the contents of the txtWeek control to a number, the method should assign the number to the `decWeek3` variable rather than to the `decWeek2` variable. Click **Debug** on the menu bar, then click **Stop Debugging**.

9. Change `decWeek2` in the third TryParse method to **decWeek3**.

10. Now you can remove the breakpoint. Right-click the **statement containing the breakpoint**, point to **Breakpoint**, then click **Delete Breakpoint**.

11. Save the solution, then start the application. Enter the number **1** in each of the four text boxes, then click the **Calculate** button. The interface shows that the total number of hours is 4.

12. On your own, test the application using other values for the hours worked in each week. When you are finished testing, click the **Exit** button to end the application. Close the Code Editor window, then close the solution.

Index

Note: Page numbers referencing key terms appear in **bold**. Page numbers referencing figures are *italicized* and followed by an *f*.

D

E

F

T

U

V